P9-DFV-443

GREAT EVENTS FROM HISTORY

Great Events from History

Worldwide
Twentieth Century Series

Volume 3
1971-1979

Edited by
FRANK N. MAGILL

Associate Editor
Edward P. Keleher

SALEM PRESS, Incorporated
Englewood Cliffs, New Jersey

LIBRARY OF CONGRESS CATALOG CARD NUMBER: 72-86347

Complete Set: ISBN   0-89356-116-9
Volume 3:   ISBN   0-89356-115-0

FIRST EDITION
First Printing

PRINTED IN THE UNITED STATES OF AMERICA

LIST OF EVENTS IN VOLUME THREE
Worldwide Twentieth Century Series

1971	Devaluation of the Dollar	1097
1971	Reform of the International Monetary System	1104
1971	Admission of the People's Republic of China to the United Nations	1110
1972	"Bloody Sunday" in Ulster	1117
1972	*Rapprochement* with the People's Republic of China	1124
1972-1974	The Watergate Affair	1131
1973-1974	Arab Oil Embargo and the Energy Crisis	1137
1973	Great Britain Joins the Common Market	1146
1973	The United States Supreme Court Rules on State Anti-abortion Laws	1154
1973	End of American Involvement in the Vietnam War	1161
1973	Diplomatic Relations Established Between East and West Germany	1167
1973	The United States Supreme Court Rules on Obscenity	1174
1973	The Yom Kippur War	1182
1973	Resignation of Vice-President Spiro T. Agnew	1188
1974	The Cyprus Crisis	1193
1974	Collapse of the Nixon Administration	1200
1974	Charter of the Economic Rights and Duties of States	1206
1975	The Fall of Cambodia to the Khmer Rouge	1212
1975-1976	The Civil War in Angola and the Intervention of Cuba	1219
1975	The Fall of South Vietnam	1227
1975-1976	The Lebanese Civil War	1235
1975-1976	The Reunification of Vietnam	1243
1975	The OAS Suspends the Embargo Against Cuba	1251
1975	The Helsinki Agreement	1257
1976	Deaths of Mao Tse-tung and Chou En-lai	1264

1976	Black Nationalist Movement in South Africa . . .	1272
1976	The United States Supreme Court Rules on the Death Penalty	1279
1976	The Bicentennial Celebration	1287
1976	The *Viking* Landings on Mars	1294
1976	Election of Carter to the Presidency in 1976	1302
1977 *ff*	The Spaceflights of *Voyagers I* and *II*	1311
1977-1978	The Struggle for the Horn of Africa	1317
1977-1978	Birth of the First Human Conceived *in Vitro* . . .	1324
1978	Ratification of the Panama Canal Treaties	1331
1979	The Iranian Revolution	1338
1979	Vietnam's Conquest of Cambodia	1346

LIST OF INDEXES

VOLUMES ONE, TWO, AND THREE
Worldwide Twentieth Century Series

Alphabetical List of Events	1357
Key Word Index for Events	1360
Category Index for Type of Event	1366
Principal Personages	1371
Pertinent Literature Reviewed	1380
Literature for Additional Recommended Reading . .	1389

REPRINTS
OF ALL INDEXES
FROM
GREAT EVENTS FROM HISTORY
Ancient and Medieval Series

Alphabetical List of Events	1419
Key Word Index for Events	1423
Category Index for Type of Event	1428
Principal Personages	1438
Pertinent Literature Reviewed	1451
Literature for Additional Recommended Reading . .	1466

Modern European Series

Alphabetical List of Events 1501
Key Word Index for Events 1505
Category Index for Type of Event 1511
Principal Personages 1519
Pertinent Literature Reviewed 1538
Literature for Additional Recommended Reading . . 1552

American Series

Alphabetical List of Events 1585
Key Word Index for Events 1590
Category Index for Type of Event 1600
Principal Personages 1608
Pertinent Literature Reviewed 1626
Literature for Additional Recommended Reading . . 1643

INITIALS IDENTIFYING CONTRIBUTORS OF SIGNED ARTICLES

A.C.R.	Anne C. Raymer	J.R.B.	John R. Broadus
A.G.G.	Alan G. Gross	J.R.H.	John R. Hanson, II
A.M.	Anne Millbrooke	J.R.P.	John R. Phillips
A.O.B.	Anita O. Bowser	J.R.S.	Jane R. Shoup
B.F.	Barry Faye	J.S.A.	J. Stewart Alverson
C.C.H.	Cabot C. Holmes	J.W.P.	James W. Pringle
C.E.C.	Charles E. Cottle	L.H.D.G.	Leonard H. D. Gordon
C.K.	Clive Kileff	L.R.M.	Lincoln R. Mui
C.W.J.	Charles W. Johnson	L.S.	Leon Stein
C.W.T.	Carol Whyte Talabay	M.G.	Manfred Grote
D.D.D.	Daniel D. DiPiazza	M.S.S.	Margaret S. Schoon
D.F.P.	Doris F. Pierce	M.W.B.	Meredith William Berg
D.W.T.	David W. Talabay	P.A.	Paul Ashin
E.A.Z.	Edward A. Zivich	P.D.M.	Paul D. Mageli
E.F.	Elizabeth Fee	P.M.	Paul Monaco
E.G.D.	E. Gene DeFelice	P.R.P.	Philip R. Popple
E.P.K.	Edward P. Keleher	R.A.G.	Roger A. Geimer
F.B.C.	Frederick B. Chary	R.E.	Rand Edwards
G.J.F.	George J. Fleming	R.H.S.	Richard H. Sander
G.R.M.	George R. Mitchell	R.J.C.	Ronald J. Cima
G.R.M.	Gordon R. Mork	R.L.L.	Richard L. Langill
H.H.B.	Henry H. Bucher, Jr.	R.R.	Richard Rice
J.A.B.	James A. Berlin	S.L.	Saul Lerner
J.C.C.	John C. Carlisle	S.V.D.	Stuart Van Dyke, Jr.
J.C.N.	John C. Neeley	T.A.B.	Terry Alan Baney
J.D.R.	John D. Raymer	T.D.	Tyler Deierhoi
J.G.U.	Jonathan G. Utley	T.D.C.	Thomas D. Crouch
J.H.	Jean Harber	T.M.S.	Thomas M. Smith
J.H.M.	John H. Morrow, Jr.	T.R.K.	Thomas R. Koenig
J.J.H.	James J. Herlan	V.N.	Victor Namias
J.L.C.	Jack L. Calbert	W.S.	Walter Schultz
J.M.F.	Jonathan M. Furdek		

DEVALUATION OF THE DOLLAR

Type of event: Economic: policy action in a monetary crisis
Time: August 15 and December 18, 1971
Locale: The United States

Principal personages:
RICHARD MILHOUS NIXON (1913-   ), thirty-seventh President of the United States, 1969-1974
KARL SCHILLER (1911-   ), West German Economics Minister
ARTHUR BURNS (1904-   ), Chairman of the Federal Reserve System
PIERRE-PAUL SCHWEITZER (1912-   ), Managing Director of the International Monetary Fund

Summary of Event

During the Great Depression of the 1930's and the political unrest and tumult generated by World War II, foreign exchange rates were uncertain and highly unstable. The leading nations of the world, with the exception of Soviet Russia, met in July, 1944, at Bretton Woods, New Hampshire, to address the problems of foreign exchange. An agreement intended to stabilize international exchange was reached. This agreement, known as the Bretton Woods agreement, established international standards for official foreign exchange. By this agreement, the American dollar became the key currency for international exchange. The dollar was a dominant world currency utilized as a standard for trade arrangement between many countries and as a reserve to "back" the currencies of many underdeveloped countries. The underdeveloped countries in Africa, Asia, Europe, and Latin America were anxious for American capital in order to expand their industrial development, while capitalists in the industrially developed countries, who were reluctant to risk ventures in foreign currencies, were seeking the stability of an international order. It was largely expected that the dollar would emerge as *the* international currency.

The major accomplishment of the Bretton Woods conference was defining parities of currencies for international exchange and finance. These parities were defined not only in terms of gold, but simultaneously in terms of the American dollar pegged at the equivalent of 1/35th ounce of gold per dollar. Official changes in the parity value of any currency were permissible under the agreement as a method of dealing with a disequilibrium in a nation's balance of payments. The World Bank and the International Monetary Fund (IMF) were also established by the Bretton Woods agreement as supportive measures to international monetary stability. It was this established order that governed international finance and exchange until August 15, 1971, when President Richard M. Nixon of the United States suspended the agreement.

A series of events and building pressures led to the collapse of the Bretton Woods agreement and to international monetary reform. By the 1950's and through the 1960's, the European community experienced balance of payments surpluses, while the United States balance of payments ran an average deficit of $1.5 billion per year. This chronic deficit situation for the United States was not alarming in view of the large amounts of dollars involved in foreign exchange. Even to the more pessimistic critics, the role of the dollar as a worldwide reserve currency for a growing world economy appeared successful.

But by 1965, the United States balance of payments deficit began to increase, and the increases in the deficit quickly escalated. It was apparent that the United States foreign exchange deficit was a major problem. In early 1971, a large movement of funds from the United States to Europe began to create difficulties in maintaining parity between the dollar and other currencies. In March and April of 1971, overt speculation in foreign exchange markets became newsworthy to the extent that by May 4, 1971, *Bundesbank* had absorbed a capital inflow of one billion dollars in one day, and, after forty minutes of trading on May 5, had absorbed another billion dollars and had then suspended support of the American dollar. By July, 1971, the United States reserves deficit had soared to

more than eleven billion dollars and the official United States gold stock had fallen to nearly ten billion dollars. A congressional subcommittee called for a general realignment of exchange rates, and President Richard M. Nixon responded on Sunday, August 15, 1971, by announcing a major new program which included a ninety-day freeze on wages and prices, new tax measures, a temporary surcharge on imports, and the suspension of the conversion of dollars into gold. Consequently, this action ended the twenty-seven-year Bretton Woods agreement and the formal role of the United States dollar as the world reserve currency.

Many factors contributed to the United States' balance of payments problem and the eventual demise of the Bretton Woods agreement. American military expenditures and generous aid programs continued after World War II. The expensive Cold War programs, including the Korean conflict, the Vietnam War, and the NATO Alliance contributed to an expanding volume of American dollars abroad. Funding the Vietnam conflict through extended debt rather than taxation contributed unanticipated pressures on the United States' balance of payments.

In addition, increasing productivity in other countries brought about significant problems for the United States' balance of payments. Remarkable increases in productivity in Western European countries and Japan dramatically changed the position of the United States in world trade. These countries were increasingly able to produce for themselves and to rely less on goods from the

United States. With increasing productivity, these countries were able to compete effectively with the United States in international markets and even to capture significant shares of markets within the United States. The Western European countries were most anxious to advocate changes in the international monetary order with Karl Schiller, West Germany's Economics Minister, among the most articulate and outspoken advocates of establishing floating exchange rates.

The development of the European Common Market strengthened the competitive position of the European economies and presented the opportunity for a more unified front in the international financial scene. Pierre-Paul Schweitzer, Director of the International Monetary Fund, was a leading spokesman for the European communities and encouraged a continuation of the convertibility of dollars into gold. The increasing productivity in European economies was creating attractive opportunities for American investors, and the European community did not favor any additional impediments to this important flow of capital.

Domestic inflation in the United States and a growing lack of trust in the dollar were also contributing factors to the balance of payments problem. In the early 1960's, the European economies were rapidly approaching full employment. European wage and other money costs were rising at a faster pace than those in America. But as the sluggish American economy approached full employment in the mid-1960's, this situation changed to the point that money costs in America grew at rates

comparable to those in the European economies. The financial advantages were obliterated and the chronic deficits in the balance of payments became alarmingly apparent. A general apprehension that the American dollar would depreciate in value relative to other currencies became prevalent. Many individuals and governments attempted to liquidate holdings of American dollars in favor of gold, thereby contributing to an escalated "gold drain" for the United States in the late 1960's.

Generally, a country may attempt to adjust to a persistent balance of payments deficit through internal deflation, through a devaluation in its exchange rate, or through restrictive controls on trade, investment, and exchange. The United States had instituted a series of programs throughout the 1960's that attempted to control investment abroad. In 1963, the interest equalization tax attempted to reduce the flow of dollars to foreign countries. In 1965, the voluntary restraint program was designed to limit direct investments abroad. In 1968, mandatory investment controls were instituted by the United States government. "Swap agreements" were made between the Federal Reserve System and the central banks of Europe, and bonds were issued by the United States Treasury that were payable in dollars or in a specific foreign currency. These programs were not successful in reducing the balance of payments deficit, but they did lessen the drain of gold from the United States and impacted the speculation on the dollar in international exchange markets.

By mid-1971, the United States

deficit had become acute. In one week, more than four billion dollars moved into foreign reserves in spite of the view that the dollar was overvalued and would be depreciated. Arthur Burns, Chairman of the Federal Reserve System, reported to the Joint Economic Committee the failure to deal with domestic inflation and the deficit in payments and recommended stringent action. On August 15, 1971, President Richard M. Nixon announced the suspension of gold convertibility of dollars as part of a plan to deal with inflation and chronic deficit of payments. By this action, the order established by the Bretton Woods agreement was ended. Nixon's move, which in effect amounted to a devaluation of the dollar, was officially confirmed in the international Smithsonian Agreement of December 18, 1971.

Pertinent Literature

Solomon, Robert. *The International Monetary System, 1945-1976: An Insider's View*. New York: Harper & Row Publishers, 1977.

Robert Solomon provides insights into the international financial situation that are unique because of his participation in these international monetary affairs and his past affiliation with the Federal Reserve System. In researching his study, Solomon interviewed key individuals directly involved to obtain significant interpretations and insights of international financial experts.

What emerges, then, is a well-documented account of the significant events in the development of the international monetary system from the agreement at Bretton Woods in 1944, when the United States took a leading and dominant role in international financial matters, through the present uncertain situation of the mid-1970's. A major portion of this work focuses on the sequence of events that led directly to the termination of the Bretton Woods agreement in 1971 when President Richard M. Nixon suspended the conversion of dollars into gold. But with the international financial system in a state of change and not fully resolved, the author identifies trends developing in the early 1970's and speculates on the possible consequences and final resolution of the international financial order.

As the economies of the world recovered from the ravages of World War II and developed competitive, peace-time economic systems, the deficiencies of the Bretton Woods agreement soon became apparent. The author lucidly describes a series of minor monetary crises which themselves reveal the difficulties of attempting to make a fixed exchange rate system function effectively in a world of quickly changing economies. Solomon expertly illustrates the inadequacies of policies and actions designed to contend with these monetary crises within the framework of the Bretton Woods agreement.

The author focuses on two major efforts in the postwar years that led to the eventual collapse of the international monetary system. The effort to rebuild the economies of Europe and Japan after World War II strengthened the competitive position as well as the balance of payments of these countries. The effort by the United States to maintain alliances through costly military aid programs had inflationary consequences. The author is able to relate these efforts to events in the international financial setting and provides an explanation of a complex financial and political process.

The chronological nature of Solomon's book is its chief limitation. The technically more complex and theoretically more difficult aspects of international finance are omitted. Such important developments during this period as the European Common Market, the Eurodollar, and the World Bank are important to examine for a complete understanding of the international financial situation in the postwar era. These developments, each of which is of sufficient importance to be dealt with in an independent study, are largely ignored by the author.

More importantly, there are several significant factors that are necessary for an understanding of the demise of the international financial system in 1971. These factors are domestic inflation in the United States, accelerated technical growth and increased productivity in the European community and Japan, and investment in foreign securities and firms. Solomon chooses to treat these factors only in a passing fashion.

In the first two chapters, Solomon examines the relative financial stability during the 1950's and identifies forces that signal problems in the future. In the subsequent two chapters, the author focuses on the problems confronting the United States and other countries, pointing out the interests in international monetary reform which involved analysis of the policies adopted and actions taken during the early 1960's.

In the next three chapters, Solomon examines the budding monetary crises in Great Britain, the United States, Germany, and Japan, culminating in the great gold rush of 1967-1968. The development of the Special Drawing Rights or SDR's of the International Monetary Fund as an acceptable instrument of international financial settlement, the currency crises faced by France and Germany, and the growing concern for a revision of the exchange rate system, all in the late 1960's, are the focus of the following three chapters. The next chapter describes in detail the events that immediately led to the decision to abandon the Bretton Woods agreement.

Solomon's viewpoint is international and is sensitive to the issues of national interest in the development of the Devaluation of the Dollar. Particularly valuable is the correlation which he establishes between the international financial arrangements and domestic economic concerns.

Mundell, Robert A. and Alexander K. Swoboda, eds. *Monetary Problems of the International Economy*. Chicago: University of Chicago Press, 1969.

The 1960's was a period when the leading nations of the world were trying to preserve order in the realm of international exchange by maintaining the agreement reached at Bretton Woods, New Hampshire, in 1944, in spite of its apparent defects and unmanageability. In other words, a major effort of the monetary leaders was to preserve a system of exchange based on a gold standard until a suitable plan to reform the international monetary system could be developed and agreed upon. In September, 1966, a conference was held in Chicago, bringing together many of the experts and younger theorists in the field of international finance, to ponder and debate the difficult theoretical issues surrounding monetary reform and the direction it should take. R. A. Mundell with H. G. Johnson constructed the conference and A. K. Swoboda transcribed and summarized the sessions. This book is a detailed account of that conference and provides interesting insights into the understanding of this significant era in international monetary history.

The opening address is by the Honorable Valéry Giscard d'Estaing, then the leader of the Independent Republican Party in France and an articulate proponent of reform of the gold exchange system. In this address, Valéry Giscard d'Estaing reviews past solutions to international monetary problems focusing on six periods since international monetary issues were of concern. The important aspect of this address is the identification of three goals: balance of payments stability, a liquidity system based on needs, and establishment of a monetary union. The problems relative to these goals are in the realm of diplomacy rather than theory.

The ensuing debates brought out many practical issues and fascinating insights concerning international monetary reform at a time immediately preceding the worldwide monetary crisis. A number of specific problems and issues are addressed. Included are the three major issues posed at meetings held in Ballagio, Italy, in 1964: (1) the problem of payment adjustments; (2) the problem of international liquidity; (3) the problem of confidence in the reserve media. Other topics of discussion are the use of reserves by countries, balance of payments disequilibria, variable exchange rates, international assets, and the role of institutions such as the International Monetary Fund.

Many of the formal presentations recorded in this work are of a theoretical and technical nature and would be of interest to the more serious and sophisticated analysts of international monetary crises. The discussions summarized from these sessions provide valuable insights into concerns and developments in international monetary systems. A key paper, with comments and discussion, concerns the economic institutions and problems with these institutions in the international monetary system. This paper by R. Z. Aliber, entitled "Improving the Bretton Woods System," was written in 1966 before the development of Special Drawing Rights, capital controls by the United States, and other important events that were to follow. A second paper, by A. C. L. Day, concerns the institutional constraints and the international monetary system.

Taken as a whole, this book provides important insights into the early problems and the eventual collapse of the Bretton Woods agreement in 1971. — *J.M.F.*

Additional Recommended Reading

Gardner, Richard N. *Sterling Dollar Diplomacy*. New York: McGraw-Hill Book Company, 1969. A study of how international policies are formed and developed, with a section devoted to the Bretton Woods agreement.

Hirsch, Fred. *Money International*. Garden City, N.Y.: Doubleday & Company, 1969. An interesting and realistic description of postwar institutional development.

International Monetary Problems. Washington, D.C.: American Enterprise Institute for Public Policy Research, 1972. A conference by the American Enterprise Institute for Public Policy Research which includes several papers, comments and discussion on issues of international monetary reform.

Kindleberger, Charles P. *The Dollar Shortage*. Cambridge, Mass.: MIT Press, 1950. A scholarly study of the causes and impact of this postwar problem.

Roosa, Robert V. *Monetary Reform for the World Economy*. New York: Harper & Row Publishers, 1965. This concise work identifies the defects and problems of international monetary systems and reviews some alternatives.

Triffin, Robert. *Gold and the Dollar Crisis: The Future of Convertibility*. New Haven, Conn.: Yale University Press, 1961. A historical approach identifying forces creating instability in the Bretton Woods system and proposals for reform.

——————— . *Our International Monetary System: Yesterday, Today and Tomorrow*. New York: Random House, 1968. Provides a historical background of the forces affecting the international monetary system.

REFORM OF THE INTERNATIONAL MONETARY SYSTEM

Type of event: Economic: arriving at a new international monetary order
Time: August 15, 1971 to the present
Locale: Washington, D.C., and the world

Principal personages:
>VALÉRY GISCARD D'ESTAING (1926-), French Minister of Finance
>SIR CHRISTOPHER (JEREMY) MORSE (1928-), the representative of the Bank of England
>RICHARD MILHOUS NIXON (1913-), thirty-seventh President of the United States, 1969-1974
>PAUL A. VOLCKER (1927-), United States Under Secretary of the Treasury for Monetary Affairs
>ALI WARDHANA (1928-), Indonesian Minister of Finance

Summary of Event

On August 15, 1971, President Richard M. Nixon, responding to international market pressures, suspended gold convertibility of the dollar, imposed a temporary surcharge on imports, and announced a ninety-day freeze on wages and prices. This action, in effect devaluating the dollar, suspended the agreements for international currency parity established at the international conference at Bretton Woods, New Hampshire, in 1944. By breaking with the Bretton Woods agreement, the world was faced with the immediate alternatives of accepting an inconvertible dollar standard or allowing a freely competitive, market-determined currency exchange rate. For the strong currencies, accepting inconvertible dollars meant continued accumulation of dollars indefinitely, while market-determined exchange rates posed the threat of falling exports and rising imports, and thus of unemployment.

In some instances, central banks intervened and exchanged for dollars. France, however, under the direction of Finance Minister Valéry Giscard d'Estaing, reacted by declaring a market-determined or floating exchange rate.

In the ensuing period of confusion and uncertainty of an appropriate parity structure, the "Group of Ten" agreed to meet and attempt to resolve the problem and arrive at international monetary reform. The "Group of Ten" were industrial countries that agreed to provide supplemental funds to the International Monetary Fund which in turn would offer compensatory financial assistance to participating countries when faced with a temporary deficit in the balance of payments.

When the Group of Ten met in 1968, an agreement was reached whereby all gold payments were suspended from official central banks to the London market. In this way, a two-tier gold exchange system was established. The official tier established parities between the currencies of countries affiliated with the International Monetary Fund (IMF). The free market tier was outside the influence of the IMF countries, where gold was treated as a market commodity, attaining a market price in terms of specific currencies.

But this remedy was recognized to be only a temporary solution. Without expanding currencies, expanding foreign trade would be thwarted. After the United States suspended gold convertibility of the dollar, the Group of Ten agreed to meet in order to reach a more permanent agreement for international finance. After several meetings, the Smithsonian Agreement of December 18, 1971, was reached. By this agreement, seven nations of the Group of Ten changed the par value of their currencies with respect to gold and in terms of the Special Drawing Rights or SDR's (a novel form of international reserve asset created in 1970) of the IMF. A widened "band" above and below the declared parity value of the currency was also established by this agreement, allowing for fluctuations in exchange rates of as much as 4½ percent. By this agreement, currencies were realigned, and the United States formally confirmed the devaluation of the dollar, which had occurred four months earlier, by changing the gold price from $35.00 per ounce to $38.00.

This new agreement did not survive through the 1970's when changing economic conditions were seemingly incompatible with stable exchange rates. The Smithsonian Agreement, however, was an achievement of international monetary cooperation. The United States did not experience any alleviation of the balance of payments deficit, and on February 12, 1973, moved to devalue the dollar an additional ten percent, raising the official price of gold to $42.22 per ounce and consequently abandoning the realigned system of exchange rates agreed upon in the Smithsonian Agreement.

The effort to reconstruct the international monetary system and resolve the international monetary crisis continued. A plan for reorganization was proposed by United States Under Secretary of the Treasury for Monetary Affairs, Paul Volcker. The proposal was put forth by the United States and addressed by the IMF. In July, 1972, the Board of Governors of the IMF created the "Committee of Twenty," made up of the financial ministers of twenty participating nations; this committee set out to resolve the monetary crisis. Ali Wardhana, Indonesia's Minister of Finance, was elected chairman, and Jeremy Morse of the Bank of England became Chairman of the Deputies.

By 1974, it became apparent that a fully reformed monetary system would not be negotiated, largely because of world events and differences in national views. In June of 1974, the Committee of Twenty presented its final report with recommendations: to establish an interim advisory committee; to strengthen the procedures of the IMF in surveilling currency adjustments; to establish guidelines to manage floating exchange rates; to avoid trade restrictions for the purpose of balance of payments; and to revalue SDR's in terms of sixteen commodities rather than gold or U.S. dollars.

The bad experience with exchange rate parities that were fixed or "pegged" in a world of rapidly changing economic conditions had created an atmosphere antagonistic to fixed rates of exchange. The difficulties experienced with equilibrium of the dollar, the central international currency, cast doubts upon a system dependent on a single national currency. The long-run inadequacy of the traditional monetary role of gold is a static reality; consequently, the international monetary system has evolved to respond to these international monetary inadequacies.

If the agreements of the Committee of Twenty remain intact, Special Drawing Rights will replace the dollar as the principal international reserve asset. The continuing discussions lend to interesting speculation regarding the eventual evolution of the new international monetary order. It is not yet clear if SDR's will arrive as the international replacement for the dollar or whether the dollar might be used as an intervention currency. The growth of reserves by creating SDR's is determined by agreement among IMF members and permanent agreements on this process as well as the allocation of reserve increments among participating companies must be solidified. The potential to establish a link between this new reserve creation and development aid has become a timely topic of discussion.

The persistent problem of imbalance in capital flows has not been resolved; however, possible remedies, such as adjusting reserve requirements, two-tier foreign exchange markets, and forward exchange, have been suggested and attempted.

Pertinent Literature

Solomon, Robert. *The International Monetary System, 1945-1976: An Insider's View*. New York: Harper & Row Publishers, 1977.

Robert Solomon, when affiliated with the Federal Reserve System, had responsibilities that involved international monetary affairs. His book is a thoroughly researched and documented account of events affecting international monetary policy and the international monetary system from the Bretton Woods agreement in 1944 to the present. In many instances, Solomon provides a firsthand account of the events, especially developments in the United States. The book concludes with an evaluation of the present international monetary system, the problems, and the anticipated evolution of newly created institutions.

One valuable aspect of this work is its emphasis on the importance of the international monetary system on all our lives and on the need for familiarity with the background of the system in order to understand the present crisis. The author recounts and analyzes historic episodes from an international viewpoint and provides insight into the conflicting perceptions and purposes of policymakers.

Solomon devotes a major portion of his study to recent developments in a new order for international finance. President Richard M. Nixon's announcement of August 15, 1971, affecting the dollar surprised the financial community, and the following four months were a period of turmoil. Solomon traces the developments during this brief period which culminated in a realignment of exchange rates at a meeting at the Smithsonian Institution. The author focuses not only on the financial market reactions but also on the political and economic relations among the countries. Concentrating on the activities of Secretary of the Treasury John Connally, the author traces the negotiations and developments at the meeting of the Ministers and Governors of the Group of Ten on September 15-16, 1971, at Lancaster House in London. The Lancaster House meeting sought to arrive at an agreement on a new pattern of exchange rates and to address the issues of the size of the improvement sought in the United States balance of payments, the United States contribution to the realignment by a devaluation of the dollar, and the continued uses of capital controls by the United States. Having succeeded only in identifying these problems, suggesting procedures to deal with them, and generating greater antagonism, the Group of Ten made little headway.

The author focuses on the development of these issues, particularly the gold price question and the negotiations that followed, which culminated in the meeting of the Min-

isters and Governors of the Group of Ten at the Smithsonian Institution in December, 1971. The agreement reached at the Smithsonian meeting resulted in a realignment of currencies, including devaluation of the dollar. Solomon recognizes that the growing economic strength of Europe and Japan made the Bretton Woods agreement obsolete. In his view, the absence of a systematic adjustment to a new order was intolerable. Consequently, the inevitable result of disappointment with an arrangement that fell far short of a system to restore a sustainable balance was the cause of further turmoil.

The Smithsonian Agreement gave the United States the currency realignment it sought in return for a modest devaluation of the dollar. Solomon examines the reasons for the rapid deterioration of the Smithsonian Agreement and the subsequent efforts of the Committee of Twenty to achieve a more durable international monetary reform. The inability of the Committee to reach any durable agreement is largely due, in Solomon's analysis, to contrasting attitudes toward reform between the United States and the European nations. The world had undergone significant changes between the time when the committee first convened in 1972 and when the committee submitted its final report on monetary reform in 1974. The goal of the Committee of Twenty was to arrive at a durable and workable realignment of currencies and the establishment of par values. With floating exchange rates effectively in practice, the purpose for such reform had evaporated. Solomon effectively blends the activities of the Committee of Twenty with the events on the international monetary scene.

The author pursues a discussion of floating exchange rates in a world afflicted with energy crises and worldwide inflation and recession. He examines movements in exchange rates and improvements in balance of payments and focuses attention on the continuing evolution of the International Monetary System.

Willett, Thomas D. *Floating Exchange Rates and International Monetary Reform.* Washington, D.C.: American Enterprise Institute for Public Policy Research, 1977.

Thomas D. Willett is the Horton Professor of Economics at Claremont Graduate School and Claremont Men's College. As an academic economist in the field of international finance, he has been affiliated with Cornell University, Harvard University, and the University of West Virginia. As a professional economist in government service, he has been a senior staff economist for the Council of Economic Advisors, Deputy Assistant Secretary for International Research and Planning for the United States Treasury Department, and Director of International Monetary Research at the United States Treasury. He is thus eminently qualified to analyze the problems of floating exchange rates and international monetary reform.

Willett's book focuses on the new order for an international monetary system. On January 8, 1976, in Kingston, Jamaica, representatives from more than one hundred nations reached an agreement to amend the International Monetary Fund Articles of Agreement. This new agreement effectively ratified floating exchange rates as the basis of the international monetary system. Floating exchange rates simply mean that the relative price of a currency is determined by the supply and demand conditions for the currency. Figuratively, the rates are allowed to seek their own level, or "float."

The author begins by examining the gold convertibility system adopted in 1944 at Bretton Woods and the deficiencies of that system. He then traces the evolutionary process leading to floating exchange rates by focusing on events as well as advances in economic analysis that contributed to this process. More specifically, he studies the reasons for this substantial shift in view on the basis for international exchange, the nature of the solidity of the new system, and the contention that further basic monetary reforms are necessary. These questions are treated in relation to the historical patterns of academic as well as official views on exchange rate arrangements and in relation to the patterns of international postwar monetary system adjustments.

Willett addresses more sophisticated problems and issues than other authors. He examines, for instance, the problem of speculative capital flows under the Bretton Woods system and the identification of a par value system with international financial cooperation, by contrasting academic perspectives and official omissions. He also analyzes the evolution of floating exchange rates resulting from reactions to changing economic conditions and experimentations, and he points to underlying economic forces and an anticlimactic role of formal agreements.

Willett recognizes the contrast between actual performance and academic ideals, yet considers the performance of floating exchange rates to be far better than expected by critics. He recognizes that international cooperation is a basic tenet of the Jamaica agreement and emphasizes the need to make strides in the further development of that cooperation. — *J.M.F.*

Additional Recommended Reading

Aliber, Robert Z., ed. *National Monetary Policies and the International Financial System*. Chicago: University of Chicago Press, 1974. Taken from the proceedings of a national seminar, July, 1972, in Racine, Wisconsin, on this topic, this book contains a collection of scholarly papers dealing with specific issues of international financial policy.

——————————. *The Political Economy of Monetary Reform*. New York: Universe Press, 1977. Based on the proceedings of an international conference held in 1974 on this topic; institutional as well as theoretical issues are considered.

Fournier, Henri and J. E. Wadsworth, eds. *Floating Exchange Rates: The Lessons of Recent Experience*. Leyden, The Netherlands: Sijthoff, 1976. A collection of papers from the fifth colloquium of the Société Universitaire Europeene de Recherches Financières (SUERF) in Venice, 1974.

Grubel, Herbert G. *The International Monetary System*. Baltimore, Md.: Penguin Books, 1969. Contains a section on international monetary reform and on centrally created reserves.

Guindey, Guillaume. *The International Monetary Tangle: Myths and Realities*. New York: M. E. Sharpe, 1977. A translation of the original French text that examines monetary policies since the Bretton Woods agreement from a European focus.

Meier, Gerald M. *Problems of a World Monetary Order*. New York: Oxford University Press, 1974. A wide-ranging discussion of international monetary reform.

ADMISSION OF THE PEOPLE'S REPUBLIC OF CHINA TO THE UNITED NATIONS

Type of event: Diplomatic: international recognition of the People's Republic of China by its admission to the United Nations
Time: October 25, 1971
Locale: United Nations, New York

Principal personages:

CHIANG KAI-SHEK (1887-1975), late President of the Republic of China on Taiwan whose government represented China in the United Nations until 1971

CH'IAO KUAN-HUA (1914-   ), Deputy Foreign Minister of the People's Republic of China and representative to the United Nations General Assembly in 1971

CHOU EN-LAI (1898-1976), late Premier of the People's Republic of China and major official concerned with Chinese foreign affairs

HUANG HUA (1913-   ), Ambassador to Canada from the People's Republic of China, made representative to the United Nations Security Council in 1971

HENRY ALFRED KISSINGER (1923-   ), Special Assistant for National Security Affairs to President Richard M. Nixon

RICHARD MILHOUS NIXON (1913-   ), thirty-seventh President of the United States, 1969-1974

Summary of Event

The historic vote that admitted the People's Republic of China into the United Nations on the night of October 25, 1971, resulted in an unprecedented emotional approval by that organization's General Assembly. China's admission, however, also represented the failure of the twenty-two year effort led by the United States to keep China out of the world body. The story of China's admission began on November 18, 1949, when the Foreign Minister of the newly created People's Republic of China sent a message to the President of the General Assembly questioning the legal authority of the Chinese Na-tionalist delegation to represent all the Chinese people in the United Nations. The Soviet representative in the United Nations Security Council supported China's claim on December 29, 1949, but nothing was done to unseat the Nationalists.

The matter was considered by the Security Council once again in 1950; but the issue was then transferred to the General Assembly. The "Chinese participation question" was brought up annually in proposals to include it on the agenda, and it was consistently rejected under this strategy during the years 1951-1960, considered a "moratorium period." The United

States had a "mechanical majority" in this decade which gradually declined, however, as new independent nations, professing a "nonaligned policy," entered the United Nations.

Beginning in 1961, the strategy changed, and the China question confronted United Nations members directly. Many nations now saw increasing justification for granting representation to the mainland Chinese. It was reasoned that "China" should be represented by a government which controlled the vast land mass on the mainland to assure that the UN would fulfill its Charter obligations; that it was unrealistic to ignore one-fourth of the world's population; that all nations should be represented in the United Nations; that broader participation was necessary if the United Nations was to perform effectively; that problems of world peace and security could not realistically be solved without Chinese Communist participation; and that China would be less belligerent and more responsive to world opinion as a member of the United Nations than as an outcast.

Members sympathetic to the American position and the Republic of China on Taiwan, however, held contrary views and continued to oppose the Chinese Communist government's admission. They argued that the Communist government did not truly represent the will of the Chinese people; that it was not necessary for the Chinese Communists to be in the United Nations because negotiations have taken place with them elsewhere; that only "peace-loving" nations could be expected to fulfill obligations of the United Nations

Charter; that irresponsible nations such as Communist China would be a disruptive force in the UN; that to replace the Nationalists with the Communists would give the latter a "hunting license" to conquer Taiwan; and finally, that an aggressive Chinese Communist government in the United Nations would destroy it.

In order to stem the tide of increasing support for the Communist People's Republic of China, the United States submitted a Five-Power Draft Resolution to the General Assembly in 1961 to consider Chinese "representation" to be an "important question." Passage of this resolution meant that the admission of the People's Republic would have to be approved by a two-thirds majority of the General Assembly. The vote favored the American position: sixty-one yes, thirty-four no, and nine abstentions. The Soviets submitted their own proposal both to seat the Communist government and simultaneously to oust the Nationalists. By contrast, that vote was thirty-seven yes, forty-eight no, and nineteen abstentions. From 1961 to 1965, however, a trend toward increasing support for the People's Republic of China was established. By 1965, the vote on the Soviet resolution appeared to reverse the trend, with forty-seven yes, forty-seven no, and twenty-three abstentions. China's temporary setback was probably due to several causes, including turmoil inside China and moves in the United Nations itself to explore alternative approaches to admission. American opinion regarding China had also become less hostile.

By 1970, an Albanian resolution to seat the People's Republic in place of the Chinese Nationalist delegation had received a majority vote: fifty-one yes, forty-nine no, and twenty-five abstained; yet it remained short of the two-thirds majority required. During the following year, a shift in American policy towards the People's Republic of China further encouraged the mounting support for admission: the United States relaxed rules forbidding American travel and trade with China, and China invited a United States ping-pong team to make a goodwill tour in April 1971. By June, Presidential Special Assistant, Henry Kissinger, had made a secret trip to China to confer with Premier Chou En-lai, and the next month, the United States and China announced that President Richard M. Nixon would visit Peking. These rapid developments culminated in an August, 1971 announcement that the United States would no longer oppose seating the People's Republic of China in the United Nations but maintained its opposition to expelling the Chinese Nationalists.

The scene was now set for China's admission. The autumn debate centered on an Albanian-led resolution both to seat the People's Republic of China and to expel the Nationalists. Sponsoring delegates agreed to call for a vote immediately following the final speech on the night of October 25, 1971. The first vote to be taken was on the American parliamentary point: whether the China representation issue was an "important question." The roll-call vote, completed at 9:47 P.M. resulted in a dramatic defeat for the United States: fifty-five yes, fifty-nine no, and fifteen abstentions. It was the first time in eleven years that the United States had lost this crucial vote, meaning that only a simple majority was now required to determine China's admission and the expulsion of the Nationalist government on Taiwan.

When the jubilant ovation and dancing in the aisle by the Tanzanian delegation had subsided, the Albanian resolution was voted on and easily passed: seventy-six yes, thirty-five no, and seventeen abstentions. Henry Kissinger was still in Peking when news of the United Nations decision reached China's capital. Chou En-lai was clearly pleased with the news, but President Chiang Kai-shek on Taiwan was despondent and declared his continued intention to reconquer the Chinese mainland.

The People's Republic of China sent its representative, Deputy Foreign Minister Ch'iao Kuan-hua, to present his credentials to the United Nations on November 14, 1971; the following day, he took his seat in the UN General Assembly. Huang Hua, China's Ambassador to Canada, was made representative to the UN Security Council.

Pertinent Literature

Weng, Byron S. *Peking's UN Policy: Continuity and Change*. New York: Frederick A. Praeger, 1972.

Published just after the People's   Republic of China entered the United

Nations in 1971, Byron S. J. Weng's study is the most thorough analysis of China's United Nations policy development available. The book is a systematic study of China's attitudes and approaches toward the United Nations throughout the twenty-two year period from China's "liberation" of the mainland in 1949 to United Nations admission in 1971. Until this study was published, most writers had viewed the subject of China and the UN from the standpoint of the United Nations or the United States, not Communist China.

The author contends that China's policy toward the United Nations changed periodically but that the People's Republic always had a UN policy before admission. While China was concerned that United Nations membership would become a politically and militarily restrictive force because of the arms control movement, the Communists also realized that they might have more to gain economically from UN aid or expanded trade because of an end of the American embargo. Moreover, China would regain the world prestige which she had lost when branded an aggressor by the Security Council during the Korean War. The advantages of UN admission were clearly seen by China.

The problem that caused a twenty-two-year delay in China's admission to the United Nations was continuation of the Nationalist government on Taiwan. Had the Communists captured Taiwan, Weng believes, China would have been admitted early. After June, 1950, the United States entered the Korean War and prevented the Chinese Communist government from seizing Taiwan, and the People's Republic made Taiwan's removal from the United Nations a condition of its membership. The United Nations membership, however, wanted a two-China's solution, and this issue alone was a major obstacle to China's admission.

In reviewing the period 1949-1971, Weng describes several changes in China's approach and attitude toward the United Nations. He perceptively observes that changes which took place in China's behavior reflected changes in the UN itself as perceived by Chinese leaders. The first major change in China's approach toward the United Nations after June, 1950, was a switch from a defensive to an offensive role. China, for example, denounced the United Nations for coming under American dominance and declared that UN decisions without the People's Republic were illegal. China believed that international questions could not be solved without her involvement, blatantly condemned the American "armed invasion of Taiwan," and wanted the United Nations to do something about it.

In the years 1954-1957, Weng states that China adopted a long-term strategy that was more sophisticated than that used in earlier years. An effort now was made to bring about a change in the UN membership and wait for the United Nations to invite China in. Consequently, China began both to support and to be supported by Third World nations. China then entered a new stage of "protracted struggle" in its domestic and international programs (1958-1961), but this struggle only resulted in international economic disaster and external setbacks.

While China sought to resurrect herself from these problems during the years 1962-1965, she became less enamored with the United Nations. Unable to solve the Taiwan issue and concerned about Big Power domination of the United Nations, China began to seek a substitute and considered a rival "revolutionary UN" of Third World countries. By 1965, China became openly hostile to the United Nations and made strong demands to expel the Chinese Nationalists, admit the People's Republic in its place, reorganize the United Nations to decrease American influence, and admit "independent states" (Communist portions of divided nations).

During the Cultural Revolution period, 1966-1969, China was initially hostile and offensive but gradually returned to a conciliatory policy. Weng believes that at some time between April, 1969, and August, 1970, a high-level policy decision was made for "revolutionary pragmatism" which stressed coexistence and negotiation. By the fall of 1970, China began a global campaign to enter the United Nations within a year; it was in this period that China assumed a less belligerent stance in dealing with both the Soviet Union and the United States.

Finally, Weng sees the twenty-two-year period before 1971 as an era in which China's overall policy toward the United Nations was dominated by three factors: the People's Republic declared that it had a legal claim as the sole representative government of all China, including Taiwan, to be given a seat in the UN; China's political attitude toward the UN was highly expedient, viewing it variously in terms of its value to China; and China's ideological and psychological approach to the UN were reflected in the thoughts of Mao Tse-tung as long as he continued to live. Weng's theme of continuity and change, moreover, is clearly supported by his narrative and analysis.

Chen, Lung-chu and Harold D. Laswell. *Formosa, China, and the United Nations: Formosa in the World Community*. New York: St. Martin's Press, 1967.

This study considers the international debate over the admission of the People's Republic of China into the United Nations and focuses special attention on Formosa (Taiwan). In their analysis, Chen and Laswell are concerned less with a narrative of events than with an examination of the decision process in government and society. At the time the book was published (1967), they anticipated that the United Nations would soon begin a new drive to admit the Chinese Communist government despite continued opposition from the United States.

The authors clearly consider the status of Formosa and the legitimacy of the Nationalist government on the island as major problems in obtaining United Nations representation for the mainland Chinese. Their solution to the dilemma was to propose a "one China, one Formosa" formula. By this arrangement, the Chinese Communist government would occupy

China's seats in the General Assembly and the Security Council instead of the Nationalist government. Formosa, they proposed, would be admitted to the United Nations after attaining independence through self-determination; a plebiscite would be required to accomplish this end. The authors counted on both governments being willing to accept each other's right to exist; the Nationalists, in particular, would resist breaking their power monopoly on Formosa.

In their support of the "one China, one Formosa" solution, Chen and Laswell discredit the "two Chinas" proposal which had been popular among advocates of Communist China's admission to the United Nations. The latter concept would leave the legal status of Formosa undetermined and subject to dispute over which of the Chinas would be eligible to occupy the "China seat" in the Security Council. The authors believe that Formosa should be separated from the mainland both in name and in fact. Once an independent Formosa had been established, they anticipated that the new state would be admitted as a new member to the United Nations. This general process of change, involving a transition of Formosa to an independent status followed by the construction of a viable Formosan nation, is discussed by the authors in detail.

The authors' optimism that the Communist government of China would soon be admitted to the United Nations (in 1967) was based on a gradual diminution of the factors that were responsible for keeping her out. The overwhelming influence of the United States on other United Nations members was considered paramount (especially up to 1960) in preventing a change in UN representation. Earlier decisive votes were also conditioned by the UN condemnation of Communist China's "aggression in Korea," and UN members' concern about China's durability. By the late 1960's, however, the importance of these factors decreased significantly.

Chen and Laswell regard seating the Chinese Communist government in the United Nations as very important to the international scene. The need to control nuclear weapons required the presence of Communist China in the United Nations. Excluded from membership, China could be expected to reject international agreements affecting her welfare; as a member of the UN, it would hopefully be easier to persuade her to comply with the United Nations Charter and to gain support from other nations to control nuclear arms. The authors further point out that the founders of the United Nations had representation of the mainland Chinese, not of Taiwan, in mind when establishing Big Power representation. Since the major powers are also nuclear powers, it becomes even more imperative that the Chinese Communist government be included.

In addition to the United Nations issue, the authors also discuss what they envision should take place after Nationalist rule is terminated and Formosa becomes independent. They see a new viable nation growing on Formosa which could actively contribute to the development of the Pacific community of nations. As Formosa's new status became stabilized and accepted, the authors believed that the drive to incorporate Formosa into the People's Republic of China would fade away.

Although actual events surrounding Communist China's admission to the United Nations have not materialized in the manner that the authors recommend, their study represents a thorough and incisive analysis of China and its effort to enter the United Nations; their emphasis on Formosa and a "one China, one Formosa" formula was rational but not in accord with the prevailing sentiments of the nations that comprised the United Nations by 1971. — *L.H.D.G.*

Additional Recommended Reading

Appleton, Sheldon. *The Eternal Triangle? Communist China, the United States and the United Nations*. East Lansing: Michigan State University Press, 1961. A historical and an analytical study of United States policy concerning Communist China's representation in the United Nations made after eleven years of UN Security Council discussion.

Brook, David. *The U.N. and the China Dilemma*. New York: Vantage Press, 1956. A dispassionate review of the salient factors in China's representation in the United Nations, concluding that a committee of jurists should decide such questions.

Brown, Benjamin H. and Fred Greene. *Chinese Representation: A Case Study in United Nations Political Affairs*. New York: Woodrow Wilson Foundation, 1955. Contains two brief accounts of the early relations of the People's Republic of China and the United Nations (1949-1954), emphasizing the Korean conflict (1950-1953) and subsequent negotiations.

Grew, Joseph Clark. *Invasion Alert! The Red China Drive for a UN Seat*. Baltimore, Md.: Maran Publishers, 1956. A strong plea explaining the author's reasons why the People's Republic of China should not be admitted into the United Nations.

Kim, Samuel S. *China, the United Nations, and World Order*. Princeton, N.J.: Princeton University Press, 1979. A study of Chinese global politics and how they have been expressed through China's activities in the United Nations.

Poole, Peter A. *China Enters the United Nations: A New Era Begins for the World Organization*. New York: Franklin Watts, 1974. An excellent brief review of events leading up to the admission of the People's Republic of China to the United Nations, including a historical account of China's relations with the United Nations and the United States since World War II, and concluding that China has assumed a serious and moderate role in the UN enhancing the prospects for peace.

"BLOODY SUNDAY" IN ULSTER

Type of event: Sociological: Irish rally that leads to a violent confrontation with British troops
Time: January 30, 1972
Locale: Ulster, Northern Ireland

Principal personages:

BRIAN FAULKNER (1921-   ), Prime Minister of Northern Ireland, 1970-1972

BERNADETTE DEVLIN (1947-   ), a student leader, 1967-1969; and a member of Parliament, 1969-1974

EDWARD HEATH (1916-   ), Prime Minister of Great Britain, 1970-1974

WILLIAM CRAIG (1924-   ), leader of the Vanguard Unionist Party in Northern Ireland

WILLIAM WHITELAW (1918-   ), Secretary of State for Northern Ireland following the dissolution of the Northern Ireland Parliament, 1972-1973

REVEREND IAN PAISLEY (1926-   ), leader of the Democratic Unionist Party in Northern Ireland

Summary of Event

On January 30, 1972, a protest rally organized by the Northern Ireland Civil Rights Association (NICRA) in Londonderry, Northern Ireland, to demand an end to the internment without trial of suspected terrorists resulted in a clash with British troops. Thirteen of the protestors, all Catholics, died, and twelve other persons were wounded. The event, which quickly became known as "Bloody Sunday," led to claims that the British had fired without provocation, a charge rejected by the official British investigation called the Widgery Report though confirmed by various eyewitnesses.

Shocking as the deaths were to the Irish and British people, they were only part of a long, complex, and continuing struggle in Northern Ireland, which may be said to have begun anew with the Civil Rights movement of 1967-1968, but which lays deep in the history of the "damnable question" of Anglo-Irish relations over many generations.

Northern Ireland came into existence on December 6, 1921, as a result of the Anglo-Irish Treaty, a pragmatic compromise negotiated by Prime Minister Lloyd George in the wake of the Easter Rising of 1916; the electoral victory of the Sinn Fein over the Parliamentary Party in the elections of 1918; and the establishment by the Sinn Fein of an independent Irish Parliament in 1919. The political division of Ireland corresponded neither to historical reality (the old Province of Ulster) nor to religious differences, but rather represented the maximum area over which those elements favorable to

Britain held political control. The six northern counties of Ireland were granted limited local autonomy under the North Ireland Parliament meeting at Stormont.

By the middle of the twentieth century, the area contained within the borders of Northern Ireland held a Protestant population of about a million and a Catholic population of about half a million. The religious division was accentuated by an economic division, for while two distinct "classes" cannot be said to exist in the society, there was a clear tendency for Protestants to be wealthier and more politically powerful, and for Catholics to be poorer and politically weak. The divisions were further marked by the inclination of Protestants to favor continued British rule, and of many Catholics, on the other hand, to favor union with the Republic of Ireland.

The chain of events leading to the confrontation of 1972 began with the emergence of the Civil Rights movement as early as 1964. This movement took as its model the civil rights marches of the American South, and endorsed the nonviolent tactics of Mohandas K. Gandhi and the Reverend Martin Luther King, Jr. During the late 1960's, Bernadette Devlin, a leader of the Student People's Democracy group, became one of the most vocal critics of British rule in Northern Ireland. In 1968, the Northern Ireland Civil Rights Association, espousing a nonsectarian unity of disadvantaged Protestants and Catholics, organized a series of marches, the first of which took place at Dungannon without incident. Then in October, 1969, the first violent clash between marchers, police, and militant Protestant groups occurred in Londonderry. Confrontations became increasingly frequent in late 1968 and into 1969. In August, 1969, British troops assumed riot duty for the first time. In December, 1969, the Irish Republican Army, the traditional though now illegal armed force favoring union of all Ireland, split into "official" and "provisional" factions over the question of tactics. The "officials" supported the nonviolent methods of NICRA and indeed provided marshals and other assistance during the marches. The "provisionals" advocated more violent means and ultimately took the initiative from all other groups with an argument that appealed to the Catholics, who formed the bulk of the ostensibly nonsectarian Civil Rights movement. They argued that only violent resistance could protect the Catholic minority from the Protestant-leaning "B Special" police militia, and later, as they began to take form, from the various Protestant paramilitary groups.

Faced with escalating violence, the Northern Ireland Parliament introduced the internment without trial of suspected terrorists in August, 1971. This measure, permitted under the Special Powers Act of 1922, was declared necessary by Prime Minister Brian Faulkner to bring the increasingly militant I.R.A. under control. The internments elicited responses from both foreign and domestic critics, and soon observers alleged that the internees were being kept under brutal conditions. Those charges provided the immediate occasion for the demonstration of January 30, 1972.

At mid-afternoon of that day, six thousand demonstrators marched from Bishop's Fields, their point of assembly, toward the Bogside district of Londonderry. To avoid an impending confrontation, the march was diverted from its original course toward the Guildhall, and redirected toward an alternate rally site at Free Derry Corner. One of the highlights of the rally was to have been a speech by Bernadette Devlin, who, since 1969, had held a seat in Parliament. At about 3:30 P.M., however, a group of Derry youths broke away from the main column and confronted the three army barricades which had been erected to contain the march. British paratroopers were pelted with stones and bottles, and they responded with tear gas and fire hoses. Shortly thereafter at least one shot was fired in the direction of the troops. The paratroopers then crossed the barricades, in what had been intended as a move to arrest demonstrators, and began firing their weapons into the crowd.

The thirteen deaths on Bloody Sunday brought shock and rage to the Irish, many of whom saw the British cast in a role which they had played so often in Irish history, that of a repressive force against the Irish people. The Irish ambassador was withdrawn from London; and the British Embassy in Dublin was firebombed.

The I.R.A. increased its activities, and indeed may have overreached itself in the next several months, for parallel with the rage against Britain came another current, one of exhaustion and rejection of violence as a political tactic. The I.R.A. declared a three-day truce in March, but later resumed its activities.

On March 24, 1972, British Prime Minister Edward Heath announced plans for a solution of the problems of Northern Ireland which included the resignation of Prime Minister Faulkner and the effective dissolution of the Stormont government. William Whitelaw was appointed Secretary of State for Northern Ireland. The dissolution was approved by the Catholic community, which had little love for the Protestant-dominated Stormont, but it was ill-received by such Protestant leaders as William Craig of the Vanguard Unionist Party, who desired independence for Northern Ireland. Another group of Protestants, of which the Reverend Ian Paisley was the spokesman, received the news of direct rule by England with moderate satisfaction, seeing in it a step toward full union with Britain and protection against "popery." However, a satisfactory solution to the political and social problems of Northern Ireland has not yet been achieved.

Pertinent Literature

O'Brien, Conor Cruise. *The States of Ireland*. New York: Pantheon Books, 1972.

"This is not a book about Ireland," Conor Cruise O'Brien states in the prologue. Instead, it is a book about the relations between Protestants and Catholics on that island, a relation which infuses Irish society but which, he cautions, should not be made to seem the whole of Irish life. The author is a Catholic with strong ties to the Protestant community, a member of the Republic of Ireland Dail (Assembly) who has met often with Irish, English, and American leaders. An eyewitness to many of the troubles of Northern Ireland both from the viewpoint of the conference table and that of the streets, O'Brien is well equipped to write a fascinating autobiography, a political treatise, or a history of contemporary Ireland. He has done all three in a book that is without doubt the best introduction to the Ireland of the late 1960's and early 1970's available to the general reader.

While he is a Catholic, O'Brien is also a democratic socialist; and for that reason he differs from his more extreme Catholic contemporaries on several points. He does not advocate a forced union of all Ireland if it is achieved against the will of the Protestant community, and he grants the Protestants the right to live in Northern Ireland on the basis of equality with the native Catholic population. He seeks to defuse the loaded question of religion by advocating a nonsectarian solution within the context of peaceful Irish constitutionalism.

Written between 1969 and 1972, *The States of Ireland* reflects O'Brien's increasing concern that a sectarian civil war was impending in Ireland; it was intended to show that renewed cooperation between the two communities was still possible. For all his objectivity in the treatment of events, the author writes with a purpose, and that purpose must be kept in mind while reading the book.

O'Brien divides the work into three parts. He first presents a summary of Anglo-Irish relations from the time of Parnell to the Easter Rising of 1916, with frequent backward glances into the earlier past as far as the colonization movement of the sixteenth century. Throughout this section, he emphasizes the complexity of Anglo-Irish and Protestant-Catholic relations, taking care to question all easy generalizations about Irish history. Parnell, he reminds his readers, was both a powerful advocate of Home Rule and a Protestant; and a significant number of Irish Protestants agreed with him. In discussing the Gaelic literary revival of the late nineteenth and early twentieth centuries, he attacks the notion of an Irish "race" as well as an unduly stereotypical view of the colonists and those colonized in Ireland. Rather, he finds—referring to J. M. Synge's *Playboy of the Western World*—six Irish subgroups: West country peasants, anglicized peasantry, an anglicized middle- and lower-class urban group, a Protestant settler group which rejects Unionism, settlers who defend the Union, and the English themselves. Relations among these groups are not to be reduced to a mere Protestant-Catholic dichotomy. Finally, taking a passage from Machiavelli as his theme, he notes that the Irish, though scattered widely, even across the Atlantic, were never totally defeated. A condition of incomplete colonization has characterized Ireland since the sixteenth century.

O'Brien next discusses the development of the two states of post-Home Rule Ireland, finding in the South an ostensibly secular polity but one in which Protestants may participate only on terms of good behavior, and in Northern Ireland a movement toward an "institutionalized caste system" from 1921 to 1969. As he enters the twentieth century, he mixes his historical narrative with recollections of personal experience: from his youth in the lovely political and social atmosphere of the Sheehy and Skeffington households of Dublin, to his education in a Protestant secondary school and at Trinity College, to his marriage into a Belfast Presbyterian family.

In the third section, he describes the progress of the Civil Rights movement and its eventual, although to O'Brien not inevitable, disintegration into sectarian violence. His partisanship as a member of the Irish Labour Party emerges in some of his statements, as when he attacks John Lynch, the Republican Taoiseach (Prime Minister), for his manipulation of Catholic anti-Communist sentiment in the election of 1969, and for his alleged aid to the I.R.A. O'Brien also assails such supposed "non-sectarians" as Bernadette Devlin and the members of the "official" I.R.A. for their tendency to make "the people" synonymous with "the Catholic people." Once again, his point is clear: violence is the result of increased religious and caste identification, and can only be avoided as those sentiments decrease. He closes with an appeal for nonviolence in the face of what he fears is an impending civil war.

Devlin, Bernadette. *The Price of My Soul.* New York: Alfred A. Knopf, 1969.

Bernadette Devlin is without doubt the most flamboyant personality to emerge from the troubles in Northern Ireland in the mid-twentieth century. Beginning with her days as a student revolutionary, she attempts in this autobiography to explain how the "complex of economic, social, and political problems of Northern Ireland threw up the phenomenon of Bernadette Devlin," as well as to trace the development of the Civil Rights movement from 1967 to 1969.

There are many parallels between Devlin's book and O'Brien's. Both are personal records of political actors which blend experiences with insights and offer proposed solutions to the Irish conflict. The two authors are so dissimilar in their lives and in the solutions they propose that the two books complement each other.

O'Brien is a constitutionalist, an advocate of gradual and peaceful political change. Devlin, though elected to the Westminster Parliament in 1969, declares that the "Parliamentary system has broken down." O'Brien roots his narrative in a historical interpretation and theoretical analysis of the situation in Northern Ireland; Devlin admits that she "gets lost" in theoretical discussion, and is consciously ahistorical in her approach.

While O'Brien grew up in an upper-middle-class Dublin home, Devlin began her life among the Catholic poor of Cookston where her grandfather was a roadsweeper and her father a carpenter. In Devlin's youth, Cookston, with its inner city dominated by the Protestant community and its outer sections by Catholics, was a microcosm of the religious division of Northern Irish society, and she retains memories of the tension between the two groups. "While some of my friends' daddies were disappearing . . . to lie low," she writes, "other people's daddies were setting out armed after them."

While she was a student at Queens University in Belfast from 1965 to 1969, her mother died, and Bernadette became head of her family. At the university she became one of the leaders of the People's Democracy group, a student organization loosely connected with the Civil Rights Association. She tells of her struggle in those student years to hold her family together, and of her political and intellectual progress through the Civil Rights movement. She describes her first protest march at Dungannon in August, 1968, as a carnivalesque affair, a sort of holiday for marchers overwhelmed by the novelty of the event.

Then at Londonderry in October, 1968, she found the mood changed, and she met the hard reality of "men who had no work." This perception led her increasingly toward a Marxist orientation. She saw the Irish conflict as a class struggle between the wealthy and the disadvantaged rather than between Protestants and Catholics. She now regarded the religious question as only a "medieval" attitude that would be left behind as "forward looking people" succeeded in educating their compatriots in the class struggle. However, as Devlin moved toward this position, many of her associates moved toward violence.

The People's Democracy group, seeking to expand its base, developed closer ties with NICRA in 1969 and created local headquarters throughout the six provinces. The group also became involved in electoral politics. Increasing decentralization, combined with the purely academic pressure of examinations and the end of the school term, however, forced the dissolution of People's Democracy as an active political force—but not before Devlin herself had gained election to the British Parliament, where she became its youngest member.

At the close of her narrative in late 1969, Devlin is left in a contradictory position. Although a Member of Parliament, she rejects parliamentary methods; an advocate of nonviolence, she has assisted in the making of petrol bombs for the "defense" of Londonderry against British troops in the summer of 1969. She takes pride in a remark made by a British taxi driver as he drove her to the House of Commons for her debut. She was, he said, one of the "two honest people" ever to enter that body; the other was Guy Fawkes.

Devlin's book is a valuable historical document, capturing the complex amalgam of civil rights idealism, international student Marxism, religious particularism, and economic and social turmoil that so troubled Northern Ireland in the mid-twentieth century. — *J.W.P.*

Additional Recommended Reading

MacEoin, Gary. *Northern Ireland: Captive of History*. New York: Holt, Rinehart and

Winston, 1974. Combines a perceptive historical study with a discussion of the period 1968-1972.

Beckett, James C. *The Making of Modern Ireland, 1603-1923*. New York: Alfred A. Knopf, 1966. A historical study of Ireland from the seventeenth to the twentieth century.

Budge, Jan and Cornelius O'Leary. *Belfast: Approach to Crisis*. London: Macmillan and Company, 1973. Attempts to analyze the social tension in Belfast on the basis of its history, recent political and economic trends, and the use of political surveys of the authors' own devising.

Hastings, Max. *Barricades in Belfast: The Fight for Civil Rights in Northern Ireland*. New York: Taplinger Publishing Company, 1970. An account of the Civil Rights movement from 1968 to 1970 by a reporter for the *London Evening Standard*.

Lyons, F. S. *Ireland Since the Famine*. London: Weidenfeld and Nicolson, 1971. A solid synthetic work on the history of Ireland in the last 120 years, particularly useful for the twentieth century and the postwar period.

Magee, John. *Northern Ireland: Crisis and Conflict*. Boston: Routledge and Kegan Paul, 1974. A collection of documents illustrating the major problems of post-Home Rule Northern Ireland.

O'Neil, Terence. *Ulster at the Crossroads*. London: Faber and Faber, 1969. An interpretation by its then Prime Minister of the political situation in Northern Ireland during the civil rights movement.

Van Voris, William H. *Violence in Ulster: An Oral Documentary*. Amherst: University of Massachusetts Press, 1975. A collection of taped interviews with a wide variety of participants in the crisis in Northern Ireland from 1972 to 1974.

RAPPROCHEMENT WITH THE PEOPLE'S REPUBLIC OF CHINA

Type of event: Diplomatic: realignment of two world powers
Time: February 21, 1972
Locale: Peking, China

Principal personages:
RICHARD MILHOUS NIXON (1913-   ), thirty-seventh President of the United States, 1969-1974
MAO TSE-TUNG (1893-1976), Chairman of the Chinese Communist Party and effective ruler of China, 1949-1976
HENRY ALFRED KISSINGER (1923-   ), Special Assistant for National Security Affairs to President Nixon, 1969-1973; United States Secretary of State, 1973-1977
CHOU EN-LAI (1898-1976), Mao Tse-tung's lieutenant and Premier of China, 1949-1976

Summary of Event

In the eyes of the world, the harmony that emerged between the People's Republic of China and the United States in 1972 came with stunning swiftness. For the past generation the two countries had been the deadliest of enemies: Americans had regarded Chinese Communism as even more hateful than Russian and maintained an almost belligerent defense of Taiwan; mainland China was filled with attacks against the "paper tiger" of American capitalism. In less than a year all of this changed—or even reversed course. An American table tennis team touring Japan received and accepted an invitation to visit the People's Republic of China in April, 1971. Three months later Henry Kissinger was in Peking, acting as a special emissary from the President and arranging for United States leaders to make a state visit to China. And in February, 1972, the actual visit occurred in a welcome, almost effusive atmosphere. Ten months was very little time for so dramatic a realignment of national friendships, but its way had been prepared by years of developments.

Rapprochement between China and America followed a slow change in the logic of world affairs. In the early 1960's, the setting of foreign policies was established and straightforward. The United States and the Soviet Union represented two opposite societies and dominated the rest of the world through overwhelming military and economic strength. World maps showed a wide swath of red stretching from central Europe to Southeast Asia: the Communist "monolith," under the leadership of Russia. Western Europe, North America, and Japan were closely coordinated in their opposition to further Communist gains, and the poor nations of the Southern Hemisphere were still largely subservient to Western guidance. Almost all important diplomacy was geared to the Cold War struggle between these two spheres of power.

Over the decade which followed, the two opposing sides each loosened somewhat, and the unquestioned power of their leaders gradually slipped. As the free countries of Europe's Common Market recovered and identified their interests more closely, the economic and political leadership of the United States declined noticeably. Japan developed from a very junior partner of America to being a rival economic power. American interventions in Cuba, in the Dominican Republic, and above all in Vietnam caused widespread resentment against such free use of military might, and encouraged the appearance of Third World nations that opposed the influence of American capitalism. By 1970 the United States had less influence in the world than at any time since World War II.

Soviet influence had declined even further. The postwar spread of Communism had come to an end by the mid-1950's. Underdeveloped countries tended to be as wary of Russia as they were of America, and the ruthless Soviet suppression of Czechoslovakia in 1968 testified to the restiveness of the Communist satellites in Eastern Europe. Finally, there was the problem of China. As it had prospered and stabilized after long decades of revolution, the People's Republic showed signs of marking its own course. Soviet aid and technology were welcomed, but party chairman Mao Tse-tung and Premier Chou En-lai insisted on freedom from Russian influence. Chinese Communism became very different from that prevailing in the U.S.S.R.; there was a greater emphasis on the social and mental life of the people, and less concern with immediate industrial growth. Russian attempts to apply pressure only estranged the two countries; a border dispute was revived, and each nation began to view the other as a dangerous ideological opponent.

By 1966 or 1967, these changes were pushing China and America toward mutual recognition. The People's Republic was dangerously isolated; the economic trade and diplomatic prestige afforded by closer relations with the United States were clearly needed. The United States, for its part, could use China as a counterweight against Russia, as a buttress to the alliance with Japan (which sought trade with China), and as a bolster to its darkened image as a friend of the Third World. Richard M. Nixon, writing in the prestigious journal *Foreign Affairs* in October, 1967, admitted as much: the fight against Communism, he argued, must accommodate itself to a more realistic approach. But other problems hindered any thawing of relations. The Vietnam War was raging, and both China and the United States feared clashes between their troops. Ideological anger in the two countries was still very great, and a liberal President such as Lyndon Johnson would be especially susceptible to charges of pro-Communism if he risked an approach to the People's Republic. And at the same time, the Chinese were passing through the upheaval of the Cultural Revolution, turning the nation inward and very much away from cooperation with capitalist nations.

Within a few years, all of these barriers had disappeared. President Nixon's formidable reputation as an anti-Communist could survive *détente*. Within a few months of taking office, he sent out feelers to China and received encouraging responses. The Cultural Revolution wound down in 1969, and a sobered Peking sought to solidify its international position. By 1971, when a gradually withdrawing United States did not support a South Vietnamese invasion of Laos, the Chinese were satisfied that they had nothing to fear from America. Invitations soon followed.

Both the Nixon entourage and their Chinese hosts set modest goals for the February visit, and these were easily achieved. The two countries agreed to extend diplomatic, economic, and cultural ties, and arranged for further visits of American leaders to China. More important than specific exchanges, however, were the symbolic acts of friendship: the handshakes, discussions, toasts, and the famous photograph of Mao and Nixon chatting together. The visit was surrounded with a certain aura of wonder, as both sides found they could like those who had so recently been deadly enemies. American journalists and diplomats expressed surprise at the serene order of Chinese society; the Chinese, for their part, were eager to share ideas with the Americans. Both sides were pleased that friendship came so easily.

Subsequent years witnessed a growth and widening of American-Chinese cooperation, although there were no major diplomatic achievements. The chief obstacle to full relations was the existence of Nationalist China, and on this issue the two nations agreed to disagree. China sent gymnasts, students, scientists, and ping-pong players to the United States both to perform and observe. Thousands of Americans went to China and came away impressed. Boeing negotiated the sale of several jets to the People's Republic, and the United States government arranged for large shipments of wheat and corn. Ideological tensions remained and showed no sign of going away, but this only made the achievement and implications of Sino-American *détente* all the more impressive. After twenty-five years of Cold War, the world seemed to be moving away from the "war of ideas."

Pertinent Literature

Barnett, A. Doak. "The Changing Strategic Balance in Asia," in *Sino-American Détente and Its Policy Implications*. Edited by Gene T. Hsiao. New York: Frederick A. Praeger, 1974, pp. 22-45.

Although an observer of the past can find assorted motives leading up to a given historical decision, it is a more difficult matter to understand the way that decision was conceived at the time. The conceptions of Henry Kissinger, who prominently assisted President Nixon in bringing about *détente* with China, may be easier to decipher than most. Steeped in the traditions of "academic" international relations, Kissinger had often advocated a shift in the structure of world affairs from "bipolarity" to "multipolarity." A. D. Barnett has written on the implications of this view.

The theory of bipolarity is an adaptation of earlier conceptions of a balance of power to the postwar world. At the turn of the century, the important diplomatic struggles were between five or six Great Powers, all roughly comparable in strength, who maneuvered for influence through shifting alliances. In the aftermath of World War II, the number of Great Powers fell to two—the United States and the U.S.S.R. Since neither nation was willing to accept the losses involved in directly attacking the other, balance and maneuvering was sought through two rival spheres of influence, thus creating a bipolar system. Such a system had its advantages: because of the "balance of terror" imposed by the threat of nuclear war, each side was protected from major attack by the other. In spite of (and because of) fears of a disastrous World War III, no such war came about. But bipolarity had serious disadvantages as well. The slightest change in the *status quo* could be interpreted as a crucial change in the delicate two-way balance. As a result, regional wars were escalated into international struggles for power in Korea, Cuba, and the Mideast. And the danger that tension could spill over into all-out war was always there.

This line of theoretical argument suggested that multipolarity could be more stable. With more participants, conflict might increase; but a concensus on cooperation would insure that

these conflicts would be settled amiably. The Far East, as Barnett points out, offers a setting in which these ideas can be examined. In the 1950's, bipolarity was ascendant: Japan and Southeast Asia were closely bound to the United States through trade and treaties of mutual defense, while even closer bonds unified the Communist countries of Asia to the Soviet Union. Interchange between the two spheres was limited, and conflicts of large proportions arose over such irrelevant matters as possession of the tiny island of Quemoy, off the Chinese coast.

A generation later, bipolarity had largely crumbled. The Communist monolith was decisively fragmented between China and the Soviet Union, and even a smaller country—North Vietnam—set a clearly independent course. Japan, though still militarily dependent on America, was an important rival economically, and other Asian nations had loosened their ties with the West. The emergence of a multipolar system was hindered by one crucial obstacle—American refusal to acknowledge the existence of the People's Republic. Without this recognition, China was dangerously isolated. The problems of a looser international system (with increased opportunity for conflict) were present without the commensurate benefits of a new balance.

According to Barnett, Sino-American *détente* ushered in a period of multipolar harmony. The structure of Asian power revolved around four great nations: the United States, Russia, China, and Japan. Each country had unique interests and capabilities which favored cooperation. Japan was almost defenseless in military terms and dependent on imports; hence, it desired peace and expanded trade in all events. Through immense economic strength it could sway events toward its own preferences. China had an impressive army and nuclear weapons, but was still struggling to develop and stabilize its own society. Its leadership in the Third World was largely dependent on hostility toward imperialism, so China was hardly likely to become openly imperialistic itself. The Soviet Union and the United States, slowly being upstaged by newer powers, sought to maintain their influence and interests in Asia through persuasion and aid rather than force. Each nation was interested not only in peace, but also in maintaining close relations with the other major powers.

Barnett sees one major threat to this multipolar balance for peace: division between the United States and Japan. The two nations sell similar products to the same countries, and competitive rivalry is inevitable. Moreover, the massive trade between the two is tilting increasingly in favor of Japan, leaving the United

States with mounting deficits in its balance of payments. As these problems increase, it becomes more and more tempting for American leaders to ease the military commitment to Japan, giving that country responsibility for its own defense (and probably slower economic growth) while slowing the flow of dollars to the East. Such a change, Barnett warns, might fatally disrupt the Asian balance. A Japan cast free of American ideology and armaments might revive the goals it sought in World War II— a broad Pacific empire based on Tokyo. Outright war would be unlikely, but as Japanese influence shifted from economic to political matters in small Asian countries, opportunities for conflict would multiply. Renewed rivalry between China and Japan could lead to a free-for-all in Southern Asia. All of this seems very plausible; Barnett and the theory of multipolarity are able to cast the nature of the Asian problem. But a solution is not provided, and the question remains: can the United States and Japan maintain their fragile interdependence as the threat of Communism recedes?

Archer, Jules. *The Chinese and the Americans*. New York: Hawthorn Books, 1976.

A women's delegation that visited the People's Republic of China soon after the new *détente* included a firm anti-Communist from Texas. Upon the return of the group, Archer reports, the lady observed of the Chinese, "I want to know why these people are so happy!"

The incident typifies this study of Sino-American interaction in more ways than one. Archer consistently

struggles against the conception that China is little more than one part of a wide Communist monolith, and he attributes the breakthroughs in recent American diplomacy to the recognition of China's uniqueness. He points out that American attitudes toward the Chinese have alternated between periods of animosity and strong admiration. The two nations seem to rub in an odd way, generating a relationship that oscillates between love and hate.

The twentieth century began with the "Open Door" notes sent to European governments by then-American Secretary of State John Hay. The notes encouraged the nations to join in cooperatively trading freely with China through an "Open Door," and played a key role in maintaining China's territorial integrity during its weakest years. After the Chinese Revolution of 1911, many in the United States expressed admiration for the new leader, Sun Yat-sen. But a few years later the United States allied with Japan in World War I, and only returned to actively supporting the Chinese after Japan invaded the country in 1931. Considerable hostility towards the United States arose in China during the ensuing years of struggle, since American aid was fluctuating and undependable, especially during World War II. With the victory over Japan, however, relations between the two nations seemed to have reached a new peak, only to be quickly shattered after the United States backed the losing side in the Nationalist-Communist civil war.

In tracing these changes in relations between the two countries, Archer finds the recent *détente* to be by far the most dramatic shift. For years China was vigorously hated by the vast bulk of laymen and officials in the United States. The mysterious aspect of the Orient was translated into something fearful and forbidding; Chinese Communism seemed not only wrong, but sinister. Their possession of a single nuclear bomb in 1964 inspired more panic than the entire Soviet arsenal. Yet with the coming of relaxed relations, fear has become fascination. Increasing numbers of visitors come away praising the achievements of the People's Republic; Chinese-Americans have developed a renewed pride in their homeland; discoveries about Chinese civilization such as acupuncture become consuming fads.

Archer is optimistic that this new burst of interest between the two countries will bring enough understanding to overcome the enormous differences in thought and ways of life. Only if less mystery and more understanding come will the swing toward admiration harden into lasting friendship between China and America. — *R.H.S.*

Additional Recommended Reading

Buss, Claude A. *The People's Republic of China and Richard Nixon.* Stanford, Calif.: Stanford Alumni Association, 1972. A general history of the foreign and domestic policies of Communist China.

Dulles, Foster Rhea. *American Policy Toward Communist China, 1949-1969.* New York: Thomas Y. Crowell Company, 1971. A critical study by a respected historian of America's hostility toward the People's Republic over its first twenty years of existence.

Oksenberg, Michel and Robert B. Oxnam, eds. *Dragon and Eagle.* New York: Basic Books, 1978. A collection of articles assessing the implications and consequences of *détente* between China and the United States, focusing on the impact of Sino-

American friendship upon other Asian countries.

Paterson, Thomas G., J. Garry Clifford and Kenneth J. Hagan. *American Foreign Policy: A History*. Lexington, Mass.: D. C. Heath, 1977. An excellent survey of American diplomatic history, detailing and placing in context the Nixon visit to Peking.

United States Foreign Policy, 1972. Washington, D.C.: U.S. Government Printing Office, 1973. The official report on *détente* with China and other foreign affairs.

THE WATERGATE AFFAIR

Type of event: Political: scandal that led to the first resignation from the presidency of the United States
Time: June 17, 1972-August 9, 1974
Locale: The United States

Principal personages:
RICHARD MILHOUS NIXON (1913-   ), thirty-seventh President of the United States, 1969-1974
JOHN WESLEY DEAN III (1938-   ), counsel to the President
JOHN NEWTON MITCHELL (1913-   ), Attorney General of the United States and campaign manager for Nixon's 1972 reelection
SAMUEL JAMES ERVIN (1896-   ), Chairman of the Senate Watergate Committee
JOHN JOSEPH SIRICA (1904-   ), United States District Court Judge for the District of Columbia
HARRY R. (BOB) HALDEMAN (1926-   ), White House Chief of Staff
JOHN DANIEL EHRLICHMAN (1925-   ), Assistant to the President for Domestic Affairs
LEON JAWORSKI (1905-   ), Special Prosecutor

Summary of Event

On June 17, 1972, five men were arrested during a bungled break-in at the Democratic campaign headquarters at the Watergate hotel-apartment-office complex in Washington, D.C. Their action was later found to be at the behest of the Committee to Reelect the President, and to involve major figures in the Administration of Richard M. Nixon in conspiracy and an attempted cover-up. When in 1974 definitive proof was made public of Richard Nixon's involvement in the cover-up of the break-in, if not the break-in itself, he became the first president in American history to resign from office. The United States had weathered perhaps its greatest constitutional crisis.

The break-in of June 17, 1972, in the Watergate office complex had precedents in Nixon's earlier (anti-Communist) political career. He had risen politically with the first few years of the Cold War, during the period of concerted anti-Communism that dominated United States politics after 1945. Nixon had used blunt attacks on Jerry Voorhis and Helen Gahagan Douglas to win seats, respectively, in the House and Senate, beating both opponents by accusing them of being "soft on Communism." As a member of the House Un-American Activities Committee, Nixon gained national prominence in ferreting out Alger Hiss, a member of the Communist Party during the 1930's, from the State Department. The 1948 Hiss case propelled Nixon into the vice-presidency under Dwight Eisenhower for two terms (1953-1961). Nominated by the Republicans for the presidency in 1960, Nixon lost an extremely close election to John F. Kennedy. After an abortive gubernatorial campaign in California in 1962, he made a steady comeback in national politics, attaining the Republican presidential nomination in 1968. With the Democrats deeply divided over the issue of American military involvement in Vietnam and with the violence by police and antiwar demonstrators at the Democratic national convention in Chicago acting as negative factors, Nixon won the 1968 election.

Nixon's first term was marked by a foreign policy aimed at scaling down American involvement in Vietnam while bombing the North Vietnamese into negotiations to end the conflict. *Détente* with the Soviet Union and attempted solutions of problems in the Middle East, coupled with reestablished contacts with Red China, marked the achievements of Nixon and Henry Kissinger in foreign affairs.

Domestic politics under Nixon were clearly related to the Watergate break-in and cover-up. Elected on a "law-and-order" platform in the turbulent years of the late 1960's, Nixon's domestic policies hinted at repression, real and threatened. When secret bombing missions against Vietcong supply routes in Cambodia were disclosed in the press in May, 1969, the President, believing these leaks to be subversive, authorized seventeen wiretaps on newsmen and his own White House aides for "national security" purposes. In July, 1970, the President approved the Huston Plan, which called for major expansion of intelligence-gathering within the United States. Nixon reversed his public support for this controversial plan a few days after its adoption, yet events clearly indicated that his Administration was intent on destroying the influence of domestic opponents to the regime. The Justice Department under Attorney General John N. Mitchell stepped up surveillance of the growing antiwar movement, as did the Central Intelligence Agency in a clear departure from its mandated purposes. Antiwar demonstrators faced increased arrests and detention, along with disruption and spying by paid informants and government operatives. For Nixon and his team, the "security threat" had been a central concern since the Cold War years. In power, Nixon, Mitchell, and the others were in the process of eliminating domestic "security threats" through repressive moves; and it is in this context that the Watergate break-in must be placed.

In the 1972 presidential campaign, Nixon faced Democratic nominee Senator George McGovern, who stood clearly to the left of most of his own party. His grassroots campaign for the nomination was directly pitched at groups opposing the Nixon Administration—antiwar students, black militants, and feminists. For the Nixon team, the Democratic campaign fell under the rubric of "security threat"; White House aides had already used the burglary techinque on their opponents. In September, 1971, E. Howard Hunt, Jr., and G. Gordon Liddy burgled the office of a psychiatrist who had treated Daniel Ellsberg, in an attempt to smear Ellsberg, who had illegally "leaked" the controversial "Pentagon Papers" (a Defense Department study of the Vietnam War) to the press. On June 17, 1972, burglary, involving Hunt and Liddy, was again used, this time against the Democrats. Irony abounded in the situation. The break-in which would ultimately topple Nixon occurred in a campaign that the President was virtually assured of winning. McGovern had alienated substantial numbers of Democrats with his left-liberal views, and his ideological isolation brought defeat as sure as the defeat of conservative ideologue Barry Goldwater in 1964. Thus, the break-in was totally unnecessary, since the reelection of Nixon seemed assured anyway. In addition, the very "law-and-order" issue used so effectively by Nixon would become the basis of a campaign to remove him from office.

On June 20, 1972, Nixon reacted to the arrests in a telephone conversation with Mitchell. There is no record of what was said, since the call was not taped by Nixon's now-fabled recording system. That same day, Nixon discussed the burglary with White House Chief of Staff H. R. Haldeman in a conversation recorded by the President, but later found to have an 18½-minute gap, an erasure he blamed on mechanical failure; the contents of that key discussion were thus lost. On June 23, 1972, Nixon and Haldeman held a recorded conversation in which the President and Haldeman agreed to order the CIA (against its legally mandated activities) to impede an FBI investigation of the break-in—a clear order for ob-

struction of justice. By September, 1972, Hunt, Liddy, and the five burglars were indicted. In the public view, the linkage with the President and his highest advisers on the Watergate affair was not known. Nixon won the November, 1972, election handily. In January, 1973, the seven men directly involved in the burglary were convicted.

But the Watergate affair refused to go away, and February, 1973, saw the U.S. Senate establish a select committee under Sam J. Ervin's chairmanship to investigate the break-in. Also in that month, the President and his counsel, John W. Dean III, made arrangements to cover up the involvement of the Administration in the break-in, using "hush money" as the method to keep those convicted from talking. On March 23, 1973, Judge John J. Sirica, of the District of Columbia read a letter from James W. McCord, one of those convicted, indicating that their trial had been fixed through pressures to plead guilty and that the burglary was approved by the highest Nixon advisers. By April 15, 1973, Dean was talking to federal prosecutors, and on April 30, 1973, H. R. Haldeman, White House Chief of Staff; John D. Ehrlichman, Assistant to the President for Domestic Affairs; and recently appointed Attorney General Richard Kleindienst tendered their resignations in the face of widening controversy. John Dean was fired by the President that same day. By May, 1973, Dean was openly providing the Sirica grand jury with documentation, and by June, 1973, he was testifying to the Senate against the President, charging him with participating in the cover-up.

In July, 1973, the Watergate Affair entered a new phase when the existence of the tapes was revealed to the Senate committee. Special Prosecutor Archibald Cox and Judge Sirica opened a drive to subpoena the tapes as evidence. The President appealed Sirica's ruling, only to lose again in the Court of Appeals in October, 1973. Through all of this Nixon consistently claimed his innocence while refusing to release the tapes. Suspicion was fanned by the infamous "Saturday Night Massacre" of October 20, 1973, when Cox was fired by the President. In the flurry of activity that followed, the Administration was under immense pressure to turn over the tapes, and on October 23, 1973, Nixon promised to give them to Sirica's court. The new Special Prosecutor, Leon Jaworski, and the House Judiciary Committee both pursued the tapes as evidence, receiving most of the transcripts by April, 1974. When the President refused to release the sensitive tape of June 23, 1972, Jaworski took the matter to the Supreme Court, which ruled that Nixon must turn over all tapes to Jaworski. By late July, 1974, the House had voted three separate articles of impeachment against Nixon. On August 5, 1974, the White House released the transcripts of the key June 23, 1972, conversations.

Thus, the end had arrived; Nixon had lied to the public, to his supporters, and to his own family for more than a year, and his supporters at last deserted him in anger or disappointment. His authority was gone, and on August 9, 1974, Richard M. Nixon became the first President of the United States to resign from office.

Pertinent Literature

Bernstein, Carl and Bob Woodward. *The Final Days*. New York: Simon and Schuster, 1976.

A massive amount of material has been written about the Watergate scandal and its aftermath, but, for the professional historian, the record is not yet complete. What we currently possess is a literature dominated by journalistic accounts, on the one hand, and, on the other, by the personal accounts of individuals who played some role in the dramatic undoing of Nixon's presidency. These documents, produced by people involved in the actual event and its unveiling, are not what historians consider to be primary sources. The considered judgment of professional historians is still missing from the current literature; political historians in the future will use the present sources for documentation in their long-range assessment of Watergate and its importance.

Clearly, the key journalistic account of the tragedy of Watergate is Woodward and Bernstein's *The Final Days*. These two journalists more than any others broke the Watergate affair through their *Washington Post* stories which followed the break-in, and in their full-length description of their investigation in *All the President's Men. The Final Days* is an inside look at the Nixon presidency as it crumbled.

The portrait that emerges is tragic indeed. Nixon saw his presidency eroded, his authority vanishing, his place in history forever tarnished— all as the result of the misguided break-in and his own undoubted complicity in the cover-up. What Woodward and Bernstein present is a president breaking under the strain of events. Nixon withdrew from the outside world and from the duties of his office during the final few months, as the fateful tape transcripts were being released; he retreated into the company of his family. It is reported that Nixon often seemed preoccupied, that his mind sometimes wandered from the topic of conversation, and that he seemed to be convinced of his own innocence, contrary to what he knew was contained on his tapes. Nixon had apparently been living the lie he had repeatedly told the American public, his loyal congressional supporters, and trusting members of his own family.

In effect, *The Final Days* is a factual moral play, since readers are shown the results of guilt at the highest level of American power. The book's greatest strength lies in its being fact rather than fiction. Woodward and Bernstein are scrupulous in protecting the anonymity of their sources—a standard procedure for investigative reporters that will annoy future historians. Yet, without that anonymity, it is doubtful that anyone would have talked as candidly with the reporters as they did, and the resulting work would have suffered. This book will undoubtedly remain important in the area of political history.

White, Theodore H. *Breach of Faith: The Fall of Richard Nixon.* New York: Atheneum Publishers, 1975.

Theodore H. White has been one of the key political reporters and analysts of recent presidential history. He is most famous for his series of books describing "the making of the presidents"—presidential elections— since 1960.

White begins his book with the unanimous Supreme Court decision of July 24, 1974, which ordered President Nixon to surrender transcripts of all of the tapes subpoenaed by Special Prosecutor Leon Jaworski. He then assesses the staggering impact of the public revelation of the June 23, 1972, tapes, which contained clear evidence of Nixon's involvement in obstruction of justice and a cover-up. Nixon's base of popular support eroded virtually overnight; his congressional supporters suffered extreme disillusionment and also deserted him. The general public now had evidence for what it had suspected for some time—that the President had lied. Key Republican leaders called for the President's resignation. Yet, as White documents, the decision to resign was not made for certain until two days before the actual resignation. Against the overwhelming pressure to resign, it even seemed conceivable that the President, supported by his loyal family, might fight his impeachment in a Senate trial.

White's book next shifts to modern presidential history and the national career of Richard M. Nixon. Of all the authors on Watergate, White takes the long view of the scandal. Nixon, reared in a poor family, came to desire power at any price. He was ruthless in his Cold War congressional campaigns, setting the Nixon style for the future—a frontal attack in the quest for power. Also during the Cold War, he developed his obsession with "national security." Finally, in the 1960's, Nixon added "law and order" to his political repertoire and developed the concept of his "team"— loyal advisers with allegiance to him alone. This background clearly contributed to the Watergate break-in and cover-up, engineered by members of the team in an almost ludicrous security effort.

White's book, though another work of reportage, is clearly and soundly historical and interpretive throughout; his sources are interviews with key personages. At present, *Breach of Faith* constitutes the best general account of Watergate and its antecedents. — *E.A.Z.*

Additional Recommended Reading

Bernstein, Carl and Bob Woodward. *All the President's Men*. New York: Simon and Schuster, 1974. A dramatic account of how these *Washington Post* reporters broke the original story behind the break-in.

Jaworski, Leon. *The Right and the Power*. New York: Reader's Digest Press, 1976. The account of the Special Prosecutor of the Watergate case.

Haldeman, H. R. and Joseph DiMona. *The Ends of Power*. New York: *Times* Books, 1978. An account by the former White House Chief of Staff.

Rather, Dan and Gary Paul Gates. *The Palace Guard*. New York: Harper & Row Publishers, 1974. Nixon's arch-foe in the broadcast media describes the Watergate years.

Dean, John Wesley, III. *Blind Ambition: The White House Years*. New York: Simon and Schuster, 1976. An important book by the first key "team" member at the White House level to testify about Nixon's direct involvement in the cover-up and his obstruction of justice.

Drew, Elizabeth. *Washington Journal: The Events of 1973-1974*. New York: Random House, 1975. Excellent, clear journalist's diary of events for the Watergate years.

ARAB OIL EMBARGO AND THE ENERGY CRISIS

Type of event: Economic: oil embargo and the turmoil it causes in the industrialized world
Time: 1973-1974
Locale: The United States

Summary of Event

On April 18, 1977, President Jimmy Carter—two days before presenting his energy proposals to a joint session of Congress—addressed the American people in what one aide described as a "the sky is falling" speech. Calling the energy problem "unprecedented in our history" and the "moral equivalent of war," Carter warned that if we delay, we will constantly live in fear of embargoes that could "endanger our freedom as a sovereign nation" and would "threaten our free institutions." But the public remained unmoved and unconvinced.

Gallup polls taken a few weeks before and after the President's energy message showed only a marginal increase in the percentage of people believing that the energy situation in the United States was "very serious," and even this slight increase vanished as public opinion quickly returned to the roughly forty percent level that had existed prior to the energy speech, and that still existed one year later. It is true that professional and business people are considerably more likely to see a serious energy situation than are clerical, sales, and manual workers; but Republicans, Democrats, and Independents exhibit little if any difference among their views. More to the point, perhaps, is the issue of the public's perception of whether our energy problems are really genuine. In July, 1977, October, 1977, and January, 1978, the *New York Times*-CBS News Poll asked its scientifically selected sample: "Do you think the shortage is real or are we just being told there are shortages so oil and gas companies can charge higher prices?" In each case, the public was sharply polarized. For every four out of ten respondents who accepted shortages as a fact, there were five who did not. Furthermore, this polarization of the public on energy issues is nothing new. In March of 1974, toward the end of the Arab oil embargo, *Business Week* published the results of an opinion poll showing that slightly more than a third of those sampled held the government collectively most responsible for the energy shortage, while nearly a third blamed the oil companies. Separating fact from fiction is thus a task that any account of the political economy of recent energy events cannot afford to ignore.

Was the Arab oil embargo of October, 1973-March, 1974, and its accompanying fourfold increase in oil prices, an action that was motivated primarily by the war against Israel during Yom Kippur? Charles Doran argues that the war was merely the catalyst that brought about a move by OPEC which worldwide political and economic forces had been pushing toward for some time. Was the energy shortage during the embargo real? Some authors argued that it was, because even those who insisted that it was contrived by the oil companies had to wait in line for their gasoline in the winter of 1973-1974.

What about those gasoline lines? They were avoidable, say two authors who reach the same conclusion by somewhat contrasting arguments. Christopher Rand focuses on the fact that during the embargo the nation's refineries were running at ten percent below their normal capacity rate of ninety-three percent and, more important, at five percent below the rate that the domestic and imported raw feedstock for gasoline was accumulating. "America's refineries," he says, "were dragging their feet." If the refineries had been operating up to a level that used the daily surplus without eating into existing inventories of crude oil and natural liquid gas (that is, at eighty-eight percent of capacity, with about fifty-three percent of the yield as gasoline), there would have been "no cause for cutbacks, gasless weekends, damped thermostats, talk of rationing, or zany price hikes." As far as Rand is concerned, then, the lines would never have occurred if it had not been for the American oil industry's "true act of deception."

Richard Mancke agrees that the long lines at the gas stations were not necessary, but he places the blame in the public sector instead of the private. Using the American Petroleum Institute's weekly reports on stocks of crude oil and refined products as reported in the *Oil and Gas Journal*, he shows that although we entered the embargo period with petroleum stocks three percent below what they were a year earlier, we emerged at its end with stocks nearly seven percent above the earlier figure. In other words, even with our importing 130 million barrels of oil less than we would have (assuming the continuation of preembargo levels), we nevertheless wound up with an inventory of eighty million barrels *more* than the same time a year before. Mancke then goes on to argue that the "surplus" was the result of policies framed not by the oil industry but by the Federal Energy Office. The FEO sought an increased inventory, and it was "successful." It is this surplus that Mancke believes could and should have been used to eliminate the gasoline shortages. And it is this same surplus, of course, that Rand identifies as not having been processed by the nation's refineries. So it appears that the oil industry was simply following the government's lead.

Yet it should be remembered that gasoline shortages had occurred in the spring and summer *before* the embargo and, moreover, that domestic oil production was *reduced* by 3.4 percent from the second half of 1973 to the first half of 1974. Also, according to industry figures, oil imports for October-December, 1973, were actually thirty-two percent *higher* than for the same period of 1972. But what is probably most relevant to any attempt to refute Mancke's casting of the FEO as the villain is Rand's own contention that, because federal energy agencies are "literally riddled with oil company executives," the oil industry has "decisive control" over government energy policy. In any case, regardless of who might be culpable, a review of the situation should suffice to show that the mere fact of having to wait in line does not tell us a thing about why, and the failure to avoid a shortage does not tell us it was unavoidable. All we can agree on is that for awhile there was a shortage of gasoline during the embargo.

But what about today? Is Carter's warning that we are now running out of gas and oil warranted by the facts? Just prior to the President's energy speech to Congress in April, 1977, the CIA released an analysis predicting oil shortages by 1985; a few days after the speech, the UN released a report predicting enough oil and gas for another century or more. A Mobil ad running in a January, 1977, issue of the *Wall Street Journal* reaffirmed its numerous previous warnings about the worsening gas shortage, while an August, 1977, editorial in the same newspaper cited government studies to support the claim that there are 1,001 years of natural gas left in America alone. Confusing? Not really. In July, 1977, Mobil made a *volte-face* that illuminated what was transpiring when it asserted in bold headlines: "We'd like to challenge those who say we have to live with a long-term shortage of energy." The oil industry's new position obviously conflicts with the administration's present one, and the reason was succinctly, if sarcastically, stated by energy czar James Schlesinger: "It was the majors that said for a decade, 'We are running out of oil.' Finally, the government said O.K., we are; the companies proposed higher prices and profits, as befits a time of national emergency; the government responds that they are not needed on existing fields; some of the companies then suddenly suggest, 'We don't have an emergency, after all.'"

To put it another way, disagreement over whether there is an oil shortage today—like the earlier disagreement over why there was a gasoline shortage during the embargo—is a good deal more than merely a matter of neutral, factual interpretation. Issues of political economy are inextricably involved. The choice of policies will be largely determined by the beliefs about reality (the myths, if you will) that are chosen. If we assume that there are physical shortages of oil, then the administration's policy of conservation underpinned by suitable taxes on petroleum products and/or profits seems to be called for. On the other hand, if the oil is assumed to be there, just waiting to be extracted when sufficiently profitable, then the alternative strategy advanced by the oil companies, namely, letting them obtain higher profits, appears to be in order. Either way, though, there would be more inflation; thus the prospect of a further depreciating dollar indicates that neither way makes much economic sense.

Pertinent Literature

Commoner, Barry. *The Poverty of Power: Energy and the Economic Crisis*. New York: Alfred A. Knopf, 1976.

In Commoner's earlier best seller   *The Closing Circle* (1971), he pointed out that "a business enterprise that pollutes the environment is . . . being subsidized by society" and thus "the emergence of a full-blown crisis in the ecosystem can be regarded, as well, as the signal of an emerging crisis in the economic system." Although he is certainly not the first to write about the link between economics and the environment—the economist William Kapp, for example, elaborated on the link in *The Social Costs of Private Enterprise* as early as 1950—Commoner's latest book leaves no doubt that he is the first to have successfully interwoven economic and environmental problems with the problem of energy; and in the process he has written a readable work.

The Poverty of Power emphasizes oil, though there are also chapters on coal, nuclear fission, and solar energy. The first major issue examined is whether the declining rate of domestic oil discovery is due to physical depletion of accessible deposits or to decisions by oil companies to invest less in the search. There are two common methods of determining the number of accessible but as yet undetected oil fields in the United States. The Hubbert method measures the amount of oil found per year, while the Zapp method relies on the amount of oil found per foot of exploratory drilling. Although the former measure shows that the domestic amount of annually discovered oil decreased by nearly thirty percent during 1956-1969, the Zapp finding ratio has actually increased slightly since 1953. There is no conflict between these results, the author notes; they merely reflect the fact that the number of domestic exploratory wells drilled an-

nually between the mid-1950's through the early 1970's declined greatly, even though the oil returns per unit of effort were not diminishing.

The reason why oil companies decided to invest less in the domestic search for oil, continues Commoner, is to be found in terms of relative profitability. Between 1947 and 1956 the profitability of the domestic oil industry remained fairly constant, at a rate of return of roughly fifteen percent on the stockholder's equity. During the same period, however, the rate of profitability of U.S. oil companies on their *foreign* operations increased from about fifteen percent on equity to nearly thirty percent. Naturally, domestic oil companies went abroad. Conversely, we could sharply increase our annual rate of oil production if we were just as sharply to raise the price of oil—and thereby the profits of the oil companies. But the price of oil would then have to rise disproportionately more than the increase in production, because productivity of invested capital (the amount of oil produced per dollar invested) declines as the annual rate of oil production goes up. Still, if the consumers were willing to pay the price, Commoner estimates that we could be oil self-sufficient for fifty to sixty years.

It would be the consumers rather than the oil companies who would have to pay the steep price for oil self-sufficiency, because even if the oil companies were willing to absorb the costs (a highly unlikely assumption), they are becoming less and less able to do so. As one Gulf Oil official is quoted as saying, "Unless the industry can earn a 15-20 percent rate of return after taxes, it will neither be able to generate the needed funds internally nor will it be able to borrow them at attractive rates." And according to a 1975 New York Stock Exchange report, this capital squeeze extends beyond the energy industry. Whereas during 1950 to 1955, United States industry supplied an average of about seventy percent of its capital from its own profits, by 1970-1974 it supplied only about twenty-five percent. The rest, of course, was obtained primarily by one form or another of borrowing.

Yet the general problem of having to go into debt increasingly in order to obtain capital—a sort of deficit financing in the private sector—is specifically grounded, argues Commoner, in the dependence of United States industry on oil. This is most clearly seen in the petrochemical industry (essentially consisting of petroleum refining and the concomitant synthetics industry) because of its heavy use of nonrenewable, high-heat sources of energy to make non-biodegradable products. Not only does the cost of controlling environmental pollution thereby soar, but so also does the expense of obtaining each additional unit of energy. Both input and output are making increasing demands on available capital; and the same development exists in other industries as well. Generally, a low efficiency in the use of energy relative to output indicates a correspondingly low efficiency in the use of capital. The author furthermore shows that in agriculture and transportation (and, of course, in the petrochemical industry as well), there has been a general decline in energy productivity accompanied by an increase in *labor* productivity; that is, it takes increasingly more energy and increasingly *less* labor to produce a given product or move it a certain distance. In short, while the final use value of what is produced has not significantly changed, the means of production have.

The change in production, in turn, leads to Commoner's final conclusion: this change is at the root of our contemporary economic crisis of *stagflation* (simultaneously high inflation and high unemployment). The doubling in production output from 1950 to 1970 was largely due to the doubling of labor productivity. As long as high growth rates could compensate for the loss of labor needed per unit of output by the creation of new jobs, unemployment rates were relatively low. But now in the 1970's, with depressed growth rates, the accumulation of needed capital through high labor productivity contributes to unemployment. Furthermore, to the extent that the needed capital is sought through the borrowing of high-interest funds or the selling of high-priced goods, inflation will get worse. Hence the author's belief that the present system of production is "inherently self-defeating and must eventually fail."

We might add that any attempt to capitalize production costs by cutting real wages is also self-defeating, for it only lessens the consumer's ability to pay the higher prices needed to step up the profits available for internal capital.

Doran, Charles F. *Myth, Oil, and Politics: Introduction to the Political Economy of Petroleum*. New York: The Free Press, 1977.

Doran, a political science professor at Rice University, has written what is probably the most wide-ranging scholarly account of energy affairs to be published in the postembargo era. Six interrelated theses, each occupying a separate chapter, allow the reader to begin where he is initially most interested and then proceed to various other topics. The political economy approach is used by the author to defend the following theses: that the war with Israel had little to do with OPEC's hiking the price of oil during the Arab oil embargo directed at the United States; that the organization of petroleum importing countries is not likely to be effective; that the OPEC cartel is not at all likely to maintain the unity it has shown so far; that the quadrupled price of OPEC oil may be equitable; that the more than eighty percent rise in oil company net profits from 1973 to 1974—the largest gain in the history of *Fortune*'s recordkeeping—was "normal" rather than "obscene"; and that the proposal to decrease concentration within the oil industry will neither weaken OPEC nor strengthen the American standard of living. Many readers—perhaps most—will find much to disagree with among the arguments in support of these propositions; but all will surely benefit from the information and interpretations presented.

Unfortunately, however, the entire question of possibly excessive political influence on the part of the major oil companies is absent from *Myth, Oil, and Politics*. Thus Robert En-gler's *The Brotherhood of Oil* (1977), which focuses on the domestic political implications of oil policy, should be read in conjunction with Doran's internationally oriented account. (Another reason for reading the two books together is that Doran's chapter on divestiture provides the international implications that need to be considered when assessing Engler's elaborate last-chapter prescriptions for public ownership of the energy industry and national planning of energy policy.) Yet *Myth, Oil, and Politics* more than makes up for any omissions, not only by how much it does include, but also by the author's awareness of how much our beliefs about reality affect that reality. Believing, for example, that OPEC prices are unjustly high and are the outcome of United States support for Israel will induce us to strive for oil self-sufficiency and to sell sophisticated arms to the Arabs. Or, believing that all oil profits are obscene and the result of too much concentration in the oil industry will contribute to the call, at the least, for divestiture, and at the most, for public ownership. And nowhere, perhaps, is the impact of our beliefs on the reality of our economy more critical than in how we shall fare in the future *vis-à-vis* other nations— an issue that deserves our most careful consideration.

Taking up an "outrageous" (given the current climate of opinion) hypothesis, Doran speculates: "A historian reflecting on the last quarter of the twentieth century is perhaps likely to ascribe to the energy crisis not the beginning of decline for the United States as a world power but an indication of the relative strength of the United States in its ability to sustain its leadership role." In other words, the United States may ultimately be viewed as the nation that most benefited (or alternatively, least suffered) from the so-called energy crisis.

The author's case for the United States' potential to benefit relative to its competitors rests on three considerations. First, we are nowhere near as dependent on OPEC oil as Western Europe and, especially, Japan are; second, OPEC will want to spend and invest its petrodollars disproportionately more in the country with the biggest, best, most secure economy in the world (ours); and third, the "threat" from OPEC can stimulate our already advanced technology to new levels of innovation (witness *Sputnik*). The author goes on to use a number of analogies to convey his point, especially noting similarities between the respective situations of seventeenth century Great Britain and twentieth century America. Spain's bullion and booty obtained from the New World did her little good. She spent it on nonproductive naval forces while paying other countries, notably Great Britain, for wares that allowed the British to develop their own productive home industry literally at Spain's expense. The outrageous hypothesis is thus quite plausible; yet Doran's discussion lacks any supporting statistics.

Available data do, however, support the existence of America's potential to remain the world's predominant power because of, rather than in spite of, the energy events following the Arab oil embargo. For example: (1) Since 1973 the value of the dollar as measured against nearly a dozen major foreign currencies has generally improved, being strengthened by about ten percent (*U.S. News & World Report*, August, 1977). (2) Since 1973 the United States growth rate has been above the average for the twenty-four member Organization of Economic Co-operation and Development, whereas it had been below average in the prior decade (*Washington Post*, July, 1977). (3) In the fifteen years before 1973, the United States share of manufactured exports in the world declined from twenty-eight to nineteen percent, but now that share has begun to grow again (*Washington Post*, July, 1977). (4) The dollar value of United States exports to Saudi Arabia and Iran—the two largest oil exporters, accounting for more than half of the oil exported by OPEC—was greater than that of any other industrial nation's exports to each of these nations (GAO, January, 1978). (5) Almost a fifth of OPEC's stock portfolios and government treasury bonds are in the United States (UPI, June, 1978). And (6) From 1974 to 1977, although the United States purchased $106 billion worth of goods and services from OPEC countries, while OPEC purchases from the United States totaled "only" $70 billion, OPEC invested at least $38 billion in the United States— in other words, more money came into the United States from OPEC than went out (*Survey of Current Business*, April, 1978). Of course, whether the full United States potential to capitalize on postembargo conditions will in fact be realized depends largely on whether Americans choose to believe in the theory that the world's energy "crisis" is actually their golden opportunity. — *E.G.D.*

Additional Recommended Reading

Adelman, Morris A. "Is the Oil Shortage Real? Oil Companies as OPEC Tax Collectors," in *Foreign Policy*. IX (February, 1973), pp. 69-107. Professor Adelman, in this preembargo publication, was the first to argue seriously for the thesis indicated in the title, a thesis which has since become incorporated in one way or another in most interpretations of the embargo.

Blair, John. *The Control of Oil*. New York: Random House, 1976. Guides the reader gracefully through the petroleum industry's maze of interlocking corporate relationships, vertical integrations, and governmental interventions designed to limit the supply of oil.

Engler, Robert. *The Brotherhood of Oil*. Chicago: University of Chicago Press, 1977. Journalistic account of domestic oil company operations and dealings with one another and with various agencies of government, including the area of campaign contributions.

Greider, William and J. P. Smith. "Fuel Crisis a Matter of Perception," in *Washington Post*. (July 24, 1977). Useful summary of the contrasting interpretations that underlie conflicting perceptions of fuel shortages.

Mancke, Richard. *Squeaking By*. New York: Columbia University Press, 1976. Short update of Mancke's equally short *Failure of U.S. Energy Policy*. Examines United States energy policies since the Arab oil embargo (the most interesting being the policy "responsible" for the gasoline lines) and defends the oil industry against charges of excessive profits and excessive market power.

Pugh, Dave and Mitch Zimmerman. "The 'Energy Crisis' and the Real Crisis Behind It," in *The Economic Crisis Reader*. Edited by David Mermelstein. New York: Random House, 1975. Provides some enlightening figures in the course of arguing that the real crisis was "a profit crisis for the big oil companies."

Rand, Christopher T. *Making Democracy Safe for Oil*. Boston: Little, Brown and Company, 1975. Sparkling if partly polemical account of oil industry interactions with government, including one chapter devoted to the embargo itself.

Sampson, Anthony. *The Seven Sisters*. New York: The Viking Press, 1975. History of the seven largest international oil firms (six of which are among the top eight in the United States): Exxon, Mobil, Standard of California, Texaco, Gulf, Royal Dutch Shell, and British Petroleum. Includes a step-by-step story of the embargo and its aftermath.

Szulc, Tad. *The Energy Crisis*. New York: Franklin Watts, 1974. Dry compilation of facts and figures barely held together by journalistic narrative and organized by chapter headings. Useful for reference.

Tanzer, Michael. *The Energy Crisis: World Struggle for Power and Wealth*. New York: Monthly Review Press, 1974. A brief historical account of international competition in the field of energy, with one chapter placing the embargo in this perspective.

U.S. General Accounting Office. "More Attention Should Be Paid to Making the U.S. Less Vulnerable to Foreign Oil Price and Supply Decisions." Washington, D.C.: U.S. Government Printing Office, January 3, 1978. Highly informative report to the Congress which argues that "an illusion of U.S. impotence has been created by U.S. policymakers' fixation on its marketplace weakness, rather than on its many strengths outside the trade of dollars for oil." Calls for greater governmental involvement in negotiations between U.S. oil companies and the members of OPEC.

GREAT BRITAIN JOINS THE COMMON MARKET

Type of event: Economic: step toward economic unity among European nations
Time: January 1, 1973
Locale: Great Britain and Western Europe

Principal personages:
HAROLD MACMILLAN (1894-   ), Prime Minister of Great Britain, 1957-1963
EDWARD HEATH (1916-   ), Prime Minister of Great Britain, 1970-1974
JAMES HAROLD WILSON (1916-   ), Prime Minister of Great Britain, 1964-1970
CHARLES ANDRÉ JOSEPH MARIO DE GAULLE (1890-1970), President of the French Republic, 1958-1969
GEORGES JEAN RAYMOND POMPIDOU (1911-   ), President of the French Republic, 1969-1974

Summary of Event

On January 1, 1973, after years of hesitancy and doubts, the United Kingdom formally became a partner in the European Economic Community (EEC), or, as it is usually called, the Common Market.

The genesis of the Common Market goes back to the period just after World War II. With American Marshall Plan assistance, Western Europe in the postwar period had accomplished a remarkable economic and social rebuilding. At the same time, however, the Continent was dividing ideologically into two hostile camps: the Communist East and the non-Communist West. Led by the Soviet Union, the Communist bloc nations of Eastern Europe in 1949 formed a Council for Mutual Economic Assistance (COMECON) to coordinate and integrate their national economies. In Western Europe, men such as Jean Monnet of France envisioned similar integration of the non-Communist nations into a common economic unit. Several Western leaders, including Winston Churchill, Konrad Adenauer, and Alcide de Gasperi, hoped that economic consolidation would be the foundation for eventual political unification into a United States of Europe.

Several organizations aiming at closer integration of Western Europe came into being by the early 1950's; one of these was the Council of Europe. Seventeen nations, including Great Britain, joined the Council and participated in its deliberations. The purpose of the Council was to formulate plans for the full political unification of Europe. However, nationalist sentiments, particularly on the part of Britain, continually thwarted the supranational hopes of the Europeanists on the Council.

Another organization formed in 1952 for cooperation and coordination among the Europeans proved more successful than the Council of Europe, in large measure because its goals were less sweeping. This was the European Coal and Steel Community (ECSC). Devised by Monnet and Robert Schuman, French Foreign Minister, the ECSC set up a common market for coal, iron ore, and steel among the states of France, West Germany, Italy, and the Benelux countries. External tariffs among those nations in those commodities would be aligned, as would prices and transportation rates. A supranational High Authority was given the power to make all decisions regarding the operation of the ECSC; the first effective step toward the integration of Europe had begun.

The United Kingdom did not join the European Coal and Steel Community for several reasons: the partial loss of sovereignty which membership would entail, a desire to maintain its ties with the British Commonwealth nations and with the United States, and the suspicion among British socialists that the ECSC was a scheme to benefit European capitalists.

The British, for some of the same reasons, also refused to participate in a French-inspired plan for the setting-up of an integrated, supranational European Defence Community for Western Europe. In 1958, on the other hand, the United Kingdom did agree to become part of European Atomic Energy Community (Euratom), an organization designed to promote the development of nuclear energy for peaceful purposes.

Encouraged by the success of the Coal and Steel Community, representatives of the six member nations met at Messina, Italy, in 1955 to discuss plans for further integration of their national economies. Another two years of negotiation followed. Then, in 1957, the six nations signed the Treaty of Rome which brought the European Economic Community into being. The Treaty provided for a common market in agricultural and industrial commodities by steadily reducing all customs barriers and internal restrictions on the movement of trade, and for the building of external tariff walls around the EEC. The Common Market would be administered by a Commission elected from the member states. There would also be a Council composed of the foreign ministers of the members and a Court of Justice to arbitrate disputes. A fourth body, the European Parliament, made up of delegates from the parliaments of the member states, was seen as the agency through which a politically united Europe might ultimately emerge.

Britain stood aloof from the Common Market and instead took the lead in the formation of a European Free Trade Area (EFTA) in 1960 to counter EEC. Sweden, Denmark, Norway, Portugal, Switzerland, and Austria agreed to participate in EFTA; they, with Britain, became known as the "Outer Seven" in contrast with the "Inner Six" of the Common Market. EFTA has been described as a "salvage operation" by which Britain tried to uphold free trade against the tariff walls of the Common Market, and to retain its influence and its trade in Europe. The effort failed; the Outer Seven did more trading with the Common Market than with one another, and the Inner Six outstripped Britain in industrial production and in growth rates.

By the early 1960's, economic conditions in the United Kingdom had worsened to the point that British leaders began to reconsider their earlier refusal to join the Common Market. From the United States, the "Kennedy Round" of tariff negotiations resulted in a sharp lowering of duties between the United States and Europe, and the Americans were urging the British to look to the advantages of applying for Common Market membership. It was pointed out that if Britain came into the EEC, a huge market would be opened to British goods, foreign investments in Britain would multiply, and British influence in Western Europe would be enhanced.

Prime Minister Harold Macmillan concurred. Calling it a "gigantic opportunity," he announced in the summer of 1961 that Britain would apply for full membership in the EEC. Immediately, Labour Party leader Hugh Gaitskill objected, saying that entry into the Common Market would mean the "end of the Commonwealth and a thousand years of history" for Britain. Commonwealth leaders also objected to Macmillan's decision, primarily on the ground that British entry would destroy the preferential agricultural trade arrangements the Commonwealth had with the United Kingdom.

But the Conservative Party, most British newspapers, and the majority of the British public sided with Macmillan on the issue. Edward Heath was dispatched to Brussels to meet with the EEC ministers and begin the arrangements of British entry. Fourteen months of very difficult negotiations followed. By the end of 1962,

it was evident that West Germany, Belgium, and the Netherlands wanted to accept British membership, but it was equally clear that French President de Gaulle had become opposed to British entry.

In January, 1963, President de Gaulle abruptly announced that France would veto British membership in the EEC, and the French foreign minister requested that the negotiations be terminated. "One day," de Gaulle said, "perhaps England will be admitted to Europe after it has detached itself from its ties with the Commonwealth and the United States." De Gaulle's veto caused dismay in Britain and forced the resignation of the Conservative government of Macmillan. Both major parties were, however, committed to eventual British membership in EEC, and each subsequent government continued to work toward that end. Thus, in 1967, Labourite Harold Wilson, with the approval of a large majority in the Commons, again formally applied for admission, but was again rebuffed by President de Gaulle.

Changing circumstances in 1969 made the acceptance of British membership more favorable. President de Gaulle resigned in that year, and his successor Georges Pompidou, less ultranationalistic than de Gaulle, suggested that French opposition to British membership was no longer as adamant as it had been. Sir Alec Douglas-Home went to Brussels to renew negotiations in April, 1970; these new talks continued for nearly a year. They culminated in a personal conference between Prime Minister Heath and President Pompidou in May, 1971, at which Heath agreed to give up certain privileges regarding the protection of British agriculture. With that concession, the terms of British entry were acceptable. Edward Heath had brought Britain into the Common Market.

It still remained for the British House of Commons to approve. Through the summer and early fall of 1971, the momentous question was debated. Harold Wilson, to hold the labor unions and the Socialists in the Labour Party, now came out against British entry and instructed the Labourites to vote against it. But Heath, confident that the majority in Commons were in favor of membership, gave the Conservatives a "free vote," meaning they could vote their consciences. Heath judged correctly. By a division of 356 to 244, the House of Commons approved Britain's entry into the Common Market.

Further arrangements to incorporate the United Kingdom into the Common Market were worked out during 1971 and 1972. A common external tariff system was begun, and a common agricultural policy formulated. The British would convert their coinage to the decimal system and switch to the centigrade system of heat measurement. A European-style "value added" tax would replace the British sales tax.

January 1, 1973, was selected as the date for formal British entry into the Common Market. At that time, two other nations, Ireland and Denmark, were also accepted as full members of the European Economic Community.

Pertinent Literature

Camps, Miriam. *Britain and the European Community, 1955-1963*. Princeton, N.J.: Princeton University Press, 1964.

In the preface to this monograph, the author informs her readers that she had, during the previous twenty years, been in circumstances which enabled her to observe rather closely the events and developments here recounted. First, she was employed for almost ten years by the United States Department of State and was directly concerned with European organizations. Then, moving to London in 1954, she studied and wrote on European institutions of the postwar era, particularly on the European Economic Community. She often spoke with British leaders in these years about British plans and policies regarding the Common Market, and

she also made frequent visits to EEC headquarters, talking to officials there. Bringing her experiences and the materials of her investigations together, Camps then wrote this lengthy and very detailed study of the antecedents and the first several years of the Common Market, and of British relationship to the EEC.

The book essentially commences with the Messina Conference of 1955, where representatives of the six nations which would later form the Common Market came together to discuss and formulate certain basic objectives. As laid down by the Messina conferees, those objectives would be the progressive fusion of their national economies, harmonization of their social policies, the creation of a common market, and ultimately the unification of Europe. Work toward attainment of those grand goals went forward, culminating in the Treaty of Rome, which marked the most important stage in what Camps calls the "re-launching of Europe."

The central and major portion of this book is concerned with British responses to the Treaty of Rome. Camps deals at length with the attitudes and actions of British political leaders and the British public as the question of British entry into Europe moved to the fore. She explains British efforts to counter the Common Market by organizing the European Free Trade Association, and how that experiment proved less than successful.

At last, in the summer of 1961, Prime Minister Macmillan announced that Britain had decided to apply for Common Market membership. Long and often frustrating negotiations followed, ending with the veto of British membership by President de Gaulle in 1963.

At this point, Camps concludes her study of nearly a decade of British relations with the European community and offers some personal conclusions. One is that during the first years following World War II, Britain missed a fine opportunity to play a determining role in shaping the new postwar Europe, "defining its scope, setting its institutions, and its ethos." But for several reasons, of which the two most important were that Britain failed to recognize the profound impulse for unity stirring among many Europeans, and that Britain was more

concerned with non-European problems, the British did not exercise sufficient leadership to bring into being the kind of Europe they might have wanted. Britain allowed others, primarily the French, to set the pace and to innovate in organizing the kind of Europe they wanted. At the same time, British foot-dragging along with the ill-fated efforts to counteract the Common Market with the EFTA, led to greater consolidation and cohesion among the Common Market nations against Britain.

Camps views the "making of Europe" as having two intertwining strands. The first strand is the emphasis on gradual denationalization and the sharing of sovereignty by the member units, such as in the Coal and Steel Community. The second strand is the building of a new political entity: a federal state of Europe much like the United States, with the retention of some sovereignty by each member, even in the future. On the whole the British have inclined toward the first strand while the Continental states have favored the second. These are not mutually exclusive approaches, however, and over time some nations have moved in one direction, then another. Camps also observes that the British have been less imaginative and more timid and halfhearted than the Europeans in working out any new patterns toward European unity.

This book was written only six months after the fateful rejection of British membership into the Common Market. Nevertheless, Camps tended to think that this rejection was not the last word, and that Britain would probably apply again under more favorable conditions. She believed, in 1964, that a rough parity of power existed between Britain and France, and that equilibrium should make it easier for the French to accept the British into Europe, and easier for the British to become "Europeans" in the near future.

Britain and the European Community, 1955-1963 may be studied as a useful survey of the complexities and the pitfalls which confronted the British and Continental diplomats in trying to deal with an idea whose time had come: the unification of Europe.

Hoepli, Nancy L., ed. *The Common Market.* New York: The H. W. Wilson Company, 1975.

This book consists of thirty-six newspaper and magazine articles, excerpts from books, and printed speeches brought together and edited by the Senior Editor of the Foreign Policy Association and issued as part of a reprint series on current affairs called the Reference Shelf.

The Common Market is divided into five sections. The opening section, entitled "In the Beginning," includes an article on the origins of a united Europe as imagined by such men as Paul-Henri Spaak of Belgium, and another article on the formation of Euratom, the European Coal and Steel Community, and the European Economic Community. There follows a selection showing how one of the component bodies of the European Community, the European Parliament, works. The first section of the book finishes with two articles on the significance of enlargement of the Common Market in 1973 for the member states, and for the rest of the world.

Section II, "A Tumultuous Transition," explains the period of adjustment after the admission of Britain, Ireland, and Denmark to the EEC. Despite the euphoria and the high hopes which enlargement of the

Market appeared to portend, there came instead a "state of crisis—a crisis of confidence, of will, and of clarity of purpose" in the EEC headquarters and in the member states in 1974. The articles of this section, contemporary with the crisis, take contrasting views as to the prospects for the unification of Europe. A West German journalist is optimistic that the drive toward unity will continue, particularly with the encouragement of the two new leaders, Helmut Schmidt of West Germany and Valéry Giscard d'Estaing of France, both Europeanists and pragmatists. The British publication, *The Economist*, was more gloomy about the future of European unity, and the *Wall Street Journal* thought that the drive was clearly slowing down. Renewal of war in the Middle East, the oil embargo against some European nations, and rampant inflation all appeared, at the time, to militate against unification.

The articles in the third section of the book are called "Unfinished Business." They offer perspectives on the many problems which must be surmounted if the political unification of Europe is to be attained by the target date of 1980. Chief among those problems must be the development of an agricultural policy which will be acceptable to all members of the Common Market. An equally urgent problem is the formulation of a common energy policy, particularly as regards oil. On the latter problem, one of the articles delineates the overall energy needs and resources of Europe, while another explains why a common energy policy has been so difficult to attain.

"The American Connection" section indicates that, while the United States has officially long supported the idea of European union, most Americans have no real knowledge of the Common Market and its operations. Other articles in this section explain American efforts to bring harmony among the Europeans at the time of the 1973-1974 crises, including a call by Henry Kissinger for a new Atlantic Charter of renewed and closer partnership between the United States and Europe. Another article of this section, taken from *U.S. News & World Report*, reviews the relations of the United States with the Common Market nations and concludes with the observation that further progress of the Europeans toward political and economic union will depend in large measure upon cooperation—not rivalry—with the United States.

The final section, "Looking Ahead to 1980," offers a mixture of gloomy and hopeful prognostications about the future of the Common Market and European unity. Articles by correspondents for the *Wall Street Journal* and the *Washington Post* are pessimistic that the European community can advance much beyond what it is already—an economic and commercial arrangement—and fear that the Common Market will do well merely to survive until 1980. Reprints of articles and speeches by certain prominent Europeans, on the other hand, show more confidence that a strong European community will ultimately emerge. It appears now, three or four years later, that the doubters have so far been more nearly correct. The hope of attaining full political and social unification of Europe by 1980 seems unlikely.

Besides being a judicious selection of well-written, illuminating articles, *The Common Market* also has a fifteen-page bibliography of pertinent books, documents, and pamphlets for further reading, and a short glossary of terms and acronyms which adds to its value. — *J.W.P.*

Additional Recommended Reading

Shanks, Michael and John Lambert. *The Common Market Today—and Tomorrow*. New York: Frederick A. Praeger, 1962. Published just when Britain made its first application for membership in the EEC, and before it was rejected, this book deals with the origins of the European Economic Community and presents arguments for and against British entry.

Krause, Lawrence B. *The Common Market: Progress and Controversy*. Englewood Cliffs, N.J.: Prentice-Hall, 1964. Written shortly after France first vetoed British entry, this work discusses the Market's accomplishments to date and predicts further cooperation and unity of the Europeans with Britain.

Calmann, John, ed. *The Common Market: The Treaty of Rome Explained*. London: Anthony Blond, 1967. Intended for British readers, this book is a close analysis, article by article, of the Treaty of Rome; it explains the functioning of the Common Market and describes the problems faced by the British government in respect to the EEC.

Hallstein, Walter. *Europe in the Making*. Translated by Charles Roetter. London: Allen and Unwin, 1972. The former President of the executive committee of the European Economic Community traces the background of the Common Market and explains the forces which, in his view, are leading to the goal of a united Europe.

Gurland, Robert and Anthony MacLean. *The Common Market: A Common Sense Guide for Americans*. New York: Paddington Press, 1974. Intended as a reference work for Americans doing business in Europe, this book by two international lawyers also provides material for the historian of the EEC.

THE UNITED STATES SUPREME COURT RULES ON STATE ANTIABORTION LAWS

Type of event: Legal: judicial decision on abortion
Time: January 22, 1973
Locale: Washington, D.C.

Principal personages:

JANE ROE, the name assigned to protect the anonymity of the plaintiff in the District Court case and the appellant in the United States Supreme Court case

HENRY WADE, District Attorney in the Texas District where Jane Roe filed suit and defendant in case

HARRY ANDREW BLACKMUN (1908-   ), Associate Justice of the United States Supreme Court and author of the majority opinion

WARREN EARL BURGER (1907-   ), Chief Justice of the United States Supreme Court and author of the concurring opinion

WILLIAM ORVILLE DOUGLAS (1898-1980) and

POTTER STEWART (1915-   ), Associate Justices of the United States Supreme Court and authors of the concurring opinion

BYRON RAYMOND WHITE (1917-   ) and

WILLIAM HUBBS REHNQUIST (1924-   ), Associate Justices of the United States Supreme Court and authors of the dissenting opinion

Summary of Event

In response to the popularity of civil rights issues, more permissive sexual mores, and the women's movement, the 1960's and early 1970's was a period during which contending forces collided over the abortion issue. On the one side were those who argued that women should have total control over their bodies, and that this right should include the freedom to terminate medically a pregnancy. On the other side were those who maintained that the right to abortion was contrary to Western moral values and religious principles. The issue finally reached the United States Supreme Court in the case of *Roe* v. *Wade*, and was decided in January, 1973.

Jane Roe was an unmarried pregnant woman who wanted to terminate her pregnancy by abortion in Texas, a state which prohibited abortion except in cases where medical advice held that the life of the mother was otherwise endangered. She first brought suit in the United States District Court for the Northern District of Texas, naming a district attorney, Henry Wade, as defendant. She received a judgment essentially in her favor when the Texas abortion statute was found unconstitutional. Both parties then appealed the decision to higher federal courts, and ultimately the case was argued before the United States Supreme Court.

By a majority decision of seven to two, the Supreme Court affirmed the decision of the United States District Court in all important matters. The majority opinion was written by Justice Harry Blackmun. Concurring opinions were written by Chief Justice Warren Burger and by Justices William O. Douglas and Potter Stewart. The majority in its decision made the following significant points. The Court first held that, although there was no direct mention of abortion in the United States Constitution, a constitutional right was involved. This was the right to personal liberty protected by the due process clause of the Fourteenth Amendment. In support of this position, the Court cited several earlier decisions which maintained that an individual's right over matters pertaining to one's self-interest was usually superior to that of the state. One earlier decision, as an example, had held that the states were prohibited from passing laws restricting the individual's right to marry whomever he or she chose regardless of race.

Having determined that the Constitution afforded women the right to determine whether to continue or terminate a pregnancy, the Court then dealt with the question of whether a state could overrule the constitutional right of the individual by demonstrating a compelling reason or reasons why it should pass laws regulating abortions.

In the one critical area which has produced much heated debate over the abortion issue, the Court ruled in favor of the woman. The State of Texas had argued that it had a compelling reason to regulate abortion to protect the life of the unborn child. The Court held, however, that "the unborn are not included within the definition of 'person' as used in the Fourteenth Amendment." Historically, the Court stated, Americans have never treated the rights of persons after birth the same as those of persons before birth. The Constitution, for example, only regards "persons born or naturalized" as citizens. There is no provision for an income tax deduction for the unborn. Property rights usually begin at birth, and the unborn has no rights of inheritance. Thus, the fetus, by law, was not a person, and the state had no compelling reason to pass laws to protect it.

The Court went further than establishing the constitutionality of abortion and laid down regulations regarding the performing of abortions. By issuing these regulations, the Court acted in a way that has caused it to be accused of legislating—a charge which has some truth. The Court, however, felt that it was justified in this case. First, it was dealing with a matter affecting the life and health of the pregnant woman and the potential for life of the unborn. Second, the Court sought to provide guidelines for state legislatures in the drafting of abortion statutes in order to help stem the tide of future abortion cases in the federal courts.

The majority opinion stated that a woman did not have an absolute right to an abortion. The state did have a legitimate interest in protecting a woman's health and potential human life and in maintaining proper standards. Before the end of the first trimester of pregnancy the state could do nothing to prevent an abortion that had been decided upon by a physician licensed by the state in consultation with his patient. "From and after the end of the first trimester, and until the point in time when the fetus becomes viable," that is, able to live independently of the mother, the state could regulate the abortion procedure only to preserve and protect the life of the mother. After the fetus became viable, however, the state could prohibit abortions altogether, except in cases where the life or health of the mother was endangered.

Minority opinions written by Justice Byron White and Justice William Rehnquist presented the antiabortion position. Justice White asserted that the Court's decision had sustained the position that the convenience of the prospective mother was superior to "the life or potential life that she carries. The Court," he continues, without constitutional sanction, "simply fashions and announces a new constitutional right for pregnant mothers" and, in so doing, "invests that right with sufficient substance to override most existing state abortion statutes." White concludes by holding that the Court had incorrectly interfered with the legislative processes of the states. Abortion, he states, is an issue that "should be left with the people and to the political processes the people have devised to govern their affairs."

Justice Rehnquist held that there is no historical foundation for the Court's position that the right to abortion was to be found in the Fourteenth Amendment. History, he argued, established the fact that a majority of states have had abortion laws for at least a century, and that the legislatures which passed these laws represented the sentiments of the citizenry. There is, then, no historical support for Roe's argument of the universal acceptability of a woman's "right" to an abortion.

The Court left many issues relating to abortion undecided because they had not been contested in this case. A victory, however, had been won by those who favored freedom of choice on the woman's part in regard to the continuation or termination of a pregnancy. Abortion on demand, which had been advocated by more radical spokesmen of the proabortion movement, had been prohibited, however; this part of the ruling gave some small hope to the antiabortion, right-to-life groups, which now began to talk of a campaign to secure a constitutional amendment prohibiting abortion.

Pertinent Literature

Andrikopoulos, Bonnie and Warren M. Hearn, eds. *Abortion in the Seventies: Proceedings of the Western Regional Conference on Abortion*. New York: National Abortion Federation, 1977.

Abortion in the Seventies is the product of an interagency and organization meeting held on the subject of abortion in Denver, Colorado, in 1976. It consists of a large number of individual presentations by professionals and discussions on various problems related to abortion, and, as a result, is one of the most authoritative and comprehensive works presently available on the subject. The topics treated are numerous, with three to four presentations on each topic. Subject areas include legal, medical, public health, counseling, psychological, economic, health, legislative and political aspects of abortion, evaluation of abortion services, abortion nursing, and education and information. Also included are the discussions of the participants in two workshops on religious and ethical aspects of abortion and on teenagers and abortion.

Without question the most helpful presentation in understanding the Supreme Court's ruling in *Roe* v. *Wade* is the introduction to this section by Sarah Weddington. A Texas state representative and President of the National Rights Action League, Weddington served as counsel for Jane Roe in arguing her case before the Supreme Court and is therefore intimately acquainted with the subject. Her writing style is marked by a clarity seldom found in complex verbal legal presentations.

Weddington begins with a brief statement about the main point of the decision and then proceeds to clarify some areas of confusion. She first indicates how the Court turned to earlier judicial decisions to demonstrate that the abortion question was a con-

stitutional one. Then she explains how the Court determined the unconstitutionality of the argument of the State of Texas that it had the right to protect the rights of the unborn, since the Court showed by citing earlier decisions that courts and legislatures did not recognize the rights of the unborn. Weddington continues by explaining the other significant points of the decision and indicates that the Court's reason for including them was to establish guidelines upon which state legislatures could model abortion legislation in the future. She concludes by indicating some additional questions which were not decided in *Roe* v. *Wade*, such as minors' rights, spouses' rights, Medicaid responsibilities, and the responsibilities of public hospitals.

By far the longest presentation in this section is by Cyril C. Means, Jr., entitled "Recent Trends in the Legal Status of Abortion." Means is a professor at the New York Law School and is an expert on the origins of abortion laws and the significance of abortion statutes and judicial decisions. Admittedly, the subject that he treats is very complex, and verbal presentations usually do not enjoy the clarity of written ones, but this article is difficult for the nonexpert to follow and appreciate fully. Nevertheless, a brief discussion of part of Mean's presentation is necessary since he treats cases that arose after *Roe* v. *Wade* which have clarified, or will help to clarity, this Supreme Court decision.

The first case he reviews is *Connecticut* v. *Menillo*, in which the Supreme Court, by interpreting itself, clarified *Roe* v. *Wade*, emphasizing its idea that an abortion performed by a surgeon or physician during the first trimester is safer than childbirth. Thus the state would have to show a compelling state interest in order to take the greater risk of childbirth. The next case discussed is *Planned Parenthood Federation of Central Missouri* v. *Danforth*, a case which had not been decided at the time of Means's presentation. In it the prosecution raised a number of questions about the Missouri abortion act, including the preciseness of the definition of "viable," the questions of parental or spousal consent, and the state's proscribing of saline procedures in inducing abortions, which, in effect, means that the legislature deprives the physician of the arrangement of treatment choices.

Two other cases, *Klein* v. *Nassau County Medical Center* and *Doe* v. *Bede*, deal with the question of Medicaid reimbursement for abortions. In both cases the Supreme Court is interested not only in statuatory questions regarding HEW Title XIX but also in constitutional questions. Neither case had been decided, but Means believed that if the Court deals fully with the way Title XIX is constructed, it may never have to deal with the constitutional question.

In addition, Means says, there have been a series of cases on public hospitals and abortions. All lower courts deciding such cases have ruled that public hospitals which perform childbirth services must also provide abortion services. With private hospitals the decisions also have been quite consistent: that they cannot be compelled to perform abortions.

Two more articles are included in this section of the book. Jean Dubofsky's "Legal Status of Abortion in Colorado and other Rocky Mountain States" deals primarily with the question of minors' rights and spousal consent. The other article, "U.S. Commission on Civil Rights Report," is by Carol Bonosaro, the Director of the U.S. Civil Rights Commission. It reviews the findings and recommendations of the Commission found in its report, "Constitutional Aspects of the Right to Limit Childbearing." Both articles are helpful in understanding the present legal picture regarding abortion.

In conclusion, *Abortion in the Seventies* is an excellect interdisciplinary study on abortion. Although only the section dealing with the legal aspects of abortion is reviewed here, this book would be helpful in understanding the other facets of the question.

Callahan, Daniel. *Abortion: Law, Choice and Morality*. New York: The Macmillan Company, 1970.

This book is a comprehensive treatment of the numerous facets of the abortion controversy. The author, Daniel Callahan, is eminently qualified for his task. Holding a Ph.D. in philosophy from Harvard, he is Director of the Institute of Society, Ethics and the Life Sciences. From 1961 to 1968 he served as executive editor of *Commonweal*, and as a visiting professor at Brown University, the University of Pennsylvania, and other institutions. The author of several books, he has contributed to numerous periodicals, including *Harpers*, *Atlantic Monthly*, and the *New York Times Magazine*. *Abortion: Law, Choices and Morality* is the product of four years of research and preparation, partially funded by research grants from the Population Council and the Ford Foundation. Since he traveled extensively to study abortion globally, Callahan is able to provide a multinational view of the subject which places the situation in the United States in perspective.

In his introduction, Callahan treats the conflict of values inherent in the abortion question and states his aim in writing the book. His major focus, he states, is on the moral questions related to abortion, which, he asserts, must not be studied in isolation but in their relation to medical, social, and legal questions; furthermore, practicality must be determined as well as theory. Therefore he has buttressed his thesis with a mass of medical, social, and legal data from around the world. Considering that the moral justification for abortion differs with the value systems of groups and individuals, Callahan believes that he can find a basis for consensus among the conflicting parties. He holds that this consensus is threefold: a belief "that life should be protected and enhanced"; a conviction "that human rights come into direct play in abortion decisions"; and the acceptance of the idea "that people should be morally responsible for the choices they make on abortion." If he is correct in his assumption, Callahan believes, the mass of data which he has collected and interpreted can help the reader, regardless of his conviction, to reach an informed and judicious decision about the morality of abortion.

In order to aid the reader in arriving at this decision, the author divides the remainder of his book into four sections which are subdivided into chapters. In the first section, "Ethics and 'Indications' Policy," he discusses medical indications and hazards, psychiatric indications and consequences, and fetal indications. Section II, "Establishing a Legal Policy," contains chapters on nations with restrictive legal codes, such as the United States before the *Roe* v. *Wade* decision, India, and countries in Latin America, the moderate legal codes of the Scandinavian countries, and the permissive legal systems characteristic of the Soviet Union and other Soviet-dominated Eastern European countries and of Japan. He concludes this section with a chapter on the social and legal patterns and probabilities of abortion. The third section, "Establishing a Moral Policy," includes chapters on the sanctity of life, and philosophical and biological considerations and data on the "beginning" of human life. The final section, "Implementing a Moral Policy," is devoted to a lengthy treatment of the Roman Catholic position on abortion, abortion on request, legal reform, and a concluding chapter on making abortion decisions.

On the whole Callahan has provided a balanced, thoroughly documented study of the abortion issue. Although he has not provided a bibliography, he has included notes at the end of each chapter which serve much the same purpose. He has also provided more than a score of tables which are most helpful. This is a book which, although it is now somewhat dated, must be read by anyone desiring an informed knowledge of the subject. — *J.S.A.*

Additional Recommended Reading

Dedek, John F. *Human Life: Some Moral Issues*. New York: Sheed and Ward, 1972. Contains two chapters on abortion by a Catholic theologian which are helpful in explaining the history of the Roman Catholic Church's position on the issue.

Dollen, Charles. *Abortion in Context: A Select Bibliography*. Metuchen, N.Y.: Scarecrow Press, 1970. A helpful bibliography on birth control, contraception and prevention, and abortion.

Kluge, Eike-Henner W. *The Practice of Death*. New Haven, Conn.: Yale University Press, 1975. Dealing with suicide, euthanasia, infanticide, and genocide, Kluge provides a clear and valuable chapter on abortion in which he delineates the various arguments for and against it.

Nolen, William A. *The Baby in the Bottle: An Investigative Review of the Edelin Case and Its Larger Meanings for the Controversy over Abortion Reform*. New York: Coward, McCann and Geoghegan, 1978. After examining the legal and moral ramifications of the Edelin abortion case, the noted surgeon William Nolen, although accepting the fact of legalized abortion, cautions against its larger ramifications regarding the sanctity of human life and suggests means by which the incidence of abortion can be lessened.

Smith, David T., ed. *Abortion and the Law: Essays by B. James George, Jr., and Others*. Cleveland, Oh.: Press of Western Reserve University, 1967. A collection of helpful essays by knowledgeable jurists originally printed in the Western Reserve Law Review.

Williams, Glanville Llewelyn. *The Sanctity of Life and the Criminal Law*. New York: Alfred A. Knopf, 1957. A series of five lectures delivered at the Columbia University School of law, including two on abortion: one dealing with the laws on abortion in Britain and the United States before *Roe* v. *Wade* and another treating religious attitudes, social difficulties, and the experiences of countries that have largely legalized abortion.

END OF AMERICAN INVOLVEMENT IN THE VIETNAM WAR

Type of event: Diplomatic: construction of a negotiated peace
Time: January 27, 1973
Locale: South Vietnam and Paris

Principal personages:

RICHARD MILHOUS NIXON (1913-   ), thirty-seventh President of the United States, 1969-1974

HENRY ALFRED KISSINGER (1923-   ), Special Assistant for National Security Affairs to President Nixon, 1969-1973; chief negotiator of secret talks for the United States

LE DUC THO (1912-   ), North Vietnamese revolutionary and later high government official, chief negotiator of secret talks for North Vietnam

NGUYEN VAN THIEU (1923-   ), President of South Vietnam

Summary of Event

In the American past, only the Civil War has aroused so many conflicting emotions among citizens, officials, and soldiers as has the Vietnam War. Debate in the United States began in the early 1960's over what means should be used to protect the Republic of South Vietnam. Division spread with time to questions of ends: what sort of peace was being sought in Asia? Were the Viet Cong really worse than the South Vietnamese government? The war posed such dilemmas that the government was soon caught up in a charade of truth, obscuring issues and purposes even further. Thus, it is understandable that the nature of the peace settlement ending American involvement in the war is still shrouded in mystery. We still do not know which side made the crucial concessions necessary for peace, or how seriously any country treated the treaty provisions, or whether the United States strongly suspected that within two years of its departure from South Vietnam, the country would fall entirely under Communist control.

From the time Richard M. Nixon became President in 1969, he was chiefly dependent upon the negotiating table for bringing the peace he had promised. His bargaining position was weak. With half a million American troops in South Vietnam, the Viet Cong and North Vietnamese forces could not win a direct offensive, but their guerrilla techniques insured that they could not lose, either. The war was essentially a waiting game, and the stakes were so much higher for the Communists that they could afford to wait longer. Nor did the Communists need a negotiated peace as much as Nixon did. The massive opposition at home to continued war required him to deescalate; but strong popular support of American intervention made total withdrawal an equally unacceptable policy.

Nonetheless, Communist initiatives brought the first real breakthroughs in discussions over peace. Since May, 1968, formal negotiations had been carried on in Paris, but these talks produced little more than rhetoric and repeatedly broke down in frustration. In June of 1971, Hanoi backed away from two earlier demands and agreed to discuss an in-place ceasefire and the conduct of "internationally supervised" elections without prior abolition of the Saigon government. Shortly afterwards the Viet Cong (South Vietnamese Communists) made similar concessions, showing a conciliatory attitude towards the West. With these concessions, a second level of negotiations began, held secretly between Le Duc Tho, a prominent North Vietnamese official, and the ever-present Henry Kissinger, Nixon's key aide for foreign affairs.

The American side made several minor concessions in the ensuing discussions, but little real progress was made. President Nixon was feeling the pressure of election year, and American troop levels in Vietnam dropped rapidly, weakening his leverage at the talks. In May, 1972, he tried a bold maneuver: he ordered the bombing of North Vietnam stepped up, and the ports of the country mined and blockaded (bringing economic crisis to the Communists); but at the same time he offered great modifications of the United States bargaining position. For the first time, the United States was willing to permit North Vietnamese troops to remain in South Vietnam after a cease-

fire, and to modify the Saigon government before elections. Intensive talks between Kissinger and Le Duc Tho resumed, with special incentives for both sides. The Nixon Administration had to prove that its gambled escalation of the war was effective, and the North Vietnamese, watching the increasing likelihood of Nixon's reelection, wanted to reach an agreement before a safer Nixon became tougher.

Barely two weeks before the election, North Vietnam announced that a peace agreement had been reached, and that it would be signed within a few days. It was then, on October 26, 1972, that Kissinger conceded before the American press that "peace is at hand," though he cautioned that certain disagreements remained. Nixon won his election, and over the ensuing weeks the seemingly final talks first stalled, and then became bitter. In mid-December they broke down completely. One can only speculate on the reasons for this collapse. It is likely that the North Vietnamese made sacrifices in their eagerness to arrive at a preelection treaty, and announced the terms to pressure the United States to sign; but after receiving credit for ending the war, the Nixon Administration toughened its terms and alienated Hanoi. When the talks collapsed, Nixon tried one more bold stroke and ordered the "Christmas bombing" of North Vietnam. Dozens of B-52 bombers were set upon the largest cities of the country, widely destroying industry. But the Communist antiaircraft defense was so vigorous, and American anger at the attack so powerful, as to make the success of the bombing very questionable. It was stopped in less than two weeks, and war-weary negotiators returned to Paris.

On January 27, 1973, peace accords were signed by North Vietnam, the Viet Cong, the United States, and a reluctant South Vietnam. The provisions of the treaty were substantially the same as those of the October agreement. By March 27, the United States was to withdraw its troops from Vietnam; exchanges of prisoners would go on during those two months. All Vietnamese forces would remain in place, and a cease-fire would be supervised by United Nations forces. All parties concurred on Vietnam's sovereignty and right of self-determination, and a Council was established with responsibility for developing and executing plans for an open election.

There is room for doubt concerning how seriously the treaty was taken by any of the concerned nations. Cease-fire lines were never clearly established, many of the provisions were vague and invited violation, and both sides broke the treaty almost as soon

as it was signed. The United States quickly withdrew, regained its captured prisoners, and could claim "peace with honor." But both President Thieu of South Vietnam and the scattered Communist forces seemed to believe that their best prospects lay in renewed fighting. By the end of 1973, open war had returned to the nation. American aid continued to flow to South Vietnam, and Thieu controlled a well-trained army of one million men. But the Viet Cong and North Vietnamese seemed to have gained some critical psychological edge on their enemy, and their successes were self-reinforcing. During 1974, the Communist positions were generally strengthened, and at the outset of 1975 they launched a last major offensive. After a major direct victory at Hue, Communist forces drove rapidly over South Vietnam, pursuing an utterly demoralized army. By the end of April, Saigon was captured; the last American advisers abandoned the country; the "Vietnam era" of American history was truly at an end.

Pertinent Literature

Brown, Weldon A. *The Last Chopper: The Denouement of the American Role in Vietnam, 1963-1975*. Port Washington, N.Y.: Kennikat Press, 1976.

In covering a subject as divisive as the Vietnam War, even the driest repetition of textbook facts can sound partisan, foundering on events buried with conflicting accounts and moral interpretations. Weldon Brown's account of American involvement in Southeast Asia largely succeeds in the feat of objectively narrating in some detail the motives and actions

governing policy. At the same time, Brown has a distinctive view of the lessons to be learned from the war.

The Last Chopper expresses much of the conventional wisdom about the "Communist struggle." The domino theory is correct to a limited degree. The Soviet Union and other Communists sought, after World War II, to expand their realm of power, and their ambitions would be fed by success, until America was turned into the "armed fortress" Harry Truman predicted when he left office in 1953. Hence, Brown insists, it was necessary to make a stand at some point. The problem was that Vietnam was the wrong place to make such a stand—wrong in almost every way. When American defense began, Vietnam was already a deeply divided country: between North and South, Communist and anti-Communist, Buddhist and Christian. As the United States belatedly realized towards the end of the 1960's, the conflict in South Vietnam was not caused by military invasion, but by a civil war. Even more problematic were the governments America aided. Neither Ngô Dinh Diem nor Thieu could be considered the head of democratic governments, and their credentials as defenders of freedom were, at best, questionable. One of the most undermining sources of declining American support for the war was the unopposed "reelection" of President Thieu in 1971. Finally, the military conditions of Vietnam insured that the United States could never win the war. Guerrilla tactics from the Viet Cong frustrated American generals schooled in conventional warfare; even if a direct victory was won, Communist forces lost little by retreating and waiting for a new opportunity to harass and surprise.

In Brown's view, we have not yet paid the full price of our folly in Vietnam. He points out that the Communist takeover in South Vietnam was followed by cruelties greater than any perpetrated by the United States; yet certain observers have criticized American actions so long that the Communists, by default, appear to be good. Such attitudes will inhibit any future effort to "fight Communism" where it resurfaces. This conclusion is no doubt correct—the question is whether this is a good or bad thing.

Thorough and fair as *The Last Chopper* is on the military and political side of the war, its perspective is narrowed by a neglect or misunderstanding of social forces. Although Brown chides the West for choosing to defend Vietnam, he still makes simple contrasts between the "free" and "Communist" worlds, as though each sphere were homogenous. He blames the South Vietnamese people for the failure of the Vietnam War, without reflecting on their attitude towards Thieu, towards Communism, and towards the prospect of endless war. Nor does he consider the underlying causes of sympathy among American liberals for the North Vietnamese. But perhaps this lack of depth in social analysis, this tendency to take things at face value, is just what makes Weldon Brown such a good reporter.

Burchett, Wilfred. *Grasshoppers and Elephants: Why Vietnam Fell*. New York: Urizen Books, 1977.

Through all the differing perspectives thrust upon Americans during the debate over Vietnam, one was noticeably (and understandably) lacking: the North Vietnamese point of view. Wilfred Burchett is all too eager to fill that gap. As an Australian, he had more freedom of movement during the war than most American journalists. Sympathetic to the Viet Minh during their final struggles against the French, he remained in contact with the Communists over the ensuing generation, and fully absorbed unquestioningly their experience and opinions of the war.

To Burchett, the moral superiority of the North Vietnamese was obvious. They had fought for more than thirty years for independence from colonial control—against the Chinese, Japanese, and the French. They had adopted Communism freely, as the best means towards regenerating the country, and Burchett freely testified to the benefits of the system. In touring the country, all he could see was prosperity, self-reliance, and endless determination; were these not sufficient proof that Communism was working? If there was anything bad to be seen, it was a consequence of the war: dim underground hideouts, militarism, the burned-out shell of an American bomber resting on display in Hanoi Zoo. The obvious conclusion was that the United States and the Saigon regimes were responsible for all evil.

Through such a perspective, Burchett is able to fit every event into a pattern of Communist heroism. If offensives falter and fail in South Vietnam, it is not because the local populations fail to sympathize and help the Viet Cong, but because the enemy is heavily financed and armed by capitalism. If only fifteen hundred people were killed in the Christmas bombings of Hanoi and Haipong, it is not because the American bombers avoided civilian "targets," but because the North Vietnamese government managed an almost total evacuation of the two cities. If the government accomplished remarkable feats, the credit rested with its popularity, not its coerciveness.

In discussing the Paris peace talks, the complete innocence Burchett attributes to the North Vietnamese government begins to break down. He suggests that their terms changed very little throughout the talks, but the United States gradually accepted their terms. Actually, the early proposals from North Vietnam asked for something approaching surrender; it seems fairly clear that during the early years of the talks, they felt their best chance lay in waiting out their opponents. Secret talks only made significant headway after Hanoi announced a new position in mid-1971. Likewise, the breakdown of talks in early 1972 probably had more to do with Communist plans to launch a new offensive than did American intransigence. When the Easter Offensive failed, talks again made rapid progress. Finally, Burchett consistently portrays the Saigon government as nothing more than a puppet of the Americans. In fact, however, Thieu became steadily more independent of the United States as withdrawals continued. By the end of 1972, when he balked at the proposed peace plan and helped to drag out the talks further, Thieu had very little to lose from ignoring American pleas for cooperation—it was very unlikely they would stop aiding his government in any case.

Because of its clear devotion to one side of the debate, *Grasshoppers and*

Elephants is more a polemic than a work of history. But it is still an interesting and important work, for it is sincere. Burchett believes what he is saying, and he reflects the viewpoint widely held by our enemies in the war. A great many American officials (and even more of the people) believed throughout the war that the Communists were sinister and diabolical. Because the United States often failed to understand the Communist point of view, and the good and earnest aspects of their cause, it took many years for the American government to understand the very nature of the war it was fighting. Burchett reveals a better understanding when he quotes Ho Chi Minh: "Our mountains will always be, our rivers will always be, our people will always be. The American invaders defeated, we will rebuild our land ten times more beautiful." — *R.H.S.*

Additional Recommended Reading

Dawson, Alan. *Fifty-five Days: The Fall of South Vietnam.* Englewood Cliffs, N.J.: Prentice-Hall, 1977. A fair and dramatic narrative of the Communist victory in Vietnam during March and April, 1975.

Jones, Alan M., Jr., ed. *U.S. Foreign Policy in a Changing World: The Nixon Administration, 1969-1973.* New York: David McKay, 1973. A collection of excellent articles largely concerned with assessing the consequences of withdrawal from Vietnam; features complete texts of the peace accords and earlier agreements.

Lake, Anthony, ed. *The Legacy of Vietnam.* New York: New York University Press, 1976. An informative series of articles evaluating the impact of Vietnam upon domestic and international affairs; contributors include Senators, officials, and academics.

Thompson, Sir Robert. *Peace Is Not at Hand.* London: Chatto and Windus, 1974. A conservative account of declining American involvement in Vietnam which criticizes heavily the "strategic surrender" of the United States in signing the 1973 peace agreement.

Thompson, W. Scott. *The Lessons of Vietnam.* New York: Crane-Russak Company, 1977. A combination of essays, interviews, and panel discussions are used to evaluate the war.

DIPLOMATIC RELATIONS ESTABLISHED BETWEEN EAST AND WEST GERMANY

Type of event: Diplomatic: efforts toward normalization of relations in central Europe
Time: June 21, 1973
Locale: Bonn and East Berlin

> *Principal personages:*
> WILLY BRANDT (HERBERT FRAHM) (1913-   ), Chancellor of the Federal Republic of Germany (FRG, "West Germany"), 1969-1974; and Chairman of the Social Democratic Party (SPD)
> WILLI STOPH (1914-   ), Chairman of the Council of Ministers of the German Democratic Republic (GDR, "East Germany")
> EGON BAHR (1922-   ), State Secretary in the Federal Chancery of the FRG and principal negotiator in Berlin, 1969-1972
> MICHAEL KOHL (1929-   ), State Secretary to the Council of Ministers of the GDR and plenipotentiary in Bonn

Summary of Event

The Treaty on the Basis of Relations Between the Federal Republic of Germany and the German Democratic Republic, the so-called Basic Treaty, entered into force on June 21, 1973. It was the instrument through which the two German states formally recognized each other as sovereign entities. The termination of the strict nonrecognition policy pursued by the FRG opened the door for the worldwide *de jure* recognition of the GDR. The establishment by the German states of mere "permanent representations" in each other's capitals, instead of full embassies, was a concession to the West German position on the state of the German nation. This position insisted on the continued existence of two German states within one German nation. Accordingly, the relationship between the two German states would have to be of a special nature, for the two entities could not deal with each other as if they were foreign states.

The Basic Treaty was a significant milestone in Chancellor Willy Brandt's innovative Eastern policy, aiming toward normalization of affairs with the East and the softening of the harsh impact of the division of Germany. The new Eastern policy represented a complete turn-about from the earlier West German posture, expressed by the so-called Hallstein Doctrine. This doctrine pursued as its principal objective the prevention of diplomatic recognition of the GDR by the non-Communist world. Bonn's earlier position maintained that Germany continued to exist in its 1937 borders. It was claimed that the German state, continuing as a subject before international law, was recognized in reorganized form in 1949 as the FRG. This legal standpoint, according to which the FRG represented the whole of the German nation, assumed that the borders of the former German Reich of 1937 maintained full validity in the legal sense, in spite of the fact that the constitution of the FRG could not be extended over the same area. A further deduction was that the FRG should pursue a foreign policy which would enable the other parts of Germany to enter into the realm of the Basic Law of the FRG. Thus, reunification of Germany within the 1937 borders was among the expressed goals of the FRG.

The new West German flexibility began to emerge with the "Grand Coalition" government in November, 1966, formed by the two largest West German parties, the Christian Democrats and the Social Democrats (SPD). As a junior partner in the coalition, the SPD was able to play a significant role in outlining a common denominator for the new West German policy thrust toward achieving normalized relations with Eastern Europe. The foremost goal would continue to be the finding of a satisfactory solution to the German problem, but the approach would be changed. Later, the parliamentary elections of 1969 enabled the SPD to form the government, in coalition with the Free Democratic Party (FDP), and to determine the basic guidelines of public policy. The new government, led by Willy Brandt, fully conceded the reality of the two German states and abandoned the earlier legal claims. The new formulation regarding the German national question was: "Two states within one

nation." This formulation, although not totally eliminating the core of the earlier posture, buried Bonn's claim of superiority over the East German regime.

Bonn's new position, making both states equal, was consistent with an earlier East German position respecting the German question. The East German Socialist Unity Party of Germany (SED) had often expressed its commitment to the reestablishment of national unity. However, when Brandt began his new Eastern policy initiatives, the GDR changed its position. Where it had spoken of itself as a socialist state of German nation before, the reference would now be a "socialist German nation-state." The new East German posture was designed to make possible a sharper ideological demarcation, to protect against possible undermining influences resulting from increased contacts with the West. With Moscow's course set on *détente*, more Western contacts became inescapable for the GDR. The East German regime had little choice but to respond to the West German policy initiatives, lest it face the prospect of isolation within the Communist camp.

Toward the end of 1969, the GDR expressed readiness for talks with the FRG, no longer insisting on its earlier pre-condition of formal diplomatic recognition. These developments led to the historic meeting between Brandt and Willi Stroph, Chairman of the Council of Ministers of the GDR, in Erfurt, on March 19, 1970. The subsequent negotiations between the two German states were very difficult and often intractable. Simultaneously, Bonn conducted talks with other

Warsaw Pact states. Treaties with Moscow and Warsaw were concluded, entailing the acceptance of the existing frontiers in central Europe, importantly including the Oder-Neisse Line, thereby formally conceding the loss of the former German eastern territories. In return, the East was expected to accept certain realities as well, such as West Berlin being a *de facto* part of the FRG. To some extent, Bonn's concerns regarding the security of West Berlin were accommodated by the Four Power Agreement on Berlin of September 3, 1971. Essentially, this agreement reaffirmed West Berlin's special status. In addition, it made possible the achievement of practical improvements involving civilian traffic between West Germany and West Berlin, the facilitating and simplifying of border clearance, and the general expansion of freedom of movement for West Berliners, all to be settled through specific arrangements between the governments of the GDR and the FRG or the Senate of West Berlin.

On November 8, 1972, State Secretaries Egon Bahr and Michael Kohl, the two principal negotiators in the German-German talks, initialed the Basic Treaty. The document provided for relations based on sovereign equality, peaceful settlement of disputes, respect for the signatories' territorial integrity, mutual support of arms control and disarmament, resolution of all problems of a practical and humanitarian nature, and the establishment of permanent missions in the respective capitals. A considerable number of issues, varying in importance and scope, were treated in

supplementary protocols. These included the resolution of problems relating to the border line, the creation of additional border crossings, the easing of travel restrictions for West Germans, the reuniting of families, the improvement of traffic in non-commercial goods, the working conditions for journalists, and the simultaneous application for membership in the United Nations.

The question regarding the continuing existence of the German nation was not settled by the Basic Treaty; it merely made it possible for both sides to maintain their differing legal positions. For Bonn it was imperative to uphold the concept of one German nation, to insist that the relationship between the two German states is of a special kind. There was no formal reference anywhere in the document to *diplomatic* relations. The substantial trade between the two states was to continue to be conducted on the basis of existing agreements. These have considered it to be inner-German, rather than foreign trade. The GDR quietly accepted this arrangement, for it provided substantial economic benefits. Nevertheless, the Basic Treaty entailed the mutual recognition of the signatories as sovereign states, irrespective of the specific terminology. The subsequent wave of *de jure* diplomatic recognitions of the GDR by Western and Third World countries and the existence of two German ambassadors in the capitals of the world legitimized and finalized the partition of Germany. In that sense, the German problem appears to have been solved. Reunification, in the form of joining the two states, has become at best a rather vague hope for the very distant future. In turn, a tolerable co-existence, rather than hostile confrontation, was given precedence. In short, the normali-zation of affairs and the attendent easing of the daily lives of the people was made possible.

Pertinent Literature

Birnbaum, Karl E. *East and West Germany: A Modus Vivendi.* Lexington, Mass.: D. C. Heath, 1973.

This slim volume, with its concise review and astute analysis of the East-West agreements of 1970-1972, including the texts of the treaties and some of the relevant diplomatic correspondence, represents a handy reference work for the developments leading to the new accommodations in central Europe. Karl E. Birnbaum, affiliated with the Swedish Institute of International Affairs, considers this phase of East-West relations to be highly significant in implication and potential. He feels that these developments have moved the ultimate elimination of the division of Europe with the realm of the possible.

Birnbaum suggests that between 1970 and 1971 Soviet leaders decided to give up some of their original options in Europe, in order to be able to exercise new and more promising ones. Accordingly, they adopted a posture more conciliatory toward the West. They specifically intended to improve relations with the FRG, which was most opportune for the West German endeavors toward Eastern Europe. In August, 1970, the Soviet Union and the FRG signed a treaty providing for normalization of their relations. It included the formal acceptance of the existing political and territorial *status quo* in central Europe. As Birnbaum points out, to Bonn the Moscow treaty was desirable for its dynamic potential as a starting point to transform the general nature of East-West relations in Europe, while Moscow places more importance on such static elements as the guarantee of the inviolability of the existing frontiers. More significantly, however, this treaty represented a basic change in Moscow's official view of the FRG. By implication, West Germany was now grouped among the peace-loving states, rather than the militarist and revanchist state it was previously portrayed as being. For the policymakers in Bonn it was particularly important to remove the West German bogey from the East European scene. In the past the Soviet Union had invariably invoked the "German menace" to promote cohesion in Eastern Europe, the last major occasion having been the Czechoslovak crisis in 1968. Bonn was, therefore, willing to make the substantial concession of formal acceptance of the existing conditions in central Europe, to acquire, as it were, the attribute "peaceful" and thus to arrive at a "package deal." Such a deal included the explicit Soviet acceptance of the *status quo* in Berlin.

The major objective of Bonn's Eastern policy was to break the impasse in inter-German relations. The

SPD leadership sought to bring about gradual change through *rapprochement* with the GDR. This constituted a policy of small steps, instead of the earlier all-or-nothing posture. The new West German government under Willy Brandt and Walter Scheel was convinced that through bilateral negotiations with Eastern European states the structure of confrontation could be dismantled. However, this step required the renunciation of claims previously upheld by the FRG. By 1969, when the new government took charge, the occasion was ripe for such a step, for the Eastern policy initiatives were in line with the new thrust of United States foreign policy.

Soviet and East German interests seemed to diverge, however, and there was a distinct East German apprehension over the Moscow-Bonn treaty. The SED leadership, more than before, had to choose between two equally distasteful alternatives: isolation within its own camp or increased exposure to Western influence and possible erosion of the SED power basis. The SED opted for the second, while skillfully moving to gain more maneuverability for its own negotiations with the West and protecting its power base through strict ideological demarcation in all contacts with the West.

The Basic Treaty ended a period of direct hostile confrontation in central Europe. Whether the formal coexistence would yield to genuine cooperation would depend on how it would be implemented and on the general process of increased interaction between East and West in Europe. After five years it is still not possible to state with confidence that genuine cooperation has been achieved. Still, Birnbaum's generally positive assessment is justified. Many practical improvements have been made and negotiations on various levels continue, entailing the prospect for more.

Schweigler, Gebhard Ludwig. *National Consciousness in Divided Germany*. Beverly Hills, Calif.: Sage Publications, 1975.

Gebhard Schweigler's valuable study puts the mutual formal recognition of the two German states into appropriate perspective. It addresses itself directly and thoroughly to the question of the German nation. Is there today one German people or are there two? Is there today one German nation or are there two? As noted above, the formal acceptance of two German states as sovereign entities has, in effect, legitimized and finalized the division of Germany. Is this step also shared by the people in each state? The answers to these questions would entail some highly relevant suggestions regarding the future of the formally established German-German relations. Schweigler is attempting to find such answers, even if only tentative. The range of his research is impressive, incorporating a considerable amount of statistical data about actual behavior.

When Germany capitulated in May, 1945, it ceased being one nation-state. However, the legal fiction of the continuing all-German nation-state was upheld until 1969, when the Brandt-Scheel government launched its Eastern policy. Recognizing the existence of two separate states, Brandt, nevertheless, insisted on the continuing existence of a formidable all-German national consciousness. Schweigler's point of departure is an expression of doubt regarding the validity of Brandt's assertion, and his study provides the evidence to the contrary. Since the end of World War II, Germans living in the FRG and in the GDR have not shared the same social, political, and economic institutions, and the channels of communication, all of which were once used to define the German nation-state. Perhaps this situation is reversible, for the most brutal border in the world has forced the severance. However, this reversibility depends on the will to be one German community. The cultural determinants do not appear to be very relevant, and even here there is evidence of the development of separate cultural patterns. Brandt was correct, according to Schweigler, in referring to national consciousness as the most meaningful concept in determining the existence of nationhood. The two states initially pursued similar policies regarding the German question by accepting the continuing existence of the all-German nation. Each pursued a policy of strength, to exert enough attraction for the other side to join it within the framework of its model for Germany. However, as each state became so successful in its own right, it became a new source of identification for its citizens.

Schweigler probes for all-German national consciousness and specific FRG and GDR national consciousness respectively. In turning to the

GDR, he finds evidence of a growing GDR nation-state consciousness, which, in the long run, could have the desirable impact of permitting the SED a policy of openness toward the West. He then analyzes the abundance of public opinion poll data available for West Germany on the German national question. To Schweigler the evidence is clear that the national goal of reunification, once vigorously defended, is no longer pursued by a majority of West Germans. Most West Germans now focus their attention on the FRG because of the failure of reunification policies and the shortcomings of the other great alternative: integration into a United States of Europe.

First on a purely instrumental level, but then, increasingly, on a sentimental level as well, sixty percent of the West German population share a specific West German national consciousness today. Thus, the FRG has truly become a nation-state in its own right. Important in this development were certain identifiable social processes, such as generational changes, the growth of prosperity, and social mobilization. Schweigler's methodologically impressive cross-section analysis suggests, in effect, that the German question has been answered by the forces of social and political development. Unfortunately, Schweigler was not able to apply the same thorough analysis to the GDR, because of the unavailability of public opinion data sets. Nevertheless, he feels there is enough evidence to suggest a pronounced specific GDR nation-state consciousness as well, and the question might be asked whether the two states are still compatible enough to be joined, even if it were possible otherwise.

After the Basic Treaty entered into force, massive construction projects were begun in both German capitals. This was especially the case in Bonn, which was for many years merely the "provisional" capital, but is now to be turned into one representative of West Germany's status. Other new symbols of national independence, such as United Nations membership and the permanent missions, have appeared on the scene. As people become used to such political facts, they will shed whatever remnants of an all-German consciousness they might yet retain. Schweigler's simple conclusion is that there are two Germanies, not one. — *M.G.*

Additional Recommended Reading

Dean, Robert W. *West German Trade with the East: The Political Dimension*. New York: Frederick A. Praeger, 1974. An excellent analysis of the politics of trade between East and West Germany and a discussion of the process of accommodation between the two states.

Merkl, Peter H. *German Foreign Policies, West and East: On the Threshold of a New European Era*. Santa Rosa, Calif.: ABC-Clio Press, 1974. An analysis of the individual foreign policies of the two German states against a one-hundred year background of German policies and attitudes.

Planck, Charles R. *The Changing Status of German Reunification in Western Diplomacy, 1955-1966*. Baltimore, Md.: The Johns Hopkins University Press, 1967. An interesting essay on the major junctures in East-West diplomacy showing increasing disagreement over the importance of German unity.

Plischke, Elmer. *Contemporary Governments of Germany*. Boston: Houghton Mifflin Company, 1969. Provides solid information on the political systems of the two German states.

Schütz, Wilhelm W. *Rethinking German Policy: New Approaches to Reunification*. New York: Frederick A. Praeger, 1967. A strong advocate of reunification recommending West German diplomatic initiatives to break the deadlock on the issues.

THE UNITED STATES SUPREME COURT RULES ON OBSCENITY

Type of event: Legal: judicial decision setting forth guidelines on obscenity
Time: June 21, 1973
Locale: The United States

Principal personage:
WARREN EARL BURGER (1907-   ), Chief Justice of the
United States Supreme Court, 1969-

Summary of Event

WASHINGTON, June 21—The Supreme Court handed down today a new set of guidelines on obscenity that will enable states to ban books, magazines, plays and motion pictures that are offensive to local standards, even if they might be acceptable elsewhere.

So read the lead sentence of the *New York Times* front-page story detailing the 1973 Court's five "rule-tightening" obscenity decisions, each the result of a five-to-four vote split among the Justices (with the four Nixon appointees, including the Chief Justice, in the majority). Unfortunately, however, this sentence contained a crucial inaccuracy that raised a false alarm: after the word "ban," the *Times* should have inserted the controlling phrase "hard-core pornographic."

True, in the principal case of *Miller* v. *California* (1973), Chief Justice Burger made absolutely no mention of the "hard-core" restriction in setting forth these basic guidelines to be used in determining a work's obscenity: whether "the average person, applying contemporary community standards" would find that the work, taken as a whole, appeals to the prurient interest; whether the work depicts or describes, in a patently offensive way, sexual conduct specifically defined by the applicable state law; and whether the work, taken as a whole, lacks serious literary, artistic, political, or scientific value. Furthermore, Burger held that the existence of unvarying First Amendment limitations on state powers did not "mean that there are, or should or can be, fixed uniform national standards of precisely what appeals to the 'prurient interest' or 'patently offensive.' "

But although Burger did not use the qualifying term "hard-core" in setting forth the obscenity guidelines, he did use that term at least four times elsewhere in the course of his opinion, and in contexts that made it fairly clear that the trier-of-fact guidelines applied to only a certain class of pornography, not simply to anything pornographic. He even gave fairly specific examples of what a state legislature could legislate against: "patently offensive representations or descriptions of ultimate sexual acts, normal or perverted, actual or simulated" and "patently offensive representations or descriptions of masturbation, excretory functions, and lewd exhibition of the genitals."

1174

So, although there may have been some ambiguity in the Court's opinion, there was certainly not enough to warrant the omission from the *New York Times* account of the "hardcore" limitation on what states and localities could ban.

In any event, the Court soon made its meaning in *Miller* v. *California* perfectly clear by its 1974 ruling in *Jenkins* v. *Georgia*. Jenkins had been convicted for violating a state statute by showing the film *Carnal Knowledge*, which had some nudity and scenes that implied the occurrence of "ultimate sex acts," and starred Candice Bergen, Art Garfunkel, Jack Nicholson, and Ann-Margret, who was nominated for an Academy Award for her performance. The Court unanimously reversed the lower court decision, saying that it had taken "pains in *Miller* to 'give a few plain examples of what a state statute could define for regulation.' " Then, after repeating those examples and noting that they were "certainly intended to fix substantive constitutional limitations," the majority opinion continued: "It would be wholly at odds with this aspect of *Miller* to uphold an obscenity conviction based on a defendant's depiction of a woman with a bare midriff, even though a properly charged jury unanimously agreed on a verdict of guilty."

What the Court had evidently sought to do in 1973 was to give more (though by no means a great deal more) discretion to states and localities to regulate obscenity so that it could largely be relieved of having to serve as a national board of censors—a role it assumed in 1957 by virtue of the *Roth* case, at the height of a period of obscenity prosecutions of respected works of literature. To shed its adopted role of national censor, however, required at least two moves on the Court's part. First, as already noted, the standard involving "the average person, applying contemporary community standards," had to be interpreted as no longer requiring that the contemplated community be national. The second move was a bit more tricky, because a presidential commission report had to be disregarded without at the same time denying its serious scientific value.

The Commission on Obscenity and Pornography had previously concluded in 1970 that no evidence of harmful effects from exposure to sexual materials had been found, and that "federal, state, and local legislation prohibiting the sale, exhibition, or distribution of sexual materials to consenting adults should be repealed." The Court now had to deal with these conclusions; the only question was how. The answer came in the 1973 *Paris Theatre* case, which involved the showing of two films at a theater whose entrance was without pictures but which had a sign that read: "Adult Theatre—You must be 21 and able to prove it. If viewing the nude body offends you, Please Do Not Enter." The films themselves depicted, in the Court's words, "simulated fellatio, cunnilingus, and group sex intercourse." Thus, the issue was clearly drawn. Could any, even hardcore pornographic, materials be legally denied consenting adults? If not, the "two-level speech" theory propounded in *Roth* (whereby material deemed obscene is not protected by the First Amendment) would be effectively overturned.

Many thought that the Court under the prior Chief Justice, Earl Warren, was headed toward just such a reversal. Since the 1966 *Memoirs* (*Fanny Hill*) case, wherein only works "utterly without redeeming social value" might be judged obscene, no banning of a book had been sustained; and in the 1969 *Stanley* v. *Georgia* case, which upheld the right to possess privately so-called obscene films, a Court opinion stated: "If the First Amendment means anything, it means that a state has no business telling a man, sitting alone in his own house, what books he may read or what films he may watch." Also, reversing *Roth* would be one way to shed the role of censor. So perhaps, though there were some significant signs to the contrary, the Warren Court would have taken this route—especially in the light of the obscenity commission report. But this was the Burger Court, and the five-to-four opinion stated that even adults who consent can be prohibited from viewing hard-core pornography if so decided by a legislature. The Chief Justice argued that, "although there is no conclusive proof of a connection between antisocial behavior and obscene material, the legislature of Georgia could quite reasonably determine that such a connection does or might exist." Thus, the commission report was disregarded until the case of *Hamling* v. *United States*.

In the 1974 *Hamling* case, the Court affirmed a conviction for mailing and conspiring to mail an obscene advertising brochure containing photographs appearing in an illustrated version of the obscenity commission report. By the now-familiar five-to-four voting pattern, the Court ruled in effect that the advertisement selling the illustrated report lacked any serious scientific value. This subtle backhand slap at the commission report did not go unnoticed. "If officials may constitutionally report on obscenity," said a dissenting Justice, then there is "nothing in the First Amendment that allows us to bar the use of a glossary factually to illustrate what the report discusses." But whatever secondary maneuverings may have been going on among the Justices, one thing was certain—any attempt by the Court to escape the role of national censor board through its 1973 decisions was thoroughly thwarted by its own 1974 decisions.

As Justice William J. Brennan said bluntly in a concurring opinion in *Jenkins*: "It is clear that as long as the *Miller* test remains in effect 'one cannot say with certainty that material is obscene until at least five members of this Court, applying inevitably obscure standards, have pronounced it so.'" In short, another route will have to be found if the Court's case-by-case obscenity quagmire is ever to be circumvented.

Pertinent Literature

Schauer, Frederick F. *The Law of Obscenity*. Washington, D.C.: Bureau of National Affairs, 1976.

Although intended primarily for   lawyers, this handbook also provides a thorough overview and analysis of obsenity law for the layman. In a mere three hundred pages of well-written text, Schauer covers the historical background of obscenity law (Chapters 1-3), the main substantive concepts of obscenity law (Chapters 4-8), the mid-1970's state and federal obscenity regulations (Chapters 9 and 10), and the procedural considerations and practical problems relevant to obscenity litigation (Chapters 11-17). In another one hundred pages of appendixes, the author has reprinted United States statutes and major U.S. Supreme Court decisions pertaining to obscenity.

Frustratingly, however, the dissenting (as well as separate concurring) opinions are completely omitted; all the reader gets is "the opinion of the Court," with all its paraphrasing of and swipes at the other opinions. This is frustrating, indeed, yet not at all unexpected, for the author tells us plainly that his volume takes the existence of obscenity law as given and, even where the law is unclear, treats only the relatively narrow legal problems. "This book is not," understates Schauer, "an appropriate vehicle for suggesting entirely new directions in obscenity law." In short, the two-level theory of free speech is not at all questioned. Within these parameters, however, it is no exaggeration to say that *The Law of Obscenity* offers the layman as well as the lawyer an extremely informative treatise on an area of speech that is not presently protected by the First Amendment. But the book's stated limitations must always be kept in mind, lest the reader come away mistaking the part for the whole.

For, as John Stuart Mill noted, hearing only one side of an argument deprives the citizen not only of knowing the other side or sides, but also of fully comprehending the side heard. This is not to say that the book should have been primarily an argument either for or against obscenity laws, or even a catalogue of the arguments; but the book should not simply espouse the view of the Court majority as it does.

For example, in discussing the case of *Ginsburg* (1968) the author goes to great lengths (giving extensive Court quotes) to refute the dissenters' opinion (never quoted) that the Court had created a new crime, one of "pandering," which was not a crime at the time the defendant distributed the materials under review. Then, again, in discussing the 1973 decisions, the majority's "specificity requirements" in *Miller* (with quotes supplied) are implicitly put forth as an effective rebuttal of Justice Brennan's dissent in *Paris Theatre* (with quotes omitted), wherein he criticized the two-level free speech theory.

Further instances of what appear to be judicial infallibility involve the Court's five-man majority move toward local community standards and also its move away from the "utterly without redeeming social value" test. In the latter move, Schauer regards the replacement of "lacks serious . . . value" for "utterly without . . . value" as now allowing juries and courts to get beneath the claimed import and to the intent; the rejection of "social value" as eliminating an ambiguous concept; and the enumeration of "literary, artistic, political, or scientific" as including everything it should while excluding nothing it should not. The move toward local standards is similarly sacrosanct. Local standards are seen by the author as being more ascertainable than national ones, as giving vitality without losing anything, and as having the beneficial effect (if any) of creating "new opportunities for proof which may be as advantageous to the defense as to the prosecution." Thus the author tries to have it both ways: good riddance to the "social value" concept because its ambiguity presumably hurts the adversaries; welcome to the "local standards" test because its ambiguity can help them.

Now, to be sure, there is nothing inherently wrong with seeking to put the best face possible on the so-called supreme law of the land, and most lawyers (especially prosecutors) will be well served by such an approach. Hence it should be repeated that *The Law of Obscenity* is an extremely useful book in its own right. Nevertheless, from the standpoint of constitutional law, it is very incomplete. Because it fails to provide a complete picture, dissents and all, of where obscenity law is at present, it cannot (as recognized by the author) suggest "new directions" for the future. This means that the book can aid the lawyer operating under current (1974) constitutional criteria, but it will be obsolete as soon as the Court takes a new direction. And it means, furthermore, that the book lacks precisely what the counsel for the defense needs to know in order to shape tomorrow's new direction by changing the Court's opinion today.

Kalven, Harry, Jr. "The Metaphysics of the Law of Obscenity," in *The Supreme Court and the Constitution*. Edited by Philip B. Kurland. Chicago: University of Chicago Press, 1965.

Kalven's classic forty-five-page treatise on obscenity was originally published in *The Supreme Court Review* in 1960. As such, it obviously cannot recount the history of obscenity law leading up to *Miller* and the companion cases of 1973. Yet—because of the careful and complete analysis of the Court's obscenity cases between 1956 and 1959, especially *Roth*—it can and does predict the general direction of the Court's position on obscenity through 1969, to *Stanley*. Indeed, the treatise is still helpful today in understanding the new directions that the Court has taken in the 1970's.

Kalven begins his study by noting that there are primarily two kinds of constitutional problems in obscenity law. The first involves the ambiguity of the word "obscenity"; the second derives from the "clear and present danger" test applied to speech. In the latter problem, his analysis reveals four possible dangers that obscenity laws were meant to avoid: the incitement to antisocial sexual conduct; the excitement produced by sexual imagery; the arousal of disgust and revulsion; and the advocacy of improper sexual values. "All present difficulties," says the author, as he concisely cuts through to the difficulty in each instance:

It is hard to see why the advocacy of improper sexual values should fare differently, as a constitutional matter, from any other exposition in the realm of ideas. Arousing disgust and revulsion in a voluntary audience seems an impossibly trivial base for making speech a crime. The incitement of antisocial conduct . . . evaporates in the light of the absence of any evidence to show a connection between the written word and overt sexual behavior. There remains the evil of arousing sexual thoughts short of action. There is no doubt that the written word can excite the imagination. What puzzled Judge Bok and amused Judge Frank was the idea that the law could be so solemnly concerned with the sexual fantasies of the adult population.

With this preliminary framework established, Kalven gets down to cases. *Butler* (1956), in which Michigan's statute banning books having a deleterious effect on minors was unanimously struck down because it would have reduced the state's adult population to reading "only what is fit for children," provides the immediate background for the landmark decision of *Roth* (1957). In *Roth* the constitutional issue revolving around the question of a "clear and present danger" was quickly disposed of by an extension of the doctrine first appearing in *Chaplinsky* (1942) and given full status in *Beauharnais* (1952), namely the two-level free-speech theory. "All ideas having even the slightest redeeming social importance," said the majority through Justice Brennan, are protected by the First Amendment; obscenity, however, is "utterly without redeeming social importance." Thus did the Court dehorn the dilemma of having to ban

obscenity in the absence of a clear and present danger.

But the Brennan opinion thereby made the ambiguity of "obscenity" an even greater constitutional problem, for now the classification of a work as obscene or not would determine whether it were protected or not. True, the Court attempted to clarify the concept of obscenity by adopting the definition in the American Law Institute's model penal code: "Whether to the average person, applying contemporary community standards, the dominant theme of the material taken as a whole appeals to prurient interest." But as Kalven points out after examining the meaning of the key word "prurient," this latest definition of obscenity was still basically a tautology: the obscene is that which appeals to an interest in the obscene. Therefore, as the author further points out, Justice Harlin exposed the central weakness of the majority decision when he argued that grave *constitutional* questions of free speech cannot be settled by *factual* answers arrived at by lower courts depending on a category as ambiguous as obscenity. The Court would constantly be called upon to render its judgment on this or that particular material—that is, to serve as a national board of censors caught in a case-by-case mire.

Furthermore, since the majority in *Roth* justified the unprotected status of obscenity on the basis of its being utterly without social importance, the Court would have to review independently lower-court judgments on obscenity. Otherwise it might find itself trapped into absurdly affirming that a work such as *Ulysses* or the *Deca-*

meron was utterly without social importance simply because a lower court had pronounced the work obscene. In view of these tensions, Kalven predicted in 1960 that Harlan's dissenting opinion regarding the need for independent Court review would triumph as soon as the occasion arose, and that the *Roth* decision would have the effect of liberalizing the enforcement of obscenity statutes—restricting obscenity to something akin to "hard-core" pornography. And that is what transpired.

In *Memoirs* (1966), which reversed a lower court's decision that *Fanny Hill* was obscene, Brennan declared, "A book cannot be proscribed unless it is found to be *utterly* without redeeming social value." A six-year period of so-called *Redrup* reversals (more than thirty cases involving mostly *per curiam* reversals of lower-court obscenity convictions) then followed. Even the Court's 1973-1974 decisions still retain the requirement that obscenity be restricted to the pornographically hard-core. Yet the recent change in the obscenity definition does go somewhat against Kalven's prediction, for the two-level speech doctrine evidently rests now on the weaker foundation represented by the argument that obscenity is unprotected merely because it has no *serious* literary, artistic, political, or scientific value. No doubt this change largely explains Burger's attempt in *Paris Theatre* to establish some sort of "clear and present danger" rationale for state legislation, as well as his opinion that a book can be banned because it may fall into the hands of children.

At any rate, the Court seems to be returning to the *Butler-Roth* era, at least temporarily. Only this time, with Harlan gone, it is Brennan in a separate opinion who is warning of the inevitable "institutional stress upon the judiciary" that will result from decisions that fail to "extricate us from the mire of case-by-case determinations of obscenity." And this time it is a lack of serious value only, rather than a lack of any value whatsoever, that the Court need worry about being trapped into affirming by some lower court. Thus the tensions in *Roth* discerned by Kalven may once again generate pressures on the Justices to escape the entanglements of obscenity statutes by liberalizing their enforcement. — *E.G.D.*

Additional Recommended Reading

Lewis, F. F. *Literature, Obscenity, and Law*. Carbondale: Southern Illinois University Press, 1976. A liberal account of the history of legal censorship of literary works which later came under the protection of the First Amendment, emphasizing the position that narrative representations of sexual behavior should never be banned.

Report of the Commission on Obscenity and Pornography. Washington, D.C.: U.S. Government Printing Office, 1970. The report that recommended the lifting of all restrictions on pornographic materials, resulting in its repudiation by Congress and President Nixon.

Sunderland, Lane V. *Obscenity: The Court, the Congress, and the President's Commission*. Washington, D.C.: American Enterprise Institute, 1975. A conservative interpretation of the Court's 1973-1974 obscenity rulings, with emphasis on dissenting reports of the obscenity commission and on philosophical arguments favoring obscenity restrictions.

Young, Mayor of Detroit et al. v. *American Mini Theaters Inc. et al.* 427 U.S. 50, 49 L. Ed. 2d 310, 96 S. Ct. 2440 (1976). A serious attempt by the Court, in a five-to-four decision, to avoid the dilemmas of case-by-case censorship judgments by permitting X-rated theaters to be subject to restrictive zoning.

THE YOM KIPPUR WAR

Type of event: Military: use of force to attain political and territorial objectives
Time: October, 1973
Locale: Israel, Egypt, and Syria

Principal personages:
HAFEZ AL-ASSAD (1930-), Syrian head of state who cooperated in the joint attack on Israel
GOLDA MEIR (1898-1978), Prime Minister of Israel, 1969-1974
ANWAR EL-SADAT (1918-), President of Egypt, 1970-
MOSHE DAYAN (1915-), Israeli Minister of Defense
HENRY ALFRED KISSINGER (1923-), United States Secretary of State, 1973-1977
AHMED ISMAIL (1923-), Egyptian military commander
MAJOR GENERAL ARIEL SHARON (1928-), Israeli military commander

Summary of Event

Before studying the Yom Kippur War itself, it is necessary to understand something of the geography and political history of that area of the Middle East which includes and surrounds Israel. When its territorial gains in Sinai are included, Israel is shaped like a pitcher: the Sinai is the body of the vessel, and to the east, extending well above the lip, is the oblong handle—the state of Israel more or less as it was after the 1948 War of Independence. Israel is surrounded by Arab states, except to the north, where it borders the Mediterranean. In the Yom Kippur War, Israel's two major enemies were Syria to the northeast and Egypt, across the Suez Canal, west of Sinai.

As a result of the Six-Day War in June, 1967, Israel had gained the Sinai from Egypt and the Golan Heights from Syria. The Arab armies had been swiftly crushed and humiliated by Israeli tanks supported by airpower. This humiliation strengthened the resolve of the Egyptian and Syrian governments. They assessed Israel's military strength and their own, and after years of planning, they decided to mount a surprise attack on two fronts—an invasion across to the east bank of the Suez Canal and into the Golan Heights in the north. They had meticulously planned and trained for this coordinated attack, which would result, they thought, in two static, set-piece battles where a mass of well-trained troops would render ineffectual Israel's superiority in a war of movement.

Arab plans also took advantage of Israeli euphoria following the Jews' incredible victory in the Six-Day War. Because of this victory the Israelis thought of themselves as invincible, and the Arabs did everything they could to encourage this Israeli belief. As a result, the Israelis were lulled into a sense of security that lacked substance. Military training was allowed to deteriorate, and the logistics of warfare-readiness were well below par. The plan for calling up military reserves in the event of war was cumbersome, due in part to the lack of railroad lines. This deficiency also impeded the flow of equipment and supplies, depots of which were in many cases very poorly placed. Finally, the military lacked unified command, was wracked by dissention, and was undermined by an absurdly rigid early retirement policy within the officer corps.

The Arabs derived additional leverage from a study of Israeli tactics. The Israelis depended for swift victory on a war of movement—tanks supported by airplanes. Their artillery support was light and they regarded infantry as secondary. In the Six-Day War, these tactics proved effective, but now the Arabs had two classes of Soviet-made weapons which were designed to neutralize the tank and the airplane. With the aid of the portable Sagger missile, a single infantryman could destroy a tank with relative ease. Israeli aircraft would be vulnerable to a combination of surface-to-air (SAM) missiles backed up by the latest Soviet antiaircraft gun.

October 6, 1973, was Yom Kippur—the holiest and most important day of the Jewish year, a time of prayer and atonement when all ordinary activities cease and Orthodox Jews spend the day fasting and praying in synagogues. In Israel on Yom Kippur, no one travels except on foot, and there are no radio or television broadcasts. On the Bar-Lev line (the line of static Israeli defenses on the east bank of the Suez Canal),

overage reservists were waiting out their tour of duty, while on the Golan Heights, undermanned units observed Yom Kippur.

Without warning, at two o'clock in the afternoon, the Egyptians and Syrians mounted a coordinated attack on two fronts. The Egyptians crossed to the east bank of the Suez Canal on a broad front, bypassed and later neutralized the Bar-Lev line, and established a shallow but firm beachhead in the Sinai. On the Golan, Syrian armor and infantry, supported by aircraft and artillery, crumpled Israeli defenses. A Syrian commando attack captured a key Israeli observation post. Vastly outnumbered defenders fought a fierce but seemingly losing battle. Early Israeli counterattacks, mounted with optimism, failed. The Egyptians and the Syrians had calculated correctly. The heat-seeking SAM missiles downed Israeli fighters, while the Sagger missiles destroyed their tanks on the ground.

The Israelis were eventually victorious, however. They broke through at the Golan Heights and Israeli tanks came within close range of Damascus, the Syrian capital. Moreover, Israeli bombings severely damaged the Syrian economic machine. On the Egyptian front, General Ariel Sharon invaded the west bank of the Canal, formed a bridgehead, and destroyed the SAM batteries. Once the Israeli air force no longer had to contend with a missile threat, it could offer adequate air cover to tanks and troops. At the call of the ceasefire the Egyptian Third Army was completely surrounded; there is every reason to believe that it would have had to surrender in a matter of days.

Israel succeeded, but at great cost. The dollar amounts needed to prosecute the war and to build up the military in the postwar period were staggering. The war had lasted a little more than two weeks, and in that period Israel had lost eight hundred tanks and 115 aircraft. In addition, 2,523 Israelis had been killed in combat. Worse perhaps than these heavy losses in men and matériel was Israel's changed position as a military power in the Middle East. Israel had won—this time; but there were to be no more easy victories. No longer could the Arab armies be dismissed with a shrug and a joke.

In men and matériel the Arab costs were greater. They lost two thousand tanks and some 450 planes, and the Syrian economy was severely damaged. However, these severe losses were balanced by a political victory of great proportions. No longer could Arab military strength be casually dismissed; the balance of power in the Middle East had changed forever.

This change in the balance of power was accelerated by the Arabs' discovery of oil as a political weapon. Never before had they thought of using their vast oil reserves to influence the eventual settlement, but now they used this weapon very effectively. Western Europe and Japan, virtually dependent on Arab oil, were completely intimidated. Even the United States, although less dependent, had to take Arab demands seriously into consideration.

The issue of oil places the Arab-Israeli conflict squarely in the international arena, which in 1973 was dominated by the two superpowers—the Soviet Union and the United States. The United States supplied arms to Israel, the Soviet Union to the Arab states. Since it was in neither superpower's interest to have a clearcut Arab or Israeli victory, weaponry was doled out with a careful eye toward stalemate. In a larger sense, therefore, the Yom Kippur War was not so much a war between Israel and the Arabs as a confrontation of the superpowers in which Jews and Arabs were only pawns. *Détente* had to be preserved and global nuclear war avoided; in these matters Israeli and Arab positions counted very little.

Pertinent Literature

The Insight Team of the London Sunday *Times*. *The Yom Kippur War*. Garden City, N.Y.: Doubleday & Company, 1974.

A balanced view of the Yom Kippur War, this collaboration of experienced London-based journalists attempts to be fair to both the Egyptians and the Israelis; the Soviet Union and the United States; and to the military and the political aspects of the conflict. It takes us behind the scenes to show us the leaders of nations and demonstrate how, for these leaders, the War finally became inextricably enmeshed in and controlled by international politics—the politics of *détente*. Behind the Armageddon rhetoric of the Egyptians and the Israelis were very human leaders with understandable motivations. Egypt's President, Anwar el-Sadat, took over the reins of government in the shadow of Nasser's charisma and in the wake of the humiliation of the Six-Day War. He had to do something to establish his credibility, and Egypt's. A successful war seemed the only answer. As Commander in Chief, Sadat appointed Ahmed Ismail, a brilliant and meticulous planner. Ismail took advantage of three crucial factors: the numerical superiority of the Egyptian army, the new tactics made possible by Egypt's acquisition of Soviet missiles, and the Israeli myth of invincibility.

Golda Meir, the Israeli Prime Minister, was a woman of seventy-five with enormous personal reserves that belied her years. She had to deal with a military without a unified command structure, and a parliamentary government pieced together by the most fragile of coalitions, at a time when Israel was on the edge of disaster. Attacked on two fronts, the Israeli army was falling back with staggering casualties. Worse, the Israeli tactics which were so successful in the Six-Day War were largely ineffectual. Golda Meir's determination, along with the courage and ingenuity of the Israeli military, snatched victory from defeat. Still, although Israel won on the battlefield, it lost in the game of international politics whose chief player was Henry Kissinger.

Kissinger, a German Jew by heritage, was a conservative diplomat by inclination and training. His overriding concern and key instrument in the search for peace was *détente* between the United States and the Soviet Union. His success as a diplomat was based on his considerable skill and intelligence and on his complete faith in pragmatism. His goal was to have Egypt and Israel stop fighting and yet allow both to leave the battlefield with their honor intact.

On matters of political pragmatism, the Soviet Union and the United States agreed. Each superpower was interested in preserving its sphere of influence in the Middle East, and to this end, each side was willing to supply one of the contestants with sophisticated arms. The Soviet and American military establishments looked on carefully to see what effect all this new weaponry had, tested under actual combat conditions. But from the Yom Kippur War one overriding political lesson was learned: the conflict of client states must not lead to superpower confrontation— and the brink of nuclear war.

The book gives considerable space to the military aspects of the war; the strategy and tactics of both sides are discussed in considerable detail. Israeli and Egyptian tactics are carefully analyzed. Each important battle is covered. There is even an extensive pictorial essay comparing the Soviet weaponry used by the Egyptians to the American weaponry used by the Israelis. The important message of the book, however, is that military force is merely an extension of politics. Before the outbreak of the war, Israel enjoyed a reputation for invincibility and for the apparently unswerving support of the United States; after the war, her victory was essentially subverted by the sudden emergence of the Arabs as a substantial military power and the uncomfortable revelation of the conditional nature of American support.

Herzog, Chaim. *The War of Atonement, October, 1973*. Boston: Little, Brown and Company, 1975.

This volume by a retired Israeli Major General is a military history strictly from the Israeli point of view. Although it attempts to be fair to the Arabs, it does not treat Arab tactics and strategy in detail.

A great deal of the book is a detailed account of the various battles that make up the Yom Kippur War. Of most interest to the general reader, perhaps, are the final two chapters. The first of these is entitled "The Air and Naval War." In the air war, as a result of their experience in the War of Attrition (March, 1969, to August, 1970) and their contact with Soviet technical expertise, the Egyptians decided to create an air defense consisting mainly of missiles—a combined system of SAM's 2, 3, 6, and 7. Added to this was the multibarreled ZSU 23, a Soviet antiaircraft gun. This combination was to prove deadly to the Israeli air force. Especially effective was the combination of SAM 6 and SAM 2, because to seek out the former, one had to enter the range of the latter. Although this formidable Arab weaponry should have been the Israeli air force's priority target, such targeting was not possible initially because of the early successes of the Arab ground forces. Early in the war, the Israeli air force was called upon to give close support to ground forces, with minimal effect and at a terrible cost. As the war went on, the Israeli air and ground forces were able to neutralize many missile sites, and the Israelis gained relative

mastery of the air. Still, it is clear that, as a result of missile sophistication, air power will have limited usefulness in the tactics of future battles.

The naval war was definitely a sideshow, but was not without significance. The Israelis relied entirely on maneuverable small missile boats with crews of forty. These boats, Israeli-built and armed with the Israeli Gabriel missile, overpowered the Egyptian and Syrian navies and throughout the war maintained mastery over the Mediterranean and the Gulf of Suez. The Arabs lost nineteen naval vessels in the conflict, including ten missile boats, while Israel did not lose a single boat. It is clear from the success of the Israelis that navies of a conventional type are of limited usefulness in closed seas.

Herzog's last chapter, "Lessons and Implications," is also aimed at the general reader. As a result of their successful experience during the Six-Day War, the Israeli military emphasized the plane and the tank to the detriment of infantry and artillery. But the plane and the tank were vulnerable to missile attack and relatively useless in night fighting. What the Israeli military needs is a balanced force with high mobility. Infantry must be used more effectively, and artillery rather than airplanes must be employed in close support. The author offers two other criticisms of the Israeli military. First, before and during the war, intelligence was defective. Second, Israel's faith in the ability of its skeleton border forces to fend off early Arab attacks was unrealistic.

The Arabs fought better than they ever had. The Egyptian infantry especially had learned to excel in defensive warfare and in the set-piece attack, such as the initial invasion of Sinai by crossing the Suez Canal. In addition, the Egyptian strategy at high levels was excellent, and its intelligence, in many cases, superb. The Syrians fought bravely and their military was well-disciplined, but the competence of Syrian forces has been much exaggerated. Their initial success was based on surprise and on overwhelming superiority of numbers rather than on competence. —*A.G.G.*

Additional Recommended Reading

Golan, Matti. *The Secret Conversations of Henry Kissinger: Step-by-Step Diplomacy in the Middle East.* Translated by Ruth Geyra Stern and Sol Stern. New York: Quadrangle/New York Times Book Company, 1976. A diplomatic correspondent for a leading Israeli newspaper gives a behind-the-scenes account of Kissinger's shuttle diplomacy during the Yom Kippur War.

Hazan, Baruch A. *Soviet Propaganda: A Case Study of the Middle East Conflict.* New York: John Wiley & Sons, 1976. A study of pro-Arab propaganda in which the state of Israel plays a scapegoat role.

Orni, Efraim and Elisha Efrat. *Geography of Israel.* New York: American Heritage Press, 1971. Deals with the geology, morphology, climate, population, history, and economy of Israel with special emphasis on the interrelationships among these fields.

Rosenfeld, Alvin. *The Plot to Destroy Israel: The Road to Armageddon.* New York: G. P. Putnam's Sons, 1977. A veteran foreign correspondent places the Yom Kippur War in a chain of events which, he says, has as its goal the destruction of Israel.

RESIGNATION OF VICE-PRESIDENT
SPIRO T. AGNEW

Type of event: Political: resignation of a Vice-President of the United States
Time: October 10, 1973
Locale: Washington, D.C.

Principal personages:

SPIRO THEODORE AGNEW (1918-   ), thirty-ninth Vice-President of the United States, 1969-1973

RICHARD MILHOUS NIXON (1913-   ), thirty-seventh President of the United States, 1969-1974

ELLIOT LEE RICHARDSON (1920-   ), Attorney General of the United States, 1973

GEORGE BROOKE BEALL (1926-   ), United States Attorney for Baltimore

WALTER EDWARD HOFFMAN (1907-   ), United States District Judge of the Fourth District

Summary of Event

With the exception of John C. Calhoun, who resigned the Vice-Presidency of the United States in 1832 for political reasons, Spiro T. Agnew is the only other person to have resigned from that office. Virtually unknown outside his native state of Maryland prior to 1968 when he was selected by Richard M. Nixon for the Republican vice-presidential nomination, his name quickly became a household word following his election. Agnew identified himself with the Nixon Administration's pursuit of the war in Indochina, and he vehemently denounced the forces of protest and disorder that opposed continued American involvement in that conflict. This stance earned him many enemies, particularly in the intellectual community and among members of the press—chief targets of Agnew's verbal attacks. However, it made him a hero among supporters of the war and throughout conservative, middle-class America, which felt that the nation's social fabric was coming unraveled at the hands of radicals who favored peace abroad at any price and violent protest at home.

Both Nixon and Agnew were reelected in a landslide victory in 1972, which seemed to indicate that the public generally supported the Administration's gradual withdrawal from the Indo-Chinese conflict. Agnew was securely established within the Administration and enjoyed a national following which was convinced that he stood for the forces of stability, law and order, and the whole gamut of middle-class, suburban, small-town American social values, which he articulated in his public speeches and pronouncements. For these reasons the resignation of Agnew from the Vice-Presidency in October, 1973, after pleading no contest to a federal income tax charge, left his supporters and much of the nation amazed.

The United States Attorney for

Baltimore, George Beall, and his staff rather routinely uncovered evidence of criminal activity on Agnew's part while pursuing a number of old political corruption cases in Maryland. This evidence, indicating that Agnew as a Maryland public official had awarded state contracts in exchange for personal payments, was turned over to the Attorney General of the United States, Elliot L. Richardson, who perceived the case against Agnew to be overwhelming and unquestionable. This alone made the matter very delicate; the problem was compounded by the fact that the Watergate scandal, which had plagued the Nixon Administration since the spring of 1973, was moving toward a climax, and in the event that the President was impeached and convicted, Agnew would be next in line for the presidency. Richardson was convinced that this must not be allowed to happen, since evidence in his possession necessitated that the Vice-President be indicted, and the nation could not run the risk of a convicted felon acceding to the presidency. Richardson thus determined to plea bargain with Agnew in order to secure his voluntary resignation.

Agnew, when presented with the charges, which already had been leaked to the press and the public, at first vehemently denied any wrongdoing and vowed to fight for his integrity. He eventually appealed to the leadership of the House of Representatives to investigate the charges against him and even to impeach him if that body found him guilty of the charges in question. The leadership failed to oblige the Vice-President, leaving Agnew with the decision of the Justice Department that a sitting Vice-President could be indicted and tried. President Nixon meanwhile had taken a very neutral position, since he knew the evidence against Agnew to be overwhelming. Eventually he, along with Richardson, committed himself to securing Agnew's resignation as the easiest way out for what was obviously a very touchy situation.

These events built up during the summer and autumn of 1973, and while Agnew promised his supporters that he would fight to the end for his reputation, he in fact had already decided to have his lawyers begin plea bargaining with the Justice Department. The House and the President had both failed him, and he had no choice but to face the Attorney General. Richardson eventually secured the resignation of the Vice-President in exchange for Agnew's plea, before Fourth District United States Judge Walter E. Hoffman, of no contest to a charge of evading federal income taxes on a payment made to him by a state contractor. Judge Hoffman then gave Agnew a suspended prison sentence and a $10,000 fine, and allowed the Justice Department to publish a statement of its charges against the defendant which were then dropped. This settlement, achieved by secret plea bargaining, took the public by surprise; under ordinary circumstances, it would have created considerable public interest and shock. However, within the larger context of the Watergate scandal, attention tended to be fixed on President Nixon, who was moving toward his own resignation.

Pertinent Literature

Cohen, Richard M. and Jules Witcover. *A Heartbeat Away*. New York: The Viking Press, 1974.

This work is the only existing study of the Agnew scandal and resignation and is the result of research pursued by two journalists who covered the Agnew case as it developed. Great detail is given to the unfolding scandal with a narrative of events provided chronologically on a daily basis. Since the resignation of the Vice-President is perceived by the authors to have had its origins in the background and career of Agnew, considerable space is devoted to a biography of the Vice-President.

Born the son of a Greek immigrant, Agnew served as an army officer in Europe during World War II and afterward studied law at the University of Baltimore. In 1947 he began to practice law in a Baltimore suburb, where he also pursued various business schemes and held several business positions. Agnew was always well-dressed, gregarious, and articulate, though probably a bit "lazy"—a quality later alluded to by Richard Nixon in his *Memoirs*. Agnew eventually determined to go into politics as a Republican—a wise decision, since Maryland was overrun with Democrats seeking office. Appointed to the Baltimore County Zoning Board of Appeals in 1957 and elected Baltimore County Executive in 1962, Agnew ultimately was elected governor of Maryland in 1967. His record was one of progressivism in civil rights, in graduated income tax legislation, and in antipollution laws. As the Civil Rights crusade of the 1960's grew in intensity and became violent, however, Agnew backed away from his progressive stance and sought additional police powers and welfare and health expenditure cuts.

Originally a supporter of New York's Governor Nelson Rockefeller for the Republican presidential nomination in 1968, Agnew was nevertheless selected by the victorious Republican presidential candidate, Richard M. Nixon, as his running mate, probably because of his increasing coolness toward militant Civil Rights and antiwar protest movements. Elected Vice-President when Nixon won the election, Agnew found his role in the new Administration to be not that of expert on state and local government, where he had spent his career, but of spokesman for the Administration's pursuit of "peace with honor" in Southeast Asia. Agnew attacked the "effete corps of impudent snobs" and the "nattering nabobs of negativism" which besieged the Administration from all sides in the conflict over the Indochina war and which brought protest to increasingly violent levels. For his efforts he earned the respect of President Nixon and of much of "middle America," which perceived the nation to be threatened by defeat, social crisis, and anarchy.

A major portion of the book is devoted to the story of how Agnew fell so quickly from so lofty a perch. Routine investigations in the United States Attorney's office in Baltimore established that Agnew for years had been involved in a very old-fashioned form of graft; he had taken kickback money from persons awarded state contracts. Attorney General Richardson soon concluded that Agnew was guilty and that the most accommodating way out was to secure his resignation; and President Nixon soon reached the same conclusion. While Agnew publicly denied all the charges circulating against him, he privately wanted to stay out of prison at any cost and accepted the invitation of the Justice Department to begin plea bargaining. The plea bargaining involved extensive legal maneuvering with Agnew threatening to make his case public by going either to the House of Representatives or to the courts, thus further paralyzing an Administration already sunk in the mire of Watergate.

In the end Agnew pleaded no contest to one count of income tax evasion, on money he had received illegally from a contractor, and the Justice Department was allowed to make a statement in court regarding the evidence it possessed, arguing that Agnew had for years run up a criminal record in his relations with Maryland contractors. The Attorney General asked leniency for Agnew, citing his office and personal hardships. Agnew denied participation in the multitude of kickback schemes with which the Justice Department charged him, and insisted that all contracts during his Maryland terms had gone to deserving contractors. Judge Walter E. Hoffman, Fourth District United States Judge, concluded that the plea bargaining agreement between the Justice Department and Agnew prevented the truth of the government's charges ever being known, but ruled that the government's case was convincingly in the national interest. Agnew was put on three years probation and fined $10,000.

Agnew's resignation hit the public, already numbed by daily Watergate developments, like a bombshell; even his closest friends and supporters, including his staff, were dumbfounded, since they only had access to leaks in the press concerning the case and were not privy to Agnew's secret plea bargaining strategies. Generally the public greeted the news of the resignation cynically, feeling that justice was in no way served, particularly since Agnew continued to live in his usual comfortable and lavish Washington life style.

Nixon, Richard M. *RN: The Memoirs of Richard Nixon*. New York: Grosset and Dunlap, 1978.

When nominated a second time by the Republican Party for the presidency in 1968, Nixon, together with his New York law partner, John N. Mitchell, decided that Maryland Governor Spiro T. Agnew would make the ideal running mate. Agnew possessed excellent credentials in the areas of local and state government as well as in urban problems, which Nixon claims became a major concern of his Administration.

Nixon asserts that when the Justice Department's charges against Agnew were first brought to his attention, he knew the Attorney General to be a political enemy of Agnew and hence was suspicious; but as the case was laid out before him he became more cautious. He was told, in fact, that the government had an "open and shut" case against the Vice-President. Nixon personally felt sorry for Agnew, and he deplored the continuing press leaks about the case, but after Speaker Carl Albert declined to bring the House of Representatives into the situation, and the Justice Department ruled that a sitting Vice-President could be indicted (they had doubts about a President, however), Nixon concluded that the only way out of the developing quagmire was to secure Agnew's resignation.

The resignation was ultimately secured by the Justice Department. Agnew requested help from Nixon in securing another position of some sort, but Nixon felt he was in no position to do anything for him, and he specifically vetoed an idea put to him by his aides requesting that he secure a sinecure for Agnew in the government so that the latter might collect on his pension rights. — *J.L.C.*

Additional Recommended Reading

Agnew, Spiro T. *The Canfield Decision*. Chicago: Playboy Press, 1976. The only thing written by the principal participant in the resignation, a work of fiction, and perhaps a clue to Agnew's makeup.

Bernstein, Carl and Bob Woodward. *The Final Days*. New York: Simon and Schuster, 1976. Claims that Nixon wanted to get Agnew out of office quickly, in order to devote his energies to getting rid of Watergate Special Prosecutor Archibald Cox.

Lukas, J. Anthony. *Nightmare: The Underside of the Nixon Years*. New York: The Viking Press, 1976. A contemporary history of the Nixon Administration as one of scandal, with appropriate space given to the Agnew part of that scandal.

Richardson, Elliot L. *The Creative Balance*. New York: Holt, Rinehart and Winston, 1976. Richardson makes a case for having gotten Agnew out of office regardless of the cost to justice, arguing that the nation could not gamble on undertaking the impeachment and trial of the Vice-President with the possibility of the impeachment of the President following immediately on its heels; both houses of Congress would have been paralyzed by this unprecedented litigation.

White, Theodore H. *Breach of Faith: The Fall of Richard Nixon*. New York: Atheneum Publishers, 1975. A well-written and entertaining account of the fall of the Nixon Administration with some treatment of the Agnew resignation as one part of the collapse.

THE CYPRUS CRISIS

Type of event: Military: armed intervention into the affairs of Cyprus
Time: July 15-August 16, 1974
Locale: Cyprus

Principal personages:
> ARCHBISHOP MAKARIOS III (1913-1977), President of Cyprus, 1960-1974
> NIKOS SAMPSON (1935-   ), President of Cyprus, July 15-23, 1974
> COLONEL GEORGIUS PAPADOPOULOS (1919-   ), Dictator of Greece, 1967-1973
> GENERAL DIMITRIOS IOANNIDES, head of the Greek Military Police and *de facto* Dictator of Greece, 1973-1974
> KONSTANTINOS G. KARAMANLIS (1907-   ), Premier of Greece, 1955-1963 and again after July 23, 1974
> BÜLENT ECEVIT (1925-   ), Premier of Turkey, January 25-September 18, 1974
> RICHARD MILHOUS NIXON (1913-   ), thirty-seventh President of the United States, 1969-1974
> HENRY ALFRED KISSINGER (1923-   ), United States Secretary of State, 1973-1977

Summary of Event

The Cyprus Crisis of July and August, 1974, was an extremely grave event in the recent history of the Eastern Mediterranean region. It caused the overthrow of both the Cyprus Settlement of 1959 and of the Greek dictatorship of the "Colonels," which had ruled in Athens since 1967. It also represented the first major diplomatic defeat for the United States Secretary of State, Henry A. Kissinger, hitherto known as "Super-K."

The island of Cyprus, with a population of about eighty percent Greek and eighteen percent Turkish, has long been a center of turmoil in the Eastern Mediterranean. During its long years as part of the Byzantine Empire, the island had been exclu-sively Greek in speech and Greek Orthodox in religion. The conquest by the Crusaders in 1192 ushered in a period of Western Roman Catholic rule. From 1489 until its conquest by the Ottoman Turks in 1571, the island was ruled by the Italian city-state of Venice. During the Turkish period, which lasted from 1571 until 1878, a substantial Turkish colony was settled on the island. After 1878, Cyprus was governed by Great Britain.

By the late 1950's, widespread unrest in the island had made further British rule impossible. The ethnic Greeks of the island demanded *Enosis* (union) with Greece, while the ethnic Turks were equally vehement in opposing the concept. Meanwhile,

1193

the governments of Greece and Turkey cheered their respective ethnic brethren from the sidelines.

Among the Greek Cypriots, the anti-British movement took both violent and nonviolent forms. The nonviolent campaign for *Enosis* was led by the Greek Orthodox Archbishop of Cyprus, Makarios. During the long years of rule by the Roman Catholic Venetians and Muslim Turks, the local Orthodox Church had come to be seen by the ethnic Greeks of Cyprus as the truest representative of their interests as an ethnonational group. To many of the impatient Greek Cypriot youth, more violent tactics were necessary than those used by Makarios. After 1955, many young Cypriots joined the guerrillas, the EOKA (National Organization of Cypriot Fighters), in waging a campaign of terror against the British Army. These guerrillas were led by General George Grivas, a Greek Cypriot who had once served in the Army of mainland Greece.

In 1959, the Greek and Turkish governments finally reached a settlement which allowed the British to withdraw from the struggle at last. By the terms of the agreement, Cyprus was to become an independent republic. The Greek Cypriots were to receive seventy percent of all bureaucratic posts and National Assembly seats, while the Turks were to receive thirty percent. Archbishop Makarios would become President, while his Vice-President would be a Turkish Cypriot. In August, 1960, Cyprus became independent.

The new Republic, which nobody had really wanted, rested on a precarious base right from the begin-ning. Relations between Greek Cypriots and Turkish Cypriots remained as tense as they had been under British rule. The carefully contrived constitution soon proved to be unworkable. In 1964, and again in 1967, the eruption of bloody inter-ethnic rioting prompted the government of Turkey to threaten armed intervention. At the time, however, nothing came of these threats.

There were two reasons why Greek Cypriots were spared a Turkish invasion in the 1960's. First of all, President Makarios had been able to establish close relations with the Soviet Union and with the Arab states, and could threaten Turkey with Soviet or Arab reprisals if she dared intervene. The second shield against the Turks was the United States, who feared that a Greco-Turkish War would weaken the North Atlantic Treaty Organization (NATO) to which both countries belonged. In both the 1964 and 1967 crises, President Lyndon Johnson sent State Department official Cyrus Vance to argue the Turks out of taking any drastic action.

By 1967, Makarios, while still unwilling to renounce definitely *Enosis*, no longer saw it as an immediately practical alternative. In his view, the aid of the Soviet Union was absolutely necessary if the threat from Turkey was to be warded off. The Soviets, he feared, would not support the Greek Cypriots against Turkey if they chose to unite with NATO member Greece. Makarios' reluctance to push for *Enosis*, coupled with his pro-Soviet foreign policy, angered both nationalist extremists among the Greek Cypriots and government circles in Greece itself. Relations between Makarios and the Greek government became especially bad after the *coup d'état* of April 21, 1967, which installed a military dictatorship in Athens led by Colonel Georgius Papadopoulos.

In any conflict with Makarios, the Greek government had one key advantage. Makarios had never been able to create a strong, reliable defense force of his own. After the riots of 1964, he had been forced to hire officers from Greece to train a new Cypriot National Guard. This National Guard soon became a hotbed of intrigue against the Archbishop. Local Greek Cypriot nationalist extremists were quite willing to cooperate with the Greek officers. By the summer of 1974, the new Dictator of Greece, General Dimitrios Ioannides, had decided that the time had come to strike.

On July 15, 1974, the Greek Cypriot National Guard, acting at the instigation of the Athens junta, carried out a lightning *coup d'état* which forced Makarios to flee into hiding. Nikos Sampson, a veteran of the 1955-1959 terrorist campaign who had taken over the leadership of the Cypriot extremists after the death of Grivas in January, 1974, became the new President of Cyprus. Neither the Athens junta nor Sampson seemed to remember one obvious geographic reality: Turkey was only forty miles away from Cyprus. They must have thought that the Turks would, as in 1964 and 1967, threaten and bluster, but finally do nothing. The world had changed a great deal since those years, however. The Soviets had supported Makarios, but they would not support the Sampson regime, which

was right-wing and extremely anti-Communist.

The United States could no longer be relied on to rescue the Greek Cypriots, either. She was weaker than she had been seven years earlier, and the long and frustrating war in Vietnam had soured most Americans on any involvement abroad. The rampaging inflation of 1974, caused by sharp increases in the price of food and oil, had weakened American economic power over other countries. The presidency itself had been shaken by the resignation of President Richard Nixon on August 8, 1974, in the wake of the Watergate scandal. For Turkey, American disapproval was no longer something to be feared.

For the Turks, the appearance of a known terrorist as President of Cyprus was just the excuse that they needed to intervene militarily. On July 20, 1974, the Premier of Turkey, Bülent Ecevit, ordered Turkish troops to land on the northern coast of Cyprus. On July 22, a tentative ceasefire was arranged, and Greco-Turkish talks began in Geneva on July 25. After these talks broke down on August 14, the Turks resumed their offensive. By the time they had ceased operations on August 16, the Turks had occupied the whole northeastern section of the island, or about forty percent of its entire area. The invasion had a shattering effect on the Cypriot economy. Streams of Greek Cypriots from the north fled south, while Turkish Cypriots fled north. Thus, there came to be a *de facto* partition of the island.

Many Greeks and Greek Cypriots were angry not only at Turkey, but also at the United States. The failure of Secretary of State Henry Kissinger to try to restrain the Turks was especially resented. On August 19, 1974, in the course of an anti-American demonstration in the capital city of Nicosia, United States Ambassador Rodger Davies was shot and killed by a Greek Cypriot extremist.

By the autumn of 1974, anger against Kissinger's policies had spread to the United States Congress as well. In February, 1975, the United States Congress, paying heed to the protests of Greek-American ethnic organizations, voted to cut off all arms aid to Turkey until a settlement of the Cyprus question was reached. Congress passed this measure over Kissinger's vocal opposition, despite the fact that Turkey was an ally of the United States and a fellow member of NATO. It was not until the summer of 1978 that the arms embargo was finally repealed.

The shock of the Turkish invasion dealt a heavy blow to the extreme right wing of Greek Cypriot politics. On July 23, 1974, Nikos Sampson resigned, and was replaced by the more moderate politician, Glafkos John Clerides. On December 7, 1974, Archbishop Makarios returned to Cyprus and resumed the office of the Presidency of the rump republic of Cyprus.

There was one unambiguously positive outcome of the Cyprus Crisis. The Turkish invasion of Cyprus had been a humiliating blow to the prestige of the Greek dictatorship. On July 23, 1974, the Greek Dictator Ioannides was forced by his fellow officers to resign. The officers then voluntarily handed over power to the moderate conservative elder statesman Konstantinos G. Karamanlis, who had been Premier from 1955 to 1963. Greek democracy was thus reborn.

As the decade of the 1970's drew to a close, no final solution of the Cyprus problem seemed to be in sight. The ceasefire had been restored, but no permanent settlement had been achieved. The Turkish occupation of the northeastern part of the island now seemed like an established fact.

Pertinent Literature

Markides, Kyriacos C. *The Rise and Fall of the Cyprus Republic*. New Haven, Conn.: Yale University Press, 1977.

The author of this book, a Greek Cypriot by birth and upbringing who teaches sociology at the University of Maine, was on a research sabbatical in Cyprus at the time the crisis broke out in 1974. Despite his Greek name and Cypriot origins, Markides has written a scholarly and objective account. Though he does condemn the Turkish invasion of the island in 1974, he is equally critical of those Greek Cypriot extremists who demanded *Enosis* (union with Greece) at any cost. He also takes a very negative view of the right-wing military dictatorship which ruled Greece from 1967 to 1974.

Markides does not focus his attention on the policies followed by the United States or any other Great

Power at the time of the crisis. Instead, he deals chiefly with the internal political reasons for the decline and fall of the Cyprus republic. He concerns himself with international issues relating to the Cyprus question only to the extent that they are necessary for understanding what was happening inside Cyprus itself. It is the author's contention that it was the internal political weakness of independent Cyprus that made foreign intervention possible.

In the first chapter, the author gives the reader the historical background of the Cyprus Crisis from the earliest times to 1974. He shows how the impact of British colonialism on traditional Cypriot institutions led to the rise of a conservative Church-led anticolonialist movement, demanding union with Greece. In the second chapter, examining what he calls the "traditional, charismatic, and legal-rational" bases of his rule, Markides discusses the reasons for the extraordinary power and popularity of that consummate politician, the President of Cyprus, Archbishop Makarios. Markides also shows how the violence and extremism of the pro-*Enosis* Right had the paradoxical result of converting the local Communist Party into a bastion of moderation and support for the *status quo*. Markides' work is the first major work of scholarship to analyze in depth the political role of the Archbishop.

The third chapter studies the origins, development, social base, and structure of the pro-*Enosis* opposition, which, aided and encouraged by the Greek dictatorship, finally succeeded in overthrowing the government of Archbishop Makarios; the fourth chapter examines the connections between the Greek dictatorship and Cyprus during the years 1967-1974, showing how the "Colonels" managed to subvert the Makarios government. It also tries to explain why Makarios was unable to ward off such foreign interference. To Markides, the fall of the Makarios regime is simply one example of the problem, in political sociology, of the "breakdown" of democratic regimes.

This book contains excellent maps of Cyprus, a list of commonly used abbreviations, several numerical tables, and a short chronological listing of key events. Unfortunately, the book lacks a cumulative bibliography, though there are footnote references. There are no photographs of the personalities involved in the crisis.

Stern, Laurence. *The Wrong Horse: The Politics of Intervention and the Failure of American Diplomacy*. New York: Time Books, 1977.

The author of this compact, 170-page book is a former reporter for the *Washington Post*. Though his book covers the whole period of American involvement in the Eastern Mediterranean, from the Truman Doctrine of 1947 right up to 1977, it is to United States policy during the Cyprus Crisis of July-August, 1974, that the author devotes most of his attention. Stern is strongly critical of that policy, and of the role played by Secretary of State Henry A. Kissinger in shaping it.

The first half of the book deals with United States policy towards the dictatorship of the "Colonels" in Greece, which lasted from 1967 to 1974. Stern strongly condemns both the Johnson and Nixon Administrations for having lent American support to a regime which he views as having been brutal and despotic. He stresses the role of the American CIA in helping to prop up the Greek dictatorship. The second half of the book deals with the Cyprus Crisis itself, and with Kissinger's reaction to it. Stern has especially harsh words for what he regards as Kissinger's sins, both of commission and omission.

According to Stern, Kissinger had a natural predilection for supporting strong, authoritarian regimes, believing that only such regimes could be reliable allies of the United States. This belief, Stern argues, led to several major blunders. The first such blunder was the failure to warn the "Colonels" strongly enough about the dangers involved in subverting the government of Archbishop Makarios. Kissinger, Stern argues, not only failed to warn against a *coup* he knew was being prepared, but also failed to speak out against it once Makarios had been deposed. Stern sees Kissinger's failure to speak up as a form of tacit encouragement of Makarios' enemies; he feels that Kissinger looked with distrust upon the diplomatic acrobatics of the Archbishop, whom he regarded as "the Castro of the Mediterranean."

The second major blunder, the author believes, was Kissinger's support for the Turkey of Bülent Ecevit; Kissinger should have tried harder to argue the Turks out of invading Cyprus. Even after the Turks had openly broken the first ceasefire and devoured the whole northeastern part of the island, Kissinger still failed to take any drastic action to make them change their policy. Stern sees Kissinger's policy as one of "tilting" towards Turkey, since he believed that a stable, militarily strong Turkey was more necessary as an ally of the United States than was the unstable democracy born in Athens on July 23, 1974.

Stern, a hard-hitting investigative reporter, bases many of his assertions on inside information given him by unnamed officials of the State Department who were, in private, strong critics of Kissinger's policies towards Greece and Cyprus. This book has been praised by most reviewers, but a few have criticized it for being too journalistic and for drawing extreme conclusions not warranted by the evidence presented. *The Wrong Horse* is, in any case, the only work available on United States policy during the Cyprus Crisis of 1974. — *P.D.M.*

Additional Recommended Reading

Xydis, Stephen George. *Cyprus: Reluctant Republic*. The Hague: Mouton, 1973. A rather lengthy account, based on published documents, memoirs, and private papers, of the negotiations which led to the Greco-Turkish compromise of 1959 over Cyprus.

Adams, Thomas W. *AKEL: The Communist Party of Cyprus*. Stanford, Calif.: Hoover

Institute Press, 1971. The only available study of the history and organization of one of the major Greek Cypriot political parties.

Kyriakides, Stanley. *Cyprus: Constitutionalism and Crisis Government*. Philadelphia: University of Pennsylvania Press, 1968. A good analysis of the constitutional problems of independent Cyprus.

Vanezis, P. N. *Makarios: Faith and Power*. London: Abelard-Schuman, 1971. One of the few biographies of the Greek Cypriot leader.

Clogg, Richard and George Yannopoulos, eds. *Greece Under Military Rule*. New York: Basic Books, 1972. A series of essays dealing with political and economic conditions in Greece under the regime of the Colonels, which fell as a result of the Cyprus debacle of 1974.

Ahmad, Feroz. *The Turkish Experiment in Democracy, 1950-1975*. Boulder, Colo.: Westview Press, 1977. Chapter 12, "Emergence of Bülent Ecevit," gives a good picture of Turkish domestic politics at the time of the Cyprus Crisis of 1974.

Tamkoc, Metin. *The Warrior Diplomats: Guardians of the National Security and Modernization of Turkey*. Salt Lake City: University of Utah Press, 1976. An evaluation of Turkish policy during the Cyprus Crisis of 1974 which finds it to have been both fair and reasonable.

COLLAPSE OF THE NIXON ADMINISTRATION

Type of event: Political: scandal and constitutional crisis
Time: August 9, 1974
Locale: Washington, D.C.

Principal personages:

RICHARD MILHOUS NIXON (1913-   ), thirty-seventh President of the United States, 1969-1974

GERALD RUDOLPH FORD (1913-   ), fortieth Vice-President of the United States, 1973-1974

JOHN JOSEPH SIRICA (1904-   ), United States District Judge of the District of Columbia

LEON JAWORSKI (1905-   ), Watergate Special Prosecutor

PETER WALLACE RODINO, JR. (1909-   ), Chairman of Judiciary Committee within the United States House of Representatives

JAMES D. ST. CLAIR, Special Counsel to the President

ALEXANDER MEIGS HAIG, JR. (1924-   ), White House Chief of Staff

Summary of Event

On August 9, 1974, Richard M. Nixon became the first President in the history of the United States to resign that office, subsequently retiring to his estate in California. Nixon's resignation and the collapse of his Administration were an outgrowth of the so-called Watergate Affair which occupied increasing amounts of his time after it first came to the fore in the winter of 1972-1973, reaching a climax in the summer of 1974 and resulting in the resignation of the President.

The Watergate scandal grew out of the arrest and conviction of five men who in 1972 broke into the national headquarters of the Democratic party at the Watergate office-apartment complex in Washington. Gradually others were implicated in the burglary because of the persistence of United States District Judge John J. Sirica, and the chain of conspirators eventually reached into the White House and the Justice Department, entangling the President himself, who, according to his own taped conversations, participated in an attempt to cover up the true nature of the burglary from proper law enforcement agencies.

The burglary was first investigated by the Senate Select Committee on Presidential Campaign Activities, chaired by Senator Sam J. Ervin, Jr., while crusading *Washington Post* reporters Bob Woodward and Carl Bernstein persisted in their attempts to get to the bottom of the situation. The President's personal lawyer, John Wesley Dean III, in sworn testimony before the Ervin Committee, stated that the President and his advisers had tried to cover up for the burglars. This testimony launched a slow but steady momentum in the press, the Congress, the courts, and the Justice Department to get to the bottom of the affair. Eventually Dean's testimony was substantiated by the Presidential tapes.

The President accepted the resignations of his principal aides, H. R. Haldeman and John D. Ehrlichman, in April, 1973, following the early portions of Dean's damaging testimony; Dean himself was dismissed. Attorney General Richard G. Kleindienst and L. Patrick Gray III, acting director of the FBI and the President's nominee for the permanent appointment, also resigned shortly thereafter. The new Attorney General, Elliot L. Richardson, appointed a special Watergate prosecutor, Harvard University law professor Archibald Cox, with full authority to pursue the case wherever it might lead.

Professor Cox fought a battle in the courts to force the President to surrender his taped conversations as material evidence, and when it appeared that Cox was winning the judicial battle for the tapes, he was abruptly dismissed by the President in October, 1973. This brought about the resignation of Attorney General Richardson and his deputy, William D. Ruckelshaus, both of whom refused to carry out the President's order to fire Cox. These events brought on a public uproar and reaction against the President, and the House Judiciary Committee on February 6, 1974, began formal impeachment proceedings against him. The President meanwhile relented and appointed a new special Watergate prosecutor,

Leon Jaworski, who continued the battle to acquire the tapes.

The struggle on the part of the House Judiciary Committee under its chairman, Peter W. Rodino, Jr., and Jaworski to gain access to the entirety of the President's taped conversations took many turns during the spring and summer of 1974, but ended with an eight to nothing decision by the Supreme Court on July 24, that the President must surrender completely all the evidence in his possession. The high court's decision marked a total defeat for Nixon and his special counsel, James D. St. Clair, one of the best trial lawyers in the country. Meanwhile, the Judiciary Committee had begun nationally televised hearings looking toward impeachment. The committee eventually approved three articles of impeachment, charging Nixon with obstruction of justice in the Watergate scandal, abuse of Presidential powers, and attempting to impede the impeachment process by defying committee subpoenas for evidence. The committee recessed on July 30.

At the insistence of St. Clair the President released on August 5 three taped conversations covered by the Supreme Court decision, which clearly indicated that he had tried to obstruct justice and cover up for the Watergate conspirators. The President's position was now destroyed in both houses of Congress, and even prominent conservative Republicans and longtime Nixon supporters such as Senator Barry M. Goldwater privately urged the President to face reality. White House Chief of Staff Alexander M. Haig, Jr., devoted his energies and position to convincing the

President that resignation was now the only way out. The President wavered for days, but on August 8, 1974, he went on nationwide television to announce that he would resign as President the following day, saying that his political base in Congress had eroded to the point that there was no longer any point in continuing the struggle.

Nixon's successor, Gerald R. Ford, granted his predecessor a full and complete pardon for all federal crimes he might have committed as President. Nixon then issued a formal statement accepting the pardon and only expressed regret that he had not been more forthright and decisive in dealing with the Watergate scandal. A considerable public outcry arose, the feeling being that, as in the case of the earlier resignation of Vice-President Agnew, justice had not been served.

Pertinent Literature

White, Theodore H. *Breach of Faith: The Fall of Richard Nixon.* New York: Atheneum Publishers, 1975.

Essentially this book takes a historical approach to the tragic demise of Nixon, arguing that the seeds of his destruction went back to his youth. Nixon was brought up in poverty in California, but was a very hardworking student and did manage to graduate from Whittier College in his hometown of Whittier, California, where his very high marks enabled him to win a scholarship to Duke University Law School. At Duke his studious ways again earned him high marks, but graduating during the Depression he found employment opportunities very limited, particularly in prestigious and snobbish New York City law firms. Nixon returned to Whittier where he became a small-town lawyer, well-known in the community and dabbling in the social life, politics, and business schemes common to such places. Like many Americans living in small towns during the Depression, he was rescued from this dreariness by the onset of World War II. Nixon first secured a

position in Washington with the Office of Price Administration, where he acquired a distaste for government bureaucracy, and then served in the Navy in several Eastern cities and eventually in the South Pacific.

Returning to postwar America in 1946 Nixon was, as were millions of other veterans, at loose ends. Miraculously at this point his Whittier connections, and also those of his mother, provided him with the opportunity to seek the Republican nomination for the California House seat held for years by a liberal Democrat, H. Jerry Voorhis. Nixon, a veteran, in a time when war veterans were heroes, unleashed an aggressive campaign against Voorhis, winning the seat. From this point his political career shot rapidly ahead; in 1950, he defeated veteran United States Senator Helen Gahagan Douglas. In the Senate he developed into a full-fledged anti-Communist crusader and earned a national reputation pursuing the Alger Hiss case. This was the era of the emerging Cold War between the United States and the Soviet Union. It was a time when the United States was not only increasingly obsessed by the aggressive nature of Stalinist Communism, but was also beginning to be bogged down in a war against North Korean and Communist Chinese aggression on the Korean peninsula. Nixon, together with such personalities as Senator Joseph R. McCarthy of Wisconsin, was able to generate considerable political capital out of the complexities and fears of the Cold War era.

In 1952 the Republican party rejected the candidacies of General Douglas MacArthur and Senator Robert A. Taft and turned instead to the hero of World War II, and a political moderate, General Dwight D. Eisenhower. Apparently as a sop thrown to the then politically important right-wing anti-Communist movement, Eisenhower selected Richard Nixon as his running mate. The Eisenhower-Nixon ticket won in 1952 and again in 1956.

Eisenhower always maintained firm control of policy in the final analysis, and while his Secretary of State, John Foster Dulles, might boast of having carried the nation "to the brink" of nuclear war and Nixon might engage in similar rhetoric, the country remained at peace during the eight years of the Eisenhower Administration. The President always kept some distance between himself and his young, outspoken, jingoistic Vice-President, and the fact that Eisenhower preferred the company of important, millionaire friends and supporters and shunned Nixon socially was a matter of some pain to the Vice-President. Nevertheless, Eisenhower did support Nixon for the Republican Presidential nomination in 1960, which he secured easily, losing the election narrowly to the Democratic candidate, John F. Kennedy. Nixon returned to California where he lost a bid to become governor in 1962, after which he vowed to retire from politics forever.

Nixon journeyed to New York City, where he now possessed sufficient connections to enter the lucrative world of prestigious law firms that had been closed to him earlier in life. Here Nixon prospered, but the anonymity of New York life distressed him, and he commenced a political comeback within the Republican Party by publically supporting the hopeless Presidential campaign of Barry M. Goldwater in 1964. Following Goldwater's disastrous defeat the Republican party was left in shambles, and Nixon was present to pick up the pieces; during the years 1965 to 1968 he traveled throughout the country speaking at every possible Republican function, and in 1968 he again secured the Republican Presidential nomination. He handily defeated the Democratic candidate, Hubert H. Humphrey, in a tumultuous campaign which focused on the nation's seemingly interminable involvement in the war in Indochina.

Nixon's first administration pursued a very gradual withdrawal from Indochina, a "peace with honor," a phrase Nixon borrowed from the nineteenth century British statesman (some would say politician) Benjamin Disraeli. The pace of this disengagement was entirely too slow for the antiwar movement which had built up during the 1960's, and for most of the liberal and intellectual establishment, so that Nixon was increasingly harassed from all sides. The President and his advisers eventually concluded that the antiwar movement was employing illegal and violent means to gain its ends, and they decided to reply in like manner. This decision set up a climate in the White House that spread down through Republican Party machinery and which meant to keep the President and his policies in power at any cost to honesty, integrity, and constitutional government. Nixon in fact set up an ambience where his subordinates broke the law, and then he tried to cover up for them.

The most precise expression of this policy was the infamous Watergate break-in, where the arrest of five men for breaking and entering the national headquarters of the opposition Democratic Party eventually and naturally led to a set of conspirators in the White House, the Justice Department, and to the President himself. Nixon fought the process of justice in the Watergate case doggedly feeling that he was once more under siege by an enemy that was out to "get" him, just as earlier Eastern employers, liberals "soft" on Communism, people unwilling to go "to the brink" of nuclear warfare, and opponents of continued involvement in Indochina had conspired to deny him his way with things.

Nixon should have realized that over the years he had built up a powerful set of enemies who, now that they had a case against him, would press it to the point of his destruction. Perhaps he did realize just that, which would explain his struggle to stay in office long after he had any chance of remaining there under even the most dishonorable of conditions. In the process of the struggle to stay in power Nixon saw his Vice-President resign in disgrace, the whole ugly story of corporate campaign contributions to the Republican party aired, whatever remained of the integrity of the Defense Department besmeared by its falsified reports on the bombing of Cambodia, and Congress rise up in wrath over Presidential impoundment of money for legitimately approved projects. Such a record did indeed enable Nixon's enemies to "get" him.

Bernstein, Carl and Bob Woodward. *The Final Days*. New York: Simon and Schuster, 1976.

The unrelenting account of the final days of the Nixon Administration by two prize-winning reporters who pursued the Watergate scandal from start to finish in the *Washington Post* rests upon interviews with scores of participants in the Watergate affair. While Richard M. Nixon declined to be interviewed, the central figure in the story is Nixon himself, and the result is a most unflattering portrait of the thirty-seventh President of the United States.

The taped conversations of Nixon's Administration, which the Supreme Court finally ordered turned over to the House Judiciary Committee and the Special Watergate Prosecutor, reveal a weak and confused President. Nixon was surrounded by quarreling subordinates, Secretary of State Henry A. Kissinger among them. The President failed to lead and instead allowed Watergate events to drift until it was too late to save himself and his Administration. More decisive action probably would have worked had it been done skillfully and early enough, according to the authors. Eventually it was just too late to do anything, but his staff was afraid to advise him that all was lost.

Nixon's behavior lays bare a President whose character somehow gave way under the stress of a Presidency caught up in domestic and international turmoil and the greatest scandal in American political history. It is not a picture in keeping with the earlier aggressive Nixon, so sure of himself in the most dangerous and awkward situations of the Cold War, and hence we glimpse still another Nixon, always an enigma and an essentially secretive person. — *J.L.C.*

Additional Recommended Reading

Ben-Veniste, Richard and George Frampton, Jr. *Stonewall*. New York: Simon and Schuster, 1977. The inside story of the Watergate prosecution by the Justice Department's lawyers.

Bernstein, Carl and Bob Woodward. *All the President's Men*. New York: Simon and Schuster, 1974. The first book of investigative reporting by the crusading *Washington Post* reporters who opened and kept open the Watergate story.

Dash, Samuel. *Chief Counsel*. New York: Random House, 1976. Inside the Ervin Committee by its chief counsel.

Dean, John Wesley, III. *Blind Ambition: The White House Years*. New York: Simon and Schuster, 1976. The Watergate story by Nixon's personal White House attorney, originally told to the Ervin committee and later substantiated by the tapes.

Haldeman, H. R and Joseph DiMona. *The Ends of Power*. New York: *Times* Books, 1978. Watergate by Nixon's crony and Chief of Staff.

Jaworski, Leon. *The Right and the Power*. New York: Reader's Digest Press, 1976. The story of the second Watergate Special Prosecutor who together with the House Judiciary Committee and the Supreme Court forced Nixon to turn over the tapes that destroyed his credibility and his Administration.

Lukas, J. Anthony. *Nightmare: The Underside of the Nixon Years*. New York: The Viking Press, 1976. A contemporary history of the Nixon-Agnew Administration described as one of scandal.

Nixon, Richard M. *RN: The Memoirs of Richard Nixon*. New York: Grosset and Dunlap, 1978. Recollections and reminiscences that present yet another Nixon.

CHARTER OF THE ECONOMIC RIGHTS AND DUTIES OF STATES

Type of event: Diplomatic: agreement governing economic relations between developed and developing nations
Time: December 12, 1974
Locale: New York City

Principal personages:

LUIS ECHEVERRÍA ALVAREZ (1922-), President of Mexico, 1970-

JORGE CASTANEDA, chairman of working groups drafting charter

RAUL PREBISCH (1901-), a Third World spokesman and former Secretary General of the United Nations Conference on Trade and Development (UNCTAD)

Summary of Event

Economic contacts between today's rich (or developed) nations and today's poor (or developing) nations go back hundreds of years. For a long time, especially during the nineteenth century, many nations in the latter group were colonies of countries in the former group, an experience the developing countries now view with distaste. The late Dr. Kwame Nkrumah, Prime Minister and President of Ghana, has written that ". . . the imperialists were all rapacious; they all subserved the needs of the subject lands to their own demands; they all circumscribed human rights and liberties; they all repressed and despoiled, degraded and oppressed." Sentiments such as these have become part and parcel of the rhetoric of international relations in the modern world. The rejoinder that the imperial powers brought law and order, roads, railways, educational systems, modern financial methods, and so forth to their colonies does not appeal to the developing world (or Third World, as it is often called). Thus, General Principle XIV of the 1964 meeting of the United Nations Conference on Trade and Development (UNCTAD), which is dominated by the Third World, states the following: "The liquidation of the remnants of colonialism . . . is a necessary condition of economic development."

The developing nations also criticize the international economic order that emerged after World War II, saying that the "rules of the game" are biased in favor of the developed countries and often accusing these countries of so-called "neo-colonialism" (that is, exploitation without the existence of formal empire).

Immediately following the war, the industrial nations, especially the United States and the United Kingdom, were instrumental in setting up several new international economic institutions whose task it would be to help foster stability and growth in the world economy. The two most important of these were the International Monetary Fund (IMF), which makes loans to countries having deficits in their balance of payments, and the International Bank for Reconstruction and Development (IBRD, that is, World Bank), which makes long-term loans for the purpose of helping countries increase their basic productive capacity. Another important organization introduced in 1967 was the General Agreement on Tariffs and Trade (GATT), the purpose of which is to promote free trade. The main principle embodied in the charters of IMF, IBRD, and GATT is a belief in the free market as the most efficient means of allocating resources. Interference with the market is to be tolerated only if it is selective and temporary. Although membership in these organizations is by no means limited to the industrialized countries and although many developing nations receive aid from the IMF and IBRD, the policies of the main international economic organizations are largely determined by the major powers.

This, Third World spokesmen often argue, is inconsistent with the long-run needs of the developing countries. It is said, for example, that a permanent tendency exists for the primary product exports of the less developed countries to command less and less in the way of manufactured imports from the developed countries (that is, there is a secular decline in the "terms of trade"). It is argued that, within the existing economic framework, a "brain drain" exists, in which highly trained people emigrate to the rich countries instead of staying home to help with the development effort. It is argued that multinational corporations exert undue influence on the economic, political, and social life of developing nations. The rich countries are also accused of violating the principles of free trade and laissez-faire when it suits their purposes, while at the same time urging these principles on others. One of the most influential exponents of these ideas is Raul Prebisch, a former Secretary General of UNCTAD.

Through UNCTAD, the Group of 77 (a coalition of seventy-seven developing nations), and various *ad hoc* committees and organizations, the developing nations have pressed for a restructuring of the international economic system. In 1968, for example, Luis Echeverría Alvarez, President of Mexico, proposed that a document specifying the economic rights and duties of nations be formulated. Subsequently, forty-nation working groups from UNCTAD, working under the chairmanship of Jorge Castaneda from Mexico, met in Geneva, Switzerland (1973, 1974), and also in Mexico City (June, 1974) to draft a document for submission to the United Nations General Assembly. The Charter of the Economic Rights and Duties of States was adopted overwhelmingly by the General Assembly, in which developing nations have the lion's share of votes, on December 12, 1974. Only six countries voted no.

According to the preamble, "The Charter shall constitute an effective instrument toward the establishment of a new system of international economic relations based on equity, sovereign equality, and interdependence of the interests of developed and developing countries." Other

1207

goals are a narrowing of the income gap between developed and developing countries, protection of the environment, and international cooperation regardless of political systems. Chapter I proclaims general principles; Chapter II contains the articles specifying rights and duties of states; Chapter III deals with common responsibilities toward the international community. The charter endorses specific techniques, such as international commodity cartels, that the developing countries might use to turn international economic relationships to their advantage. Thus, the charter is not based on principles of free trade and laissez-faire.

Several related proposals appeared almost simultaneously with approval of the charter. The most highly publicized of these is the Integrated Programme for Commodities, which was approved by UNCTAD in September, 1974. Sometimes called the Corea Plan, after Gamani Corea, current Secretary General of UNCTAD, the plan proposes, among other things,

an elaborate mechanism for protecting developing countries from large fluctuations in the prices of the primary products exported by them. So far the Corea Plan has not been accepted by the developed countries. However, the countries of the European Economic Community (that is, the Common Market) have reached an agreement with forty-six developing nations to reimburse partially these countries for large fluctuations in export revenues. This plan is called STABEX, and, although the sums of money involved are not especially large and although the United States does not yet participate, it is symbolic of the increased sympathy for the point of view of developing nations that has appeared in the developed world during the 1970's. Nonetheless, many economists question the economic soundness of these plans and predict that, even if they are implemented, the long-run effect on the standard of living of the poor people of the world will be negligible.

Pertinent Literature

Rangarajan, L. N. *Commodity Conflict*. Ithaca, N.Y.: Cornell University Press, 1978.

This book deals with the question of international policy toward international trade in primary commodities, placing the issue against the background of the larger matrix of relationships between rich and poor countries. The book is an extremely thorough treatment of the essential elements of international commodity negotiations, stressing not only economic considerations but also political considerations. The author, in

fact, believes that an appreciation of the political factor is essential to an understanding of the process by which commodity agreements are reached or, as is more often the case, not reached. The author bluntly (and correctly) asserts that developed countries preach free trade to the developing nations but violate free trade principles when it suits their interests as defined by domestic politics. He is not, however, an ardent believer in free trade and free markets, which in theory are supposed to foster efficiency in the production and distribution of products, but argues instead that other goals, such as equity, should sometimes take precedence. He also believes that the existing economic order is not a neutral set of rules but an arrangement which favors developed countries at the expense of poor ones. Thus, he calls for the establishment of a New International Economic Order.

The first three chapters in the book are the most useful. They spell out in detail the basic historical and factual background necessary to understand the current "dialogue" between the North (that is, the developed countries) and South (that is, the developing countries). The history of the international economic order that emerged after World War II is described clearly, fully, and reasonably objectively, given the sympathies of the author for the demands the developing world is making on the developed world. The history of several commodity agreements is briefly explained, and a short but useful statis-

tical description of international trade in commodities is given.

The middle chapters (four through twelve) explore in great depth the problems that arise in concluding successful commodity agreements. Some of these chapters are overburdened with minutiae, and the author's personal views are more explicitly (and sometimes stridently) stated. Nonetheless, these chapters contain much valuable reference material.

The final two chapters offer a none-too-rosy prognosis for the future of commodity agreements. The best part deals with the Integrated Programme for Commodities, or Corea Plan, proposed by UNCTAD in 1974 but not yet implemented. The discussion of the background of the Corea Plan, the specifics of the plan, and the problems with it is extremely meaty. As in the other chapters, the discussion is colored by the author's allegiance to the developing countries.

The Appendix contains some basic primary documents (including the Integrated Programme), some useful statistics, and an annotated bibliography.

Bauer, Peter T. *Dissent on Development*. Cambridge, Mass.: Harvard University Press, 1976.

This book was written by one of the most distinguished specialists in the field of economic development in the world today. The style is highly literate and is accessible to the educated person. Although Bauer has gone out of his way to avoid technical language and mathematics, some knowledge of economics is required for a full appreciation of the discussion.

Bauer's point of view is iconoclastic, as the title of the book suggests. In general, he believes that the developing nations have deluded themselves about the causes of their poverty and, what is worse, that adherence to their policy recommendations would lead to a large waste of resources while leaving the populations of the developing world no better off than before. Bauer is especially scornful of the propensity of the developing nations to blame external circumstances (for example, the developed countries, unstable commodity markets) for their condition, and he rejects the argument that the terms of trade of the developing nations perpetually decline. Bauer claims that more often than not the inability of a developing country to achieve material advancement stems from domestic conditions, and he cites many cases in which wise domestic policies and aggressive entrepreneurial spirit helped countries to develop economically. His success stories are derived not only from the experience of now-developed countries, but also from the experience of some of the more rapidly progressing poor nations. Bauer's views are unpopular in the developing world, but he is taken seriously nonetheless.

The book has eight chapters, each of which deals with an important issue in development policy. No issue of importance in economic development is left untouched. Chapter 1, for example, deals with the size of the gap in standards of living between rich and poor nations and with the assertion that the gap is widening. A widening gap is one basis of the poor countries' call to action, but Bauer, while not denying that the developing nations have lower per capita incomes than developed countries, believes that the matter has been overdone. Bauer points out, among other things, that a downward bias exists in national income measurements in developing nations.

Chapter 2 is a critique of economic planning as a tool of development policy. Bauer generally believes that comprehensive centralized planning is more likely to obstruct progress than advance it. He also ties foreign aid, of which he is suspicious, into the discussion.

Chapter 3 attacks the view that past colonial status is necessarily a cause of economic backwardness. Bauer is well known for pointing out that several former colonies (for example, the United States and Canada) are among the world's richest countries today. Chapter 4 examines the appeal of Marxism in developing nations and criticizes the policies implicit in Marxism-Leninism.

Chapters 5 and 6 criticize some of the leading prescriptions for promoting economic development in poor countries. Gunnar Myrdal, the Swedish social scientist, and the UNCTAD staff are special targets for Bauer's barbs.

The final two chapters are more reflective and contain Bauer's ideas on how orthodox economics is relevant to the problems of the developing nations. Given the strident tone of the current dialogue between rich and poor nations, this is by no means a bland position to take.

According to one reviewer, ". . . it is no longer possible to discuss development economics intelligently without coming to grips with the many arguments P. T. Bauer has marshalled in this extraordinary work." — *J.R.H.*

Additional Recommended Reading

Beckford, George. *Persistent Poverty*. London: Oxford University Press, 1972. A

Third World perspective on poverty in plantation economies.

Bhagwati, Jagdish. *The New International Economic Order: The North-South Debate*. Cambridge, Mass.: MIT Press, 1977. A book of articles by economists about international economic policy toward the Third World.

Brookfield, Harold. *Interdependent Development*. London: Methuen, 1975. A careful description and analysis of modern theories of economic development.

Cohen, Benjamin J. *The Question of Imperialism: The Political Economy of Dominance and Dependence*. New York: Basic Books, 1973. A lucid treatment of colonialism, neocolonialism, and the different attitudes toward North-South relationships that exist in the world today.

Meier, Gerald M. *Leading Issues in Economic Development*. New York: Oxford University Press, 1976. A book of well-chosen readings about economic development.

Kindleberger, Charles P. and B. Herrick. *Economic Development*. New York: McGraw-Hill Book Company, 1977. A textbook on economic development by two leading international economists.

THE FALL OF CAMBODIA TO THE KHMER ROUGE

Type of event: Political: Communist revolution and war in Cambodia
Time: 1975
Locale: Cambodia (Kampuchea)

Principal personages:

KHIEU SAMPHAN (1931-   ), Cambodian Marxist who joined the Communist movement in 1967, and led Khmer Rouge military; Minister of Defense, Commander in Chief, and Chairman of the State Presidium and head of state of Democratic Kampuchea, 1976-1978

PRINCE NORODOM SIHANOUK (1922-   ), abdicated as King of Cambodia in 1955 but ruled as Prince until deposed in 1970, then led a government in exile until his return to Cambodia as nominal head of state under the Khmer Rouge until forced to retire in 1976

LON NOL (1913-   ), participated in *coup* against Prince Sihanouk in March, 1970; Prime Minister, Commander in Chief, and head of state of Khmer Republic, 1970-1975

CHENG HENG (1916-   ), Cambodian head of state when right-wing government was elected in 1966, but was forced to resign when Lon Nol assumed full political control in March, 1972

CREIGHTON WILLIAMS ABRAMS (1914-   ), Commander of United States forces in Vietnam, 1968-1972

RICHARD MILHOUS NIXON (1913-   ), thirty-seventh President of the United States, 1969-1974

HENRY ALFRED KISSINGER (1923-   ), Special Assistant for National Security Affairs, 1969-1973; and United States Secretary of State, 1973-1977

LE DUC THO (1912-   ), chief negotiator for North Vietnam at the Paris peace talks which concluded on January 27, 1973

POL POT (1928-   ), Cambodian Marxist who joined the Communist movement in 1963; Secretary General of the Central Committee of the Communist Party of Kampuchea, 1963-1978; and Prime Minister of Democratic Kampuchea, 1976-1978

Summary of Event

The fall of Cambodia to the Communist Khmer Rouge guerrilla forces in 1975 was an episode in Southeast Asian history that involved a Communist-Nationalist movement, a weakened and discredited imperial government, and American and Vietnamese military action.

Cambodia first entered the Communist movement as a branch of the Indochinese Communist Party created by Ho Chi Minh in 1930. The Indochinese Communist Party was dominated by Chinese and Vietnamese, but after World War II, the Communist movement in Cambodia took on a Khmer flavor. A leading figure was Khieu Samphan, who ultimately became Commander in Chief of the Khmer Rouge and later head of state. His thesis submitted at the University of Paris in 1959 became the foundation of Cambodian Communist economic thought. Writing on Cambodia's economic and industrial development, he emphasized the need to make Cambodia self-sufficient by thoroughly developing the country's agriculture and then its industry. To do so, it would be necessary to move Cambodia's population to the countryside. This tactic, he proposed, should be accomplished by persuasion, but other Communists later engaged in a forceful method.

With a false sense of confidence in 1966, the Cambodian leader, Prince Norodom Sihanouk, allowed an open slate of candidates for a national election. A right-wing legislature won, and Lon Nol became Prime Minister and Cheng Heng was made head of state. To balance this unexpected turn of events, Prince Sihanouk attempted to bring Khieu Samphan into a loyal opposition. It did not work, and the peasants of Battambang province in western Cambodia revolted in 1967. This uprising was a turning point in the Cambodian revolution, and the Revolutionary Army of Kampuchea was formed, which Prince Sihanouk named "les Khmer Rouges." The period from the Battambang uprising to March 18, 1970, when Prince Sihanouk was deposed while on a trip to Moscow and Peking by a right-wing *coup* which led to Lon Nol's becoming Prime Minister and Cheng Heng head of state is considered the "civil war" by the Khmer Rouge.

It was during this period, especially 1966-1967, that a weakened Prince Sihanouk allowed the Vietnamese Communists to use Cambodian border areas to transmit their supplies to the Viet Cong guerrillas in South Vietnam and to land supplies at the port of Sihanoukville (Kompong Som). The United States, which had broken relations with Cambodia on May 3, 1965, protested; but American and South Vietnamese troops made only small raids into Cambodia in an effort to stop the Communist supplies.

By early February, 1969, Creighton Abrams, Commander of the United States forces in South Vietnam, requested permission to make B-52 bombing raids on Communist base camps in Cambodia. This request was approved by President Richard M. Nixon in mid-March, but the raids were not reported publicly until May 9, 1969, in *The New York Times*. It was considered a "secret war" and became the center of controversy in the United States involving the President and his Special Assistant for National Security Affairs, Henry A. Kissinger. In the following year, on April 30, 1970, President Nixon announced that American and South Vietnamese troops had attacked Communist bases in Cambodia. This escalation of American involvement on Cambodian territory led to congressional prohibition on future operations. Meanwhile, President Nixon had announced on June 30, 1970, that the "incursion" into Cambodia had been "successful" because of the amount of supplies captured.

Before the American pursuit of North Vietnamese troops and supplies in Cambodia in 1969 and 1970 was over, Prince Sihanouk in Peking had begun to ally with his former enemies, the Khmer Rouge, and formed a government in exile. His actual participation in revolutionary activities from afar was minimal. In Cambodia, the Lon Nol government was weakening. The Prime Minister had a stroke and left for treatment in Hawaii February 13, 1971, and stayed two months. By the end of the year, Lon Nol's forces had abandoned major positions to the Khmer Rouge and experienced heavy losses. In March, 1972, Cheng Heng resigned, and Lon Nol assumed all executive, legislative, and military powers. His failing health, however, diminished his effectiveness.

After extensive negotiation by Kissinger and Le Duc Tho of the Democratic Republic of Vietnam, a peace agreement was signed at Paris on January 27, 1973, to end the Vietnam War. Kissinger tried to obtain a ceasefire in Cambodia as well, but Le Duc Tho claimed that the North Vietnamese did not have control over the Khmer Rouge to guarantee their cooperation. In less than two weeks after the peace agreement was signed, massive B-52 and F-111 bombing raids resumed over Cambodia and were not to cease until August 15, 1973. Once again, the United States Congress intervened, now by blocking funds to continue the bombing.

After the Paris peace agreement, the Khmer Rouge launched their own military operations, depending upon the North Vietnamese only for logistical support. They also began to implement a policy of concentrating on agricultural development. In early January, 1974, the Khmer Rouge began a dry-season offensive against the northwest perimeter of Phnom Penh, Cambodia's capital, using big artillery that reached the city. The following year, at 1:00 A.M. on January 1, 1975, the Khmer Rouge launched another offensive that was to be fatal for the forces of Lon Nol. In a month, the Communists closed off the Mekong river traffic, preventing food, fuel, and ammunition from reaching the beleaguered capital. The fall came quickly. On April 1, 1975, Lon Nol and some supporters left for Hawaii; and on April 17, 1975, the Khmer Rouge entered triumphantly into Phnom Penh. Within hours, the new Communist government began to empty the city of its people to inaugurate a forceful policy of agricultural development.

The new government, led by Pol Pot, isolated itself from the world; but enough refugee accounts of oppressive rule filtered out, indicating that an extreme form of Communism was implemented to make Cambodia entirely self-sufficient and egalitarian. Renewed foreign intervention, however, rather than revolution, brought another change in government. The Socialist Republic of Vietnam, backed by the Soviet Union, invaded Pol Pot's Republic of Democratic Kampuchea, backed by China, on December 25, 1978, and soon set up a new government sympathetic to   Vietnam.

Pertinent Literature

Shawcross, William. *Sideshow: Kissinger, Nixon and the Destruction of Cambodia.* New York: Simon and Schuster, 1979.

Although a generation may pass before all the documentation on American military action in Cambodia becomes available for public scrutiny, William Shawcross has managed to obtain selected American records to produce the first book-length account of events in Cambodia up to the Khmer Rouge takeover in 1975. While concentrating on the American bombing and subsequent "incursions" into Cambodia to eliminate Vietnamese sanctuaries, he also considers the political upheaval inside Cambodia including the Communist insurgency, the rule of Prince Norodom Sihanouk, and the conservative government of General Lon Nol.

Shawcross is highly critical of the American decision in 1969 to bomb Vietnamese outposts in Cambodia, particularly what he considers to be the surreptitious way in which it was made. He believes that a deliberate effort was made to conceal the bombing; he also believes that records were constructed to show "that it had never happened." The author also notes that early "search and destroy" operations into Cambodia failed to accomplish anything substantial. He is particularly critical of the role of Secretary of State Henry A. Kissinger, who, as Nixon's Special Assistant for National Security Affairs, aggressively pursued the course of bombing raids. Kissinger's rationale is that the

raids saved many American military personnel from being killed by Vietnamese using the sanctuaries inside the Cambodian border.

Unsatisfied with Shawcross' presentation of his views, Kissinger later explained his justification for the bombing raids in a letter to *The Economist* (September 8-14, 1979, issue) which reappeared in part in *The New York Times* (September 23, 1979, E19). The Secretary views the raids as a response to the earlier Vietnamese incursion into Cambodia, violating a 1968 understanding whereby the United States stopped bombing North Vietnam. Kissinger justifies the "double bookkeeping" or distorted records that showed the bombing raids took place over Vietnam as part of the "practical implementation of the decision for secrecy." While admitting that some legislators were misled, Kissinger declares that it was not the Nixon Administration's intention. The question of keeping congressional leaders informed is also a controversy between Shawcross and Kissinger. While the author believes that the entire Congress should have been kept informed because it was Congress' constitutional right to pass on questions of military action, the Secretary believes that informing approximately twenty-five congressional leaders adequately fulfilled the Administration's responsibility.

The 1969 bombing raids, and later

incursions and more bombings, were very destructive to the Cambodian economy, morale, and political stability in that beleaguered country. Food became scarce in Phnom Penh after mid-1972; drugs were brought into the country; refugees and poverty mounted; and graft and corruption overtook Cambodian officials. The effect on the American government of the bombing decision was equally disturbing to Shawcross. He writes at some length about the "spying" of one branch upon another and the passing of information gotten surreptitiously. The Department of Defense, the Joint Chiefs of Staff, and the National Security Council were involved.

The attention given to the narrative of events is matched by the author's concern for personalities. His portrait of Prince Sihanouk is that of a complex man, vain, sometimes irrational, sometimes charming and seemingly intelligent. Basically, Shawcross views him as unstable and often manipulative in behavior. Kissinger is also given close scrutiny, and Shawcross depicts him as deceptive with a thirst for power and control. He sees Kissinger as attempting to ingratiate himself with President Nixon and his staff by assuming policy positions more firm and determined than those of the President himself, who is seen as hard and determined to take a "tough" stand for the best possible effect. By contrast, the Secretary of State, William Rogers, and the Secretary of Defense, Melvin Laird, appear conciliatory and more moderate in determining the extent to which American incursions into Cambodia should be made.

The limits of available documentation necessarily leave this account incomplete. By the author's own admission, for example, the extent of American involvement in the *coup* over Sihanouk by Lon Nol remains in doubt. For the questions these limitations raise and the accusatory tone concerning America's "secret war" in Cambodia, *Sideshow* has quickly become a highly controversial book.

Ponchaud, François. *Cambodia: Year Zero.* Translated by Nancy Amphoux. New York: Holt, Rinehart and Winston, 1978.

When the city of Phnom Penh was seized by the Communist Khmer Rouge on April 17, 1975, the country suddenly fell behind a wall of silence. To tell the world of the bizarre and frightening events that took place during the weeks that followed, François Ponchaud, a French Catholic missionary, reports on conversations and written accounts from many refugees about their experiences.

Ponchaud had lived in Cambodia for ten years, from November 8, 1965, to his departure on May 8, 1975, about three weeks after the Khmer Rouge entered Phnom Penh. Half of this period was spent under the government of Prince Sihanouk and half under the regime of Lon Nol. Ponchaud knew the Khmer people well, having spent the first three years of his life in Cambodia learning the language, culture, and Buddhist religion of the Khmers. During his early years, he lived in various places in the rural districts and towns, later moving to Phnom Penh. As the revolution progressed, Ponchaud's early belief in its necessity changed as the conflict became more bloody.

Having witnessed the Khmer Rouge entrance into Phnom Penh, Ponchaud describes the response of the people. The guerrilla army was initially welcomed, but not enthusiastically. It was difficult for many to realize that the long years of fighting had finally come to an end. Relief, however, soon changed to astonishment and finally to fear. Within hours, the process of emptying the city of Phnom Penh of all its people had begun. Hospitals were to be evacuated first. Those who could walk did so; those who could not had to be carried; others had to be pushed in their beds. The explanation given to the people by the soldiers was that the Americans were expected to bomb the city. The people were advised to take little with them as they were told that they would return in two or three days. The forced march to the countryside led to scenes of horror and death. Masses of people were herded in a slow march out of the city, with few personal possessions and little to eat. Objects of wealth were taken by the armed Khmer Rouge who, it was reported, would punish disobedience by shooting. People were only ordered to return to the town of their origin and take up farming. The plan to force nearly the entire population of Cambodia into rice production was quickly unfolding without warning.

The revolution left nothing to chance and methodically began to eliminate the former civilian and military establishment once Phnom Penh had been occupied and evacuated of its residents. Reports were given that this macabre policy was achieved by shooting those associated with the Lon Nol government. In a thorough effort to eliminate any remnant of the former governing class, wives and children of the old establishment were also eliminated. No effort was made to reeducate associates of the former regime as had been done in China and Vietnam. Foreigners, in accord with Democratic Kampuchea's policy of self-reliance, would not be allowed the convenience of planes and were trucked to the border of Thailand.

The new society of Kampuchea emphasized the long hours of farming under the supervision of armed Khmer Rouge soldiers who would not tolerate delays or resistance. Local organization and the emphasis of continuous struggle was patterned after the Chinese Communist experience under Mao. At the root of the revolutionary fervor was Cambodian Nationalism that drove the Khmer Rouge with a fanatical zeal—a zeal which, according to Ponchaud's informants, led to unending labor with a limited food supply and in wretched sanitary conditions. Terror and summary executions to eliminate opposition became commonplace. It was estimated that in the first year of "peace" about one million people may have died. Ponchaud points out, however, that Lon Nol's government treated captured Khmer Rouge soldiers just as savagely as they were now treating their enemy.

The purpose of these excesses, Ponchaud notes, was to satisfy the desire for complete self-sufficiency and to stress that economic growth is important to the achievement of real independence. To accomplish this, the government established by the Khmer Rouge declared that all the nation's resources must be mobilized for rice production, for when rice can be exported, currency can be obtained—providing capital that would be applied to industrial development. Cambodia, unfortunately, is not blessed with good soil or mineral wealth.

The revolutionary government, Ponchaud observes, sought to bring about its great economic development by fashioning an egalitarian society that emphasizes service, personal sacrifice, and continuous struggle. This experiment in utopia, however, was interrupted at the end of 1978 by an invasion of the Vietnamese in concert with dissident forces in Cambodia, an event that brought another round of disorder and horror to the Khmer people, once known for their gentle manner. — *L.H.D.G.*

Additional Recommended Reading

Caldwell, Malcolm and Lek Tan. *Cambodia in the Southeast Asian War*. New York: Monthly Review Press, 1973. Account before the fall of Cambodia.

Kissinger, Henry A. *The White House Years*. Boston: Little, Brown and Company, 1979. Kissinger's account of the Cambodian policy of the United States.

Lukas, J. Anthony. *Nightmare: The Underside of the Nixon Years*. New York: The Viking Press, 1976. This book about the Watergate episode includes references to American policy pertaining to Cambodia.

Nixon, Richard M. *RN: The Memoirs of Richard Nixon*. New York: Grosset and Dunlap, 1978. Nixon's account of the American Cambodian policy.

Safire, William. *Before the Fall: An Inside View of the Pre-Watergate White House*. Garden City, N.Y.: Doubleday and Company, 1975. Written by a Nixon speech writer and journalist, the author recounts his view of the Cambodian decision.

Szulc, Tad. *The Illusion of Peace: Foreign Policy in the Nixon Years*. New York: The Viking Press, 1978. Includes a dispassionate account of the decision-making process regarding Cambodia.

THE CIVIL WAR IN ANGOLA AND THE INTERVENTION OF CUBA

Type of event: Military: armed intervention in the internal affairs of an African nation by a Western Hemisphere country
Time: 1975-1976
Locale: Angola

Principal personages:

ANTONIO AGOSTINHO NETO (1922-   ), leader of the Popular Movement for the Liberation of Angola (MPLA), and after November, 1976, President of the People's Republic of Angola

ROBERTO HOLDEN (1925-   ), President of the National Front for the Liberation of Angola (FNLA)

JONAS SAVIMBI (1934-   ), founder of the National Union for the Total Independence of Angola (UNITA)

MOBUTU SESE SEKO (1930-   ), President of the Republic of Zaïre (formerly the Belgian Congo) and supporter of his relative by marriage, Roberto Holden

Summary of Event

The Bakongo people at the mouth of the Congo river had been a kingdom for about one century when they first encountered Portuguese sailors in 1482. A permanent trading/military post was established in 1575. Until 1836 Portugal was primarily engaged in the slave trade and Christian missions along the coast, especially in Luanda and Benguela. After slavery was abolished in 1856, Portugal expanded inland in search of new sources of income. Competition with Britain led to a treaty in 1891 which created the boundaries of today's Angola.

Portugal considered all of her "provinces" (as her colonies were called after 1951) as a source of labor and natural materials for the benefit of three groups in the following priority: Portuguese in Portugal, settlers in Angola from Portugal, and Africans. Africans who met certain educational and social standards became *assimilados* entitled to Portuguese citizenship, but most men were conscripted as laborers for the mines (diamond, manganese, petroleum, iron ore), plantations (especially coffee and cotton), and other businesses. Between World War II and 1975, Portuguese settlement rose from 50,000 to 500,000, thus increasing the demand for African labor. Portuguese settlers were primarily the poor and uneducated of Portugal, Europe's least developed nation.

Angola's first political party was formed in 1956 under the leadership of educated *assimilados*, and Mbundu people in and around the capital city of Luanda. After 1962, Dr. Agostinho Neto assumed leadership of the Popular Movement for the Liberation of Angola (MPLA) which represented

1219

about twenty-three percent of the country's population. In 1957, the Union of the Populations of Northern Angola was founded in Leopoldville (now called Kinshasa) uniting the Bakongo people of the then Belgian Congo with the Bakongo of northern Angola, who represented thirteen percent of the country's people. In 1958, the Union changed its name and by 1961 Roberto Holden took charge, merged it with other political groups, and formed in 1962 the National Front for the Liberation of Angola (FNLA). Regional, ethnic, personal, and political differences divided the two parties although occasional alliances underlined their basic and common goal—ending more than four centuries of Portuguese colonialism.

After 1959, Portugal's policy was to arrest the political leaders and openly suppress any show of popular solidarity. In June, 1960, Portuguese soldiers killed thirty and wounded two hundred Angolans in Neto's village during a protest of his arrest. By February of the next year, the MPLA took up arms in the belief that a violent struggle was the only viable option. Portugal had the military advantage in arms. Support from her NATO allies allowed her to employ aerial bombings and sophisticated techniques of antiguerrilla warfare, including the use of napalm. Both the MPLA and the FNLA directed their operations from Kinshasa, Zaïre (formerly Leopoldville, Belgian Congo), where the FNLA began receiving covert United States backing in December, 1962. In 1963, the Organization of African Unity (OAU) recognized the FNLA as the legiti-

mate liberation movement and the MPLA was expelled from Zaïre. By July, 1964, Jonas Savimbi resigned from the FNLA because he considered it too dominated by the Bakongo and did not favor American support. Savimbi formed his own front, the National Union for the Total Independence of Angola (UNITA) whose base was among the Ovimbundu people of the south, representing thirty-eight percent of Angola's population.

Although splits within and between the FNLA, MPLA, and UNITA were barely below the surface, each carried out their own military operations against the common enemy, the Portuguese, in the north, center, and south, respectively. Zaïre, France, and the United States supported the FNLA; the U.S.S.R. backed the MPLA; and certain Portuguese business interests, South Africa, the Peoples' Republic of China, and to a limited extent, the United States, assisted UNITA. Washington's renewal of the Azores Agreement with Portugal (part of a $435 million aid contract) in 1971 and the investments of Gulf Oil Company placed many American interests on the side of continued Portuguese rule, but this was only one of many contradictions in the Angolan intervention.

Competition among the three liberation movements decidedly intensified after April, 1974, when Portugal's dictatorship was overthrown in a *coup* by army officers who wanted Portugal to free her colonies. While South Africa and white Angolans supported Savimbi as a moderate, the new Portuguese government signed the Alvor Agreement on January 15,

1975, promising all three groups that they would be equally represented in a transitional coalition government. In addition, elections were to take place in October, 1975, leading to independence on November 11 of that year. Officially the major powers and the OAU were pledged to support this period of "peaceful transition" but the United States immediately stepped up its covert support of FNLA and UNITA. In June, 250 Cubans arrived to advise MPLA forces, who had Russian-made weapons. White mercenaries from Europe and the United States were being recruited to help the FNLA.

The turning point of the no-longer "civil" war was the invasion of Angola through Namibia (South West Africa) by some four or five thousand white South African troops on October 20 in collaboration with Savimbi's forces. Heavily armored South African columns joined UNITA, and some FNLA troops, to inflict serious defeats on the MPLA. But South African intervention immediately placed most African nations on the side of the MPLA, which, on November 11, 1975, declared the People's Republic of Angola independent as stipulated in the Alvor Agreement. Thirty nations recognized the Agree-

ment; none recognized the Democratic Republic of Angola declared jointly by the FNLA/UNITA forces.

The arrival of three thousand Cuban troops in Luanda in mid-November signaled the beginning of the retreat of the South African forces. In December, 1975, the United States Senate passed the Tunney Amendment to the Defense Appropriation Bill cutting off further covert aid to the FNLA and UNITA forces. The House confirmed the Amendment in January, as MPLA units, reinforced by more Cuban troops and Soviet weapons, continued their offensive. By February, 1976, most African states recognized the MPLA and welcomed the Peoples' Republic of Angola into the OAU as its forty-seventh member. The forces of UNITA and FNLA, however, did not disappear. Regional animosity, discontent among the major powers over the outcome of the Angolan civil war, and the destruction of Angola's cities and countryside were only three of the many obstacles facing the new republic. Limited discontent continued to plague the new government into the late 1970's and several major powers continued to hope for the renaissance of their defeated clients.

Pertinent Literature

Stockwell, John. *In Search of Enemies: A CIA Story*. New York: W. W. Norton and Company, 1978.

John Stockwell, who was chief of the CIA Angola Task Force, deals primarily with two major concerns: first, how and why our Angola intervention was ill-conceived and poorly carried out; and second, why the CIA's clandestine operations should be discontinued in all parts of the world.

Regarding the Angolan intervention, which he reluctantly led after returning disillusioned from CIA operations in Vietnam, Stockwell describes how the United States actually helped to spread the civil war by arming the FNLA during the period pledged to "peaceful transition" until the October elections of 1975. Washington's main purpose then was "to make a MPLA victory more costly." Because this was in violation of official American policy, the entire operation was a secret, no-win, economy-size war carried out on a budget of 24.7 billion dollars; but it was "the only war we had."

Stockwell visited the Angolan front and provides intimate and illustrative insights into what was happening on the ground with the FNLA and UNITA forces in Angola and Zaïre. Savimbi (UNITA), he concludes, was not a Marxist, capitalist, or black revolutionary; he was an Ovimbundu patriot willing to accept help for his cause from any quarters—even from South Africa. Stockwell points out that Savimbi embarrassed the United States at one point by sending feelers to the MPLA for a negotiated peace. UNITA's army was better than the FNLA's, and Savimbi was the most organized and courageous of the three liberation leaders. The author notes that "in retreat, Mobutu's finest forces raped and pillaged in Angolan villages until the Bakongo of northern Angola prayed for the early arrival of the MPLA and Cuban liberators." Stockwell claims that he argued for a full American backing of the UNITA/FNLA coalition or full withdrawal. He also contrasts American covert activity (a necessity given our official position) to Cuba's open intervention announced before the General Assembly of the United Nations.

Stockwell uses the Angolan intervention to criticize the CIA. With his own broad experience with the inner thinking of the "master chessplayers" (Henry Kissinger, William Colby, and others), he draws into his text parallel examples of past CIA bungling and illegal operations all over the world. Everyone knew the chessplayers, he asserts, but even the CIA leaders were unaware of any master plan. Stockwell details how CIA propaganda on Angola infiltrated the world press (including the unsuspecting *Washington Post*), and how the CIA hosted the FNLA in New York (on money laundered in Europe) and even wrote their position paper delivered at the United Nations. For the CIA, it was a great success, convincing even to American black leaders such as Roy Ennis of CORE.

The disclosure of American collaboration with white South Africa's invasion of Angola added humiliation to the defeat that soon followed with the MPLA/Cuban advance. In desperation, Washington switched to a win policy, but it was too late to convince an angry Congress (reacting to exposed CIA deceptions) to appropriate more funds. Stockwell devotes an entire chapter to the friendly duel between the CIA and Congress. He points out that Senators, briefed by the CIA only after taking an oath of secrecy, could not expose CIA deceptions and had only one legal recourse—the cutting or limiting of the CIA budget. This was the basis for the support behind the Tunney Amendment. The assassination of a

CIA agent in Greece during the controversy with Congress convinced many members of the danger of exposing CIA agents and operations, thus giving the CIA more or less of a free hand again in Angola. National security reasons were also important in bringing more initiative back into the CIA operations. Stockwell notes that the attempt to recruit mercenaries covered the globe. Vietnamese, anti-Castro Cubans, Brazilians, Filipinos, and others were approached, but only Portuguese and South Africans responded in appreciable numbers. American cooperation with South Africa would have been even greater, he concludes, had the United States Ambassador in Pretoria not threatened resignation.

Stockwell concludes that the clandestine operations of the CIA (not the CIA itself) constitute an unneeded "shadowy alter ego" and should be abolished for several reasons. Such operations are costly, in terms of human lives as well as dollars; there is great loss of life among the participants, and even the lives of United States citizens abroad who are suspected of being agents are in jeopardy. Stockwell considers such involvement unworthy of a great nation such as the United States. The role of the United States in Angola, he resolves, was only made possible by the apathy and naïveté of most Americans.

In his appendixes, Stockwell provides a chronology of the events in Angola, a chart of the control and direction of United States Foreign Intelligence (no names of agents are given for reasons of their own safety), and several lists of United States arms and matériel delivered to various groups in Angola. The last appendix is a long letter from Stockwell to Admiral Stansfield Turner, Director of the CIA, explaining his long involvement in Africa, his disillusionment with the agency, and his reasons for resigning. To date, this is one of the few books published in English after the victory of the MPLA in Angola. Many others of varying opinion will certainly follow.

Houser, George, Jennifer Davis, Herbert Shore and Susan Rogers. *No One Can Stop the Rain*. New York: Africa Fund (Associated with the American Committee on Africa), 1976.

This booklet begins on independence day (November 11, 1975) with the MPLA in Luanda and the FNLA/UNITA coalition in Huambo simultaneously claiming leadership of a new Angola freed from over four hundred years of Portuguese rule. In spite of rapid recognition of the MPLA by some thirty countries (not one country recognized the FNLA/UNITA claims), the graffiti on the wall was all too correct: "a luta armada continua" or "the armed struggle continues." In some forty pages, the authors succinctly answer the most obvious question: Why and how did victory gained at such cost now evolve into civil strife with alliances of Western European, American, South African, and conservative African forces lining up against the MPLA?

Beginning with the Portuguese

presence ten years before Columbus reached North America, they briefly describe the kingdom of Congo, the Mbundu kingdom of Ndongo, and the long resistance (1578-1680) of the Mbundu to Portuguese intrusion. A brief section describes the slave trade which ended effectively in 1878. Most of the slaves were sent to Brazil, the Portuguese territory through which Angola was administered. As the Portuguese expanded into the interior of Angola, the people resisted in heroic struggles, the accounts of which are still alive in the collective memory of many communities. Needing labor for the maintenance and growth of their colony, the Portuguese instituted forced labor after the abolition of slavery and encouraged more Portuguese to settle. By 1975, there were 400,000 Europeans and six million Angolans.

After summarizing the negative effects of Portuguese rule on Angola, the authors outline the history of the various political organizations and the ultimate emergence of the MPLA as the leading group. The success of the MPLA signaled that reformist channels provided no answer to Portuguese repression. The authors explain the ties of the MPLA to the movements and leaders in other Portuguese colonies; namely, Mozambique and Guinea Bissau.

A brief biography of Dr. Agostinho Neto is helpful. This son of a Methodist pastor had just opened his medical practice when he was imprisoned as a leader in the MPLA. The protests of his people led to a massacre by Portuguese soldiers which sparked the rising belief in armed struggle. From his prison cell, Neto wrote poetry. A section from "Here in Prison" provided the title of this book:

> Here in prison
> rage contained in my breast
> I patiently wait
> for the clouds to gather
> blown by the wind of history
>
> No one
> can stop the rain

A good portion of the book is given to explaining the political differences of various Angolan parties, the progress of the civil war and the many abortive attempts at unity. A very important section spells out the MPLA program, which basically called for the liquidation of colonialism and a wider alliance of progressive forces around the world in support of the struggle of the Angolan people. A basic goal was an egalitarian society without distinction of ethnic group, class, political beliefs, or religious faith. The MPLA program supported freedom of speech, conscience, press, and assembly, and called for universal suffrage. Supporting the end of privileges derived from the colonial system, the platform also guaranteed the protection of industry and private enterprise. Agrarian reform promised land to those who worked the soil. Internationally, the MPLA advocated nonalignment.

The MPLA platform was more than promises on paper. Concrete programs had been set up in areas liberated from Portuguese control. Trained medical personnel already ran a successful health service which was free for all the people. Agricultural collectives were set up that were based on self-reliance, and schools were opened in liberated areas.

The authors place the struggle in Angola in its international context. Within a month of his election to the presidency of MPLA, Neto traveled to the United States to present the MPLA's case to anyone who would listen. He met with many people and organizations but gained little support. By then the United States had already decided to support Roberto Holden and the FNLA, which coincided more or less with American policy in Zaïre. The return of Angolans training abroad (primarily in Algeria) seemed far more promising than any hope of support from the United States of America. The authors show the direct relationship between the *coup* in Lisbon (April 25, 1974) and the turn of events in Angola soon afterward. They describe the direct support for Portugal to the very end from conservative forces in Africa and the West.

The last section carefully details the civil war and international interference in a muddled situation. This section, which the researcher will want to read most carefully, was written at the moment that MPLA victory was evident. But the authors and the Angolans they are writing about know that the battle is not yet over, either literally or figuratively. The rebuilding of Angola is ahead, as is the liberation of other parts of the continent. The book closes with a poem by Neto's wife, Eugenia, underlining hope in the future:

As you will see, my brother
There will be no more wars in Angola

The hands of guerrillas will leave their weapons
The hands of the Portuguese soldiers
Will go to till the soil
And cover it with flowers

And one day
Not far from that moment
Men who once killed each other
Can build in unity
The future of mankind

No One Can Stop the Rain suggests additional readings and provides a glossary of organizations involved in Angola between 1913 and 1974 and their acronyms. — *H.H.B.*

Additional Recommended Reading

Abshire, D. M. and M. A. Samuels, eds. *Portuguese Africa: A Handbook*. New York: Frederick A. Praeger, 1969. A background for understanding Angola is provided within the context of Portuguese colonialism on the continent.

Barnett, Don and Roy Harvey. *The Revolution in Angola: MPLA, Life Histories and Documents*. Indianapolis: Bobbs-Merrill, 1972. The authors, who traveled with MPLA soldiers, describe the struggle for independence and consider it as part of a wider revolution.

Davidson, Basil. *In the Eye of the Storm: Angola's People*. Garden City, N.Y.: Doubleday & Company, 1972 (Penguin edition, 1975). An eminent Africanist provides a scholarly summary of Angola's history including the beginnings of the war against Portugal.

Minter, William. *Imperial Network and External Dependency: The Case of Angola*.

Beverly Hills, Calif.: Sage Publications, 1972. An Africanist (sociologist) offers unusual insight into Angola in this series of the Sage Professional Papers in International Studies.

Marcum, John. *The Angolan Revolution.* Vol. I: *The Anatomy of an Explosion, 1950-1962.* Cambridge, Mass.: MIT Press, 1969. A scholar specializing in Angola provides sources for and a history of the beginnings of the civil war, focusing on the roots of rebellion among the three major ethnic groups.

Vansina, Jan. *Kingdoms of the Savannah.* Madison: University of Wisconsin Press, 1968. An internationally recognized Africanist concentrates on several central African kingdoms before European arrival.

THE FALL OF SOUTH VIETNAM

Type of event: Military: North Vietnamese strategy to defeat South Vietnamese regime
Time: January 7-April 30, 1975
Locale: Saigon, South Vietnam

Principal personages:

LE DUAN (1908-   ), First Secretary of the North Vietnamese Communist Party

GENERAL VAN TIEN DUNG (1917-   ), North Vietnamese Army Chief of Staff and military planner of the 1975 Communist offensive

NGUYEN VAN THIEU (1923-   ), President of the Republic of (South) Vietnam

TRAN VAN HUONG (1903-   ), Vice-President of the Republic of (South) Vietnam

DUONG VAN (BIG) MINH (1916-   ), last President of the Republic of (South) Vietnam who surrendered to the Communists

GERALD RUDOLPH FORD (1913-   ), thirty-eighth President of the United States, 1974-1977

HENRY ALFRED KISSINGER (1923-   ), United States Secretary of State, 1973-1977

GRAHAM ANDERSON MARTIN (1912-   ), United States Ambassador to South Vietnam

Summary of Event

On January 27, 1973, the United States and the Democratic Republic of Vietnam (North Vietnam) signed the Paris Peace Accords bringing to an end American military participation in the Vietnam War. By separating the military and political issues of the war, the Administration of President Richard M. Nixon had found a graceful way of extricating the United States from this unpopular war. The major political issue of who would rule South Vietnam, however, was left up to the Vietnamese to resolve. There was probably never any chance that Hanoi and Saigon could agree on the composition of a postwar government acceptable to both parties; the issues dividing them were too fundamental to be capable of peaceful resolution. The Nixon Administration and that of President Gerald R. Ford nevertheless believed that the regime of South Vietnam President Nguyen Van Thieu was strong enough to weather whatever political or military challenges it faced from the Communists. United States Ambassador to South Vietnam, Graham Martin, held out hope to Thieu that Congress and the American people would eventually approve his requests for more aid. Within two years, however, that hope proved illusionary and the Thieu regime collapsed faster than anybody thought possible.

The events leading up to the fall of Saigon began in December, 1974, when the North Vietnamese Army (NVA) launched a major offensive against the South, attacking Phuoc Long province bordering Cambodia. By January 7, 1975, the capital of this province, Phuoc Binh, had fallen into the hands of the Communists. Although Phuoc Binh was of marginal military value, its loss was a psychologically devastating blow to the South Vietnamese government. Other reversals in Tay Ninh province strained the morale of the South Vietnamese Army, and these Communist victories proved to be a major turning point in the war. Not only did they convince the North Vietnamese Politburo, headed by Le Duan, First Secretary of the North Vietnamese Communist Party, that the time was ripe for a major military offensive against the South, but they also convinced the Communist leadership that the United States would not intervene militarily to prop up the Thieu regime.

On March 4, 1975, the Communists opened an attack on the Central Highlands making it appear that Pleiku was their major target. Then, when Thieu rushed elements of the 23rd Division from Ban Me Thuot to defend Pleiku, the North Vietnamese attacked Ban Me Thuot in full force, overrunning the city by March 12. The Communists had completely outwitted the Thieu regime, capturing large quantities of arms, munitions, and vehicles that would be used in the campaign to "liberate" Saigon. By March 15, the military situation was so precarious that Thieu decided

upon a "tactical withdrawal" from the Central Highlands. The decision to abandon this region had a devastating effect on the morale of the South Vietnamese as thousands of refugees jammed the highways to reach the coast for safety.

The South Vietnamese government came under increasing pressure by mid-March as rumors floated around Saigon about plots to kill Thieu and replace his regime with one that could conduct the war more effectively. Fearful of a *coup d'état* against him, Thieu ordered the 1st Airborne Division from Quang Tri province in the North to protect his position in the South. The Communists took full advantage of this confused situation by attacking the old imperial city of Hue. By March 26, Hue fell into Communist hands without a major fight. Three days later the Communists followed up these victories by attacking Danang, the second largest city in South Vietnam. The scene in Danang was one of total panic as South Vietnamese Army units trampled over men, women, and children to secure evacuation on American aircraft.

The Thieu government attempted to build a new defense perimeter in the South stretching from Tay Ninh in the West to Nha Trang on the coast. This defense perimeter was supposed to be strong enough to withstand any attack by the Communists. The South Vietnamese government hoped that with the onset of the monsoon rains, the Communist advance against Saigon could be blunted. What the Thieu regime failed to take into account was the mobility and firepower of the enemy. Using vehicles and tanks captured from the South Vietnamese Army, Communist units rolled along the highways of Central Vietnam without encountering much opposition. A three-pronged attack against this defense perimeter was ordered by General Van Tien Dung, Commander of the North Vietnamese Army and military planner of the 1975 offensive. The major battle of this campaign was fought at Xuan Loc, thirty-seven miles east of Saigon. After three weeks of heavy fighting, Xuan Loc was overrun by the Communists on April 21, 1975, and the road to Saigon now lay completely open.

Paralleling the military collapse on the battlefield was the political collapse of the Thieu regime. In February, 1975, Father Tran Huu Thanh, the leader of the Popular Anti-Corruption Movement, issued a call for Thieu's removal, accusing him of "high treason" and "undermining the nationalist cause for financial gain." He warned that more territory on the battlefield would be lost if the corrupt Thieu regime continued in power. By April other leading South Vietnamese politicians had joined in opposition to the Thieu government. Even the pro-Thieu Senate called for his resignation. Thieu reacted to these pressures by firing his Prime Minister, Tran Thien Khiem, and replacing him with a new military government composed of his close supporters, but this government would not last long. After the fall of Xuan Loc on April 21, 1975, Thieu's political position became so untenable that he was forced to step down from the presidency to make way for a candidate more capable of negotiating peace with the Communists.

In his television speech to the nation, Thieu blamed the United States government for his predicament. He recounted how he had opposed the Paris Peace Accords, and how he only agreed to sign them after President Nixon personally promised to use military force to stop any major Communist attack against the South. Thieu charged that Nixon and Henry A. Kissinger, United States Secretary of State, told him that Congress would cut off all military and economic aid if he did not sign these accords. Now, in the hour of greatest need, the United States refused to honor these commitments. At the end of the speech Thieu announced his resignation and turned the government over to his Vice-President, Tran Van Huong.

As a member of the "Thieu clique," Tran Van Huong was no more acceptable to the Communists than President Thieu, and they demanded his ouster in favor of ex-General Duong Van (Big) Minh. On the verge of panic, the National Assembly complied with Communist wishes naming "Big Minh" as the new President. By April 30, 1975, Minh ordered all government troops to observe a cease fire. He pledged himself to work out an orderly transfer of power to the Communists to minimize further bloodshed. Shortly after noon on April 30, the first Communist troops entered Saigon and proceeded to the Presidential Palace where they accepted the surrender of South Vietnam's government.

The fall of Saigon brought an end to thirty years of war against the French, the Americans, and the South

Vietnamese government. The triumph of the North Vietnamese exposed the weaknesses of the containment doctrine which had guided American foreign policy since World War II. It called for a reexamination of United States foreign policy around the world. The way was now clear for the reunification of the two Vietnams on Communist terms.

Pertinent Literature

Snepp, Frank. *Decent Interval*. New York: Random House, 1977.

Decent Interval by Frank Snepp is an extremely detailed account of the fall of the Thieu government in South Vietnam, focusing on the period between the signing of the Paris Peace Accords in January, 1973, and the fall of Saigon in April, 1975. During this period, Snepp served as the CIA's Chief Strategy Analyst in Vietnam. He was thus in a unique position to observe and interpret the events which eventually led to the collapse of the South Vietnamese government.

The literature on the fall of Saigon focuses on two basic questions. First, despite massive doses of American military and economic aid, why did the Thieu regime collapse so quickly and what factors were responsible for the demise of South Vietnam? Second, how should the American role in Vietnam be evaluated: was this role an honorable one during the course of the war and during the last dying days of the regime?

Snepp maintains that the underlying reasons for the fall of Saigon are complex. Years of military and economic dependence upon the United States sapped the inner strength of the South Vietnamese regime. Assurances of unconditional support for the Thieu government by Presidents Nixon and Ford postponed the difficult choices that had to be made by the Saigon government. Thieu continued to believe that he could count on United States financial assistance despite evidence of growing congressional skepticism about the war. Ambassador Graham Martin and other United States Embassy officials reassured Thieu that Congress and the American people would eventually come around to approve new aid requests. When this failed to happen, the South Vietnamese regime was not psychologically prepared to continue the struggle by itself.

A second major problem which helped pave the way for defeat was the insidious problem of corruption which undermined the legitimacy of the South Vietnamese government. Although President Thieu repeatedly assured his critics that he would ferret out corruption in the ranks of the military and government, steps against the worst offenders were never undertaken. Snepp charges that Thieu could not bring himself to prosecute old friends and cronies in the military. He was more afraid of the possibility of a backlash against him by other corrupt generals than he was of eradicating the corruption which was necessary to prosecute the war against the Communists effectively.

Finally, some of Thieu's biggest mistakes occurred in the military realm. Once the Communist offensive began, Thieu committed a series of military blunders that crippled the morale of his troops and contributed to the psychology of defeat which gripped the South Vietnamese Army. After the loss of Ban Me Thuot in the Central Highlands, he embarked on a strategy of "light at the top, heavy at the bottom"—in effect, writing off large portions of the North and Central part of the country in order to defend Saigon and the Delta region. Snepp points out that this fundamental military decision was taken without much thought or discussion as to its consequences. The practical problems of implementing such an important scheme were never fully considered.

Snepp catalogues a host of other bad military moves Thieu made during this crucial period. For example, the retreat of the 23rd Division commanded by General Pham Van Phu was botched by the selection of an old logging road which was scarcely passable in many parts; apparently, nobody had considered checking to determine the condition of this vital escape route. Thieu's decision to pull the 1st Airborne Division out of the North to protect Saigon against a possible *coup d'état* weakened the defense of Hue and Danang. The conflicting military orders Thieu gave to his northern commander, General Ngo Quang Truong, only served to make the situation worse in the North. At first, Thieu told General Truong to concentrate his troops on defending Danang rather than Hue. After Thieu was told by close associates that he needed a spectacular victory to remain in power, he then ordered Truong to defend the former imperial capital of Hue at all costs.

The Ford Administration and right-wing critics of United States foreign policy blamed congressional aid cutbacks for the disaster in Vietnam. Snepp takes issue with this charge, laying most of the blame on the "shoddy leadership" of the Thieu regime. He is frankly quite bitter about the manner in which the American pullout from Vietnam was handled. Snepp charges that Ambassador Graham Martin, CIA Chief Polgar, and Secretary of State Henry Kissinger all subscribed to the "fatal illusion" that negotiations with the Communists to end the war were still possible even though the Communists had won a series of military victories on the battlefield and United States intelligence sources indicated that they would press their advantage to the fullest. Martin, in particular, refused to take any action to evacuate American and Vietnamese personnel—a move which might be interpreted as a sign that the United States did not think that the Thieu government would fall.

By delaying the evacuation until the last minute, Snepp indicates that thousands of Vietnamese who worked for the United States were callously abandoned to face the wrath of the Communists. American intelligence officials did not even have time to destroy personnel files and intelligence dossiers of those who had cooperated with the Americans over the years. In Snepp's view, this was inexcusable. More than five billion dollars in United States military equipment including sophisticated jet fighters, tanks, artillery pieces, and other war matériel was simply aban-

1231

doned to the Communists.

What troubled Snepp more than anything else was that after the evacuation was complete, United States government officials tried to cover up the story of what actually happened in South Vietnam. It was this coverup that eventually drove Snepp to write this fascinating account, violating the oath of secrecy all CIA employees take upon joining the agency.

Lewy, Guenter. *American in Vietnam*. New York: Oxford University Press, 1978.

The record of American involvement in Vietnam is plagued by factual as well as moral ambiguities and Guenter Lewy's *American in Vietnam* attempts to provide a record of American actions in Vietnam that strips away the myths that both "hawk" and "dove" factions have propounded about the war. In addition to consulting all the standard sources on the subject, Lewy makes extensive use of classified records of the United States Army, Air Force, and Marine Corps. The perspective that emerges is a distinctive one not based on personal experience—the author is a Professor of Political Science at the University of Massachusetts—but rather based on the reports of military personnel in the field.

In the first half of the book, Lewy attacks the strategy and tactics used by the Americans to fight the war. The American military under General William Westmoreland fought a highly technological war in the rice paddies of Vietnam using enormous destructive power to crush the enemy. Unfortunately according to Lewy, the United States probably inflicted more damage on the helpless rural peasantry than they did on the Viet Cong. Instead of winning the war for the hearts and minds of the rural peasantry, American military operations undermined the efforts of the South Vietnamese regime to win the allegiance of its own people. Destructive engagements such as Operation "Masher White Wing" in Binh Dinh province contributed significantly to the war-weariness of the Vietnamese people.

Lewy also considers the reasons for the collapse of the South Vietnamese regime. Shortages of war supplies brought about by cuts in the aid budget certainly hurt the war effort, but these were not sufficient by themselves to bring about the final collapse of the regime. All things being equal, poor leadership rather than a lack of supplies was the main reason for the defeat of the South Vietnamese Army.

During the period of Vietnamization of the war, the United States turned over large quantities of sophisticated military equipment to the South Vietnamese Army. Lewy points out, however, that there were few Vietnamese who possessed the technical expertise to service and maintain this equipment. As a result, planes and helicopters were grounded not because of a lack of fuel, but because they could no longer fly. The South Vietnamese Army found it difficult to handle even routine transportation and logistic problems because of bureaucratic red tape.

In Lewy's view, the most serious shortcoming of the regime which ultimately contributed to its demise was the lack of strong dynamic leadership capable of mobilizing the rural masses. Military units in South Vietnam seldom trained or drilled in the field. Military commanders were too frequently selected on the basis of personal loyalty and political reliability rather than command effectiveness. Given this orientation it is not surprising that the Thieu regime found it difficult to stand up to the superior forces of North Vietnam.

In the end Lewy maintains that the average South Vietnamese soldier in the field did not believe that the regime was worth saving and was not prepared to die for a government riddled by corruption and ineptitude. The Thieu regime did not inspire the sense of trust and confidence that was necessary to prosecute the war effectively.

After exploring the history of United States involvement in the Vietnam War, Lewy examines the conduct of the war from a moral and legal perspective. He repudiates the charge of antiwar activists such as Noam Chomsky, Richard Falk, and Bertrand Russell that the United States engaged in a genocidal war in Vietnam. Lewy points out that the population of South Vietnam actually increased from sixteen million in 1965 to almost twenty million by 1973. There was no systematic policy of genocide in Vietnam.

Lewy also charges that critics of United States policy had a distorted picture of the battlefield situation in Vietnam. United States military authorities did not sanction the indiscriminate killing of innocent civilians. Atrocities such as My Lai undoubtedly occurred, but they were infrequent and not deliberate, and the individuals who perpetrated them were punished. Since there was never any intent to destroy the civilian population as a matter of policy, the charge of genocide in Vietnam is totally unwarranted.

In conclusion, what Guenter Lewy calls for is a more evenhanded treatment of the moral and legal aspects of the Vietnam War. He suggests that it is grossly unfair to label American military actions as genocide while the acts of terrorism by the Viet Cong and North Vietnamese are not also morally condemned. — *R.L.L.*

Additional Recommended Reading

Terzani, Tiziano. *Giai Phong!: The Fall and Liberation of Saigon*. New York: St. Martin's Press, 1976. A detailed account of the fall of Saigon by an Italian journalist who remained in the country after the Americans pulled out; contains particularly good chapters on how the "liberation" forces behaved immediately after seizing power.

Fanning, Louis A. *Betrayal in Vietnam*. New Rochelle, N.Y.: Arlington House Publishers, 1976. A conservative, right-wing interpretation of the fall of Saigon which places blame on "liberals" in the United States Congress for losing Vietnam.

Dawson, Alan. *Fifty-five Days: The Fall of South Vietnam*. Englewood Cliffs, N.J.: Prentice-Hall, 1977. A descriptive account of the fall of South Vietnam by the head of United Press International in Saigon; contains excellent chapters on how the system of corruption worked in Vietnam.

Dung, General Van Tien. *Our Great Spring Victory*. New York: Monthly Review Press, 1977. A semiofficial account of how North Vietnam masterminded the victory over the Thieu regime, written by the Commander of the North Vietnamese Army.

Gelb, Leslie H. and Richard K. Betts. *The Irony of Vietnam: The System Worked*. Washington, D.C.: The Brookings Institution, 1979. A scholarly examination of the events which led to the fall of South Vietnam.

Chanda, Nayan. "Suddenly Last Spring," in *Far Eastern Economic Review*. LXXXIX (September 12, 1975), pp. 35-39. A short but detailed account of the 55-Day Spring Offensive.

Goodman, Allan E. "South Vietnam: War Without End?," in *Asian Survey*. XV (January, 1975), pp. 70-84. An examination of the political, economic, and military factors which led to the fall of the Thieu government.

THE LEBANESE CIVIL WAR

Type of event: Military: civil war involving extra-national forces to the point of threatening world peace
Time: April 13, 1975-November 10, 1976
Locale: Lebanon

Principal personages:
SULEIMAN FRANJIEH, Maronite Christian President of Lebanon, 1970-1976
RASHID KARAMI, Sunnite Muslim Prime Minister of Lebanon
PIERRE GEMAYEL, Christian leader of the Kataib (Phalangist) Party
KAMAL JUMBLATT, Druze leader of the Progressive Socialist Party and the Muslim alliance, the National Movement
CAMILLE CHAMOUN (1900-   ), Christian leader of the Party of Liberal Nationalists (PNL)
YASIR ARAFAT (MOHAMMED ABED AR'OUF ARAFAT) (1929-   ), President of the Executive Committee of the Palestine Liberation Organization (PLO)
JIMMY (JAMES EARL) CARTER (1924-   ), thirty-ninth President of the United States, 1977-

Summary of Event

The Civil War in Lebanon, to be fully understood, must be set against the national development and political makeup of Lebanon and the Palestinian diaspora. When Lebanon became independent in 1943 under the sponsorship of the British, the country already had experienced five years as a republic under the French Mandate (1936-1941). The National Covenant, an unwritten agreement supplementing the Constitution, governed political life and established that the President should be a Maronite Christian and the Prime Minister a Sunnite Muslim. Other confessional communities in Lebanon, such as Druzes, Shiite Muslims, Greek Orthodox, were to be represented in the national government.

For a long time the Maronites were probably the most aggressive group politically. They preserved the school of thought that Lebanon is an Arab country and has to cooperate with neighboring Arab states to retain its unique character. Coalitions crossed confessional lines. Kamal Jumblatt, a Druze, organized his Progressive Socialist Party in 1949, and in 1952 cooperated with Christian leaders to depose Bisharah al-Khuri, replacing him with Camille Chamoun as new President of Lebanon.

After the Six-Day War in 1967, when Israel occupied the West Bank and the Gaza strip, a Palestinian nationalism began to develop politically and militarily. The Palestine Liberation Organization (PLO) came out into the open with its new leader Yasir Arafat. The Popular Front for the Liberation of Palestine (PFLP) emerged as a Marxist group, devel-

1235

oping strong ties with Communist countries. Numerous other Palestinian groups arose, including as-Saiqa, a Palestinian organization under Syrian control.

When the Arab League had organized the PLO in 1964, Lebanon had insisted that there be no bases of the Palestine Liberation Army on its territory. This directive was never honored. Lebanese efforts to control the Palestinian military presence in fact ended in clashes until the secret Cairo Agreement of November 3, 1969, allowing for arms inside the refugee camps. Following the expulsion in 1971 of the Palestinians from Jordan, where the organization had threatened the stability of the government, Lebanon became host to more than a million Palestinian refugees. A natural sympathy between the Lebanese Muslim population and the Palestinians thrived. In this tiny country with a population of two million, the scales were tipped.

In 1970 the presidency went to Suleiman Franjieh, who took a tough stance against the presence of armed Palestinians inside Lebanon. In 1971, Franjieh appointed a Commander in Chief of the military, Iskander Ghanem, who was similarly persuaded concerning the armed presence. Lebanese Muslims felt just the opposite, partly because of their grievances against the military. The majority of officers were Christians, and when the armed forces were used in 1973 to quell a disturbance between the Lebanese and the Palestinians, Muslims were alienated. The government fell and the cabinet resigned.

By 1975 the powder keg was ready to explode. Probably the fuse was lit when, in late February and early March, violence broke out in Sidon during a strike by fishermen who had been protesting a monopoly granted by the government to a company owned by Chamoun. The ensuing deaths of Sidon political leader Marouf Saad and an army corporal in a confrontation between the army and the demonstrators were "a signal for all political fronts in the country to go into action," stated Professor Salibi, of the American University in Beirut. On a Sunday morning, April 13, 1975, the first round of the Civil War began when an assassination attempt was made on the Kataib (Phalangist) leader Pierre Gemayel at a church he was helping to dedicate. Four persons, including two members of the Kataib militia, were killed, but Gemayel escaped unhurt. Early that afternoon a busload of Palestinians who had been attending a commemorative event and were returning to their camp, Tall az-Zaatar, were ambushed by Christian elements. A total of twenty-seven were killed.

Street fighting broke out between the Palestinians and the Kataib; Kataib headquarters, shops, and factories were attacked. Camille Chamoun's Party of Liberal Nationalists (PNL) joined in the fighting, throwing their support behind the Kataib. To further complicate matters, Kamal Jumblatt's National Movement took up arms against the PNL. By April 16, 120 had been killed before a ceasefire was arranged; yet on April 17 snipers were in action, apparently disrupting the agreement. Fifteen persons were killed mostly by snipers during the ceasefire. Property damage was estimated at 100 million dollars.

A crisis in government came next, and Prime Minister Rashid Solh resigned on May 15, as armed clashes broke out in northern Beirut. By June 30 a government was finally formed with Rashid Karami as Prime Minister. Karami also became Minister of Defense, thus gaining control over the Army; Chamoun, ally of the Kataib, was appointed Minister of the Interior, thus holding control over the Security Forces.

By late summer the so-called Round Four had begun. In the east a Lebanese-Syrian incident in Zahle started the confrontation between armed sides. In the north Christians and Muslims fought one another, while in the mountains near Jumblatt's fiefdom, Druzes fought Christians.

Saudi Arabia and Egypt called for the other Arab countries to come to Cairo for discussions on ending the Lebanese crisis. Syria, the PLO, and Libya boycotted the meeting. When it was apparent that the Cairo talks were a failure, fighting broke out in downtown Beirut. Two Americans on their way to work were among the hundreds who were kidnaped by both sides. By October 25, the Kataib and an independent Nasserist group, the Murabitoun, were fighting in western Beirut where the American and British communities lived. The American Embassy, as well as the West European and other embassies, advised nationals to leave the country. Kataib and Murabitoun fought over the Holiday Inn in the tourist section of the city. Universities and colleges, some of which had never opened for fall semester, closed down completely. Foreigners fled Beirut, crowding the

airport as soon as a safe route could be found from town to the terminal.

By November 3, with the formation of a Higher Coordination Committee, which was to investigate all breaches of the ceasefires, fighting began to subside. Karami had the support of Syria and the PLO and had an agreement with Franjieh. Downtown Beirut had been virtually destroyed, being now a no-man's land between a newly divided city of Christians in the east and Muslims in the west.

Karami and Jumblatt continued to press the Maronites for political reforms. Vatican and French mediators offered their services. All efforts led only to a Fifth Round of fighting which began November 29. This time the clash began in an entirely different area: a Druze and a Maronite town began exchanging fire with each other in the mountains on the outskirts of Beirut. The Kataib rounded up one hundred Muslims and massacred them in retaliation for the murders of four Kataib Party members. Murabitoun and Kataib again fought in the area of the Holiday Inn. Under pressure from the Syrians and the PLO, a new ceasefire was put into effect on December 15.

Up to this point, the PLO had remained politically in the background. Maronites, however, convinced that the Palestine commando presence was the cause of the war, besieged two refugee camps, Tall az-Zaatar and Jisr al-Basha in January, 1976. Removal of the two camps would establish a long stretch of Christian territory from Kataib and PNL headquarters east of no man's land to approximately ten miles beyond the northern outskirts of the city. The outlook for partition between a Muslim and Christian state would gain strength. Syria, opposed to such an idea, brought about a ceasefire on January 20. By this time Damour, a Christian village south of Beirut, had been overrun, and in exchange a Muslim sector, al-Karantina, a slum area by the slaughterhouses near the port of Beirut, was leveled.

In March a large number of Lebanese Muslim soldiers deserted and formed a new army (the Lebanese Arab Army) under Lieutenant Ahmad al-Khatib. A military government was proclaimed by Brigadier General Abdel Aziz al-Ahdab on March 10; he broadcast his appeal for the resignation of the President. Nothing came of the desertions and the attempted *coup d'état*, except that others took up the call for Franjieh's resignation. Two-thirds of the members of parliament demanded that the President step down. Franjieh was shelled in the presidential palace at Baabda on March 25; the rebel army forced him and his family to flee. Finally, Franjieh signed a formal document, and a ten-day truce was declared for presidential elections. Of the two candidates, Raymond Eddé was supported by Lebanese Muslims and Elias Sarkis had Syrian support.

L. Dean Brown of the United States and George Gorse of France in the meanwhile continued mediation efforts. Early in April, Syria and the Palestine commandos reached an accord on a seven-point program to end the war, but this was rejected by Chamoun as meddling in Lebanese affairs. At the same time Syrian troops began crossing the border into

Lebanon, holding up near the Lebanese border station at Masnaa.

In May Sarkis was elected President, a victory for Syria and the Christian bloc. As Syria's army moved deeper into Lebanese territory, France offered to send troops. In June token peacekeeping troops arrived from the Sudan; however, Syria had won the role of providing the major peacekeeping force. United States-Lebanese relations were shaken when, on June 16, the new United States Ambassador, Francis Meloy, Jr., and his economic adviser, Robert Waring, along with their chauffeur, Zoheir Moghrab, were murdered crossing no-man's land in central Beirut. President Ford two days later ordered the evacuation of all Americans from Lebanon. As Americans and other foreigners were leaving by overland routes and by sea, Syrian and Libyan peacekeeping troops were building forces. By June 22, the Christians were once again attacking the two Palestinian camps, Jisr al-Basha and Tall az-Zaatar, that stood in the way of partition. Estimates were that one thousand died in eight days of fighting, mostly within the camps.

Tall az-Zaatar held up during the summer's heat and the unending attack, long after Jisr al-Basha fell. Finally, on August 13, Tall az-Zaatar was overrun, sustaining thousands of casualties. Not even the Red Cross had been allowed to evacuate four thousand wounded earlier because the Christian attack had been so fierce. The Palestinians were virtually deserted by their earlier Syrian allies, for Syria wished not to have a Palestinian neighbor replacing Christian-dominated Lebanon. Finally, on

September 23, Elias Sarkis was inaugurated, and on November 10, Syrian troops and tanks entered Beirut without a shot being fired. An estimated 35,000 people were killed in nineteen months of armed clashes among the several groups.

As a postscript, fighting erupted in 1978 between the Syrian peacekeeping forces and the Kataib and PNL armies. President Sarkis threatened to resign but was persuaded to remain in office. The fighting continued to flare up. Finally, in October, 1978, following intensive shelling of the Christian areas by Syrian troops, President Jimmy Carter brought to bear the power and prestige of his office to force Syria to disengage its forces. He contacted Syrian President Hafez al-Assad and other world leaders with a stake in Lebanon, including Soviet leader Leonid Brezhnev, French President Valéry Giscard d'Estaing, and Prime Minister Menachem Begin of Israel. Syrian resolve quickly evaporated in the face of such pressure. Within a short time, Assad pulled back his forces from strategic locations in the Christian areas and resumed Syria's role as a peacekeeper in Lebanon.

Pertinent Literature

Salibi, Kamel Suleiman. *Crossroads to Civil War: Lebanon, 1958-1976.* Delmar, N.Y.: Caravan Books, 1976.

Professor Salibi teaches history at the American University in Beirut and is the author of *The Modern History of Lebanon*, which stands alone in its field and is a good base study for the Civil War.

The work is indexed but has no table of contents. Chapters 1 and 2 sum up the founding of the modern republic of Lebanon and its first twenty years. The Lebanese course, influenced by the Egyptian leader, Gamal Abdel Nasser toward pan-Arabism, was changed in 1958. Camille Chamoun invited the United States Marines to the shores of Lebanon to stem threats to Lebanese sovereignty. Chamoun was able to finish his presidency, and the Commander of the Lebanese Army, Fuad Shihab, succeeded him in office. Shihab worked hard to incorporate the Lebanese Muslims within the constitutional system which favored the Christians.

Once out of power Chamoun organized his Party of Liberal Nationalists (PNL), which played a prominent role in the Civil War. The Kataib, or Phalangists, supported Shihab and lost credibility among Christians for nearly a decade. A rival to the Phalangists was the National Bloc, headed by Raymond Eddé, whose father had been President of Lebanon under the French Mandate (1936-1941). Greek Orthodox and Maronites supported both Raymond Eddé and his brother Pierre. Raymond took up the cause of anti-militarism, whereas his father had been against pan-Arabism. As an opponent of Shihab, Eddé and Chamoun became natural allies. Especially repugnant to Shihab's rivals was his considerable use of the military espionage system *(Deuxième Bureau)*.

Shihab in fact encouraged his army intelligence to link up with Nasserists in order for him to keep control of the situation.

Demographic discussions also are an important part of the history of the first two decades. The cities of the coast, particularly Beirut, were draining the villages of the mountains and the Bekaa valley of human power. Maronite Christian peasants and Shiite Muslims were drawn to the cities. Palestinian refugees, mostly Sunnite Muslims, were added to the urban population along the coast. Migrant workers from Syria and Kurdish refugees peopled the slums near the port of Beirut, al-Karantina.

Chapters 3 to 6 are devoted to the 1960's in Lebanon. The Palestinian factor is seen growing in importance. One example was the fall of the flourishing, Palestinian-controlled Intra Bank, which was denied credit by native Lebanese-owned banks. A Shihabist, Elias Sarkis, was appointed Governor of the Central Bank of Lebanon following the Intra collapse.

In the meantime, concern at the growing Palestinian commando movement brought an alliance of Gemayel's Kataib, Chamoun's PNL, and Eddé's National Bloc. They saw the radical politics of the Palestinians as bringing in systems opposed to the Lebanese establishment—for example, Communism, and Baath Socialism of Syria and Iraq, to mention a few. The Palestinians were supported by Kamal Jumblatt, whose Druze followers were allied with the Sunnite Muslims. Shiite Muslims under the dynamic leadership of Imam Musa as-Sadr grew in political sophistication.

The presidency of Suleiman Franjieh is described in the next two chapters and actually covers the circumstances leading to the war and the war itself. There were efforts at reform, including the appointment of younger men (the Youth Cabinet). The Palestinian political movement came in full force to Lebanon in 1970 at the beginning of Franjieh's presidency. Yet there seemed little that anyone could do to control the mounting confusion of domestic and international problems during the early 1970's.

The last two chapters are devoted to the events of the Civil War. (This is less than half the space given over to events leading up to the civil war.) Salibi is correct in plumbing the political depths leading to the war, for there is little understanding of the war outside Lebanon and circles of experts. Television and newspaper journalism have not had the time to interpret the war in depth. Americans are often left with the impression that the Lebanese Civil War was basically a religious war involving Christians against Muslims.

Salibi is to be admired for telling the story as objectively as he does. He is obviously part of the events: his university was closed down; his livelihood was interrupted; and personal loss was no doubt part of the experience. Yet the author, a Christian and a nationalist, does not resort to emotionalism or finger-pointing. He remains loyal to his discipline—history. He is a Tacitus, reporting and describing. This contemporary history is the only book available in English on the topic. The prose is journalistic; the work is rapidly read;

there are photographs that are helpful and appendixes of political documents and political structures. A great deal of effort has gone into its timely publication.

Kelidar, Abbas and Michael Burrell. *Lebanon: The Collapse of a State*. London: Institute for Conflict Studies, 1976.

The collaborators of this work, Dr. Kelidar and Mr. Burrell, both teach at the School of Oriental and African Studies, London University, and rely heavily on Salibi's *The Modern History of Lebanon* and *Crossroads to Civil War*. This is an interpretive work, enjoying the benefit of being far removed from the scene of the conflict. This monograph is the seventy-fourth in the *Conflict Studies* series and is nineteen pages in length. However, the writers have summarized and condensed so that the result is a highly compact and compressed description. There is a Foreword of background essentials (statistical data, the Ottoman political organization which is the legacy of Lebanon, and economic information).

The authors begin accurately enough by stating, "The conflict in Lebanon is complex, multidimensional and therefore one that does not lend itself easily to a simple definition." More than half their work is devoted to factors leading to the Civil War. They include Syrian objectives, the birth of the Kataib Party, the Palestinian intrusion, and Jumblatt's left front.

Franjieh's presidency never satisfied Christians alarmed at the Palestinian armed presence in the country nor Muslims incensed at disproportionate power in the government and military. His problems were intensified when Syria, after splitting from Egypt following Kissinger's peace initiative, drew close to Jordan. This meant that the Rejection Front (Iraq and Libya) supported the radical movements inside Lebanon. After the Civil War began, Franjieh appointed a military cabinet, an action which proved to be disastrous politically. One result was the strengthening of the determination of the opposition; Jumblatt drew close to the conservative Muslim leaders.

For the Civil War narration the authors continue to focus on national political institutions and international alliances. Lebanon's international role is first of all closely tied to Syria, which later provided the peacekeeping troops that ended the war. The presence of the Palestinians, the authors show, antagonized the conflict. Both Chamoun and Gemayel prolonged the destruction, hoping to gain the government's use of the military. The armed forces never entered the war. Thus, the breakdown of the rule by law was so pervasive that nonpolitical gangsters were able to take advantage of the lack of security and extort protection money from apartment owners and dwellers.

Elias Sarkis, Franjieh's successor, is supported by the Syrians. Kelidah and Burrell close on an uncertain note: "If the manifold conflicting interests persist in hard-line policies that frustrate the chance of a new beginning, the scene is open for continued tragedy with ever-increasing complications." — *J.H.*

Additional Recommended Reading

Karpat, Kemal H., ed. *Political and Social Thought in the Contemporary Middle East.* New York: Frederick A. Praeger, 1968. A collection, unique in its field in the English language, of speeches and essays of statesmen and intellectuals of the modern Middle East.

Markham, James M. "Lebanon: The Insane War," in *The New York Times.* LXIV (August 15, 1976), p. 6. A feature article updating the war by a correspondent who followed it from its early stages; stresses the international dimension of the conflict which, at the time Markham was writing, was causing Syrians to turn against the Palestinians.

Moughrabi, Fouad and Naseer Aruri, eds. *Lebanon: Crisis and Challenge in the Arab World.* Detroit, Mich.: Association of Arab-American University Graduates, 1977. A series of nine wide-ranging and probing essays by mostly American professors of Arab ancestry.

Judis, John. "Report from Lebanon: A Mini World War," in *In These Times.* (May 17-23, 1978), Detroit, Mich.: Association of Arab-American University Graduates, 1977. A journalist's summing up of the past and his impressions of the present which reveals that the war issues have not abated, but rather seem to have crystallized.

Makdisi, Samir A. "An Appraisal of Lebanon's Postwar Economic Development and a Look to the Future," in *Middle East Journal.* XXXI, no. 3 (Summer, 1977), pp. 267-280. Argues that the Lebanese economic future, dependent on reconstruction and human resources available, will only succeed if political factors are favorable.

Hijazi, Ihsan. "New Allies, Old Woes for Moslems in Lebanon," in *The New York Times.* LXVI (July 30, 1978), p. 2. An updating of the fresh outbreak of the Civil War.

THE REUNIFICATION OF VIETNAM

Type of event: Political: reunification of a divided country
Time: April 30, 1975-June 24, 1976
Locale: Hanoi, Vietnam

Principal personages:

GIA LONG (NGUYEN PHUC ANH) (1762-1820), Emperor of Vietnam who briefly unified the country in 1802

HO CHI MINH (1890-1969), late President of North Vietnam who launched the Vietnamese Revolution

LE DUAN (1908-   ), head of the Vietnamese Communist Party

PHAM VAN DONG (1906-   ), Premier of the Socialist Republic of Vietnam

CHINH TRUONG (1907-   ), Chairman of the Standing Committee of the Vietnamese National Assembly

PHAM HUNG (1912-   ), a member of the North Vietnamese Politburo who directed the Party's Southern Bureau

GENERAL VO NGUYEN GIAP (1912-   ), Commander who defeated the French at Dien Bien Phu

NGÔ DINH DIEM (1901-1963), President of South Vietnam, 1954-1963

Summary of Event

The reunification of Vietnam brought about by thirty years of protracted war against the French, the Americans, and the South Vietnamese government is an event of great historical significance to the people of Vietnam and Southeast Asia. Since the beginning of Vietnamese history more than two thousand years ago, the Vietnamese have attempted to create a unified political community capable of exercising power throughout the whole country. They have been frustrated in realizing this dream by a host of internal and external factors—divisions and conflicts among the ruling elite; the power of their northern neighbor, China; the imposition of French colonial rule; and more recently, American military intervention.

In the modern period, the goal of establishing a unified political system began in 1802 with the suppression of the Tay Son Rebellion. After the suppression of this rebellion, the Emperor Gia Long governed the whole country from the imperial capital of Hue. This brief period of unification, however, was brought to an end by the arrival in the mid-nineteenth century of the French, who imposed their colonial rule, first in the Delta region of the south known as Cochin China and later in the central and northern part of the country known as Annam and Tonkin. The uneven pattern of French colonial rule perpetuated the myth that Vietnam was really three separate countries rather than one country. In fact, the French outlawed the name "Viet Nam," which had been used by Gia Long to describe the country. The nationalistic overtones of this name worried the French.

During the 1920's the quest for independence was spearheaded by the Vietnamese Nationalist Party (VNQDD), modeled after Sun Yatsen's Chinese Nationalist Party. The VNQDD had the potential to unify the country, but the French suppressed the party before it had the chance to carry out plans for revolution. With the demise of the VNQDD, the mantle of nationalist leadership fell to the Indochina Communist Party led by Ho Chi Minh.

The invasion of Southeast Asia by the Japanese in World War II provided the next opportunity for the Vietnamese to establish a unified, independent country. Ho Chi Minh confidently looked forward to American help in establishing the independence of the country from the French. After all, Ho had worked closely with the Allies by supplying information on Japanese troop movements in the area, rescuing American pilots shot down in the Gulf of Tonkin, and fighting the Japanese. The death of President Franklin D. Roosevelt, however, changed United States policy toward Vietnam. The Administration of President Harry S Truman was more interested in maintaining good relations with the French than with the Vietnamese, so the French were allowed to reimpose colonial rule in Vietnam. The result of this action was the outbreak late in 1945 of the First Indochina War, fought between the Vietminh (a nationalist front group led by the Communists) and the French.

By 1954 the war against the Vietminh was going badly. Any hopes that the French had of remaining in Vietnam were dashed by the decisive defeat they suffered at the hands of General Vo Nguyen Giap on May 7, 1954, in the battle of Dien Bien Phu, inflicted just one day before the opening of the Geneva Conference. The way appeared clear to unify the country under Ho Chi Minh's leadership, but these plans were thwarted again, this time by the Major Powers.

The Geneva Agreements provided for the establishment of two provisional states: the Democratic Republic of Vietnam in the North and the State of Vietnam in the South, with the 17th parallel fixed as a temporary demarcation line between these two regimes. General elections to be held two years later were to provide the basis for a reunited state called Vietnam. These elections, however, were never held, and Vietnam remained a divided state. Ho Chi Minh consolidated his political position in North Vietnam; Ngô Dinh Diem established an autocratic, anti-Communist state in South Vietnam aided by substantial American military and financial assistance.

By 1960 the National Liberation Front (Vietcong), a southern-based guerrilla organization, was founded with the aim of overthrowing the South Vietnamese government and providing the basis for the gradual reunification of the country. For twenty-five years the United States and South Vietnam had struggled to prevent this goal from being realized on Communist terms. With American military withdrawal from the

Vietnam War in 1973 and the collapse of the South Vietnamese regime two years later, the Communist-led Vietnamese were finally in a position to implement their long-cherished goal.

The new Communist leadership in Vietnam did not move immediately to reunify the country although they did lower many of the barriers that had prevented contact between the peoples of Vietnam. Initially it appeared that formal reunification might take as long as five years to complete. After many years of separation, the two Vietnams had taken vastly different political and economic paths. In the North, a socialist economic system had been established emphasizing centralized planning, state-owned enterprises, and collectivized agriculture. The South had evolved along capitalist lines with a *comprador* class exercising great political and economic power. Although many members of this class had fled the country taking their wealth with them upon the fall of Saigon, old bourgeois attitudes still remained strong in the South.

The question for the new regime now became whether they should act quickly to establish a socialist state throughout the whole country or should allow the regime a period of several years to reeducate the population of the South to the goals of the Revolution. This problem was the main topic of an important meeting held in the former South Vietnamese capital of Saigon (renamed Ho Chi Minh City) from November 15 to 21, 1975. At this conference, Chinh Truong, Chairman of the Standing Committee of the National Assembly, argued persuasively for the early

reunification of Vietnam along socialist lines. The final communique of this meeting reflected his views. It was decided to hold nationwide elections to select a new National Assembly for the whole country. These elections were held on April 24, 1976. When the new National Assembly convened on June 24, 1976, it formally declared Vietnam to be reunified, renaming the country the Socialist Republic of Vietnam. The National Assembly also selected a Constitutional Drafting Committee to write a new constitution for the country. It approved a major change in the administrative units of Vietnam, dividing the country into thirty-five provinces.

Several prominent positions in the new government were assigned to southern revolutionaries, including Pham Hung, a member of the North Vietnamese Politburo and head of the Party's Southern Bureau; Nguyen Huu Tho, the former President of the National Liberation Front; and Huyuh Tan Phat, former President of the Provisional Revolutionary Government in the South. Most high governmental offices, however, went to North Vietnamese leaders such as Le Duan, First Secretary of the Vietnamese Communist Party; Pam Van Dong, Premier of the Government; and Chinh Truong, Chairman of the Standing Committee of the National Assembly.

Since 1976 the Socialist Republic of Vietnam has moved to rehabilitate the war-torn economy of the country. Years of struggle took a heavy economic toll in both the North and the South; the enormous destruction in North Vietnam during the war crippled the government's ability to implement its economic plans, while in the South the dislocations brought about by the war are still being felt. Unemployment exacerbated by the disbanding of the South Vietnamese Army constitutes a formidable economic problem. The lack of spare parts, draught animals, and irrigation facilities has hampered agricultural production in the South.

Under the latest five-year plan scheduled to run between 1976 and 1980, both industry and agriculture are to receive attention. In terms of economic tasks, the role of the South will be to concentrate on increasing agricultural production and light industry, while the North will focus on the development of heavy industry. This division of labor makes good economic sense and corresponds to the natural strengths of each region.

Whether political unification will bring about economic prosperity is hard to say at this point. It will depend on many factors—the ability to raise capital at home and abroad, the mobilization of the people behind the government's programs, and the exercising of capable leadership. None of the country's economic problems will be easily solved.

Pertinent Literature

Terzani, Tiziano. *Giai Phong!: The Fall and Liberation of Saigon*. New York: St. Martin's Press, 1976

Since the fall of Saigon on April 30, 1975, several journalistic accounts have described the decline and fall of the Thieu regime. Unfortunately, few Americans stayed around to see what the North Vietnamese would do after the liberation of the country; virtually all Americans were evacuated from South Vietnam just before the liberation forces marched triumphantly into Saigon. The important feature of this book is that the author, an Italian journalist who worked for *Der Spiegel*, returned to South Vietnam just before the military collapse of the Thieu regime and describes in great detail the last three days of the old regime and the first three months of the new one. The perspective of life that emerges from this account is important even though it may be overly sympathetic to the new regime.

Once the South Vietnamese Army was defeated on the battlefield, Terzani vividly describes the sense of panic that gripped the American and Vietnamese population eager to flee the country. He points out that for years the Thieu regime and its American supporters had carefully nurtured the idea that a bloodbath would follow a Communist takeover of the country. These officials thought that stories about Communist atrocities would discredit the enemy and strengthen the will of the South Vietnamese to resist. In the end Terzani maintains that these propaganda ploys came back to haunt the United States and the Thieu regime, accelerating the demise of the South Vietnamese government rather than helping to stem the tide of battle.

The first Communist tanks filtered through the streets of Saigon just after noon on April 30, 1975, making their way to the Presidential Palace where Duong Van Minh, the last President of South Vietnam, was waiting to surrender to the Communists. It was "Big Minh" who had asked the soldiers of South Vietnam to lay down their arms and end all hostilities against the enemy. This difficult decision had averted much needless bloodshed and saved the city of Saigon from certain destruction. As tanks and other armored vehicles moved through the streets of Saigon, small groups of people congregated along the way to catch a glimpse of the victors. Youths from the National Liberation Front riding these vehicles shouted, "Giai Phong! Giai Phong!" (Liberation! Liberation!)

Initially there was great fear and apprehension among the people as to what the Communist victory meant in South Vietnam; within a short period of time, Terzani maintains that in most cases this fear gave way to a sense of hope for the future. During the war the enemy had been described as cruel, ruthless, and barbaric. Now that the South Vietnamese people had an opportunity to observe the "faceless Vietcong" at close range, they found them to be simple patriotic youths uncorrupted by the fast life of the city.

Once these youthful soldiers, known as *bo doi*, entered Saigon, they sought out old friends and relatives who were living in the South. Many *bo doi* carried messages and letters from the North which were given to members of families displaced by years of war. Terzani describes several incidences

of fathers, sons, brothers, or friends being tearfully reunited after liberation. The establishment of these relations between the army and people of the South had a calming effect on the population of Saigon and facilitated Communist rule.

Some of the most intriguing chapters of the book describe the process of handling former South Vietnamese soldiers, officers, and officials. It was this segment of the population that had the most to fear from the new government. Within a week after liberation, all former "puppets" of the Thieu regime were ordered to register with local authorities. Initially, all South Vietnamese soldiers were required to explain their role in the war, why they had joined the army, what they thought about liberation, and what expectations they had for the future. Once registration with local neighborhood committees was complete, they were issued identity cards which allowed them to circulate freely among the people. The process of *hoc tap* or political reeducation, however, did not stop there; a more extensive course in revolutionary rehabilitation was prescribed for all soldiers and officials of the old regime.

Terzani describes the content of these courses, which in most cases lasted for three days. The first day was devoted to the study of the Vietnamese Revolution and the life of Ho Chi Minh. The second day was consumed by personal confessions as each participant was asked to explain what crimes against the people he had committed. On the final day, political cadres from the National Liberation Front discussed the policies of the new government, stressing the need to rebuild the country after the ravages of war. The experience of *hoc tap* was designed to provide a new beginning for officials of the old regime. Old bourgeois capitalist values were to be purged in favor of a new socialist orientation to politics. Those who appeared genuinely converted to the new faithful were classified as reeducated and released from custody. Others whose sincerity was suspected were ordered to remain for further training.

Former officials of the government were not the only ones to undergo *hoc tap*. Virtually the whole population was provided with political instruction in their homes, fields, or places of employment. In a sense, the whole nation was transformed into a school where new revolutionary values were inculcated. Terzani leaves the impression that the new Communist rulers of Vietnam were quite successful in their reeducation efforts. The subsequent mass exodus of refugees out of the country since 1975, however, suggests that these training courses were not completely successful.

At the end of the book Terzani attempts to evaluate what peace meant to the Vietnamese people after thirty years of constant struggle. Peace was a luxury few Vietnamese had had a chance to experience during their lifetimes. The people paid an enormous price to achieve national independence and reunification of the country. During the period immediately following the Revolution, they seemed to be enjoying a world free of war. Whether they continue to enjoy peace will be determined by the behavior and policies of the new government; however, there is already considerable evidence to suggest that the honeymoon period of the Vietnamese Revolution has long since passed.

Turley, William S. "Vietnam Since Reunification," in *Problems of Communism*. XXVI, no. 2 (March-April, 1977), pp. 36-54.

Since the fall of Saigon, Vietnam has all but passed out of the consciousness of the American people; today, the Vietnam War is seen as a bad dream which most people would like to forget. Although a few stories about Vietnam have appeared in the American press, coverage of that country has been spotty to nonexistent. Fortunately, there are a handful of American Vietnam scholars who are still keeping a close eye on contemporary developments within the country. One such scholar is William Turley, a professor of Political Science at Southern Illinois University, Carbondale, who has written numerous articles on Vietnam. Turley's article "Vietnam Since Reunification" represents one of several contemporary assessments of Vietnamese politics since 1975; in it, the author attempts to show what part the theme of reunification played in Vietnamese politics, how the present leadership of the country has evolved, what plans for economic reconstruction the new leaders have proposed, and what significant problems remain to be solved in order to build a prosperous socialist state.

Turley examines the theme of reunification in Vietnamese politics showing how this theme has figured prominently in the political life of the country. He points out the significance of changing the name of the party from the Vietnam Worker's Party to the Vietnamese Communist Party, a change which took place at the Fourth Party Congress held December 14-20, 1976. Turley maintains that this name change was designed to highlight the importance of national unification in Vietnam and to pay tribute to the father of Vietnamese nationalism, Ho Chi Minh.

In examining the current leadership of the Vietnamese Communist Party, Turley finds great continuity at the highest echelons of the Party, even though the membership of the Central Committee had more than doubled since 1960. A major effort has been made to bring new blood into the leadership of the party. Turley maintains that political and economic reasons account for these changes. On one hand, the regime wanted to reward those who distinguished themselves in the revolutionary struggle to liberate the South. Equally important, however, was the need to strengthen the Party's leadership in the economic area. Implementing the new five-year plan for economic reconstruction of the country will require a host of economic specialists to administer the program.

Turley also discusses the origins and background of the present Vietnamese leadership. For many years Western scholars have debated the "northern" *versus* "southern" roots of the Communist leadership in Vietnam. Was the North Vietnamese Communist Party essentially a north-ern-based organization which kept the leaders of the National Liberation Front in a subordinate position, or were the revolutionary front organizations in the South really autonomous centers of power which merely cooperated with the Hanoi regime to accomplish the same goal? Turley takes the position that both of these extremes are wrong. The basic decision to step up the guerrilla campaign in the South was taken by leaders of North Vietnam, but southern revolutionaries participated in this decision within the framework of democratic centralism imposed by the Party. In summary, Turley believes that the whole debate surrounding the "northern" and "southern" leadership of the Vietnamese Communist Party has been exaggerated. These were simply two parts of the same movement working toward the common goal of independence and unification of the country.

Economic problems of reconstruction and development in Vietnam are also discussed at length in this article. Based on decisions taken at the Fourth Party Congress, Turley suggests that the new regime will concentrate on promoting industry and agriculture simultaneously, though greater attention will be devoted to raising agricultural production in order to feed the population. Industry and agriculture are seen as complementary sectors which can help each other develop. During the present planning period, most investment in heavy industry will be channeled into the production of agricultural equipment. In this way the development of agriculture will serve as the basis for further industrial development.

In order to achieve the lofty economic targets of the current five-year development plan, new sources of capital will have to be found. During the war a substantial amount of foreign aid poured into North Vietnam from the Communist bloc countries. Now that the war is over, Turley doubts that adequate financing can be secured for important industrial projects.

Turley sees additional economic problems on the horizon. With a scarcity of trained manpower, the new regime has mobilized the army to work on a wide variety of projects.

This plan has apparently produced a strong reaction from military leaders such as Defense Minister Vo Nguyen Giap and others, who see these tasks as weakening the morale and combat readiness of the troops in the field. Managerial problems have also complicated the task of economic reconstruction in the South. Reports of widespread corruption and mismanagement there have deeply worried Vietnam's leaders. Unless Hanoi's new leaders can solve these major problems, they will have difficulty fulfilling the economic targets of the five-year plan. — *R.L.L.*

Additional Recommended Reading

McAlister, John T., Jr. *Vietnam: The Origins of Revolution.* Garden City, N.Y.: Doubleday & Company, 1971. Places the origins of the Vietnamese Revolution in historical perspective by showing how the goal of reunification has been a constant theme in Vietnamese politics.

Fall, Bernard. *The Two Viet Nams: A Political and Military Analysis.* New York: Frederick A. Praeger, 1964. The separate development of North and South Vietnam are traced in this book by a leading Vietnam expert.

Elliot, David. "North Vietnam Since Ho," in *Problems of Communism.* XXIV, no. 4 (July-August, 1975), pp 35-52. An extensive survey of policy debates that have taken place within the North Vietnamese Politburo.

Pike, Douglas. "Vietnam During 1976: Economics in Command" in *Asian Survey.* XVII, no. 1 (January, 1977), pp. 34-42. Summary of political and economic events in Vietnam during 1976 with particularly good chapters on the economic decisions taken at the Fourth Party Congress.

Porter, Gareth. "Vietnam's Long Road to Socialism," in *Current History.* LXXI, no. 422 (December, 1976), pp. 209-212 and 226-228. Discussion of the political and economic ramifications of unifying North and South Vietnam.

Thayer, Carlyle A. "Dilemmas of Development in Vietnam," in *Current History.* LXXV, no. 442 (December, 1978), pp. 221-225. The problems of promoting socialism in Vietnam are explored; the author believes that Vietnam faces complex choices in order to stimulate technology transfers necessary for development.

Smith, Ralph. "Vietnam's Fourth Party Congress," in *World Today.* XXXIII, no. 5. (May, 1977), pp. 195-202. Examination of the decisions taken at the Fourth Party Congress held in Hanoi from December 14 to 20, 1976.

THE OAS SUSPENDS THE EMBARGO AGAINST CUBA

Type of event: Diplomatic: lifting of sanctions placed on Cuba by the OAS
Time: July 29, 1975
Locale: San Jose, Costa Rica

Principal personages:

ALEJANDRO ORFILA (1925-   ), Secretary General of the Organization of American States

RAUL ROA Y GARCIA (1907-   ), Foreign Minister of Cuba

WILLIAM SOMERS MAILLARD (1917-   ), United States Ambassador to the Organization of American States

FIDEL CASTRO (1927-   ), Premier of Cuba, 1959-

HENRY ALFRED KISSINGER (1923-   ), United States Secretary of State, 1973-1977

Summary of Event

On July 29, 1975, the ambassadors to the Organization of American States (OAS) voted to lift the political and economic sanctions which had been placed on Cuba eleven years earlier; this vote was viewed by most to be an action which merely formalized the recognition of an already existing state of affairs. At the time of the vote, nine members of the OAS had diplomatic and trade relations with Cuba. While it is questionable whether the sanctions against Cuba ever had any adverse effects on that nation, it was clear by July, 1975, that their continuance would constitute a retreat from the realities of Latin American affairs.

The sanctions against Cuba were imposed in July, 1964, as a result of charges presented to the OAS by Venezuela. Early in 1964, Venezuela charged that Cuba had made an overt attempt to disrupt the Venezuelan national elections in December, 1963. Furthermore, it was alleged that the Cuban regime of Fidel Castro had aided and abetted Communist terrorists who planned to overthrow the government of Venezuela. As an immediate response to the Venezuelan charges, the OAS gave the Cuban government a chance to respond, and a list of the charges was forwarded to the Cuban Foreign Minister, Dr. Raul Roa y Garcia. As they appeared in the *New York Times* the charges were: "1) a systematic campaign of subversive propaganda; 2) recruitment and training for guerrilla and other war operations; 3) the financing of an insurrectionist movement; and, 4) the presence of arms and subversive plans." The Cuban response repudiated the charges and cynically noted that the OAS had never accused the United States of hemispheric subversion despite its support of the Bay of Pigs invasion in 1961.

On July 26, 1964, the OAS voted to impose political and economic sanctions against Cuba under the provisions of the Inter-American Treaty of Reciprocal Assistance (the Rio Treaty of 1947)—the mutual defense treaty of the organization. Article

Seventeen of the Rio Treaty stipulated that such decisions could be made only by a two-thirds majority of the eligible signatories. Cuba already had been suspended from participation by an earlier action at Punta del Este, Uruguay, in 1962, and Venezuela was excluded because it was an interested party to the dispute. The remaining signatories voted fifteen to four in favor of the sanctions. Voting against the resolution were Bolivia, Chile, Mexico, and Uruguay.

The resolution against Cuba called for three major actions by the signatories to the Rio Treaty: severance of diplomatic relations with Cuba; the suspension of most trade with Cuba (food and medicine excepted); and the suspension of maritime transportation. Although the governments of Bolivia, Chile, and Uruguay disagreed with the imposition of sanctions against Cuba, they indicated they would go along with the OAS decision, and later during 1964 these three nations did break diplomatic relations with Cuba. Mexico, however, refused to abide by the OAS action because it violated Mexico's foreign policy stance of nonintervention in the domestic affairs of other nations. The 1964 action was not expected to have severe adverse economic effects on Cuba; Cuba's economic ties to the Soviet Union and Eastern Europe at that point were strong enough to prevent serious economic setbacks produced by an embargo from Latin American nations.

By 1975 the political and economic conditions were right for revoking the sanctions imposed eleven years ear-lier. In the political sphere, the United States position toward Cuba was softening. This more relaxed posture was indicated by the actions of administration figures such as Secretary of State Henry Kissinger, the OAS Ambassador, William S. Maillard, and several senators. In March, Senators Edward Kennedy and Jacob Javits called upon the Ford Administration to normalize relations with Cuba. In May, Senator George McGovern traveled to Cuba on a fact-finding mission, and Senator Charles Percy advocated lifting the United States embargo against Cuba regardless of the action taken by the OAS. Nine countries in Latin America had restored diplomatic ties with Cuba and were actively pursuing trade relations with the Castro regime. Venezuela, for example, was anxious to sell oil to Cuba. In return for industrial commodities and certain raw materials, Cuba was anxious to sell its sugar on the world market for $.50 a pound rather than to the Soviet Union for only $.20 a pound under previous agreements.

Suspending the embargo, however, was not accomplished without some difficulties. In November, 1964, at Quito, Ecuador, only twelve states supported such a move. This number fell short of the two-thirds vote required by the Rio Treaty. Subsequent to the Quito meeting, efforts to lift the embargo focused first on revising the Rio Treaty so that a simple majority could suspend the embargo. The prospects for accomplishing the treaty revision were clouded by a deadlock in the election of a new Secretary General of the OAS. The two candidates for the post were Victor

Gomez Berger of the Dominican Republic and Alejandro Orfila of Argentina. The final choice of Orfila as the new Secretary General helped pave the way toward the suspension of the embargo because Argentina was one of the nine countries which currently ignored the 1964 sanctions.

On July 26, 1975, the ambassadors to the OAS, acting as plenipotentiaries, unanimously approved the necessary revisions of the Rio Treaty, thus making it possible to settle the Cuban question with a simple majority. Three days later the embargo was suspended with sixteen members of the OAS voting in favor of the resolution. Unlike the 1964 resolution, which included "mandatory" provisions against Cuba, the 1975 resolution stated that member nations were free to pursue their own course with respect to Cuba.

Pertinent Literature

Lowenthal, Abraham F. "Cuba: Time for a Change," in *Foreign Policy*. XX (Fall, 1975), pp. 65-86.

Written immediately after the OAS decision to suspend the embargo against Cuba, this article calls for a renewal of United States political and economic ties with the Castro regime. Lowenthal argues that the OAS decision freed the United States "to determine its own stance toward Cuba," and, consequently, that the United States should have proceeded immediately by lifting its own embargo.

Several arguments are marshaled to encourage a change in United States foreign policy toward Cuba. First, Lowenthal maintains that the original four goals of political and economic sanctions have not been obtained, or that they are no longer an issue. These four goals were the desire to thwart Cuba's export of revolution; the desire to break Cuban military ties with the Soviet Union; the desire to undermine Cuba's appeal as a developmental model for the Third World; and the desire to aid in the eventual collapse of the Castro government. Writing from the vantage point of September, 1975, the author asserts that none of these goals "provides a defensible basis for U.S. policy." Cuba has given up its policy of aiding Latin American insurrection; the Soviets are permanently installed in Cuba; Cuba's appeal as a developmental model has not materialized; and future "Cubas" in Latin America are not likely to arise. Finally, even Cuban immigrants in the United States no longer believe that the Cuban government will fall.

Second, Lowenthal maintains that the United States should soften its stance because it has no real interest in maintaining "perpetual antagonism" toward Cuba. He argues that a normalization of relations with Cuba would actually benefit the United States' national interest for several reasons. First, it would be a signal to Latin America that the United States is willing to deal with its southern neighbors on a new footing—one which entails a respect for their sovereignty. Such a position would enhance United States chances of maintaining a positive influence in Latin America. Second, there would be worthwhile economic benefits to be derived from the normalization of relations. Next, a renewal of political and economic ties between the United States and Cuba might lessen Cuba's dependence upon the Soviet Union. Dismissing official Cuban statements which affirm continued loyalty to the Soviet Union, Lowenthal feels that Cuba desires to diversify its trade relationships.

A third reason for normalizing relations between the United States and Cuba is that normalization would offer the opportunity to solve some long-standing disputes. The United States still has $1.8 billion in claims against the Cuban government which might be settled, and a release of political prisoners in Cuban jails might also be obtained. In return, Cuba might obtain some United States concessions on the status of the Guantanamo naval base. Fourth, Lowenthal argues that a continuance of nonrecognition of Cuba serves to isolate not Cuba, but rather the United States. To impose an embargo on Cuba while protesting the OPEC embargo against the United States weakens the United States position.

Lowenthal is realistic enough to cite numerous reasons why the United States might not proceed with a program to ease tensions with Cuba. Paramount among these is the simple fact that the United States is preoccupied elsewhere with foreign affairs of such importance that attention to Cuban policy may get slighted. Progress toward renewed ties between the United States and Cuba stalled between 1975 and 1978 because of Cuban military activities in Africa. During the summer of 1978, however, informal governmental ties were established between the two nations.

Petras, James F. "The U.S.-Cuban Policy Debate," in *Monthly Review*. XXVI, no. 9 (February, 1975), pp. 22-33.

Although Petras' article appeared before the OAS suspension of the embargo against Cuba, it offers valuable insights into the international context in which the OAS action occurred. This is true despite Petras' primary concern of examining the foundation of United States policy toward the Castro regime.

Petras argues that two distinct United States perspectives toward Cuba were prevalent in 1975. The first was a "conservative" position favoring a continuance of United States attempts to isolate Cuba within the hemisphere through diplomatic nonrecognition and economic embargo. This position was developed for the most part by Secretary of State Henry Kissinger. Opposing the United States State Department's conservatism was a "liberal" position, advocated by significant congressional figures, favoring the normalization of diplomatic relations with Cuba and the elimination of the trade embargo. While these two camps favored different approaches to United States relations with Cuba, Petras notes that they nevertheless shared a significant area of consensus. Both were hostile "to socialism, to the Cuban leadership, and to the extension of socialism to the Latin American mainland."

Interestingly, Petras suggests that the conservative position was consonant with the United States policy of *détente* with the Soviet Union. United States-Soviet *détente* recognized the division of the world into spheres of influence which each major power could police. Thus, Kissinger's policy of *détente* permitted a United States relaxation of tension toward Cuba's patron state, but not toward Cuba itself.

The liberal position rested on different foundations. The liberals judged the conservative policies as failures; they felt that continued diplomatic and economic sanctions against Cuba were isolating the United States from the rest of the hemisphere, rather than isolating and undermining the Cuban government. The liberal position was based on a "new definition of reality" for hemispheric politics. Petras describes this new reality as involving the rise of "establishment nationalism" in Latin America; the rising price of oil; the growing importance of the Organization of Petroleum Exporting Countries; and Mexican actions to establish closer economic ties with Latin America.

Thus, the hemisphere was diversifying both politically and economically and consequently reducing United States hegemony in the area.

The Cuban response to the realities perceived by the liberals furthered the erosion of United States influence in Latin America. Petras argues that Cuba changed its foreign policy in Latin America "from one of revolutionary bi-polar politics toward a more regionalist-bloc strategy for isolating the United States." Cuba's policy of exporting its revolution to the Latin American mainland had failed, and future prospects for leftist regimes were not good. Also, because Cuba sought to expand and diversify its economic ties, it was encouraged to adopt a foreign policy based on "ideological and economic pluralism."

Petras concludes that a continuance of conservative United States policies would prove counterproductive to the interests of United States corporate capitalism in Latin America. Consequently, an alliance of business, the liberals, and the liberal media in the United States would probably force Kissinger and the State Department to move toward a normalization of relations with Cuba despite the policy of *détente* with the Soviet Union. — *C.E.C.*

Additional Recommended Reading

Ball, M. Margaret. *The OAS in Transition*. Durham, N.C.: Duke University Press, 1969. An excellent text detailing the organizational structure and the history of the OAS; includes a lengthy discussion of Cuba's relation to the organization since the advent of the Castro regime, as well as a text of the Rio Treaty.

Del Rio, Eduardo (RIUS), ed. *Cuba for Beginners: An Illustrated Guide for Americans*. New York: Pathfinder Press, 1970. A humorous pro-Cuban account of the Cuban revolution which details the strain and eventual break in U.S.-Cuban diplomatic and economic relations.

"Cuba, Sí!" in *Newsweek*. LXXXVI, no. 6 (August 11, 1975), p. 40. A summary report detailing the OAS suspension of the embargo against Cuba.

Orfila, Alejandro. "Cuba - and Beyond," in *Saturday Review*. II (September 6, 1975), pp. 18-19. An explanation of the meaning of the OAS suspension of the embargo against Cuba from the Secretary General of the OAS.

Thomas, Hugh. *Cuba: The Pursuit of Freedom, 1762-1969*. New York: Harper & Row Publishers, 1971. This history of Cuba provides an objective account of the deterioration of U.S.-Cuban relations as well as significant background material on Cuba's expulsion from the OAS.

"Back of U.S. Switch on Cuba," in *U.S. News & World Report*. LXXIX, no. 5 (August 4, 1975), p. 44. An explanation of benefits for the United States to be derived from United States support of the OAS resolution to suspend the embargo against Cuba.

THE HELSINKI AGREEMENT

Type of event: Diplomatic: establishment of a European system for security and cooperation
Time: August 1, 1975
Locale: Helsinki, Finland

Principal personages:

GERALD RUDOLPH FORD (1913-   ), thirty-eighth President of the United States, 1974-1977

HENRY ALFRED KISSINGER (1923-   ), United States Secretary of State, 1973-1977

LEONID ILICH BREZHNEV (1906-   ), First Secretary of the Communist Party of the Soviet Union, 1964-

VALÉRY GISCARD d'ESTAING (1926-   ), President of France, 1974-

HELMUT SCHMIDT (1918-   ), Chancellor of the Federal Republic of Germany, 1974-

Summary of Event

The Conference on Security and Cooperation in Europe (CSCE), held in Helsinki, invites comparison with the Congress of Vienna in 1815. Unlike the latter, the "Congress" of Helsinki never danced, but it was a similarly momentous diplomatic undertaking and may be considered the beginning of a new era. The gathering of such ranking world statesmen as President Gerald Ford, Secretary of State Henry Kissinger, President Leonid Brezhnev, President Valéry Giscard d'Estaing, Chancellor Helmut Schmidt, and the many others representing the thirty-five participating states during the final ceremonies, gave fleeting form to a vision of Europe free of confrontations and divisions. The CSCE formally opened at the foreign ministers level on July 3, 1973, in Helsinki and concluded there on August 1, 1975, when the national leaders of the United States, Canada, the Soviet Union, and thirty-two European countries (including the ministates) signed the Final Act. The actual working phase of the CSCE was held in Geneva from September, 1973, to July, 1975. The Final Act, the so-called Helsinki Agreement, must be regarded as a political statement of intent, rather than a legally binding treaty.

The Soviet Union had first proposed such a conference as early as 1954, but at that time the United States and its allies were not receptive to the idea. The subject was again broached in July, 1966, by the Bucharest Declaration of the Warsaw Pact members. Although the relaxation of tensions between East and West in the 1960's made the prospect for such a conference less remote, the Soviet-led invasion of Czechoslovakia in 1968 foreclosed serious Western consideration of the proposal at that time. Moscow continued to pursue the matter. The need to convene an all-European conference on security and cooperation was a dominant theme in Soviet statements concerning European affairs. The keen Soviet interest in the CSCE was, obviously, based on the fact that such a conference could serve the Soviet Union most beneficially in several different ways. One of these was the possible furtherance of the long-standing objective of driving a wedge between the United States and Western Europe. While campaigning for the CSCE, the Soviets depicted the United States as the main obstacle to peace and security in Europe. American opposition to the conference unless certain conditions were met was decried as evidence of the incompatibility of basic American and European interests.

Eventually the Warsaw Pact states accepted the conditions imposed by the United States and Canada in the conference; an agreement on Berlin providing for improved conditions; and the holding of talks for the mutual reduction of armed forces. Thus, multilateral preparatory talks began in November, 1972, and established sufficient common ground to justify the convocation of the CSCE. As to the actual holding of the conference, Moscow was most anxious to secure multilateral recognition of the prevailing conditions in Central and Eastern Europe. On the basis of such a consolidated position, the Soviet leaders then intended to pursue more economic and technological cooperation with the major Western nations and to entertain considerations on mutual force reductions in Central Europe. The United States and West-

ern Europe saw an opportunity in Moscow's strong interest in the CSCE to facilitate progress in the human rights area; concessions by the East on human rights issues were to be the *quid pro quo* for the formal acknowledgment by the West of prevailing circumstances.

The Helsinki Agreement consists of a declaration of principles guiding the relations between the signatories and three main sections, referred to by the term "basket." Basket 1 contains so-called confidence-building measures, security, and disarmament. Outlined in this section are ways and means by which military confidence can be strengthened and tension reduced, thereby diminishing the danger of war between the signatories. Basket 2 contains a variety of measures which are expected to enhance economic, scientific, technical, and environmental cooperation. Such areas as commercial exchanges, industrial cooperation, and the promotion of tourism are referred to. Basket 3 includes cooperation in humanitarian and other fields. In this section are to be found statements advocating the freer movement of people, ideas, and information; family reunification and visits; binational marriages; travel; access to printed, broadcast, and filmed information; improved working conditions for journalists; and increased cultural and educational exchanges.

The Western emphasis regarding the Helsinki Agreement has been on *improvement*, not on the freezing of the *status quo*. The United States, in particular, has pressed the Soviet Union and other East European states to follow through on implementing the provisions of the Final Act. Basket 3 has drawn the most public attention in the United States, which has been engaged in an intensified campaign for human rights during the presidency of Jimmy Carter. However, three years after the signing of the Final Act, the Warsaw Pact nations have taken only modest and rather limited steps to fulfill their commitments regarding increased and freer movement of people, ideas, and information. The United States has been monitoring the process of implementation very closely. In June, 1976, Congress established the Commission of Security and Cooperation in Europe, composed of twelve members of Congress and three Executive Branch appointees, to which the President must issue semiannual reports.

The signatory nations themselves have had an opportunity to review the process of implementation in the first follow-up meeting to the CSCE, held in Belgrade from October 4, 1977, to March 9, 1978. This meeting was not to conduct negotiations for new provisions, but to find means for improving the implementation of the Helsinki Agreement. At this time the United States and the Western European states voiced their concern over the record of the Soviet Union and other Warsaw Pact states, registering the specific shortcomings in the area of human rights. Indeed, at Western insistence, human rights was a major agenda item at Belgrade. Western participants sought to impress upon the Warsaw Pact states that human rights was a fundamental and integral part of the Helsinki Agreement and that full implementation would be essential for security and cooperation in Europe. Moreover, specific implementation failures were to be pointed out and publicly criticized, rejecting the argument that such action would constitute unwarranted intervention into the internal affairs of the states. The next such follow-up meeting is to be held in Madrid in 1980.

The Helsinki Agreement came under strong criticism immediately after the signing. The principal argument of the opponents was that Moscow made rich gains, while the West obtained only meager ones at best. It was charged that, by agreeing to the inviolability of the existing frontiers, the stamp of legitimacy was put on the Soviet annexations of territory, including the former Baltic states of Estonia, Latvia, and Lithuania. Along with exiled Soviet writer Alexander Solzhenitsyn, opponents warned that any concessions to the Soviet Union would only help consolidate the oppressive regime; they saw the Soviet Union deceitfully using *détente* to lull the West into complacency.

Continued vigilance regarding the Soviet Union may well be called for, but such arguments rejecting the CSCE are unfounded. Nothing was given away at Helsinki that was not, in effect, already lost. Meanwhile, a new stage of "businesslike cooperation" in Europe, having supplanted the Cold War, holds open the enticing promise of genuine improvement of the living conditions for all peoples on the Old Continent.

Pertinent Literature

Russell, Harold S. "The Helsinki Declaration: Brobdingnag or Lilliput?," in *American Journal of International Law*. LXX, no. 2 (April, 1976), pp. 242-272.

Harold Russell, Assistant Legal Adviser for European Affairs in the Department of State, was the principal United States negotiator for that part of the Helsinki Agreement covering the principles guiding the relations between the participating states. In this article he reviews succinctly and interestingly various aspects of the Final Act of the CSCE from a legal perspective. His insider's account enables the reader to gain an appreciation of the difficulties involved in negotiating such a lengthy and complex document, which adds up to some sixty pages. Russell points out that the United States tried to play down or understate the importance of certain aspects of the Final Act. Specifically, the Ford Administration seemed to be concerned about the emergence of a euphoric spirit which might increase public pressure for the withdrawal of American troops from Europe. The United States and most of the other participating states did not want a legally binding document. For obvious political reasons it was important that the Final Act of the CSCE not be considered the equivalent of a peace treaty. Reflecting on the legal nature of the document, Russell notes that it is morally compelling, but legally not binding. In international practice, the reference "final act" normally connotes an intention or a declaration, but not a *legal* commitment such as a treaty. Nevertheless, Russell feels that this declaration may have considerable potential impact on international law.

One aspect of the CSCE which has been widely and very critically noted by the American press was the alleged recognition of the existing frontiers in Europe. Inasmuch as the Helsinki Agreement declares the inviolability of the existing frontiers in Europe, the press wrongly concluded that Soviet supremacy in Eastern Europe was formally recognized and that the Final Act was tantamount to a World War II peace treaty. Many of these press accounts suggested that such a ratification of the frontiers amounted to a disastrous loss of prestige for the United States. Russell believes that this attitude was rather unfortunate, noting that the language of the document does not depart materially from any previous international agreements and does not, in fact, accord legal validity to the existing frontiers. He recalls that the Soviets bargained very hard to obtain different language and only grudgingly gave ground on the inviolability issue. In the end they accepted a formulation which departed substantially from that which they originally sought. Regrettably, what the Soviets failed to achieve in the negotiations in this respect, they almost totally recouped through the assessments made in the North American press, according to Russell.

The article affords some interesting insights into the semantic difficulties of drafting the document and the squabbles over acceptable words in the five official languages. Another highly problematic issue which the negotiators had to tackle while drafting the declaration of principles pertained to the so-called Brezhnev Doctrine. The Soviets endeavored to have this doctrine, which imposes limits on the sovereignty of socialist states and justifies intervention by sister socialist states in the internal affairs of another to "protect socialist gains," upheld by the declaration of principles. The Western powers, of course, were determined to prevent any possible justification of the Brezhnev Doctrine, and they succeeded in using appropriate terms prohibiting the kind of intervention the Soviets envisioned. However, as Russell notes, the practical effect might be marginal, for the Soviet Union is not likely to be deterred by the prohibitions contained in the Final Act, once it has decided on the need to intervene. Moreover, it can always contrive to enter by "invitation." In defining the principle of nonintervention in the internal affairs of states, Western negotiators faced a tricky problem: they wanted to uphold the principle unequivocally and thereby undercut the Brezhnev Doctrine, while at the same time make it possible under the terms to pressure the Warsaw Pact states on human rights.

A similarly difficult situation arose out of the need not to have the Final Act of the CSCE be considered a surrogate peace treaty. This meant most importantly that it had to leave unaffected all four-power rights in Germany as a whole and in Berlin, while at the same time include Berlin in the various provisions. The lawyers were apparently sufficiently astute to find the proper clauses and disclaimers. In defining the basic principles guiding the relations between the signatories, the fundamental problem throughout was to discover a wording with which all states could feel comfortable. This problem by no means solely involved the resolution of differences in attitude and interpretation between Eastern and Western states. On occasion members of the Western alliance would insist on reservations and exceptions regarding otherwise noncontroversial principles, such as the principle calling for refraining from the threat and use of force. Nevertheless, in general the Final Act of the CSCE gave substance to the concept of *détente*. Russell rightly notes that *détente* is a process still in its early stages; full implementation of the provisions of the Helsinki Agreement would constitute major progress in the development of that process.

Birnbaum, Karl E. "Human Rights and East-West Relations," in *Foreign Affairs*. LV, no. 4 (July, 1977), pp. 783-799.

Karl E. Birnbaum, a Research Fellow of the Swedish Institute of International Relations, discusses the growing interest in the human dimension of world politics, which he considers a healthy reaction to the former emphasis on power politics. According to Birnbaum, the advocacy of human rights and fundamental freedoms in the widest sense has two implications. The first refers to the safeguarding of the individual in his given society, and the second deals with the collective rights of peoples for self-determination and equal status. The CSCE has had a significant impact in both respects. Birnbaum notes the growing assertiveness of dissenters and human rights groups in such countries as the Soviet Union, Poland, Czechoslovakia, and the German Democratic Republic. In accordance with the explicit commitment, the major government and party-controlled newspapers in these countries have had to publish the text of the Final Act of the CSCE. Western expectations that the wide circulation of this text might initiate an internal process has been fulfilled.

Birnbaum notes several manifestations of this process, such as tens of thousands of East Germans seeking to assert their rights under the Helsinki Agreement by applying to leave the GDR legally. All of this has, of course, raised Eastern suspicions considerably; developments have reached a point where they could jeopardize *détente*. Birnbaum believes that the West must be on guard against this possibility, for *détente* has produced important benefits, and promises more positive results in the future. He cautions against an overzealous pressing of the human rights issue. There have been some tangible improvements in the human condition. More could follow, but a severe reaction and setback could also be possible. Obviously, the frequent invoking of the Helsinki Agreement by the dissenters is most disconcerting to the Communist regimes. Basket 3 of the Final Act is perceived by the

Warsaw Pact states as a growing threat to their systems, and doubt about the benefits of *détente* is increasing. Birnbaum suggests that in the matter of human rights, the Carter Administration has caused some bewilderment in official circles and the media of Western European countries as well. Ironically, the strong American stand on human rights seems to move people in the United States and Western Europe to question their governments' decisions regarding long-term cooperation with those countries failing to meet the Helsinki provisions on human rights.

In view of the need for continued businesslike cooperation, Birnbaum deems it essential to convey to the Warsaw Pact states that Western support for human rights movements in their area does not reflect an aspiration to upset the political and social systems there. His analysis calls for patience; it suggests that the first priority is the reduction of tensions. The CSCE process has led to some improvements and still entails the prospect for more. The Communist regimes appear to be considerably more self-conscious and consequently are more likely to refrain from the most severe forms of repression. Thus, the United States faces a policy dilemma in that the strong and consistent stand on human rights, designed to counter charges of hypocrisy, interferes with efforts to reduce tensions and to achieve more success, especially in the vital Strategic Arms Limitations Talks. It remains to be seen whether the stand on human rights can be softened without being compromised. — *M.G.*

The Helsinki Agreement

Additional Recommended Reading

Ball, George W. "Capitulation in Helsinki," in *Newsweek*. LXXXVI (August 4, 1975), p. 13. The former Under Secretary of State strongly criticizes the *détente* policy of the Ford Administration.

Flieger, Howard. "Beyond the Summit," in *U.S. News & World Report*. LXXIX (August 11, 1975), p. 72. Another critical statement on the Helsinki Agreement for putting the seal of approval on Soviet conquests.

Fraser, Donald M. "Freedom and Foreign Policy," in *Foreign Policy*. XXVI (Spring, 1977), pp. 140-156. An argument on behalf of giving more active support to human rights.

Gati, Charles, ed. *The International Politics of Eastern Europe*. New York: Frederick A. Praeger, 1976. Deals in part with the question of what the West can expect to achieve through "peaceful engagement" in Eastern Europe and discusses the impact of the CSCE.

King, Robert R. and Robert W. Dean, eds. *East European Perspectives on European Security and Cooperation*. New York: Frederick A. Praeger, 1974. Staff members of Radio Free Europe analyze East-West negotiations and relations in Europe.

Korbel, Josef. *Détente in Europe: Real or Imaginary*. Princeton, N.J.: Princeton University Press, 1972. A good background study of the policy of *détente* in Europe, leading to changes in the configuration of political, economic, and cultural forces.

Solzhenitsyn, Alexander. *Détente: Prospects for Democracy and Dictatorship*. New Brunswick, N.J.: Transaction Books, 1976. Major public statements appealing to the West to wake up to the perils of Communism and stop helping the Soviet regime, plus critical commentaries by Western observers.

DEATHS OF MAO TSE-TUNG AND CHOU EN-LAI

Type of event: Political: China's change in leadership and policy
Time: January 8 (death of Chou), and September 9, 1976 (death of Mao)
Locale: China

Principal personages:

MAO TSE-TUNG (1893-1976), late Chairman of the Chinese Communist Party and first head of state in the People's Republic of China

CHOU EN-LAI (1898-1976), late Vice Chairman of the Chinese Communist Party and Prime Minister of the People's Republic of China

HUA KUO-FENG (1921-   ), Chairman of the Chinese Communist Party and Prime Minister of the People's Republic of China after Mao

TENG HSIAO-P'ING (1904-   ), Vice Chairman of the Chinese Communist Party and Deputy Prime Minister of the People's Republic of China

YEH CHIEN-YING (1898-   ), a member of the Politburo of the Chinese Communist Party and Minister of Defense until March, 1978

CHU TEH (1886-1976), founder and Marshal of the Red Army; former member of the Standing Committee of the Politburo of the Chinese Communist Party; and sole Vice Chairman of the People's Republic of China, September, 1954 - April, 1959

CHIANG CH'ING (1914-   ), widow of Mao Tse-tung, leader in the Cultural Revolution, 1966-1969; and member of the "Gang of Four"

CHANG CH'UN CH'IAO (1912-   ), member of the Politburo of the Chinese Communist Party; leader of the abortive Shanghai Commune, 1967; and member of the "Gang of Four"

WANG HUNG-WEN (1935-   ), Shanghai cotton-mill worker who was second to Mao in the party hierarchy by August, 1973, and youngest member of the "Gang of Four"

YAO WEN-YUAN (1931-   ), Shanghai journalist, member of the Politburo of the Chinese Communist Party, and member of the "Gang of Four"

Summary of Event

The Year of the Dragon (1976) was one in which China experienced dramatic changes in leadership, setting the stage for new directions in political and economic policies. These changes resulted from the deaths and purges of major prominent officials in the Communist hierarchy, a process begun several years earlier. At the Chinese Communist Party Congress in 1973, for example, the Politburo had twenty-two members. By August, 1977, five had been purged, four had died, and one was very ill; and among these, nine were on the Politburo's eleven-member Standing Committee, a body reserved for the top echelon of the Communist Party. Consequently, nearly half of China's leading Communists had departed.

The death of Chou En-lai on January 8, 1976, from cancer at the age of seventy-eight began a year in which China experienced its greatest losses. Since 1922, Chou had been in the Communist Party, where he played a leading role in the revolutionary movement as a political organizer, and during the government years as a specialist on foreign affairs. Despite his bourgeois background, Chou was always loyal to the Communist cause. His intelligence and urbane manner endeared him to his colleagues and the public, and he survived political crises where lesser men failed.

There was a great expression of public grief over Chou's departure. Nearly a million Chinese and foreigners paid their respects by viewing Chou's portrait and ashes at the old imperial palace in Peking. The period of mourning, however, broke with rising political turmoil between Teng Hsiao-p'ing, a close associate of Chou and a moderate advocating pragmatic policies, and left-wing extremists stressing ideological purity. Without Chou's presence, the two groups began to polarize and maneuver for control of the party and government led now by an ill and aging Mao Tse-tung.

The squabbling resulted in a compromise replacement for Chou. Hua Kuo-feng, who was once a Communist Party leader in Mao's home district in Hunan province, was chosen as Acting Premier. He had only reached the national scene in 1969 when he was elected to the Central Committee of the Chinese Communist Party. As Minister of Public Security in 1976, he was the sixth in a line of twelve Deputy Prime Ministers. The five Deputies passed over were all better-known and more experienced.

In April, 1976, Hua was designated to the full office of Prime Minister, and the internal struggle between the pragmatists and the ultra-leftists resulted in the second purge of Teng Hsiao-p'ing. After being dismissed from public office (1967) in the leftist-dominated Cultural Revolution, Teng was restored in 1973 and again occupied responsible positions. After Chou's death in January, 1976, Teng disappeared from public view; he formally lost his posts in April. His enthusiasm for modernization and his disparagement of class struggle and continuing policies of the Cultural Revolution brought him into disfavor with influential radicals. The catalyst for Teng's dismissal was a riot in Peking's T'ien-an-men Square that resulted from a protest demonstration against the sudden removal of memorial wreaths honoring Chou En-lai. While there was no evidence that Teng organized the disturbance, the crowd's antileftist mood gave the radicals in government the rationale to strike against him.

The death of another Communist leader and a natural disaster soon brought further convulsions to China. Chu Te, who worked closely with Mao Tse-tung in building the Red Army, died on July 6, 1976, at the age of ninety. A participant in the Nanchang Uprising (1927) and the Long March (1934-1935), Chu's exploits brought him to positions of leadership. At the time of his death, he was a member of the Standing Committee of the Politburo and chairman of the Standing Committee of the National People's Congress.

A few weeks later on July 28 a violent earthquake, reaching a magnitude of 7.5, struck the Tangshan-Fengnan area of eastern Hopei province. Although no casualty figures were issued, extremely severe damage and extensive losses were reported to have occurred in the industrial city of Tangshan, with destruction spreading to Tientsin and Peking. China's economy was seriously interrupted with the closing of the Kailuan Coal Mine and the Tangshan Iron and Steel Company. Rescue and reconstruction teams came quickly from distant places in China, and both enterprises were reopened in a month.

The greatest shock to China's stability in this agonizing year was the death of Mao Tse-tung on September 9, 1976, at the age of eighty-two. It came as no surprise, as the aging party Chairman had been ill for some time with Parkinson's disease and was becoming politically inactive. The week-long mourning services in his honor culminated in a national tribute paid on September 18 in which all China stopped work for three minutes. Eight months after Mao's death, a huge memorial structure was erected in his honor. Mao had been leader of the Communist Party, the army, and the government, often concurrently, for most of his revolutionary career. His success as a military and political planner and organizer gave him a reputation that could not be challenged or condemned, even after his death.

With Mao gone, leftist leaders quickly tried to gain power. Known as the "Gang of Four," they included Chiang Ch'ing, Mao's widow and a leading representative of the Cultural Revolution; Chang Ch'un-ch'iao, a former Shanghai journalist, considered the "brain" of the group; Wang Hung-wen, a Shanghai cotton-mill worker whom Mao had elevated to high office while still in his thirties; and Yao Wen-yuan, a pamphleteer with family ties to Mao. Before they could maneuver into control positions, Hua ordered their arrest on the night of October 6, 1976, and they were jailed in southwest Peking.

In the following weeks, the Gang of Four was mercilessly vilified, being condemned for every imaginable crime against Chinese society. This thorough purge of leftist leadership allowed the emergence of moderate, pragmatic policies that stressed China's modernization through economic development. To help lead these policies, Teng Hsiao-p'ing was restored to all his former posts in July, 1977. By early 1978, Teng stood in stature almost coequal to Hua Kuo-feng. The tumult of 1976 had passed, and a stable, moderate course returned to the Chinese scene.

Pertinent Literature

Terrill, Ross. *The Future of China After Mao*. New York: Delacorte Press, 1978.

In this first comprehensive analysis of the traumatic events that shook China from the beginning of 1976 to mid-1977, Ross Terrill succinctly explains how the emphasis in Chinese objectives has shifted from ideological purity to modernization. Despite changes in Chinese leadership through deaths and purges, disorder caused by earthquakes and slackened production, and the threat of Russian interference, the author believes that China successfully weathered the experience and emerged a model of stability.

The new leaders, Terrill believes, reflect the aspirations of China's youth who had not lived through the anguish of pre-revolution days. They yearn for an improved standard of living and a more relaxed life, unhindered by Mao Tse-tung's emphasis on constant revolution and struggle. China's growing demand for better times and the people's continued adulation for the late Chairman Mao, however, pose a dilemma for Hua Kuo-feng, China's new leader. Terrill correctly points out that the shift to the right, away from Maoist rigidity, was quickly and deftly handled by the publication of Mao's earlier pronouncements from the late 1950's in which he emphasized the need for greater production.

The symbols of the ideological struggle that dominated leadership changes in 1976 were Teng Hsiao-p'ing, the twice purged and twice restored pragmatist whose views on modernization ultimately prevailed, and the Gang of Four, the ultra-left advocates of continued class struggle, led by Mao's widow, Chiang Ch'ing. Terrill contends that the outcome of this conflict was determined by the fact that Chou En-lai died before Mao. With Chou gone and Mao's illness restricting his effectiveness, polarization between the two extremes resulted. Teng sympathizers eventually prevailed. Had Chou been alive in this critical period, the conflict might have been prevented and pro-Maoist policies retained.

A development intriguing to Terrill and other specialists is the emergence of Hua Kuo-feng as Mao's successor. When Hua became acting premier in February, 1976, after Mao's death, very little was known about him. He reached the national scene only in 1969 when he was elected to the Central Committee of the Chinese Communist Party after a successful career as Governor of an important province, Mao's native Hunan. Here again, the fact that Chou's death preceded Mao's became a fateful determinant in China's political leadership. Terrill speculates that had Mao died before Chou, Chou's protégé, Teng Hsiao-p'ing, would have become premier. In his evaluation of Hua's potential, Terrill sees him as a "traditional figure" and "a humble footnote to the era of Mao." Teng appears to have become the real power despite his second-place billing.

As the political crisis settled, it became clear that Hua had accepted the pragmatist line, and he was sharing his leadership role with Teng and with Yeh Chien-ying, Minister of Defense, who yielded in March, 1978, to Hsu Hsiang-ch'ien. The quick elimination of the Gang of Four's influence on October 6, 1976, a month after Mao's death, confirmed the triumvirate's success and their cause for a less stringent form of Communism.

In the future, Terrill believes Hua will give primary emphasis to China's industrialization, thus finally implementing the earlier policies of Mao and Chou; but agriculture will remain the primary production. This emphasis and an increased willingness to resort to foreign assistance will raise the standard of living. Because of China's huge population, Terrill foresees a continuation of austerity for the Chinese and projects only a $600-$700 per capita annual income by the year 2000. China, Terrill declares will remain basically Maoist, but there will be greater reliance on settled political institutions rather than on ideological dogma; but as modernization advances, equality is likely to lose ground.

A major concern to the author is the nonrecognition of the People's Republic of China by the United States. He argues that the Shanghai Communiqué of 1972 is a commitment for eventual normalization and that its fulfillment could be advantageous to the United States, particularly as leverage in its relations with the Soviet Union. Unlike other writers, Terrill downgrades the significance of the Taiwan issue as a hindrance to peace. Eagerly proposing normalization, he regards 1978 as a critical year in Sino-American relations. Further delays might result in both nations losing interest and a return to less cordial exchanges.

On the vital issue of China's relations with the Soviet Union, Terrill believes that the border disputes could be settled easily and tensions eased, if the parties desired. He concludes that a degree of *détente* eventually will occur but that the two nations "will not return to their old intimacy and military partnership." In most respects, however, Terrill's view of China's prospects for domestic growth and international harmony is optimistic.

Hsu, Kai-yu. *Chou En-lai: China's Gray Eminence*. Garden City, N.Y.: Doubleday & Company, 1968.

Although Mao Tse-tung had emerged as the undisputed leader of China's Communist revolution, much of his success was due to the political craftsmanship of Chou En-lai. His superior talent in organization and administration had given the revolution a vital thrust toward fruition which made Chou's role in the movement indispensable. This biography of Chou's life outlines his revolutionary career and clearly illustrates his contributions to the major developments of the Chinese Communist movement and government until 1968, near the end of the Cultural Revolution. The author adds insight into Chou's character and personality that explains his ability to surmount fractional division which plagued the Communist movement. In this personal account, Chou is portrayed as a brilliant tactician with amazing stamina and grace.

Chou En-lai's path to Communism came not from peasant roots but from his bourgeois, intellectual experience as a student: first at the Nankai Middle School in Tientsin, which had an antitradition reputation, then in Japan, where he was exposed to the Marxian teachings of Hajimi Kawakami at Kyoto University. His link to Communism was solidified later by his brief contact with a Russian, Sergei A. Polevoy, who served briefly in China both as a Russian teacher at Peking University and as the cultural liaison for the Comintern. It was in France in 1920, however, that Chou received practical training in political organization meeting with Chinese students and laborers already planning a Chinese Communist Youth Corps.

His organizational ability, developed during his student days, served Chou well as a Communist Party member back in China. During the period of the Kuomintang-Communist alliance (1923-1927), when Chou was on the staff of Chiang Kai-shek's Whampoa Military Academy, he actively recruited soldiers into the Chinese Communist Party. In addition to these infiltration tactics, Chou En-lai was instrumental in planning and leading several revolts in Shanghai, in an abortive effort to set up a Soviet-style government in the spring of 1927, and in Nanchang. Despite these setbacks, Chou's success at infiltrating the Kuomintang organization, coupled with his persuasive arguments, his devotion to the cause, and his obvious ability as a strategist, earned for him the respect and rec-

ognition of his comrades. He was soon elevated to the Central Committee of the Chinese Communist Party where he assumed a leadership role.

Important to Chou's career was his close collaboration with Mao Tse-tung. This began in 1934 when they agreed to retreat from the Kiangsi Soviet which led to the Long March. At the Kiangsi experiment and after, Chou had been very active in organizing, training, and disciplining the Red Army. Unlike other writers, Hsu gives more credit to Chou than the Red Army's founder, Chu Teh, for the army's organizational development, pointing out that Chu was busy commanding units in the field. Thus, by the mid-1930's, Chou En-lai had developed recognized talents in political organization and leadership and in military strategy.

The art of diplomacy and tactical maneuvering was skillfully developed by Chou in his efforts to bring about a United Front with the Nationalists against the Japanese invaders. The need to alleviate pressure on the Communist headquarters at Yenan was paramount as the war progressed; and although the United Front plan was never fully successful, Chou's efforts forestalled a Nationalist onslaught while the Communists were able to expand and strengthen their position in northern China. Chou was both the chief architect of the United Front plan and its leading diplomat. His ability to negotiate, maneuver, and persuade his adversaries of his sincerity led him to become the main link of the People's Republic of China to the world. Although not always successful in foreign affairs, Chou had been responsible for China's growing stature and increased recognition.

Chou's ability to deal with contrasting personalities, according to the author, began when he was a young boy shifting between relatives. He developed a composure and cordiality that disarmed those with whom he dealt. His eloquent speech and charisma enabled him to survive even the most sudden and dramatic political shifts of policy and power, always endearing himself to Mao. Chou was clearly a practitioner and not a theoretician. Ever loyal to traditional Marxist-Leninist principles, he concentrated his promotion of the Communist cause on advancing its power and position. In doing so, he alternated his tactics, compromised on principle, and sacrificed his own advancement allowing others to be appointed before him for the sake of harmony. Such loyalty to Communist objectives reflected Chou's thorough commitment to Chinese Communism. The biographical picture that Hsu has painted is that of an indispensable leader credited with much of Communism's success in China. — *L.H.D.G.*

Additional Recommended Reading

Archer, Jules. *Chou En-lai.* New York: Hawthorn Books, 1973. A brief, readable account of Chou's life, exploring his personality and character, based on secondary sources.

Barnett, A. Doak. *Uncertain Passage: China's Transition to the Post-Mao Era.* Washington, D.C.: The Brookings Institution, 1974. An analytical essay focusing on selected major problems the author expected China to face after Mao's demise; he concludes with implications of China's post-Mao situation on United States policy.

Ch'en, Jerome. *Mao and the Chinese Revolution.* New York: Oxford University Press, 1966. The first commendable and well-documented account of Mao's career and thought up to the Cultural Revolution.

Fitzgerald, C. P. *Mao Tse-tung and China.* New York: Pelican Books, 1977. A brief, factual account of Mao's life, revolutionary rise to power, and leadership of China by a noted Sinologist.

Karnow, Stanley. *Mao and China: From Revolution to Revolution.* New York: The Viking Press, 1972. This objective and readable account of Mao's direction of the Cultural Revolution (1966-1969) by a noted journalist gives many insights into the nature of Chinese Communism.

Meisner, Maurice. *Mao's China: A History of the People's Republic.* New York: The Free Press, 1977. In this history of China's Communist government, the author evaluates its successes and failures in terms of Chinese Communist goals.

Pye, Lucian W. *Mao Tse-tung: The Man in the Leader.* New York: Basic Books, 1976. This study of Mao the man is from the viewpoint of psychohistory and examines Mao's personality and the effect it had on his thoughts and actions.

Roots, John McCook. *Chou: An Informal Biography of China's Legendary Chou En-lai.* New York: Doubleday, 1978. A personal account of Chou by a journalist friend who also describes his own childhood in China.

Schram, Stuart R. *The Political Thought of Mao Tse-tung*. New York: Frederick A. Praeger, 1970. An analysis of the development of Mao's political thinking which illustrates how Marxism in China was shaped both by Mao's personality and by China's internal revolutionary conditions.

Uhalley, Stephen, Jr. *Mao Tse-tung: A Critical Biography*. New York: New Viewpoints, 1975. An interpretive history of Mao's character and revolutionary career in which the author implies that Mao had surpassed other leaders in his experiments in social engineering to achieve his idealistic goals.

Wakeman, Frederic, Jr. *History and Will: Philosophical Perspectives of Mao Tse-tung's Thought*. Berkeley: University of California Press, 1973. A highly analytical examination of Mao's thoughts which traces the origins and influences on his ideology.

BLACK NATIONALIST MOVEMENT IN SOUTH AFRICA

Type of event: Sociological: internal interracial conflict
Time: Summer, 1976
Locale: Johannesburg area, Union of South Africa

Principal personages:

BALTHAZAR JOHANNES VORSTER (1915-   ), Prime Minister of the Union of South Africa, 1966-

DR. Alfred B. XUMA (1893-1962), President-General of the African National Congress (ANC), 1940-1949

DR. JAMES MOROKA, President-General of the African National Congress, 1949-1953

CHIEF ALBERT JOHN LUTHULI (1898-1967), President-General of the African National Congress, 1953-1960; and winner of the Nobel Peace Prize for 1960

ROBERT SOBUKWE, one of the founders of the Pan-Africanist Congress (PAC)

CHIEF GATSHA BUTHELEZI (1928-   ), Bantustan leader

Summary of Event

On June 16, 1976, black students in South West Township (Soweto), a black ghetto near Johannesburg, gathered to protest the government requirement that some high school courses in black schools be taught in Afrikaans, a language of Dutch origin. The protest developed into a full-scale riot when ten thousand school children clashed with police. Other township dwellers joined the riot, which spread to seven other townships by the end of the week. During this time 176 people were killed, buses were stoned, and state beer halls, schools, and liquor stores were burned. As a result, the government quickly dropped its insistence on the use of Afrikaans in black schools. Not since the Sharpeville deaths in 1960, when sixty-nine blacks were shot in a racial disturbance, had such large-scale violence occurred in South Africa.

Authorities were unable to quell the disturbances, which erupted again in August when twenty thousand blacks, most of them students, began a march to Johannesburg to demand the release of four students arrested since the June violence. Demonstrators were joined by workers commuting to jobs in the city. The throng was eventually halted by police bullets. Crowds of people stopped commuters from going to work, stoned buses, and tore up sections of railway lines linking the black townships with Johannesburg. The summer's unrest dealt a powerful blow to the prestige of South African Prime Minister Balthazar Johannes Vorster, the staunch upholder of Apartheid, the system of racial segregation.

The riots and violence in South African cities in 1976 were a result of the blacks's spontaneous outburst of anger over their living conditions and

1272

the South African political system. Although the immediate cause of the conflict was the Afrikaans language issue, the Black Nationalist Movement in South Africa was quick to mobilize and channel this anger in an effort to change the system. This movement had its roots in the African National Congress (ANC), which was originally founded in 1912 under the name of the South African Native National Congress. The ANC is Black Africa's oldest political party, and its goals are to eliminate racial discrimination, create African unity, and establish a democratic system within the party and within South Africa. Although the party was led by mission-educated, Western-oriented blacks, they tried to include the traditional chiefs in their party. The strategies and tactics of the ANC changed with time. Initially the moderate leaders merely sought to influence the racial policies by trying to consult with white government leaders. This nonconfrontation strategy included requests for the enlargement of the reservations rather than for their outright abolishment. It called for rights of land ownership in the black townships instead of a total change in which blacks could purchase land anywhere, including in white residential and commercial areas. This policy of moderation was labeled realistic by some observers on the grounds that any demands for radical change would only be futile, while requests for changes within the system which did not destroy the segregationist structure would have a better chance of success.

As time passed, the strategy of the ANC changed from consultation with the authorities to noncollaboration, then to passive resistance, and finally to organization of mass protests. Different methods of trying to change the system were tried, including appealing to Britain and the United States. A major policy shift came after World War II when the ANC leader, Dr. Alfred B. Xuma, departed from a conciliatory stance and rejected the entire South African segregation system. Part of this more strident pose came from the members of the ANC Youth League, who demanded quick action. It was from this same organization that several black leaders emerged, including Nelson Mandela, a leader of the African National Congress; Oliver Tambo, acting President of the African National Congress after the organization was banned; Robert Sobukwe, President of the Pan-Africanist Congress; and Chief Gatsha Buthelezi, the most militant of the Bantustan leaders.

The impatience of the ANC Youth League led to periodic changes in the leadership of the parent organization. Thus, in December, 1949, the ANC Youth League employed some skillful political maneuvers to replace the relatively moderate Dr. Xuma (as President-General) with Dr. James Moroka, an active participant in the movement since 1935. Moroka played an important role in leading the Defiance Campaign in 1952 against the Pass Laws (which required black Africans to carry a permit or pass at all times) and other legal mainstays of the Apartheid system. Some of Moroka's views, however, alienated the ANC Youth League, which, as a consequence, in 1953 supported the popular Chief Albert Luthuli as head of the African National Congress. Luthuli remained at the helm of the ANC until 1960, when the organization was banned by the South African government in the wake of the Sharpeville tragedy. Thereafter, the ANC went underground to continue its activities on behalf of black liberation in South Africa. As a tribute to Albert Luthuli and what was called the "indestructible spirit" of the African National Congress, he was presented with the Nobel Peace Prize for 1960.

The leadership changes described above reflected policy differences within the ANC despite attempts to maintain unity. Certain members favored a nonracist doctrine, whereas others supported a Black Power approach. Another split occurred between the pro-Communists and the anti-Communists, while another area of conflict centered on whether the independent African states were to be asked to help in the struggle. Some members of the ANC believed that developing self-sufficiency would have the greatest impact on the South African political scene, whereas others believed that the only way they could influence so powerful an adversary as the South African government was to seek foreign aid. In addition to these policy differences, there still existed the unanswered question of strategy mentioned above. Could change be achieved more readily by conciliation or by confrontation? Even life style became a point of disagreement in the Black Nationalist Movement. Some members frowned on drinking and sex as pleasures which diverted people from the revolutionary goal of changing the system, while others did not see the relevance of these matters to the political scene.

It was inevitable, with this range of views within the Black Nationalist Movement, that factions would appear. In 1959 the Pan-Africanist Congress (PAC), under the leadership of Robert Sobukwe, broke away from the ANC. PAC members were critical of the African National Congress stand on party membership. The ANC employed nonracist principles and accepted nonblacks as members, provided that they shared the beliefs and goals of the party. PAC members, however, believed that in order to foster black pride and self-sufficiency, only blacks should become members of the movement. In addition, the PAC decried what it called the left-wing trend within the ANC. On the day of the Sharpeville tragedy, Sobukwe was arrested and imprisoned on Robben Island. In 1969 he was released from prison, but remains restricted to the town of Kimberly. The PAC, banned like the ANC after Sharpeville, has its external headquarters in Tanzania under the leadership of Potlaka Leballo and is recognized by the Organization of African Unity.

Despite the apparent strength of the PAC, the ANC is still the dominant and most widely recognized black nationalist party in South Africa. Although the role of the ANC in the 1976 South African riots is difficult to assess, it is clear that both ideologically and materially the ANC will lend its support to any attempt to destroy South Africa's Apartheid system.

1274

Pertinent Literature

Benson, Mary. *The African Patriots: The Story of the African National Congress of South Africa*. Chicago: Encyclopedia Britannica Press, 1963.

Mary Benson's book on the African National Congress provides the reader with a thorough analysis of the Black Nationalist Movement in South Africa. Her knowledge of the movement is based upon her research in South Africa as well as upon her friendship with some of the members and former leaders of the ANC. This friendship and empathy with members of the ANC has resulted in a highly personalized and committed book.

Benson takes up the story of black nationalism in the early 1880's, at which time the first African political group, Imbumba Yama Afrika (Union of Africans), was created. But a few blacks had voted in the Cape Colony as early as 1854. By 1880, some black families had had two generations of missionary education, and had become acquainted with Western ideas of democracy. As more blacks began voting, the settlers raised the qualifications for voter eligibility; and by the turn of the century only 4.7 percent of the electorate in the Cape Colony was black. In other areas of South Africa, blacks had even fewer rights. In Natal, for example, the Zulus were being moved onto reservations to make way for sugar plantations.

The Anglo-Boer War of 1899-1902 resulted in further problems for blacks in South Africa. They generally supported the British against the Boers; and after the war the Boers remembered and treated them with distrust.

This gave further impetus to the formation of black political organizations, among them, in 1902, the Natal Native Congress led by Martin Luthuli, uncle of Chief Albert Luthuli, and the African Peoples Organization in the Cape Colony. M. K. Gandhi had already set up the Natal Indian Congress in 1894, and he first utilized the method of passive resistance when he defied the authorities by organizing an Indian resistance to the pass laws.

Benson continues her account by focusing on specific historical events and relating the effects that these events had on the black population. She describes in considerable detail the often futile efforts of blacks to protect their interests. When it was discovered that Britain was to hand over control of South Africa to the resident white minority, three black newspaper editors tried to get black voting rights written into the new constitution. A delegation went to Britain in an effort to get the British Parliament to withhold ratification of the South African Bill. However, the Bill passed, and from 1910 on the blacks in South Africa were under the direct control of the white minority. Hence, whereas Britain at a later date could grant independence to blacks in Ghana, Kenya, and other British colonies, they lost their power to do so in South Africa because they had already transferred power to the South African whites. Several blacks in South Africa realized the significance of the formation of the South African Union in 1910, which placed them under the power of the white minority, and took quick action. In 1912 they organized a huge meeting of blacks from all over South Africa. In keeping with the platform of national unity, a cross-section of blacks, including townsmen, countrymen, chiefs, and commoners, attended. The meeting resulted in the formation of South African Native National Congress (SANNC), the first organization of its kind in Africa. The newly formed organization, later to become the famous African National Congress, ANC, determined to put an end to segregation and racial discrimination.

One of the first issues which the newly formed organization confronted was that of land distribution. They protested the Native Land Bill which allocated ninety percent of the land in South Africa to the three million whites and restricted the four million blacks to ownership of only 7.3 percent. The SANNC sent petitions to the government and delegations to England in efforts to change the Land Bill. They were unsuccessful, however, and thousands of blacks were characterized as squatters and evicted from their homes.

During World War I the SANNC supported Britain. After the war, this same group requested that Britain not hand over the High Commission Territories, Swaziland, Basutoland, and Bechuanaland, to South Africa.

The British honored the request, and one of the organization's first successes was achieved.

In the years following the war, the ANC, as the black organization became known, helped organize labor strikes despite the threat of imprisonment. In this area they had a minor local success when the ANC members accused of inciting violence were acquitted and wages were raised. Another target of the ANC since its foundation was South Africa's pass laws, which not only degraded blacks but limited their freedom. If a black lost his pass, he was classified as a vagrant, could not get a job, could not travel, and was subject to a fine and imprisonment. In addition to the more active resistance of mass demonstrations, the ANC organized campaigns in which sacks were filled with passes and left at pass law offices. However, the police ignored such passive protests and forcefully broke up all demonstrations, with the result that the pass laws remained.

Benson continues her history of the ANC by tracing each action of the organization as it responded to various government moves. The major leaders are discussed with empathy and thoroughness up to the time when the ANC was banned in 1960. Benson concludes with a tribute to the "indestructible spirit" of the ANC. Her chronicle of this organization is remarkable for its clarity and detail and is indispensable to scholars of Black Nationalism in South Africa.

Davenport, T. R. H. *South Africa: A Modern History*. Toronto: University of Toronto Press, 1977.

In any history of South Africa, the ideology of the author is pertinent.

Davenport is quick to characterize his philosophy, labeling himself a liberal

Africanist and describing his stance as somewhere between reactionary conservative and violent revolutionary. As such, he is open to criticism from both sides. However, despite Davenport's self-confirmed, middle-of-the-road views, his book is factually informative. He begins his account of South Africa's history in the seventeenth century, relating the population distribution to the weather, soil, and migration patterns. A good example of his objectivity and reliance on facts rather than emotions is his treatment of the controversy over the early settlers of South Africa. On the one hand, many people believe that the whites settled the southern portion of South Africa at the same time that blacks entered from the North; others believe that blacks inhabited the territory long before whites arrived, and hence the area morally belongs to them. Davenport cites archaeological data supporting the view that blacks arrived in the area, known today as the Transvaal, in the fifth century A.D. He also gives evidence pointing to the existence of a prior community of Iron Age blacks which was dependent upon mining and trading.

Davenport describes the precursor of the black/white conflict by detailing the historic factors which drew the two opposing forces together. From the North, as a result of the *Mfecane* (a Nguni word meaning "crushing" and conveying the idea of "total war") came blacks pushed by wars and population pressures. From the South came the Boers who participated in the Great Trek (late 1830's),

seeking independence from British Administration in the Cape. Davenport discusses the different South African groups struggling for power—the blacks, Boers, Griquas, and British. Since the blacks were militarily weaker than the whites, a focal point of conflict was the struggle between the Boers and the British. The Boers had tried to avoid the conflict by moving away from areas of British control and setting up their own administrative areas. Davenport describes this process in detail and discusses the succession of British High Commissioners and their attitudes towards the Boer requests for independence. The Boers and British finally reached a stage where it became impossible to settle their differences over the conference table, and the Anglo-Boer War broke out in 1899. Davenport treats the war in greater depth than Benson does, describing the factors leading up to the conflict, together with its subsequent repercussions; he also notes the hardships suffered by the blacks, who were placed in concentration camps during the war. Benson, however, writes about the Anglo-Boer War largely from the perspective of the impact it had on the blacks, with less emphasis on the political maneuverings of the British and the Boers.

Davenport brings his history of South Africa up to 1976. His analysis is valuable because of its inclusion of political, economic, and geographical data, and is essential reading for anyone wishing to understand the forces which created contemporary South Africa. — *C.K.*

Additional Recommended Reading

Van den Berghe, Pierre. *South Africa, A Study in Conflict*. Berkeley: University of California Press, 1970. A perceptive analysis of interaction between the races in South Africa.

Carter, Gwendolen M. "The Black Experience in South Africa," in *The Wilson Quarterly*. I (Spring, 1977), pp. 51-63. A brief overview of what blacks in South Africa have undergone since their first contacts with the Dutch in the seventeenth century.

Feit, Edward. *South Africa: The Dynamics of the African National Congress*. New York: Oxford University Press, 1962. An indispensable book for any student of the South African Black Nationalist Movement.

Johnson, Richard William. *How Long Will South Africa Survive?* New York: Oxford University Press, 1977. A readable account of emerging international and internal developments in Southern Africa, examining the domestic implications of international events.

Lacour-Gayet, Robert. *A History of South Africa*. Translated by Stephen Hardman. London: Cassell and Company, 1977. An account of South Africa from the point of view of a liberal European, with a good index and bibliography.

Munger, Edwin S. *Afrikaner and African Nationalism: South African Parallels and Parameters*. New York: Oxford University Press, 1967. Provides valuable insights into both Afrikaner and African nationalism.

Ngubane, Jordan K. *An African Explains Apartheid*. New York: Frederick A. Praeger, 1963. Ngubane makes no claims of objectivity, yet writes about whites with empathy and about blacks with insight.

Shepherd, George W. J. *Anti-Apartheid: Transnational Conflict and Western Policy in the Liberation of South Africa*. Westport, Conn.: Greenwood Press, 1977. An overview of the influence of the outside world on South Africa, documenting the support that Black Nationalists in South Africa receive both directly and indirectly.

Walshe, Peter. *The Rise of African Nationalism in South Africa*. London: C. Hurst and Company, 1970. Remarkable for its detailed information on the African National Congress, Walshe's sources include minutes of the Congress conferences, articles, newspapers, government publications, manuscripts, theses, books, and interviews.

THE UNITED STATES SUPREME COURT RULES ON THE DEATH PENALTY

Type of event: Legal: judicial decision on the death penalty
Time: July 2, 1976
Locale: Washington, D.C.

Principal personages:

WILLIAM H. FURMAN, petitioner in *Furman* v. *Georgia*, 1972, heard with *Jackson* v. *Georgia* and *Branch* v. *Texas*

LUCIOUS JACKSON, JR., petitioner in *Jackson* v. *Georgia*, 1972

ELMER BRANCH, petitioner in *Branch* v. *Texas*, 1972

WILLIAM ORVILLE DOUGLAS (1898-1980) and

WILLIAM JOSEPH BRENNAN, JR. (1906-   ), Associate Justices of the United States Supreme Court and the authors of the concurring majority opinion in *Furman* v. *Georgia* and other 1972 cases

TROY LEON GREGG, petitioner in *Gregg* v. *Georgia*, 1976

POTTER STEWART (1915-   ), Associate Justice of the United States Supreme Court, and the author of the concurring majority opinion in *Furman* v. *Georgia* and others, and coannouncer of the decision in the case of *Gregg* v. *Georgia*

LEWIS FRANKLIN POWELL (1907-   ) and

JOHN P. STEVENS (1920-   ), Associate Justices of the United States Supreme Court, and the coannouncers of the decision in the case of *Gregg* v. *Georgia*

Summary of Event

The death penalty is a method of punishment which historically has been applied globally for both serious and relatively minor crimes against state, person, and property. During the medieval and early modern periods of European history, the death sentence was used as punishment for a large number of crimes, and usually was administered in public, often accompanied by torture of the most painful and gruesome kind. The greatest abuse of the use of the death penalty was probably reached in eigh-teenth century England when it was decreed, although not regularly applied, for several hundred offenses, most representing crimes against property.

The increased utilization of the death penalty and the resulting public desensitization, accompanied by the humanitarian movement in the West known as the Age of Enlightenment, led to a growing reaction to its use, especially among the intellectuals of the age. The most famous early attack on the death penalty came from an Italian, Cesare Beccaria, whose *Essay on Crimes and Punishments* (1764) led to a rapidly growing demand for reform. The results were quick to come. During the French Revolution, for instance, the guillotine was utilized as a more humane instrument of execution than the less swift and sure ax or sword. By the 1830's, the number of cases in England for which the death penalty could be imposed had been reduced from the hundreds of a few decades earlier to fifteen. The same trends followed in the United States, although the death penalty had never been imposed as widely there.

By the middle of the twentieth century the use of the death penalty had declined even further throughout most of the world, especially in Europe and the Americas. However, a large majority of the states in the United States still legislated its potential use in court sentences, although it was seldom actually imposed. A continuous attack on the imposition of the death penalty in criminal cases accompanied this decline in capital punishment. The opponents of the death penalty were never a majority, however, and all their arguments were countered by its proponents.

Generally, arguments for and against capital punishment can be divided into two basic categories— one based upon religious belief and emotions, and the other founded on utilitarian or practical arguments. Supporters have argued, for example, that it is ordained by God as a means by which men act as God's agents in ridding the world of the grossly undesirable, whereas opponents have held that justice belongs

to God alone and cannot be delegated to men. In the category of practicality, supporters have held that capital punishment is a deterrent, protecting the community, prison staffs, and fellow prisoners from dangerous criminals. They also argue that those prisoners who receive the penalty of life imprisonment instead of death are an economic liability to the state. Opponents have countered these arguments by asserting that there is no proof that the threat of death deters criminals for committing capital offenses; that rehabilitation in prison rather than punishment could mitigate the problem of the dangerous criminal to society, prison staff and prisoners; and that in well-run prisons, prisoners can be economic assets instead of liabilities. Most importantly, they have argued that judicial error can and has led to the execution of innocent persons, and that the imposition of the death penalty often has been socially and racially arbitrary and discriminatory. It was essentially on these arguments that the United States Supreme Court made its decisions on the death penalty in 1972, and 1976.

In 1972, two petitioners from Georgia, William H. Furman and Lucious Jackson, Jr., and a petitioner from Texas, Elmer Branch, brought suit in federal court against their respective states. Furman and Jackson had been convicted by juries in Georgia state courts of murder and rape respectively, and had been sentenced to death by juries which had discretion over whether or not to impose the death penalty. Their sentences had been upheld by the Georgia Supreme Court. Branch had been sentenced to death for rape in Texas by a jury with the same discretionary power, and his sentence had been upheld by the Texas Court of Criminal Appeals. The United States Supreme Court, in a five-to-four decision, reversed the judgment of the state courts and remanded the cases for further proceedings.

Justices William O. Douglas, William Brennan, Potter Stewart, Byron White, and Thurgood Marshall, who composed the majority, held that the death penalty, as it had been applied in these cases, violated the Eighth and Fourteenth Amendments' prohibition of cruel and unusual punishment because, under the laws of Georgia and Texas, juries had an untrammeled discretion to impose or withhold the death penalty. In his opinion, Justice Douglas held that the death penalty was cruel and unusual because, since it was imposed at the discretion of the jury, it had been applied selectively in a discriminatory fashion to members of a minority. Justice Brennan, probably in an attempt to counter strict constructionists of the Constitution, held that the Eighth Amendment's prohibition of cruel and unusual punishment should not be considered as limited to torture or to punishments considered cruel and unusual at the time the Eighth Amendment was ratified. The prohibition should include all punishments which did not comport with the concept of human dignity held by society as a whole. Since society, according to Brennan, did not regard so severe a punishment as acceptable, its imposition represented a violation of the Eighth Amendment. It was now up to Georgia and Texas and

states with similar death penalty laws either to abolish capital punishment or to draft new laws which would be in agreement with the Supreme Court's decision in these three cases.

After the United States Supreme Court's decision in *Furman* v. *Georgia*, the Georgia legislature amended its laws regarding imposition of the death penalty and attempted to make them fair, nondiscriminatory, and nonarbitrary. Under the new law, guilt or innocence was to be determined either by a jury, or by a trial judge, in a case where there was no jury. In the jury trial the judge was required to instruct the jury on lesser included offenses supported by the evidence. After either a verdict, finding, or plea of guilty, a presentence hearing was to be conducted at which the jury or judge would hear arguments and additional evidence in order to arrive at the nature of punishment. At least one of two aggravating circumstances specified in the laws had to be found to exist beyond a reasonable doubt and had to be stated in writing before a jury or judge could impose the death penalty. The death sentence was then to be appealed automatically to the Supreme Court of Georgia which would determine if the sentence had been imposed under the influence of passion, prejudice, or any other arbitrary factor; whether the evidence supported the finding of a legally aggravating circumstance; and whether the sentence was excessive or disproportionate to the penalty imposed in similar cases. Finally, if the Georgia Supreme Court affirmed the death sentence, its decision was required to include reference to similar cases that the court considered.

A case to test these revised Georgia statutes, *Troy Leon Gregg* v. *State of Georgia*, was argued before the United States Supreme Court in March, 1976, and decided on July 2, 1976. The petitioner, Troy Gregg, had been convicted by a jury in a Georgia state court of two counts of armed robbery and two counts of murder. Throughout the trial and in the appeals process the new Georgia statutes had been followed. The Georgia Supreme Court affirmed the conviction and the imposition of the death sentence for murder, although it vacated the sentence for the two counts of armed robbery.

The United States Supreme Court, in its decision on *Gregg* v. *Georgia*, affirmed the decision of the Georgia Supreme Court. In a decision announced by Justices Potter Stewart, Lewis Powell, and John P. Stevens, seven of the nine justices held that in this case the imposition of the death penalty did not violate the prohibition of the infliction of cruel and unusual punishment under the Eighth and Fourteenth Amendments.

Thus the right of states to impose and implement the death penalty had been affirmed, so long as the statutes of these states were fair, nondiscriminatory, and nonarbitrary, and thus did not violate the constitutional prohibition against cruel and unusual punishment.

Pertinent Literature

Beccaria, Cesare Bonesana. *On Crimes and Punishments*. Translated with an Introduction by Henry Paolucci. Indianapolis: Bobbs-Merrill Company, 1963.

Indispensable in approaching a study of the historical controversy over the death penalty is Cesare Beccaria's *On Crimes and Punishments*, originally published in 1764. A product of the Enlightenment, it is a masterpiece of eighteenth century liberalism which, according to historian Leo Gershoy, ". . . served as the inspiration for all subsequent writings [on penal reform] and most of the practical reforms of [Beccaria's] and the following century."

A member of the nobility of Milan, Beccaria (1738-1794) had a disappointing career as a student at the Jesuit college at Parma and at the University of Padua. While at the latter, however, he became interested in Montesquieu's writings on comparative law and soon after associated himself with a group of young intellectuals from Milan who were committed to effecting liberal change with deeds as well as words. Led by two brothers, Pietro and Alessandro Verri, the group appropriately called itself the Society of Fists and began to publish a periodical. Under Pietro's guidance, Beccaria immersed himself in the writings of the leading authors of his day, including Voltaire and Rousseau, whose ideas he later incorporated into his own writings on penal reform. Previously somewhat apathetic, Beccaria was finally moved to write because of the prodding of his friends, the influence exerted upon him by his reading, and occasional visits to the prisons in Milan.

His first effort, an unimpressive book on currency reform, was followed by his only memorable work, *On Crimes and Punishments*, written when he was only twenty-six. First published anonymously because of Beccaria's fear of prosecution by Milanese political authorities, anonymity was quickly discarded when the reception of the treatise was positive. It was translated into French in 1766 and into English one year later. After the publication of the French translation, Beccaria was invited to come to Paris, the intellectual hub of the Enlightenment, where he was honored by members of Parisian intellectual society. Beccaria, unaccustomed to French society, made a bad impression and soon returned to Milan, where he spent his remaining days, first as a college professor and later as a public official. Having laid the groundwork for penal reform through his application of Enlightenment thought to the subject of physical punishment by society, Beccaria retired, leaving his successors to implement his theories in real situations.

On Crimes and Punishments is an indictment of, and an impassioned call for the reform of, the criminal justice and penal system which Beccaria believed then prevailed in Europe. Expressing a generally accepted premise of his day, he argued that just laws should be based upon reason and the laws of nature rather than upon custom and tradition. People, however, were suffering from laws composed of a blending of statutes dating back to the sixth century, including Roman law, the Justinian Code, and early German tribal law. The purpose of law was to protect society and guarantee the greatest happiness to the greatest number by preventing criminals from performing their deeds. Punishment should be in consonance with the severity of the crime, and since this was not the case in eighteenth century Europe, the whole scale of penalties was badly in need of revision.

Just and well-publicized punishments, Beccaria held, would deter people from committing crimes. This assumption was based upon the eighteenth century belief that men were, by nature, rational creatures. Therefore, a rational person, by knowing in advance the punishment for a particular crime, could weigh the possible benefits of a given crime against the severity of punishment, decide that the latter outweighed the former, and thus be deterred from committing that crime. Beccaria further argued that the certainty of punishment was much more important than its severity, that treatment of the imprisoned should be humane, and that judicial procedures should be carried out in public so that they might serve as a deterrent. He roundly condemned the use of torture on the grounds that it was inhumane, and was inherently unreliable as a means of arriving at the truth. In a brief concluding chapter, Beccaria summarizes his position with the following statement: "In order for punishment not to be, in every instance, an act of violence of one or many against a private citizen, it must be essentially public, prompt, necessary, the least possible in the given circumstances, proportionate to the crimes, dictated by the laws."

Beccaria begins his chapter on the

death penalty by defining it as ". . . the war of a nation against a citizen whose destruction it judges to be necessary or useful." Beccaria, determined to demonstrate that the death penalty is neither necessary nor useful, held that there are two reasons for believing it to be necessary. The first is to eliminate one who, even if deprived of his liberty, might endanger the security of the nation by fomenting revolution. In a well-governed state in which the government is supported by the consent of the people as a whole, such a necessity would not present itself. The other reason is that the death of one criminal might restrain others from committing crimes. History has shown, Beccaria asserts, that this is simply not the result, and thus the death penalty is unnecessary. But is it useful? Beccaria once again responds negatively, citing: ". . . it is not the intensity of punishment that has the greatest effect on the human spirit, but its duration." The greatest deterrent to the potential criminal is not achieved by forcing him to witness a public execution, for although that may make an initial forceful impression, it is momentary. Much more effective

is to witness the example of a man perpetually deprived of his liberty and required through hard labor to atone for his crime against society. "The advantage of penal servitude," Beccaria states, "is that it inspires terror in the spectator more than in the sufferer, for the former considers the entire sum of unhappy moments, while the latter is distracted from the thought of future misery by that of the present moment."

There is much in Beccaria's work that can be criticized. Through overgeneralization he at times exaggerates the abuses of the criminal justice and penal systems of his day. His conclusions are sometimes narrowly restricted by his slavish adherence to the now partially-discredited assumptions of Enlightenment philosophy. The treatise is also a one-sided argument; intended as such, it is subjective and lacking in supportive documentation. However, it remains one of the most influential works in Western literature. It has had a direct effect in producing badly needed criminal justice and penal reforms, and many of its arguments are still voiced by those favoring further reform.

Black, Charles L., Jr. *Capital Punishment: The Inevitability of Caprice and Mistake*. New York: W. W. Norton and Company, 1974.

Charles L. Black is Luce Professor of Jurisprudence at Yale University, and has also taught at the Yale Law School and at Yale College. He has published many books on constitutional law; he is the coauthor of the standard treatise on American law of Admiralty; and he has often argued cases before the United States Su-

preme Court. Written after the United States Supreme Court's decision in *Furman* v. *Georgia* but before *Gregg* v. *Georgia*, his *Capital Punishment: The Inevitability of Caprice and Mistake*, as the subtitle indicates, is an attack on capital punishment on the very grounds indicated by the Supreme Court in 1972. In the process

Black also seeks to discredit two of the other reasons that have been advanced to justify the death penalty: retribution and deterrence. In addition, Black would be dissatisfied also with the Supreme Court's ruling in *Gregg* v. *Georgia*, for he holds that no amount of safeguards can guarantee that an innocent person will not suffer, and that all guilty persons will suffer the same punishment at the hands of the courts.

Black's central thesis is that the complex series of decisions that have to be made by the legal system from the time the accused criminal is arrested to the time he is executed is so open to mistake, and the standards governing these choices are so vague or nonexistent as to render them arbitrary, that it is unthinkable to impose the death sentence on anyone. Mistakes and arbitrariness ". . . are not fringe problems, susceptible to being mopped up by refinements in concept and technique, but are at the very heart of the matter and are insoluble by any methods now known or now foreseeable." Had Black written after *Gregg* v. *Georgia*, he would have found the state of Georgia's statutory revisions inadequate and the United States Supreme Court's decision unacceptable. He notes, quite correctly, that the death penalty is unique to all other penalties. It is unique because it provides for extinction; it creates the unique agony of anticipating extinction; it destroys all hope; and it is, most of all, irrev-ocable. The innocent person convicted wrongly can be compensated for all other wrongful punishments but not for death. The greater the punishment, the greater the standards of clarity and certainty have to be. In the case of death the standards must be perfect, which is impossible.

The author devotes the greater part of his book to demonstrating the various points in the legal process at which mistakes and arbitrariness can exist even under the most favorable conditions. He devotes great attention to the decisions that must be made by the prosecutor in charging the accused; the plea-bargaining process when the most skillful defense attorney is needed; the trial itself and the verdict; the wide degree of latitude left to the jury or judge in the choice of sentences; the postsentencing process such as appeals and clemency, and the disadvantages inherent in the poverty or race of the accused. Here he notes the usual inability of the accused to secure the best counsel because of lack of funds and the significance of conscious and unconscious prejudice.

Black has provided a tightly argued treatise against capital punishment. However, it is an argument, not a history, and should be balanced with a contrary opinion. The work would also have benefited from documentation, although this cannot be expected from what is essentially a personal essay. — *J.S.A.*

Additional Recommended Reading

Bedau, Hugo Adam, ed. *The Death Penalty in America: An Anthology*. Chicago: Aldine Publishing Company, 1968. A collection of writings on the death penalty with a helpful bibliography.

Cohen, Bernard Lande. *Law Without Order: Capital Punishment and the Liberals*. New Rochelle, N.Y.: Arlington House, 1970. A forceful argument in favor of the death penalty by a respected lawyer, businessman, and author.

Isenberg, Irwin, ed. *The Death Penalty*. New York: The H. W. Wilson Company, 1977. A helpful compilation of recent writings on the constitutional, legal, ethical, and philosophical aspects of capital punishment, taken from a wide variety of sources, mainly periodicals.

McCafferty, James, ed. *Capital Punishment*. Chicago: Aldine-Atherton, 1972. A fairly recent collection of essays and lectures on the subject.

St. John-Stevas, Norman. *The Right to Life*. New York: Holt, Rinehart and Winston, 1964. The scope of this book is broad since it treats euthanasia, abortion, and suicide as well as capital punishment.

THE BICENTENNIAL CELEBRATION

Type of event: Cultural: United States celebrates her two hundredth birthday
Time: July 4, 1976
Locale: The United States

Principal personages:

ELIZABETH II (1926-   ), Queen of Great Britain who with Prince Philip, Duke of Edinburgh, spent six days touring the United States in honor of the Bicentennial and in Philadelphia, presented a Bicentennial Bell as a birthday gift

ARTHUR FIEDLER (1894-1979), celebrated conductor of the Boston Pops Orchestra who staged a July 4th concert on the banks of the Charles river featuring the "1812 Overture"

GERALD RUDOLPH FORD (1913-   ), thirty-eighth President of the United States and chief executive during the Bicentennial

LYNDON BAINES JOHNSON (1908-1973), thirty-sixth President of the United States (1963-1969) who established the American Revolution Bicentennial Commission (ARBC) in 1966

JOHN W. WARNER (1927-   ), head of the Federal American Revolution Bicentennial Administration

Summary of Event

America welcomed her Bicentennial day in a joyous mood, with renewed hope for the future of the nation. Watergate was over, and most of its ghosts had been forgotten. The recessions, racial strife, wars, energy shortages, assassinations, and presidential crises that plagued America for thirteen years were behind us, leaving a revitalized people to celebrate July 4, 1976.

America's Bicentennial day officially began in a tiny Maine potato-growing town where, at 4:31 A.M., the sun rose on a sleeping continent. At Mars Hill Mountain, National Guardsmen took part in a flag-raising ceremony and an accompanying fifty-gun salute that set the stage for the many activities to follow from coast to coast.

Boston, the cradle of American liberty, led the impressive salute to the United States' first two hundred years. On the banks of the Charles river, Arthur Fiedler's Boston Pops Orchestra performed for a crowd of 40,000 people. The grand finale of the program was Tchaikovsky's "1812 Overture," which had its own climax: five howitzers echoed forty blasts, eighty bells in a nearby church rang out, and fireworks, the gift of a local philanthropist, illuminated the sky for twenty-three minutes.

New York surpassed Boston in her spectacular display. 225 tall ships, sixteen of them among the world's larg-

1287

est, journeyed from thirty nations and filled the New York harbor for a magnificent Bicentennial parade, part of "Operation Sail." From the harbor's Verrazano-Narrows Bridge, all ships were in full view of the largest American flag ever lofted—a 193 by 366½-foot display that was crafted in Massachusetts at a cost of $45,000. The parade began at noon, leaving the harbor and proceeding up the Hudson River to the reviewing ship, *U.S.S. Forrestal*. At the reviewing stand, each craft raised sail in triumphant salute to America. Witnessing the majestic sight were the dignitaries aboard the *Forrestal*: Secretary of State Henry Kissinger, Commerce Secretary Elliot Richardson, Princess Grace of Monaco, and Congresswoman Bella Abzug of New York. A band played "Hail to the Chief" and "The Star Spangled Banner" as President Gerald Ford's helicopter landed on board. President Ford tolled the ship's Bicentennial bell thirteen times in honor of the original colonies. Nationwide, other bells joined in as the parade continued to the George Washington Bridge and back through Manhattan. Viewing the extravaganza were five million spectators on the New York and New Jersey sides of the river. Celebrants paid twenty-five dollars per bleacher seat in a South Manhattan landfill, while others cheered from the Wall Street towers, which were opened to friends and employees for the occasion. The parade's end was signaled by a fireworks exhibition over the Statue of Liberty to the delight of cheering throngs.

More than a million people celebrated in Washington, D.C., where parades, traffic jams, and fireworks were prominent features of the day. Thirty-three and a half tons of fireworks were detonated at four locations around the Washington Monument, the Tidal Basin, and the Lincoln Memorial. The $200,000 fireworks display was conceived by *Établissement Ruggieri*, a French firm which had managed a fireworks exhibition witnessed by Thomas Jefferson in 1786. As a further Bicentennial commemorative, the Declaration of Independence was on display in the nation's capital for seventy-six hours, and was read to the assembled crowd. Washington was also the site of the dedication of the new Air and Space Museum and the Smithsonian Institution's Centennial Exhibition of 1876.

Other demonstrations were part of Philadelphia's celebration, where President Ford addressed an audience in front of Independence Hall, and many historic sites were open for public inspection. A five-hour parade marched down a main street, which wore a newly painted coat of red, white, and blue and "76" for the occasion. Parading into nearby Valley Forge on July 3, and addressed by President Ford on July 4, were sixty Conestoga wagons and two thousand travelers from all of the fifty states.

In Baltimore, Maryland, thirty thousand people witnessed a reenactment of the Fort McHenry bombing, the occasion for Francis Scott Key's "The Star Spangled Banner" in 1814. There was also an authentic dramatization of the Battle of Gettysburg by volunteer armies in Pennsylvania.

Celebrations, however, were by no means limited to major cities. From parades to fireworks, pie-eating contests, frog-jumping marathons, balloon races, bike parades, and the swearing in of new American citizens, bits of Americana were celebrated in regional ways. While these jubilees lacked the glamor of the tall ships on the Hudson and the excitement of Tchaikovsky on the Charles river, they were no less characterized by enthusiasm.

The Bicentennial did not begin and end with the day of July 4, 1976, but encompassed an entire year. John W. Warner, head of the Federal American Revolution Bicentennial Administration, called the celebration "the most massive volunteer undertaking in peacetime America." Years were given to its planning and preparation, by nations as well as by individuals. Twelve residents of a Kansas nursing home wove a commemorative tapestry depicting an American eagle and presented their six-weeks' effort to the White House. An Atlanta, Georgia, man spent a thousand hours engraving a Marlin rifle with significant Americana: depictions of the moon landing, the Liberty Bell, Abraham Lincoln. A Girl Scout troop in Wisconsin re-created the Declaration of Independence in miniature macaroni letters. In the state of Washington, an elementary school community constructed a pioneer village. Time capsules were planned and sealed, not to be opened until America's Tricentennial.

Not only in America were United States citizens celebrating. In West Germany, the United States Ambassador, Martin Hillenbrand, held a Bicentennial reception; and the American government underwrote an exhibition featuring two hundred years of American art. Americans in England were able to attend a John Philip Sousa concert, a fireworks display, and a religious service at George Washington's ancestral home. In France, the American School of Paris held a Bicentennial picnic. Americans in Belgium and Rome picnicked, too, on hot dogs, ice cream, corn-on-the-cob, beer, and soda pop.

While some remained in Europe for the celebration, others crossed oceans to celebrate in the United States. The most notable visitors to the nation were Queen Elizabeth II of Great Britain and her husband, Prince Philip, whose six-day American tour included a presentation in Philadelphia of a seven-ton Bicentennial Bell inscribed "Let Freedom Ring." Other foreign visitors included Queen Margrethe II of Denmark, President Valéry Giscard d'Estaing and his wife of France, King Carl XVI Gustaf of Sweden, King Baudouin and Queen Fabiola of Belgium, King Hussein of Jordan, and King Juan Carlos I and Queen Sophia of Spain. The impressive list of dignitaries numbered several dozen by the end of America's Bicentennial year.

The Bicentennial can best be labeled an exciting, spectacular, and extravagant birthday party that spanned the American continent. Everyone celebrated the achievements of the past, and almost everyone looked to the future with optimism. As President Gerald Ford said, "I have not the slightest doubt that our Third Century will be yet more glorious than our first 200 years." America's Tricentennial celebration will undoubtedly surpass the pagean-try of America's Bicentennial.

Pertinent Literature

Hartje, Robert G. *Bicentennial USA: Pathways to Celebration.* Nashville: The American Association for State and Local History, 1973.

Because Hartje felt strongly that the Bicentennial was a "once-in-a-lifetime opportunity for Americans," he undertook a study of centennial celebrations, compiling a list of what most successful commemoratives have in common. He also explored the roots of America's celebrations to honor the signing of the Declaration of Independence, as well as presenting the plans under way as long ago as 1973 for the Bicentennial. While Hartje intended his study to be used by regional, state, and local planners as they prepared for July 4, 1976, it is also useful now. Not only is this study a history of America's Bicentennial planning, it is also a yardstick by which Americans can measure the success of their Bicentennial celebration and explain why, perhaps, they felt the day to be either so memorable, or so ordinary. Hartje's study ponders why Americans might or might not become keenly involved in the festivities. Would America's Bicentennial be all that it might be? Would it meet all the criteria for a meaningful celebration? Would Bicentennial planners "recognize man's search for identity, his needs for festivity, and his innate urge to create"? Would the Bicentennial be merely a social affair, or would it reawaken the deep spirit of patriotism inspired by the original revolution?

July 4, 1776, has been celebrated with fireworks, speeches, and festiv-ities since the early nineteenth century; Federal troops even paused in the middle of the Civil War to commemorate the day. John Adams originally suggested a day of homage, and a 1783 Boston town meeting encouraged the same. When, on July 4, 1826, John Adams and Thomas Jefferson died, fifty years after the Declaration of Independence, further significance was attached to the day.

America's first Centennial celebration, July 4, 1876, did more than commemorate the signing of the Declaration of Independence: it also celebrated one hundred years of American achievement. By 1876, America had acquired international status and had made strides in science and art, and was well on the way to becoming an industrial power. The nation celebrated with an exposition in Philadelphia, the "highlight of a year of glamorous and sometimes meaningful pageantry."

As early as July 4, 1966, America's Bicentennial planning began when President Lyndon Johnson established the American Revolution Bicentennial Commission (ARBC) "to plan, encourage, develop, and coordinate the commemoration of the American Revolution Bicentennial." On July 3, 1971, President Richard Nixon, Chief Justice Warren Burger, and House Speaker Carl Albert met at the National Archives to mark the beginning of the Bicentennial Era in a nationally televised ceremony.

America had ten years from the establishment of the ARBC to plan her national birthday. The celebration would commemorate more than America's aging; it would signify achievement and growth and remind Americans that past, present, and future are inseparable. In only a decade, America would have to prepare for an occasion that, because of its very nature, must be far more significant than mere pageantry.

Hartje seeks to answer the question "Where should America begin as she plans?" His study of successful commemoratives, from the Canadian Centennial to the Civil War Centennial to the New Jersey Tercentenary to local celebrations, is America's answer to that question. Significantly, Hartje found common factors in all successful celebrations: a historical group to undertake education and "historical understanding"; a citizen's group to give the celebration firm direction; economic resources; the presence of civic pride; a historical event of local significance to unify the local with the greater historical occasion; and cooperative public relations activities.

In guiding America as she planned her Bicentennial, Hartje's book suggested that once the above six criteria have been secured, programs, projects, and events need to be balanced among five general categories. The most meaningful celebrations have covered the areas of heritage, ethnic affairs, fine arts, service, and pageantry, with heritage being the most important. In all programs, in all areas, on local, state, and national levels, however, personal involvement and commitment are essential ingredients to make any of the above criteria and guidelines workable.

How well did America measure up to Hartje's standards? Heritage was definitely emphasized, as in the reading of the Declaration of Independence in Washington and the opening of historic sites in Philadelphia. Local celebrations abounded in regional and ethnic flavor, as in the Calaveras County frog-jumping contest. In Philadelphia, the Afro-American Historical and Cultural Museum was opened, a short distance from Independence Hall. America's achievements in the fine arts were on view, from the American painting exhibit in West Germany to symphony concerts in London and Boston. Service and community action programs were undertaken, from local and national beautification programs to the re-creating of a pioneer village in the state of Washington. Pageantry, of course, was plentiful. The tall ships, fireworks, and parades were probably the most memorable parts of the Bicentennial celebration for very young Americans. How well did America measure up to Hartje's expectations? She followed his guidelines well, and undoubtedly *Bicentennial USA* contributed to the success of America's two hundredth birthday.

Linton, Calvin D., ed. *The Bicentennial Almanac.* Nashville: Thomas Nelson, 1975.

The Bicentennial Almanac is an important tool for the study of the Bicentennial celebration of 1976, for it is only through a knowledge of history that Americans can comprehend the richness of the legacy left them by the signers of the Declaration of Independence. *The Bicentennial Almanac* is indeed an almanac in the traditional sense of the word. It is complete with official portraits of thirty-eight United States presidents and pictures of the signers of the Declaration of Independence. Reprints of the Declaration of Independence and the Constitution, complete with amendments, comprise part of the work. The real value of the volume, however, lies in its excellent synopsis of events year by year, month by month, and sometimes day by day, from 1776 through the spring of 1975, the official opening of the Bicentennial Era.

To understand the significance of the Bicentennial, the "1776" entry must be read. It was in this year that Thomas Paine's *Common Sense* converted multitudes to the revolutionary cause. It was also in 1776 that the Thomas Jefferson draft of the Declaration of Independence was accepted, after which time, the almanac reports, battles became more intense. Students of the Bicentennial will want to read the entries up to 1789, the year in which the real impact of the Declaration of Independence began to be felt worldwide.

The Bicentennial celebration can be further appreciated through a study of 1876, America's Centennial year. The almanac's "1876" entry is complete with a photograph of the Horticultural Hall in Philadelphia, home of the Centennial Exposition that included entries from fifty countries. The display was largely one of American ingenuity, however, as the telephone, typewriter, and refrigerator car were featured. The almanac reveals, however, that the Centennial year was not solely a time of national pride in industrial achievement; it was also a time of national strife. The presidential contest between Samuel Tilden and Rutherford Hayes was filled with dispute and clouded the year. The Sioux and the federal government were at war and the Battle of Little Bighorn was fought. Political corruption on all levels was abundant. But there was a brighter side to the Centennial year, too. Not only had America become an industrial power, but she also had inventors such as Alexander Graham Bell, who that year patented his telephone. Furthermore, in 1876 America expanded her own territory by admitting Colorado into the union.

Like the year of the Centennial, the years preceding America's Bicentennial were difficult ones, filled with the tension of race riots, assassinations, Watergate, presidential collapse, and economic instability. However, as America entered her Bicentennial Era, Watergate had vanished, inflation was being attacked, and the U.S.S.R. and the United States were cooperating on a joint space project.

The Bicentennial Almanac is an attempt to re-create factually United States history; but it does more than that. It suggests the mood that surrounded the event, giving the reader an accurate portrayal of the happening as well as its spirit. While the student of the Bicentennial will want to skip lightly over most of the contents, he will also want to concentrate on certain entries that illuminate Amer-

ica's beginning, her Centennial year,   tennial. — *C.W.T.*
and the years approaching her Bicen-

Additional Recommended Reading

Brown, Dee. *The Year of the Century: 1876.* New York: Charles Scribner's Sons, 1966. An exploration of the year of America's Centennial celebration.

Randel, William P. *Centennial: American Life in 1876.* Philadelphia: Chilton Book Company, 1969. Provides a look at the American people and how they celebrated their Centennial.

"The Best Birthday," in *Newsweek.* LXXXVIII (July 19, 1976), pp. 48-55. A picture essay of the fireworks, tall ships, parades, and battles worth investigating for its detailed photographic and journalistic look at how America celebrated her two hundredth birthday.

"Birthday Issue," in *Time.* CVIII (July 5, 1976), pp. 8-90. A close-up look at "The Big 200th Bash" which has exceptional photo coverage.

"Special 1776 Issue," in *Time.* CV (July 4, 1776), pp. 3-77. A combination of history and journalism in news magazine format, this issue is devoted to reporting on the first days of July, 1776.

"Special Bicentennial Issue," in *Time.* CVII (September 26, 1789), pp. 3-71. Written as a sequel to the "1776 Issue," this special issue reports the news as it might have been reported in 1789, the year the Declaration of Independence began to have meaning for America and the world. It provides excellent insight into what the Bicentennial really means.

"Special Bicentennial Supplement," in *U.S. News & World Report.* LXXXI (July 5, 1976), pp. 37-80. A report which looks ahead into the third century with predictions by economists, sociologists, and politicians, and includes an essay by Gerald Ford.

"This Land of Ours," in *National Geographic.* CL (July, 1976), pp. 1-158. A beautifully illustrated and narrated look at America then, now, and in the future which includes "A First American's View" and "How Are We Using Our Land?"

THE *VIKING* LANDINGS ON MARS

Type of event: Scientific: controlled unmanned soft landings on a distant planet
Time: July 20, and September 3, 1976
Locale: Mars

Principal personages:
JAMES MARTIN, *Viking* Project Manager
MICHAEL CARR, head of the *Orbiter* Imaging Team
HUGH H. KIEFFER, head of the Thermal Mapping Team
THOMAS MUTCH, head of the *Lander* Imaging Team
HAROLD P. KLEIN, head of the *Viking* Biology Team

Summary of Event

Mars, the last of the four inner or terrestrial planets, appears habitable when viewed from earth. White polar caps, dark regions of possible organic life, and myriad canals crisscrossing a red glowing surface conjure up visions of a vegetated and volcanic landscape of abundant waterways. However, the American *Mariner IX* and twin *Viking* probes revealed Mars as a rock-strewn, channeled and cratered, cold, dry world, inhospitable to macroscopic life.

The most detailed survey of the Martian globe was made by *Mariner IX* in 1971; but clearer topographic pictures were relayed by the *Viking* probes five years later. Fewer dust storms and improved camera imaging, developed under the guidance of Dr. Thomas Mutch, head of the Thermal Mapping Team, and Michael Carr, head of the *Orbiter* Imaging Team, enabled the *Vikings* to assemble sharp pictures of craters, channels, mesas, and sand drifts at different times of day and night. Color accuracy in the pictures beamed back by the landing crafts was good and established the hue of the Martian sky as a salmon pink. None of

the previous fly-by and orbital missions to Mars had captured surface detail relief in color. *Viking* Project Manager James Martin was very gratified with the results.

Conceived in the mid-1960's for post-*Mariner* missions, the *Vikings* were named after Norse explorers who allegedly visited the Americas five hundred years before Columbus. Each identical craft consisted of two parts, an *Orbiter* and a *Lander*. Weighing less than a ton each, the *Orbiter* measured eight feet across and 10.8 feet high, while the *Lander* measured ten feet across and seven feet high. They were considered small-dimensional craft and were solar-powered through space. Both parts traveled together across four hundred million miles of interplanetary space into closed Martian orbit. The *Lander* separated from the *Orbiter* upon electronic command from earth and gently descended to a preselected landing site. All automatic processes worked well, although there were some temporary transmission relay problems within the *Viking II Orbiter*. On July 20, 1976, the first *Lander* touched ground and beamed back the

1294

first close-up picture of Mars one minute later which was received on earth after a nineteen-minute signal reception delay. The second *Lander* set down successfully on a rougher surface on September 3, 1976, and American scientists congratulated themselves on an unprecedented political as well as aerospace achievement.

Although the *Orbiter* was easy to construct, since it was but an improved and modified *Mariner*-type craft with similar Guidance and Attitude Control Electronics Systems, the *Lander* had to be specially designed. The existence of a Martian atmosphere necessitated the modification of equipment used in the lunar landings, and the need for on-board laboratories to detect native microbes compounded developmental difficulties.

When completed and vigorously sterilized, the *Orbiters* and *Landers* were expected to carry out separate programmed operations. The primary responsibility of each *Orbiter* was to pinpoint the safest resting site for the *Lander* and then to relay *Lander* transmissions, map the surface temperature (a procedure developed under the auspices of Dr. Hugh H. Kieffer, head of the Thermal Mapping Team), monitor atmospheric water vapor content, and photograph the global surface. Photographs were also made of Phobos and Deimos, the two Martian moons. *Orbiter I* especially scanned the western slopes of the Chryse Planitia region of the Southern Hemisphere, the targeted landing area for *Lander I*. *Orbiter II* investigated the vast plains of Utopia Planitia in the Northern Hemisphere, a latitude outside the radar tracking range at Arecibo, Puerto Rico. Selecting an ideal location was crucial since the *Landers* were delicately constructed and could rupture if they did not land smoothly and upright on level ground. The great abundance of rocks on Mars made any landing attempt risky.

After separation from the *Orbiter*, the *Lander* descended onto Mars encapsulated in a conical, aluminum alloy aero-shell and a base cover. Not until the atmosphere was felt at about 150 miles above ground did the capsule turn so that the aero-shell and heat shield faced the direction of travel. This maneuver enabled the parachute to be properly deployed at nineteen thousand feet, when the aero-shell could be discarded and the craft slowed significantly. At about 3,900 feet, the parachute was jettisoned, the three *Lander* legs were extended, and three descent engines were fired. By the final stage, *Lander* speed was between five to six miles per hour, an ideal speed for soft-surface landing. Descent onto the Martian surface was more complicated than that onto earth's moon because Mars has an atmosphere.

Since the *Lander* passed through the entire Martian atmosphere, instruments were attached to the aero-shell to collect scientific data which were relayed immediately to earth. The most important post-landing tasks were to find a sample of Martian life and then to gather data on the peculiar properties of the Martian rocks, soil, and atmosphere. Various biological, geological, mineralogical, magnetic, and meterological experiments were conducted with major interest focused on the three soil experiments that tested for biological activity. These three experiments were the particular concern of Dr. Harold P. Klein, the head of the *Viking* Biology Team.

The first experiment, Pyrolitic Release, tested the soil under Martian conditions. A sample was treated with artificial light and carbon dioxide from earth which contained radioactive carbon-14 particles, a detectable tracer. A Martian atmosphere was simulated inside a closed chamber for five days where the treated soil sample was heated to induce photosynthesis. An incubation period followed when the soil was kept in the dark; carbon dioxide molecules were then flushed away and the sample reheated. Theoretically, organic compounds or pyrolysis should have broken up and produced carbon dioxide which could be identified through the release of carbon-14. Radioactivity was detected, but in wildly fluctuating concentrations, a puzzling, unexpected reaction that made all results inconclusive.

The second experiment, Labelled Release, assumed that Martian organisms might prefer earth conditions. A soil sample was moistened with a nutrient solution of simple carbon substances and carbon-14 in water. The chamber was void of light and the atmosphere above was monitored for radioactivity which would occur if live organisms released a gas containing carbon-14. Carbon-14 was detected but the levels behaved unpredictably. Consequently, neither life nor the absence of life could be confirmed.

The last experiment tested for a gas exchange and assumed that Martian life would be similar to terrestrial. It was carried out in the dark but did not involve carbon-14. Based on the principle that living organisms exchange gases with the atmosphere, a soil sample treated with a nutrient was tested to see if it would release gases to alter the atmosphere inside the closed chamber. A water solution at the base of the chamber first released water vapor to the sample, then wetted it. Results indicated a gas exchange initially, but the wetted sample released no oxygen, a surprising reaction and untypical of earth soil. As a result, organic compounds could neither be detected nor ruled out. Chemical reactions definitely took place, but not in a way expected of life. The best summarizing statement that could be made was that Mars may have only the potential to support life.

All soil samples were collected by a scoop or cup attached to the end of a retractable arm on the *Lander* for analysis on board. While the life-seeking experiments proved inconclusive, other experiments yielded hard data. The soil proved comparable to earth's in its high concentrations of silicon and oxygen, but richer in iron and sulfur and poorer in aluminum, sodium, and potassium. The higher iron content probably gives the surface its rusty hue. Water was evident in the form of permafrost (the *Orbiters* identified permafrost even at the equator), but not in the liquid state. However, past fluvial action was surmised by *Orbiter* pictures of the intricate tributary nature of the Martian channels. Much of the soil was magnetic, and elements with atomic numbers higher than sodium were plentiful.

Carbon dioxide was the most abundant gas found in the atmosphere and was followed in low percentages by nitrogen, argon, and traces of oxygen and water vapor, an unbreathable mixture for humans. The weather was frigid with low surface pressure. Aeolian action which resulted in dust storms that occasionally swept around the planet was not corrosive or severe in force though some material was windblown. From all appearances, Mars seemed locked in an ice age.

Because the *Landers* reported data based on landing site terrain, it is possible that some of the information, for example the salient topographic details, may not be typical of the entire globe. The data relayed from both sites were basically the same; though there were unique bedrock outcrops near *Lander I*, most of the rocks around *Lander II* were pitted while only a few pitted rocks were detected around *Lander I*. Such minor dissimilarities may be the only distinguishable local features.

In general, Mars's surface seems to be the product of periods of volcanism. Sand concentration is low, while a thin veneer of dust envelops the planet. Water once flowed abundantly along now dried-up waterways. Much of that water is locked up in the Martian poles and in the ground as permafrost. A denser atmosphere once existed, which could exist again.

While the *Vikings* transmitted billions of bits of information, more than any previous robot probes, they raised and left unanswered questions. In addition, they did not explore Mars's interior. Future unmanned missions to Mars may resolve some of the puzzles; for the present, however, Mars and its complex history remain an enigma.

Pertinent Literature

Arvidson, Raymond E., *et al.* "The Surface of Mars," in *Scientific American.* CCXXXVIII (March, 1978), pp. 76-89.

Considerable geological data were collected by the *Mariner IX* and two *Viking* probes to Mars. In this very analytical article, the authors, by interpreting the data, attempt to explain how the Martian surface was formed. Many comparisons are made between Martian terrain and that of the earth and earth's moon. The hypotheses presented still remain to be verified though they comprise the best scientific opinions on the subject based on current information.

Mariner IX's global coverage revealed that the planet is divided into two distinct hemispheres: a rugged, heavily cratered and channeled Southern Hemisphere, and a lightly cratered, volcanic Northern Hemisphere. Adding to this knowledge, the *Viking Orbiters* revealed smooth crater definition, perhaps the result of numerous ancient lava flows. Lunar craters are more sharply defined, but appear to be of comparable age, which strongly suggests that about half of Mars consists of larger land forms unchanged for billions of years.

These craters were probably formed by interstellar debris left over from the formation of the solar system, because for the most part there is no evidence of recent high velocity impact cratering from meteorites. The Martian atmosphere, though very thin, could still break up meteors before they hit the surface, while earth's moon has no such shield.

While cratering is extensive, fluvial action was probably the most important agent in shaping the Martian surface. The many crisscrossed channels observed by *Mariner IX* were photographed with much greater clarity by *Viking* vidicon cameras which beamed back images of an extensive and integrated drainage system. Only rain runoff and polar melting could have produced such an elaborate network. Further analysis indicated that since the present thin atmosphere with its low surface pressure could not support running water, Mars must have had a denser atmosphere in the past. This theory is supported by *Orbiter* evidence of the significant amount of water ice frozen at Mars's poles. Since the ice caps are not composed of carbon dioxide as had been conjectured from the *Mariner IX* data, water could once again flow on Mars under the proper conditions. The planet is not as dead nor as lunar-featured as originally suspected.

Viking also updated *Mariner* reports on wind erosion. Crisp, topographic details captured by *Orbiter* and *Lander* images indicated little breakdown of rock and redistribution of debris, though dust was carried away by the wind. While dust storms often sweep around the planet (particularly after perihelion), only small and light particles appear to be transported by the wind. Bedrock and darker, less-weathered material are exposed by movement of dust, but these outcrops do not appear to erode—much unlike such exposures on earth. Winds on Mars may not be as severe as previously conjectured, and sand deposits may stay put because particle aggregates are not as easily transported as sand on earth. The layering of sand and water ice at the Martian North Pole strongly supports this idea. Sand may gather in dunes, but not be light enough to be weathered. All results demonstrate that Mars's climatic history was certainly dissimilar to earth's.

Soil samples analyzed on board the *Viking Landers* and observed in *Lander* vicinity emphasized further the uniqueness of Mars's history. The rocks and soil from both sites were of similar spectral shape and mineral composition and were covered with a smooth dust. They appeared to be volcanic in origin and were rich in magnesium and iron. One convincing theory is that they were derived from mafic igneous rocks that crystallized from a large melt. Polygonal surface fracturing indicated repeated water evaporation and the formation of what is known on earth as duricrust. However, at this time it is not possible to determine the age of the planet's terrain with certainty based on the varied accumulated evidence, nor how much material is blown from one hemisphere to another.

The authors point out that two distinct landing sites were selected by *Viking* planners so that Mars's history could be studied in greater complexity. Ironically, while surface dissimilarities were confirmed, no conclusions could be reached on direction of wind currents though streaking of fine grained material on the lee side of most rocks indicated a north to south airflow. The Chryse Planitia, *Lander I*'s base in the Southern Hemisphere, compared to a rocky earth desert, while the Utopia Planitia in the Northern Hemisphere was more a vast plain. Such dissimilarities were not significant enough data to shed light on the planet's puzzling thermal history and hypothetical periods of weather fluctuations.

The abundance of unanswered questions has led the authors to conclude that further exploration of Mars is needed. While certain evolutionary and geological processes are comparable enough to earth's and our moon's to provide for meaningful evaluations, Mars's unique history can only be conjectured about. Scientists need samples of Martian materials at hand and data about Mars's interior to understand why the planet's appearance is so different from the earth's.

Washburn, Mark. *Mars at Last*. New York: G. P. Putnam's Sons, 1977.

In *Mars at Last*, Mark Washburn chronicles the history of man's observations of Mars. Dwelling on man's long fascination with the red planet, he highlights the speculations of early astronomers such as Galileo and Copernicus and the imaginings of science fiction writers. The continuum climaxes with a description and competent appraisal of the 1976 twin *Viking* missions. Washburn's often journalistic style is peppered with popularly written biographical sketches, and he surveys the topic well in a very readable format that summarizes fact and fiction regarding Mars.

In Part IV, "Visit to a Small Planet," the author dramatically re-creates the events and engineering feats leading up to the actual *Viking* landings, then summarizes and appraises vehicle operations and data collected.

According to Washburn, *Viking* was the brainchild of a committee of NASA planners who were very economy-minded. The Jet Propulsion Laboratory designed and constructed the *Orbiter* while the prime contractor for the *Lander* was Martin-Marietta of Denver. The biology experiments carried out by both *Landers* were the hardest to develop, but crucial for project support. Various key people worked diligently, both in the political and scientific spheres, to make the *Viking* launches a reality.

While similar in construction to the early *Mariner* probes, the *Viking Orbiter* was a more sophisticated craft. Equipped with a *Mariner*-type imaging system, two television cameras mounted side by side on a movable scan platform, the *Orbiter* assembled pictures via an electron beam and vidicon tube. Improved computer interpretation and the addition of color filtering yielded clearer and more accurate pictures than previously. Also, a Mars Atmospheric Water Detector and an Infrared Thermal Mapper enabled scientists to deduce more about the nature of the Martian surface.

The *Lander*, the first robot probe to visit another planet, was a scientific triumph. Small in size and equipped with delicate instrumentation, it was rigorously sterilized and had to be protected from temperatures as high as 2,700 degrees Fahrenheit. After a complex descent to the Martian surface, it had to keep in touch with earth through a UHF relay link with the *Orbiter* and a direct S-Bank link with earth. Everything on board had to be controlled by a guidance, control, and sequencing computer. A different imaging system from the *Orbiter*'s had to be constructed that could rotate 360 degrees and capture an entire panorama. All these specifications were met, and both *Landers* performed beautifully despite all Mission Control apprehension and the seismometer failure on *Lander I*.

After the final mating of a *Viking Orbiter* and *Lander*, a *Titan III-C* missile launched the probe from Cape Kennedy. *Viking* was tracked by radio and solar-powered by panels that also acted like sails in the solar wind. The probe used a visual as well as a radio navigational system. The visual system was important in keeping the spaceship on trajectory, providing an alternate contact frequency, and determining a safe ground base for the *Lander*. Earth-based radar reduced hazard possibility by monitoring the flight path area for obstacles.

The author's detailing of the actual *Viking* orbiting of Mars and the *Lander*'s descents are as competent as other reports, and even more entertaining. A play-by-play account that captures the anxiety and tenseness of NASA personnel gives the layman a feeling of the mission's complexity. This factor increases the significance of the experiments performed and data received.

While searching for life or conducting other scientific investigations, both *Landers* carried on unprecedented operations that proved Mars to be a much more different world than our own. Dry and very cold with some seismic activity, but with no detectable biological life, the planet is both somewhat terrestrial and somewhat lunar but also uniquely Martian in appearance. Washburn briefly describes the experiments and conclusions that attempt to solve any surface anomaly; he includes engaging speculation on the types of Martian probes that will attempt to answer specifics. Such imaginative, visionary treatment makes for a pleasantly informative introduction to the planet of Mars. — *A.C.R.*

Additional Recommended Reading

Asimov, Isaac. *Mars, the Red Planet*. New York: Lothrop, Lee & Shepherd, 1977. Covers human interest in Mars from the speculations of early man to the revelations of the two *Viking* probes, focusing much attention on the significance of the *Mariner* missions.

Bradbury, Ray, *et al. Mars and the Mind of Man*. New York: Harper & Row Publishers, 1973. An intriguing philosophical approach to the subject.

Moore, Patrick. *Guide to Mars*. New York: W. W. Norton and Company, 1977. A celebrated astronomer overviews telescopic observations of Mars throughout history and summarizes the findings of interplanetary probes.

Sagan, Carl. *The Cosmic Connection: An Extraterrestrial Perspective*. Garden City, N.Y.: Doubleday & Company, 1973. A famous interstellar researcher ponders the mysteries of the red planet.

ELECTION OF CARTER TO THE PRESIDENCY IN 1976

Type of event: Political: election of a president
Time: November, 1976
Locale: The United States

Principal personages:
JIMMY (JAMES EARL) CARTER (1924-   ), former governor of Georgia and Democratic presidential nominee
GERALD RUDOLPH FORD (1913-   ), thirty-eighth President of the United States and Republican presidential nominee
RONALD WILSON REAGAN (1911-   ), former governor of California

Summary of Event

Jimmy Carter took the presidency from Gerald Ford by a popular vote margin of only two percent—the same figure that one year earlier represented the miniscule proportion of Democrats who preferred the former Georgia governor as their party's presidential nominee. It was the first time that an incumbent president had been defeated in forty-four years. Carter had come a long way, indeed; but just barely. Not only did Carter receive a bare majority of the popular vote and carry a minority of the states, he gained a mere margin of fifty-six electoral votes. It was the narrowest victory since Woodrow Wilson defeated Charles Evans Hughes by twenty-three electoral votes in 1916.

The very geography of the electoral vote seemed to reflect this narrow victory by presenting a symmetrical picture of a nation split roughly down the middle, with a solid South opposing a granite West. Yet the closeness of the national vote was really a closeness found mostly within rather than between the states. Hence, relatively slight shifts of the popular vote in a few states could easily have altered the election results substantially. Thus, for example, Martin Plissner conjectures that—in view of the facts that first, Eugene McCarthy's vote in Iowa, Maine, Oklahoma, and Oregon was greater than Ford's plurality over Carter, and second, polls have consistently shown the great majority of McCarthy's support coming from Democrats—the Georgian would very likely have carried at least Oregon and Maine if McCarthy had not run there, and possibly Iowa and Oklahoma also. But this conjecture neglects to consider whom these McCarthy Democrats preferred between Ford and Carter. The importance of this consideration is nicely illustrated in respect to the 1968 election, when a number of journalists concluded that George Wallace's candidacy may well have cost Hubert Humphrey the election because Wallace voters were mainly Democrats. They neglected the possibility, which was borne out by later research, that most of these Wallace Democrats pre-

1302

ferred not Humphrey but Richard Nixon. And even if, in 1976, most of the McCarthy Democrats had preferred Carter to Ford, it is doubtful whether these voters were enough to overcome the actual Ford plurality plus those McCarthyites preferring the President. Without McCarthy on the ballot, then, Carter's victory would probably have been just as close.

Another speculation involves the fifty-one electoral votes of Texas and Ohio, which might have been denied the Carter-Mondale ticket if Ford's running mate had been Ronald Reagan instead of Robert Dole. There is little doubt that as the Republican vice-presidential candidate, Dole was more of a liability than an asset to Ford's campaign. An NBC News poll taken in late October found, for example, that while half the voters would choose Walter Mondale over Dole for vice-president, only a third would choose Dole. In fact, about two weeks before the Republican convention, Ford's campaign strategists delivered a 120-page memorandum to him that implicity rejected Dole for the number two spot because of his televised personal attack on Carter as being "Southern-fried McGovern." Yet Dole was picked and Reagan was not.

According to Jules Witcover's account of the pursuit of the presidency, Reagan was not asked to join the ticket because his campaign manager in effect told Ford's chief of staff that the Californian would meet with the President "only on the firmest condition that he not be asked." According to Lloyd Shearer's more recent report, however, Reagan has himself now said he would have run

with Ford, "Only I was never asked!" As a matter of fact, Reagan says that, *after* losing the nomination, one of his supporters informed several of Ford's top staff that he was available as a running mate, and so he half expected to be offered the vice-presidency when he met Ford. Still, Reagan's campaign manager maintains that, *before* the nomination, he explained to Ford's staff that the vice-presidency should not be offered to Reagan, who did not want to embarrass the President by an outright refusal. And there is Reagan's handwritten note to his own California delegation: ("There is no circumstance whatsoever under which I would accept the nomination for Vice-President. That is absolutely final.") Because, Reagan says, the Ford people on the convention floor were promising the uncommitted delegates that Reagan would be on the ticket if Ford won, the Californians had to be assured it was not true. Nevertheless, Reagan now says that even though he did not want the job, *if* Ford had twisted his arm by claiming an obligation to party and country, "It would have been an impossibility to say no." In any event, if Reagan had run on the ticket, and Texas and Ohio had gone Republican, and no state for Ford defected, the only difference in the final outcome would have been an even closer race—with Carter winning by a hairline electoral vote margin of five. Then we would really have been inundated with speculations.

It is doubtful, though, that Ohio would have switched. As Gerald Pomper points out, the Democratic victory there "could be properly attributed to the union campaign." Nationwide, Carter held a nearly twenty-five percent lead over his opponent among voters from union households. And this union support (which McGovern lacked in 1972) reflected the fact that trivial matters—such as the campaign's semantic slips involving "ethnic purity"—had little if any lasting impact. Rather, for the first time in a generation, the electorate was sharply divided along partisan lines that ran parallel to the New Deal alignment. Four of every five Democrats voted for Carter, and almost nine of every ten Republicans for Ford. Since there are about twice as many Democrats as Republicans among the roughly two-thirds of the electorate identifying with a party, the reappearance of loyal party voting was critical to Carter's close victory. Not that the return to partisan voting should be seen as a return to the issueless party loyalties of the 1950's and early 1960's. For as Pomper argued prior to 1976, the causal influence of issue preferences on the vote and on party identification has become quite substantial since the mid-1960's. And Norman Nie, Sidney Verba, and John Petrocik have estimated that the proportion of pure issueless partisans has declined drastically, from forty-two percent in 1960 to twenty-three percent in 1972.

What *was* the 1976 issue most frequently on the voter's minds, even if only rarely on their candidate's lips? In a word, *stagflation*: rampant inflation eating at incomes while an exasperating rate of unemployment lengthened the relief rolls. The middle class was suffering. In response, the Democratic platform first observed the obvious and then promised the improbable:

> Fighting inflation by curtailing production and increasing unemployment has done nothing to restrain it. With the current level of capacity utilization, we can increase production and employment without rekindling inflation.

In the first of the debates between the candidates, the economy again occupied the Democrats as Carter called the present tax structure a "disgrace" and a "welfare program for the rich." To be sure, most voters doubtlessly never got these messages—Thomas Patterson's study of news coverage of the campaign revealed that only some twenty percent was devoted to issue positions—but the voters *did* harken back to the partisanship that characterized former hard times. Nearly two-thirds of the least economically advantaged voters (income under $8,000) supported Carter; a like percentage among those with the highest incomes (over $20,-000) voted for Ford. And at a time when the official unemployment rate was eight percent, NBC estimated that Carter won seven of eight votes from persons who viewed unemployment to be the major issue.

In short, since the days of Franklin D. Roosevelt the voters have believed that the Democrats were better able to handle problems of the economy, and in the election of 1976 they sought to test their secular faith once again.

1304

Pertinent Literature

Pomper, Gerald M., *et al. The Election of 1976: Reports and Interpretations*. New York: David McKay Company, 1977.

Seven essays cover the presidential, congressional, state, and local elections of 1976 in this timely volume written by five Rutgers political scientists. Most of the essays focus on various aspects of Carter's victory, with Pomper's opening study of the nominating contests and conventions being perhaps the most useful.

Describing the Democratic also-rans, Pomper suggests that each of the initial front-runners "seemed fixated" by an earlier Democratic nomination. Thus Henry Jackson appeared to be trying to repeat John Kennedy's 1960 successful formula, Hubert Humphrey harked back to the 1968 campaign, George Wallace remembered the 1972 nomination, and so forth. Each thereby failed to recognize that the political terrain had changed. Each failed to see that the spread of primaries, requirements of proportional representation, and public declarations of delegates' preferences meant that strategies based on a few states would no longer work. Each also failed to realize that strategies relying on older power groups, large contributions, or specific issues would not work either. Carter, on the other hand, recognized that with delegates available everywhere, an effort was needed in every state. (He ran in twenty-nine of the thirty primaries, winning eighteen.) Moreover, while the other contestants continued to have official duties, Carter had been free to concentrate on getting the nomination ever

since his term as governor of Georgia ended in 1974.

The result of Carter's ubiquitous battle for delegates was that even in defeat, he won. For example, on May 25, he won only three of the six primaries, yet he captured 107 of the 179 delegates chosen. The overall outcome of the primaries is usefully presented by the author in a chronological table which clearly shows that Carter reached and held an impressive cumulative popular vote of about forty percent after only five primaries. And by May-June, he became the favorite nominee of more than forty percent of the Democratic rank and file. Another table, presenting the single roll call for the nomination, demonstrates the scope of Carter's support, which amounted to nearly three-fourths of the delegate votes. As Pomper says, this roll call "did no more than record formally a predestined result." So, what was supposed to have been a brokered convention—"'Brokered convention' may be the campaign cliché of the year," said a January 1976 issue of *Congressional Quarterly*—turned out after all to be just one more nomination effectively decided beforehand, in the period of preconvention politics.

But the Republican convention, maintains Pomper, stands out as the exception to the rule that has existed since 1952; namely, that "the winner of the nomination has been determined before the convention actually convened." Reagan's challenge to the incumbent President is thus seen by the author as a "virtual victory" and needs to be explained. Watergate's impact on the prestige of the presidency, Ford's pardon of Nixon, the new campaign finance laws, Reagan's freedom from official duties, the shift in Republican delegate apportionment, the spread of primaries, the lack of proportional representation, Reagan's espousal of conservative policies—all are seen as factors explaining why the Republican nomination was "in doubt" until the convention roll calls. But was it really in doubt? As the state conventions chose the last delegates, says the author, the Republican contest "came to resemble a sudden-death playoff," with 47.9 percent of the delegates pledged to Ford and 45.4 percent to Reagan. In other words, Ford had a 51.3 to 48.7 percent lead among the delegates prior to the convention.

At the convention, as it turned out, Ford won the nomination by 1187 votes to 1070, by 52.6 percent to 47.4—a margin twice what it had been preceding the convention. Pomper and others view the convention contest as a genuine cliff-hanger, one which put the fear of the right wing into Ford. For instance, Jules Witcover opines that an unsatisfactory choice of vice-president could have triggered "a runaway convention, demanding a draft of Reagan and repudiating the President who it had so narrowly, even niggardly, nominated." And Pomper, while avoiding such extreme interpretations, does speak about Dole's selection in terms of conciliating and placating the conservatives by not only giving Reagan a virtual veto over the designation but also by following his recommendation. Yet Reagan says he simply offered Ford a one-sentence opinion on each of the names mentioned to him, and when the President mentioned Dole, he merely said, "I've never heard anyone say anything against him, and he's obviously popular with his associates."

In any case, it is hard to see what Ford supposedly feared so much. Surely since the 1952 election, when those Republicans who had preferred Taft as their nominee supported Eisenhower *more* than did those Republicans who had preferred Eisenhower, it has been known that there is practically no danger of losing conservative Republican voters, who are among the strongest party identifiers and thus constitute the party's most stalwart supporters. So the roughly one-third of the Republican voters who preferred Reagan to Ford were most unlikely to be lost on Election Day. Then too, there is the fact that the closeness of the convention vote does not necessarily mean its outcome was very doubtful. It should be remembered that the two candidates' delegate counts had been relatively close throughout the preconvention campaign, but *Ford's had been consistently greater than Reagan's*. Certainly CBS had few doubts concerning who would be the winner, as the network's last preconvention poll of delegates showed 1189 for the President and 1068 for the challenger—almost to a man the actual convention result. More to the point, perhaps, is the fact that an NBC poll, two months before the delegates convened, had forecast a 115 vote lead by Ford (putting him only fourteen

votes short of sewing up the nomination).

In 1976, then, it seems that the
Republican convention may have been
no more of an exception to the rule
of predestined presidential nominee
choices than was the Democratic.

Ladd, Everett C., Jr. and Charles D. Hadley. *Transformations of the American
Party System: Political Coalitions from the New Deal to the 1970s.* New York: W. W.
Norton and Company, 1978.

Two considerations prompted the
authors to revise *Transformations of
the American Party System* only two
years after their first edition. One was
to update the various figures and tables to reflect the 1976 election. But
the main one was to refute the widely
held interpretation of Carter's victory
found in such prestigious publications
as *Newsweek*, the *Congressional
Quarterly*, and the *New York Times*,
which held that American electoral
politics was once again to be understood in terms of the New Deal coalition. This view, say the authors, is
"nonsense." And through their access to impressive inventories of data,
they attempt to show why they think
so.

In the first edition, and repeated
here, Ladd and Hadley argued that
the 1960's ushered in an electoral
alignment that has mostly, not completely, supplanted the configurations
of the Roosevelt era. Here, the authors come to the defense of their
earlier thesis, against the charge that
they overextrapolated from recent
short-term movements by launching
a four-pronged attack designed to
show that the New Deal alignment
explains Carter's election very poorly,
at best. Their attack involves looking
at the South, selected social groups,
the tendency toward "class inversion," and the Democrats as the

"everyone party." Beginning with the
South, the authors gladly concede
that Carter's four percent regional
advantage of the popular vote was a
sharp reversal of the 1964-1972 vote
distribution, though they are quick to
point out that it was still nowhere
near the Democratic advantage enjoyed from 1932 to 1944. Moreover,
they continue, the upsurge must
largely be accounted for by the fact
that Carter came from the Deep
South. And more important, Carter
failed to win a majority among Southern whites; even with one of their
own running for President, Southern
white Protestants were five percentage points less Democratic than the
national electorate. Newly enfran-
chised blacks provided the winning
edge. So the 1976 vote is regarded by
Ladd and Hadley as simply an extension of the departure, begun in earnest in 1960, of Southern whites from
the New Deal fold.

What the authors neglect to mention, however, is that each presidential election between 1960 and 1972
had some major short-term element
that either attracted Southern white
Protestants toward or else repelled
them from the Democratic ticket. In
1960, there was Kennedy's Catholi-
cism; in 1964, Goldwater's "southern
strategy"; in 1968, Wallace's third-
party candidacy; and in 1972, Mc-

Govern's "new liberalism." True, since the New Deal the South has evidently been becoming more like the rest of the nation in its underlying partisanship—less solidly Democratic. But this partisan movement has been glacially slow and largely the result, as demonstrated by Philip Converse, of population migration rather than generational replacement or individual conversion. That is to say, much of the convergence between the South and the non-South in their voting behavior (which includes the direction of the vote, turnout, and class voting patterns) can be accounted for by the contrasting streams of migration. Specifically, the South is not only losing Democrats but is gaining Republicans—and the Republicans gained are actually *more* strongly Republican than the voters they leave behind.

After having looked at the South, Ladd and Hadley focus on selected social groups such as white blue-collar workers, urban white Catholics, and urban white blue-collar workers. These groups, according to the authors' statistics, did for the most part move back toward the Democratic candidate in 1976 as compared to 1972, but generally not as far back as in 1960 to 1968. In other words, the electoral standing of the groups "remained consonant with that of the last decade and a half."

Class inversion, the next item in the authors' arsenal of arguments supporting their transformation thesis, refers to the "unexpected" phenomenon of high socioeconomic status groups being more liberal than middle-to-lower status groups. Lou Harris called this phenomenon "Karl Marx upside down": a reversal of po-

sitions that finds the fifth of the population earning over $15,000 to be more, or at least as, liberal as the fifth making under $5,000 in the early 1970's. "If Marx has been stood on his head," say Ladd and Hadley, then the top of the socioeconomic pyramid should give more support to the national Democratic Party than to its Republican opposition. No such transposal occurred in 1976, however; at both the congressional and presidential levels, the New Deal pattern of increasing Democratic support as one glances down the socioeconomic-status (SES) ladder was in evidence. So much so, in fact, that the partisan voting gap separating high-SES from low-SES voters was thirteen percentage points in the congressional race and twelve in the presidential. "Gallup data data [*sic*] do confirm" admit the authors, "that there was a drawing back from the sharp tendency toward inversion of 1968 and 1972." Yet, just how sharp that tendency was, immediately prior to 1976, is itself quite problematic. At the congressional level, for example, the low-SES whites were seen to be thirteen, six, and ten percentage points more Democratic than in 1968, 1972, and 1974, respectively. Granted, at the *presidential* level in 1968 and 1972, there was little if any gap between these SES groups; but we would expect presidential elections to be more open to short-term forces, hence less stable and less reliable as an indicator of what is happening below the surface statistics.

Furthermore, even if presidential voting were to be a good indicator of underlying shifts in party alignments, we would still be left without knowing whether the shift is toward class inversion, as the authors maintain, or else is simply a matter of what might be labeled "class dispersion." Perhaps, in other words, the decline in class distinctiveness in voting—if it exists—is nothing more than that. Perhaps it is merely a reflection of the authors' fourth and final prong in their case for partisan transformation; namely, the predominant presence of Democrats throughout nearly all the socioeconomic strata of the electorate. Be that as it may, there is no doubt the Democrats are found in force everywhere. Wage workers are still more Democratic in their party identification than businessmen and executives; but a plurality of even the latter identify with the Democrats now. Again, self-described moderates, liberals, and radicals are still more than conservatives; but a plurality of self-described conservatives think of themselves as Democrats today. The Democrats are in this sense clearly the party of "everyone" in the 1970's.

It is, then, in the context of a significantly changing voter base that the election of Jimmy Carter must be placed in order to be fully understood. Whether we are indeed witnessing the transformation of the American party system into the post-New Deal direction that Ladd and Hadley see, however, remains to be determined by the course of future events, both political and economic. — *E.G.D.*

Additional Recommended Reading

Educational Broadcasting Corporation. "The MacNeil/Lehrer Report—Roper Poll." Transcript of Show #2041, Library #285 (aired November 1, 1976, and available from WNET in New York). Discussion of Roper's final pre-election survey in which it was predicted that Carter would win by fifty-one to forty-seven percent.

Institute for Social Research, University of Michigan. "Debates Increased Awareness," in *ISR Newsletter*. Vol. 6, no. 1 (1978). Survey analysis of reaction to the Carter-Ford debates.

_____ . "Election Study Notes New Trends in Voter Behavior, Attributes Close Race to Well-Run Campaign," in *ISR Newsletter*. Vol. 5, no. 1 (1977). Survey analysis of why the vote went the way it did.

Patterson, Thomas E. "Press Coverage of the Presidential Campaign, 1976," in *Washington Post*. (December 5, 1976), p. 1. A year-long study involving a panel of 1,100 voters in Los Angeles and Erie, Pennsylvania—who were interviewed seven times—and an analysis of the campaign content of television newscasts in both cities, the *Los Angeles Times*, the *Erie Times*, *Newsweek*, and *Time*.

Plissner, Martin, *et al. Campaign '76*. New York: Arno Press, 1977. A CBS News reference book with official vote returns, biographies of presidential primary candidates, and an eleven-page campaign overview by Plissner.

Polsby, Nelson W., *et al.* "Politics, Parties and 1976," in *National Journal Reprint*. 1976. Usefully conveys the flavor of campaign journalism—its insights as well as shortcomings.

Schram, Martin. *Running for President, 1976: The Carter Campaign*. New York: Stein and Day, 1977. A sort of poor man's version of *Marathon*, which is to say it is a journalistic campaign narrative whose quality is second to only one.

Shearer, Lloyd. "Intelligence Report—Behind the Scenes," in *Parade*. July 2, 1978. Report on Reagan's and Ford's recollections of selected events surrounding the choice for Vice-President.

Strong, Donald. *Issue Voting and Party Realignment*. Tuscaloosa: University of Alabama Press, 1977. Provides a clear and concise account of what the academic community has recently written about voting behavior.

Witcover, Jules. *Marathon: The Pursuit of the Presidency 1972-1976*. New York: The Viking Press, 1978. A breathtakingly encyclopedic masterpiece which, unfortunately, fails to reprint extended excerpts from some extremely important campaign staff memos that *are* found in Schram's book.

THE SPACEFLIGHTS OF *VOYAGER I* AND *II*

Type of event: Scientific: exploration of distant planets
Time: 1977 to the present
Locale: Earth, Jupiter, Saturn, Uranus, and beyond

Principal personage:
CARL SAGAN (1934-   ), Chairman of the NASA Voyager
Record Committee

Summary of Event

In March and July, 1979, *Voyager I* and *Voyager II* sent back to the earth photographs of Jupiter and its surrounding moons that startled and delighted the scientific community. The *Voyagers* had been launched eighteen months earlier by the National Aeronautics and Space Administration (NASA) from Cape Canaveral with the Jet Propulsion Laboratory at California Institute of Technology in Pasadena, California, as mission control. As part of a continuing investigation of the more distant planets of the solar system, a series of launches had begun with *Pioneer X* and *Pioneer XI* which had been sent up in 1971 and 1972. The *Pioneer* mission was to photograph features of Jupiter, Saturn, and Uranus in preparation for the *Voyager I* and *Voyager II* flights.

Pioneer XI in particular sent back photographs of Jupiter's Giant Red Spot that, while far less clear than those taken by the *Voyagers*, were much more detailed than anything taken from the earth. The NASA scientists expected *Voyager I* and *Voyager II* to reveal details of the turbulence in the layers of the Jovian atmosphere and much better data on the largest of the satellite moons that rotate around the planet.

Voyager I was launched September 5, 1977, following a path close to Jupiter and to the Jovian moons Io and Ganymede which also offers a fairly good view of the moon Callisto. The flight plan calls for *Voyager I* to proceed from Jupiter to Saturn with close encounters with Saturn's moons Titan, Dione, and Rhea. From the earth eighteen months are required to reach Jupiter and another seventeen to reach Saturn. From Saturn the spacecraft will proceed to Uranus, which will take approximately five years to reach.

Voyager II was launched on August 20, 1977, and was to act as a substitute should something go wrong with the first craft, especially as it passed through the flux tube between Jupiter and Io which contains an electrical current of 400,000 watts. *Voyager II* also was following a trajectory that would provide a better look at Callisto and Ganymede and good photographs of the Jovian moon Europa. It should, when it reaches Saturn, come very close to Saturn's moons Enceladus, Mimas, and the rings of Saturn. It too is scheduled to move on to Uranus.

Although the conditions around the planets are harsh, it is hoped that at least one of the *Voyagers* will continue to move out of our solar system, reaching areas untold light years away. Many scientists are of the opinion that it is possible for some form of life to exist in other solar systems around other stars, although they often feel that it is more likely that such life would be radically different from anything that we now know. The possibility that such life might be contacted by a *Voyager* that successfully escaped our solar system so intrigued the NASA scientists that they decided that some sort of communication should be carried on board the spacecraft to explain our civilization to another that might encounter it hurling through space.

Some attempt in this regard had been made with the *Pioneer* spacecraft. Carl Sagan, a Professor of Astronomy and Space Sciences at Cornell University, designed a six-inch by nine-inch gold-anodized aluminum plaque. One was affixed to *Pioneer X* and another to *Pioneer XI*. The plaques included some information on our location and the time of the launch in scientific language, as well as representations of two human beings. Sagan was asked to design something for the *Voyagers*, and the form and content of the communication that resulted was considerably more complex. It was a gold phonograph record in an aluminum cover which included both sounds and visual images, all carefully chosen by a team of experts. In all, there were twenty-seven musical selections, nineteen sounds of the earth such as wind, rain, and surf, fifty-four messages in different languages, and one hundred and sixteen photographs chosen by a team to represent and explain as much about human civilization as possible.

Just as the *Voyager* greetings to other planets were more complex than those of *Pioneer*, so were the spacecraft. The *Voyagers* included eleven scientific instrument packages on board. Each of the packages has its own team of scientists and engineers on earth—specialists in imaging science, radio science, plasma waves, infrared spectroscopy, radiometry, and several other fields—who will interpret returning data to give a better picture of the composition of the planets, and, hence, of their origins and activities.

As *Voyager I* reached Jupiter on March 5, 1979, an amazing pictorial record began to emerge. Much closer pictures of the Giant Red Spot than had ever been taken before revealed unexpected levels of turbulence. Io was shown to have a brilliant yellow, red, and black surface with no craters visible anywhere. This posed questions about its age in regard to lack of erosional features, until one of the scientists noticed that there are numerous volcanoes, the dust from which was probably covering the rougher features. The other major discovery of this flyby was the presence of a ring around Jupiter. Photographs were taken of the moons Amalthea, Ganymede, Europa, and Callisto, although none but those of Callisto were particularly impressive. Callisto was shown to be covered with craters with ripplelike marks emanating from them.

The findings of *Voyager I* were still being digested as *Voyager II* began to send back images on July 8, 1979. *Voyager II* scanned Europa at closer range, observed areas of Callisto and Ganymede that were not visible to *Voyager I*, and monitored Io for more volcanic plumes.

Europa was shown to be surprisingly smooth, etched with canallike streaks. The pictures of Callisto primarily confirmed those taken by *Voyager I*, but those taken of Ganymede showed a far more varied surface than expected, indicative of a complicated geologic history. *Voyager II*'s flight plan was altered so that further observations could be made of the ring that *Voyager I* had discovered.

Voyager II's pictures of the ring were very bright and distinct.

By comparing the photographs made by *Voyager II* against those taken by *Voyager I*, it became apparent that Io is intensely volcanic. The NASA scientists found it puzzling that the second *Voyager* should encounter intense radiation when the first one did not. Many years of analysis will probably elapse before all of the information gathered by the *Voyagers* can be correlated and integrated into a definitive body of knowledge.

Pertinent Literature

Beatty, J. Kelly. "The Far-Out Worlds of *Voyager I*-Part 1," in *Sky and Telescope*. LVII, no. 5 (May, 1979), pp. 423-427.

_____. "The Far-Out Worlds of *Voyager I*-Part 2," in *Sky and Telescope*. LVII, no. 6 (June, 1979), pp. 516-520.

_____. "*Voyager*'s Encore Performance," in *Sky and Telescope*. LVIII, no. 3 (September, 1979), pp. 206-216.

While the total significance of the findings of *Voyager I* and *Voyager II* will not be apparent for many years and after much study, this series of articles represents the first fairly official interpretations of the data. The first article, in the May issue, emphasizes the photographic record and the more easily observed phenomena, starting with clear color pictures of the Jovian moons Amalthea, Io, Ganymede, and Europa. There follow both time-lapse and close-up color photographs of the Giant Red Spot of Jupiter, which illustrate the changes that occur in its cloud patterns over a relatively short period of time as well as the enormous amount of turbulence present. Close views of the surface reveal that Callisto is dotted with craters and covered with ripplelike markings. The photograph that first displayed traces of a ring around Jupiter is reproduced, although the phenomenon is seen more clearly in the September issue photographs from *Voyager II*. There are also photographs of the brightly colored Jovian surface as well as of Io.

The second article, published in June, is somewhat more technical, delineating less and delving more, although, of course, still only based on a preliminary digest of the eighteen thousand photographs and the results of eleven experiments performed on board. Some preliminary observations regarding the experiments are included, but final judgment on the results is reserved until a much more thorough study can be made. Enough time had passed since the flyby that the NASA scientists had been able to study the photographs of Io more closely, and as a result, several discoveries had been made. Io shows evidence of several volcanoes. However, careful study of the photographs does not show any craters. The speculation in this article is that there are great amounts of material being spewed out onto the surface of the moon, perhaps at such a rapid rate as to cover the evidence of the craters. There are also further observations on the other moons that have resulted from examination of the data. Europa is noted to be both larger in diameter than expected and less dense, while Ganymede shows a more active history than was previously suspected.

The third article, written for the September issue after the *Voyager II* flyby, is both a delineation of the findings of *Voyager II* and a summary of the information accumulated by both of the *Voyagers*. In addition, this article contains a fairly well illustrated record of the major findings of the *Pioneer* flights correlated with those of *Voyager I* and *Voyager II* to emphasize the importance of successive missions as mechanisms for the observation of patterns over time.

In the same spirit, there is a projection of the possible *Voyager I* and *Voyager II* findings on Saturn, although the speculations are void of the benefits of the information gathered by *Pioneer XI*, which had not yet reached Saturn at the time of Beatty's writing.

Much of the information presented in the September summary from the *Voyager I* flight is repeated from the June issue in order to correlate it with the further findings of *Voyager II*. The volcanoes on Io were the objects of special observation as were the turbulence patterns on the Jovian surface, especially around the Giant Red Spot, for the NASA scientists hope that some patterns over a measured amount of time could be observed. A series of photographs showing the newly discovered ring quite clearly are included, as are the very close views of the smooth but streaked surface of Europa.

Although the information in these articles may eventually be supplanted by more comprehensive analyses, they convey quite well the sense of immediacy and excitement felt by the scientific community at their initial scan of the data.

Sagan, Carl, *et al. Murmurs of Earth: The Voyager Interstellar Record*. New York: Random House, 1978.

After *Voyager I* and *Voyager II* have gathered data from Jupiter, Saturn, Uranus, and the areas surrounding them, they will continue on their outward journey beyond our solar system. Because their journey may take them to other stars, particularly other stars containing planets with civilizations, the National Aeronautics and Space Administration asked Carl Sagan, a Professor of Astronomy and Space Sciences at Cornell University, to design an appropriate message to such civilizations to be placed aboard the *Voyager* space-craft.

Sagan had designed a message to be affixed to both *Pioneer* spacecraft, a six-inch by nine-inch gold-anodized aluminum plaque bearing a visual message about our location as well as representations of two human beings.

The effort for the *Voyager* space-craft was to be much more compre-hensive, however. Sagan asked a team consisting of Philip Morrison of the Massachusetts Institute of Tech-nology, Frank Drake of the National Astronomy and Ionosphere Center at Cornell University, A. G. W. Cameron of Harvard University, Les-lie Orzel of the Salk Institute for Bi-ological Research, B. M. Oliver of the Hewlett-Packard Corporation, and Steve Toulmin of the University of Chicago for advice on what should be included in the *Voyager* message. Sa-gan also discussed the question with Isaac Asimov, Arthur Clarke, and Robert Heinlein, since he felt that some science fiction writers with backgrounds in the sciences might have been imagining such a situation for some time and consequently might have some ready answers.

The suggestions that he received were as diverse as the respondents. While there was some emphasis on sending scientific data, there was a considerable interest in sending in-formation on human society and the arts as well. The next basic question was the physical form that should carry the message. Messages encoded on magnetic tape would deteriorate over time, and a solid plaque such as that used on the *Pioneer* spacecraft had insufficient area to carry the amount of information that Sagan

wanted to include. A phonograph record was finally chosen to solve both of these problems and because it could carry both audio and video messages.

In the introductory chapters, Sagan tells the story of all that was involved in making the decisions about what to include in this historic recording. Each of the chapters which follow is written about one aspect of the mes-sage by the persons from Sagan's committee who were responsible for the selection. These chapters delin-eate what was chosen, and what was not, including an explanation of how and why the decision was made.

The scientific messages and dia-grams that were chosen are well pre-sented, but it is in the selections of photographs and audio messages that the immense task of representing the diverse cultures found on the earth can be better appreciated by the lay-man. The final sequence of photo-graphs as included on the record is reproduced, with a thorough discus-sion on the artistic and informational merit of the choices as well as the logic behind their sequence. A chart of the greetings in fifty-four different languages, both written and oral, pre-sents the enormous cultural diversity which the team hoped to represent. There is also a complete listing of the musical works that were included on the record, with each of them dis-cussed at length in regard to struc-ture, performance, and cultural sig-nificance.

Sagan ends the volume with an ex-planation of the information that the *Voyager* flights hope to gather as well as the scientific instruments on board to do the gathering. Throughout the work Sagan and the team very carefully document their sources through acknowledgments and bibliographies, and in so doing present to the reader a comprehensive picture of what an enormous undertaking their message involved. When one considers what a small part of the space program this message really was, it is, perhaps, easier to imagine the great amount of effort on the part of many people that is required to launch even one vehicle into space. — *M.S.S.*

Additional Recommended Reading

"There's a Ring, By Jupiter," in *Time*. CXIII (March 19, 1979), pp. 86-87. Good background and general information for the *Voyager I* findings, including color photographs.

Science. CXCVII (September 16, 1977), pp. 1163-1165. A highly technical but comprehensive discussion of the equipment aboard the *Voyager* craft.

"Jupiter's World," in *Science News*. CXV, no. 10 (March 10, 1979), pp. 147-149.

"*Voyager I*: Active Io, Jolting Jupiter," in *Science News*. CXV, no. 11 (March 17, 1979), pp. 165 and 172.

"Jupiter and Io: Competing Stars," in *Science News*. CXV, no. 23 (June 9,1979), pp. 371-372. Three articles which deal with the weekly unfolding of the *Voyager I* findings as the data were interpreted.

"The Worlds of Jupiter," in *Science News*. CXVI, no. 3 (July 21, 1979), pp. 35-37. A brief discussion of the specific findings of *Voyager II*.

Newsweek. XCIV (July 23, 1979), p. 69. A preliminary summary of the findings of *Voyager II* which includes color photographs.

THE STRUGGLE FOR THE HORN OF AFRICA

Type of event: Political: contemporary expansion of Communist influence into East
 Africa
Time: 1977-1978
Locale: The Horn of Africa on the Red Sea

> *Principal personages:*
> LIEUTENANT COLONEL MENGISTU HAILE MARIAM
>   (1937-   ), head of the government of Ethiopia
> MUHAMMAD SIAD BARRE (1919-   ), President of Somalia
> JIMMY (JAMES EARL) CARTER (1924-   ), thirty-ninth President of the United States, 1977-
> FIDEL CASTRO (1927-   ), Premier of Cuba, 1959-
> GENERAL VASILY IVANOVICH PETROV, Commander in Chief
>   of Soviet military operations in the Horn of Africa

Summary of Event

To many casual observers of world conditions, the so-called "Horn" of Africa may lack the familiarity usually associated with East-West confrontations. The key nation of Ethiopia, around which so much of the current apprehension centers, is often referred to in contemporary historical terms as the land of Emperor Haile Selassie whose primitive society was victimized by Fascist Italy as a prelude to World War II.

Today, however, the Horn region in general, and Ethiopia in particular, are significant ingredients in what has become an apparently calculated strategic gamble on the part of the Soviet Union and her Cuban allies. Not only is the stability of the area no longer viable, but a substantial threat is building towards the neighboring moderate Arab states (Sudan, Egypt, Saudi Arabia), as well as to the West's oil lifelines through the Red Sea and the Indian Ocean.

The absence of a direct United States involvement in physical terms may account partially for the struggle's lowered profile. Yet, while this view may be true in Western eyes, the struggle is seen in more profound terms from the Soviet vantage point. Since late November, 1977, there has been a relentless build-up of Russian weapons, advisers, and supplies to assist Ethiopia's Marxist government headed by Lieutenant Colonel Mengistu Haile Mariam in Addis Ababa, the Ethiopian capital. Some 1.6 billion dollars in Soviet aid has been extended, including four hundred tanks, fifty MIG jet fighters, fifteen hundred Russian military advisers, and roughly sixteen thousand Cuban combat troops organized into three brigades. Of particular note to the apparent importance Russia attaches to this enterprise is the presence of four Soviet generals directing operations, led by General Vasily Ivanovich Petrov, Deputy Commander in Chief of all Soviet ground forces and former head of the Russian Far East Command.

The rationale given for this massive array of military strength is to lend support to Mengistu's government in its struggle with neighboring Somalia over the disputed Ogaden territory which lies between the two African nations. In truth, the Ogaden area was initially seized by Somali forces, making them the technical aggressors. President Muhammad Siad Barre of Somalia had staked his own political future on reuniting the entire Somali people, millions of whom live outside the nation itself in Ethiopia, Kenya, and the Ogaden. Barre had even received arms shipments himself from the Soviets in 1974 in exchange for bases on the Somali coast, but in 1977 he ousted the Russians and turned to the United States for his principal aid. Assistant Secretary of State Richard Moose visited Barre in March, 1978, and allegedly offered United States economic assistance, but little if any arms hardware was forthcoming. Rather ironically, Moose's visit coincided with Somalia's complete withdrawl from the Ogaden.

The paucity of United States military aid may hold true for the immediate future as Moose indicates in an article published in the *Department of State Bulletin* in April, 1978. According to Moose, "the African program we propose for next year is consistent with the President's directive of May 19, 1977, to restrict arms transfers." In addition, Moose notes that, "the foreign military sales credit proposed for sub-Saharan countries is slightly less than the appropriation we received from the Congress for fiscal year 1978."

Clearly the United States, in its post-Vietnam attitude, does not relish direct involvement of American military contingents in politically unstable areas of the "less developed countries," as they now prefer to be termed. United States Secretary of Defense Harold Brown in a July 17, 1978, interview given to *U.S. News & World Report* may have summed up the extent of the Carter Administration's response when he stated that, "I don't see a role for U.S. combat forces. I think the best way to try to deal with that problem is diplomatically as well as economically, and with the military capability of the Africans themselves."

For his part, President Jimmy Carter has repeatedly denounced the Soviet and Cuban activities in Africa, and administration officials have hinted that the progress of the Strategic Arms Limitation Talks (SALT) between the United States and Russia could be adversely affected if the current patterns do not change. On the whole, however, President Carter has restricted his response concerning the African issue to hopeful rhetoric.

Still, those remain who see the Horn of Africa as a crisis of sizable proportions. Frank Carlucci, Deputy Director of the CIA, told a Senate subcommittee: "the degree of Soviet and Cuban military activity in sub-Saharan Africa is unprecedented. We are witnessing the most determined campaign to expand foreign influence in this troubled region since it was carved up by the European powers in the late nineteenth century." Rashna Writer of London's prestigious International Institute for Strategic Studies elaborates by adding that, "the Soviets are using the Cubans as a reminder that they have caught up with the U.S. and are now a superpower with a global reach. A lot of their moves in Africa are based on testing the U.S. reaction—or lack of it."

The Cuban presence in the Horn of Africa has been a matter of particular conjecture. While many view the Cuban role as a fisted glove of Moscow, correspondent Carl J. Migdail reports from Havana that, "Castro still is convinced that this Communist nation has a 'revolutionary duty' to help African countries throw off the yoke of 'undemocratic' rule." Today, Fidel Castro, Cuba's head of state, is proving his dedication with some forty-two thousand of his nation's best-trained personnel in fourteen African countries, sixteen thousand of whom are in Ethiopia. This deployment amounts to about one-fourth of Cuba's total armed forces, with reservist men in their forties now being tapped.

With the Ethiopians now holding the upper hand in the Ogaden region against Somali troops, and the ongoing Soviet-Cuban support being channeled into Ethiopia's present conflict with bordering Eritrea, it is suggested that a Communist-controlled Horn of Africa would not be an end in itself. Rather, it may pave the way for a broader Soviet push into mineral-rich southern Africa. Here, Soviet-Cuban efforts may even be welcomed by black elements against the white minority regimes. Both Rhodesia and South Africa are already facing guerrilla opposition which is at least indirectly aided by Soviet and Cuban cadres.

The struggle in the Horn, then, is critical to more than the immediate scope of Ethiopian expansionism. The implications are vast even if the public awareness remains questionable.

Pertinent Literature

Connell, Dan. "Eritrean Battlefront: The Cubans Move In," in *The Nation*. CCXXVI, no. 17 (May 6, 1978), pp. 530-533.

Inasmuch as the heated struggles in the Horn of Africa involving United States, Russian, and Cuban interests are of relatively recent origin, there are really no definitive works yet compiled. While the background conditions can easily be sought out and are a matter of record, the crisis in this part of the globe is a situation in the making. It remains difficult to fix a true perspective on either the incidents or the designs of the parties involved in an event so contemporary.

Dan Connell, a correspondent for *The Nation*, spent roughly six months during 1977 touring the region of Eritrea, the much-disputed northern land mass which borders the Red Sea and Ethiopia; Eritrea has been the site for what might be termed "Phase II" of the current Soviet-Cuban activity in the Horn. Connell's essay in *The Nation* in May, 1978, is therefore much more than eyewitness observation of the conditions. The author takes pains not only to provide a fairly extensive background to the

Eritrean-Ethiopian dispute (stretching back to 1951), but also to analyze the up-to-the-minute military status of the adversaries as well as their political justifications.

While remaining relatively unbiased in his presentation of the problems, Connell does imply that, despite United States fears, the Soviet-Cuban assistance to Ethiopia's efforts has not dampened the Eritrean independence movement. In fact, he suggests that the Eritrean political and military groups could provide Moscow with a "mini-Vietnam dilemma in the Horn."

Eritrea, an Italian colony for fifty-five years (and Egyptian-controlled prior to that), was affixed to Ethiopia by the United Nations in 1952. Nine years later, Eritrean nationalists began a concerted armed struggle to secure independence. Shortly thereafter Ethiopian Emperor Haile Selassie used force to annex the region in 1962; today, Eritrea claims itself to be a free state in the Horn while Ethiopia views it as a secessionist province.

Ironically, both the United States and Israel originally sided with the Ethiopians in exchange for Red Sea bases as early as 1953. Commitments were made to assist in the upgrading of the Ethiopian armed forces as well. However, the changing strategic circumstances throughout the Horn area have altered the picture substantially. Today, United States involvement is negligible, while the Russians and Cubans have become Ethiopia's primary backers; some assistance in military personnel also comes from South Yemen.

Remarkably, the Eritrean effort seems to have prospered at least on the battlefield. After some seventeen years of fighting (the longest ongoing armed conflict in Africa), the Eritreans held the upper hand as of May, 1978, the time of Connell's report. Numerous towns and strongholds once held by Ethiopian troops in Eritrea have been overrun or placed under siege, including Barentu, Adi Caieh, the key Red Sea ports of Massawa and Assab, and Asmara. In Asmara, the Eritrean capital, some twenty-thousand Ethiopian troops and 200,000 civilian residents have been encircled since October, 1977. According to Connell, Ethiopian troop morale is low with desertions running to about fifteen or twenty daily. Apparently, all attempts to break out of the besieged city have failed and about one hundred Ethiopian soldiers have been executed for criticizing their own commander's actions.

Connell does add, however, that the Eritrean cause is not without its own problems. Other African states have avoided taking sides in the conflict largely because of the controversial political issues involved. The absence of genuine international recognition of their independence claims has meant that the Eritreans have not received the aid necessary for long-term survival. Potentially dangerous too for the Eritreans is the fact that their military gains have stretched their own lines to the point where a coordinated Ethiopian counteroffensive could reverse the battlefield positions appreciably. Since the time of Connell's story in *The Nation*, Ethiopian advances against the Eritreans have been reported.

Just such a strike may be the reasoning behind Cuban troops remaining active in the Horn. Already three thousand Cubans have been airlifted to Asmara, and airstrips have been constructed around Makele, a town only eighty miles from Eritrea's border with Ethiopia. Some Cuban units have been flown in from as far away as Angola.

The picture, then, as Connell paints it, is anything but a settled matter. The Russian involvement would seem to see the Eritrean ports as one more piece in the puzzle of Soviet domination of the Horn, while placing added dangers to neighboring Arab and African states. What, if any, may be the future involvement of the United States, or even the United Nations, remains to be seen.

Deming, Angus, *et al.* "The Cubans in Africa," in *Newsweek.* XCI, no. 11 (March 13, 1978), pp. 36-42.

During the period from February to June, 1978, the American press lavished substantial attention on the problems of Soviet and Cuban involvement in the Horn of Africa. Periodicals ranging from *U.S. News & World Report* to *Business Week* printed articles highlighting the growing Communist buildup in Ethiopia and its unsettling possibilities for the future of *détente*. While many of these articles essentially restated the same particulars, only a few took pains to look behind the scenes to survey the actual participants and their motivations.

The May 13, 1978, issue of *Newsweek* featured an impressive cover story focusing on the Cuban element; the article functions as a primer on the topic, but includes also a wider theme regarding the overall Soviet threat to the Carter Administration in that part of the world.

For the uninitiated, *Newsweek* graphically depicts on a helpful abstract map of the African continent the extent of the Cuban operations and provides approximate figures on the number of Cuban personnel (including noncombatants) in the various countries. A commentary on the Cuban role attempts to explain its whys and wherefores in human terms.

The suggestion is made that ideological goals and revolutionary designs on the part of Cuban Premier Fidel Castro may not be the full reason for Cuba's African policies. Some, of course, have reasoned that Russia is simply obligating Cuba to assist in building Moscow's influence in Africa as partial payment for the sizable aid Russia has granted to Castro over the years. However, *Newsweek* adds that domestic Cuban economic realities may also be a root cause. Low world market prices for Cuban-grown sugar have produced food shortages and limited consumer goods on the Caribbean island. Most notably, there is a critical unemployment picture, especially among young males. Some thirty-eight thousand of the Cuban forces sent to assorted African areas come from this pool of manpower.

Newsweek reports also that the African program may have aroused some antiwar sentiment among Cuban students similar to university protests in the United States during the Vietnam conflict. One unnamed twenty-one-year-old Havana University student is quoted as saying, "Why should Cuba fight in Africa when there are so many things that have to be done here first? I don't want to go to Africa. It's a crazy place. When my friends come back, they are crazy."

The Russian portion of the African equation is perhaps no less enigmatic. Although such Carter Administration officials as Secretary of State Cyrus Vance have lobbied hard to keep *détente* from being swallowed in a renewed "Cold War," Soviet leaders may be playing the game with a unique set of rules. In 1976, the Soviet leader Leonid Brezhnev told his Party Congress: "We make no secret of the fact that we see *détente* as the way to create more favorable conditions for peaceful socialist and Communist construction. *Détente* does not in the slightest abolish . . . the laws of the class struggle."

Washington's view of the Horn of Africa issue may be the least clearly defined of all. Aside from the *détente*-minded Vance, there are other noteworthy State Department officials (Richard Moose, Marshall Shulman, Anthony Lake) who have pointed out that the Somalis, after all, were the aggressors in the Ogaden. In addition, former United States Ambassador to the United Nations Andrew Young (perhaps the Carter team's most controversial and outspoken diplomat) once defined the Cuban presence in Africa as a "stabilizing" influence. Aside from President Carter's more idealistic concern for human rights violations, only na-tional security adviser Zbigniew Brzezinski seems inclined to view the Horn of Africa in more harshly realistic terms.

One further element of the *Newsweek* article may be particularly worth noting—brief profiles of Cuban General Arnaldo Ochoa and Soviet General Vasily Ivanovich Petrov. Respectively, these two commanders function as the military directors of their nation's combat contingents in the Horn. Ochoa, a close friend of Fidel Castro's brother, Raúl, also serves as Deputy Minister of Defense in Cuba and is a member of the Cuban Central Committee. In one respect, Ochoa may be termed Cuba's highest ranking African veteran, having gained experience in the Cuban operations in Angola.

General Petrov, on the other hand, is a more mysterious figure. The top-level Soviet military figure with experience in the 1969 border skirmishes between Russia and China, he also stands next in line for the position of command of all Soviet ground forces. However, the uncertainty surrounding Petrov stems from what *Newsweek* intriguingly notes as a tendency for Russian officers to use pseudonyms when serving in distant locales such as Africa.

In any event, *Newsweek*'s capsule view of the wide-ranging personalities, motives, and strategic considerations is both an easily readable article and an effective introduction to the still-undetermined outcome of the raging conflict in the Horn of Africa. — *T.A.B.*

Additional Recommended Reading

"Russia's Grand Design," in *Newsweek*. XCI, no. 7 (February 13, 1978), pp. 47-48. Includes excerpts from an interview, edited by A. DeBorchgrave, with Somali President Muhammad Siad Barre about his country's disputes with Ethiopia.

"Havana on the Horn," in *Newsweek*. XCI, no. 10 (March 6, 1978), p. 36. An early look at the introduction of Cuban forces in support of Ethiopia.

Legum, Colin. "Next: Eritrea," in *New Republic*. CLXXVIII, no. 14 (April 8, 1978), pp. 13-15. With the at least temporary conclusion of Ogaden hostilities, this article looks at the prospects for Ethiopian assaults to subdue the Eritrean independence movement with Soviet and Cuban assistance.

"Turmoil in Africa: Will Carter Act?," in *U.S. News & World Report*. LXXXIV, no. 21 (May 29, 1978), pp. 17-19. A rundown of the current situation in the Horn and an implied suggestion that time to alter the situation for the Carter Administration may be running out.

Deming, Angus, *et al*. "A New Cold War?," in *Newsweek*. XCI, no. 24 (June 12, 1978), pp. 26-37. A good look at national security adviser Zbigniew Brzezinski and the overall state of United States-Soviet relations.

"Soviet's Dangerous Game on Africa's Horn," in *Business Week*. (February 13, 1978), p. 52. A focus on the Russian aspect of the Horn crisis and the threat it poses to the future of *détente* with the United States.

BIRTH OF THE FIRST HUMAN CONCEIVED *IN VITRO*

Type of event: Scientific: significant advance in genetic engineering technology
Time: November, 1977-July 25, 1978
Locale: Oldham, England

Principal personages:
DR. ROBERT G. EDWARDS, the physiologist
DR. PATRICK C. STEPTOE, the obstetrician and gynecologist
GILBERT JOHN BROWN, the father
LESLEY BROWN, the mother
LOUISE JOY BROWN, the baby girl

Summary of Event

Occasionally during the twentieth century scientific achievement has overtaken science fiction, sometimes at a precisely determined point in time. One such moment was 11:47 P.M., July 25, 1978, when Louise Joy Brown was born in the northwestern English mill town of Oldham. Hers was the first documented birth of a human being conceived *in vitro* (Latin for "within glass," meaning that fertilization had occurred not in the mother's body, but in laboratory equipment; hence, the press's sensational but inappropriate phrase, "test-tube" baby). Delivered by Cesarean section, Louise weighed in at 2,700 grams (five pounds, twelve ounces) and "came out crying her head off . . . a beautiful, normal baby," according to the obstetrician, Dr. Patrick C. Steptoe.

Although the father, Gilbert John Brown, had a daughter from a previous marriage, the mother, Lesley Brown, was infertile because of occlusions (blockages) of her Fallopian tubes. A previous operation to correct this dysfunction had proven unsuccessful, and attempts by the Browns to adopt a child had run into exten-sive and frustrating delays. The couple was referred to Steptoe, who was collaborating with the Cambridge University physiologist, Dr. Robert G. Edwards, in *in vitro* technology.

Prior to attempting such experimentation on Mrs. Brown, Steptoe surgically removed her tubes. They were of no further use to her and their presence could impare future surgical procedures; furthermore, if the tubes were not removed and Mrs. Brown bore a child, suspicions would linger that the child had been conceived in the natural manner and did not result from an experimental procedure. A series of hormones was administered to Mrs. Brown to stimulate follicle development and egg maturation. On November 10, 1977, at Dr. Kershaw's Cottage Hospital in Oldham, Steptoe, in order to illuminate her ovaries, inserted a laparoscope (a type of medical telescope and flashlight using fiber optics) through a small abdominal incision. He then employed an aspiration (suction) needle to extract ova (eggs), which were transferred to glass vessels which Edwards had prepared with nutrients and blood sera. This was followed by deposition of spermatozoa from Mr. Brown. After fertilization within the glass vessel (hence the term *in vitro*) was verified, Edwards transferred the fertilized egg, now called a zygote, to a second culture dish containing a different combination of media. Within approximately fifty hours the zygote divided three times by cleavage to form an eight-celled embryo.

Meanwhile, Mrs. Brown had been given a second hormone treatment to prepare the wall of the uterus for implantation of the young embryo. (Earlier, unsuccessful attempts at implantation had involved older embryos of sixty-four cells or more.) This embryo, about the size of a typewriter dot, was drawn into a narrow plastic tube called a cannula, inserted through the vagina into the cervix, and gently expelled into the uterus.

Although it soon became evident that the embryo had indeed been implanted and was flourishing in the uterus, the first announcement concerning the uniqueness of the Brown pregnancy was withheld until April, 1978. Regardless of attempts to protect the Browns's privacy, the press was insistent in its clamor for details. As a result, the Browns negotiated publication rights with the *London Daily Mail*, and by mid-July, the world press was fully aware of the impending birth and converged on Oldham.

At this time Mrs. Brown developed a mild case of preeclamptic toxemia associated with hypertension, whereupon Steptoe decided to deliver the child by Cesarean section, thirty-eight weeks and five days after her last menstrual period. The ten minute operation, utilizing a conventional horizontal "bikini cut," resulted in the delivery of a 2,700 gram baby girl at 11:47 P.M., July 25, 1978, at District General Hospital in Oldham. A motion picture of the event was made to document the birth.

Steptoe and Edwards had been collaborating for the previous twelve years, Steptoe pioneering techniques in laparoscopic examination and aspiration and Edwards devising a multitude of *in vitro* culturing techniques. The first mammalian *in vitro* fertilization had been achieved with rabbits in 1936 by Gregory Pincus (who gained worldwide recognition for his work in developing oral contraceptives), but such fertilization on a consistent basis was not achieved until the 1960's, by M. C. Chang and C. R. Austin. John Rock first reported successful *in vitro* human development in 1944, but many authorities were convinced that the few cells he observed represented abnormal asexual (parthenogenetic) growth. A decade later, Landrum Shettles claimed *in vitro* human development to the sixth day. (Ironically, at the time of Louise Brown's birth, Shettles' former department head, Raymond L. Vande Wiele, was successfully sued by an American couple for arbitrary destruction in 1972 of their *in vitro* embryo which Shettles had achieved for them.)

Claims in 1961 by Daniele Petrucci of the University of Bologna that he had kept an embryo alive in the laboratory for twenty-nine days, and had witnessed a regular heartbeat, were met with strong criticism, especially from the Roman Catholic Church. He thereupon abandoned his research. Steptoe and Edwards described in 1970 various combinations of hormone treatments necessary for superovulation; a subsequent study appeared in 1975. Meanwhile, Douglas Bevis claimed in 1974 that three women had given birth to "test-tube" babies, but he refused to document the births. The resulting furor apparently caused Steptoe and Edwards to proceed with more caution than they would otherwise have used. One of their few reports described how a blastocyst (an embryonic hollow sphere containing about a hundred cells) was injected into an infertile patient. Unfortunately, the embryo became implanted in the tubes (an ectopic pregnancy) and had to be terminated at thirteen weeks.

Therefore, although the public was largely ignorant of the continuing efforts of Steptoe and Edwards, the scientific community eagerly anticipated the results. The birth of Louise Brown was met with universal and resounding congratulations—a scientific milestone had been achieved.

Pertinent Literature

Howard, Ted and Jeremy Rifkin. *Who Should Play God? The Artificial Creation of Life and What It Means for the Future of the Human Race*. New York: Dell Publishing Company, 1977.

The birth of Louise Brown is only one in a sequence of accomplishments that will undoubtedly result in a biomedical technology sophisticated enough to create artificial human life. The book, written prior to Louise's birth, explores not only *in vitro* fertilization and gestation, but also the more inclusive realm of genetic engineering. The historical perspective and ethical implications of such research are discussed more intelligently than the melodramatic title would suggest. The inclusion of a good index and thirty-three pages of citations and references is especially appreciated, but the serious reader is advised to use an introductory genetics text in conjunction with this book. Furthermore, caution is required, since several technical errors (usually inadvertent, but still irritating) exist. For example, the statement that "genetic disorders are inherited in one of two ways—through either recessive or dominant genes"—ignores chromosomal defects, some of which the authors have already discussed. In addition, "Sickle cell anemia is a disease that affects only black people" and "carriers have no health problems, victims die" are gross oversimplifications. Although the sickling hemoglobin mutation originated in some African populations, it has since spread through miscegenation and migration; furthermore, carriers can, under conditions of oxygen stress, exhibit moderate sickling reactions. Despite several such misstatements, *Who Should Play God?* is well worth reading.

Genetic engineering can be defined as the manipulation (in any manner) of the gene, the reproductive cells, or the fetus, at any stage of their development, to modify (in any manner) the pattern of that development. The theoretical framework and practical applications of such techniques are discussed in the first chapter. Examples of currently employed procedures cited include the fusion of cells from two different species into a single hybrid cell (such fusions have already resulted in cultures containing hybrid human-ape, human-mouse, and even human-tobacco cells); the cracking of the DNA code and isolation of single genes; and the artificial synthesis of human genes from stockroom chemicals that function normally when inserted into living cells. The authors emphasize recombinant-DNA research, in which genes are removed from one organism and "spliced" into another organism, often of an unrelated species. (The latter technique has caused such concern that one municipality—Cambridge, Massachusetts—has legally restricted such research within its limits.)

The authors next describe the social philosophies of eugenics, programs for improving the genetic "quality" of the human race, either by "removal" of the material declared "undesirable" or by promoting the reproduction of individuals defined as "superior." Detracting from this generally objective analysis is a superficial and biased approach to the hoary question of whether criminal and antisocial behavior is genetically or socially determined.

The fourth chapter, "Life in the Laboratory," is the most relevant to the topic of *in vitro* fertilization and gestation. Techniques currently in use are artificial insemination of a woman by her husband (AIH) or by an anonymous donor (AID) and,

now, *in vitro* fertilization and reimplantation of the embryo. Potential techniques include: (1) implantation of embryos in surrogate mothers (a well-publicized experiment involved the air shipment of a hundred embryonic sheep from England to the United States, all implanted within the uterus of a single living rabbit); (2) extracorporeal or *in vitro* gestation from fertilization to "birth"; (3) parthenogenesis, literally "virgin birth," the development of a child from an unfertilized egg (several claims exist, including one which is reasonably well documented, of children born to virgins); (4) chimeras, or embryo-fusion (cells from two separate mouse embryos are commonly combined into a single embryo which develops into an adult that possesses not two, but four, parents); and (5) cloning, or the asexual reproduction of a sexually reproducing organism (although Rorvik's controversial book *In His Image* remains unsubstantiated at this date and is therefore widely considered a hoax, many geneticists anticipate that a human being will be cloned within thirty to thirty-five years).

A discussion of genetic screening, its historical perspectives and moral and legal dilemmas, follows. One must wonder whether it is perhaps not the screening *per se* that causes social repercussions, but rather the scientific ignorance or bureaucratic clumsiness of the well-meaning screeners. The authors do stress a point that cannot be overemphasized: genetic variability is not genetic abnormality. Indeed, such variability is our richest natural resource.

The chapter on biofutures explores

a spectrum of problems which can be corrected if not cured by genetic manipulation. Although some of these speculations sound extreme (such as "shopping" for fetuses which have been deep-frozen for future revival), our thinking is sobered by the knowledge that biologists today do create functional genes "from scratch" and insert these genes into living cells which reproduce daughter cells containing the new heredity. Such techniques are sure to attract the attention of those industries which feel that they can profit by offering such services to the public. Recent news releases indicate that drug companies have recently been given the right to secure patents for any forms of artificial life created in their laboratories.

The Howard and Rifkin book is, then, a generally serious and sobering exploration, sometimes melodramatic, of the benefits and problems deriving from genetic engineering and related research interests.

Edwards, Robert G. and P. C. Steptoe. "Induction of Follicular Growth, Ovulation and Luteinization in the Human Ovary," in *Journal of Reproduction and Fertility*. Supplement 22 (1975), pp. 121-163.

At this writing (within six weeks of Louise Brown's birth), there has been insufficient time for Patrick Steptoe and Robert Edwards to write their own account of the birth. To date they have published only a brief letter in the British medical journal *Lancet* (August 12, 1978, p. 366). Consequently the article reviewed here is a somewhat earlier description of their experimental procedures. It is technical and requires concentration on the part of the general reader, but it does provide a description of the hormonal treatments employed to induce ovulation in infertile women.

More than sixty patients were exposed to one of three different regimes, depending on the type of infertility they were experiencing. Those patients who menstruated regularly but were unable to conceive (apparently Lesley Brown's situation) were treated with human chorionic gonadotrophin (HCG). This hormone is normally secreted by the developing embryo in the uterus of pregnant women and has properties similar to the luteinizing hormone (LH). Large amounts of LH are normally secreted by the anterior pituitary gland at the base of the brain at about midcycle, that is, the thirteenth or fourteenth day. The resulting surge in LH levels seems to stimulate the ovarian follicle to rupture and release the egg which has been maturing within. A single dose of 5,000 international units of HCG was administered to these women six to twelve hours prior to the anticipated naturally occuring LH surge. (The hormonal cycle of each of these women had been monitored through urinalysis during several earlier menstrual periods in order to estimate accurately the proper time for HCG injection.) Following ovulation, the ruptured follicle fills with blood and the follicular cells enlarge to form a structure called the corpus luteum, which must be maintained in the ovary if a pregnancy is to be successful. One of the functions of HCG secreted by the embryo is to help in the maintenance of the corpus luteum and therefore to help assure the full-term development of the fetus.

Another regime was employed with anovulatory patients (those who do not normally ovulate). Beginning on the second or third day of their menstrual cycle these women were given several injections of human menopausal gonadotrophin (HMG, a hormone that induces follicular growth). This treatment was repeated at intervals of forty-eight to fifty hours for six to nine days and was followed, within eight more days, by a single 5,000 international unit injection of HCG.

A different regime was followed in amenorrheic women (those suffering from rare or irregular menstrual cycles). Instead of HMG, they were given fifty milligram tablets of clomiphene for a period of five days, beginning on the second or third day of their cycle, to induce follicular growth. As above, this series of treatments was then followed by a 5,000 international unit injection of HCG on the twelfth or thirteenth day.

In all three regimes, a laparoscopic examination of the ovary was made by Steptoe approximately thirty-two to forty-two hours after the administration of the HCG. The number and size of the follicles observed were recorded; these proved to be extremely variable, a factor discussed by the authors. Follicles were then aspirated, yielding not only the oocyte (an egg in the latter stages of maturation), but also some granulosa cells from the follicular lining, and follicular fluids as well. An analysis of several different aspects of the data follows, including follicular growth after treatment with HMG-HCG, clomiphene-HCG, and HCG alone; timing of follicular rupture after the single injection of HCG; anatomical and physiological development of the follicle and oocyte; constitution and properties of the follicular fluids; and a description of luteinization (the formation of the corpus luteum after ovulation).

The interval between the HCG injection and rupture of the follicle is "astonishingly regular" in all species of mammals so far investigated. Although the nature of the regulation of follicle growth is unclear, substances called chalones (or coylones, chemicals which are produced by one organ, released into the bloodstream and sent to a different organ where they act as inhibitory agents) apparently interfere with mitotic division of follicular stem cells. Many investigators attribute follicular growth patterns to a wide variety of other factors; but, however regulated, follicles are produced in a sequential progression and not in clusters. In many mammals, possibly including man, several waves of follicles are formed during each cycle.

Ovulation normally occurs some thirty hours after the natural surge of LH. If HCG is administered prior to the LH surge, ovulation is usually delayed for an additional seven hours. The significance of this rather consistent time lag remains unclear. The authors also indicate that factors other than LH influence the mechanics of ovulation, such as estradiol, progesterone, and other steroids; the autonomic nervous system and the adrenal secretions; and, perhaps, cyclic AMP, the nucleotide known to regulate some aspects of DNA activity.

Relationships between the rhythm method of contraception and follicular dynamics and ovulation are explored. Needless to say, the implications of using knowledge gained from these studies to alleviate infertility are explored as well—explorations that were to lead, three years later, to the technology that resulted in the birth of Louise Joy Brown. — *J.C.N.*

Additional Recommended Reading

Edwards, Robert G. and David J. Sharpe. "Social Values and Research in Human Embryology," in *Nature*. CCXXXI (May 14, 1971), pp. 87-91. An exploration of some social and legal issues arising from *in vitro* experimentation, including the alleviation of infertility, determination of embryonic sex, modification of embryological development, and the legal regulation of scientific research.

Frankel, Charles. "The Specter of Eugenics," in *Commentary*. LVII (March, 1974), pp. 25-33. An objective discussion by the Columbia University philosopher of the troubling ramifications of biomedical research and the practical application of such research to complex social issues.

Goodfield, Jane. *Playing God: Genetic Engineering and the Manipulation of Life*. New York: Random House, 1977. A recent study of the social and ethical implications of genetic research, with special emphasis on the potential for political regulation of genetic engineering.

Ramsey, Paul. "Shall We 'Reproduce'?," in *Journal of the American Medical Association*. CCXX (June 5 and June 14, 1972), pp. 1346-1350 and 1480-1485. A two part essay (the first on the medical ethics of *in vitro* fertilization and the second on rejoinders and future forecast) by the Princeton theologian.

Taylor, Gordon Rattray. *The Biological Time Bomb*. New York: New American Library, 1968. A wide-ranging exploration of a variety of experimental techniques contemplated by biomedical scientists and their potential influences on humanity.

Edwards, Robert G., P. C. Steptoe and J. M. Purdy. "Fertilization and Cleavage in Vitro of Preovulator Human Oocytes," in *Nature*. CCXXVII (September 26, 1970), pp. 1307-1309. An earlier paper describing experimental techniques for *in vitro* growth of embryos to the eight- and sixteen-celled stages.

RATIFICATION OF THE PANAMA CANAL TREATIES

Type of event: Diplomatic: achievement of new agreements on the use and control of the Panama Canal
Time: March 16 and April 18, 1978
Locale: Washington, D.C.

Principal personages:

GERALD RUDOLPH FORD (1913-   ), thirty-eighth President of the United States, 1974-1977

JIMMY (JAMES EARL) CARTER (1924-   ), thirty-ninth President of the United States, 1977-

HENRY ALFRED KISSINGER (1923-   ), United States Secretary of State, 1973-1977

CYRUS ROBERTS VANCE (1917-   ), United States Secretary of State in the Carter Administration

OMAR TORRIJOS HERRERA (1929-   ), Chief of State of Panama and Commander of the National Guard

JUAN ANTONIO TACK (1934-   ), Foreign Minister of Panama, 1970-1976

ROBERT CARLYLE BYRD (1917-   ), Majority Leader of the United States Senate

HOWARD HENRY BAKER (1925-   ), Minority Leader of the United States Senate

Summary of Event

The Senate's ratification of the Treaty Concerning the Permanent Neutrality and Operation of the Panama Canal and the Panama Canal Treaty in the spring of 1978 was the culmination of a long and often dramatic effort to achieve mutually satisfactory new agreements between the United States and the Republic of Panama on one of the most vital waterways in the world. Opponents fought the treaties with conviction and determination, leaving the outcome in doubt until the day of the vote. The Panama Canal had become a major political issue, and the debate was charged with emotion and intensity.

The history of the Canal has been colorful and long; one can trace its conception back to the year 1513, when Vasco Núñez de Balboa first sighted the Pacific Ocean. The discovery that the territory called Darien was a relatively narrow land bridge between two great oceans prompted the Spanish Emperor Charles V to order a survey for a possible canal across the isthmus. Periodically, the concept was revived, but not until the latter part of the nineteenth century could actual efforts toward its realization be made. Indeed, not even an efficient overland crossing was possible until the 1850's, when an American company built the Panama Railroad. In 1880, a French company under the direction of Ferdinand de Lesseps, the celebrated builder of the Suez Canal, decided to build the Panama Canal. However, the enterprise proved to be enormously more difficult than had been anticipated. Malaria, yellow fever, and financial ruin brought the French effort to a humiliating end.

American interest in the gigantic project grew after the Spanish-American War of 1898, leading to the development of specific plans. Before buying out the French company's rights and resuming construction, the United States intended to insure its complete control over the future canal. At the time, the Panamanian territory was a part of the Republic of Colombia, which was unwilling to make the kind of concessions sought by the United States. Thus, the United States saw its interests well served by assisting a Panamanian nationalist faction in forming the independent Republic of Panama in 1903. Two weeks after the independence proclamation, a treaty was signed between the new republic and the United States, granting the latter "in perpetuity" the use, occupation, and control of a ten-mile-wide strip of land across the isthmus. In return Panama received ten million dollars and subsequent annual rent payments.

The building of the Panama Canal through the center of the Zone required ten years, at a cost of $310 million and approximately four thousand lives. It was formally opened to traffic on August 15, 1914. Superlatives have been lavished on the fifty-one-mile-long "Big Ditch," but it is no exaggeration to refer to it as one of the greatest engineering achievements of all time. It rises eighty-five feet above sea level to cross a continental divide through the astounding Gaillard Cut. Ships are raised or lowered for crossing in a six-step sequence of double locks. Over the years the Canal has been immensely important for maritime transport and enormously beneficial to the Panamanian economy. Approximately eleven thousand Panamanians are directly employed in the operation and related services in the Canal Zone. In addition to this factor one must consider the personal spending of American residents of the Zone and the corollary benefits of a busy international waterway, which have turned the cities of Panama and Colón into centers of international banking and commerce.

However, the fundamental issue for Panama was the fact that it did not control its major resource. A growing nationalistic sentiment generated vehement resentment of the "neocolonial enclave." Finally, a bloody confrontation in January, 1964—precipitated by an attempt of Panamanian students to hoist their national flag in the Zone and resulting in two dozen deaths and hundreds of injuries—convinced American governmental leaders of the need to enter into negotiations with Panama for a new treaty. Three years of deliberations followed, leading to three draft treaties in 1967 which dealt with jurisdiction over the Canal, defense and status of the military forces, and the possibility of a new sea-level canal; but these tentative agreements were subsequently repudiated by Panama. The negotiations resumed in June, 1971, but remained intractable. Meanwhile, Panama succeeded in drawing worldwide attention to, and critical scrutiny of, the Canal controversy. In March, 1973, the United Nations Security Council held a special meeting in Panama. A resolution calling for a "just and equitable" solution to the dispute and "effective sovereignty" for Panama over all its territory was introduced. The United States defeated the motion through the exercise of its veto power. Nevertheless, these actions gave Panama an important propaganda victory.

Leading American officials now felt that new accommodations were inescapable. Consequently, on February 7, 1974, Secretary of State Henry Kissinger and Panamanian Foreign Minister Juan Antonio Tack met in Panama City and signed a joint statement of principle to serve as a framework for a new round of negotiations. The mutual goal was to arrive at a new treaty satisfying the basic concerns of both nations. This effort reached a successful conclusion on September 7, 1977, when the new Panama Canal Treaty and the Treaty Concerning the Permanent Neutrality and Operation of the Panama Canal were signed in Washington. They were to enter into force simultaneously on a specified date subsequent to the exchange of ratification instruments.

One treaty governs the operations and defense of the Canal through December 31, 1999; the other guarantees the permanent neutrality of the Canal. They replace the 1903 treaty and the supplementary provisions of 1936 and 1955. In essence, the treaties provide for the orderly complete transfer of jurisdiction over the Canal and the Zone from the United States to Panama by the year 2000. Until that time, the United States will manage and operate the Canal and assume the primary responsibility to protect and defend it. A new United States government agency, the Panama Canal Commission, will operate the Canal for the rest of the century. Its board of directors will be composed of five Americans and four Panamanians; an American will be the administrator until 1990 and a Panamanian the deputy; thereafter the roles will be reversed.

The new treaties encountered formidable opposition from conservative and rightist elements and required an intense public relations campaign, as well as vigorous lobbying, to assure ratification by the United States Senate. President Jimmy Carter, his Secretary of State, Cyrus Vance, and other leading Administration officials made every effort to persuade the country that the treaties were in the national interest. Rather than undermining national security, as the opposition charged, they argued that the new treaties strengthened it. The agreements were presented as constituting a better defense against possible sabotage and terrorist attacks, for they gave the Panamanian people a greater stake in keeping the Canal open. They provided for the major American objective: an open, secure, and efficiently operated canal. Moreover, the treaties were designed to promote a constructive, positive relationship between the United States and the other nations of the Western Hemisphere; a failure to ratify them could be expected to lead to an increasingly hostile, anti-American atmosphere. President Carter talked of "fairness, not force" in our dealings with other nations, positing this not as a mere moral imperative, but as an element of a pragmatic foreign policy.

The Senate Foreign Relations Committee endorsed the treaties in January, 1978, on condition that they be modified to insure more clearly American defense and transit rights after 2000. Majority Leader Robert C. Byrd worked very hard on behalf of the President, who had staked his prestige on the successful passage. Several Democratic Senators, whose votes were vital, were holding out for concessions from the Administration on the substance of the treaties and on certain domestic issues. Apparently the President had no choice but to make the necessary political deals, earning him the charge of buying votes.

The Senate ratified the Neutrality Treaty on March 16, 1978, by a vote of 68-32. Two "reservations," instead of amendments, which might have required a repetition of the ratification process in Panama, were added. The first of these was introduced by Senator Dennis De Concini of Arizona, providing for American armed intervention in Panama in the event the Canal was closed. The second was introduced by Senator Sam Nunn of Georgia, allowing for the United States and Panama to agree on stationing American troops in Panama after 1999. Panamanian spokesmen indicated acceptance of these changes, but there was growing opposition in Panama to the Senate's efforts to alter the negotiated terms. The Panama Canal Treaty was ratified on April 18, 1978, again by a vote of 68-32. The added reservations included another by De Concini, allowing for American troops to reopen the Canal if operations were disrupted. Relieved that the long and intense process had finally come to an end, President Carter and Panamanian leader Omar Torrijos Herrera hailed the ratifications and predicted a new and amicable relationship between their countries.

Pertinent Literature

Lernoux, Penny. "Face-off in Panama: U.S. Imperialists, Old and New," in *At Issue: Politics in the World Arena*. Edited by Steven L. Spiegel. New York: St. Martin's Press, 1977.

Penny Lernoux advances the intriguing thesis about an old and a new camp of empire builders opposing each other over the future of the Panama Canal. It was a confrontation between the traditional military expansionists and the community of executives representing the multinational corporations and international banks. From this latter group's perspective, the question was whether the Canal was worth risking the multinationals' holdings in Latin America. Lernoux's account intimates that the American government was rather more responsive to the interests of the multinationals.

Both the American and the Panamanian governments knew that the stakes were political and economic, not military; yet, it was the defense of the Canal which became one of the major items of contention during the lengthy negotiations. As Lernoux points out, the Canal cannot be defended against nuclear attack or guerrilla warfare, nor can one envision realistically the use of United States troops stationed in the Canal Zone as a strike force for military intervention elsewhere in Latin America. Nevertheless, the old camp insisted on a continued presence of a strong American military force in Panama. This obstinacy was beginning to pose a real threat to the operations of the multinational corporations and banks.

Panama's national leader, Omar Torrijos Herrera, had managed to turn the dispute with the United States over a new treaty into the single most important issue in Latin America. Irrespective of the differences and antagonisms, on the question of Panamanian sovereignty over the Canal the nations of the hemisphere pulled together. The camp of the multinationals feared that such political solidarity could have dire consequences for their interests in Latin America, should matters ever get out of hand in Panama. Panama itself, having become the financial and commercial center for the Americas, was important enough. However, potentially the total economic stake in all of Latin America was threatened. An accommodating new treaty was the obvious answer to the problem, and an effective public relations campaign was launched.

The Torrijos regime was exceptionally tolerant of foreign business activities. The corporate and banking interests, keenly aware of how strongly public opinion in Panama was fixed on sovereignty over the Canal and the inability of the government to back away from the issue, simply wanted to protect their investments. Thus it came about, according to Lernoux, that the multinationals championed the Panamanian cause and encouraged the United States government in its efforts to provide for an orderly transition of control over the Canal. The resultant demonstration of political pragmatism, fortunately, seems to have strengthened the long-range interests of the United States in Latin America.

Crane, Philip M. *Surrender in Panama: The Case Against the Treaty*. New York: Dale Books, 1978.

Congressman Philip Crane, a prominent and highly articulate advocate of conservative causes, wrote this book to rally sufficient opposition to defeat the treaties. Obviously, in this purpose he failed. However, his strongly stated case against the treaties puts the issues into clear focus for the reader and helps to illuminate the total situation.

Crane believes the original Panama Canal Treaty of 1903 contains incontrovertible language regarding the sovereignty of the United States over the Canal Zone. Under Article Two of this treaty, Panama grants the United States "in perpetuity the use, occupation and control of a zone . . .";

and Article Three grants the United States "all rights, power and authority within the zone . . . which the United States would possess and exercise if it were the sovereign of the territory. . . ." To Crane, the 1903 treaty is an ironclad legal basis for American possession of the Canal and the Zone. This, of course, stands in direct opposition to the government's position that Panama's fundamental sovereignty remained intact; the Zone was, in effect, leased and not owned. Administration spokesmen pointed out that the United States was making annual rent payments, suggesting that one normally does not pay rent on what one owns.

In positing full American sovereignty over the Canal Zone, Crane and other opponents of the new treaties sought to establish a role for the House of Representatives in determining the fate of the treaties. According to the Constitution, it is the Congress, not the Senate only, which has the power to dispose of United States territory and property. Indeed, Crane's case was bolstered by the fact that there was precedence for House participation in implementing legislation, when small alterations in the Canal Zone were effected in the past. But for Congressman Crane the moral issue at stake in Panama was even more important than such issues of constitutionality. He felt that in the face of encroachments on America's power the world over, it is of vital importance that the United States assume a strong and determined posture. Giving up the Canal would be an unforgivable sign of irresolution and weakness.

The Panama Canal, extremely im-

portant in its own right, is even more important as a symbol of American resolution, according to Crane. Giving it up would lead to an irreparable loss of dignity and self-respect; it would be another "step in a descent to ignominy." Crane talks about the glorious past of the Theodore Roosevelt era in terms suggesting that it should be a guide to action today. His polemics about the "strategic cost of surrender" are the weakest part of his argument. In this connection, the gratuitous disparagement of foreign leaders and countries does not strengthen his case. To be sure, Panama joined the ranks of sovereign Latin American republics comparatively late, and it has an unstable political heritage of revolution and strongman rule, interspersed with short-lived experiments in democracy. Today, General Omar Torrijos Herrera's personalized dictatorship is in the *caudillo* tradition. However, Torrijos is popular with most of his compatriots, through a combination of charisma and defiance of United States "imperialism." Similar to Fidel Castro of Cuba, he skillfully played the Latin David standing up to the Yankee Goliath. But for a man accused of having strong Communist sympathies, Torrijos has been amazingly friendly to American business and has shown a remarkable preference for capitalism. Whether one likes him or not, one must recognize some uncommon leadership qualities in Torrijos. It was he, after all, who cleverly manipulated the Canal issue and turned it into a *cause célèbre* for all of Latin America.

If Crane, Ronald Reagan, and the Senate members of the so-called "truth squad" had prevailed, America's standing and influence in the Western Hemisphere and most of the Third World would probably be diminished. The new treaties were a demonstra-tion of the rational use of power. The national interest of the United States was identified by relating to today's realities and the foreseeable future prospects. — *M.G.*

Additional Recommended Reading

"After Carter's Panama Victory," in *U.S. News & World Report*. LXXIX (May 1, 1978), pp. 25-27. A concise review of the process of transition envisioned by the treaties.

"How the Treaty Was Saved," in *Time*. LXXXIII (May 1, 1978), pp. 12-15. A review of the last-minute efforts to get the necessary votes for ratification.

Biesanz, John and Mavis Biesanz. *The People of Panama*. New York: Columbia University Press, 1955. An excellent general background study of Panama.

Haskin, Frederic J. *The Panama Canal*. Garden City, N.Y.: Doubleday, Page & Company, 1913. A fascinating early treatment of the story of the Panama Canal.

McCullough, David. *The Path Between the Seas: The Creation of the Panama Canal, 1870-1914*. New York: Simon and Schuster, 1977. A timely, definitive study of the building of the Canal.

THE IRANIAN REVOLUTION

Type of event: Political: overthrow of Iranian government which results in international
  ramifications
Time: 1978-1979
Locale: Iran

Principal personages:
  MOHAMMED RIZA PAHLAVI (1919-   ), the last Shah of
  Iran, 1941-1979
  AYATOLLAH RUHOLLAH KHOMEINI (1900-   ), exiled Is-
  lamic leader, 1963-1979; and unofficial ruler of revolution-
  ary Iran, 1979-
  JIMMY (JAMES EARL) CARTER (1924-   ), thirty-ninth Pres-
  ident of the United States, 1977-

Summary of Event

The average American has become
an expert on the revolution in Iran.
In a time when *coups d'état*, military
takeovers, and collapsing governments seem almost a routine matter,
the Iranian Revolution of 1979 has
startled the world. Part of the attention focused on Iran has stemmed
from the American embassy crisis,
and from the fear of a new, broader
war in the Middle East. But behind
these concerns is an awareness that
the changes in Iran are not typical of
those occurring elsewhere in the Third
World, but instead reflect that country's anomalous status and pattern of
development over the past fifty years.

Iran today is a major country. With
forty million people, a land mass as
large as Western Europe (or one-
fourth the size of the continental
United States), an abundance of sophisticated military technology, and
a wealth of natural resources, Iran
ranks just below such major powers
as France and India. Over the past
generation, Iran has made more rapid
strides towards industrialization than

any country since Japan in the late
nineteenth century. Like most large
countries, Iran is composed of many
different peoples, and culture varies
from one region to the next; but the
nation is bound together by a long
history of successful independence.

Until this century, Iran was known
as Persia, the heart and remnant of
an empire which in its heyday during
the fifth century B.C. stretched from
Greece to India. The Persian Empire
was conquered by Alexander the
Great in 327 B.C., and over the next
two thousand years was successively
attacked by Parthians, Muslims, Ot-
tomans, and Mongols; but Persia consistently succeeded in eventually ab-
sorbing its masters and reasserting its
national identity. In the nineteenth
century, this struggle for sovereignty
took the form of resistance to imperialism. Delicately balanced between
the Russian Empire to the north, the
Ottoman Empire to the west, and
British India to the east, the Persian
shahs had little choice but to play
these powers off against one another

and to convince each that their best interest lay in Persia's independence. Their strategy was remarkably successful, and the area remained one of the few in Asia that avoided colonial status. In 1907, however, the British and Russians concluded an entente formally establishing defined spheres of interest in the country.

What was left of Persian independence collapsed under the pressure of World War I. Fearful that the Turks (allied with Germany) would gain a strategic advantage, the British established informal control over part of the country during the war years. The ruling Persian dynasty was too weak to create much resistance, and after the war it signed an agreement to use British advisers to modernize the government, the army, and the oil industry—in effect, to preserve British control. This obvious surrender to foreign domination aroused fervent nationalism among the educated classes and the army and encouraged local "tribal" chiefs to revolt against the central government. A young nationalist general named Reza Khan Pahlavi successfully staged a *coup* in 1921. Over the next three years, he managed to consolidate power within the central government, abolish the British contracts, put down the regional revolts, and have himself declared the new Shah of "Iran"—a word with more traditional and patriotic connotations than "Persia."

The Reza Shah was primarily concerned with the modernization of Iran. He replaced the British experts with politically powerless Germans, expanded the oil industry, and imported machines for both agriculture and industry. Change came slowly, but the interwar years gave Iran a crucial head start that most of the Third World, still under European control, could not follow.

World War II again brought instability to the region. With the Nazi rise to power in Germany, the British looked with increasing suspicion upon the Germans in Iran. When Hitler invaded the Soviet Union in the summer of 1941, the newly allied British and Russians desperately needed a supply route to prevent a Russian collapse. Only one route seemed possible—through Iran. After token negotiations with the Shah, the British and Russians invaded Iran and forced almost immediate surrender. Convinced that the Reza Shah was secretly a Nazi sympathizer, they agreed to permit Iranian independence only on one condition—that the Shah abdicate in favor of his young son, the twenty-two-year-old Reza Muhammed Pahlavi, who has been known ever since simply as the Shah of Iran.

The new Shah was idealistic and inexperienced. He had been educated in Europe and was familiar with (and sympathetic to) current Western ideas of how modernization should occur in undeveloped countries. He was determined to mold a strong, independent, modern, and reformed Iran under his leadership.

But he first faced a long apprenticeship. The first twelve years of the Shah's rule were consumed in struggles for power. Shortly after his accession, Iran was essentially forced to agree to a Tripartite Treaty of Alliance with Great Britain and the U.S.S.R. and to give formal support to the war against the Axis. Throughout the war, the Shah struggled with the Allies for control over the Iranian bureaucracy. Despite reassurances from the Allies, foreign domination continued and the credibility of the Shah declined. Even at the end of the war with the removal of American and British forces, it was clear that the U.S.S.R. intended to maintain control over a small northwestern province with avowed Communist sympathies. At the height of Soviet-Iranian tension, the Truman Doctrine was announced (March, 1947); and though aimed chiefly at Greece and Turkey, the U.S.S.R. interpreted it as support for Iran and quickly withdrew its forces.

With a relaxed international situation, the Shah was quickly confronted with domestic troubles. Political movements both of reaction and radicalism demanded an array of changes in the government and a reduction in the Shah's power. This the Shah was determined not to yield—he considered the success of his plans inseparable from his own authority. After an assassination attempt in 1949 succeeded only in wounding the Shah, he took advantage of the surge in his personal popularity by securing broader powers from Parliament. In 1950, he won further support from his distribution of royal lands to small landowners. The alarmed conservatives in government accused the Shah of being a tool of foreigners, nationalized the British oil company, and staged a *coup d'état* which actually forced the Shah from the country for a brief period in August, 1953. With the aid of the American Central Intelligence Agency (CIA), however, the Shah had anticipated the *coup*

d'état; he had carefully planned a series of countermoves and triumphantly returned to Iran. By the end of 1953, his power was immense and secure.

The Shah was still idealistic, but experience had lent sophistication to his plans for Iran. He developed a three-cornered strategy for Iranian policy. In foreign policy, he threw his fortunes in with the United States. He feared Russian expansionism and encouraged the United States to place military forces in Iran and to provide advice on Iranian policies. America, in return, came to view Iran as one of the "key" nations in the free world and willingly strengthened the country with military equipment and technology. This led to the second corner of the Shah's strategy—modernization. Instead of building roads and dams and encouraging business, as many other countries did, the Shah sought to promote directly modern factories, a balanced national economy, and widespread education. To achieve all this, he sold Iranian oil for Western machines and Western advisers. As the economy progressed, the Shah planned to implement the third part of his strategy—political reform. As the country became less poor and better educated, he would gradually extend political freedoms and redistribute wealth. Power would be decentralized. If insurgents threatened instability, there was always American support to back him up. Within a generation or two, Iran would be an industrial democracy in the front rank of nations.

Such was the plan, and for a long while it succeeded spectacularly. Iran's military power steadily increased, and the nation was unthreatened by war. Iran's economic success was unparalleled. By the end of the 1950's, industrial output had more than doubled; by the early 1970's, it had doubled twice more. Per capita income frequently rose ten percent in a single year. From a few thousand students after World War II, the Iranian educational system grew to include nearly one million students in the mid-1960's, and more than seven million students—virtually the entire school-age population—by the mid-1970's. In 1961, the Shah launched a "revolution" of agrarian reform, seizing the lands of the large landholders and dividing it up among tenant farmers. Political restrictions were eased, provincial departments of the government were granted greater authority, and signs of a cultural renaissance began to appear. Financing all this improvement, always in the background, was oil. Oil revenues rose from $200 million in the 1950's to some $5 billion in the mid-1970's.

But despite its outward success, the Shah's rule was authoritarian, elitist, and ruthless when necessary. The benefits of progress were wildly uneven in their distribution. The rising urban middle class enjoyed a life style comparable to that of the middle class in the United States while rural families continued in grinding poverty. Foreign experts were paid large salaries to come and teach their skills; the aura of money and privilege around them created tension and resentment among Iranians. Pro-American policies, such as Iran's sale of oil to Israel, seemed like slavish obedience to the American will and anti-Islam in purpose. The Shah's government was neither oppressive enough to stifle dissent, nor tolerant enough to permit vocal opposition. To an increasingly articulate and educated population, such rigid control was unsatisfactory. An angry but quiet consensus of opinion against the Shah began to build.

In 1978, smouldering dissent erupted from the conservative Muslim leadership of Iran. Widespread corruption among the Shah's relatives was exposed, and riots and demonstrations began to occur. Early in the year, the Ayatollah Ruhollah Khomeini, who had been expelled from Iran in 1963, was now expelled from Iraq. He went to Paris and quickly became the symbolic leader of the dissent within Iran. Tension seemed to lessen in the early summer, but the burning of a crowded theater in early August, killing more than four hundred people, sparked new and more violent demonstrations. The Shah promised democratic reforms and appointed a moderate prime minister, but the violence continued.

By September, it was evident that dissent within Iran was remarkably broad-based. Throughout industry, and particularly in the oil fields, a massive and coordinated slowdown created increasing economic chaos. By the beginning of November, oil production was at a virtual standstill. The Shah reversed himself, declaring martial law and appointing a general as prime minister, but the demonstrations steadily grew, seeming to feed on every move the Shah made.

By January of 1979, the Shah faced essentially two options: he could restore a semblance of order by force, or he could leave the country. Perhaps hoping to duplicate his successful return to power in 1953, he chose the latter course. The government was turned over to the conciliatory Shahpur Bakhtiar, and the Shah traveled to Egypt. The Ayatollah Khomeini soon returned to Iran, declaring that he bore "no hostility" to countries giving the Shah asylum, but demanding a new government. The Bakhtiar government collapsed, leading to a succession of Khomeini-appointed ministers.

The Iranian Revolution followed a troubled course in 1979. Workers returned to work and order was restored to the economy, but the revolution produced serious economic problems. The leadership of Khomeini was uncertain, and no consensus of national purpose or goals seemed to emerge. While devout Muslims called for a return to traditional values, many students and others sought a more leftist regime, and provincial leaders reasserted their old grievances against the central Tehran government. Violence continued against those formerly in power, and threats were made against those who aided the deposed Shah now in exile in Panama. When President Jimmy Carter permitted the Shah to undergo medical treatment in the United States, radical students in Tehran responded by seizing the American embassy.

The seizure of hostages in the American embassy in November crystallized a long series of anti-American demonstrations and brought the revolution into a new phase. The students guarding the embassy became a critical new force in Iranian politics, and the hostages became a clear issue for national debate. Hence, at the end of 1979, the question of the hostages remained as unclear as the shape of Iranian political life.

Pertinent Literature

Tocqueville, Alexis de. *The Old Regime and the French Revolution*. Translated by Stuart Gilbert. Garden City, N.Y.: Doubleday & Company, 1955.

To know the events that lead up to a revolution is not to understand the revolution itself. The Iranian Revolution in years to come will be explained by any number of theories and underlying forces hardly visible to us today. But probably one of the most persuasive of these theories will resemble the work of a French bureaucrat writing more than a century ago.

Alexis de Tocqueville has been called the first "social scientist." Writers in the early nineteenth century were just beginning to observe the impact of abstract social forces upon the course of change in society. Tocqueville's two-volume work, *Democracy in America*, has always been recognized as a masterpiece of this type of social observation. After many years in French government, he retired to write a more complex book on the French Revolution. The only part of this work that he completed was *The Old Regime and the French Revolution*, which was published in 1856, three years before Tocqueville died.

The Old Regime and the French Revolution is full of insightful observations about France and about methods for discovering the past, but the underlying theme of the book has to do with the nature of social and political change. The author views society as normally in a state of equilibrium which in France was thoroughly disrupted during the generation preceding the Revolution. Under the reign of Louis XVI, which began in 1774, the French government launched a variety of new enterprises designed to expand the economy which succeeded in raising the general standard of living throughout France. But this increased activity by itself both attracted more attention to the workings of government and significantly raised expectations about what government could accomplish. When depression struck France in 1788, a wide array of groups adamantly demanded reform in the government. The Revolution began the following year.

There is a remarkable degree of similarity between the Iranian and the French Revolutions. Both countries experienced remarkable economic growth after a period of stagnation; both were advancing from rural, feudal economies toward more urban and industrial ones. In both cases, a new middle class was beginning to develop which was the main beneficiary of the new economic advance, but which was unhappy that monetary gain did not bring political power and social prestige to match. Both governments were brought down not by physical force or armies but through a broad national consensus for fundamental change.

The analogies between the two countries can easily be extended beyond the beginning of revolution. The course of revolution in France was long and unstable. Once the old government was undermined, the legitimacy of any new government was seriously in question, and successive governments fell fairly rapidly. Louis XVI occupied a steadily less important role, but hatred of his rule led to his execution in 1793. The extreme fluctuations of the government under the "Reign of Terror" of Maximilien de Robespierre eventually provoked a national reaction oriented toward a more moderate and stable government.

Much of this social agitation can be seen in Iran. During the Shah's final months, a succession of ministers enacted reforms designed to appease protest but which succeeded only in further mobilizing the revolution. The present government is seriously plagued by a lack of legitimate authority. Since the Shah is gone from Iran, the frustration at the failure of revolution that in France led to the King's execution has in Iran led to the seizure of the American embassy. Even the provincial revolts in Iran have their counterparts in the "Vendee" revolt during the French Revolution.

Although such analogies do not allow one to predict the course of revolution in Iran, they do strongly suggest that fundamental and unchanging social processes are at work in Iran; and few have analyzed these processes better than Tocqueville.

Maclean, John, *et al.* "How America Stumbled in Iran," in *Chicago Tribune*. (December 16, 1979), pp. 17-18.

Comparisons of the Iranian and French revolutions suggest that domestic forces were the prime movers of revolution. This differs strongly from those who argue, particularly in the case of Iran, that revolution instead springs out of an international diplomatic situation.

"How America Stumbled in Iran," written by the Washington staff of the *Chicago Tribune*, is one of the best examples of this argument applied to Iran. The basic premise of the argument is that international order is a prerequisite for domestic order. When relations between nations become undependable, the power of each nation is lessened, and in critical times they become less capable of dealing with their own domestic problems.

In the case of Iran, the argument runs that the Carter Administration, beginning in 1977, created an unstable situation for American allies. The official position of the United States began to run toward declarations of human rights, the need for limiting arms sales, and the desirability of democracy. All of these positions could have two negative effects on Iran. First, they indirectly criticized the harsh, undemocratic policies of the Shah and paved the way for internal criticism. Second, they threw into question, both in the Shah's mind and in the minds of his people, the reliability of Iran's alliance with the United States. If Iran needed America, could it count on support, or would the United States instead deliver moral criticisms?

Other American actions can also be interpreted as causes of the revolution in Iran. During the early 1970's, the Shah bought increasing amounts of arms from the United States. This fact raises the question of whether such action created an artificial dependency on America. During the early stages of the revolution, the Carter Administration steadily urged the Shah to pursue a moderate course. It could be argued that if the Shah had "cracked down" on the revolution at its outset, it never would have occurred.

Such arguments are weakened by their vagueness. It is possible to argue in retrospect that almost any international event contributed in some way to a later event; but such actions, however they may have added to instability, cannot explain how such powerful instability began in the first place. These arguments do, however, point out an interesting dilemma of American foreign policy. In many places in the world, the United States is actively supporting governments whose policies run directly counter to the democratic, free values of American society. This fact creates an underlying tension in our foreign policy, and the resulting contradictions weaken both the logic and the strength of American policies. — *R.H.S.*

Additional Recommended Reading

Avery, Peter. *Modern Iran*. London: Ernest Benn, 1965. An excellent survey of

Iranian history over the last two hundred years, though now somewhat dated by events.

Paydarfar, Ali A. *Social Change in a Southern Province of Iran*. Chapel Hill: University of North Carolina Press, 1974. One of the few studies of the impact of industrialization upon the Iranian people.

Sanghvi, Ramesh. *The Shah of Iran*. New York: Stein and Day, 1969. An interesting political history of recent Iran, although obviously told from the Shah's perspective.

Zonis, Marvin. *The Political Elite of Iran*. Princeton, N.J.: Princeton University Press, 1971. Examines the effect that a loss of political power has had upon the "political elite" in Iran during the Shah's reign and comes up with a number of interesting insights.

VIETNAM'S CONQUEST OF CAMBODIA

Type of event: Military: armed conflict between two adjacent countries
Time: 1979
Locale: Cambodia (Kampuchea)

Principal personages:

POL POT (1928-   ), Prime Minister and Secretary of the
Cambodian Communist Party (Khmer Rouge) of Demo-
cratic Kampuchea (the Cambodian Communist name for
Cambodia)

HENG SAMRIN, President and head of the Central Committee
of the Kampuchean National United Front for National
Salvation of the People's Republic of Kampuchea (Cambodia)

PRINCE NORODOM SIHANOUK (1922-   ), deposed head of
state of Cambodia

GENERAL VAN TIEN DUNG (1917-   ), Army Chief of Staff
of Vietnam

Summary of Event

Historically, Indochina has long symbolized human unrest and suffering, whether resulting from outside forces of colonialism, "neocolonialism" and occupation, or domestic turmoil. With little respite from the throes of Japanese occupation during World War II, the First Indochina War was launched late in 1945 by Vietnamese Nationalist/Communist forces against the French, the area's colonial masters since the mid-nineteenth century. The war ended rather inconclusively in 1954 with the partitioning of Vietnam into a Communist North and non-Communist South, and the "neutralization" of both Laos and Cambodia. Although the war rather pronouncedly forced the exit of France, it also witnessed the vicarious entrance of the United States, which, acting under perceptions conceived by Cold War arguments, initiated increasing United States in-

volvement in the 1960's in what later came to be known as the Second Indochina War. This war ended in April, 1975, with Communist victories in both South Vietnam and Cambodia.

With the Communists finally in control it was generally believed that some manner of stability would prevail in the area. It was therefore surprising when, late in 1977, local skirmishes on the Vietnamese-Cambodian border suddenly erupted into large-scale battles between these two Communist nations that were once allies. The seriousness of the conflict was underlined when Cambodia (now called Democratic Kampuchea) officially suspended relations with Vietnam on December 31, 1977.

Apparently, fierce fighting had occurred regularly in the border area almost from the time of the Communist conquests. The border itself traditionally had been a point of contention as it was originally established by the French; greater attention was given to administrative concerns than to the conscientious accounting for population location or topographical features. In relatively few places was the border clearly marked, and authoritative maps accurately defining it were nonexistent. More recently, the sea boundary as well had been a reason for controversy, since division of the territorial waters of the two nations had never been mutually agreed to and the possibility of an oil-rich seabed underlying the Gulf of Thailand made the staking of claims in that area a particularly pressing concern.

The developing conflict, however, did not long remain confined to border areas. Although the Cambodians are believed to have initiated the fighting, forcing the Vietnamese at first to evacuate large areas along the frontier, over a period of time the Vietnamese response increased enormously in scale. At the end of December, 1978, in support of a token Cambodian rebel element known as the Kampuchean National United Front for National Salvation (KNUFNS), Vietnamese forces led by General Van Tien Dung, Army Chief of Staff, launched a massive invasion of Cambodia and captured its capital, Phnom Penh. The incumbent Democratic Kampuchea regime, led by Prime Minister and Secretary of the Cambodian Communist Party (Khmer Rouge), Pol Pot, was forced to retreat to mountainous areas along Cambodia's western border with Thailand, where, for a short time, its fighting forces were able to carry on

successful guerrilla warfare against KNUFNS and Vietnamese units. A renewed Vietnamese drive in April, 1979, however, located the mountain base areas and seriously impaired the capacity of Democratic Kampuchean troops to carry on effectively. In Phnom Penh, the Vietnamese established a KNUFNS regime under the leadership of a Pol Pot defector, Heng Samrin, President and head of the Central Committee of KNUFNS. Renaming Cambodia the People's Republic of Kampuchea, the new government retained a tenuous hold on the country in spite of Vietnamese support. Having consolidated its position in mostly depopulated urban centers, its struggle to control the countryside continues.

Vietnam's invasion of Cambodia paradoxically provoked official condemnation from a majority of the world's nations at the same time that many were unofficially expressing their profound relief at Pol Pot's demise. The Democratic Kampuchean regime, once ensconced in Phnom Penh in 1975, had withdrawn Cambodia from the world community. The little information that escaped its self-imposed isolation reflected an inward-looking, intensely xenophobic government intent upon remaking Cambodian society into a rigid model of peasant socialism. The reported draconian tactics used in forcibly evacuating entire urban populations to the countryside and in eliminating "threatening elements" in the population alarmed many nations. A few, such as the United States and Great Britain, legislated formal resolutions condemning Cambodia for its human rights violations. Vietnam's invasion was therefore greeted internationally with mixed feelings: on the one hand it had clearly violated international law by militarily encroaching on the territory of a sovereign nation, while on the other, it had also perpetrated a humanitarian act in ridding the nation of a terrorist regime.

However, to understand fully the current Vietnam-Cambodia situation it is necessary to balance the contemporary circumstances of the two countries with their past patterns of interaction. Historically, the two states have engaged in extended rivalry and have regarded each other with suspicion and hostility. At one time, the Khmer Empire, of which Cambodia is the present-day descendant, extended across much of what is now the southern region of Vietnam. However, in the fifteenth century the empire fell into decline and consistently began to lose territory to its increasingly powerful neighbors— Thailand to the west and Vietnam to the east. By the latter part of the seventeenth century, settlers from Vietnam were beginning to move in large numbers into the Mekong Delta region of southern Vietnam, then under Khmer authority. Vietnamese expansion continued with little contest until the arrival of the French in the nineteenth century. While the introduction of French colonialism put a halt to the continued dismemberment of the Khmer Empire, it did not alleviate the enmity with which the two peoples continued to regard each other. Even later, when the two countries faced a common enemy (the United States), the brief period of cooperation that resulted never quite displaced the ancient fears and

hatreds. In initiating border attacks on Vietnam in 1975, the Pol Pot government was reviving ancient Cambodian fears of a territorially ambitious Vietnam intent upon establishing hegemony over the whole of Indochina. Similarly, Vietnam's invasion of Cambodia was a reversion to historical Vietnamese behavior patterns in attempting to dominate Cambodia both militarily and politically.

The implications of the situation, however, are greater than the local concerns of the Vietnamese and Cambodians would at first glance indicate. On January 8, 1978, President Carter's Adviser for National Security Affairs, Zbigniew Brzezinski, stated that the Vietnamese-Cambodian conflict was the first instance of a "proxy war" between China and the Soviet Union. While the statement ignored the very pertinent differences between the Cambodians and Vietnamese that contributed to hostilities, it introduced the equally important Sino-Soviet dimension of the conflict.

The prospect of direct Chinese or Soviet intervention in Cambodia is significant. Although neither country is particularly anxious to be drawn into the conflict, the prestige of each rests with the outcome. In the beginning, China attempted to maintain a balanced position by continuing diplomatic relations with both Phnom Penh and Hanoi; the Soviet Union, finding it difficult to gain favor with Pol Pot because of having once maintained relations with the regime that preceded him, moved immediately to support the Vietnamese. China, having nurtured the Cambodian government under deposed leader Prince

Norodom Sihanouk during its years in exile (1970-1975), became its protégé's only ally, and as the Soviet buildup of arms in Vietnam became more pronounced, the Chinese position of neutrality transformed into open support of the Cambodians. Since then, Sino-Vietnamese relations have disintegrated entirely and Sino-Soviet competition for influence in Southeast Asia has grown more intense.

Although Phnom Penh's decision to break diplomatic ties with Hanoi in December, 1977, took the Vietnamese by surprise, it was interpreted as confirmation of their view that the problem with Cambodia was not merely a bilateral issue but the result of Chinese machinations designed to check Vietnamese power in the area. Based on this evaluation, the decision was made to intervene militarily in Cambodia ten months before the invasion took place. At the same time it was decided to join the Soviet bloc's COMECON (Council of Economic Mutual Assistance) in order to insure adequate economic assistance for the anticipated period of crisis that would likely follow the invasion. As insurance against a possible Chinese counterattack, a twenty-five-year treaty of friendship and cooperation was signed with Moscow. The Vietnamese calculated, however, that the Chinese would be unlikely to go to war with Vietnam for the sake of saving Pol Pot.

Nevertheless, on February 17, 1979, between 200,000 and 300,000 Chinese troops struck at Vietnam from several points along the 480-mile Sino-Vietnamese frontier. The Chinese explained that their actions were intended to "teach Vietnam a lesson" and were in response to Vietnamese-instigated incidents along the border that had been taking place for more than a year. Actually, their motivations were more complex, as the invasion was as much a response to Vietnam's Moscow ties and actions in Cambodia as it was to Vietnamese activity along the Sino-Vietnamese border. Vietnam's military thrust into Cambodia in essence represented but one more Vietnamese action openly demonstrating its defiance of China. When grouped with the others, it proved irritating enough to provoke the Chinese into taking military action even at the risk of invoking Soviet retaliation. Although the Soviets refrained from intervening and the Chinese withdrew after two weeks, a precedent for the use of military force had been established and the situation remains a volatile one on all sides.

Among Indochina's Southeast Asian neighbors, Vietnamese and Chinese actions have once again engendered an aged preoccupation with the threat of Communist aggression. Overall, however, Asians appear to have sided with Peking against Hanoi. This is particularly true in the case of Thailand, where Vietnamese forces, having pushed through Cambodia, remain camped on the Thai border. The five members of the Association of Southeast Asian Nations—Thailand, Malaysia, Singapore, Indonesia, and the Philippines—are strongly anti-Communist and not disposed to favor either China or Vietnam. They have decided, however, that Vietnam is a direct threat and China is not.

For the time being, however, Communist hostilities are directed inwardly. The conflict in the region is that of one Communist nation toward another. The "domino theory," having once claimed that Southeast Asia would eventually succumb to Communism, is today no closer to realization than before. The Communist world's internal wars reflect instead both the schism dividing Communism's two largest powers as well as long-dormant nationalist sentiments emerging to prevail over commonly held ideological beliefs.

Despite Vietnamese battlefield successes against the Democratic Kampuchean forces, the current conflict will not end easily. Vietnam faces overwhelming problems of reconstruction and consolidation at home as well as the threat of renewed Chinese attacks along its northern border. In conquering Cambodia, Vietnam has assumed additionally the problems of a nation severely weakened by the policies of its previous regime. The Khmer Rouge, in their fervor to discard the previous social, political, and economic fabric of their country, undertook a campaign of widespread domestic destruction that in the end destroyed the nation itself. To restore order in Cambodia and begin the process of rebuilding will simply require more resources than Vietnam is currently able to provide.

Statements from the surviving elements of Democratic Kampuchea make it clear that they are intending to continue fighting for what they perceive to be the survival of Cambodia's nationhood. Preservation of Cambodia's territorial integrity remains fundamental to the Pol Pot forces and the strength with which they hold the resolve may in part explain the ferocity with which they are continuing to carry it out.

The People's Republic of Kampuchea under Heng Samrin exists on the strength of Vietnamese military support alone. Despite the incredibly destructive record of the previous regime, it was still a Cambodian government staffed by Cambodians operating independently of foreign control. Heng Samrin's association with Vietnam will continue to taint all he accomplishes. Regardless of his intentions to institute reforms or the needs they may fill, it is unlikely that he will be able to overcome his subordinate relationship to Vietnam.

As is the situation in any war, it is the people inadvertently found in its path and left in its wake who bear the greatest suffering. The instability in the countryside that the war has created has prevented Cambodians from planting a crucial rice crop. Because rice stores are practically nonexistent, the likelihood of a famine appears imminent. The situation is critical because the war continues with no end in sight. Pol Pot's forces, although severely weakened, still retain the guns as well as the will necessary to prevent the Heng Samrin government from securing the countryside. Although Pol Pot has small chance for victory he is still effective enough to keep the rural areas unsafe for farming and food production.

No one knows how many Cambodians there are. The population exceeded six million when Pol Pot took over in 1975, but most estimates claim that at least one million have died since then, whether by war, execution, malnutrition, or disease; some guesses put the current population at only four million. Because the prospects for resolution of the present conflict are poor, those who remain in Cambodia face unrelenting hunger and deprivation. The future is, in many ways, likely to repeat the past.

Pertinent Literature

Osborne, Milton. "Kampuchea and Vietnam: A Historical Perspective," in *Pacific Community*. IX, no. 3 (April, 1978), pp. 249-263.

Milton Osborne's analysis of the situation between Cambodia (Kampuchea) and Vietnam as of April, 1978, reviews historical precedent as well as contemporary circumstances in attempting to arrive at a satisfactory explanation of the conflict. It briefly details Cambodia's historic role, derived from its geographic position, separating the more powerful kingdoms of Thailand and Vietnam from each other. Although both were a threat to Cambodia, Osborne points out that the relationships each maintained with that country were significantly different. While Cambodia shared a common religion and culture with Thailand, its culture clashed with that of Vietnam. Thailand and Cambodia had both been enormously influenced by India; Vietnam, on the other hand, had derived much of its culture from its neighbor to the north, China. The differences were particularly manifest with regard to their varying perceptions concerning the nature of borders. For Thailand and Cambodia borders were never clearly delineated. Each state, rather, conceived its territory to end whenever it became clear that the population, either in language or appearance, was foreign. Vietnam, having assimilated Chinese administrative procedures,

saw its border as more clearly established. Osborne observes that these differences were exacerbated by the French in the late nineteenth century when, for their own administrative purposes, they followed border policies that were closer to the Vietnamese way of thinking than to the Cambodian.

Yet it was also the French who undertook to establish Cambodia as a protectorate and to halt any further Vietnamese advances into its territory. In many ways, however, it was already too late, for Vietnamese claims by that time included regions where a large number of Cambodians continued to live. Many of these territorial incursions had been completed during the 1830's, a period Osborne singles out as particularly bitter in Cambodian-Vietnamese relations and still very much a part of the Cambodian national consciousness.

In discussing relations between the two countries during the First Indochina War (1945-1954), Osborne suggests that the Cambodian view of the Vietnamese remained essentially unchanged. Although both shared the goal of achieving independence from the French, the Cambodians continued to be suspicious of Vietnamese territorial ambitions.

Osborne next reviews the period of peace immediately following the signing of the 1954 Geneva Accords and concludes that Cambodian attitudes continued to persist. It was during this time that Prince Sihanouk accurately accused both Communist and non-Communist sides in the Vietnam War of aiding Cambodian exile groups who wished to see him deposed.

Despite continued distrust, agreements concerning the border were arrived at in 1967, instituting the French-delineated border as the true boundary. Osborne notes that this decision left several problems unresolved, the chief among them being the distribution of ethnic minorities along the border. The French, in determining the border, had failed to account for the location of minority populations. Accepting their boundary meant unavoidably placing certain minorities on the "wrong side" of the border.

Briefly, in the 1970's, it appeared that a shared ideology might overcome the ancient hatreds. Osborne writes that when the overthrow of Prince Sihanouk in March, 1970, opened the way for the Cambodian Communists to make a bid for power, their resources were limited and they had no alternative but to rely on Vietnamese aid. He cautions, however, that it would be an error to think that Vietnamese assistance lessened antipathy, since almost immediately following Communist victories in each country, clashes along the border began.

Osborne speculates that there were probably still Vietnamese Communist troops stationed in Cambodia at the war's end, and that, with the possible exception of "the Parrot's Beak" (an area of Cambodia that juts into Vietnam) and some of the offshore islands, these troops were left there for strategic reasons and not for the purpose of occupation. He argues that until 1977, the policy of the Vietnamese government was to station untrained troops along its southern border with Cambodia, a procedure which in itself would suggest that the Vietnamese were not planning an invasion. He concludes, therefore, that it was the Cambodians who made the border an issue. The issue to the Cambodians, however, was not simply the border, but the survival of their territorial integrity.

Should the current conflict follow historical precedents, Osborne believes that a solution will not come about easily. Yet, he writes, history could at the same time guide the way, for in the past Cambodia has remained at peace when its neighbors have conceded its right to exist. The possibility of a Thai-Vietnamese *rapprochement* could act to initiate such an understanding. However, there currently exist substantial differences from the past as well, and Osborne points out that although Cambodia was always weaker than its neighbors and remains so, in the nineteenth century it could also be described as "fragile." Only time will tell if that particular description continues to apply.

Pike, Douglas. *Vietnam-Cambodia Conflict*. Report prepared at the request of the Subcommittee on Asian and Pacific Affairs, Committee on International Relations. Washington, D.C.: U.S. Government Printing Office, 1978.

In discussing the Vietnam-Cambodia border war, Douglas Pike reviews the history of Vietnamese-Cambodian relations and notes that the historical antipathy between the two peoples is as deep and pervasive as between any two peoples in the world, including the Arabs and the Jews. Even in the light of more contemporary events during which the two countries appeared united by a shared ideology, Pike writes that the unity was tenuous at best, while the mutual enmity remained virtually undiminished. He goes on to suggest that the border war really has very little to do with the delineation of the border itself, but, rather, is derived from Cambodia's fear for its integrity as a nation in the face of past Vietnamese behavior.

History has revealed Cambodia to be a small nation bordered by larger, more powerful nations who, more times than not, have proved to be enemies. Whereas in other instances countries similarly situated have often survived by adeptly playing a game of balance-of-power politics and setting one nation against the other, Pike writes that in Cambodia's experience, such an approach never worked. Thus, in explaining Cambodia's seemingly irrational behavior toward Vietnam in the border war, he concludes that in the light of historical experience it may not be irrational at all but rather a deliberate strategy which simply holds more promise than a battle plan with a more rational appearance. Pike terms

Cambodia's strategy "the small bristly dog gambit" and likens it to a small dog bristling its fur in the face of bigger dogs to appear more troublesome. He also notes that the Vietnamese for this particular conflict shunned their proven guerrilla tactics for the highly technological, Western-style warfare favored by their former foe, the United States. Indeed, Pike points out that the military operation they launched in January, 1978, very much resembled the American invasion of Cambodia in the spring of 1970.

Aside from discussing the tactics of either side, Pike presents a chronology of the major developments occurring in the border war as a further aid to understanding the conflict. Beginning with the Communist victories in both Cambodia and Vietnam in April and May, 1975, he lists significant occurrences initiated by both sides up to and including the large-scale Vietnamese thrust into Cambodia in January, 1978.

Pike devotes considerable space to an analysis of possible directions the war might take. One prospect he views as unlikely is the establishment within Cambodia of a Vietnamese client state. Ironically, this is exactly what happened early in 1979. But the consequences that Pike feels would result if such an event took place have already come to pass for the most part. Thus, he observes that such a blatantly aggressive move could very well nudge China, Cambodia's ally, to intervene actively as well as trigger

1353

Vietnam's ally, the Soviet Union, to take action. There is additionally the problem of any client regime necessarily having to be associated with Vietnam and therefore irreversibly tainted in the eyes of the Cambodians. — *R.J.C.*

Additional Recommended Reading

Barron, John and Anthony Paul. *Murder of a Gentle Land: The Untold Story of Communist Genocide in Cambodia.* New York: Reader's Digest Press, 1977. A revealing glimpse of internal Cambodia under the Democratic Kampuchean regime based on interviews with Cambodian refugees.

Bonavia, David. "Changing the Course of History," in *Far Eastern Economic Review.* III, no. 9 (March 2, 1979), pp. 8-10.

——————— ."Sowing the Seeds of a Bigger War," in *Far Eastern Economic Review.* III, no. 10 (March 9, 1979), pp. 12-13. Two articles analyzing China's "punitive" attack on Vietnam and the implications for Soviet intervention.

Carney, Timothy Michael. *Communist Party Power in Kampuchea (Cambodia): Documents and Discussion.* Ithaca, N.Y.: Cornell University Press, 1977. A study of the origins and ideology of the Communist Party of Kampuchea.

Hildebrand, George C. and Gareth Porter. *Cambodia: Starvation and Revolution.* New York: Monthly Review Press, 1976. A description of the difficulties facing the Cambodian Communists upon assuming power in 1975, and a defense of the domestic policies they proceeded to employ.

Jackson, Karl D. "Cambodia 1978: War, Pillage, and Purge in Democratic Kampuchea," in *Asian Survey.* XIX, no. 1 (January, 1979), pp. 72-84. A survey of events in Cambodia in 1978.

Leighton, Marian Kirsch. "Perspectives on the Vietnam-Cambodia Border Conflict," in *Asian Survey.* XVIII, no. 5 (May, 1978), pp. 448-457. A brief outline of developments along the Vietnam-Cambodia border from mid-1977 to March, 1978, including a discussion of the Soviet and Chinese roles in the conflict.

Mendenhall, Joseph. "Communist Vietnam and the Border War: Victim or Aggressor," in *Strategic Review.* Washington, D.C.: United States Strategic Institute. (Summer, 1978), pp. 56-61. The author concludes that the current conflict in Cambodia is a continuation of historic Vietnamese hegemonic tendencies.

Ponchaud, François. *Cambodia: Year Zero.* Translated by Nancy Amphoux. New York: Holt, Rinehart and Winston, 1978. A vivid description, based on refugee accounts, of conditions in Cambodia following the Communist victory.

Zasloff, Joseph J. and MacAlister Brown. "The Passion of Kampuchea," in *Problems of Communism.* (January-February, 1979), pp. 28-44. A discussion summarizing recent events in Cambodia beginning with the imposition of Communist rule in 1975 and extending to the Vietnamese invasion.

INDEXES

VOLUMES ONE, TWO, AND THREE

Worldwide Twentieth Century Series

Admission of Alaska and Hawaii into the Union   II-790

Admission of the People's Republic of China to the United Nations   III-1110

Adolf Hitler Publishes *Mein Kampf*   I-188

Antitotalitarian Literature of the 1930's and Early 1940's   I-241

Arab Oil Embargo and the Energy Crisis   III-1137

Arnold Toynbee Publishes *A Study of History*   I-329

Atomic Research   I-246

Attempts to Contact Intelligent Beings in Space   II-827

Battle of Britain, The   I-430

Battle of Germany, The   II-577

Battle of Midway, The   I-472

Battle of the Atlantic, The   I-404

Bay of Pigs Invasion Repulsed, The   II-926

Bertrand Russell and Alfred North Whitehead Publish *Principia Mathematica*   I-79

Bicentennial Celebration, The   III-1287

Birth of the First Human Conceived *in Vitro*   III-1324

"Black Hole" Investigations   II-835

Black Insurgency Movements in Zimbabwe/ Rhodesia   II-981

Black Nationalist Movement in South Africa   III-1272

"Bloody Sunday" in Ulster   III-1117

Building of the Alaska Pipeline   II-1022

Castro Seizes Power in Cuba   II-743

Cellular Research   I-501

César Chávez Organizes the Farm Workers   II-842

Chaco War, The   I-289

Chadwick Discovers the Neutron   I-283

Changing Attitudes Toward Religion in America   I-507

Changing Patterns in Education   I-513

Changing Social Contract, The   II-848

Charter of the Economic Rights and Duties of States   III-1206

Chinese Revolution of 1911, The   I-92

Civil Rights Act of 1964, The   II-965

Civil Rights Acts of the 1960's, The   II-806

Civil War in Angola and the Intervention of Cuba, The   III-1219

Civil War in China, The   I-211

Collapse of the Nixon Administration   III-1200

Communications and Meteorological Satellites   II-751

Communist *Coup* in Czechoslovakia, The   II-626

Congress Passes the Formosa Resolution   II-709

Continuing Search for Peace in the Middle East, The   I-145

Creation of the Federal Republic of Germany and the German Democratic Republic, The   II-647

Crisis of Railroad Transportation, The   I-520

Cyprus Crisis, The   III-1193

Death of Franco and the Restoration of the Monarchy   II-1043

Deaths of Mao Tse-tung and Chou En-lai   III-1264

Decision by the United States to Construct an Atomic Bomb   I-389

Demise of the Puritan Ethic in America, The   I-526

Détente with the Soviet Union   II-1050

Devaluation of the Dollar   III-1097

Development of Radar   I-324

Development of the Teletype   I-1

Digital Computers and the Information Revolution   II-535

Diplomatic Relations Established Between East and West Germany   III-1167

Discovery of Pulsars   II-1009

Discovery of Quasars   II-899

Discovery of the Dead Sea Scrolls   II-598

Dissent Among Soviet Intellectuals   II-988

Dissolution of the Habsburg Monarchy, The   I-158

Economic Crisis of Stagflation, The   II-1062

Eisenhower Doctrine on the Middle East Enunciated, The   II-757

Election of Carter to the Presidency in 1976   III-1302

Emergence of Consumer Awareness   II-856

Emergence of the American Indian Reform Movement   II-865

Emergence of the Drug Culture   II-814

Emigration of European Intellectuals to America   I-295

End of American Involvement in the Vietnam War   III-1161

Environmental Legislation Passed Since 1960   II-872

Establishment of the Democratic Republic of Vietnam, The   II-696

Establishment of the Organization of Petroleum Exporting Countries (OPEC)   II-912

Establishment of the Southeast Asia Treaty Organization (SEATO)   II-703

Establishment of the Union of South Africa   I-87

Existentialism in Literature   I-252
Explosion of the First Hydrogen Bomb   II-683
Expulsion of Yugoslavia from the Cominform   II-640

Fall of Cambodia to the Khmer Rouge, The   III-1212
Fall of Khrushchev, The   II-974
Fall of South Vietnam, The   III-1227
First Heart Transplant Operation, The   II-1016
First Major Arab Attack on the Jews in Palestine, The   I-231
First Superfortress Bombing Raid on Japan, The   I-487
Foreign Policy of John Foster Dulles, The   II-690
Formation of the Arab League   I-494
Formation of the Commonwealth of Australia and the Dominion of New Zealand, The   I-14
Founding of the National Organization for Women   II-998
Friedrich Meinecke Publishes *Cosmopolitanism and the National State*   I-54
Fritz Fischer Publishes *Germany's Aims in the First World War*   II-918

Gallipoli Campaign, The   I-129
General MacArthur Administers the Reconstruction of Japan   II-584
Genetic Research   I-7
Geneva Disarmament Conference, The   I-276
Geneva Summit Conference, The   II-721
German Invasion of Russia   I-450
Germany and Italy Declare War on the United States   I-465
Germany Invades the Balkans   I-444
Germany Remilitarizes the Rhineland   I-348
Germany Renounces the Versailles Treaty   I-342
Great Armenian Massacre, The   I-107
Great Britain Issues the 1939 White Paper Restricting Jewish Emigration to Palestine   I-411
Great Britain Joins the Common Market   III-1146
Great Russian Civil War, The   I-152
Growth of the Separatist Movement in Quebec   II-820

Helsinki Agreement, The   III-1257
Hitler Comes to Power in Germany   I-311
Hitler Establishes Control of the Diplomatic and Military Hierarchy   I-375

Impact of Television on Society, The   II-669
India-Pakistan War and the Creation of Bangladesh, The   II-1091
Inflation and Labor Unrest   II-572
International Geophysical Year, The   II-764
Invention of the Jet Engine   I-355
Invention of the Laser   II-881
Invention of the Transistor   II-612
Invention of Xerography   I-382
Iranian Revolution, The   III-1338
Italy Enters World War I   I-138

Japan Occupies Indochina   I-438
Japan Occupies the Dutch East Indies, Singapore, and Burma   I-457
Japan Presents China with the Twenty-One Demands   I-121
Japanese Military Campaigns in China   I-361
John A. Hobson Publishes *Imperialism: A Study*   I-31
John Steinbeck Publishes *The Grapes of Wrath*   I-418

Khrushchev Denounces Stalin   II-736

Landing of United Nations Forces at Inchon, The   II-676
Lebanese Civil War, The   III-1235
Little Rock School Desegregation Crisis, The   II-770
Locarno Conference, The   I-197

Manchurian Crisis and the Rise of Japanese Militarism, The   II-269
Max Weber Publishes *The Protestant Ethic and the Spirit of Capitalism*   I-38
Merger of the AFL and the CIO   II-730
Mexican Revolution, The   I-69
Mohandas K. Ghandi Leads the Nonviolent Indian Reform Movement   I-175
Moroccan Crises, The   I-46

Nazi Extermination of the Jews   I-396
Nazi Persecution of the Jews   I-303
Nigerian Civil War, The   II-1003
Nuclear Test Ban Treaty, The   II-955

OAS Suspends the Embargo Against Cuba, The   III-1251
Opening of the St. Lawrence Seaway   II-783

Paris Peace Conference, The   II-591
Partition of India, The   II-605
Philosophical Efforts Toward an Objective View of Planet Earth   II-1069
Polar Explorations   I-63
Political Terrorism   II-1028
Population Shift to the Sunbelt, The   II-1077
Pressure for Prison Reform   II-886

Pressure of Minorities for Personal Equality   II-893
Proclamation of an Independent Jewish State   II-634
Proclamation of the People's Republic of China   II-654
Public Awareness of Environmental Dangers   III-542
Publication of the Cambridge Histories   I-24
Publication of the Kinsey Reports   II-619

Quantum Physics Research   I-166

Rachel Carson Publishes *Silent Spring*   II-942
Rapprochement with the People's Republic of China   III-1124
Ratification of the Panama Canal Treaties   III-1331
Reform of the International Monetary System   III-1104
Reform Program of Mustafa Kemal, The   I-225
Research into the Origins of Man   I-218
Resignation of Vice-President Spiro T. Agnew   III-1188
Reunification of Vietnam, The   III-1243
Rise of the Megalopolis, The   II-550
Russia Invades East Prussia   I-101

Signing of the Antarctic Treaty   II-798
Signing of the Warsaw Pact   II-715
Soviet Invasion of Eastern Europe   I-479
Soviet Union Launches *Sputnik*, The   II-776
Spaceflights of *Voyagers I* and *II*, The   III-1311
Stalin Begins the Purge Trials   I-336
Strategic Arms Limitation Talks (SALT) with the Soviet Union   II-1054
Struggle for the Horn of Africa, The   III-1317

Synthesis of DDT for Use as an Insecticide, The   I-425

"Third World's" Struggle for Equality, The   II-557
Treaty of Trianon   I-181

United States Establishes a Two-Ocean Navy, The   I-368
United States Establishes Diplomatic Relations with the Soviet Union, The   I-319
United States Establishes the Good Neighbor Policy Toward Latin America, The   I-260
United States Invades Cambodia, The   II-1083
United States Puts a Man in Space, The   II-934
United States Supreme Court Rules Against Bible Reading in Public Schools, The   II-949
United States Supreme Court Rules on Obscenity, The   III-1174
United States Supreme Court Rules on State Antiabortion Laws, The   III-1154
United States Supreme Court Rules on the Death Penalty, The   III-1279
U-2 Incident and the Collapse of the Paris Summit Conference, The   II-906

Vernon Louis Parrington Publishes *Main Currents in American Thought*   I-205
Viet Cong Tet Offensive   II-1036
Vietnam's Conquest of Cambodia   III-1346
Viking Landings on Mars, The   III-1294

Watergate Affair, The   III-1131
William Appleman Williams Pioneers Cold War Revisionist Historiography   II-663
Worldwide Attempts at Nuclear Disarmament and Nonproliferation   II-564

Yom Kippur War, The   III-1182

Admission of Alaska and Hawaii into the Union   II-790
Admission of the People's Republic of China to the United Nations   III-1110
AFL and the CIO, Merger of the   II-730
Africa, Black Nationalist Movement in South   III-1272
Africa, Establishment of the Union of South   I-87
Africa, The Struggle for the Horn of   III-1317
Agnew, Resignation of Vice-President Spiro T.   III-1188
Alaska and Hawaii into the Union, Admission of   II-790
Alaska Pipeline, Building of the   II-1022
America, Changing Attitudes Toward Religion in   I-507
America, The Demise of the Puritan Ethic in   I-526
American Indian Reform Movement, Emergence of the   II-865
American Involvement in the Vietnam War, End of   III-1161
Angola and the Intervention of Cuba, The Civil War in   III-1219
Antarctic Treaty, Signing of the   II-798
Antiabortion Laws, The United States Supreme Court Rules on State   III-1154
Antitotalitarian Literature of the 1930's and Early 1940's   I-241
Arab Attack on the Jews in Palestine, The First Major   I-231
Arab League, Formation of the   I-494
Arab Oil Embargo and the Energy Crisis   III-1137
Armenian Massacre, The Great   I-107
Atlantic, The Battle of the   I-404
Atomic Research   I-246
Attempts to Contact Intelligent Beings in Space   II-827
Australia and the Dominion of New Zealand, The Formation of the Commonwealth of   I-14

Balkans, Germany Invades the   I-444
Battle of Britain, The   I-430
Battle of Germany, The   II-577
Battle of Midway, The   I-472
Battle of the Atlantic, The   I-404
Bangladesh, The India-Pakistan War and the Creation of   II-1091
Bay of Pigs Invasion Repulsed, The   II-926
Bible Reading in Public Schools, The United States Supreme Court Rules Against   II-949
Bicentennial Celebration, The   III-1287
Birth of the First Human Conceived *in Vitro*   III-1324

"Black Hole" Investigations   II-835
Black Insurgency Movements in Zimbabwe/Rhodesia   II-981
Black Nationalist Movement in South Africa   III-1272
"Bloody Sunday" in Ulster   III-1117
Britain, The Battle of   I-430
Burma, Japan Occupies the Dutch East Indies, Singapore, and   I-457

Cambodia, The United States Invades   II-1083
Cambodia, Vietnam's Conquest of   III-1346
Cambodia to the Khmer Rouge, The Fall of   III-1212
Cambridge Histories, Publication of the   I-24
Carson Publishes *Silent Spring*, Rachel   II-942
Carter to the Presidency in 1976, Election of   III-1302
Castro Seizes Power in Cuba   II-743
Cellular Research   I-501
Chaco War, The   I-289
Chadwick Discovers the Neutron   I-283
China, Japanese Military Campaigns in   I-361
China, Proclamation of the People's Republic of   II-654
China, *Rapprochement* with the People's Republic of   III-1124
China, The Civil War in   I-211
China to the United Nations, Admission of the People's Republic of   III-1110
China with the Twenty-One Demands, Japan Presents   I-121
Chinese Revolution of 1911, The   I-92
Chou En-lai, Deaths of Mao Tse-tung and   III-1264
CIO, Merger of the AFL and the   II-730
Civil Rights Act of 1964, The   II-965
Civil Rights Acts of the 1960's, The   II-806
Civil War, The Great Russian   I-152
Civil War, The Lebanese   III-1235
Civil War, The Nigerian   II-1003
Civil War in Angola and the Intervention of Cuba, The   III-1219
Civil War in China, The   I-211
Cold War Revisionist Historiography, William Appleman Williams Pioneers   II-663
Cominform, Expulsion of Yugoslavia from the   II-640
Common Market, Great Britain Joins the   III-1146
Communications and Meteorological Satellites   II-751
Communist *Coup* in Czechoslovakia, The   II-626

Computers and the Information Revolution, Digital   II-535

Congress Passes the Formosa Resolution   II-709

Consumer Awareness, Emergence of   II-856

Cosmopolitanism and the National State, Friedrich Meinecke Publishes   I-54

Cuba, Castro Seizes Power in   II-743

Cuba, The Civil War in Angola and the Intervention of   III-1219

Cuba, The OAS Suspends the Embargo Against   III-1251

Cyprus Crisis, The   III-1193

Czechoslovakia, The Communist *Coup* in   III-626

DDT for Use as an Insecticide, The Synthesis of   I-425

Dead Sea Scrolls, Discovery of the   II-598

Death of Franco and the Restoration of the Monarchy   II-1043

Death Penalty, The United States Supreme Court Rules on the   III-1279

Deaths of Mao Tse-tung and Chou En-lai   III-1264

Desegregation Crisis, The Little Rock School   II-770

Détente with the Soviet Union   II-1050

Devaluation of the Dollar   III-1097

Development of Radar   I-324

Development of the Teletype   I-1

Digital Computers and the Information Revolution   II-535

Diplomatic Relations Established Between East and West Germany   III-1167

Diplomatic Relations with the Soviet Union, The United States Establishes   I-319

Disarmament Conference, The Geneva   I-276

Discovery of Pulsars   II-1009

Discovery of Quasars   II-899

Discovery of the Dead Sea Scrolls   II-598

Dissent Among Soviet Intellectuals   II-988

Dissolution of the Habsburg Monarchy   I-158

Doctrine on the Middle East Enunciated, The Eisenhower   II-757

Dollar, Devaluation of the   III-1097

Drug Culture, Emergence of the   II-814

Dulles, The Foreign Policy of John Foster   II-690

Dutch East Indies, Singapore, and Burma, Japan Occupies   I-457

Earth, Philosophical Efforts Toward an Objective View of Planet   II-1069

Eastern Europe, Soviet Invasion of   I-479

Economic Crisis of Stagflation, The   II-1062

Economic Rights and Duties of States, Charter of the   III-1206

Education, Changing Patterns in   I-513

Eisenhower Doctrine on the Middle East Enunciated, The   II-757

Election of Carter to the Presidency in 1976   III-1302

Embargo Against Cuba, The OAS Suspends the   III-1251

Embargo and the Energy Crisis, Arab Oil   III-1137

Emigration of European Intellectuals to America   I-295

Energy Crisis, Arab Oil Embargo and the   III-1137

Environmental Dangers, Public Awareness of   II-542

Environmental Legislation Passed Since 1960   II-872

Equality, Pressure of Minorities for Personal   II-893

Establishment of the Democratic Republic of Vietnam, The   II-696

Establishment of the Organization of Petroleum Exporting Countries (OPEC)   II-912

Establishment of the Southeast Asia Treaty Organization (SEATO)   II-703

Establishment of the Union of South Africa   I-87

Existentialism in Literature   I-252

Explosion of the First Hydrogen Bomb   II-683

Expulsion of Yugoslavia from the Cominform   II-640

Fall of Cambodia to the Khmer Rouge, The   III-1212

Fall of Khrushchev, The   II-974

Fall of South Vietnam, The   III-1227

Farm Workers, César Chávez Organizes the   II-842

Federal Republic of Germany and the German Democratic Republic, The Creation of the   II-647

First Heart Transplant Operation, The   II-1016

Fischer Publishes *Germany's Aims in the First World War*, Fritz   II-918

Formation of the Arab League   I-494

Formation of the Commonwealth of Australia and the Dominion of New Zealand, The   I-14

Formosa Resolution, Congress Passes the   II-709

Foreign Policy of John Foster Dulles, The   II-690

Founding of the National Organization for Women   II-998

Franco and the Restoration of the Monarchy, Death of   II-1043

Gallipoli Campaign, The   I-129

Genetic Research   I-7

Geneva Disarmament Conference, The   I-276

Geneva Summit Conference, The   II-721

Geophysical Year, The International   II-764

German Democratic Republic, The Creation of the Federal Republic of Germany and the   II-647

German Invasion of Russia   I-450

Germany, Diplomatic Relations Established Between East and West   III-1167

Germany, Hitler Comes to Power in   I-311

Germany, The Battle of   II-577

Germany and Italy Declare War on the United States   I-465

Germany Invades the Balkans   I-444

Germany Remilitarizes the Rhineland   I-348

Germany Renounces the Versailles Treaty   I-342

Germany's Aims in the First World War, Fritz Fischer Publishes   II-918

Ghandi Leads the Nonviolent Indian Reform Movement, Mohandas K.   I-175

Good Neighbor Policy Toward Latin America, The United States Establishes the   I-260

Grapes of Wrath, John Steinbeck Publishes *The*   I-418

Great Armenian Massacre, The   I-107

Great Britain Issues the 1939 White Paper Restricting Jewish Emigration to Palestine   I-411

Great Britain Joins the Common Market   III-1146

Great Russian Civil War, The   I-152

Habsburg Monarchy, Dissolution of the   I-158

Hawaii into the Union, Admission of Alaska and   II-790

Heart Transplant Operation, The First   II-1016

Helsinki Agreement, The   III-1257

Hitler Comes to Power in Germany   I-311

Hitler Establishes Control of the Diplomatic and Military Hierarchy   I-375

Hitler Publishes *Mein Kampf*, Adolf   I-188

Hobson Publishes *Imperialism: A Study*, John A.   I-31

Horn of Africa, The Struggle for the   III-1317

Hydrogen Bomb, Explosion of the First   II-683

Imperialism: A Study, John A. Hobson Publishes   I-31

in Vitro, Birth of the First Human Conceived   III-1324

Inchon, The Landing of the United Nations Forces at   II-676

India, The Partition of   II-605

India-Pakistan War and the Creation of Bangladesh, The   II-1091

Indian Reform Movement, Emergence of the American   II-865

Indian Reform Movement, Mohandas K. Ghandi Leads the Nonviolent   I-175

Indochina, Japan Occupies   I-438

Inflation and Labor Unrest   II-572

Information Revolution, Digital Computers and the   II-535

Insecticide, The Synthesis of DDT for Use as an   I-425

Intellectuals to America, Emigration of European   I-295

International Geophysical Year, The   II-764

Invention of the Jet Engine   I-355

Invention of the Laser   II-881

Invention of the Transistor   II-612

Invention of Xerography   I-382

Iranian Revolution, The   III-1338

Italy Declare War on the United States, Germany and   I-465

Italy Enters World War I   I-138

Japan, General MacArthur Administers the Reconstruction of   II-584

Japan, The First Superfortress Bombing Raid on   I-487

Japan Occupies Indochina   I-438

Japan Occupies the Dutch East Indies, Singapore, and Burma   I-457

Japan Presents China with the Twenty-One Demands   I-121

Japanese Military Campaigns in China   I-361

Japanese Militarism, The Manchurian Crisis and the Rise of   I-269

Jet Engine, Invention of the   I-355

Jewish Emigration to Palestine, Great Britain Issues the 1939 White Paper Restricting   I-411

Jewish State, Proclamation of an Independent   II-634

Jews, Nazi Extermination of the   I-396

Jews, Nazi Persecution of the   I-303

Jews in Palestine, The First Major Arab Attack on the   I-231

Kemal, The Reform Program of Mustafa   I-225

Khmer Rouge, The Fall of Cambodia to the   III-1212

Khrushchev, The Fall of   II-973

Khrushchev Denounces Stalin   II-736

Kinsey Reports, Publication of the   II-619

Labor Unrest, Inflation and   II-572

Landing of United Nations Forces at Inchon, The   II-676

Laser, Invention of the   II-881

Latin America, The United States Establishes the Good Neighbor Policy Toward   I-260

Lebanese Civil War, The   III-1235

Little Rock School Desegregation Crisis, The   II-770

Locarno Conference, The   I-197

MacArthur Administers the Reconstruction of Japan, General   II-584

Main Currents in American Thought, Vernon Louis Parrington Publishes   I-205

Manchurian Crisis and the Rise of Japanese Militarism, The   I-269

Mao Tse-tung and Chou En-lai, Deaths of   III-1264

Mars, The *Viking* Landings on   III-1294

Megalopolis, The Rise of the   II-550

Mein Kampf, Adolf Hitler Publishes   I-188

Meinecke Publishes *Cosmopolitanism and the National State*, Friedrich   I-54

Meteorological Satellites, Communications and   II-751

Mexican Revolution, The   I-69

Middle East, The Continuing Search for Peace in the   I-145

Middle East Enunciated, The Eisenhower Doctrine on the   II-757

Midway, The Battle of   I-472

Monetary System, Reform of the International   II-1104

Moroccan Crises, The   I-46

Mustafa Kemal, The Reform Program of   I-225

National Organization for Women, Founding of the   II-998

Navy, The United States Establishes a Two-Ocean   I-368

Nazi Extermination of the Jews   I-396

Nazi Persecution of the Jews   I-303

Neutron, Chadwick Discovers the   I-283

New Zealand, The Formation of the Commonwealth of Australia and the Dominion of   I-14

Nigerian Civil War, The   II-1003

1939 White Paper Restricting Jewish Emigration to Palestine, Great Britain Issues the   I-411

Nixon Administration, Collapse of the   III-1200

Nonviolent Indian Reform Movement, Mohandas K. Ghandi   I-175

Nuclear Disarmament and Nonproliferation, Worldwide Attempts at   II-564

Nuclear Test Ban Treaty, The   II-954

OAS Suspends the Embargo Against Cuba, The   III-1251

Obscenity, The United States Supreme Court Rules on   III-1174

Organization of Petroleum Exporting Countries (OPEC), Establishment of the   II-911

Origins of Man, Research into the   I-218

Palestine, Great Britain Issues the 1939 White Paper Restricting Jewish Emigration to   I-411

Palestine, The First Major Arab Attack on the Jews in   I-231

Panama Canal Treaties, Ratification of the   III-1331

Paris Peace Conference, The   II-591

Paris Summit Conference, The U-2 Incident and the Collapse of the   II-906

Parrington Publishes *Main Currents in American Thought*, Vernon Louis   I-205

Partition of India, The   II-605

People's Republic of China, Proclamation of the   II-654

People's Republic of China, *Rapprochement* with the   III-1124

People's Republic of China to the United Nations, Admission of the   III-1110

Petroleum Exporting Countries (OPEC), Establishment of the Organization of   II-912

Philosophical Efforts Toward an Objective View of Planet Earth   III-1069

Pipeline, Building of the Alaska   II-1022

Planet Earth, Philosophical Efforts Toward an Objective View of   III-1069

Polar Explorations   I-63

Political Terrorism   II-1028

Population Shift to the Sunbelt, The   III-1077

Presidency in 1976, Election of Carter to the   III-1302

Principia Mathematica, Bertrand Russell and Alfred North Whitehead Publish   I-79

Prison Reform, Pressure for   II-885

Proclamation of an Independent Jewish State   II-634

Proclamation of the People's Republic of China   II-654

Protestant Ethic and the Spirit of Capitalism, Max Weber Publishes *The*   I-38

Prussia, Russia Invades East   I-101

Publication of the Cambridge Histories   I-24

Publication of the Kinsey Reports   II-619

Pulsars, Discovery of   II-1009

Purge Trials, Stalin Begins the   I-336

Puritan Ethic in America, The Demise of the   I-526

Quantum Physics Research   I-166

Quasars, Discovery of   II-899

Quebec, Growth of the Separatist Movement in   II-820

Radar, Development of   I-324

Railroad Transportation, The Crisis in   I-520

Rapprochement with the People's Republic of China   III-1124

Ratification of the Panama Canal Treaties   III-1331

Reform of the International Monetary System   III-1104

Reform Program of Mustafa Kemal, The   I-225

Religion in America, Changing Attitudes Toward   I-507

Resignation of Vice-President Spiro T. Agnew   III-1188

Reunification of Vietnam, The   III-1243

Revisionist Historiography, William Appleman Williams Pioneers Cold War   II-663

Revolution, The Mexican   I-69

Revolution of 1911, The Chinese   I-92

Rhineland, Germany Remilitarizes the   I-348

Russell and Alfred North Whitehead Publish *Principia Mathematica*, Bertrand   I-79

Russia, German Invasion of   I-450

Russia Invades East Prussia   I-101

St. Lawrence Seaway, Opening of the   II-783

Satellites, Communications and Meteorological   II-751

Separatist Movement in Quebec, Growth of the   II-820

Signing of the Antarctic Treaty   II-798

Signing of the Warsaw Pact   II-715

Silent Spring, Rachel Carson Publishes   II-942

Singapore, and Burma, Japan Occupies the Dutch East Indies   I-457

Social Contract, The Changing   II-848

South Africa, Black Nationalist Movement in   III-1272

South Africa, Establishment of the Union of   I-87

Southeast Asia Treaty Organization (SEATO), Establishment of the   II-703

Soviet Intellectuals, Dissent Among   II-988

Soviet Invasion of Eastern Europe   I-479

Soviet Union, *Détente* with the   II-1050

Soviet Union, Strategic Arms Limitation Talks (SALT) with the   II-1054

Soviet Union, The United States Establishes Diplomatic Relations with the   I-319

Soviet Union Launches *Sputnik*, The   II-776

Space, Attempts to Contact Intelligent Beings in   II-827

Space, The United States Puts a Man in   II-934

Spaceflights of *Voyagers I* and *II*, The   III-1311

Sputnik, The Soviet Union Launches   II-776

Stagflation, The Economic Crisis of   II-1062

Stalin, Khrushchev Denounces   II-736

Stalin Begins the Purge Trials   I-336

Steinbeck Publishes *The Grapes of Wrath*, John   I-418

Strategic Arms Limitation Talks (SALT) with the Soviet Union   II-1054

Study of History, Arnold Toynbee Publishes *A*   I-329

Summit Conference, The Geneva   II-721

Summit Conference, The U-2 Incident and the Collapse of the Paris   II-906

Sunbelt, The Population Shift to the   II-1077

Superfortress Bombing Raid on Japan, The First   I-487

Teletype, Development of the   I-1

Television on Society, The Impact of   II-669

Terrorism, Political   II-1028

Tet Offensive, Viet Cong   II-1036

"Third World's" Struggle for Equality, The   II-557

Toynbee Publishes *A Study of History*, Arnold   I-329

Transistor, Invention of the   II-612

Treaties, Ratification of the Panama Canal   III-1331

Treaty, Germany Renounces the Versailles   I-342

Treaty, Signing of the Antarctic   II-798

Treaty, The Nuclear Test Ban   II-955

Treaty of Trianon   I-181

Trianon, Treaty of   I-181

Two-Ocean Navy, The United States Establishes a   I-368

Ulster, "Bloody Sunday" in   III-1117

United Nations, Admission of the People's Republic of China to the   II-1110

United Nations Forces at Inchon, The Landing of   II-676

United States, Germany and Italy Declare War on the   I-465

United States Establishes a Two-Ocean Navy, The   I-368

United States Establishes Diplomatic Relations with the Soviet Union, The   I-319

United States Establishes the Good Neighbor Policy Toward Latin America, The   I-260

United States Invades Cambodia, The   II-1083

United States Puts a Man in Space, The   II-933

United States Supreme Court Rules Against Bible Reading in Public Schools, The   II-949

United States Supreme Court Rules on Obscenity, The   III-1174

United States Supreme Court Rules on State Antiabortion Laws, The   III-1154

United States Supreme Court Rules on the Death Penalty, The   III-1279

United States to Construct an Atomic Bomb, Decision by the   I-389

U-2 Incident and the Collapse of the Paris Summit Conference, The   II-905

Versailles Treaty, Germany Renounces the   I-342
Viet Cong Tet Offensive   II-1036
Vietnam, The Establishment of the Democratic Republic of   II-696
Vietnam, The Fall of South   III-1227
Vietnam, The Reunification of   III-1243
Vietnam War, End of American Involvement in the   III-1161
Vietnam's Conquest of Cambodia   III-1346
Viking Landings on Mars, The   III-1294
Voyagers I and *II*, The Spaceflights of   III-1311

Warsaw Pact, Signing of the   II-715
Watergate Affair, The   III-1131
Weber Publishes *The Protestant Ethic and the Spirit of Capitalism*, Max   I-38

Whitehead Publish *Principia Mathematica*, Bertrand Russell and Alfred North   I-79
Williams Pioneers Cold War Revisionist Historiography, William Appleman   II-663
Women, Founding of the National Organization for   II-998
World War I, Italy Enters   I-138

Xerography, Invention of   I-382

Yom Kippur War, The   III-1182
Yugoslavia from the Cominform, Expulsion of   II-640

Zimbabwe/Rhodesia, Black Insurgency Movements in   II-981

CONSTITUTIONAL

Admission of Alaska and Hawaii into the Union   II-790

Chinese Revolution of 1911, The   I-92

Civil Rights Act of 1964, The   II-965

Civil Rights Acts of the 1960's, The   II-806

Collapse of the Nixon Administration   III-1200

Communist *Coup* in Czechoslovakia, The   II-626

Death of Franco and the Restoration of the Monarchy   II-1043

Dissolution of the Habsburg Monarchy, The   I-158

Establishment of the Democratic Republic of Vietnam, The   II-696

Establishment of the Union of South Africa   I-87

Formation of the Commonwealth of Australia and the Dominion of New Zealand, The   I-14

General MacArthur Administers the Reconstruction of Japan   II-584

Great Russian Civil War, The   I-152

Growth of the Separatist Movement in Quebec   II-820

Hitler Comes to Power in Germany   I-311

India-Pakistan War and the Creation of Bangladesh, The   II-1091

Little Rock School Desegregation Crisis, The   II-770

Mexican Revolution, The   I-69

Proclamation of an Independent Jewish State   II-634

Reform Program of Mustafa Kemal, The   I-225

United States Supreme Court Rules Against Bible Reading in Public Schools, The   II-949

United States Supreme Court Rules on Obscenity, The   III-1174

United States Supreme Court Rules on State Antiabortion Laws, The   III-1154

United States Supreme Court Rules on the Death Penalty, The   III-1279

Watergate Affair, The   III-1131

CULTURAL

Antitotalitarian Literature of the 1930's and Early 1940's   I-241

Arnold Toynbee Publishes *A Study of History*   I-329

Bicentennial Celebration, The   III-1287

Changing Attitudes Toward Religion in America   I-507

Changing Patterns in Education   I-513

Changing Social Contract, The   II-848

Civil Rights Act of 1964, The   II-965

Civil Rights Acts of the 1960's, The   II-806

Civil War in China, The   I-211

Crisis in Railroad Transportation, The   I-520

Demise of the Puritan Ethic in America, The   I-526

Emergence of the American Indian Reform Movement   II-865

Emergence of the Drug Culture   II-814

Emigration of European Intellectuals to America   I-295

Existentialism in Literature   I-252

Friedrich Meinecke Publishes *Cosmopolitanism and the National State*   I-54

General MacArthur Administers the Reconstruction of Japan   II-584

Great Britain Issues the 1939 White Paper Restricting Jewish Emigration to Palestine   I-411

Growth of the Separatist Movement in Quebec   II-820

Impact of Television on Society, The   II-669

Little Rock School Desegregation Crisis, The   II-770

Pressure of Minorities for Personal Equality   II-893

Publication of the Kinsey Reports   II-619

Reform Program of Mustafa Kemal, The   I-225

Research into the Origins of Man   I-218

Rise of the Megalopolis, The   II-550

United States Supreme Court Rules on Obscenity, The   III-1174

Vernon Louis Parrington Publishes *Main Currents in American Thought*   I-205

DIPLOMATIC

Admission of the People's Republic of China to the United Nations   III-1110

Arab Oil Embargo and the Energy Crisis   III-1137

Charter of the Economic Rights and Duties of States   III-1206

Congress Passes the Formosa Resolution   II-709

Continuing Search for Peace in the Middle East, The   I-145

Creation of the Federal Republic of Germany and the German Democratic Republic, The   II-647

Détente with the Soviet Union   II-1050

Diplomatic Relations Established Between East and West Germany   III-1167

Eisenhower Doctrine on the Middle East Enunciated, The   II-757

End of American Involvement in the Vietnam War   III-1161
Establishment of the Southeast Asia Treaty Organization (SEATO)   II-703
Expulsion of Yugoslavia from the Cominform   II-640
Foreign Policy of John Foster Dulles, The   II-690
Formation of the Arab League   I-494
Geneva Disarmament Conference, The   I-276
Geneva Summit Conference, The   II-721
Germany Renounces the Versailles Treaty   I-342
Great Britain Issues the 1939 White Paper Restricting Jewish Emigration to Palestine   I-411
Great Britain Joins the Common Market   III-1146
Helsinki Agreement, The   III-1257
India-Pakistan War and the Creation of Bangladesh, The   II-1091
International Geophysical Year, The   II-764
Japan Presents China with the Twenty-One Demands   I-121
Locarno Conference, The   I-197
Moroccan Crises, The   I-46
Nuclear Test Ban Treaty, The   II-955
OAS Suspends the Embargo Against Cuba, The   III-1251
Paris Peace Conference, The   II-591
Rapprochement with the People's Republic of China   III-1124
Ratification of the Panama Canal Treaties   III-1331
Signing of the Antarctic Treaty   II-798
Signing of the Warsaw Pact   II-715
Strategic Arms Limitation Talks (SALT) with the Soviet Union   II-1054
Treaty of Trianon   I-181
United States Establishes Diplomatic Relations with the Soviet Union, The   I-319
United States Establishes the Good Neighbor Policy Toward Latin America, The   I-260
U-2 Incident and the Collapse of the Paris Summit Conference, The   II-906
Worldwide Attempts at Nuclear Disarmament and Nonproliferation   II-564

ECONOMIC

Arab Oil Embargo and the Energy Crisis   III-1137
Building of the Alaska Pipeline   II-1022
Charter of the Economic Rights and Duties of States   III-1206
Crisis in Railroad Transportation, The   I-520
Devaluation of the Dollar   III-1097
Economic Crisis of Stagflation, The   II-1062
Establishment of the Organization of Petroleum Exporting Countries (OPEC)   II-912
Great Britain Joins the Common Market   III-1146
Inflation and Labor Unrest   II-572
Japan Occupies Indochina   I-438
Japan Occupies the Dutch East Indies, Singapore, and Burma   I-457
Merger of the AFL and the CIO   II-730
Moroccan Crises, The   I-46
Nazi Persecution of the Jews   I-303
OAS Suspends the Embargo Against Cuba, The   III-1251
Opening of the St. Lawrence Seaway   II-783
Polar Explorations   I-63
Population Shift to the Sunbelt, The   II-1077
Reform of the International Monetary System   III-1104
United States Establishes the Good Neighbor Policy Toward Latin America, The   I-260

EDUCATIONAL

Changing Patterns in Education   I-513
Little Rock School Desegregation Crisis, The   II-770

INTELLECTUAL

Antitotalitarian Literature of the 1930's and Early 1940's   I-241
Arnold Toynbee Publishes *A Study of History*   I-329
Bertrand Russell and Alfred North Whitehead Publish *Principia Mathematica*   I-79
Dissent Among Soviet Intellectuals   II-988
Existentialism in Literature   I-252
Friedrich Meinecke Publishes *Cosmopolitanism and the National State*   I-54
Fritz Fischer Publishes *Germany's Aims in the First World War*   II-918
John A. Hobson Publishes *Imperialism: A Study*   I-31
Max Weber Publishes *The Protestant Ethic and the Spirit of Capitalism*   I-38
Philosophical Efforts Toward an Objective View of Planet Earth   II-1069
Publication of the Cambridge Histories   I-24
Rachel Carson Publishes *Silent Spring*   II-942
Vernon Louis Parrington Publishes *Main Currents in American Thought*   I-205
William Appleman Williams Pioneers Cold War Revisionist Historiography   II-663

LEGAL

Admission of Alaska and Hawaii into the Union   II-790

Civil Rights Act of 1964, The   II-965
Civil Rights Acts of the 1960's, The   II-806
Collapse of the Nixon Administration   III-1200
Environmental Legislation Passed Since 1960   II-872
Resignation of Vice-President Spiro T. Agnew   III-1188
United States Supreme Court Rules Against Bible Reading in Public Schools, The   II-949
United States Supreme Court Rules on Obscenity, The   III-1174
United States Supreme Court Rules on State Antiabortion Laws, The   III-1154
United States Supreme Court Rules on the Death Penalty, The   III-1279
Watergate Affair, The   III-1131

LITERARY

Adolf Hitler Publishes *Mein Kampf*   I-188
Antitotalitarian Literature of the 1930's and Early 1940's   I-241
Arnold Toynbee Publishes *A Study of History*   I-329
Bertrand Russell and Alfred North Whitehead Publish *Principia Mathematica*   I-79
Existentialism in Literature   I-252
Friedrich Meinecke Publishes *Cosmopolitanism and the National State*   I-54
Fritz Fischer Publishes *Germany's Aims in the First World War*   II-918
John A. Hobson Publishes *Imperialism: A Study*   I-31
John Steinbeck Publishes *The Grapes of Wrath*   I-418
Max Weber Publishes *The Protestant Ethic and the Spirit of Capitalism*   I-38
Publication of the Cambridge Histories   I-24
Rachel Carson Publishes *Silent Spring*   II-942
Vernon Louis Parrington Publishes *Main Currents in American Thought*   I-205

MILITARY

Battle of Britain, The   I-430
Battle of Germany, The   II-577
Battle of Midway, The   I-472
Battle of the Atlantic, The   I-404
Bay of Pigs Invasion Repulsed, The   II-926
Castro Seizes Power in Cuba   II-743
Chaco War, The   I-289
Chinese Revolution of 1911   I-92
Civil War in Angola and the Intervention of Cuba, The   III-1219
Civil War in China, The   I-211
Cyprus Crisis, The   III-1193
Fall of South Vietnam, The   III-1227

First Superfortress Bombing Raid on Japan, The   I-487
Gallipoli Campaign, The   I-129
General MacArthur Administers the Reconstruction of Japan   II-584
German Invasion of Russia   I-450
Germany and Italy Declare War on the United States   I-465
Germany Invades the Balkans   I-444
Germany Remilitarizes the Rhineland   I-348
Hitler Establishes Control of the Diplomatic and Military Hierarchy   I-375
India-Pakistan War and the Creation of Bangladesh, The   II-1091
Italy Enters World War I   I-138
Japan Occupies Indochina   I-438
Japan Occupies the Dutch East Indies, Singapore, and Burma   I-457
Japanese Military Campaigns in China   I-361
Landing of United Nations Forces at Inchon, The   II-676
Lebanese Civil War, The   III-1235
Manchurian Crisis and the Rise of Japanese Militarism, The   I-269
Nigerian Civil War, The   II-1003
Russia Invades East Prussia   I-101
Soviet Invasion of Eastern Europe   I-479
United States Establishes a Two-Ocean Navy, The   I-368
United States Invades Cambodia, The   II-1083
Viet Cong Tet Offensive   II-1036
Vietnam's Conquest of Cambodia   III-1346
Yom Kippur War, The   III-1182

PHILOSOPHICAL

Attempts to Contact Intelligent Beings in Space   II-827
Existentialism in Literature   I-252
Philosophical Efforts Toward an Objective View of Planet Earth   II-1069

POLITICAL

Admission of Alaska and Hawaii into the Union   II-790
Antitotalitarian Literature of the 1930's and Early 1940's   I-241
Bay of Pigs Invasion Repulsed, The   II-926
Bicentennial Celebration, The   III-1287
Black Nationalist Movement in South Africa   III-1272
"Bloody Sunday" in Ulster   III-1117
Castro Seizes Power in Cuba   II-743
César Chávez Organizes the Farm Workers   II-842
Changing Social Contract, The   II-848

Chinese Revolution of 1911, The   I-92
Civil War in Angola and the Intervention of Cuba, The   III-1219
Civil War in China, The   I-211
Collapse of the Nixon Administration   III-1200
Communist *Coup* in Czechoslovakia, The   II-626
Congress Passes the Formosa Resolution   II-709
Continuing Search for Peace in the Middle East, The   I-145
Creation of the Federal Republic of Germany and the German Democratic Republic, The   II-647
Death of Franco and the Restoration of the Monarchy   II-1043
Deaths of Mao Tse-tung and Chou En-lai   III-1264
Decision by the United States to Construct an Atomic Bomb   I-389
Dissent Among Soviet Intellectuals   II-988
Dissolution of the Habsburg Monarchy, The   I-158
Election of Carter to the Presidency in 1976   III-1302
Emergence of Consumer Awareness   II-856
Emergence of the American Indian Reform Movement   II-865
Environmental Legislation Passed   II-872
Establishment of the Democratic Republic of Vietnam, The   II-696
Establishment of the Union of South Africa   I-87
Fall of Cambodia to the Khmer Rouge, The   III-1212
Fall of Khrushchev, The   II-974
First Major Arab Attack on the Jews in Palestine, The   I-231
Formation of the Commonwealth of Australia and the Dominion of New Zealand, The   I-14
Founding of the National Organization for Women   II-998
Great Armenian Massacre, The   I-107
Great Russian Civil War, The   I-152
Growth of the Separatist Movement in Quebec   II-820
Hitler Comes to Power in Germany   I-311
Hitler Establishes Control of the Diplomatic and Military Hierarchy   I-375
India-Pakistan War and the Creation of Bangladesh, The   II-1091
Iranian Revolution, The   III-1338
Italy Enters World War I   I-138
Japan Occupies Indochina   I-438
Japan Occupies the Dutch East Indies, Singapore, and Burma   I-457
Khrushchev Denounces Stalin   II-736
Lebanese Civil War, The   III-1235
Merger of the AFL and the CIO   II-730

Mexican Revolution, The   I-69
Mohandas K. Ghandi Leads the Nonviolent Indian Reform Movement   I-175
Moroccan Crises, The   I-46
Nazi Extermination of the Jews   I-396
Nazi Persecution of the Jews   I-303
Nigerian Civil War, The   II-1003
Partition of India, The   II-605
Political Terrorism   II-1028
Pressure for Prison Reform   II-886
Pressure of Minorities for Personal Equality   II-893
Proclamation of an Independent Jewish State   II-634
Proclamation of the People's Republic of China   II-654
Public Awareness of Environmental Dangers   II-542
Reform Program of Mustafa Kemal   I-225
Resignation of Vice-President Spiro T. Agnew   III-1188
Reunification of Vietnam, The   III-1243
Stalin Begins the Purge Trials   I-336
Struggle for the Horn of Africa, The   III-1317
"Third World's" Struggle for Equality, The   II-557
United States Establishes a Two-Ocean Navy, The   I-368
United States Establishes the Good Neighbor Policy Toward Latin America, The   I-260
Watergate Affair, The   III-1131

RELIGIOUS

"Bloody Sunday" in Ulster   III-1117
Changing Attitudes Toward Religion in America   I-507
Continuing Search for Peace in the Middle East, The   I-145
Discovery of the Dead Sea Scrolls   II-598
First Major Arab Attack on the Jews in Palestine, The   I-231
India-Pakistan War and the Creation of Bangladesh, The   II-1091
Iranian Revolution, The   III-1338
Lebanese Civil War, The   III-1235
Max Weber Publishes *The Protestant Ethic and the Spirit of Capitalism*   I-38
Nazi Extermination of the Jews   I-396
Partition of India, The   II-605
Proclamation of an Independent Jewish State   II-634

SCIENTIFIC

Atomic Research   I-246
Attempts to Contact Intelligent Beings in Space   II-827
Birth of the First Human Conceived *in Vitro*   III-1324

"Black Hole" Investigations   II-835
Cellular Research   I-501
Chadwick Discovers the Neutron   I-283
Digital Computers and the Information Revolution   II-535
Discovery of Pulsars   II-1009
Discovery of Quasars   II-899
Explosion of the First Hydrogen Bomb   II-683
First Heart Transplant Operation, The   II-1016
Genetic Research   I-7
International Geophysical Year, The   II-764
Invention of the Laser   II-881
Invention of the Transistor   II-612
Polar Explorations   I-63
Publication of the Kinsey Reports   II-619
Quantum Physics Research   I-166
Rachel Carson Publishes *Silent Spring*   II-942
Research into the Origins of Man   I-218
Soviet Union Launches *Sputnik*, The   II-776
Spaceflights of *Voyagers I* and *II*, The   III-1311
Synthesis of DDT for Use as an Insecticide, The   I-425
United States Puts a Man in Space, The   II-934
Viking Landings on Mars, The   III-1294

SOCIOLOGICAL

Adolf Hitler Publishes *Mein Kampf*   I-188
Bicentennial Celebration, The   III-1287
Birth of the First Human Conceived *in Vitro*   III-1324
Black Insurgency Movements in Zimbabwe/Rhodesia   II-981
Black Nationalist Movement in South Africa   III-1272
"Bloody Sunday" in Ulster   III-1117
César Chávez Organizes the Farm Workers   II-842
Changing Social Contract, The   II-848
Civil Rights Act of 1964, The   II-965
Civil Rights Acts of the 1960's, The   II-806
Civil War in China, The   I-211
Crisis in Railroad Transportation, The   I-520
Cyprus Crisis, The   III-1193
Demise of the Puritan Ethic in America, The   I-526
Dissolution of the Habsburg Monarchy, The   I-158
Emergence of Consumer Awareness   II-856
Emergence of the American Indian Reform Movement   II-865
Emergence of the Drug Culture   II-814
Emigration of European Intellectuals to America   I-295
First Major Arab Attack on the Jews in Palestine, The   I-231
Founding of the National Organization for Women   II-998
Great Armenian Massacre, The   I-107
Growth of the Separatist Movement in Quebec   II-820
Impact of Television on Society, The   II-669
John Steinbeck Publishes *The Grapes of Wrath*   I-418
Little Rock School Desegregation Crisis, The   II-770
Max Weber Publishes *The Protestant Ethic and the Spirit of Capitalism*   I-38
Mohandas K. Gandhi Leads the Nonviolent Indian Reform Movement   I-175
Nazi Extermination of the Jews   I-396
Nazi Persecution of the Jews   I-303
Population Shift to the Sunbelt, The   II-1077
Pressure for Prison Reform   II-886
Pressure of Minorities for Personal Equality   II-893
Public Awareness of Environmental Dangers   II-542
Publication of the Kinsey Reports   II-619
Rise of the Megalopolis, The   II-550
"Third World's" Struggle for Equality, The   II-557
United States Supreme Court Rules Against Bible Reading in Public Schools, The   II-949
United States Supreme Court Rules on Obscenity, The   III-1174
United States Supreme Court Rules on State Antiabortion Laws, The   III-1154
United States Supreme Court Rules on the Death Penalty, The   III-1279

TECHNOLOGICAL

Communications and Meteorological Satellites   II-751
Decision by the United States to Construct an Atomic Bomb   I-389
Development of Radar   I-324
Development of the Teletype   I-1
Digital Computers and the Information Revolution   II-535
Explosion of the First Hydrogen Bomb   II-683
Invention of the Jet Engine   I-355
Invention of the Laser   II-881
Invention of the Transistor   II-612
Invention of Xerography   I-382
Opening of the St. Lawrence Seaway   II-783
Soviet Union Launches *Sputnik*, The   II-776
Spaceflights of *Voyagers I* and *II*, The   III-1311
United States Puts a Man in Space, The   II-934
Viking Landings on Mars, The   III-1294

Abdul-Hamid II (1842-1918)   I-411
Abdullah, ibn-Husein (1882-1951)   I-494
Abernathy, Ralph (1926-   )   II-865
Abrams, Creighton Williams (1914-   )   II-1083; III-1212
Acheson, Dean Gooderham (1893-1971)   II-564
Acton, First Baron (see Dalberg-Acton, Lord John Emerich Edward)
Adenauer, Konrad (1876-1967)   II-647,690
Agnew, Spiro Theodore (1918-   )   III-1188
Alexander, Sir Harold Rupert Leofric George (1891-1969)   I-457
Alfonso, Perez   II-912
Altizer, Thomas Jonathon Jackson (1927-   )   I-507
Alvarez, Luis Echeverría (see Echeverría Alvarez, Luis)
Alvarez, Luis Walter (1911-   )   II-683
Amann, Max   I-188
Amundsen, Roald E. (1872-1928)   I-63
Apfelbaum, Hirsch (see Zinoviev, Grigori Evseevich)
Apponyi, Albert György (1846-1933)   I-181
Arafat, Yasir (Mohammed Abed Ar'ouf Arafat) (1929-   )   I-145; II-1028; III-1235
Arango, Doroteo (see Villa, Francisco)
Arias Navarro, Carlos   II-1043
Arnold, Henry Harley (Hap) (1886-1950)   I-487
Assad, Hafez al- (1930-   )   III-1182
Ayala, Eusebio (1875-1942)   I-289

Baade, Wilhelm Heinrich Walter (1893-1960)   II-1009
Baader, Andreas (1943-1977)   II-1028
Bahr, Egon (1922-   )   III-1167
Baker, Howard Henry (1925-   )   III-1331
Balewa, Sir Abubakar Tafawa   II-1003
Balfour, Lord Arthur James (First Earl of Balfour) (1848-1930)   I-231, 411
Banks, Dennis   II-865
Bao Dai (1911-   )   II-696
Baranov, Aleksandr (1747-1819)   II-790
Bardeen, John (1908-   )   II-612
Barnard, Christian Neethling (1922-   )   II-1016
Barton, Sir Edmund (1849-1920)   I-14
Barton, James   I-107
Baruch, Bernard Mannes (1870-1965)   II-564
Basov, Nikolai Gennadievich (1922-   )   II-881
Bates, Daisy (1920-   )   II-770
Batista y Zaldivar, Fulgencio (1901-1973)   II-743
Baudot, Jean Marie Emile   I-1

Baxter, Richard (1615-1691)   I-38
Beall, George Brooke (1926-   )   III-1188
Beauvoir, Simone de (1908-   )   I-252
Begin, Menachem (1913-   )   I-145
Bell (Burnell), Jocelyn   II-1009
Beneš, Eduard (1884-1948)   II-626
Ben-Gurion, David (1886-1973)   II-634
Bennett, William Ralph, Jr. (1930-   )   II-881
Beria, Lavrenti Pavlovich (1899-1953)   II-736
Berkner, Lloyd Viel (1905-1967)   II-764
Bernadotte Af Wisborg, Count Folke (1895-1948)   II-634
Bethlen, Stephen (1874-1947)   I-181
Bethmann-Hollweg, Theobald von (1856-1921)   I-46
Bevin, Ernest (1884-1951)   II-591
Bhutto, Zulfikar Ali (1928-1979)   II-1091
Bidault, Georges (1899-   )   II-591
Bismarck-Schönhausen, Count Otto (Eduard Leopold) von (1815-1898)   I-54
Bissell, Richard Mervin (1909-   )   II-926
Black, Hugo LaFayette (1886-1971)   I-507
Blackmun, Harry Andrew (1908-   )   II-1154
Blomberg, Werner von (1878-1946)   I-375
Blossom, Virgil T.   II-770
Bock, Fedor von (1880-1945)   I-450
Bohr, Niels (1885-1962)   I-166, 246; II-881
Boris III, of Saxe-Coburg (1894-1943)   I-444
Botha, Louis (1862-1919)   I-87
Bourgault, Pierre   II-820
Bradley, Omar Nelson (1893-1979)   II-577
Branch, Elmer   III-1279
Brandt, Willy (Herbert Frahm) (1913-   )   III-1167
Brattain, Walter Houser (1902-   )   II-612
Brauchitsch, Heinrich Alfred Hermann Walther von (1881-1948)   I-375, 450
Braun, Wernher von (1912-1976)   II-751,-776, 934
Brennan, William Joseph, Jr. (1906-   )   III-1279
Brezhnev, Leonid Ilyich (1906-   )   II-974, 988, 1050, 1054; III-1257
Briand, Aristide (1862-1932)   I-197
Bridges, Calvin Blackman (1889-1938)   I-7
Broglie, Louis Victor de (1892-   )   I-166
Bronstein, Leib Darydovich (see Trotsky, Leon)
Brooke, Sir Alan Francis (1883-1963)   I-430
Broom, Robert (1866-1951)   I-218
Brown, Gilbert John   III-1324
Brown, Lesley   III-1324
Brown, Louise Joy   III-1324
Bruce, Victor Alexander (Ninth Earl of Elgin) (1849-1917)   I-14

Brüning, Heinrich (1885-1970)   I-276
Bryan, William Jennings (1860-1925)   I-121
Bryce, Viscount James (1838-1922)   I-107
Bukharin, Nikolai Ivanovich (1888-1938)   I-336
Bulganin, Nikolai Aleksandrovich (1895-1975)   II-715, 721
Bülow, Prince Bernhard von (1849-1929)   I-46
Burger, Warren Earl (1907-   )   I-513; III-1154, 1174
Burnell, Jocelyn (*see* Bell, Jocelyn)
Burns, Arthur (1904-   )   III-1097
Bush, Vannevar (1890-   )   I-389
Buthelezi, Gatsha (1928-   )   III-1272
Byrd, Robert Carlyle (1917-   )   III-1331
Byrnes, James Francis (1879-1972)   II-591, 647

Calles, Plutarco Elías (1877-1945)   I-69
Calvin, John (1509-1564)   I-38
Camus, Albert (1913-1960)   I-252
Carden, Sir Sackville Hamilton (1857-1930)   I-129
Cardona, José Miró (1901-1974)   II-926
Carey, James Barron (1911-   )   II-730
Carlson, Chester F.   I-382
Carol II, of Hohenzollern-Sigmaringen (1893-1953)   I-444
Carr, Michael   III-1294
Carranza, Venustiano (1859-1920)   I-69
Carrero Blanco, Luis   II-1043
Carson, Rachel Louise (1907-1964)   I-425; II-542, 942, III-1069
Carter, Jimmy (James Earl) (1924-   )   I-145; II-872, 988, 1050, 1054; III-1235, 1302, 1317, 1331, 1338
Carter, W. G.   I-355
Casson, Dollier de   II-783
Castaneda, Jorge   III-1206
Castro, Fidel (1927-   )   II-743, 926; III-1251, 1317
Chadwick, James (1891-1974)   I-246, 283
Chaikovsky, Nikolai Vasilievich (1850-1926)   I-152
Chamberlain, Sir Austen (1863-1937)   I-197
Chamberlain, Joseph (1836-1914)   I-14, 87
Chamoun, Camille (1900-   )   II-758; III-1235
Chancellor, Sir John Robert (1870-1952)   I-231
Chang Ch'un-ch'iao (1912-   )   III-1264
Chang Hsüeh-liang (1898-   )   I-211
Chapman, Sydney (1888-1970)   II-764
Charles I (Charles Francis Joseph), of Austria (1887-1922)   I-158
Chávez, César (1927-   )   II-842
Chehab, Fuad (*see* Shehab, Fuad)
Cheng Heng (1916-   )   III-1212
Chetverikov, Sergei S. (1880-1959)   I-7
Chevrier, Lionel   II-783

Chiang Ch'ing (1914-   )   III-1264
Chiang Kai-shek (1887-1975)   I-211, 361; II-654, 690, 709; III-1110
Ch'iao Kuan-hua (1914-   )   III-1110
Ch'in Teh-ch'un   I-361
Chiu, Hong-Lee   II-899
Chou En-lai (1898-1976)   II-654, 709; III-1110, 1124, 1264
Chu Teh (1886-1976)   I-211; III-1264
Ch'un, Prince (1882-   )   I-92
Churchill, Sir Winston Leonard Spencer (1874-1965)   I-129, 404, 457; II-577
Clarenbach, Kathryn (1920-   )   II-998
Clark, Thomas Campbell (1899-   )   II-949
Clarke, Arthur C. (1917-   )   II-751
Claude, Albert (1899-   )   I-501
Clay, Lucius Du Bignon (1897-   )   II-647
Clifford, Clark McAdams (1906-   )   II-1036
Collins, Joseph Lawton (1896-   )   II-676
Commoner, Barry (1917-   )   II-542
Conant, James Bryant (1893-   )   I-389
Cooper, Kent   I-1
Cousteau, Jacques (1910-   )   II-1069
Cox, Harvey Gallagher, Jr. (1929-   )   I-507
Craig, William (1924-   )   III-1117
Cripps, Sir Richard Stafford (1889-1952)   II-605
Curcio, Renato   II-1028

Dalberg-Acton, Lord John Emerich Edward (First Baron Acton) (1834-1902)   I-24
Daniels, Paul Clement (1903-   )   II-798
D'Annunzio, Gabriele (1863-1938)   I-138
Dart, Raymond Arthur (1893-   )   I-218
Darvall, Denise   II-1016
Darvall, Edward   II-1016
Dayan, Moshe (1915-   )   III-1182
Deakin, Alfred (1856-1919)   I-14
Dean, John Wesley, III (1938-   )   III-1131
De Forest, Lee (1873-1961)   II-612
de Gaulle, Charles André Joseph Mario (1890-1970)   II-1003; III-1146
Deloria, Vine, Jr. (1933-   )   II-865
Denikin, Anton Evanovich (1872-1947)   I-152
Dessauer, John H.   I-382
De Vaux, Roland (1903-   )   II-598
Devlin, Bernadette (1947-   )   III-1117
Díaz, Porfirio (1830-1915)   I-69
Diem, Ngô Dinh (1901-1963)   II-696; III-1243
Dimitrov, Georgi (1882-1949)   II-640
Dingell, John David, Jr. (1926-   )   II-872
Dirac, Paul Andre Marie (1902-   )   I-166
Dirksen, Everett McKinley (1896-1969)   II-806, 965
Dixon, Robert   II-827
Djemal Pasha, Ahmed (1872-1922)   I-107

Djevdet Bey   I-107
Dobrynin, Anatoly Fedorovich (1919-
)   II-1054
Dodge, Joseph   II-584
Dole, Sanford (1844-1926)   II-790
Dönitz, Karl (1891-   )   I-404
Doorman, Karel W. F. M. (1889-1942)   I-457
Douglas, William Orville (1898-1980)   III-1154, 1279
Dowding, Sir Hugh Caswall (1882-1970)   I-430
Drake, Frank Donald (1930-   )   II-827
Dulaney, R. G.   II-1022
Dulles, Allen (1893-   )   II-926
Dulles, John Foster (1888-1959)   I-260, 690, 703, 709
Dung, Van Tien (1917-   )   III-1227, 1346
Duve, Christian Rene de (1917-   )   I-501
Dzhugashvili, Iosif Vissarionovich (*see* Stalin, Joseph)

Ecevit, Bülent (1925-   )   III-1193
Echeverría Alvarez, Luis (1922-   )   III-1206
Eckert, John Presper (1919-   )   II-535
Eckford, Elizabeth   II-770
Eden, Sir Robert Anthony (1897-1977)   I-348, 494; II-721
Edison, Thomas Alva (1847-1931)   I-1
Edwards, Robert G.   III-1324
Edwardsen, Charlie   II-1022
Egan, William Allen (1914-   )   II-1022
Ehrlich, Paul Ralph (1932-   )   II-542, 1069
Ehrlichman, John Daniel (1925-   )   III-1131
Eichmann, Adolf (1906-1962)   I-303, 396
Einstein, Albert (1879-1955)   I-295; II-835, 881
Eisenhower, Dwight David (1890-1969)   I-260; II-564, 577, 690, 703, 709, 721, 758, 770, 776, 783, 790, 798, 906, 934
Eki, Hioki   I-121
Elizabeth II, of Great Britain (1926-   )   III-1287
Enver Pasha (1881?-1922)   I-107, 129
Ervin, Samuel James (1896-   )   III-1131
Estigarribia, Jóse Félix (1888-1940)   I-289
Everett, Robert R. (1921-   )   II-535

Fabrikant, V. A.   II-881
Faubus, Orval E. (1910-   )   II-770
Faulkner, Brian (1921-   )   III-1117
Faure, Edgar (1908-   )   II-721
Fermi, Enrico (1901-1954)   I-246
Ferrell, Robert H. (1921-   )   II-663
Feuchtwanger, Lion (1884-1958)   I-241
Fiedler, Arthur (1894-1979)   III-1287
Filov, Bogdan (1883-1945)   I-444
Fischer, Fritz (1908-   )   II-918

Fisher, Sir John Arbuthnot (1841-1920)   I-129
Fisher, Ronald A. (1890-1962)   I-7
Flandin, Pierre Étienne (1889-1958)   I-348
Fletcher, Frank Jack (1885-   )   I-472
Ford, Gerald Rudolph (1913-   )   I-513; II-1054; III-1200, 1227, 1257, 1287, 1302, 1331
Forrester, Jay W. (1928-   )   II-535
Frahm, Herbert (*see* Brandt, Willy)
Francis Ferdinand (1863--1914)   I-158
Francis Joseph I, of Austria (1830-1916)   I-158
Franco, Francisco (1892-1975)   II-1043
Franjieh, Suleiman   III-1235
Frederick William IV, of Prussia (1795-1861)   I-54
Friedan, Betty (1921-   )   II-893, 998
Friendly, Fred W. (1915-   )   II-669
Fritsch, Werner von (1880-1939)   I-375
Fumimaro, Prince Konoye (1891-1945)   I-361
Furman, William H.   III-1279

Gandhi, Indira (1917-   )   II-1091
Gandhi, Mohandas Karamchand (1869-1948)   I-175, II-605
Gebhard, Paul H. (1917-   )   II-619
Gemayel, Pierre   III-1235
George, Walter F. (1878-1957)   II-709
Gia Long (Nguyen Phuc Anh) (1762-1820)   III-1243
Giap, Vo Nguyen (1912-   )   II-696; III-1243
Gilruth, Robert R. (1913-   )   II-934
Giolitti, Giovanni (1842-1928)   I-138
Giscard d'Estaing, Valéry (1926-   )   III-1104, 1257
Goddard, Robert Hutchings (1882-1945)   II-751
Goebbels, Joseph (1897-1945)   I-311
Goerdeler, Carl (1884-1945)   I-375
Gold, Thomas (1920-   )   II-1009
Goldberg, Arthur Joseph (1908-   )   II-730
González, Felipe   II-1043
Göring, Hermann (1893-1946)   I-303, 311, 375, 396, 430
Gottwald, Klement (1896-   )   II-626
Gould, Gordon (1920-   )   II-881
Gowon, Yakubu (1934-   )   II-1003
Grandes, Muñoz   II-1043
Grau San Martín, Ramón (1887-1969)   II-743
Greenstein, Jessie Leonard (1909-   )   II-899
Gregg, Troy Leon   III-1279
Grey, Sir Edward (1862-1933)   I-121
Gromyko, Andrei A. (1909-   )   II-564, 955, 1054
Gropius, Walter (1883-1969)   I-295

Gruening, Ernest Henry (1887-) II-790

Guderian, Heinz (1886-1954)   I-479

Gun, Hashimoto   I-361

Habash, George (1925-)   II-1028

Hahn, Otto (1879-1968)   I-246

Haig, Alexander Maigs, Jr. (1924-)   III-1200

Hailsham, Lord   II-955

Haldane, J. B. S. (1892-1964)   I-7

Haldeman, Harry R. (Bob) (1926-)   III-1131

Halifax, Earl of (*see* Irwin, Lord)

Halmos, Charles   I-181

Hamilton, Sir Ian Standish Monteith (1853-1947)   I-129

Harding, G. Lankester (1901-)   II-598

Harriman, William Averell (1891-)   II-955

Harris, La Donna (1931-)   II-865

Haushofer, Karl (1869-1946)   I-188

Hawking, Stephen William (1942-)   II-835

Hays, Brooks   II-770

Hazard, Cyril   II-899

Heath, Edward (1916-)   III-1117, 1146

Hebrang, Andreya   II-640

Hegel, Georg Wilhelm Friedrich (1770-1831)   I-54

Heidegger, Martin (1889-1976)   I-252

Heineman, Ben Walter (1914-)   I-520

Heinkel, Ernst (1888-1958)   I-355

Heisenberg, Werner (1901-1977)   I-166

Hemingway, Ernest (1899-1961)   I-241

Heng Samrin   III-1346

Henry, E. William   II-669

Herriot, Édouard (1872-1957)   I-276

Herriott, Donald   II-881

Hertz, Heinrich (1857-1894)   I-324

Herzl, Theodor (1860-1904)   I-411; II-634

Hess, Walther Richard Rudolf (1894-)   I-188

Heuss, Theodor (1884-1963)   II-647

Hewish, Anthony   II-1009

Heydrich, Reinhard (1904-1942)   I-303, 396

Hickel, Walter J. (1919-)   II-1022

Hills, William   II-942

Himmler, Heinrich (1900-1945)   I-303, 375, 396

Hindenburg, Paul von (Paul Ludwig Hans Anton von, Beneckendorff und von Hindenburg) (1847-1934)   I-101, 311

Hitler, Adolf (1889-1945)   I-188, 276, 295, 303, 311, 342, 348, 375, 396, 444, 450, 465, 479; II-577

Ho Chi Minh (1890-1969)   II-696, 703; III-1243

Hobson, John Atkinson (1858-1940)   I-31

Hoffman, Walter Edward (1907-)   III-1188

Holden, Roberto (1925-)   III-1219

Holstein, Friedrich von (1837-1909)   I-46

Home, Sir Alec Douglas- (1903-)   II-955

Hoover, Herbert Clark (1874-1964)   I-260

Hope, Victor Alexander John (*see* Linlithgow, Lord)

Horthy, Miklós von Nagybánya (1868-1957)   I-181

Hossbach, Friedrich (1894-)   I-375

Hoxha, Enver (1908-)   II-640

Hsüan T'ung (*see* P'u-yi, Henry)

Hua Kuo-feng (1921-)   III-1264

Huang Hsing (1873-1916)   I-92

Huang Hua (1913-)   III-1110

Huerta, Adolfo de la (?-1955)   I-69

Huerta, Dolores (1930-)   II-842

Huerta, Victoriano de la (1854-1916)   I-69

Hull, Cordell (1871-1955)   I-260, 438, 465

Humphrey, Hubert Horatio (1911-1978)   II-806, 893, 965

Huong, Tran Van (1903-)   III-1227

Husayni, Hajj Amin al- (1893-)   I-231

Hutchinson, Roy Coryton (1907-)   I-241

Huxley, Aldous (1894-1963)   I-241

Iida, Shojiro (1888-)   I-457

Imada, Shintarō   I-269

Inönü, Ismet (1884-1973)   I-225

Ioannides, Dimitrios   III-1193

Ironsi, Johnson Aguiyi- (1924-1966)   II-1003

Irwin, Lord (Earl of Halifex) (Edward Frederick Lindley Wood) (1881-1959)   I-175

Ishihara, Kanji (1889-1949)   I-269

Ismail, Ahmed (1923-)   III-1182

Itagaki, Seishirō (1885-1948)   I-269

Itliong, Larry   II-842

Jabotinsky, Vladimir (1880-1940)   I-231

Jackson, Henry M. (1912-)   II-872

Jackson, Lucious, Jr.   III-1279

Javabu, J. T.   I-87

Javin, Ali (1926-)   II-881

Jaworski, Leon (1905-)   III-1131, 1200

Jinnah, Mohammed Ali (1876-1948)   I-175; II-605

John XXIII, Pope (1881-1963)   I-507

Johnson, Lyndon Baines (1908-1973)   II-806, 856, 965, 1036; III-1287

Jordan, John Newell   I-121

Juan, Don   II-1043

Juan Carlos (1938-)   II-1043

Jumblatt, Kamal   III-1235

Kaku, Mori   I-269

Kamehameha I, of Hawaii (1758?-1819)   II-790

Kamehameha II, of Hawaii (1797-1824)   II-790

Karageorgevich (*see* Paul, Prince)

Karageorgevich (*see* Peter II, of Yugoslavia)
Karami, Rashid   III-1235
Karamanlis, Konstantinos G. (1907-
) III-1193
Kato, Baron Takaakira (1859-1926)   I-121
Kefauver, Estes (1903-1963)   II-856
Kelly, Mervin   II-612
Kelly, Thomas E. (1931-   )   II-1022
Kemal Atatürk, Mustafa (1881-1938)   I-107,
    129, 225
Kennedy, John Fitzgerald (1917-1963)   I-
    260, 507; II-806, 856, 926, 934, 955, 965
Kerr, Roy P.   II-835
Kesselring, Albert (1887-1960)   I-430
Khaled, Leila (1945-   )   II-1028
Khan, Yahya (1917-   )   II-1091
Khomeini, Ayatollah Ruhollah (1900-
) III-1338
Khrushchev, Nikita Sergeevich (1894-
    1971) II-715, 721, 736, 776, 906, 955,
    974, 988
Kiderlen-Wächter, Alfred von (1852-1912)   I-
    46
Kieffer, Hugh H.   III-1294
Kierkegaard, Sören Aabye (1813-1855)   I-
    252
Kinderlen-Wäechter, Alfred von (1852-
    1912) I-46
King, Ernest Joseph (1878-1956)   I-404
King, Martin Luther, Jr. (1929-1968)   I-507;
    II-806, 893, 965
Kinsey, Alfred Charles (1894-1956)   II-619
Kirov, Sergei (1886-1934)   I-336
Kissinger, Henry Alfred (1923-   )   I-145,
    260; II-1050, 1054, 1083; III-1110, 1124, 1161,
    1182, 1193, 1212, 1227, 1251, 1257, 1331
Kitchener, Horatio Herbert (Earl Kitchener of
    Khartoum and of Broome) (1850-1916)   I-
    87, 129
Klein, Harold P.   III-1294
Knowland, William F. (1908-   )   II-709
Koestler, Arthur (1905-   )   I-241
Kohl, Michael (1929-   )   III-1167
Kolchak, Aleksandr Vasilievich (1874-
    1920) I-152
Kolko, Gabriel (1932-   )   II-663
Konev, Ivan Stepanovich (1897-1973)   II-
    577, 715
Kornei, Otto   I-382
Kornilov, Lavr Georgievich (1870-1918)   I-
    152
Korolov, Sergei Pavlovich   II-776
Kosygin, Aleksei Nikolaevich (1904-
) II-974
Krum, Charles   I-1
Krum, Howard   I-1
Kundt, Hans (1869-1939)   I-289
Kunstler, William   II-865
Kuwatli, Shukri al- (1891-1967)   I-494
Kuznetsov, Vasili (1901-   )   II-798

LaFeber, Walter (1933-   )   II-663
Lansing, Robert (1864-1928)   I-121
Lasley, R. E.   I-355
Laval, Pierre (1883-1945)   I-342
Lawrence, Ernest Orlando (1901-1958)   II-
    683
Leakey, Louis Seymour Bazett (1903-
    1972) I-218
Leathes, Stanley (1830-1900)   I-24
Le Duan (1908-   )   III-1227, 1243
Leeb, Wilhelm Joseph Franz von (1876-
    1956) I-450
Lenin, Vladimir Ilich (Ulyanov) (1870-
    1924) I-152; II-736
Lepsius, Johannes (1858-1926)   I-107
Lévesque, René (1922-   )   II-820
Lewis, John Llewellyn (1880-1969)   II-572
Liang Ch'i-ch'ao (1873-1929)   I-92
Lilienthal, David Eli (1899-   )   II-564
Liliuokalani, Lydia (1838-1917)   II-790
Liman von Sanders, Otto (1855-1929)   I-
    107, 129
Linlithgow, Lord (Victor Alexander John Hope)
    (1887-1951) II-605
Litvinov, Maksim Maksimovich (1876-
    1951) I-219
Lovell, James (1928-   )   II-1069
Luthuli, Albert John (1898-1967)   III-1272

MacArthur, Douglas A. (1880-1964)   II-584,
    676
McClintock, Robert (1909-   )   II-758
McCullough, Father Thomas   II-842
McDonald, David John (1902-   )   II-730
McDonnell, Father Donald   II-842
Machado y Morales, Gerardo (1871-1939) II-
    743
McLuhan, Herbert Marshall (1911-   )
    II-1069
McMahon, Brien (1903-   )   II-683
Macmillan, Harold (1894-   )   II-955; III-
    1146
Madero, Francisco Indalecio (1873-1913)   I-
    69
Maillard, William Somers (1917-   )   III-
    1251
Maiman, Theodore Harold (1927-   )   II-
    881
Makarios III, Archbishop (1913-1977)   III-
    1193
Makhno   I-152
Malraux, André (1901-1976)   I-241
Mann, Thomas (1875-1955)   I-295
Mansfield, Michael Joseph (Mike) (1903-
) II-703
Manstein, Eric von   I-479
Mao Tse-tung (1893-1976)   I-211, 361; II-
    654, 1050; III-1124, 1264
Mariam, Mengistu Haile (1937-   )   III-
    1317

Marshall, George Catlett (1880-1959)   I-211, 260

Martin, Clyde E.   II-619

Martin, Graham Anderson (1912-   )   III-1227

Martin, James   III-1294

Marx, Karl (1818-1883)   I-38

Masaryk, Jan Garrigue (1886-1948)   II-626

Masaryk, Tomáš Garrigue (1850-1937)   I-158

Matsui, Iwane (1878-   )   I-361

Matsuoka, Yasuke (1880-1946)   I-438

Matthews, Thomas   II-899

Mauchly, John W. (1907-   )   II-535

Maxwell, James Clerk (1831-1879)   I-324

Mead, Sidney Earl (1904-   )   I-507

Means, Russell   II-865

Meany, George (1894-1980)   II-730

Medvedev, Roy   II-988

Meinecke, Friedrich (1862-1954)   I-54

Meinhof, Ulrike (1934-1976)   II-1028

Meir, Golda (1898-1978)   III-1182

Meitner, Lise (1878-1968)   I-246

Mendès-France, Pierre (1907-   )   II-696

Merritt, William Hamilton (1793-1862)   II-783

Mikoyan, Anastas Ivanovich (1905-1970)   II-736

Milner, Sir Alfred (First Viscount Milner) (1854-1925)   I-87

Minh, Duong Van (Big) (1916-   )   III-1227

Minow, Newton   II-669

Mitchell, John Newton (1913-   )   III-1131

Mohammed Abed Ar'ouf Arafat (*see* Arafat, Yasir)

Mohammed Riza Pahlevi (Shah of Iran) (1919-   )   II-912; III-1338

Molotov, Vyacheslav Mikhailovich (Skryabin) (1890-   )   II-591, 715

Momaday, N. Scott (1934-   )   II-865

Monro, Sir Charles Carmichael (1860-1929)   I-129

Montgomery, Bernard Law (First Viscount Montgomery of Alamein) (1887-1976)   II-577

Montini, Giovanni Battista (*see* Paul VI, Pope)

Morgan, Thomas Hunt (1866-1945)   I-7

Morgenthau, Henry, Sr. (1856-1946)   I-107

Morin, Claude (1929-   )   II-820

Moro, Aldo (1916-1978)   II-1028

Moroka, James   III-1272

Morrison, Philip (1938-   )   II-827

Morse, Sir Christopher (Jeremy) (1928-   )   III-1104

Morton, Joy (1855-1934)   I-1

Mountbatten, Lord Louis (First Earl Mountbatten of Burma) (1900-1979)   II-605

Mugabe, Robert Gabriel (1925-   )   II-981

Mueller, Paul Hermann (1899-1965)   I-425

Muhammad adh-Dhib   II-598

Muller, Hermann Joseph (1890-1967)   I-7

Murphy, Robert Daniel (1894-   )   II-758

Murray, John Courtney (1904-   )   I-507

Murray, Philip (1886-1952)   II-572

Murrow, Edward R. (1908-1965)   II-669

Muskie, Edmund Sixtus (1914-   )   II-872

Mussolini, Benito (1883-1945) I-138, 342, 348, 444, 465

Mustafa el-Nahas Pasha (1876-1965)   I-494

Mustafa Kemal Atatürk (*see* Kemal Atatürk, Mustafa)

Mutch, Thomas   III-1294

Muzorewa, Abel Tendekayi (1925-   )   II-981

Nader, Ralph (1934-   )   II-856

Nadolny, Rudolf   I-276

Nagao, Ariga   I-121

Nagumo, Chuichi (1887-1944)   I-472

Nasser, Gamal Abdel (1918-1970)   II-690, 758

Nehru, Jawaharlal (1889-1964)   I-175, 605

Neto, Antonio Augustino (1922-   )   III-1219

Neumann, John von (1903-1957)   II-535, 683

Neurath, Konstantin von (1873-1956)   I-276, 348, 375

Nguyen Phuc Anh (*see* Gia Long)

Nicholas II, of Russia (Nikolai Aleksandrovich) (1868-1918)   I-101

Niebuhr, Helmut Richard (1894-1962)   I-507

Nietzsche, Friedrich Wilhelm (1844-1900)   I-38

Nimitz, Chester William (1885-1966)   I-472

Nixon, Richard Milhous (1913-   )   I-513; II-865, 872, 988, 1050, 1054, 1083, 1091; III-1097, 1104, 1110, 1124, 1131, 1161, 1188, 1193, 1200, 1212

Nkomo, Joshua (1917-   )   II-981

Nol, Lon (1913-   )   II-1083; III-212

Nuri as-Said (1888-1958)   I-494

Oberth, Hermann (1894-   )   II-751

Obregón, Álvaro (1880-1928)   I-69

Ohain, Hans-Joachim Pabst von   I-355

Ojukwu, Chukwuemeka Odumegwu (1933-   )   II-1003

Okyar, Ali Fethi (1880-1943)   I-225

Oppenheimer, Julius Robert (1904-1967)   II-683, 835, 1009

Orfila, Alejandro (1925-   )   III-1251

Page, Robert M. (1903-   )   I-324

Pahlevi, Mohammed Riza (*see* Mohammed Riza Pahlevi)

Paisley, Reverend Ian (1926-   )   III-1117

Palade, George Emil (1912-   )   I-501

Paléologue, Maurice (1859-1944)   I-181

Paley, William S. (1901-   )   II-669
Palmer, Patrick Edward (1940-   )   II-827
Papadopoulos, Georgius (1919-   )   III-1193
Papen, Franz von (1879-1969)   I-311
Parizeau, Jacques   II-820
Park, Keith R. (1892-1975)   I-430
Parkes, Sir Henry (1815-1896)   I-14
Parrington, Vernon Louis (1871-1929)   I-205
Paul, Prince (Karageorgevich) (1893-   )   I-444
Pauli, Wolfgang (1900-1958)   I-166
Peary, Robert Edwin (1856-1920)   I-63
Peel, Lord (William Robert Wellesley Peel) Earl (1867-1937)   I-411
Peñaranda, Enrique Costillo (1892-   )   I-289
Percival, Arthur Ernest (1887-1966)   I-457
Peter II, of Yugoslavia (Karageorgevich) (1923-1970)   I-444
Petrov, Vasily Ivanovich   III-1317
Pham Hung (1912-   )   III-1243
Pham Van Dong (1906-   )   III-1243
Phan Boi Chau (1867-1940)   II-696
Phleger, Herman (1890-   )   II-798
Plumer, Lord (Herbert Charles Onslow) (1857-1932)   I-231
Pol Pot (1928-   )   III-1212, 1346
Pomeroy, Wardell B. (1913-   )   II-619
Pompidou, Georges Jean Raymond (1911-   )   III-1146
Poorten, Hein ter (1887-   )   I-457
Porter, Keith R. (1912-   )   I-501
Powell, Lewis Franklin (1907-   )   III-1279
Powers, Francis Gary (1929-   )   II-906
Prebisch, Raul (1901-   )   III-1206
Prokhorov, Aleksandr Mikhaylovich (1916-   )   II-881
Prothero, George Walter (1848-1922)   I-24
P'u-yi, Henry (Hsüan T'ung) (1906-1967)   I-92

Quwatli, Shukri al- (*see* Kuwatli, Shukri al-)

Raeder, Erich (1876-1960)   I-430
Rahman, Sheik Mujibur (1922-   )   II-1091
Ranke, Leopold von (1795-1886)   I-54
Reagan, Ronald Wilson (1911-   )   III-1302
Rees, Martin John (1942-   )   II-835
Reeves, William Pember (1857-1932)   I-14
Rehnquist, William Hubbs (1924-   )   III-1154
Reid, Sir George Houston (1845-1918)   I-14
Reinsch, Paul Samuel (1869-1923)   I-121
Rennenkampf, Pavel Karlovich (1854-1918)   I-101
Reuss, Henry Schoellkopf (1912-   )   II-872

Reuther, Walter Philip (1907-1970)   II-572, 730
Rhee, Syngman (1875-1965)   II-676
Rhodes, Cecil John (1853-1902)   II-981
Ribbentrop, Joachim von (1893-1946)   I-375
Ribicoff, Abraham A. (1910-   )   II-856
Richards, James P. (1894-   )   II-709
Richardson, Elliot Lee (1920-   )   III-1188
Ridgway, Matthew Bunker (1895-   )   II-584
Ritter, Gerhard (1888-1967)   II-918
Roa y Garcia, Raul (1907-   )   III-1251
Robeck, John de   I-129
Rochefort, Joseph J., Jr.   I-472
Rodino, Peter Wallace, Jr. (1909-   )   III-1200
Roe, Jane   III-1154
Röhm, Ernst (1887-1934)   I-311
Rokossovski, Konstantin K. (1896-1968)   II-577
Roosevelt, Franklin Delano (1882-1945) I-260, 319, 368, 389, 404, 418, 438, 465, 487
Roosevelt, Theodore (1858-1919)   II-790
Ross, Fred   II-842
Rouhani, Fuad (1907-   )   II-912
Rundstedt, Karl Rudolf Gerd von (1875-1953)   I-450; II-577
Rusk, Dean (1909-   )   II-955, 1036
Russell, Bertrand Arthur William (1872-1970)   I-79
Rutherford, Ernest (1871-1937)   I-246, 283
Ryle, Sir Martin (1918-   )   II-899

Sachs, Alexander   I-389
Sadat, Anwar el- (1918-   )   I-145; III-1182
Sagan, Carl (1934-   )   II-827; III-1311
St. Clair, James D.   III-1200
Sakharov, Andrei Dimitrievich (1921-   )   II-988
Salamanca, Daniel (1869-1935)   I-289
Salandra, Antonio (1853-1931)   I-138
Samphan, Khieu (1931-   )   III-1212
Sampson, Nikos (1935-   )   III-1193
Samsonov, Aleksandr Vasilievich (1859-1914)   I-101
Samuel, Archbishop Athansius Yeshue   II-598
Samuel, Sir Herbert Louis (1870-1963)   I-231
Sanchez, Ilitch Ramirez ("Carlos") (1949-   )   II-1028
Sandage, Allan Rex (1926-   )   II-899
Sanders, Otto Liman von (*see* Liman von Sanders, Otto)
Sarnoff, David (1891-1971)   II-669
Sartre, Jean-Paul (1905-   )   I-252
Saunders, LaVerne (Blondie) (1903-   )   I-487
Saunders, Stuart Thomas (1909-   )   I-520

Savimbi, Jonas (1934-) III-1219
Schaffert, Roland Michael I-382
Schawlow, Arthur Leonard (1921-) II-881
Schempp, Edward II-949
Schempp, Sidney II-949
Schiller, Karl (1911-) III-1097
Schleicher, Kurt von (1882-1934) I-311
Schmidt, Helmut (1918-) III-1257
Schmidt, Maartin (1929-) II-899
Schnitzler, William F. (1904-) II-730
Schrödinger, Erwin (1887-1961) I-166
Schwartze, E. W. II-942
Schwarzschild, Karl II-835
Schweitzer, Pierre-Paul (1912-) III-1097
Scott, Robert Falcon (1868-1912) I-63
Seddon, Richard John (1845-1906) I-14
Seko, Mobutu Sese (1930-) III-1219
Shackleton, Ernest Henry (1874-1922) I-63
Shah of Iran (*see* Mohammed Riza Pahlevi)
Shakura, Nikolai II-835
Sharon, Ariel (1928-) III-1182
Shehab, Fuad (1902-1973) II-758
Shepard, Alan Bartlett, Jr. (1923-) II-934
Sherman, Forrest Percival (1896-) II-676
Shihab, Fuad (*see* Shehab, Fuad)
Shockley, William Bradford (1910-) II-612
Shumway, Norman Edward (1923-) II-1016
Siad Barre,Muhammad (1919-) III-1317
Sihanouk, Prince Norodom (1922-) II-1083; III-1212, 1346
Silone, Ignazio (1900-1978) I-241
Simon, Sir John Allsebrook (1873-1954) I-276
Simović, Dušan (1882-1962) I-444
Sinclair, Upton Beall (1878-1968) I-241; II-942
Sirica, John Joseph (1904-) III-1131, 1200
Sithole, Reverend Ndabaningi (1920-) II-981
Smith, H. Alexander (1880-) II-703
Smith, Ian Douglas (1919-) II-981
Smith, Oliver P. (1893-) II-676
Smuts, Jan Christian (1870-1950) I-87
Sobukwe, Robert III-1272
Solzhenitsyn, Alexander Isayevich (1918-) II-988
Sombart, Werner (1863-1941) I-38
Sperrle, Hugo (1885-1953) I-430
Spruance, Raymond Ames (1886-1969) I-472
Stalin, Joseph (Iosif Vissarionovich Dzhugashvili) (1879-1953) I-319, 336, 444, 450, 479; II-577, 626, 640, 736
Stark, Harold Raynsford (1880-1972) I-368, 404

Steinbeck, John Ernst (1902-1968) I-418
Steptoe, Patrick C. III-1324
Stevens, John P. (1920-) III-1279
Stevenson, Adlai Ewing (1900-1965) II-926
Stewart, Potter (1915-) II-949; III-1154, 1279
Stimson, Henry Lewis (1867-1950) I-465
Stoph, Willi (1914-) III-1167
Strauss, Lewis L. (1896-) II-683
Stresemann, Gustav (1878-1929) I-197, 342
Sturtevant, Alfred H. (1891-1971) I-7
Suárez, González Adolfo (1932-) II-1043
Sukenik, E. L. (1889-) II-598
Sun Yat-sen (1866-1925) I-92, 211; II-654
Sung Chiao-jen I-92
Sunyaev, Rashid II-835
Suslov, Mikhial Andreevich (1902-) II-974
Szilard, Leo (1898-1964) I-389

Tack, Juan Antonio (1934-) III-1331
Tadashi, Hanaya I-269
Talaat Pasha, Mehmet (1872-1921) I-107
Tardieu, André Pierre Gabriel Amédée (1876-1945) I-276
Tariki, Abdullah (1919-) II-912
Teleki, Paul (1879-1941) I-181
Teller, Edward (1908-) II-683
Teng Hsiao-p'ing (1904-) III-1264
Thieu, Nguyen Van (1923-) III-1161, 1227
Tho, Le Duc (1912-) III-1161, 1212
Tillich, Paul (1886-1965) I-295, 507
Tito, Josip Broz (1892-) II-640
Tizard, Henry Thomas (1885-1959) I-324
Todd, Reginald Stephen Garfield (1908-) II-981
Toro, David (1892-) I-289
Torrijos Herrera, Omar (1929-) III-1331
Townes, Charles Hard (1915-) II-881
Toynbee, Arnold Joseph (1889-1975) I-107
Trammel, Park (1876-1936) I-368
Troitsky, Vsevolod II-827
Trotsky, Leon (Leib Davydovich Bronstein) (1879-1940) I-152, 336
Trudeau, Pierre Elliott (1919-) II-820
Truman, Harry S (1884-1972) I-260; II-572, 584, 683, 783
Truong, Chinh (1907-) III-1243
Tsai Feng (*see* Ch'un, Prince)
Tsuji, Masanobu (1902-) I-457
Turing, Alan M. (1912-1954) II-535
Tz'u-hsi (1835-1908) I-92

Ulam, Stanislaw Marcin (1909-) II-683
Ulbricht, Walter (1893-1973) II-647
Ulyanov, Vladimir Ilich (*see* Lenin, Vladimir Ilich)

Van Allen, James Alfred (1914-) II-764

Van Buren, Paul Matthews (1924-) I-507

Vance, Cyrus Roberts (1917-) II-1054; III-1331

Vandenberg, Hoyt (1899-) II-683

Van Dyke, Fred II-842

Verschuur, Gerrit L. (1937-) II-827

Victoria, Queen of England (1819-1901) I-14

Villa, Francisco (Pancho) (Doroteo Arango) (1877-1923) I-69

Vinson, Carl (1883-) I-368

Volcker, Paul A. (1927-) III-1104

Vorster, Balthazar Johannes (1915-) III-1272

Vyshinsky, Andrei (1883-1954) I-336

Wade, Henry III-1154

Wallace, George J. (1906-) II-942

Wallace, Henry Agard (1888-1965) II-572

Wang Ching-wei (1884-1944) I-361

Wang Hung-wen (1935-) III-1264

Wangenheim, Hans von I-107

Ward, Sir Adolphus William (1837-1924) I-24

Ward, Sir Joseph George (1856-1930) I-14

Wardhana, Ali (1928-) III-1104

Warner, John W. (1927-) III-1287

Warren, Earl (1891-1974) I-513; II-893, 949

Washkansky, Louis II-1016

Watson-Watt, Robert Alexander (1892-) I-324

Wavell, Sir Archibald Percival (1883-1950) I-457

Weber, Max (1864-1930) I-38

Weizmann, Chaim (1874-1952) I-231; II-634

Welles, Sumner (1892-1961) I-260; II-743

Westmoreland, William Childs (1914-) II-1036

Wheeler, Earle Gilmore (1908-) II-1036

White, Byron Raymond (1917-) III-1154

Whitehead, Alfred North (1861-1945) I-79

Whitelaw, William (1918-) III-1117

Whittle, Frank I-355

William II (Friedrich Wilhelm Viktor Albert), Emperor of Germany and King of Prussia (1859-1941) I-46

Williams, William Appleman (1921-) II-663

Wilson, James Harold (1916-) III-1146

Wilson, Joseph C. I-382

Wilson, Richard II-865

Wilson, Thomas Woodrow (1856-1924) I-107, 121 158

Wolfe, Kenneth B. (1896-1971) I-487

Wolfe, Thomas (1900-1938) I-241

Wolff-Metternich, Paul (1853-1934) I-107

Woll, Joseph Albert (1904-) II-730

Wood, Edward Frederick Lindley (*see* Irwin, Lord)

Woodhead, Sir John Ackroyd (1881-1973) I-411

Wrangel, Pëtr Nikolaevich (1878-1928) I-152

Wright, Sewall (1889-) I-7

Xuma, Alfred B. (1893-1962) III-1272

Yadin, Yigael (1917-) II-598

Yamagata, Prince Aritomo (1838-1922) I-121

Yamamoto, Isoroku (1884-1943) I-472

Yamashita, Tomoyuki (1885-1946) I-457

Yao Wen-yuan (1931-) III-1264

Yeh Chien-ying (1898-) III-1264

Yevtushenko, Yevgeny (1933-) II-988

Yezhov, Nikolai Ivanovich (1895-1939?) I-336

Yoshida, Shigeru (1878-1967) II-584

Young, Leo C. (1926-) I-324

Young, Robert I-520

Yüan, Shih-k'ai (1859-1916) I-92, 121

Yuderich, Nikolai Nikolaevich (1862-1933) I-152

Zapata, Emiliano (1877?-1919) I-69

Zeidler, Othmar I-425

Zhukov, Georgi Konstantinovich (1895-1974) I-479; II-577

Zhuyovich-Tsrni, Streten II-640

Zinoviev, Grigori Evseevich (Hirsch Apfelbaum) (1833-1936) I-336

Ziolkovsky, Konstantin Eduardovich (1857-1935) II-751, 776

Zuckerman, Benjamin Michael (1943-) II-827

Zwicky, Fritz II-1009

Abbazia, Patrick
Mr. Roosevelt's Navy: The Private War of the U.S. Atlantic Fleet, 1939-1942 I-408
Abdullah ibn-Husein, Amir of Transjordan
Memoirs of King Abdullah of Transjordan I-496
"Acton and the *C. M. H.*: Republication and Reassessment," in *The Times Literary Supplement* I-28
Adler, Richard and Douglass Cater, eds.
Television as a Cultural Force II-673
Allen, William Sheridan
Nazi Seizure of Power: The Experience of a Single German Town 1930-1935, The I-316
Amundsen, Roald
South Pole: An Account of the Norwegian Antarctic Expedition in the "Fram," 1910-1912, The I-66
Andrikopoulos, Bonnie and Warren M. Hearn, eds.
Abortion in the Seventies: Proceedings of the Western Regional Conference on Abortion III-1156
Antarctic Treaty, The. Hearings Before the Committee on Foreign Relations II-803
Archer, Jules
Chinese and the Americans, The III-1128
Arvidson, Raymond E. *et al.*
"Surface of Mars, The," in *Scientific American* III-1297
Asimov, Isaac
Collapsing Universe: The Story of Black Holes, The II-838

Bairoch, Paul
Economic Development of the Third World Since 1900, The II-559
Ball, William E.
"Religion and Public Education: The Post-Schempp Years," in *Religion and Public Education* II-952
Barghoorn, Frederick C.
Détente and the Democratic Movement in the U.S.S.R. II-995
Barnard, Christian N.
Heart Attack: You Don't Have to Die II-1020
"Transplants: Will Future Vindicate the Failures?," in *Chicago Sun Times* II-1019
Barnett, A. Doak
"The Changing Strategic Balance in Asia," in *Sino-American Détente and Its Policy Implications* III-1126
Barnouw, Erik
Tube of Plenty: The Evolution of American Television II-671

Bates, Daisy
Long Shadow of Little Rock: A Memoir, The II-772
Bauer, Peter T.
Dissent on Development III-1209
Beatty, J. Kelly
"Far-Out Worlds of *Voyager I*—Part 1, The," in *Sky and Telescope* III-1313
"Far-Out Worlds of *Voyager I*—Part 2, The," in *Sky and Telescope* III-1313
"*Voyager*'s Encore Performance," in *Sky and Telescope* III-1313
Beccaria, Cesare Bonesana
On Crimes and Punishments III-1282
Bell, J. Bowyer
Time of Terror: How Democratic Societies Cope with Terrorism, A II-1032
Bell, Joseph
Seven into Space II-937
Bell, Oliver, ed.
America's Changing Population II-1081
Benson, Mary
African Patriots: The Story of the African National Congress of South Africa, The III-1275
Bernstein, Carl and Bob Woodward
Final Days, The III-1134, 1204
Berry, Mary Clay
Alaska Pipeline: The Politics of Oil and Native Land Claims, The II-1024
Birnbaum, Karl E.
East and West Germany: A Modus Vivendi III-1170
"Human Rights and East-West Relations," in *Foreign Affairs* III-1261
Bishop, James, Jr. and Henry Hubbard
Let the Seller Beware II-862
Black, Charles L., Jr.
Capital Punishment: The Inevitability of Caprice and Mistake III-1284
Blossom, Virgil T.
It Has Happened Here II-773
Blumberg, Stanley A. and Gwinn Owens
Energy and Conflict: The Life and Times of Edward Teller II-686
Boles, Donald E.
Bible, Religion, and the Public Schools, The II-951
Boudurant, Joan V.
Conquest of Violence I-178
Bova, Ben
In Quest of Quasars: An Introduction to Stars and Starlike Objects II-901
Boyers, Robert, ed.
Legacy of the German Refugee Intellectuals, The I-299
Braestrup, Peter
Big Story: How the American Press and Tele-

vision Reported and Interpreted the Crisis of Tet 1968 in Vietnam and Washington II-1040
Brenner, Anita
Wind That Swept Mexico: The History of the Mexican Revolution, 1910-1942, The I-76
Brinkley, B. R. and Keith Porter, eds.
International Cell Biology, 1976-1977 I-506
Brinkley, George A.
Volunteer Army and the Allied Intervention in South Russia, 1917-1921, The I-154
Brooks, John
Telephone: The First Hundred Years II-616
Brown, Judith M.
Gandhi and Civil Disobedience I-178
Brown, Weldon A.
Last Chopper: The Denouement of the American Pole in Vietnam, 1963-1975, The III-1163
Bueler, William M.
U.S. China Policy and the Problem of Taiwan II-712
Bunker, Gerald E.
Peace Conspiracy: Wang Ching-wei and the China War, 1937-1941, The I-365
Burchett, Wilfred
Grasshoppers and Elephants: Why Vietnam Fell III-1164
Burr, Robert N.
Our Troubled Hemisphere: Perspectives on United States-Latin American Relations I-266
Burrows, Millar
Dead Sea Scrolls, The II-601

Caidin, Martin
Red Star in Space II-780
Callahan, Daniel
Abortion: Law, Choice and Morality III-1158
Campbell, John C.
Tito's Separate Road: America and Yugoslavia in World Politics II-644
Camps, Miriam
Britain and the European Community, 1955-1963 III-1149
Carlson, Elof Axel
Gene: A Critical History, The I-10
Carr, Edward Hallett
History of Soviet Russia. Vol. I-III: The Bolshevik Revolution, 1917-1923, A I-322
Carson, Rachel Louise
Silent Spring I-428
Chamberlin, William Henry
Russian Revolution, 1917-1921, The I-155
Charques, Richard
Twilight of Imperial Russia, The I-105

Chen, Lung-chu and Harold D. Laswell
Formosa, China, and the United Nations: Formosa in the World Community III-1114
Chennault, Claire Lee
Way of a Fighter I-491
Chevrier, Lionel
St. Lawrence Seaway, The II-787
Chi, Madeleine
China Diplomacy, 1914-1918 I-126
Choudhury, G. W.
Last Days of United Pakistan, The II-1094
Churchill, Winston S.
World Crisis. Vol. II: 1915, The I-135
Cicchetti, Charles J.
Alaskan Oil: Alternative Routes and Markets II-1025
Clark, G. N.
"Origin of the Cambridge Modern History, The," in *The Cambridge Historical Journal* I-27
Clarke, Arthur C.
Promise of Space, The II-754
Clubb, Oliver Edmund, Jr.
United States and the Sino-Soviet Bloc in Southeast Asia, The II-707
Cohen, Richard M. and Jules Witcover
Heartbeat Away, A III-1190
Commoner, Barry
Closing Circle: Nature, Men and Technology, The II-545
Poverty of Power: Energy and the Economic Crisis, The III-1139
Compton, James V.
Swastika and the Eagle: Hitler, the United States, and the Origins of World War II, The I-469
Connell, Dan
"Eritrean Battlefront: The Cubans Move In," in *The Nation* III-1319
Conquest, Robert
Great Terror: Stalin's Purge of the Thirties, The I-338
Copp, Anthony R.
Regulating Competition in Oil II-915
Crane, Philip M.
Surrender in Panama: The Case Against the Treaty III-1335
Cranshaw, Edward
Khrushchev: A Career II-739
Craven, Wesley Frank and James Lea Cate, eds.
Army Air Forces in World War II. Vol. V: The Pacific: Matterhorn to Nagasaki, June 1944 to August 1945, The I-489
Crozier, Brian
South-East Asia in Turmoil II-705
Cumberland, Charles Curtis
Mexican Revolution: The Constitutionalist Years I-74

Davenport, T. R. H.
   South Africa: A Modern History   III-1276
Davies, John Paton, Jr.
   Dragon by the Tail: American, British, Japanese, and Russian Encounters with China and One Another   II-660
Davis, Gavan
   Shoal of Time: A History of the Hawaiian Islands   II-794
Davis, George T.
   Navy Second to None: The Development of Modern American Naval Policy, A   I-372
Davis, John H.
   Evasive Peace: A Study of the Zionist-Arab Problem, The   I-149
Davis, Nuel Pharr
   Lawrence and Oppenheimer   II-687
Deák, Francis
   Hungary at the Paris Peace Conference: The Diplomatic History of the Treaty of Trianon   I-183
Dean, Arthur H.
   Test Ban and Disarmament: The Path of Negotiation   II-960
Decolonization   II-985
Dedijer, Vladimir
   Battle Stalin Lost: Memoirs of Yugoslavia, 1948-1953, The   II-642
De Kiewiet, C. W.
   History of South Africa, Social and Economic, A   I-90
Deming, Angus, *et al.*
   "The Cubans in Africa," in *Newsweek*   III-1321
Des Pres, Terrence
   Survivor: An Anatomy of Life in the Death Camps, The   I-400
Dessauer, John H.
   My Years with Xerox: The Billions Nobody Wanted   I-384
De St. Jorre, John
   Brothers' War, Biafra & Nigeria, The   II-1005
Deutsch, Albert, ed.
   Sex Habits of American Men: A Symposium on the Kinsey Report   II-623
Deutsch, Harold C.
   Hitler and His Generals: The Hidden Crisis, January–June 1938   I-378
Deutscher, Isaac
   Stalin: A Political Biography   I-340
Devlin, Bernadette
   Price of My Soul, The   III-1121
Divine, Robert A.
   Reluctant Belligerent: American Entry into World War II, The   I-467
Donohue, Agnes McNeill, ed.
   Casebook on The Grapes of Wrath*, A*   I-421

Doran, Charles F.
   Myth, Oil, and Politics: Introduction to the Political Economy of Petroleum   III-1142

Edwards, Robert G. and P. C. Steptoe
   "Induction of Follicular Growth, Ovulation and Luteinization in the Human Ovary," in *Journal of Reproduction and Fertility*   III-1328
Emmerson, James Thomas
   Rhineland Crisis of 7 March, 1936: A Study in Multilateral Diplomacy, The   I-350
Epstein, William
   Last Chance: Nuclear Proliferation and Arms Control, The   II-567
Ernst, Morris Leopold and David Loth
   American Sexual Behavior and the Kinsey Report   II-622
Esherick, Joseph W.
   Reform and Revolution in China: The 1911 Revolution in Hunan and Hubei   I-97
Eubank, Keith
   Summit Conferences, 1919-1960, The   II-725

Fagen, M. D., ed.
   History of Engineering and Science in the Bell System: The Early Years, 1875-1925, A   I-4
Falk, Richard A.
   This Endangered Planet: Prospects and Proposals for Human Survival   II-1072
Feis, Herbert
   Road to Pearl Harbor, The   I-440
Ferrell, Robert H.
   "Truman Foreign Policy: A Traditional View," in *The Truman Period as a Research Field: A Reappraisal*   II-665
Ferris, Timothy
   "Seeking an End to Cosmic Loneliness," in *New York Times*   II-831
Feuchtwanger, Lion
   Oppermanns, The   I-244
Fieldhouse, D. K.
   "Imperialism: An Historiographical Revision," in *The Economic History Review*   I-35
Fischer, Fritz
   War of Illusions: German Policies from 1911 to 1914   I-51; II-923
   World Power or Decline: The Controversy over Germany's Aims in the First World War   II-921
Fleming, Donald and Bernard Bailyn, eds.
   Intellectual Migration: Europe and America, 1930-1960, The   I-297
Fontaine, André
   History of the Cold War: From the Korean War to the Present   II-727

Fontenrose, Joseph
John Steinbeck: An Introduction and Interpretation   I-422
Friedman, Herbert
Amazing Universe, The   II-1013
Fuchida, Mitsuo and Masatake Okumiya
Midway: The Battle That Doomed Japan   I-476

Gallo, Max
Spain Under Franco: A History   II-1045
Gamow, George
Thirty Years That Shook Physics   I-169
Gans, Herbert J.
Levittowners, The   II-552
Gatland, Kenneth
Manned Spacecraft   II-939
Gaustad, Edwin Scott
Religious History of America, A   I-509
Gendzier, Irene L., ed.
Middle East Reader, The   I-147
Gerson, Louis L.
American Secretaries of State and Their Diplomacy. Vol. XVII: John Foster Dulles, The   II-694
Geyl, Pieter
Debates with Historians   I-331
Gimbel, John
American Occupation of Germany: Politics and the Military, 1945-1949, The   II-650
Glazer, Nathan
Affirmative Discrimination: Ethnic Inequality and Public Policy   II-897, 970
Goitein, S. D.
Jews and Arabs: Their Contacts Through the Ages   I-414
Goldberg, Arthur J.
AFL-CIO: Labor United   II-732
Gonzalez, Edward
Cuba Under Castro: The Limits of Charisma.   II-747
Goulden, Joseph C.
Meany: A Biography of the Unchallenged Strong Man of American Labor   II-733
Graber, Doris A.
"Truman and Eisenhower Doctrines in the Light of the Doctrine of Non-Intervention, The, in Political Science Quarterly   II-761
Grabill, Joseph L.
Protestant Diplomacy and the Near East: Missionary Influence on American Policy, 1810-1927   I-114
Gruening, Ernest
Battle for Alaska Statehood, The   II-795
Guderian, Heinz
Panzer Leader   I-484
Gurley, John G.
China's Economy and the Maoist Strategy   II-561

Hacker, Andrew
End of the American Era, The   I-531
Halpern, Ben
Idea of the Jewish State, The   II-637
Hammer, Ellen Joy
Struggle for Indochina, The   II-700
Hardy, Peter
Muslims of British India, The   II-609
Hartje, Robert G.
Bicentennial USA: Pathways to Celebration   III-1290
Hartmann, Frederick H.
Germany Between East and West: The Reunification Problem   II-651
Haskins, James S.
Consumer Movement, The   II-860
Hechinger, Fred M. and Grace Hechinger
Growing Up in America   I-515
Heisenberg, Werner
Physics and Beyond: Encounters and Conversations   I-249
Herzog, Chaim
War of Atonement, October, 1973, The   III-1186
Hewlett, Richard G. and Oscar E. Anderson, Jr.
History of the United States Atomic Energy Commission. Vol. I: The New World, 1939-1946, A   I-391
Hilberg, Raul
Destruction of the European Jews, The   I-399
Hoepli, Nancy L., ed.
Common Market, The   III-1151
Hofstadter, Richard
Progressive Historians: Turner, Beard, Parrington, The   I-207
Hoopes, Townsend
Devil and John Foster Dulles, The   II-693
Houser, George, Jennifer Davis, Herbert Shore and Susan Rogers
No One Can Stop the Rain   III-1223
Howard, Ted and Jeremy Rifkin
Who Should Play God? The Artificial Creation of Life and What It Means for the Future of the Human Race   III-1326
Hsu, Kai-yu
Chou En-lai: China's Gray Eminence   III-1268
Hyland, William and Richard Wallace Shryock
Fall of Khrushchev, The   II-978

Insight Team of the London Sunday Times, The
Yom Kippur War, The   III-1184

Jackson, Robert Victor
South Asian Crisis: India, Pakistan and Bangladesh. A Political and Historical Analysis of the 1971 War   II-1095

Jenks, Christopher and David Riesman
Academic Revolution, The   I-517
Johnson, Chalmers A.
Peasant Nationalism and Communist Power: The Emergence of Revolutionary China, 1937-1945   I-214, 363
Johnson, Haynes
Bay of Pigs: The Leaders' Story of Brigade 2506, The   II-929

Kahn, Frenz D. and Henry P. Palmer
Quasars, Their Importance in Astronomy and Physics   II-902
Kahn, Herman, *et al.*
Next 200 Years: A Scenario for America and the World, The   II-547
Kalven, Harry, Jr.
"Metaphysics of the Law of Obscenity, The," in *The Supreme Court and the Constitution*   III-1178
Kaufmann, William J.
Relativity and Cosmology   II-839
Kawai, Kazuo
Japan's American Interlude   II-586
Kelidar, Abbas and Michael Burrell
Lebanon: The Collapse of a State   III-1241
Kennan, George Frost
Russia and the West Under Lenin and Stalin   I-322
Kirby, S. Woodburn
Singapore: The Chain of Disaster   I-460
Kovrig, Bennett
Myth of Liberation, The   II-595

Lacouture, Jean
Ho Chi Minh: A Political Biography   II-698
Ladd, Everett Carll, Jr. and Charles D. Hadley
Transformations of the American Party System: Political Coalitions from the New Deal to the 1970s   III-1307
LaFeber, Walter
America, Russia, and the Cold War, 1945-1975   II-1052
La Nauze, John Andrew
Making of the Australian Constitution, The   I-20
Laqueur, Walter Ze'ev
History of Zionism, A   I-239
Israel-Arab Reader, The   I-413
Terrorism   II-1034
Leakey, Richard E. and Roger Lewin
Origins   I-222
Lebra, Joyce C.
Japanese-Trained Armies in Southeast Asia: Independence and Volunteer Forces in World War II   I-461
Leckie, Robert
Conflict: The History of the Korean War, 1950-1953   II-678

Lenin, V. I.
Imperialism, the Highest Stage of Capitalism: A Popular Outline   I-34
Lernoux, Penny
"Face-off in Panama: U.S. Imperialists, Old and New," in *At Issue: Politics in the World Arena*   III-1334
Levitan, Sar A., William B. Johnston and Robert Taggart
Still A Dream   II-811
Lewis, Bernard
Emergence of Modern Turkey, The   I-227
Lewy, Guenter
American in Vietnam   III-1232
Liddell Hart, B. H.
German Generals Talk, The   I-482
Linton, Calvin D., ed.
Bicentennial Almanac, The   III-1291
Liroff, Richard A.
National Policy for the Environment: NEPA and Its Aftermath, A   II-876
Locke, Raymond Friday, ed.
"History, Red Power and the New Indian," in *The American Indian*   II-868
London, Joan and Henry Anderson
So Shall Ye Reap   II-845
Lorch, Netanel
Edge of the Sword: Israel's War of Independence, The   II-636
Lord, Walter
Incredible Victory   I-474
Lovell, Bernard
Out of the Zenith: Jodrell Bank, 1957-1970   II-1011
Lowe, Peter
Great Britain and Japan, 1911-1915: A Study of British Far Eastern Policy   I-125
Lowenthal, Abraham F.
"Cuba: Time for a Change," in *Foreign Policy*   III-1253
Lu, David J.
From Marco Polo Bridge to Pearl Harbor: Japan's Entry into World War II   I-441

Macartney, Carlile Aylmer
Hungary and Her Successors: The Treaty of Trianon and Its Consequences, 1919-1937   I-185
Macdonald, Robert W.
League of Arab States: A Study in the Dynamics of Regional Organization, The   I-498
McKelvey, Blake
American Prisons: A History of Good Intentions   II-888
Maclean, John, *et al.*
"How America Stumbled in Iran," in *Chicago Tribune*   III-1344
McLoughlin, William G. and Robert N. Bellah, eds.
Religion in America   I-511

Malloy, James M.
  Bolivia: The Uncompleted Revolution   I-291
Margenau, Henry
  Nature of Physical Reality: Philosophy of Modern Physics, The   I-172
Markides, Kyriacos C.
  Rise and Fall of the Cyprus Republic, The   III-1196
Marshall, Samuel L., ed.
  Laser Technology and Applications   II-883
Maser, Werner
  Hitler's Mein Kampf: *An Analysis*   I-191
Massey, Harrie and Norman Feather
  "James Chadwick," in *Biographical Memoirs of Fellows of the Royal Society*   I-287
May, Arthur J.
  Passing of the Habsburg Monarchy, 1914-1918, The   I-161
Mazlish, Bruce
  Kissinger   II-1052
Meisler, Stanley
  "Spain's New Democracy," in *Foreign Affairs*   II-1047
Meisner, Maurice
  Mao's China: A History of the People's Republic   II-658
Meyer, Karl E. and Tad Szulc
  Cuban Invasion: The Chronicle of a Disaster, The   II-931
Middleton, Drew
  Sky Suspended: The Battle of Britain, The   I-436
Mikdashi, Zuhayr
  Community of Oil Exporting Countries, The   II-914
Miller, Arthur H.
  "Political Issues and Trust in Government: 1964-1970," in *American Political Science Review*   II-852
Miller, Marshall Lee
  Bulgaria During the Second World War   I-447
Millis, Harry A. and Emily Clark Brown
  From the Wagner Act to Taft-Hartley: A Study of National Labor Policy and Labor Relations   II-575
Mitford, Jessica
  Kind and Usual Punishment: The Prison Business   II-889
Mitzman, Arthur
  Iron Cage: An Historical Interpretation of Max Weber, The   I-43
Montagu, Ashley, ed.
  Toynbee and History   I-333
Moorehead, Alan
  Gallipoli   I-133
Morison, Samuel Eliot
  History of United States Naval Operations in World War II. Vol. I: *The Battle of the Atlantic, September 1939-May 1943*   I-407
Morse, Arthur D.
  While Six Million Died: A Chronicle of American Apathy   I-306
Mowshowitz, Abbe
  Conquest of Will: Information Processing in Human Affairs, The   II-538
Mumford, Lewis
  Urban Prospect, The   II-554
Mundell, Robert A. and Alexander K. Swoboda, eds.
  Monetary Problems of the International Economy   II-1101
Muse, Benjamin
  American Negro Revolution from Nonviolence to Black Power, The   II-808
Myrdal, Alva
  Game of Disarmament: How the United States and Russia Run the Arms Race, The   II-569, 1058

National Organization for Women
  NOW Origins: A Summary Description of How 28 Women Changed the World by Reviving a Revolution Everyone Thought Was Dead!   II-1001
Neville, Leslie E. and Nathaniel F. Silsbee
  Jet Propulsion Progress: The Development of Aircraft Gas Turbines   I-358
Newhouse, John
  Cold Dawn: The Story of SALT   II-1059
Newman, William J.
  Balance of Power in the Interwar Years, 1919-1939, The   I-200
Nisbet, Robert
  Twilight of Authority   II-896
Nixon, Richard M.
  RN: The Memoirs of Richard Nixon   III-1191
Noble, David F.
  America by Design: Science, Technology, and the Rise of Corporate Capitalism   II-614

O'Brian, Conor Cruise
  States of Ireland, The   III-1119
O'Connor, James
  Fiscal Crisis of the State, The   II-850
Ogata, Sadako N.
  Defiance in Manchuria: The Making of Japanese Foreign Policy, 1931-1932   I-274
O'Meara, Patrick
  Rhodesia: Racial Conflict or Coexistence?   II-984
Opie, Redvers, *et al.*
  Search for Peace Settlements, The   II-593
Orfield, Gary
  Reconstruction of Southern Education, The   II-968

Osborne, Milton
"Kampuchea and Vietnam: A Historical Perspective," in *Pacific Community* III-1351
O'Shea, Donald C., *et al.*
Introduction to Lasers and Their Applications, An II-884

Paul, Günter
Satellite Spin-Off: The Achievements of Space Flight, The II-755
Peary, Robert Edwin
North Pole, Its Discovery in 1909 Under the Auspices of the Peary Arctic Club, The I-65
Pepper, Suzanne
Civil War in China: The Political Struggle, 1945-1949 I-215
Peterson, Merril D.
"Parrington and American Liberalism," in *Virginia Quarterly Review* I-209
Petras, James F.
"U.S.-Cuban Policy Debate, The," in *Monthly Review* III-1254
Philips, C. H. and Mary Doreen Wainwright, eds.
Partition of India: Policies and Perspectives, 1935-1947, The II-607
Pike, Douglas
Vietnam-Cambodia Conflict III-1353
Poats, Rutherford
Decision in Korea II-680
Pogue, Forrest C.
"Decision to Halt at the Elbe, The," in *Command Decisions* II-582
Pois, Robert A.
Friedrich Meinecke and German Politics in the Twentieth Century I-59
Pomper, Gerald M., *et al.*
Election of 1976: Reports and Interpretations, The III-1305
Ponchaud, François
Cambodia: Year Zero III-1216
Poole, Peter A.
Expansion of the Vietnam War into Cambodia: Action and Response by the Governments of North Vietnam, South Vietnam, Cambodia, and the United States, The II-1086
Porath, Yehoshuah
Emergence of the Palestinian-Arab National Movement, 1918-1929, The I-237
Provencher, Jean
René Lévesque: Portrait of a Québécois II-824
Pylyshyn, Zenon W., ed.
Perspectives on the Computer Revolution II-540

Quarles, John
Cleaning Up America II-878

Qubain, Fahim I.
Crisis in Lebanon II-760

Radar, A Report on Science at War I-326
Rangarajan, L. N.
Commodity Conflict III-1208
Rappard, William E.
Quest for Peace Since the World War, The I-280
Ray, Oakley S.
Drugs, Society and Human Behavior II-816
Remington, Robin Alison
Warsaw Pact: Case Studies in Communist Conflict Resolution, The II-717
Rhoads, Edward J. M.
China's Republican Revolution: The Case of Kwangtung, 1895-1913 I-95
Rich, Norman
Friedrich von Holstein: Politics and Diplomacy in the Era of Bismarck and Wilhelm II I-49
Ridpath, Ian
Worlds Beyond: A Report on the Search for Life in Space II-832
Roberts, Chalmers M.
Nuclear Years: The Arms Race and Arms Control, 1945-1970, The II-961
Rothberg, Abraham
Heirs of Stalin: Dissidence and the Soviet Regime, 1953-1970, The II-994
Rovere, Richard H.
"Letter from Washington," in *The New Yorker* II-713
Rowe, Albert Percival
One Story of Radar I-327
Rublowsky, John
Stoned Age—A History of Drugs in America, The II-818
Rudd, Robert L.
Pesticides and the Living Landscape II-946
Ruiz, Ramón Eduardo
Cuba: The Making of a Revolution II-746
Russell, Bertrand
Mysticism and Logic I-84
Russell, Harold S.
"Helsinki Declaration: Brobdingnag or Lilliput?, The," in *American Journal of International Law* III-1260

Sagan, Carl, *et al.*
Murmurs of Earth: The Voyager Interstellar Record III-1314
Salibi, Kamel Suleiman
Crossroads to Civil War: Lebanon, 1958-1976 III-1239
Salomone, Arcangelo William
Italian Democracy in the Making: The Political Scene in the Giolittian Era, 1900-1914 I-141

Samuelsson, Kurt
Religion and Economic Action   I-41
Saywell, John
Rise of the Parti Québécois 1967-1976, The   II-822
Schaffert, Roland Michael
Electrophotography   I-386
Schandler, Herbert
Unmaking of a President: Lyndon Johnson and Vietnam, The   II-1038
Schauer, Frederick F.
Law of Obscenity, The   III-1176
Schleunes, Karl A.
Twisted Road to Auschwitz: Nazi Policy Toward German Jews, 1933-1939, The   I-308
Schonland, Sir Basil
Atomists (1805-1933), The   I-285
Schweigler, Gebhard Ludwig
National Consciousness in Divided Germany   III-1171
Seabury, Paul
Wilhelmstrasse: A Study of German Diplomats Under the Nazi Regime, The   I-379
Seaton, Albert
Russo-German War, 1941-1945, The   I-452
Seidman, Joel
American Labor from Defense to Reconversion   II-574
Shannon, Claude E. and Warren Weaver
Mathematical Theory of Communication, The   I-5
Shaw, Stanford J. and Ezel Kural Shaw
History of the Ottoman Empire and Modern Turkey. Vol. II: Reform, Revolution, and Republic: The Rise of Modern Turkey, 1808-1975   I-228
Shawcross, William
"Cambodia: The Verdict Is Guilty on Nixon and Kissinger," in *Far Eastern Economic Review*   II-1088
"Cambodia: When the Bombing Finally Stopped," in *Far Eastern Economic Review*   II-1088
Sideshow: Kissinger, Nixon and the Destruction of Cambodia   III-1215
Shelton, William
Soviet Space Exploration: The First Decade   II-779
Sherman, Howard J.
Stagflation: A Radical Theory of Unemployment and Inflation   II-1066
Shusky, Ernest
Right to Be Indian, The   II-869
Simon, William E.
Time for Truth, A   II-1064
Sinclair, Keith
Imperial Federation: A Study of New Zealand Policy and Opinion, 1880-1914   I-21
Smith, G. Geoffrey
Gas Turbines and Jet Propulsion for Aircraft   I-359
Smyth, Henry DeWolf
Atomic Energy for Military Purposes: The Official Report on the Development of the Atomic Bomb Under the Auspices of the United States Government, 1940-1945   I-250, 393
Snepp, Frank
Decent Interval   III-1230
Solomon, Robert
International Monetary System, 1945-1976: An Insider's View, The   III-1100, 1106
"South Today, The," in *Time*   II-1079
Southerland, Thomas C., Jr. and William McCleery
Way to Go: The Coming Revival of U.S. Rail Passenger Service, The   I-524
Spaight, James M.
Battle of Britain, 1940, The   I-434
Spanos, William V., ed.
Casebook on Existentialism, A   I-255
Sprigge, Cecil Jackson Squire
Development of Modern Italy, The   I-140
Sterling, Claire
Masaryk Case, The   II-631
Sterling, Richard W.
Ethics in a World of Power: The Political Ideas of Friedrich Meinecke   I-57
Stern, Laurence
Wrong Horse: The Politics of Intervention and the Failure of American Diplomacy, The   III-1197
Stockwell, John
In Search of Enemies: A CIA Story   III-1221
Stover, John F.
Life and Decline of the American Railroad, The   I-522
Stremlau, John J.
International Politics of the Nigerian Civil War, 1967-1970, The   II-1007
Sturtevant, A. H.
History of Genetics, A   I-12
Sullivan, Walter
Assault on the Unknown: The International Geophysical Year   II-766
Swanson, Carl P. and Peter L. Webster
Cell, The   I-504
Sypher, Wylie
Loss of the Self   I-257

Tatu, Michel
Power in the Kremlin: From Khrushchev to Kosygin   II-909, 977
Taubenfeld, Howard J.
Treaty for Antarctica, A   II-802

Taylor, A. J. P.
  Origins of the Second World War, The   I-202, 344

Taylor, Ronald B.
  Chávez and the Farm Workers   II-846

Terrill, Ross
  Future of China After Mao, The   III-1267

Terzani, Tiziano
  Giai Phong!: The Fall and Liberation of Saigon   III-1246

Thoumin, Richard
  First World War, The   I-103

Tocqueville, Alexis de
  Old Regime and the French Revolution, The   III-1342

Toland, John
  Last Hundred Days, The   II-580

Trumpener, Ulrich
  Germany and the Ottoman Empire, 1914-1918   I-117

Tuleja, Thaddeus V.
  Statesmen and Admirals: Quest for a Far Eastern Naval Policy   I-371

Turley, William S.
  "Vietnam Since Reunification," in *Problems of Communism*   III-1248

Ulam, Adam B.
  Rivals: America and Russia Since World War II, The   II-910

Van Creveld, Martin
  Hitler's Strategy 1940-1941: The Balkan Clue   I-446

Waite, Robert G. L.
  Psychopathic God: Adolf Hitler, The   I-193

Ward, Barbara and René Dubos
  Only One Earth: The Care and Maintenance of a Small Planet   II-1074

Washburn, Mark
  Mars at Last   III-1299

Weinberg, Gerhard L.
  Foreign Policy of Hitler's Germany: Diplomatic Revolution in Europe, 1933-1936, The   I-346, 352

Weng, Byron S. J.
  Peking's UN Policy: Continuity and Change   III-1112

West, T. F. and G. A. Campbell
  DDT: And Newer Persistent Insecticides   I-427

Whaley, Barton
  Codeword Barbarossa   I-454

Wheaton, Eliot B.
  Prelude to Calamity: The Nazi Revolution 1933-35, with a Background Survey of the Weimar Era   I-314

Wheeler-Bennett, John W.
  Disarmament Deadlock, The   I-278

White, Theodore H.
  Breach of Faith: The Fall of Richard Nixon   III-1135, 1202

Whitehead, Alfred North
  Science and the Modern World   I-83

Whorton, James
  Before Silent Spring: Pesticides and Public Health in Pre-DDT America   II-944

Whyte, William H., Jr.
  Organization Man, The   I-530

Willett, Thomas D.
  Floating Exchange Rates and International Monetary Reform   III-1108

Williams, William Appleman
  Contours of American History, The   II-667

Willoughby, William R.
  St. Lawrence Waterway: A Study in Politics and Diplomacy, The   II-786

Wilson, Edmund
  Dead Sea Scrolls, 1947-1969, The   II-602

Wilson, Edward O.
  Sociobiology: The New Synthesis   I-220

Wilson, John Tuzo
  I.G.Y., the Year of the New Moons   II-768

Wilson, Monica and Leonard Thompson, eds.
  Oxford History of South Africa, The   I-89

Wolfe, Bertram D.
  Khrushchev and Stalin's Ghost   II-740

Wolfe, Thomas
  You Can't Go Home Again   I-244

Wolfe, Thomas W.
  Role of the Warsaw Pact in Soviet Policy   II-719

Women: Their Changing Roles   II-1000

Wood, Bryce
  Making of the Good Neighbor Policy, The   I-264

Yoshida, Shigeru
  Yoshida Memoirs: The Story of Japan in Crisis, The   II-588

Yoshihashi, Takehiko
  Conspiracy at Mukden: The Rise of Japanese Military   I-273

Zeman, Z. A. B.
  Break-Up of the Habsburg Empire, 1914-1918: A Study in National and Social Revolution, The   I-163

Zinner, Paul
  Communist Strategy and Tactics in Czechoslovakia, 1918-1948   II-629

Zook, David Hantzler, Jr.
  Conduct of the Chaco War, The   I-293

Abshire, D. M. and M. A. Samuels, eds.
Portuguese Africa: A Handbook   III-1225
Ackerman, Bruce A., Susan Rose-Ackerman, James W. Sawyer, Jr., and Dale W. Henderson
Uncertain Search for Environmental Quality, The   II-879
Adamic, Louis
Eagle and the Roots, The   II-645
Adams, Thomas W.
AKEL: The Communist Party of Cyprus   III-1198
Adams, Walter, ed.
Brain Drain, The   I-301
Adelman, Morris A.
"Is the Oil Shortage Real? Oil Companies as OPEC Tax Collectors." in *Foreign Policy*   III-1144
World Petroleum Market, The   II-916
Adelman, Morris A., Paul G. Bradley and Charles A. Norman
Alaskan Oil Costs and Supplies   II-1027
"After Carter's Panama Victory," in *U.S. News & World Report*   III-1337
Agnew, Spiro T.
Canfield Decision, The   III-1192
Ahlstrom, Sydney E.
Religious History of the American People, A   I-534
Ahmad, Feroz
Turkish Experiment in Democracy, 1950-1975, The   III-1199
Aiken, Howard
"Proposed Automatic Calculating Machine," in *Spectrum*   I-541
Ainszstein, Reuben
Jewish Resistance in Nazi-Occupied Eastern Europe: With a Historical Survey of the Jew as a Fighter and Soldier in the Diaspora   I-403
Akpan, N. V.
Struggle for Secession, 1966-1970, The   II-1008
Albertini, Luigi
Origins of the War of 1914, The   I-52; II-924
Albertini, Rudolf von
Decolonization   II-563
Albrecht-Carrié, René
Diplomatic History of Europe Since the Congress of Vienna, A   I-52
Alexander, Yonah, ed.
International Terrorism: National, Regional, and Global Perspectives   II-1035
Ali, Chaudhri Muhammad
Emergence of Pakistan, The   II-611
Aliber, Robert Z., ed.
National Monetary Policies and the International Financial System   III-1109
Political Economy of Monetary Reform, The   III-1109
"All Together," in *The New Yorker*   II-735
Allen, Garland E.
Life Science in the Twentieth Century   I-506
Allen, Lawrence
Trans-Alaska Pipeline South to Valdez, The   II-1027
Allen, Richard
Imperialism and Nationalism in the Fertile Crescent: Sources and Prospects of the Arab-Israeli Conflict   I-240
Alliuyeva, Sveltana
Twenty Letters to a Friend   II-742
Allman, T. D.
"Cambodia: Into an Iceberg War," in *Far Eastern Economic Review*   II-1090
"Ever Wider," in *Far Eastern Economic Review*   II-1089
Alsop, Stewart
"Lessons of the Cuban Disaster, The," in *Saturday Evening Post*   II-932
American Assembly, Columbia University, The
Future of American Transportation, The   I-524
Amodia, J.
Franco's Political Legacy: From Dictatorship to Facade Democracy   II-1049
Anabtawi, M. F.
Arab Unity in Terms of Law   I-500
Anderson, Eugene Nelson
First Moroccan Crisis, 1904-1906, The   I-52
"Meinecke's *Ideengeschichte* and the Crisis in Historical Thinking," in *Medieval and Historiographical Essays in Honor of James Westfall Thompson*   I-62
Anderson, Irvine, H., Jr.
Standard Vacuum Oil Company and United States East Asian Policy, 1933-1941, The   I-443
Andrade e Silva, J. and G. Lochak
Quanta   I-174
Andrist, Ralph K.
Long Death, The   II-871
"Angry American Indian Starting Down the Protest Trail, The," in *Time*   II-871
Ansari, Mohammad Iqbal
Arab League 1945-1955, The   I-499
Ansel, Walter
Hitler Confronts England   I-437
Antoni, Carlo
From History to Sociology: The Transition in German Historical Thinking   I-61

Antonius, George
  Arab Awakening, The   I-417
Appleton, Sheldon
  Eternal Triangle? Communist China, the United States and the United Nations, The   III-1116
Apponyi, Albert
  Memoirs of Count Apponyi, The   I-187
Archer, Jules
  Chou En-lai   III-1270
Area Handbook for Southern Rhodesia   II-987
Arlen, Michael J.
  Passage to Ararat   I-119
Armstrong, Harold C.
  Grey Wolf: Mustafa Kemal, an Intimate Study of a Dictator   I-229
Armstrong, Hamilton Fish
  Tito and Goliath   II-646
Arrighi, G.
  Political Economy of Rhodesia, The   II-987
Ashmore, Harry S.
  Arkansas: A Bicentennial History   II-775
Asimov, Isaac
  Collapsing Universe: The Story of Black Holes, The   II-905
  Mars, the Red Planet   III-1300
Aspin, Les
  "SALT or No SALT," in *The Bulletin of the Atomic Scientists*   II-1061
Atkins, Burton M. and Henry R. Glick, eds.
  Prisons, Protest, & Politics   II-891
Atyeo, Henry C.
  "United States in the Middle East, The" in *Current History*   II-763
Auty, Phyllis A.
  Tito: A Biography   II-646
Avery, Peter
  Modern Iran   III-1344
Avnery, Uri
  Isreal Without Zionists: A Plea for Peace in the Middle East   I-150
Aziz, M. A.
  Japan's Colonialism and Indonesia   I-463

"Back of U.S. Switch on Cuba," in *U.S. News & World Report*   III-1256
Balfour, Patrick (Lord Kinross)
  Atatürk: The Rebirth of a Nation   I-229
Ball, George W.
  "Capitulation in Helsinki," in *Newsweek*   III-1263
Ball, M. Margaret
  OAS in Transition, The   III-1255
Barber, James
  Rhodesia: The Road to Rebellion   II-987
Barker, Elizabeth
  British Policy in South-East Europe in the Second World War   I-448

Barlow, Ima Christina
  Agadir Crisis, The   I-52
Barnaby, Frank and Ronald Huiske
  Arms Uncontrolled   I-570
Barnett, A. Doak
  Uncertain Passage: China's Transition to the Post-Mao Era   III-1270
Barnett, Don and Roy Harvey
  Revolution in Angola: MPLA, Life Histories and Documents, The   III-1225
Barraclough, Geoffrey
  Survey of International Affairs, 1955-1956   II-729
Barron, John and Anthony Paul
  Murder of a Gentle Land: The Untold Story of Communist Genocide in Cambodia   III-1354
Barros, James and Douglas M. Johnston
  International Law of Pollution, The   II-880
Basset, R.
  Democracy and Foreign Policy: A Case History of the Sino-Japanese Dispute, 1931-1933   I-275
Baxter, William
  People or Penguins: The Case for Optimal Pollution   II-880
Beal, John Robinson
  John Foster Dulles   II-695
Beals, Carleton
  Porfirio Díaz, Dictator of Mexico   I-78
Becker, Jillian
  Hitler's Children: The Story of the Baader-Meinhof Gang   II-1035
Becker, Wayne, M.
  Energy and the Living Cell: An Introduction to Bioenergetics   I-506
Beckett, James C.
  Making of Modern Ireland, 1603-1923, The   III-1123
Beckford, George
  Persistent Poverty   III-1210
Bedau, Hugo Adam, ed.
  Death Penalty in America: An Anthology, The   III-1285
Beers, Burton F.
  Vain Endeavor: Robert Lansing's Attempts to End the American-Japanese Rivalry   I-127
Beloff, Max
  Foreign Policy of Soviet Russia, 1929-1941, The   I-323
Belote, James H. and William M. Belote
  Titans of the Sea: The Development and Operations of Japanese and American Carrier Task Forces During World War II, The   I-478
Bemis, Samuel Flagg
  Latin American Policy of the United States, The   I-267

Benda, Harry J.
Crescent and the Rising Sun: Indonesian Islam Under the Japanese Occupation, 1942-1945, The   I-463
Bendix, Reinhard
Max Weber: An Intellectual Portrait   I-45
Beneš, Eduard
My War Memoirs   I-157
Ben-Gurion, David
Israel: A Personal History   II-639
Ben-Veniste, Richard and George Frampton, Jr.
Stonewall   III-1205
Berger, Carl
Korea Knot: A Military-Political History, The   II-680
Berger, Elmer
Partisan History of Judaism, A   I-151
Berkowitz, Eliezen
Judaism: Fossil of Ferment?   I-334
Berman, William C.
Politics of Civil Rights in the Truman Administration, The   II-898
Bernstein, Barton J., ed.
Politics and Policies of the Truman Administration   II-668
Bernstein, Carl and Bob Woodward
All the President's Men   III-1136, 1205
Final Days, The   III-1192
Berry, Adrian
Iron Sun: Crossing the Universe Through Black Holes, The   II-841
Berry, Brian J. L., et al.
Land Use, Urban Form and Environmental Quality   II-880
"Best Birthday, The," in *Newsweek*   III-1293
Bethlen, Stephen
Treaty of Trianon and European Peace: Four Lectures Delivered in London in November, 1933, The   I-187
Bhagwati, Jagdish
New International Economic Order: The North-South Debate, The   III-1211
Biesanz, John and Mavis Biesanz
People of Panama, The   III-1337
Billion Dollar Story: The International St. Lawrence Seaway and Power Development, The   II-789
Binion, Rudolph
Hitler Among the Germans   I-196
Bird, Caroline
Case Against College, The   I-518
"Birthday Issue," in *Time*   III-1293
Blair, John
Control of Oil, The   III-1144
"Market Power and Inflation," in *Journal of Economic Issues*   II-1068
Blasier, Cole
Hovering Giant: United States Responses to

Revolutionary Change in Latin America, The   I-267
Bloch, Sidney and Peter Reddaway
Psychiatric Terror: How Soviet Psychiatry Is Used to Suppress Dissent   II-996
"Blood-Hungry Red Brigades, The" in *Time*   II-1035
Bloom, Sandra C. and Stanley E. Degler
Pesticides and Pollution   I-429
Bloomfield, Lincoln P., W. C. Clemens, Jr. and Franklyn Griffiths
Khrushchev and the Arms Race: Soviet Interests in Arms Control and Disarmament, 1954-1964   II-964
Bonavia, David
"Changing the Course of History," in *Far Eastern Economic Review*   III-1354
"Sowing the Seeds of a Bigger War," in *Far Eastern Economic Review*   III-1354
Bonsal Philip W.
Cuba, Castro, and the United States   II-932
Bowman, Larry W.
Politics in Rhodesia: White Power in an African State   II-987
Boyer, Richard and Herbert Morais
Labor's Untold Story   II-576
Boyle, John Hunter
China and Japan at War, 1937-1945: The Politics of Collaboration   I-366
Bracher, Karl Dietrich
German Dictatorship: The Origins, Structure, and Effects of National Socialism, The   I-318
Bradbury, Ray, et al.
Mars and the Mind of Man   III-1300
Bradley, General Omar N.
Soldier's Story, A   II-583
Brauer, Jerald C., ed.
Essays in Divinity. Vol. V: Reinterpretation in American Church History   I-512
Braun, Wernher von and Frederick I. Ordway
History of Rocketry and Space Exploration, A   II-756
Breckenfeld, Gurney
"Business Loves the Sunbelt (and Vice Versa)," in *Fortune*   II-1082
Bree, Germaine
Camus and Sartre: Crisis and Commitment   I-259
Brinton, Crane
History of Western Morals, A   I-533
Brodie, Bernard
Sea Power in the Machine Age   I-374
Broglie, Louis, Prince de
Revolution in Physics: A Non-Mathematical Survey of Quanta, The   I-173
Bromberg, Joan
"Impact of the Neutron: Bohr and Heisenberg, The" in *Historical Studies in the Physical Sciences*   I-288

Brook, David
U.N. and the China Dilemma, The III-1116
Brookfield, Harold
Interdependent Development III-1211
Brooks, Harvey
Government of Science, The II-618
Brown, Anthony C. and Charles B. MacDonald
Secret History of the Atomic Bomb, The I-395
Brown, Benjamin H. and Fred Greene
Chinese Representation: A Case Study in United Nations Political Affairs III-1116
Brown, Dee
Bury My Heart at Wounded Knee II-871
Year of the Century: 1876, The III-1293
Brown, F. Lee and A. O. Lebeck
Cars, Cans and Dumps II-880
Brown, James F.
New Eastern Europe: The Khrushchev Era and After, The II-720
Brown, Judith M.
Gandhi's Rise to Power: Indian Politics, 1915-1922 I-179
Bruce, Robert V.
Bell: Alexander Graham Bell and the Conquest of Solitude II-618
Bruce-Lockhart, Robert H.
Jan Masaryk II-632
Brumberg, Abraham, ed.
Russia Under Khrushchev: An Anthology from Problems of Communism II-742, 979
Brzezinski, Zbigniew K.
Permanent Purge, The I-341
Soviet Bloc: Unity and Conflict, The II-720
Buckley, Marie
Breaking into Prison: A Citizen Guide to Volunteer Action II-891
Budge, Ian and Cornelius O'Leary
Belfast: Approach to Crisis III-1123
Bullock, Alan
Hitler: A Study in Tyranny I-195, 318, 380
Burbidge, Geoffrey and Margaret Burbidge
Quasi-Stellar Objects II-905
Burg, David and George Feiffer
Solzhenitsyn II-996
Burns, E. L. M.
Seat at the Table: The Struggle for Disarmament, A II-963
Burns, Richard Dean
Bibliography, A II-570
Burns, Richard Dean and Edward M. Bennett, eds.
Diplomats in Crisis: United States-Chinese-Japanese Relations, 1919-1941 I-443
Burr, Robert N.
Critical Bibliography of Religion in America, A I-512
Burrows, Millar
More Light on the Dead Sea Scrolls: New Scrolls and New Interpretations II-604
Burton, Anthony
Urban Terrorism: Theory, Practice and Response II-1035
Buss, Claude A.
People's Republic of China and Richard Nixon, The III-1129
Southeast Asia and the World Today II-708
Byrd, Richard E.
Alone I-67

Caldwell, Malcolm and Lek Tan
Cambodia in the Southeast Asian War II-1090; III-1218
Calmann, John, ed.
Common Market: The Treaty of Rome Explained, The II-1153
Cambridge, History of the British Empire Vol. VIII: South Africa, Rhodesia and the High Commission Territories, The* I-91
Cameron, E. R.
Prologue to Appeasement: A Study in French Foreign Policy, 1933-1936 I-203
Campbell, Ernest Q. and Thomas F. Pettigrew
Christians in Racial Crisis: A Study of Little Rock's Ministry II-775
Campbell, R. W.
Economics of Soviet Oil and Gas, The II-916
Carney, Timothy Michael
Communist Party Power in Kampuchea (Cambodia): Documents and Discussion III-1354
Carpenter, B. E. and R. W. Doran
"Other Turing Machine, The," in *The Computer Journal*. II-541
Carper, Robert S.
Focus: The Railroad in Transition I-524
Carson, Rachel Louise
Silent Spring II-549
Carter, Gwendolen M.
"Black Experience in South Africa, The," in *The Wilson Quarterly*. III-1278
Carter, Gwendolen M. and Patrick O'Meara, eds.
Southern Africa: The Continuing Crisis I-91
Carter, Robert L., Dorothy Kenyon, Peter Marcuse and Loren Miller
Equality II-972
Carter, Robert M., Daniel Glaser and Leslie T. Wilkins
Correctional Institutions II-892
Castelnuovo-Tedesco, Pietro
Psychiatric Aspects of Organ Transplantation II-1021

Cawelti, John G.
Apostles of the Self-Made Man   I-533
Chamberlin, William Henry
Ukraine: A Submerged Nation, The   I-157
Chambers, F. P.
War Behind the War, 1914-1918: A History of the Political and Civilian Fronts, The   I-143
Chanda, Nayan
"Four Year Coup, The," in *Far Eastern Economic Review*   II-1090
"Suddenly Last Spring," in *Far Eastern Economic Review*   III-1234
Chapman, Sydney
I.G.Y.: Year of Discovery   II-769
Charschan, S. S., ed.
Lasers in Industry   II-885
Chase, George C.
"History of Mechanical Computing Machinery," in *Proceedings of the Association for Computing Machinery*   II-541
Chaudhury, P. C. Roy
Gandhi and His Contemporaries   I-179
Ch'en, Jerome
Mao and the Chinese Revolution   III-1270
Choudhury, G. W.
India, Pakistan, Bangladesh, and the Major Powers: Politics of a Divided Sub-Continent   II-1096
Chouraqui, André
History of Judaism, A   I-416
Christenson, Cornelia V.
Kinsey, A Biography   II-624
Churchill, Winston S.
Second World War. Vol. I: *The Gathering Storm, The*   I-347
Second World War. Vol. IV: *The Hinge of Fate, The*   I-463
Second World War. Vol. II: *Their Finest Hour, The*   I-437
Second World War. Vol. VI: *Triumph and Tragedy, The*   II-583
Churchward, L. G.
Soviet Intelligentsia: An Essay on the Structure and Roles of the Soviet Intellectuals During the 1960's, The   II-996
Ciano, Galeazzo
Ciano Diaries, 1939-1943, The   I-449
Clark, Alan
Barbarossa: The Russian-German Conflict, 1941-1945   I-456, 485
Clarke, Arthur C.
Report on Planet Three and Other Speculations   II-1075
Voices from the Sky: Previews of the Coming Space Age   II-757
Clendenen, Clarence C.
United States and Pancho Villa: A Study in Unconventional Diplomacy, The   I-78
Clogg, Richard and George Yannopoulos, eds.
Greece Under Military Rule   III-1199

Clutterbuck, Richard
Living with Terrorism   II-1034
Coates, W. P. and Zelda K. Coates
Armed Intervention in Russia, 1918-1922   I-157
Cochran, William Gemmell, *et al.*
Statistical Problems of the Kinsey Report on Sexual Behavior in the Human Male   II-624
Cogley, John, ed.
Religion in America: Original Essays on Religion in a Free Society   I-512
Cohen, Benjamin J.
Question of Imperialism: The Political Economy of Dominance and Dependence, The   I-37; III-1211
Cohen, Bernard Lande
Law Without Order: Capital Punishment and the Liberals   III-1286
Cohn, Norman
Warrant for Genocide: The Myth of the Jewish World-Conspiracy and the Protocols of the Elders of Zion   I-310
Collier, Basil
Battle of Britain, The   I-437
War in the Far East, 1941-1945: A Military History, The   I-463
Collier, David S. and Kurt Glaser, eds.
Conditions for Peace in Europe: Problems of Détente and Security, The   II-596
Collins, Larry and Dominique Lapierre
O Jerusalem!   II-639
Combs, Jerald A., ed.
Nationalist, Realist, and Radical: Three Views of American Diplomacy   II-668
Commoner, Barry
Science and Survival   II-549
Compton, Arthur Holly
Atomic Quest: A Personal Narrative   I-394; II-689
Connell-Smith, Gordon
Inter-American System, The   I-268
Conquest, Robert
Power and Policy in the U.S.S.R.: The Struggle for Stalin's Succession 1945-1960   II-979
Consumer Protection: Gains and Setbacks   II-864
Cooley, John K.
Green March, Black September: The Story of the Palestinian Arabs   II-1035
Coombs, Norman
Black Experience in America, The   II-813
Coombs, Robert H., *et al.*, eds.
Socialization in Drug Abuse   II-819
Cormier, Frank J. and William J. Eaton
Reuther   II-735
Cortina, Frank Michael
Stroke a Slain Warrior   II-819
Cottrell, Alvin J.
"Eisenhower Era in Asia, The," in *Current*

History II-708
Court, W. H. B., ed.
British Economic History, 1870-1914: Commentary and Documents I-37
Cousins, Norman
Improbable Triumvirate: John F. Kennedy, Pope John, Nikita Khrushchev, The II-964
Cox, Arthur Macy
Dynamics of Détente: How to End the Arms Race, The II-570
Craig, Gordon A.
Politics of the Prussian Army, 1640-1945, The I-380
Craig, Gordon A. and Felix Gilbert, eds.
Diplomats: 1919-1939, The I-347
Crankshaw, Edward
Fall of the House of Habsburg, The I-165
Crew, F. A. E.
Foundations of Genetics, The I-13
Croce, Benedetto
History of Italy, 1871-1915, A I-144
Cronjé, Suzanne
World and Nigeria, The III-1008
Cropper, William H.
Quantum Physicists, and an Introduction to Their Physics, The I-174
Crowley, James B.
"Reconsideration of the Marco Polo Bridge Incident," in *Journal of Asian Studies.* I-367
Crozier, Brian and Eric Chou
Man Who Lost China: The First Full Biography of Chiang Kai-shek, The II-662
Cruttwell, C. R. M. F.
History of the Great War, 1914-1918, A I-136
"Cuba, Sí!," in *Newsweek* III-1256
Cumberland, Charles Curtis
Mexican Revolution, Genesis Under Madero I-77
Curtis, Charles P.
Oppenheimer Case: The Trial of a Security System, The II-689
Czechoslovak Academy of Sciences, Mathematico-physical Section
International Geophysical Year and Cooperation in Czechoslovakia 1957-1959 II-769

Dallin, Alexander
German Rule in Russia, 1941-1945: A Study of Occupation Policies I-456
Dalziel, Raewyn M.
Origins of New Zealand Diplomacy: The Agent-General in London, 1870-1905, The I-23
Daniloff, Nicholas
Kremlin and the Cosmos, The II-781
Dash, Samuel
Chief Council III-1205

Daughen, Joseph R. and Peter Binzen
Wreck of the Penn Central, The I-525
David, Nina
Reference Guide for Consumers II-864
Davidson, Basil
In the Eye of the Storm: Angola's People III-1225
Dawidowicz, Lucy S.
War Against the Jews, 1933-1945, The I-310, 403
Dawson, Alan
Fifty-five Days: The Fall of South Vietnam III-1166, 1233
Dawson, Christopher
Dynamics of World History I-335
Day, Mark
Forty Acres: César Chávez and the Farm Workers II-847
Deadline Date on World Affairs
Soviet Union: Khrushchev's Fall II-979
Dean, Arthur H.
"United States Foreign Policy and Formosa," in *Foreign Affairs* II-714
Dean, John Wesley, III
Blind Ambition: The White House Years III-1136, 1205
Dean, Robert W.
West German Trade with the East: The Political Dimension III-1173
Debo, Angie
History of the Indians of the United States, A II-871
DeCaux, Len
Labor Radical: From the Wobblies to CIO, a Personal History II-576
DeConde, Alexander
Herbert Hoover's Latin American Policy I-268
Dedek, John F.
Human Life: Some Moral Issues III-1160
Deloria, Vine, Jr.
Custer Died for Your Sins II-871
Del Rio, Eduardo (RIUS), ed.
Cuba for Beginners: An Illustrated Guide for Americans II-749; III-1255
Deming, Angus, *et al.*
"New Cold War?, A," in *Newsweek.* III-1323
Denikin, Anton I.
White Army, The I-157
Dessauer, John H. and H. E. Clark, eds.
Xerography and Related Processes I-387
Djemal Pasha, Ahmed
Memories of a Turkish Statesman, 1913-1919 I-120
Dobson, Christopher and Ronald Payne
Carlos Complex: A Study in Terror, The II-1035
Dollen, Charles
Abortion in Context: A Select Bibliography III-1160

Donaldson, Robert H.
Soviet Policy Toward India: Ideology and Strategy II-1095
Dore, Ronald P.
Land Reform in Japan II-590
Dornberg, John
Two Germanys, The II-653
Dorpalen, Andreas
Hindenburg and the Weimar Republic I-318
Dorsen, Norman
Discrimination and Civil Rights II-813
Draper, Theodore
Castro's Revolution: Myths and Realities II-750
"Cuba and U.S. Policy," in *New Leader* II-932
Drew, Elizabeth
"Argument over Survival, An," in *New Yorker* II-1061
Washington Journal: The Events of 1973-1974 III-1136
Dubofsky, Melvyn and Warren Van Tine
John L. Lewis II-576
Duerig, W. H. and J. F. Jenkins, *et al.*
Notes on Transistor Physics and Electronics II-618
Duker, Sam
Public Schools and Religion: The Legal Context, The II-954
Dull, Paul S.
Battle History of the Japanese Navy (1941-1945), A I-478
Dulles, Foster Rhea
American Policy Toward Communist China, 1949-1969 III-1129
Dulles, John Foster
War or Peace II-695
Dumont, Fernand
Vigil of Quebec, The II-826
Dumont, René and B. Rosier
Hungry Future, The II-563
Dung, General Van Tien
Our Great Spring Victory III-1234
Dupré, Joseph Stefan and Stanford A. Lakoff
Science and the Nation: Policy and Politics II-618
Duus, Peter
Party Rivalry and Political Change in Taishō Japan I-128

Eames, Charles and Ray Eames
Computer Perspective, A I-541
Eastman, Lloyd E.
Abortive Revolution: China Under Nationalist Rule, 1927-1939, The I-217
"Eavesdropping on the Galaxy," in *Intellect* II-834
Eberhart, Jonathan
"Giving Ourselves Away," in *Science News* II-834

Edib, Halidé (Adivar)
Turkey Faces West: A Turkish View of Recent Changes and Their Origin I-230
Educational Broadcasting Corporation
"MacNeil/Lehrer Report—Roper Poll, The," III-1309
Edwards, Robert G., P. C. Steptoe and J. M. Purdy
"Fertilization and Cleavage in Vitro of Preovulator Human Oocytes," in *Nature* III-1330
Edwards, Robert G. and David J. Sharpe
"Social Values and Research in Human Embryology," in *Nature* III-1330
Effects of Pesticides in Water: A Report to the States. II-848
Ehrlich, Paul
Population Bomb, The II-549
Einstein, Albert and Leopold Infield
Evolution of Physics, The I-173
Eisenhower, Dwight D.
Crusade in Europe II-583
Mandate for Change, 1953-1956 II-707, 714, 729
White House Years: Waging Peace, 1956-1961, The II-763, 911
Eisenhower, Milton S.
Wine Is Bitter: The United States and Latin America, The I-268
Eklund, Carl D. and Joan Beckman
Antarctica, Polar Research, and Discovery During the International Geophysical Year II-769
Elkins, Michael
Forged in Fury I-403
Elliot, David
"North Vietnam Since Ho," in *Problems of Communism* III-1250
Emme, Eugene M.
History of Space Flight, A II-941
Engelenburg, F. V.
General Louis Botha I-91
Engler, Robert
Brotherhood of Oil, The III-1144
Enloe, Cynthia H.
Politics of Pollution in a Comparative Perspective: Ecology and Power in Four Nations, The II-880
Environmental Protection Agency Efforts to Remove Hazardous Pesticides from the Channels of Trade. II-948
Epstein, William
Last Chance: Nuclear Proliferation and Arms Control, The II-964

Faber, Doris
Enough! The Revolt of the American Consumer II-864
Fagen, M. D., ed.
History of Engineering and Science in the Bell

System: The Early Years, 1875-1925, A   II-618

Fainsod, Merle
Smolensk Under Soviet Rule   I-341

Fall, Bernard B.
Street Without Joy   II-702
Two Viet-Nams: A Political and Military Analysis, The   III-1250
Viet-Minh Regime: Government and Administration in the Democratic Republic of Vietnam, The   II-702

Falls, Cyril
Great War: 1914-1918, The   I-136

Fanning, Louis A.
Betrayal in Vietnam   III-1233

Farrell, R. Barry
Jugoslavia and the Soviet Union, 1948-1956: An Analysis with Documents   II-645

Fearey, Robert A.
Occupation of Japan, Second Phase: 1948-1950, The   II-590

Feather, Norman
"History of Neutrons and Nuclei, A" in Contemporary Physics.   I-288

Feingold, Henry L.
Politics of Rescue: The Roosevelt Administration and the Holocaust, 1938-1945, The   I-403

Feit, Edward
South Africa: The Dynamics of the African National Congress   III-1278

Fermi, Laura
Atoms in the Family: My Life with Enrico Fermi   I-301

Fest, Joachim C.
Hitler   I-195

Filov, Bogdan
"Diary of Bogdan Filov, The," in Southeastern Europe.   I-449

Finch, Volney C.
Jet Propulsion Turbojets   I-360

Fine, Lenore and Jesse A. Remington
United States Army in World War II: The Technical Services; The Corps of Engineers; Construction in the United States, The   I-493

Finer, Herman
Dulles over Suez   II-695

"First Human Hearts Transplanted," in Science News.   II-1021

Fisher, Sidney Nettleton
Middle East: A History, The   I-229

Fitzgerald, C. P.
Mao Tse-tung and China   II-662; III-1270

Fleming, Peter
Operation Sea Lion   I-437

Flieger, Howard
"Beyond the Summit," in U.S. News & World Report   III-1263

Florinsky, Michael T.
End of the Russian Empire, The   I-106

Foda, Ezzeldin
Projected Arab Court of Justice, The   I-500

Fodell, Beverly
César Chávez and the United Farm Workers: A Selective Bibliography   II-847

Fogel, David
". . . We Are the Living Proof . . ." The Justice Model for Corrections   II-892

Footman, David
Civil War in Russia   I-157

Fournier, Henri and J. E. Wadsworth, eds.
Floating Exchange Rates: The Lessons of Recent Experience   III-1109

Fraenkel, Osmond K.
Rights We Have, The   II-898

Frank, Pat and Joseph D. Harrington
Rendezvous at Midway: U.S.S. Yorktown and the Japanese Carrier Fleet   I-478

Frankel, Charles
"Specter of Eugenics, The," in Commentary   III-1330

Fraser, Donald M.
"Freedom and Foreign Policy," in Foreign Policy   III-1263

Fraser, Sir Ronald
Once Round the Sun   II-769

French, Warren
John Steinbeck   I-424

Freund, Julien
Sociology of Max Weber, The   I-45

Friedlaender, Saul
Prelude to Downfall: Hitler and the United States, 1939-1941   I-471

Friedman, Herbert
Amazing Universe, The   II-841

Friedman, Isaiah
Question of Palestine, 1914-1918: British-Jewish-Arab Relations, The   I-240

Friedman, Leon, ed.
Civil Rights Reader, The   II-813

Friedman, Otto
Break-up of Czech Democracy, The   II-633

Friedman, Saul S.
No Haven for the Oppressed: United States Policy Toward Jewish Refugees, 1933-1945   I-301, 310

Friendly, Fred W.
Due to Circumstances Beyond Our Control   II-674
Good Guys, the Bad Guys, and the First Amendment: Free Speech Versus Fairness in Broadcasting, The   II-675

Futrell, Robert Frank
United States Air Force in Korea, 1950-1953, The   II-681

Gabriel, Mordecai L. and Seymour Fogel, eds.
Great Experiments in Biology   I-13

Gabriel, Ralph H.
"Vernon Louis Parrington," in *Pastmasters: Some Essays on American Historians*   I-210

Gaedeke, Ralph M. and Warren W. Etcheson
Consumerism: Viewpoints from Business, Government, and the Public Interest   II-864

Galbraith, John K.
Economics and the Public Purpose   II-1068

Gallup, George H.
Gallup Poll: Public Opinion 1972-1977, The   II-854

Gardner, Lloyd C.
Architects of Illusion: Men and Ideas in American Foreign Policy   II-668

Gardner, Richard N.
Sterling Dollar Diplomacy   III-1103

Gargan, Edward T., ed.
Intent of Toynbee's History, The   I-334

Gasster, Michael
Chinese Intellectuals and the Revolution of 1911: The Birth of Modern Chinese Radicalism   I-99

Gati, Charles, ed.
International Politics of Eastern Europe, The   III-1263

Geddes, Donald Porter, ed.
Analysis of the Kinsey Reports on Sexual Behavior in the Human Male and Female, An   II-624

Geer, Andrew
New Breed: The Story of the U.S. Marines in Korea, The   II-681

Geertz, Clifford
Interpretation of Cultures, The   I-223

Gelb, Leslie H. and Richard K. Betts
Irony of Vietnam: The System Worked, The   III-1234

George, Margaret
Hollow Men: An Examination of British Foreign Policy Between the Years 1933 and 1939, The   I-354

Gilbert, Felix
History: Choice and Commitment   I-62

Gilbert, Felix, ed.
Hitler Directs His War: The Secret Records of His Daily Military Conferences   I-486

Gilbert, M. and R. Gott
Appeasers, The   I-203

Gillispie, Charles Coulson, ed.
Dictionary of Scientific Biography   I-288

Glasstone, Samuel
Sourcebook on Atomic Energy   I-251

Glazer, Nathan
Remembering the Answers: Essays on the American Student Revolt   I-518

Glicksberg, Charles I.
Modern Literature and the Death of God   I-259

Goebbels, Joseph
My Part in Germany's Fight   I-318

Golan, Matti
Secret Conversations of Henry Kissinger: Step-by-Step Diplomacy in the Middle East, The   III-1187

Goldberg, Alfred, ed.
History of the United States Air Force: 1907-1957, A   I-493

Golden, Frederic
Quasars, Pulsars, and Black Holes   II-841, 905, 1015

Goldfarb, Ronald
Jails: The Ultimate Ghetto   II-892

Goldman, Leon and R. James Rockwell, Jr.
Lasers in Medicine   II-885

Goldsby, Richard A.
Cells and Energy   I-506

Goldsen, Joseph M., ed.
Outer Space in World Politics   II-781

Goldston, Robert
Suburbia: Civic Denial   II-556

Gollan, Robin
Radical and Working Class Politics: A Study of Eastern Australia, 1850-1910   I-23

Gompert, David C., Michael Mandelbaum, Richard L. Garwin and John H. Barton
Nuclear Weapons and World Politics: Alternatives for the Future   II-570

Gooch, George P.
History and Historians in the Nineteenth Century   I-29

Good, Robert C.
U.D.I. The International Politics of the Rhodesian Rebellion   II-987

Goodfield, Jane
Playing God: Genetic Engineering and the Manipulation of Life   III-1330

Goodman, Allan E
"South Vietnam: War Without End?," in *Asian Survey*   III-1234

Goold-Adams, Richard
John Foster Dulles: A Reappraisal   II-695

Gordon, Donald C.
Dominion Partnership in Imperial Defense, 1870-1914, The   I-23

Graebner, Norman A.
Cold War Diplomacy: American Foreign Policy, 1945-1960   II-597

Gramling, Oliver
AP: The Story of News   I-6

Grant, Jonathan S., *et al.*
Cambodia: The Widening War in Indochina   II-1090

Gray, George W.
Frontiers of Flight: The Story of NACA Research   I-360

Greenwood, Ted
"Reconnaissance and Arms Control," in *Sci-*

entific American II-1061

Gregor, Arthur
Bell Laboratories: Inside the World's Largest Communications System II-618

Greider, William and J. P. Smith
"Fuel Crisis a Matter of Perception," in *Washington Post* III-1144

Grew, Joseph Clark
Invasion Alert! The Red China Drive for a UN Seat III-1116

Gribbin, John
White Holes: Cosmic Gushes in the Universe II-905

Griffith, Alexander
Ship to Remember, A I-478

Grinspoon, Lester and Peter Hedblom
Speed Culture—Amphetamine Use and Abuse in America, The II-819

Groueff, Stephane
Manhattan Project: The Untold Story of the Making of the Atomic Bomb I-394

Grubel, Herbert G.
International Monetary System, The II-1109

Gruen, Victor
Heart of Our Cities, The II-556

Gruening, Ernest
State of Alaska, The II-797

Guevara, Ernesto Che
Episodes of the Revolutionary War II-750

Guhin, Michael A.
John Foster Dulles: A Statesman and His Times II-695

Guindey, Guillaume
International Monetary Tangle: Myths and Realities, The III-1109

Gurland, Robert and Anthony MacLean
Common Market: A Common Sense Guide for Americans, The III-1153

Hadawi, Sami
Bitter Harvest: Palestine Between 1914-1967 I-417

Halberstam, David
HO II-702

Haldeman, H. R. and Joseph DiMona
Ends of Power, The III-1136, 1205

Hallstein, Walter
Europe in the Making III-1153

Halperin, Maurice
Rise and Decline of Fidel Castro: An Essay in Contemporary History, The II-932

Halperin, S. William
Italy and the Vatican at War I-144

Hancock, W. K.
Smuts: The Sanguine Years, 1870-1919 I-91

Harcave, Sidney
Russia: A History I-106

Harlow, Alvin F.
Old Wires and New Waves I-6

Harris, Louis
Confidence and Concern: Citizens View American Government II-854

Hartley, Joseph R.
Effect of the St. Lawrence Seaway on Grain Movements, The II-789

Hartshorne, Thomas L.
Distorted Image: Changing Conceptions of the American Character Since Turner, The I-533

Hartunian, Abraham H.
Neither to Laugh Nor to Weep: A Memoir of the Armenian Genocide I-119

Harvey, James C.
Black Civil Rights During the Johnson Administration II-972

Haskin, Frederic J.
Panama Canal, The III-1337

Hassouna, Hussein A.
League of Arab States and Regional Disputes, The I-500

Hastings, Max
Barricades in Belfast: The Fight for Civil Rights in Northern Ireland III-1123

Haugland, Vern
AAF Against Japan, The I-493

"Havana on the Horn," in *Newsweek* III-1323

Hawking, Stephen
"Quantum Mechanics for Black Holes, The," in *Scientific American* II-841

Hays, Brooks
Southern Moderate Speaks, A II-775

Hayton, Robert D.
National Interests in Antarctica II-805

Hazan, Baruch A.
Soviet Propaganda: A Case Study of the Middle East Conflict III-1187

Hecht, Selig
Explaining the Atom I-251

Heiden, Konrad
Der Fuehrer: Hitler's Rise to Power I-196

Heinemann, Frederick
Existentialism and the Modern Predicament I-259

Henkin, Harmon, Martin Merta and James Staples
Environment, the Establishment, and the Law, The I-429

Herberg, Will
Protestant-Catholic-Jew: An Essay in American Religious Sociology I-512

Herr, Michael
Dispatches II-1042

Herring, James M. and Gerald C. Gross
Telecommunications, Economics and Regulation I-6

Hersey, John R.
Hiroshima I-251

Hertzberg, Arthur, ed.
Zionist Idea: A Historical Analysis and Reader, The   I-150; II-639
Hewish, Anthony
"Pulsars and High Density Physics," in *Science*   II-1015
Hewish, Anthony and Jocelyn Bell, *et al.*
"Observation of a Rapidly Pulsating Radio Source," in *Nature*   II-1015
Hey, J. S.
Evolution of Radio Astronomy, The   II-905, 1015
Higgins, Trumbull
Korea and the Fall of MacArthur: A Precis in Limited War   II-681
Higham, John, ed.
Reconstruction of American History, The   I-533
Higham, John
"Study of American Intellectual History, The," in *Writing American History: Essays on Modern Scholarship*   I-210
Hijazi, Ihsan
"New Allies, Old Woes for Moslems in Lebanon," in *The New York Times*   III-1242
Hilberg, Raul, ed.
Documents of Destruction   I-310
Hildebrand, George C. and Gareth Porter
Cambodia: Starvation and Revolution   III-1354
Hildebrand, Klaus
Foreign Policy of the Third Reich, The   I-354
Hildreth, C. H. and B. C. Nalty
1001 Questions Answered About Aviation History   I-360
Hillson, Norman
Geneva Scene   I-282
Hilton, Bruce
Highly Irregular   II-1008
Himelhoch, Jerome and Sylvia Fava, eds.
Sexual Behavior in American Society: An Appraisal of the First Two Kinsey Reports   II-624
Himmelfarb, Gertrude
Lord Acton: A Study in Conscience and Politics   I-29
Hirsch, Fred
Money International   III-1103
Hitti, Philip K.
Lebanon in History, from the Earliest Times to the Present   II-763
Hodson, H. V.
Great Divide: Britain, India, Pakistan, The   II-611
Hoffman, Frederick John
Modern Novel in America, 1900-1950, The   I-424
Hogye, Michael
Paris Peace Conference of 1946: Role of the Hungarian Communists and of the Soviet Union, The   II-597
Hoopes, Townsend
Limits of Intervention, The   II-1042
Horne, Charles F., ed.
Source Records of the Great War   I-136
Horwitz, Robert H. and Norman Meller
Land and Politics in Hawaii   II-797
Hotz, Robert
"MR3 in Perspective," in *Aviation Week*   II-941
"How the Treaty Was Saved," in *Time*   III-1337
Howard, Harry N.
"Regional Pacts and the Eisenhower Doctrine, The," in *Annuals of the American Academy of Political and Social Science*   II-763
Howard, Leon
Literature and the American Tradition   I-424
Huang, Philip C.
Liang Ch'i-ch'ao and Modern Chinese Liberalism   I-99
Hudgins, H. C., Jr.
Warren Court and the Public Schools, The   II-954
Hughes, Donald J.
Neutron Story, The   I-288
Hughes, Everett C.
French Canada in Transition   II-826
Hughes, Henry Stuart
Consciousness and Society: The Reorientation of European Social Thought, 1890-1930   I-45, 62
Humphrey, Hubert
Beyond Civil Rights   II-813
Hyams, Edward
Terrorists and Terrorism   II-1035
Hyde, Margaret O.
Exploring Earth and Space   II-769
Hyma, Albert
Renaissance to Reformation   I-45
Hyamson, Albert Montefiore
Palestine Under the Mandate   I-240

Iggers, Georg G.
German Conception of History: The National Tradition of Historical Thought from Herder to the Present, The   I-61
"In the Wake of the Siege at Wounded Knee," in *U.S. News & World Report*   II-871
"Indians: Return to Wounded Knee," in *Newsweek*   II-871
Institute for Social Research, University of Michigan
"Debates Increased Awareness," in *ISR Newsletter*   III-1309
"Election Study Notes New Trends in Voter Behavior, Attributes Close Race to Well-

Run Campaign," in *ISR Newsletter*   III-1309

"Political Trust Stays Low as Economic Attitudes Worsen," in *ISR Newsletter*   II-854

"Watergate Crisis Had Indirect Impact on Deteriorating Trust in Government," in *ISR Newsletter*   II-854

International Monetary Problems   III-1103

Ionescu, Ghita
Break-Up of the Soviet Empire in Eastern Europe, The   II-720

Isenberg, Irwin, ed.
Death Penalty, The   III-1286

Israel, Jerry
Progressivism and the Open Door: America and China, 1905-1921   I-128

Jäckel, Eberhard
Hitler's Weltanschauung: A Blueprint for Power   I-196

Jackson, Karl D.
"Cambodia 1978: War, Pillage, and Purge in Democratic Kampuchea," in *Asian Survey*   III-1354

Jacobs, Jane
Death and Life of Great American Cities, The   II-556

Jameson, Storm
In the Second Year   I-245

Jammer, Max
Philosophy of Quantum Mechanics, The   I-174

Jaszi, Oscar
Dissolution of the Habsburg Monarchy, The   I-165
Revolution and Counter-Revolution in Hungary   I-187

Jaworski, Leon
Right and the Power, The   III-1136, 1205

Jensen, Lloyd
Return from the Nuclear Brink   II-570

John, Laurie, ed.
Cosmology Now   II-841

Johnson, Bruce D.
Marihuana Users and Drug Subcultures   II-819

Johnson, Richard William
How Long Will South Africa Survive?   III-1278

Jolly, Alison
Evolution of Primate Behavior, The   I-223

Jones, Alan M., Jr., ed.
U.S. Foreign Policy in a Changing World: The Nixon Administration, 1969-1973   III-1166

Jones, Maldwyn Allen
American Immigration   I-302

Judis, John
"Report from Lebanon: A Mini World War,"
in *In These Times*   III-1242

Jungk, Robert
Brighter Than a Thousand Suns: A Personal History of the Atomic Scientists   II-689

"Jupiter & Io: Competing Stars," in *Science News*   III-1316

"Jupiter's World," in *Science News*   III-1316

Kain, Ronald Stuart
"Behind the Chaco War," in *Current History*   I-294

Kaiser, Robert G.
Russia: The People and the Power   II-996

Kalb, Marvin and Bernard Kalb
Kissinger   II-1053

Karnow, Stanley
Mao and China: From Revolution to Revolution   III-1270

Karpat, Kemal
Turkey's Politics: The Transition to a Multi-Party System   I-229

Karpat, Kemal H., ed.
Political and Social Thought in the Contemporary Middle East   I-150; III-1242

Karunakaran, K. P.
New Perspectives on Gandhi   I-179

Kasner, Edward and James Newman
Mathematics and the Imagination   I-85

Kataoka, Tetsuya
Resistance and Revolution in China: The Communists and the Second United Front   I-217

Kaufmann, Walter A., ed.
Existentialism from Dostoevsky to Sartre   I-259

Kaufmann, William J.
Cosmic Frontiers of General Relativity, The   II-841

Kazin, Alfred
On Native Grounds: An Interpretation of Modern American Prose Literature   I-424

Keller, Werner
Diaspora: The Post-Biblical History of the Jews   II-639

Kelley, Neil D.
"Xerography: The Greeks Had a Word for It," in *Infosystems*   I-387

Kelly, Alfred H. and Winfred A. Harbison
American Constitution: Its Origins and Development, The   II-954

Kelly, Mervin J.
"First Five Years of the Transistor, The," in *Bell Telephone Magazine.*   II-618

Kemal Atatürk, Mustafa
Speech Delivered by Ghazi Mustafa Kemal, President of the Turkish Republic, October 1927, A   I-229

Kennan, George Frost
Russia and the West Under Lenin and Stalin   I-157

Khadduri, Majid
"Towards an Arab Union," in *American Political Science Review*   I-499
Khouri, Fred J.
Arab-Israeli Dilemma, The   I-416
Khrushchev, Nikita S.
Khrushchev Remembers   II-729, 742, 911, 979
Kieve, Jeffrey
Electric Telegraph in the U.K., The   I-6
Kim, Samuel S.
China, the United Nations, and World Order   III-1116
Kimmich, Christopher M.
Germany and the League of Nations   I-282
Kindleberger, Charles P. and B. Herrick
Economic Development   III-1211
Kindleberger, Charles P.
Dollar Shortage, The   III-1103
King, Ernest J. and Walter M. Whitehill
Fleet Admiral King: A Naval Record   I-410
King, Robert R. and Robert W. Dean, eds.
East European Perspectives on European Security and Cooperation   III-1263
Kirby, S. Woodburn
War Against Japan, Vol. I: The *Loss of Singapore*; Vol. II: *India's Most Dangerous Hour, The*   I-463
Kirk, George
Middle East in the War, The   I-499
Kirwan, Laurence P.
History of Polar Exploration, A   I-67
Kissinger, Henry A.
American Foreign Policy   II-1053
White House Years, The   III-1218
Klebanow, Diana, Franklin L. Jonas and Ira M. Leonard
Urban Legacy   II-556
Kluge, Eike-Henner W.
Practice of Death, The   III-1160
Koebner, Richard and Helmut Dan Schmidt
Imperialism: The Story and Significance of a Political World, 1840-1960   I-37
Koestler, Arthur
Darkness at Noon   I-341
Kohl, Herbert
36 Children   I-518
Kolcum, Edward
"Atlas Tests Key to Manned Orbital Flight," in *Aviation Week*   II-941
"Mercury-Redstone Procedures Simplified," in *Aviation Week*   II-941
Kolko, Gabriel
Politics of War: The World and United States Foreign Policy, 1943-1945, The   II-653
"Working Wives," in *Science and Society*   II-855
Korbel, Josef
Communist Subversion of Czechoslovakia,
1938-1948: The Failure of Coexistence, The   II-633
Détente in Europe: Real or Imaginary   III-1263
Kovarsky, Irving and William Albrecht
Black Employment   II-972
Krause, Lawrence B.
Common Market: Progress and Controversy, The   III-1152
Kuklick, Bruce
American Policy and the Division of Germany   II-653
Kulischer, Eugene M.
Europe on the Move: War and Population Changes, 1917-1947   I-301
Kyriakides, Stanley
Cyprus: Constitutionalism and Crisis Government   III-1199

Labor Research Association
Research in Economic Trends   II-1068
Lacour-Gayet, Robert
History of South Africa, A   III-1278
LaFeber, Walter
America, Russia, and the Cold War, 1945-1975   II-729, 781, 971
Lake, Anthony, ed.
Legacy of Vietnam, The   III-1166
Lamont, Lansing
Day of Trinity   I-251, 395
La Nauze, John Andrew
Alfred Deakin: A Biography   I-23
Lancaster, Donald
Emancipation of French Indochina, The   II-702
Landau, David
Kissinger: The Uses of Power   II-1053
Langer, William L. and S. Everett Gleason
Undeclared War, 1940-1941, The   I-443, 471
Langguth, A. J.
"Dear Prince: Since You Went Away," in *The New York Times Magazine*   II-1090
Lapp, Ralph E.
Roads to Discovery   I-251
Lasers and Light: Readings from Scientific American   II-885
Laurence, William L.
Men and Atoms   I-394
Lawrence, Nathaniel
Alfred North Whitehead   I-85
Lazo, Mario
Dagger in the Heart: American Policy Failures in Cuba   II-932
Leasor, James
Singapore: The Battle That Changed the World   I-464
Lederer, Ivo J.
Yugoslavia at the Paris Peace Conference: A Study in Frontiermaking   I-187

Lee, Dwight E.
  Europe's Crucial Years: The Diplomatic Background of World War I, 1902-1914   I-52;   II-924
Legum, Colin
  "Next: Eritrea," in *New Republic*   III-1323
Lehmbeck, Donald R.
  "Electrophotographic Processes and Systems," in *Neblette's Handbook of Photography and Reprography*   I-388
Leighton, Marian Kirsch
  "Perspectives on the Vietnam-Cambodia Border Conflict," in *Asian Survey*.   III-1345
Lenchek, Allen, ed.
  Physics of Pulsars, The   II-1015
Lengyel, Bela A.
  "Evolution of Masers and Lasers," in *American Journal of Physics*   II-885
Lens, Sidney
  Crisis of American Labor, The   II-576
Lerner, I. Michael and William J. Libby
  Heredity, Evolution, and Society   I-13
Leuchtenburg, William E.
  Franklin D. Roosevelt and the New Deal, 1932-1940   I-323
Leutze, James R.
  Bargaining for Supremacy: Anglo-American Naval Collaboration, 1937-1941   I-410
Lévesque, René
  Option for Quebec, An   II-826
Levin, Nora
  Holocaust: The Destruction of European Jewry, 1933-1945, The   I-310, 403
Lewis, Bernard
  Middle East and the West, The   I-150
Lewis, F. F.
  Literature, Obscenity, and Law   III-1180
Ley, Willy
  Events in Space   II-941
  "Jet Propulsion: From Fancy to Fact," in *Aviation*   I-360
  Rockets, Missiles and Men in Space   II-756
Li, T'ien-i
  Woodrow Wilson's China Policy, 1913-1917   I-127
Lichtheim, George
  Imperialism   I-37
Liddell Hart, B. H.
  History of the Second World War   I-456
Liew, Kit Siong
  Struggle for Democracy: Sung Chiao-jen and the 1911 Chinese Revolution   I-99
Lind, Andrew W.
  Hawaii's People   II-797
Linden, Carl A.
  Khrushchev and the Soviet Leadership, 1957-1964   II-980
Lindsay, Michael

Unknown War: North China 1937-1945, The   I-367
Lindsay, Robert B. and Henry Margenau
  Foundations of Physics   I-173
Liu, Frederick F.
  Military History of Modern China, 1924-1949, A   I-217
Lockard, Duane
  Toward Equal Opportunity   II-898
Lodal, Jan M.
  "Assuring Strategic Stability: An Alternative View," in *Foreign Affairs*   II-1061
London, Kurt, ed.
  Eastern Europe in Transition   II-720
  Soviet Union: A Half-Century of Communism, The   II-720
Loney, Martin
  White Rhodesia and Imperial Response   II-987
Loosbrock, John F. and Richard M. Skinner, eds.
  Wild Blue, The   I-477
  Lore of Flight, The   I-360
Loshak, David
  Pakistan Crisis   II-1095
Lovell, Bernard
  Out of the Zenith: Jodrell Bank, 1957-1970   II-905
Low, Alfred D.
  Soviet Hungarian Republic and the Paris Peace Conference, The   I-187
Lowenthal, Abraham F.
  "United States and Latin America: Ending the Hegemonic Presumption, The," in *Foreign Affairs*   I-268
Lu, David J.
  From the Marco Polo Bridge to Pearl Harbor: Japan's Entry into World War II   I-367
Lukacs, John A.
  Great Powers and Eastern Europe, The   II-597
Lukas, J. Anthony
  Nightmare: The Underside of the Nixon Years   III-1192, 1205, 1218
Lyons, F. S.
  Ireland Since the Famine   III-1123
Lytle, Clifford M.
  Warren Court and Its Critics, The   II-954

Mabee, Carleton
  Seaway Story, The   II-789
Mabon, Prescott C.
  Mission Communications: The Story of Bell Laboratories   II-618
McAlister, John T., Jr.
  Viet Nam: The Origins of Revolution   II-702; III-1250
MacArthur Memorial, The
  Occupation of Japan: Proceedings, The   II-590

McBride, James Hubert
  Test Ban Treaty: Military, Technological, and Political Implications, The   II-964
McCafferty, James, ed.
  Capital Punishment   III-1286
McCarry, Charles
  Citizen Nader   II-864
McCord, William
  Mississippi: The Long Hot Summer   II-972
McCullough, David
  Path Between the Seas: The Creation of the Panama Canal, 1870-1914, The   III-1337
McElroy, William D. and Carl P. Swanson
  Modern Cell Biology   I-506
MacEoin, Gary
  Northern Ireland: Captive of History   III-1122
MacLeod, Murdo, Jr.
  "Bolivia and Its Social Literature, Before and After the Chaco War: An Historical Study of Social and Literary Revolution"   I-294
McWilliams, Carey
  Factories in the Field: The Story of Migratory Farm Labor in California   II-847
Maddox, John
  Doomsday Syndrome, The   II-549
Magee, John
  Northern Ireland: Crisis and Conflict   III-1123
Majdalany, Fred
  Fall of Fortress Europe, The   I-486
Makdisi, Samir A.
  "Appraisal of Lebanon's Postwar Economic Development and a Look to the Future, An," in *Middle East Journal*   III-1242
Maki, John M.
  Japanese Militarism, Its Causes and Cure   I-275
Mamatey, Victor S.
  United States and East Central Europe, 1914-1918: A Study in Wilsonian Diplomacy and Propaganda, The   I-165
Manchester, Richard and Joseph Taylor
  Pulsars   II-1015
Manchester, William
  Glory and the Dream: A Narrative History of America, 1932-1974, The   I-533
Mancke, Richard
  Squeaking By   III-1144
Mansfield, Peter
  Arab World: A Comprehensive History, The   I-416
Mansoor, Menahem
  Dead Sea Scrolls: A College Textbook and a Study Guide, The   II-604
Marcum, John
  Angolan Revolution. Vol. I: *The Anatomy of an Explosion, 1950-1962, The*   III-1226

Marine Traffic Control: St. Lawrence River   II-789
Markham, James M.
  "Lebanon: The Insane War," in *The New York Times*   III-1242
Marlowe, John
  Seat of Pilate, The   I-240
Marshack, Alexander
  World in Space, The   II-769
Marshall, S. L. A.
  World War I   I-136
Martin, Edwin M.
  Allied Occupation of Japan, The   II-590
Martin, James
  Telecommunications and the Computer   I-6
  Teleprocessing Network Organization
Marty, Martin E.
  New Shape of American Religion, The   I-512
Masefield, John
  Gallipoli   I-136
Matthews, Herbert L.
  Fidel Castro   II-750
Matthiessen, Peter
  Sal Si Puedes: César Chávez and the New American Revolution   II-847
May, Ernest R.
  "Alliance for Progress in Historical Perspective, The" in *Foreign Affairs*.   I-268
Mead, Sidney E.
  Lively Experiment: The Shaping of Christianity in America, The   I-512
Meadows, D., et al.
  Limits to Growth, The   II-549
Mecham, J. Lloyd
  United States and Inter-American Security, 1889-1960, The   I-268
Meier, Gerald M.
  Leading Issues in Economic Development   III-1211
  Problems of a World Monetary Order   III-1109
Meisner, Maurice
  Mao's China: A History of the People's Republic   III-1270
Melby, John F.
  Mandate of Heaven: Record of a Civil War, China 1945-49, The   I-217
Mellanby, Kenneth
  Pesticides and Pollution   II-948
Mellenthin, Friedrich Wilhelm von
  Panzer Battles: A Study of the Employment of Armor in the Second World War   I-486
Mendenhall, Joseph
  "Communist Vietnam and the Border War: Victim or Aggressor," in *Strategic Review*.   III-1354
Menon, V. P.
  Transfer of Power in India, The   II-611

Merkl, Peter H.
  German Foreign Policies, West and East: On the Threshold of a New European Era   III-1173
  Origin of the West German Republic, The   II-653
Merleau-Ponty, Jacques and Bruno Morando
  Rebirth of Cosmology, The   II-905
Mermelstein, David, ed.
  Economic Crisis Reader, The   II-1068
Meyer, Michael C.
  Huerta: A Political Portrait   I-78
Miller, Douglas T. and Marion Nowak
  Fifties: The Way We Really Were, The   I-533
Miller, Ronald and David Sawers
  Technical Development of Modern Aviation, The   I-360
Milne, Lorus J.
  Ecology Out of Joint   II-1075
Milner, Henry
  Politics in the New Quebec   II-826
Minear, Richard H.
  Victors' Justice: The Tokyo War Crimes Trial   II-590
Minter, William
  Imperial Network and External Dependency: The Case of Angola   III-1225
Mitchell, John G. and Constance Stallings, eds.
  Ecotactics: The Sierra Club Handbook for Environment Activists   II-1076
Momaday, N. Scott
  House Made of Dawn   II-871
Montagu, Ashley
  Nature of Human Aggression, The   I-223
Montgomery of Alamein, Field Marshal
  Memoirs   II-583
Moon, Penderel
  Divide and Quit   II-611
Moore, Patrick
  Guide to Mars   III-1300
Moore, Patrick and Iain Nicolson
  Black Holes in Space   II-841
Morgan, Elaine
  Descent of Woman, The   I-223
Morgan, Robin, ed.
  Sisterhood Is Powerful: An Anthology of Writings from the Women's Liberation Movement   II-1002
Morgenthau, Henry, Sr.
  Ambassador Morgenthau's Story   I-120, 137
Morison, Samuel Eliot
  History of United States Naval Operations in World War II. Vol. III: *The Rising Sun in the Pacific, 1931-April 1942*   I-443
  History of United States Naval Operations in World War II. Vol. IV: *Coral Sea, Midway and Submarine Actions, May 1942-August 1942*   I-477

  History of United States Naval Operations in World War II. Vol. X: *The Atlantic Battle Won, May 1943-May 1945*   I-410
Morris, Robert M.
  "Economic Progress in the Americas," in *Bolivia*.   I-294
Morrison, Donald M.
  "What Hath Xerox Wrought?," in *Time Magazine*   I-387
Moses, John A.
  Politics of Illusion: The Fischer Controversy in German Historiography, The   II-925
Mosley, Hugh
  "Is There A Fiscal Crisis of the State?," in *Monthly Review*.   II-855
Mosley, Leonard
  Dulles: A Biography of Eleanor, Allen, and John Foster Dulles and Their Family Network   II-695
Moss, Norman
  Men Who Play God: The Story of the H-Bomb and How the World Came to Live with It   II-689
Mott, Frank L.
  News in America, The   I-6
Moughrabi, Fouad and Naseer Aruri, eds.
  Lebanon: Crisis and Challenge in the Arab World   III-1242
Mueller, George E. and Eugene R. Spangler
  Communication Satellites   II-757
Mueller, John E.
  War, Presidents and Public Opinion   II-1042
Muller, Herbert J.
  Uses of the Past   I-334
Mumford, Lewis
  City in History: Its Origins, Its Transformations, and Its Prospects, The   II-556
Munger, Edwin S.
  Afrikaner and African Nationalism: South African Parallels and Parameters   III-1278
Murphy, Irene Lyons
  Public Policy on the Status of Women: Agenda and Strategy for the 70's   II-1002
Murray, Bruce, *et al.*
  "Extraterrestrial Intelligence: An Observational Approach," in *Science*   II-834
  "Searches for Intelligence Beyond Earth Continue," in *Physics Today*   II-834
  "Six Searches for Extraterrestrial Civilizations," in *Science News*   II-834
Murray, Robert K.
  Red Scare: A Study in National Hysteria, 1919-1920   I-323
Myrdal, Gunnar
  Asian Drama, The   II-563

Nadel, Mark V.
  Politics of Consumer Protection, The   II-864

Nalbandian, Louise
  Armenian Revolutionary Movement: The Development of Armenian Political Parties Through the Nineteenth Century, The   I-120
Namier, Sir Lewis B.
  Europe in Decay: A Study of Disintegration, 1936-1940   I-354
Nash, Henry T.
  Nuclear Weapons and International Behavior   II-570
Nash, Roderick
  Wilderness and the American Mind   II-549
National Commission on Marihuana and Drug Abuse. *Drug Use in America: Problem in Perspective*   II-819
  Marihuana: A Signal of Misunderstanding   II-819
Neuhaus, Richard
  In Defense of People   II-549
"New Milestone in the Shift to the Sunbelt, A," in *Nation's Business*   II-1082
Newsweek   III-1316
Ngubane, Jorden K.
  African Explains Apartheid, An   III-1278
Niven, Sir Rex
  War of Nigerian Unity, 1967-1970, The   II-1008
Nixon, Richard M.
  RN: The Memoirs of Richard Nixon   II-1053; III-1205, 1218
Nkrumah, Kwame
  Neo-colonialism   II-563
Nobel Lectures, Including Presentation Speeches and Laureates' Biographies: Physics, 1922-1941   I-288
Nobel Lectures, Physics, 1963-70   II-885
Nolen, William A.
  Baby in the Bottle: An Investigative Review of the Edelin Case and Its Larger Meanings for the Controversy over Abortion Reform, The   III-1160
Norris, R.
  Emergent Commonwealth: Australian Federation, Expectations and Fulfilment, 1889-1910, The   I-23
Nwanko, Arthur and Samuel Ifejika
  Biafra, The Making of a Nation   II-1008

O'Ballance, Edgar
  Indo-China War, 1945-54: A Study in Guerilla Warfare, The   II-702
Oberdorfer, Don
  Tet!   II-1042
Odell, Peter R.
  Oil and World Power   II-916
Ojukwu, C. Odumegwu
  Biafra   II-1008
Oksenberg, Michel and Robert B. Oxnam, eds.

  Dragon and Eagle   III-1129
Olney, Ross R.
  Americans in Space: A History of Manned Space Travel   II-941
O'Neil, Terence
  Ulster at the Crossroads   III-1123
O'Neill, Robert J.
  German Army and the Nazi Party, 1933-1939, The   I-380, 381
O'Neill, William L.
  Coming Apart: An Informal History of America in the 1960's   I-533
Oppenheim, Edward Phillips
  Last Train Out   I-245
Oppenheimer, J. Robert
  Open Mind, The   II-689
Orfila, Alejandro
  "Cuba—and Beyond," in *Saturday Review*   III-1256
Orni, Efraim and Elisha Efrat
  Geography of Israel   III-1187
Ortega y Gasset, José
  Interpretation of Universal History, An   I-334
Orwell, George
  Nineteen Eighty-Four   I-341
Ostriker, Jeremiah
  "Nature of Pulsars, The," in *Scientific American.*   II-1015
Owen, Denis Frank
  What Is Ecology?   II-1076

Page, Martin
  Day Khrushchev Fell, The   II-980
Page, Robert M.
  "Early History of Radar, The," in *Annual Report of the Smithsonian Institution (1962)*   I-328
Panter-Downes, Mollie
  London War Notes, 1939-1945   I-437
Paradis, Adrian A.
  Labor in Action: The Story of the American Labor Movement   II-576
Pares, Bernard
  Fall of the Russian Monarchy: A Study of the Evidence, The   I-106
Patterson, Thomas E.
  "Press Coverage of the Presidential Campaign, 1976," in *Washington Post*   III-1309
Paterson, Thomas G., Garry J. Clifford and Kenneth J. Hagan
  American Foreign Policy: A History   III-1130
Patterson, Thomas G., ed.
  Cold War Critics   II-668
Paydarfar, Ali A.
  Social Change in a Southern Province of Iran   III-1345
Payne, Stanley G.
  Falange: A History of Spanish Fascism   II-

1049

Peattie, Mark R.
Ishiwara Kanji and Japan's Confrontation with the West I-367

Pechman, Joseph and Benjamin Okner
Who Bears the Tax Burden? II-855

Pedigree of Champions I-493

Pelz, Stephen E.
Race to Pearl Harbor: The Failure of the Second London Naval Conference and the Onset of World War II I-374

Penrose, Roger
"Black Holes," in *Scientific American* II-841

Percival, General Arthur E.
War in Malaya, The I-464

Pesticides: Actions Needed to Protect the Consumer from Defective Products II-948

Peterson, Mary Bennett
Regulated Consumer, The II-864

Pfeiffer, John E.
Emergence of Man, The I-223

Pick, Robert
Last Days of Imperial Vienna, The I-164

Pike, Douglas
"Vietnam During 1976: Economics in Command," in *Asian Survey* III-1250

Planck, Charles R.
Changing Status of German Reunification in Western Diplomacy, 1955-1966, The III-1173

Plischke, Elmer
Contemporary Governments of Germany III-1173
Summit Diplomacy: Personal Diplomacy of the President of the United States II-729

Plissner, Martin, *et al.*
Campaign '76 III-1309

Ploeg, J. van der
Excavations at Qumran: A Survey of the Judean Brotherhood and Its Ideas, The II-604

Polsby, Nelson W.; *et al.*
"Politics, Parties and 1976," in *National Journal Reprint* III-1309

Pomeroy, Wardell B.
Dr. Kinsey and the Institute for Sex Research II-624

Ponchaud, François
Cambodia: Year Zero III-1354

Pool, Ithiel de Sola, ed.
Social Impact of the Telephone, The II-618

Poole, Peter A.
China Enters the United Nations: A New Era Begins for the World Organization III-1116

Popper, Karl
Open Society and Its Enemies, The I-335

Porter, Gareth
"Vietnam's Long Road to Socialism," in *Current History* III-1250

Potter, G. R., *et al.*, eds.
New Cambridge Modern History, The I-30

Pounds, Norman J. G.
Divided Germany and Berlin II-653

Power Development

Powers, Francis Gary and Curt Gentry
Operation Overflight: The U-2 Spy Pilot Tells His Story for the First Time II-911

Preston, Paul, ed.
Spain in Crisis: The Evolution and Decline of the Franco Regime II-1049

Price, Alfred
Instruments of Darkness: The History of Electronic Warfare I-328

Prittie, Terence
Germany Divided: The Legacy of the Nazi Era II-653

Proffitt, Nicholas
"Texas! The Superstate," in *Newsweek* II-1082

Pryde, Lucy T.
Pesticides, Food, and Drugs II-948

Pugh, Dave and Mitch Zimmerman
"The 'Energy Crisis' and the Real Crisis Behind It," in *The Economic Crisis Reader* III-1144

Purcell, Edward M., Norman Feather, Emilio Segrè and James Chadwick
"Symposium III: The Discovery of the Neutron and Its Effects upon History," in *Proceedings of the Tenth International Congress of the History of Science* I-288

Pye, Lucian W.
Mao Tse-tung: The Man in the Leader III-1270

Quandt, William B., Fuad Jabber and Ann Mosely Lesch
Politics of Palestinian Nationalism, The I-240

Quester, George H.
Offense and Defense in the International System II-570

Quirk, Robert E.
Mexican Revolution, 1914-1915: The Convention at Aquascalientes, The I-78

Rabi, I. I., Robert Serber, Victor F. Weisskopf, Abraham Pais and Glenn Seaborg
Oppenheimer II-689

Ramachandran, G. and T. K. Mahadevan
Gandhi: His Relevance for Our Times I-179

Ramsey, Paul
"Shall We 'Reproduce'?," in *Journal of the American Medical Association* III-1330

Rand, Christopher T.
Making Democracy Safe for Oil III-1144

Randel, William P.
Centennial: American Life in 1876   III-1293
Rangel, Carlos
Latin Americans: Their Love-Hate Relationship with the United States, The   I-268
Rankin, Karl Lott
China Assignment   II-714
Rapoport, Roger
Great American Bomb Machine, The   II-689
Rather, Dan
Camera Never Blinks: Adventures of a TV Journalist, The   II-675
Rather, Dan and Gary Paul Gates
Palace Guard, The   III-1136
Rauschning, Hermann
Revolution of Nihilism: Warning to the West, The   I-196
Ravenal, Earl C.
"Toward Nuclear Stability: A Modest Proposal for Avoiding Armageddon," in *Atlantic*   I-1061
Ray, Sibnarayan, ed.
Gandhi, India and the World: An International Symposium   I-179
Record, Wilson and Jane Cassels Record, eds.
Little Rock: U.S.A.   II-774
Redmond, Kent C. and Thomas M. Smith
"Lessons from Project Whirlwind," in *Spectrum*   II-541
Reinsch, Paul Samuel
American Diplomat in China, An   I-127
Reitlinger, Gerald
House Built on Sand: The Conflicts of German Policy in Russia, 1939-1945, The   I-456
Religion in the Public Schools   II-954
Remak, Joachim
Origins of World War I, 1871-1914, The   I-52; II-924
Report of the Commission on Obscenity and Pornography   III-1180
Report of the National Advisory Commission on Civil Disorders   II-813
Rhodes, Robert I., ed.
Imperialism and Underdevelopment: A Reader   II-563
Rich, Norman
Hitler's War Aims   I-471
Hitler's War Aims. Vol. I: *Ideology, the Nazi State, and the Course of Expansion*   I-347, 381
Richardson, Elliot L.
Creative Balance, The   III-1192
Ridenour, Louis N., ed.
Radar System Engineering   I-328
Rienow, Robert and Leona Rienow
Moment in the Sun   II-549
Riesman, David, Revel Denney and Nathan Glazer

Lonely Crowd: A Study of the Changing American Character, The   I-533
Rioux, Marcel
Quebec in Question   II-826
Ripka, Hubert
Czechoslovakia Enslaved   II-633
Ristić, Dragiša N.
Yugoslavia's Revolution of 1941   I-449
Ritter, Gerhard
Sword and the Scepter: The Problem of Militarism in Germany, The   I-52; II-924
Roberts, Chalmers M.
"Planning of Asia Thrust Began in Late March," in *The Washington Post*   II-1090
Robertson, E. M.
Hitler's Pre-War Policy and Military Plans, 1933-1939   I-347, 354
Robertson, E. M., ed.
Origins of the Second World War: Historical Interpretation, The   I-347
Robertson, H. M.
Aspects of the Rise of Economic Individualism: Criticism of Max Weber and His School   I-45
Robinson, Francis
Separatism Among Indian Muslims: The Politics of the United Provinces' Muslims, 1860-1923   II-611
Rodinson, Maxime
Israel and the Arabs   I-151
Rogers, George, ed.
Change in Alaska: People, Petroleum, and Politics   II-797
Rohan, Bedrich
What Happened in Czechoslovakia   II-633
Romanus, Charles F. and Riley Sunderland
United States Army in World War II: China-Burma-India Theater; Stilwell's Command Problems, The   I-493
Rondot, Pierre
Changing Patterns of the Middle East, The   II-763
Roosa, Robert V.
Monetary Reform for the World Economy   II-1003
Roots, John McCook
Chou: An Informal Biography of China's Legendary Chou En-lai   III-1270
Roscow, James P.
800 Miles to Valdez: The Building of the Alaska Pipeline   II-1027
Rose, Norman
Gentile Zionists, The   I-240
Rosen, Saul
"Electronic Computers: A Historical Survey," in *Computing Surveys*   II-541
Rosenfeld, Alvin
Plot to Destroy Israel: The Road to Armageddon, The   III-1187

Rosinger, Lawrence K.
  China's Wartime Politics, 1937-1944   I-217
Roskill, Stephen W.
  Naval Policy Between the Wars. Vol. II: *The Period of Reluctant Rearmament, 1930-1939*   I-374
  Navy at War, 1939-1945, The   I-410
Ross, Frank, Jr.
  Partners in Space: A Study of the International Geophysical Year   II-769
Ross, Stanley R., ed.
  Is the Mexican Revolution Dead?   I-78
Roth, Cecil
  Dead Sea Scrolls: A New Historical Approach, The   II-604
Rouveral, Jean
  Pancho Villa: A Biography   I-78
Ruge, Friedrich
  Sea Warfare, 1939-1945   I-410
Ruland, Richard
  Rediscovery of American Literature: Premises of Critical Taste, 1900-1940, The   I-210
Rusinow, Dennison
  Yugoslav Experiment, 1948-1974, The   II-646
Ruskin, A. H.
  "AFL-CIO: A Confederation or, Federation? Which Road for the Future?" in *Annals of the American Academy of Political and Social Sciences: The Crisis in the American Trade Union Movement*   II-735
Russell, Bertrand
  Autobiography of Bertrand Russell, The   I-86
  Introduction to Mathematical Philosophy   I-86
  "Russia's Grand Design," in *Newsweek*   III-1323
Rutherford, Ernest
  "Bakerian Lecture: Nuclear Constitution of Atoms," in *Proceedings of the Royal Society of London*   I-288
Ryan, Cornelius
  Last Battle, The   I-485; II-583
Rybczynski, T. M.
  Economics of the Oil Crisis, The   II-916

Sachs, Ignacy
  Discovery of the Third World, The   II-563
Safire, William
  Before the Fall: An Inside View of the Pre-Watergate White House   III-1218
Sagan, Carl
  Cosmic Connection: An Extraterrestrial Perspective, The   III-1301
Saint John, Robert
  Ben-Gurion: A Biography   I-416
St. John-Stevas, Norman
  Right to Life, The   III-1286

Salisbury, Harrison E.
  900 Days: The Siege of Leningrad, The   I-456
Salisbury, William T. and James D. Theberge, eds.
  Spain in the 1970's: Economics, Social Structure, Foreign Policy   II-1049
Sampson, Anthony
  Seven Sisters, The   II-917; III-1144
  Sovereign State of I.T.T., The   II-618
Sanghri, Ramesh
  Shah of Iran, The   III-1345
Sayegh, Fayez A.
  Arab Unity: Hope and Fulfillment   I-500
Scalapino, Robert A.
  Democracy and the Party Movement in Prewar Japan: The Failure of the First Attempt   I-275
Schapiro, Leonard
  Communist Party of the Soviet Union, The   I-341; II-742
Schawlow, A. L. and C. H. Townes
  "Infrared and Optical Masers," in *The Physical Review*   II-885
Schiffrin, Harold Z.
  Sun Yat-sen and the Origins of the Chinese Revolution   I-99
Schiller, Herbert I.
  Mass Communications and American Empire   II-618
Schlesinger, Arthur M., Jr.
  Thousand Days: John F. Kennedy in the White House, A   II-933, 964
Schoenberger, Walter S.
  Decision of Destiny   I-394
Schoenberner, Gerhard
  Yellow Star: The Persecution of the Jews in Europe, 1933-1945, The   I-310
Schor, P. S.
  "Dust in the Chaco," in *The Living Age*   I-294
Schram, Martin
  Running for President, 1976: The Carter Campaign   III-1309
Schram, Stuart R.
  Political Thought of Mao Tse-tung, The   III-1271
Schroeder, Paul W.
  Axis Alliance and Japanese-American Relations, 1941, The   I-443, 471
Schroeter, Leonard
  Last Exodus, The   II-996
Schuettinger, Robert L.
  Lord Acton: Historian of Liberty   I-29
Schuman, F. L.
  War and Diplomacy in the French Republic: An Inquiry into Political Motivations and the Control of Foreign Policy   I-203
Schütz, Wilhelm W.
  Rethinking German Policy: New Approaches to Reunification   III-1173

Schwartz, Bernard, ed.
  Civil Rights. Vol. II,: *Statutory History of the United States*   II-972
Science   III-1316
Scott, George
  Rise and Fall of the League of Nations, The   I-282
Scott, Robert Falcon
  Scott's Last Expedition: The Journals of Captain R. F. Scott   I-68
Seaton, Albert
  Russo-German War, 1941-1945, The   I-486
Seaway in Canada's Transportation: An Economic Analysis, The   II-789
Selden, Mark
  Yenan Way in Revolutionary China, The   I-217
Sellin, Johan Thorsten and Richard D. Lambert, eds.
  Prisons in Transformation   II-892
Selsam, J. P.
  Attempts to Form an Anglo-French Alliance, 1919-1924, The   I-203
Sender, Ramón José
  Seven Red Sundays   I-245
Serrell, R., M. M. Astrahan, G. W. Patterson and I. B. Pyne
  "Evolution of Computing Machines and Systems, The" in *Proceedings of the IRE*   II-541
Seton-Watson, Hugh
  Decline of Imperial Russia, 1855-1914, The   I-106
Seymour, James D.
  China: The Politics of Revolutionary Reintegration   II-662
Shackleton, Edward
  "Antarctica, the Case of Permanent International Controls," in *World Affairs*   II-805
Shackleton, Ernest H.
  Heart of the Antarctic: Being the Story of the British Antarctic Expedition, 1907-1909, The   I-67
Shanks, Michael and John Lambert
  Common Market Today—and Tomorrow, The   III-1152
Shapiro, Leonard
  Communist Party of the Soviet Union, The   II-742
Shaplen, Robert
  Road from War: Vietnam, 1965-1970, The   II-1042
Shaw, Bruno, ed.
  Selected Works of Mao Tse-tung   II-662
Shaw, Stanford J. and Ezel Kural Shaw
  History of the Ottoman Empire and Modern Turkey. Vol. II: *Reform, Revolution, and Republic: The Rise of Modern Turkey, 1808-1975*   I-119

Shearer, Lloyd
  "Intelligence Report—Behind the Scenes," in *Parade*   III-1310
Sheldon, Walt
  Honorable Conquerors: The Occupation of Japan, 1945-1952, The   II-590
Shelton, William
  American Space Exploration: The First Decade   II-781
Shepherd, George W. J.
  Anti-Apartheid: Transnational Conflict and Western Policy in the Liberation of South Africa   III-1278
Sherrill, Robert
  Gothic Politics in the Deep South: Stars of the New Confederacy   II-774
Siddiqui, Kalim
  Conflict, Crisis, and War in Pakistan   II-1095
"Siege of Wounded Knee, The," in *Newsweek*   II-871
Silberman, Charles E.
  Crisis in the Classroom: The Remaking of American Education   I-518
Silberman, Charles E.
  Crisis in the Classroom: The Remaking of American Education   I-518
Sills, David L., ed.
  International Encyclopedia of the Social Sciences   I-30
Simon, John Allsebrook
  Retrospect: The Memoirs of Viscount Simon   I-282
Simpich, Frederick
  Anatomy of Hawaii   II-797
Simson, Brigadier Ivan
  Singapore: Too Little, Too Late: Some Aspects of the Malayan Disaster in 1942   I-464
Sizer, Theodore R., ed.
  Religion and Public Education   II-954
Skotheim, Robert Allen
  American Intellectual Histories and Historians   I-210
Smith, Bernard
  "Parrington's *Main Currents of American Thought*," in *Books That Changed Our Minds*   I-210
Smith, D. M.
  Italy: A Modern History   I-144
Smith, David T., ed.
  Abortion and the Law: Essays by B. James George, Jr., and Others   III-1160
Smith, Francis Graham
  Pulsars   II-1015
Smith, Hedrick
  "Cambodian Decision: Why President Acted," in *The New York Times*   II-1090
  Russians, The   II-996

Smith, Ralph
"Vietnam's Fourth Party Congress," in *World Today*   III-1250
Smith, Richard Austin, *et al.*
Frontier States: Alaska and Hawaii, The   II-797
Smith, Sara R.
Manchurian Crisis, 1931-1932: A Tragedy in International Relations, The   I-275
Smith, William Ward
Midway: Turning Point of the Pacific   I-477
Snow, Edgar
Battle for Asia, The   I-367
Red China Today: The Other Side of the River   II-662
Red Star over China   II-662
Snyder, Louis L.
German Nationalism: The Tragedy of a People   I-62
Solinger, Dorothy J.
Regional Government and Political Integration in Southwest China, 1949-1954: A Case Study   II-662
Solzhenitsyn, Alexander
Détente: Prospects for Democracy and Dictatorship   III-1263
Gulag Archipelago, The   I-341
Sorensen, Theodore C.
Kennedy   II-933; 964
Southern Africa Literature List   II-987
"Soviet's Dangerous Game on Africa's Horn," in *Business Week*.   III-1323
"Special Bicentennial Issue," in *Time*.   III-1283
"Special Bicentennial Supplement," in *U.S. News & World Report*   III-1293
"Special 1776 Issue," in *Time*   III-1293
Stafford, Edward P.
Big E: Story of the U.S.S. Enterprise, The   I-478
"State of Emergency Declared!" in *MS*   II-1002
Stern, Fritz
Failure of Illiberalism: Essays on the Political Culture of Modern Germany, The   II-924
Stern, Philip
Rape of the Taxpayer, The   II-855
Stevens, Leonard A.
Equal!: The Case of Integration vs. Jim Crow   II-898
Storry, Richard
Double Patriots: A Study of Japanese Nationalism, The   I-275
Stover, John F.
American Railroads   I-524
Strachey, Lytton
Eminent Victorians: Cardinal Manning, Dr. Arnold, Florence Nightingale, General Gordon   I-86

Strong, Donald
Issue Voting and Party Realignment   III-1310
Stuart, J.
History of the Zulu Rebellion, 1906, and of Dinuzulu's Arrest, Trial and Expatriation, A   I-91
Sturtevant, A. H. and G. W. Beadle
Introduction to Genetics, An   I-12
Sullivan, Walter
Black Holes: The Edge of Space and Time   II-841
Sullivan, W. T., III, *et al.*
"Eavesdropping: The Radio Signature of the Earth," in *Science*   II-834
Sunderland, Lane V.
Obscenity: The Court, the Congress, and the President's Commission   III-1180
"Surgery: Fascination and Lessons," in *Time*   II-1021
Sykes, Christopher
Crossroads to Israel   I-240
Szulc, Tad
Energy Crisis, The   III-1144
Illusion of Peace: Foreign Policy in the Nixon Years, The   III-1218

Taber, Robert
M-26, The Biography of a Revolution   II-750
Taft, Phillip A.
Organized Labor in American History   II-735
Talbott, Strobe
"Who Concealed What to Whom," in *Time*   II-1061
Tamkoc, Metin
Warrior Diplomats: Guardians of the National Security and Modernization of Turkey, The   III-1199
Tanham, George K.
Communist Revolutionary Warfare: From the Vietminh to the Viet Cong   II-702
Tansill, Charles Callan
Back Door to War: The Roosevelt Foreign Policy, 1933-1941   I-471
Tanzer, Michael
Energy Crisis: World Struggle for Power and Wealth, The   III-1144
Tate, Merze
United States and Armaments, The   I-374
Tawney, R. H.
Religion and the Rise of Capitalism: A Historical Study   I-45
Taylor, A. J. P.
Habsburg Monarchy, 1809-1918: A History of the Austrian Empire and Austria-Hungary, The   I-165
Origins of the Second World War, The   I-354, 381
Second World War, The   I-437

Struggle for Mastery in Europe, 1848-1918, The   *I-53, 144*
Taylor, Gordon Rattray
   Biological Time Bomb, The   III-1330
Taylor, John G.
   Black Holes: The End of the Universe?   II-841
Tedlock, Ernest Warnock
   Steinbeck and His Critics: A Record of Twenty-five Years   I-424
Teller, Edward and Allen Brown
   Legacy of Hiroshima, The   II-689
Temperley, A. C.
   Whispering Gallery of Europe, The   I-282
Terzani, Tiziano
   Giai Phong!: The Fall and Liberation of Saigon   III-1233
Thayer, Carlyle A.
   "Dilemmas of Development in Vietnam," in *Current History*   III-1250
Theoharis, Athan
   Seeds of Repression: Harry S Truman and the Origins of McCarthyism   II-668
"There's a Ring, By Jupiter," in *Time*   III-1316
"This Land of Ours," in *National Geographic*   III-1293
Thomas, Hugh
   Cuba: The Pursuit of Freedom, 1762-1969   II-749, 933; III-1256
   Spanish Civil War, The   II-1049
Thompson, Leonard Monteath
   Unification of South Africa, 1902-1910, The   I-91
Thompson, Sir Robert
   Peace Is Not at Hand   III-1166
Thompson, W. Scott
   Lessons of Vietnam, The   III-1166
Thompson, Wayne C.
   "September Program: Reflections on the Evidence, The," in *Central European History*   II-925
Thomsen, Dietrick E.
   "Looking for LGM's," in *Science News*   II-834
Thorne, Christopher
   Limits of Foreign Policy: The West, the League and the Far Eastern Crisis of 1931-1933, The   I-275
Thorne, Kip
   "Search for Black Holes, The," in *Scientific American*   II-841
Thornton, A. P.
   Imperial Idea and Its Enemies: A Study in British Power, The   I-37
Tibor, Méray
   Thirteen Days That Shook the Kremlin   II-742
Tien, Hung-mao
   Government and Politics in Kuomintang China, 1927-1937   I-217

Tihany, Leslie Charles
   Baranya Dispute, 1918-1921: Diplomacy in the Vortex of Ideologies, The   I-187
Tobias, Fritz
   Reichstag Fire, The   I-318
Tökes, Rudolf L., ed.
   Dissent in the U.S.S.R.: Politics, Ideology and People   II-997
Toland, John
   Adolf Hitler   I-318, 380
   Last 100 Days, The   I-485
"Too Many Too Soon?," in *Time*   II-1021
Trenn, Thaddeus, J.
   "Rutherford and Recoil Atoms: The Metamorphosis and Success of a Once Stillborn Theory," in *Historical Studies in the Physical Sciences*   I-288
Triffin, Robert
   Gold and the Dollar Crisis: The Future of Convertibility   III-1103
   Our International Monetary System: Yesterday, Today and Tomorrow   III-1103
Trilling, Lionel
   "Reality in America," in *The Liberal Imagination: Essays on Literature and Society*   I-210
Trunk, Isaiah
   Judenrat: The Jewish Councils in Eastern Europe Under Nazi Occupation   I-403
Trythall, J. W. D.
   El Caudillo: A Political Biography of Franco   II-1049
Tsuji, Masanobu
   Singapore: The Japanese Version   I-464
Tsurumi, Kazuko
   Social Change and the Individual: Japan Before and After Defeat in World War II   II-590
Tuchman, Barbara W.
   Stilwell and the American Experience in China, 1911-1945   I-367
Tuleja, Thaddeus V.
   Climax at Midway   I-478
"Turmoil in Africa: Will Carter Act?" in *U.S. News & World Report*   III-1323
Turner, Leonard Charles Frederick
   Origins of the First World War   II-924
Turner, Robert F.
   Vietnamese Communism, its Origins and Development   II-702
Tussing, Arlon R., G. W. Rogers and V. Fischer
   Alaska Pipeline Report   II-1027
Tyler, Poyntz
   Outlook for the Railroads   I-524
Uhalley, Stephen, Jr.
   Mao Tse-tung: A Critical Biography   III-1271
Ulam, Adam B.
   Expansion and Coexistence: The History of Soviet Foreign Policy, 1917-1967   II-911
   Rivals: America and Russia Since World War

II, The   II-668, 729
Titoism and the Cominform   II-646
"Ultimate Operation, The," in *Time*   II-1021
U.S. Department of Commerce
  Survey of Current Business   II-1068
U.S. Department of Labor, Bureau of Labor Statistics
  Employment and Earnings   II-1068
  Handbook of Labor Statistics 1974   II-1068
United States Department of State
  Conference on Antarctica: Washington, October 15-December 1, 1959, The   II-805
  "Multilateral Antarctic Treaty, The" in *United States Treaties and Other International Agreements*   II-805
  United States Foreign Policy, 1972   III-1130
U.S. General Accounting Office
  "More Attention Should Be Paid to Making the U.S. Less Vulnerable to Foreign Oil Price and Supply Decisions."   III-1145
United States Strategic Bombing Survey, The
  Air Campaigns of the Pacific War   I-493
  Summary Report: (Pacific War).   I-493
  The Strategic Air Operations of Very Heavy Bombardment in the War Against Japan (Twentieth Air Force)   I-493
Utley, Jonathan G.
  "Upstairs, Downstairs at Foggy Bottom: Oil Exports and Japan, 1940-41," in *Prologue, the Journal of the National Archives*   I-443

Valiani, Leo
  End of Austria-Hungary, The   I-164
Van den Berghe, Pierre
  South Africa, A Study in Conflict   III-1278
Van der Waerden, B. L., ed.
  Sources of Quantum Mechanics, Classics of Science   I-173
Vandenbosch, Amry and Richard Butwell
  Changing Face of Southeast Asia, The   II-707
Vanezis, P. N.
  Makarios: Faith and Power   III-1199
Van Pelt, W. F., *et al.*
  Laser Fundamentals and Experiments   II-885
Vansina, Jan
  Kingdoms of the Savannah   III-1226
Van Slyke, Lyman P.
  Enemies and Friends: The United Front in Chinese Communist History   I-217
Van Voris, William H.
  Violence in Ulster: An Oral Documentary   III-1123

Verghese, B. G.
  End to Confrontation (Bhutto's Pakistan): Restructuring the Sub-Continent, An   II-1096
Vernon, Raymond
  Oil Crisis, The   II-917
Vital Speeches   II-714
Von Laue, Theodore H.
  Why Lenin? Why Stalin? A Reappraisal of the Russian Revolution, 1900-1930   I-106
"*Voyager I*: Active Io, Jolting Jupiter," in *Science News*   III-1316

Wade, Mason
  French Canadians 1760-1967, The   II-826
Wagner, Richard H.
  Environment and Man   II-1076
Wagner, Susan
  "NOW Campaigns for Law to Bar Sex Bias in Texts," in *Publishers Weekly*   II-1002
Wahl, Jean
  Short History of Existentialism, A   I-259
Wakeman, Frederic, Jr.
  History and Will: Philosophical Perspectives of Mao Tse-tung's Thought   III-1271
Walshe, Peter
  Rise of African Nationalism in South Africa, The   III-1278
Walters, Francis Paul
  History of the League of Nations, A   I-282
Wandycz, P. S.
  France and Her Eastern Allies, 1919-1925: French-Czechoslovak-Polish Relations from the Paris Peace Conference to Locarno   I-203
Ward, A. W., G. W. Prothero and Stanley Leathes, eds.
  Cambridge Modern History, Planned by Lord Acton, The   I-30
Ward, Barbara
  Spaceship Earth   II-1076
Ward, John M.
  Colonial Self-Government: The British Experience, 1759-1856   I-23
Ward, Richard J., Don Peretz and E. M. Wilson
  Palestine State: A Rational Approach, The   I-417
Warren, Harris Gaylord
  "Political Aspects of the Paraguayan Revolution, 1936-1940," in *The Hispanic American Historical Review*   I-294
Warren, Robert Penn
  Who Speaks for the Negro?   II-898
Warshofsky, Fred
  Control of Life in the 21st Century, The   II-1021
Watson, Francis
  Trial of Mr. Gandhi, The   I-180

Watson-Watt, Robert Alexander
  *Pulse of Radar: The Autobiography of Sir
  Robert Watson-Watt, The*   I-328
Weber, William T.
  "Kissinger as Historian: A Historiographical
  Approach to Statesmanship," in *World
  Affairs, A Quarterly Review of Interna-
  tional Problems*   II-1090
Weinberg, Gerhard L.
  *Foreign Policy of Hitler's Germany: Diplo-
  matic Revolution in Europe, 1933-1936,
  The*   I-282
  *Germany and the Soviet Union, 1939-
  1941*   I-449
Weizmann, Chaim
  *Trial and Error: The Autobiography of Chaim
  Weizmann*   I-240
Wendt, Herbert
  From Ape to Adam   I-224
Werth, Alexander
  Russia at War, 1941-1945   I-456
Westmoreland, William C.
  Soldier Reports, A   II-1042
Wheeler, Gerald
  *Prelude to Pearl Harbor: The United States
  Navy and the Far East, 1921-1931*   I-
  374
Wheeler-Bennett, John W.
  *Nemesis of Power: The German Army in
  Politics, 1918-1945, The*   I-354,380
Whelan, Kenneth
  *How the Golden Age of Television Turned
  My Hair to Silver*   II-675
Whitaker, Arthur P.
  *Western Hemisphere Idea: Its Rise and De-
  cline, The*   I-268
Whitaker, John
  *Striking a Balance: Environment and Natural
  Resources Policy in the Nixon-Ford
  Years*   II-880
White, Theodore H.
  *Breach of Faith: The Fall of Richard
  Nixon*   III-1192
Whitney, Courtney
  MacArthur: His Rendezvous with History
  II-682
Whorton, James
  Before Silent Spring: *Pesticides and Public
  Health in Pre-DDT America*   I-429
Widger, William N.
  Meteorological Satellites   II-757
Wildes, Harry Emerson
  *Typhoon in Tokyo: The Occupation and Its
  Aftermath*   II-590
Wilhoit, Francis M.
  Politics of Massive Resistance, The   II-774
Wilk, Max
  *Golden Age of Television: Notes from the
  Survivors, The*   II-675
Williams and Wilkins v. *the United States. Su-
  preme Court Review*   I-388

Williams, Glanville Llewelyn
  *Sanctity of Life and the Criminal Law,
  The*   III-1160
Williams, William Appleman
  Tragedy of American Diplomacy, The   I-
  471
Willoughby, Charles A. and John Chamberlain
  MacArthur 1941-1951   II-682
Wilmot, Chester
  Struggle for Europe, The   I-437; II-583
Wilson, Edmund
  Scrolls from the Dead Sea, The   II-604
Winks, Robin W., ed.
  Age of Imperialism, The   I-37
Wise, David and Thomas B. Ross
  U-2 Affair, The   II-911
Witcover, Jules
  *Marathon: The Pursuit of the Presidency
  1972-1976*   III-1310
Witkin, Richard
  Challenge of the Sputniks, The   II-781
Wolfe, Thomas W.
  Soviet Power and Europe, 1945-1970   II-
  720
Wolfers, Arnold, ed.
  *Changing East-West Relations and the Unity
  of the West*   II-597
Wolff, Robert Lee
  Balkans in Our Time, The   II-645
Wolpert, Stanley
  New History of India, A   II-611
Womack, John
  Zapata and the Mexican Revolution   I-78
"Women vs. ABC," in *Newsweek*   II-1002
Wren, Jack
  Great Battles of World War I, The   I-137
"Worlds of Jupiter, The," in *Science News*
  III-1316
Wukelic, George E., ed.
  *Handbook of Soviet Space Science Re-
  search*   II-781
Wylie, I. A. R.
  To the Vanquished   I-245

Xydis, Stephen George
  Cyprus: Reluctant Republic   III-1198

Yen, Ch'ing-huang
  *Overseas Chinese and the 1911 Revolution,
  The*   I-99
Young, Ernest P.
  *Presidency of Yüan Shih-k'ai: Liberalism
  and Dictatorship in Early Republican China,
  The*   I-99, 128
Young, Mayor of Detroit et al. v. *American Mini
  Theaters Inc. et al.*   III-1181
Youngblood, Gene
  *Expanded Cinema: The Audio-Visual Exten-
  sions of Man*   II-675

Zaretsky, Irving I. and Mark P. Leone, eds.

Religious Movements in Contemporary America   I-512

Zasloff, Joseph J. and MacAlister Brown
"Passion of Kampuchea, The," in *Problems of Communism*   III-1354

Zinn, Howard

SNCC: The New Abolitionists   II-973

Ziring, Lawrence
Ayub Khan Era: Politics in Pakistan, 1958-1969, The   II-1096

Zonis, Marvin
Political Elite of Iran, The   III-1345

REPRINTS

OF ALL INDEXES

FROM

GREAT EVENTS FROM HISTORY

Ancient and Medieval Series
Modern European Series
American Series

INDEXES

VOLUMES ONE, TWO, AND THREE

Ancient and Medieval Series

ALPHABETICAL LIST OF EVENTS

Abélard Writes *Sic et Non*   III-1313
Accession of Basil II   III-1215
Adoption of the Heavy Plow   II-1099
Advances in Hellenistic Astronomy   I-398
Aeschylus Writes the *Oresteia*   I-248
Alexander's Victory at Gaugamela   I-358
Anselm Writes the *Cur Deus Homo*   III-1291
Appearance of the Gilgamesh Epic   I-40
Appearance of the Intertestamental Jewish Apocrypha   I-443
Appearance of the Sibylline Books   I-200
Appearance of the Waldensians   III-1381
Appearance of the *Zohar*   III-1559
Appearance of Zoroastrian Ditheism   I-163
Apollo's Revelations at Delphi   I-120
Aristotle Writes the *Politics*   I-343
Aristotle's Isolation of Science as a Discipline   I-363
Athenian Invasion of Sicily   I-308
Augustine Writes the *City of God*   II-940
Augustine Writes the *Contra Julianum*   II-946
Avicenna Compiles the *Canon of Medicine*   III-1226

Battle of Actium   I-551
Battle of Adrianople   II-898
Battle of Chaeronea   I-338
Battle of Châlons   II-975
Battle of Hastings   III-1248
Battle of Kadesh   I-70
Battle of Manzikert   III-1253
Battle of Tours   II-1117
Battle of Zama   I-437
Beginning of the Rome-Constantinople Schism   III-1237
Beginnings of Metaphysics   I-231
Beginnings of Renaissance Sculpture   III-1665
Beginnings of Trigonometry   II-716
Birth of Islam   II-1075
Birth of Jesus   I-567
Boethius Writes the *Consolation of Philosophy*   II-1018
Building of Santa Sophia   II-1040
Building of the Appian Way   I-373
Building of the Great Pyramid   I-25
Building of the Parthenon   I-276
Building of the Roman Aqueducts   II-626
Building of the Slavic Alphabet   II-1173
Building of the Temple   I-101

Caesar's Conquest of Gaul   I-516
Calling of the Albigensian Crusade   III-1441
Calling the Council of Constance   III-1680
Capture of Constantinople by the Crusaders   III-1436
Cato Writes the *De Agri Cultura*   I-465

Celebration of the Eleusinian Mysteries   I-158
Celebration of the Last Supper   II-595
Chartres' Preservation of Classical Learning   III-1231
Chaucer Writes the *Canterbury Tales*   III-1655
Cicero Writes the *De Officiis*   I-541
Cicero Writes the *De Oratore*   I-521
Cicero Writes the *De Republica*   I-526
Clement of Rome Addresses the Corinthians   II-667
Codification of the Canon Law   III-1491
"Commissioning" of the Septuagint   I-418
Commissioning of the Vulgate   II-909
Compilation of the Muratorian Canon   II-767
Compilation of the *Summa Theologiae*   III-1544
Compilation of the Talmud   II-985
Completion of the Augustan Settlement   I-562
Composition of Egyptian Wisdom Literature   I-35
Composition of the Book of Genesis   I-96
Composition of the *Defensor Pacis*   III-1608
Composition of the Nibelungenlied   III-1405
Composition of the *Romance of the Rose*   III-1467
Composition of the *Song of Roland*   III-1308
Conception of the Apostolic Succession, The   II-742
Conception of Mechanistic Atomism   I-264
Condemnation of Christian Averroism   III-1564
Condemnation of Jesus   II-601
Condemnation of Wycliffe   III-1640
Conduct of the Ministry of Jesus   II-589
Conquests of Genghis Khan   III-1462
Consolidation of France   III-1733
Conversion of Clovis   II-995
Conversion of Constantine   II-846
Conversion of Hungary   III-1210
Conversion of Ireland   II-969
Conversion of Lithuania   III-1650
Conversion of Northumbria   II-1081
Conversion of Russia   III-1205
Coronation of Pepin   II-1131
Creation of the Athenian Empire   I-242
Creation of the "Holy Roman Empire"   III-1195
Creation of the Imperial Bureaucracy   II-621
Creation of the New Comedy   I-368
Creation of the Sexagesimal System   I-21
Crystallization of the *Code of Barcelona*   III-1514
Crystallization of the New Testament   II-779

Culmination of the Synthesis of Islamic and Greek Thought   III-1395
Cultivation of Polyphony   III-1409
Cultural Development at the Court of Harun al-Rashid   II-1142
Cybele's Introduction into Rome   I-432

Dante Writes the *Divine Comedy*   III-1598
Death of Socrates   I-318
Declaration of the First Punic War   I-408
Declaration of the Pragmatic Sanction of Bourges   III-1703
Dedication of Aelia Capitolina   II-702
Defeat in Teutoburger Forest   II-578
Deification of Ptolemy Philadelphus   I-403
Delineation of the Seven Sacraments   III-1338
Destruction of Pompeii   II-659
Destruction of the Golden Horde   III-1742
Destruction of the Serapeum   II-924
Development of Gothic Architecture   III-1416
Development of Lenses   III-1555
Development of Scientific Cattle Breeding   III-1426
Development of the Antiochene Episcopacy   II-681
Development of the Christian Calendar   II-877
Development of the Guilds of Florence   III-1303
Development of the Miracle Play   III-1221
Development of the Penitential System   II-762
Discoveries of Archimedes   I-422
Discovery of America   III-1756
"Discovery" of Iron   I-58
Discussion of the Date of Easter   II-857
Dissemination of the *Book of the Dead*   I-52
Domestication of the Camel   I-30
Domestication of the Horse   I-1
Drafting of the *Breviarium* of Alaric II   II-1005

Editing of the Chronicles of Julius Africanus   II-789
Election of Hugh Capet to the Throne of France   III-1200
Election of Pope Clement VII   III-1644
Emergence of Austria   III-1364
Emergence of Greek Medicine   I-302
Emergence of Modern Western Painting   III-1587
Emergence of Papal Decretals   II-914
Emergence of Perspective in Painting   III-1691
Emergence of "Theology" as a Concept   II-757
Emergence of the Common Law in England   III-1386

Emergence of the English Vernacular   III-1287
Enactment of the Canuleian Law   I-281
Enactment of the Julian Law   I-506
Enactment of the "Provisions of Oxford"   III-1528
Enactment of the Statute of Winchester   III-1569
Enforcement of Clerical Celibacy   III-1257
Enunciation of the *Dictatus Papae*   III-1263
Enunciation of the "Golden Bull"   III-1635
Establishment of Alcuin's Palace School   II-1136
Establishment of Castile's School of Translation   III-1524
Establishment of the *Cursus Honorum*   I-448
Establishment of the Julian Calendar   I-536
Establishment of the Kingdom of Israel   I-106
Establishment of the Liturgical Year   II-1091
Establishment of the Rhine-Danube Frontier   II-584
Establishment of the School of Prince Henry the Navigator   III-1686
Establishment of the See of Canterbury   II-1058
Establishment of the United Kingdom   I-90
Establishment of Vivarium   II-1046
Establishment of Yahweh's Covenant with Israel   I-84
Eusebius Writes His *Ecclesiastical History*   II-840
Excommunication of Theodosius   II-920
Exegesis of Maimonides   III-1391
Exploitation of the Arch   I-501
Expulsion of the Jews from Spain   III-1752

Failure of Akhenaten's Cultural Revival   I-64
Failure of Julian's Pagan Revival   II-888
Failure of the Seventh Crusade   III-1496
Fall of Acre   III-1574
Fall of Babylon   I-179
Fall of Constantinople   III-1718
Fall of Granada   III-1747
"Fall" of Rome   II-980
Flourishing of the Court of Cordoba   II-1189
Flowering of Late Medieval Physics   III-1614
Forging of the "Donation of Constantine"   II-1121
Formalization of Geometry   I-383
Formalization of the Idea of Usury   III-1519
Formalization of the Liturgy of the Mass   II-1069
Formation of the Roman Symbol   II-752
Formation of the Scipionic Circle   I-453
Formulation of Logic   I-348
Formulation of the Multiple-Element Hypothesis   I-270
Formulation of the Nicene Creed   II-867

Formulation of the "Twelve Tables" of Roman Law   I-253
Formulation of Ulpian's Dictum   II-784
Founding of Alexandria   I-353
Founding of Cluny   II-1184
Founding of Constantinople   II-862
Founding of Luxeuil and Bobbio   II-1052
Founding of Monte Cassino and the Rule of Saint Benedict   II-1029
Founding of Syracuse   I-129
Founding of the Alexandrian School of Exegesis   II-795
Founding of the Franciscans   III-1447
Founding of the Platonic Academy of Florence   III-1723
Founding of the Pythagorean Brotherhood   I-194
Founding of the University of Paris   III-1400

Gaius' Edition of the *Institutes* of Roman Law   II-721
Gelasius' Statements on Church-State Relationships   II-989
Genesis of the Trivium and Quadrivium   II-1000
Granting of the Charter of Lorris   III-1323
Gregory's Recognition of "Vulgar Christianity"   II-1063
Growth of Manichaean Gnosticism   II-807
Growth of the Fairs of Champagne   III-1421

Hebrew Exodus from Egypt   I-75
Hesiod's Composition of the *Theogony*   I-139
Homer's Composition of the *Iliad*   I-110

Imperial Visit to Canossa   III-1269
Improvements in Horse Transportation   II-1169
Improvements in Shipbuilding and Navigation   III-1503
Inauguration of the Dominate   II-829
Inauguration of the Feast of Christmas   II-884
Inauguration of the Olympic Games   I-115
Inception of Christian Apologetics   II-707
Inception of Church-State Problems   II-852
Innovations in Medieval Prosody   III-1349
Institution of the Formulary System   I-491
Institution of the Inquisition   III-1484
Institution of the Plebeian Tribunate   I-221
Introduction of Arabic Numerals   III-1282
Introduction of Christianity into Germany   II-1126
Introduction of the Wheel   I-5
Invasion of the Black Death   III-1625
Invention of Bronze   I-16
Invention of Coinage   I-144
Invention of Gunpowder   III-1509
Invention of Printing   III-1713
Isidore of Seville Writes the *Etymologies*   II-1086

Issuance of Draco's Code   I-153
Issuance of the Decree *Licet Juris*   III-1620
Issuance of the *Lex Hortensia*   I-393
Institution of the Alimentary System   II-675
Ivan III's Organization of the "Third Rome"   III-1738

Jerome Writes the *Contra Vigilantium*   II-929
Joan of Arc's Relief of Orléans   III-1697
John of Damascus Writes the Fountain of Knowledge   II-1111
John of Salisbury's Expression of Political Theory   III-1370
Judah Halevi Writes the *Kuzari*   III-1334

Legislation of Solon   I-168
Leonardo da Vinci Paints the *Last Supper*   III-1761
Lucretius Writes the *De Rerum Natura*   I-511

March of the Ten Thousand   I-313
Marcus Aurelius Writes the *Meditations*   II-725
Marius' Creation of the Private Army   I-496
Martyrdom of Ignatius of Antioch   II-696
Martyrdom of Saint Peter in Rome   II-643
Medical Writings of Rhazes   II-1179
Meeting of the Fourth Lateran Council   III-1457
Misidentification of Dionysius the Areopagite   II-1011
Murder of Thomas à Becket   III-1375

Naval Law of Themistocles, The   I-226
Nero's Persecution of the Christians   II-638
Nicholas of Cusa Writes *De Docta Ignorantia*   III-1708

Origen's Teaching on the Natural Law   II-801
Origin of *Municipia*   I-333
Origin of Writing   I-10
Outbreak of the Decian Persecution   II-812
Outbreak of the Nestorian Controversy   II-952
Ovid Writes the *Metamorphoses*   II-573

Paul Writes His Letter to the Romans   II-632
Penetration of the Baltic by the Teutonic Knights   III-1472
Perfection of the Greek Choral Lyric   I-215
Persian Invasion of Greece   I-237
Phidias Creates the Statue of Zeus at Olympia   I-297
Philo's Hellenization of Judaism   II-612
Plato Develops the Theory of Ideas   I-323
Pliny the Elder Compiles the *Natural History*   II-653

Plotinus' Conception of Neoplatonism   II-823

Plutarch's Popularization of Biography   II-686

Popularization of Experimental Science   III-1539

Porphyry's Commentaries of the *Categories* of Aristotle   II-834

Postulation of the Geocentric System   II-712

Postulation of the Logos   I-210

Preaching of John Huss, The   III-1675

Preaching of the First Crusade   III-1276

Preaching of the Pentecostal Gospel   II-607

Presentation of Leo's *Tome*   II-963

Presentation of the Recapitulation Theory   II-747

Priscian Writes the *Institutiones Grammaticae*   II-1023

Professionalization of History   I-259

Promulgation of Hammurabi's Code   I-45

Promulgation of Justinian's *Code*   II-1035

Promulgation of Theodosius' Edicts   II-904

Promulgation of the Statute of Praemunire   III-1630

Pronouncement of the Bull *Unam Sanctam*   III-1592

Proscriptions of the Second Triumvirate   I-546

Publication of Celsus' *True Word*   II-731

Publication of Galen's Medical Writings   II-737

Radbertus' Discussion of the Eucharist   II-1164

Rationalization of Ethics   I-328

Recognition of the University of Salerno   III-1478

Re-Creation of Western Empire   II-1146

Refinement of Latin Prose   I-531

Refinements in Banking   III-1359

Reform of the Spanish Church   III-1728

Reforms of Cleisthenes, The   I-205

Regularization of Papal Elections   III-1243

Return from the Captivity   I-189

Revelation of Jeremiah, The   I-149

Revenue Laws of Ptolemy Philadelphus   I-413

Revival of Classical Themes in Painting   III-1766

Revival of Roman Law   III-1344

Revolt of the Maccabees   I-459

Rise of Courtly Love   III-1296

Rise of Parthia   I-427

Rise of Philosophy   I-173

Rise of the Christian Platonists   II-773

Rise of the Hansa   III-1430

Rise of the Pharisees   I-477

Roman Conquest of Britain   II-616

Roman Destruction of the Temple at Jerusalem   II-648

Sack of Rome, The   II-935

Saint Bernard's Expression of Mysticism   III-1329

Settlement of the Iconoclastic Struggle   II-1152

Signing of Magna Carta   III-1452

Signing of the Concordat of Worms   III-1318

Skepticism of the Middle Academy   I-471

Spartan Conquest of Messenia   I-134

Statement of Trajan's Religious Policy   II-692

Stephen's Use of the Primacy Text   II-818

Stoic Conception of Natural Law   I-388

Summoning of the Council of Sardica   II-872

Summoning of the Model Parliament   III-1581

Swiss Victory at Morgarten   III-1603

Synod of Jamnia   II-664

Tarik's Crossing into Spain   II-1105

Teaching of Amos, The   I-125

Teaching of Euhemerus, The   I-378

Teaching of Second Isaiah, The   I-184

Teachings of the Sophists, The   I-286

Thomas à Kempis Writes the *Imitation of Christ*   III-1670

Thucydides Writes the *History of the Peloponnesian War*   I-292

Transference of Pergamum to Rome   I-486

Transmission of the Alphabet   I-80

Travels of Marco Polo   III-1550

Treaty of Verdun   II-1158

Tribunate of Tiberius Sempronius Gracchus   I-481

Turkish Conquest of Serbia   III-1660

Upsurge of Venetian Trade with the East   III-1354

Vandal Seizure of Carthage   II-958

Vergil Writes the *Aeneid*   I-556

Vincent of Beauvais Compiles the *Speculum Maius*   III-1533

Writing of Basil the Great's Theological Works   II-893

KEY WORD INDEX FOR EVENTS

Acre, Fall of   III-1574
Actium, Battle of   I-551
Adrianople, Battle of   II-898
Aelia Capitolina, Dedication of the   II-702
Aeneid, Vergil Writes the   I-556
Africanus, Editing of the Chronicles of Julius II-789
Akhenaten's Cultural Revival, Failure of I-64
Alcuin's Palace School, Establishment of II-1136
Alexandria, The Founding of   I-353
Alexandrian School of Exegesis, Founding of the II-795
Alimentary System, Institution of the   II-675
Alphabet, Transmission of the   I-80
America, Discovery of   III-1756
Amos, The Teaching of   I-125
Antiochene Episcopacy, Development of the II-681
Apologetics, Inception of Christian   II-707
Apostolic Succession, The Conception of II-742
Appian Way, Building of the   I-373
Aqueducts, Building of the Roman   II-626
Arabic Numerals, Introduction of   III-1282
Arch, Exploitation of the   I-501
Archimedes, Discoveries of   I-422
Aristotle, Porphyry's Commentaries on the *Categories* of   II-834
Astronomy, Advances in Hellenistic   I-398
Athenian Empire, Creation of the   I-242
Augustan Settlement, Completion of the   I-562
Austria, Emergence of   III-1364
Averroism, Condemnation of Christian   III-1564

Babylon, Fall of   I-179
Banking, Refinements in   III-1359
Basil the Great's Theological Works, Writing of II-893
Basil II, Accession of   III-1215
Benedict, Founding of Monte Casino and the Rule of Saint   II-1029
Biography, Plutarch's Popularization of   II-686
Black Death, Invasion of the   III-1625
Bobbio, Founding of Luxeuil and   II-1052
Book of the Dead, Dissemination of the   I-52
Breviarium of Alaric II, Drafting of the   II-1005
Britain, Roman Conquest of   II-616
Bronze, Invention of   I-16
Bureaucracy, Creation of the Imperial   II-621

Calendar, Development of the Christian   II-877
Camel, Domestication of the   I-30
Canon Law, Codification of the   III-1491
Canossa, Imperial Visit to   III-1269
Canterbury, Establishment of the See of   II-1058
Canterbury Tales, Chaucer Writes the   III-1655
Canuleian Law, Enactment of the   I-281
Capet to the Throne of France, Election of Hugh III-1200
Captivity, Return from the   I-189
Carthage, Vandal Seizure of   II-958
Castile's School of Translation, Establishment of III-1524
Categories of Aristotle, Porphyry's Commentaries on the   II-834
Cattle Breeding, Development of Scientific III-1426
Celibacy, Enforcement of Clerical   III-1257
Chaeronea, Battle of   I-338
Châlons, Battle of   II-975
Charter of Lorris, Granting of the   III-1323
Choral Lyric, Perfection of the   I-215
Christian Platonists, Rise of the   II-773
Christians, Nero's Persecution of the   II-638
Christmas, Inauguration of the Feast of   II-884
Church-State Problems, Inception of   II-852
Church-State Relationships, Gelasius' Statements on   II-989
City of God, Augustine Writes the   II-940
Classical Learning, Chartres' Preservation of III-1231
Cleisthenes, The Reforms of   I-205
Clement VII, Election of Pope   III-1644
Clovis, Conversion of   II-995
Cluny, Founding of   II-1184
Code of Barcelona, Crystallization of the III-1514
Code, Promulgation of Justinian's   II-1035
Coinage, Invention of   I-144
Common Law in England, Emergence of the III-1386
Concordat of Worms, Signing of the   III-1318
Consolation of Philosophy, Boethius Writes the II-1018
Constantine, Conversion of   II-846
Constantinople, Fall of   III-1718
Constantinople, Founding of   II-862
Contra Julianum, Augustine Writes the   II-946
Contra Vigilantium, Jerome Writes the   II-929
Cordoba, Flourishing of the Court of   II-1189

Corinthians, Clement of Rome Addresses the II-669
Council of Constance, Calling the   III-1680
Courtly Love, Rise of   III-1296
Crusade, Calling of the Albigensian   III-1441
Crusade, Failure of the Seventh   III-1496
Crusade, Preaching of the First   III-1276
Crusaders, Capture of Constantinople by the III-1436
Cur Deus Homo, Anselm Writes the   III-1291
Cursus Honorum, Establishment of the   I-448
Cybele's Introduction into Rome   I-432

De Agri Cultura, Cato Writes the   I-465
De Docta Ignorantia, Nicholas of Cusa Writes III-1708
De Officiis, Cicero Writes the   I-541
De Oratore, Cicero Writes the   I-521
De Republica, Cicero Writes the   I-526
De Rerum Natura, Lucretius Writes the   I-511
Decian Persecution, Outbreak of the   II-812
Defensor Pacis, Composition of the   III-1608
Delphi, Apollo's Revelations at   I-120
Dictatus Papae, Enunciation of the   III-1263
Dionysius the Areopagite, Misidentification of II-1011
Divine Comedy, Dante Writes the   III-1598
Dominate, Inauguration of the   II-829
"Donation of Constantine," Forging of the II-1121
Draco's Code, Issuance of   I-153

Easter, Discussion of the Date of   II-857
Ecclesiastical History, Eusebius Writes His II-840
Egyptian Wisdom Literature, Composition of I-35
Eleusinian Mysteries, Celebration of the   I-158
Ethics, Rationalization of   I-328
Etymologies, Isidore of Seville Writes the II-1086
Eucharist, Radbertus' Discussion of the   II-1164
Euhemerus, The Teaching of   I-378
Exodus from Egypt, Hebrew   I-75
Experimental Science, Popularization of   III-1539

Fairs of Champagne, Growth of the   III-1421
Formulary System, Institution of the   I-491
Fountain of Knowledge, John of Damascus Writes the   II-1111
Fourth Lateran Council, Meeting of the   III-1457
France, Consolidation of   III-1733
Franciscans, Founding of the   III-1447

Galen's Medical Writings, Publication of II-737
Gaul, Caesar's Conquest of   I-516
Gaugamela, Alexander's Victory at   I-358
Genesis, Composition of the Book of   I-96
Genghis Khan, Conquests of   III-1462
Geocentric System, Postulation of the   II-712
Geometry, Formalization of   I-383
Germany, Introduction of Christianity into II-1126
Gilgamesh Epic, Appearance of the   I-40
Gnosticism, Growth of Manichaean   II-807
"Golden Bull," Enunciation of the   III-1635
Golden Horde, Destruction of the   III-1742
Gospel, Preaching of the Pentecostal   II-607
Gothic Architecture, Development of   III-1416
Gracchus, Tribunate of Tiberius Sempronius I-481
Granada, Fall of   III-1747
Guilds of Florence, Development of the   III-1303
Gunpowder, Invention of   III-1509

Hammurabi's Code, Promulgation of   I-45
Hansa, Rise of the   III-1430
Harun al-Rashid, Cultural Development at the Court of   II-1142
Hastings, Battle of   III-1248
History of the Peloponnesian War, Thucydides Writes the   I-292
History, Professionalization of   I-259
"Holy Roman Empire," Creation of the   III-1195
Horse, Domestication of the   I-1
Horse Transportation, Improvements in   II-1169
Hungary, Conversion of   III-1210
Huss, The Preaching of John   III-1675

Iconoclastic Struggle, Settlement of the   II-1152
Ignatius of Antioch, Martyrdom of   II-696
Iliad, Homer's Composition of the   I-110
Imitation of Christ, Thomas à Kempis Writes the III-1670
Inquisition, Institution of the   III-1484
Institutes of Roman Law, Gaius' Edition of the II-721
Institutiones Grammaticae, Priscian Writes the II-1023
Intertestamental Jewish Apocrypha, Appearance of   I-443
Invasion of Greece, Persian   I-237
Ireland, Conversion of   II-969
Iron, "Discovery" of   I-58
Islam, Birth of   II-1075
Islamic and Greek Thought, Culmination of the Synthesis of   III-1395

Jamnia, Synod of   II-664

Jeremiah, The Revelation of   I-149
Jesus, Birth of   I-567
Jesus, Condemnation of   II-601
Jesus, Conduct of the Ministry of   II-589
Jews from Spain, Expulsion of the   III-1752
Joan of Arc's Relief of Orléans   III-1697
Judaism, Philo's Hellenization of   II-612
Julian Calendar, Establishment of the   I-536
Julian Law, Enactment of the   I-506
Julian's Pagan Revival, Failure of   II-888

Kadesh, Battle of   I-70
Kingdom of Israel, Establishment of the   I-106
Kuzari, Judah Halevi Writes the   III-1334

Last Supper, Celebration of the   II-595
Last Supper, Leonardo da Vinci Paints the   III-1761
Latin Prose, Refinement of   I-531
Lenses, Development of   III-1555
Leo's *Tome*, Presentation of   II-963
Lex Hortensia, Issuance of the   I-393
Licet Juris, Issuance of the   III-1620
Lithuania, Conversion of   III-1650
Liturgical Year, Establishment of the   II-1091
Logic, Formulation of   I-348
Logos, Postulation of the   I-210
Luxeuil and Bobbio, Founding of   II-1052

Maccabees, Revolt of the   I-459
Magna Carta, Signing of   III-1452
Maimonides, Exegesis of   III-1391
Manichaean Gnosticism, Growth of   II-807
Manzikert, Battle of   III-1253
Marco Polo, Travels of   III-1550
Mass, Formalization of the Liturgy of the   II-1069
Mechanistic Atomism, Conception of   I-264
Medicine, Avicenna Compiles the *Canon of*   III-1226
Medicine, Emergence of Greek   I-302
Meditations, Marcus Aurelius Writes the   II-725
Messenia, Spartan Conquest of   I-134
Metamorphoses, Ovid Writes the   II-573
Metaphysics, Beginnings of   I-231
Middle Academy, Skepticism of the   I-471
Miracle Play, Development of the   III-1221
Monte Casino and the Rule of Saint Benedict, Founding of   II-1029
Morgarten, Swiss Victory at   III-1603
Multiple-Element Hypothesis, Formulation of the   I-270
Municipia, Origin of   I-333
Muratorian Canon, Compilation of the   II-767
Mysticism, Saint Bernard's Expression of   III-1329

Natural History, Pliny the Elder Compiles the   II-653
Natural Law, Origen's Teaching on the   II-801
Natural Law, Stoic Conception of   I-388
Naval Law of Themistocles, The   I-226
Navigation, Improvements in Shipbuilding and   III-1503
Neoplatonism, Plotinus' Conception of   II-823
Nestorian Controversy, Outbreak of the   II-952
New Comedy, Creation of the   I-368
New Testament, Crystallization of the   II-779
Nicene Creed, Formulation of the   II-867
Nibelungenlied, Composition of the   III-1405
Northumbria, Conversion of   II-1081

Olympic Games, Inauguration of the   I-115
Oresteia, Aeschylus Writes the   I-248

Painting, Emergence of Modern Western   III-1587
Painting, Emergence of Perspective in   III-1691
Painting, Revival of Classical Themes in   III-1766
Papal Decretals, Emergence of   II-914
Papal Elections, Regularization of   III-1243
Paris, Founding of the University of   III-1400
Parliament, Summoning of the Model   III-1581
Parthenon, Building of the   I-276
Parthia, Rise of   I-427
Penitential System, Development of the   II-762
Pepin, Coronation of   II-1131
Pergamum to Rome, Transference of   I-486
Peter in Rome, Martyrdom of Saint   II-643
Pharisees, Rise of the   I-477
Philosophy, Rise of   I-173
Physics, Flowering of Late Medieval   III-1614
Platonic Academy of Florence, Founding of the   III-1723
Platonists, Rise of the Christian   II-773
Plebeian Tribunate, Institution of the   I-221
Plow, Adoption of the Heavy   II-1099
Political Theory, John of Salisbury's Expression of   III-1370
Politics, Aristotle Writes the   I-343
Polyphony, Cultivation of   III-1410
Pompeii, Destruction of   II-659
Pragmatic Sanction of Bourges, Declaration of the   III-1703
Primacy Text, Stephen's Use of the   II-818
Printing, Invention of   III-1713
Private Army, Marius' Creation of the   I-496

Proscriptions of the Second Triumvirate   I-546

Prosody, Innovations in Medieval   III-1349

"Provisions of Oxford," Enactment of the   III-1528

Ptolemy Philadelphus, Deification of   I-403

Ptolemy Philadelphus, Revenue Laws of   I-413

Punic War, Declaration of the First   I-408

Pyramid, Building of the Great   I-25

Pythagorean Brotherhood, Founding of the   I-194

Quadrivium, Genesis of the Trivium and   II-1000

Recapitulation Theory, Presentation of the   II-747

Rhazes, Medical Writings of   II-1179

Rhine-Danube Frontier, Establishment of the   II-584

Roman Law, Revival of   III-1344

Roman Symbol, Formation of the   II-752

Romance of the Rose, Composition of the   III-1467

Romans, Paul Writes His Letter to the   II-632

Rome, "Fall" of   II-980

Rome, The Sack of   II-935

Russia, Conversion of   III-1205

Salerno, Recognition of the University of   III-1478

Santa Sophia, Building of   II-1040

Sardica, Summoning of the Council of   II-872

Schism, Beginning of the Rome-Constantinople   III-1237

School of Prince Henry the Navigator, Establishment of the   III-1686

Science as a Discipline, Aristotle's Isolation of   I-363

Scipionic Circle, Formation of the   I-453

Sculpture, Beginnings of Renaissance   III-1665

Second Isaiah, The Teaching of   I-184

Septuagint, "Commissioning" of the   I-418

Serapeum, Destruction of the   II-924

Serbia, Turkish Conquest of   III-1660

Seven Sacraments, Delineation of the   III-1338

Sexagesimal System, Creation of the   I-21

Shipbuilding and Navigation, Improvements in   III-1503

Sibylline Books, Appearance of the   I-200

Sic et Non, Abélard Writes   III-1313

Sicily, Athenian Invasion of   I-308

Slavic Alphabet, Building of the   II-1173

Socrates, Death of   I-318

Solon, Legislation of   I-168

Song of Roland, Composition of the   III-1308

Sophists, The Teachings of the   I-286

Spain, Tarik's Crossing into   II-1105

Spanish Church, Reform of the   III-1728

Speculum Maius, Vincent of Beauvais Compiles   III-1533

Statue of Zeus at Olympia, Phidias Creates the   I-297

Statute of Praemunire, Promulgation of the   III-1630

Statute of Winchester, Enactment of the   III-1569

Summae Theologiae, Compilation of the   III-1544

Syracuse, Founding of   I-129

Talmud, Compilation of the   II-985

Temple at Jerusalem, Roman Destruction of the   II-648

Temple, Building of the   I-101

Ten Thousand, March of the   I-313

Teutoburger Forest, Defeat in   II-578

Teutonic Knights, Penetration of the Baltic by   III-1472

Theodosius' Edicts, Promulgation of   II-904

Theodosius, Excommunication of   II-920

Theogony, Hesiod's Composition of the   I-139

"Theology" as a Concept, Emergence of   II-757

Theory of Ideas, Plato's Development of the   I-323

"Third Rome," Ivan III's Organization of the   III-1738

Thomas à Becket, Murder of   III-1375

Tours, Battle of   II-1117

Trade with the East, Upsurge of Venetian   III-1354

Trajan's Religious Policy, Statement of   II-692

Trigonometry, Beginnings of   II-716

Trivium and Quadrivium, Genesis of the   II-1000

True Word, Publication of Celsus'   II-731

"Twelve Tables" of Roman Law, Formulation of the   I-253

Ulpian's Dictum, Formulation of   II-784

Unam Sanctam, Pronouncement of the Bull   III-1592

United Kingdom, Establishment of the   I-90

Usury, Formalization of the Idea of   III-1519

Verdun, Treaty of   II-1158

Vernacular, Emergence of the English   III-1287

Vivarium, Establishment of   II-1046

"Vulgar Christianity," Gregory's Recognition of   II-1063

Vulgate, Commissioning of the   II-909

Waldensians, Appearance of the   III-1381
Western Empire, Re-Creation of   II-1146
Wheel, Introduction of the   I-5
Writing, Origin of   I-10
Wycliffe, Condemnation of   III-1640

Yahweh's Covenant with Israel, Establishment
   of   I-84

Zama, Battle of   I-437
Zohar, Appearance of the   III-1559
Zoroastrian Ditheism, Appearance of   I-163

ARTISTIC

Beginnings of Renaissance Sculpture   III-1665
Building of Santa Sophia   II-1040
Building of the Great Pyramid   I-25
Building of the Parthenon   I-276
Development of Gothic Architecture   III-1416
Emergence of Modern Western Painting   III-1587
Emergence of Perspective in Painting   III-1691
Leonardo da Vinci Paints the *Last Supper* III-1761
Phidias Creates the Statue of Zeus at Olympia I-297
Revival of Classical Themes in Painting   III-1766

CONSTITUTIONAL

Completion of the Augustan Settlement I-562
Creation of the Athenian Empire   I-242
Creation of the Imperial Bureaucracy   II-621
Drafting of the *Breviarium* of Alaric II   II-1005
Emergence of the Common Law in England III-1386
Enactment of the Canuleian Law   I-281
Enactment of the Julian Law   I-506
Enactment of the "Provisions of Oxford" III-1528
Enactment of the Statute of Winchester   III-1569
Enunciation of the *Dictatus Papae*   III-1263
Enunciation of the "Golden Bull"   III-1635
Establishment of the *Cursus Honorum*   I-448
Formulation of the "Twelve Tables" of Roman Law   I-253
Formulation of Ulpian's Dictum   II-784
Gaius' Edition of the *Institutes* of Roman Law II-721
Inauguration of the Dominate   II-829
Institution of the Formulary System   I-491
Institution of the Plebeian Tribunate   I-221
Issuance of Draco's Code   I-153
Issuance of the Decree *Licet Juris*   III-620
Issuance of the *Lex Hortensia*   I-393
Ivan III's Organization of the "Third Rome" III-1738
Legislation of Solon   I-168
Promulgation of Hammurabi's Code   I-45
Promulgation of Justinian's Code   II-1035
Promulgation of Theodosius' Edicts   II-904
Promulgation of the Statute of Praemunire III-1630
Re-Creation of Western Empire   II-1146

Reforms of Cleisthenes, The   I-205
Tribunate of Tiberius Sempronius Gracchus I-481

CULTURAL

Abélard Writes *Sic et Non*   III-1215
Aeschylus Writes the *Oresteia*   I-248
Anselm Writes the *Cur Deus Homo*   III-1291
Apollo's Revelations at Delphi   I-120
Appearance of the Gilgamesh Epic   I-40
Appearance of the Intertestamental Jewish Apocrypha   I-443
Appearance of the Sibylline Books   I-200
Appearance of the *Zohar*   III-1559
Appearance of Zoroastrian Ditheism   I-163
Aristotle Writes the *Politics*   I-343
Aristotle's Isolation of Science as a Discipline I-363
Augustine Writes the *City of God*   II-940
Augustine Writes the *Contra Julianum*   II-946
Avicenna Compiles the *Canon of Medicine* III-1226
Beginnings of Metaphysics   I-231
Beginnings of Renaissance Sculpture   III-1665
Boethius Writes the *Consolation of Philosophy* II-1018
Building of Santa Sophia   II-1040
Building of the Great Pyramid   I-25
Building of the Parthenon   I-276
Building of the Slavic Alphabet   II-1173
Cato Writes the *De Agri Cultura*   I-465
Celebration of the Eleusinian Mysteries   I-158
Chartres' Preservation of Classical Learning III-1231
Chaucer Writes the *Canterbury Tales*   III-1655
Cicero Writes the *De Officiis*   I-541
Cicero Writes the *De Oratore*   I-521
Cicero Writes the *De Republica*   I-526
Compilation of the *Summa Theologiae*   III-1544
Compilation of the Talmud   II-985
Completion of the Augustan Settlement   I-562
Composition of Egyptian Wisdom Literature I-35
Composition of the Book of Genesis   I-96
Composition of the *Defensor Pacis*   III-1608
Composition of the *Nibelungenlied*   III-1405
Composition of the *Romance of the Rose* III-1467
Composition of the *Song of Roland*   III-1308
Conception of Mechanistic Atomism   I-264

Condemnation of Christian Averroism   III-1564

Creation of the New Comedy   I-368

Creation of the Sexagesimal System   I-21

Crystallization of the New Testament   II-779

Culmination of the Synthesis of Islamic and Greek Thought   III-1395

Cultivation of Polyphony   III-1410

Cultural Development at the Court of Harum al-Rashid   II-1142

Cybele's introduction into Rome   I-432

Dante Writes the *Divine Comedy*   III-1598

Dedication of the Aelia Capitolina   II-702

Development of Gothic Architecture   III-1416

Development of the Christian Calendar   II-877

Development of the Guilds of Florence   III-1303

Development of the Miracle Play   III-1221

Dissemination of the *Book of the Dead*   I-52

Editing of the Chronicles of Julius Africanus   II-789

Emergence of Modern Western Painting   III-1587

Emergence of Perspective in Painting   III-1691

Emergence of the English Vernacular   III-1287

Establishment of Alcuin's Palace School   II-1136

Establishment of Castile's School of Translation   III-1524

Establishment of the Julian Calendar   I-536

Establishment of the School of Prince Henry the Navigator   III-1686

Establishment of Vivarium   II-1046

Establishment of Yahweh's Covenant with Israel   I-84

Eusebius Writes His *Ecclesiastical History*   II-840

Exegesis of Maimonides   III-1391

Failure of Akhenaten's Cultural Revival   I-64

Failure of Julian's Pagan Revival   II-888

Flourishing of the Court of Cordoba   II-1189

Formalization of the Liturgy of the Mass   II-1069

Formation of the Scipionic Circle   I-453

Formulation of Logic   I-348

Formulation of the Multiple-Element Hypothesis   I-270

Founding of Alexandria   I-353

Founding of Luxeuil and Bobbio   II-1052

Founding of Monte Cassino and the Rule of Saint Benedict   II-1029

Founding of the Alexandrian School of Exegesis   II-795

Founding of the Platonic Academy of Florence   III-1723

Founding of the Pythagorean Brotherhood   I-194

Founding of the University of Paris   III-1400

Genesis of the Trivium and Quadrivium   II-1000

Gregory's Recognition of "Vulgar Christianity"   II-1063

Growth of the Fairs of Champagne   III-1421

Hesiod's Composition of the *Theogony*   I-139

Homer's Composition of the *Iliad*   I-110

Inauguration of the Feast of Christmas   II-884

Innovations in Medieval Prosody   III-1349

Isidore of Seville Writes the *Etymologies*   II-1086

Jerome Writes the *Contra Vigilantium*   II-929

John of Damascus Writes the *Fountain of Knowledge*   II-1111

John of Salisbury's Expression of Political Theory   III-1370

Judah Halevi Writes the *Kuzari*   III-1334

Leonardo da Vinci Paints the *Last Supper*   III-1761

Lucretius Writes the *De Rerum Natura*   I-511

Marcus Aurelius Writes the *Meditations*   II-725

Nicholas of Cusa Writes *De Docta Ignorantia*   III-1708

Origen's Teaching on the Natural Law   II-801

Origin of Writing   I-10

Ovid Writes the *Metamorphoses*   II-573

Perfection of the Greek Choral Lyric   I-215

Phidias Creates the Statue of Zeus at Olympia   I-297

Philo's Hellenization of Judaism   II-612

Plato Develops the Theory of Ideas   I-323

Pliny the Elder Compiles the *Natural History*   II-653

Plotinus' Conception of Neoplatonism   II-823

Plutarch's Popularization of Biography   II-686

Popularization of Experimental Science   III-1539

Porphyry's Commentaries of the *Categories* of Aristotle   II-834

Presentation of Leo's *Tome*   II-963

Priscian Writes the *Institutiones Grammaticae*   II-1023

Professionalization of History   I-259

Publication of Celsus' *True Word*   II-731

Publication of Galen's Medical Writings   II-737

Refinement of Latin Prose   I-531

Revelation of Jeremiah, The   I-149

Revival of Classical Themes in Painting   III-1766

Revival of Roman Law   III-1344

Rise of Courtly Love   III-1296
Rise of Philosophy   I-173
Rise of the Christian Platonists   II-773
Stoic Conception of Natural Law   I-388
Teaching of Amos, The   I-125
Teaching of Euhemerus, The   I-378
Teaching of Second Isaiah, The   I-184
Teachings of the Sophists, The   I-286
Thomas à Kempis Writes the *Imitation of Christ*
III-1670
Thucydides Writes the *History of the Peloponnesian War*   I-292
Transmission of the Alphabet   I-80
Travels of Marco Polo   III-1550
Vergil Writes the Aeneid   I-556
Vincent of Beauvais Complies the *Speculum Maius*   III-1533
Writing of Basil the Great's Theological Works
II-893

ECONOMIC

Crystallization of the *Code of Barcelona*   III-1514
Development of the Guilds of Florence   III-1303
Formalization of the Idea of Usury   III-1519
Growth of the Fairs of Champagne   III-1421
Invention of Coinage   I-144
Refinements in Banking   III-1359
Revenue Laws of Ptolemy Philadelphus   I-413
Rise of the Hansa   III-1430
Upsurge of Venetian Trade with the East
III-1354

INTELLECTUAL

Abélard Writes *Sic et Non*   III-1313
Advances in Hellenistic Astronomy   I-398
Aeschylus Writes the *Oresteia*   I-248
Anselm Writes the *Cur Deus Homo*   III-1291
Appearance of the Gilgamesh Epic   I-40
Appearance of the Intertestamental Jewish Apocrypha   I-443
Appearance of the *Zohar*   III-1559
Aristotle Writes the *Politics*   I-343
Aristotle's Isolation of Science as a Discipline   I-363
Augustine Writes the *City of God*   II-940
Augustine Writes the *Contra Julianum*   II-946
Avicenna Compiles the *Canon of Medicine*   III-1226
Beginnings of Metaphysics   I-231
Beginnings of Trigonometry   II-716
Boethius Writes the *Consolation of Philosophy*   II-1018
Building of the Slavic Alphabet   II-1173
Cato Writes the *De Agri Cultura*   I-465

Chartres' Preservation of Classical Learning
III-1231
Chaucer Writes the *Canterbury Tales*   III-1655
Cicero Writes the *De Officiis*   I-541
Cicero Writes the *De Oratore*   I-521
Cicero Writes the *De Republica*   I-526
Compliation of the *Summa Theologiae*   III-1544
Compilation of the Talmud   II-985
Composition of Egyptian Wisdom Literature
I-35
Composition of the *Defensor Pacis*   III-1608
Composition of the *Nibelungenlied*   III-1405
Composition of the *Romance of the Rose*
III-1467
Composition of the *Song of Roland*   III-1308
Conception of Mechanistic Atomism   I-264
Creation of the New Comedy   I-368
Creation of the Sexagesimal System   I-21
Culmination of the Synthesis of Islamic and Greek Thought   III-1395
Dante Writes the *Divine Comedy*   III-1598
Development of the Miracle Play   III-1221
Dissemination of the *Book of the Dead*   I-52
Editing the Chronicles of Julius Africanus
II-789
Emergence of Greek Medicine   I-302
Emergence of the English Vernacular   III-1287
Establishment of Alcuin's Palace School   II-1136
Establishment of Castile's School of Translation
III-1524
Establishment of the School of Prince Henry the Navigator   III-1686
Establishment of Vivarium   II-1046
Eusebius Writes His *Ecclesiastical History*
II-840
Exegesis of Maimonides   III-1391
Flowering of Late Medieval Physics   III-1614
Formalization of Geometry   I-383
Formation of the Scipionic Circle   I-453
Formulation of Logic   I-348
Formulation of the Multiple-Element Hypothesis   I-270
Founding of Luxeuil and Bobbio   II-1052
Founding of the Alexandrian School of Exegesis
II-795
Founding of the Platonic Academy of Florence
III-1723
Founding of the Pythagorean Brotherhood
I-194
Founding of the University of Paris   III-1400
Gaius' Edition of the *Institutes* of Roman Law
II-721
Genesis of the Trivium and Quadrivium   II-1000
Hesiod's Composition of the Theogony   I-139

Homer's Composition of the *Iliad*   I-110
Innovations in Medieval Prosody   III-1349
Introduction of Arabic Numerals   III-1282
Isidore of Seville Writes the *Etymologies*   II-1086
Jerome Writes the *Contra Vigilantium*   II-929
John of Damascus Writes the *Fountain of Knowledge*   II-1111
John of Salisbury's Expression of Political Theory   III-1370
Judah Halevi Writes the *Kuzari*   III-1334
Lucretius Writes the *De Rerum Natura*   I-511
Marcus Aurelius Writes the *Meditations*   II-725
Medical Writings of Rhazes   II-1179
Nicholas of Cusa Writes the *De Docta Ignorantia*   III-1708
Origen's Teaching on the Natural Law   II-801
Origin of Writing   I-10
Ovid Writes the *Metamorphoses*   II-573
Perfection of the Greek Choral Lyric   I-215
Plato Develops the Theory of Ideas   I-323
Pliny the Elder Compiles the *Natural History*   II-653
Plotinus' Conception of Neoplatonism   II-823
Plutarch's Popularization of Biography   II-686
Popularization of Experimental Science   III-1539
Porphyry's Commentaries of the *Categories* of Aristotle   II-834
Postulation of the Geocentric System   II-712
Postulation of the Logos   I-210
Priscian Writes the *Institutiones Grammaticae*   II-1023
Professionalization of History   I-259
Publication of Celsus' *True Word*   II-731
Publication of Galen's Medical Writings   II-737
Radbertus' Discussion of the Eucharist   II-1164
Rationalization of Ethics   I-328
Recognition of the University of Salerno   III-1478
Refinement of Latin Prose   I-531
Revival of Roman Law   III-1344
Rise of Courtly Love   III-1296
Rise of Philosophy   I-173
Rise of the Christian Platonists   II-773
Saint Bernard's Expression of Mysticism   III-1329
Skepticism of the Middle Academy   I-471
Stoic Conception of Natural Law   I-338
Teaching of Euhemerus, The   I-378
Teachings of the Sophists, The   I-286
Thomas à Kempis Writes the *Imitation of Christ*   III-1670

Thucydides Writes the *History of the Peloponnesian War*   I-292
Transmission of the Alphabet   I-80
Vergil Writes the *Aeneid*   I-556
Vincent of Beauvais Compiles the *Speculum Maius*   III-1533
Writing of Basil the Great's Theological Works   II-893

LEGAL

Completion of the Augustan Settlement   I-562
Declaration of the Pragmatic Sanction of Bourges   III-1703
Drafting of the *Breviarium* of Alaric II   II-1005
Emergence of the Common Law in England   III-1386
Enactment of the Canuleian Law   I-281
Enactment of the Julian Law   I-506
Enactment of the "Provisions of Oxford"   III-1528
Enactment of the Statute of Winchester   III-1569
Enunciation of the *Dictatus Papae*   III-1263
Enunciation of the "Golden Bull"   III-1635
Establishment of the *Cursus Honorum*   I-448
Establishment of Yahweh's Covenant with Israel   I-84
Formulation of Ulpian's Dictum   II-784
Formulation of the "Twelve Tables" of Roman Law   I-253
Forging of the "Donation of Constantine"   II-1121
Gaius' Edition of the *Institutes* of Roman Law   II-721
Granting of the Charter of Lorris   III-1323
Inauguration of the Dominate   II-829
Institution of the Formulary System   I-491
Institution of the Plebeian Tribunate   I-221
Issuance of Draco's Code   I-153
Issuance of the *Licet Juris*   III-1620
Issuance of the *Lex Hortensia*   I-393
Legislation of Solon   I-168
Naval Law of Themistocles, The   I-226
Promulgation of Hammurabi's Code   I-45
Promulgation of Justinian's *Code*   II-1035
Promulgation of the Statute of Praemunire   III-1630
Reforms of Cleisthenes, The   I-205
Signing of Magna Carta   III-1452

LITERARY

Abélard Writes the *Sic et Non*   III-1313
Aeschylus Writes the *Oresteia*   I-248
Anselm Writes the *Cur Deus Homo*   III-1291
Appearance of the Gilgamesh Epic   I-40
Appearance of the Intertestamental Jewish Apocrypha   I-443

Appearance of the *Zohar*   III-1559
Aristotle Writes the *Politics*   I-343
Augustine Writes the *City of God*   II-940
Augustine Writes the *Contra Julianum*   II-946
Boethius Writes the *Consolation of Philosophy* II-1018
Building of the Slavic Alphabet   II-1173
Cato Writes the *De Agri Cultura*   I-465
Chartres' Preservation of Classical Learning III-1231
Chaucer Writes the *Canterbury Tales*   III-1655
Cicero Writes the *De Officiis*   I-541
Cicero Writes the *De Oratore*   I-521
Cicero Writes the *De Republica*   I-526
"Commissioning" of the Septuagint   I-418
Commissioning of the Vulgate   II-909
Compilation of the Muratorian Canon   II-767
Compilation of the *Summa Theologiae*   III-1544
Compilation of the Talmud   II-985
Composition of Egyptian Wisdom Literature I-35
Composition of the Book of Genesis   I-96
Composition of the *Defensor Pacis*   III-1608
Composition of the *Nibelungenlied*   III-1405
Composition of the *Romance of the Rose* III-1467
Composition of the *Song of Roland*   III-1308
Creation of the New Comedy   I-368
Crystallization of the New Testament   II-779
Culmination of the Synthesis of Islamic and Greek Thought   III-1395
Cultural Development at the Court of Harun al-Rashid   II-1142
Dante Writes the *Divine Comedy*   III-1598
Development of the Miracle Play   III-1221
Dissemination of the *Book of the Dead*   I-52
Editing of the Chronicles of Julius Africanus II-789
Emergence of the English Vernacular   III-1287
Establishment of Alcuin's Palace School   II-1136
Establishment of Castile's School of Translation III-1524
Establishment of Vivarium   II-1046
Eusebius Writes His *Ecclesiastical History* II-840
Exegesis of Maimonides   III-1391
Flourishing of the Court of Cordoba   II-1189
Formation of the Scipionic Circle   I-453
Founding of Luxeuil and Bobbio   II-1052
Founding of Monte Cassino and the Rule of Saint Benedict   II-1029
Founding of the Alexandrian School of Exegesis II-795
Founding of the Platonic Academy of Florence III-1723

Founding of the University of Paris   III-1400
Genesis of the Trivium and Quadrivium   II-1000
Hesiod's Composition of the *Theogony*   I-139
Homer's Composition of the *Iliad*   I-110
Innovations in Medieval Prosody   III-1349
Isidore of Seville Writes the *Etymologies*   II-1086
Jerome Writes the *Contra Vigilantium*   II-929
John of Damascus Writes the *Fountain of Knowledge*   II-1111
John of Salisbury's Expression of Political Theory   III-1370
Judah Halevi Writes the *Kuzari*   III-1334
Lucretius Writes the *De Rerum Natura*   I-511
Marcus Aurelius Writes the *Meditations*   II-725
Medical Writings of Rhazes   II-1179
Nicholas of Cusa Writes *De Docta Ignorantia* III-1708
Origen's Teaching on the Natural Law   II-801
Origin of Writing   I-10
Ovid Writes the *Metamorphoses*   II-573
Paul Writes His Letter to the Romans   II-632
Perfection of the Greek Choral Lyric   I-215
Pliny the Elder Compiles the *Natural History* II-653
Plotinus' Conception of Neoplatonism   II-823
Plutarch's Popularization of Biography   II-686
Porphyry's Commentaries of the *Categories* of Aristotle   II-834
Presentation of Leo's *Tome*   II-963
Priscian Writes the *Institutiones Grammaticae* II-1023
Professionalization of History   I-259
Publication of Celsus' *True Word*   II-731
Refinement of Latin Prose   I-531
Revelation of Jeremiah, The   I-149
Rise of Courtly Love   III-1296
Saint Bernard's Expression of Mysticism III-1329
Teaching of Amos, The   I-125
Teaching of Second Isaiah, The   I-184
Thomas à Kempis Writes the *Imitation of Christ* III-1670
Thucydides Writes the *History of the Peloponnesian War*   I-292
Transmission of the Alphabet   I-80
Vergil Writes the *Aeneid*   I-556
Vincent of Beauvais Compiles the *Speculum Maius*   III-1533

MILITARY

Alexander's Victory at Gaugamela   I-358
Athenian Invastion of Sicily   I-308

Battle of Actium   I-551
Battle of Adrianople   II-898
Battle of Chaeronea   I-338
Battle of Châlons   II-975
Battle of Hastings   III-1248
Battle of Kadesh   I-70
Battle of Manzikert   III-1253
Battle of Tours   II-1117
Battle of Zama   I-437
Building of the Appian Way   I-373
Caesar's Conquest of Gaul   I-516
Calling of the Albigensian Crusade   III-1441
Capture of Constantinople by the Crusaders III-1436
Conquests of Genghis Khan   III-1462
Consolidation of France   III-1733
Creation of the Athenian Empire   I-242
Creation of the "Holy Roman Empire"   III-1195
Creation of the Imperial Bureaucracy   II-621
Declaration of the First Punic War   I-408
Defeat in Teutoburger Forest   II-578
Destruction of the Golden Horde   III-1742
Destruction of the Serapeum   II-924
Establishment of the Rhine-Danube Frontier II-584
Establishment of the United Kingdom   I-90
Failure of the Seventh Crusade   III-1496
Fall of Acre   III-1574
Fall of Babylon   I-179
Fall of Constantinople   III-1718
Fall of Granada   III-1747
"Fall" of Rome   II-980
Founding of Alexandria   I-353
Ivan III's Organization of the "Third Rome" III-1738
Invention of Gunpowder   III-1509
Joan of Arc's Relief of Orléans   III-1697
March of the Ten Thousand   I-313
Marius' Creation of the Private Army   I-496
Naval Law of Themistocles, The   I-226
Penetration of the Baltic by the Teutonic Knights   III-1472
Persian Invasion of Greece   I-237
Proscriptions of the Second Triumvirate   I-546
Re-Creation of Western Empire   II-1146
Revolt of the Maccabees   I-459
Rise of Parthia   I-427
Roman Conquest of Britain   II-616
Roman Destruction of the Temple at Jerusalem II-648
Sack of Rome, The   II-935
Spartan Conquest of Messenia   I-134
Swiss Victory at Morgarten   III-1603
Tarik's Crossing into Spain   II-1105
Turkish Conquest of Serbia   III-1660
Vandal Seizure of Carthage   II-958

NATURAL PHENOMENON

Destruction of Pompeii   II-659

PHILOSOPHICAL

Abélard Writes *Sic et Non*   III-1313
Anselm Writes the *Cur Deus Homo*   III-1291
Aristotle Writes the *Politics*   I-343
Augustine Writes the *City of God*   II-940
Augustine Writes the *Contra Julianum*   II-946
Beginnings of Metaphysics   I-231
Boethius Writes the *Consolation of Philosophy* II-1018
Chartres' Preservation of Classical Learning III-1231
Compilation of the *Summa Theologiae*   III-1544
Composition of Egyptian Wisdom Literature I-35
Conception of Mechanistic Atomism   I-264
Culmination of the Synthesis of Islamic and Greek Thought   III-1395
Establishment of Castile's School of Translation III-1524
Formulation of Logic   I-348
Formulation of the Multiple-Element Hypothesis   I-270
Founding of the Platonic Academy of Florence III-1723
Founding of the Pythagorean Brotherhood I-194
Founding of the University of Paris   III-1400
Genesis of the Trivium and Quadrivium   II-1000
Jerome Writes the *Contra Vigilantium*   II-929
John of Damascus Writes the *Fountain of Knowledge*   II-1111
Lucretius Writes the *De Rerum Natura*   I-511
Marcus Aurelius Writes the *Meditations*   II-725
Nicholas of Cusa Writes *De Docta Ignorantia* III-1708
Origen's Teaching on the Natural Law   II-801
Outbreak of the Nestorian Controversy   II-952
Philo's Hellenization of Judaism   II-612
Plato Develops the Theory of Ideas   I-323
Plotinus' Conception of Neoplatonism   II-823
Porphyry's Commentaries of the *Categories* of Aristotle   II-834
Postulation of the Logos   I-210
Rationalization of Ethics   I-328
Rise of Philosophy   I-173
Rise of the Christian Platonists   II-773

Skepticism of the Middle Academy   I-471
Stoic Conception of Natural Law   I-388
Teaching of Euhemerus, The   I-378
Teachings of the Sophists, The   I-286
Vincent of Beauvais Compiles the *Speculum Maius*   III-1533

POLITICAL

Accession of Basil II   III-1215
Aristotle Writes the *Politics*   I-343
Augustine Writes the *City of God*   II-940
Cicero Writes the *De Officiis*   I-541
Cicero Writes the *De Republica*   I-526
Completion of the Augustan Settlement   I-562
Composition of the *Defensor Pacis*   III-1608
Conquests of Genghis Khan   III-1462
Consolidation of France   III-1733
Coronation of Pepin   II-1131
Creation of the Athenian Empire   I-242
Creation of the "Holy Roman Empire"   III-1195
Creation of the Imperial Bureaucracy   II-621
Death of Socrates   I-318
Declaration of the First Punic War   I-408
Declaration of the Pragmatic Sanction of Bourges   III-1703
Destruction of the Golden Horde   III-1742
Election of Hugh Capet to the Throne of France   III-1200
Emergence of Austria   III-1364
Emergence of the Common Law in England   III-1386
Enactment of the "Provisions of Oxford"   III-1528
Establishment of the Rhine-Danube Frontier   II-584
Establishment of the United Kingdom   I-90
"Fall" of Rome   II-980
Formation of the Scipionic Circle   I-453
Founding of Alexandria   I-353
Founding of Constantinople   II-862
Founding of Syracuse   I-129
Granting of the Charter of Lorris   III-1323
Inauguration of the Dominate   II-829
Institution of the Plebeian Tribunate   I-221
Issuance of the Decree *Licet Juris*   III-620
Ivan III's Organization of the "Third Rome"   III-1738
John of Salisbury's Expression of Political Theory   III-1370
Legislation of Solon   I-168
Origin of *Municipia*   I-333
Proscriptions of the Second Triumvirate   I-546
Re-Creation of Western Empire   II-1146
Reforms of Cleisthenes, The   I-205
Revolt of the Maccabees   I-459
Rise of Parthia   I-427
Signing of Magna Carta   III-1452

Summoning of the Model Parliament   III-1581
Transference of Pergamum to Rome   I-486
Treaty of Verdun   II-1158

POLITICO-RELIGIOUS

Appearance of the Sibylline Books   I-200
Calling of the Albigensian Crusade   III-1441
Capture of Constantinople by the Crusaders   III-1436
Condemnation of Jesus   II-601
Condemnation of Wycliffe   III-1640
Conversion of Clovis   II-995
Conversion of Constantine   II-846
Coronation of Pepin   II-1131
Deification of Ptolemy Philadelphus   I-403
Election of Pope Clement VII   III-1644
Enunciation of the *Dictatus Papae*   III-1263
Establishment of the Kingdom of Israel   I-106
Excommunication of Theodosius   II-920
Forging of the "Donation of Constantine"   II-1121
Gelasius' Statement on Church-State Relationships   II-989
Imperial Visit to Canossa   III-1269
Inception of Church-State Problems   II-852
Institution of the Inquisition   III-1484
Murder of Thomas à Becket   III-1375
Nero's Persecution of the Christians   II-638
Outbreak of the Decian Persecution   II-812
Penetration of the Baltic by the Teutonic Knights   III-1472
Promulgation of Theodosius' Edicts   II-904
Pronouncement of the Bull *Unam Sanctam*   III-1592
Return from the Captivity   I-189
Revolt of the Maccabees   I-459
Signing of the Concordat of Worms   III-1318
Statement of Trajan's Religious Policy   II-692

RELIGIOUS

Abélard Writes *Sic et Non*   III-1313
Anselm Writes the *Cur Deus Homo*   III-1291
Appearance of the Intertestamental Jewish Apocrypha   I-443
Appearance of the Sibylline Books   I-200
Appearance of the Waldensians   III-1381
Appearance of the *Zohar*   III-1559
Appearance of Zoroastrian Ditheism   I-163
Apollo's Revelations at Delphi   I-120
Augustine Writes the *City of God*   II-940
Augustine Writes the *Contra Julianum*   II-946
Beginning of the Rome-Constantinople Schism   III-1237
Birth of Islam   II-1075
Birth of Jesus   I-567

Building of Santa Sophia   II-1040
Building of the Great Pyramid   I-25
Building of the Parthenon   I-276
Building of the Temple   I-101
Calling the Council of Constance   III-1680
Celebration of the Eleusinian Mysteries   I-158
Celebration of the Last Supper   II-595
Clement of Rome Addresses the Corinthians   II-669
Codification of the Canon Law   III-1491
"Commissioning" of the Septuagint   I-418
Commissioning of the Vulgate   II-909
Compilation of the Muratorian Canon   II-767
Compilation of the *Summa Theologiae*   III-1544
Compilation of the Talmud   II-985
Composition of the Book of Genesis   I-96
Condemnation of Christian Averroism   III-1564
Condemnation of Wycliffe   III-1640
Conduct of the Ministry of Jesus   II-589
Conception of Apostolic Succession, The   II-742
Conversion of Clovis   II-995
Conversion of Constantine   II-846
Conversion of Hungary   III-1210
Conversion of Ireland   II-969
Conversion of Lithuania   III-1650
Conversion of Northumbria   II-1081
Conversion of Russia   III-1205
Crystallization of the New Testament   II-779
Culmination of the Synthesis of Islamic and Greek Thought   III-1395
Cybele's Introduction into Rome   I-432
Deification of Ptolemy Philadelphus   I-403
Delineation of the Seven Sacraments   III-1338
Destruction of the Serapeum   II-924
Development of the Antiochene Episcopacy   II-681
Development of the Christian Calendar   II-877
Development of the Penitential System   II-762
Discussion of the Date of Easter   II-857
Dissemination of the *Book of the Dead*   I-52
Editing of the Chronicles of Julius Africanus   II-789
Election of Pope Clement VII   III-1644
Emergence of Papal Decretals   II-914
Emergence of "Theology" as a Concept   II-757
Enforcement of Clerical Celibacy   III-1257
Enunciation of the *Dictatus Papae*   III-1263
Establishment of the Kingdom of Israel   I-106
Establishment of the Liturgical Year   II-1091
Establishment of the See of Canterbury   II-1058

Establishment of Vivarium   II-1046
Establishment of Yahweh's Covenant with Israel   I-84
Eusebius Writes His *Ecclesiastical History*   II-840
Excommunication of Theodosius   II-920
Exegesis of Maimonides   III-1391
Expulsion of the Jews from Spain   III-1752
Failure of Akhenaten's Cultural Revival   I-64
Failure of Julian's Pagan Revival   II-888
Formalization of the Idea of Usury   III-1519
Formalization of the Liturgy of the Mass   II-1069
Formation of the Roman Symbol   II-752
Formulation of the Nicene Creed   II-867
Founding of Cluny   II-1184
Founding of Luxeuil and Bobbio   II-1052
Founding of Monte Cassino and the Rule of Saint Benedict   II-1029
Founding of the Alexandrian School of Exegesis   II-795
Founding of the Franciscans   III-1447
Founding of the Pythagorean Brotherhood   I-194
Gregory's Recognition of "Vulgar Christianity"   II-1063
Growth of Manichaean Gnosticism   II-807
Hesiod's Composition of the *Theogony*   I-139
Inauguration of the Feast of Christmas   II-884
Inauguration of the Olympic Games   I-115
Inception of Christian Apologetics   II-707
Institution of the Inquisition   III-1484
Introduction of Christianity into Germany   II-1126
Jerome Writes the *Contra Vigilantium*   II-929
Leonardo da Vinci Paints the *Last Supper*   III-1761
Martyrdom of Ignatius of Antioch   II-696
Martyrdom of Saint Peter in Rome   II-643
Meeting of the Fourth Lateran Council   III-1457
Misidentification of Dionysius the Areopagite   II-1011
Nicholas of Cusa Writes *De Docta Ignorantia*   III-1708
Origen's Teaching on the Natural Law   II-801
Outbreak of the Decian Persecution   II-812
Outbreak of the Nestorian Controversy   II-952
Paul Writes His Letter to the Romans   II-632
Phidias Creates the Statue of Zeus at Olympia   I-297
Philo's Hellenization of Judaism   II-612
Preaching of John Huss, The   III-1675
Preaching of the First Crusade   III-1276
Preaching of the Pentecostal Gospel   II-607
Presentation of Leo's *Tome*   II-963

Presentation of the Recapitulation Theory II-747
Publication of Celsus' *True Word*   II-731
Radbertus' Discussion of the Eucharist   II-1164
Reform of the Spanish Church   III-1728
Regularization of Papal Elections   III-1243
Revelation of Jeremiah, The   I-149
Rise of the Christian Platonists   II-773
Rise of the Pharisees   I-477
Roman Destruction of the Temple at Jerusalem II-648
Saint Bernard's Expression of Mysticism III-1329
Settlement of the Iconoclastic Struggle   II-1152
Stephen's Use of the Primacy Text   II-818
Summoning of the Council of Sardica   II-872
Synod of Jamnia   II-664
Teaching of Amos, The   I-125
Teaching of Second Isaiah, The   I-184
Thomas à Kempis Writes the *Imitation of Christ* III-1670
Writing of Basil the Great's Theological Works II–893

RELIGIOUS AND SOCIAL

Appearance of the Sibylline Books   I-200
Celebration of the Eleusinian Mysteries   I-158
Commissioning of the Vulgate   II-909
Conduct of the Ministry of Jesus   II-589
Cybele's Introduction into Rome   I-432
Destruction of the Serapeum   II-924
Dissemination of the *Book of the Dead*   I-52
Establishment of Yahweh's Covenant with Israel I-84
Expulsion of the Jews from Spain   III-1752
Failure of Akhenaten's Cultural Revival I-64
Gregory's Recognition of "Vulgar Christianity" II-1063
Hebrew Exodus from Egypt   I-75
Nero's Persecution of the Christians   II-638
Return from the Captivity   I-189
Revolt of the Maccabees   I-459
Statement of Trajan's Religious Policy   II-692

SCIENTIFIC

Advances in Hellenistic Astronomy   I-398
Aristotle's Isolation of Science as a Discipline I-363
Avicenna Compiles the *Canon of Medicine* III-1226
Beginnings of Trigonometry   II-716
Conception of Mechanistic Atomism   I-264
Creation of the Sexagesimal System   I-21

Culmination of the Synthesis of Islamic and Greek Thought   III-1395
Development of Lenses   III-1555
Development of Scientific Cattle Breeding III-1426
Discoveries of Archimedes   I-422
Discovery of America   III-1756
Emergence of Greek Medicine   I-302
Establishment of Castile's School of Translation III-1524
Establishment of the School of Prince Henry the Navigator   III-1686
Flowering of Late Medieval Physics   III-1614
Formalization of Geometry   I-383
Formulation of the Multiple-Element Hypothesis   I-270
Founding of the Pythagorean Brotherhood I-194
Introduction of Arabic Numerals   III-1282
Invention of Gunpowder   III-1509
Medical Writings of Rhazes   II-1179
Popularization of Experimental Science   III-1539
Postulation of the Geocentric System   II-712
Publication of Galen's Medical Writings   II-737
Recognition of the University of Salerno   III-1478
Vincent of Beauvais Compiles the *Speculum Maius*   III-1533

SOCIOLOGICAL

Conduct of the Ministry of Jesus   II-589
Development of the Guilds of Florence   III-1303
Domestication of the Camel   I-30
Domestication of the Horse   I-1
Establishment of Yahweh's Covenant with Israel I-84
Expulsion of the Jews from Spain   III-1752
Failure of Akhenaten's Cultural Revival I-64
Failure of Julian's Pagan Revival   II-888
Gregory's Recognition of "Vulgar Christianity" II-1063
Growth of the Fairs of Champagne   III-1421
Institution of the Alimentary System   II-675
Invasion of the Black Death   III-1625
Invention of Printing   III-1713
Transmission of the Alphabet   I-80
Travels of Marco Polo   III-1550

TECHNOLOGICAL

Adoption of the Heavy Plow   II-1099
Building of Santa Sophia   II-1040
Building of the Great Pyramid   I-25
Building of the Parthenon   I-276

ANCIENT/MEDIEVAL

Category Index for Events

Building of the Roman Aqueducts   II-626

Development of Gothic Architecture   III-1416

Development of Lenses   III-1555

Discoveries of Archimedes   I-422

Discovery of America   III-1756

"Discovery" of Iron   I-58

Exploitation of the Arch   I-501

Improvements in Horse Transportation   II-1169

Improvements in Shipbuilding and Navigation   III-1503

Introduction of the Wheel   I-5

Invention of Bronze   I-16

Invention of Gunpowder   III-1509

Invention of Printing   III-1713

PRINCIPAL PERSONAGES

Abd-al-Rahman I (731-788)   II-1117; 1189
Abd-al-Rahman II (788-852)   II-1189
Abd-al-Rahman III (891-961)   II-1189
Abélard, Peter (1079-1142)   III-1313; 1329; 1400
Abner (*fl.* 11th Cent. B.C.)   I-90
Abrabanel, Isaac (1437-1508)   III-1752
Abraham bar Hiyya (*see* bar Hiyya)
Abraham ben David (*see* ben David)
Abraham ibn-Ezra (*see* ibn-Ezra)
Abraham Senior (*fl.* 15th Cent.)   III-1752
Abu Bakr (573-634)   II-1075
abū-Bakr Muhammad ibn-Zakarīyā' al-Rāzi (*see* Rhazes)
Abu-Nuwas (756?-?810)   II-1142
Abu Talib (*fl.* 7th Cent.)   II-1075
Acacius (*fl.* 5th Cent.)   II-989
Accursius (1182-1260)   II-784; III-1344; 1519
Adalbert (c.1000-1072)   III-1210
Adam of St. Victor (c.1110-c.1180)   III-1349
Adda(i) (*fl.* 3rd Cent. B.C.)   II-807
Adelard of Bath (1079-1143)   III-1524
Adelbero of Rheims (?-c.1030)   III-1200
Adhemar de Monteil (?-1098)   III-1276
Adimantus (*fl.* 5th Cent. B.C.)   I-237
Adolf of Nassau (1250?-1298)   III-1603
Aemilius Lepidus, Marcus (*see* Lepidus)
Aeschylus (c.526-456 B.C.)   I-248
Aetius (396?-454)   II-975
Africanus, Sextus Julius (c.170-c.240)   II-789
Agricola (37-93 A.D.)   II-616
Agrippa II, Herod (*see* Herod Agrippa II)
Agrippa, Marcus Vipsanius (63 B.C.-A.D. 12)   I-551
Agrippa, Menenius (*fl.* 5th Cent. B.C.)   I-221
Ahijah (*fl.* 10th Cent. B.C.)   I-106
Aidan (*fl.* 7th Cent. B.C.)   II-1081
Akhenaten (Amenhotep IV) (*fl.* 14th Cent. B.C.)   I-64
Akiba ben Joseph (*see* ben Joseph)
Alaric (370?-410)   II-935; 940
Alaric II (*fl.* 5th-6th Cent.)   II-1005
Al-ashraf al-Khalil (*fl.* 13th Cent.)   III-1574
Albategnius (c.850-929)   II-716
Albert of Hapsburg (?-1308)   III-1603
Albert of Saxony (*fl.* 14th Cent.)   III-1614
Albert the Great (1193-1280)   III-1544
Alberti, Leon Battista (1404-1472)   III-1665; 1691
Albinus (*fl.* 2nd Cent. A.D.)   II-731
Albinus, Lucius (*fl.* late 5th Cent. B.C.)   I-221
Alcibiades (c.450-404 B.C.)   I-308; 318
Alcimus (*see* Eliachim)
Alcmaeon of Croton (*fl.* c.500 B.C.)   I-194; 302
Alcuin (735-804)   II-1136; 1146

Alessandro Filipepi (*see* Botticelli)
Alexander III (*see* Alexander the Great)
Alexander III (Pope) (?-1181)   III-1243; 1257; 1375; 1381
Alexander IV (Pope) (?-1261)   III-1528
Alexander VI (Pope) (1431?-1503)   III-1728
Alexander, Bishop of Alexandria (?-328)   II-867
Alexander of Neckam (*fl.* 13th Cent.)   III-1503
Alexander of Villedieu (c.1170-c.1250)   II-1023
Alexander the Great (356-323 B.C.)   I-338; 353; 358; 403
Alexius I Comnenus (1048-1118)   III-1276; 1354
Alexius III (?-1210)   III-1436
Alexius IV (?-1204)   III-1436
Al-Farabi (870-950)   III-1395
Alfasi, Isaac (1013-1103)   III-1334; 1391
Alfonso X (1226?-1284)   III-1524
Alfonso, Pedro (1062-c.1140)   III-1524
Alfred the Great (849-899)   II-1063
Al-Ghazzali (1058-1111)   III-1395
Al-Hakim II (913?-976)   II-1189
Alhazen (Ibn al-Haitham) (c.965-1039)   III-1555
Ali (600?-661)   II-1075
Alighieri, Dante (*see* Dante)
Al-Khowarizmi (780-c.850)   III-1282
Al-Kindi (*fl.* 9th Cent.)   III-1395
Al-Mansur (939-1002)   II-1189
Alparslan (1029-1072)   III-1253
Alphanus of Salerno (c.1015-1085)   III-1478
Alphonse of Poitiers (1220-1271)   III-1496
al-Rashid, Harun (764?-809)   II-1142
al-Rāzi, abū-Bakr Muhammad ibn Zakarīyā (*see* Rhazes)
Alyattes (c.610-560 B.C.)   I-144
Amaziah (*fl.* 8th Cent. B.C.)   I-125
Ambiorix (*fl.* 1st Cent. B.C.)   I-516
Ambrose (340?-397)   II-852; 920
Amenhotep III (*fl.* 14th Cent. B.C.)   I-64
Amenhotep IV (*see* Akhenaten)
Amos (*fl.* 8th Cent. B.C.)   I-125
Amphilochius (c.340-c.394)   II-893
Anastasius I (430?-518)   II-989
Anaxagoras of Clazomenae (c.500-428 B.C.)   I-270
Anaximander of Miletus (611-547 B.C.)   I-173
Anaximenes of Miletus (*fl.* 585-524 B.C.)   I-173
Andragoras (*fl.* 3rd Cent. B.C.)   I-427
Angelo, Brother (*fl.* 13th Cent.)   III-1447
Anicius Manlius Severinus Boethius (*see* Boethius)
Annas of Ananus (*fl.* 1st Cent. A.D.)   II-601

Anne of Brittany (1477-1514)   III-1733
Anselm (1033-1109)   III-1291
Anthemius of Tralles (*fl.* 6th Cent.)   II-1040
Antiochus III (242-187 B.C.)   I-427
Antiochus IV (c.215-163 B.C.)   I-459
Antiphon the Sophist (c.480-410 B.C.)   I-286
Antoninus, Marcus Aurelius (*see* Marcus Aurelius)
Antoninus Pius (A.D. 86-161)   II-616
Antonius, Marcus (*see* Mark Antony)
Antonius Merenda, Titus (*see* Merenda)
Anytus (5th-4th Cent. B.C.)   I-318
Apollonius (*fl.* 3rd Cent. B.C.)   I-413
Apollonius of Chalcedon (*fl.* 2nd Cent.)   II-725
Apollonius of Perga (265-190 B.C.)   I-422
Appius Claudius (*see* Claudius, Appius)
Appius Claudius Caudex (*see* Claudius Caudex)
Appius Claudius Crassus Caecus (*see* Claudius Crassus)
Aquila (Biblical Translator) (*fl.* c.130)   I-418
Aquila (Christian Convert) (*fl.* 1st. Cent. A.D.)   II-632
Aquillius, Manlius (*fl.* 2nd Cent. B.C.)   I-486
Aquinas, Thomas (1225-1274)   III-1395; 1519; 1544; 1564
Aquitaine, Duke of (*see* William the Pious)
Arcesilaus (c.315-241 B.C.)   I-471
Archias (*fl.* 8th Cent. B.C.)   I-129
Archimedes (c.287-212 B.C.)   I-422
Archytas of Tarentum (*fl.* 4th Cent. B.C.)   I-194
Aristarchus of Samos (c.310-230 B.C.)   I-398; II-712
Aristides (c.520-468 B.C.)   I-226; 242
Aristides of Athens (*fl.* 2nd Cent.)   II-707
Aristonicus (?-128 B.C.)   I-486
Aristo of Pella (*fl.* 2nd Cent.)   II-707
Aristophanes (c.448-c.385 B.C.)   I-318
Aristotle of Stagira (384-322 B.C.)   I-328; 343; 348; 363; II-712
Arius (?-336)   II-867
degli Armati, Salvino (?-1367)   III-1555
Arminius (17 B.C.-A.D. 21)   II-578; 584
Arnard-Amalric (c.1160-1225)   III-1441
Arsaces (*fl.* 3rd Cent. B.C.)   I-427
Artaxerxes II (?-359 B.C.)   I-313
Asclepas (*fl.* 4th Cent.)   II-872
Asclepius *(no dates)*   I-302
Ashurbanipal (?-626 B.C.)   I-40
Asprenas (?-A.D. 30)   II-578
Athanasius (c.293-373)   II-767; 779; 852; 862; 872; 888
Athenagoras (*fl.* 2nd Cent.)   II-707
Atilus Regulus, Marcus (*see* Regulus)
Attalus I (Soter) (269-197 B.C.)   I-432; 486
Attalus II (220-138 B.C.)   I-486
Attalus III (171-133 B.C.)   I-486
Attila (406?-453)   II-975
Augustine of Canterbury (?-605)   II-1029; 1058

Augustine of Hippo (354-430)   II-757; 852; 935; 940; 946; III-1338
Augustulus, Romulus (*see* Romulus)
Augustus (*see* Caesar Augustus)
Aulus Manlius (*see* Manlius)
Aurelius Antoninus, Marcus (*see* Marcus Aurelius)
Aurelius Commodus, Lucius Aelius (*see* Commodus)
Aurelius Valerius Diocletianus, Gaius (*see* Diocletian)
Aurelius Valerius Maxentius, Marcus (*see* Maxentius)
Aurelius Valerius Maximianus, Marcus (*see* Maximian)
Avempace (?-1138)   III-1395
Averröes (1126-1198)   III-1395
Avicenna (908-1037)   III-1226; 1391; 1395; 1478

Bacchylides (c.505-c.450 B.C.)   I-215
Bacon, Roger (1214-1292)   III-1509; 1539; 1555
Bahram I (*fl.* 3rd Cent.)   II-807
Bakr, Abu (*see* Abu Bakr)
Baldus de Ubaldis (c.1320-1400)   II-784; III-1344
Balke, Hermann (?-1239)   III-1472
di Banco, Nanni (1374-c.1420)   III-1665
Barabbas (*fl.* 1st Cent. A.D.)   II-601
Barca, Hamilcar (c.270-229 B.C.)   I-408
Barca, Hasdrubal (?-207 B.C.)   I-437
Bardas Scleros (*see* Scleros)
bar Hiyya, Abraham (c.1065-c.1136)   III-1524
bar Kokhba, Simon (*fl.* 2nd Cent.)   II-702
Bartolomi de las Casas (*fl.* 15th Cent.)   III-1756
Bartolus of Sassoferrato (1314-1357)   II-784; III-1344
Baruch (*fl.* 7th-6th Cent. B.C.)   I-149
Basil (330?-?379)   II-893
Basil II Bulgaroctonus (985?-1025)   III-1215
Basil the Eunuch (*fl.* 10th Cent.)   III-1215
Batu (?-1255)   III-1462
Bayazid I (1347-1403)   III-1660
Becket, Thomas à (1118-1170)   III-1375
Bede, The Venerable (673-735)   II-877; 1091
Bedford, Duke of (1389-1435)   III-1697
Behem, Martin (c.1459-c.1507)   III-1503
Belshazzar (*fl.* 6th Cent. B.C.)   I-179
ben David, Abraham (1120-1198)   III-1391
ben Giora, Simon (?-A.D. 71)   II-648
ben Joseph, Akiba (A.D. c.40-c.135)   II-702
Ben Maimon, Moses (*see* Maimonides)
ben Zakkai, Johanan (A.D. c.10-115)   II-664
Benedict XII (?-1342)   III-1620
Benedict XIII (c.1328-1422/3)   III-1680
Benedict of Aniane (c.750-821)   II-1029
Benedict of Nursia (c.480-c.550)   II-1029

Berenquer III, Ramon (*fl.* 12th Cent.)   III-1514

Bernard, Saint (*see* Saint Bernard)

Bernard of Chartres (c.1080-1167)   III-1231

Bernard of Clairvaux (1091-1153)   III-1313

Bernard of Cluny (*fl.* 12th Cent.)   III-1349

Bernard of Pavia (*fl.* late 12th Cent.)   III-1491

Bernard of Quintavalle (*fl.* 13th Cent.)   III-1447

Berno of Baume (c.850-927)   II-1029; 1184

Bertha (*fl.* 6th Cent.)   II-1058

Bessus (*fl.* 4th Cent.)   I-358

Bigod, Hugh (?-1176)   III-1528

Black Berthold (*see* Schwarz, Berthold)

Blanche of Castile (1187?-1252)   III-1496

Boabdil (*fl.* 15th Cent.)   III-1747

Boethius, Ancius Manlius Severinus (c.480-c.524)   II-834; 1000; 1018; III-1410

Boethius of Dacia (*fl.* 13th Cent.)   III-1564

di Bondone, Giotto (*see* Giotto)

Boniface (c.672-754)   II-1126

Boniface, Count (*fl.* 5th Cent.)   II-958

Boniface VIII (1235?-1303)   III-1491; 1592

Boniface of Montferrat (c.1155-1207)   III-1436

Boris (?-907)   III-1205

Boso (*fl.* 12th Cent.)   III-1291

Botticelli, Sandro (Alessandro Filipepi) (c.1444-1510)   III-1723; 1766

de Bracton, Henry (c.1200-1268)   II-784

Bradwardine, Thomas (1290?-1349)   III-1614

Brother Angelo (*see* Angelo)

Brother Giles (*see* Giles)

Brother Leo (*see* Leo)

Brother Rufino (*see* Rufino)

Brunelleschi, Filippo (c.1377-1446)   III-1665; 1691

Bulan (*fl.* 8th Cent.)   III-1334

di Buoninsegna, Duccio (*see* Duccio)

Burgundio of Pisa (?-1190)   II-1111

Buridan, John (*fl.* 14th Cent.)   III-1614

Burrhus (*fl.* 1st-2nd Cent.)   II-696

Cadwallon (?-634)   II-1081

Caecilian (*fl.* 4th Cent.)   II-857

Caesar Augustus (Gaius Julius Caesar Octavianus) (63 B.C.-14 A.D.)   I-546; 551; 556; 562; II-578; 584; 621

Caesar, Gaius Julius (100-44 B.C.)   I-516; 531; 536; 541; II-584; 616

Caesar, Lucius Julius (?-87 B.C.)   I-506

Caeso, Duillius (*see* Duillius)

Caiaphas, Joseph (*fl.* 1st Cent. A.D.)   II-601

Calixtus II (?-1124)   III-1257; 1318

Callicrates (*fl.* 5th Cent. B.C.)   I-276

Callistus (Freedman) (*fl.* 1st Cent.)   II-621

Callistus (Pope) (*fl.* 3rd Cent.)   II-762

Can Grande della Scala (*see* Scala)

Canuleius, Gaius (*fl.* 5th Cent. B.C.)   I-281

Capet, Hugh (940?-996)   III-1200

Carneades (214-129 B.C.)   I-471

Casimir IV Jagiello (1427-1492)   III-1650; 1742

Cassiodorus (477-570)   II-1000; 1046

Cato, "Censorius" Marcus Porcius (*see* Cato the Elder)

Cato the Elder (Cato, "Censorius" Marcus Porcius (234-149 B.C.)   I-448; 465; 531

Cavallini, Pietro (c.1250-c.1330)   III-1691

Caxton, William (c.1422-1491)   III-1713

Celestine I (?-432)   II-914; 952; 969

Celestine V (1215-1296)   III-1592

Celestius (*fl.* 5th Cent.)   II-946

Celsus (*fl.* 2nd Cent.)   II-731

Cerularius, Michael (*fl.* 11th Cent.)   III-1237

Cesarini, Julian (1398-1444)   III-1708

Charlemagne (742-814)   II-1136; 1142; 1146; III-1308

Charles IV (1436-1481)   III-1733

Charles IV of Luxemburg (1316-1378)   III-1620; 1635

Charles V (1337-1380)   III-1644

Charles VII of Valois (1403-1461)   III-1703; 1733

Charles VIII of Valois (1470-1498)   III-1723

Charles Martel (*see* Martel)

Charles of Anjou (1227-1285)   III-1496

Charles of Berry (1446-1472)   III-1723

Charles of Hapsburg (1500-1558)   III-1723

Charles of Lorraine (*fl.* 10th Cent.)   III-1200

Charles of Luxemburg (*see* Charles IV)

Charles the Bald (823-877)   II-1158

Charles the Bold (1433-1477)   III-1723

Chaucer, Geoffrey (c.1343-1400)   III-1655

Cheops (*fl.* 23rd Cent. B.C.)   I-25

Childeric III (*fl.* 8th Cent.)   II-1121; 1131

Christian (*fl.* 13th Cent.)   III-1472

Chrysippus of Soloi (280-207)   I-388

Cicero, Marcus Tullius (the Elder) (106-43 B.C.)   I-521; 526; 531; 541; 546

Cicero, Marcus Tullius (the Younger) (65-c.25 B.C.)   I-541

Cimabue (c.1240-c.1302)   III-1587

Cimon (c.512-449 B.C.)   I-158; 242

de Cisneros, Cardinal Jiménez (1437-1517)   III-1728

de Clare, Richard (*see* Gloucester, Earl of)

Clare, Saint (*see* Saint Clare)

Claudius (10 B.C.-A.D. 54)   II-616; 621

Claudius, Appius (*fl.* 5th Cent.)   I-253

Claudius Crassus, Appius (surnamed Caecus) (*fl.* 4th-3rd Cent. B.C.)   I-373; II-636

Claudius Caudex, Appius (*fl.* 3rd Cent. B.C.)   I-408

Claudius Drusus, Nero (*see* Nero, Claudius Drusus)

Claudius Drusus Germanicus, Nero (*see* Nero, Claudius Drusus Germanicus

Claudius Marcellus, Marcus (*see* Marcellus)

Claudius Nero, Tiberius (*see* Nero, Tiberius Claudius)

Claudius Ptolemaeus (*see* Ptolemy)

Cleanthes of Assos (331-232 B.C.)   I-388

Clearchus (c.450-401 B.C.)   I-313

Cleisthenes (*fl.* 6th Cent. B.C.)   I-205

Clemens, Titus Flavius (*see* Flavius Clemens)

Clement VI (1291-1352)   III-1620

Clement VII (1478-1534)   III-1644

Clement of Alexandria (c.150-c.215)   II-757; 773; 795; 801

Clement of Rome (c.30-c.100 A.D.)   II-669; 681

Cleomenes (*fl.* 6th-5th Cent. B.C.)   I-205

Cleopatra VII (69-30 B.C.)   I-551

Clotilde (c.470-545)   II-995

Clovis (466?-511)   II-995; 1005

de Coëtquis, Philippe (1376-1441)   III-1703

Columban (c.543-615)   II-1052

Columbus, Christopher (c.1446-1506)   III-1756

Commodus, Lucius Aelius Aurelius (161-192) II-725

Conon of Samos (*fl.* 3rd Cent. B.C.)   I-422

Conrad III (1093-1152)   III-1364

Conrad of Masovia (1187-1247)   III-1472

Constans (323?-350)   II-852

Constantine I (Constantine the Great) (*see* Constantine, Flavius)

Constantine V (719-775)   II-1152

Constantine XI (1404-1453)   III-1718

Constantine, Flavius Valerius (280?-337)   II-846; 852; 857; 862; 867; 884; 1121

Constantine the African (c.1020-c.1087)   III-1478

Constantius (250?-306)   II-829

Constantius Chlorus, Flavius Valerius (*see* Constantius)

Constantius II (317-361)   II-852

Cornelius (*fl.* 3rd Cent.)   II-812

Cornelius Fronto, Marcus (*see* Fronto)

Cornelius Maluginensis, Marcus (*fl.* 5th Cent. B.C.)   I-253

Cornelius Tacitus (*see* Tacitus)

Cosimo de Medici (*see* Medici)

Cosmas (*fl.* 8th Cent.)   II-1111

Coster, Laurens Janszoon (*fl.* 15th Cent.) III-1713

de Courçon, Robert (*fl.* 13th Cent.)   III-1400

Crassus "Caecus," Appius Claudius (*see* Claudius, Appius Claudius "Caecus")

Crassus, Lucius Licinius (140-91 B.C.)   I-521

Crassus, Marcus Licinius (c.115-53 B.C.)   I-516

Crispin, Gilbert (?-1117)   III-1291

Critias (*fl.* 5th Cent. B.C.)   I-318

Crito (*fl.* 6th Cent. B.C.)   I-318

Croesus (?-546 B.C.)   I-144

Curiatius, Publius (*fl.* 5th Cent. B.C.)   I-253

Cyprian (?-258)   II-762; 812; 818

Cyril (376-444)   II-888; 952; 1173

Cyrus II (*see* Cyrus the Great)

Cyrus the Great (Cyrus II) (600?-529 B.C.) I-179; 184; 189; 313

Damasus I (304?-384)   II-893; 909; 914

Damian, Peter (1007-1072)   III-1269

Dandolo, Enrico (1108?-1205)   III-1436

Dante Alighieri (1265-1321)   III-1598

Darius VII (?-330 B.C.)   I-358

Dauphin, The (1403-1461)   III-1697

David (?-973 B.C.)   I-90; 101

David, Abraham ben (*see* ben David)

Decius (201-251)   II-812

Delfini, Gil (*fl.* 15th Cent.)   III-1728

Demeter *(no dates)*   I-158

Demetrius of Phaleron (c.345-283 B.C.)   II-924

Democritus of Abdera (c.460-370 B.C.)   I-264

Demosthenes (384-322 B.C.)   I-308; 338

Dinocrates of Macedonia (*fl.* 4th Cent.)   I-353

Diocletian (245-313)   II-829

Dionysius (*fl.* 3rd Cent.)   II-812; 818

Dionysius Exiguus (c.500-c.550)   II-877; 914; 1091

Dionysius the Areopagite (*fl.* 1st Cent. A.D.) II-1011

Dioscoros (*fl.* 5th Cent.)   II-952

Dioscurus (*fl.* 5th Cent.)   II-963

Diphilus (*fl.* 4th-3rd Cent. B.C.)   I-368

Dominic of Guzman (1170-1221)   III-1441

Dominic, Saint (*see* Saint Dominic)

Domitian (51-96 A.D.)   II-669

Domitius Ulpianus (*see* Ulpian)

Donatello (c.1386-1466)   III-1665

Donatus (*fl.* 4th Cent.)   II-857

Draco (*fl.* 7th Cent. B.C.)   I-153

Drusus, Marcus Livius (*fl.* 2nd Cent. B.C.) I-506

Drusus, Nero Claudius (*see* Nero)

Duccio di Buoninsegna (c.1255-1319)   III-1587; 1691

Duillius, Caeso (*fl.* 5th Cent. B.C.)   I-253

Dumbleton, John (*fl.* 14th Cent.)   III-1614

Duns Scotus, Johannes (*see* Scotus)

Durand of Huesca (*fl.* 12th Cent.)   III-1381

Eadmer (c.1055-1124)   III-1291

Earl of Gloucester (*see* Gloucester)

Earl of Northumberland (*see* Percy, Henry)

Eckhart, Meister Johannes (c.1260-1327) III-1670

Edward I (1239-1307)   III-1386; 1528; 1569; 1581

Edward III (1312-1377)   III-1630

Edward, Prince of Portugal (1391-1438)   III-1686

Edward the Confessor (1002?-1066)   III-1248

Edwin (585-632)   II-1081

Einhard (c.770-840)   II-1136
Eleazar the Priest (c.75-c.150)   II-702
Eliachim (Alcimus) (*fl.* 2nd Cent. B.C.)   I-459
Elohist, The (c.950 B.C.)   I-96
Empedocles of Acragas (c.493-443 B.C.)   I-270
Ennius, Quintus (239-170 B.C.)   I-378; 453
Epicurus of Samos (342-270 B.C.)   I-264; 511
Erasistratus (*fl.* 3rd Cent. B.C.)   II-737
Eratosthenes of Cyrene (c.275-194 B.C.)   I-398
Erigena, Johannes Scotus (*see* Johannes Scotus)
Ethelbert (*fl.* 6th Cent.)   II-1058
Ethelburga (*fl.* 7th Cent.)   II-1081
Etheria (*fl.* 6th Cent.)   II-877; 1091
Étienne Tempier (*see* Tempier)
Euclid (323-285 B.C.)   I-383; 422
Eudes (665-?735)   II-1117
Eudoxus (c.408-355 B.C.)   I-383; II-712
Eugene III (?-1153)   III-1329
Eugenius IV (1383-1477)   III-1338; 1703
Euhemerus (*fl.* 4th Cent. B.C.)   I-378; 403
Eumenes II (?-?160 B.C.)   I-486
Eunomius (c.335-c.394)   II-893
Euric (?-484)   II-1005
Eurybiades (*fl.* 5th Cent. B.C.)   I-237
Eusebius of Caesarea (c.260-c.340)   II-767; 779; 840; 867
Eusebius of Nicomedia (?-342)   II-867
Eutyches (375?-?454)   II-952; 963
Evrard of Béthune (*fl.* 13th Cent.)   II-1023
Ezra (*fl.* 5th Cent. B.C.)   I-189; II-664
Ezra, Abraham ibn- (*see* ibn-Ezra)

Fabian (*fl.* 3rd Cent.)   II-812
Fabius Vibulanus, Quintus (*fl.* 5th Cent. B.C.)   I-253
Falier, Ordelafo (*fl.* early 12th Cent.)   III-1354
Faliero I Vitale (*see* Vitale)
Farabi, Al- (*see* Al-Farabi)
Felix II (?-365)   II-989
Ferdinand (1452-1516)   III-1728; 1747; 1752; 1756
Fibonacci (*see* Leonard of Pisa)
Ficino, Marsilio (1433-1499)   III-1723; 1766
Filipepi, Alessandro (*see* Botticelli)
Filotheus (*fl.* 16th Cent.)   III-1738
Fiorelli, Giuseppe (1823-1896)   II-659
Firmilian (*fl.* 3rd Cent.)   II-818
Firuz (*fl.* 5th Cent.)   II-985
Flavian (390?-449)   II-963
Flavius Clemens, Titus (*fl.* 1st Cent. A.D.)   II-669
Flavius Sabinus Vespasianus, Titus (*see* Vespasian)
Flavius Valerius Constantine (*see* Constantine)
Flavius Valerius Constantius Chlorus (*see* Constantius)

Florus, Gessius (*fl.* 1st Cent. A.D.)   II-648
Foliot, Gilbert (*fl.* 12th Cent.)   III-1375
Francis of Assisi, Saint (*see* Saint Francis)
Frederick I Barbarossa (1123?-1190)   III-1364
Frederick II (1194-1250)   III-1457; 1472; 1478; 1484
Frederick III (1286?-1330)   III-1603; 1620
Frederick the Handsome of Hapsburg (*see* Frederick III)
Fritigern (*fl.* 4th Cent.)   II-898
Frontinus, Sextus Julius (*fl.* 1st Cent. A.D.)   II-626
Fronto, Marcus Cornelius (*fl.* 2nd Cent.)   II-725
Fulbert of Chartres (c.960-1028)   III-1231
Fust, Johann (1400?-?1466)   III-1713

Gabirol, Solomon ibn- (*see* ibn-Gabirol)
Gaetani, Benedict (*see* Boniface VIII)
Gaiseric (?-477)   II-958; 975
Gaius (*fl.* 2nd Cent.)   II-721
Gaius Aurelius Valerius Diocletianus (*see* Diocletian)
Gaius Canuleius (*see* Canuleius)
Gaius Galerius Valerius Maximianus (*see* Galerius)
Gaius Julius (*see* Julius, Gaius)
Gaius Julius Caesar (*see* Caesar, Gaius Julius)
Gaius Julius Caesar Octavianus (*see* Caesar Augustus)
Gaius Laelius (*see* Laelius)
Gaius Licinius (*see* Licinius)
Gaius Maecenas (*see* Maecenas)
Gaius Marius (*see* Marius)
Gaius Memmius (*see* Memmius)
Galen (*fl.* 2nd Cent.)   II-737
Galerius Valerius Maximianus, Gaius (*see* Maximian)
Gall (c.560-c.615)   II-1052
Galla Placidia (388-450)   II-958; 975
Ganelon (?-778)   III-1308
Gedymin (*fl.* 14th Cent.)   III-1650
Gelasius (*fl.* 5th Cent.)   II-989
Genghis Khan (1162-1227)   III-1462
Genucius, Titus (*fl.* 5th Cent. B.C.)   I-253
Gerard of Cremona (c.1114-1187)   III-1524
Gerbert of Aurillac (*later* Pope Sylvester II) (c.940-1003)   III-1200; 1231
Gerento (*fl.* 11th Cent.)   III-1276
Gessius Florus (*see* Florus)
Geza (*fl.* 10th Cent.)   III-1210
Ghazzali, Al- (*see* Al-Ghazzali)
Ghiberti, Lorenzo (1378-1455)   III-1665
Giles, Brother (*fl.* 13th Cent.)   III-1447
Giora, Simon ben (*see* ben Giora)
Giotto di Bondone (c.1276-c.1337)   III-1587; 1691
Girey, Mengli (c.1440-c.1515)   III-1742
Giustiniani, John (*fl.* 15th Cent.)   III-1718
Gleb (*fl.* 10th Cent.)   III-1205

Gloucester, Earl of (Richard de Clare) (1222-1262)   III-1528
Gnaeus Pompeius Magnus (*see* Pompey)
Gnaeus Pompeius Strabo (*see* Strabo)
Godwinson, Harold (*fl.* 11th Cent.)   III-1248
Gomez, Diego (*fl.* 15th Cent.)   III-1686
Gongylus (*fl.* 5th Cent. B.C.)   I-308
Gonsaluez, Anton (*fl.* 15th Cent.)   III-1686
Gonsaluez, John (*fl.* 15th Cent.)   III-1686
Gorgias of Leontini (c.483-376 B.C.)   I-286
Gracchus, Tiberius Sempronius (163-133 B.C.)   I-481; 486
Gratian (359-383)   II-852; 898; 904
Gratian (*fl.* 12th Cent.)   III-1491
Gregory I (*see* Gregory the Great)
Gregory II (?-731)   II-1126
Gregory IV (?-844)   II-1158
Gregory VII (Hildebrand) (1020?-1085)   III-1257; 1263; 1269; 1318
Gregory IX (1147?-1241)   III-1400; 1441; 1472; 1491
Gregory X (1210-1276)   III-1550
Gregory XI (1331-1378)   III-1644; 1680
Gregory XIII (1502-1585)   II-1091
Gregory of Nazianus (c.330-c.390)   II-893
Gregory of Nyssa (c.335-c.394)   II-893
Gregory of Tours (538?-593)   II-995
Gregory the Great (Gregory I) (540?-604)   II-1058; 1063; 1069; III-1243; 1257
Groote, Gerhard (1340-1384)   III-1670
Grosseteste, Robert (1175-1253)   III-1539; 1555
Guillaume de Lorris (*see* Lorris)
Guillaume de Machaut (*see* Machaut)
Guillaume de Poitiers (*see* Poitiers)
Gundebad (*fl.* 5th-6th Cent.)   II-995
Gutenberg, Johann (c.1400-1468)   III-1713
Gylippus (c.450-400 B.C.)   I-308

Hacen, Muley (*fl.* 15th Cent.)   III-1747
Hadrian (76-138)   II-616; 621; 702
Haggai (*fl.* 6th Cent. B.C.)   I-189
Haitham, Ibn al- (*see* Ibn al-Haitham)
Hakim II, Al- (*see* Al-Hakim)
Halevi, Judah (c.1075-1141)   III-1334; 1391
Hamilcar Barca (*see* Barca)
Hammurabi (*fl.* 2nd Millen.)   I-45
Ha Nasi, Judah (135-193)   II-985
Hannibal (248-182 B.C.)   I-437
Hardrada, Harold (*fl.* 11th Cent.)   III-1248
Hasdai ibn-Shaprut (*see* ibn-Shaprut)
Hasdrubal Barca (*see* Barca)
Hecataeus of Miletus (*fl.* 6th Cent. B.C.)   I-259
Hecataeus of Teos (*fl.* 4th Cent. B.C.)   I-378
Hegesippus (*fl.* 2nd Cent.)   II-742
Henry I (1068-1135)   III-1195; 1291; 1386
Henry II (1133-1189)   III-1375; 1386
Henry II (Cyprus & Jerusalem) (*fl.* 13th Cent.)   III-1574
Henry III (1207-1272)   III-1452; 1528

Henry IV (1050-1106)   III-1263; 1269; 1318
Henry V (1081-1125)   III-1318
Henry VI (1165-1197)   III-1436
Henry VI (1421-1471)   III-1697
Henry VII of Luxemburg (1275?-1313)   III-1603
Henry de Bracton (*see* Bracton)
Henry of Lausanne (*fl.* 12th Cent.)   III-1329
Henry of Portugal (the Navigator) (1394-1460)   III-1503; 1686
Henry the Lion (1129-1195)   III-1364
Henry the Proud (c.1108-1139)   III-1364
Heracles (*fl.* 3rd Cent.)   II-795
Heraclitus of Ephesus (c.530-470 B.C.)   I-210
Hermas (*fl.* 2nd Cent.)   II-762
Hermocrates (c.455-407 B.C.)   I-308
Herod Agrippa II (27-?100 A.D.)   II-648
Herodotus (484-c.425 B.C.)   I-259
Herophilus (*fl.* 3rd Cent. B.C.)   II-737
Hesiod (c.750-700 B.C.)   I-139
Heytesbury, William (*fl.* 14th Cent.)   III-1614
Hiero I of Syracuse (478-466 B.C.)   I-408
Hiero II of Syracuse (c.308-215 B.C.)   I-422
Hilary (*fl.* 4th Cent.)   II-852
Hildebrand (*see* Gregory VII)
Hilduin of Saint-Denis (c.775-c.855)   II-1011
Hillel (c.30 B.C.-A.D. 30)   I-477
Hipparchus of Nicaea (c.190-c.120)   I-398; II-712; 716
Hippocrates of Chios (*fl.* 5th Cent. B.C.)   I-383
Hippocrates of Cos (460?-?377 B.C.)   I-302
Hippias of Elis (c.475-400 B.C.)   I-286
Hippolytus (*fl.* 3rd Cent.)   II-742; 752; 757; 762; 1069
Hiram (989?-936 B.C.)   I-101
Hiyya, Abraham bar (*see* bar Hiyya)
Honorius (384-423)   II-935; 940
Honorius III (?-1227)   III-1441
Hortensius, Quintus (114-50 B.C.)   I-393
Hosius of Cordova (?-358)   II-867; 872; III-1257
Hostiensis (c.1200-1271)   II-784
Hugh of Cluny (1024-1109)   III-1269
Hugh of St. Victor (c.1096-1141)   III-1338
Humbert, Cardinal (c.1000-1061)   III-1237
Humbert of Silva Candida (?-1061)   III-1269
Huss, John (c.1369-1415)   III-1675; 1680
Hypatia (?-415)   II-924
Hyrcanus, John (?-104 B.C.)   I-477

Iamblichus (?-333)   II-888
Ibn al-Haitham (*see* Alhazen)
ibn-Bajjah (*see* Avempace)
ibn-Ezra, Abraham (1092-1167)   III-1334
ibn-Gabirol, Solomon (1021-1069)   III-1334; 1559
ibn Nusair, Musa (c.660-c.714)   II-1105
ibn-Rushid (*see* Averröes)
ibn-Shaprut, Hasdai (912-961)   III-1334

ibn-Sina (*see* Avicenna)
ibn-Tibbon, Samuel (1150-1230)   III-1391
ibn-Zakarīyā' al-Rāzi, abū-Bakr Muhammad
    (*see* Rhazes)
ibn Ziyad, Tarik (?-720)   II-1105
Ictinus (*fl.* 5th Cent. B.C.)   I-276
Ignatius (*fl.* 1st-2nd Cent.)   II-681; 696
Innocent I (?-417)   II-914
Innocent II (?-1143)   III-1329
Innocent III (1161-1216)   III-1381; 1436;
    1441; 1447; 1457; 1484; 1491
Innocent IV (?-1254)   III-1484
Innocent VI (?-1362)   III-1630
Irenaeus (c.130-202)   II-742; 747; 757; 767;
    779
Irene (752-803)   II-1146; 1152
Irnerius (c.1050-1130)   III-1344
Isaac II (?-1204)   III-1436
Isabella (1451-1504)   III-1728; 1747; 1752;
    1756
Isagoras (*fl.* 6th Cent. B.C.)   I-205
Isaiah, First (*fl.* 8th Cent. B.C.)   I-184
Isaiah, Second (*fl.* 6th Cent. B.C.)   I-184
Ishbaal (*fl.* 11th-10th Cent. B.C.)   I-90
Isidore of Seville (560?-636)   II-1086
Isidorus of Miletus (*fl.* 6th Cent.)   II-1040
Isocrates (436-338 B.C.)   I-338
Ivan III (1440-1505)   III-1738; 1742
Ivo of Chartres (c.1040-1115)   III-1231

Jadwiga of Anjou (1370-1399)   III-1650
Jagiello, Casimir IV (*see* Casimir IV)
Jagiello, Vladislav II (*see* Vladislav)
James I ("The Conqueror") (1208-1276)   III-
    1514
Jaroslav the Wise (*fl.* 10th Cent.)   III-1205
Jasomirgott of Babenberg, Henry (?-1177)
    III-1364
Jazdegerd II (*fl.* 5th Cent.)   II-985
Jehoiakim (615?-?560 B.C.)   I-149
Jeremiah (c.645-580 B.C.)   I-149
Jeroboam I (?-912? B.C.)   I-106
Jeroboam II (?-744? B.C.)   I-125
Jerome (c.342-420)   II-779; 909; 929; 935
Jerome of Prague (c.1370-1416)   III-1675
Jesus (Jason) (*fl.* 2nd Cent. B.C.)   I-459
Jesus of Nazareth (the Christ) (4 B.C.-A.D. 29)
    I-477; 567; 589; II-595; 601
Jesus (son of Sirach) (*fl.* 200 B.C.)   I-443
Joab (*fl.* c.1000 B.C.)   I-90
Joan of Arc (1412-1431)   III-1697
Joan of Navarre (1370?-1437)   III-1421
Johanan ben Zakkai (*see* ben Zakkai)
Johannes Duns Scotus (*see* Scotus)
Johannes Eckhart (*see* Eckhart)
Johannes Scotus Erigena (c.810-c.877)   II-
    1011
John, Disciple of Jesus (?-c.100 A.D.)   II-607
John Hyrcanus (*see* Hyrcanus)
John Lackland (1167?-1216)   III-1452; 1457
John XII (938?-964)   III-1195

John XXI (?-1277)   III-1564
John XXII (1249-1334)   III-1410; 1564;
    1608; 1620
John XXIII (?-1415)   III-1680
John I of Avis (?-1433)   III-1686
John of Damascus (c.676-752)   II-1011;
    1111; 1152
John of Ephesus (?-c.100 A.D.)   II-681
John of Gishala (*fl.* 1st Cent. A.D.)   II-648
John of Salisbury (c.1115-1180)   III-1231;
    1370
John of Villiers (*fl.* late 13th Cent.)   III-1574
John, Patriarch of Jerusalem (?-966)   II-1111
John the Baptist (c.10 B.C.-A.D. 29)   I-477;
    II-589
John the Evangelist (*fl.* 1st Cent. A.D.)   I-210
de Joinville, Jean (c.1224-1317)   III-1496
Jonas (c.600-c.665)   II-1052
Jonathan (*fl.* 2nd Cent. B.C.)   I-459
Joseph, Akiba ben (*see* ben Joseph)
Josephus (37-?100 A.D.)   II-648
Joshua (*fl.* c.1200 B.C.)   I-84
Josiah (?-?608 B.C.)   I-149; II-664
Juchi (*fl.* 13th Cent.)   III-1462
Judah Ha Nasi (*see* Ha Nasi)
Judas Maccabaeus (*see* Maccabaeus)
Judas of Kerioth (?-29 A.D.)   II-601
Jugurtha (?-104 B.C.)   I-496
Julian of Eclanum (c.386-454)   II-946
Julian, Count (*fl.* 8th Cent.)   II-1105
Julian the Apostate (331-363)   II-731; 888
Julius (?-352)   II-872
Julius Africanus, Sextus (*see* Africanus)
Julius Caesar (*see* Caesar, Gaius Julius)
Julius Frontinus, Sextus (*see* Frontinus)
Julius, Gaius (*fl.* 5th Cent.)   I-253
Julius Nepos (?-480)   II-980
Julius Severus, Sextus (*see* Severus)
Junius Rusticus (*see* Rusticus)
Justin Martyr (c.100-c.165)   II-707; 731; 757;
    779; 1069
Justinian (483-565)   II-721; 1035; 1040

Kalavun (*fl.* 13th Cent.)   III-1574
Kempis, Thomas à (1380-1471)   III-1670
Khadija (570-632)   II-1075
Khairzuran (*fl.* 8th-9th Cent.)   II-1142
Khalil, Al-ashraf al- (*see* Al-ashraf al-Khalil)
Khan Akhmad (*fl.* 15th-16th Cent.)   III-
    1742
Kokhba, Simon bar (*see* bar Kokhba)
Khowarizmi, Al- (*see* Al-Khowarizmi)
Kilwardby, Robert (?-1279)   III-1564
Kindi, al- (*see* al-Kindi)
Koberger, Anthony (*fl.* 15th Cent.)   III-1713
Kublai Khan (c.1215-1294)   III-1550

Ladislas I (1040?-1095)   III-1210
Laelius, Gaius (*fl.* 2nd Cent. B.C.)   I-437
Laevinius, Marcus Valerius (*fl.* 3rd Cent. B.C.)
    I-432

Lanfranc (c.1005-1089)   III-1291
Lazar I of Hrebelyanovich (?-1389)   III-1660
Lazarevich, Stephen (?-1427)   III-1660
Leander of Seville (550?-?601)   II-1063; 1086
Leicester, Earl of (*see* Montfort, Simon de)
Leo I (*see* Leo the Great)
Leo III (680?-741)   II-1111; 1146; 1152
Leo V (?-820)   II-1152
Leo IX (1002-1054)   III-1237; 1243; 1257
Leo, Brother (*fl.* 13th Cent.)   III-1447
Leo the Great (Leo I) (400?-474)   II-952; 963; III-1257
Leonardo da Vinci (*see* Vinci, Leonardo da)
Leonard of Pisa (c.1180-1250)   III-1282
de Leon, Mosed (1250-1305)   III-1559
Leonidas (*fl.* 5th Cent. B.C.)   I-237
Leonin (*fl.* 12th Cent.)   III-1410
Leopold of Hapsburg (?-1326)   III-1603
Lepidus, Marcus Aemilius (?-77 B.C.)   I-546
Leucippus of Miletus (*fl.* 5th Cent. B.C.) I-264
Liberius (?-366)   II-914
Licinius, Gaius (*fl.* 5th Cent. B.C.)   I-221
Licinius, Valerius (270?-325)   II-846
Livius, Titus (*see* Livy)
Livy (Titus Livius) (59 B.C.-A.D. 17)   I-531
Lombard, Peter (*see* Peter the Lombard)
Lorenzetti, Ambrogio (1300-c.1348)   III-1691
Lorenzo de Medici (*see* Medici)
de Lorris, Guillaume (?-c.1235)   III-1467
Lothair (795?-855)   II-1158
Louis IV of Bavaria (1287?-1347)   III-1603; 1608; 1620
Louis VI (1081-1137)   III-1323
Louis VII (1121?-1180)   III-1323; 1375
Louis IX (1214-1270)   III-1496; 1533
Louis XI of Valois (1423-1483)   III-1733
Louis the German (*fl.* 9th Cent.)   II-1158
Louis the Pious (778-840)   II-1158
Lucius Aelius Aurelius Commodus (*see* Commodus)
Lucius Albinus (*see* Albinus)
Lucius Annaeus Seneca (*see* Seneca the Younger)
Lucius Julius Caesar (*see* Caesar, Lucius Julius)
Lucius Licinius Crassus (*see* Crassus, Lucius Licinius)
Lucius Minucius (*see* Minucius)
Lucius Veturius (*see* Veturius)
Lucius Villius (*see* Villius)
Lucretius (Titus Lucretius Carus) (94-55 B.C.) I-264; 511
Lull, Raymond (c.1235-1315)   III-1503
Lupicinus (*fl.* 4th Cent.)   II-898
Luria, Isaac (1534-1572)   III-1559
de Luzarches, Robert (*fl.* 13th Cent.)   III-1416
Luzzato, Hayim (1707-1747)   III-1559

Maccabaeus, Judas (?-160 B.C.) I-459

de Machaut, Guillaume (c.1300-c.1377)   III-1410
Machet, Gérard (1380-1448)   III-1703
Maecenas, Gaius (70?-8 B.C.)   I-556
Maffeo, Polo (*see* Polo, Maffeo)
Maimonides (1135-1204)   III-1391; 1478
Maluginensis, Marcus Cornelius (*see* Cornelius Maluginensis)
Manetti, Antonio (1423-1497)   III-1691
Mani (Manichaeus) (216-277)   II-807
Manius Rabuleus (*see* Rabuleus)
Manius Valerius (*see* Valerius)
Manlius Aquillius (*see* Aquillius)
Manlius, Aulus (*fl.* 5th Cent. B.C.)   I-253
Manlius Torquatus, Titus (*see* Torquatus)
Mansur, Al- (*see* Al-Mansur)
Manutius, Aldus (1450-1515)   III-1713
Mar 'Ammo (*fl.* 3rd Cent.)   II-807
Marcellinus (*fl.* 5th Cent.)   II-940
Marcellus, Marcus Claudius (c.265-208 B.C.) I-422
Marcellus (?-c.374)   II-752; 872
Marcian (392-457)   II-952; 963
Marcion of Sinope (*fl.* 2nd Cent.)   II-767; 779
Marcius Rex, Quintus (*see* Rex)
Marco Polo (*see* Polo, Ser Marco)
Marcus Aemilius Lepidus (*see* Lepidus)
Marcus Antonius (*see* Mark Antony)
Marcus Atilus Regulus (*see* Regulus)
Marcus Aurelius Antoninus (188-217)   II-725; 731
Marcus Aurelius Valerius Maxentius (*see* Maxentius)
Marcus Aurelius Valerius Maximianus (*see* Maximian)
Marcus Caecilius Metellus (*see* Metellus, Marcus Caecilius)
Marcus Claudius Marcellus (*see* Marcellus)
Marcus Cornelius Fronto (*see* Fronto)
Marcus Cornelius Maluginensis (*see* Cornelius Maluginensis)
Marcus Fabius Quintilianus (*see* Quintilian)
Marcus Licinius Crassus (*see* Crassus)
Marcus Livius Drusus (*see* Drusus)
Marcus Porcius Cato (*see* Cato the Elder)
Marcus Sergius (*see* Sergius)
Marcus Tullius Cicero (Elder) (*see* Cicero, Marcus Tullius)
Marcus Tullius Cicero (Younger) (*see* Cicero, Marcus Tullius)
Marcus Ulpius Traianus Augustus (*see* Trajan)
Marcus Valerius Laevinius (*see* Laevinius)
Marcus Vipsanius Agrippa (*see* Agrippa, Marcus Vipsanius)
Marguerite of Provence, Queen (c.1221-1295) III-1496; 1533
Marius, Gaius (157-86 B.C.)   I-496
Mark Antony (143-87 B.C.)   I-521; 541; 546; 551
Maroboduus (18 B.C.?-?41 A.D.)   II-584

Marsiglio of Padua (c.1275-1342)   III-1608; 1640
Martel, Charles (c.688-741)   II-1117
Mary (mother of Jesus) (*fl.* 1st Cent. B.C.-1st Cent. A.D.)   I-567
Mary of Burgundy (1457-1482)   III-1733
Masaccio (1401-1428)   III-1665; 1691
Massinissa (c.240-148 B.C.)   I-473
Matilda of Tuscany (1046-1115)   III-1269
Mattathias (?-166 B.C.)   I-459
Maurice (539?-602)   II-1063
Maxentius, Marcus Aurelius Valerius (?-312)   II-846
Maximian (?-310)   II-829
Maximilian of Hapsburg (1459-1519)   III-1733
Maximus (*fl.* 4th Cent.)   II-888
Maximus the Confessor (580-662)   II-1011
de Medici, Cosimo (1389-1464)   III-1723
de Medici, Lorenzo (the Magnificent) (1449-1492)   III-1723; 1766
Medinaceli, Duke of (*fl.* 5th Cent.)   III-1756
Meletus (*fl.* 5th-4th Cent. B.C.)   I-318
Memmius, Gaius (before 85-after 49 B.C.)   I-511
Menander (342-291 B.C.)   I-368
de Mendoza, Cardinal Pedro González (1428-1495)   III-1728
Menelaus (*see* Onias)
Menelaus of Alexandria (*fl.* 1st Cent. A.D.)   II-716
Menenius Agrippa (*see* Agrippa, Menenius)
de Meun, Jean (c.1250-c.1305)   III-1467
Merenda, Titus Antonius (*fl.* 5th Cent. B.C.)   I-253
Merneptah (*fl.* 13th Cent. B.C.)   I-75
Metellus, Marcus Caecilius (*fl.* 3rd Cent. B.C.)   I-432
Methodius (c.815-885)   II-1173
Michael the Scot (?-c.1235)   III-1524
Miltiades (?-310)   II-857
Mindaugas (*fl.* 13th Cent.)   III-1650
Minucius, Lucius (*fl.* 5th Cent. B.C.)   I-253
Della Mirandola, Pico (1463-1494)   III-1723; 1766
Mishra (*fl.* 3rd Cent.)   II-807
Mithridates I (?-302 B.C.)   I-427
Mohammed (c.570-632)   II-1075
Mohammed II the Great (1430-1481)   III-1660; 1718
Montanus from Phrygia (*fl.* 2nd Cent.)   II-767
de Montfort, Simon (Earl of Leicester) (1208-1265)   III-1441; 1457; 1528
Mosed de Léon (*see* Léon)
Moses (*fl.* 13th Cent. B.C.)   I-75; 84
Müller, Johannes (1436-1476)   II-716
Murad I (1319-1389)   III-1660
Murat, Joachim (1767?-1815)   II-659
Musa ibn Nusair (*see* ibn Nusair)
Muwatallish (*fl.* 14th-13th Cent. B.C.)   I-70

Nabonidus (?-539? B.C.)   I-179
Nahmanides (c.1190-1270)   III-1559
Nanni di Banco (*see* Banco)
Narcissus (*fl.* 1st Cent. A.D.)   II-621
Nasica, Publius Cornelius Scipio (*see* Scipio Nasica)
Nasica Serapio, Publius Cornelius Scipio (*see* Scipio Nasica Serapio)
Nathan (*fl.* 10th Cent. B.C.)   I-101
Nebuchadrezzar (*fl.* 12th Cent. B.C.)   I-179
Necho (*fl.* 7th Cent. B.C.)   I-149
Nefertiti (*fl.* 14th Cent. B.C.)   I-64
Nehemiah (*fl.* 5th Cent. B.C.)   I-189
Nepos, Julius (*see* Julius Nepos)
Nero Claudius Drusus (38 B.C.-A.D. 9)   II-584
Nero Claudius Drusus Germanicus (38-9 B.C.)   II-584
Nero, Claudius Caesar Drusus Germanicus (37-68 A.D.)   II-638
Nero, Tiberius Claudius (42 B.C.-37 A.D.)   II-584
Nerva (35-98 A.D.)   II-675
Nestor (1056-1114)   III-1205
Nestorius (?-451)   II-952
di Niccolo Bardi, Donato (*see* Donatello)
Nicholas II (980?-1061)   III-1243; 1263
Nicholas of Cusa (1401-1464)   III-1708
Nicias (c.470-413 B.C.)   I-308
Nicolo Polo (*see* Polo, Nicolo)
Novatian (*fl.* 3rd Cent.)   II-812
Nusair, Musa ibn (*see* ibn Nusair)
Nuwas, Abu- (*see* Abu-Nuwas)

Octavianus, Gaius Julius Caesar (*see* Caesar Augustus)
Octavius, Marcus (*fl.* 2nd Cent. B.C.)   I-481
Odilo (*fl.* 10th-11th Cent.)   II-1184
Odo (*fl.* 10th Cent.)   II-1184
Odovacar (c.434-493)   II-980
Ogadai (1185-1241)   III-1462
Olga (?-969)   III-1205
Olgerd (?-1377)   III-1650
Omar (581?-644)   II-1075
Onesimus (*fl.* 2nd Cent.)   II-696
Onias (Menelaus) (*fl.* 2nd Cent. B.C.)   I-459
Onias III (*fl.* 2nd Cent. B.C.)   I-459
Oppius Cornicen, Spurius (*fl.* 5th Cent. B.C.)   I-253
d'Orbais, Jean (*fl.* 13th Cent.)   III-1416
Oresme, Nicole (1330?-1382)   III-1614
Origen (185-254)   I-418; II-731; 757; 762; 773; 779; 795; 801
Oswald (604-642)   II-1081
Otto I (912-973)   III-1195
Ovid (43 B.C.-A.D. 17)   II-573

Palaeologus, Sophia (Zoe) (*fl.* 15th Cent.)   III-1738
Pallas (*fl.* 1st Cent. A.D.)   II-621

Panaetius of Rhodes (c.185-109 B.C.)   I-453; 541
Panainos (*fl.* 5th Cent. B.C.)   I-297
Pannartz, Arnold (*fl.* 15th Cent.)   III-1713
Pantaenus (*fl.* 2nd-3rd Cent.)   II-795
Parmenides of Elea (5th Cent. B.C.)   I-231
Parmenion (*fl.* 4th Cent. B.C.)   I-358
Paschasius Radbertus (*see* Radbertus)
Pasha, Zagan (*fl.* 15th Cent.)   III-1718
Patik (*fl.* 2nd-3rd Cent.)   II-807
Paulinus (*fl.* 7th Cent.)   II-1081
Paul of Tarsus (?-67 A.D.)   II-607; 632; 638
Paul the Deacon (*fl.* 8th Cent.)   II-1136
Pausanias (*fl.* 5th Cent. B.C.)   I-237
Pedro III (1236-1285)   III-1514
Pedro Alfonso (*see* Alfonso, Pedro)
Pelagius (360?-?420)   II-946
Pellicioli, Mauro (*fl.* 20th Cent.)   III-1761
Penda (c.600-654)   II-1081
Pepin I (803?-838)   II-1158
Pepin III (*see* Pepin the Short)
Pepin the Short (Pepin III) (c.714-768)   II-1121; 1131
Percy, Henry (Earl of Northumberland) (1342-1408)   III-1640
Pérez, Juan (*fl.* 15th Cent.)   III-1756
Pericles (c.495-429 B.C.)   I-158; 226; 242; 276
Perotin (c.1183-c.1238)   III-1410
Peroz (*fl.* 5th Cent.)   II-807
Persephone (*no dates*)   I-158
Peter (*fl.* 1st Cent. A.D.)   II-638; 643; 681
Peter II of Aragon (?-1213)   III-1441
Peter of Murrone (*see* Celestine V)
Peter of Spain (c.1145-c.1190)   III-1524
Peter, Prince (*fl.* 15th Cent.)   III-1686
Peter the Great (1672-1725)   II-1173
Peter the Hermit (c.1050-1115)   III-1276
Peter the Lombard (c.1100-1160)   III-1338; 1400
Peter the Venerable (1092?-1156)   II-1184
Petrus Helias (*fl.* 12th Cent.)   II-1023
Phidias (475-430 B.C.)   I-276; 297
Philagathus, John (*fl.* 10th Cent.)   III-1215
Philemon (c.361-262 B.C.)   I-368
Philip (the Deacon) (*fl.* 1st Cent. A.D.)   II-607
Philip II (of Macedon) (382-336 B.C.)   I-338
Philip II (Philip Augustus) (1165-1223)   III-1323; 1400
Philip IV (1268-1314)   III-1421; 1581; 1592
Philip VI of Valois (1293-1350)   III-1620
Philip Augustus (*see* Philip II)
Philip of Swabia (1180?-1208)   III-1436
Philip the Good, Duke of Burgundy (1396-1467)   III-1697
Philippa (*fl.* 14th Cent.)   III-1686
Philo of Alexandria (c.30 B.C.-A.D. 45)   I-210; II-612
Philolaus of Croton (*fl.* 5th Cent. B.C.)   I-194
Phocas, Bardas (*fl.* 10th Cent.)   III-1215

Pico Della Mirandola (*see* Mirandola)
Pilate, Pontius (*fl.* 1st Cent. A.D.)   II-601
Pilgrim (?-991)   III-1210
Pindar (c.518-c.453 B.C.)   I-215
Pisistratus (?-527 B.C.)   I-158
Placidia, Galla (*see* Galla)
Plato (c.427-347 B.C.)   I-318; 323; 328; 383; II-612
Pletho, Gemistus (c.1335-c.1450)   III-1723
Pliny the Elder (23-79 A.D.)   II-653; 659
Pliny the Younger (62-113 A.D.)   II-659; 692
Plotinus (205-270)   II-823
Plotius Tucca (*see* Tucca, Plotius)
Plutarch (46?-?120 A.D.)   II-686
Poetelius, Quintus (*fl.* 5th Cent. B.C.)   I-253
de Poitiers, Guillaume (1071-1127)   III-1296
da Polenta, Guido (*fl.* 14th Cent.)   III-1598
Polo, Nicolo (*fl.* 13th-14th Cent.)   III-1550
Polo, Maffeo (*fl.* 13th-14th Cent.)   III-1550
Polo, Ser Marco (1254-1324)   III-1550
Polybius (c.203-c.120 B.C.)   I-453
Polycarp (69?-?155)   II-681; 696
Pompaedius, Silo (*fl.* 1st Cent. B.C.)   I-506
Pompeius Magnus, Gnaeus (*see* Pompey)
Pompey (Gnaeus Pompeius Magnus) (106-48 B.C.)   I-516
Pontius Pilate (*see* Pilate, Pontius)
Porphyry (c.232-c.304)   II-731; 834
Postumius, Spurius (*fl.* 5th Cent. B.C.)   I-253
Priestly Writer, The (*fl.* 6th Cent. B.C.)   I-96
Priscian (*fl.* 6th Cent.)   II-1023
Priscilla (*fl.* 1st Cent. A.D.)   II-632
Proclus (c.410-485)   I-383
Prodicus of Ceos (c.470-400 B.C.)   I-286
Protagoras of Abdera (c.481-411 B.C.)   I-286
Protogenes (*fl.* 4th Cent.)   II-872
Pseudo-Dionysius (*fl.* 1st Cent. A.D.)   II-1011
Ptolemaeus, Claudius (*see* Ptolemy)
Ptolemy (Claudius Ptolemaeus) (*fl.* 2nd Cent.)   II-712; 716
Ptolemy I (Soter) (367?-283 B.C.)   I-353; 403; II-924
Ptolemy II (Philadelphus) (309-246 B.C.)   I-353; 403; 413; 418
Publius Cornelius Scipio Aemilianus (*see* Scipio Aemilianus)
Publius Cornelius Scipio Africanus Major (*see* Scipio Africanus Major)
Publius Cornelius Scipio Nasica (*see* Scipio Nasica)
Publius Cornelius Scipio Nasica Serapio (*see* Scipio Nasica Serapio)
Publius Curiatius (*see* Curiatius)
Publius Quintilius Varus (*see* Varus)
Publius Sestius (*see* Sestius, Publius)
Publius Sulpicius (*see* Sulpicius, Publius)
Publius Terentius Afer (*see* Terence)
Publius Vergilius Maro (*see* Vergil)
Pulcheria (399-453)   II-963
Purbach, Georg (1423-1461)   II-716

Pyrrho of Elis (c.360-c.270)   I-471
Pythagoras of Samos (572-c.500 B.C.)   I-194;
383

Quadratus (*fl.* 2nd Cent.)   II-707
Quintilian (Marcus Fabius Quintilianus) (A.D. 39-95)   I-531
Quintilianus, Marcus Fabius (*see* Quintilian)
Quintilius Varus, Publius (*see* Varus)
Quintus Ennius (*see* Ennius)
Quintus Fabius Vibulanus (*see* Fabius Vibulanus)
Quintus Hortensius (*see* Hortensius)
Quintus Marcius Rex (*see* Rex)
Quintus Poetelius (*see* Poetelius, Quintus)

Rab (175-247)   II-985
Rabbina II (474-499)   II-985
Rabuleus, Manius (*fl.* 5th Cent. B.C.)   I-253
Radbertus, Paschasius (c.785-c.860)   II-1164
Rahman I, Abd-al- (*see* Abd-al-Rahman I)
Rahman II, Abd-al- (*see* Abd-al-Rahman II)
Rahman III, Abd-al- (*see* Abd-al-Rahman III)
Raimundo (*fl.* 12th Cent.)   III-1524
Ralph of Beauvais (*fl.* 12th Cent.)   II-1023
Ralph of Royaumont (*fl.* 13th Cent.)   III-1533
Ramses II (1292-1225 B.C.)   I-70; 75
Rashid, Harun al- (*see* al-Rashid)
Ratramnus (?-868)   II-1164
Raymond IV of Toulouse (c.1043-1105)   III-1276
Raymond VI (1156-1222)   III-1441
Raymond VII (?-1247)   III-1441
Raymond Lull (*see* Lull)
Raymond of Peñafort (c.1180-1275)   III-1491; 1544
Recceswinth (*fl.* 7th Cent.)   II-1005
Reginald of Piperno (?-1290)   III-1544
Regulus, Marcus Atilus (?-c.250 B.C.)   I-408
Rehoboam (?-917 B.C.)   I-106
Rex, Quintus Marcius (*fl.* 2nd Cent. B.C.)   II-626
Rhazes (abū-Bakr Muhammad ibn-Zakarīyā' al-Rāzi) (850-923)   II-1179
Robert de Courçon (*see* Courçon)
Robert de Luzarches (*see* Luzarches)
Robert of Arbrissel (c.1055-1117)   III-1276
Robert of Artois (*fl.* 13th Cent.)   III-1496
Robert of Molesme (c.1029-1111)   II-1029
Roderick (?-?711)   II-1105
Roger of York (?-1181)   III-1375
Roland (?-778)   III-1308
Romanus IV Diogenes (?-1071)   III-1253
Romilius, Titus (*fl.* 5th Cent. B.C.)   I-253
Romulus Augustulus (461-c.476)   II-980
Rotislav (*fl.* 9th Cent.)   II-1173
Rudolf of Hapsburg (1218-1291)   III-1603
Rufino, Brother (*fl.* 13th Cent.)   III-1447
Rufinus (*fl.* 4th-5th Cent.)   II-752
Rufus, Tineius (*fl.* 2nd Cent.)   II-702

Rufus, Varius (*fl.* 1st Cent. B.C.)   I-556
Rufus, William (?-1100)   III-1291
Rusticus, Junius (*fl.* 2nd Cent.)   II-725

Saint Bernard (1090-1152)   III-1329
Saint Clare (1194-1253)   III-1447
Saint Colman (c.605-676)   II-969
Saint Columba (521-597)   II-969
Saint Columban (543-615)   II-969
Saint Dominic (c.1170-1221)   III-1457
Saint Finnian (c.470-c.552)   II-969
Saint Francis of Assisi (1181/2-1226)   III-1447; 1457
Saint Patrick (c.389-c.461)   II-969
Salisbury, Earl of (*see* William, Earl of Salisbury)
Samuel (*fl.* 11th Cent. B.C.)   I-90
Samuel ibn-Tibbon (*see* ibn-Tibbon)
Samuel (Rabbi) (180-257)   II-985
Samuel (Tsar) (980-1014)   III-1215
Sanballat (*fl.* 5th Cent. B.C.)   I-189
Saul (*fl.* 11th Cent. B.C.)   I-90
della Scala, Can Grande (1291-1329)   III-1598
Schoeffer, Peter (*fl.* 15th Cent.)   III-1713
Schwarz, Berthold (Black Berthold) *(no dates)*   III-1509
Scipio Aemilianus, Publius Cornelius (185-129 B.C.)   I-453; 531
Scipio Africanus Major, Publius Cornelius (236-184 B.C.)   I-437; 448; 453
Scipio Nasica, Publius Cornelius (*fl.* 2nd Cent. B.C.)   I-432
Scipio Nasica Serapio, Publius Cornelius (*fl.* 2nd Cent. B.C.)   I-481
Scleros, Bardas (*fl.* 10th Cent.)   III-1215
Scotus Erigena, Johannes (*see* Johannes Scotus)
Scotus, Johannes Duns (c.1264-1308)   III-1564
Sebastian (*fl.* 4th Cent.)   II-898
Sebokhut, Severus (?-667)   III-1282
Seljuk (*fl.* 10th Cent.)   III-1253
Sempronius Gracchus, Tiberius (*see* Gracchus)
Seneca the Younger (Lucius Annaeus Seneca) (4 B.C.-A.D. 65)   I-531
Sergius, Marcus (*fl.* 5th Cent. B.C.)   I-253
Sestius, Publius (*fl.* 5th Cent. B.C.)   I-253
Severus, Sextus Julius (*fl.* 2nd Cent.)   II-702
Severus (c.465-538)   II-1011
Sextus Julius Africanus (*see* Africanus)
Sextus Julius Frontinus (*see* Frontinus)
Sextus Julius Severus (*see* Severus)
Sforza, Ludovico (1451-1508)   III-1761
Shammai (*fl.* 2nd Cent. B.C.)   I-477
Shapur 1 (241-272)   II-807
Sheba (*fl.* 10th Cent. B.C.)   I-106
Sicinius (*fl.* 5th Cent. B.C.)   I-221
Siger of Brabant (c.1235-c.1284)   III-1564
Sigismund (1467-1548)   III-1675; 1680
Silo Pompaedius (*see* Pompaedius, Silo)
Simon ben Giora (*see* ben Giora)
Simon bar Kokhba (*see* bar Kokhba)

Simon de Montfort (*see* Montfort)
Simon Peter (?-?67 A.D.)　II-589; 607
Simonides of Ceos (c.556-468 B.C.)　I-215
Simplicius (*fl.* 5th Cent.)　II-989
Siricius (*fl.* 4th Cent.)　II-914; III-1257
Socrates (469-399 B.C.)　I-318; 323; 328
Solomon (?-c.933 B.C.)　I-101; 106
Solomon ibn-Gabirol (*see* ibn-Gabirol)
Solon (c.638-c.559)　I-168
Sophia (Zoe) Palaeologus (*see* Palaeologus)
Sosigenes (*fl.* 1st Cent. B.C.)　I-536
Sostratus of Cnidus (*fl.* 3rd Cent. B.C.)　I-353
Spurius Postumius (*see* Postumius, Spurius)
Stephen (Bishop of Rome) (?-257)　II-818
Stephen (Deacon) (?-c.35 A.D.)　II-607
Stephen (King of Hungary) (*fl.* 10th-11th Cent.) III-1210
Stephen II (?-757)　II-1121; 1131
Stilicho (359?-408)　II-935
Strabo, Gnaeus Pompeius (*fl.* 1st Cent. B.C.) I-506
Sudbury, Archbishop (?-1381)　III-1640
Suger (1081?-1151)　III-1416
Sulpicius, Publius (*fl.* 5th Cent. B.C.)　I-253
Sweinheim, Konrad (*fl.* 15th Cent.)　III-1713
Swineshead, Richard (*fl.* 14th Cent.)　III-1614
Syagrius (430?-486)　II-995
Sylvester II (*see also* Gerbert of Aurillac) (940?-1003)　II-857; 1121; III-1210

Tacitus, Cornelius (A.D. 55-120)　I-531
Talib, Abu (*see* Abu Talib)
Tarik ibn Ziyad (*see* ibn Ziyad)
Tarquinius Superbus (*fl.* 6th Cent. B.C.)　I-200
Tatian (*fl.* 2nd Cent.)　II-707
Tempier, Étienne (1162-1227)　III-1544; 1564
Temujin (*see* Genghis Khan)
Terence (Publius Terentius Afer) (195-159 B.C.) I-453
Terentius Afer, Publius (*see* Terence)
Tertullian (c.155-220)　II-742; 757; 762; 767; 818; III-1338
Thales of Miletus (c.640-c.548 B.C.)　I-173; 383
Themistocles (c.528-462 B.C.)　I-226; 237
Theobald (?-1161)　III-1375
Theodora (*fl.* 9th Cent.)　II-1152
Theodore (*fl.* 9th Cent.)　II-1152
Theodoric (?-451)　II-975; 1018
Theodoric II (426-466)　II-1052
Theodosius (Russian Patriarch) (*fl.* 10th Cent.) III-1205
Theodosius I (*see* Theodosius the Great)
Theodosius II (401-450)　II-952; 963
Theodosius the Great (Theodosius I) (346?-395) II-852; 904; 920; 924
Theodotion (*fl.* 2nd Cent.)　I-418
Theodulph (?-821)　II-1136

Theophilus (*fl.* 2nd Cent.)　II-707; 924
Theophrastus (c.370-c.287 B.C.)　I-348
Theopompus (c.380-?)　I-134
Thierry of Chartres (c.1100-1156)　III-1231
Thomas à Becket (*see* Becket)
Thomas à Kempis (*see* Kempis)
Thomas Aquinas (*see* Aquinas)
Thomas of Celano (c.1200-1255)　III-1349
Thucydides (c.485-c.425 B.C.)　I-242; 292
Tibald of Champagne, Count (?-1201)　III-1436
Tibbon, Samuel ibn- (*see* ibn-Tibbon)
Tiberius Claudius Nero (*see* Nero, Tiberius Claudius)
Tiberius Sempronius Gracchus (*see* Gracchus)
Tineius Rufus (*see* Rufus)
Tiridates (*fl.* 3rd Cent. B.C.)　I-427
Tissaphernes (*fl.* 5th Cent. B.C.)　I-313
Titus (40?-81 A.D.)　II-648
Titus Antonius Merenda (*see* Merenda)
Titus Flavius Clemens (*see* Flavius Clemens)
Titus Flavius Sabinus Vespasianus (*see* Vespasian)
Titus Genucius (*see* Genucius)
Titus Livius (*see* Livy)
Titus Lucretius Carus (*see* Lucretius)
Titus Manlius Torquatus (*see* Torquatus)
Titus Romilius (*see* Romilius)
Tomás de Torquemada (*see* Torquemada)
Torquatus, Titus Manlius (?-202 B.C.) I-333
de Torquemada, Tomás (1420?-1498)　III-1752
Traianus Augustus, Marcus Ulpius (*see* Trajan)
Trajan (Marcus Ulpius Traianus Augustus) (52-117 A.D.)　I-373; II-675; 692; 696
Triptolemus *(no dates)*　I-158
Tristam, Nuno (*fl.* 15th Cent.)　III-1686
Tucca, Plotius (*fl.* 1st Cent. B.C.)　I-556
Tughril (*fl.* 1037-1063)　III-1253
Turoldus (*fl.* 12th Cent.)　III-1308
Tvrtko I (?-1391)　III-1660
Twelve Disciples of Jesus, The *(no dates)* II-595
Tyrtaeus (*fl.* 7th Cent. B.C.)　I-134

Ugolino, Cardinal (*fl.* 13th Cent.)　III-1447
Ugolino of Orvieto (c.1375-c.1455)　III-1410
Ulpian (Domitius Ulpianus) (c.170-228)　II-784
Ulpianus, Domitius (*see* Ulpian)
Urban II (1042?-1099)　III-1257; 1276; 1354
Urban VI (1318-1389)　III-1644

Valens (328?-378 A.D.)　II-893; 898
Valentinian II (372-392)　II-904
Valentinus (*fl.* 2nd Cent. B.C.)　II-747
Valerian (?-269)　II-812
Valerius Constantius Chlorus, Flavius (*see* Constantius)

Valerius Diocletianus, Gaius Aurelius (*see* Diocletian)
Valerius Laevinius, Marcus (*see* Laevinius)
Valerius, Licinius (*see* Licinius)
Valerius, Manius (*fl.* 5th Cent. B.C.)   I-221
Valerius Maxentius, Marcus Aurelius (*see* Maxentius)
Valerius Maximianus, Gaius Galerius (*see* Galerius)
Valerius Maximianus, Marcus Aurelius (*see* Maximian)
Varius Rufus (*see* Rufus)
Varus, Publius Quintilius (?-9 A.D.)   II-578; 584
Vassian, Bishop (*fl.* late 15th Cent.)   III-1742
Vercingetorix (*fl.* 1st Cent. B.C.)   I-516
Vergil (Publius Vergilius Maro) (70-19 B.C.)   I-556
Vergilius Maro, Publius (*see* Vergil)
Vespasian (Titus Flavius Sabinus Vespasianus)   II-648
Veturius, Lucius (*fl.* 5th Cent. B.C.)   I-253
Vibulanus, Quintus Fabius (*see* Fabius Vibulanus)
Vigilantius (*fl.* 5th Cent.)   II-929
Villius, Lucius (*fl.* 2nd Cent. B.C.)   I-448
Vincent of Beauvais (c.1190-c.1264)   III-1533
da Vinci, Leonardo (1452-1519)   III-1761; 1766
Vipsanius Agrippa, Marcus (*see* Agrippa, Marcus)
del Virgilio, Giovanni (*fl.* 14th Cent.)   III-1598
Vishtaspa (*fl.* 7th Cent. B.C.)   I-163
Vitale, Faliero I (*fl.* 11th Cent.)   III-1354
Vitale, Michieli (*fl.* 11th Cent.)   III-1354
Viten (*fl.* 13th-14th Cent.)   III-1650
Vitold (*fl.* 15th Cent.)   III-1650
Vladimir of Kiev (c.956-1015)   III-1205; 1215
Vladislav II Jagiello (1350-1434)   III-1650
von Salza, Hermann (1170-1239)   III-1472

Waldo, Peter (*fl.* 12th Cent.)   III-1381
Wallia (*fl.* 5th Cent.)   II-958
Waraka (*fl.* 7th Cent.)   II-1075

Wenceslaus (?-1419)   III-1675
William of Auxerre (?-c.1231)   III-1338
William of Beaujeau (?-1291)   III-1574
William of Conches (c.1090-1154)   III-1231
William of Moerbeke (c.1215-1286)   III-1544
William of Nogaret (*fl.* 13th-14th Cent.)   III-1592
William of Ockham (c.1285-1349)   III-1564; 1640
William, Duke of Normandy (1035-1087)   III-1248
William, Earl of Salisbury (c.1212-1250)   III-1496
William the Pious, Duke of Aquitaine (*fl.* 9th-10th Cent.)   II-1184
Willibrord (658-739)   II-1126
Witiza (*fl.* 7th-8th Cent.)   II-1105
Wycliffe, John (c.1320-1384)   III-1640; 1675
Wynfrith (*see* Boniface)

Xenophanes (Atenophanes) (*fl.* 6th Cent. B.C.)   I-153
Xenophanes of Colophon (c.579-c.475 B.C.)   I-173
Xenophon (c.434-c.355 B.C.)   I-313
Xerxes (519?-465 B.C.)   I-237

Yawist, The (*fl.* 10th Cent.)   I-96

Zacharias (?-752)   II-1121; 1131
Zadok (*fl.* 1st Cent. B.C.-A.D. 1st Cent.)   I-477
Zakkai, Johanan ben (*see* ben Zakkai)
Zechariah (*fl.* 6th-5th Cent. B.C.)   I-189
Zedekiah (*fl.* 6th Cent. B.C.)   I-149
Zeno (*fl.* late 5th Cent.)   II-980
Zeno of Citium (335-263 B.C.)   I-210; 388; 403
Zeno of Elea (*fl.* 5th Cent. B.C.)   I-231
Zeno the Isaurian (426-491)   II-989
Zerubbabel (*fl.* 6th Cent. B.C.)   I-189
Ziyad, Tarik ibn (*see* ibn Ziyad)
Zoroaster (660-590 B.C.)   I-163
Zosimas (*fl.* 15th Cent.)   III-1738
Zosimus (?-418)   II-946
Zubaidha (*fl.* 8th Cent.)   II-1142

Abbo, John A.
Sacred Cannons, The   II-917
Abbott, Frank Frost
History and Description of Roman Political Institutions, A   I-396
Abbott, Nabia
Two Queens of Baghdad: Mother and Wife of Harun al-Rashid   II-1144
Abelson, Paul
Seven Liberal Arts: A Study in Mediaeval Culture, The   II-1001
Adcock, F. E.
Athens, 478-401 B.C. Vol. V of The Cambridge Ancient History   I-244
"Draco", in The Cambridge Ancient History I-155
Greek and Macedonian Art of War, The I-311
Thucydides and His History   I-295
Adler, Morris
World of the Talmud, The   II-987
Afnan, Soheil M.
Avicenna: His Life and Works   III-1227
Alt, Albrecht
"Formation of the Israelite State in Palestine, The," in Essays on Old Testament History and Religion   I-92
Andrewes, A.
Greek Tyrants, The   I-136
Ashby, Thomas
Roman Campagna in Classical Times, The I-374
Astin, A. E.
Scipio Aemilianus   I-456
Aulen, Gustaf
Christus Victor: An Historical Study of the Three Main Types of the Atonement   III-1293

Badian, E.
Foreign Clientelae (264-70 B.C.)   I-336
Baer, Yitzhak
History of the Jews in Christian Spain, A III-1754
Bailey, Cyril
Phases in the Religion of Ancient Rome I-433
Bainton, Roland H.
"Patristic Christianity," in The Idea of History in the Ancient Near East   II-793
Baldry, H. C.
Unity of Mankind in Greek Thought, The I-390; 455
Banner, W. A.
"Origen and the Tradition of Natural Law Concepts," in Dumbarton Oaks Papers II-804
Barker, Ernest

Politics of Aristotle, The. Translated with an Introduction, Notes and Appendixes   I-346
Barnard, L. W.
Justin Martyr. His Life and Thought   II-710
Barraclough, Geoffrey
History in a Changing World   III-1198
Origins of Modern Germany, The   III-1366; 1475; 1623; 1638
Barrett, Helen M.
Boethius: Some Aspects of His Times and Work II-1020
Barrow, Reginald Haynes
Plutarch and His Times   II-688
Barthold, W.
Turkestan Down to the Mongol Invasion III-1255
Baugh, Albert C.
History of the English Language, A   III-1288
Beazley, C. Raymond
Prince Henry, the Navigator   III-1688
Bede, The Venerable
Opera de Temporibus   II-860
Bell, Sir H. Idris
Egypt from Alexander the Great to the Arab Conquest   I-416
Bergin, Thomas G.
Dante   III-1601
Berkouwer, G. C.
Sacraments, The   III-1341
Bevan, Edwyn Robert
History of Egypt Under the Ptolemaic Dynasty, A   I-406
Stoics and Sceptics   I-473
Bigg, Charles
Christian Platonists of Alexandria, The II-735
Bilmanis, Alfred
History of Latvia, A   III-1474
Birley, A. R.
Marcus Aurelius   II-728
Blank, Sheldon H.
Jeremiah, Man and Prophet   I-151
Prophetic Faith in Israel   I-185
Blinzler, Josef
Trial of Jesus, The   II-603
Bloomfield, Morton W.
Linguistic Introduction to the History of English, A   III-1289
Boase, Thomas Sherer
Boniface VIII   III-1594
Bourne, Frank C.
"Roman Alimentary Program and Italian Agriculture, The," in Transactions and Proceedings of the American Philological Association   II-678

Bowra, C. M.
  Tradition and Design in the Iliad   I-112
Brandon, S. G. F.
  Fall of Jerusalem and the Christian Church, The   II-651
  History, Time and Deity   II-792
Breasted, James Henry
  Battle of Kadesh, The   I-72
  Development of Religion and Thought in Ancient Egypt   I-55
Brehaut, Ernest
  Encyclopedist of the Dark Ages: Isidore of Seville, An   II-1088
Brehier, Emile
  History of Philosophy: The Hellenistic and Roman Age, The   I-474
Bridges, J. H.
  Life and Works of Roger Bacon, The   III-1541
Bromhead, C. N.
  From Early Times to the Fall of the Ancient Empires. Vol. I of *A History of Technology*   I-17
Brooke, Zachery N.
  "Lay Investiture and Its Relation to the Conflict of Empire and Papacy," in *Proceedings of the British Academy*   III-1320
Brown, Peter
  Augustine of Hippo: A Biography   II-948
Bruce-Boswell, Alexander
  "Poland and Lithuania in the Fourteenth and Fifteenth Centuries," in Vol. VIII of *The Cambridge Medieval History*   III-1652
Bruckberger, R. L.
  History of Jesus Christ, The   I-570
Bryce, James
  Holy Roman Empire, The   III-1196; 1319
Buber, Martin
  Kingship of God   I-87
Buchan, J.
  Augustus   I-549
Bultmann, Rudolf
  Jesus and the Word   II-591
Burckhardt, Jacob
  Age of Constantine the Great, The   II-848
Burkitt, F. C.
  Religion of the Manichees, The   II-809
Burnet, John
  Early Greek Philosophy   I-272
Burroughs, Betty
  Vasari's Lives of the Artists   III-1589
Bury, J. B.
  Invasion of Europe by the Barbarians, The   II-961
Butler, Dom Edward Cuthbert
  Benedictine Monachism   II-1032
  Western Asceticism: The Teaching of SS Augustine, Gregory and Bernard on Contemplation and the Contemplative Life   III-1331
Butler, H. C.

"Roman Aqueducts as Monuments of Architecture, The," in *American Journal of Archaeology*   II-628
Butler, Pierce
  Origin of Printing in Europe, The   III-1715
Cajori, Florian
  History of Mathematical Notations, A   III-1284
  History of Mathematics, A   III-1285
Campbell, Anna M.
  Black Death and Men of Learning, The   III-1629
Campbell, Thomas L.
  Dionysius the Pseudo-Areopagite: The Ecclesiastical Hierarchy   II-1014
Campenhausen, Hans von
  Fathers of the Greek Church, The   II-775; 803; 896
Campion, Thomas
  "Obseruations in the Art of English Poesie," in *Elizabethan and Jacobean Quartos*   III-1350
Canfield, Leon H.
  Early Persecutions of the Christians, The   II-694
Capes, William W.
  English Church in the Fourteenth and Fifteenth Centuries, The   III-1632
Carlyle, R. W.
  History of Medieval Political Theory in the West, A   II-1089
Carter, Jesse Benedict
  Religion of Numa and Other Essays on the Religion of Ancient Rome, The   I-202
Cayré, Fulbert
  Manual of Patrology   II-1114
Cazamian, L.
  History of French Literature, A   III-1224
Ceram, C. W.
  Gods, Graves, and Scholars   II-661
Chadwick, Henry
  Origen: Contra Celsum. *Translated with an Introduction and Notes*   II-734
Chambers, Mortimer
  Fall of Rome: Can It Be Explained?, The   II-981
Chenu, M.D., O.P.
  Toward Understanding Saint Thomas   III-1546
Cheyney, Edward P.
  Dawn of a New Era, 1250-1453, The   III-1516
Chibnall, M.
  Historia Pontificalis of John of Salisbury, The   III-1373
Childe, V. Gordon
  "Rotary Motion," in *A History of Technology*   I-6
  What Happened in History   I-60
Chute, Marchette

Geoffrey Chaucer of England   III-1657
Cipolla, Carlo M.
  Guns, Sails, and Empires   III-1511
Clagett, Marshall
  Science of Mechanics in the Middle Ages, The
  III-1616
Clark, Kenneth
  *Leonardo da Vinci: An Account of His Develop-
  ment As an Artist*   III-1762
Clarke, W. K. Lowther
  First Epistle of Clement to the Corinthians, The
  II-671
Clay, Reginald S.
  History of the Microscope, The   III-1557
Clements, R. E.
  *God and Temple; the Presence of God in Isra-
  el's Worship*   I-102
Coghlan, H. H.
  *From Early Times to the Fall of the Ancient
  Empires.* Vol. I of *A History of Technology*
  I-17
Cohn, N.
  *World-View of a Thirteenth-Century Parisian
  Intellectual: Jean de Meun and the* Roman
  de la Rose, *The*   III-1470
Collinder, Per
  History of Marine Navigation, A   III-1507
Collingwood, R. G.
  Roman Britain and the English Settlements
  II-619
Columbus, Christopher
  Journal of Christopher Columbus, The   III-
  1759
Comba, Emilio
  *History of the Waldensians of Italy, from Their
  Origin to the Reformation*   III-1383
Congar, Yves
  *After Nine Hundred Years: The Background of
  the Schism Between the Eastern and Western
  Churches*   III-1240
Conzelmann, Hans
  *Outline of the Theology of the New Testament,
  An*   II-610
Copleston, Frederick C., S. J.
  Medieval Philosophy   II-836
  "Nicholas of Cusa," in Vol. III of *A History
  of Philosophy*   III-1711
Cornford, Francis Macdonald
  *Principium Sapientiae: The Origins of Greek
  Philosophical Thought*   I-175
Corwin, Virginia
  Saint Ignatius and Christianity in Antioch
  II-698
Coulton, George G.
  Black Death, The   III-1628
  *St. Barnard, His Predecessors and Successors,
  1000-1200.* Vol. I of *Five Centuries of Reli-
  gion*   II-1031
Court, Thomas L.
  History of the Microscope, The   III-1557
Creasy, Sir Edward S.

Twenty Decisive Battles of the World   II-
  581; 1118
Creighton, Mandell
  *History of the Papacy from the Great Schism
  to the Sack of Rome, A*   III-1595
Cullmann, Oscar
  "Origin of Christmas, The," in *The Early
  Church, Studies in Early Christian History
  and Theology*   II-885
  Peter, Disciple, Apostle, Martyr   II-644
Cumont, Franz
  Oriental Religions in Roman Paganism, The
  I-435
Curtis, D.
  "Roman Monumental Arches," in *Supple-
  mentary Papers* of the American School of
  Classical Studies in Rome   I-504

Daly, Lowrie J., S. J.
  Medieval University, The   III-1481
Daniel, Samuel
  "Defence of Rhyme, A," in *Elizabethan and
  Jacobean Quartos*   III-1352
Danielou, Jean
  Origen   II-777; 798
Dante Alighieri
  Comedy of Dante Alighieri the Florentine, The
  III-1560
Deanesly, Margaret
  *History of Early Medieval Europe, 476 to 911,
  A*   II-1162
  Pre-Conquest Church in England, The   II-
  1061
Debevoise, Neilson C.
  Political History of Parthia, A   I-429
Decarreaux, Jean
  *Monks and Civilization: From the Barbarian
  Invasions to the Reign of Charlemagne*
  II-1055
De Clercq, Victor
  *Ossius of Cordova: A Contribution to the His-
  tory of the Constantinian Period*   II-875
De Faye, Eugene
  Origen and His Work   II-759; 797
De Montmorency, J. E. G.
  Thomas à Kempis, His Age and His Book
  III-1672
De Roover, Raymond A.
  *Money, Banking and Credit in Medieval
  Bruges*   III-1360
De Santillana, Giorgio
  Prologue to Parmenides   I-233
Dewey, John
  Reconstruction in Philosophy   I-366
Dickinson, J.
  Statesman's Book of John of Salisbury, The
  III-1372
Dijksterhuis, E. J.
  Archimedes, in Vol. XII of *Acta Historica
  Scientiarum Naturalium et Medicinalium*
  I-423

Diringer, David
 Alphabet, The I-82
Dix, Dom Gregory, O. S. B.
 Shape of the Liturgy, The II-881; 1096
Dodd, C. H.
 Apostolic Preaching and Its Developments, The
  II-609
 Epistle of Paul to the Romans, The II-635
Dodge, T. A.
 Hannibal I-440
Drachmann, A. B.
 Atheism in Pagan Antiquity I-381
Dreyer, J. L. E.
 *History of Astronomy from Thales to Kepler,
 A* (formerly entitled *History of the Planetary
 Systems from Thales to Kepler*) II-714
Driver, G. R.
 Babylonian Laws, The I-47
Duchesne, Louis
 "Christian Festivals (Christmas and Epiph-
 any), The," in *Christian Worship, Its Origin
 and Evolution* II-886
Duchesne-Guillemin, Jacques
 Symbols and Values in Zoroastrianism
  I-166
Dudden, Frederick Homes
 *Gregory the Great: His Place in History and
 Thought* II-1066
 Life and Times of St. Ambrose, The II-921
Duff, A. M.
 Freedmen in the Early Roman Empire
  II-624
Duff, J. Wight
 *Literary History of Rome from the Origins to
 the Close of the Golden Age, A* I-468;
 524; 533
 *Literary History of Rome in the Silver Age from
 Tiberius to Hadrian, A* I-533; 654
Duggan, Charles
 Twelfth-century Decretal Collection II-916
Duke, John A.
 Columban Church, The II-1084
Dunbabin, T. J.
 Western Greeks, The I-130
Dvornik, Francis
 Byzantine Missions Among the Slavs II-
 1176
 Byzantium and the Roman Primacy III-
 1239
 Slavs, Their Early History and Civilization, The
  III-1208

Eddy, Samuel K.
 *King Is Dead, The. Studies in the Near Eastern
 Resistance to Hellenism, 334-31 B.C.*
 I-462
Edelstein, Ludwig
 "Greek Medicine in Its Relation to Religion
 and Magic," in *Bulletin of the Institute of
 the History of Medicine* I-304
 Meaning of Stoicism, The I-391

Editors of Time-Life Books
 World of Leonardo (1452-1519), The III-
 1764
Edwards, I. E. S.
 Pyramids of Egypt, The I-27
Ehrhardt, Arnold
 *Apostolic Succession in the First Two Centuries
 of the Church, The* II-744
 Framework of the New Testament Stories, The
  II-769
Elliott-Binns, L. E.
 *History of the Decline and Fall of the Medieval
 Papacy, The* III-1647
Else, G. F.
 Origin and Form of Early Greek Tragedy, The
 I-251
Emerton, Ephraim
 *Correspondence of Pope Gregory VII: Selected
 Letters from the Registrum, The* III-
 1265
 *Defensor Pacis of Marsiglio of Padua: A Criti-
 cal Study, The* III-1610
Ensslin, W.
 "Reforms of Diocletian, The," in Vol. XII of
 The Cambridge Ancient History II-831
Erman, Adolf
 *Ancient Egyptians: A Sourcebook of Their
 Writings, The* I-36

Fabre, Lucien
 Joan of Arc III-1699
Face, Richard D.
 *Caravan Merchants and the Fairs of Cham-
 pagne, The* III-1424
Farquharson, A. S. L.
 Marcus Aurelius: His Life and His World
  II-727
Farrar, F. W.
 Lives of the Fathers II-931
Farrington, Benjamin
 Science and Politics in the Ancient World
 I-513
Fawtier, Robert
 *Capetian Kings of France: Monarchy and Na-
 tion (987-1328), The* III-1202
Fedotov, George P.
 *Russian Religion Mind: Kievan Christianity:
 The Tenth to the Thirteenth Centuries, The*
 III-1207
Fennell, J. L. I.
 Ivan the Great of Moscow III-1739; 1743
Ferguson, John
 Pelagius II-949
Ferguson, W. S.
 "Athenian Expedition to Sicily, The," in Vol.
 V of *The Cambridge Ancient History*
 I-310
 "Fall of the Athenian Empire, The," in Vol.
 V of *The Cambridge Ancient History*
 I-310
 "Oligarchic Movement in Athens, The," in

Vol. V of *The Cambridge Ancient History*
I-310
"Leading Ideas of the New Period, The," in
Vol. V of *The Cambridge Ancient History*
I-405
Fichte, Johann Gottlieb
Addresses to the German Nation   II-587
Fichtenau, Heinrich
Carolingian Empire, The   II-1149
Figgis, John Neville
*Political Aspects of St. Augustine's "City of
God", The*   II-942
Finkelstein, Louis
Pharisees, The   I-478
Fleming, John Dick
*Israel's Golden Age: The Story of the United
Kingdom*   I-108
Fletcher, Sir Banister
*History of Architecture on the Comparative
Method, A*   III-1418
Flick, Alexander C.
Decline of the Medieval Church, The   III-
1646
Florinsky, Michael T.
Russia: A History and Interpretation   III-
1464; 1740; 1745
Folz, Robert
"Eighth Century Concepts About the Roman
Empire," in *The Coronation of Charle-
magne, What Did It Signify?*   II-1124
Forbes, Robert J.
*From Early Times to the Fall of the Ancient
Empires.* Vol. I of *A History of Technology*
I-17
"Power," in *A History of Technology*   I-7
Studies in Ancient Technology. Vol. IX
I-19; Vol. VIII & IX   I-61
Fowler, H. D.
Camels to California   I-32
Frank, Tenney
"Rome and Carthage: The First Punic War,"
in Vol. VII of *The Cambridge Ancient His-
tory*   I-410
Frankfort, H.
Ancient Egyptian Religion: An Interpretation
I-54
"Egyptian Way of Life, The," in *Ancient Egyp-
tian Religion: An Interpretation*   I-38
French, A.
Growth of the Athenian Economy, The
I-171
Frend, W. H. C.
*Martyrdom and Persecution in the Early
Church*   II-639; 814
Frere, Sheppard
Britannia: A History of Roman Britain
II-618
Friedlander, Paul
Plato, an Introduction   I-325
Frisch, Hartvig
Constitution of the Athenians, The   I-228

Frontinus
Stratagems and the Aqueducts of Rome, The
II-629
Frye, Richard N.
Heritage of Persia, The   I-430
Fuller, John F. C.
*From the Earliest Times to the Battle of
Lepanto.* Vol. I of *A Military History of the
Western World*   II-580; 978
Julius Caesar, Man, Soldier, and Tyrant
I-518
Military History of the Western World, A
II-1119
Fuller, Reginald H.
Mission and Achievement of Jesus, The
II-592
Fussell, George E.
*Farming Techniques from Prehistoric to Mod-
ern Times*   II-1171

Gabrieli, Francesco
"Transmission of Learning and Literary Influ-
ences to Western Europe," in Vol. II of *The
Cambridge History of Islam*   II-1192
Gade, John A.
*Hanseatic Control of Norwegian Commerce
During the Late Middle Ages, The*   III-
1433
Gardiner, Sir Alan H.
Egypt of the Pharaohs   I-66
Kadesh Inscriptions of Ramesses II, The
I-73
Gelb, I. J.
Study of Writing, A   I-11
Gewirth, Alan
*Marsilius of Padua and Medieval Political
Philosophy.* Vol. I of *Marsilius of Padua:
The Defender of Peace*   III-1611
Gibbon, Edward
*History of the Decline and Fall of the Roman
Empire, The*   II-983
Gierke, Otto
Political Theories of the Middle Ages   II-
786
Gilson, Étienne
*Christian Philosophy of St. Thomas Aquinas,
The*   III-1547
*History of Christian Philosophy in the Middle
Ages*   II-836
Mystical Theology of Saint Bernard, The
III-1332
Reason and Revelation in the Middle Ages
III-1397; 1566
Gleason, H. A.
Introduction to Descriptive Linguistics, An
I-13
Glubb, General Sir John
Lost Centuries, The   III-1578
Godfrey, John
Church in Anglo-Saxon England, The   II-
1060; 1083; 1128

Gomme, A. W.
Historical Commentary on Thucydides, A
I-293
Gomperz, Theodor
Greek Thinkers: A History of Ancient Philosophy I-288
Goodenough, Erwin R.
Introduction to Philo Judaeus, An II-614
Goodspeed, Edgar Johnson
History of Early Christian Literature, A II-699
New Solutions of New Testament Problems II-782
Story of the Apocrypha, The I-445
Gossage, A. J.
"Plutarch," in *Latin Biography* II-689
Goudge, Elizabeth
My God and My All: The Life of St. Francis of Assisi III-1449
Graham, A. J.
Colony and Mother City in Ancient Greece I-132
Graves, Edgar B.
"Legal Significance of the Statute of Praemunire of 1353, The," in *Anniversary Essays in Medieval History* III-1632
Greenidge, Abel H. J.
Roman Political Life I-451
Roman Public Life I-222
Greenslade, S. L.
Church and State from Constantine to Theodosius II-855
Gregory, Bishop of Tours
History of the Franks II-997
Griffith, G. T.
Hellenistic Civilization I-341
Grillmeier, Aloys, S.J.
Christ in Christian Tradition: From the Apostolic Age to Chalcedon II-965
Guarducci, Margherita
Tomb of St. Peter—New Discoveries in the Sacred Grottoes of the Vatican, The II-645
Guérard, Albert
France: A Modern History III-1705
Guérdan, René
Byzantium: Its Triumphs and Tragedy III-1720
Gunkel, Hermann
Legends of Genesis: The Biblical Saga and History, The I-98
Guthrie, W. K. C.
Greeks and Their Gods, The I-161
Gwatkin, Henry Melvill
Christian Roman Empire and the Foundation of the Teutonic Kingdoms, The. Vol. I of *The Cambridge Medieval History* II-959

Hadas, Moses
History of Greek Literature, A I-113; 262
History of Latin Literature, A I-534
Hadzsits, George Depue
Lucretius and His Influence I-514
Halecki, Oscar
"From the Union with Hungary to the Union with Lithuania: Jadwiga 1374-99," in *The Cambridge History of Poland. From the Origins to Sobieski (to 1696)* III-1653
Hamarneh, Sami K.
"Arabic Historiography as Related to the Health Professions in Medieval Islam," in *Medical History* III-1228
"Climax of Chemical Therapy in the 10th Century Arabic Medicine, The," in *Der Islam* II-1181
"Climax of Medieval Arabic Professional Pharmacy, The," in *Bulletin of the History of Medicine* II-1181; III-1228
Index of Arabic Manuscripts on Medicine and Pharmacy at the National Library of Cairo III-1228
"Medical Education and Practice in Medieval Islam," in O'Malley's *The History of Medical Education* II-1181; III-1228
"Sources and Development of Arabic Medical Therapy and Pharmacology," in *Sudhoffs Archiv.* II-1181; III-1228
"Surgical Developments in Medieval Arabic Medicine," in *Viewpoints: American Friends of the Middle East* III-1228
Hamilton, Edith
"Pindar: The Last Greek Aristocrat," in *The Great Way to Western Civilization* I-218
Hammond, B. G. L.
History of Greece to 322 B.C., A I-340
Hammond, Mason
Augustan Principate in Theory and Practice During the Julio-Claudian Period, The I-564
City-State and World State I-509
Hannan, Jerome D.
Sacred Canons, The II-917
Hansen, Esther V.
Attalids of Pergamon, The I-488
Hanson, R. P. C.
St. Patrick: A British Missionary Bishop II-971
Hardie, W. F. R.
Aristotle's Ethical Theory I-331
Harnack, Adolph
History of Dogma, The II-869
Origin of the New Testament, The II-781
Harris, H. A.
Greek Athletes and Athletics I-118
Hart, Henry H.
Venetian Adventurer III-1552
Hauser, Arnold
Social History of Art, The III-1590
Havelock, Eric A.
Preface to Plato I-326
Hawkins, D. J. B.
Of Learned Ignorance III-1710
Hazeltine, Harold Dexter

"Roman and Canon Law in the Middle Ages," in Vol. V of *The Cambridge Medieval History*   III-1494

Head, Barclay V.
Historia Numorum   I-145

Heath, Sir Thomas L.
Archimedes   I-424
Aristarchus of Samos: The Ancient Copernicus I-399
History of Greek Mathematics, A   I-385
Thirteen Books of Euclid's Elements, The I-386

Henderson, Bernard W.
Five Roman Emperors   II-677

Herford, Robert Travers
Pharisees, The   I-479

Herodotus
Histories, The   I-239

Hess, Hamilton
Canons of the Council of Sardica, The   II-874

Hignett, C. H.
History of the Athenian Constitution to the End of the Fifth Century, B.C., A   I-156; 206
Xerxes' Invasion of Greece   I-240

Hirmer, Max
Egypt. Architecture, Sculpture, Painting in Three Thousand Years   I-28
Greek Coins   I-147
Greek Sculpture   I-278

Hirst, Leonard B.
Conquest of Plague, The   III-1627

Hitti, Philip K.
History of the Arabs   II-1077; 1107

Hoepffner, Ernest
Troubadours dans leur vie et dans leurs oeuvres, Les   III-1300

Holland, D. Larrimore
"Earliest Text of the Old Roman Symbol: A Debate with Hans Leitzmann and J. N. D. Kelly, The," in *Church History*   II-755

Holmes, Thomas Rice
Caesar's Conquest of Gaul   I-518

Holt, J. C.
Magna Carta   III-1453

Hooper, William Davis
Marcus Porcius Cato, On Agriculture; Marcus Terentius Varro, On Agriculture   I-467

How, W. W.
"Cicero's Ideal in His De Republica," in *Journal of Roman Studies*   I-529

Hughes, Barnabas, O. F. M.
Regiomontanus on Triangles   II-718

Hughes, Kathleen
Church in Early Irish Society, The   II-972

Hughes, Philip
Church in Crisis: A History of the General Councils 325-1870, The   III-1460

Hunt, H. A. K.
Humanism of Cicero, The   I-543

Hunt, Richard W.

"Studies on Priscian in the Twelfth Century: The School of Ralph of Beauvais," in *Medieval and Renaissance Studies*   II-1026

Huttmann, Maude Aline
Establishment of Christianity and the Proscription of Paganism, The   II-907

Huxley, G. L.
Early Sparta   I-137

Hyatt, J. Philip
Jeremiah: Prophet of Courage and Hope I-151

Innes, Mary M., trans.
Metamorphoses of Ovid, The   II-574

Irving, Washington
Chronicle of the Conquest of Granada, A III-1750

Jacobs, E. F.
"Innocent III," in Vol. VI of *The Cambridge Medieval History*   III-1459

Jaeger, Werner W.
"Aristocracy: Conflict and Transformation, The," in *Paideia*   I-116
Aristotle, Fundamentals of the History of His Development   I-330
"Memory of Socrates, The," in *Paideia: The Ideals of Greek Culture*, in 3 vols.   I-321
Paideia: The Ideals of Greek Culture, in 3 vols. I-289

Jalland, T. G.
Church and the Papacy, The   II-820

Jerimias, Joachim
Eucharistic Words of Jesus, The   II-599

Jenkins, Romilly
Byzantium: The Imperial Centuries, A.D. 610-1071   III-1217

Join-Lambert, Michel
Jerusalem   I-103

Jolowicz, H. F.
Historical Introduction to the Study of Roman Law   I-256; 493

Jones, A. H. M.
Athenian Democracy   I-208
Constantine and the Conversion of Europe II-849
Greek City from Alexander to Justinian, The I-355
Later Roman Empire 284-602—A Social, Economic, and Administrative Survey, The II-936

Jones, G. F.
Ethos of the Song of Roland, The   III-1310

Jones, H. Stuart
"Primitive Institutions of Rome, The," in Vol. VII of *The Cambridge Ancient History* I-284

Jones, Leslie Webber
Introduction to Divine and Human Readings by Cassiodorus Senator, An   II-1048

Jungmann, Joseph A., S. J.
Mass of the Roman Rite: Its Origins and Development, The   II-1071

Kähler, Heinz
Hagia Sophia   II-1043
Kalmer, Joseph
Warrior of God   III-1677
Kantorowicz, Ernst
King's Two Bodies, The   III-1345
Kapelrud, A. S.
Central Ideas in Amos   I-126
Kayser, Rudolf
Life and Time of Jehuda Halevi, The   III-1336
Kelly, J. N. D.
Early Christian Creeds   II-753; 870
Early Christian Doctrines   II-750
Keyes, G. L.
Christian Faith and the Interpretation of History   II-944
King, N. Q.
Emperor Theodosius and the Establishment of Christianity, The   II-906
Kirk, G. S.
Heraclitus, the Cosmic Fragments   I-212
Presocratic Philosophers: A Critical History with a Selection of Texts, The   I-267
Kitch, M. J.
Capitalism and the Reformation   III-1522
Knowles, David
Evolution of Medieval Thought, The   III-1526
Kohn, Hans
Nationalism and Liberty: The Swiss Example   III-1606
Kraay, C. M.
Greek Coins   I-147
Kristeller, Paul Oscar
Philosophy of Marsilio Ficino, The   III-1725
Kuttner, Stephen
"Cardinalis: The History of a Canonical Concept," in *Traditio*   III-1245

Labarge, Margaret Wade
Simon de Montfort   III-1530
Laistner, Max L. W.
Thought and Letters in Western Europe, A.D. 500 to 900   II-1139
Lanchester, H. C. O.
"Sibylline Oracles," in *Encyclopaedia of Religion and Ethics*   I-203
Lane, Frederic C.
"Andrea Barbarigo Merchant of Venice 1418-1449" in *Johns Hopkins University Studies in Historical and Political Science*   III-1355
Lange, K.
Egypt. Architecture, Sculpture, Painting in Three Thousand Years   I-28

Last, Hugh
"Tiberius Gracchus," in Vol. IX of *The Cambridge Ancient History*   I-483
Lawson, John
Biblical Theology of Saint Irenaeus, The   II-749
Lea, Henry Charles
History of Sacerdotal Celibacy in the Christian Church   III-1259
History of the Inquisition of the Middle Ages, The   III-1486
Lechler, Gotthard
John Wycliffe and His English Precursors   III-1642
Leclerq, Jean
Love of Learning and the Desire for God, The   II-1049
Leff, Gordon
Heresy in the Later Middle Ages   III-1384
Lekai, Louis J.
White Monks, The. A History of the Cistercian Order   III-1427
Leonard, A. G.
Camel: Its Uses and Management, The   I-31
Levarie, Siegmund
Guillaume de Machaut   III-1413
Lewis, C. S.
Allegory of Love: A Study in Medieval Tradition, The   III-1300
Lightfoot, J. B.
"Christian Ministry, The," in *Saint Paul's Epistle to the Philippians*   II-683
Lindars, Barnabas
New Testament Apologetic   II-707
Lindberg, David C.
"Cause of Refraction in Medieval Optics, The," in *The British Journal for the History of Science*   III-1556
Linforth, Ivan M.
Solon the Athenian   I-169
Lods, Adolphe
Israel from Its Beginnings to the Middle of the Eighth Century   I-107
Long, Herbert S.
"Unity of Empedocles Thought, The," in *American Journal of Philology*   I-273
Longfellow, W. P. P.
Column and the Arch, The   I-502
Lot, Ferdinand
End of the Ancient World and the Beginnings of the Middle Ages, The   II-864; 998
Lowell, Francis C.
Joan of Arc   III-1700
Lullies, R.
Greek Sculpture   I-278
Lutzow, Count
Life and Times of Master John Hus, The   III-1678
Lyon, Bryce

Constitutional and Legal History of Medieval England, A   III-1531; 1572

McArthur, A. Allan
Evolution of the Christian Year, The   II-880; 1095
McDonnell, Sir John
Great Jurists of the World. Vol. II of *Continental Legal History Series.*   II-723
McGregor, M. F.
Athenian Tribute Lists, The   I-245
McIlwain, Charles Howard
Constitutionalism: Ancient and Modern   II-787; III-1387
MacKendrick, Paul
Greek Stones Speak: The Story of Archaeology in Greek Lands, The   I-300
McKenzie, John L.
"Gospel According to Matthew, The," in *The Jerome Biblical Commentary*   I-569
MacKinney, Loren C.
Bishop Fulbert and Education at the School of Chartres   III-1234
McShane, Roger B.
Foreign Policy of the Attalids of Pergamum, The   I-489
Madaule, Jacques
Albigensian Crusade, The   III-1443
Mahaffy, J. P.
Progress of Hellenism in Alexander's Empire, The   I-315
Maimonides
Guide for the Perplexed, The   III-1392
Maitland, Frederick William
Constitutional History of England, The   III-1570
History of English Law Before the Time of Edward I, The   III-1389
Manson, Edward
Great Jurists of the World, Vol. II of *Continental Legal History Series*   II-723
Marcellinus, Ammianus
Histories, The   II-900
Martin, Paul E.
"Swiss Confederation in the Middle Ages, The," in Vol. VII of *The Cambridge Medieval History*   III-1605
Martins, J. P. Oliveira
Golden Age of Prince Henry, the Navigator, The   III-1689
Marxsen, W.
Introduction to the New Testament   II-634
Maryon, Herbert
From Early Times to the Fall of the Ancient Empires. Vol. I of *A History of Technology*   I-17
Matthews, D. J. A.
Norman Conquest, The   III-1251
Mattingly, Harold B.
Imperial Civil Service of Rome, The   II-623

"Imperial Recovery, The," in Vol. XI of *The Cambridge Ancient History*   II-831
Mendenhall, George E.
Law and Covenant in Israel and in the Ancient Near East   I-86
Meritt, Benjamin D.
Athenian Tribute Lists, The   I-245
Merton, Reginald
Cardinal Jiménes and the Making of Spain   III-1730
Metzger, B. M.
Introduction to the Apocrypha, An   I-446
Meyerhoff, Max
"Philosophy of the Physician ar-Razi, The," in *Islamic Culture*   II-1182
Michels, A. K.
Calendar of the Roman Republic, The   I-539
Miles, John C.
Babylonian Laws, The   I-47
Miller, Townsend
Castles and the Crown, The   III-1749
Minar, Edwin L.
Early Pythagorean Politics in Practice and Theory   I-196
Mitchell, Lt. Col. Joseph B.
Twenty Decisive Battles of the World   II-581; 1118
Molland, A. G.
"Geometrical Background to the 'Merton School': An Exploration into the Application of Mathematics to Natural Philosophy in the Fourteenth Century, The," in *The British Journal for the History of Science*   III-1617
Molland, Einar
"Irenaeus of Lugdunum and the Apostolic Succession," in *Journal of Ecclesiastical History*   II-745
Molmenti, Pompeo
Venice, Its Individual Growth from the Earliest Beginnings to the Fall of the Republic   III-1357
Momigliano, Arnaldo
Conflict Between Paganism and Christianity in the Fourth Century, The   II-927
Mommsen, Theodore
History of Rome, The   I-283
Montalembert, Charles Forbes René
Saint Columban   II-1054
Moorhouse, Alfred C.
Triumph of the Alphabet, The   I-82
Moravcsik, Gy
"Hungary and Byzantium in the Middle Ages," in Vol. IV of *The Cambridge Medieval History*   III-1213
Morgenstern, Julian
Amos Studies   I-127
Morison, Samuel Eliot
Admiral of the Ocean Sea   III-1758
Morrison, Karl Frederick

"Canossa: A Revision," in *Traditio* III-1271

Rome and The City of God II-854

Mullin, Francis A.
History of the Work of the Cistercians in York-shire 1131-1300, A III-1428

Mundy, John H.
Medieval Town, The III-1326

Murray, A. Victor
Abélard and St. Bernard: A Study in 12th Century Modernism III-1316

Muscatine, Charles
Chaucer and the French Tradition III-1658

Myers, John L.
Herodotus, Father of History I-261

Mylonas, George E.
Eleusis and the Eleusinian Mysteries I-160

Myres, J. N. L.
Roman Britain and the English Settlements II-619

Naumann, Hans
"Nibelungenlied: eine stauffische Elegie oder ein Deutsches Nationalepos?, Das," in *Dichtung und Volkstum* III-1406

Nelson, Benjamin N.
Idea of Usury, The III-1521

Nelson, N. E.
"Cicero's *de Officiis* in Christian Thought: 300-1300," in *University of Michigan Essays and Studies in English and Comparative Literature* I-544

Neugebauer, Otto
Exact Sciences in Antiquity, The I-23; II-715

Neuman, Abraham
Jews in Spain, The III-1754

Newmark, Leonard
Linguistic Introduction to the History of English, A III-1289

Nicholas, Barry
Introduction to Roman Law, An II-1036

Nilsson, Martin P.
History of Greek Religion, A I-121
Primitive Time-Reckoning I-537

North, Christopher R.
Suffering Servant in Deutero-Isaiah, The I-186

Norwood, Gilbert
Pindar I-217

Noth, Martin
Exodus: A Commentary I-78
History of Israel, The I-94; 191

Nussbaum, G. B.
Ten Thousand, The. A Study in Social Organization and Action in Xenophon's Anabasis I-316

Oborn, George T.
"Why Did Decius and Valerian Proscribe Christianity?" in *Church History* II-815

O'Donnell, Joseph M.
Canons of the First Council of Arles, 324 A.D., The II-859

Oesterley, W. O. E.
Jewish Background of the Christian Liturgy, The II-596

Oppenheim, A. Leo
Ancient Mesopotamia: Portrait of a Dead Civilization I-43

Ostrogorsky, George
History of the Byzantine State II-1155

Oswald, John Clyde
History of Printing, A III-1716

Otis, Brooks
Virgil. A Study in Civilized Poetry I-559

Ottley, R. R.
Handbook to the Septuagint, A I-420

Pain, Nesta
King and Becket, The III-1377

Painter, Sidney
Reign of King John, The III-1455

Pais, Ettore
Ancient Italy I-255

Panofsky, Erwin
Renaissance and Renascences in Western Art III-1693

Panzer, Friedrich
Nibelungenlied: Entstehung und Gestalt, Das III-1407

Paredi, Angelo
Saint Ambrose—His Life and Times II-922

Parke, H. W.
Delphic Oracle, The I-123

Parsch, Pius
Liturgy of the Mass, The II-1072

Parsons, Edward Alexander
Alexandrian Library: Glory of the Hellenic World, The II-925

Patrick, John
Apology of Origen in Reply to Celsus, The II-733

Pears, Edwin
Destruction of the Greek Empire and the Story of the Capture of Constantinople by the Turks, The III-1720

Perowne, John James Stewart
Death of the Roman Republic I-497
End of the Roman World, The II-938
Hadrian II-704

Petit-Dutaillis, Charles
Feudal Monarchy in France and England from the Tenth to the Thirteenth Century, The III-1203
"France: Louis XI," in Vol. VIII of *The Cambridge Medieval History* III-1735

Pfeiffer, Robert H.
Introduction to the Old Testament II-666

Philby, H. St. John
Harun al-Rashid II-1144

Philip, J. A.
  Pythagoras and Early Pythagoreans   I-197
Picard, Collette
  Life and Death of Carthage, The   I-411
Picard, Gilbert Charles
  Life and Death of Carthage, The   I-411
Pirenne, Henri
  "Carolingian Coup d'Etat and the Volte-Face of the Papacy, The," in *Mohammed and Charlemagne*   II-1133
  Economic and Social History of Medieval Europe   III-1362
  Medieval Cities   II-1133
Plenderleith, H. J.
  From Early Times to the Fall of the Ancient Empires. Vol. I of *A History of Technology*   I-17
Plucknett, Theodore F. T.
  Taswell-Langmead's English Constitutional History   III-1584
Pollock, Sir Frederick
  History of English Law Before the Time of Edward I, The   III-1389
Polo, Marco
  Travels of Marco Polo, The   III-1553
Pope-Hennessy, John
  Italian Renaissance Sculpture   III-1668
Pöschl, Viktor
  Art of Vergil: Image and Symbol in the Aeneid, The   I-558
Poschmann, Bernhard
  Penance and the Anointing of the Sick   II-765
Post, Gaines
  Studies in Medieval Legal Thought   III-1346
Post, L. A.
  From Homer to Menander   I-369
Postan, M. M.
  Agrarian Life of the Middle Ages, The. Vol. I. of *The Cambridge Economic History*   III-1325
  Trade and Industry in the Middle Ages. Vol. II of *The Cambridge Economic History*   III-1517
Pourrat, Rev. Pierre
  Christian Spirituality   II-932
Powicke, Frederick M.
  Thirteenth Century, 1216-1307, The   III-1583
Previte-Orton, Charles W.
  Late Roman Empire to the Twelfth Century, The. Vol. I of *The Shorter Cambridge Medieval History*   II-976; 1160
Procter, Evelyn S.
  Alfonso X of Castile, Patron of Literature and Learning   III-1525

Quasten, Johannes
  Beginnings of Patristic Literature, The. Vol. I of *Patrology*   II-672

Quine, Willard Van Orman
  From a Logical Point of View   II-837

Rackham, H.
  Cicero, De Oratore   I-522
Radbertus, Paschasius
  Lord's Body and Blood, The   II-1165
Ramsay, William M.
  Church in the Roman Empire, The   II-641
  "Pliny's Report and Trajan's Rescript," in *The Church in the Roman Empire*   II-693
Rand, E. K.
  Founders of the Middle Ages   II-1021
Randall, John Herman
  Aristotle   I-365
Ranking, G. S. A.
  "Life and Works of Rhazes, The," in *Proceedings of the 17th International Congress of Medicine*   II-1182
Rashdall, Hastings
  Salerno—Bologna—Paris. Vol. I of *The Universities of Europe in the Middle Ages*   III-1493
  Universities of Europe in the Middle Ages, The (in 3 vols.)   III-1402
Ratramnus
  Lord's Body and Blood, The   II-1166
Raven, J. E.
  Presocratic Philosophers: A Critical History with a Selection of Texts, The   I-267
Reynolds, Robert L.
  Europe Emerges   II-1102; III-1305; 1424
Ricciotti, Guiseppe
  Julian the Apostate   II-891
Rice, Tamara Talbot
  Seljuks in Asia Minor, The   III-1254
Rich, E. E.
  Cambridge Economic History, The (in 6 vols.)   III-1517
  Trade and Industry in the Middle Ages. Vol. II of *The Cambridge Economic History*   III-1517
Richardson, G. W.
  "Actium," in *The Journal of Roman Studies*   I-554
Richter, Gisela M. A.
  Sculpture and Sculptors of the Greeks, The   I-299
Riesenberg, Peter
  Medieval Town, The   III-1326
Riesman, David
  Story of Medicine in the Middle Ages, The   III-1480
Rist, John M.
  Plotinus: The Road to Reality   II-826
Robertson, D. S.
  Handbook of Greek and Roman Architecture, A   I-279
Rogers, E. F.

Peter Lombard and the Sacramental System
III-1340
Rolt, C. E.
*Dionysius the Areopagite on the Divine Names
and the Mystical Theology* II-1013
Rörig, Fritz
Medieval Town, The III-1432
Rose, Lynn C.
Aristotle's Syllogistic I-350
Rostovtzeff, Mikhail I.
Rome. Vol. II of *A History of the Ancient
World* II-832
*Social and Economic History of the Hellenistic
World, The* I-414
Roubiczek, Paul
Warrior of God III-1677
Rowley, H. H.
*From Joseph to Joshua: Biblical Traditions in
the Light of Archaeology* I-77
Growth of the Old Testament, The II-667
Runciman, Steven
"Crusader States, 1243-1291, The," in *The
Later Crusades 1189-1311.* Vol. II of Set-
ton's *A History of the Crusades* III-1576
*First Crusade and the Foundation of the King-
dom of Jerusalem, The.* Vol. I of Setton's *A
History of the Crusades* III-1280
History of the First Bulgarian Empire, A
III-1218
Kingdom of Acre and the Later Crusades, The.
Vol. III of Setton's *A History of the Crusades*
III-1439; 1498
*Medieval Manichee: A Study of the Christian
Dualist Heresy, The* III-1444

Sabatier, Paul
Life of St. Francis of Assisi III-1450
Sabine, George Holland
*One of the Commonwealth of Marcus Tullius
Cicero* I-527
Saggs, H. W. F.
Greatness That Was Babylon, The I-181
Sägmüller, Johannes Baptist
"Cardinal," in *The Catholic Encyclopedia*
III-1246
Saint John of Damascus
Writings II-1113
Sale, William
"Dual Vision of the *Theogony,* The," in *Arion*
I-142
Sanders, N. K.
Epic of Gilgamesh, The I-42
Sandys, John Edwin
*From the Sixth Century B.C. to the End of the
Middle Ages.* Vol. I of *A History of Classical
Scholarship* I-356; II-1025; III-1233
Sarkissian, Karekin
*Council of Chalcedon and the Armenian
Church, The* II-966
Sarton, George
Galen of Pergamum II-739

*Hellenistic Science and Culture in the Last
Three Centuries B.C.* Vol. II of *A History of
Science* I-401
Saunders, J. J.
History of Medieval Islam, A II-1079
Schevill, Ferdinand
*History of the Balkan Peninsula, The. From the
Earliest Times to the Present Day* III-
1663
Schnürer, Gustav
Church and Culture in the Middle Ages: Vol.
I: *350-814* II-1129
Scholem, Gershom G.
*Jewish Gnosticism, Markabah Mysticism, and
Talmudic Tradition* III-1562
Major Trends in Jewish Mysticism III-
1561
Schürer, Emil
*History of the Jewish People in the Time of
Jesus Christ, The* II-650
Scott, J. F.
History of Mathematics, A II-719
Scullard, H. H.
Roman Politics 220-150 B.C. I-449
Scipio Africanus: Soldier and Politician
I-439
Seay, Albert
Music in the Medieval World III-1412
Seebohm, M. E.
Evolution of the English Farm, The II-1171
Seidler, Grzegorz Leopold
Political Doctrine of the Mongols, The III-
1465
Sellar, W. Y.
*Roman Poets of the Augustan Age: Horace and
the Elegiac Poets, The* II-576
Sellers, R. V.
Council of Chalcedon, The II-954
Setton, Kenneth M.
First Hundred Years, The. Vol. I of *A History
of the Crusades* III-1278
Later Crusades, 1189-1311, The. Vol. II: *A
History of the Crusades* III-1500
Seymour, Charles, Jr.
Sculpture in Italy: 1400-1500 III-1667
Seznec, Jean
*Survival of the Pagan Gods: The Mythological
Tradition and Its Place in Renaissance Hu-
manism and Art, The* III-1769
Sherwin-White, Adrian N.
Roman Citizenship, The I-335; 508
Siegel, Rudolph E.
Galen's System of Physiology and Medicine
II-740
Sigerist, Henry E.
History of Medicine, A I-305
Sikes, J. G.
Peter Abailard III-1314
Silver, Daniel J.
*Maimonidean Criticism and the Maimonidean
Controversy, 1180-1240* III-1393

Simpson, George Gaylord
Horses: The Story of the Horse Family in the Modern World and Through Sixty Million Years of History   I-3
Singer, Charles
Mediterranean Civilization and the Middle Ages, The. Vol. II of A History of Technology   I-229
Sinor, Denis
History of Hungary   III-1211
Smith, Lucy Margaret
Early History of the Monastery of Cluny, The   II-1186
Smith, R. E.
Failure of the Roman Republic, The   I-484; 499
Smith, Stanley B.
On the Commonwealth of Marcus Tullius Cicero   I-527
Snell, Bruno
Discovery of the Mind: The Greek Origins of European Thought, The   I-176
"Myth and Reality in Greek Tragedy," in The Discovery of the Mind: The Greek Origins of European Thought   I-250
Sohm, Rudolph
Institutes, A Textbook of the History and System of Roman Private Law, The   II-1006
Solmsen, Friedrich
"Dialectic Without the Forms," in Aristotle on Dialectic   I-351
Southern, R. W.
Saint Anselm and His Biographer: A Study of Monastic Life and Thought, 1059-c.1130   III-1294
Sparks, H. F. D.
"Latin Bible, The," in The Bible in Its Ancient and English Versions   II-911
Speiser, E. A.
"Authority and Law in Mesopotamia," in Journal of the American Oriental Society   I-49
Sperry, Willard L.
Strangers and Pilgrims   III-1673
Spinka, Matthew
John Hus at the Council of Constance   III-1682
Spooner, F. C.
"Reformation in Difficulties: France, 1519-1559, The," in Vol. II of The New Cambridge Modern History   III-1704
Stacey, John
John Wyclif and Reform   III-1643
Stahl, William H.
Roman Science: Origins, Development, and Influence to the Later Middle Ages   II-656
Stavrianos, L. S.
Balkans Since 1453, The   III-1661
Stenton, F. M.
Anglo-Saxon England   III-1250
Strack, Hermann L.

Introduction to the Talmud and Midrash   I-986
Strayer, Joseph R.
Western Europe in the Middle Ages: A Short History   II-1148
Streeter, B. H.
Primitive Church, The   II-683
Stuhlmueller, Carroll, C. P.
"Gospel According to Luke, The," in The Jerome Biblical Commentary   I-569
Sundberg, A. C.
"Towards a Revised History of the New Testament Canon," in Studia Evangelica IV: Texte und Untersuchengen   II-770
Sutton, E. W.
Cicero, De Oratore   I-522
Sweeney, Leo
"Another Interpretation of Enneads," in Modern Schoolman   II-825
"Infinity in Plotinus," in Gregorianum   II-825
Swete, H. B.
Introduction to the Old Testament in Greek, An   I-419
Swift, Emerson Howland
Hagia Sophia   II-1042
Syme, Ronald
"Northern Frontier Under Augustus, The," in Vol. X of The Cambridge Ancient History   II-586
Roman Revolution, The   I-547; 565

Tanzer, Helen H.
Common People of Pompeii: A Study of the Graffiti, The   II-662
Taran, Leonardo
Parmenides: A Text with Translation, Commentary and Critical Essays   I-234
Tarn, Sir William W.
Alexander the Great   I-361
"Battle of Actium, The," in The Journal of Roman Studies   I-553
Hellenistic Civilization   I-341
Hellenistic Military and Naval Developments   I-359
Taylor, A. E.
Socrates   I-320
Taylor, Henry Osborn
Mediaeval Mind: A History of the Development of Thought and Emotion in the Middle Ages, The   II-1003
Taylor, L. R.
"Forerunners of the Gracchi," in Journal of Roman Studies   I-224
Tcherikover, Victor
Hellenistic Civilization and the Jews   I-461
Thompson, E. A.
Visigoths in the Time of Ulfila, The   II-902
Thompson, James Westfall
Economic and Social History of the Middle Ages (300-1300), An   III-1423

Feudal Germany   III-1367

Thorndike, Lynn
  History of Magic and Experimental Science, A.
  Vol. II   III-1542
  "Vincent of Beauvais," in Vol. II of *A History
  of Magic and Experimental Science During
  the First Thirteen Centuries of Our Era*
  III-1535

Thuasne, L.
  Roman de la Rose, Le   III-1468

Thurian, Max
  Marriage and Celibacy   III-1260

Tocqueville, Alexis de
  Old Regime and the Revolution, The   III-
  1736

Tod, Marcus N.
  Athens, 478-401 B.C. Vol. V of *The Cambridge
  Ancient History*   I-244

Trend, J. B.
  "Spain and Portugal," in *The Legacy of Islam*
  II-1108

Turner, J. W. Cecil
  Introduction to the Study of Roman Law
  I-494

Ullman, B. L.
  "Project for a New Edition of Vincent of
  Beauvais, A," in *Speculum*   III-1536

Ullmann, Walter
  *Growth of Papal Government in the Middle
  Ages, The*   II-991; 1122; 1132; III-1266;
  1273
  Origins of the Great Schism, The   III-1683

Vacandard, E.
  *Inquisition: A Critical and Historical Study of
  the Coercive Power of the Church, The*
  III-1488

Valency, Maurice
  *In Praise of Love: An Introduction to the Love-
  Poetry of the Renaissance*   III-1299

Vance, E.
  Reading the Song of Roland   III-1311

Van Der Waerden, B. L.
  Science Awakening   I-23

Van Melsen, Andrew G.
  From Atomos to Atom   I-266

Varende, Jean de la
  Cherish the Sea   III-1506

Vasiliev, A. A.
  History of the Byzantine Empire, 324-1453
  II-863; 890; 1154; III-1438

Venables, Edmund
  "Basilius of Caesareia," in *A Dictionary of
  Christian Biography*   II-895

Vernadsky, George
  Origins of Russia, The   II-1175

Vignaux, Paul
  Philosophy in the Middle Ages: An Introduction
  III-1567

Villari, Pasquale

First Two Centuries of Florentine History, The
  III-1305

Vinogradoff, Paul
  Roman Law in Medieval Europe   II-1008

Voegelin, Eric
  Plato and Aristotle. Vol. III of *Order and History*   I-345

Von Fritz, Kurt
  "Reorganization of the Roman Government
  in 366 B.C. and the So-called Licinio-Sex-
  tian Laws, The," in *Historia*   I-394

Von Hagen, Victor W.
  Roads That Led to Rome, The   I-376
  Roman Roads   I-376

Von Hefele, the Rev. Dr.
  Life of Cardinal Ximenes   III-1731

Von Hügel, Friedrich
  *Reality of God and Religion and Agnosticism,
  The*   I-380

Von Rad, Gerhard
  "Form-Critical Problem of the Hexateuch,
  The," (1938), reprinted in *The Problem of
  the Hexateuch and Other Essays*   I-99

Von Simson, Otto
  *Gothic Cathedral: Origins of Gothic Architec-
  ture and the Medieval Concept of Order, The*
  III-1419

Wade-Gery, H. T.
  Athenian Tribute Lists, The   I-245

Walker, D. P.
  *Spiritual and Demonic Magic from Ficino to
  Campanella*   III-1726

Walker, E. M.
  Athens, 478-401 B.C. Vol. V of *The Cambridge
  Ancient History*   I-244

Wallace, R.
  World of Leonardo (1452-1519), The   III-
  1764

Wallace-Hadrill, D. S.
  Eusebius of Caesarea   II-843

Wallace-Hadrill, J. M.
  Barbarian West, 400-1000, The   II-1138

Watkins, Oscar D.
  History of Penance, A   II-764

Watt, W. Montgomery
  History of Islamic Spain, A   II-1191

Waugh, W. T.
  "Germany: Charles IV," in Vol. VII of *The
  Cambridge Medieval History*   III-1636
  "Germany: Lewis the Bavarian," in Vol. III
  of *The Cambridge Medieval History*   III-
  1622

Waxman, Meyer
  History of Jewish Literature, A   III-1335

Webster, T. B. L.
  Art and Literature in Fourth Century Athens
  I-371

Welch, Adam C.
  Post-Exilic Judaism   I-190

Weltin, E. G.

"Ancient Popes, The," in *The Popes Through History*   II-821
Ancient Popes, The   II-955
West, M. L.
Hesiod's Theogony. Edited with *Prolegomena and Commentary*   I-140
Wheelwright, Philip
Heraclitus   I-213
White, H. J.
"Vulgate," in *A Dictionary of the Bible*   II-912
White, John
Birth and Rebirth of Pictorial Space, The   III-1694
White, Leslie A.
Science of Culture: A Study of Man and Civilization, The   I-68
White, Lynn, Jr.
Medieval Technology and Social Change   II-1101; 1170; III-1512
Whitney, J. P.
Christian Roman Empire and the Foundation of the Teutonic Kingdoms, The. Vol. I of *The Cambridge Medieval History*   II-959
Wickham, Glynne W.
Early English Stages, 1300-1660   III-1222
Widegren, George
Mani and Manichaeism   II-810
Wieruszowski, H.
Medieval University, The   III-1403
Wilken, Robert L.
"Bishop's Maiden, The," in *The Myth of Christian Beginnings*   II-842
Wilson, W. R.
Execution of Jesus: A Judicial and Historical Investigation, The   II-604
Wind, Edgar
Pagan Mysteries in the Renaissance   III-1768
Winston, Richard

Thomas Becket   III-1378
Wohil, Howard
"Note on the Fall of Babylon, A," in *Journal of the Ancient Near Eastern Society of Columbia University*   I-182
Wolff, Hans Julius
Roman Law: An Historical Introduction   II-1037
Wolfson, Harry A.
Philo   II-613
Philosophy of the Church Fathers, The   II-759
Workman, Herbert B.
Evolution of the Monastic Ideal, The   II-1187
Wormell, D. E. W.
Delphic Oracle, The   I-123

Yadin, Yigael
"Finding Bar Kokhba's Despatches: The Exciting Story of an Archaeological Expedition Among the Dead Sea Caves," in *Illustrated London News*   II-705

Zaehner, R. C.
Teachings of the Magi, The   I-165
Zedler, Beatrice H.
Averroës' Destructio Destructionum Philosophiae Algazelis *in the Latin Version of Calo Calonymos*   III-1398
Zeuner, Friedrich E.
History of Domesticated Animals, A   I-3
Ziegler, A. K.
"Pope Gelasius and His Teaching on the Relation of Church and State," in *Catholic Historical Review*   II-992
Zimmerman, Odo John
Saint Gregory the Great: Dialogues   II-1065
Zulueta, Francis de
Institutes of Gaius, The   II-722

Abbott, Edwin A.
St. Thomas of Canterbury   III-1380
Abbott, Frank Frost
History and Description of Roman Political Institutions, A   I-452
Municipal Administration in the Roman Empire   I-337
Abbott, Walter M.
Documents of Vatican II, The   III-1262
Abelson, Paul
Seven Liberal Arts, The   III-1235
Abraham, Gerald
New Oxford History of Music, The (in 4 vols.)   III-1415
Abrahams, Israel
Maimonides   III-1394
Studies in Pharisaism and the Gospels   I-480
Adams, G. B.
Council and Courts in Anglo-Norman England   III-1390
Adams, Henry
Mont-Saint-Michel and Chartres   III-1420
Adcock, F. E.
Augustan Empire, 44 B.C.-A.D. 70, The. Vol. X of *The Cambridge Ancient History*   II-583; 625
"Conquest of Central Italy, The," in *The Cambridge Ancient History*   I-337; 377
Roman Art of War Under the Republic, The   I-500
Roman Political Ideas and Practice   I-452
Roman Republic, 133-44 B.C., The. Vol. IX of *The Cambridge Ancient History*   I-500
Adendy, Walter F.
"Waldenses," in *Encyclopedia of Religion and Ethics*   III-1385
Agus, Jacob B.
"Yehuda Halevi," in *Great Jewish Books and Their Influence on History*   III-1337
Aikan, Pauline
Various Articles in *Speculum,* X, XIII, and XVII; also in *Studies of Philology*   III-1537
Aitchison, Leslie
History of Metals, A   I-63
Aland, Kurt
Problem of the New Testament Canon, The   II-783
Alberti, Leon Battista
On Painting   III-1695
Albright, W. F.
Biblical Period from Abraham to Ezra, The   I-109
Aldis, Harry G.
Printed Book, The   III-1717
Aldred, Cyril
Egypt to the End of the Old Kingdom   I-29

Egyptians, The   I-57; 69
Kingship and Gods: A Study of Ancient Near Eastern Religion as the Integration of Society and Nature   I-69
Alexander, Paul J.
Patriarch Nicephorus of Constantinople: Ecclesiastical Policy and Image Worship in the Byzantine Empire, The   II-1156
Alfoldi, A.
Conversion of Constantine and Pagan Rome, The   II-850
Allen, Agnes
Story of the Book, The   III-1717
Al-Makkari, Ahmed ibn Mohammed
History of the Mohammedan Dynasties in Spain, The   II-1194
Alt, Albrecht
"God of the Fathers, The," in *Essays on Old Testament History and Religion*   I-100
"Origins of Israelite Law, The," in *Essays on Old Testament History and Religion*   I-88
Altamira, Rafael
History of Spain, A   II-1194
Altaner, Berthöld
Patrology   II-700; 1067
Ambrose
Letter 51. Early Latin Theology   II-923
Amiot, François
History of the Mass   II-1073
Anderson, J. G. C.
"Genesis of Diocletian's Provincial Re-Organization, The," in *Journal of Roman Studies*   II-833
Anderson, J. K.
Military Theory and Practice in the Age of Xenophon   I-317
Anderson, W.
Man's Quest for Political Knowledge. The Study and Teaching of Politics in Ancient Times   I-530
André, Marius
Columbus   III-1759
Andreades, A. M.
History of Greek Public Finance, A   I-247
Andreski, Stanislav
Military Organization and Society   I-500
Anonymous
Little Flowers of Saint Francis, The   III-1451
Anton, John P.
Aristotle's Theory of Contrariety   I-367
Aquinas, Thomas
Summa Theologiae   III-1549
Arberry, A. J.
Revelation and Reason in Islam   III-1398
Spiritual Physick of Rhazes, The   II-1182

Armstrong, A. H.
Cambridge History of Later Greek and Early Medieval Philosophy, The II-827
Plotinus with an English Translation II-827
Armstrong, Gregory T.
"Imperial Church Building and Church-State Relations, A.D. 313-363," in *Church History* II-856
Ashby, Thomas
Aqueducts of Ancient Rome, The II-631
Astin, A. E.
Lex Annalis Before Sulla, The I-452
Scipio Aemilanus I-485
Atiya, Asiz
Crusade, Commerce, and Culture III-1281
Crusade: Historiography and Bibliography, The III-1502
Atkins, J. W. H.
Literary Criticism in Antiquity I-535
Audisio, Gabriely
Harun al-Rashid II-1145
Augur, Helen
Book of Fairs, The III-1425
Azo, R. F.
"Chemistry in Iraq and Persia in the Tenth Century A.D.," in *Memoirs of the Royal Asiatic Society of Bengal* II-1182
Azurara, Gomes Eannes
Conquests and Discoveries of Henry the Navigator III-1690

Badawi, A.
"Muhammad ibn Zakariya al-Razi," in Vol. I of *A History of Muslim Philosophy* II-1183
Badcock, F. J.
History of the Creeds, The II-756
Badian, E.
Foreign Clientelae *(264-70 B.C.)* I-510
Baeck, Leo
Pharisees and Other Essays, The I-480
Bailey, Cyril
Greek Atomists and Epicurus, The I-268
Legacy of Rome, The II-630
Phases in the Religion of Ancient Rome I-204
"Roman Religion and the Advent of Philosophy," in *The Cambridge Ancient History* I-204
Titi Lucreti Cari De Rerum Natura *Libri Sex* I-515
Bailey, K. C.
Elder Pliny's Chapters on Chemical Subjects, The II-657
Baker, G. P.
Hannibal I-442
Baldwin, Charles Sears
Medieval Rhetoric and Poetic to 1400 III-1353

Baldwin, Marshall
Alexander III and the Twelfth Century III-1380
Ball, W. W. Rouse
Short Account of the History of Mathematics, A II-720; III-1286
Balsdon, J. P.
Julius Caesar I-520
Bammel, Ernst
Trial of Jesus, The II-606
Bang, Martin
"Expansion of the Teutons (to A.D. 378)," in *The Cambridge Medieval History* II-903
Barber, Richard
Henry Plantagenet III-1380
Barker, Ernest
Political Thought of Plato and Aristotle, The I-347
Barker, Stephen F.
Philosophy of Mathematics I-387
Baron, Salo Wittmayer
Social and Religious History of the Jews, A I-464; II-652
Barraclough, Geoffrey
Medieval Germany 911-1250. Vol. I of *Studies in Medieval History* III-1322
Medieval Germany 911-1250: Essays by German Historians. Vol. I: *Introduction.* Vol. II: *Essays* III-1267
Medieval Papacy, The II-994; 1125; 1134; III-1247; 1267; 1274; 1322; 1596; 1648
Origins of Modern Germany, The III-1199
Barrett, C. K.
Commentary on the Epistle to the Romans, A II-637
Barrett, Helen M.
Boethius: Some Aspects of His Times and Work II-1004
Barrett, W. P.
Trial of Jeanne d'Arc, The III-1702
Barron, John P.
"Religious Propaganda of the Delian League," in *Journal of Hellenic Studies* I-247
Barry, Nicholas
Introduction to Roman Law, An II-724
Barth, Karl
Epistle to the Romans II-636
Bartok, Josef Paul
John Hus at Constance III-1679
Barton, G. A.
Archaeology and the Bible I-39
Baus, Karl
From the Apostolic Community to Constantine. Vol. I of *Handbook of Church History* II-700
Baynes, Norman H.
"Constantine the Great and the Christian Church," in *The Proceedings of the British Academy* II-850
"Dynasty of Valentinian and Theodosius the Great, The," in *The Cambridge Medieval*

History II-903
Beamish, Tufton
  Battle Royal III-1532
Beare, F. W.
  "Canon of the New Testament," in *The Inter-
    preter's Dictionary of the Bible* II-772
  "Letter to the Romans," in *The Interpreter's
    Dictionary of the Bible* II-637
Bede, The Venerable
  History of the English Church and People, A
    II-1062; 1085
Bekker, Hugo
  Nibelungenlied: A Literary Analysis, The
    III-1409
Belkin, Samuel
  Philo and the Oral Law II-615
Bell, Harold Idris
  *Egypt: From Alexander the Great to the Arab
    Conquest* II-928
Bemont, Charles
  Simon de Montfort Earl of Leicester 1208-1265
    III-1532
Benardete, M. J.
  *Hispanic Culture and Character of the Sephar-
    dic Jews* III-1755
Benecke, P. V. M.
  "Rome and the Hellenistic States," in *The
    Cambridge Ancient History* I-490
Bengtson, Hermann
  Hellenism and the Rise of Rome I-412
Bennett, H. S.
  "Chaucer and the Fifteenth Century," in *The
    Oxford History of English Literature*
    III-1659
Bennett, J. A. W.
  Early Middle English Verse and Prose III-
    1290
Benson, E. F.
  Life of Alcibiades, The I-312
Bentwich, Norman
  Philo II-615
Benvenisti, J. L.
  *Iniquitous Contract: An Analysis of Usury and
    Maldistribution, The* III-1523
Benz, Ernst
  Eastern Orthodox Church, The III-1242
Berenson, Bernard
  Italian Painters of the Renaissance, The
    III-1591; 1770
Bernard, L. W.
  "St. Clement of Rome and the Persecution of
    Domitian," in *Studies in the Apostolic Fa-
    thers and Their Background* II-673
Betrams, Wilhelm
  Celibacy of the Priest, The III-1261
Bethune-Baker, J. F.
  *Introduction to the Early History of Christian
    Doctrine, An* II-761
Bett, H.
  Nicholas of Cusa III-1712
Bevan, Edwyn Robert

House of Seleucus, The I-407
  Jerusalem Under the High Priests I-193
  Stoics and Sceptics I-392
  "Syria and the Jews," in *The Cambridge An-
    cient History* II-652
Beye, Charles Rowan
  Iliad, the Odyssey, and the Epic Tradition, The
    I-114
Bickermann, Elias
  Maccabees, The I-464
Bieber, Margarete
  History of the Greek and Roman Theater, The
    I-372
Bieler, Ludwig
  History of Roman Literature I-470; 525
  Ireland: Harbinger of the Middle Ages
    II-973
Bigg, Charles
  Christian Platonists of Alexandria, The
    II-735; 778; 799; 805
Bihlmeyer, Karl
  Church History II-892
  Middle Ages, The II-1168
Billings, Thomas Henry
  Platonism of Philo Judaeus, The II-615
Billington, James H.
  *Icon and the Axe: An Interpretative History of
    Russian Culture, The* III-1209
Blake, Warren E.
  Menander's Dyscolus I-372
Blau, Joseph L.
  *Christian Interpretation of the Cabala in the
    Renaissance, The* III-1563
Blenkinsopp, Joseph
  Celibacy, Ministry, Church III-1262
Bloch, Marc
  Growth of the Ties of Independence, The, and
    Social Classes and Political Organization.
    Vols. I-II of *Feudal Society* III-1327
Block, Edward A.
  John Wycliffe, Radical Dissenter III-1643
Blondel, Maurice
  St. Augustine II-945
Blötzer, Joseph
  "Inquisition," in *The Catholic Encyclopedia*
    III-1490
Boak, Arthur E. R.
  History of Rome to A.D. 565, A II-939; 979
Boardman, J.
  Greek Art and Architecture I-301
Boase, Thomas Shesser Ross
  St. Francis of Assisi III-1451
Bochenski, I. M.
  Problem of Universals, The II-839
Boissier, Gaston
  Cicero and His Friends I-545
Boissonnade, Prosper
  Life and Work in Medieval Europe III-
    1307; 1429; 1518
Bokser, Ben Zion
  From the World of the Cabbalah III-1563

Legacy of Maimonides, The   III-1394

Bolgar, R. R.
Classical Heritage and Its Beneficiaries from the Carolingian Age to the End of the Renaissance, The   III-1235

Bolkenstein, H.
Economic Life in Greece's Golden Age   I-148

Bonner, Gerald
St. Augustine of Hippo: Life and Controversies   II-950

Bonner, Robert J.
Administration of Justice from Homer to Aristotle, The   I-157

Bony, Jean
French Cathedrals   III-1420

Borchsenius, Paul
Three Rings, The   III-1755

Boren, Henry C.
"Numismatic Light on the Gracchan Crisis," in *American Journal of Philology*   I-485

Bornkamm, Günther
Jesus of Nazareth   I-571; 599

Botsford, George W.
Roman Assemblies, The   I-397

Bourke, Vernon J.
Augustine's Quest of Wisdom   II-761

Bourne, Edward G.
Prince Henry, the Man   III-1690

Bowra, C. M.
Oxford Book of Greek Verse in Translation, The   I-219

Boyd, William K.
Ecclesiastical Edicts of the Theodosian Code, The   II-908

Boyer, Carl B.
History of Mathematics, A   I-24

Bradeen, Donald W.
"Popularity of the Athenian Empire, The," in *Historia*   I-246

Brandon, S. G. F.
Trial of Jesus of Nazareth, The   II-606

Branner, Robert
Gothic Architecture   III-1420

Breasted, James Henry
"Age of Ramses II, The," in *The Cambridge Ancient History*   I-74
Ancient Records of Egypt   I-74
Development of Religion and Thought in Ancient Egypt   I-39

Brehaut, Ernest
Cato the Censor on Farming   I-470
"Occupational Development of Roman Society About the Time of the Elder Cato," in *Essays in Intellectual History Dedicated to James Harvey Robinson*   I-470

Bréhier, Émile
Philosophhy of Plotinus, The   II-827

Bréhier, Louis
"Attempts at Reunion of the Greek and Latin Churches," in *The Cambridge Medieval History*   III-1242

Bright, John
Early Israel in Recent History Writing   I-109
"From Tribal Confederacy to Dynastic State," in *A History of Israel*   I-95
History of Israel, A   I-79
Jeremiah   I-152

Brinker, R.
Influence of Sanctuaries in Early Israel, The   I-104

Brock, A. J.
Galen On the Natural Faculties   II-741

Brokelmann, Carl
History of the Islamic Peoples   II-1110

Brown, Frank E.
Roman Architecture   I-505

Brown, J. R.
Temple and Sacrifice in Rabbinic Judaism   I-105

Brown, Peter
Augustine of Hippo   II-945

Brown, Ruth Martin
Study of the Scipionic Circle, A   I-457

Browne, L. E.
From Babylon to Bethlehem   I-193

Bruce, F. F.
Books and the Parchments, The   II-912

Brucker, Gene A.
Florentine Politics and Society, 1343-1378   III-1306

Brundage, James A.
Crusades: A Documentary Survey, The   III-1281; 1439
Crusades: Motives and Achievements, The   III-1281

Brunt, P. A.
"Persian Accounts of Alexander's Campaigns," in *Classical Quarterly*   I-362
"Thucydides and Alcibiades," in *Revue de études grecques*   I-296; 312

Bryce, James
Holy Roman Empire, The   II-1151

Buber, Martin
Moses: The Revelation and the Covenant   I-79; 88

Buchan, John
Augustus   I-566

Buckland, William W.
Manual of Roman Private Law, A   I-495
Textbook of Roman Law from Augustus to Justinian, A   I-495; II-724; 1039

Buckler, F. W.
Harun'l-Rashid and Charles the Great   II-1120; 1145

Bukofzer, Manfred F.
"Speculative Thinking in Medieval Music," in *Speculum (XVII)*   III-1415

Bullough, Donald
Age of Charlemagne, The   II-1120

Bultmann, Rudolf

Form Criticism: Two Essays in New Testament Research II-593
Theology of the New Testament II-611
Burckhardt, Jacob
Age of Constantine the Great, The II-866
Burn, A. E.
Council of Nicaea, The II-871
Introduction to the Creeds, An II-756
Burn, Andrew R.
Persia and the Greeks I-241
World of Hesiod, The I-143
Burn-Murdoch, A.
Development of the Papacy, The II-674; 822; 919
Burnet, John
Early Greek Philosophy I-177; 268
Bury, J. B.
Ancient Greek Historians, The I-263
Cambridge Medieval History, The III-1312
History of Greece to the Death of Alexander the Great, A I-317
History of the Later Roman Empire from the Death of Theodosius I to the Death of Justinian (A.D. 305 to A.D. 565) II-956; 984; 999
Invasion of Europe by the Barbarians, The II-903
Life of St. Patrick and His Place in History, The II-973
"Roman Emperors from Basil II to Isaac Komnenos," in *Selected Essays of J. B. Bury* III-1220
Bussell, Frederick William
Marcus Aurelius and the Later Stoics II-730
Butchvarov, Panayot
Resemblance and Identity. An Examination of the Problem of Universals II-839
Butler, Denis
1066: The Story of a Year III-1252
Butler, Dom Cuthbert
St. Benedict's Rule for Monasteries II-1034
Western Mysticism: The Teaching of SS Augustine, Gregory, and Bernard on Contemplation and the Contemplative Life II-1067
Butler, H. E.
Letters III-1374

Canfield, L. H.
Early Persecutions of the Christians, The II-642
Cadiou, René
Origen, His Life at Alexandria II-800
Cadoux, C. J.
Ancient Smyrna. A History from the Earliest Times to 324 A.D. I-357
Early Church and the World, The II-711; 736
Cajori, Florian

History of Mathematics, A I-387; II-720
Calahan, Harold Augustin
Sky and the Sailor, The III-1508
Calisse, Carlo
History of Italian Law III-1347
Calmette, Joseph
"France: The Reign of Charles VII and the End of the Hundred Years' War," in *The Cambridge Medieval History* III-1707
Cambridge Medieval History, The. Vol. V, chapters xvii, xix; Vol. VI, chapters ix, x III-1204
Campenhausen, Hans von
Fathers of the Greek Church II-845
Men Who Shaped the Western Church II-913
Cantor, Norman F.
Church, Kinship and Lay Investiture in England, 1089-1135 III-1295
"Crisis of Western Monasticism, 1050-1130, The," in *The American Historical Review* III-1275
English Tradition: Modern Studies in English History, The III-1585
Medieval History: The Life and Death of a Civilization II-1163
Capitolinus, Julius
"Marcus Antonius Philosophus," in *The Scriptores Historiae Augustae* II-730
Carey, Kenneth M.
Historic Episcopate, The II-746
Carli, Enzo
Giotto and His Contemporaries III-1591
Carlyle, A. J.
History of Medieval Political Theory in the West, A. Vol. I II-994
History of Medieval Political Theory in the West, A. Vol. IV. *The Theories of the Relation of the Empire and the Papacy from the Tenth Century to the Twelfth* III-1268
History of Medieval Political Theory in the West, A. Vol. VI. *Political Theory from 1306 to 1600* III-1612
Carlyle, R. W.
History of Medieval Political Theory in the West, A. Vol. IV. *The Theories of the Relation of the Empire and the Papacy from the Tenth Century to the Twelfth* III-1268
History of Medieval Political Theory in the West, A. Vol. VI. *Political Theory from 1306 to 1600* III-1612
Carpenter, Rhys
Folk Tale, Fiction, and Saga in the Homeric Epics I-114
Carrington, Philip
Christian Apologetics of the Second Century II-711
Carter, Jesse Benedict
Religion of Numa and Other Essays on the Religion of Ancient Rome, The I-436
Cary, Max

"Callias o Laccoplutos," in *Classical Review* I-230

History of the Greek World from 323 to 146 B.C. I-342

History of Rome Down to the Reign of Constantine, A I-550; 588

Oxford Classical Dictionary, The I-220

Case, Shirley Jackson
Christian Philosophy of History, The II-794

Cassidy, Frederick C.
Development of Modern English, The III-1290

Castro, Américo
Structure of Spanish History, The II-1110; 1193

Cave, Roy C.
Source Book for Medieval Economic History, A III-1425

Cawley, Arthur C.
Wakefield Pageants in the Townley Cycle, The III-1225

Ceram, C. W.
"Battle of Kadesh, The," in *The Secret of the Hittites* I-74

Chadwick, Henry
Early Christian Thought and the Classical Tradition II-736; 800
"Origen, Celsus and the Stoa," in *Journal of Theological Studies* II-805

Chadwick, Nora K.
Age of the Saints in the Early Celtic Church, The II-973

Chajes, Zebi Hirsch
Student's Guide Through the Talmud, The II-988

Chambers, Sir Edmund K.
"Medieval Drama," in *English Literature at the Close of the Middle Ages* III-1225

Chambers, Mortimer
Fall of Rome—Can It Be Explained?, The II-939

Charles, R. H.
Apocrypha and Pseudepigrapha, The I-447

Charlesworth, M. P.
Augustan Empire, 44 B.C.-A.D. 70, The. Vol. X of *The Cambridge Ancient History* II-583; 625
"Gaius and Claudius," in *The Cambridge Ancient History* II-625
Roman Republic, 133-44 B.C., The. Vol. IX of *The Cambridge Ancient History* I-500
"War of the East Against the West, The," in *The Cambridge Ancient History* I-555

Chase, Richard
Quest for Myth I-382

Cheyney, Edward P.
Dawn of a New Era, 1250-1453, The. Vol. I of *The Rise of Modern Europe* series III-1648; 1654; 1663

Chiera, W.

They Wrote on Clay I-14

Childe, V. Gordon
"Wheeled Vehicles," in *A History of Technology* I-9

Chrimes, K. M. T.
Ancient Sparta: A Reëxamination of the Evidence I-138

Chroust, Anton-Hermann
Aristotle: Protrepticus, A Reconstruction I-332

Chubb, Thomas Caldecott
Dante and His World III-1602

Church, Alonzo
Problem of Universals, The II-839

Cizevsky, Dmitry
Outline of Comparative Slavic Literatures II-1177

Clagett, Marshall
Archimedes in the Middle Ages I-426
Giovanni Marliani and Late Medieval Physics III-1619
Greek Science in Antiquity I-426; II-715
Medieval Science of Weights, The III-1619
Twelfth Century Europe and the Foundation of Modern Society III-1404

Clapham, J. H.
"Commerce and Industry in the Middle Ages," in *The Cambridge Medieval History* III-1363

Clark, James M.
Abbey of St. Gall as A Center of Literature and Art, The II-1057

Clayton, Joseph
Saint Anselm: A Critical Biography III-1295

Cleator, P. E.
Lost Languages I-14

Clough, Shepard B.
Economic History of Europe III-1307; 1358
European Economic History: The Economic Development of Western Civilization III-1327; 1358

Coggins, Jack
By Star and Compass: The Story of Navigation III-1508

Cole, Charles W.
Economic History of Europe III-1307 1358

Coleman, Christopher B.
Treatise of Lorenzo Valla on the Donation of Constantine, The II-1125

Coleman-Norton, P. R.
Twelve Tables Prefaced, Arranged, Translated, Annotated, The I-258

Colón, Fernando
Discovery of America, The III-1759

Commager, Steele
Virgil. A Collection of Critical Essays I-561

Compton, Piers
Turbulent Priest, The III-1380

Conant, Levi
  Number Concept, The. Its Origin and Development   I-24
Cook, J. M.
  Greeks in Ionia and the East   I-317
Cook, S. A.
  Augustan Empire, 44 B.C.-A.D. 70, The. Vol. X of *The Cambridge Ancient History* II-583
  Cambridge Ancient History, The   II-625
  Imperial Crisis and Recovery, A.D. 193-324. Vol. XII of *The Cambridge Ancient History* II-816
  Roman Republic, 133-44 B.C., The. Vol. IX of *The Cambridge Ancient History*   I-500
Copleston, Frederick, S. J.
  Aquinas   III-1549
  History of Philosophy, A. Vol. III: *Ockham to Suarez*   III-1613
  Medieval Philosophy   II-1016
Corbett, P. E.
  Sculpture of the Parthenon, The   I-280
Cornford, Francis Macdonald
  Before and After Socrates   I-322
  Plato and Parmenides   I-235
  Principium Sapientiae: The Origins of Greek Philosophical Thought   I-143
Corevin, Virginia
  St. Ignatius and Christianity in Antioch II-684
Cottrell, Leonard
  Guide to Roman Britain, A   II-620
  Hannibal, Enemy of Rome   I-442
Coulson, Herbert H.
  Source Book for Medieval Economic History, A   III-1425
Coulton, George Gordon
  Inquisition and Liberty   III-1385; 1445; 1489
Count, Earl W.
  "Mother and Child in Quest of a Birthday, A," in *4000 Years of Christmas*   II-887
Covensky, Milton
  Ancient Near Eastern Tradition, The   I-44
Cowell, F. R.
  Cicero and the Roman Republic   I-530
  Revolutions of Ancient Rome, The   I-550
Craig, H.
  English Religious Drama in the Middle Ages III-1225
Cram, Ralph Adams
  Substance of Gothic: Six Lectures on the Development of Architecture from Charlemagne to Henry VIII, The   III-1420
Cranz, F. Edward
  "Kingdom and Polity in Eusebius of Caesarea," in *Harvard Theological Review* II-856
Crawfurd, Raymond
  Plague and Pestilence in Literature and Art III-1629

Creasy, Sir Edward S.
  Fifteen Decisive Battles of the World from Marathon to Waterloo, The   II-588
  Twenty Decisive Battles of the World   III-1252
Crehan, Joseph
  Early Christian Baptism and the Creed II-756
Creighton, Charles
  History of Epidemics in Britain, A. (in 2 vols.) Vol. I: *From A.D. 664 to the Great Plague* III-1629
Crombie, A.C.
  Augustine to Galileo: The History of Science A.D. 400-1650   III-1619
  Robert Grosseteste and the Origins of Experimental Science   III-1558
Crombie, I. M.
  Examination of Plato's Doctrines, An. Vol. II: *Plato on Knowledge and Reality*   I-327
Crook, John A.
  Law and Life of Rome   I-495; II-1039
Croon, J. H.
  "Mysteries," in *Oxford Classical Dictionary* I-162
Crosby, Sumner McK.
  Helen Gardner's Art Through the Ages III-1591
Cross, F.L.
  Oxford Dictionary of the Christian Church, The   III-1707
Cross, S. H.
  Russian Primary Chronicle, The   III-1209
Crosse, G.
  "Praemunire," in *A Dictionary of English Church History*   III-1634
Crowley, Theodore
  Roger Bacon   III-1543
Cumont, Franz
  Astrology and Religion Among the Greeks and Romans   I-402
  Oriental Religions in Roman Paganism, The II-928
Cunningham, Robert L.
  "Etymologies, The," in *Masterpieces of Catholic Literature*   II-1090
Curley, Sr. Mildred
  Conflict Between Boniface VIII and Philip IV, the Fair, The   III-1596
Curwen, E. C.
  Plough and Pasture: The Early History of Farming   II-1103
Cust, Robert
  Botticelli   III-1770

Dahl, Nils A.
  "Particularity of the Pauline Epistles as a Problem in the Ancient Church, The," in *Neotestamentica et Patristica*   II-772
Dalmais, I. H.
  Introduction to the Liturgy   II-1073

Daly, Lowrie, S. J.
 Benedictine Monasticism: Its Formation and Thought Through the Twelfth Century II-1034; 1188
Dancy, J. C.
 Commentary on I Maccabees, A I-464
Daniel-Rops, Henri
 Bernard of Clairvaux III-1333
 Church in the Dark Ages, The II-1156
Dante Alighieri
 Convivio III-1601
 Monarchy and Three Political Letters III-1601
D'Arcy, Martin C., S. J.
 St. Augustine II-945
 Thomas Aquinas III-1548
Dark, Sidney
 St. Thomas of Canterbury III-1380
Daube, David
 Exodus Pattern in the Bible, The I-79
Davidson, Samuel
 Canon of the Bible, The II-668
Davies, J. G.
 Early Christian Church, The II-892
 Origin and Development of Early Christian Church Architecture, The II-1045
Davies, Reginald Trevor
 Golden Century of Spain, 1501-1621, The III-1732
Davies, W. D.
 Paul and Rabbinic Judaism II-636
Davis, Harold T.
 Alexandria, the Golden City II-928
Davis, Henry
 St. Gregory the Great, Pastoral Care II-1067
Davis, Simon
 Race Relations in Ancient Egypt I-357
Dawson, Christopher
 Making of Europe: An Introduction to the History of European Unity, The II-1134; 1151
De Beer, Gavin
 Hannibal I-442
De Boer, T. J.
 History of Philosophy in Islam, The III-1229; 1398
DeBray, Reginald G.
 Guide to the Slavonic Languages, A II-1178
DeCamp, L. Sprague
 Ancient Engineers I-377
De Coulanges, Fustel
 Ancient City, The I-285
De Faye, Eugene
 "Influence of Greek Scepticism on Greek and Christian Thought in the First and Second Centuries, The," in *Hibbert Journal* I-475
De Labriolle, Pierre
 History and Literature of Christianity from Tertullian to Boethius II-1022
De Lacy, Phillip
 "On Mallon and the Antecedents of Ancient Scepticism," in *Phronesis* I-476
De Marco, Angelus A., O. F. M.
 Tomb of St. Peter, A Representative and Annotated Bibliography of the Excavations, The II-646
De Paor, Liam
 Early Christian Ireland II-974
De Paor, Maire
 Early Christian Ireland II-974
De Romilly, Jacqueline
 Thucydides and Athenian Imperialism I-296
De Roover, Raymond A.
 Medici Bank: Its Organization, Management, Operation, and Decline, The III-1518
 Money, Banking, and Credit in Mediaeval Bruges: Italian Merchant Bankers, Lombards and Money Changers, a Study in the Origins of Banking III-1518
 "Organization of Trade, The," in *The Cambridge Economic History of Europe* III-1434
 San Bernardino of Siena and Sant' Antonino of Florence: The Two Great Economic Thinkers of the Middle Ages III-1518; 1523
De Rougemont, Denis
 Love in the Western World III-1301
De Vaux, Roland
 "Israelite Concept of the State, The," in *Ancient Israel* I-95
DeVogel, C. J.
 Pythagoras and Early Pythagoreanism I-198
De Wulf, M.
 History of Mediaeval Philosophy III-1568
Deane, S. W.
 Saint Anselm: Basic Writings III-1295
Deanesly, Margaret
 Pre-Conquest Church in England, The II-1085; 1130
Decarreaux, Jean
 Monks and Civilization II-1034; 1050
Deck, John N.
 Nature, Contemplation and the One: A Study in the Philosophy of Plotinus II-828
Dempsey, Bernard W.
 Interest and Usury III-1523
Den Boer, W.
 Laconian Studies I-138
Derry, T. K.
 Short History of Technology from the Earliest Times to A.D. 1900, A I-63
Dhalla, M. N.
 History of Zoroastrianism I-167
Dibelius, Martin
 From Tradition to Gospel II-593
Dickinson, J. C.

Great Charter, The   III-1456
Diehl, Charles
  Byzantium: Greatness and Decline   II-866;
  1156; III-1721
  "Fourth Crusade and the Latin Empire, The,"
  in *The Cambridge Medieval History*   III-
  1439
Dijksterhuis, E. J.
  Mechanization of the World Picture, The
  III-1619
Dill, Sir Samuel
  Roman Society from Nero to Marcus Aurelius
  II-680
  Roman Society in Gaul in the Merovingian Age
  II-999; 1009
  *Roman Society in the Last Century of the West-
  ern Empire*   II-928
Dinsmoor, W. B.
  Architecture of Ancient Greece, The   I-
  280
Dinsmore, Wayne
  History of the Percheron Horse   II-1172
Diringer, David
  *Alphabet: A Key to the History of Mankind,
  The*   I-14; II-1177
  Writing   I-14
Dix, Dom Gregory, O.S.B.
  Shape of the Liturgy, The   II-599; 1073
Dobb, Maurice H.
  Studies in the Development of Capitalism
  III-1307
Doblhofer, Ernst
  *Voices in Stone: The Decipherment of Ancient
  Scripts and Writings*   I-14; 83
Dodd, B. E.
  Early Christians in Britain, The   II-1062;
  1085
Dodd, C. H.
  "Historical Problem of the Death of Jesus,
  The," in *More New Testament Studies*
  II-606
Dodds, E. R.
  "Blessings of Madness, The," in *The Greeks
  and the Irrational*   I-124; 402
  Pagan and Christian in an Age of Anxiety
  II-730; 928
Dodge, Thomas A.
  *Caesar: A History of the Art of War Among the
  Romans*   I-519
Doerries, Hermann
  Constantine and Religious Liberty   II-850
Donaldson, E. T., ed.
  *Chaucer's Poetry: An Anthology for the Modern
  Reader*   III-1659
Donaldson, James
  Ante-Nicene Fathers, The   II-794
Donovan, Mortimer J.
  "Priscian and the Obscurity of the Ancients,"
  in *Speculum*   II-1028
Dorey, T. A.
  Cicero   I-545

Dossat, Y.
  "Waldenses," in *New Catholic Encyclopedia*
  III-1385
Dougherty, Raymond P.
  Nabonidus and Belshazzar   I-183
Douglas, A. E.
  Cicero   I-545
Douglas, David C.
  *William the Conqueror: The Norman Impact
  upon England*   III-1252
Downey, Glanville
  History of Antioch in Syria, A   I-357
Downs, Norton
  Basic Documents in Medieval History   III-
  1624; 1639
Dozy, Reinhart Pieter Anne
  *Spanish Islam: A History of the Moslems in
  Spain*   II-1079; III-1526; 1751
Drew, Katherine Fischer
  "Barbarian Kings as Lawgivers and Judges,
  The," in *Life and Thought in the Early Mid-
  dle Ages*   II-1009
Driver, Godfrey R.
  Semitic Writing   I-83
Driver, Samuel R.
  Book of the Prophet Jeremiah, The   I-152
Dubois, Marguerite Marie
  *Saint Columban: A Pioneer of Western Civili-
  zation*   II-1057
Duby, Georges
  Europe of the Cathedrals, The   III-1420
  *Rural Economy and Country Life in the Me-
  dieval West*   II-1103
Duchesne-Guillemin, J.
  Western Response to Zoroaster, The   I-167
Duchesne, Louis
  Christian Worship, Its Origin and Evolution
  II-882; 1097
Duckett, Eleanor Shipley
  *Alcuin, Friend of Charlemagne: His World and
  His Work*   II-1141
  Anglo-Saxon Saints and Scholars   II-1130
  *Carolingian Portraits: A Study of the Ninth
  Century*   II-1141
  Death and Life in the Tenth Century   III-
  1214
  Monasticism: Gateway to the Middle Ages
  II-1051; 1056
Duckworth, W. L. H.
  *Galen on Anatomical Procedures, The Later
  Books*   II-741
Duggan, Alfred
  Thomas Becket of Canterbury   III-1380
Dutton, William S.
  One Thousand Years of Explosives   III-
  1513
Dvornik, Francis
  Early Christian and Byzantine Philosophy
  II-994
  Ecumenical Councils, The   III-1461

Making of Central and Eastern Europe, The
III-1214; 1368; 1654
Slavs in European History and Civilization, The
III-1654; 1664

Easton, Stewart C.
*Roger Bacon and His Search for a Universal
Science* III-1543
Eastwood, Bruce S.
"Grosseteste's Quantitative Law of Refrac-
tion: A Chapter in the History of Non-
Experimental Science," in *Journal of the
History of Ideas* III-1558
Edelstein, E. J.
Asclepius I-306
Edelstein, L.
Asclepius I-306
Hippocratic Oath, The I-306
Edgerton, Samuel Y.
"Alberti's Perspective: A New Discovery and
a New Evaluation," in *The Art Bulletin*
III-1696
Ehler, Sydney Z.
*Church and State Through the Centuries: A
Collection of Historic Documents with Com-
mentaries* III-1268
Ehrhardt, Arnold
"Gospels in the Muratorian Fragment, The,"
in *The Framework of the New Testament
Stories* II-772
Ehrlich, Ernst Ludwig
Concise History of Israel, A I-95
Eimerl, Sarel
World of Giotto, The III-1591
Ekholm, Gordon F.
"Transpacific Contacts," in *Prehistoric Man in
the New World* I-9
Eliot, T. S.
Murder in the Cathedral III-1380
Ellard, Gerald, S. J.
*Master Alcuin, Liturgist: A Partner of Our
Piety* II-1073; 1141
Elliott, John Huxable
Imperial Spain, 1469-1716 III-1751
Elliott-Binns, L. E.
Innocent III III-1445
Emeleus, Vera M.
Composition of Greek Silver Coins, The
I-148
Emerson, William
"Hagia Sophia, Istanbul: Preliminary Report
of a recent Examination of the Structure,"
in *American Journal of Archaeology* II-
1044
"Hagia Sophia: The Collapse of the First
Dome" and "The Construction of the Sec-
ond Dome and Its Later Repairs," in *Ar-
chaeology* II-1044
Emerton, Ephraim
"Germanic Ideas of Law," in *An Introduction*

to the Study of the Middle Ages II-
1010
Encyclopedia of World Art, Vol. VI III-1591
d'Entreves, Alexander Passerin
Dante as a Political Thinker III-1602
*Medieval Contribution to Political Thought,
The* III-1613
Entwistle, W. J.
Russian and the Slavonic Languages II-
1178
Ergang, Robert
Renaissance, The III-1771
Eusebius
History of the Church, The Book 10 II-850
Life of Constantine. Vol. I of *The Nicene and
Post-Nicene Fathers, The* II-850
Evans, Ivan
Cluniac Art of the Romanesque Period
II-1188
*Romanesque Architecture of the Order of
Cluny, The* II-1188
Evelyn-White, H. G.
Hesiod, the Homeric Hymns and Homerica
I-124
Eversull, Harry K.
Temples in Jerusalem, The I-104

Farmer, W. R.
*Maccabees, Zealots, and Josephus: An Inquiry
into Jewish Nationalism in the Greco-Roman
Period* I-464
Farnell, Lewis Richard
Cults of the Greek States, The I-124; 436
Farrington, Benjamin
Greek Science: Its Meaning for Us I-402;
426
Science and Politics in the Ancient World
I-402
Fedotov, G. P.
Russian Spirituality III-1209
Ferguson, Wallace K.
Europe in Transition, 1300-1520 III-1639;
1674; 1707; 1737
Ferm, Robert L.
Reading in the History of Christian Thought
II-1125
Fichtenau, Heinrich
Carolingian Empire, The II-1134
Ficker, Rudolf
"Polyphonic Music of the Gothic Period," in
Musical Quarterly III-1415
Filson, Floyd V.
*New Testament History: The Story of the
Emerging Church, A* I-571
Which Books Belong to the Bible? II-668
Finegan, Jack
Handbook of Biblical Chronology II-794
Finkel, Asher
Pharisees and the Teacher of Nazareth, The
I-480
Finkelstein, Louis

Akiba: Scholar, Saint and Martyr   II-706

Finley, M. I.
Thucydides   I-296

Flick, A. C.
Decline of the Medieval Church, The   III-1596

Foakes-Jackson, F. J.
Eusebius Pamphili   II-845
Josephus and the Jews   II-845

Forbes, Robert J.
"Hydraulic Engineering and Sanitation," in *A History of Technology*   I-9
Man the Maker: A History of Technology and Engineering   I-63
Metallurgy in Antiquity   I-20
"Roads and Land Travel," in *A History of Technology*   I-377
"Water Supply," in *Studies in Ancient Technology*   II-630

Fowler, W. Warde
"Greek Philosophy and Roman Religion," in *The Religious Experience of the Roman People*   I-457
Julius Caesar   I-519
Religious Experience of the Roman People, The   I-204; 436

Fox, M. M.
Life and Times of St. Basil the Great as Revealed in His Works, The   II-897

Frank, Tenney
Economic Survey of Ancient Rome, An   I-258
Life and Literature in the Roman Republic   I-525
"Rome," in *The Cambridge Ancient History*   I-452

Frankfort, H.
"Egypt: The Values of Life," in *The Intellectual Adventure of Ancient Man*   I-39

Frankfort, H. A.
"Egypt: The Values of Life," in *The Intellectual Adventure of Ancient Man*   I-39
"Good Life, The," in *The Intellectual Adventure of Ancient Man: An Essay on Speculative Thought in the Ancient Near East*   I-44
Intellectual Adventure of Ancient Man: An Essay on Speculative Thought in the Ancient Near East, The   I-57

Frankfort, Henri
Ancient Egyptian Religion: An Interpretation   I-69
"Good Life, The," in *The Intellectual Adventure of Ancient Man: An Essay on Speculative Thought in the Ancient Near East*   I-44
Intellectual Adventure of Ancient Man: An Essay on Speculative Thought in the Ancient Near East, The   I-50; 57

Fränkel, Hermann
"Heraclitus on God and the Phenomenal World," in *Transactions and Proceedings of the American Philological Association*   I-214
Ovid: A Poet Between Two Worlds   II-577

Frazer, J. G.
Growth of Plato's Ideal Theory, The   I-327

Freeman, Kathleen
Ancilla to the Pre-Socratic Philosophers   I-268; 290
Work and Life of Solon, The   I-172

Fremantle, Anne
Age of Belief, The. The Medieval Philosophers   II-839

French, Robert Dudley
Chaucer Handbook, A   III-1659

Frend, W. H. C.
Donatist Church, The   II-945
Martyrdom and Persecution in the Early Church   II-695

Friedrich, J.
Extinct Languages   I-14

Frothingham, Arthur L.
"Memorial Arch," in *Dictionary of Architecture and Building*   I-505

Fry, Christopher
Curtmantle   III-1380

Fuller, John F. C.
Armament and History   III-1513
Generalship of Alexander the Great, The   I-362

Fuller, Reginald H.
New Testament in Current Study, The   II-593

Funck-Brentano, F.
Earliest Times, The   II-999

Furneaux, Rupert
Invasion 1066   III-1252

Gabrieli, Francesco
Mohammed and the Conquests of Islam   II-1110

Gadd, C. J.
Hammurabi and the End of His Dynasty   I-50

Gadol, Joan
"Unity of the Renaissance: Humanism, Natural Science, and Art, The," in *From the Renaissance to the Counter Reformation*   III-1770

Gardiner, Sir Alan H.
Egypt of the Pharaohs   I-39; 74

Gardiner, E. Norman
Athletics of the Ancient World   I-119
Greek Athletic Sports and Festival   I-119
History and Remains of Olympia   I-119
Olympia: Its History and Remains   I-301

Gardiner, R.
"Enfranchisement of Italy, The," in *The Cambridge Ancient History*   I-510

Garraty, John A.
Nature of Biography, The   II-690

Gasquet, Francis A.
Black Death of 1348 and 1349, The III-1629
Gaster, Theodor H.
Oldest Stories in the World, The I-44
Gavin, F.
Jewish Antecedents of the Christian Sacraments, The III-1343
Geanakoplos, Deno J.
Byzantine East and Latin West: Two Worlds of Christendom in Middle Ages and Renaissance III-1242
"Church and State in the Byzantine Empire: A Reconsideration of the Problem of Caesaropapism," in *Church History* II-856
Gelzer, Matthias
Caesar: Politician and Statesman I-519
Gersheson, Daniel E.
Anaxagoras and the Birth of Physics I-274
Ghirshman, R.
Iran from the Earliest Times to the Islamic Conquest I-167; 431
Gibb, H. A. R.
Arab Conquests in Central Asia, The III-1256
Gibbon, Edward
Decline and Fall of the Roman Empire, The II-928
Gibbons, Herbert A.
Foundations of the Ottoman Empire, The III-1256
Gibson, George M.
Story of the Christian Year, The II-883; 1098
Giles, E.
Documents Illustrating Papal Authority, A.D. 96-454 II-822
Giles, Frederick J.
Ikhnaton: Legend and History I-69
Gill, Joseph
Eugenius IV Pope of Christian Union III-1707
Gilliard, Charles
History of Switzerland, A III-1606
Gilmore, Myron P.
World of Humanism, 1453-1517, The Vol. II of *The Rise of Modern Europe* series III-1663; 1737
Gilson, Étienne
History of Christian Philosophy in the Middle Ages, The II-1016; III-1548; 1568
Ginzberg, Louis
"Akiba ben Joseph," in *The Jewish Encyclopedia* II-706
Glasfurd, Alec
Antipope, Peter de Luna 1342-1423, The III-1684
Glatzer, Nahum N.
Jerusalem and Rome. The Writings of Josephus II-652
Glob, P. V.

Ard and Plough in Prehistoric Scandinavia II-1103
Godolphin, Francis R. B.
Greek Historians, The I-263
Goldman, Solomon
Jew and the Universe, The III-1394
Goldscheider, Ludwig
Leonardo da Vinci III-1765
Goldstein, N. W.
"Cultivate Pagans and Ancient Antisemitism," in *Journal of Religion* I-464
Golino, C. Q.
Galileo and His Precursors III-1619
Gombosi, Otto
"Machaut's *Messe Notre Dame*," in *Musical Quarterly* III-1415
Gomme, A. W.
"End of the City-State, The," in *Essays in Greek History and Literature* I-342
Population of Athens in the Fifth and Fourth Centuries B.C. I-209
Gontard, Friedrich
Chair of Peter: A History of the Papacy, The III-1461
Goodchild, R. G.
"Roads and Land Travel," in *A History of Technology* I-377
Goodenough, Erwin R.
"Political Philosophy of Hellenistic Kingship, The" in *Yale Classical Studies* I-407
Theology of Justin Martyr, The II-711
Goodman, Nelson
Problem of the Universals, The II-839
Goodrich, Norma Loore
Ways of Love: Eleven Romances of Medieval France, The III-1471
Goodspeed, Edgar Johnson
Introduction to the New Testament, An I-571
Gordon, Benjamin Lee
Medieval and Renaissance Medicine III-1483
Gordon, C. D.
Age of Attila, The II-979
Gordon, Cyrus
Hammurabi's Code: Quaint or Forward-Looking? I-50
Gore, Charles
Church and the Ministry, The II-684
Leo the Great II-968
Görres, Ida Friedericke
Is Celibacy Outdated? III-1262
Grabmann, Martin
Thomas Aquinas: His Personality and Thought III-1548
Graetz, H.
History of the Jews I-193
Grant, A. J.
Early Lives of Charlemagne by Einhard and the Monk of St. Gall II-1151
Grant, Michael

Ancient Mediterranean, The   I-412
From Imperium *to* Auctioritas: *A Historical Study of* Aes *Coinage in the Roman Empire 49 B.C.-A.D. 14*   I-566
Julius Caesar   I-520
Grant, Robert M.
Apostolic Fathers, The   II-673
Formation of the New Testament, The   II-772; 783
Sword and the Cross, The   II-695; 816
Gratz, H.
History of the Jews   III-1755
Gray, John
Archaeology and the Old Testament World   I-79
Greenaway, George W.
St. Boniface   II-1130
Greenberg, Daniel A.
Anaxagoras and the Birth of Physics   I-274
Greenidge, Abel H. J.
Handbook of Greek Constitutional History, A   I-157
History of Rome During the Later Republic and Early Principate, A   I-485
Roman Public Life   I-566
Greenslade, S. L.
Church and State from Constantine to Theodosius   II-908; 923
Schism in the Early Church   II-956
Gregoire, Henri
"Question of the Diversion of the Fourth Crusade, The," in *Byzantion*   III-1440
"Reign of Basil II, The," in *The Cambridge Medieval History*   III-1220
Gregorovius, Ferdinand
Emperor Hadrian: A Picture of the Graeco-Roman World in His Time, The   II-706
Grene, Marjorie
Portrait of Aristotle, A   I-332
Grenfell, B. P.
Revenue Laws of Ptolemy Philadelphus, The   I-417
Grenier, Albert
Roman Spirit in Religion, Thought and Art, The   I-458
Grimal, Pierre
Hellenism and the Rise of Rome   I-412
Grosset, René
Empire of the Steppes, The. A History of Central Asia   III-1466
Gruen, Erich
"Political Prosecutions in the 90's B.C.," in *Historia*   I-510
Guérard, Albert
France: A Modern History   III-1737
Guerdan, René
Byzantium—Its Triumphs and Tragedy   II-1157
Gurney, Oliver R.
Hittites, The   I-63

Gusmann, Pierre
Mural Decorations of Pompeii   II-663
Guterman, S. L.
Religious Toleration and Persecution in Ancient Rome   II-692
Guthrie, W. K. C.
History of Greek Philosophy, A   I-177; 198; 269; 274
Gwatkin, Henry Melvill
Cambridge Medieval History, The. Vol. I: *The Christian Roman Empire and the Foundation of the Teutonic Kingdoms*   II-939
Studies of Arianism   II-871; 876

Hadas, Moses
Hellenistic Culture: Fusion and Diffusion   I-133
History of Greek Literature, A   I-219
History of Latin Literature, A   I-470; II-577; 657
Hadrill, Wallace
Long Haired Kings, The   II-999
Hale, Edwyn Andalus
Spain Under the Muslims   III-1751
Halecki, Oscar
Borderlands of Western Civilization. A History of East Central Europe   III-1214; 1654; 1663; 1741; 1746
Hall, A. R.
History of Technology, A. Vol. I: *From Early Times to the Fall of Ancient Empires*   I-63
Halliday, W. A.
Lectures on the History of Roman Religion   I-204; 436
Hallward, B. L.
"Scipio and Victory," in *The Cambridge Ancient History*   I-441
Hamilton, Earl J.
"The Role of Monopoly in the Overseas Expansion and Colonial Trade of Europe Before 1800," in "Papers and Proceedings of the American Economic Association," Supplement, *American Economic Review*   III-1690
Hamilton, Edith
"Herodotus, the First Sight-Seer," in *The Greek Way*   I-263
Hansen, E. V.
Attalids of Pergamum, The   I-407
Hanson, R. P. C.
Acts in the Revised Standard Version, The   II-611
Hardy, Edward R.
Christianity and the Roman Government. A Study in Imperial Administration   II-642; 695
Christology of the Later Fathers   II-967
Haring, N. M.
"Paschasius Radbertus," in *New Catholic Encyclopedia*   II-1168

Harnack, Adolph
Constitution and the Law of the Church in the
First Two Centuries, II-684; 736
History of Dogma, The II-751; 761; 766
Harper, William R.
Amos and Hosea I-128
Hartshorne, Charles
Anselm's Discovery: A Re-Examination of the
Ontological Proof for God's Existence
III-1295
Hartt, Frederick
"Art and Freedom in Quattrocento Florence,"
in Essays in Memory of Karl Lehman
III-1669
History of Italian Renaissance Art III-
1696
Haskell, H. J.
This Was Cicero: Modern Politics in a Roman
Toga I-525
Haskins, Charles Homer
Renaissance of the Twelfth Century, The
II-1004; III-1236; 1483
Rise of the Universities, The III-1404
Haslehurst, R. S. T.
Some Accounts of the Penitential Discipline of
the Early Church II-766
Hastings, James
"Euhemerism," in Encyclopedia of Religion
and Ethics I-382
Hatch, Edwin
Organization of the Early Christian Churches,
The II-684
Hatt, G.
Plough and Pasture: The Early History of
Farming II-1103
Havelock, Eric A.
Liberal Temper in Greek Politics, The I-
230; 290
Havighurst, Alfred F.
Pirenne Thesis: Analysis, Criticism, and Revi-
sion, The II-1134; III-1327
Hayward, F. H.
Marcus Aurelius: A Saviour of Men II-
730
Hazeltine, H. D.
"Gaius," in Encyclopaedia of the Social
Sciences II-724
Hazlitt, W. Carew
Venetian Republic, Its Rise, Its Growth, and Its
Fall, 421-1797, The III-1358
Heath, Sir Thomas L.
Aristarchus of Samos II-715
Greek Astronomy I-402
"Hellenistic Science and Mathematics," in
The Cambridge Ancient History I-426
History of Greek Mathematics, A I-426; II-
720
Manual of Greek Mathematics, A I-426
Heaton, Herbert
Economic History of Europe III-1307;
1363; 1518

Hecker, Justus F. C.
Black Death, The III-1629
Heer, Friedrich
Holy Roman Empire, The III-1322; 1368
Medieval World: Europe from 1100 to 1350,
The III-1317
Heichelheim, Fritz M.
History of the Roman People, A II-588
Heidel, Alexander
Babylonian Genesis, The I-100
Gilgamesh Epic and Old Testament Parallels,
The I-44
Heidel, William A.
Hippocratic Medicine I-307
"Pythagoreans and Greek Mathematics,
The," in American Journal of Philology
I-198
Heitland, William E.
Agricola II-680
Roman Republic, The I-225; 337; 412
Henderson, Bernard W.
Life and Principles of the Emperor Hadrian,
A.D. 76-138, The II-706
Henry, Desmond Paul
Logic of Saint Anselm, The III-1295
Henry of Livonia
Chronicle, The III-1476
Herben, Jan
Hus and His Followers III-1679
Herford, Robert Travers
Talmud and Apocrypha II-998
Heritage, T. C.
Early Christians in Britain, The II-1062;
1085
Herodotus
History of the Persian Wars I-263
Persian Wars, The I-183
Herschel, Clemens
Two Books on the Water Supply of the City of
Rome of Sextus Julius Frontinus, Water
Commissioner of the City of Rome A.D. 97,
The II-630
Hertz, Frederick
Development of the German Public Mind, The.
A Social History of German Political Senti-
ments, Aspirations and Ideas III-1624;
1639
Hertzberg, Hans Wilhelm
I & II Samuel: A Commentary I-95
Herzstein, R. E.
Holy Roman Empire in the Middle Ages, The.
Universal State or German Catastrophe?
III-1199
Hewson, J. B.
History of the Practice of Navigation, A
III-1508
Heydenreich, Ludwig H.
Leonardo da Vinci III-1765
Hicks, Robert Drew
Stoic and Epicurean I-392
Higginbotham, John

Cicero on Moral Obligation   I-545

Higham, T. F.
Oxford Book of Greek Verse in Translation, The   I-219

Highet, Gilbert
Classical Tradition, The   II-577

Hill, G. F.
Development of Arabic Numerals in Europe, The   III-1286

Hill, George
History of Cyprus   III-1579

Hitchcock, F. R. M.
Irenaeus of Lugdunum   II-751

Hitti, Philip K.
History of the Arabs   II-1194

Hodgkin, R. H.
History of the Anglo-Saxons, A   II-1062; 1085

Hodgkin, T.
Italy and Her Invaders   II-999

Holborn, Hajo
History of Modern Germany, A. The Reformation   III-1639

Holdsworth, W. S.
History of English Law   III-1390

Hole, Edwyn
Andalus: Spain Under the Muslims   II-1079; 1194; III-1527

Holmes, T. Rice
Ancient Britain and the Invasions of Julius Caesar   II-620
Architect of the Roman Empire, The   I-555; 566; II-625

Holmes, Urban T., Jr.
History of Old French Literature, A   III-1225

Holmyard, E. J.
History of Technology, A. Vol. I: *From Early Times to the Fall of Ancient Empires* I-63

Holt, Elizabeth G.
Documentary History of Art, A   III-1695

Holt, J. C.
Magna Carta   III-1456

Honeycutt, Roy Lee
Amos and His Message   I-128

Houben, Heinrich Hubert
Christopher Columbus: The Tragedy of a Discoverer   III-1760

Hourani, George F.
On the Harmony of Religion and Philosophy III-1398

How, W. W.
Commentary on Herodotus, A   I-241

Howorth, Henry H.
History of the Mongols   III-1466

Huby, Pamela
Greek Ethics   I-332

Hughes, Dom Anselm
New Oxford History of Music, The (in 4 vols.) III-1415

Hughes, Philip
Church in Crisis: A History of the General Councils, 325-1870, The   II-957; III-1684
History of the Church, A   II-1116; III-1597

Huizinga, J.
Waning of the Middle Ages: A Study in the Forms of Life, Thought and Art in France and the Netherlands in the XIV and XV Centuries, The   III-1301

Hunt, Richard W.
"Studies on Priscian in the Eleventh and Twelfth Centuries," in *Medieval and Renaissance Studies*   II-1028

Hunt, William
English Church from Its Foundations to the Norman Conquest (597-1066), The   II-1062

Hunter, Archibald M.
Paul and His Predecessors   II-611

Hürlimann, Martin
French Cathedrals   III-1420

Husain, M. H.
"Chemistry in Iraq and Persia in the Tenth Century A.D.," in *Memoirs of the Royal Asiatic Society of Bengal*   II-1182

Husik, Isaac
History of Medieval Jewish Philosophy, A III-1337; 1399

Hussey, John M.
"Byzantine Empire in the Eleventh Century: Some Different Interpretations, The," in *Transactions of the Royal Historical Society* III-1220
Byzantine World, The   III-1721

Huxley, G. L.
Early Ionians, The   I-133

Hyde, Walter W.
"Origin of Christmas, The," in *Paganism to Christianity in the Roman Empire*   II-887

Hyma, Albert
Christian Renaissance, The   III-1674

Imamuddin, S. M.
Some Aspects of the Socio-Economic and Cultural History of Muslim Spain 711-1492 A.D.   II-1193

Inge, W. R.
Christian Mysticism   II-1016
Philosophy of Plotinus, The   II-828

Innis, George S.
Wycliffe: The Morning Star   III-1643

Irwin, K. G.
Romance of Writings, The   I-14

Jackson, A. V. Williams
Researches in Manichaeism: With Special Reference to Turfan Fragments   II-811
Zoroastrian Studies   I-167

Jacobs, Louis
  Studies in Talmudic and Methodology   II-988
Jacobsen, Thorkild
  "Good Life, The," in The Intellectual Adventure of Ancient Man: An Essay on Speculative Thought in the Ancient Near East   I-44
Jaeger, Werner W.
  Aristotle: Fundamentals of the History of His Development   I-347; 367
  "Demosthenes: The Death Struggle and Transfiguration of the City-State," in Vol. III of Paideia   I-342
  Early Christianity and Greek Paideia   II-673, 800
  "Isocrates Defends His Paideia," in Vol. III of Paideia   I-342
  "Parmenides' Mystery of Being," in The Theology of the Early Greek Philosophers   I-235
  Theology of the Early Greek Philosophers, The   I-177; 214; 275
Jagic, V.
  "Conversion of the Slavs, The," in The Cambridge Medieval History   II-1178
Jakobson, Roman
  Slavic Languages: A Condensed Survey   II-1178
Jalland, T. G.
  Life and Times of St. Leo the Great, The   II-967
James, Bruno S.
  Saint Bernard of Clairvaux: An Essay in Biography   III-1333
James, E. O.
  Cult of the Mother-Goddess, The   I-436
James, Montague R.
  "Learning and Literature till Pope Sylvester II," in The Cambridge Medieval History   II-1028
Janson, H. W.
  Sculpture of Donatello, The   III-1669
Jedin, Hubert
  Ecumenical Councils of the Catholic Church: A Historical Survey   III-1461
Jenkins, R. J. H.
  "Reign of Basil II, The," in The Cambridge Medieval History   III-1220
Jenkins, T. Atkinson
  Chanson de Roland, La   III-1312
Jennett, Sean
  Pioneers in Printing   III-1717
Jerome
  Against Vigilantius   II-933
Jespersen, Otto
  Growth and Structure of the English Language   III-1290
Jobe, Joseph
  Great Age of Sail, The   III-1508
John of Salisbury

  Metalogicon, The   III-1236
Johnson, Allan C.
  Municipal Administration in the Roman Empire   I-337
Johnson, Aubrey R.
  Sacral Kingship in Ancient Israel   I-105
Jolliffe, J. E. A.
  Constitutional History of Medieval England, The   III-1585
Jolowicz, H. F.
  Historical Introduction to the Study of Roman Law   I-225; II-1039
Jonas
  Life of Columban, The, in Translations and Reprints   II-1057
Jonas, Hans
  Gnostic Religion: The Message of the Alien God and the Beginnings of Christianity, The   II-811
Jones, A. H. M.
  "Athens of Demosthenes, The," in Athenian Democracy   I-342
  Constantine and the Conversion of Europe   II-866
  Decline of the Ancient World, The   II-583
  Herods of Judaea, The   II-652
  Later Roman Empire 284-602: A Social, Economic and Administrative Survey, The   II-833; 866; 903; 962; 984
  Studies in Roman Government and Law   I-566
Jones, Alexander
  Gospel According to St. Matthew, The   I-571
Jones, Charles W.
  Saints' Lives and Chronicles in Early England   II-1068
Jones, Henry Stuart
  "Making of a United State, The," in The Cambridge Ancient History   I-397
  "Plebeian Institutions," in The Cambridge Ancient History   I-225
  "Princeps, The," in The Cambridge Ancient History   I-566
Jones, J. Walter
  Law and Legal Theory of the Greeks: An Introduction, The   I-157
Jones, W. S.
  Hippocratic Writings   I-306
Jope, E. M.
  "Agricultural Implements," in A History of Technology   II-1103
  "Vehicles and Harness," in A History of Technology   I-9
Jordon, G. J.
  Inner History of the Great Schism of the West, The   III-1649
Jörgensen, Johannes
  St. Francis of Assisi   III-1451
Joveyni, Ala al-Din

History of the World Conqueror   III-1466

Jungmann, Joseph A. S.J.
Early Liturgy to the Time of Gregory the Great,
The   II-1074
Pastoral Liturgy   II-1074
Public Worship   II-1074

Kahn, Charles H.
Anaximander and the Origins of Greek Cos-
mology   I-177

Kantoworicz, Ernst
Frederick the Second 1194-1250   III-1477

Kapp, Ernst
Aristotle's Constitution of Athens   I-209

Karpinski, L. D.
Hindu-Arabic Numerals   III-1286

Karrer, Otto
Peter and the Church, An Examination of Cull-
mann's Thesis   II-646

Katz, Peter
Philo's Bible   I-421

Keck, Leander E.
Studies in Luke-Acts   II-611

Kelley, D. H.
Alphabet and the Ancient Calendar Signs, The
I-15

Kellner, K. A. Heinrich
Heortology, A History of the Christian Festivals
from Their Origin to the Present Day
II-882, 1097

Kelly, J. N. D.
Early Christian Doctrines   II-761; 876; 897;
1168

Kendall, Paul Murray
Louis XI. The Universal Spider   III-1737

Kennedy, H. A. A.
Sources of New Testament Greek   I-421

Kenney, James F.
"Columban," in *The Sources for the Early His-*
tory of Ireland   II-1057

Kenyon, Frederic G.
Books and Readers in Ancient Greece and
Rome   I-357

Kern, Fritz
Kingship and Law in the Middle Ages   II-
788; 1134

Kidd, B. J.
Roman Primacy, The   II-822; 919

Kilpatrick, G. D.
Trial of Jesus, The   II-606

King, Archdale A.
Liturgy of the Roman Church   II-1074

King, N. Q.
Emperor Theodosius and the Establishment of
Christianity, The   II-923

King, Wilson
Chronicles of Three Free Cities   III-1434

Kingsford, C. L.
"Sir Otho de Grandson, 1238?-1328," in
Transactions of the Royal Historical Society
III-1579

Kirk, G. S.
Presocratic Philosophers: A Critical History
with a Selection of Texts, The   I-178;
198; 214; 236; 275

Kirk, Kenneth E.
Apostolic Ministry, The   II-746

Kirschbaum, Engelbert, S. J.
Tombs of St. Peter and St. Paul, The   II-
646

Kitto, H. D. F.
Greek Tragedy: A Literary Study   I-252

Kittredge, George L.
Chaucer and His Poetry   III-1659

Klausner, Joseph
Jesus of Nazareth, His Life, Times and Teach-
ing   II-594

Klein, Carol
Credo of Maimonides, The   III-1394

Kleist, James A.
Epistles of Saint Clement of Rome and Saint
Ignatius of Antioch, The   II-673, 700

Kluchevsky, V. O.
History of Russia, A   III-1741

Kneale, Martha
Development of Logic, The   I-352

Kneale, William
Development of Logic, The   I-352

Knight, W. F. Jackson
Roman Vergil   I-561

Knowles, David, O.S.B.
Cistercians and Cluniacs   II-1188
Evolution of Medieval Thought, The   II-
1016; III-1317
Great Historical Enterprises and Problems in
Monastic History   II-1034
Monastic Order in England, The   II-1034
Religious Orders in England, The   II-1034

Know, Wilfred L.
St. Paul and the Church of the Gentiles
II-636

Knox, John
Marcion and the New Testament   III-783

Kourouniotes, K.
"Pnyx of Athens, The," in *Hesperia*   I-209

Kraay, Colin M.
"Archaic Owls of Athens: Classification and
Chronology, The," in *Numismatic Chroni-*
cle   I-172
Composition of Greek Silver Coins, The
I-148

Kraemer, C. J.
"Bureaucracy and Petty Graft in Ancient
Egypt," in *Classical Weekly*   I-417

Kramer, Samuel Noah
History Begins at Sumer   I-44
Sumerian Mythology: A Study of Spiritual and
Literary Achievements in the Third Millen-
nium B.C.   I-44
Sumerians: Their History, Culture and Char-
acter, The   I-50

Kramer, Werner
  Christ, Lord, Son of God   II-611
Kraus, S.
  "Bar Kokhba and Bar Kokhba War," in *The Jewish Encyclopedia*   II-706
Krautheimer, Richard
  Early Christian and Byzantine Architecture II-1045
  Lorenzo Ghiberti   III-1669; 1695
Krautheimer-Hess, Trude
  Lorenzo Ghiberti   III-1669; 1695
Krey, A. C.
  First Crusade: The Accounts of Eye-Witnesses and Participants   III-1281
  "Urban's Crusade, Success or Failure?" in *American Historical Review*   III-1281
Kristeller, Paul Oscar
  Studies in Renaissance Thought and Letters III-1727
Krober, A. L.
  Anthropology   I-9
Kuhn, Thomas S.
  Copernican Revolution, The. Planetary Astronomy in the Development of Western Thought II-715
Kundsin, Karl
  Form Criticism: Two Essays in New Testament Research   II-593
Kushyar ibn Labban
  Hindu Reckoning   III-1286
Kyball, Blastimil
  Francis of Assisi   III-1451

Laidlaw, W. A.
  History of Delos, A   I-246
Laing, Gordon J.
  Survivals of Roman Religion   II-934
Laistner, Max L. W.
  History of the Greek World from 479 to 323 B.C., A   I-246
  Thought and Letters in Western Europe, A.D. 500 to 900   II-1004; 1022; 1051; 1090
Lake, Kirsopp
  "Baptism (Early Christian and Later Christian)," in *Encyclopedia of Religion and Ethics*   II-822
  Eusebius, The Ecclesiastical History   II-845
Lane, Edward W.
  Arabian Nights in the Middle Ages   II-1145
Lane, Frederic C.
  Enterprise and Secular Change   III-1363
  Venetian Ships and Shipbuilders of the Renaissance   III-1358
Lane-Poole, Stanley
  Story of the Moors in Spain, The   II-1080; III-1751
Last, Hugh
  "Enfranchisement of Italy, The," in *The Cambridge Ancient History*   I-510
  "Making of a United State, The," in *The Cambridge Ancient History*   I-397

"Servian Reforms, The," in *Journal of Roman Studies*   I-285
  "Wars of Marius, The," in Vol. IX of *The Cambridge Ancient History*   I-500
Latourette, Kenneth Scott
  History of Christianity, A   II-1068
Lattimore, Richmond
  Iliad of Homer, The   I-114
  Odes of Pindar, The   I-119
Lauterback, J. Z.
  Pharisees and Their Teachings, The   I-480
Lawrence, C. H.
  English Church and the Papacy in the Middle Ages, The   III-1634
Lawson, John
  Theological and Historical Introduction to the Apostolic Fathers, A   II-674
Lea, Henry Charles
  History of the Inquisition in Spain   III-1490
Leathes, Stanley
  "France," in *The Cambridge Modern History* III-1707; 1737
Lebreton, Jules
  History of the Primitive Church, The   II-822
Leclerq, Jean
  Love of Learning and the Desire for God, The II-1068
Lee, Norman E.
  Travel and Transport Through the Ages II-1172
Leeman, A. D.
  Orationis Ratio. The Stylistic Theories and Practice of the Roman Orators, Historians and Philosophers   I-535
Leeming, Bernard, S. J.
  Principles of Sacramental Theology   III-1343
Leeper, A. W. A.
  History of Medieval Austria, A   II-588; III-1214; 1368
Leff, Gordon
  Heresy in the Later Middle Ages   III-1445
  Medieval Thought: St. Augustine to Ockham II-1016; III-1548
Le Gentil, Pierre
  Chanson de Roland, The   III-1312
Leeper, F. A.
  Trajan's Parthian War   I-431
Leppmann, Wolfgang
  Pompeii in Fact and Fiction   II-663
Leserth, Johann
  Wycliffe and Hus   III-1643
Lesky, Albin
  History of Greek Literature, A   I-114; 220; 263; II-690
Leslie, Elmer A.
  Jeremiah   I-152
LeStrange, Guy
  Baghdad During the Abbasid Caliphate II-1145

Lever, Katherine
Art of Greek Comedy, The   I-372
Levin, Richard
Question of Socrates, The   I-322
Levin, Saul
"St. Paul's Ideology for the Urbanized Roman Empire," in *Concordia Theological Monthly* III-1262
Levison, Wilhelm
England and the Continent in the Eighth Century   II-1130
Levy, Reuben
Baghdad Chronicle, A   II-1145
Lewis, Archibald R.
Naval Power and Trade in the Mediterranean, A.D. 500-1100   II-1120
Lewis, Bernard
Arabs in History, The   II-1110
Lewis, Clive Staples
Allegory of Love: A Study in Medieval Tradition, The   III-1471
Lewis, Ewart K.
Medieval Political Thought   II-788
Lewis, Naphtali
Roman Civilization. Vol. I: *The Republic* I-225
Liebeschütz, H.
Mediaeval Humanism in the Life and Writings of John of Salisbury   III-1374
Lietzmann, Hans
Era of the Church Fathers, The. Vol. IV of *A History of the Early Church*   II-897; 908; 923
Mass and Lord's Supper   II-600
Liddell Hart, B. H.
Greater than Napoleon: Scipio Africanus, A I-441
Lightbody, C. W.
Judgements of Joan: Joan of Arc, a Study in Cultural History, The   III-1702
Lindsay, Jack
Byzantium into Europe   II-1157
Lindsay, T. M.
Church and the Ministry in the Early Centuries, The   II-685
Linforth, Ivan M.
Solon the Athenian   I-157
Linscott, Robert N.
Notebooks of Leonardo da Vinci, The   III-1765
Lintott, A. W.
Violence in Republican Rome   I-225
Lissner, Ivar
Caesars—Might and Madness, The   II-583
Lister, Richard Percival
Genghis Khan   III-1466
Little, A. G.
Roger Bacon: Essays   III-1543
Lloyd, G. E. R.
Aristotle: The Growth and Structure of His Thought   I-352

Lloyd, R. B
Peter Abélard: The Orthodox Rebel   III-1317
Lloyd, William Bross
Waging Peace. The Swiss Experience   III-1607
Locke, Clinton
Age of the Great Western Schism, The   III-1648
Loetscher, Frederick W.
"St. Augustine's Conception of the State," in *Church History*   II-856
Lohse, Eduard
History of the Suffering and Death of Jesus Christ   II-606
Loomis, Louis Ropes
See of Peter, The   II-822; 919
Loomis, Louise Ropes
Council of Constance, The   III-1685
Longden, R. P.
"Nerva and Trajan," in *The Cambridge Ancient History*   II-679
Lopez, Robert S.
Birth of Europe, The   II-1125
Medieval Trade in the Mediterranean World III-1518
Lot, Ferdinand
End of the Ancient World and the Beginnings of the Middle Ages, The   II-939; 979; 984
Lowes, John Livingston
Convention and Revolt in Poetry   III-1353
Lucas, A.
Ancient Egyptian Materials and Industries I-20
Luchaire, Achille
Social France at the Time of Philip Augustus III-1204
Lucretius
Nature of the Universe, The   I-515
Lukasiewicz, Jan
Aristotle's Syllogistic from the Standpoint of Modern Formal Logic   I-352
Lupton, Joseph
"St. John Damascene," in *A Dictionary of Christian Biography*   II-1116
Luther, Martin
"Babylonian Captivity of the Church, The," in *Luther's Works*   III-1343
Judgment of Martin Luther on Monastic Vows, The   II-933
Lydekker, R.
Horse and Its Relatives, The   I-4
Lyons, M. C.
Galen on Anatomical Procedures, The Later Books   II-740

McClintock, John
Cyclopedia of Biblical, Theological, and Ecclesiastical Literature   II-1116
McEwan, C. W.

Oriental Origin of Hellenistic Kingship, The
I-407
McGiffert, Arthur C.
Apostles' Creed, The II-756
Church History of Eusebius II-844
History of Christian Thought, A II-751;
950
McIlwain, Charles Howard
Growth of Political Thought in the West, The
II-788
McIntyre, John
*St. Anselm and His Critics: A Re-Interpretation
of the* Cur Deus Homo III-1295
McKechnie, W. S.
*Magna Carta: A Commentary on the Great
Charter of King John* III-1456
McKisack, May
Fourteenth Century 1307-1399, The III-
1634
McNally, Robert, S. J.
Old Ireland II-974
McNeal, Edgar
"Fourth Crusade, The," in *The Later Cru-
sades.* Vol. II of Setton's *A History of the
Crusades* III-1440
Macartney, Carlile Aylmer
Magyars in the Ninth Century, The III-
1214
Macdonald, D.
*Development of Muslim Theology, Jurispru-
dence and Constitutional Theory* III-
1398
MacManus, Francis
Saint Columban II-1056
Madaule, Jacques
Albigensian Crusade, The III-1489
Madden, Marie R.
"*Lex Visigothorum* or the *Forum Iudiciorum,*
The," in *Political Theory and Law in Medie-
val Spain* II-1010
Magie, David
*Roman Rule in Asia Minor to the End of the
Third Century After Christ* I-490
"Rome and the City-States of Western Asia
Minor from 200 to 133 B.C.," in *Anatolian
Studies Presented to William H. Buckler*
I-490
Mahaffy, J. P.
Revenue Laws of Ptolemy Philadelphus, The
I-417
Major, R. H.
Life of Henry of Portugal, The III-1690
Malden, R. H.
Apocrypha, The I-447
Manson, T. W.
Church's Ministry, The II-746
Mantius, M.
"Teutonic Migrations, 378-412, The," in *The
Cambridge Medieval History* II-903
Marcus Aurelius Antoninus
Communings with Himself, The II-730

Marcus, Ralph
"Antisemitism in the Hellenistic World," in
Essays on Antisemitism I-417
Mariejol, Jean Hippolyte
Spain of Ferdinand and Isabella, The III-
1732; 1751
Marriott, J. A. R.
*Eastern Question, The. An Historical Study in
European Diplomacy* III-1663
Marrou, Henri I.
History of Education in Antiquity, A I-357;
II-1004
Marsh, Frank Burr
*History of the Roman World from 146 to 30
B.C., A* I-485; 525
Marshall, Arthur
Explosives. Vol. I: *History and Manufacture*
III-1513
Martin, Henry Desmond
*Rise of Chingis Khan and His Conquest of
North China, The* III-1466
Martyn, J. Louis
Studies in Luke-Acts II-611
Marzials, F.
*Memoirs of the Crusades by Villehardouin and
De Joinville* III-1502
Mason, W. A.
History of the Art of Writing, A I-14
Masson, John
Lucretius, Epicurean and Poet I-515
Mattingly, Harold B.
Christianity in the Roman Empire II-
695
"Growth of Athenian Imperialism, The," in
Historia I-246
Roman Coins I-148
Roman Imperial Civilization II-625
Maurer, A.
Medieval Philosophy III-1712
May, Margaret T.
Galen on the Usefulness of the Parts of the Body
II-741
Maynard, Theodore
Richest of the Poor III-1451
Meadows, Dennis
Saint and a Half, A III-1317
Meecham, Henry G.
Epistle to Diognetus, The II-711
Meek, Theophile James
Hebrew Origins I-79
"Origins of Hebrew Law, The," in *Hebrew
Origins* I-88
Mercer, Samuel A. B.
Religion of Ancient Egypt, The I-57
Meritt, Benjamin D.
"Alliance Between Athens and Egesta, The,"
in *Bulletin de correspondence hellénique*
I-312
"Dating of Documents to the Mid-Fifth Cen-
tury, The," in *Journal of Hellenic Studies*
I-246

Mertz, Barbara
   Red Land, Black Land: The World of the Ancient Egyptians   I-57
   Temples, Tombs and Hieroglyphs   I-57
Metlake, George
   Life and Writings of Saint Columban, The   II-1057
Metz, René
   What Is Canon Law?   III-1495
Metzger, Bruce Manning
   New Testament: Its Background, Growth, and Content, The   I-572
Meyers, Jacob M.
   Chronicles   I-192
   Ezra and Nehemiah   I-192
Michell, Humphrey
   Economics of Ancient Greece, The   I-148
   Sparta   I-138
Migg, Walter
   Warriors of God: The Great Religious Orders and Their Founders   III-1333
Milburn, R. L. P.
   Early Christian Interpretations of History   II-794
Miller, Edward
   Cambridge Economic History of Europe, The. Vol. III: *Economic Organization and Policies in the Middle Ages*   III-1328
Miller, Elizabeth Jane
   Science of Columbus, The   III-1760
Miller, W. J.
   Letters   III-1374
Minadeo, Richard
   Lyre of Science: Form and Meaning in Lucretius' De Rerum Natura, *The*   I-515
Minar, F. L.
   "Logos of Heraclitus, The," in *Classical Philology*   I-214
Minkin, Jacob S.
   Abrabanel and the Expulsion of the Jews from Spain   III-1755
   World of Maimonides, The   III-1394
Minor, A. C.
   "Roman Calendar, The," *Masters Thesis*   I-540
Mitchell, Lt. Col. Joseph B.
   Twenty Decisive Battles of the World   III-1252
Mollat, G.
   Popes at Avignon, The   III-1648
Momigliano, Arnaldo
   Claudius the Emperor and His Achievement   II-625
   Conflict Between Paganism and Christianity in the Fourth Century, The   II-892; 908
Monan, J. Donald
   Moral Knowledge and Its Methodology in Aristotle   I-332
Moody, Ernest
   Medieval Science of Weights, The   III-1619
Mooney, William M.

Travel Among the Ancient Romans   I-377
Moore, Charles Herbert
   Development and Character of Gothic Architecture   III-1420
Moore, Clifford H.
   Religious Thought of the Greeks, The   I-382
Moore, George Foote
   Judaism   II-988
Moore, Samuel
   Historical Outlines of English Sounds and Inflections   III-1290
Moorhouse, A.C.
   Triumph of the Alphabet, The   I-15
Moorman, John R. H.
   History of the Church in England, A   III-1634
Moran H. A.
   Alphabet and the Ancient Calendar Signs, The   I-15
Morgan, B. Q.
   Socratic Enigma, The   I-322
Morgenstern, Julian
   Book of Genesis: A Jewish Interpretation, The   I-100
Morison, W. A.
   Russian and the Slavonic Languages   II-1178
Morrall, John B.
   Church and State Through the Centuries: A Collection of Historic Documents with Commentaries   III-1268
Morris, J.
   "Pelagian Literature," in *Journal of Theological Studies*   II-950
Morrison, J. S.
   "Notes on Certain Greek Nautical Terms," in *Classical Quarterly*   I-230
Morrison, Karl Frederick
   "Cardinal," in *New Catholic Encyclopedia*   III-1247
   Rome and the City of God: An Essay on the Constitutional Relationships of the Empire and Church in the Fourth Century   II-923
   Two Kingdoms; Ecclesiology in Carolingian Political Thought, The   II-1163
Mortimer, R. C.
   Origins of Private Penance in the Western Church, The   II-766
Moss, H. St. L. B.
   Birth of the Middle Ages, 395-814, The   II-999
Moule, C. F. D.
   Birth of the New Testament, The   II-783
Moulton, J. H.
   Early Zoroastrianism   I-167
Mullett, Charles F.
   Bubonic Plague and England, The   III-1629
Mullinger, James Bass

Schools of Charles the Great and the Restoration of Education in the Ninth Century, The II-1141

Munro, Dana C.
"Fourth Crusade, The," in *Translations and Reprints from the Original Sources* III-1440
"Speech of Pope Urban II at Clermont, The," in *American Historical Review* III-1281

Murdoch, John E.
"Medieval Science of Propositions: Elements of the Interaction with Greek Foundations and the Development of New Mathematical Techniques, The," in *Scientific Change* III-1619

Murphy, Francis X. C.Ss.R.
Monument to Saint Jerome, A II-913; 933

Murray, Gilbert
Aeschylus, the Creator of Tragedy I-252
Five Stages of Greek Religion I-382
Literature of Ancient Greece, The I-220

Murray, Margaret
Splendor That Was Egypt, The I-69

Musurillo, Herbert A.
Acta Alexandrinorum. The Acts of the Pagan Martyrs I-417
Fathers of the Primitive Church, The II-701
"Recent Revival of Origen Studies," in *Theological Studies* II-778

Myers, Eugene A.
Arabic Thought and the Western World in the Golden Age of Islam II-1194

Myendorff, John
Orthodox Church: Its Past and Its Role in the World Today, The III-1242

Nash, E. Gee
Hansa, Its History and Romance, The III-1434

Nasr, Seyyed Hossein
"Book of al-Mansur, The," in *Science and Civilization in Islam* II-1182
Science and Civilization in Islam III-1229

Nef, John U.
Industry and Government in France and England III-1513

Neugebauer, Otto
Exact Sciences in Antiquity, The I-402
Mathematical Cuneiform Texts I-24

Neunheuser, Burkhard
"Sacraments," in Sacramentum Mundi, *An Encyclopedia of Theology* III-1343

Neusner, Jacob
History of the Jews in Babylonia, A II-988

Neumark, David
Essays in Jewish Philosophy III-1337
Juheda Hallevi's Philosophy in Its Principles III-1337

Newman, James R.
World of Mathematics, The III-1286

New Testament Accounts of the Last Supper: I Corinthians 11:23-26; John 13; Luke 22:7-38; Mark 14:12-26; Matthew 26:17-30 II-599

Nicholas, Barry
Introduction to Roman Law, An I-495; II-724

Nichols, Stephen G., Jr.
Formulaic Diction and Thematic Composition in the Chanson de Roland III-1312
Roman de la Rose *de Guillaume de Lorris, Le* III-1471

Nickerson, Hoffmann
Inquisition: A Political and Military Study of Its Establishment, The III-1489

Nilsson, M. P.
Imperial Rome II-680
"Introduction of Hoplite Tactics at Rome: Its Date and Its Consequences, The," in *Journal of Roman Studies* I-285
"Legalism and Superstition; Hell" and "Seers and Oracles," in *Greek Popular Religion* I-124
"Mysteries," in *Oxford Classical Dictionary* I-162

Nock, Arthur Darby
"Notes on Ruler-Cult, I-IV," in *Journal of Hellenic Studies* I-407
St. Paul II-636

Nohl, Johannes
Black Death, The III-1629

Noonan, John T. Jr.
Contraception: A History of Its Treatment by the Catholic Theologians and Canonists II-811
Scholastic Analysis of Usury, The III-1523

North, Christopher R.
Second Isaiah: Introduction, Translation and Commentary to Chapters 15-55, The I-187

Norwood, Gilbert
Greek Comedy I-372

Noth, Martin
History of Israel, The I-109
"Laws in Pentateuch: Their Assumption and Meaning, The," in *The Laws of the Pentateuch and Other Studies* I-89

Nunn, H. P. V.
"St. Peter's Presence in Rome—The Monumental Evidence," in *Evangelical Quarterly* II-647

Oates, Whitney J.
Stoic and Epicurean Philosophers, The I-392

Obolensky, Dimitri
Byzantine Commonwealth, The III-1220; 1722
"Byzantium, Kiev, and Moscow: A Study in Ecclesiastical Relations," in *Dumbarton*

Oaks Papers   III-1209
Oesterley, W. O. E.
 History of Israel, A   I-193
 Introduction to the Books of the Apocrypha, An
  I-446
 *Introduction to the Books of the Old Testa-
  ment, An*   II-668
 *Jews and Judaism During the Greek Period,
  The*   I-480
Ogg, George
 "Tabella Appended to the Pseudo-Cyprianic
  De Pascha Computus in the *Codex Remen-
  sis*, The," in *Vigilia Christiana*   II-861
Ogg, Oscar
 26 Letters, The   I-15; 83
O'Leary, De Lacy
 Arabic Thought and Its Place in History
  III-1398
 How Greek Science Passed to the Arabs
  III-1229
Olmstead, Arthur T.
 History of the Persian Empire, A   I-183;
  241
Olschki, Leonardo
 *Marco Polo's Asia: An Introduction to His "De-
  scription of the World Called 'Il Millione' "*
  III-1554
O'Malley, C. C.
 *Leonardo's Legacy: An International Sym-
  posium*   III-1765
Oman, Sir Charles
 *History of the Art of War in the Middle Ages,
  A*   II-1120
 Seven Roman Statesmen of the Later Republic
  I-485
Ordnance Survey, H. M.
 Map of Roman Britain   II-620
Orlinsky, Harry
 Ancient Israel   I-109
Ortego y Gosset, José
 Invertebrate Spain   II-1079
Osborn, E. F.
 Philosophy of Clement of Alexandria, The
  II-778
Ostborn, G.
 *Cult and Canon: A Study in the Canonization
  of the Old Testament*   II-668
Ostrogorsky, George
 History of the Byzantine State   II-866; III-
  1220; 1242; 1256; 1440
Otis, Brooks
 Ovid As an Epic Poet   II-577

Page, Denys L.
 History and the Homeric Iliad   I-114
Painter, Sidney
 Rise of Feudal Monarchies, The   III-1204
Palanque, J. R.
 Church in the Christian Roman Empire, The
  II-897
Palmer, E. H.

*Caliph Haroun Alrashid and Saracen Civiliza-
 tion, The*   II-1145
Palmieri, A.
 "Two Masters of Byzantine Mysticism:
  Dionysius the Areopagite and Maximus the
  Confessor," in *American Catholic Quarterly
  Review*   II-1016
Panofsky, Erwin
 *Abbot Suger on the Abbey Church of St.-Denis
  and Its Art Treasures*   III-1420
Pares, Bernard
 History of Russia, A   III-1741; 1746
Parke, H. W.
 *Greek Mercenary Soldiers. From the Earliest
  Times to the Battle of Ipsus*   I-317
Parker, H.
 "Seven Liberal Arts, The," in the *English His-
  torical Review*   II-1004
Parker, Henry M.
 *History of the Roman World from A.D. 138 to
  337, A*   II-850
 Roman Legions, The   I-500
Parker, T. M.
 *Christianity and the State in the Light of His-
  tory*   II-994; III-1274; 1322
Parrot, André
 Temple of Jerusalem, The   I-104
Parry, J. H.
 Europe and a Wider World, 1415-1715
  III-1690
Parsons, Edward A.
 Alexandrian Library, The   I-357
Partington, James R.
 History of Greek Fire and Gunpowder, A
  III-1513
Pastor, Ludwig
 History of the Popes, The   III-1648
Patch, Howard Rollin
 Tradition of Boethius, The   II-1022
Patrick, Mary Mills
 Greek Sceptics, The   I-475
Patterson, Warner Forrest
 Three Centuries of French Poetic Theory
  III-1353
Patzig, Gunther
 Aristotle's Theory of The Syllogism   I-352
Paulinus the Deacon
 Life of St. Ambrose, The   II-923
Payne, Robert
 *Holy Sword, the Story of Islam from Mo-
  hammed to the Present, The*   II-1079
Pearson, Lionel I. C.
 Early Ionian Historians, The   I-263
Pease, A. S.
 "Notes on the Delphic Oracle and the Greek
  Colonization," in *Classical Philology*   I-
  124
Pelikan, J.
 "Eusebius: Finality and Universality in His-
  tory," in *The Finality of Jesus Christ in an
  Age of Universal History*   II-845

Perkins, John
Shrine of St. Peter and the Vatican Excavations, The II-646
Pernoud, Régine
Crusades, The III-1502
Joan of Arc: By Herself and Her Witnesses III-1702
Perowne, John James Stewart
Caesars and Saints: The Evolution of the Christian State A.D. 180-313 II-730; 816
End of the Roman World, The II-962
Hadrian II-625
Later Herods, The. The Political Background of the New Testament II-652
Perrin, Bernadotte
Plutarch's Themistocles and Aristides I-230
Perroy, Edouard
Hundred Years' War, The III-1702
Peters, F. E.
Aristotle and the Arabs III-1229
Petry, Ray C.
Francis of Assisi, Apostle of Poverty III-1451
Pfeiffer, Robert H.
History of New Testament Times with an Introduction to the Apocrypha I-446; II-652
Philip A.
Calendar, The I-540
Philips, Margaret Mann
Erasmus and the Northern Renaissance III-1674
Pindar
Odes of Pindar, The I-220
Pinsent, John
"Original Meaning of *Municeps*, The" in *Classical Quarterly* I-337
Pirenne, Henri
Economic and Social History of Medieval Europe III-1328; 1425
Medieval Cities: Their Origin and the Revival of Trade III-1327
Pirenne, M. H.
"Scientific Basis of Leonardo da Vinci's Theory of Perspective, The," in *The British Journal for the Philosophy of Science* III-1695
Pistorius, P. V.
Plotinus and Neoplatonism: An Introductory Study II-828
Plato
Protagoras, Gorgias I-291
Plucknett, T.F.T.
Legislation of Edward I III-1573
Statutes and Their Interpretation in the First Half of the Fourteenth Century III-1390
Plunket, Ierne Arthur Lifford
Isabel of Castile and the Making of the Spanish Nation, 1451-1504 III-1732
Plutarch
Lives II-690

Podlecki, Anthony J.
Political Background of Aeschylean Tragedy, The I-252
Pollack, Sir Frederick
Expansion of Common Law, The III-1390
Pollard, Albert F.
Evolution of Parliament, The III-1634
Polo, Marco
Marco Polo's Account of Japan and Java III-1554
Poole, Reginald Lane
"Beginning of the Year in the Middle Ages, The," in *Studies in Chronology and History* II-883; 1098
"Earliest Use of the Easter Cycle of Dionysius, The," in *Studies in Chronology and History* II-882; 1098
Illustrations of the History of Medieval Thought and Learning III-1404
Portalie, Eugene
Guide to the Thought of St. Augustine, A II-950
Post, G.
Twelfth Century Europe and the Foundation of Modern Society III-1404
Postan, M. M.
Cambridge Economic History of Europe, The. Vol. III: *Economic Organization and Policies in the Middle Ages* II-1103; III-1328
Pound, Ezra
Spirit of Romance, The III-1301
Powell, James M.
Innocent III: Vicar of Christ or Lord of the World? III-1461
Power, Eileen E.
Wool Trade in English Medieval History, The III-1429
Powicke, Frederick M.
Christian Life in the Middle Ages, The III-1597
King Henry III and the Lord Edward III-1532; 1585
Ways of Medieval Life and Thought: Essays and Addresses III-1585
Prawdin, Michael (Michael Charol)
Mongol Empire, The. Its Rise and Legacy III-1466
Prescott, H. W.
Development of Virgil's Art, The I-561
Prescott, William Hickling
History of the Reign of Ferdinand and Isabella the Catholic III-1732
Press, Alan R.
Anthology of Troubadour Lyric Poetry III-1301
Prestige, G. L.
God in Patristic Thought II-897
Previté-Orton, C. W.
"*Defensor Pacis*" *of Marsilius of Padua, The* III-1613

Shorter Cambridge Medieval History, The.
Vol. I: *The Later Roman Empire to the Twelfth Century* II-939
Price, H. H.
Thinking and Experience II-839
Price, Ira Maurice
Ancestry of Our English Bible, The II-913
Pringsheim, F.
"Character of Justinian's Legislation, The," in *Law Quarterly Review,* LVI (1940), II-1039
Pritchard, James B.
Ancient Near East—An Anthology of Texts and Pictures, The I-51
Ancient Near Eastern Texts Relating to the Old Testament I-39; 74; 143; 183
Procopius
Buildings II-1045
Psellus, Michael
"Fourteen Byzantine Rulers," in *The* Chronographia III-1220
Putnam, M. C. J.
Poetry of the Aeneid, The I-561
Pyles, Thomas
Origins and Developments of the English Language, The III-1290

Quasten, Johannes
Patrology II-701; 778; 794; 806; 957
Quesnell, Quentin
"Made Themselves Eunuchs for the Kingdom of Heaven," in *Catholic Biblical Quarterly* III-1262
Quick, C. Oliver
Christian Sacraments, The III-1343

Raab, Clement, O. F. M.
Twenty Ecumenical Councils of the Catholic Church, The III-1461
Radin, Max
Jews Among the Greeks and the Romans, The II-615
Rait, R. S.
Life in the Medieval University III-1404
Rand, E. K.
Ovid and His Influence II-577
Randall, John Herman, Jr.
Aristotle I-347
Rashdall, Hastings
Universities of Europe in the Middle Ages, The III-1483
Raven, J. E.
Presocratic Philosophers: A Critical History with a Selection of Texts, The I-178; 198; 214; 236; 275
Pythagoreans and Eleatics I-199; 236
Reagan, J. N.
Preaching of Peter: The Beginning of Christian Apologetic, The II-711
Reese, Gustave
Music in the Middle Ages III-1415

Reid, James S.
Municipalities of the Roman Empire, The I-337
Reinhold, Meyer
Roman Civilization. Vol. I: *The Republic* I-225
Rescher, Nicholas
"Avicenna on the Logic of Questions," in *Studies in Arabic Philosophy* III-1230
Galen and the Syllogism III-1229
Reynolds, R.
Twelfth Century Europe and the Foundation of Modern Society III-1404
Reynolds, Robert L.
Europe Emerges: Transition Toward an Industrial World-Wide Society, 600-1750 II-1172
Ricciotti, Giuseppe
Life of Christ, The II-594
Rich, E. E.
Cambridge Economic History of Europe, The. Vol. III: *Economic Organization and Policies in the Middle Ages* III-1328
Richardson, H. G.
Governance of Medieval England from the Conquest to Magna Carta, The III-1586
Richmond, I.A.
"Commemorative Arches and City Gates in the Augustan Age," in *The Journal of Roman Studies* I-505
Ridge, F. Morgan
Prophet Amos, The I-128
Ridgeway, W.
Origin and Influence of the Thoroughbred Horse, The I-4
Ries, J.
"Manichaeism," in *The New Catholic Encyclopedia* II-811
Riesenberg, Peter
Inalienability of Sovereignty in Medieval Political Thought III-1347
Rigaux, Beda
Letters of Paul: Modern Studies, The II-636
Rist, John M.
Eros and Psyche: Studies in Plato, Plotinus, and Origen II-828
Ritter, S. M.
"Formation of the Eusebian Christian Historical Tradition, The," *Masters Thesis* II-845
Robb, Nesca Adeline
Neoplatonism of the Italian Renaissance III-1727
Robert of Clari
Conquest of Constantinople, The III-1440
Roberts, Alexander
Ante-Nicene Fathers, The II-794
Robertson, Stuart
Development of Modern English, The III-1290

Robinson, H. Wheeler
History of Israel, The   I-109
Robinson, R. S.
Sources for the History of Greek Athletics
    I-119
Robinson, Theodore H.
Book of Amos, The   I-128
Decline and Fall of the Hebrew Kingdoms, The
    I-109
History of Israel, A   I-193
Introduction to the Books of the Old Testament, An   II-668
Rodenwaldt, G.
Acropolis, The   I-280
Roebuck, Carl A.
Ionian Trade and Colonization   I-133
Rogers, Robert W.
History of Babylonia and Assyria, A   I-183
Rolfe, John C.
Ammianus Marcellinus   II-892
Cicero and His Influence   I-545
Romilly, Jenkins
Byzantium, the Imperial Centuries: 610-1071
    III-1256
Rörig, Fritz
"Hanseatic League," in *Encyclopedia of the
    Social Sciences*   III-1434
Rose, A. C.
"Via Appia in the Days When All Roads Led
    to Rome," in *Annual Report of Board of
    Regents*   I-377
Rose, H. J.
Ancient Greek Religion   I-382
Handbook of Greek Mythology, A   I-162
"Patricians and Plebeians at Rome," in *Journal of Roman Studies*   I-285
Ross, Sir David
Aristotle   I-347; 352
Plato's Theory of Ideas   I-327
Rossetti, Dante Gabriel
Dante and His Circle   III-1602
Rostovtzeff, Mikhail I.
Iranians and Greeks in South Russia   I-133
*Large Estate in Egypt in the Third Century
    B.C., A*   I-417
"Notes on the Economic Policy of the Pergamene Kings," in *Anatolian Studies Presented to Sir William Ramsay*   I-490
"Pergamum," in *The Cambridge Ancient History*   I-490
Rome   I-550
*Social and Economic History of the Hellenistic
    World, The*   I-490
*Social and Economic History of the Roman
    Empire, The*   II-663; 679
Roth, Cecil
History of the Marranos, A   III-1755
Spanish Inquisition, The   III-1490
Roux, Georges
Ancient Iraq   I-183

Rowell, Henry Thompson
Rome in the Augustan Age   I-566
Rowley, H. H.
Servant of the Lord, The   I-187
Runciman, Steven
Byzantine Civilization   III-1721
Eastern Schism, The   III-1242
Fall of Constantinople 1453, The   III-1721
History of the Crusades, A. (in 3 vols.)
    III-1256
Kingdom of Acre and the Later Crusades, The
    Vol. III of *A History of the Crusades.*
    III-1579
*Medieval Manichee: A Study of the Christian
    Dualist Heresy, The*   II-811
Russell, Francis H.
"Battlefield of Zama, The," in *Archaeology*
    I-441
Rutledge, Dom Denis
*Cosmic Theology, The Ecclesiastical Hierarchy
    of Pseudo-Denys: An Introduction*   II-1017
Ryan, J. J.
"Ratramnus of Corbie," in *The New Catholic
    Encyclopedia*   II-1168
Ryan, John, S. J.
Irish Monasticism   II-974
Rypins, Stanley I.
Book of Thirty Centuries, The   II-668

Sabra, A. I.
Theories of Light from Descartes to Newton
    III-1558
Sachs, A.
Mathematical Cuneiform Texts   I-24
Saint Croix, G. E. M. de
"Character of the Athenian Empire, The," in
    Historia   I-246
Saintsbury, George E.
History of English Prosody, A   III-1353
Salter, Frederick M.
Medieval Drama in Chester   III-1225
Saltet, Louis
"Jerome," in *The Catholic Encyclopedia*
    II-933
Sanders, Alvin Howard
History of the Percheron Horse   II-1172
Sandmel, Samuel
Philo's Place in Judaism   II-615
Sandys, J. E.
Companion to Latin Studies, A   I-540
Santillana, Giorgio de
Age of Adventure, The   III-1712
"Role of Art in the Scientific Renaissance,
    The," in *The Rise of Science in Relation to
    Society*   III-1771
Sarachek, Joseph
Faith and Reason   III-1394
Sarton, George
"Vincent of Beauvais," in *Introduction to the
    History of Science*   III-1537

Sartoria, Enrico
Brief History of the Waldensians, A III-1385
Sayles, G. O.
Governance of Medieval England from the Conquest to Magna Carta, *The* III-1586
Schaeffer, C. F. A.
"Appearance and Spread of Metal, The," in *Larousse Encyclopedia of Prehistoric and Ancient Art* I-20
Schillebeeck, E.
Celibacy III-1261
Schmemann, Alexander
Historical Road of Eastern Orthodoxy, The III-1209
Schmidt, Ludwig
"Teutonic Kingdoms in Gaul," in *The Cambridge Medieval History* II-1010
Schneemelcher, Wilhelm
"History of the New Testament Canon, The," in Edgar Hennecke's *New Testament Apocrypha* II-772
Schoeck, Richard J.
Chaucer Criticism: The Canterbury Tales III-1659
Schoeps, H. J.
Paul. The Theology of the Apostle in the Light of Jewish Religious History II-636
Scholem, Gershom G.
On the Kabbalah and Its Symbolism III-1563
Schreiber, Hermann
Teuton and Slav III-1368; 1477
Schroeder, H. J., O. P.
Disciplinary Decrees of the General Councils: Text, Translation, and Commentary II-957; III-1461; 1685
Schulte, J. F. von
"Curia," in *The New Schaff-Herzog Encyclopedia of Religious Knowledge* III-1247
Schulz, Fritz
Classical Roman Law I-495
Principles of Roman Law II-1039
Schürer, Emil
History of the Jewish People in the Time of Jesus Christ, A I-447; II-706
Schwarze, William Nathaniel
John Hus, The Martyr of Bohemia III-1679
Scott, J. F.
History of Mathematics, A I-387
Scott, Samuel Parsons
History of the Moorish Empire in Europe II-1080
Scullard, H. H.
From the Gracchi to Nero: A History of Rome from 133 B.C. to A.D. 68 I-550
Sedgwick, Henry Dwight
Marcus Aurelius II-730
Segal, Charles P.

"Gorgias and the Psychology of the Logos," in *Harvard Studies in Classical Philology* I-291
Sellers, E.
Elder Pliny's Chapters on the History of Art, The II-657
Sellers, R. V.
Council of Chalcedon: A Historical and Doctrinal Survey, The II-967
Seltman, Charles
Greek Coins I-148
Setton, Kenneth M.
Christian Attitude Toward the Emperor in the Fourth Century II-805; 856
"900 Years Ago: The Norman Conquest," in *National Geographic* III-1252
Shaw, R. Dykes
"Fall of the Visigothic Power in Spain, The," in *English Historical Review* II-1110
Sheldon-Williams, I. P.
"Pseudo-Dionysius, The," in *The Cambridge History of Later Greek and Early Medieval Philosophy* II-1017
Sherbowitz-Wetzor, O. P.
Russian Primary Chronicle, The III-1209
Sherley-Price, Leo, Trans.
Saint Francis of Assisi, His Life and Writings III-1451
Sherrard, Philip
Greek East and the Latin West, The III-1242
Sherwin-White, Adrian N.
"Trajan's Replies to Pliny: Authorship and Necessity," in *Journal of Roman Studies* II-695
"Trial of Jesus, The," in *Historicity and Chronology in the New Testament* II-606
Shor, Jean Bowie
After You, Marco Polo III-1554
Shotwell, James T.
History of History, The I-263
See of Peter, The II-822; 919
Silverberg, Tom
Who Was Socrates? I-322
Simons, J.
Jerusalem in the Old Testament I-105
Simpson, George G.
Horses II-1172
Sinclair, T. E.
History of Greek Political Theory, A I-530
Singer, Charles
From Magic to Science III-1483
Galen on Anatomical Procedures II-741
History of Technology, A. Vol. I: *From Early Times to the Fall of Ancient Empires* I-63
Short History of Science to the Nineteenth Century, A II-657
Sinnigen, William B. G.
History of Rome to A.D. 565, A II-939; 979
Sitwell, Gerald, O.S.B.

St. Odo of Cluny   II-1188
Smart, J. D.
  History and Theology in Second Isaiah
  I-188
Smith, David Eugene
  Hindu-Arabic Numerals   III-1286
  History of Mathematics   I-24; 387; II-720
Smith, Gertrude
  *Administration of Justice from Homer to Aris-
  totle, The*   I-157
Smith, Lucy Margaret
  Cluny in the Eleventh and Twelfth Centuries
  II-1188
Smith, R. E.
  Cicero the Statesman   I-530
  Failure of the Roman Republic, The   I-510
Smith, Sidney
  *Isaiah Chapters XL-LV: Literary Criticism and
  History*   I-187
Smith, Vincent Edward
  Science and Philosophy   I-367
Smith, W. Stevenson
  *Art and Architecture of Ancient Egypt, The.
  Pelican History of Art*   I-29
Smithers, G. V.
  Early Middle English Verse and Prose   III-
  1290
Snow, A., O.S.B.
  Saint Gregory the Great, His Work and Spirit
  II-1068
Solmsen, Friedrich
  Aristotle's System of the Physical World
  I-367
  "Greek Philosophy and the Discovery of the
  Nerves," in *Museum Helveticum*   II-741
  Hesiod and Aeschylus   I-143; 252
Sordo, Enrique
  Moorish Spain   II-1193
Souter, Alexander
  Text and Canon of the New Testament, The
  II-772
Southern, R. W.
  Making of the Middle Ages, The   III-1527
Sozomen
  Church History, Vol. 2, series 2, of *Nicene and
  Post-Nicene Fathers*   II-923
Speiser, E. A.
  Anchor Bible: Genesis, The   I-100
Spiegelberg, Herbert
  Socratic Enigma, The   I-322
Spinka, Matthew
  Advocates of Reform. Vol. XIV of *The Library
  of Christian Classics*   III-1649
  John Hus and the Czech Reformation   III-
  1679
Stapleton, H. E.
  "Chemistry in Iraq and Persia in the Tenth
  Century A.D.," in *Memoirs of the Royal
  Asiatic Society of Bengal*   II-1182
Stauffer, Ethelbert
  Christ and the Caesars   II-816

Staverly, E. S.
  "Tribal Assemblies Before the *Lex Hor-
  tensia*," in *Athenaeum*   I-397
Stecchini, Livio C.
  Athenaion Politeia: The Constitution of Athens
  I-209
Steinmann, Jean
  Saint Jerome and His Times   II-933
Stenton, F. M.
  Anglo-Saxon England   II-1062; 1085
Stevens, G. P.
  Restorations of Classical Buildings   I-280
Stevenson, G. H.
  "Imperial Administration, The," in Vol. XI of
  The Cambridge Ancient History,   II-625
Stevenson, J.
  *Creeds, Councils and Controversies: Docu-
  ments Illustrative of the Church A.D. 337-
  461*   II-967
Steward, H. F.
  Boethius: An Essay   II-1022
Stewart, J. A.
  Plato's Doctrine of Ideas   I-327
Stone, Darwell
  *History of the Doctrine of the Holy Eucharist,
  A*   II-1168
Stones, E. L. G.
  Edward I   III-1573
Strong, James
  *Cyclopedia of Biblical, Theological, and Ec-
  clesiastical Literature*   II-1116
Stroud, Ronald Sidney
  Drakon's Law on Homicide   I-157
Stuart, Duane Reed
  Epochs of Greek and Roman Biography
  II-690
Stubbs, William
  Constitutional History of England, The
  III-1573; 1634
  Germany in the Early Middle Ages, 476-1250
  III-1199
Swete, H. B.
  *Apostles' Creed: Its Relation to Primitive Chris-
  tianity, The*   II-756
  Old Testament in Greek, The   I-421
Swindler, W. F.
  Magna Carta, Legend and Legacy   III-
  1456
Syme, Ronald
  Roman Revolution, The   I-525

Talbot, C. H.
  *Anglo-Saxon Missionaries in Germany: Being
  the Lives of SS. Willibrord, Boniface, Sturm,
  Leoba and Lebuin, Together with the Hodo-
  eporicon of St. Willibald and a Selection
  from the Correspondence of St. Boniface,
  The*   II-1130
Tarn, Sir William W.
  Greeks in Bactria and India, The   I-431
  "Hellenistic Ruler-Cult and the Daemon,

The," in *Journal of Hellenic Studies* I-407

"War of the East Against the West, The," in *The Cambridge Ancient History* I-555

Taton, René
History of Science, A. Vol. 2: *The Beginnings of Modern Science* III-1558

Taylor, Eva Germaine R.
Haven Finding Art, The III-1508

Taylor, Henry Osborn
Mediaeval Mind, The II-1022

Taylor, Jerome
Chaucer Criticism: The Canterbury Tales III-1659

Tcherikover, Avigdor
Hellenistic Civilization and the Jews I-421

Teall, John L.
"Enigma of the Fourth Crusade, The," in Spitz's *Major Crises in Western Civilization* III-1440

Telfer, W.
Forgiveness of Sins, The II-766

Tellenbach, Gerd
Church, State, and Christian Society at the Time of the Investiture Contest II-994; 1135; III-1268; 1274; 1322

Temkin, Owsie
"Medieval Translation of Rhazes' Clinical Observations, A," in *Bulletin of the History of Medicine*, (XII) II-1183

Thackery, Henry St. John
Septuagint and the Jewish Worship, The I-421
Some Aspects of the Greek Old Testament I-421

Thayer, William Roscoe
Art of Biography, The II-690

Thompson, E. A.
Early Germans, The II-588
History of Attila and the Huns, A II-903; 979

Thompson, Faith
First Century of Magna Carta: *Why It Persisted as a Document, The* III-1456
Magna Carta: *Its Role in the Making of the English Constitution, 1300-1629* III-1456

Thompson, H. A.
"Pnyx of Athens, The," in *Hesperia* I-209

Thompson, James Westfall
Economic and Social History of Europe in the Middle Ages (300-1300), An III-1363
Feudal Germany III-1199; 1477
History of Historical Writing III-1537

Thomson, George
Aeschylus and Athens I-252

Thomson, S. Harrison
Europe in Renaissance and Reformation III-1654; 1707; 1737

Thorndike, Lynn
"Arabic Occult Science," in *A History of*

Magic and Experimental Science, Vol. I II-1183
History of Magic and Experimental Science During the First Thirteen Centuries of Our Era, A II-657
"Other Early Medieval Learning: Boethius, Isidore, Bede, Gregory the Great," in *A History of Magic and Experimental Sciences During the First Thirteen Centuries of Our Era* II-1090
University Records and Life in the Middle Ages III-1483

Thoy, Macy
Study of the Nibelungenlied, The III-1409

Throop, Palmer A.
Criticism of the Crusade: A Study of Public Opinion and Crusade Propaganda, A III-1502

Thucydides
Peloponnesian War, The I-296

Tierney, Brian
"Bracton on Government," in *Speculum* II-788
Crisis of Church and State 1050-1300, The II-994; 1125; III-1274; 1322; 1597
Foundations of the Conciliar Theory: The Contribution of the Medieval Canonists from Gratian to the Great Schism III-1613; 1649; 1685

Tilley, A.
Medieval France III-1204

Tod, Marcus N.
Selection of Greek Historical Inscriptions to the End of the Fifth Century B.C., A I-157

Torrey, C. C.
Apocryphal Literature, The I-446
Second Isaiah, The I-187

Tout, Thomas Frederick
Edward the First III-1573

Towers, B.
Galen on Anatomical Procedures, The Later Books II-740

Toynbee, Arnold J.
"Creation of a Literature in Latin on the Pattern of Literature in Greek, The," in *Hannibal's Legacy: The Hannibalic War's Effects on Roman Life* I-458
Hannibal's Legacy: The Hannibalic War's Effects on Roman Life I-412

Toynbee, Jocelyn
"Graffiti Beneath St. Peter's: Professor Guarducci's Interpretations," in *The Dublin Review* II-647
Shrine of St. Peter and the Vatican Excavations, The II-646

Tracy, Sterling
Philo Judaeus and the Roman Principate II-615

Trattner, Ernest R.
Understanding the Talmud II-988

Treharne, R. F.

Baronial Plan of Reform 1258-1263, The
  III-1532
Trench, Richard Chenevix
  Plutarch: His Life, His Lives, and His Morals
  II-691
Tuberville, A. S.
  Medieval Heresy and Inquisition   III-1385;
  1446; 1489
Tüchle, Hermann
  Church History   II-892
  Middle Ages, The   II-1168
Turner, C. H.
  "Apostolic Succession," in *Essays on the Early
  History of the Church and the Ministry*
  II-746
  History and Use of Creeds and Anathemas, The
  II-871
Turner, H.E.W.
  Patristic Doctrine of Redemption, The   II-
  751

Ullman, B. L.
  Ancient Writings and Its Influence   I-83
Ullman, Walter
  *History of Political Thought: The Middle Ages,
  A*   III-1268
Ullmann, M.
  Medizin in Islam, Die.   II-1182
Ullmann, Walter
  *Growth of Papal Government in the Middle
  Ages: A Study in the Ideological Relation of
  Clerical to Lay Power, The*   III-1247;
  1322; 1495
  *Medieval Idea of Law as Represented by Lucas
  de Penna, The. A Study in Fourteenth-Cen-
  tury Legal Scholarship*   III-1348
  *Medieval Papalism: The Political Theories of
  the Medieval Canonists*   III-1268
  Origins of the Great Schism   III-1648
  *Principles of Government and Politics in the
  Middle Ages*   II-788
Untersteiner, Mario
  Sophists, The   I-291
Utechin, S. V.
  Russian Political Thought. A Concise History.
  III-1741; 1746

Valentin, Veit
  *German People: Their History and Civilization
  from the Holy Roman Empire to the Third
  Reich, The*   III-1606; 1624; 1639
Van Bath, B. H.
  *Agrarian History of Western Europe, A.D. 500-
  1850, The*   II-1104
Van Deman, Esther Boise
  Building of the Roman Aqueducts, The
  II-630
Van der Meer, Frederick
  Augustine the Bishop   II-945; 951
Van Nice, Robert L.
  "Hagia Sophia, Istanbul: Preliminary Report

of a Recent Examination of the Structure,"
  in *American Journal of Archaeology*   II-
  1044
"Hagia Sophia: The Collapse of the First
  Dome" and "The Construction of the Sec-
  ond Dome and Its Later Repairs," in *Ar-
  chaeology*   II-1044
Van Sickle, C. E.
  "Diocletian and the Decline of the Roman
  Municipalities," in *Journal of Roman Stud-
  ies*   II-833
Van Steenberghen, Fernand
  *Philosophical Movement in the Thirteenth Cen-
  tury, The*   III-1568
Van Zijil, Rev. Theodore P., S.V.D.
  *Gerhard Groote, Ascetic and Reformer, 1340-
  1384*   III-1674
Vasiliev, A. A.
  History of the Byzantine Empire, 324-1453
  III-1220; 1242; 1721
Vernadsky, George
  Ancient Russia   II-1178
Vernon, Arthur
  History and Romance of the Horse, The
  II-1172
Versenyi, Laszlo
  Socratic Humanism   I-322
Vesey-Fitzgerald, B.
  Book of the Horse, The   I-4
Vickers, Kenneth H.
  England in the Later Middle Ages   III-
  1633
Vignaux, Paul
  Philosophy in the Middle Ages   III-1317
Villehardouin, Geoffrey de
  "Conquest of Constantinople, The," in
  Chronicles of the Crusades   III-1439
Vinogradoff, Paul
  Roman Law in Medieval Europe   III-1348
Vlastes, Gregory
  "Ethics and Physics in Democritus," in *Philo-
  sophical Review*   I-269
Vogt, Joseph
  *Decline of Rome, The. The Metamorphosis of
  Ancient Civilization*   II-833; 984
Von Fritz, Kurt
  Aristotle's Constitution of Athens   I-209
  *Theory of the Mixed Constitution in Antiquity,
  The*   I-530
Von Grunebaum, Gustave E.
  Medieval Islam   III-1230; 1527
Von Hefele, Karl J.
  *History of the Councils of the Church from the
  Original Documents, A*   II-861; 876
Von Rad, Gerhard
  Genesis: A Commentary   I-100
Von Ranke, Leopold
  History of the Popes of Rome   III-1648
Von Treitschke, Heinrich
  Origins of Prussianism, The   III-1477

Vryonis, Speros
  Byzantium and Europe   III-1358

Waddell, Helen
  Wandering Scholars, The   III-1404
Wade-Gery, H. T.
  "Dating of Documents to the Mid-Fifth Century, The," in *Journal of Hellenic Studies*
  I-246
Wailes, Rex
  "Windmills," in *A History of Technology*
  I-9
Waite, Arthur E.
  Holy Kabbalah, The   III-1563
Walford, Cornelius
  Fairs, Past and Present   III-1425
Walker, Adrian
  St. Bernard of Clairvaux   III-1333
Wallace-Hadrill, J. M.
  Barbarian West: The Early Middle Ages, A.D. 400-1000   II-1051; 1134; 1151
Wallach, Luitpold
  Alcuin and Charlemagne: Studies in Carolingian History and Literature   II-1141
Walsh, William T.
  Characters of the Inquisition   III-1490
Walshe, Maurice O'Connell
  Medieval German Literature: A Survey
  III-1409
Walter, Gerard
  Caesar: A Biography   I-519
Walzer, R.
  Greek into Arabic   III-1230
Wand, J. W. C.
  Development of Sacramentalism, The   III-1343
  Doctors and Councils   II-897
Ware, Timothy
  Orthodox Church, The   III-1242
Warmington, Brian Herbert
  Carthage   I-412; 442
  North African Provinces from Diocletian to the Vandal Conquest, The   II-945
Warmington, E. H.
  Lucilius: The Twelve Tables in Vol. III of *Remains of Old Latin*   I-258
Warner, H. J.
  Albigensian Heresy, The   III-1446
Watson, Harry
  Kabbalah and Spinoza's Philosophy, The
  III-1563
Watt, W. Montgomery
  History of Islamic Spain, A   III-1527
Watts, J. D. W.
  Vision and Prophecy in Amos   I-128
Waugh, W. T.
  "Great Statute of *Praemunire*, The," in *English Historical Review*   III-1534
Webb, C. C. J.
  John of Salisbury   III-1374
Webb, Geoffrey

St. *Bernard of Clairvaux*   III-1333
Weber, Leonhard M.
  "Celibacy," in *Sacramentum Mundi*   III-1262
Webster, T. B. L.
  Studies in Menander   I-372
Weigall, Arthur E. P. B.
  Life and Times of Cleopatra, Queen of Egypt, The   I-555
  Life and Times of Marc Antony, The   I-550
Weiner, A.
  "Hansa, The," in *The Cambridge Medieval History*   III-1434
Weisheip, J. A.
  "Vincent of Beauvais," in *The New Catholic Encyclopedia*   III-1538
Welch, A. C.
  Jeremiah   I-152
Wellhausen, Julius
  Arab Kingdom and Its Fall, The   II-1110
  Prolegomena to the History of Ancient Israel
  I-100; II-668
Wells, J. A.
  Commentary on Herodotus, A   I-241
Weltin, E. G.
  Ancient Popes, The   II-674; 876; 919
  "Concept of Ex-opere-operato Efficacy in the Fathers as an Evidence of Magic in Early Christianity, The," in *Greek-Roman-and-Byzantine Studies*   II-1168; III-1343
  "Some Animadversions on Early Church Government," in *Concordia Theological Monthly*   II-822
Wenley, Robert Mark
  Stoicism and Its Influence   I-392
Werblowsky, R. J. Zwi
  Joseph Karo, Lawyer and Mystic   III-1563
Werfel, Franz
  Hearken Unto the Voice   I-152
Werthman, Michael S.
  English Tradition: Modern Studies in English History, The   III-1585
West, David
  Imagery and Poetry of Lucretius, The   I-515
Westcott, B. F.
  General Survey of the History of the Canon of the New Testament, A   II-783
Westermann, W. L.
  "Ptolemies and the Welfare of Their Subjects, The," in *American Historical Review*   I-417
Westlake, H. D.
  "Athenian Aims in Sicily, 427-424 B.C.," in *Historia*   I-312
Wethered, H. N.
  Mind of the Ancient World: A Consideration of Pliny's Natural History, The   II-658
Whall, W. B.
  Rovers of the Deep   III-1508
White, John

Birth and Rebirth of Pictorial Space, The
III-1669
Whitney, J. P.
Hildebrantine Essays III-1274
Wilcken, Ulrich
Alexander the Great I-362
William, Watkin
St. Bernard: The Man and His Message
III-1333
Williams, Schafer
*Gregorian Epoch: Reformation, Revolution,
Reaction?, The* III-1274; 1322
Williams, Trevor I.
*Short History of Technology from the Earliest
Times to A.D. 1900, A* I-63
Wilson, John A.
Culture of Ancient Egypt, The I-39; 57; 69
"Egypt: The Values of Life," in *The Intellectual Adventure of Ancient Man: An Essay on
Speculative Thought in the Ancient Near
East* I-39
"The Good Life," in *The Intellectual Adventure of Ancient Man: An Essay on Speculative Thought in the Ancient Near East*
I-44
*The Intellectual Adventure of Ancient Man: An
Essay on Speculative Thought in the Ancient
Near East* I-57
Winsor, Justin
*Christopher Columbus and How He Received
and Imported the Spirit of Discovery* III-1759
Winspear, Alban Dewes
Lucretius and Scientific Thought I-515
Who Was Socrates? I-322
White, Lynn, Jr.
Transformation of the Roman World, The
II-984
Whitely, D. E. H.
Theology of St. Paul, The II-636
Withington, E. T.
Hippocratic Writings I-306
Whitney, J. P.
*Cambridge Medieval History, The. Vol. I: The
Christian Roman Empire and the Foundation of the Teutonic Kingdoms* II-939
Winsor, Justin
*Christopher Columbus and How He Received
and Imported the Spirit of Discovery* III-1759
Wittek, Paul
Rise of the Ottoman Empire, The III-1256
Whittingham, W. R.
Book of Ratram II-1168
Wilkinson, L. P.
Ovid Recalled II-577
Williams, G. H.
"Christology and Church-State Relations in
the Fourth Century," in *Church History,*
XX II-856
Wingren, Gustav

Man and the Incarnation II-751
Winter, M. M.
Saint Peter and the Popes II-919
Winter, Paul
On the Trial of Jesus II-606
Woldering, Irmgard
Art of Egypt, The. The Time of the Pharaohs.
I-29
Wolfe, Rolland E.
Meet Amos and Hosea, the Prophets of Israel
I-128
Wolff, Hans Julius
Roman Law. An Historical Introduction.
I-225; 258; 724
Wolff, Robert L.
"Fourth Crusade, The," in *The Later Crusades.* Vol. II of Setton's *A History of the
Crusades* III-1440
Wood, Charles T.
Philip the Fair and Boniface VIII III-1597
Wood, H. G.
"Baptism (Early Christian and Later Christian)," in *Encyclopedia of Religion and Ethics* II-822
Woodbridge, Frederick
Aristotle's Vision of Nature I-367
Woodhouse, William J.
Solon the Liberator I-172
Woodruff, F. Winthrop
Roger Bacon: A Biography III-1543
Wooley, Sir Leonard
Beginnings of Civilization, The I-51
Woolf, C. N. S.
Bartolus of Sassoferrato III-1348
Wordsworth, W. A.
*En-Roeh: The Prophecy of Isaiah the Seer with
Habakkuk and Nahum* I-187
Workman, Herbert B.
Dawn of the Reformation, The III-1679
Evolution of the Monastic Ideal, The II-1050
*John Wycliffe: A Study of the English Medieval
Church* III-1643
Martyrs of the Early Church, The II-642
Persecution of the Early Church II-642;
817
Wren, Melvin C.
Course of Russian History, The III-1741;
1746
Wulf, M. de
History of Medieval Philosophy III-1712

Xenophon
Anabasis I-317

Yadin, Yagael
*Finds from the Bar Kokhba Period in the Cave
of Letters, The* II-706
Yates, Frances Amelia

Giordano Bruno and the Hermetic Tradition
III-1727
Yellin, David
Maimonides III-1394
Yeo, Cedric A.
"Founding and Function of Roman Colonies,
The," in *The Classical World* I-337
History of the Roman People, A II-588
Young, George
Portugal, Old and Young III-1690
Young, Karl
Drama of the Medieval Church, The III-
1225

Zabeeh, Farhang
Universals. A New Look at an Old Problem.
II-839
Zaehner, R. C.
Dawn and Twilight of Zoroastrianism, The
I-167
Zandee, J.
Death as an Enemy According to Ancient Egyptian Conceptions I-57

Zeiller, Jacques
History of the Primitive Church, The II-
822
Zeller, Edward
Stoics, Epicureans, and Sceptics, The I-475
Zeller, Hubert Van, O.S.B.
Benedictine Idea, The II-1034
*Holy Rule: Notes on St. Benedict's Legislation
for Monks, The* II-1034
Zeller, Mary Claudia
Development of Trigonometry from Regiomontanus to Pitiscus II-720
Zernov, Nicholas
Eastern Christendom III-1209; 1721
Zeuner, Frederick E.
History of Domesticated Animals, A I-34
Ziada, Mustafa M.
"Mamluk Sultans to 1293, The," in *The Later
Crusades.* Vol. II of Setton's *A History of the
Crusades, 1189-1311* III-1579
Zimmern, Helen
Hansa Towns, The III-1435
Zubov, V. P.
Leonardo da Vinci III-1765

INDEXES

VOLUMES ONE, TWO, AND THREE

Modern European Series

Abdication of Charles V   I-153
Abdication of Edward VIII   III-1420
Abolition of Slavery in the British Colonies II-715
Accession of Charles III of Spain   I-442
Accession of Frederick the Great   I-414
Accession of Frederick William I of Prussia I-396
Act of Settlement   I-385
Act of Supremacy   I-103
Act of Union   II-551
Adam Smith Publishes *The Wealth of Nations* I-485
Adoption of the Weimar Constitution   III-1295
Advent of the Labour Government in Great Britain   III-1517
Algeria Wins Its Independence   III-1628
Allied Invasion of France   III-1491
Anschluss, The   III-1425
Appearance of the "False Dimitry"   I-231
Arab-Israeli War   III-1654
Austria Annexes Bosnia and Hercegovina III-1202
Austrian *Ausgleich,* The   II-939

Bach Pioneers Modern Music   I-380
Baghdad Railway Concession   II-1133
Balkan Wars, The   III-1240
Battle of Aboukir Bay   I-538
Battle of Austerlitz   II-568
Battle of Blenheim   I-390
Battle of Dien Bien Phu   III-1577
Battle of El Alamein   III-1467
Battle of Jutland   III-1266
Battle of Lepanto   I-180
Battle of Marengo   II-556
Battle of Marston Moor   I-313
Battle of Mohács   I-87
Battle of Narva   I-376
Battle of Pavia   I-82
Battle of the Bulge   III-1496
Battle of the Nations   II-590
Battle of Verdun   III-1262
Battle of Waterloo   II-618
Beccaria Publishes *On Crimes and Punishments* I-456
Beginning of Extensive Submarine Warfare III-1254
Beginning of the Chartist Movement   II-741
Beginning of the *Fronde*   I-324
Belgian Revolution   II-686
Bergson Publishes *Creative Evolution*   III-1183
Berlin Airlift   III-1543
Berlin Conference on African Affairs   II-1048

Bismarck Becomes Minister-President of Prussia II-880
Bloody Sunday   III-1156
Boer War, The   II-1128
Boulanger Crisis, The   II-1053
Brandt Wins West German Elections   III-1690
British Evacuation from Dunkirk   III-1456
Building of the Berlin Wall   III-1624
Building of the Maginot Line   III-1359
Building of the Suez Canal   II-818

Caetano Becomes Premier of Portugal   III-1673
Calling of the States-General by Louis XVI I-502
Calvin Publishes *Institutes of the Christian Religion*   I-116
Carlist Wars in Spain   II-726
Casablanca Conference, The   III-1477
Catherine the Great's *Instruction* for Radical Social Reform   I-464
Charles I Ascends the Throne of Spain   I-40
Charles VIII of France Invades Italy   I-21
Churchill's "Iron Curtain" Speech   III-1526
Civil Constitution of the Clergy   I-516
Collapse of France   III-1451
Collapse of the Fourth French Republic   III-1607
Columbus Lands in America   I-16
Common Market Formed by Western European Nations   III-1601
Communists Lose Italian Elections   III-1538
Completion of the H.M.S. *Dreadnought*   III-1187
Comte Publishes *Positive Philosophy*   II-803
Concordat of Bologna   I-44
Congo Crisis   III-1613
Congress of Berlin   II-1007
Conquest of Mexico   I-59
Copernicus Publishes *De Revolutionibus Orbium Coelestium*   I-138
Coronation of Napoleon as Emperor   II-564
Council of Trent   I-143
Crimean War, The   II-813
Crystal Palace Exhibition   II-799
Czechoslovakia Invaded by Russians   III-1666

Daguerre Develops the First Permanent Photograph   II-747
Daily Telegraph Episode   III-1207
Daimler Develops the Gasoline Internal Combustion Engine   II-1033
Darwin Publishes *On the Origin of Species* II-855
Davy Invents the Arc Lamp   II-560
"Day of Dupes", The   I-278

Death of Charles II of Spain   I-372
Death of Stalin   III-1566
Decembrist Revolt, The   II-665
Defeat of the Spanish Armada   I-193
Defenestration of Prague   I-250
De Gaulle Steps Down   III-1683
Descartes Publishes *Discourse on Method*   I-294
Dias Rounds the Cape of Good Hope   I-11
Diplomatic Revolution, The   I-437
Discovery of the Neanderthal Man   II-822
Discovery of the Structure of DNA   III-1572
Dos de Mayo Insurrection in Spain   II-581
Dreyfus Affair, The   II-1075

Edict of Nantes   I-214
Edit of Restitution   I-270
Einstein Publishes *Special Theory of Relativity*   III-1160
Election of Charles V as Emperor   I-64
Election of Michael Romanov as Tsar   I-247
Elizabeth I Is Excommunicated by Pius V   I-174
Emancipation Acts of 1828 and 1829   II-669
Emancipation of the Serfs   II-866
Ems Telegram, The   II-949
Enabling Act of 1933, The   III-1382
Entente Cordiale, The   III-1152
Establishment of the Commonwealth in England   I-329
Establishment of the League of Nations   III-1289
Establishment of the Russian Patriarchate   I-198
Establishment of the Third French Republic   II-974
Establishment of Tudor Rule in England   I-6
Execution of Louis XVI   I-520
Explosion of the First Nuclear Bomb   III-1561

Fall of La Rochelle   I-259
Fall of Robespierre   I-529
Faraday Develops the Electric Motor and Generator   II-649
Fashoda Incident, The   II-1113
"Fatti di Maggio" Riots   II-1109
First Battle of the Marne   III-1249
First Five-Year Plan in Russia   III-1329
First Hague Peace Conference   II-1123
First Manned Lighter-Than-Air Assent   I-496
First Meeting of the Duma   III-1179
First Polish Rebellion   II-691
First Popular Front Ministry in France   III-1411
First Thousand-Bomber Raid on Germany   III-1461
Flaubert Publishes *Madame Bovary*   II-827
Fleming Discovers Penicillin   III-1335
Formation of the First International   II-897

Formation of the German Empire   II-963
Formation of the League of Cambrai   I-31
Formation of the North German Confederation   II-918
Formation of the Russian Social Democratic Labor Party   II-1105
Formation of the Schmalkaldic League   I-91
Formation of the Three Emperors' League   II-988
Formation of the United Nations   III-1507
Formation of the World Council of Churches   III-1550
Founding of Moscow University   I-432
Founding of the Jesuits   I-96
France Withdraws from NATO   III-1648
Franchise Act of 1884   II-1038
Francis Bacon Publishes *Novum Organum*   I-254
Franco-Prussian War, The   II-954
Franco-Russian Alliance   II-1070
French Governmental Crisis of 1934   III-1386
Freud Publishes *The Interpretation of Dreams*   III-1139

Galileo Publishes *Dialogue on the Two Great World Systems*   I-285
Garibaldi's Thousand "Redshirts" Land in Italy   II-860
General Strike of 1926 in Great Britain   III-1324
German Invasion of Norway   III-1446
German Invasion of Poland   III-1440
German Peasants' War   I-76
"Glorious Revolution", The   I-357
Great Blood Purge, The   III-1391
Great Britain Purchases Suez Canal Shares   II-998
Great Britain Strengthens the Royal Navy   II-1057
Great Britain Withdraws from the Concert of Europe   II-654
Grove's First Incandescent Electric Lamp   II-753

Henry IV Ascends the Throne of France   I-202
Hungarian Revolution   III-1595

Invasion of Italy   III-1486
Invention of the Diesel Engine   II-1100
Irish Famine and the Great Emigration   II-757
Irish Home Rule Bill   III-1233
Italian Defeat at Adowa and the Downfall of Crispi   II-1094
Italian Ethiopian Campaign   III-1401
Italian Parliament Passes the Law of Papal Guarantees   II-978
Italy Annexes Tripoli   III-1228
Italy Is Proclaimed a Kingdom   II-870

James I Becomes King of England and Scotland I-224

James Watt Develops His Steam Engine I-460

Jean-Paul Sartre Publishes *Being and Nothingness* III-1482

John Stuart Mill Publishes *On Liberty* II-843

John Wesley's Conversion I-409

Joseph II's Reforms I-480

Jubilee Year of 1500 and Renaissance Papacy, The I-26

July Revolution in France II-682

Jung Publishes *Psychological Types* III-1310

Kay Invents His Flying Shuttle I-405

Kepler Publishes *The New Astronomy* I-236

Keynes Publishes *The General Theory of Employment, Interest, and Money* III-1406

Koch Receives the Nobel Prize for Service to Medicine III-1174

Kulturkampf II-969

Laying of the First Transatlantic Cable II-834

Legalization of French Trade Unions II-1044

Lenin's New Economic Policy III-1304

Lister and Antiseptic Surgery II-935

Loss of Spanish Colonies to the United States II-1119

Louis XIV Invades the Netherlands I-345

Louis XIV Moves the French Court to Versailles I-349

Louis Napoleon Bonaparte Becomes Emperor of France II-808

Luther Posts His Ninety-Five Theses I-54

Lyell Publishes *The Principles of Geology* II-678

Machiavelli Writes *The Prince* I-35

Magellan Expedition Circumnavigates the Globe I-68

Malthus Publishes *An Essay on the Principle of Population* I-533

Marconi Develops Wireless Telegraphy II-1080

Maria Theresa Succeeds to the Austrian Throne I-419

Marriage of Ferdinand and Isabella I-1

Marshall Plan Is Announced, The III-1532

Massacre of St. Bartholomew's Day I-184

Maudslay Develops the Slide Rest I-524

Mazzini Founds "Young Italy" II-697

Mendel Announces His Laws on Genetics II-908

Mexican Adventure of Maximilian II-876

Miguel Seizes the Portuguese Throne II-675

Milton Publishes *Areopagitica* I-317

Munich Crisis, The III-1429

Municipal Corporations Act II-737

Murder of Dollfuss III-1395

Mussolini Formulates The Doctrine of Fascism III-1299

Mussolini's "March on Rome" III-1319

Napoleon Rises to Power in France I-547

Napoleon's Invasion of Russia II-585

Napoleon III and Cavour Meet at Plombières II-838

Napoleon III and the Emperor Francis Joseph Meet at Villafranca II-849

National Insurance Act III-1223

Nazi-Soviet Pact, The III-1433

Neapolitan Revolution of 1820 II-638

"New Laws" of Spain, The I-129

New Poor Law, The II-730

Nietzsche Publishes *Thus Spake Zarathustra* II-1024

North Atlantic Treaty Organization Pact Signed III-1555

Norway Becomes Independent III-1164

Nuremberg Trials, The III-1522

Oath of the Tennis Court I-506

October Manifesto, The III-1169

October Revolution, The III-1271

Opening of the Stockton and Darlington Railway II-660

Organization of the German Confederation II-602

Outbreak of the Civil War in Spain III-1416

Outbreak of World War I III-1245

Panama Canal Scandal in France II-1066

Paris Commune, The II-984

Paris Revolution of 1848 II-786

Parliament Act of 1911 III-1214

Partitioning of Poland I-469

Passage of Anti-Socialist Legislation in Germany II-1013

Peace of Augsburg I-148

Peace of Karlowitz I-368

Peace of Paris, The I-451

Peace of the Pyrenees I-341

Peace of Westphalia I-308

Petition of Right I-263

Philip II of Spain Becomes King of Portugal I-189

Pius IX Publishes the *Syllabus of Errors* II-902

Pontificate of Pope Pius IX II-770

Pope Paul VI Publishes *Humanae Vitae* III-1659

Portugal Gains Independence Under the Braganzas I-304

Portuguese Revolution of 1820 II-645

Potato-Growing in Europe I-424

Potsdam Conference, The III-1512

Proclamation of the Republic of Portugal III-1219

Proclamation of the Second Spanish Republic III-1368

Prussian Reform After Defeat at Jena   II-572
Prussian Revolution of 1848   II-790
Publication of Kant's Three *Critiques*   I-491
Publication of the *Communist Manifesto*   II-781
Publication of the *Encyclopédie*   I-428
Publication of the King James Bible   I-241

Reform Act of 1867: Disraeli's "Leap in the Dark", The   II-929
Reform Act of 1832   II-704
Reforms of Peter the Great   I-364
Reichstag Fire, The   III-1377
Renan Publishes *Life of Jesus*   II-892
Repeal of the Corn Laws   II-764
Restoration of Charles II   I-337
Restoration of Ferdinand VII to the Throne of Spain   II-594
Restoration of Maria II to the Throne of Portugal   II-722
Restoration of the French Bourbon Kings   II-598
Revocation of the Edict of Nantes   I-353
Revolt of the Catalans   I-299
Revolutions of 1848 in Italy   II-775
Rhodesian Declaration of Independence   III-1642
Ricardo Publishes *Principles of Political Economy*   II-629
Roentgen Discovers X Rays   II-1084
Rome Becomes the Capital of Italy   II-958
Rosenberg Publishes *The Myth of the Twentieth Century*   III-1363
Rousseau Publishes *La Nouvelle Héloïse*   I-446
Russia Puts a Man in Space   III-1618
Russo-Japanese War   III-1148

Second Hague Peace Conference   III-1192
Second Peace of Paris   II-623
Second Polish Rebellion   II-886
Second Vatican Council   III-1633
Senefelder Invents Lithography   I-542
Separation of the Church and the State in France   III-1143
Sergei Witte Begins the Industrialization of Russia   II-1062
Seven Weeks' War, The   II-912
Shakespeare Writes His Dramas   I-208
Sidney B. Fay Publishes *Origins of the World War*   III-1340
Sir Thomas More Publishes *Utopia*   I-49

Six Articles of Henry VIII, The   I-123
Social Insurance Laws in Germany   II-1028
Socialist Congress at Gotha   II-992
Soviet-Chinese Border War   III-1678
Soviet-Chinese Dispute and China's Detonation of an Atomic Bomb   III-1583
Spain Declares Neutrality in World War I   III-1259
Spanish Constitution of 1876   II-1003
Spanish Revolution of 1868   II-945
Spanish Revolution of 1820   II-634
Spengler Publishes *Decline of the West*   III-1279
Stand at Stalingrad, The   III-1472
Statute of Westminster   III-1372
Stephenson Adapts the Steam Engine for the Railroad   II-608
Storming of the Bastille   I-510
Suez Canal Seized by Egypt   III-1589
Suppression of the Monasteries in England   I-110
Sweden Enters the Thirty Years' War   I-274
Swiss Confederation Formed   II-794

Theodor Herzl Publishes *Der Judenstaat*   II-1089
Thirty-Nine Articles of the Church of England, The   I-168
Treaty of Câteau-Cambrésis   I-158
Treaty of Kuchkuk Kainarji   I-475
Treaty of 1921 Between Britain and Ireland   III-1314
Treaty of Prague   I-290
Treaty of Utrecht   I-400
Treaty of Versailles   III-1283
Treaty of Vervins   I-220
Triple Alliance, The   II-1019
Triple Entente, The   III-1197
Trotsky Sent into Exile   III-1347

Uprising of the Comuneros   I-72

Vatican Treaty, The   III-1354
Venetia Is Ceded to Italy   II-923
Vesalius Publishes *On the Fabric of the Human Body*   I-133
Vienna Settlement, The   II-612
War of the Three Henrys   I-162

Yalta Conference, The   III-1501

Zollverein, The   II-711

Aboukir Bay, Battle of   I-538
Act, Municipal Corporations   II-737
Act, National Insurance   III-1223
Act of 1884, Franchise   II-1038
Act of 1867: Disraeli's "Leap in the Dark", The Reform   II-929
Act of 1832, Reform   II-704
Act of 1911, Parliament   III-1214
Act of 1933, The Enabling   III-1382
Act of Union   II-551
Acts of 1828 and 1829, Emancipation   II-669
Adowa and the Downfall of Crispi, Italian Defeat at   II-1094
African Affairs, Berlin Conference on   II-1048
Airlift, Berlin   III-1543
Algeria Wins Its Independence   III-1628
Alliance, Franco-Russian   II-1070
Alliance, The Triple   II-1019
America, Columbus Lands in   I-16
An Essay on the Principle of Population, Malthus Publishes   I-533
Anschluss, The   III-1425
Antiseptic Surgery, Lister and   II-935
Anti-Socialist Legislation in Germany, Passage of   II-1013
Arc Lamp, Davy Invents the   II-560
Areopagitica, Milton Publishes   I-317
Armada, Defeat of the Spanish   I-193
Articles of Henry VIII, The Six   I-123
Articles of the Church of England, The Thirty-Nine   I-168
Augsburg, Peace of   I-148
Ausgleich, The Austrian   II-939
Austerlitz, Battle of   II-568
Austria Annexes Bosnia and Hercegovina   III-1202
Austrian Throne, Maria Theresa Succeeds to the   I-419

Bach Pioneers Modern Music   I-380
Bacon Publishes *Novum Organum,* Francis   I-254
Baghdad Railway Concession   II-1133
Balkan Wars, The   III-1240
Bartholomew's Day, Massacre of St.   I-184
Bastille, Storming of the   I-510
Beccaria Publishes *On Crimes and Punishments*   I-456
Being and Nothingness, Jean-Paul Sartre Publishes   III-1482
Bergson Publishes *Creative Evolution*   III-1183
Berlin Conference on African Affairs   II-1048
Berlin, Congress of   II-1007
Berlin Wall, Building of the   III-1624
Bible, Publication of the King James   I-241

Bismarck Becomes Minister-President of Prussia   II-880
Blenheim, Battle of   I-390
Bloody Sunday   III-1156
Boer War, The   II-1128'
Bologna, Concordat of   I-44
Bosnia and Hercegovina, Austria Annexes   III-1202
Boulanger Crisis, The   II-1053
Bourbon Kings, Restoration of the French   II-598
Braganzas, Portugal Gains Independence Under the   I-304
Brandt Wins West German Elections   III-1690
Britain and Ireland, The Treaty of 1921 Between   III-1314
British Colonies, Abolition of Slavery in the   II-715
Bulge, Battle of the   III-1496

Cambria, Formation of the League of   I-31
Cape of Good Hope, Dias Rounds the   I-11
Carlist Wars in Spain   II-726
Casablanca Conference, The   III-1477
Catalans, Revolt of the   I-299
Câteau-Cambrésis, Treaty of   I-158
Catherine the Great's *Instruction* for Radical Social Reform   I-464
Cavour Meet at Plombières, Napoleon III and   II-838
Charles VIII of France Invades Italy   I-21
Charles V, Abdication of   I-153
Charles V as Emperor, Election of   I-64
Charles I Ascends the Throne of Spain   I-40
Charles II of Spain, Death of   I-372
Charles II, Restoration of   I-337
Charles III of Spain, Accession of   I-442
Chartist Movement, Beginning of the   II-741
Church and the State in France, Separation of the   III-1143
Churches, Formation of the World Council of   III-1550
Church of England, The Thirty-Nine Articles of the   I-168
Civil War in Spain, Outbreak of the   III-1416
Collapse of France   III-1451
Columbus Lands in America   I-16
Common Market Formed by Western European Nations   III-1601
Commonwealth in England, Establishment of the   I-329
Commune, The Paris   II-984
Comuneros, Uprising of the   I-72
Concert of Europe, Great Britain Withdraws from the   II-654
Confederation Formed, Swiss   II-794
Congo Crisis, The   III-1613

Constitution of 1876, Spanish   II-1003
Constitution of the Clergy, Civil   I-516
Copernicus Publishes *De Revolutionibus Orbium Coelestium*   I-138
Corn Laws, Repeal of the   II-764
Creative Evolution, Bergson Publishes   III-1183
Crisis of 1934, French Governmental   III-1386
Crisis, The Munich   III-1429
Crispi, Italian Defeat at Adowa and the Downfall of   II-1094
Critiques, Publication of Kant's Three   I-491
Czechoslovakia Invaded by Russians   III-1666

Daguerre Develops the First Permanent Photograph   II-747
Daily Telegraph Episode   III-1207
Daimler Develops the Gasoline Internal Combustion Engine   II-1033
Darwin Publishes *On the Origin of Species*   II-855
Davy Invents the Arc Lamp   II-560
Decline of the West, Spengler Publishes   III-1279
Defenestration of Prague   I-250
De Gaulle Steps Down   III-1683
De Revolutionibus Orbium Coelestium, Copernicus Publishes   I-138
Descartes Publishes *Discourse on Method*   I-294
Dialogue on the Two Great World Systems, Galileo Publishes   I-285
Dias Rounds the Cape of Good Hope   I-11
Dien Bien Phu, Battle of   III-1577
Diesel Engine, Invention of the   II-1100
Dimitry", Appearance of the "False   I-231
Discourse on Method, Descartes Publishes   I-294
DNA, Discovery of the Structure of   III-1572
Doctrine of Facism, Mussolini Formulates The   III-1299
Dollfuss, Murder of   III-1395
Dreadnought, Completion of the H.M.S.   III-1187
Dreyfus Affair, The   II-1075
Duma, First Meeting of the   III-1179
Dunkirk, British Evacuation from   III-1456
Dupes", The "Day of   I-278

Economic Policy, Lenin's New   III-1304
Edward VIII, Abdication of   III-1420
Einstein Publishes *Special Theory of Relativity*   III-1160
El Alamein, Battle of   III-1467
Electric Lamp, Grove's First Incandescent   II-753
Electric Motor and Generator, Faraday Develops the   II-649

Elizabeth I Is Excommunicated by Pius V   I-174
Emigration, Irish Famine and the Great   II-757
Encyclopédie, Publication of the   I-428
England, Establishment of Tudor Rule in   I-6
England, Suppression of the Monasteries in   I-110
Entente Cordiale, The   III-1152
Entente, The Triple   III-1197
Ethiopian Campaign, Italian   III-1401
Excommunicated by Pius V, Elizabeth I Is   I-174
Exhibition, Crystal Palace   II-799

Famine and the Great Emigration, Irish   II-757
Faraday Develops the Electric Motor and Generator   II-649
Fashoda Incident, The   II-1113
Fay Publishes *Origins of The World War,* Sidney B.   III-1340
Ferdinand and Isabella, marriage of   I-1
Ferdinand VII to the Throne of Spain, Restoration of   II-594
Five-Year Plan in Russia, First   III-1329
Flaubert publishes *Madame Bovary*   II-827
Fleming Discovers Penicillin   III-1335
France, Allied Invasion of   III-1491
France, Collapse of   III-1451
France, First Popular Front Ministry in   III-1411
France, Henry IV Ascends the Throne of   I-202
France, Louis Napoleon Bonaparte Becomes Emperor of   II-808
France, Napoleon Rises to Power in   I-547
France, Panama Canal Scandal in   II-1066
France, Separation of the Church and the State in   III-1143
France Withdraws from NATO   III-1648
Francis Joseph Meet at Villafranca, Napoleon III and the Emperor   II-849
Frederick the Great, Accession of   I-414
Frederick William I of Prussia, Accession of   I-396
French Governmental Crisis of 1934   III-1386
French Republic, Collapse of the Fourth   III-1607
French Republic, Establishment of the Third   II-974
Freud Publishes *The Interpretation of Dreams*   III-1139
Fronde, Beginning of the   I-324

Galileo Publishes *Dialogue on the Two Great World Systems*   I-285
Gasoline Internal Combustion Engine, Daimler Develops the   II-1033
General Theory of Employment, Interest, and

Money, Keynes Publishes *The*   III-1406

Genetics, Mendel Announces His Laws on II-908

German Confederation, Formation of the North II-918

German Confederation, Organization of the II-602

German Elections, Brandt Wins West   III-1690

German Empire, Formation of the   II-963

German Invasion of Norway   III-1446

German Invasion of Poland   III-1440

Germany, First Thousand-Bomber Raid on III-1461

Germany, Passage of Anti-Socialist Legislation in   II-1013

Germany, Social Insurance Laws in   II-1028

Globe, Magellan Expedition Circumnavigates the   I-68

"Glorious Revolution", The   I-357

Gotha, Socialist Congress at   II-992

Great Britain, Advent of the Labour Government in   III-1517

Great Britain, General Strike of 1926 in   III-1324

Great Britain Purchases Suez Canal Shares II-998

Great Britain Strengthens the Royal Navy II-1057

Hague Peace Conference, First   II-1123

Hague Peace Conference, Second   III-1192

Henry VIII, The Six Articles of   I-123

Henry IV Ascends the Throne of France I-202

Hercegovina, Austria Annexes Bosnia and III-1202

Herzl Publishes *Der Judenstaat,* Theodor II-1089

Home Rule Bill, Irish   III-1233

Humanae Vitae, Pope Paul VI Publishes III-1659

Industrialization of Russia, Sergei Witte Begins the   II-1062

Institutes of the Christian Religion, Calvin Publishes   I-116

Instruction for Radical Social Reform, Catherine the Great's   I-464

International, Formation of the First   II-897

Interpretation of Dreams, Freud Publishes The III-1139

Invasion of France, Allied   III-1491

Invasion of Italy   III-1486

Ireland, The Treaty of 1921 Between Britain and III-1314

"Iron Curtain Speech", Churchill's   III-1526

Isabella, Marriage of Ferdinand and   I-1

Italian Elections, Communists Lose   III-1538

Italy Annexes Tripoli   III-1228

Italy, Charles VIII of France Invades   I-21

Italy, Garibaldi's Thousand "Redshirts" Land in II-860

Italy, Invasion of   III-1486

Italy Is Proclaimed a Kingdom   II-870

Italy, Rome Becomes the Capital of   II-958

Italy, Venetia Is Ceded to   II-923

James I Becomes King of England and Scotland I-224

Jena, Prussian Reform After Defeat at   II-572

Jesuits, Founding of the   I-96

Joseph II's Reforms   I-480

Judenstaat, Theodor Herzl Publishes *Der* II-1089

Jung Publishes *Psychological Types*   III-1310

Jutland, Battle of   III-1266

Kant's Three *Critiques,* Publication of   I-491

Karlowitz, Peace of   I-368

Kay Invents His Flying Shuttle   I-405

Kepler Publishes *The New Astronomy*   I-236

Keynes Publishes *The General Theory of Employment, Interest, and Money*   III-1406

Kingdom, Italy Is Proclaimed a   II-870

King James Bible, Publication of the   I-241

Koch Receives the Nobel Prize for Service to Medicine   III-1174

Kuchkuk Kainarji, Treaty of   I-475

Kulturkampf   II-969

Labour Government in Great Britain, Advent of the   III-1517

La Nouvelle Héloïse, Rousseau Publishes   I-446

La Rochelle, Fall of   I-259

League of Nations, Establishment of the   III-1289

"Leap in the Dark", The Reform Act of 1867: Disraeli's   II-929

Lenin's New Economic Policy   III-1304

Lepanto, Battle of   I-180

Life of Jesus, Renan Publishes   II-892

Lighter-Than-Air Ascent, First Manned   I-496

Lister and Antiseptic Surgery   II-935

Lithography, Senefelder Invents   I-542

Louis XIV Invades the Netherlands   I-345

Louis XIV Moves the French Court to Versailles I-349

Louis XVI, Calling of the States-General by I-502

Louis XVI, Execution of   I-520

Luther Posts His Ninety-Five Theses   I-54

Lyell Publishes *The Principles of Geology* II-678

Machiavelli Publishes *The Prince*   I-35

Madame Bovary, Flaubert Publishes   II-827

Magellan Expedition Circumnavigates the Globe I-68

Maginot Line, Building of the   III-1359

Malthus Publishes *An Essay on the Principle of Population*   I-533

Manifesto, Publication of the Communist II-781

Manifesto, The October   III-1169

"March on Rome", Mussolini's   III-1319

Marconi Develops Wireless Telegraphy   II-1080

Marengo, Battle of   II-556

Maria Theresa Succeeds to the Austrian Throne I-419

Maria II to the Throne of Portugal, Restoration of   II-722

Marne, First Battle of the   III-1249

Marshall Plan Is Announced, The   III-1532

Marston Moor, Battle of   I-313

Maudslay Develops the Slide Rest   I-524

Maximilian, Mexican Adventure of   II-876

Medicine, Koch Receives the Nobel Prize for Service to   III-1174

Mendel Announces His Laws on Genetics II-908

Mexico, Conquest of   I-59

Miguel Seizes the Portuguese Throne   II-675

Mill Publishes *On Liberty*, John Stuart   II-843

Milton Publishes *Areopagitica*   I-317

Mohács, Battle of   I-87

Monasteries in England, Suppression of the I-110

More Publishes *Utopia*, Sir Thomas   I-49

Moscow University, Founding of   I-432

Music, Bach Pioneers Modern   I-380

Mussolini Formulates The Doctrine of Fascism III-1299

Mussolini's "March on Rome"   III-1319

Myth of the Twentieth Century, Rosenberg Publishes *The*   III-1363

Nantes, Edict of   I-214

Nantes, Revocation of the Edict of   I-353

Napoleon as Emperor, Coronation of   II-564

Napoleon Bonaparte Becomes Emperor of France, Louis   II-808

Napoleon Rises to Power in France   I-547

Napoleon's Invasion of Russia   II-585

Napoleon III and Cavour Meet at Plombières II-838

Napoleon III and the Emperor Francis Joseph Meet at Villafranca   II-849

Narva, Battle of   I-376

Nations, Battle of the   II-590

NATO, France Withdraws from   III-1648

Neanderthal Man, Discovery of the   II-822

Netherlands, Louis XIV Invades the   I-345

Neutrality in World War I, Spain Declares III-1259

New Astronomy, Kepler Publishes *The*   I-236

"New Laws" of Spain, The   I-129

Nietzsche Publishes *Thus Spake Zarathustra* II-1024

Ninety-Five Theses, Luther Posts His   I-54

North Atlantic Treaty Organization Pact Signed III-1555

Norway Becomes Independent   III-1164

Norway, German Invasion of   III-1446

Novum Organum, Francis Bacon Publishes I-254

Nuclear Bomb, Explosion of the First Soviet III-1561

Nuremberg Trials, The   III-1522

On Crimes and Punishments, Beccaria Publishes I-456

On Liberty, John Stuart Mill Publishes   II-843

On the Fabric of the Human Body, Vesalius Publishes   I-133

On the Origin of Species, Darwin Publishes II-855

Origins of The World War, Sidney B. Fay Publishes   III-1340

Pact, The Nazi-Soviet   III-1433

Papacy, The Jubilee Year of 1500 and Renaissance   I-26

Papal Guarantees, Italian Parliament Passes The Law of   II-978

Paris, Second Peace of   II-623

Paris, The Peace of   I-451

Partitioning of Poland   I-469

Patriarchate, Establishment of the Russian I-198

Paul VI Publishes *Humanae Vitae*, Pope   III-1659

Pavia, Battle of   I-82

Penicillin, Fleming Discovers   III-1335

Peter the Great, Reforms of   I-364

Philip II of Spain Becomes King of Portugal I-189

Photograph, Daguerre Develops the First Permanent   II-747

Pius IX, Pontificate of Pope   II-770

Pius IX Publishes the *Syllabus of Errors*   II-902

Plombières, Napoleon III and Cavour Meet at II-838

Poland, Partitioning of   I-469

Poland, The German Invasion of   III-1440

Poor Law, The New   II-730

Popular Front Ministry in France, First   III-1411

Portugal, Caetano Becomes Premier of   III-1673

Portugal Gains Independence Under the Braganzas   I-304

Portugal, Philip II of Spain Becomes King of I-189

Portugal, Proclamation of the Republic of III-1219

Portugal, Restoration of Maria II to the Throne of   II-722

Portuguese Throne, Miguel Seizes the   II-675

Positive Philosophy, Comte Publishes   II-803

Potato-Growing in Europe   I-424

Potsdam Conference, The   III-1512

Prague, Defenestration of   I-250

Prague, Treaty of   I-290

Prince, Machiavelli Publishes *The*   I-35

Principles of Geology, Lyell Publishes *The* II-678

Principles of Political Economy, Ricardo Publishes   II-629

Prussia, Accession of Frederick William I of I-396

Prussia, Bismarck Becomes Minister-President of   II-880

Psychological Types, Jung Publishes   III-1310

Purge, The Great Blood   III-1391

Pyrenees, Peace of the   I-341

Raid on Germany, First Thousand-Bomber III-1461

Railroad, Stephenson Adapts the Steam Engine for the   II-608

Rebellion, First Polish   II-691

Rebellion, Second Polish   II-886

"Redshirts" Land in Italy, Garibaldi's Thousand II-860

Reforms, Joseph II's   I-480

Reichstag Fire, The   III-1377

Renan Publishes *Life of Jesus*   II-892

Restitution, Edict of   I-270

Restoration of Charles II   I-337

Revolt, The Decembrist   II-665

Revolution, Belgian   II-686

Revolution, Hungarian   III-1595

Revolution in France, July   II-682

Revolution of 1848, Paris   II-786

Revolution of 1848, Prussian   II-790

Revolution of 1868, The Spanish   II-945

Revolution of 1820, Neapolitan   II-638

Revolution of 1820, Portuguese   II-645

Revolution of 1820, Spanish   II-634

Revolution, The Diplomatic   I-437

Revolution", The "Glorious   I-357

Revolution, The October   III-1271

Revolution of 1848, Italian   II-775

Rhodesian Declaration of Independence   III-1642

Ricardo Publishes *Principles of Political Economy*   II-629

Right, Petition of   I-263

Riots, "Fatti di Maggio"   II-1109

Robespierre, Fall of   I-529

Roentgen Discovers X Rays   II-1084

Romanov as Tsar, Election of Michael   I-247

Rome Becomes the Capital of Italy   II-958

Rosenberg Publishes *The Myth of the Twentieth Century*   III-1363

Rousseau Publishes *La Nouvelle Héloïse*   I-446

Royal Navy, Great Britain Strengthens the II-1057

Russia, First Five-Year Plan in   III-1329

Russia, Napoleon's Invasion of   II-585

Russians, Czechoslovakia Invaded by   III-1666

Russian Social Democratic Labor Party, Formation of the   II-1105

Russia, Sergei Witte Begins the Industrialization of   II-1062

St. Bartholomew's Day, Massacre of   I-184

Sartre Publishes *Being and Nothingness,* Jean-Paul   III-1482

Scandal in France, Panama Canal   II-1066

Schmalkaldic League, Formation of the   I-91

Scotland, James I Becomes King of England and I-224

Senefelder Invents Lithography   I-542

Serfs, Emancipation of the   II-866

Settlement, Act of   I-385

Shakespeare Writes His Dramas   I-208

Shuttle, Kay Invents His Flying   I-405

Slavery in the British Colonies, Abolition of II-715

Slide Rest, Maudslay Develops the   I-524

Smith Publishes *The Wealth of Nations,* Adam I-485

Social Insurance Laws in Germany   II-1028

Soviet-Chinese Dispute and China's Detonation of an Atomic Bomb   III-1583

Space, Russia Puts a Man in   III-1618

Spain, Accession of Charles III of   I-442

Spain, Carlist Wars in   II-726

Spain, Charles I Ascends the Throne of   I-40

Spain Declares Neutrality in World War I III-1259

Spain, *Dos de Mayo* Insurrection in   II-581

Spain, Outbreak of the Civil War in   III-1416

Spain, Restoration of Ferdinand VII to the Throne of   II-594

Spanish Colonies to the United States, Loss of II-1119

Spanish Republic, Proclamation of the Second III-1368

Special Theory of Relativity, Einstein Publishes III-1160

Stalin, Death of   III-1566

Stalingrad, The Stand at   III-1472

States-General by Louis XVI, Calling of the I-502

Statute of Westminister   III-1372

Steam Engine for the Railroad, Stephenson Adapts the   II-608

Steam Engine, James Watt Develops His   I-460

Stephenson Adapts the Steam Engine for the Railroad   II-608

Stockton and Darlington Railway, Opening of the   II-660
Strike of 1926 in Great Britain, General   III-1324
Submarine Warfare, Beginning of Extensive   III-1254
Suez Canal, Building of the   II-818
Suez Canal Seized by Egypt   III-1589
uez Canal Shares, Great Britain Purchases   II-998
Sunday, Bloody   III-1156
Supremacy, Act of   I-103
Sweden Enters the Thirty Years' War,   I-274
Syllabus of Errors, Pius IX Publishes the   II-902

Telegram, The Ems   II-949
Tennis Court, Oath of the   I-506
Thirty Years' War, Sweden Enters the   I-274
Three Emperors' League, Formation of the   II-988
Three Henrys, War of the   I-162
Thus Spake Zarathustra, Nietzsche Publishes   II-1024
Trade Unions, Legalization of French   II-1044
Transatlantic Cable, Laying of the First   II-834
Trent, Council of   I-143
Treaty of 1921 Between Britain and Ireland, The   III-1314
Treaty, The Vatican   III-1354
Tripoli, Italy Annexes   III-1228
Trotsky Sent into Exile   III-1347
Tudor Rule in England, Establishment of   I-6

Union, Act of   II-551
United Nations, Formation of the   III-1507
United States, Loss of Spanish Colonies to the   II-1119
Utopia, Sir Thomas More Publishes   I-49
Utrecht, Treaty of   I-400

Vatican Council, Second   III-1633
Venetia Is Ceded to Italy   II-923
Verdun, Battle of   III-1262

Versailles, Louis XIV Moves the French Court to   I-349
Versailles, Treaty of   III-1283
Vervins, Treaty of   I-220
Vesalius Publishes *On the Fabric of the Human Body*   I-133
Vienna Settlement, The   II-612
Villafranca, Napoleon III and the Emperor Francis Joseph Meet at   II-849

War, Arab-Israeli   III-1654
War, German Peasants'   I-76
War of the Three Henrys   I-162
War I, Outbreak of World   III-1245
War, Russo-Japanese   III-1148
War, Soviet-Chinese Border   III-1678
War, The Boer   II-1128
War, The Crimean   II-813
War, The Franco-Prussian   II-954
War, The Seven Weeks'   II-912
Wars, The Balkan   III-1240
Waterloo, Battle of   II-618
Watt Develops His Steam Engine, James   I-460
Wealth of Nations, Adam Smith Publishes *The*   I-485
Weimar Constitution, Adoption of the   III-1295
Wesley's Conversion, John   I-409
Westphalia, Peace of   I-308
Wireless Telegraphy, Marconi Develops   II-1080
Witte Begins the Industrialization of Russia, Sergei   II-1062
World Council of Churches, Formation of the   III-1550
World War I, Outbreak of   III-1245
World War I, Spain Declares Neutrality in   III-1259

X Rays, Roentgen Discovers   II-1084

Yalta Conference   III-1501
"Young Italy", Mazzini Founds   II-697

Zollverein, The   II-711

MODERN EUROPEAN

CATEGORY INDEX FOR TYPE OF EVENT

CONSTITUTIONAL

Abdication of Charles V   I-153
Abdication of Edward VIII   III-1420
Abolition of Slavery in the British Colonies   II-715
Act of Settlement   I-385
Act of Supremacy   I-103
Act of Union   II-551
Adoption of the Weimar Constitution   III-1295
Belgian Revolution   II-686
Calling of the States-General by Louis XVI   I-502
Collapse of the Fourth French Republic   III-1607
Coronation of Napoleon as Emperor   II-564
Death of Charles II of Spain   I-372
Edict of Restitution   I-270
Emancipation Acts of 1828 and 1829   II-669
Enabling Act of 1933, The   III-1382
Establishment of the Commonwealth in England   I-329
Establishment of the Third French Republic   II-974
Establishment of Tudor Rule in England   I-6
Formation of the German Empire   II-963
Formation of the North German Confederation   II-918
Franchise Act of 1884   II-1038
"Glorious Revolution", The   I-357
Irish Home Rule Bill   III-1233
Italian Parliament Passes The Law of Papal Guarantees   II-978
James I Becomes King of England and Scotland   I-224
Louis Napoleon Bonaparte Becomes Emperor of France   II-808
Municipal Corporations Act   II-737
National Insurance Act   III-1223
Neapolitan Revolution of 1820   II-638
"New Laws" of Spain, The   I-129
New Poor Law, The   II-730
Organization of the German Confederation   II-602
Parliament Act of 1911   III-1214
Passage of Anti-Socialist Legislation in Germany   II-1013
Petition of Right   I-263
Proclamation of the Republic of Portugal   III-1219
Proclamation of the Second Spanish Republic   III-1368
Reform Act of 1867: Disraeli's "Leap in the Dark", The   II-929
Reform Act of 1832   II-704
Restoration of Charles II   I-337

Revocation of the Edict of Nantes   I-353
Rhodesian Declaration of Independence   III-1642
Social Insurance Laws in Germany   II-1028
Spanish Constitution of 1876   II-1003
Statute of Westminster   III-1372
Swiss Confederation Formed   II-794
Treaty of 1921 Between Britain and Ireland   III-1314

CULTURAL

Bach Pioneers Modern Music   I-380
Crystal Palace Exhibition   II-799
Founding of Moscow University   I-432
Jubilee Year of 1500 and Renaissance Papacy, The   I-26
Publication of the *Encyclopédie*   I-428
Publication of the King James Bible   I-241
Shakespeare Writes His Dramas   I-208

DIPLOMATIC

Anschluss, The   III-1425
Berlin Airlift   III-1543
Berlin Conference on African Affairs   II-1048
Casablanca Conference, The   III-1477
Concordat of Bologna   I-44
Congress of Berlin   II-1007
Daily Telegraph Episode   III-1207
Diplomatic Revolution, The   I-437
Ems Telegram, The   II-949
Entente Cordiale, The   III-1152
Establishment of the League of Nations   III-1289
First Hague Peace Conference   III-1123
Formation of the League of Cambrai   I-31
Formation of the Three Emperors' League   II-988
Formation of the United Nations   III-1507
France Withdraws from NATO   III-1648
Franco-Russian Alliance   II-1070
Great Britain Withdraws from the Concert of Europe   II-654
Jubilee Year of 1500 and Renaissance Papacy, The   I-26
Marriage of Ferdinand and Isabella   I-1
Munich Crisis, The   III-1429
Napoleon III and Cavour Meet at Plombières   II-838
Napoleon III and the Emperor Francis Joseph Meet at Villafranca   II-849
North Atlantic Treaty Organization Pact Signed   III-1555
Peace of Karlowitz   I-368
Peace of Paris, The   I-451

1511

Peace of the Pyrenees   I-341
Peace of Westphalia   I-308
Potsdam Conference, The   III-1512
Second Hague Peace Conference   III-1192
Second Peace of Paris   II-623
Treaty of Câteau-Cambrésis   I-158
Treaty of Kuchkuk Kainarji   I-475
Treaty of Prague   I-290
Treaty of Utrecht   I-400
Treaty of Versailles   III-1283
Triple Alliance, The   II-1019
Triple Entente, The   III-1197
Vatican Treaty, The   III-1354
Vienna Settlement, The   II-612
Yalta Conference, The   III-1501

ECONOMIC

Abolition of Slavery in the British Colonies   II-715
Adam Smith Publishes *The Wealth of Nations*   I-485
Baghdad Railway Concession   II-1133
Building of the Suez Canal   II-818
Columbus Lands in America   I-16
Common Market Formed by Western European Nations   III-1601
Dias Rounds the Cape of Good Hope   I-11
Emancipation Acts of 1828 and 1829   II-669
Emancipation of the Serfs   II-866
"Fatti di Maggio" Riots   III-1109
First Five-Year Plan in Russia   III-1329
Formation of the First International   II-897
Great Britain Purchases Suez Canal Shares   II-998
Invention of the Diesel Engine   II-1100
Irish Famine and the Great Emigration   II-757
Italian Parliament Passes The Law of Papal Guarantees   II-978
James Watt Develops His Steam Engine   I-460
Kay Invents His Flying Shuttle   I-405
Keynes Publishes *The General Theory of Employment, Interest, and Money*   III-1406
Lenin's New Economic Policy   III-1304
Magellan Expedition Circumnavigates the Globe   I-68
Malthus Publishes *An Essay on the Principle of Population*   I-533
Marshall Plan Is Announced, The   III-1532
Maudslay Develops the Slide Rest   I-524
Municipal Corporations Act   II-737
Opening of the Stockton and Darlington Railway   II-660
Publication of the *Communist Manifesto*   II-781
Repeal of the Corn Laws   II-764
Ricardo Publishes *Principles of Political Economy*   II-629

Sergei Witte Begins the Industrialization of Russia   II-1062
Stephenson Adapts the Steam Engine for the Railroad   II-608
Zollverein, The   II-711

INTELLECTUAL

Beccaria Publishes *On Crimes and Punishments*   I-456
Bergson Publishes *Creative Evolution*   III-1183
Calvin Publishes *Institutes of the Christian Religion*   I-116
Comte Publishes *Positive Philosophy*   II-803
Copernicus Publishes *De Revolutionibus Orbium Coelestium*   I-138
Darwin Publishes *On the Origin of Species*   II-855
Descartes Publishes *Discourse on Method*   I-294
Einstein Publishes *Special Theory of Relativity*   III-1160
Francis Bacon Publishes *Novum Organum*   I-254
Freud Publishes *The Interpretation of Dreams*   III-1139
Galileo Publishes *Dialogue on the Two Great World Systems*   I-285
Jean-Paul Sartre Publishes *Being and Nothingness*   III-1482
John Stuart Mill Publishes *On Liberty*   II-843
Jung Publishes *Psychological Types*   III-1310
Kepler Publishes *The New Astronomy*   I-236
Lyell Publishes *The Principles of Geology*   II-678
Machiavelli Writes *The Prince*   I-35
Malthus Publishes *An Essay on the Principle of Population*   I-533
Milton Publishes *Areopagitica*   I-317
Pius IX Publishes the *Syllabus of Errors*   II-902
Pope Paul VI Publishes *Humanae Vitae*   III-1659
Publication of Kant's Three *Critiques*   I-491
Publication of the *Communist Manifesto*   II-781
Publication of the *Encyclopédie*   I-428
Publication of the King James Bible   I-241
Ricardo Publishes *Principles of Political Economy*   II-629
Rosenberg Publishes *The Myth of the Twentieth Century*   III-1363
Sidney B. Fay Publishes *Origins of the World War*   III-1340
Spengler Publishes *Decline of the West*   III-1279
Theodor Herzl Publishes *Der Judenstaat*   II-1089

LEGAL

Abolition of Slavery in the British Colonies II-715
Act of Settlement   I-385
Act of Supremacy   I-103
Act of Union   II-551
Adoption of the Weimar Constitution   III-1295
Anschluss, The   III-1425
Dreyfus Affair, The   II-1075
Emancipation Acts of 1828 and 1829   II-669
Emancipation of the Serfs   II-866
Enabling Act of 1933, The   III-1382
Establishment of the League of Nations   III-1289
Formation of the German Empire   II-963
Formation of the United Nations   III-1507
Franchise Act of 1884   II-1038
Irish Home Rule Bill   III-1233
Italian Parliament Passes The Law of Papal Guarantees   II-978
Legalization of French Trade Unions   II-1044
"New Laws" of Spain, The   I-129
New Poor Law, The   II-730
Parliament Act of 1911   III-1214
Passage of Anti-Socialist Legislation in Germany II-1013
Peace of Karlowitz   I-368
Peace of Paris, The   I-451
Peace of the Pyrenees   I-341
Peace of Westphalia   I-308
Reform Act of 1867: Disraeli's "Leap in the Dark", The   II-929
Reform Act of 1832   II-704
Social Insurance Laws in Germany   II-1028
Statute of Westminster   III-1372
Treaty of Câteau-Cambrésis   I-158
Treaty of Kuchkuk Kainarji   I-475
Treaty of 1921 Between Britain and Ireland III-1314
Treaty of Prague   I-290
Treaty of Utrecht   I-400
Treaty of Versailles   III-1283
Treaty of Vervins   I-220
Vatican Treaty, The   III-1354
Vienna Settlement, The   II-612

LITERARY

Adam Smith Publishes *The Wealth of Nations* I-485
Beccaria Publishes *On Crimes and Punishments* I-456
Bergson Publishes *Creative Evolution*   III-1183
Calvin Publishes *Institutes of the Christian Religion*   I-116
Comte Publishes *Positive Philosophy*   II-803

Copernicus Publishes *De Revolutionibus Orbium Coelestium*   I-138
Darwin Publishes *On the Origin of Species* II-855
Descartes Publishes *Discourse on Method* I-294
Einstein Publishes *Special Theory of Relativity* III-1160
Flaubert Publishes *Madame Bovary*   II-827
Francis Bacon Publishes *Novum Organum* I-254
Freud Publishes *The Interpretation of Dreams* III-1139
Galileo Publishes *Dialogue on the Two Great World Systems*   I-285
Jean-Paul Sartre Publishes *Being and Nothingness*   III-1482
John Stuart Mill Publishes *On Liberty*   II-843
Jung Publishes *Psychological Types*   III-1310
Kepler Publishes *The New Astronomy*   I-236
Keynes Publishes *The General Theory of Employment, Interest, and Money*   III-1406
Lyell Publishes *The Principles of Geology* II-678
Machiavelli Writes *The Prince*   I-35
Malthus Publishes *An Essay on the Principle of Population*   I-533
Milton Publishes *Areopagitica*   I-317
Nietzsche Publishes *Thus Spake Zarathustra* II-1024
Pius IX Publishes the *Syllabus of Errors*   II-902
Pope Paul VI Publishes *Humanae Vitae*   III-1659
Publication of Kant's Three *Critiques*   I-491
Publication of the *Communist Manifesto*   II-781
Publication of the *Encyclopédie*   I-428
Publication of the King James Bible   I-241
Renan Publishes *Life of Jesus*   II-892
Ricardo Publishes *Principles of Political Economy*   II-629
Rosenberg Publishes *The Myth of the Twentieth Century*   III-1363
Rousseau Publishes *La Nouvelle Héloïse*   I-446
Shakespeare Writes His Dramas   I-208
Sidney B. Fay Publishes *Origins of the World War*   III-1340
Sir Thomas More Publishes *Utopia*   I-49
Spengler Publishes *Decline of the West*   III-1279
Theodor Herzl Publishes *Der Judenstaat*   II-1089
Vesalius Publishes *On the Fabric of the Human Body*   I-133

MILITARY

Allied Invasion of France   III-1491
Arab-Israeli War   III-1654

Category Index for Type of Event

Austrian *Ausgleich*, The   II-939
Balkan Wars, The   III-1240
Battle of Aboukir Bay   I-538
Battle of Austerlitz   II-568
Battle of Blenheim   I-390
Battle of Dien Bien Phu   III-1577
Battle of El Alamein   III-1467
Battle of Jutland   III-1266
Battle of Lepanto   I-180
Battle of Marengo   II-556
Battle of Marston Moor   I-313
Battle of Mohács   I-87
Battle of Narva   I-376
Battle of Pavia   I-82
Battle of the Bulge   III-1496
Battle of the Nations   II-590
Battle of Verdun   III-1262
Battle of Waterloo   II-618
Beginning of Extensive Submarine Warfare   III-1254
Belgian Revolution   II-686
Boer War, The   II-1128
British Evacuation from Dunkirk   III-1456
Building of the Maginot Line   III-1359
Carlist Wars in Spain   II-726
Charles VIII of France Invades Italy   I-21
Collapse of France   III-1451
Completion of the H.M.S. *Dreadnought*   III-1187
Conquest of Mexico   I-59
Crimean War, The   II-813
Czechoslovakia Invaded by Russians   III-1666
Decembrist Revolt, The   II-665
Defeat of the Spanish Armada   I-193
Dos de Mayo Insurrection in Spain   II-581
Fall of La Rochelle   I-259
Fashoda Incident, The   II-1113
First Battle of the Marne   III-1249
First Polish Rebellion   II-691
First Thousand-Bomber Raid on Germany   III-1461
Formation of the German Empire   II-963
Formation of the Schmalkaldic League   I-91
Franco-Prussian War, The   II-954
German Invasion of Norway   III-1446
German Invasion of Poland   III-1440
German Peasants' War   I-76
"Glorious Revolution", The   I-357
Great Blood Purge, The   III-1391
Great Britain Strengthens the Royal Navy   II-1057
Hungarian Revolution   III-1595
Invasion of Italy   III-1486
Italian Ethiopian Campaign   III-1401
Italy Annexes Tripoli   III-1228
July Revolution in France   II-682
Louis XIV Invades the Netherlands   I-345
Napoleon's Invasion of Russia   II-585
Neapolitan Revolution of 1820   II-638
October Revolution, The   III-1271

Outbreak of the Civil War in Spain   III-1416
Outbreak of World War I   III-1245
Paris Revolution of 1848   II-786
Portuguese Revolution of 1820   II-645
Prussian Revolution of 1848   II-790
Revolt of the Catalans   I-299
Revolutions of 1848 in Italy   II-775
Rome Becomes the Capital of Italy   II-958
Russo-Japanese War   III-1148
Second Polish Rebellion   II-886
Seven Weeks' War, The   II-912
Soviet-Chinese Border War   III-1678
Spanish Revolution of 1868   II-945
Spanish Revolution of 1820   II-634
Stand at Stalingrad, The   III-1472
Storming of the Bastille   I-510
Sweden Enters the Thirty Years' War   I-274
Uprising of the Comuneros   I-72
War of the Three Henrys   I-162

PHILOSOPHICAL

Adam Smith Publishes *The Wealth of Nations*   I-485
Bergson Publishes *Creative Evolution*   III-1183
Calvin Publishes *Institutes of the Christian Religion*   I-116
Comte Publishes *Positive Philosophy*   II-803
Darwin Publishes *On the Origin of Species*   II-855
Descartes Publishes *Discourse on Method*   I-294
Francis Bacon Publishes *Novum Organum*   I-254
Jean-Paul Sartre Publishes *Being and Nothingness*   III-1482
John Stuart Mill Publishes *On Liberty*   II-843
Machiavelli Writes *The Prince*   I-35
Milton Publishes *Areopagitica*   I-317
Nietzsche Publishes *Thus Spake Zarathustra*   II-1024
Publication of Kant's Three *Critiques*   I-491
Publication of the *Communist Manifesto*   II-781
Publication of the *Encyclopédie*   I-428
Sir Thomas More Publishes *Utopia*   I-49
Spengler Publishes *Decline of the West*   III-1279

POLITICAL

Abdication of Charles V   I-153
Abdication of Edward VIII   III-1420
Accession of Charles III of Spain   I-442
Accession of Frederick the Great   I-414
Accession of Frederick William I of Prussia   I-396
Act of Settlement   I-385
Act of Union   II-551

MODERN EUROPEAN

Category Index for Type of Event

Adoption of the Weimar Constitution   III-1295

Advent of the Labour Government in Great Britain   III-1517

Anschluss, The   III-1425

Appearance of the "False Dimitry"   I-231

Algeria Wins Its Independence   III-1628

Austria Annexes Bosnia and Hercegovina   III-1202

Balkan Wars, The   III-1240

Beginning of the *Fronde*   I-324

Berlin Airlift   III-1543

Berlin Conference on African Affairs   II-1048

Bismarck Becomes Minister-President of Prussia   II-880

Bloody Sunday   III-1156

Boulanger Crisis, The   II-1053

Brandt Wins West German Elections   III-1690

Building of the Berlin Wall   III-1624

Caetano Becomes Premier of Portugal   III-1673

Calling of the States-General by Louis XVI   I-502

Carlist Wars in Spain   II-726

Casablanca Conference, The   III-1477

Charles I Ascends the Throne of Spain   I-40

Churchill's "Iron Curtain" Speech   III-1526

Collapse of the Fourth French Republic   III-1607

Communists Lose Italian Elections   III-1538

Concordat of Bologna   I-44

Congo Crisis   III-1613

Congress of Berlin   II-1007

Coronation of Napoleon as Emperor   II-564

Daily Telegraph Episode   III-1207

"Day of Dupes", The   I-278

Death of Charles II of Spain   I-372

Death of Stalin   III-1566

Decembrist Revolt, The   II-665

Defenestration of Prague   I-250

De Gaulle Steps Down   III-1683

Diplomatic Revolution, The   I-437

Dos de Mayo Insurrection in Spain   II-581

Dreyfus Affair, The   II-1075

Edict of Restitution   I-270

Election of Charles V as Emperor   I-64

Election of Michael Romanov as Tsar   I-247

Emancipation Acts of 1828 and 1829   II-669

Ems Telegram, The   II-949

Enabling Act of 1933, The   III-1382

Entente Cordiale, The   III-1152

Establishment of the Commonwealth in England   I-329

Establishment of the League of Nations   III-1289

Establishment of the Third French Republic   II-974

Establishment of Tudor Rule in England   I-6

Execution of Louis XVI   I-520

Fall of Robespierre   I-529

First Hague Peace Conference   II-1123

First Meeting of the Duma   III-1179

First Polish Rebellion   II-691

First Popular Front Ministry in France   III-1411

Formation of the First International   II-897

Formation of the German Empire   II-963

Formation of the League of Cambrai   I-31

Formation of the North German Confederation   II-918

Formation of the Russian Social Democratic Labor Party   II-1105

Formation of the Three Emperors' League   II-988

Formation of the United Nations   III-1507

France Withdraws from NATO   III-1648

Franchise Act of 1884   II-1038

Franco-Russian Alliance   II-1070

French Governmental Crisis of 1934   III-1386

Garibaldi's Thousand "Redshirts" Land in Italy   II-860

Great Blood Purge, The   III-1391

Great Britain Withdraws from the Concert of Europe   II-654

Henry IV Ascends the Throne of France   I-202

Irish Home Rule Bill   III-1233

Italian Defeat at Adowa and the Downfall of Crispi   II-1094

Italy Is Proclaimed a Kingdom   II-870

James I Becomes King of England and Scotland   I-224

Josephs II's Reforms   I-480

July Revolution in France   II-682

Legalization of French Trade Unions   II-1044

Loss of Spanish Colonies to the United States   II-1119

Louis XIV Moves the French Court to Versailles   I-349

Louis Napoleon Bonaparte Becomes Emperor of France   II-808

Maria Theresa Succeeds to the Austrian Throne   I-419

Marriage of Ferdinand and Isabella   I-1

Mazzini Founds "Young Italy"   II-697

Mexican Adventure of Maximilian   II-876

Miguel Seizes the Portuguese Throne   II-675

Milton Publishes *Areopagitica*   I-317

Munich Crisis, The   III-1429

Municipal Corporations Act   II-737

Murder of Dollfuss   III-1395

Mussolini Formulates The Doctrine of Fascism   III-1299

Mussolini's "March on Rome"   III-1319

Napoleon III and Cavour Meet at Plombières   II-838

Napoleon III and the Emperor Francis Joseph Meet at Villafranca   II-849

MODERN EUROPEAN

Category Index for Type of Event

Napoleon Rises to Power in France   I-547
Nazi-Soviet Pact, The   III-1433
"New Laws" of Spain, The   I-129
North Atlantic Treaty Organization Pact Signed III-1555
Norway Becomes Independent   III-1164
Nuremberg Trials, The   III-1522
Oath of the Tennis Court   I-506
October Manifesto, The   III-1169
October Revolution, The   III-1271
Organization of the German Confederation II-602
Outbreak of World War I   III-1245
Panama Canal Scandal in France   II-1066
Paris Commune, The   II-984
Paris Revolution of 1848   II-786
Parliament Act of 1911   III-1214
Partitioning of Poland   I-469
Passage of Anti-Socialist Legislation in Germany II-1013
Peace of Karlowitz   I-368
Peace of Paris, The   I-451
Peace of the Pyrenees   I-341
Peace of Westphalia   I-308
Petition of Right   I-263
Philip II of Spain Becomes King of Portugal I-189
Portugal Gains Independence Under the Braganzas   I-304
Portuguese Revolution of 1820   II-645
Potsdam Conference, The   III-1512
Proclamation of the Republic of Portugal III-1219
Proclamation of the Second Spanish Republic III-1368
Prussian Reform After Defeat at Jena   II-572
Prussian Revolution of 1848   II-790
Publication of the *Communist Manifesto*   II-781
Reform Act of 1867: Disraeli's "Leap in the Dark", The   II-929
Reform Act of 1832   II-704
Reichstag Fire, The   III-1377
Restoration of Charles II   I-337
Restoration of Ferdinand VII to the Throne of Spain   II-594
Restoration of Maria II to the Throne of Portugal   II-722
Restoration of the French Bourbon Kings II-598
Revolt of the Catalans   I-299
Revolutions of 1848 in Italy   II-775
Rhodesian Declaration of Independence   III-1642
Second Hague Peace Conference   III-1192
Second Peace of Paris   II-623
Second Polish Rebellion   II-886
Socialist Congress at Gotha   II-992
Soviet-Chinese Dispute and China's Detonation of an Atomic Bomb   III-1583

Spain Declares Neutrality in World War I III-1259
Spanish Constitution of 1876   II-1003
Spanish Revolution of 1868   II-945
Spanish Revolution of 1820   II-634
Statute of Westminster   III-1372
Storming of the Bastille   I-510
Suez Canal Seized by Egypt   III-1589
Swiss Confederation Formed   II-794
Theodor Herzl Publishes *Der Judenstaat*   II-1089
Treaty of Câteau-Cambrésis   I-158
Treaty of Kuchkuk Kainarji   I-475
Treaty of 1921 Between Britain and Ireland III-1314
Treaty of Prague   I-290
Treaty of Utrecht   I-400
Treaty of Versailles   III-1283
Treaty of Vervins   I-220
Triple Alliance, The   II-1019
Triple Entente, The   III-1197
Trotsky Sent into Exile   III-1347
Vatican Treaty, The   III-1354
Venetia Is Ceded to Italy   II-923
Vienna Settlement, The   II-612
War of the Three Henrys   I-162
Yalta Conference, The   III-1501

POLITICO-ECONOMIC

Common Market Formed by Western European Nations   III-1601
"Fatti di Maggio" Riots   II-1109
First Five-Year Plan in Russia   III-1329
Great Britain Purchases Suez Canal Shares II-998
Lenin's New Economic Policy   III-1304
Marshall Plan Is Announced, The   III-1532
Repeal of the Corn Laws   II-764

POLITICO-RELIGIOUS

Act of Supremacy   I-103
Calvin Publishes *Institutes of the Christian Religion*   I-116
Civil Constitution of the Clergy   I-516
Elizabeth I Is Excommunicated by Pius V I-174
Italian Parliament Passes The Law of Papal Guarantees   II-978
Kulturkampf   II-969
Massacre of St. Bartholomew's Day   I-184
Pontificate of Pope Pius IX   II-770
Revocation of the Edict of Nantes   I-353
Separation of the Church and the State in France III-1143

RELIGIOUS

Council of Trent   I-143
Edict of Nantes   I-214

Establishment of the Russian Patriarchate
I-198
Formation of the World Council of Churches
III-1550
Founding of the Jesuits   I-96
John Wesley's Conversion   I-409
Jubilee Year of 1500 and Renaissance Papacy,
The   I-26
Luther Posts His Ninety-Five Theses   I-54
Peace of Augsburg   I-148
Pius IX Publishes the *Syllabus of Errors*   II-902
Pope Paul VI Publishes *Humanae Vitae*   III-1659
Publication of the King James Bible   I-241
Renan Publishes *Life of Jesus*   II-892
Second Vatican Council   III-1633
Six Articles of Henry VIII, The   I-123
Suppression of the Monasteries in England
I-110
Thirty-Nine Articles of the Church of England,
The   I-168

SCIENTIFIC

Bergson Publishes *Creative Evolution*   III-1183
Building of the Suez Canal   II-818
Copernicus Publishes *De Revolutionibus Orbium
Coelestium*   I-138
Daguerre Develops the First Permanent Photo-
graph   II-747
Daimler Develops the Gasoline Internal Com-
bustion Engine   II-1033
Darwin Publishes *On the Origin of Species*
II-855
Davy Invents the Arc Lamp   II-560
Dias Rounds the Cape of Good Hope   I-11
Discovery of the Neanderthal Man   II-822
Discovery of the Structure of DNA   III-1572
Einstein Publishes *Special Theory of Relativity*
III-1160
Explosion of the First Soviet Nuclear Bomb
III-1561
Faraday Develops the Electric Motor and Gen-
erator   II-649
First Manned Lighter-Than-Air Ascent   I-496
Fleming Discovers Penicillin   III-1335
Francis Bacon Publishes *Novum Organum*
I-254
Freud Publishes *The Interpretation of Dreams*
III-1139
Galileo Publishes *Dialogue on the Two Great
World Systems*   I-285
Grove's First Incandescent Electric Lamp
II-753
Invention of the Diesel Engine   II-1100
James Watt Develops His Steam Engine   I-460
Jung Publishes *Psychological Types*   III-1310

Kay Invents His Flying Shuttle   I-405
Kepler Publishes *The New Astronomy*   I-236
Koch Receives the Nobel Prize for Service to
Medicine   III-1174
Laying of the First Transatlantic Cable   II-834
Lister and Antiseptic Surgery   II-935
Lyell Publishes *The Principles of Geology*
II-678
Magellan Expedition Circumnavigates the Globe
I-68
Marconi Develops Wireless Telegraphy   II-1080
Maudslay Develops the Slide Rest   I-524
Mendel Announces His Laws on Genetics
II-908
Opening of the Stockton and Darlington Railway
II-660
Roentgen Discovers X Rays   II-1084
Russia Puts a Man in Space   III-1618
Senefelder Invents Lithography   I-542
Sergei Witte Begins the Industrialization of
Russia   II-1062
Stephenson Adapts the Steam Engine for the
Railroad   II-608
Vesalius Publishes *On the Fabric of the Human
Body*   I-133

SOCIOLOGICAL

Abolition of Slavery in the British Colonies
II-715
Beginning of the Chartist Movement   II-741
Catherine the Great's *Instruction* for Radical So-
cial Reform   I-464
Crystal Palace Exhibition   II-799
Irish Famine and the Great Emigration   II-757
Malthus Publishes *An Essay on the Principle of
Population*   I-533
Potato-Growing in Europe   I-424

SOCIO-POLITICAL

Arab-Israeli War   III-1654
Belgian Revolution   II-686
Boer War, The   II-1128
Columbus Lands in America   I-16
Crimean War, The   II-813
Emancipation of the Serfs   II-866
Franco-Prussian War, The   II-954
General Strike of 1926 in Great Britain   III-1324
German Peasants' War   I-76
"Glorious Revolution", The   I-357
Hungarian Revolution   III-1595
National Insurance Act   III-1223
Neapolitan Revolution of 1820   II-638
New Poor Law, The   II-730
Reforms of Peter the Great   I-364
Russo-Japanese War   III-1148

Seven Weeks' War, The   II-912
Social Insurance Laws in Germany   II-1028
Soviet-Chinese Border War   III-1678
Uprising of the Comuneros   I-72

TECHNOLOGICAL

Daguerre Develops the First Permanent Photograph   II-747
Daimler Develops the Gasoline Internal Combustion Engine   II-1033
Explosion of the First Soviet Nuclear Bomb   III-1561
First Manned Lighter-Than-Air Ascent   I-496
Grove's First Incandescent Electric Lamp   II-753

Invention of the Diesel Engine   II-1100
James Watt Develops His Steam Engine   I-460
Kay Invents His Flying Shuttle   I-405
Laying of the First Transatlantic Cable   II-834
Marconi Develops Wireless Telegraphy   II-1080
Maudslay Develops the Slide Rest   I-524
Opening of the Stockton and Darlington Railway   II-660
Russia Puts a Man in Space   III-1618
Senefelder Invents Lithography   I-542
Sergei Witte Begins the Industrialization of Russia   II-1062
Stephenson Adapts the Steam Engine for the Railroad   II-608

PRINCIPAL PERSONAGES

Abbas, Ferhat (*fl.* 1960)   III-1628
Abbott, Henry (*fl.* 1733-1735)   I-405
Abdul-Hamid II (1842-1918)   II-1133
Abeken, Heinrich (*fl.* 1870)   II-949
Aberdeen, Earl of (George Hamilton Gordon), (1784-1860)   II-813
Abrial, Admiral Jean (*fl.* 1940)   III-1456
de Acuña, Antonio (*fl.* 1521)   I-72
Adenauer, Konrad (1876-1967)   III-1601; 1624; 1690
Adler, Alfred (1870-1937)   III-1310
Adoula, Cyrille   III-1613
Adrian of Utrecht (*fl.* 1506)   I-40; 72
von Aehrenthal, Count Alois Lexa (1854-1912)   III-1202; 1228
Albert, Archduke of Austria (1559-1621)   I-220
Albert Francis Charles Augustus Emmanuel of Saxe-Coburg-Gotha, Prince (1819-1861)   II-799
Albert, Friedrich Wilhelm Viktor (*see* William II)
Albert, Jacques Victor, Duc de Broglie (1821-1901)   II-974
d'Albret, Jeanne (1528-1572)   I-184
de Alcántara Borbon, Dom Antonio Pedro (1798-1834)   II-645
Alekseev, Admiral Eugeni Ivanovich (1845-?1917)   III-1148
d'Alembert, Jean Le Rond (1717?-1783)   I-428
Alençon, Duke of (*see* Francis, Duke of Anjou)
Alexander I, of Russia (1777-1825)   II-568; 585; 598; 612; 623; 654
Alexander II, of Russia (1818-1881)   II-813; 866; 886; 988; 1007; 1062
Alexander III, of Russia (1845-1894)   II-1062; 1070
Alexander VI, Pope (Roderigo Borgia) (1431?-1503)   I-21; 26
Alexander, General Sir Harold Rupert Leofric George (1891-1969)   III-1467
Alexander, General Sir Henry (*fl. c.* 1943)   III-1477
Alfonso XII (1857-1885)   II-1003
Alfonso XIII (1886-1941)   III-1368
de Alhuemas, Marqués (Manual Garcia Prieto) (1860-1938)   III-1259
Ali, Uluch (*fl.* 1571)   I-180
Allemane, Jean (*fl.* 1890)   II-1044
Althorp, Viscount (*see* Spencer, George John)
Alula, Ras (*fl.* 1887)   II-1094
Alva, Duke of (1508-1582)   I-153
von Alvensleben, Albrecht (1803-1881)   II-711
d'Amboise, Cardinal Georges (1460-1510)   I-31
Anderson, Thomas (*fl.* 1864)   II-935

Andrássy, Count Gyula (1823-1890)   II-939; 988; 1007
André, Frederick (*fl.* 1800)   I-542
Andrewes, Lancelot (1555-1626)   I-241
Anglesey, Marquis of (*see* Paget, Henry William)
Anne (1665-1714)   I-385
Anne of Austria (1601-1666)   I-278; 324; 341; 349
Anne of Cleves (1515-1557)   I-123
Antonelli, Cardinal Giacomo (1806-1876)   II-770; 902; 978
Antonelli, Count Pietro (*fl.* 1889)   II-1094
Antonio (1531-1594)   I-189
Aosta, Duke of (*see* di Savoia, Amadeo)
Apfelbaum, Hirsch (*see* Zinoviev, Grigori Evseevich)
Arago, Dominique François Jean (1786-1853)   II-649; 747
Aranda, Count of (1718-1799)   I-442
Aretin, Baron (1773?-1824)   I-542
d'Arlandes, Marquis (*fl.* 1783)   I-496
Armand, Jules, Prince of Polignac (1780-1847)   II-682
Arouet, François Marie (*see* Voltaire)
de Arriaga, Manuel José (1842-1917)   III-1219
d'Artois, Comte de Chambord, Duc de Bordeaux (Henri Charles Ferdinand Marie Dieudonné) (1820-1883)   II-974
Artois, Count of (*see* Charles, Count of Artois)
Aske, Robert (*fl.* 1535)   I-110
Asquith, Herbert Henry (1852-1928)   III-1214; 1223; 1233
Attlee, Clement Richard (1883-1967)   III-1512; 1517
Attwood, Thomas (1783-1856)   II-704; 741
Auchinleck, General Sir Claude John Eyre (1884-   )   III-1467
August of Saxony (1526-1586)   I-148
Augustus II of Wettin (1670-1733)   I-376
de Austria, Mariana (1634-1696)   I-372
Azaña y Diaz, Manuel (1880-1940)   III-1368; 1416

Bach, Johann Sebastian (1685-1750)   I-380
Bacon, Francis (1561-1626)   I-254
Badoglio, Pietro (1871-1956)   III-1401; 1486
Bagration, Pëtr Ivanovich, Prince (1765-1812)   II-585
Bailly, Jean-Sylvain (1736-1793)   I-510
Bakunin, Mikhail Aleksandronovich (1814-1876)   II-897
Balbo, Italo (1896-1940)   III-1319
Baldwin, Stanley (1867-1947)   III-1324; 1420
Balfour, Arthur James (1848-1930)   III-1214; 1372
Bancroft, Richard (1544-1610)   I-241
Baptiste, Gaston Jean, Duke of Orléans (1608-

1660)   I-278; 324
Baratieri, General Oreste (1841-1901)   II-1094
Barbarizo, Augustino (*fl.* 1571)   I-180
Barberet, Joseph (*fl.* 1871)   II-1044
Barclay, Sir Thomas (1853-1941)   III-1152
Barone, Domenico (*fl.* 1926)   III-1354
Bava-Beccaris, General Fiorenzo (*fl.* 1898)   II-1109
Bavaria, Duke of (*see* Maximilian of Wittelsbach)
Bazaine, Marshal Achille François (1811-1888)   II-954
Bea, Cardinal Augustin (*fl.* 1965)   III-1633
Beaconsfield, Earl of (*see* Disraeli, Benjamin)
Beatty, Vice-Admiral Sir David (1871-1936)   III-1266
Beauchamp, Lord (1539?-1621)   I-224
Bebel, August (1840-1913)   II-992; 1013; 1028
di Beccaria, Marchese (*see* Bonesana, Cesare)
Beck, Józef (1894-1944)   III-1440
Becquerel, Antoine Henri (1852-1908)   II-1084
Beddoes, Dr. Thomas (1760-1808)   II-560
Bedford, Duke of (*see* Russell, John)
Beekman, Isaac (*fl.* 1618)   I-294
Bekkers, William (*fl.* 1963)   III-1659
Bellarmine, Cardinal Robert (1542-1621)   I-285
de Bellegarde, Elisabeth-Sophie, Mme. d'Houdetot (1730-1813)   I-446
de Belle-Isle, Duc (*see* Fouquet, Marshall Charles)
de Bellievre, Pompone (*fl.* 1598)   I-220
von Benedek, General Ludwig (*fl.* 1866)   II-912
Benedetti, Count Vincente (1817-1900)   II-949; 954
Beneš, Eduard (1884-1948)   III-1429
Bénévente, Prince of (*see* Talleyrand)
Ben-Gurion, David (1886-   )   III-1589
Bennigsen, Count Levin August Theophil (1745-1826)   II-590
Bentham, Jeremy (1748-1832)   I-456
Bentinck, Lord George (1802-1848)   II-764
von Berchtold, Count Leopold (1863-1942)   III-1240; 1245; 1340
Beresford, Captain Lord Charles William de la Poer (1846-1919)   II-1057
Beresford, William Carr, Viscount Beresford (1768-1854)   II-645
Bergson, Henri (1859-1941)   III-1183
Beria, Lavrenti Pavlovich (1899-1953)   III-1566
Berlichingen, Götz von (1480-1562)   I-76
Bernadotte, Jean Baptiste (1763?-1844)   II-590
de Berulle, Pierre (1575-1629)   I-294
Bestuzhev-Ryumin, Mikhail (*fl.* 1825-1826)   II-665

von Bethmann-Hollweg, Theobald (1856-1921)   III-1245; 1340
de Béthune, Maximilien, Duc de Sully (1560-1641)   I-214; 353
von Beust, Count Friedrich Ferdinand (1809-1886)   II-939
Bevin, Ernest (1884-1951)   III-1512; 1532; 1555
de Bèze, Théodore (1519-1605)   I-241
Bianchi, Michele (*fl.* 1920's)   III-1319
Bidault, Georges (1899-   )   III-1532
von Bieberstein, Baron Adolf Herman Marschall (1842-1912)   II-1133
von Bismarck-Schönhausen, Count Otto Eduard Leopold (1815-1898)   II-880; 912; 918; 923; 949; 954; 963; 969; 988; 992; 1007; 1013; 1019; 1028; 1048; 1070
Björnson, Björnstjerne (1832-1910)   III-1164
Black, Joseph (1728-1799)   I-460
Blanc, Louis (1811-1882)   II-786
Blanqui, Louis Auguste (1798-1854)   II-786; 897; 984
Blenkinsop, John (1783-1831)   II-608
von Blomberg, General Werner (1878-1946)   III-1391
Bloody Mary (*see* Mary I)
von Blücher, General Gebhard Leberecht (1742-1819)   II-590; 618
Blum, Léon (1872-1950)   III-1411
von Bodelschwingh, Ernst (*fl.* 1842-1848)   II-711
Bodin, Jean (1530-1596)   I-202
Böhler, Peter (1712-1775)   I-409
de Boisdeffre, General Le Mouton (*fl.* 1892)   II-1070
Boleyn, Anne (1507-1536)   I-103
Bolingbroke, Viscount Henry St. John (1678-1751)   I-400
Bonaparte, Joseph (1768-1844)   II-581; 594
Bonaparte, Lucien (1775-1840)   I-547
Bonaparte, Napoleon (1769-1821)   I-538; 547 II-556; 564; 568
Bonesana, Cesare, Marchese di Beccaria (1738-1794)   I-456
Bonnet, Georges (1889-   )   III-1429; 1440
de Borbón, Joaquina Carlota (1775-1830)   II-645; 675
de Bordeaux, Duc (*see* d'Artois, Henri)
Borden, Sir Robert Laird (1854-1937)   III-1372
Borgia, Cesare (1475/1476-1507)   I-26; 35
Borgia, Francis, Duke of Gandia (*fl.* 1546)   I-96
Borgia, Giovanni (?-1497)   I-26
Borgia, Lucrezia (1480-1519)   I-26
Borgia, Roderigo (*see* Alexander VI, Pope)
Bormann, Martin Ludwig (1900-1973)   III-1522
Boström, Erik Gustaf (*fl.* 1904-1905)   III-1164

Botha, Louis (1862-1919)   II-1128
Boulanger, Georges Ernest Jean Marie (1837-1891)   II-1053
Boulton, Matthew (1728-1809)   I-460
de Bourbon, Antoine (1518-1562)   I-162
de Bourbon-Condé, Louis Antoine Henri, Duc d'Enghien (1772-1804)   II-564
Bourbon, Duke of (*see* Charles, Duke of Bourbon)
Bourgeois, Léon Victor Auguste (1851-1925)   II-1123; III-1289
von Boyen, Hermann (1771-1848)   II-572
Bradley, General Omar Nelson (1893-   )   III-1496
Braga, Teófilo (1843-1924)   III-1219
de Bragança, Dom Miguel Maria Evaristo (1802-1866)   II-645
Braganza, Duke of (*see* John, Duke of Braganza)
Brahe, Tycho (1546-1601)   I-236
Bramah, Joseph (1748-1814)   I-524
von Brandenburg, Count Friedrich Wilhelm (*fl.* 1848)   II-790
Brandt, Willy (Herbert Frahm) (1913-   )   III-1624; 1690
Branly, Édouard (1844-1940)   II-1080
Bray, Count (*fl.* 1870)   II-963
Brent, Charles Henry (1862-1929)   III-1550
Brentano, Lujo (1844-1931)   II-1028
Breuer, Josef (1842-1925)   III-1139
Brezhnev, Leonid Ilich (1906-   )   III-1666
Briand, Aristide (1862-1932)   III-1143
Bright, John (1811-1889)   II-764; 929
Broca, Paul (1824-1880)   II-822
von Brockdorff-Rantzau, Count Ulrich (1869-1928)   III-1283
de Broglie, Duc (*see* Albert, Jacques Victor)
Bronstein, Leib Davydovich (*see* Trotsky, Leon)
Brooke, General Sir Alan Francis (1883-1963)   III-1467; 1477
Broome, Earl of (*see* Kitchener, General Horatio)
Brougham, Henry Peter (1778-1868)   II-654; 715; 799
Broughton, Hugh (*fl.* 1604)   I-241
Brown, Samuel (*fl.* 1823)   II-1033
van den Bruck, Mueller (*fl.* 1910-1930)   III-1363
Brueys, Admiral F. P. (*fl.* 1798)   I-538
Brugha, Cathal (*fl.* 1921)   III-1314
Brunel, Sir Marc Isambard (1769-1849)   I-524; II-834
Brunswick, Duke of (*see* Karl Wilhelm Ferdinand)
Bucer, Martin (1491-1551)   I-116
Buchanan, George (1506-1582)   I-224
Buckingham, Duke of (*see* Villiers, George)
Buckland, William (1784-1856)   II-678
Bukharin, Nikolai Ivanovich (1888-1938)   III-1304; 1329
Bulganin, Nikolai Aleksandrovich (1895-   )   III-1589

von Bülow, General Karl (1846-1921)   III-1249
von Bülow, Prince Bernhard (1849-1929)   III-1202; 1207
Bulwer, Sir Henry (1801-1872)   II-818
Buonarroti (*see* Michelangelo Buonarroti)
Burbage, Richard (?-1597)   I-208
Burdett, Sir Francis (1770-1844)   II-669
Burns, Major General E. L. M. (*fl.* 1956)   III-1589
Busch, Adolphus (*fl.* 1857-1893)   II-1100
Bute, Earl of (*see* Stuart, John)
Buxton, Thomas Fowell (1786-1845)   II-715
Byrnes, James Francis (1879-   )   III-1512; 1526

Caballero, Francisco Largo (*see* Largo Caballero, Francisco)
Cabral, Amilcar (*fl.* 1968)   III-1673
Cabreira, Colonel Sebastian de Brito (*fl.* 1820)   II-645
Caetano, Marcello Jose De Neves Alves (*fl.* 1968)   III-1673
Cajetan, Cardinal Thomas (1469-1534)   I-54
van Calcar, Stephen (1499?-?1550)   I-133
de Calonne, Charles Alexandre (1734-1802)   I-502; 516
Calvin, John (1509-1564)   I-116
Cambó, Francisco (*fl.* 1915)   III-1259
Cambon, Pierre Paul (1843-1924)   III-1152
Campbell, Admiral Henry H. (*fl.* 1914)   III-1254
Campbell-Bannerman, Sir Henry (1836-1908)   III-1192
Camphausen, Ludolf (1803-1890)   II-790
Campion, Edmund (1540-1581)   I-174
Campochiaro, Duke of (*fl.* 1821)   II-638
de Campomanes, Pedro Rodríquez, Count of Campomanes (1723-1802)   I-442
Campos, General Arsenio Martínez (1834-1900)   II-1003
Caneva, Carlo (1845-1922)   III-1228
Canisius, Peter (1521-1597)   I-96
Canning, George (1770-1827)   II-654; 715
Canning, Stratford (Viscount de Redcliffe) (1786-1880)   II-794; 813; 818
del Cano, Juan Sebastián (?-1526)   I-68
Cano, Melchor (1509-1560)   I-96
Canrobert, General François Certain (1809-1895)   II-813
Cão, Diogo (*fl.* 1480-1486)   I-11
Carlos I (1863-1908)   III-1219
Carlos I, Don (1788-1855)   II-726
Carlota (Marie Charlotte Amelie Augustine Victoire Clémentine Léopoldine) (1840-1927)   II-876
Carlstadt, Andreas (1480?-1541)   I-76
Carnot, Nicolas Léonard Sadi (1796-1832)   II-1100
Carr, Robert (?-1645)   I-224

Carson, Edward Henry (1854-1935) III-1233

de las Casas, Bartolomé (1503-1556) I-129

de Castelnau, General Nöel Marie Joseph Édouard de Curières (1851-1944) III-1262

de los Castillejos, Marqués (*see* Prim y Prats, General Juan)

del Castillo, Antonio Cánavos (?1828-1897) II-1003; 1119

Castlereagh, Viscount (Robert Stewart) (1769-1822) II-612; 623; 638; 654

Catherine II, the Great (1729-1796) I-414; 456; 464; 469; 475

Catherine of Aragon (1485-1536) I-103

Catherine the Great (*see* Catherine II)

Caussidière, Maro (*fl.* 1840's) II-786

Cavaignac, General Louis Eugène (1802-1857) II-786

Cavendish, Spencer Compton (*see* Devonshire, Duke of)

Cavendish, William, Marquis of Newcastle (1592-1676) I-313

di Cavour, Count Camillo Benso (1810-1861) II-770; 838; 849; 860; 870

Cecil, Lord Robert (Edgar Algernon Robert Cecil) (1864-1958) III-1289

Cecil, Robert (1563?-1612) I-224

Cecil, William (1520-1598) I-174

Černík, Oldrich (1921-) III-1666

Chadwick, Edwin (1800-1890) II-730

Chain, Ernst Boris (1906-) III-1335

Challe, General (*fl.* 1961) III-1628

Chamberlain, Arthur Neville (1869-1940) III-1429; 1433; 1440

Chamberlain, Houston Stewart (1855-1927) III-1363

Chamberlain, Joseph (1836-1914) II-1038; 1128

de Chambord, Comte (*see* d'Artois, Henri)

Charles (1788-1855) II-726

Charles I, of Spain (*also* Charles V, Holy Roman Emperor) (1500-1558) I-40; 72; 129

Charles I, of England (1600-1649) I-259; 263; 313; 329

Charles II, of England (1630-1685) I-337

Charles II, of Spain (1661-1700) I-372

Charles III, of Spain (1716-1788) I-442

Charles IV (1748-1819) II-581

Charles V, Holy Roman Emperor (*also* Charles I of Spain) (1500-1558) I-54; 64; 68; 76; 82; 87; 91; 103; 123; 143; 148; 153; 158

Charles VI, Holy Roman Emperor (1685-1740) I-400; 405

Charles VII, Holy Roman Emperor (1697-1745) I-419

Charles VIII, of France (1470-1498) I-21; 26; 82

Charles IX, of France (1550-1574) I-162; 184

Charles X (1757-1836) II-682

Charles XII of Vasa (1682-1718) I-376

Charles Albert (1798-1849) II-697; 775

Charles, Archduke of Austria (1685-1740) I-372

Charles, Count of Artois (1757-1836) II-598

Charles, Duke of Bourbon (1490-1527) I-82

Charles, Lord Howard of Effingham (1536-1624) I-193

Charles of Lannoy (*fl.* 1525) I-82

Charles of Mayenne (1554-1611) I-202

Charles, Jacques Alexandre César (*fl.* 1783) I-496

de Chateaubriand, Duc (1768-1848) II-654

Chiang Kai-shek (1887-) III-1583

Chiappe, Jean (1878-1940) III-1386

de Chievres, Sieur (*see* de Croy, Guillaume)

Chlopicki, General Joséf (1771-1854) II-691

Choate, Joseph Hodges (1832-1917) II-1123; III-1192

de Choiseul, Duc (*see* François Étienne)

Chou En-lai (1898?-) III-1678

Christina (1626-1689) I-294

Churchill, John, Duke of Marlborough (1650-1722) I-390; 400

Churchill, Lord Randolph (Randolph Henry Spencer Churchill) (1849-1895) II-1038

Churchill, Sir Winston Leonard Spencer (1874-1965) III-1223; 1233; 1324; 1420; 1446; 1451; 1456; 1461; 1467; 1477; 1486; 1491; 1501; 1507; 1512; 1517; 1526

Ciano, Galeazzo (Ciano di Cortellazzo) (1903-1944) III-1440

De Cisneros, Cardinal Jiménez (1437-1517) I-1; 40

Clarendon, Earl of (*see* Hyde, Edward)

Claris, Pau (*fl.* 1640) I-299

Clark, General Mark Wayne (1896-) III-1486

Clay, General Lucius D. (1897-) III-1543

Clemenceau, Georges (1841-1929) II-984; 1053; III-1283

Clement VII, Pope (1478-1534) I-91; 103

Clement VIII, Pope (1536-1605) I-214; 220; 224

Clément, Jacques (1567?-1589) I-202

Cluseret, Gustave (1823-1900) II-984

Coasta, Joaquín (*fl.* 1898) II-1119

Cobbett, William (1763-1835) I-424; II-704

Cobden, Richard (1804-1865) II-764

Cogny, Major General René (*fl.* 1953) III-1577

Cohn, Ferdinand Julius (1828-1898) III-1174

Coke, Sir Edward (1552-1634) I-224; 263

Colbert, Jean Baptiste, Marquis de Torcy (1619-1683) I-345; 400

Cole, Henry (1808-1882) II-799

Coligny, Admiral (1519-1572) I-162

de Coligny, Gaspard (1584-1646) I-184

Collins, Michael (1890-1922) III-1314

Colonna, Marco Antonio (?-1584) I-180

Columbus, Christopher (1451-1506)   I-16
Combes, Justin Louis Émile (1835-1921)   III-1143
de Commines, Philippe (1447?-?1511)   I-21
Comte, Isidore Auguste Marie François (1798-1857)   II-803
Condé, Prince of (*see* Henry, Prince of Condé)
Condé, Prince of (*see* Louis, Prince of Condé)
Condé, Prince of (1530-1569)   I-162
Condell, Henry (?-1627)   I-208
de Condorcet, Marquis (1743-1794)   I-533
Conneau, Doctor (*fl.* 1858)   II-838
Constantine, Grand Duke (Nikolaevich) (1827-1892)   II-886
Constantine, Grand Duke (Pavlovich) (1779-1831)   II-691
Contarini, Gaspar (1483-1542)   I-96
Cop, Nicholas (*fl.* 1533)   I-116
Copernicus, Nicholas (1473-1543)   I-26; 138
Copley, John Singleton (*see* Lyndhurst, Baron)
de Córdoba, Gonsalo Fernández (1453-1515)   I-1
Cornwallis, Charles (First Marquis Cornwallis) (1738-1805)   II-551
di Cortellazzo, Ciano (*see* Galeazzo, Ciano)
Cortés, Hernán (1485-1547)   I-59; 129
da Costa, Afonso Augusto (1871-   )   III-1219
Coty, René Jules Gustave (1882-1962)   III-1607
Couthon, Georges (1755-1794)   I-529
Cranmer, Thomas (1489-1556)   I-103; 123; 168
Crick, Francis Harry Compton (1916-   )   III-1572
Crispi, Francesco (1819-1901)   II-860; 1094; 1109
de la Croix de Castries, Brigadier General Christian Marie Ferdinand (*fl.* 1953)   III-1577
Cromwell, Oliver (1599-1658)   I-313; 329
Cromwell, Richard (1626-1712)   I-329
Cromwell, Thomas (1485?-1540)   I-6; 103; 110; 123
Crookes, Sir William (1832-1919)   II-1084
de Croy, Guillaume (Sieur de Chièvres) (*fl.* 1506)   I-40; 72
Cuauhtémoc (1495?-1525)   I-59
Czartoryski, Prince Adam (1770-1861)   II-691

Daguerre, Louis Jacques Mandé (1787-1851)   II-747
Daimler, Gottlieb (1834-1900)   II-1033
Daladier, Édouard (1884-1970)   III-1359; 1386; 1411; 1429; 1433; 1440
Danton, Georges Jacques (1759-1794)   I-529
Darwin, Charles Robert (1809-1882)   II-678; 855; 908
Darwin, Erasmus (1731-1802)   II-855
Dauch, Martin (*fl.* 1789)   I-506
Daudet, Léon (1867-1942)   III-1386

Davis, Jameson (*fl.* 1899)   II-1080
Davout, Marshal Louis Nicholas (1770-1823)   II-568
Davy, Sir Humphry (1778-1829)   II-560; 649; 753
Dawson, Geoffrey (1874-1944)   III-1420
Dayan, Moshe (1915-   )   III-1589; 1654
Deák, Ferencz (1803-1876)   II-939
Dearden, John F. (1907-   )   III-1659
De Bono, Emilio (*fl.* 1922)   III-1319
De Gaulle, General Charles Andre Joseph Marie (1890-1970)   III-1477; 1512; 1607; 1628; 1648; 1654; 1683
Delaroque, Colonel (*fl.* 1936)   III-1411
Delbecque, Léon (*fl.* 1958)   III-1607
Délcassé, Théophile (1852-1923)   II-1113; III-1152
Delescluze, Charles (1809-1871)   II-984
Depretis, Agostino (1813-1887)   II-1019
Derby, Earl of (Edward Henry Smith Stanley) (1826-1893)   II-998
Derby, Lord (Edward George Geoffrey Smith Stanley) (1799-1869)   II-929
Déroulède, Paul (1846-1914)   II-1053
Descartes, René (1596-1650)   I-294
D'Estaing, Giscord (*fl.* 1960's)   III-1683
De Valera, Eamon (1882-   )   III-1314
Devereux, Robert, Earl of Essex (1566-1601)   I-224
Devonshire, Duke of (Spencer Compton Cavendish, Marquis of Hartingdon) (1833-1908)   II-1038
De Vries, Hugo (1848-1935)   II-908
De Wet, Christiaan Rudolph (1854-1922)   II-1128
Diderot, Denis (1713-1784)   I-428
Diebitsch-Zabalkanski, Field Marshal Ivan (1785-1831)   II-691
Diesel, Rudolf (1858-1913)   II-1100
Dietrich, General Sepp (*fl.* 1945)   III-1496
de Dieu Soult, Marshal Nicholas Jean (1769-1851)   II-568
Dimitrov, Georgi (*fl.* 1933)   III-1377
Dimitry, the pretender or "false" tsar (*fl.* early fifteenth century)   I-231
Disraeli, Benjamin, Earl of Beaconsfield (1804-1881)   II-730; 764; 929; 998; 1007
Doenitz, Karl (1891-   )   III-1522
Dollfuss, Engelbert (1892-1934)   III-1395; 1425
von Döllinger, Johann Joseph Ignaz (1770-1841)   II-902; 969
y Dominguez, General Francisco Serrano (*see* Serrano y Dominguez)
Don Carlos I (*see* Carlos I, Don)
Döpfner, Cardinal Julius (1913-   )   III-1659
Doria, Giovanni Andria (1468?-1560)   I-180
Doumergue, Gaston (1863-1937)   III-1411
Drake, Sir Francis (1540?-1596)   I-193

Dreyfus, Captain Alfred (1859-1935) II-1075; 1089

Drucki-Lubecki, Prince Ksawery (*fl.* 1829-1830) II-691

Drummond, Sir Eric (1876-1951)   III-1289

Drumont, Édouard (*fl.* 1890's)   II-1066; 1075

Dubček, Alexander (1921-   )   III-1666

Dubois, Marie Eugène F. T. (1858-1940)   II-822

Dubrovin, Alexander (*fl.* 1905)   III-1169

Dufour, Colonel William Henry (1787-1875) II-794

Dulles, John Foster (1888-1959)   III-1589

Dupanloup, Félix Antoine Philibert (1802-1878) II-902

Duplessis-Normay, Philippe (1549-1623)   I-214

Dzhugashvili, Iosif Vissarionovich (*see* Stalin, Joseph)

Ebert, Friedrich (1871-1925)   III-1295

Eck, John (1486-1543)   I-54

Eden, Sir Robert Anthony (1897-   )   III-1456; 1501; 1512; 1589

Edison, Thomas Alva (1847-1931)   II-753

Edward VI (1537-1553)   I-123; 168

Edward VII (Albert Edward, the Peacemaker) (1841-1910)   III-1152; 1197; 1214

Edward VIII (Duke of Windsor) (Edward Albert Christian George Andrew Patrick David) (1894-1972)   III-1420

Effingham, Lord Howard of (*see* Charles, Lord Howard)

Einaudi, Luigi (1874-   )   III-1538

Einstein, Albert (1879-1955)   III-1160

Eisenhower, General Dwight David (1890-1969) III-1477; 1486; 1491; 1496; 1589; 1624

Eliot, Sir John (1592-1632)   I-263

Elizabeth I (1533-1603)   I-158; 162; 168; 174; 184; 193; 202; 224

Elizabeth Petrovna (1709-1762)   I-414; 432

Engels, Friedrich (1820-1895)   II-781

d'Enghien, Duc (*see* Louis de Bourbon-Condé)

Erasmus, Desiderius (1466?-1536)   I-49

Erhard, Ludwig (1897-   )   III-1690

Ernst, Friedrich Wilhelm Viktor August (*see* William)

Eshkol, Levi (Shkolnik) (1895-1969)   III-1654

Espartero, Baldomero (1792-1879)   II-726

Essex, Earl of (*see* Devereux, Robert)

Esterhazy, Major Marie Charles Ferdinand Walsin (1847-1923)   II-1075

de Estrada, José Maria Gutierrez (*fl.* 1861-1864) II-876

Eugène, Prince of Savoy (1663-1736)   I-368; 390

Eustachio, Bartolommeo (1524?-1574)   I-133

Eythin, Lord (*fl.* 1640's)   I-313

Facta, Luigi (1861-1930)   III-1319

Fairfax, Sir Thomas (1612-1671)   I-313

Falk, Adalbert (1827-1900)   II-969

von Falkenhayn, General Erich (1861-1922) III-1262

von Falkenhorst, General Nikolaus (1885-1968) III-1446

Falloux, Vicomte Frédéric Pierre (1811-1886) II-786

Faraday, Michael (1791-1867)   II-560; 649

Farel, William (1489-1565)   I-116

Favre, Peter (1506-1546)   I-96

Fawkes, Guy (1570-1606)   I-224

Fay, Sidney Bradshaw (1876-1967)   III-1340

Felici, Archbishop Pericle (*fl.* 1965)   III-1633

Fels, Baron Colona (*fl.* early seventeenth century)   I-250

Felton, John (*fl.* 1570)   I-174

Ferdinand I, of Aragon; Holy Roman Emperor (1503-1564)   I-40; 64; 76; 87; 91; 148; 153; 174

Ferdinand I, of the Two Sicilies (1751-1825) II-638

Ferdinand II, of Aragon (*also* Ferdinand V of Castille) (1452-1516)   I-1; 16; 31; 40

Ferdinand II, of Austria; Holy Roman Emperor (1578-1637)   I-250; 270; 274; 290; 357

Ferdinand II, of the Two Sicilies (1810-1859) II-775

Ferdinand III, Holy Roman Emperor (1608-1657)   I-308

Ferdinand V, of Castile (*see* Ferdinand II, of Aragon)

Ferdinand VII, of Spain (1784-1833)   II-581; 594; 634; 726

Ferdinand of Saxe-Coburg (1861-1948)   III-1240

Ferretti, Giovanni Maria Mastai (*see* Pius IX, Pope)

Ferry, Jules François Camille (1832-1893) II-1048

Fey, Emil (1888-1938)   III-1395

Field, Cyrus West (1819-1892)   II-834

Field, Winston (*fl.* 1962-1964)   III-1642

Fielden, John (*fl.* 1837)   II-730

de Figueroa y de Torres, Alvaro (*see* de Romanones, Conde)

Filaret, early Patriarch of Russian Church (1619-1633)   I-247

Filaret, Metropolitan Patriarch of Moscow (*fl.* 1858-1861)   II-866

Fisher, Admiral Sir John Arbuthnot (1841-1920) III-1187

Fisher, John (1459-1535)   I-103

Flaubert, Gustave (1821-1880)   II-827

Fleming, Sir Alexander (1881-1955)   III-1335

de Flesselles, Jacques (*fl.* 1789)   I-510

Fleury, Cardinal André Hercule (1653-1743) I-419

Florey, Sir Howard Walter (1898-1968)   III-1335

Floridablanca, Count of (*see* Moñino, José)

Forbes, Admiral Sir Charles (*fl.* 1940)   III-1446

Ford, John (*fl.* 1967)   III-1659

Fouquet, Marshal Charles Louis Auguste, Duc de Belle-Isle (1684-1761)   I-419

Frahm, Herbert (*see* Brandt, Willy)

Franchet d'Esperey, General Louis Felix Marie François (1856-1942)   III-1249

Francis I, of France (1494-1547)   I-44; 64; 82; 87; 91; 116; 123; 143

Francis I, Holy Roman Emperor (1708-1765)   I-419

Francis II, of France (1544-1560)   I-162

Francis II, Holy Roman Emperor (1768-1835)   II-568

Francis, Duke of Anjou (Duke of Alençon) (1554-1584)   I-184; 202

Francis Ferdinand, Archduke (1863-1914)   III-1245; 1340

Francis Joseph I, of Austria (1830-1916)   II-849; 912; 939; 988

Franco, General Francisco (1892-   )   III-1416

François, Étienne, Duc de Choiseul (1719-1785)   I-451

Franklin, Rosalind E. (*fl.* 1953)   III-1572

Frederick I, of Prussia (1657-1713)   I-396

Frederick II, the Great of Prussia (1712-1786)   I-396; 414; 419; 437; 469; 475

Frederick II, The Wise of Five Electors of the Palatinate (1482-1556)   I-54

Frederick III, of Prussia (1831-1888)   II-1013

Frederick III, The Pious of Five Electors of the Palatinate (1515-1576)   I-148

Frederick IV, of Denmark and Norway (1671-1730)   I-376

Frederick V, of Five Electors of the Palatinate (1596-1632)   I-250; 290

Frederick Charles, Prince (1828-1885)   II-912

Frederick, John (1529-1595)   I-91

Frederick of Prussia, Crown Prince (1831-1888)   II-912; 963

Frederick William I, of Prussia (1688-1740)   I-396; 414

Frederick William II, of Prussia (1744-1797)   I-469

Frederick William III, of Prussia (1770-1840)   II-572; 711

Frederick William IV, of Prussia (1795-1861)   II-790

French, Field Marshal Sir John Denton Pinkstone (1852-1925)   III-1249

Freud, Sigmund (1856-1939)   III-1139; 1310

Frey, Roger (*fl.* 1960's)   III-1683

de Freycinet, Charles Louis de Saulces (1828-1923)   II-1053

Friedland, Duke of (*see* Wallenstein, Albrecht)

Frings, Cardinal Josef (1887-   )   III-1633

Fuhlrott, Johann Carl (*fl.* 1856)   II-822

Furrer, Jonas (1805-1861)   II-794

Gagarin, Yuri Alekseyevich (1934-1968)   III-1618

Gaismaier, Michael (*fl.* 1825)   I-76

Galen (*fl.* Second century A.D.)   I-133

Galilei, Galileo (1564-1642)   I-236; 285

Gallieni, General Joseph Simon (1849-1916)   III-1249

Galton, Sir Francis (1822-1911)   III-1310

Gambetta, Léon (1838-1882)   II-954; 974

Gamelin, General Maurice Gustave (1872-1958)   III-1451

Gandia, Duke of (*see* Borgia, Francis)

Gapon, Father Georgi Appollonovich (1870?-1906)   III-1156

Gardiner, Stephen (1483-1555)   I-123

Garibaldi, Giuseppe (1807-1882)   II-860; 870; 923; 958

Gascoyne-Cecil, Robert Arthur Talbot (*see* Salisbury, Marquis of)

Gasparri, Cardinal Pietro (1852-1934)   III-1354

de Gasperi, Alcide (1881-1954)   III-1538; 1601

y Gassett, José Ortega (*see* Ortega y Gassett, José)

Gattinara, Mercurino (*fl.* 1519-1520)   I-64

Gentile, Giovanni (1875-1944)   III-1299

George I, of Great Britain (1660-1727)   I-385

George II, of Great Britain (1683-1760)   I-419; 437

George III, of Great Britain (1738-1820)   I-451; II-551

George IV, of Great Britain (1762-1830)   II-669

George V, of Great Britain (1865-1936)   III-1214

George VI, of Great Britain (1895-1952)   III-1517

George, David Lloyd (1863-1945)   III-1214; 1223; 1283; 1289; 1314; 1372

George, John (1585-1656)   I-270; 274; 290

Gerö, Erno (*fl.* 1948-1953)   III-1595

Geyer, Florian (*fl.* 1524)   I-76

Giap, General Vo Nguyen (*fl.* 1953)   III-1577

de Giers, Nikolai Karlovich (1820-1895)   II-1070

Giese, Tiedemann (*fl.* 1542)   I-138

Ginzberg, Asher (*see* Haam, Achad)

Giolitti, Giovanni (1842-1928)   II-1094; 1109; III-1228

Giraud, General Henri Honoré (1879-1949)   III-1477

Gizenga, Antoine (*fl.* 1960's)   III-1613

Gizzi, Cardinal (*fl.* 1846)   II-770

Gladstone, William Ewart (1809-1898)   II-929; 1038; 1048
Glass, Fridolin (*fl.* 1934)   III-1395
Gleissner, Franz (*fl.* 1792-1798)   I-542
von Gneisenau, August Neithardt (1760-1831)   II-572
de Godoy, Manuel (1767-1851)   II-581
Godunov, Boris Feodorovich (1551?-1605)   I-198; 231
Godwin, William (1756-1836)   I-533
Goebbels, Joseph Paul (1897-1945)   III-1377; 1382; 1391
Gooch, Sir Daniel (1816-1889)   II-834
Gorchakov, Prince Aleksandr Mikhailovich (1798-1883)   II-988; 1007
Gordon, George Hamilton (*see* Aberdeen, Earl of)
Gordon, Patrick (1635-1699)   I-364
Goremykin, Ivan Longinovich (1839-1917)   III-1179
Goring, George (*fl.* 1640's)   I-313
Göring, Hermann (1893-1946)   III-1377; 1391; 1456; 1472; 1522
Gort, General Lord John Standish Surtees Prendergast Vereker (1886-1946)   III-1456
de Gramont, Antoine Alfred Agenor, Duc de Guiche (1819-1880)   II-954
de Granvelle, Cardinal Antoine Perrenot (1517-1586)   I-189
Grattan, Henry (1746-1820)   II-551
Graziani, Marshal Rodolfo (di Neghelli) (1882-1955)   III-1467
Gregory XIII, Pope (1502-1585)   I-174
Grenville, Sir John (*fl.* 1660)   I-337
Grey, Earl Charles (1764-1845)   II-704; 715
Grey, Sir Edward (1862-1933)   III-1192; 1197; 1202; 1240; 1245; 1340
Griffith, Arthur (1872-1922)   III-1314
Grimaldi, Marquis of (*fl.* 1761-1776)   I-442
de Grouchy, Marquis Emmanuel (1766-1847)   II-618
Grove, Sir William Robert (1811-1896)   II-753
von Grumbkow, General Frederick William (*fl.* 1723)   I-396
Guchkov, Aleksandr Ivanovich (1861?-1936)   III-1179
Guesde, Jules (Mathieu Bastile) (1845-1922)   II-1044
Guicciardini, Francesco (1483-1540)   I-35
de Guiche, Duc (*see* de Gramont, Antoine)
Guise, Duke of (1519-1563)   I-162
Guiton, Jean (*fl.* 1628)   I-259
Gustavus Adolphus (*also* Gustavus II, of Sweden) (1594-1632)   I-270; 274
de Guzmán, Don Alonzo Pérez (*see* Medina-Sidonia, Duke of)
de Guzmán, Eugénie Marie de Montijo (1826-1920)   II-849
de Guzmán, Gaspar, Count-Duke of Olivares (1587-1645)   I-299; 304

de Guzman, Luisa (1613-1666)   I-304

Haakon VII (1872-1957)   III-1164
Haam, Achad (Asher Ginzberg) (1856-1927)   II-1089
Habicht, Theo (*fl.* 1934)   III-1395
Hácha, Emil (1872-1945)   III-1429
Haile Selassie (*see* Selassie, Haile)
Halifax, Earl of (Edward Frederick Lindley Wood) (1881-1959)   III-1440
Hamid II, Abdul (*see* Abdul-Hamid II)
Hamilton, Lord George Francis (1845-1927)   II-1057
Hammarskjöld, Dag (1905-1961)   III-1589; 1613
de Harcourt, Marquis (1654-1718)   I-372
von Hardenberg, Prince Karl August (1750-1822)   II-572; 612; 623
Hardinge, Sir Charles (1858-1944)   III-1197
Häring, Bernard (*fl.* 1967)   III-1659
de Haro, Luís (1598-1661)   I-299; 341
Harris, Sir Arthur Travers, Air Chief Marshal (1892-   )   III-1461
Hartingdon, Marquis of (*see* Devonshire, Duke of)
Harvey, Daniel (*fl.* 1838)   II-741
Harvey, William (1578-1657)   I-254
Helen, Grand Duchess (*fl.* 1857)   II-866
Heminge, John (1556?-1630)   I-208
Henle, Friedrich Gustav Jacob (1809-1885)   III-1174
Henry II, of France (1519-1559)   I-153; 158; 162
Henry III, of France (1551-1589)   I-202
Henry IV, of France (1553-1610)   I-202; 214; 220; 353
Henry VII, of England (1457-1509)   I-6
Henry VIII, of England (1491-1547)   I-6; 49; 64; 103; 110; 123
Henry of Anjou (1551-1589)   I-184
Henry, Cardinal, of Portugal (1512-1580)   I-189
Henry of Guise (1519-1563)   I-184; 202
Henry, Joseph (1797-1878)   II-649
Henry of Navarre (1553-1610)   I-184
Henry, Patrick (*see* Pearse, Padhraic)
Henry, Prince of Condé (1552-1588)   I-184
Henry the Navigator, Prince (1394-1460)   I-11
Henry, Major Hubert Joseph (1846-1898)   II-1075
von Herder, Johann Gottfried (1744-1803)   I-480
Hertz, Heinrich Rudolph (1857-1894)   II-1080
Hertzog, James Barry Munnik (1866-1942)   III-1372
Herz, Dr. Cornelius (*fl.* 1888)   II-1066
Herzl, Theodor (1860-1904)   II-1089
Hess, Richard Rudolf (1894-   )   III-1522

Himmler, Heinrich (1900-1945)   III-1391
von Hindenburg, Paul (Paul Ludwig Hans von Beneckendorff und von Hindenburg) (1847-1934)   III-1382
von Hipper, Vice-Admiral Franz (1863-1932)   III-1266
Hitler, Adolf (1889-1945)   III-1363; 1377; 1382; 1391; 1395; 1416; 1425; 1429; 1433; 1440; 1446; 1451; 1456; 1467; 1472; 1486; 1491; 1496
Hoare, Sir Samuel John Gurney (1880-1959)   III-1401
Ho Chi Minh (1890-1969)   III-1577
Hodel, Max (*fl.* 1878)   II-1013
Hodges, General Courtney Hicks (1887-1966)   III-1496
't Hooft, W. A. Visser (*fl.* 1966)   III-1550
Hopkins, Harry Lloyd (1890-1946)   III-1477; 1501; 1512
von Hötzendorf, Count Franz Conrad (1852-1925)   III-1228
d'Houdetot, Mme. (*see* de Bellegarde, Elisabeth-Sophie)
House, "Colonel" Edward Mandell (1858-1938)   III-1289
Howard, Catherine (1520?-1542)   I-123
Howard, John (1726?-1790)   I-424
Howard, Thomas (1473-1554)   I-123
Hughes, William Morris (1864-1952)   III-1372
Hull, Cordell (1871-1955)   III-1507
Humbert I, of Italy (1844-1900)   II-1019; 1094
von Humboldt, Wilhelm (1769-1859)   II-572
Hume, David (1711-1776)   I-485
Husák, Gustav (*fl.* 1969)   III-1666
Hussein (Ibn Talal) (1935-   )   III-1654
Hutcheson, Francis (1694-1746)   I-485
Hutton, James (1726-1797)   II-678
Huxley, Thomas Henry (1825-1895)   II-822; 855
Hyde, Edward, Earl of Clarendon (1609-1674)   I-337

Ibn Talal (*see* Hussein)
Ignatiev, Nikolai Pavlovich (1832-1908)   II-1007
Ignatius of Loyola (1491-1556)   I-9
Innocent XI, Pope (1611-1689)   I-368
Iradier, Eduardo Dato (*fl.* 1913-1917)   III-1259
Isabella I, of Spain (1451-1504)   I-1; 16; 40
Isabella II, of Spain (1830-1904)   II-726; 945
Isidor, Metropolitan of Russian Orthodox Church (*fl.* 1436-1441)   I-198
Ismail I, Khedive of Egypt (1830-1895)   II-998
Ivan IV, The Terrible (1530-1584)   I-198
Ivanovich, Dimitry (1581-1591)   I-231
Ivanovich, Feodor (1557-1598)   I-231

Izvolski, Aleksandr Petrovich (1856-1919)   III-1192; 1197; 1202

Jagiello, Anne (*fl.* 1515)   I-87
Jagiello, Louis II (1506-1526)   I-87
James I, of Great Britain (*also* James VI of Scotland) (1566-1625)   I-224; 241; 254; 329
James II, of Great Britain (1633-1701)   I-357; 385
James VI, of Scotland (*see* James I of Great Britain)
de Jaucourt, Louis Chevalier (1704-1779)   I-428
Jaurès, Jean Léon (1859-1914)   II-1044; III-1143
Jellicoe, Admiral Sir John Rushworth (1859-1935)   III-1266
Jenkinson, Robert Banks, Lord Liverpool (1776-1828)   II-654
Jeremiah (*fl.* 1588)   I-198
Joachim of Brandenburg (1505-1571)   I-148
Joanna (1479-1555)   I-40
Job (*fl.* 1589)   I-198
Joffre, General Joseph Jacques Césaire (1852-1931)   III-1249; 1262; 1359
John II, of Portugal (1455-1495)   I-11
John III, of Portugal (1502-1557)   I-189
John III Sobieski, of Poland (1624-1696)   I-368
John IV, of Ethiopia (Yohannis IV) (1872-1889)   II-1094
John VI, of Portugal (1769-1767?-1826)   II-645; 675
John XXIII, Pope (1881-1963)   III-1633; 1659
John, Duke of Braganza (1605-1656)   I-304
John, Elector of Saxony (1503-1554)   I-91
Johnson, Lyndon Baines (1908-1973)   III-1648
Jonson, Ben (1573?-1637)   I-208
Joseph I, Holy Roman Emperor (1678-1711)   I-400
Joseph II, Holy Roman Emperor (1741-1790)   I-414; 469; 480
Joseph, Father (François Le Clerq Du Tremblay) (1577-1638)   I-278
Joseph Ferdinand, of Bavaria (?-1699)   I-372
Joxe, Louis (*fl.* 1960)   III-1628
Joynson-Hicks, Sir William (1865-1932)   III-1324
Juan, Don, of Austria (1547-1578)   I-180
Juárez, Benito Pablo (1806-1872)   II-876
Julius II, Pope (Giuliano della Rovere) (1443-1513)   I-26; 31; 44; 143
Jung, Carl Gustav (875-1961)   III-1310

Kaas, Ludwig (*fl.* 1933)   III-1382
Kádár, Janos (*fl.* 1960's)   III-1595
Kahn, R. F. (*fl.* 1920-1930's)   III-1406
Kakhovsky, Peter (*fl.* 1825)   II-665

Kálnoky, Count Gustav Siegmund (1832-1898) II-1019
Kamenev, Lev Borisovich (Rosenfeld) (1883-1936) III-1347
Kant, Immanuel (1724-1804)   I-491
Karl Wilhelm Ferdinand, Duke of Brunswick (1735-1806)   I-520
Kasavubu, Joseph (*fl.* .1960's)   III-1613
von Kaunitz-Rietberg, Prince Wenzel Anton (1711-1794)   I-437; 469; 480
Kay, John (*fl.* 1733-1764)   I-405
Kay, Robert (*fl.* 1760)   I-405
Kennan, George (1845-1924)   III-1532
Kennedy, John Fitzgerald (1917-1963)   III-1618; 1624
Kepler, Johannes (1571-1630)   I-236
Kerenski, Aleksandr (1881-1970)   III-1271
Kesselring, Field Marshall Albert (1887-1960) III-1486
von Ketteler, Bishop Wilhelm Emmanuel (1811-1877)   II-1028
Keynes, John Maynard (1883-1946)   III-1406
Khalifa Abdullah et Taaisha, The (1846?-1899) II-1113
Khartoum, Earl of (*see* Kitchener, General Horatio)
ben Khedda, Youssef (*fl.* 1962)   III-1628
Khrushchev, Nikita Sergeevich (1894-1971) III-1566; 1595; 1618; 1624
von Kiderlen-Waechter, Alfred (1852-1912) III-1228
King, Fleet Admiral Ernest Joseph (1878-1956) III-1477
Kitchener, General Horatio Herbert (Earl Kitchener of Khartoum and of Broome) (1850-1916)   II-1113; 1128
Klehment, Reinhold (*fl.* 1908)   III-1207
von Kluck, General Alexander (1846-1934) III-1249
von Knobelsdorf, General Schmidt (*fl.* 1916) III-1262
Koch, Robert (1843-1910)   III-1174
Kornilov, General Lavr Georgievich (1870-1918)   III-1271
Kosciuszko, Thaddeus (1746-1817)   I-469
Kosygin, Aleksei Nikolaevich (1904-   ) III-1666; 1678
Kremer, Alexander (*fl.* 1897)   II-1105
Kretschmer, Ernst (1888-1964)   III-1310
von Krismanić, General Gideon (*fl.* 1866) II-912
Kruger, Stephanus Johannes (1825-1904)   II-1128
Kundt, August (1839-1894)   II-1084
Küng, Hans (*fl.* 1965)   III-1633
Kurbatov, Alexis (1697-1698)   I-364
Kurchatov, Igor Vasilevich (*fl.* 1938)   III-1561
Kuropatkin, General Aleksei Nikolaevich (1848-1921)   III-1148

Kutuzov, Mikhail Ilarionovich (1745-1813) II-568; 585

de Lafayette, Marquis (1757-1834)   I-510
de Lagarde, Paul Anton (1827-1891)   III-1363
de Lamartine, Alphonse (1790-1869)   II-786
Lamb, William (*see* Melbourne, Viscount)
Lambruschini, Cardinal Luigi (1776-1854) II-770
Lamormaini, William (*fl.* 1629)   I-270
Lang, Cosmo Gordon (1864-1945)   III-1420
Langiewicz, General Marjan (*fl.* 1863)   II-886
Lannes, Gustave Louis, Marquis de Montebello (1838-1907)   II-1070
Lannes, Jean (1769-1809)   II-556
Lansdowne, Marquis of (Henry Charles Keith Petty-Fitzmaurice) (1816-1866)   III-1152; 1214
Lanza, Giovanni (1810?-1882)   II-958; 978
Largo Caballero, Francisco (1869-1946)   III-1368; 1416
Lasker, Eduard (1829-1884)   II-1013
Lassalle, Ferdinand (1825-1864)   II-992
de La Tour, Françoise-Marie, Baronne de Warens (*fl. c.* 1756)   I-446
de Launay, Bernard-René (1740-1789)   I-510
Laval, Pierre (1883-1945)   III-1401
Law, Andrew Bonar (1858-1923)   III-1233
Laynez, James (1512-1565)   I-96; 143
Layton, Richard (*fl.* 1535)   I-110
Le Breton, André-François (*fl.* 1751)   I-428
Ledru-Rollin, Alexandre (1807-1874)   II-786
Legh, Thomas (*fl.* 1535)   I-110
von Leiberich, Baron Karl Mack (1752-1828) II-568
Lelewel, Joachim (1786-1861)   II-691
Le May, Lieutenant General Curtis E. (1908-   )   III-1543
Lenard, Philipp (1862-1947)   II-1084
Lenin, Nikolai (Vladimir Ilich Ultanov) (1870-1924)   II-1105; III-1271; 1304; 1347
Lenoir, Jean Joseph Étienne (1822-1900)   II-1033
Leo X, Pope (1475-1521)   I-44; 54; 64
Leo XIII, Pope (Gioacchiuo Vincenzo Pecci) (1810-1903)   II-902; 969 III-1143
Leopold I, Holy Roman Emperor (1640-1705) I-368; 372
Leopold II, of Belgium (1835-1909)   II-1048
Leopold of Anhalt-Dessau, Prince (1676-1747) I-396
Leopold of Hohenzollern-Sigmaringen, Prince (1835-1905)   II-949; 954
Leopold of Saxe-Coburg, Prince (1790-1865) II-686
Léopoldine, Marie Charlotte (*see* Carlota)
Lerroux, Alejandro (*fl.* 1914)   III-1259; 1368
Leslie, Alexander, Earl of Leven (1580?-1661) I-313

de Lesseps, Comte Charles Aimée Marie (1849-1923)   II-1066
De Lesseps, Vicomte Ferdinand Marie (1805-1894)   II-818; 998; 1066
Le Tellier, François Michel, Marquis de Louvois (1641-1691)   I-345; 353
Le Tellier, Michel (1603-1685)   I-353
Leven, Earl of (*see* Leslie, Alexander)
de Leyva, Antonio (*fl.* 1524)   I-82
de L'Hôpital, Michel (*fl.* 1562)   I-162
Liebknecht, Wilhelm (1826-1900)   II-992; 1013
Liénart, Achilles Cardinal (1884-   )   III-1633
Lilburne, John (1614?-1657?)   I-317
List, Friedrich (1789-1846)   II-711
Lister, Joseph L. (1827-1912)   II-935
Litvinov, Maksim Maksimovich (1876-1951)   III-1433; 1440
Liverpool, Lord (*see* Jenkinson, Robert Banks)
Llorenz, Juan (*fl.* 1522)   I-72
Lomonosov, Mikhail Vasilievich (1711-1765)   I-432
London, John (*fl.* 1538)   I-110
de Longueville, Duc (?-1663)   I-308
Lorentz, Hendrik Antoon (1853-1928)   III-1160
Lorraine, Cardinal of (1524-1574)   I-162
Loubet, Émile (1838-1929)   III-1152
Louis II (*see* Jagiello, Louis II)
Louis XII, of France (1462-1515)   I-31; 44; 82
Louis XIII, of France (1601-1643)   I-259; 278
Louis XIV, of France (1638-1715)   I-324; 341; 345; 349; 353; 357; 368; 372; 400
Louis XV, of France (1710-1774)   I-437
Louis XVI, of France (1754-1793)   I-496, 502, 506, 510, 516, 520
Louis XVIII, of France (1755-1824)   II-598; 634; 682
Louis Alexander, of Battenburg, Rear Admiral Prince (1854-1921)   III-1187; 1254
Louis Napoleon (*see* Napoleon III)
Louis Philippe (1773-1850)   II-682; 686; 722
Louis, Prince of Condé (1530-1569)   I-184
de Louvois, Marquis (*see* Le Tellier, François)
Lovett, Robert Abercrombie (1895-   )   III-1555
Lovett, William (*fl.* 1836)   II-741
van der Lubbe, Marinus (1910-1934)   III-1377
Ludwig II (*fl.* 1870)   II-963
Lueger, Karl (*fl.* 1882)   II-1089
Lumumba, Patrice (*fl.* 1950's)   III-1613
Luther, Martin (1483-1546)   I-54; 76; 91; 116
Lvov, Prince Georgi Evgenievich (1861-1925)   III-1271
Lyell, Sir Charles (1797-1875)   II-678; 855
Lyndhurst, Baron (John Singleton Copley) (1772-1863)   II-737

von Maassen, Karl Georg (*fl.* 1830's)   II-711
MacDonald, James Ramsay (1866-1937)   III-1372
Machiavelli, Niccolò (1469-1527)   I-35
McKinley, William (1843-1901)   II-1119
de MacMahon, Marshal Marie Edme Patrice Maurice (1808-1893)   II-954; 974
MacNeill, Eoin (*fl.* 1913)   III-1233
Magellan, Ferdinand (*c.* 1480-1521)   I-68
Maginot, André (1877-1932)   III-1359
Mahan, Captain Alfred Thayer (1840-1914)   II-1123
Malakoff, Duke of (*see* Pelissier, General Jean-Jacques)
de Malebranche, Nicholas (1638-1715)   I-294
Malenkov, Georgi Maximillianovich (1902-   )   III-1566
de Malesherbes, Chrétien-Guillaume (1721-1794)   I-428
Maléter, Colonel Pal (*fl.* 1956)   III-1595
Malthus, Daniel (*fl.* 1776)   I-533
Malthus, Thomas Robert (1766-1834)   I-424; 533; II-629
Manchester, Earl of (*see* Montagu, Edward)
Mancini, Pasquale Stanislao (1817-1888)   II-1019
von Manstein, Field Marshall (General) Erich (*fl.* 1942-1943)   III-1451; 1472
von Mantueffel, Baron Otto (1805-1882)   II-790
von Manteuffel, General Hasso (*fl.* 1945)   III-1496
Mantua, Margaret of (*fl.* 1640)   I-304
Manuel II (of Portugal) (1889-1932)   III-1219
Mao Tse-tung (1893-   )   III-1583; 1678
Marcel, Claude (*fl.* 1572)   I-184
Marchand, Captain Jean Baptiste (1863-1934)   II-1113
Marconi, Marchese Guglielmo (1874-1937)   II-1080
Margall, Francisco Pi y (*fl.* 1860's)   II-945
Margaret of Austria (1480-1530)   I-31
Marguerite of Navarre (1492-1549)   I-116
Marguerite of Valois (1553-1615)   I-184; 214
Maria II, of Portugal (1819-1853)   II-675; 722
Maria Anna of Bavaria-Neuburg (1667-1740)   I-372
Maria Carlotta, of Spain (*fl.* 1830)   II-726
María Cristina, of Spain (1806-1878)   II-726
Maria Theresa (1717-1780)   I-414; 419; 437; 469; 475
Maria Theresa, of Austria (1638-1683)   I-341
Marie Louise d'Orléans, of Spain (1662-1689)   I-372
de Marillac, Louis (1573-1632)   I-278
de Marillac, Michel (1563-1632)   I-278
Marlborough, Duke of (*see* Churchill, John)
di La Marmora, Marchese (Alfonso Ferrero) (1804-1878)   II-923

Marshall, General George Catlett (1880-1959) III-1477; 1486; 1491; 1532; 1555

de Marsin, Marchal Comte Ferdinand (*fl.* 1704) I-390

Martí, José Julian (1853-1895)   II-1119

Martinitz, Count Jaroslav (*fl.* early seventeenth century)   I-250

Martov, Julius (J. O. Zederbaum) (*fl.* 1895) II-1105

Mary I (Mary Tudor, *also* Bloody Mary of England) (1516-1558)   I-103; 123; 153; 158; 168

Mary II, of Great Gritain (1662-1694)   I-357; 385

Mary Louise, of Spain (1751-1819)   II-581

Mary Stuart, Queen of Scots (1542-1587) I-162; 174

Marx, Karl (1818-1883)   II-781; 897; 992

Massu, General Jacques (*fl.* 1958)   III-1607

Matthias (1557-1619)   I-250

Maudslay, Henry (1771-1831)   I-524

Maura y Montaner, Antonio (1853-1925) III-1259

Maurice, Duke of Saxony (1521-1553)   I-91

Maurras, Charles (1868-1952)   III-1386

Max of Baden, Prince (Maximilian Alexander Friedrich Wilhelm) (1867-1929)   III-1295

Maximilian of Austria; *also* Emperor of Mexico (Ferdinand Maximilian Joseph) (1832-1867) II-876

Maximilian I, Holy Roman Emperor (1459-1519)   I-31; 44; 64

Maximilian II, Holy Roman Emperor (1527-1576)   I-148

Maximilian II, Emanuel, of Three Electors of Bavaria (1662-1726)   I-390

Maximilian of Wittelsbach (Duke of Bavaria) (1597-1651)   I-270

Mazarin, Jules Cardinal (1602-1661)   I-324; 341; 349

Mazzini, Giuseppe (1805-1872)   II-697; 775

de Medici, Lorenzo, The Magnificent (1449-1492)   I-35; 44

de Medici, Piero (1414-1469)   I-21

de Medicis, Catherine (1519-1589)   I-162; 184; 202

de Médicis, Marie (1573-1642)   I-278

Medina-Sidonia, Duke of (Don Alonso Pérez de Guzmán) (1550-1615)   I-193

Medjid, Abdul (1832-1861)   II-813

Melanchthon, Philipp (Philipp Schwarzert) (1497-1560)   I-148; 168

von Melas, Baron Michael Friedrich Benedikt (1729-1806)   II-556

Melbourne, John (*fl.* 1835)   II-737

Melbourne, Viscount (William Lamb) (1779-1848)   II-737; 764

Mendel, Gregor Johann (1822-1884)   II-908

Mendeleev, Dmitri Ivanovich (1834-1907) II-1062

Mendizábal, Juan Álvarez (*fl.* 1833-1835) II-726

Menelik II, Emperor of Abyssinia (1844-1913) II-1094

Menshikov, Alexander (1672-1729)   I-364

Menshikov, Prince Alexander (1787-1869) II-813

Mercier, General Auguste (*fl.* 1894)   II-1075

Mercoeur, Duke of (*see* Philippe Emmanuel)

Mercoeur, Duke of (1558-1602)   I-214

Mersenne, Marin (1588-1648)   I-294

Messmer, Pierre (*fl.* 1960's)   III-1683

von Metternich, Prince Klemens Wenzel Nepomuk Lothar (1773-1859)   II-598; 602; 612; 623; 634; 638; 654; 775; 794

Meynell, Thomas (*fl.* 1818)   II-660

Michelangelo Buonarroti (1475-1564)   I-26

Michelsen, Peter Christian Hersleb Kjerschow (1857-1925)   III-1164

Michelson, Albert Abrahan (1852-1931)   III-1160

Mieroslawski, General Ludwick (1814-1878) II-886

Miguel, King of Portugal (1802-1866)   II-675; 722

Mikoyan, Anastas Ivanovich (1905-1970) III-1566

Miliukov, Paul (*fl.* 1905)   III-1169; 1179

Mill, James (1773-1836)   II-629

Mill, John Stuart (1806-1873)   II-843

Milner; Sir Alfred (1854-1925)   II-1128

Milton, John (1608-1674)   I-317

Milton, Mary Powell (*fl.* 1642-1652)   I-317

Mitterand, François (*fl.* 1969)   III-1683

Mobutu, Joseph (*fl. c.* 1965)   III-1613

Mochnacki, Maurycy (1803-1835)   II-691

Molé, Mathieu (1584-1656)   I-324

Mollet, Guy (1905-   )   III-1589; 1683

Molotov, Vyacheslav Mikhailovich (Skryabin) (1890-   )   III-1433; 1440; 1501; 1507; 1512; 1532; 1566

Von Moltke, Count Helmuth (1800-1891) II-880; 912; 949; 954; III-1249

Monck, General George (1608-1670)   I-337

Mondlane, Eduardo (*fl.* 1968)   III-1673

Monino, José, Count of Floridablanca (1728-1808)   I-442

Monnet, Jean (*fl.* 1945)   III-1601

Monson, Sir Herbert (1898-   )   II-1113

Montagu, Edward, Earl of Manchester (1602-1671)   I-313

y Montaner, Antonio Maura (*see* Mauray Montaner, Antonio)

Montebello, Marquis of (*see* Lannes, Gustave Louis)

de Montesquieu, Baron (1689-1755)   I-464

Montezuma II (1480-1520)   I-59

Montgolfier, Jacques Étienne (1745-1799)   I-496

Montgolfier, Joseph Michel (1740-1810)   I-496

de Montgomery, Gabriel (1530-1574)   I-162
Montgomery, General Bernard Law (1887-   )
    III-1467; 1486; 1491; 1496
Montini, Giovanni Battista (*see* Paul VI, Pope)
de Montmorency, Duc (*fl.* 1822)   II-654
More, Sir Thomas (1478-1535)   I-49; 103
Morley, Edward Williams (1838-1923)   III-
    1160
de Morny, Duc Charles Auguste Louis Joseph
    (*fl.* 1850's)   II-808
Morse, Samuel F. B. (1791-1872)   II-834
Mott, John Raleigh (1865-1955)   III-1550
Mounier, Jean-Joseph (1758-1806)   I-506
de Moura, Cristobal (*fl.* 1580)   I-189
Müller, Hans (*fl.* 1524)   I-76
Münzer, Thomas (1489-1525)   I-76
Murat, Marshal Joachim (1767-1815)   II-581
Muravyev, Nikolai M. (1809-1881)   III-1678
Muravyov-Apostol, Serge (*fl.* 1825)   II-665
Muravyov, Mikhail Nikolaevich (1845-1900)
    II-886
Muravyov, Nikita (*fl.* 1825)   II-665
Murchison, Roderick (1792-1871)   II-678
Murray, John Courtney (*fl.* 1965)   III-1633
de Murville, Maurice Couve (*fl.* 1966)   III-
    1648
Mussolini, Benito (1883-1945)   III-1299;
    1319; 1354; 1401; 1416; 1425; 1429; 1440;
    1451; 1486
Mustafa II, Sultan of Turkey (1664-1704)
    I-368
Mustafa III, Sultan of the Ottoman Empire (*fl.*
    1757-1774)   I-475

von Nägeli, Karl Wilhelm (1817-1891)   II-
    908
Nagy, Imre (*fl.* 1953)   III-1595
Napoleon I (1769-1821)   II-581; 585; 590;
    594; 598; 618
Napoleon III (see Louis Napoleon)
Napoleon III, of France (*also* Louis Napoleon)
    (1808-1873)   II-770; 775; 786; 808; 813;
    818; 838; 849; 860; 870; 876; 918; 923; 949;
    954; 958
Napoleon, Prince Jerome, of Westphalia (1784-
    1860)   II-838
de Narváez, Panfilo (1480-1528)   I-59
Nasmyth, James (*fl.* 1797)   I-524
Nasser, Gamal Abdel (1918-1970)   III-1589;
    1654
Navarre, General Eugène (*fl.* 1953)   III-1577
Necker, Jacques (1732-1804)   I-502; 510
di Neghelli, Marshall Rodolfo (*see* Graziani,
    Marshall)
Nelson, Horatio (1758-1805)   I-538
Nenni, Pietro (1891-   )   III-1538
Neto, Antonio Augustino (*fl.* 1968)   III-1673
Newcastle, Duke of (*see* Pelham-Holles,
    Thomas)
Newcastle, Marquis of (*see* Cavendish, William)
Newcomen, Thomas (1663-1729)   I-460

Ney, Marshal Michel (1769-1815)   II-618
Nicholas I, of Russia (1769-1855)   II-665;
    691; 813
Nicholas II, of Russia (1868-1918)   II-1062;
    1123; III-1148; 1156; 1169; 1179; 1192; 1271
Nicholson, Sir Arthur (1849-1928)   III-1197
Niépce, Isidore (*fl.* 1833)   II-747
Niépce, Joseph-Nicéphore (1765-1833)   II-
    747
Nietzsche, Friedrich Wilhelm (1844-1900)
    II-1024
Nivelle, General Robert Georges (1856-1924)
    III-1262
Nkomo, Joshua (*fl.* 1962)   III-1642
Nobiling, Dr. Karl (*fl.* 1878)   II-1013
Nordau, Max Simon (1849-1923)   II-1089
Norfolk, Duke of (*fl.* 1793)   II-669
Northcote, Sir Stafford Henry (1818-1887)
    II-1038
de Novaes, Bartholomeu Dias (1450-1500)
    I-11
Novotný, Antonín (*fl.* 1953-1968)   III-1666

Oastler, Richard (1789-1861)   II-730; 741
O'Brien, William Smith (1803-1864)   II-
    757
Obruchev, General Nikolai (*fl.* 1892)   II-
    1070
O'Connell, Daniel (1775-1847)   II-669; 741;
    757
O'Connor, Feargus Edward (1794-1855)   II-
    730; 741; 764
O'Connor, Sir Nicholas (*fl.* 1899)   II-1133
Oersted, Hans Christian (1777-1851)   II-649
Olivares, Count Duke of (*see* de Guzmán, Gas-
    par)
Oliveira, John Carlos, Duke of Saldanha (1791-
    1876)   II-675; 722
Ollivier, Émile (1825-1913)   II-808
Orange, Prince of the Netherlands (see William
    Frederik, [William I])
Orlando, Vittorio Emanuele (1860-1952)
    III-1283
Orléans, Duke of (*see* Baptiste, Gaston Jean)
d'Orléans, Louis Philippe Albert (*see* de Paris,
    Comte)
d'Orléans, Marie Louise (*see* Marie Louise d'Or-
    léans)
Orlov, Count Aleksei (1737-1809)   I-475
Orlov, Count Grigori Grigorievich (1734-1783)
    I-464
Orsini, Felice (1819-1858)   II-838
Ortega y Gassett, José (1883-1955)   II-1119
Ortoli, François-Xavier (*fl.* 1960's)   III-1683
Oscar II, of Sweden and Norway (1829-1907)
    III-1164
Osiander, Andreas (*fl.* 1543)   I-138
Ottaviani, Alfredo Cardinal (1890-   )   III-
    1633; 1659
Otto, Nikolaus August (1832-1891)   II-1033
Overton, George (*fl.* 1818)   II-660

Oxenstierna, Count Axel (1583-1654)   I-290; 308

Pacelli, Eugenio (*see* Pius XII, Pope)
Pacelli, Francesco (*fl.* 1926)   III-1354
de Padilla, Juan (1480-1528)   I-72
Paes, Sidonio Barnadino Cardosa da Silva (1872-1918)   III-1219
Paget, Henry William, Marquis of Anglesey (1768-1854)   II-669
Painlevé, Paul (1863-1933)   III-1359
Palmela, Duke of (*see* de Sousa, Pedro)
Palmer, Herbert (*fl.* 1644)   I-317
Palmerston, Viscount (Henry John Temple) (1784-1865)   II-686; 722; 794; 813; 818; 998
Panin, Count Nikita (1718-1783)   I-464
de Paris, Comte (Louis Philippe Albert d'Orléans) (1838-1894)   II-974
Parker, Matthew (1504-1575)   I-168
Parkes, Joseph (*fl.* 1835)   II-737
Parnell, Charles (1846-1891)   II-1038
Parr, Catherine (1512-1548)   I-123
Parri, Ferruccio (1890-   )   III-1538
Parsons, Robert (1546-1610)   I-174; 224
Pasha, Ali, of Turkey (*fl.* 1571)   I-180
Pasha, Mohammed Said, of Egypt (1822-1863)   II-818
Pasha, Omar, of Turkey (1806-1871)   II-813
Pashitch, Nikola (Pasic) (1845-1926)   III-1340
Paskevich-Erivanski, Field Marshal Count Ivan (1782-1856)   II-691
Pasteur, Louis (1822-1895)   II-935; III-1174
Paul III, Pope (1468-1549)   I-91; 96; 143
Paul IV, Pope (1476-1559)   I-96; 153
Paul V, Pope (1552-1621)   I-285
Paul VI, Pope (Giovanni Battista Montini) (1897-   )   III-1633; 1659
Paulus, General Friedrich (*fl.* 1942-1943)   III-1472
Pauncefote, Sir Julian (1828-1902)   II-1123
Paxton, Joseph (1801-1865)   II-799
Pearse, Padhraic (Patrick Henry) (1879-1916)   III-1233
Pease, Edward (1767-1858)   II-660
Pecci, Gioacchino Vincenzo (*see* Leo XIII, Pope)
Pedro I (Emperor of Brazil; *also* Pedro IV of Portugal) (1798-1834)   II-675
Pedro IV, of Portugal (1798-1834)   II-722
Peel, Sir Robert (1788-1850)   II-669; 704; 737; 757; 764
Pelham-Holles, Thomas, Duke of Newcastle (1693-1768)   I-437
Pelissier, General Jean-Jacques, Duke of Malakoff (1794-1864)   II-813
Pelloux, General Luigi (1839-1924)   II-1109
Pepe, Guglielmo (1783-1855)   II-638
Perrin, Claude Victor (*see* Victor, Claude)
Pescara, Marquis of (1489-1525)   I-82
Pestel, Paul (*fl.* 1825)   II-665

Petain, Marshal Henri Phillippe (1856-1951)   III-1262; 1359; 1452
Peter I, the Great, of Russia (1672-1725)   I-364; 376; 432; 464
Peter III, of Russia (1728-1762)   I-414; 464
Petty-Fitzmaurice, Henry Charles Keith (*see* Lansdowne, Marquis of)
Pflimlin, Pierre (*fl.* 1958)   III-1607
Pher, Alain (*fl.* 1960's)   III-1683
Philip I, of Spain (1478-1506)   I-40
Philip II, of Spain (1527-1598)   I-153; 158; 162; 174; 180; 189; 193; 202; 220
Philip IV, of Spain (1605-1665)   I-299; 304; 341
Philip V, of Spain (1683-1746)   I-372; 400
Philippe Emmanuel, Duke of Mercoeur (1558-1602)   I-220
Philip of Hesse (1504-1567)   I-76; 91; 148
Picquart, Major Georges (1854-1914)   II-1075
Pigafetta, Antonio (1491-1534)   I-68
Pinsker, Leo (*fl.* 1882)   II-1089
Pinzón, Martín Alonso (1440-1493)   I-16
Pitt, William, the Elder (1708-1778)   I-451
Pitt, William, the Younger (1759-1806)   I-485; II-551
Pius III, Pope (1475/76-1507)   I-26
Pius IV, Pope (1499-1565)   I-174
Pius V, Pope (1504-1572)   I-174; 180
Pius VI, Pope (1717-1799)   I-516; 520
Pius VII, Pope (1742-1823)   II-564
Pius IX, Pope (Giovanni Maria Mastar-Ferretti (1792-1878)   II-770; 775; 808; 892; 902; 923; 958; 969; 978; III-1143
Pius X, Pope (Giuseppe Melchiorre Sarto) (1835-1914)   III-1143
Pius XI, Pope (Achille Ambrogio Damiano Ratti) (1857-1939)   III-1354
Pius XII, Pope (Eugenio Pacelli) (1876-1958)   III-1659
Place, Francis (1771-1854)   II-704; 741
Planetta, Otto (*fl.* 1934)   III-1395
Plekhanov, Geori Valentinovich (1857-1918)   II-1105
du Plessis, Armand Emmanuel (*see* de Richelieu, Duc)
du Plessis, Armand Jean (*see* Richelieu, Cardinal)
Pobedonostsev, Konstantin Petrovich (1827-1907)   III-1156
Poincaré, Raymond (1860-1934)   III-1340
Polignac, Prince of (*see* Armand, Jules)
Pollio, Alberto (*fl.* 1912)   III-1228
Pompidou, Georges Jean Raymond (1911-   )   III-1648; 1683
Poniatowski, Stanislas (1732-1798)   I-469
Popov, Aleksandr Stepanovich (1859-1905)   II-1080
Portal, Sir Charles Frederick Algernon, Marshal of the Royal Air Force (1893-1971)   III-1461

de la Rue, Warren (1815-1889)   II-753
Rumford, Count (Benjamin Thompson) (1753-1814)   II-560
Runciman, Walter (1870-1949)   III-1429
von Rundstedt, Field Marshal (General) Karl Rudolf Gerd (1875-1953)   III-1451; 1456; 1491; 1496
Rupert, Prince (1619-1682)   I-313
Ruppa, Wenceslaus (*fl.* early seventeenth century)   I-250
Russell, John, Duke of Bedford (1710-1771)   I-451
Russell, Lord John (1792-1878)   II-669; 704; 737; 757; 764; 929
Rye, George (*fl.* 1730)   I-424
Rykov, Aleksei Ivanovich (1881-1938)   III-1329
Ryleiev, Kondraty (1795-1826)   II-665

Sagasta, Práxedes Mateo (1827-1903)   II-1003; 1119
Sagredo, Giovanni Francesco (*fl.* 1632)   I-285
Saigh, Patriarch Maximos IV (*fl.* 1965)   III-1633
de Saint-Arnaud, General Le Roy (1801-1854)   II-808; 813
de Saint-Just, Louis Antoine Léon (1767-1794)   I-529
de Saint-Simon, Comte (*see* de Rouvroy, Claude Henri)
Salan, General Raoul (*fl.* 1958)   III-1607
Salazar, Antonio De Oliveira (1889-1970)   III-1673
Saldanha, Duke of (*see* Oliveira, John Carlos)
Salisbury, Marquis of (Robert Arthur Talbot Gascoyne-Cecil) (1830-1903)   II-1038; 1057; 1113
von Salis-Soglio, General Johann Ulrich (*fl.* 1847)   II-794
Salmerón, Alphonse (*fl.* 1558)   I-96
Salviati, Filippo (*fl.* 1632)   I-285
Samarin, Yurii (*fl.* 1858-1861)   II-866
Samuel, Sir Herbert Louis (1870-1963)   III-1324
Sanjurjo, General José (*fl.* 1932)   III-1368
Santa Coloma, Count of (*fl.* 1639)   I-299
dos Santos, Antonio Machado (*fl.* 1908)   III-1219
Saragat, Giuseppe (1898-   )   III-1538
Sarto, Giuseppe Melchiorre (*see* Pius X, Pope)
Sarte, Jean-Paul (1905-   )   III-1482
Sauvage, Jean (*fl.* sixteenth century)   I-72
Savimba, Joseph (*fl.* 1968)   III-1673
di Savoia, Amadeo Ferdinando Maria, Duke of Aosta (1845-1890)   II-945
Savonarola, Fra Girolamo (1452-1498)   I-21
Sazonov, Sergei Dmitrievich (1866-1927)   III-1240; 1245; 1340
Scalonge, Daniel (*fl.* 1747)   I-405
Scalonge, Moses (*fl.* 1747)   I-405

Scelba, Mario (1901-   )   III-1538
Schacht, Horace Greeley Hjalmar (1877-1970)   III-1522
von Scharnhorst, Gerhard Johann (1755-1813)   II-572
Scheer, Vice-Admiral Reinhard (1863-1928)   III-1266
Scheidemann, Philipp (1865-1939)   III-1295
Schiller, Karl (*fl.* 1966)   III-1690
von Schlieffen, General Alfred (1833-1913)   III-1249
von Schoen, Baron Wilhelm Eduard (1851-1933)   III-1207
von Schön, Theodor (1772-1856)   II-572
Schumacher, Kurt (1946-1952)   III-1690
Schumann, Robert (1810-1856)   III-1601
von Schuschnigg, Kurt (1897-   )   III-1425
Schwarzenberg, Karl Philipp (1771-1820)   II-590
Schwarzert, Philipp (*see* Melanchthon, Philipp)
von Schweitzer, Johann Baptist (1834-1875)   II-992
Sebastian I, of Portugal (1554-1578)   I-189
Sedgwick, Adam (1785-1873)   II-678
Selassie, Haile (1891-   )   III-1401
Semmelweiss, Ignaz Philipp (1818-1865)   II-935
Senefelder, Alois (1771-1834)   I-542
Senior, Nassau (1790-1864)   II-730
Seripando, Jerome (*fl.* 1545)   I-143
Serrano y Dominguez, General Francisco (1810-1885)   II-945; 1003
Seymour, Jane (1509-1537)   I-123
von Seyss-Inquart, Artur (1892-1946)   III-1425
Sforza, Ludovico (1451-1508)   I-21
Shakespeare, William (1564-1616)   I-208
Shehan, Lawrence Cardinal Joseph (1898-   )   III-1659
Shkolnik (*see* Eshkol, Levi)
Shuisky, Vasily Ivanovich (*d.* 1612)   I-231
Shuvalov, I. I. (*fl.* 1754)   I-432
Sibthorp, Colonel Charles (*fl.* 1850-1851)   II-799
von Siemens, Georg (*fl.* 1888)   II-1133
Sièyes, Abbé Emmanuel Joseph (1748-1836)   I-506; 547; II-564
Simpson, James Y. (1811-1870)   II-935
Simpson, Wallis Warfield (1897-   )   III-1420
Sinclair, Sir Archibald (1890-1970)   III-1461
Sithole, Ndabaningi (*fl.* 1902)   III-1642
Skryabin (*see* Molotov, Vyacheslav)
Skrzynecki, General Jan (1787-1860)   II-691
Slavata, Count Wilhelm (*fl.* early seventeenth century)   I-250
Sloane, Sir Hans (1660-1753)   I-424
Smith, Adam (1723-1790)   I-424; 485; II-629
Smith, Ian (*fl.* 1964)   III-1642
Smith, Solomon (*fl.* 1733-1735)   I-405
Smuts, Jan Christian (1870-1950)   III-1289

de Portocarrero, Luis Cardinal (*fl.* 1696) I-372
Pound, Admiral Sir Alfred Dudley Pickman Rogers (1877-1943) III-1446
Preece, Sir William Henry (1834-1913) II-1080
Preuss, Hugo (1860-1925) III-1295
Prieto, Indalecio (*fl.* 1925-1931) III-1368
Prieto, Manual Garcia (*see* Alhuemas, Marquis de)
Primrose, Archibald Philip (*see* Rosebery, Earl of)
Prim y Prats, General Juan, Marqués de los Castillejos (1814-1870) II-945
Proudhon, Pierre Joseph (1809-1865) II-897
Pujo, Maurice (1872-1955) III-1386
Pyatakov, Grigori L. (1890-1937) III-1329

Quesnay, François (1694-1774) I-485
Quiñones, José María Gil Robles (*fl.* 1933) III-1368
Quisling, Vidkun (1887-1945) III-1446

Raeder, Grand Admiral Erich (1876-1960) III-1446; 1467
Rainolds, John (1549-1607) I-241
Raistrick, Harold (*fl.* 1920's) III-1335
Rákosi, Matyas (*fl.* 1955) III-1595
Ramsay, Admiral Sir Bertram H. (*fl.* 1940) III-1456
Ratti, Achille Ambrogio Damiano (*see* Pius XI, Pope)
Ravaillac, François (1578-1610) I-214
de Redcliffe, Viscount (*see* Canning, Stratford)
Redmond, John Edward (1856-1918) III-1233
de Reinach, Baron Jacques (*fl.* 1888) II-1066
Renan, Joseph Ernest (1823-1892) II-892
Reuter, Ernst (*fl.* 1948) III-1543
Reynaud, Paul (1878-1966) III-1451
Rheticus (1514-1576) I-138
Rhodes, Cecil John (1853-1902) II-1128
Ribbentrop, Joachim (1893-1946) III-1433; 1440; 1522
Ricardo, David (1772-1823) II-629
Rice, John Ap (*fl.* 1535) I-110
Richard III, of England (1452-1485) I-6
Richelieu, Cardinal (Armand Jean du Plessis) (1585-1642) I-259; 270; 274; 278; 290; 299; 304; 308; 353
de Richelieu, Duc (Armand Emmanuel du Plessis) (1766-1822) II-623
del Riego, Major Rafael (1785-1823) II-634
Rintelen, Dr. Anton (1876-1946) III-1395
de Rivera, General Fernando Primo (*fl.* 1874) II-1003
de Rivera, José Antonio Primo (*d.* 1939) III-1416
Robert, Aine (*fl.* 1783) I-496
Robert, Cadet (*fl.* 1783) I-496
Roberto, Holden (*fl.* 1968) III-1673

Roberts, Field Marshal Frederick Sleigh (1832-1914) II-1128
Roberts, Thomas (*fl.* 1964) III-1659
Robertson, D. H. (*fl.* 1920's) III-1406
Robespierre, Augustin (*fl.* 1793-1794) I-529
de Robespierre, Maximilien François Marie Isidore (1758-1794) I-520; 529
Robison, John (*fl.* 1763-1764) I-460
Robledo, Francisco Romero (*fl.* 1895-1897) II-1119
Rocco, Alfredo (1875-1935) III-1299
de Rochas, Alphonse Beau (*fl.* 1862) II-1033
Rochefort, Victor Henri, Marquis de Rochefort-Lucay (1830-1913) II-1053
Rock, John C. (*fl.* 1963) III-1659
Rodríguez, Simon (*fl.* 1535) I-96
Roebuck, John (1718-1794) I-460
Roentgen, Wilhelm Conrad (1845-1923) II-1084
de Rohan, Benjamin (Seigneur de Soubise) (1583-1642) I-259
Röhm, Ernst (1887-1934) III-1391
Rokossovski, General Konstantin (1896-1968) III-1472
de Romanones, Conde (Álvaro de Figueroa y de Torres) (1863-1950) III-1259
Romanov, Alexis (1690-1718) I-364
Romanov, Michael (1613-1645) I-247
Rommel, Field Marshal Erwin (1891-1944) III-1467; 1491
von Roon, Count Albrecht Theodor Emil (1803-1879) II-880; 949
Roosevelt, Franklin Delano (1882-1945) III-1406; 1477; 1486; 1491; 1501; 1507
Roosevelt, Theodore (1858-1919) III-1148; 1192
Root, Elihu (1845-1937) III-1192
de la Rosa, Francisco Martinez (1789-1862) II-634
Rosebery, Earl of (Archibald Philip Primrose) (1847-1929) III-1214
Rosenberg, Alfred (1893-1946) III-1363; 1522
Rosenfeld, Lev (*see* Kamenev, Lev Borisovich)
Rossel, Louis (*fl.* 1871) II-984
Rossi, Count Pellegrino (1787-1848) II-770
Rouher, Eugène (1814-1884) II-808
Rousseau, Jean Jacques (1712-1778) I-446
de Rouvroy, Claude Henri (Comte de Saint-Simon) (1760-1825) II-803
della Rovere, Cardinal Giuliano (1458-1501) I-21
della Rovere, Giuliano (*see* Julius II, Pope)
Rozhdestvenski, Admiral Zinovi Petrovich (1848-1909) III-1148
de Rozier, Jean François Pilâtre (1756-1789) I-496
di Rudini, Antonio (1839-1908) II-1094; 1109
Rudolf II, Holy Roman Emperor (1552-1612) I-148; 236; 250

Soares, Mario (*fl.* 1960's)   III-1673
Sobieski (*see* John III Sobieski)
Söderblom, Nathan (1866-1931)   III-1550
von Sonnenfels, Joseph (*fl.* 1775-1790)   I-480
Sophia, Electress of Hanover, (1630-1714)
    I-385
Sotelo, José Calvo (*fl.* 1936)   III-1416
de Soubise, Seigneur (*see* de Rohan, Benjamin)
de Sousa, Antonio José, Duke of Terceira (*fl.* 1829)   II-722
de Sousa, Pedro, Duke of Palmela (*fl.* 1829)   II-722
Soustelle, Jacques (*fl.* 1955-1958)   III-1607
Spaak, Paul Henri (1899-   )   III-1601; 1648
Spencer, George John, Viscount Althorp (1758-1834)   II-730
Spengler, Oswald (1880-1936)   III-1279
Stalin, Joseph (Iosif Vissarionovich Dzhugashvili) (1879-1953)   III-1271; 1329; 1347; 1411; 1416; 1433; 1440; 1472; 1477; 1491; 1501; 1507; 1512; 1566; 1583
Stanley, Edward George Geoffrey Smith (*see* Derby, Lord)
Stanley, Edward Henry Smith (*see* Derby, Earl of)
Staupitz, John (*fl.* 1507)   I-54
Stavisky, Serge Alexandre (1886-1934)   III-1386; 1411
Stead, William Thomas (1849-1912)   II-1057
Stein, Baron Heinrich Friedrich Karl vom und zum (1757-1831)   II-572; 602
von Stemrich, Wilhelm (*fl.* 1908)   III-1207
Stephens, J. R. (*fl.* 1837)   II-741
Stephenson, George (1781-1848)   II-608; 660
Stephenson, Robert (1803-1859)   II-608; 660
Stettinius, Edward Reilley, Jr. (1900-1949)   III-1501; 1507
Steyn, Martinus Theunis (1857-1916)   II-1128
Stoecker, Adolf (1835-1909)   II-1028
Stolypin, Pëtr Arkadevich (1863-1911)   III-1179; 1202
Strasser, Gregor (1892-1934)   III-1391
Strauss, David Friedrich (1808-1874)   II-892
Stuart, Ackroyd (1890-   )   II-1100
Stuart, Arabella (1575-1615)   I-224
Stuart, James Francis Edward, the "Old Pretender" (1688-1766)   I-357
Stuart, John, Earl of Bute (1713-1792)   I-451
Stuart, Mary, Queen of Scots (*see* Mary Stuart)
Stuart-Wortley, Colonel Edward James Montague (*fl.* 1908-1909)   III-1207
Sturge, Joseph (*fl.* 1831)   II-715
Suenens, Leo-Joseph Cardinal (1904-   )   III-1659
Sule iman I, The Magnificent (1496-1566)   I-87
de Sully, duc (*see* de Béthune, Maximilien)
Suvorov, Count Alexander Vasilievich (*fl.* 1760-1774)   I-475

Sverdrup, Johan (1816-1892)   III-1164
Svoboda, Ludvík (*fl.* 1968)   III-1666
Swan, Joseph Wilson (1828-1914)   II-753
Swift, Jonathan (1667-1745)   I-424

Tallard, Marshal Camille d'Hostun (1652-1728)   I-390
Talleyrand (Charles Maurice de Talleyrand-Périgord, Prince de Bénévente) (1754-1838)   I-516; 547; II-598; 612; 623
Talon, Omer (*fl.* 1648)   I-324
Tardini, Domenico Cardinal (*fl.* 1958)   III-1633
Temple, Henry John (*see* Palmerston, Viscount)
Temple, Sir William (1881-1944)   III-1550
Terceira, Duke of (*see* de Sousa, Antonio)
Tetzel, John (1465-1519)   I-54
Thant, U (1909-   )   III-1654
Theodore I, of Russia (1557-1598)   I-198
Thiers, Louis Adolphe (1797-1877)   II-974; 984
Thomas, Émile (*fl.* 1840's)   II-786
Thomaz, Americo Deus (*fl.* 1960's)   III-1673
Thompson, Benjamin (*see* Rumford, Count)
Thomson, Sir William (1824-1907)   II-834
Thurn, Count Mattias (1567-1640)   I-250
Titian (*see* Vecelli, Tiziano)
Tito, Josip Broz (1892-   )   III-1595
Togliatti, Palmiro (1893-   )   III-1538
de Tolly, Prince Mikhail Barclay (1761-1818)   II-585
Tomás, Manuel Fernandes (*fl.* 1820)   II-645
Tomsky, Mikhail Pavolovich (1880-1936)   III-1329
Tone, Wolfe (1763-1798)   II-551
de Torcy, Marquis (*see* Colbert, Jean Baptiste)
Torgler, Ernst (*fl.* 1933)   III-1377
y Torres, Niceto Alcalá Zamora (*see* Zamora y Torres)
Totleben, Count Edward Ivanovitch (1818-1884)   II-813
von Trauttmansdorff, Count Maximilian (1584-1650)   I-308
du Tremblay, François le Clerq (*see* Joseph, Father)
Trenchard, Sir Hugh Montague, Marshal of the Royal Air Force (1873-1956)   III-1461
Trevelyan, Charles Edward (1807-1886)   III-757
Trevelyan, Sir George Otto (1838-1928)   II-1038
Trevithick, Richard (1771-1833)   II-608
de Triana, Rodrigo (*fl.* 1492)   I-16
Trochu, General Louis (1815-1896)   II-954
Trotsky, Leon (Leib Davydovich Bronstein) (1879-1940)   III-1169; 1271; 1304; 1329; 1347
Trubetskoy, Prince Serge (1790-1859)   II-665
von Truchsess, George (*fl.* 1524-1525)   I-76

Truman, Harry S (1884-1973)   III-1512; 1526; 1532; 1543; 1555; 1561
Tshombe, Moise (*fl.* 1964-1965)   III-1613
Tudor, Mary (*see* Mary I)
Tunner, Lieutenant General William H. (*fl.* 1948-1949)   III-1543
Turati, Filippo (1857-1932)   II-1109
de Turenne, Vicomte (1611-1675)   I-345

Ulbricht, Walter (1893-   )   III-1624; 1666
Ulrich (1487-1550)   I-76
Ultanov, Vladimir Ilich (*see* Lenin, Nikolai)
de Unamuno y Jugo, Miguel (1864-1936)   II-1119
Urban VIII (1568-1644)   I-285

Vaillant, Édouard (1840-1915)   II-1044
Vandenberg, Arthur H., Jr. (1884-1951)   III-1555
Vannikov, General Boris Lvovich (*fl.* 1946)   III-1561
Vasa, Sigismund III, King of Sweden (1595-1648)   I-247
Vasa, Wladyslav (1595-1648)   I-247
Vasilyevich, Ivan (1530-1584)   I-231
de Vauban, Seigneur (1633-1707)   I-345
de Vaux, Clotilde (*fl.* 1850's)   II-803
Vavilov, Serfei (*fl.* 1934)   III-1561
De Vecchi, Cesare Maria (1884-   )   III-1319
Vecelli, Tiziano (Titian) (1477-1576)   I-133
Velásquez, Diego (1465-1522)   I-59
Vesalius, Andreas (1514-1564)   I-133
Veuillot, Louis François (1813-1883)   III-1143
de Veygoux, Louis Charles Antoine Desaix (1768-1880)   II-556
Victor, Claude (Claude Victor Perrin) (1766-1841)   II-556
Victor, Emmanuel II, King of Italy (1820-1878)   II-770; 838; 849; 860; 870; 923; 958
Victor, Emmanuel III, Prince of Naples (1869-1947)   III-1319; 1354; 1486
Victoria, Queen of England (1819-1901)   II-799
Villiers, Charles (1802-1898)   II-764
Villiers, George, Duke of Buckingham (1592-1628)   I-224; 259; 263
Virchow, Rudolph (1821-1902)   II-822
Visconti-Venosta, Emilio (1829-1914)   II-978
Volta, Count Alessandro (1745-1827)   II-560
Voltaire (François-Marie Arouet) (1694-1778)   I-446; 456

von Waechter, Dr. Karl Georg (1797-1880)   III-1395
Wagner, Adolf (*fl.* 1883)   II-1028
Waldeck-Rousseau, Pierre Marie René (1846-1904)   II-1044; III-1143
Walensky, Sir Roy (*fl.* 1953-1963)   III-1642
Walewski, Count (1810-1868)   II-838

Wallace, Alfred Russel (1823-1913)   II-855
Wallenstein, Albrecht, Duke of Friedland (1583-1634)   I-236; 270; 274
Walter, John (1818-1894)   II-730
Walwyn, William (*fl.* 1640)   I-317
de Warens, Baronne (*see* de La Tour, Francoise-Marie)
Watson, James Dewey (1928-   )   III-1572
Watt, James (1736-1819)   I-460
Watts, Sir Philip (1846-1926)   III-1187
Wavell, General Sir Archibald Percival (1883-1950)   III-1467
Weddigen, Lieutenant Otto (1882-1915)   III-1254
Wehner, Herbert (*fl.* 1957)   III-1690
Wellesley, Arthur, Duke of Wellington (1769-1852)   II-594; 618; 623; 654; 669; 704
Wellington, Duke of (*see* Wellesley, Arthur)
Wels, Otto (*fl.* 1933)   III-1382
Wentworth, Sir Thomas (1593-1641)   I-263
von Werther, Baron Karl (*fl.* 1870)   II-949
Wesley, Charles (1707-1788)   I-409
Wesley, John (1703-1791)   I-409
Wesley, Susanna (*fl.* 1710-1724)   I-409
Weydenhammer, Dr. Rudolf (*fl.* 1934)   III-1395
Weygand, General Maxime (1867-1965)   III-1451
Weyler, General Valeriano Nicolau (1838-1930)   II-1119
Whitefield, George (1714-1770)   I-409
Whitehead, Sir Edgar (*fl.* 1960-1961)   III-1642
Wielopolski, Count Aleksander (*fl.* 1858)   II-886
Wilkins, Maurice Hugh Frederick (1916-   )   III-1572
Willem, Frederik (William I) (Prince of Orange of The Netherlands) (1772-1843)   II-686
William (Friedrich Wilhelm Viktor August Ernst) (*fl.* 1916)   III-1262
William I (King of Netherlands) (1797-1888)   II-880; 912; 918; 949; 954; 963; 988; 993; 1013; 1028
William II (Friedrich Wilhelm Viktor Albert) (Emperor of Germany and King of Prussia) (1859-1941)   II-1013; 1070; 1123; III-1148; 1192; 1207; 1262; 1295
William III of England (*see* William of Orange)
William IV (King of Great Britain and Ireland) (1765-1837)   II-704
William of Orange (William III of England) (1650-1702)   I-357; 385
Wilberforce, William (1759-1833)   II-715
Wilson, Harold (James Harold Wilson) (1916-   )   III-1642
Wilson, James Harold (*see* Wilson, Harold)
Wilson, Thomas Woodrow (1856-1924)   III-1283; 1289
Windthorst, Ludwig (1812-1891)   II-1013
de Witt, John (1625-1672)   I-345

Witte, Count Sergei Yelievich (1849-1915)
II-1062; III-1148; 1169; 1179
Wöhler, Friedrich (1800-1882)   III-1174
Wolsey, Thomas Cardinal (1475-1530)   I-6;
103
Wood, Edward Frederick Lindley (*see* Halifax,
Earl of)
Wood, Nicholas (*fl.* 1814)   II-608
Wright, Almroth Edward (1861-1947)   III-
1335

Xavier, Francis (1506-1552)   I-96

Yeremeko, General Andrei Ivanovich (1892-
1970)   III-1472
Yohannis IV (*see* John IV of Ethiopia)

Zamora y Torres, Niceto Alcalá (*fl.* 1931-1936)
III-1368
Zamoyski, General Andrei (*fl.* 1862-1863)
II-886
Zanardelli, Giuseppe (1829-1903)   II-1109
Zápolya, John (1487-1540)   I-87
Zederbaum, J. O. (*see* Martov, Julius)
Zhukov, Marshal Georgi Konstantinovich
(1895-   III-1472
Zinoviev, Grigori Evseevich (Hirsch Apfelbaum)
(1883-1936)   III-1347
Zola, Émile (1840-1902)   II-1075
Zorilla, Manuel Ruíz (1834-1895)   II-945
Zubatov, Sergei (*fl.* 1902)   III-1156
Zumalacárregui, Tomas (1788-1835)   II-726
Zwingli, Ulrich (1484-1531)   I-116

MODERN EUROPEAN

PERTINENT LITERATURE REVIEWED

Acton, Harold
  Bourbons of Naples, 1734-1825, The   II-643
Albertini, Luigi
  Origins of the War of 1914, The   II-1021; III-1231; 1247
Alperovitz, Gar
  Atomic Diplomacy: Hiroshima and Potsdam   III-1515
Ames, Russell
  Citizen Thomas More and His Utopia   I-51
Anderson, Eugene N.
  Social and Political Conflict in Prussia, 1858-1864, The   II-883
Anderson, Fulton H.
  Francis Bacon   I-256
Anderson, M. S.
  Eastern Question, 1774-1923: A Study in International Relations, The   III-1205; 1243
Anderson, R. C.
  Naval Wars in the Levant   I-182
Andrews, Roy Chapman
  Meet Your Ancestors   II-825
Armitage, Angus
  World of Copernicus, The   I-140
Armstrong, Barbara
  Insuring the Essentials   II-1031
Aron, Raymond
  Main Currents in Sociological Thought   II-806
Artz, Frederick B.
  France Under the Bourbon Restoration   II-684
  Reaction and Revolution, 1814-1832. Vol. XIII of *The Rise of Modern Europe* series.   II-689
Ashley, Maurice
  Greatness of Oliver Cromwell, The   I-315; 333
Askew, William C.
  Europe and Italy's Acquisition of Libya, 1911-1912   III-1230
Asprey, Robert B.
  First Battle of the Marne, The   III-1251
Atkinson, Christopher T.
  Marlborough and the Rise of the British Army   I-394
Aubry, Octave
  Second Empire, The   II-810

Baer, George W.
  Coming of the Italian-Ethiopian War, The   III-1403
Bailey, Edward
  Charles Lyell   II-679
Bain, R. Nisbet
  Charles XII and the Collapse of the Swedish Empire, 1682-1719   I-377

Bainton, Roland H.
  Here I Stand: A Life of Martin Luther   I-56
Baird, Henry M.
  Huguenots and Henry of Navarre, The   I-216
Bakerville, Geoffrey
  English Monks and the Suppression of the Monasteries   I-112
Barbour, Philip L.
  Dimitry, Called the Pretender, Tsar and Great Prince of All Russia, 1605-1606   I-233
Barker, Arthur E.
  Milton and the Puritan Dilemma   I-322
Barker, Nancy Nichols
  Distaff Diplomacy: The Empress Eugénie and the Foreign Policy of the Second Empire   II-852
Barnes, Donald G.
  History of the English Corn Laws, 1660-1846, A   II-768
Barnes, Hazel
  "Translator's Introduction," in *Being and Nothingness*   III-1484
Barraclough, Geoffrey
  Origins of Modern Germany, The   I-66
Barrett, Ada L.
  George Stephenson, Father of Railways   II-610
Bart, Benjamin F.
  Flaubert   II-831
Bax, E. Belfort
  Peasants' War in Germany, The   I-79
Bennet, E. A.
  C. G. Jung   III-1312
Benoist-Méchin, Jacques
  Sixty Days That Shook the West: The Fall of France, 1940   III-1452
Bergson, Henri
  Duration and Simultaneity, with Reference to Einstein's Theory   III-1162
Berkeley, G. F. H.
  Italy in the Making, 1815-1846   II-701
Betley, J. A.
  Belgium and Poland in International Relations, 1830-1831   II-693
Binchy, Daniel
  Church and State in Fascist Italy   III-1356
Bird, Anthony
  Motor Car, 1765-1914, The   II-1034
Blake, Robert
  Disraeli   II-1000
Bleich, Alan R.
  Story of X-Rays from Roentgen to Isotopes, The   II-1087
Blond, Georges
  Verdun   III-1265
Bloomfield, Lincoln P.

Outer Space: Prospects for Man and Society
III-1620
Blum, Jerome
Lord and Peasant in Russia from the Ninth to the Nineteenth Centuries II-868
Bober, M. M.
Karl Marx's Interpretation of History II-782
Bolitho, Hector
King Edward VIII III-1423
Bolling, Klaus
Republic in Suspense: Politics, Parties, and Personalities in Postwar Germany III-1692
Bonjour, E.
Short History of Switzerland, A II-796
Boulenger, Jacques
Seventeenth Century in France, The I-281; 327
Brabant, Frank H.
Beginning of the Third Republic in France: A History of the National Assembly (February-September 1871), The II-976
Bracher, Karl Dietrich
"Technique of Nationalist Socialist Seizure of Power, The," in Eschenburg's *The Path to Dictatorship, 1918-1933* III-1384
Braithwaite, William J.
Lloyd George's Ambulance Wagon III-1225
Brandi, Karl
Emperor Charles V, The I-65
Brenan, Gerald
Spanish Labyrinth: An Account of the Social and Political Background of the Civil War, The II-1004; III-1260; 1369
Bridge, John S. C.
History of France from the Death of Louis XI, A I-22; 32
Briggs, Asa
Chartist Studies II-744
Victorian Cities II-738
Brinton, Crane
Decade of Revolution, 1789-1799, A. Vol. XI of *The Rise of Modern Europe* series I-512
Brodrick, James, S.J.
Origin of the Jesuits, The I-100
Brogan, Denis W.
France Under the Republic: The Development of Modern France, 1870-1939. Book IV: *The Republic in Danger* II-1055
France Under the Republic: The Development of Modern France, 1870-1939. Book VI: *The Republic Saved* II-975; 1068; III-1144
Brombert, Victor
Novels of Flaubert: A Study of Themes and Techniques, The II-832
Brook-Shepherd, Gordon
Anschluss: The Rape of Austria III-1426
Prelude to Infamy: The Story of Chancellor Dollfuss of Austria III-1397

Broome, J. H.
Rousseau: A Study of His Thought I-447
Bruun, Geoffrey
Europe and the French Imperium, 1799-1814. Vol. XII of *The Rise of Modern Europe* series II-566
Brzezinski, Zbigniew K.
Soviet Bloc: Unity and Conflict, The III-1598
Buckle, George E.
Life of Benjamin Disraeli, Earl of Beaconsfield, The. Vol. V: *1868-1876* II-1001
Bullock, Alan
Hitler: A Study in Tyranny III-1392; 1442
Buranelli, Vincent
Louis XIV I-348
Burckhardt, Carl J.
Richelieu: His Rise to Power I-282
Bury, J. B.
History of the Papacy in the Nineteenth Century II-906
Butler, J. R. M.
Passing of the Great Reform Bill, The II-708
Butterfield, Herbert
Statecraft of Machiavelli, The I-37

Cantimori, Delio
"Italy in 1848" in François Fejto's *The Opening Of an Era, 1848* II-779
Carell, Paul
Hitler Moves East, 1941-1943 III-1474
Carr, Raymond
Spain, 1808-1939 I-444; II-582; 595; 635; 727; 946; 1005; III-1260
Carter, Charles Howard
Secret Diplomacy of the Habsburgs, 1598-1625, The I-222
Carter, Samuel, III
Cyrus Field: Man of Two Worlds II-835
Carver, General Michael
El Alamein III-1468
Caspar, Max
Kepler, 1571-1630 I-238
Chabod, Federico
Machiavelli and the Renaissance I-37
Chace, James
Conflict in the Middle East III-1656
Chamberlain, William Henry
Russian Revolution, 1917-1921, The III-1274
Chambers, Sir Edmund K.
William Shakespeare: A Study of Facts and Problems I-210
Chandler, Albert R.
Rosenberg's Nazi Myth III-1365
Chandler, David
Campaigns of Napoleon: The Mind and Method of History's Greatest Soldier, The II-621
Chapman, Guy

Dreyfus Case: A Reassessment, The II-1077

Third Republic of France: The First Phase, 1871-1894, The II-1054; 1067

Chapman, Maybelle K.
Great Britain and the Bagdad Railway, 1888-1914 II-1136

Cherniavsky, Michael
Tsar and Empire: Studies in Russian Myths I-234

Cheyne, William Watson
Lister and His Achievement II-938

Childs, David
From Schumacher to Brandt: The Story of German Socialism, 1945-1965 III-1693

Choate, Joseph H.
Two Hague Conferences, The II-1126

Churchill, Winston S.
Marlborough, His Life, and Times I-392
Memoirs of the Second World War III-1529
Second World War, The. Vol. II: *Their Finest Hour* III-1452
Second World War, The. Vol. VI: *Triumph and Tragedy* III-1520

Clapham, J. H.
Economic Development of France and Germany, 1815-1914, The II-1046

Clark, Alan
Barbarossa: The Russian-German Conflict, 1941-1945 III-1474

Clark, George
Later Stuarts, 1660-1714, The. Vol. X of *The Oxford History of England* I-403

Clarke, Jack Alden
Huguenot Warrior: The Life and Times of Henri de Rohan, 1579-1638 I-260

Claude, Innis L. Jr.
Swords into Ploughshares III-1510

Clay, Lucius D.
Decision in Germany III-1548

Clements, Frank
Rhodesia: A Study of the Deterioration of a White Society III-1644

Codding, George A.
Federal Government of Switzerland, The II-797

Cole, G. D. H.
British Common People, 1746-1946, The II-739

Colton, Joel
Léon Blum, Humanist in Politics III-1414

Coolidge, Archibald C.
Origins of the Triple Alliance II-1022

Copleston, Frederick, S.J.
Friedrich Nietzsche, Philosopher of Culture II-1026
"Kant," in *A History of Philosophy.* Vol. VI: *Wolff to Kant* I-493

Corti, Egon Caesar

Maximilian and Charlotte of Mexico II-877

Cowles, Virginia
Kaiser, The III-1210

Cowling, Maurice
Mill and Liberalism II-846

Craig, Gordon A.
Battle of Königgrätz, The II-915
Politics of the Prussian Army, 1640-1945, The II-792

Creighton, M. M.
History of the Papacy from the Great Schism to the Sack of Rome, A I-29; 47

Cremona, P.
Italy's Foreign and Colonial Policy, 1914-1937 III-1404

Crowther, James G.
British Scientists of the Nineteenth Century II-561

Curran, Charles E.
Contraception: Authority and Dissent III-1663

Daiches, David
King James Version of the English Bible, The I-243

Dansette, Adrien
Religious History of Modern France. Vol. I: *From the Revolution to the Third Republic* I-518
Religious History of Modern France. Vol. II: *Under the Third Republic* III-1145

Davidson, Eugene
Trial of the Germans: An Account of the Twenty-Two Defendants Before the International Military Tribunal at Nuremburg, The III-1524

Davidson, Walter Phillips
Berlin Blockade: A Study in Cold War Politics, The III-1546

Davies, Godfrey
Early Stuarts, 1603-1660, The. Vol. IX of *The Oxford History of England.* I-229
Restoration of Charles II, 1658-1660, The I-338

Davies, R. Trevor
Spain in Decline, 1621-1700 I-302; 342

Davies, Rupert E.
Methodism I-412

Davis, Calvin de Armond
United States and the First Hague Conference, The II-1125

Dawson, Daniel
Mexican Adventure, The II-878

Deakin, Frederick W.
Brutal Friendship, The III-1489

De Bertier De Sauvigny, Guillaume
Bourbon Restoration, The II-599; 684

De Carmoy, Guy
Foreign Policies of France, 1944 to 1968, The III-1650

De Caulaincourt, Armand
With Napoleon in Russia   II-588
De Kruif, Paul
Microbe Hunters   III-1177
De Madariaga, Salvador
Spain: A Modern History   II-1121
Deniau, Jean François
Common Market, The   III-1603
Denny, Alice
Africa and the Victorians   II-1051
Derry, T. K.
Campaign in Norway, The   III-1448
Desan, Wilfred
Tragic Finale, The   III-1483
De Schweinitz, Karl
England's Road to Social Security   III-1226
Díaz del Castillo, Bernal
Discovery and Conquest of Mexico, The   I-62
Dickens, A. G.
English Reformation, The   I-107; 127
Dillenberger, John
Martin Luther: A Selection from His Writings   I-56
Divine, David
Broken Wing: A Study in the British Exercise of Air Power, The   III-1464
Dobb, Maurice
Soviet Economic Development Since 1917   III-1305
Dollfus, Charles
Orion Book of Balloons, The   I-500
Doolin, Paul Rice
Fronde, The   I-325
Dorn, Walter L.
Competition for Empire, 1740-1763. Vol. IX of *The Rise of Modern Europe* series   I-421; 438; 454
Drinkwater, John
Shakespeare   I-211
Dry, Avis M.
Psychology of Jung: A Critical Interpretation, The   III-1311
Duffy, James E.
Portuguese Africa   III-1675
Duke, Paul
Catherine the Great and the Russian Nobility   I-467
Dunlap, Orrin E., Jr.
Marconi: The Man and His Wireless   II-1082
Dunn, L. C.
Short History of Genetics, A   II-910

Earle, Edward M.
Turkey, the Great Powers, and the Bagdad Railway   II-1135
Eckles, Robert B.
Britain, Her Peoples, and the Commonwealth   III-1375

Eiseley, Loren
Darwin's Century   II-856
Elliott, John H.
Imperial Spain, 1469-1716   I-4; 42; 74; 156; 190; 374
Revolt of the Catalans, The   I-301; 306
Ellis, Major L. F.
War in France and Flanders, The   III-1458
Elting, John Robert
Military History and Atlas of the Napoleonic Wars, A   II-571
Elton, Geoffrey Rudolph
England Under the Tudors. Vol. IV of *A History of England*   I-7
Reformation Europe, 1517-1559   I-155
Embree, George Daniel
Soviet Union Between the 19th and 20th Party Congresses, 1952-1956, The   III-1567
Ensor, R. C. K.
England, 1870-1914   II-1061
Ergang, Robert Reinhold
Potsdam Führer: Frederick William I, Father of Prussian Militarism, The   I-398
Erlanger, Philippe
St. Bartholomew's Night   I-186
Esposito, Vincent J.
Military History and Atlas of the Napoleonic Wars, A   II-571
Eubank, Keith
Munich   III-1432
Eyck, Erich
Bismarck and the German Empire   II-966
History of the Weimar Republic, A   III-1297

Fall, Bernard B.
Hell in a Very Small Place: The Siege of Dien Bien Phu, in *Great Battles of History* series   III-1581
Farrington, Benjamin
Francis Bacon: Philosopher of Industrial Science   I-257
Fay, C. R.
Adam Smith and the Scotland of His Day   I-487
Palace of Industry, 1851: A Study of the Great Exhibition and Its Fruits.   II-801
Fay, Sidney B.
Origins of the World War, The. Vol. I: *Before Sarajevo*   II-1073; III-1154; 1195
Origins of the World War, The. Vol. II: *After Sarajevo*   III-1245
Rise of Brandenburg-Prussia to 1786, The   I-399
Feis, Herbert
Between War and Peace: The Potsdam Conference   III-1514
Churchill, Roosevelt, Stalin   III-1480; 1503
Fenton, Mildred Adams
Giants of Geology   II-681
Ferrara, Orestes

Borgia Pope: Alexander the Sixth, The   I-28
Finer, Herman
  Mussolini's Italy   III-1300
Fleming, D. F.
  Cold War and Its Origins, The. Vol. I: *1917-1950.*   III-1558
  Cold War and Its Origins, The. Vol. II: *1950-1960.*   III-1558
Flenley, Ralph
  Modern German History   II-606
Fletcher, C. R. L.
  Gustavus Adolphus and The Thirty Years War   I-276
Florinsky, Michael T.
  Russia: A History and Interpretation   I-199; 249; 366; II-1065; III-1171; 1182; 1681
Ford, Guy Stanton
  Stein and the Era of Reform in Prussia, 1807-1815   II-575
Frankland, Noble
  Strategic Air Offensive Against Germany, 1939-1945, The   III-1463
Friedjung, Heinrich
  Struggle for Supremacy in Germany, 1859-1866, The   II-915
Frost, Holloway H.
  Battle of Jutland, The   III-1268
Fuller, General J. F. C.
  Military History of the Western World, A   I-315
Fülöp-Miller, René
  Jesuits: A History of the Society of Jesus, The   I-101

Gallagher, John
  Africa and the Victorians   II-1051
Galvao, Henrique
  Santa Maria: My Crusade for Portugal   III-1676
Gardiner, C. Harvey
  History of the Conquest of Mexico   I-61
Gardiner, Samuel Rawson
  History of the Commonwealth and Protectorate, 1649-1656   I-332
Gardner, Martin
  Relativity for the Million   III-1162
Garvin, James L.
  Life of Joseph Chamberlain, The. Vol. I: *1836-1885*   II-1042
Gaxotte, Pierre
  Frederick the Great   I-416
Gehl, Jürgen
  Austria, Germany, and the Anschluss, *1931-1938*   III-1399; 1427
Geiringer, Irene
  Johann Sebastian Bach: The Culmination of an Era   I-383
Geiringer, Karl
  Johann Sebastian Bach: The Culmination of an Era   I-383
Gernsheim, Alison
  L. J. M. Daguerre: The History of the Diorama and the Daguerreotype   II-749
Gernsheim, Helmut
  L. J. M. Daguerre: The History of the Diorama and the Daguerreotype   II-749
Gershoy, Leo
  French Revolution and Napoleon, The   I-549; II-600
Geymonat, Ludovico
  Galileo Galilei   I-288
Gilbert, G. M.
  Nuremberg Diary   III-1524
Gillispie, Charles Coulston
  Diderot Pictorial Encyclopedia of Trades and Industry, A   I-430
Glasser, Otto
  Wilhelm Conrad Roentgen   II-1085
Godlee, Rickman John
  Lord Lister   II-936
Gooch, Brison D.
  New Bonapartist Generals in the Crimean War: Distrust and Decision-Making in the Anglo-French Alliance, The   II-815
Gooch, G. P.
  Before the War   II-1115
  Frederick the Great: The Ruler, the Writer, the Man   I-417
Goodall, Norman
  Ecumenical Movement: What It Is and What It Does, The   III-1553
Gordon, David C.
  Passing of French Algeria, The   III-1631
Green, V. H. H.
  John Wesley   I-411
Greene, John C.
  Darwin and the Modern World View   II-858
Greenwood, Ernest
  Amber to Amperes   II-562
Grimm, Harold J.
  Reformation Era, 1500-1650, The   I-94; 151
Grindrod, Muriel
  Rebuilding of Italy, The   III-1541
Grosser, Alfred
  French Foreign Policy Under De Gaulle   III-1651
Gwynn, Denis
  Daniel O'Connell, the Irish Liberator   II-672
  History of Partition, 1912-1925, The   III-1237
  Struggle for Catholic Emancipation, The   II-672

Hackett, Francis
  Francis the First   I-85
Halasz, Nicholas
  Captain Dreyfus: The Story of a Mass Hysteria   II-1078
Hale, Oron J.

Publicity and Diplomacy: With Special Reference to England and Germany, 1890-1914 III-1212

Hale, Richard W., Jr.
Britain, Her Peoples, and the Commonwealth III-1375

Hales, Edward E.
Mazzini and the Secret Societies II-700
Pio Nono: A Study in European Politics and Religion in the Nineteenth Century II-773; 981
Pio Nono (Pius IX) II-905

Halévy, Elie
Growth of Philosophic Radicalism, The I-536; II-631
"Rule of Democracy 1905-1914, The," in *A History of the English People in the Nineteenth Century* III-1217

Hall, A. R.
Scientific Revolution, 1500-1800, The I-136

Hallberg, Charles
Suez Canal: Its History and Diplomatic Importance, The II-820

Halle, Louis J.
Cold War as History, The III-1536

Halperin, S. William
Germany Tried Democracy III-1297
Italy and the Vatican at War II-960; 980

Hamerow, Theodore S.
Restoration, Revolution, Reaction: Economics, and Politics in Germany, 1815-1871 II-791; 884

Hammond, Barbara
Age of the Chartists II-735

Hammond, John L.
Age of the Chartists II-735

Hancock, W. K.
Survey of British Commonwealth Affairs. Vol. I: *Problems of Nationality, 1918-1936* III-1316

Hanke, Lewis
The Spanish Struggle for Justice in the Conquest of America I-131

Hare, Christopher
Charles de Bourbon: High Constable of France I-84

Hargreaves, John D.
Prelude to the Partition of West Africa II-1050

Harkness, Georgia
John Calvin: The Man and His Ethics I-120

Harris, Seymour E.
John Maynard Keynes, Economist and Policy Maker III-1409

Hart, Henry H.
Sea Road to the Indies I-12

Hart, Ivor B.
James Watt and the History of Steam Power I-462

Hartmann, Frederick H.
Germany Between East and West: The Reunification Problem III-1627

Hayes, Carleton J. H.
Generation of Materialism, 1871-1900, A. Vol. XVI of *The Rise of Modern Europe* series II-991

Heilbroner, Robert L.
Worldly Philosophers: The Lives, Times, and Ideas of the Great Economic Thinkers, The I-488

Heller, Joseph
Zionist Idea, The II-1092

Helmreich, Ernst C.
Diplomacy of the Balkan Wars, 1912-1913, The III-1242

Henderson, William Otto
Zollverein, The II-712

Hennessy, C. A. M.
Federal Republic in Spain, The II-947

Herold, J. Christopher
Bonaparte in Egypt II-539

Herr, Richard
Eighteenth Century Revolution in Spain, The I-443

Hertier, Jean
Catherine de' Médici I-160

Hertz, Frederick
Development of the German Public Mind: A Social History of German Political Sentiments, Aspirations, and Ideas, The. Vol. I: *The Middle Ages and Reformation* I-252
Development of the German Public Mind: A Social History of German Political Sentiments, Aspirations, and Ideas, The. Vol. II: *The Age of the Enlightenment* I-89; 370

Hexter, J. H.
More's Utopia: Biography of an Idea I-51

Hibbert, Christopher
Garibaldi and His Enemies II-864

Hinsley, F. H.
"British Foreign Policy and Colonial Questions, 1895-1904," in *The Cambridge History of the British Empire* III-1154
"Great Britain and the Powers, 1904-1914," in *The Cambridge History of the British Empire* III-1200

Hobhouse, Christopher
1851 and the Crystal Palace II-800

Holborn, Hajo
History of Modern Germany, A. Vol. I: *The Reformation* I-79; 89; 93; 150; 292
History of Modern Germany, A. Vol. II: *1648-1840* I-379; 483

Holt, Edgar
Boer War, The II-1130

Hoole, K.
North East England. Vol. IV of *A Regional History of the Railways of Great Britain* II-663

Horn, David Bayne
"Diplomatic Revolution, The" in *The New
Cambridge Modern History*   I-440
Horne, Alistair
Price of Glory, The   III-1264
Hoskyns, Catherine
*Congo Since Independence: January, 1960-
December, 1961, The*   III-1615
Hovell, Mark
Chartist Movement, The   II-743
Howard, Michael
*Franco-Prussian War: The German Invasion of
France, 1870-1871, The*   II-955
Hughes, H. Stuart
Oswald Spengler: A Critical Estimate   III-
1280
Hughes, Philip
Reformation in England, The   I-105; 125;
171
*Rome and the Counter-Reformation in En-
gland*   I-178
Hulme, Harold
Life of Sir John Eliot, The   I-266
Hume, Martin
Court of Philip IV, The   I-302

Iltis, Hugo
Life of Mendel   II-909
Isselin, Henri
Battle of the Marne, The   III-1252

Jackson, Gabriel
*Spanish Republic and the Civil War, 1931-
1939, The*   III-1370; 1418
Jackson, W. G. F.
Battle for Italy, The   III-1488
Jacobsen, H. A.
*Decisive Battles of World War II: The German
View*   III-1469; 1475; 1494
Jedin, Hubert
History of the Council of Trent, A   I-145
Jellinek, Frank
Paris Commune of 1871, The   II-985
Jenkins, Roy
Mr. Balfour's Poodle   III-1216
Jensen, De Lamar
*Diplomacy and Dogmatism: Bernardino de
Mendoza and the French Catholic League*
I-221
Johnson, William H. E.
Russia's Education Heritage   I-434
Jones, Ernest
Life and Works of Sigmund Freud, The
III-1141
Judson, Margaret A.
Crisis of the Constitution, The   I-267

Kafker, Frank A.
*French Revolution: Conflicting Interpretations,
The*   I-517
Kann, Robert

*Multinational Empire: Nationalism and Na-
tional Reform in the Habsburg Monarchy,
1848-1918, The.* Vol I: *Empire and Na-
tionalities*   I-482; II-941
*Study in Austrian Intellectual History: From
Late Baroque to Romanticism, A*   I-482
Kaplan, Herbert H.
First Partition of Poland, The   I-473
Keeling, S. V.
Descartes   I-296
Kemp, Betty
King and Commons, 1660-1832   I-386
Kennan, George F.
Memoirs: 1925-1950   III-1557
Russia: The Atom, and the West   III-1564
Kidd, B. J.
Counter-Reformation, 1550-1600, The   I-
146
King, Bolton
Italy Today   II-1112
Klingberg, Frank J.
*Anti-Slavery Movement in England: A Study in
English Humanitarianism, The*   II-718
Kluchevsky, Vasily O.
History of Russia, A   I-248; 466
Knowles, David, O.S.B.
Religious Orders in England, The   I-113
Knudsen, John I.
History of the League of Nations, A   III-
1293
Koenigsberger, H. G.
"Western Europe and the Power of Spain," in
The New Cambridge Modern History
I-159
Kramish, Arnold
Atomic Energy in the Soviet Union   III-
1563
Krausnick, Helmut
"Stages of 'Co-ordination'," in Eschenburg's
The Path to Dictatorship, 1918-1933   III-
1383
Kroner, Richard
Kant's Weltanschauung   I-494
Kuhn, Thomas S.
Copernican Revolution, The   I-141; 239

Lane, Carroll
Giants of Geology   II-681
Langdon-Davies, John
Carlos: The King Who Would Not Die   I-
374
Langer, William L.
Diplomacy of Imperialism, 1890-1902, The
II-1116
*European Alliances and Alignments, 1871-
1890*   II-989; 1010
Franco-Russian Alliance, 1890-1914, The
II-1072
Larsen, Karen
History of Norway, A   III-1167
Laux, James M.

French Revolution: Conflicting Interpretations, The   I-517
Learsi, Rufus (pseudonym for Israel Goldberg)
Fulfillment: The Epic Story of Zionism   II-1091
Lecky, William Edward Hartpole
History of Ireland in the Eighteenth Century, A   II-553
Lecler, Joseph, S. J.
Toleration and the Reformation   I-217
Lefebvre, Georges
Coming of the French Revolution, The   I-508; 513
French Revolution: From Its Origins to 1793, The   I-504; 522
Napoleon: From 18 Brumaire to Tilsit, 1799-1807   I-548; II-558; 565
Lekachman, Robert
Age of Keynes, The   III-1408
Le May, G. H. L.
British Supremacy in South Africa, 1899-1907   II-1131
Le Roy, Eduard
New Philosophy of Henri Bergson, The   III-1184
Leslie, R. F.
Polish Politics and the Revolution of November, 1830   II-694
Reform and Insurrection in Russian Poland, 1856-1865   II-888
Lewis, Floyd A.
Incandescent Light, The   II-754
Lewis, Michael
Armada Guns: A Comparative Study of English and Spanish Armaments   I-196
Lichtheim, George
Marxism: An Historical and Critical Study   II-784; 900
Lidtke, Vernon L.
Outlawed Party: Social Democracy in Germany, 1878-1890, The   II-994; 1015
Lipson, E.
Europe in the Nineteenth Century, 1815-1914   II-688
Livermore, Harold V.
New History of Portugal, A   I-306; II-646; 676; 723; III-1220
Lord, Robert Howard
Origins of the War of 1870, The. Harvard Historical Studies, XXVIII   II-951
Lortz, Joseph
How the Reformation Came   I-57
Lorwin, Val R.
French Labor Movement, The   II-1045
Loth, David
Royal Charles, Ruler, and Rake   I-339
Lovett, Gabriel H.
Napoleon and the Birth of Modern Spain   II-583; 596
Ludovici, L. J.
Fleming: Discoverer of Penicillin   III-1338

Luttichau, Charles V. P. von
"German Counteroffensive in the Ardennes, The" in *Command Decisions*   III-1499
Lynch, John
Spain Under the Habsburgs. Vol. I: *Empire and Absolutism, 1516-1598*   I-42; 190
Macartney, M. H. H.
Italy's Foreign and Colonial Policy, 1914-1937   III-1404
McCord, Norman
Anti-Corn Law League, 1838-1846, The   II-767
McDonald, Philip B.
Saga of the Seas: The Story of Cyrus W. Field and the Laying of the First Atlantic Cable, A   II-836
Machin, G. I. T.
Catholic Question in English Politics, 1820-1830, The   II-673
McIntosh, Thomas P.
Potato, Its History, Varieties, Culture, and Diseases, The   I-427
Macintyre, Captain Donald
Battle of the Atlantic, The   III-1257
McKay, Donald Cope
National Workshops: A Study in the French Revolution of 1848, The   II-787
Mackie, John Duncan
Earlier Tudors, 1485-1558, The. Vol. VII of *The Oxford History of England*   I-9
Mack Smith, Denis
Cavour and Garibaldi   II-873
Italy: A Modern History   II-960; 1097; 1111
Maestro, Marcello T.
Voltaire and Beccaria as Reformers of Criminal Law   I-457
Malof, Peter
Common Market: The European Community in Action, The   III-1604
Malozemoff, Andrew
Russian Far Eastern Policy, 1881-1904: With Special Emphasis on the Causes of the Russo-Japanese War   III-1151
Mammarella, Giuseppe
Italy After Fascism: A Political History, 1943-1965   III-1539
Manceron, Claude
Austerlitz: The Story of a Battle   II-570
Mann, Julia De Lacy
Cotton Trade and Industrial Lancashire, 1600-1780   I-406
Mansergh, Nicholas
Irish Question, 1840-1921, The   III-1236
Mantoux, Paul
Industrial Revolution in the Eighteenth Century, The   I-407
Marconi, Degna M.
My Father, Marconi   II-1081
Marcus, Harold G.

"Imperialism and Expansionism in Ethiopia from 1865-1900," in *Colonialism in Africa, 1870-1960.* Vol. I: *The History and Politics of Colonialism, 1870-1914*   II-1097

Marder, Arthur J.
Anatomy of British Sea Power, The. A History of British Naval Policy in the Pre-Dreadnought Era, 1880-1905   II-1059
From the Dreadnought to Scapa Flow. Vol. I: *The Road to War*   III-1189
From the Dreadnought to Scapa Flow. Vol. III: *Jutland and After*   III-1269

Mariéjol, Jean H.
Spain of Ferdinand and Isabella, The   I-3

Maritain, Jacques
Bergsonian Philosophy and Thomism   III-1185

Marlowe, John
World Ditch: The Making of the Suez Canal   II-819

Marriott, Sir J. A. R.
Eastern Question: An Historical Study in Diplomacy, The   I-477
Evolution of Prussia, The   II-605

Marshall-Cornwall, James
Napoleon as Military Commander   II-557; 591

Marshall, Samuel L.
Swift Sword: The Historical Record of Israel's Victory, June, 1967   III-1657

Marx, Karl
Critique of the Gotha Program   II-995

Mason, Edward S.
Paris Commune: An Episode in the History of the Socialist Movement, The   II-986

Mathiez, Albert
French Revolution, The   I-530

Mattingly, Garrett
Armada, The   I-195
Renaissance Diplomacy   I-24

Mauriac, François
De Gaulle   III-1686

Maurois, André
Life of Sir Alexander Fleming, The   III-1336

May, Arthur J.
Hapsburg Monarchy, 1867-1914, The   II-942

Mayer, Arno J.
Politics and Diplomacy of Peacemaking: Containment and Counterrevolution at Versailles, 1918-1919   III-1287

Mazlish, Bruce
Riddle of History, The   III-1280

Mazour, Anatole G.
First Russian Revolution: The Decembrist Revolt, The   II-667

Medlicott, W. N.
Bismarck and Modern Germany   II-920
Congress of Berlin and After: A Diplomatic History of the Near Eastern Settlement,

1878-1880, The   II-1011

Mehnert, Klaus
Peking and Moscow   III-1586

Merriman, Roger B.
Rise of the Spanish Empire in the Old World and in the New, The. Vol. II: *The Catholic Kings*   I-3
Rise of the Spanish Empire in the Old World and in the New, The. Vol. IV: *The Prudent King*   I-191

Metchnikoff, Élie (Ilya Mechnikov)
Founders of Modern Medicine, The   III-1175

Meyer, Arnold Oskar
England and the Catholic Church Under Queen Elizabeth   I-177

Meyer, Carl S.
Elizabeth I and the Religious Settlement of 1559   I-170

Michelet, Jules
History of the French Revolution   I-503; 508

Mill, John Stuart
Auguste Comte and Positivism   II-805

Miller, Townsend
Castles and the Crown, The   I-41

Moore, Barrington
Soviet Politics: The Dilemma of Power   III-1307

Morgan, George A.
What Nietzsche Means   II-1026

Morison, Samuel Eliot
Admiral of the Ocean Sea: A Life of Christopher Columbus   I-18

Moulton, J. L.
Norwegian Campaign of 1940, The   III-1449

Mowat, Charles Loch
Britain Between the Wars, 1918-1940   III-1318; 1327

Namier, Sir Lewis B.
Europe in Decay: A Study of Disintegration, 1936-1940   III-1443

Neill, Stephen Charles
History of the Ecumenical Movement, 1517-1948, A   III-1552

Newbolt, Henry
Naval Operations   III-1255

Newhall, Beaumont
Latent Image: The Discovery of Photography   II-751

Nicolaevsky, Boris I.
"Secret Societies and the First International," in Drachkovitch's *The Revolutionary Internationals, 1864-1943*   II-899

Nicolson, Harold
Congress of Vienna: A Study of Allied Unity, 1812-1822, The   II-615; 627
Portrait of a Diplomatist: Sir Arthur Nicholson, Bart. First Lord Carnock: A Study in Old

Diplomacy   III-1199

Nitske, W. Robert
Rudolf Diesel: Pioneer of the Age of Power
II-1101

Noguères, Henri
Massacre of St. Bartholomew, The   I-188

Nolte, Ernest
Three Faces of Fascism   III-1302

Noonan, John T., Jr.
*Contraception: A History of Its Treatment by
the Catholic Theologians and Canonists*
III-1662

Nove, Alec
Economic Rationality and Soviet Politics
III-1331

Nowell, Charles E.
History of Portugal, A   I-306; II-647; 677;
724; III-1221
Magellan's Voyage Around the World   I-71

Nystrom, J. Warren
*Common Market: The European Community
in Action, The*   III-1604

O'Ballance, Edgar
Algerian Insurrection, 1954-1962, The   III-
1630

O'Dea, William T.
Social History of Lighting, The   II-755

Offler, H. S.
Short History of Switzerland, A   II-794

Ogg, David
*England in the Reigns of James II and William
III*   I-388
Europe in the Seventeenth Century   I-350;
355

O'Gorman, Edmundo
*Invention of America: An Inquiry into the His-
torical Nature of the New World and the
Meaning of Its History, The*   I-19

Okey, Thomas
Italy Today   II-1112
Venice and Its Story   I-34

O'Malley, C. D.
Andreas Vesalius of Brussels, 1514-1564
I-134

Padover, Saul K.
Life and Death of Louis XVI, The   I-521

Pares, Sir Bernard
History of Russia, A   I-200

Park, Joseph
English Reform Bill of 1867, The   II-933

Parkes, Oscar
British Battleships   III-1190

Parr, Charles McKew
Ferdinand Magellan, Circumnavigator
I-70

Pastor, Ludwig
*History of the Popes from the Close of the Mid-
dle Ages, The*   I-46

Pennell, Elizabeth Robins

*Lithography and Lithographers. Some Chap-
ters in the History of the Art*   I-545

Pennell, Joseph
*Lithography and Lithographers. Some Chap-
ters in the History of the Art*   I-545

Penrose, Boies
*Travel and Discovery in the Renaissance, 1420-
1620*   I-13

Petrie, Charles
Earlier Diplomatic History, 1492-1713   I-
343

Pflanze, Otto
Bismarck and the Development of Germany
II-921

Philips, C. E. Lucas
Alamein   III-1468

Phillipson, Coleman
*Three Criminal Law Reformers: Beccaria,
Bentham, Romilly*   I-458

Pope, Hugh
English Versions of the Bible   I-245

Postgate, Raymond
British Common People, 1746-1946, The
II-739

Potter, G. R.
Short History of Switzerland, A   II-796

Prescott, William H.
History of the Conquest of Mexico   I-61

Price, Arnold H.
Evolution of the Zollverein, The   II-713

Price, Harry Bayard
Marshall Plan and Its Meaning, The   III-
1535

Pryce-Jones, David
Hungarian Revolution, The   III-1597

Radcliff, Peter
Limits of Liberty: Studies of Mill's On Liberty
II-845

Ramos Oliveira, Antonio
*Politics, Economics, and Men of Modern Spain,
1808-1946*   II-636; 728; III-1261

Reddaway, W. F.
Cambridge History of Poland, The. Vol. II:
From Augustus to Pilsudski, 1697-1935
I-471; II-889

Renouvin, Pierre
Immediate Origins of the War, The   III-
1343

Roberts, Michael
*Gustavus Adolphus: A History of Sweden, 1611-
1632.* Vol. II: *1626-1632*   I-275

Robertson, Sir Charles Grant
Evolution of Prussia, The   II-605

Robertson, Priscilla
Revolutions of 1848: A Social History   II-
788

Robertson, Terence
Crisis: The Inside Story of the Suez Conspiracy
III-1591

Robinson, G. T.

Rural Russia Under the Old Regime   II-868
Robinson, Ronald
    Africa and the Victorians   II-1051
Rodgers, William L.
    Naval Warfare Under Oars, IV to XVI Centuries   I-182
Rohwer, J.
    Decisive Battles of World War II: The German View   III-1469; 1475; 1494
Rolt, L. T. C.
    Aeronauts: A History of Ballooning, 1783-1903, The   I-498
    James Watt   I-461
    Mechanicals, The   II-1103
    Railway Revolution, The   II-609
    Short History of Machine Tools, A   I-527
Romani, George T.
    Neapolitan Revolution of 1820-1821, The   II-641
Rossi, A.
    Russo-German Alliance, August, 1939-June, 1941, The   III-1438
Roth, Guenther
    Social Democrats in Imperial Germany, The   II-1016
Rouse, Ruth
    History of the Ecumenical Movement, 1517-1948, A   III-1552
Rowe, Vivian
    Great Wall of France, The   III-1360
Rowen, Herbert H.
    Ambassador Prepares for War, The   I-346
Roy, Jules
    Battle of Dien Bien Phu, The   III-1582
Russell, Ruth B.
    History of the United Nations Charter: The Role of the United States, 1940-1945, A   III-1509
Rynne, Xavier
    Vatican Council Two   III-1638

Salaman, Redcliffe N.
    History and Social Influence of the Potato, The   I-426
Salisbury, Harrison E.
    Soviet Union: The First Fifty Years, The   III-1621
    War Between Russia and China   III-1680
Salmon, J. H. M.
    French Wars of Religion, The   I-165; 206
Salvemini, Gaetano
    Fascist Dictatorship in Italy, The   III-1321
Santillana, Giorgio de
    Crime of Galileo, The   I-287
Schapiro, Leonard
    Communist Party of the Soviet Union, The   II-1106; III-1158; 1350
Schellenger, Harold Kent, Jr.
    S. P. D. in the Bonn Republic: A Socialist Party Modernizes, The   III-1693

Schieldrop, Edgar B.
    Highway, The   II-1036
Schmitt, Bernadotte E.
    Annexation of Bosnia, 1908-1909, The   III-1204
    Coming of the War, 1914, The   III-1246; 1344
Schrier, Arnold
    Ireland and the American Emigration, 1850-1900   II-762
Schweitzer, Albert
    Quest of the Historical Jesus: A Critical Study of Its Progress from Reimarus to Wrede, The   II-894
Seaman, L. C. B.
    From Vienna to Versailles   II-851
Seaver, Henry L.
    Great Revolt in Castile, The   I-74
Senefelder, Alois
    Invention of Lithography, The   I-544
Serafian, Michael
    Pilgrim, The   III-1639
Seton-Watson, Christopher
    Italy from Liberalism to Fascism, 1870-1925   II-1097
Seton-Watson, Hugh
    Decline of Imperial Russia, 1855-1914, The   III-1181
Seymour, Charles
    Electoral Reform in England and Wales   II-706; 931; 1040
Sharlin, Harold I.
    Making of the Electrical Age, The   II-651
Shirer, William L.
    Rise and Fall of the Third Reich, The   III-1379
Silverberg, Robert
    Morning of Mankind, The   II-823
Simon, Walter M.
    Failure of the Prussian Reform Movement, 1807-1819, The   II-577
Simpson, Lesley Byrd
    Encomienda in New Spain, The   I-132
Smiles, Samuel
    Industrial Biography: Iron Workers and Tool Makers   I-526
Smith, Jean Edward
    Defense of Berlin, The   III-1626
Snell, John L.
    Meaning of Yalta, The   III-1504
Solmi, Arrigo
    Making of Modern Italy, The   II-926
Spector, I.
    "M. V. Lomonosov and the Founding of Moscow University," in *Readings in Russian History and Culture*   I-433
Spector, M.
    "M. V. Lomonosov and the Founding of Moscow University," in *Readings in Russian History and Culture*   I-433
Spitta, Philipp

Johann Sebastian Bach   I-382
Stankiewicz, W. J.
  *Politics and Religion in Seventeenth Century
  France: A Study of Political Ideas from the
  Monarchomachs to Bayle, as Reflected in the
  Toleration Controversy*   I-262
Stavenow, Ludvig
  "Scandinavia," in *The Cambridge Modern
  History*   III-1168
Stavrianos, L. S.
  Balkans Since 1453, The   I-89; 370; 476
Steefel, Lawrence D.
  *Bismarck, the Hohenzollern Candidacy, and
  the Origins of the Franco-German War of
  1870*   II-952; 956
Stephen, Sir Leslie
  English Utilitarians, The   I-535; II-631
Stern, Fritz
  *Politics of Cultural Despair: A Study in the Rise
  of the Germanic Ideology, The*   III-1366
Stern, Karl
  *Third Revolution: A Study of Psychiatry and
  Religion, The*   III-1141
Stirling-Maxwell, William
  Don Juan of Austria   I-183
Strasser, Otto
  Hitler and I   III-1393
Sulzbach, Walter
  *German Experience with Social Insurance.
  (Studies in Individual and Collective
  Security.* No. 2)   II-1030
Sumner, B. H.
  Peter the Great and the Emergence of Russia
  I-365
  Russia and the Balkans, 1870-1880   II-
  1011
Sutherland, John
  Men of Waterloo   II-620
Symons, Julian
  General Strike, The   III-1326
Szulc, Tad
  Czechoslovakia Since World War II   III-
  1671

Tanner, J. R.
  "Revolution of 1688, The" in *English Consti-
  tutional Conflicts of the Seventeenth Cen-
  tury, 1603-1689*   I-362
Tarle, E. V.
  Napoleon's Invasion of Russia   II-587
Tasca, Angelo
  Rise of Italian Fascism, The   III-1322
Taylor, A. J. P.
  Bismarck: The Man and the Statesman
  II-967; 971
  Churchill Revised: A Critical Assessment
  III-1530
  *Struggle for Mastery in Europe, 1848-1918,
  The*   II-925
Taylor, Telford
  March of Conquest, The   III-1459

Temperley, Harold W. V.
  England and the Near East: The Crimea
  II-814
  *Foreign Policy of Canning, 1822-1827: En-
  gland, the Neo-Holy Alliance, and the New
  World, The*   II-656
  "Peace of Paris, The" in *The Cambridge His-
  tory of the British Empire*   I-453
Thayer, William R.
  Life and Times of Cavour, The   II-840
Thomas, Hugh
  Spanish Civil War, The   III-1447
  Suez   III-1592
Thompson, James M.
  Napoleon Bonaparte   II-592
  Robespierre and the French Revolution   I-
  531
Thompson, James Westfall
  Wars of Religion in France, 1559-1576, The
  I-164
Thomson, David
  Democracy in France Since 1870   III-
  1413
Thomson, M. A.
  "War of the Austrian Succession, The" in *The
  New Cambridge Modern History*   I-422
Tobias, Fritz
  Reichstag Fire: Legend and Truth, The
  III-1380
Toland, John
  Battle: The Story of the Bulge   III-1498
Tomlinson, William W.
  North Eastern Railway   II-661
Trend, John B.
  Origins of Modern Spain, The   II-1121
Trevelyan, George Macaulay
  Garibaldi and The Thousand   II-862
Trotsky, Leon
  *Revolution Betrayed: What Is the Soviet Union
  and Where Is It Going?, The*   III-1349
Tuchman, Barbara W.
  Proud Tower, The   III-1194
Tucker, Robert C.
  *Soviet Political Mind: Studies in Stalinism and
  Post-Stalin Change, The*   III-1332

Ulam, Adam B.
  *Bolsheviks: The Intellectual and Political His-
  tory of the Triumph of Communism in
  Russia, The*   II-1107; III-1276
  *Expansion and Coexistence: The History of
  Soviet Foreign Policy, 1917-1967*   III-
  1437

Vandenberg, Arthur H., Jr.
  Private Papers of Senator Vandenberg, The
  III-1509
Versfeld, Marthinus
  Essay on the Metaphysics of Descartes, An
  I-297
Von Laue, Theodore H.

Sergei Witte and the Industrialization of Russia
II-1064

Wadsworth, Alfred P.
Cotton Trade and Industrial Lancashire, 1600-1780, The I-407
Wallace, Lillian Parker
Papacy and European Diplomacy, 1869-1878, The II-972
Walters, F. P.
History of the League of Nations, A III-1292
Ward, A. W.
"Outbreak of the Thirty Years' War, The," in *The Cambridge Modern History* I-253
"Peace of Utrecht and the Supplementary Pacifications, The," in *The Cambridge Modern History* I-402
"Peace of Westphalia, The," in *The Cambridge Modern History* I-311
"Protestant Collapse, 1620-1630, The," in *The Cambridge Modern History* I-272
Wardman, H. W.
Ernest Renan: A Critical Biography II-895
Warner, Oliver
Battle of the Nile, The I-540
Warth, Robert
Joseph Stalin III-1569
Watson, J. Steven
Reign of George III, 1760-1815, The II-554
Watson, James D.
Double Helix, The III-1575
Molecular Biology of the Gene III-1576
Watt, Richard M.
Kings Depart, The. The Tragedy of Germany: Versailles, and the German Revolution III-1288
Webb, Beatrice
English Local Government II-733
Webb, Sidney
English Local Government II-733
Weber, Eugen
Action Française: *Royalism and Reaction in Twentieth Century France* III-1389
Webster, Richard A.
Cross and the Fasces: Christian Democracy and Fascism in Italy, The III-1357
Webster, Sir Charles
Congress of Vienna, 1814-1815, The II-614
Foreign Policy of Castlereagh, 1812-1815, The II-626
Foreign Policy of Castlereagh, 1815-1822, The II-657
Strategic Air Offensive Against Germany, 1939-1945, The III-1463
Wedgewood, C. V.
Life of Cromwell, The I-333
Thirty Years War, The I-252; 271; 291; 310

Wendel, François
Calvin: The Origins and Development of His Religious Thought I-119
Werth, Alexander
De Gaulle: A Political Biography III-1685
De Gaulle Revolution, The III-1609
France in Ferment III-1388
Twilight of France, 1933-1940, The III-1454
Wheeler-Bennett, John W.
Munich: Prologue to Tragedy III-1431
White, John A.
Diplomacy of the Russo-Japanese War, The III-1150
Whyte, Arthur James
Evolution of Modern Italy, The II-778
Political Life and Letters of Cavour, 1848-1861, The II-841; 872
Wilkinson, Maurice
History of the League of Sainte Union, 1576-1595, A I-205
Williams, Eric
Capitalism and Slavery II-720
Williams, Francis
Socialist Britain: Its Background, Its Present, and an Estimate of Its Future III-1519
Williams, L. Pearce
Michael Faraday: A Biography II-650
Williams, Philip M.
Crisis and Compromise: Politics in the Fourth Republic III-1611
Williamson, James A.
Short History of British Expansion: The Modern Empire and Commonwealth, A III-1374
Willson, D. Harris
King James VI and I I-228
Wilmot, Chester
Struggle for Europe, The III-1479; 1493; 1503
Wilson, Arthur M.
Diderot, The Testing Years, 1713-1759 I-429
Wilson, Charles Morrow
Rudolf Diesel: Pioneer of the Age of Power II-1101
Windsor, The Duke of
King's Story, A III-1422
Winwar, Frances
Jean-Jacques Rousseau: Conscience of an Era I-449
Witte, Sergei
Memoirs of Count Witte, The III-1172
Wolf, John B.
Emergence of the Great Powers: 1685-1715, The. Vol. VII of *The Rise of Modern Europe* series I-361
Louis XIV I-351; 355
Wolfe, Don M.
Milton in the Puritan Revolution I-321
Wolfers, Arnold

Britain and France Between Two Wars   III-1361

Woodham-Smith, Cecil B.
Great Hunger, The. Ireland, 1845-1849   II-761

Woodward, E. L.
Three Studies in European Conservatism   II-771

Wren, Melvin C.
Course of Russian History, The   III-1158

Young, Crawford
Politics in the Congo   III-1616

Young, Kenneth
Rhodesia and Independence   III-1646

Zagoria, Donald S.
Sino-Soviet Conflict, 1956-1961, The   III-1585

Zeldin, Theodore
Political System of Napoleon III, The   II-811

Zeman, Zbynek A.
Prague Spring: A Report on Czechoslovakia, 1968   III-1669

Zetlin, Mikhail
Decembrists, The   II-668

LITERATURE FOR ADDITIONAL RECOMMENDED READING

Abbott, Walter M., S.J.
Documents of Vatican Two, The   III-1641
Abramovich, Raphael R.
Soviet Revolution, 1917-1939, The   III-1333; 1352
Ackerknecht, Erwin H.
Short History of Medicine, A   I-137; II-1087
Aczel, Tamas
Revolt of the Mind, The   III-1599
Ten Years After   III-1600
Adam, Arthur E.
Russian Revolution and Bolshevik Victory: Why and How?, The. Problems in European Civilization series   III-1278
Adams, Francis O.
Swiss Confederation, The   II-797
Adams, Frank Dawson
Birth and Development of the Geological Sciences, The   II-681
Ahnlund, Nils
Gustav Adolf the Great   I-277
Ahrons, E. L.
British Steam Railway Locomotive, 1825-1925, The   II-611
Albertini, Luigi
Origins of the War of 1914, The   III-1155; 1206; 1244; 1346
Albrecht-Carrie, René
Italy from Napoleon to Mussolini   II-928; 982
Alexander, Ian W.
Bergson: Philosopher of Reflection   III-1186
Allen, Ward
Translating for King James: Notes Made by a Translator of King James's Bible   I-246
Alston, Patrick L.
Education and the State in Tsarist Russia   I-435
Altamira, Rafael
History of Spain, A   I-75; 303; 375; 445; II-584; 597; 637; 729; 1122; III-1261
Altholz, Josef
Churches in the Nineteenth Century, The   II-774
Amme, Carl H., Jr.
NATO Without France: A Strategic Appraisal   III-1653
Anderson, Eugene Newton
Nationalism and the Cultural Crisis in Prussia, 1806-1815   II-579
Anderson, Fulton H.
Philosophy of Francis Bacon, The   I-258
Anderson, Ingvar
History of Sweden, A   I-277
Anderson, M. S.
*Eastern Question, 1774-1923: A Study in Inter-

national Relations, The*   I-479; II-1012
Andrade, E. N. da Costa
Approach to Modern Physics, An   II-1088
Physics for the Modern World   II-1088
Aradi, Zsolt
Pius XI, the Pope and the Man   III-1357
Arendt, Hannah
Origins of Totalitarianism   II-1079
Armitage, Angus
Copernicus: The Founder of Modern Astronomy   I-142
John Kepler   I-240
Armstrong, Edward
Emperor, Charles V, The   I-67; 95; 156
Armstrong, Hamilton Fish
When There Is No Peace   III-1432
Aron, Raymond
De Gaulle, Israel, and the Jews   III-1658
On War   III-1565
Artz, Frederick B.
Reaction and Revolution: 1814-1832. Vol. XIII of *The Rise of Modern Europe* series   II-601; 616; 644; 659; 685; 797
Ash, Bernard
Norway, 1940   III-1450
Ashley, Maurice
Greatness of Oliver Cromwell, The   I-335
Louis XIV and the Greatness of France   I-327
Oliver Cromwell and the Puritan Revolution   I-335
Asquith, Cyril
Life of Herbert Henry Asquith, Lord Oxford and Asquith, The   III-1218; 1239
Atkinson, C. T.
"War of the Austrian Succession, The," in *The Cambridge Modern History*   I-422
Atkinson, William C.
History of Spain and Portugal, A   II-677; 725; III-1222; 1677
Attlee, Clement R.
Labor Party in Perspective—and Twelve Years Later, The   III-1521
Aulard, Alphonse
French Revolution: A Political History, 1789-1804, The   I-523; 532

Badoglio, Pietro
War in Abyssinia, The   III-1405
Bailey, Thomas A.
Woodrow Wilson and the Lost Peace   III-1294
Bain, Leslie B.
Reluctant Satellites, The   III-1599
Bain, R. Nisbet
"Charles XII and the Great Northern War," in *The Cambridge Modern History*   I-379

Baird, H. M.
History of the Rise of the Huguenots   I-166
Baker, Ray Stannard
Woodrow Wilson and the World Settlement: Written from His Unpublished and Personal Material   III-1294
Baldwin, Hanson
Great Mistakes of the War   III-1481
World War I   III-1248
Ball, Margaret M.
Post-War German-Austrian Relations: The Anschluss Movement, 1918-1936   III-1399
Balz, Albert G.
Descartes and the Modern Mind   I-298
Barber, James
Rhodesia: The Road to Rebellion   III-1647
Barker, Joseph Edmund
Diderot's Treatment of the Christian Religion in the Encyclopédie   I-431
Barnes, Donald Grove
George III and William Pitt, 1783-1806   II-555
Barnes, Harry Elmer
Genesis of the World War: An Introduction to the Problem of War Guilt, The   III-1248; 1346
Barnes, John
Baldwin: A Biography   III-1328; 1424
Barnett, Corelli
Swordbearers: Studies in Supreme Command in the First World War, The   III-1265
Barnett, Lincoln
Universe and Doctor Einstein, The   III-1163
Barnett, Samuel Anthony
Century of Darwin, A   II-859
Barnhouw, Erik
Tower in Babel, A   II-1083
Barr, Stringfellow
Mazzini: Portrait of an Exile   II-702
Barraclough, Geoffrey
Origins of Modern Germany, The   I-95; 152; 293; II-607
Bartlett, C. J.
Castlereagh   II-659
Barzun, Jacques
Darwin, Marx, Wagner: Critique of a Heritage   II-785; 859
Bastian, Hartmut
And Then Came Man   II-826
Batiffol, Louis
Century of the Renaissance, The   I-34; 48
Marie de Medici and the French Court in the Seventeenth Century   I-283
Bayne, C. G.
Anglo-Roman Relations, 1558-1565   I-179
Beaglehole, J. C.
Exploration of the Pacific, The   I-71
Beatty, Charles
Ferdinand de Lesseps   II-821; 1069

Beaufre, Andre
Suez Expedition: 1956, The   III-1593
Bebel, August
My Life   II-997
Beck, Leslie J.
Metaphysics of Descartes, The   I-298
Beckett, J. C.
Making of Modern Ireland, The   III-1318
Belden, Albert David
George Whitefield, the Awakener   I-413
Belloc, Hilaire
Charles II, The Last Rally   I-340
Richelieu   I-262
Waterloo   II-622
Beloff, Max
Foreign Policy of Soviet Russia, 1929-1941, The   III-1438
Benians, E. A.
Cambridge History of the British Empire, The. Vol. VIII: *South Africa, Rhodesia and the High Commission Territories*   II-1132
Bennett, Geoffrey
Battle of Jutland, The   III-1270
Benton, Wilburn E.
Nuremberg: German Views of the War Trials   III-1525
Berkeley, George F.
Campaign of Adowa and the Rise of Menelik, The   II-1099
Italy in the Making, June 1846-January, 1848   II-780
Berkeley, J.
Italy in the Making, June 1846-January, 1848   II-780
Berlin, Isaiah
Karl Marx: His Life and Environment   II-901
Bernardini, Gilberto
Galileo and the Scientific Revolution   I-289
Berry, W. Turner
Annals of Printing: A Chronological Encylopedia from the Earliest Times to 1950   I-546
Biddle, James S.
Nazi Soviet Relations, 1939-1941. Documents from the Archives of the German Foreign Office   III-1438
Binchy, Daniel
Church and State in Fascist Italy   III-1323; 1405
Bindoff, S. T.
Tudor England. Vol. V of *The Pelican History of England*   I-10
Binkley, Robert C.
Realism and Nationalism, 1852-1871. Vol. XV of *The Rise of Modern Europe* series   II-854; 943; 962
Bird, Anthony
Antique Automobiles   II-1037
Birmingham, William

What Modern Catholics Think of Birth Control
III-1665
Birt, Henry Norbert, O.S.B.
Elizabethan Religious Settlement, The I-172
Blair, Lowell
Memoirs of Catherine the Great, The I-468
Blake, Robert
Disraeli II-934
Unknown Prime Minister: The Life and Times of Andrew Bonar Law, The III-1239
Blakiston, Noel
Roman Question, The II-962; 982
Blanchard, Jean Pierre
First Air Voyage in America: The Times, the Place, and the People of the Blanchard Balloon Voyage of January 9, 1793, (Philadelphia to Woodbury), The I-501
Blaugh, Mark
Ricardian Economics: A Historical Study II-632
Blinoff, Martha
Life and Thought in Old Russia I-435
Blitzer, Charles
Age of Power, The I-293
Bloch, Camille
Causes of the World War: An Historical Summary, The III-1346
Blond, Georges
Marne, The III-1253
Blum, J. G.
Lord and Peasant in Russia from the Ninth to the Nineteenth Century I-468
Bogardus, Emory Stephen
Development of Social Thought, The II-807
Boivin, André
Microbes III-1178
Bonham-Carter, Violet
Winston Churchill: An Intimate Portrait III-1227
Boni, Albert
Photographic Literature II-752
Bonin, Georges
Bismarck and the Hohenzollern Candidature for the Spanish Throne II-957
Bonomi, Ivanoe
From Socialism to Fascism: A Study of Contemporary Italy III-1323
Borer, Mary Cathcart
Mankind in the Making II-826
Born, Max
Einstein's Theory of Relativity III-1163
Bornkamm, Heinrich
Luther's World of Thought I-58
Bourdieu, Pierre
Algerians, The III-1632
Bourgeois, Émile
"Orleans Monarchy, The" in The Cambridge Modern History II-689
Bourne, Edward G.

Spain in America I-71
Bovill, E. W.
Battle of Alcazar, The I-192
Bowen, Charles F.
Conquest of the Seas: The History and Adventure of Seas and Ships II-1061
Sea: Its History and Romance, The II-1061
Bowle, John
Henry VIII I-108; 128
Boxer, Charles R.
Portuguese Seaborne Empire, 1415-1825, The I-14
Boyer, Richard E.
Oliver Cromwell and the Puritan Revolt: Failure of a Man or a Faith? Problems in European Civilization series I-336
Brace, Joan
Ordeal in Algeria III-1632
Brace, Richard M.
Ordeal in Algeria III-1632
Bradley, General Omar N.
Soldier's Story, A III-1500
Brady, Joseph H.
Rome and the Neapolitan Revolution of 1820-1821 II-644
Braganza-Cunha, Vicente
Revolutionary Portugal III-1222
Brandi, Karl
Emperor, Charles V, The I-43; 75; 85; 157
Brandt, Joseph A.
Towards the New Spain II-948
Brandt, Willy
My Road to Berlin III-1695
Braunthal, Julius
Tragedy of Austria, The III-1400
Brebner, John B.
Making of Modern Britain, The III-1376
Brenan, Gerald
Spanish Labyrinth: An Account of the Social and Political Background of the Civil War, The II-729; 948; 1122; III-1419
Breuil, Henri
Men of the Old Stone Age, The II-826
Bridge, John S. C.
History of France from the Death of Louis XI, A I-48
Briefs, Henry W.
NATO in Quest of Cohesion III-1559
Briggs, Asa
Age of Improvement, 1763-1867, The II-740
Victorian People: A Reassessment of Persons and Themes, 1851-1867 II-802; 934
Bright, Arthur A., Jr.
Electric-Lamp Industry: Technological Change and Economic Development from 1800-1947, The II-563; 756
Brinton, Crane
Decade of Revolution, 1789-1799, A. Vol. XI of *The Rise of Modern Europe* series

I-505; 509; 519; 523; 550
Lives of Talleyrand, The   II-601
Nietzsche   II-1026
Broad, Lewis
  Winston Churchill: The Years of Achievement
    III-1531
Broad, Roger
  Community Europe: A Short Guide to the Common Market   III-1605
Brodrick, James, S.J.
  Galileo, the Man, His Work, His Misfortunes
    I-289
  Progress of the Jesuits, 1556-1579, The   I-102
  Saint Ignatius Loyola, the Pilgrim Years
    I-102
Brogan, Denis W.
  Development of Modern France, 1870-1939, The   III-1390; 1415
  France Under the Republic, 1870-1939   II-987
Brook-Shepherd, Gordon
  Dollfuss   III-1428
Brown, Bernard E.
  De Gaulle Republic: Quest for Unity, The
    III-1688
Brown, Robert McFee
  Observer in Rome   III-1641
Bruce, F. F.
  British Bible: A History of Translations, The
    I-245
Bruford, W. H.
  "Organization and Rise of Prussia, The," in *The New Cambridge Modern History*
    I-399; 418
Brunet, Rene
  New German Constitution, The   III-1298
Bruun, Geoffrey
  Europe and the French Imperium, 1799-1814. Vol. XII of *The Rise of Modern Europe* series   II-571
  Revolution and Reaction   II-780
Bryant, Arthur
  Turn of the Tide: A History of the War Years Based on the Diaries of Field Marshal Lord Alanbrooke, The   III-1470
Bucke, Emory Stevens
  History of American Methodism, The   I-413
Buckle, George Earle
  Life of Benjamin Disraeli, Earl of Beaconsfield, The   II-934
Bull, Theodore
  Rhodesian Perspective. (Published in the U.S. as *Rhodesia: Crisis of Color.*)   III-1647
Bullock, Alan
  Hitler: A Study in Tyranny   III-1381; 1385; 1428; 1439
Burke-Gaffney, M. S., S.J.
  Kepler and the Jesuits   I-239
Burns, Arthur Lee

Peace-Keeping by U.S. Forces: From Suez to the Congo   III-1617
Burns, E. L.
  Between Arab and Israeli   III-1593
Burns, Edward McNall
  Counter Reformation, The   I-147
Burt, Alfred LeRoy
  Evolution of the British Empire and Commonwealth from the American Revolution
    II-1132; III-1376
Burton, W. G.
  Potato, The   I-427
Bury, J. B.
  History of the Papacy in the Nineteenth Century   II-773
Bury, J. P. T.
  France, 1814-1940   II-1056
  Gambetta and the National Defence   III-1146
  "Nationalities and Nationalism," in *The New Cambridge Modern History*   II-690
Busch, Moritz
  Bismarck in the Franco-Prussian War, 1870-1871   II-952
Bustin, Edouard
  "Congo, The," in *Five African States: Responses to Diversity*   III-1617
Buthman, William C.
  Rise of Integral Nationalism in France, The
    II-1056; 1069
Butler, Jeffrey
  Liberal Party and the Jameson Raid, The
    II-1132
Butler, Rohan D.
  Roots of National Socialism, 1783-1933, The
    III-1367
Butterfield, Herbert
  Origins of Modern Science, 1300-1800, The
    I-142
Butterworth, C. C.
  Literary Lineage of the King James Bible, The
    I-245
Byrnes, James F.
  Speaking Frankly   III-1511
Byrnes, Robert F.
  Antisemitism in Modern France   II-1069; 1079

Callahan, Daniel
  Catholic Case for Contraception, The   III-1665
Calman, Alvin
  Ledru-Rollin and the Second French Republic
    II-789
Calvin, John
  Institutes of the Christian Religion, The
    I-122
Campbell, William E.
  More's Utopia and Its Social Teaching   I-53
Cannon, William Ragsdale
  Theology of John Wesley, The   I-413

Capovilla, Loris
   Heart and Mind of John XXIII, The   III-1641
Cardwell, D. S. L.
   Steam Power in the Eighteenth Century   I-463
Carlson, Elof A.
   Gene: A Critical History, The   II-911
Carr, E. H.
   Bolshevik Revolution, 1917-1923, The   III-1277; 1308
   German-Soviet Relations Between the Two World Wars, 1919-1939   III-1439
   Michael Bakunin   II-901
   October Revolution: Before and After, The   III-1277
   Socialism in One Country, 1924-1926   III-1352
Carr, Herbert W.
   Henri Bergson: The Philosopher of Change   III-1185
Carr, Raymond
   Spain, 1808-1939   II-1122; III-1371
Carroll, E. Malcolm
   Germany and the Great Powers, 1866-1914: A Study in Public Opinion and Foreign Policy   III-1213
Case, Lynn M.
   French Opinion on War and Diplomacy During the Second Empire   II-816; 854; 879; 957
Cassirer, Ernst
   Philosophy of the Enlightenment   I-431
Cassirer, H. W.
   Commentary on Kant's Critique of Judgment, A   I-495
Castiglioni, Arturo
   History of Medicine, A   I-137; II-1088
Cattell, David C.
   Communism and the Spanish Civil War   III-1419
Caullery, Maurice
   History of Biology, A   II-911
Cerny, Karl H.
   NATO in Quest of Cohesion   III-1559
Chalmers, Rear Admiral W. S.
   Full Cycle   III-1460
Chamberlain, William Henry
   Russian Revolution, 1917-1921, The   II-1108; III-1159; 1182
Chambers, R. W.
   Thomas More   I-53
Chambers, Sir Edmund K.
   Elizabethan Stage, The   I-212
   Mediaeval Stage, The   I-212
Chandler, David G.
   Campaigns of Napoleon, The   II-559; 571; 593
Chapman, Charles E.
   History of Spain, A   I-223; 445
Chapman, Colin
   August Twenty First: The Rape of Czechoslo-vakia   III-1672
Chastenet, Jacques
   Godoy, Master of Spain   II-584
Chevalier, Jacques
   Henri Bergson   III-1185
Choate, Joseph H.
   Two Hague Conferences, The   III-1196
Choisy, Maryse
   Sigmund Freud: A New Appraisal   III-1142
Christie, O. F.
   Transition to Democracy, 1867-1914   II-1043
Chudoba, Bohdan
   Spain and the Empire, 1519-1643   I-86; 161
Churchill, Rogers P.
   Anglo-Russian Convention of 1907, The   III-1201
Churchill, Winston S.
   Lord Randolph Churchill   II-1043
   Second World War, The. Vol. I. *The Gathering Storm*   III-1362; 1439; 1450
   Second World War, The. Vol. III: *The Grand Alliance*   III-1471
   Second World War, The. Vol. IV: *The Hinge of Fate*   III-1481
   Second World War, The. Vol. V: *Closing the Ring*   III-1489; 1495
   Second World War, The. Vol. VI: *Triumph and Tragedy*   III-1495; 1500; 1505; 1531
   Unknown War, The   III-1253
   World Crisis, 1916-1918, The   III-1191; 1265
Chute, Marchette
   Shakespeare of London   I-212
Ciano, Count Galeazzo
   Ciano Diaries, 1939-1943, The   III-1445
Clancy, John G.
   Apostle for Our Time: Pope Paul VI   III-1641
Clapham, J. H.
   Economic Development of France and Germany, 1815-1914, The   II-714; 1032
   Economic History of Britain: The Railway Age, 1820-1850, An   II-736
Clark, George
   Later Stuarts, 1660-1714, The. Vol. X of *The Oxford History of England*   I-340; 363; 388
Clark, General Mark
   Calculated Risk   III-1489
Clark, Michael K.
   Algeria in Turmoil   III-1632
Clarke, Arthur C.
   Voice Across the Sea   II-837
Clarke, H. Butler
   Modern Spain, 1815-1898   II-597; 636; 729
Clarkson, Jesse D.
   History of Russia, A   I-235; III-1151
Claude, Inis L., Jr.
   Swords into Plowshares: The Problems and

Progress of International Organization
III-1196

Clay, Lucius D.
Germany and the Fight for Freedom   III-1549

Clemenceau, Georges
Grandeur and Misery of Victory   III-1288

Cleveland-Stevens, Edward
English Railways   II-611

Clough, Shepard B.
Economic History of Modern Italy, The
II-1112
*France: A History of National Economics,
1789-1939*   II-1047

Cohen, Israel
Zionist Movement, The   II-1093

Cohn, David L.
Combustion on Wheels   II-1037

Cole, G. D. H.
British Common People, 1746-1946, The
III-1227; 1328
Chartist Portraits   II-745
*Socialist Thought: Marxism and Anarchism,
1850-1890*   II-901; 997

Colletta, General Pietro
History of the Kingdom of Naples   II-644

Collier, Basil
Defence of the United Kingdom, The   III-1465
Second World War: A Military History, The
III-1362; 1476; 1490; 1500

Collier, Richard
Sands of Dunkirk, The   III-1460

Collins, James
History of Modern European Philosophy, A
II-1026; III-1186
"Sartre's Postulatory Atheism," in *The Existentialists*   III-1485

Collis, Maurice
Cortés and Montezuma   I-63

Colón, Fernando
*Life of the Admiral Christopher Columbus by
His Son Ferdinand*   I-20

Colton, Joel
Leon Blum, Humanist in Politics   III-1390

Columbus, Christopher
Journal of Christopher Columbus, The
I-20

Colvin, Ian
Life of Lord Carson, The   III-1239
Vansittart in Office   III-1445

Cooper, Lettice
James Watt   I-463

Cooper, Thompson
"General Monck," in the *Dictionary of National Biography*   I-340

Core, William C.
*Memoirs of the Duke of Marlborough with His
Original Correspondence*   I-394

Corley, Thomas A. B.

Democratic Despot: A Life of Napoleon III
II-812

Corrigan, Raymond, S. J.
Church and the Nineteenth Century, The
II-774; 906

Cortés, Hernán
*Fernando Cortés—His Five Letters of Relation
to the Emperor Charles V*   I-63

Costigan, Giovanni
Sigmund Freud: A Short Biography   III-1142

Cotterill, Henry B.
Italy from Dante to Tasso, 1300-1600   I-25

Cottrell, Alvin J.
Politics of the Atlantic Alliance, The   III-1560

Coulton, G. G.
Five Centuries of Religion   I-114

Coupland, Reginald
British Anti-Slavery Movement, The   II-721

Cowie, Leonard W.
Eighteenth-Century Europe   I-399; 418; 474
Seventeenth-Century Europe   I-348; 356

Crabites, Pierre
Spoliation of Suez, The   II-821

Craig, Gordon A.
Politics of the Prussian Army, 1640-1945, The
II-917; 922

Creasy, Edward S.
Fifteen Decisive Battles of the World   I-395

Cressy, Edward
Hundred Years of Mechanical Engineering, A
II-1037

Crick, Francis H. C.
"Genetic Code: II, The," in *Scientific American*   III-1576
"Genetic Code: III, The," in *Scientific American*   III-1576

Croce, Benedetto
History of Italy, 1871-1915, A   II-1099; 1112

Crocker, Lester G.
*Embattled Philosopher: A Biography of Denis
Diderot, The*   I-431

Cronin, Vincent
Louis XIV   I-328

Crook, Wilfrid H.
Communism and the General Strike   III-1328

Cropsey, Joseph
Polity and Economy   I-489

Cross, Richard K.
Flaubert and Joyce: The Rite of Fiction
II-832

Crow, John A.
Italy: A Journey Through Time   I-34
Spain: The Root and the Flower   I-303; 375;
II-597; 637

Crowe, S. E.

Berlin West Africa Conference, 1884-1885, The II-1051

Crowther, James G.
Francis Bacon, The First Statesman of Science I-258

Cummins, Clessie L.
My Days with the Diesel II-1104

Cunningham, C. D.
Swiss Confederation, The II-797

Cunningham, C. W.
Study in the Philosophy of Bergson, A III-1186

Curry, George
Edward Stettinus, Jr., 1944 to 1945 and James R. Byrnes, 1945 to 1947 III-1531

Curtis, Edmund
History of Ireland, A II-555; 763

Curtiss, John Shelton
Russian Army Under Nicholas I, 1825-1855, The II-696

Dabbs, Jack A.
French Army in Mexico, 1861-1867: A Study in Military Government, The II-879

Dahlerus, J. Birger
Last Attempt, The III-1445

Dallin, David
Rise of Russia in Asia, The III-1151

Dangerfield, George
Strange Death of Liberal England, 1910-1914, The III-1218; 1238

Daniel-Rops, Henri
Church in an Age of Revolution, 1789-1870, The II-907

Daniels, Emil
"Frederick the Great and His Successors," in *The Cambridge Modern History* I-418
"Prussia Under Frederick William I," in *The Cambridge Modern History* I-399

Daniels, Robert V.
Conscience of the Revolution: Communist Opposition in Soviet Russia, The III-1333

Davies, Godfrey
Early Stuarts, 1603-1660, The. Vol. IX of *The Oxford History of England* I-335

Davies, R. Trevor
Golden Century of Spain, 1501-1621, The I-43; 75; 192
Spain in Decline, 1621-1700 I-307; 375

Davis, H. C.
Age of Grey and Peel, The II-710; 740

Davy, Maurice J. B.
Interpretive History of Flight I-500

Dawes, Ben
Hundred Years of Biology, A II-911

Dawson, William H.
German Empire, 1867-1914, and the Unity Movement, The II-997; III-1213
Social Insurance in Germany, 1883-1911 II-1032

Dayan, Moshe
Diary of the Sinai Campaign III-1593

Deakin, F. W.
Brutal Friendship: Mussolini, Hitler, and the Fall of Italian Fascism, The III-1303

Dean, Vera Michelis
Europe in Retreat III-1432

Deane, John R.
Strange Alliance, The III-1506; 1516

De Bertier De Sauvigny, Guillaume
Metternich and His Times II-628

de Chardin, Pierre Teilhard
Appearance of Man, The II-826

Dedijer, Vladimir
Road to Sarajevo, The III-1206

De Gramont, Sanche
Age of Magnificence: Memoirs of the Court of Louis XIV by the Duc de Saint-Simon, The I-352

De Grunwald, Constantin
Tsar Nicholas I II-668; 696

De La Gorce, Paul-Marie
French Army: A Military-Political History, The III-1612

De Lubac, Henri, S.J.
Drama of Atheist Humanism, The II-807

De Madariaga, Salvador
*Christopher Columbus: Being the Life of the Very Magnificent Lord Don Cristóbal Colón, I-20
Hernán Cortés, Conqueror of Mexico I-63
Spain: A Modern History II-584; 729; 948; 1006; III-1261; 1371

De Oliveira Martins, Joaquim
History of Iberian Civilization, A II-677; 725

De Polnay, Peter
Garibaldi: The Man and the Legend II-865

Derfler, Leslie
The Dreyfus Affair, Tragedy of Errors? Problems in European Civilization series II-1079
Third French Republic, 1870-1940, The III-1415

Derleth, August W.
Saint Ignatius and the Company of Jesus I-102

De Roo, Peter
Material for a History of Pope Alexander VI I-30

Descartes, René
Discourse on Method, The I-298

Deutscher, Isaac
Prophet Armed: Trotsky, 1879-1921, The III-1352
Prophet Unarmed: Trotsky, 1921-1929, The III-1352
Stalin: A Political Biography III-1333; 1570

Devillers, Philippe
End of a War: Indochina, 1954 III-1576

Dibelius, Martin
  Jesus   II-896
Dibner, Bern
  Atlantic Cable, The   II-837
Dickens, A. G.
  English Reformation, The   I-114
  *Thomas Cromwell and the English Reforma-
    tion*   I-108; 114; 128
Dickinson, A. E. F.
  Art of Bach, The   I-384
Dickinson, G. L.
  International Anarchy, 1904-1914, The
    III-1196
  Revolution and Reaction in Modern France
    II-789; 987
Dickinson, Henry W.
  James Watt, Craftsman and Engineer   I-
    463
  Short History of the Steam Engine, A   I-463
Diderot, Denis
  Rameau's Nephew and Other Works   I-431
Dill, Marshall, Jr.
  Germany: A Modern History   II-793; 885
Dillard, Dudley D.
  Economics of John Maynard Keynes, The
    III-1410
Dinerstein, Herbert S.
  War and the Soviet Union   III-1565
Dixon, Richard Watson
  *History of the Church of England and the Abo-
    lition of the Roman Jurisdiction*   I-172
Dodds, M. H.
  *Pilgrimage of Grace, 1536-1537, and the Ex-
    eter Conspiracy, 1538, The*   I-114
Dodds, R.
  *Pilgrimage of Grace, 1536-1537, and the Ex-
    eter Conspiracy, 1538, The*   I-114
Dolan, Edward F.
  *Adventure with a Microscope: A Story of Robert
    Koch*   III-1178
Dönitz, Grand Admiral Karl
  Ten Years and Twenty Days   III-1258
Donworth, Albert B.
  Why Columbus Sailed   I-20
Doolin, Dennis J.
  *Territorial Claims in the Sino-Soviet Conflict:
    Documents and Analysis*   III-1682
Dougherty, James E.
  Politics of the Atlantic Alliance, The   III-
    1560
Douglas-Home, Charles
  Arabs and Israel: A Background Book, The
    III-1658
Draper, Theodore
  Six Weeks War, The   III-1455
Dreyer, John L.
  *History of Astronomy from Thales to Kepler,
    A*   I-142
Dubos, René
  Unseen World, The   III-1178
Dudon, Paul, S.J.

  Saint Ignatius of Loyola   I-102
Duff, Edward, S.J.
  *Social Thought of the World Council of
    Churches, The*   III-1554
Dugdale, Blanche
  Arthur James Balfour, 1906-1930   III-1218
Dunlap, Orrin E., Jr.
  Radio's 100 Men of Science   II-1083
Dunlop, Robert
  Daniel O'Connell   II-674
Durant, Ariel
  Rousseau and Revolution   I-450
Durant, Will
  Story of Civilization, The. Vol. V: *The Renais-
    sance*   I-25
  Story of Civilization, The. Vol. VI: *The Refor-
    mation*   I-85
  Story of Civilization, The. Vol. VIII: *The Age
    of Louis XIV*   I-348
  Story of Civilization, The. Vol. X: *Rousseau
    and Revolution*   I-450
Duranty, Walter
  Duranty Reports Russia   III-1333
Duroselle, Jean-Baptiste
  In Search of France   III-1689
Dwiggins, Don
  *Air Devils: The Story of Balloonists, Barnstorm-
    ers, and Stunt Pilots, The*   I-500

Earle, Edward M.
  *Modern France: Problems of the Third and
    Fourth Republics*   II-977
Eastman, Max
  Marxist: Is It Science?   II-785
Eden, Sir Anthony
  Full Circle: The Memoirs of Anthony Eden
    III-1593
Edmonds, Sir James E.
  Short History of World War I, A   III-1253
Edmundson, George
  "Brazil and Portugal," in *The Cambridge
    Modern History*   II-648; 677; 725
Edwards, R. Dudley
  *Great Famine: Studies in Irish History, 1845-
    1852*   II-762
Egner, G.
  Contraception vs. Tradition   III-1665
Ehrlich, A.
  Soviet Industrialization Debate, The   III-
    1333
Einaudi, Mario
  Early Rousseau, The   I-450
Eiseley, Loren C.
  Francis Bacon and the Modern Dilemma
    I-258
Eisenhower, General Dwight D.
  Crusade in Europe   III-1489; 1495; 1500
Eisenmann, Louis
  "Austria-Hungary," in *The Cambridge Mod-
    ern History*   II-944
Ellery, John B.

John Stuart Mill   II-848

Elliott-Binns, Leonard Elliott
Early Evangelicals: A Religious and Social Study, The   I-413

Elliott, John H.
Imperial Spain, 1469-1716   I-161; 197; 303; 307; 344

Elliot, W. Y.
New British Empire, The   III-1376

Ellis, C. Hamilton
British Railway History   II-611; 664
Trains We Loved, The   II-664

Elting, John Robert
Military History and Atlas of the Napoleonic Wars, A   II-589; 593

Elton, Geoffrey Rudolph
Revolutionary Idea in France, 1789-1891, The   II-789

Emmons, Terence
Russian Landed Gentry and the Peasant Emancipation of 1861, The   II-891

Engels, Friedrich
Peasant War in Germany, The   I-80

England, Sylvia Lennie
Massacre of St. Bartholomew, The   I-188

Ensor, Robert C.
England, 1870-1914. Vol. XIV of *The Oxford History of England*   III-1155

Epstein, Howard M.
Revolt in the Congo, 1960-1964   III-1617

Epstein, Samuel
Miracles from Microbes   III-1178; 1339

Ergang, Robert Reinhold
Myth of the All-Destructive Fury of the Thirty Years' War, The   I-312
Potsdam Führer: Frederick William I, Father of Prussian Militarism, The   I-418

Erikson, Erik H.
Young Man Luther   I-58

Erler, Fritz
Democracy in Germany   III-1695

Esper, Erwin A.
History of Psychology, A   III-1313

Esposito, Vincent J.
Concise History of World War I, A   III-1265
Military History and Atlas of the Napoleonic Wars, A   II-589; 593

Evans, Arthur F.
History of the Oil Engine, The   II-1104

Ewing, A. C.
Short Commentary on Kant's Critique of Pure Reason, *A*   I-495

Eyck, Erich
Bismarck and the German Empire   II-885; 952; 973; 1017

Falconi, Carlo
Popes in the Twentieth Century, The   III-1358

Fainsod, Merle
How Russia Is Ruled   III-1352

Falls, Cyril
Great Military Battles   I-395
Great War, 1914-1918, The   III-1248; 1253; 1265

Farrington, Benjamin
Philosophy of Francis Bacon, The   I-258

Faulkner, Harold U.
"Chartism and the Churches," in *Columbia University Studies in History, Economics, and Public Law*   II-746

Fawcett, H. W.
Fighting at Jutland, The   III-1270

Fay, C. R.
World of Adam Smith, The   I-490

Fay, Charles S.
Corn Laws and Social England, The   II-769

Fay, Sidney B.
Origins of the World War, The   II-1023; III-1201; 1206; 1244
Rise of Brandenburg-Prussia to 1786, The   I-418

Feiling, Keith
History of England, A   I-316

Feis, Herbert
Churchill, Roosevelt, and Stalin   III-1511

Ferguson, Eugene S.
"Expositions of Technology, 1851-1900," in *Technology in Western Civilization*   II-802

Fermi, Laura
Galileo and the Scientific Revolution   I-289
Mussolini   III-1303

French, Yvonne
Great Exhibition: 1851, The   II-802

Fichter, Joseph H., S.J.
James Laynez, Jesuit   I-147

Finch, James K.
Engineering and Western Civilization   I-463; II-756

Finer, Herbert
Mussolini's Italy   III-1323

Finer, S.
Life and Times of Edwin Chadwick, The   II-736

Firth, Charles H.
Last Years of the Protectorate, 1656-1658, The   I-335
Oliver Cromwell and the Rule of the Puritans in England   I-316; 335; 344
"Rupert," in the *Dictionary of National Biography*   I-316

Fischer, Fritz
Germany's Aims in the First World War   III-1346

Fisher, H. A. L.
History of England from the Accession of Henry VII to the Death of Henry VIII, The. Vol. V of *The Political History of England*   I-10

Napoleon   I-550; II-593; 622
Fitzgerald, Percy
    Great Canal at Suez, The   II-821
Fleming, D. F.
    Cold War and Its Origins, 1917-1960, The.
        Vol. I: *1917-1950*   III-1516
    Origins and Legacies of World War I, The
        III-1288
Flenley, Ralph
    Modern German History   II-885
Fletcher, Harris F.
    Intellectual Development of John Milton, The
        I-323
Fletcher, Willard Allen
    Mission of Vincent Benedetti to Berlin, 1864-
        1870, The   II-957
Florinsky, Michael T.
    Russia: A History and Interpretation   I-
        235; 379; 435; 441; 474; 478; II-695; 869;
        991; 1012; 1074; 1108; III-1159; 1201; 1206;
        1244; 1277
Flugel, John C.
    Hundred Years of Psychology, A   III-1313
Footman, David
    Ferdinand Lassalle, Romantic Revolutionary
        II-997
Forkel, Johann N.
    Über J. S. Bachs Leben, Kunst, and Kunst-
        werke   I-384
Fortescue, John W.
    History of the British Army, A   I-394
Frank, Philipp
    Einstein: His Life and Times   III-1163
Fredette, Raymond H.
    First Battle of Britain, 1917-1918, The   III-
        1466
Freidjung, Heinrich
    Struggle for Supremacy in Germany, 1859-
        1866, The   II-885; 922; 928
Frere, Walter Howard
    English Church in the Reigns of Elizabeth and
        James I, The   I-173
Friedrich, Carl J.
    Age of Power, The   I-293
    Age of the Baroque, 1610-1660, The. Vol. V of
        The Rise of Modern Europe series   I-249;
        253; 273; 312; 328
Frischauer, Paul
    Garibaldi: The Man and the Nation   II-865
    Imperial Crown: The Rise and Fall of the Holy
        Roman and Austrian Empires, The   I-
        293
Fromm, Erich
    Beyond the Chains of Illusion: My Encounter
        with Marx and Freud   III-1142
Frye, Roland Mushat
    Shakespeare: The Art of the Dramatist   I-
        212
Fuller, General J. F. C.
    Military History of the Western World, A
        I-183; 394

Second World War, 1939-1945, The   III-
    1362; 1476; 1481; 1500
Furniss, Edgar S., Jr.
    France, Troubled Ally: De Gaulle's Heritage
        and Prospects   III-1688
Fusfeld, Daniel Roland
    Age of the Economist, The   I-537; II-633

Gagnon, Paul A.
    France Since 1789   II-567; 601; 685; 977;
        1056; III-1146
Gaines, David P.
    World Council of Churches: A Study of Its
        Background and History, The   III-1554
Gairdner, James H.
    English Church in the Sixteenth Century, from
        the Accession of Henry VIII to the Death of
        Mary, 1509-1558, The   I-109; 128
Gallagher, John
    "Partition of Africa, The," in *The New Cam-*
        bridge Modern History   II-1052
Galland, Adolf
    First and the Last, The   III-1465
Gardiner, C. Harvey
    Naval Power in the Conquest of Mexico
        I-63
Gardiner, Samuel Rawson
    Constitutional Documents of the Puritan Revo-
        lution, The   I-268
    History of England from the Accession of
        James I to the Outbreak of the Civil War
        I-268
Gardner, Brian
    Year That Changed the World, 1945, The
        III-1516
Garibaldi, Giuseppe
    Memoirs of Garibaldi, The   II-865
Garnham, S. A.
    Submarine Cable, The   II-837
Garthoff, Raymond L.
    Sino-Soviet Military Relations   III-1682
Gash, Norman
    Mister Secretary Peel   II-674
    Politics in the Age of Peel   II-709
Gasquet, Francis Aidan, O.S.B.
    Henry VIII and the English Monasteries
        I-114
Gay, Peter
    Dilemma of Democratic Socialism, The   II-
        1017
Gee, Henry
    Documents Illustrative of English Church His-
        tory   I-128
    Elizabethan Clergy and the Settlement of Reli-
        gion, The   I-173
Geer, Walter
    Napoleon III: The Romance of an Emperor
        II-842
Geiringer, Karl
    Symbolism in the Music of Bach   I-384
Gernsheim, Alison

History of Photography from the Earliest Use
of the Camera Obscura in the Eleventh Cen-
tury Up to 1914, The   II-752
Gernsheim, Helmut
History of Photography from the Earliest Use
of the Camera Obscura in the Eleventh Cen-
tury Up to 1914, The   II-752
Gerschenkron, Alexander
Bread and Democracy in Germany   II-1032
Gershoy, Leo
French Revolution and Napoleon, The   I-
504; 509; 519; 532; II-559; 571; 593
From Despotism to Revolution, 1763-1789.
Vol. X of The Rise of Modern Europe series
I-445; 478; 484
Geyl, Pieter
Napoleon: For and Against   I-550; II-593
Revolt of the Netherlands, The   I-223
Gibson, Charles
Spain in America   I-132
Gide, Charles
History of Economic Doctrines, A   I-537;
II-632
Gilbert, Allan H.
Machiavelli's Prince and Its Forerunners
I-39
Gilbert, Felix
Machiavelli and Guicciardini   I-39
Gillespie, Frances E.
Labor and Politics in England, 1850-1867
II-934
Gillespie, Joan
Algeria Rebellion and Revolution   II-1632
Gillispie, Charles Coulston
Edge of Objectivity: An Essay in the History of
Scientific Ideas, The   II-859
Genesis and Geology   II-681
Gilmore, Myron P.
World of Humanism, The. Vol. II of The Rise
of Modern Europe series   I-25
Ginzberg, Eli
House of Adam Smith, The   I-490
Giolitti, Giovanni
Memoirs of My Life   III-1232
Girard, Raymond
Flaubert: A Collection of Critical Essays
II-832
Glaser, Hugo
Road to Modern Surgery, The   II-938
Glass, David Victor
Introduction to Malthus   I-537
Glasscheib, Hermann S.
March of Medicine, The   II-938; 1088
Gleason, S. Everett
Challenge to Isolation, 1937-1940, The
III-1438
Glover, Edward
Freud or Jung   III-1313
Glueck, Sheldon
Nuremberg Trial and Aggressive War, The
III-1525

Godechot, Jacques
Taking of the Bastille, July 14th, 1789   I-
515
Goguel, François
In Search of France   III-1689
Goguel, Maurice
Life of Jesus, The   II-896
Golino, Carlo L
Galileo Reappraised   I-289
Gómara, Francisco López de
Cortes: The Life of the Conqueror   I-63
Gooch, George P.
Cambridge History of British Foreign Policy,
The   II-1002
Catherine the Great and Other Studies   I-
468
"Continental Agreements," in The Cambridge
History of British Foreign Policy, 1783-1919
III-1201
Second Empire, The   II-812; 842
Goodspeed, Stephen S.
Nature and Function of International Organi-
zation, The   III-1511
Goodwin, Albert
European Nobility in the Eighteenth Century,
The   I-468
French Revolution, The   I-514
Gordon, Benjamin L.
Medieval and Renaissance Medicine   I-137
Gordon, Douglas H.
Censoring of Diderot's Encyclopédie and the
Re-Established Text, The   I-431
Gottschalk, Louis R.
Era of the French Revolution, 1715-1815, The
I-514; II-571
Goutour, Jacques R.
Algeria and France, 1830-1963   III-1632
Graham, Gerald
Politics of Naval Supremacy: Studies in British
Maritime Ascendancy, The   II-1061
Grant, A. J.
French Monarchy, 1483-1789, The   I-48
Grant, Frederick C.
Translating the Bible   I-245
Green, Robert W.
Protestantism and Capitalism: The Weber The-
sis and Its Critics   I-122
Green, William
Famous Bombers of the Second World War
III-1465
Greene, Nathaniel
Crisis and Decline: The French Socialist Party
in the Popular Front Eve   III-1415
Greenfield, Kent Roberts
Economics and Liberalism in the Risorgi-
mento: A Study of Nationalism in Lom-
bardy, 1814-1848   II-780
Greenslade, S. L.
Cambridge History of the Bible: The West from
the Reformation to the Present Day, The
I-245

Greenwood, Ernest
Amber to Amperes: The Story of Electricity
II-652
Gregg, Pauline
Social and Economic History of Britain, 1760-1950, A   II-736
Grene, Marjorie
Introduction in Existentialism   III-1485
Grew, Raymond
Sterner Plan for Italian Unity and the Italian National Society in the Risorgimento, A
II-875
Grey, Sir Edward
Twenty-Five Years, 1892-1916   III-1155; 1201
Griffith, William E.
Sino-Soviet Rift, The   III-1588
Grimm, Georg
Nuremberg: German Views of the War Trials
III-1525
Grimm, Harold J.
Reformation Era, 1500-1650, The   I-293
Grindrod, Muriel
Italy   III-1542
Grisar, Hartmann
Martin Luther: His Life and Work   I-58
Grosser, Alfred
Federal Republic of Germany, The   III-1627
Grunberger, Richard
Germany, 1918-1945   III-1298; 1381
Guérard, Albert
France: A Modern History   I-352; 356
Life and Death of an Ideal, The   I-327
Napoleon III   II-812; 854
Guillemard, F. H. H.
Life of Ferdinand Magellan and the Great Circumnavigation of the Globe, 1480-1581, The
I-71
Gulick, Charles A., Jr.
Austria: From Habsburg to Hitler   III-1399; 1428
Gulick, E. V.
"Final Coalition and the Congress of Vienna, 1813-1815, The," in *The New Cambridge Modern History*   II-617
Gurtov, Melvin
First Vietnam Crisis: Chinese Communist Strategy and United States Involvement, The
III-1582
Gwynn, Stephen
John Redmond's Last Years   III-1239
Gyorgy, Andrew
Communism in Perspective   II-785

Hackett, Francis
Francis the First   I-48
Hadfield, Robert L.
Submarine Cable, The   II-837
Haigh, Kenneth R.
Cableships and Submarine Cables   II-837

Haines, C. Grover
Origins and Background of the Second World War, The   III-1432
Haldane, Elizabeth S.
Descartes, His Life and Times   I-298
Hale, John R.
Age of Exploration   I-14
Machiavelli and Renaissance Italy   I-39
Halecki, Oscar
Borderlands of Western Civilization: A History of East Central Europe   I-90; 200; 249; 371; 478
History of Poland, A   II-891
Hales, Edward E.
Catholic Church in the Modern World, The
II-907
Revolution and Papacy, 1769-1846   I-519
Halevy, Elie
History of the English People in the Nineteenth Century, The. Vol. II: *The Liberal Awakening, 1815-1830*   II-674
History of the English People in the Nineteenth Century, The. Vol. III: *The Triumph of Reform, 1830-1841*   II-709; 736; 740
History of the English People in the Nineteenth Century, The. Vol. IV: *The Victorian Years, 1841-1895*   II-769
History of the English People in the Nineteenth Century, The. Vol. V: *Imperialism and the Rise of Labour, 1895-1905*   III-1155
History of the English People in the Nineteenth Century, The. Vol. VI: *The Rule of Democracy, 1905-1914*   III-1227
Hallberg, Charles W.
Franz Joseph and Napoleon III, 1852-1864: A Study of Austro-French Relations   II-816; 842; 853
Halle, Louis J.
Cold War as History, The   III-1531; 1560; 1627
Hallendorf, Carl
History of Sweden   I-277
Halpern, Ben
Idea of the Jewish State, The   II-1093
Hamburger, Joseph
Intellectuals in Politics: John Stuart Mill and the Philosophical Radicals   II-736
Hamerow, Theodore S.
Otto von Bismarck: A Historical Assessment
II-952
Hammer, Ellen J.
Struggle for Indochina, 1940-1955, The
III-1582
Haney, Lewis H.
History of Economic Thought   I-537; II-633
Hangen, Welles
Muted Revolution: East Germany's Challenge to Russia and the West, The   III-1627
Hankey, Lord
Politics and Errors   III-1525

Hansen, Alvin H.
  Guide to Keynes, A   III-1410
Harbage, Alfred
  Shakespeare's Audience   I-212
Harcave, Sidney
  Russia: A History   I-200
Harding, Bertita
  Phantom Crown: The Story of Maximilian and Carlota   II-879
Hardwick, Charles
  Articles of Religion, The   I-172
Hardy, W. J.
  Documents Illustrative of English Church History   I-128
Haring, C. H.
  Spanish Empire in America, The   I-132
Harlow, Alvin F.
  Old Wires and New Waves   II-1083
Harris, R. W.
  Absolutism and Enlightenment   I-356
Harrod, R. F.
  Life of John Maynard Keynes, The   III-1410
Hase, Commander Georg
  Kiel and Jutland   III-1270
Hassall, Arthur
  Mazarin   I-344
Hatch, Alden
  Man Named John, A   III-1641
Havens, George R.
  Age of Ideas, The   I-450
Hayek, Friedrich A.
  Counter-Revolution of Science: Studies on the Abuse of Reason, The   II-807
  Road to Serfdom, The   III-1410
Hayes, Carlton J. H.
  Contemporary Europe Since 1870   III-1168
  Generation of Materialism, 1871-1900, A. Vol. XVI of *The Rise of Modern Europe* series   II-1012; 1023; 1074; 1117
  Political and Social History of Modern Europe, A   II-798
Heathcote, Nina
  Peace-Keeping by U.N. Forces: From Suez to the Congo   III-1617
Heiden, Konrad
  Der Fuehrer: Hitler's Rise to Power   III-1381; 1385; 1394
Heilbroner, Robert L.
  Worldly Philosophers, The   I-537; II-633
Helmreich, Ernst C.
  Free Church in a Free State, A? The Catholic Church: Italy, Germany, France, 1864-1914. Problems in European Civilization series   II-973
Hendel, Charles W.
  Philosophy of Kant and Our Modern World, The   I-495
Henderson, Gavin B.
  Crimean War Diplomacy and Other Historical Essays   II-816

Henderson, Sir Nevile
  Failure of a Mission   III-1432
Henderson, William Otto
  Industrial Revolution in Europe, The   II-714
  State and the Industrial Revolution in Prussia, 1740-1870, The   II-714
Henriques, Robert
  One Hundred Hours to Suez: An Account of Israel's Campaign in the Sinai Peninsula   III-1593
Henriques, Ursula
  Religious Toleration in England, 1787-1833   II-674
Herold, J. Christopher
  Age of Napoleon, The   II-567
  Horizon Book of the Age of Napoleon, The   II-589
Hertslet, E.
  Map of Africa by Treaty, The   II-1051
Hertz, Frederick
  Development of the German Public Mind: A Social History of German Political Sentiments, Aspiration, and Ideas, The. Vol. I: *The Middle Ages and Reformation*   I-273; 311
  Development of the German Public Mind: A Social History of German Political Sentiments, Aspirations, and Ideas, The. Vol. II: *The Age of the Enlightenment*   I-399; 404; 418; 423; 440; 474; 484
Herz, John H.
  International Politics in the Atomic Age   III-1565
Hess, John L.
  Case for De Gaulle: An American Viewpoint, The   III-1653; 1688
Hill, Frank Ernest
  Automobile, The   II-1037
Hill, Richard L.
  Toryism and the People, 1832-1846   II-736
Hilton-Young, Wayland
  Italian Left: A Short History of Political Socialism in Italy, The   II-1112
Himmelfarb, Gertrude
  Darwin and the Darwinian Revolution   II-859
Hindemith, Paul
  J. S. Bach: Heritage and Obligation   I-384
Hindus, Maurice
  We Shall Live Again   III-1432
Hinman, Charlton
  First Folio of Shakespeare: The Norton Facsimile, The   I-212
Hiscocks, Richard
  Adenauer Era, The   III-1627
Hitchcock, William R.
  Background of the Knights' Revolt, The   I-80
Hitler, Adolf
  Mein Kampf   III-1367

Hoagland, H. E.
"Collective Bargaining in the Lithographic Industry," in *Studies in History, Economics, and Public Law*   I-546

Hobsbawm, E. J.
Age of Revolution: Europe from 1789-1848, The   I-427; 528; II-567; 685; 780

Hoffman, J. D.
Conservative Party in Opposition, 1945-1951, The   III-1521

Hoffman, Ross, J.S.
Great Britain and the German Trade Rivalry   II-1138
Origins and Background of the Second World War, The   III-1432

Hoffmann, Stanley
In Search of France: The Economy, Society, and the Political System in the Twentieth Century   III-1612; 1689

Hohman, Helen F.
Development of Social Insurance and Minimum Wage Legislation in Great Britain, The   III-1227

Holborn, Hajo
History of Modern Germany, A. Vol. I: *The Reformation*   I-67; 157; 253; 273; 312
History of Modern Germany, A. Vol. II: *1648-1840*   I-399; 404; 418; 423; 440; 474; II-579; 607
History of Modern Germany, A. Vol. III: *1840-1945*   III-1298; 1385; 1394
Political Collapse of Europe, The   III-1288

Holland, Bernard
Fall of Protection, The   II-769

Hollingdale, R. J.
Nietzsche: The Man and His Philosophy   II-1026

Holtman, Robert B.
Napoleonic Propaganda   II-559

Hooper, G. W. W.
Fighting at Jutland, The   III-1270

Horn, David Bayne
Great Britain and Europe in the Eighteenth Century   I-441; 455

Horne, Alistair
Fall of Paris: The Siege and the Commune, 1870-1871, The   II-957

Hötzsch, Otto
"Catherine II," in *The Cambridge Modern History*   I-478

Howard, Michael
Franco-Prussian War, The   II-952

Howarth, David
Waterloo: Day of Battle   II-622

Howarth, Helen E.
Source Book of Astronomy, A   I-141

Howarth, Patrick
Year Is 1851, The   II-802

Howe, Sonia E.
False Dimitry, The. A Russian Romance and

Tragedy, Described by British Eye-Witnesses   I-235

Howley, Frank
Berlin Command   III-1549

Hoyt, Robert G.
Birth Control Debate, The   III-1665

Hozier, H. M.
Seven Weeks' War: Its Antecedents and Incidents, The   II-916

Hubert, Eugène
"Joseph II," in *The Cambridge Modern History*   I-484

Hudson, Geoffrey
Sino-Soviet Dispute, The   III-1588

Hug, Lina
Story of Switzerland, The   II-798

Hughes, H. Stuart
Consciousness and Society   III-1142; 1282
Contemporary Europe: A History   III-1677
United States and Italy, The   III-1542

Hughes, Philip
Popular History of the Reformation, A   I-147
Reformation in England, The   I-115; 179

Hull, Cordell
Memoirs of Cordell Hull, The   III-1511

Hume, Martin
Court of Philip IV, The   I-307
"Spain Under Philip II," in *The Cambridge Modern History*   I-161

Hunt, R. Carew
Theory and Practice of Communism, The   II-785

Hunt, Richard N.
Creation of the Weimar Republic: Stillborn Democracy, The. Problems in European Civilization series   III-1298

Hunter, Adam M.
Teaching of Calvin, The   I-122

Hutchinson, Francis E.
Cranmer and the English Reformation   I-128
Milton and the English Mind   I-323

Hutt, William H.
Keynesianism   III-1410

Huxley, Aldous
Grey Eminence   I-283

Hyde, Harford Montgomery
Mexican Empire: The History of Maximilian and Carlota of Mexico   II-879

Irvine, William
Apes, Angels, and Victorians: The Story of Darwin, Huxley, and Evolution   II-859

Isenberg, Irwin
Outlook for Western Europe, The   III-1605

Israel, Frederick L.
Major Peace Treaties of Modern History, 1648-1966   I-403; 455; 478; III-1288

Jackman, Sydney Wayne
Romanov Relations   II-696
Jackson, Ernest
Critical Reception of Gustave Flaubert in the United States, 1860-1960, The   II-833
Jackson, Robert H.
Nürnberg Case, The   III-1525
Jackson, W. A. Douglas
Russo-Chinese Borderlands: Zone of Peaceful Contact or Potential Conflict   III-1588
Jacobsen, Dr. Hans-Adolf
"Dunkirk 1940," in *Decisive Battles of World War II*   III-1460
Jammes, André
"French Primitive Photography," in *Aperture*, XV   II-752
Jane, Fred T.
Fighting Ships   III-1191
Janelle, Pierre
Catholic Reformation, The   I-147
Janssen, Johannes
History of the German People at the Close of the Middle Ages   I-67; 80; 95; 152; 157
Jarman, T. L.
Rise and Fall of Nazi Germany, The   III-1381; 1385; 1394
Jarret, Robert
Community Europe: A Short Guide to the Common Market   III-1605
Jaspers, Karl
Nietzsche   II-1027
Jastrow, Morris
War and the Baghdad Railway, The   II-1137
Jászi, Oscar
Dissolution of the Habsburg Monarchy, The   II-943
Jeans, James
New Background of Science, The   III-1163
Jedin, Hubert
History of the Council of Trent, A   I-95
Jelavich, Barbara
Century of Russian Foreign Policy, 1814-1914, A   II-891
Jellicoe, Admiral Viscount
Grand Fleet: Its Creation, Development, and Work, The   III-1270
Jemelo, Arturo C.
Church and State in Italy, 1850-1950   II-962; III-1357
Jenkins, Arthur Hugh
Adam Smith Today   I-490
Jensen, De Lamar
Diplomacy and Dogmatism—Bernardino de Mendoza and the French Catholic League   I-207
Machiavelli: Cynic, Patriot, or Political Scientist?   I-39
Johnson, A. H.
Europe in the Sixteenth Century, 1494-1598   I-25

Johnston, Norman
Sociology of Punishment and Correction: A Book of Readings, The   I-459
Joll, James
Decline of the Third Republic, The   III-1415
Jones, Thomas
Lloyd George   III-1227
Jones, Wilbur P.
Lord Derby and Victorian Conservatism   II-934
Josephson, Matthew
Edison   II-756
Josephy, Alvin M., Jr.
American Heritage History of Flight, The   I-500
Joughin, Jean T.
Paris Commune in French Politics, 1870-1880, The   II-987

Kaiser, Robert B.
Pope, Council, and World   III-1641
Kamen, Henry
Spanish Inquisition, The   I-5
Kardelj, Edvard
Socialism and War   III-1565
Kash, Don E.
Politics of Space Cooperation, The   III-1623
Kaufman, Walter
Nietzsche: Philosopher, Psychologist, Antichrist   II-1027
Kautsky, Karl
Thomas More and His Utopia   I-53
Kayser, Jacques
Dreyfus Affair, The   II-1079
Keatley, Patrick
Politics of Partnership: The Federation of Rhodesia and Nyasaland, The   III-1647
Kecskemeti, Paul
Strategic Surrender   III-1481
Keep, J. L. H.
"Russia," in *The New Cambridge Modern History*   II-1108
Keith, Arthur
Belgian Congo and the Berlin Act, The   II-1051
Kelly, George A.
Birth Control and Catholics   III-1665
Lost Soldiers: The French Army and Empire in Crisis, 1947-1962   III-1582; 1612; 1632
Keltie, J. S.
Partition of Africa, The   II-1051
Kendrew, John
Thread of Life: An Introduction to Molecular Biology, The   III-1576
Kennan, George F.
Russia and the West Under Lenin and Stalin   III-1516
Kennedy, General Sir John Shaw
Notes on the Battle of Waterloo   II-622

Kesselring, Field Marshal Alfred
Soldier's Story, A III-1460
Kesten, Hermann
Copernicus and His World I-142
Khadduri, Mejdia D.
Arab-Israeli Impasse: Expression of Moderate Viewpoints on the Arab-Israeli Conflict by Well-Known Western Writers, The III-1658
Khouri, Fred J.
Arab-Israeli Dilemma, The III-1594; 1658
Kindleberger, Charles P.
In Search of France III-1689
King, Bolton
History of Italian Unity, A II-842
Kingdon, Robert M.
Geneva and the Coming of the Wars of Religion in France I-166
Geneva and the Consolidation of the French Protestant Movement, 1564-1572 I-188
Kinglake, Alexander William
Invasion of the Crimea, The II-816
Kirby, Richard S.
Engineering in History II-563; 1104
Kirkpatrick, Ivone
Mussolini: A Study in Power III-1357
Kissinger, Henry A.
Troubled Partnership: A Re-Appraisal of the Atlantic Alliance, The III-1653
World Restored: Metternich, Castlereagh, and the Problems of Peace, 1815-1822, A II-616; 628
Klaczko, Julian
Rome and the Renaissance: The Pontificate of Julius II I-30
Klein, Julius
Mesta: A Study in Spanish Economic History, The I-5
Kluchevsky, Vasily O.
History of Russia, A I-367
Knaplund, Paul
Britain, Commonwealth and Empire, 1901-1955 III-1376
Knapp, Wilfred
History of War and Peace, 1939-1965, A III-1516; 1536
Knappen, M. M.
Tudor Puritanism I-173
Knickerbocker, William S.
Classics of Modern Science III-1178
Knight, David C.
Johannes Kepler and Planetary Motion I-240
Knoenigsberger, H.
"Empire of Charles V in Europe, The," in *The New Cambridge Modern History* I-43
Koestler, Arthur
Watershed, The I-240
Kogan, Norman
Political History of Postwar Italy, A III-1542

Politics of Italian Foreign Policy, The III-1542
Kohn, Hans
Habsburg Empire, 1804-1918, The II-943
Prelude to Nation-States: The French and German Experience, 1789-1815 II-579
Kolnai, Aurel
War Against the West, The III-1367
Korbel, Josef
Communist Subversion of Czechoslovakia, 1938-1948: The Failure of Coexistence, The III-1672
Korner, S.
Kant I-495
Kornilov, A. A.
Modern Russian History II-589; 668; 869
Koyré, Alexandre
From the Closed World to the Infinite Universe I-142
Kraehe, Enno E.
Metternich's German Policy II-607
Kranzberg, Melvin
Siege of Paris, 1870-1871: A Political and Social History, The II-957; 987
Krause, Lawrence B.
European Economy: Integration and the United States III-1605
Krieger, Leonard
German Idea of Freedom: History of a Political Tradition, The II-579; 922
Kukiel, Marian
Czartoryski and European Unity, 1770-1861 II-696
Kulski, Wladyslaw W.
De Gaulle and the World: The Foreign Policy of the Fifth French Republic III-1653
Küng, Hans
Church and Ecumenism, The. Vol. IV of *Concilium* III-1554

Lacouture, Jean
End of a War: Indochina, 1954 III-1582
Lally, Frank E.
French Opposition to the Mexican Policy of the Second Empire II-879
Lambert, Richard S.
Railway King, The II-611
Lamour, Peter J.
French Radical Party in the 1930's, The III-1390
Landauer, Carl
European Socialism: A History of Ideas and Movements II-901
Lander, J. R.
War of the Roses, The. History in the Making series I-10
Langer, William L.
Challenge to Isolation, 1937-1940, The III-1438
Diplomacy of Imperialism, 1890-1892, The II-1074; 1138; III-1151

European Alliances and Alignments, 1871-1890   II-1023

Political and Social Upheaval, 1832-1852. Vol. XIV of *The Rise of Modern Europe* series   II-763; 798

Langford, Jerome J.
Galileo, Science, and the Church   I-289

Lantier, Raymond
Men of the Old Stone Age, The   II-826

Laqueur, Walter
Fate of the Revolution: Interpretations of Soviet History, The   III-1333

Latimer, Elizabeth Wormeley
Spain in the Nineteenth Century   II-636; 729

Latourette, Kenneth Scott
Christianity in a Revolutionary Age   II-774

Laurence, John
History of Capital Punishment, A   I-459

Lecky, William E. H.
Leaders of Public Opinion in Ireland   II-674

Lederer, Ivo J.
Versailles Settlement: Was It Foredoomed to Failure, The? Problems in European Civilization series   III-1288

Lednicki, Waclaw
Russia, Poland, and the West: Essays in Literary and Cultural History   II-891

Lee, Sir Sidney
King Edward VII   III-1218

Lefebvre, Georges
French Revolution: From Its Origins to 1793, The   I-514; 519

Legum, Colin
Congo Disaster   II-1052; III-1617

Leijonkufvud, Axel
On Keynesian Economics and the Economics of Keynes   III-1410

Lemarchand, René
Political Awakening in the Belgian Congo   III-1617

Lemoine, Jean
"Reversal of Alliances and the Family Compact, The," in *The Cambridge Modern History*   I-440

Leonhard, Wolfgang
Kremlin Since Stalin, The   III-1571

LeRoy-Beaulieu, Anatole
Empire of the Tsars and the Russians, The   II-869

Levi, Albert W.
Philosophy and the Modern World   III-1163; 1282

Lewin, Henry Grote
Railway Mania and Its Aftermath, The   II-664

Lewisohn, Ludwig
Theodor Herzl: A Portrait for This Age   II-1093

Lewitter, L. R.
"Partitions of Poland, The," in *The New Cambridge Modern History*   I-474

Liddell Hart, B. H.
"Armed Forces and the Art of War: Armies," in *The New Cambridge Modern History*   II-916

Real War, 1914-1918, The   III-1265

Lindgren, Raymond E.
Norway-Sweden: Union, Disunion, and Scandinavian Integration   III-1168

Lindsay, J. O.
"International Relations," in *The New Cambridge Modern History*   I-404; 455

Lippmann, Walter
Western Unity and the Common Market   III-1605

Lipson, E.
Europe in the Nineteenth Century, 1815-1914   II-991

History of the Woollen and Worsted Industries   I-408

Littell, Robert
Czech Black Book, The   III-1672

Livermore, Harold V.
History of Portugal, A   III-1677
History of Spain, A   I-303; 375; 445
New History of Portugal, A   I-192

Lloyd, Christopher
Nation and the Navy: A History of Naval Life and Policy, The   II-1061

Lobanov-Rostovsky, Andrei
Russia and Europe, 1789 to 1825   II-589

Lockyer, Roger
Tudor and Stuart Britain, 1471-1714   I-197

Lodge, Richard
"Austria, Poland, and Turkey," in *The Cambridge Modern History*   I-371
History of England from the Restoration to the Death of William III, 1660-1702, The. Vol. VIII of *The Political History of England*   I-363

London Times, The
History of the Times: The 150th Anniversary and Beyond, 1912-1948, The   III-1424

Lord, Robert
Second Partition of Poland, The   I-474

Lough, John
Introduction to Seventeenth Century France, An   I-284; 327

Lovell, R. I.
Struggle for South Africa, The   II-1132

Lowenthal, Richard
Sino-Soviet Dispute, The   III-1588

Luckhurst, Kenneth W.
Story of Exhibitions, The   II-801

Lumumba, Patrice
Congo, My Country   III-1617

Lyashchenko, P. I.
History of the National Economy of Russia to the 1917 Revolution   II-1065

Lynch, John
   Spain Under the Habsburgs. Vol. I: *Empire and Absolutism, 1516-1598*   I-75; 157; 197; 223
Lynd, Helen M.
   England in the 1880's   II-1043

Macardle, Dorothy
   Irish Republic, The   III-1318
McArthur, Harvey K.
   Quest Through the Centuries: The Search for the Historical Jesus, The   II-896
Macartney, Carlile A.
   "Austrian Empire and Its Problems, 1848-1867, The," in *The New Cambridge Modern History*   II-943
MacCaffrey, James
   History of the Church in the Nineteenth Century   II-774
Maccoby, Simon
   English Radicalism, 1756-1832   II-710
   English Radicalism, 1832-1852   II-746; 769
   English Radicalism, 1853-1886   II-1043
McCloskey, H. J.
   John Stuart Mill: A Critical Study   II-848
McCullum, R. B.
   British General Election of 1945, The   III-1521
McDay, Donald
   Dreyfus Case: By the Man—Alfred Dreyfus —and His Son—Pierre Dreyfus, The   II-1079
McDonagh, Michael
   Daniel O'Connell and the Story of Catholic Emancipation   II-674
MacDonald, Mary
   Republic of Austria, 1918-1934: A Study in the Failure of Democratic Government, The   III-1400
McDowell, R. B.
   Irish Public Opinion, 1750-1800   II-555
McElrath, Damian
   Syllabus of Pius IX: Some Reactions in England, The   II-907
McElwee, William L.
   Wisest Fool in Christendom, The   I-230
MacFarquhar, Roderick
   Sino-Soviet Dispute, The   III-1588
Macintyre, Captain Donald
   Fighting Under the Sea   III-1258
   Narvik   III-1450
   U-Boat Killer   III-1258
Mackenzie, Compton
   Windsor Tapestry, The   III-1424
MacKinnon, James
   Calvin and the Reformation   I-122
McManaway, James G.
   Shakespeare Quarterly   I-212
McNeill, John T.

History and Character of Calvinism, The   I-122
McNeill, William H.
   America, Britain, and Russia: Their Cooperation and Conflict, 1941-1946   III-1505
Mack Smith, Denis
   "Colonial Defeat and Political Reaction, 1893-1900," in *Italy: A Modern History*   II-928
   Italy: A Modern History   II-928; 982; 1023; III-1232; 1303; 1358; 1542
Macleod, R.
   Time Unguarded: The Ironside Diaries, 1937-1940   III-1450
Macridis, Roy C.
   De Gaulle Republic: Quest for Unity, The   III-1688
Magill, Frank N.
   Masterpieces of World Philosophy in Summary Form   I-495
Magnus, Philip
   Kitchener: Portrait of an Imperialist   II-1117
Mahan, Alfred T.
   Influence of Sea Power upon the French Revolution and Empire, 1793-1812   I-541
Mangone, Gerard J.
   Short History of International Organization, A   III-1196
Mansergh, Nicholas
   Coming of the First World War, The   III-1248
Marcham, Frederick George
   Constitutional History of Modern England, 1485 to the Present, A   I-389
Marcus, Abraham
   Power Unlimited   II-1104
Marcus, Rebecca B.
   Power Unlimited   II-1104
Marcuse, Ludwig
   Soldier of the Church   I-102
Marder, Arthur J.
   Anatomy of British Sea Power: A History of British Naval Policy in the Pre-Dreadnought Era, 1880-1905, The   II-1061
   From the Dreadnought to Scapa Flow. Vol. II: *The War Years: To the Eve of Jutland*   III-1270
Markham, Felix
   Napoleon   I-550; II-567; 593
Marriott, J. A. R.
   Eastern Question: An Historical Study in European Diplomacy, The   III-1244
   Evolution of Prussia: The Making of an Empire, The   I-399; 418; II-885
Marshall, C. F. Dendy
   History of British Railways Down to the Year 1830, A   II-664
Marshall, S. L. A.
   American Heritage History of World War I, The   III-1265

Martelli, George
  From Leopold to Lumumba   II-1052
Marti-Ibanez, Felix
  Men, Molds, and History   III-1339
Martin, Kingsley
  French Liberal Thought in the Eighteenth Century   I-450
Martin, Thomas
  Faraday's Discovery of Electro-Magnetic Induction   II-652
Masson, David
  Life of John Milton, The   I-323
Mathew, Arnold H.
  Life and Times of Rodrigo Borgia, The   I-30
Mathew, David
  James I   I-230
Mathews, J. J.
  Egypt and the Formation of the Anglo-French Entente of 1904   III-1155
Mathieson, William Law
  British Slave Emancipation, 1838-1849   II-721
  British Slavery and Its Abolition, 1823-1838   II-721
Mathiez, Albert
  French Revolution, The   I-505
Mattingly, Garrett
  Catherine of Aragon   I-109
Maurois, André
  Disraeli: A Picture of the Victorian Age   II-1002
  History of France, A   I-352; II-1056
May, Arthur J.
  Age of Metternich, 1814-1848, The   II-617; 689
  Hapsburg Monarchy, 1867-1914, The   III-1206; 1232; 1244
Mazlish, Bruce
  Riddle of History, The   III-1142
Mazour, Anatole G.
  Soviet Economic Development: Operation Outstrip, 1921-1965   III-1308
Mazzini, Joseph
  Life and Writings of Joseph Mazzini   II-702
Medlicott, W. N.
  Bismarck and Modern Germany   II-968
Mehring, Franz
  Karl Marx   II-901
Meigs, Cornelia
  Great Design, The   III-1511
Mellor, George R.
  British Imperial Trusteeship, 1783-1850   II-721
Menshutkin, B. N.
  Russia's Lomonosov, Chemist, Courtier, Physicist, Poet   I-435
Merkl, Peter H.
  Origin of the West German Republic, The   III-1627
Merriman, Roger B.
  Rise of the Spanish Empire, The   I-161; 223
  Rise of the Spanish Empire in the Old World and in the New, The. Vol. III: *The Emperor*   I-43; 75
Meyer, Alfred G.
  Communism   II-785
Michie, Allan A.
  Invasion of Europe: The Story Behind D-Day, The   III-1495
Michael, Wolfgang
  "Great Britain," in *The Cambridge Modern History*   I-455
Middlemas, Keith
  Baldwin: A Biography   III-1328; 1424
Miliukov, Paul
  Russia and Its Crisis   III-1159
Miller, D. H.
  Drafting of the Covenant, The   III-1294
Miller, Townsend
  Castle and the Crown, The   I-5
Miller, William
  "Ottoman Empire and the Balkan Peninsula, The," in *The Cambridge Modern History*   II-1012
Milmed, Bella K.
  Kant and Current Philosophical Issues   I-495
Mitford, Nancy
  Sun King, The   I-352
Mitramy, David
  Progress of International Government, The   III-1196
Moffit, Louis W.
  England on the Eve of the Industrial Revolution   I-408
"Monitor"
  Death of Stalin: An Investigation, The   III-1571
Montague, F. C.
  "National Assembly, and the Spread of Anarchy, The," in *The Cambridge Modern History*   I-514
Montgomery of Alamein, Field Marshal
  Memoirs   III-1470; 1489; 1495; 1500
Montross, Lynn
  War Through the Ages   I-395
Monypenny, William Flavelle
  Life of Benjamin Disraeli, Earl of Beaconsfield, The   II-934
Moody, Joseph N.
  Church and Society: Catholic Social and Political Thought and Movements, 1789-1950   III-1146
Moon, Parker T.
  Imperialism and World Politics   II-1118; 1137
  Labor Problem and the Social Catholic Movement in France: A Study in the History of Social Politics, The   II-1047
Moore, Barrington

Soviet Politics: The Dilemma of Power III-1352

Moore, Ruth
Earth We Live On, The II-681

Moorehead, Alan
March to Tunis: The North African War, 1940-1943, The III-1471

More, Sir Thomas
Utopia I-53

Morgan, Alfred P.
Pageant of Electricity, The II-563; 653; 756

Morgan, Roger
German Social Democrats and the First International, 1864-1872, The II-997

Morison, Samuel Eliot
History of United States Naval Operations in World War II III-1258

Morley, John
Life of Richard Cobden, The II-769
Life of William Ewart Gladstone, The II-934; 1042

Morris, Gouveneur
Diary of the French Revolution, A I-514

Morris, J. Bayard
Hernando Cortés: Five Letters, 1519-1526 I-63

Mosley, Leonard
Haile Selassie: The Conquering Lion III-1405

Mosse, George L.
Struggle for Sovereignty in England, The I-268

Mosse, W. E.
European Powers and the German Question, 1848-1871, The II-968

Mowat, Charles Loch
Britain Between the Wars, 1918-1940 III-1424

Mumford, Lewis
Technics and Civilization I-528

Murphy, Gardner
Historical Introduction to Modern Psychology III-1313

Murray, George
Letters and Dispatches of J. Churchill, First Duke of Marlborough from 1702-1712 I-394

Murray, Robert H.
Science and Scientists in the Nineteenth Century II-681

Namier, Sir Lewis B.
Diplomatic Prelude, 1938-1939 III-1438
1848: The Revolution of the Intellectuals II-793
Facing East II-890

Nathanson, Maurice
Critique of Jean-Paul Sartre's Ontology, A III-1485

Naylor, John

Waterloo II-622

Neale, J. E.
Age of Catherine de Médici, The I-167; 188; 207; 218
Queen Elizabeth I I-173; 179

Neill, Thomas P.
Makers of the Modern Mind III-1142

Nettl, J. P.
Soviet Achievement, The III-1309

Nevins, Allan
Making of Modern Britain, The III-1376

Newhall, Beaumont
History of Photography from 1839 to the Present, The II-752

Newton, A. P.
Cambridge History of the British Empire, The. Vol. VIII: South Africa, Rhodesia, and the High Commission Territories, The II-1132

Nicoll, Allardyce
Shakespeare Survey I-212

Nicolson, Harold
Diplomacy II-1118
King George V: His Life and Reign III-1218
Peacemaking, 1919 III-1288

Nimitz, Chester W.
Sea Power: A Naval History I-183

Nirenberg, Marshall W.
"Genetic Code: II, The," in Scientific American III-1576

Nissenson, Hugh
Notes from the Frontier III-1658

Nock, O. S.
Railways of Britain, The II-664

Noland, Aaron
Founding of the French Socialist Party, 1893-1905, The II-1047

Nolte, Ernst
Three Faces of Fascism: Action Française, Italian Fascism, National Socialism III-1390

Nomad, Max
Apostles of Revolution II-1018

Notestein, Wallace
English People on the Eve of Colonization, The I-230
Winning of the Initiative by the House of Commons, The I-269

Nowell, Charles E.
History of Portugal, A I-192; III-1677

Nussbaum, Frederick L.
Triumph of Science and Reason, 1660-1685, The. Vol. VI of *The Rise of Modern Europe* series I-348

Nutting, Anthony
No End of a Lesson: The Story of Suez III-1594

Oakley, Stewart
Short History of Sweden, A I-277

O'Brien, Conor Cruise
To Katanga and Back: U.S. Case History
III-1617
Ogg, David
England in the Reigns of James II and William III   I-363
Europe in the Seventeenth Century   I-253;
273; 312; 344; 371; 379; 404
Oldenbourg, Zoé
Catherine the Great   I-468
Ollivier, Emile
Franco-Prussian War and Its Hidden Causes, The   II-953
Oman, Sir Charles
History of the Peninsula War, A   II-597
Onchen, Hermann
"German Empire, The," in *The Cambridge Modern History*   II-991
O'Neill, Robert J.
General Giap: Politician and Strategist   III-1582
Ong, Walter J., S.J.
Darwin's Vision and Christian Perspectives
II-859
Ordway, Frederick I.
History of Rocketry and Space Travel   III-1622
Orsi, Rietro
Cavour   II-875
Osborn, Annie Marion
Rousseau and Burke   I-450
Outler, Albert C.
Methodist Observer at Vatican Two   III-1641

Packard, Laurence B.
Age of Louis XIV, The   I-348
Padden, R. C.
Hummingbird and the Hawk: Conquest and Sovereignty in the Valley of Mexico, 1503-1541, The   I-63
Padover, Saul K.
Life and Death of Louis XVI, The   I-352;
505; 509
Paglin, Morton
Malthus and Lauderdale: The Anti-Ricardian Tradition   I-537
Pakenham, Frank
Peace by Ordeal   III-1318
Palèologue, Maurice
Cavour   II-875
Palley, Claire
Constitutional History and Law of Southern Rhodesia, 1888-1965, The   III-1647
Palm, Franklin C.
Calvinism and the Religious Wars   I-167
Politics and Religion in Sixteenth Century France   I-207
Palmer, R. R.
Age of the Democratic Revolution: A Political History of Europe and America, 1760-1800,

The. Vol. I: *The Challenge*   I-484
Twelve Who Ruled, The   I-531
Palmstierna, C. F.
Short History of Sweden   III-1168
Pares, Sir Bernard
Fall of the Russian Monarchy, The   III-1151
History of Russia, A   I-249; 367; 436; II-869
"Reaction and Revolution in Russia," in *The Cambridge Modern History*   II-1065
"Reform Movement in Russia, The," in *The Cambridge Modern History*   III-1173; 1182
Paret, Peter
Yorck and the Era of Prussian Reform, 1807-1815   II-579
Parker, Thomas H. L.
Doctrine of the Knowledge of God: A Study in the Theology of John Calvin, The   I-122
Parris, John
Lion of Caprera, The   II-865
Parry, J. H.
Age of Reconnaissance, The   I-14
Europe and a Wider World, 1415-1715
I-71
Pastor, Ludwig
History of the Popes from the Close of the Middle Ages, The   I-30
Paton, Henry
"Alexander Leslie," in the *Dictionary of National Biography*   I-316
Paton, Herbert J.
Categorical Imperative: A Study in Kant's Moral Philosophy   I-495
Patrick, John M.
Francis Bacon   I-258
Pattee, Richard
Portugal and the Portuguese World   I-307;
II-648; 677; 725; III-1222
This Is Spain   III-1261
Pauli, W.
"Influence of Archetypal Ideas on the Scientific Theories of Kepler, The," in *The Interpretation of Nature and Psyche*   I-240
Paxton, John
Structure and Development of Common Market, The   III-1605
Payne, Robert
Rise and Fall of Stalin, The   III-1571
Payne, Stanley G.
Falange: A Study of Spanish Fascism   III-1371; 1419
Politics and the Military in Modern Spain
II-948; 1006; III-1261; 1419
Pearson, Hesketh
Dizzy: The Life and Personality of Benjamin Disraeli, Earl of Beaconsfield   II-1002
Henry of Navarre   I-207; 218
Pelikan, Jaroslav
Obedient Rebels   I-58

Penrose, Boies
Travel and Discovery in the Renaissance
I-71
People's Republic of Hungary, Information Bureau of the Council of Ministers
Counter-revolutionary Conspiracy of Imre Nagy and His Accomplices, The III-1599
Pepys, Samuel
Memoirs of Samuel Pepys I-340
Perry, V. J.
"Ottoman Empire, 1520-1566, The," in *The New Cambridge Modern History* I-90
Petrie, Sir Charles
Philip II of Spain I-192; 223
Pflanze, Otto
Bismarck and the Development of Germany II-953; 968
Phillips, W. Alison
Confederation of Europe, 1813-1823, The II-628; 658
Revolution in Ireland, 1906-1923, The III-1239
Philp, H. L.
Jung and the Problem of Evil III-1313
Pickles, Dorothy
Fifth French Republic: Institutions and Politics, The III-1688
Pinkham, Lucile
William III and the Respectable Revolution: The Part Played by William of Orange in the Revolution of 1688 I-363
Pinson, Koppel S.
Modern Germany: Its History and Civilization II-968; III-1298
Pitts, Jesse R.
In Search of France III-1689
Plamenatz, John
Revolutionary Movement in France, 1815-1871, The II-789; 987
Pollard, A. F.
Henry VIII I-109; 128
Wolsey I-109
Pollen, John H., S. J.
English Catholics in the Reign of Queen Elizabeth, The I-179
Pomfret, John E.
Struggle for Land in Ireland, 1800-1923, The II-763
Ponomaryov, Boris N.
History of the Communist Party of the Soviet Union III-1333
Poole, H. Edmund
Annals of Printing: A Chronological Encyclopedia from the Earliest Times to 1950 I-546
Porritt, A. G.
Unreformed House of Commons, The II-709
Porritt, E. A.

Unreformed House of Commons, The II-709
Porter, Sir Robert Ker
Narrative of the Campaign in Russia During the Year 1812, A II-588
Postgate, Raymond
British Common People, 1746-1946, The III-1227; 1328
Revolution from 1789 to 1906 III-1172; 1182
Story of a Year: 1848, The II-793
Potter, Elmer B.
Sea Power: A Naval History I-183
Prescott, William H.
History of the Reign of Ferdinand and Isabella I-5
Prestage, Edgar
Portuguese Pioneers, The I-14
Pribam, Alfred F.
Austrian Foreign Policy, 1908-1918 III-1206
England and the International Policy of the Great Powers, 1871-1914 II-1074; III-1155; 1201
Price, Ira Maurice
Ancestry of Our English Bible, The I-245
Protestant Episcopal Church
Book of Common Prayer, The I-172
Puleston, W. D.
Mahan: The Life and Work of Captain Alfred Mahan, U.S.N. II-1127
Puryear, Vernon J.
England, Russia, and the Straits Question, 1844-1856 II-817
Pushkarev, Serge
Emergence of Modern Russia, The II-668
Pushkin, Alexander
Boris Godunov I-235
Puzzo, Dante A.
Spain and the Great Powers, 1936-1941 III-1419

Raab, Clement, O.F.M.
Twenty Ecumenical Councils of the Catholic Church, The I-147
Raack, R. C.
Fall of Stein, The II-579
Rabb, Theodore K.
Thirty Years' War: Problems of Motive, Extent and Effect, The. Problems in European Civilization series I-253; 273; 312
Raeff, Marc
Peter the Great: Reformer or Revolutionary? Problems in European Civilization series I-367
Ragg, Laura M.
Crises in Venetian History I-34
Ramos Oliveira, Antonio
Politics, Economics and Men of Modern Spain, 1808-1946 II-584; 597; 948; 1006; 1122; III-1371; 1419

Ramsay, Anna A. W.
  Sir Robert Peel   II-769
Randall, F.
  Stalin's Russia   III-1571
Ranum, Orest A.
  Richelieu and the Councillors of Louis XIII
  I-262
Ratcliff, J. D.
  Yellow Magic: The Story of Penicillin   III-
  1339
Rayner, Robert M.
  European History, 1648-1789   I-348
Readman, A.
  British General Election of 1945, The   III-
  1521
Recouly, Raymond
  *Third Republic, The. The National History of
  France* series   III-1056
Reddaway, W. F.
  Documents of Catherine the Great   I-468
Rees, David
  *Age of Containment: The Cold War, 1945-
  1965, The*   III-1627
Reinfeld, Fred
  Miracle Drugs and the New Age of Medicine
  III-1339
Reinhardt, Kurt F.
  Germany: 2,000 Years   II-968
Relf, Frances H.
  Petition of Right, The   I-269
Remak, Joachim
  Sarajevo: The Story of a Political Murder
  III-1248
Renan, Joseph Ernest
  Life of Jesus, The   II-896
Reynaud, Paul
  In the Thick of the Fight   III-1445; 1455
Reynolds, J. A.
  *Catholic Emancipation Crisis in Ireland, 1823-
  1829, The*   II-674
Rich, E. E.
  Cambridge Economic History of Europe, The
  I-427
Rich, Norman
  *Friedrich von Holstein: Politics and Diplomacy
  in the Era of Bismarck and Wilhelm II*
  III-1213
Richards, Denis
  "Collapse in the West," in *Royal Air Force,
  1939-1945*   III-1460
  Royal Air Force, The, 1939-1945   III-1465
  "Scandinavian Misadventure," in *Royal Air
  Force, 1939-1945.* Vol I: *The Fight at Odds*
  III-1450
Richmond, Herbert
  *Navy as an Instrument of Policy, 1558-1727,
  The*   I-197
Richter, Werner
  Bismarck   II-922; 973; 1017
Riess, Curt
  Berlin Story   III-1549

Rigg, J. M.
  "Great Britain," in *The Cambridge Modern
  History*   I-455
Rist, Charles
  History of Economic Doctrines, A   I-537;
  II-632
Ritter, Gerhard
  Schlieffen Plan: Critique of a Myth, The
  III-1253
Robbins, Michael
  Railway Age, The   II-611; 664
Robertson, C. Grant
  Bismarck   II-922
  *Evolution of Prussia: The Making of an Em-
  pire, The*   I-399; 418; II-885
Robertson, Priscilla
  Revolutions of 1848: A Social History   II-
  780; 793
Robertson, Terence
  Night Raider of the Atlantic   III-1258
Robinson, H. Wheeler
  Bible in Its Ancient and English Versions, The
  I-246
Robinson, Joan
  Introduction to the Theory of Employment
  III-1410
Robinson, John M.
  *Improvement of Mankind: The Social and
  Political Thought of John Stuart Mill, The*
  II-848
Robinson, Margaret
  *Arbitration and the Hague Peace Conference
  1899 and 1907*   II-1127
Robinson, Ronald
  "Partition of Africa, The," in *The New Cam-
  bridge Modern History*   II-1052
Robson, Eric
  "Seven Years War, The," in *The New Cam-
  bridge Modern History*   I-455
Roche, O. I. A.
  Days of the Upright, The   I-262
Rock, John C.
  *Time Has Come: A Catholic Doctor's Proposals
  to End the Battle over Birth Control, The*
  III-1665
Rodes, John E.
  Germany: A History   I-423
  *Quest for Unity: Modern Germany, 1848-1870,
  The*   III-1695
Rodger, A. B.
  War of the Second Coalition, 1798-1801, The
  I-541
Rogger, Hans
  European Right: A Historical Profile, The
  III-1303; 1390
  *National Consciousness in Eighteenth Century
  Russia*   I-468; II-668
Romer, Alfred
  Restless Atom, The   II-1088
Rommel, Field Marshal Erwin
  Rommel Papers, The   III-1470; 1495

Rose, John Holland
Life of Napoleon I II-622
William Pitt and the Great War II-555
Rosenberg, Arthur
Birth of the German Republic, 1871-1918, The II-997; 1017
History of the German Republic, A III-1298
Rosenblatt, Frank F.
"Chartist Movement in Its Social and Economic Aspects, The," in *Columbia University Studies in History, Economics, and Public Law* II-746
Roskill, S. W.
War at Sea, The III-1258
War at Sea, The. Vol. I: *The Defensive* III-1460
Rowse, Alfred L.
Bosworth Field, from Medieval to Tudor England I-10
Shakespeare the Man I-213
Rubenson, Sven
"Aspects of the Survival of Ethiopian Independence, 1840-1896," in *Nineteenth Century Africa* II-1099
Rudman, Henry W.
Italian Nationalism and English Letters II-702
Russell, Bertrand
ABC of Relativity, The III-1163
Ryan, Alan
John Stuart Mill II-848
Ryan, Cornelius
Longest Day: June 6, 1944, The III-1495

Safran, Nadav
From War to War: The Arab-Israeli Confrontation, 1948-1967: A Study of the Conflict from the Perspective of Coercion in the Context of Inter-Arab and Big Power Relations III-1658
Saillens, Émile
John Milton: Man, Poet, and Polemicist I-323
St. Clair, Oswald
Key to Ricardo, A II-632
Salamone, A. W.
Italian Democracy in the Making, 1900-1914 II-1112
Salisbury, Harrison E.
War Between Russia and China III-1588
Salmon, Edward D.
Imperial Spain I-43
Salvadori, Massimo
Cavour and the Unification of Italy II-875
Italy II-703
Salvan, Jacques
To Be and Not To Be III-1485
Salvatorelli, Luigi
Concise History of Italy, A I-85
Salvemini, Gaetano

Mazzini II-702
Prelude to World War II III-1405
Sánchez, José M.
Reform and Reaction: The Politico-Religious Background of the Spanish Civil War. II-1006; III-1371
Santillana, Giorgio de
Dialogue on the Two Great World Systems I-289
Sarton, George
Six Wings: Men of Science of the Renaissance I-137
Savine, Alexander
English Monasteries on the Eve of Their Dissolutions I-115
Savitz, Leonard
Sociology of Punishment and Correction: A Book of Readings, The I-459
Schapiro, Jacob Salwyn
Social Reform and the Reformation I-81
Schapiro, Leonard
Communist Party of the Soviet Union, The III-1277; 1334
Scheer, Admiral Reinhard
Germany's High Seas Fleet in the World War III-1270
Schenk, Hans G.
Aftermath of the Napoleonic Wars: The Concert of Europe—An Experiment, The II-616; 659
Schevill, Ferdinand
Great Elector, The I-277
Medieval and Renaissance Florence. Vol. II: *The Age of the Medici and the Coming of Humanism* I-25
Schmitt, Bernadotte E.
England and Germany, 1740-1914 III-1213
Schöenbrun, David
As France Goes III-1688
Three Lives of Charles de Gaulle, The III-1612
Schonfield, Hugh J.
Suez Canal, The II-821
Schroeder, Paul W.
Metternich's Diplomacy at Its Zenith, 1820-1823 II-644; 658
Schroter, Heinz
Stalingrad III-1476
Schuck, Adolf
History of Sweden I-277
Schultz, Duane P.
History of Modern Psychology, A III-1313
Schuman, Frederick L.
Soviet Russia Since 1917 III-1352
Schumpeter, Joseph A.
Capitalism, Socialism, and Democracy II-1032
Schuschnigg, Kurt von
Austrian Requiem III-1428
My Austria III-1400

Schwartz, Harry
Prague's Two Hundred Days   III-1672
Tsars, Mandarins, and Communists: A History of Chinese-Russian Relations   III-1682
Schweitzer, Albert
J. S. Bach   I-384
Schwiebert, Ernst G.
Luther and His Times   I-58
Scott, John A.
Republican Ideas and the Liberal Tradition in France, 1870-1914   II-977
Scott, Joseph F.
Scientific Work of René Descartes, The   I-298
Scott-Moncrief, David
Veteran Motor-Car, The   II-1037
Seaman, L. C. B.
From Vienna to Versailles   II-616; 842; 1117
Sedgwick, Henry
Henry of Navarre   I-207; 219
Seebohm, Frederic
Oxford Reformers, The   I-53
Seeley, J. R.
Life and Times of Stein, or Germany and Prussia in the Napoleonic Age   II-579
Segur, Count Philippe Paul
Napoleon's Russian Campaign   II-588
Sensabaugh, George F.
Grand Whig, The   I-323
Serfaty, Simon
France, De Gaulle, and Europe: The Policy of the Fourth and Fifth Republics Toward the Continent   III-1653
Seton-Watson, Hugh
Decline of Imperial Russia, 1855-1914, The   II-1065; 1108; III-1159; 1173
Seton-Watson, R. W.
Britain and the Dictators   III-1432
Britain in Europe, 1789-1914   II-1002
Shachtman, Max
Struggle for the New Course, The   III-1352
Shakespeare, William
Complete Works, The   I-213
Shamuyarira, Nathan
Crisis in Rhodesia   III-1647
Shanahan, William O.
German Protestants Face the Social Question   II-1032
Prussian Military Reforms, 1786-1813   II-580
Shapley, Harlow
Source of Astronomy, A   I-141
Sharlin, Harold I.
Making of the Electrical Age, The   II-563; 756
Shaw, W. A.
"Commonwealth and Protectorate, 1648-1659, The," in *The Cambridge Modern History*   I-335
Shelton, William R.

Soviet Space Exploration: The First Decade   III-1623
Sherwood, Robert E.
Roosevelt and Hopkins   III-1481; 1505
Shirer, William L.
Collapse of the Third Republic, The   III-1455
Rise and Fall of the Third Reich, The   III-1385; 1394; 1476
Shirley, F. J.
Elizabeth's First Archbishop   I-173
Simon, W. M.
European Positivism in the Nineteenth Century   II-807
Germany: A Brief History   II-607
Simon, Yves
Road to Vichy, 1918-1938, The   III-1455
Simpson, Frederick A.
Louis Napoleon and the Recovery of France, 1848-1856   II-789
Singer, Charles
History of Technology, A. Vol. IV: *The Industrial Revolution, 1750-1850*   I-500; 528
Short History of Anatomy and Physiology from the Greeks to Harvey, A   I-137
Short History of Medicine, A   II-938
Sinor, Denis
History of Hungary   I-90; II-943
Slosson, William P.
"Decline of the Chartist Movement, The," in *Columbia University Studies in History, Economics, and Public Law*   II-745
Smith, Adam
Inquiry into the Nature and Causes of the Wealth of Nations, An   I-489
Smith, Gaddis
American Diplomacy During the Second World War   III-1481
Smith, H. Maynard
Henry VIII and the Reformation   I-109; 128
Smith, Howard K.
State of Europe, The   III-1536
Smith, Jean Edward
Defense of Berlin, The   III-1549
Smith, Lacey B.
Tudor Prelates and Politics   I-128
Smith, Norman Kemp
New Studies in the Philosophy of Descartes   I-298
Smith, Rhea Marsh
Spain: A Modern History   I-303; 344; 375; 445; II-584; 597; 636; 729; 1122; III-1261
Snell, John L.
Illusion and Necessity   III-1506
Nazi Revolution: Germany's Guilt or Germany's Fate?, The   III-1381
Outbreak of the Second World War, The. Design or Blunder? Problems in European Civilization series   III-1439
Snyder, Louis L.

War: A Concise History, 1939-1945, The
   III-1362; 1490
Weimar Republic, The   III-1298
Sobel, Lester A.
   Space: From Sputnik to Gemini   III-1623
Sobieszek, Robert
   "French Primitive Photography," in *Aperture,*
   XV   II-752
Society of Friends
   What Do the Churches Say on Capital Punish-
   ment?   I-459
Sokolf, Boris
   Story of Penicillin, The   III-1339
Soltau, Roger Henry
   French Political Thought in the Nineteenth
   Century   II-987; 1047; III-1147
Sontag, Raymond J.
   European Diplomatic History, 1871-1932
   II-991; 1012; 1023; 1074; III-1155; 1196;
   1201; 1206; 1244
   Nazi Soviet Relations, 1939-1941: Documents
   from the Archives of the German Foreign
   Office   III-1438
Sorokin, Pitrim A.
   Social Philosophies of an Age of Crisis   III-
   1282
Southgate, Donald
   Passing of the Whigs, 1832-1886, The   II-
   1043
Souvarine, B.
   Stalin: A Critical Survey of Bolshevism   III-
   1334
Spears, General Sir Edward L.
   Assignment to Catastrophe. Vol. II: *The Fall*
   of France   III-1455
Speidel, General Hans
   Invasion, 1944   III-1495
Spencer, Philip H.
   Politics of Belief in Nineteenth Century France,
   The   III-1147
Spender, James A.
   Life of Herbert Henry Asquith, Lord Oxford
   and Asquith   III-1218; 1239
Spiegelberg, Herbert
   Phenomenological Movement, The   III-
   1485
Stafford, Helen G.
   James VI of Scotland and the Throne of En-
   gland   I-230
Stanislawski, Daniel
   Individuality of Portugal: A Study in Histori-
   cal-Political Geography, The   III-1677
Stannard, Harold M.
   Gambetta and the Foundation of the Third
   Republic   II-977
Starkie, Enid
   Flaubert: The Making of the Master   II-833
Stavrianos, L. S.
   Balkans Since 1453, The   II-1012; III-
   1206; 1244
Stead, Richard

Story of Switzerland, The   II-798
Steinberg, Jonathan
   Yesterday's Deterrent   III-1191
Stettinius, Edward R., Jr.
   Roosevelt and the Russians: The Yalta Confer-
   ence   III-1505; 1511
Stillman, William J.
   Francesco Crispi: Insurgent, Exile, Revolution-
   ist and Statesman   II-1099
Stock, Ernest
   Israel on the Road to Sinai, 1949-1956, with a
   Sequel on the Six-Day War, 1967   III-
   1658
Stojanović, M. D.
   Great Powers and the Balkans, 1875-1878, The
   II-1012
Stolper, Gustav
   German Economy, 1870-1940: Issues and
   Trends   II-1032
Stoye, John
   Siege of Vienna, The   I-371
Straka, Gerald M.
   Revolution of 1688: Whig Triumph or Palace
   Revolution?, The. Problems in European
   Civilization series   I-363
Sturmey, S. G.
   Economic Development of Radio, The   III-
   1083
Sturtevant, Alfred Henry
   History of Genetics, A   II-911
Sturzo, Luigi
   Italy and Fascism   III-1323
Sukhanov, Nikolai Nikolayevich
   Russian Revolution, 1917: Eyewitness Account,
   The   III-1277
Sumner, B. H.
   Short History of Russia, A   III-1309
Surtz, Edward, S.J.
   Praise of Pleasure, The   I-53
   Praise of Wisdom, The   I-53
Svanström, R.
   Short History of Sweden   III-1168
Swanson, Guy E.
   Religion and Regime: A Sociological Account
   of the Reformation   I-152
Sweet, Paul R.
   Friedrich von Gentz, Defender of the Old Order
   II-628
Sykes, Percy
   History of Exploration from the Earliest Times
   to the Present, A   I-15
Szabo, Tamas
   Boy on the Rooftop   III-1599

Tate, Merze
   Disarmament Illusion: The Movement for a
   Limitation of Armaments to 1907, The
   II-1127
Tatu, Michel
   Power in the Kremlin: From Khrushchev to
   Kosygin   III-1588

Taylor, A. J. P.
  Bismarck, The Man and the Statesman
  II-917
  English History, 1914-1945   III-1318;
  1328; 1424
  *Habsburg Monarchy, 1809-1918: A History of
  the Austrian Empire and Austria-Hungary,
  The*   II-943
  "International Relations," in *The New Cam-
  bridge Modern History*   II-991
  Origins of the Second World War, The
  III-1432; 1445
  *Struggle for Mastery of Europe, 1848-1918,
  The*   II-842; 854; 962; 982; 1117; III-
  1346
Taylor, F. L.
  Art of War in Italy, 1494-1529, The   I-85
Taylor, F. Sherwood
  Galileo and the Freedom of Thought   I-289
Taylor, Frank
  Wars of Marlborough, 1702-1709, The   I-
  394
Taylor, Philip A. M.
  *Origins of the English Civil War, The. Con-
  spiracy, Crusade, or Class Conflict? Prob-
  lems in European Civilization series*   I-
  335
Temperley, Harold W.
  History of the Peace Conference of Paris, A
  III-1288
  "Revolution and Revolution Settlement in
  Great Britain, The," in *The Cambridge
  Modern History*   I-363
Tenenbaum, Joseph
  Race and Reich: The Story of an Epoch
  III-1367
Terry, C. S.
  Bach: A Biography   I-384
Thayer, John A.
  *Italy and the Great War: Politics and Culture,
  1870-1914*   II-1099
Thayer, William Roscoe
  Dawn of Italian Independence, The   II-
  644
Thomas, Hugh
  Spanish Civil War, The   III-1371
Thompson, G. S.
  *Catherine the Great and the Expansion of
  Russia*   I-468
Thompson, James M.
  French Revolution, The   I-505; 509; 519;
  523
  Louis Napoleon and the Second Empire
  II-812; 928
  Napoleon Bonaparte: His Rise and Fall
  I-541; 550; II-559; 571; 589
Thompson, James Vincent Perronet
  *Supreme Governor, a Study of Elizabethan Ec-
  clesiastical Policy and Circumstance*   I-
  173
Thompson, James Westfall

  Wars of Religion in France, 1559-1576, The
  I-188
Thomson, A. M.
  Democracy in France Since 1870   II-977
Thomson, David
  Democracy in France Since 1870   III-1147
  England in the Nineteenth Century, 1815-1914
  II-740
  *Two Frenchmen: Pierre Laval and Charles de
  Gaulle*   III-1612
Thomson, M. A.
  *Constitutional History of England, 1642-1801,
  A*   I-389
Thomson, S. Harrison
  Europe in Renaissance and Reformation
  I-90; 201; 253; 273; 312
Tibor, Meray
  Revolt of the Mind, The   III-1599
Tilley, Arthur
  French Wars of Religion, The   I-219
  Modern France   I-356
Timasheff, Nicholas S.
  *Great Retreat: The Growth and Decline of
  Communism in Russia, The*   III-1309
  Sociological Theory, Its Nature and Growth
  II-807
Tompkins, Peter
  Italy Betrayed   III-1490
Tompkins, S. R.
  Russian Mind, The   II-668
Torrance, Thomas F.
  Calvin's Doctrine of Man   I-122
Torrey, Norman L.
  Censoring of Diderot's Encyclopédie *and the
  Re-Established Text, The*   I-431
Towers, Walter K.
  From Beacon Fire to Radio   II-1083
Toynbee, Arnold
  *Survey of International Affairs, 1939-1946: The
  Eve of War, 1939*   III-1445
Toynbee, Veronica M.
  *Survey of International Affairs, 1939-1946: The
  Eve of War, 1939*   III-1445
Trease, Geoffrey
  Italian Story, The   I-34
Trend, John B.
  Origins of Modern Spain, The   II-1006
  Portugal   I-307; II-648; 677; 725; III-1222
Trenner, Anne
  Mercurial Chemist, The   II-563
Trevelyan, George Macaulay
  *British History in the Nineteenth Century and
  After, 1782-1949*   II-740
  Garibaldi and the Making of Italy   II-875
  History of England. Vol. II: *The Tudors and
  the Stuart Era*   I-340
  Lord Grey of the Reform Bill   II-709
Trimble, William Raleigh
  Catholic Laity in Elizabethan England, The
  I-179
Trotsky, Leon

History of the Russian Revolution, The III-1277

My Life: An Attempt at an Autobiography III-1352

Real Situation in Russia, The III-1352

Stalin III-1353

Suppressed Testament of Lenin: The Complete Original Text, with Two Explanatory Articles by Leon Trotsky, The III-1353

Truax, Rhoda
Joseph Lister, Father of Modern Surgery II-938

Truman, Harry S
Memoirs of Harry S Truman. Vol. II: The Years of Trial and Hope III-1531

Tuchman, Barbara W.
Guns of August, The III-1248; 1253
Proud Tower, The II-1127

Tucker, Robert C.
Soviet Political Mind, The III-1571

Turner, William P.
Machine-Tool Work, Fundamental Principles I-528

Twymen, Michael
Lithography, 1800-1850: The Techniques of Drawing on Stone in England and France and Their Application in the Works of Topography I-546

Tyler, Royall
Emperor Charles V, The I-43; 75

Ulam, Adam B.
Bolsheviks: The Intellectual and Political History of the Triumph of Communism in Russia, The III-1172

Underwood, E. Ashworth
Short History of Medicine, A II-938

United States Department of State
Conferences at Malta and Yalta, 1945, The III-1505

United States Office for Prosecution of Axis Criminality
Nazi Conspiracy and Aggression III-1525

Urwin, Derek W.
Western Europe Since 1945: A Short Political History III-1536

Usher, Abbott P.
History of Mechanical Inventions, A I-408; 528; II-1104

Utechin, S. V.
Russian Political Thought: A Concise History II-1108

Valentin, Veit
1848: Chapters in German History II-793
German People: Their History and Civilization from the Holy Roman Empire to the Third Reich, The I-293; 423; 441; II-714

Vandenberg, Arthur H., Jr.
Private Papers of Senator Vandenberg, The III-1560

Van Dyke, Paul
Catherine de Medici I-167; 188
Ignatius Loyola I-102

Van Houtte, J. A.
"Low Countries, The," in The New Cambridge Modern History II-689

Vaughan, Herbert M.
Medici Popes, Leo X and Clement VII, The I-48

Vernadsky, George
History of Russia, A I-367

Vidler, Alexander R.
Church in an Age of Revolution, The II-774

Villari, Luigi
Fascist Experiment, The III-1323

Vlahos, Olivia
Human Beginnings II-826

Vleeschauwer, Herman Jean de
Development of Kantian Thought, The I-495

Von Bismarck-Schonhausen, Otto E. Leopold
Bismarck, Man and Statesman II-1017
Memoirs, The II-973

Von Braun, Wernher
History of Rocketry and Space Travel III-1622

Von Laue, Theodore H.
Why Lenin? Why Stalin? A Reappraisal of the Russian Revolution, 1900-1930 II-1065; III-1159; 1277

Von Montgelas, Max Graf
Case for the Central Powers, The III-1346

Von Tirpitz, Alfred P.
My Memoirs III-1191

Vucinich, Alexander
Science in Russian Culture: A History to 1860 I-436

Vucinich, W. S.
Serbia Between East and West: The Events of 1903-1908 III-1206

Wahl, Nicholas
Fifth Republic: France's New Political System, The III-1612

Waite, Robert G.
Hitler and Nazi Germany III-1381

Waley, Daniel
Later Medieval Europe I-34

Walker, Eric A.
Cambridge History of the British Empire, The. Vol VIII: South Africa, Rhodesia, and the High Commission Territories. II-1132
History of Southern Africa, A II-1132

Walker, Richard L.
Edward Stettinius, Jr., 1944 to 1945 and James R. Byrnes, 1945 to 1947 III-1531

Walker, Walliston
John Calvin I-122

Wallace, D. M.
Russia II-869

Wallace, Lillian Parker
Papacy and European Diplomacy, 1869-1878, The II-962; 983
Wallas, Graham
Life of Francis Place, 1771-1854, The II-710; 746
Wallis, Charles G.
Great Books of the Western World I-141
Walsh, A. E.
Structure and Development of Common Market, The III-1605
Walsh, Warren B.
Russia and the Soviet Union III-1151
Walsh, William Thomas
Isabella of Spain I-5
Philip II, King of Spain, 1527-1598 I-161; 183; 192
Walton, Perry
Story of Textiles, The I-408
Wangermann, E.
"Habsburg Possessions and Germany, The" in *The New Cambridge Modern History* I-484
Ward, A. W.
Cambridge History of British Foreign Policy, The II-1002
Ward, Barbara
West at Bay, The III-1537
Warlimont, Walter
Inside Hitler's Headquarters, 1939-1945 III-1476
Warner, Charles K.
From the Ancient Régime to the Popular Front III-1415
Warner, Oliver
Great Sea Battles I-183
Watkins, Ernest
Cautious Revolution, The III-1521
Watson, J. Steven
Reign of George III, 1760-1815, The. Vol XII of *The Oxford History of England* I-455
Watson, Philip S.
Let God Be God I-58
Webb, Beatrice
Our Partnership III-1227
Weber, Eugen
European Right: A Historical Profile, The III-1303; 1390
Weber, Wilhelm
History of Lithography, A I-546
Webster, Sir Charles
Congress of Vienna, 1814-1815, The II-628
European Alliance, 1815-1825, The II-659
"Pacification of France, 1813-1815, The," in *The Cambridge History of English Foreign Policy* II-628
Webster, Richard A.
Cross and the Fasces: Christian Democracy and Fascism in Italy, The III-1303
Wechsberg, Joseph

Voices: Prague, 1968, The III-1672
Wedgwood, C. V.
Coffin for King Charles: The Trial and Execution of Charles I, A I-335
King's War, 1641-1647, The I-316
Oliver Cromwell I-335
Richelieu and the French Monarchy I-262; 284
Thirty Years War, The I-152
Weil, Gordon L.
Handbook of the European Economic Community, A III-1606
Weiss, John
Fascist Tradition, The III-1303
Weisskopf, Kurt
Agony of Czechoslovakia, 1938-1968, The III-1672
Welensky, Sir Roy
4000 Days: The Life and Death of the Federation of Rhodesia and Nyasaland III-1647
Werth, Alexander
Russia at War, 1941-1945 III-1476
Twilight of France, 1933-1940, The III-1390
West, Donald J.
Hundred Years of Psychology, A III-1313
West, Julius
History of the Chartist Movement, A II-745
Westermeyer, H. E.
Fall of the German Gods, The III-1367
Wetter, Gustav A.
Dialectical Materialism II-785
Weygand, Maxime
Recalled to Service III-1455
Wheeler-Bennett, John W.
Nemesis of Power: The German Army in Politics, 1918-1945, The III-1394; 1481
White, Andrew D.
History of the Warfare of Science with Theology in Christendom, A II-681
Whitehead, A. W.
Gaspard de Coligny, Admiral of France I-188
Whitfield, John H.
Machiavelli I-39
Whitney, G.
Heritage of Kant, The I-495
Whittaker, Edmund T.
History of the Theories of Aether and Electricity, A II-653
Whyte, Arthur James
Evolution of Modern Italy, The II-853; 928; 1099
Williams, Beryl
Miracles from Microbes III-1178; 1339
Williams, Charles
James I I-230
William, E. Neville
Eighteenth Century Constitution, 1688-1815, The I-388

Williams, L. Pearce
Origins of Field Theory, The   II-653
Williams, Roger
World of Napoleon III, 1851-1870, (Gaslight and Shadow), The   II-812
Williams, T. Desmond
Great Famine: Studies in Irish History, 1845-1852, The   II-762
Williamson, Hugh Ross
Historical Whodunits   I-10
Williamson, James A.
Great Britain and the Commonwealth   III-1376
Tudor Age, The   I-10
Willis, F. Roy
France, Germany, and the New Europe, 1945-1967   III-1653
Willson, David Harris
Privy Councillors in the House of Commons, 1604-1629, The   I-269
Wilmot, Chester
Struggle for Europe, The   III-1362; 1500
Wilson, C. H.
Cambridge Economic History of Europe, The   I-427
Wiltgen, Ralph M., S.V.D.
Rhine Flows into the Tiber: The Unknown Council, The   III-1641
Windell, George C.
Catholics and German Unity, 1866-1871, The   II-973
Wingfield-Stratton, Esme
Charles, King of England, 1600-1637   I-269
Wiskemann, Elizabeth
Rome-Berlin Axis: A History of the Relations Between Hitler and Mussolini, The   III-1405; 1428
Witte, Sergei
Memoirs of Count Witte, The   II-1065
Wittels, Fritz
Freud and His Time   III-1142
Wolf, Abraham
History of Science, Technology, and Philosophy in the Eighteenth Century, A   I-408
Wolf, John B.
Emergence of the Great Powers, 1685-1715, The. Vol VII of *The Rise of Modern Europe* series   I-367; 371; 404
Diplomatic History of the Baghdad Railway, The   II-1138
France, 1814-1919   II-601; 685
Louis XIV   I-404
Wolfe, Bertram
Three Who Made a Revolution   III-1277
Wolfe, Don M.
Complete Prose of John Milton, The   I-323
Wolfgang, Marvin
Sociology of Punishment and Correction: A

Book of Readings, The   I-459
Woodham-Smith, Cecil
Great Hunger: Ireland, 1845-1849, The   I-427
Woodrooffe, Thomas
Vantage at Sea: England's Emergence as an Ocean Power   I-197
Woodward, E. L.
Great Britain and the German Navy   III-1191; 1213
Woodward, Llwewllyn
Age of Reform, 1815-1870, The. Vol. XIII of *The Oxford History of England,*   II-689; 740; 763
World Council of Churches
First Assembly of the World Council of Churches: The Official Report, The   III-1554
Uppsala Report, 1968, The   III-1554
Wren, Melvin C.
Course of Russian History, The   I-200; 249; 367; 379; 478; II-1065; III-1172; 1182
Wright, Gordon
France in Modern Times: 1760 to the Present   II-567; 601; 685; 977; 1056
Wylie, Laurence
In Search of France   III-1689

Yarmolinsky, Abraham
Memoirs of Count Witte, The   II-1127
Young, Agatha
Scalpel: Men Who Made Surgery   II-938
Young, Desmond
Rommel, The Desert Fox   III-1471
Young, G. M.
Victorian England: Portrait of an Age   II-802
Young, I.
"Russia," in *The New Cambridge Modern History*   I-478
Young, Peter
World War, 1939-1945   III-1362; 1476; 1490; 1500
Yzermans, Vincent A.
American Participation in the Second Vatican Council   III-1641

Zablock, Clement J.
Sino-Soviet Rivalry: Implications for U.S. Policy   III-1682
Zimmern, Alfred
League of Nations and the Rule of Law, 1918-1935, The   III-1294
Zirkle, Conway
Evolution, Marxian Biology, and the Social Scene   II-911
Zoff, Otto
Huguenots, The   I-262

INDEXES

VOLUMES ONE, TWO, AND THREE

American Series

ALPHABETICAL LIST OF EVENTS

Acquisition of the Panama Canal Zone   II-1339

Adoption of the Articles of Confederation I-288

Adoption of the Constitution   I-330

Adoption of the Ordinance of 1785   I-306

Adoption of Virginia Statute of Religious Liberty I-318

Alexander Graham Bell Invents the Telephone II-1089

Alexis de Tocqueville's Visit to America   II-673

Algonquin Indians Sell Manhattan Island for Twenty-Four Dollars   I-80

American Intervention Short of War, 1939-1941 III-1686

American Renaissance, The   II-848

Andrew Jackson's Battle with the Second Bank of the United States   II-696

Anthracite Coal Strike   II-1329

Apollo 11 Lands on the Moon   III-1940

Appearance of the Knickerbocker School   I-481

Armory Show, The   III-1411

Arrival of the First Negroes and the Origins of Slavery in British North America   I-69

Arrival of the Indians, the First Americans I-1

Assassination of Lincoln and the End of the Civil War   II-1014

Assassination of President Kennedy   III-1899

Assassinations of Martin Luther King and Robert F. Kennedy   III-1927

Bacon's Rebellion   I-151

Baltimore and Ohio Railroad Begins Operations I-624

Bancroft Publishes *History of the United States from the Discovery of the American Continent* II-730

Battle for Leyte Gulf   III-1731

Battle of Fallen Timbers   I-383

Battle of Guadalcanal   III-1709

Battle of Lexington and Concord   I-251

Battle of New Orleans   I-533

Battle of the Little Big Horn   II-1094

Battle of Tippecanoe   I-498

Battles of Gettysburg, Vicksburg, and Chattanooga   II-997

Battles of Saratoga   I-277

Beard Publishes *An Economic Interpretation of the Constitution*   III-1426

Beginning of the Penny Press   II-713

Beginnings of Commercial Television Broadcasting   III-1674

Beginnings of Organized Labor *(Commonwealth v. Hunt)*   II-785

Beginnings of State Universities   I-312

Benjamin Franklin Writes His *Autobiography* I-236

Berkeley Student Revolt, The   III-1912

Berlin Airlift, The   III-1794

Black Sox Scandal and the Rise of Spectator Sports   III-1497

Bleeding Kansas   II-889

Bombing of Pearl Harbor   III-1697

Booker T. Washington Delivers His "Atlanta Compromise" Speech   II-1249

Boston Massacre   I-231

Boston Tea Party   I-241

British Conquest of New Netherland   I-140

Brooklyn Bridge Erected   II-1060

Burr's Conspiracy   I-461

California Gold Rush   II-843

Calling of the First General Assembly of Virginia I-65

Carnegie Publishes *The Gospel of Wealth* II-1167

Carolina Regulator Movements   I-213

Cartier and Roberval Search for a Northwest Passage   I-28

Chartering of the American Fur Company I-476

Chartering of the Second Bank of the United States   I-539

Closing of the Frontier   II-1213

Columbus Lands in the New World   I-17

Commodore Perry Opens Japan to American Trade   II-884

Completion of the Transcontinental Telegraph II-930

Compromise of 1850, The   II-854

Conclusion of Franco-American Treaties   I-282

Confederation of the United Colonies of New England   I-109

Congress of Industrial Organizations Formed III-1655

Construction of the Erie Canal   I-546

Construction of the First Transcontinental Railroad   II-969

Construction of the National Road   I-491

Convening of the First Continental Congress I-246

Convening of the Second Continental Congress I-256

Coronado's Expedition and the Founding of Santa Fe   I-40

Creation of the Confederate States of America II-941

Creation of the Office of Commissioner of Education   II-1031

Creation of the Office of Scientific Research and Development   III-1692

Creation of the Tennessee Valley Authority III-1621

"Crime of 1873," The   II-1083

Cuban Missile Crisis, The   III-1888

Declaration of Independence   I-261

Demobilization after World War I   III-1478

Demobilization and Reconversion after World War II   III-1759

Democratic Revolution of 1928   III-1566

DeSoto's Expedition and the Founding of St. Augustine   I-33

Development of Direct Democracy   II-1307

Development of the Ford Assembly Line and Adoption of the Five-Dollar-a-Day Minimum Wage   III-1421

Development of the Salk Vaccine   III-1835

Dewey Publishes *The School and Society*   II-1301

Dingley Tariff, The   II-1273

Discovery and Demonstration of an Effective Anesthetic   II-791

Discovery That Yellow Fever Is Spread by a Mosquito   II-1313

Dollar Diplomacy   III-1379

Dorr Rebellion and the Growth of Political Democracy   II-766

Dred Scott Decision on Slavery *(Dred Scott* v. *Sanford)*   II-900

Dropping of the Atomic Bomb on Hiroshima III-1753

Dust Bowl, The   III-1627

Economic Mobilization for War and Formation of the War Production Board   III-1680

Edison Demonstrates the First Practical Incandescent Lamp   II-1110

Eighteenth Amendment, The   III-1507

Election of Coolidge to the Presidency, and the Ascendancy of Big Business   III-1542

Election of 1884   II-1140

Election of 1840   II-760

Election of 1824   I-607

Election of Eisenhower to the Presidency in 1952 III-1843

Election of Franklin D. Roosevelt to the Presidency in 1932   III-1609

Election of Hayes to the Presidency, and the End of Reconstruction   II-1099

Election of Jackson to the Presidency in 1828 I-1828

Election of Jefferson to the Presidency in 1800 I-426

Election of Kennedy to the Presidency   III-1871

Election of Lincoln to the Presidency in 1860 II-935

Election of Lyndon B. Johnson to the Presidency, and the Emergence of the Great Society III-1918

Election of McKinley to the Presidency in 1896 II-1268

Election of Nixon to the Presidency in 1968 III-1933

Election of Truman to the Presidency, and the Emergence of the Fair Deal   III-1800

Election of Wilson to the Presidency in 1912 III-1405

Emancipation Proclamation   II-980

Emergence of the First Political Parties   I-350

Enactment of the G.I. Bill and Federal Aid to Education   III-1725

Entrance of the United States into World War I   III-1450

Era of the Clipper Ships   II-807

Erection of Slater's Spinning Mill at Pawtucket I-362

Ernest Hemingway Publishes *The Sun Also Rises* III-1560

Establishment of Harvard College and Enactment of the Massachusetts School Law I-103

Establishment of Oberlin College   II-708

Establishment of Separate but Equal Doctrine for Black and White Public Facilities *(Plessy* v. *Ferguson)*   II-1261

Establishment of the Independent Treasury II-748

Establishment of the United States Military Academy   I-432

Establishment of the United States Public Health Service   III-1394

Expeditions of John C. Frémont   II-795

Federal Government Assumes Control of Interstate Commerce *(Gibbons* v. *Ogden)*   I-600

First Battle of Bull Run   II-952

First Commercial Oil Well   II-912

First Inauguration of Abraham Lincoln   II-946

First Pan-American Congress   II-1190

First Showing of *The Great Train Robbery* II-1333

First Successful Voyage of the *Clermont*   I-471

First Test of a Submarine in Warfare   I-267

Formation of the American Anti-Slavery Society II-719

Formation of the Dominion of New England I-163

Formation of the Peace Corps   III-1877

Formation of the Republican Party   II-877

Formulation of the Dawes Plan   III-1537

Founding of Pennsylvania   I-157

Founding of Quebec and French Exploration of the Great Lakes   I-52

Founding of Rhode Island   I-97

Founding of San Francisco   I-272

Founding of the American Philosophical Society I-194

Founding of The Johns Hopkins University
II-1077
Founding of the Mayo Clinic   II-1178
Founding of the Moody Bible Institute   II-1173
Founding of the Smithsonian Institution   II-831
Founding of the Unitarian Church in the United States   I-570
Fourteenth Amendment, The   II-1049
Free Public School Movement, The   I-576
French and Indian War, The   I-200
French Exploration of the Mississippi Valley   I-144

German and Irish Immigration   II-754
Government Acts to Assure Loyalty at Home in Wartime   III-1703
Great Awakening, The   I-176
Great Depression, 1929-1939, The   III-1582
Great Migration, The   I-527
Great Puritan Migration, The   I-85

Half-Way Covenant, The   I-127
Harriet Beecher Stowe Publishes *Uncle Tom's Cabin*   II-859
Hartford Convention, The   I-517
Hearst-Pulitzer Circulation War   II-1243
Henry Adams Publishes *History of the United States of America During the First Administrations of Jefferson and Madison*   II-1184
Hoover-Stimson Doctine   III-1599
Howe's Invention of the Sewing Machine Heralding the Rise of Industrial Capitalism   II-837
Hudson River School of Painters, The   I-613
Humanitarian Reform Movement, The   I-642
Hundred Days, The   III-1615

Impeachment of Andrew Johnson   II-1026
Inauguration of Barnum's Circus   II-1066
Inauguration of George Washington as First President   I-341
Insular Cases, The   II-1318
Invasion of Normandy: Operation "Overlord," The   III-1721
Invasion of North Africa   III-1715
Invention of the Electric Telegraph   II-742
Issuance of Alexander Hamilton's *Report on Public Credit*   I-356

Jedediah Smith's Exploration of the Far West   I-619
John Brown's Raid on Harpers Ferry   II-918
John Hay Sends His "Open Door Notes"   II-1296
Judicial Recognition of the Doctrine of Implied Powers *(McCulloch* v. *Maryland)*   I-564
Judicial Recognition of the Doctrine of the Sanctity of Contracts *(Fletcher* v. *Peck)*   I-485

Korean War, The   III-1823

Land Law of 1820   I-582
Landing of the Pilgrims at Plymouth   I-74
Laying of the First Transatlantic Cable   II-895
Lewis and Clark Expedition   I-450
Library of Congress Occupies Its Own Building   II-1279
Lincoln-Douglas Debates   II-906
Louisiana Purchase, The   I-445

McCarthy Hearings, The   III-1817
McCormick's Invention of the Reaper   II-679
Mahan Publishes *The Influence of Sea Power upon History, 1660-1783*   II-1201
Mark Twain Publishes *The Adventures of Huckleberry Finn*   II-1146
Marshall Mission to China, The   III-1765
Mayan Calendar, The   I-5
Meeting of the Washington Disarmament Conference   III-1531
Meuse-Argonne Offensive   III-1466
Monitor v. the *Merrimack,* The   II-957
Monroe Doctrine, The   I-593
Montgomery Bus Boycott   III-1855
Mormon Migration to Utah   II-812

Nat Turner's Slavery Insurrection   II-685
National Association for the Advancement of Colored People Formed   III-1384
Negotiation of Jay's Treaty   I-389
Negotiation of Pinckney's Treaty   I-396
Negotiation of the Adams-Onís Treaty   I-558
Negotiation of the Missouri Compromise   I-552
Negotiation of the North Atlantic Treaty   III-1806
Negotiation of the Treaty of Ghent   I-552
Negotiation of the Treaty of Paris   I-300
Negotiation of the Treaty of Versailles   III-1484
Negotiation of the Treaty of Washington   II-1072
Negotiation of the Webster-Ashburton Treaty   II-801
New Harmony, Indiana, and the Communitarian Movement   I-511
New Immigration and the Establishment of Ellis Island Immigration Station, The   II-1219
New Poetry Movement, The   III-1399
Nineteenth Amendment, The   III-1513
Noah Webster Publishes *An American Dictionary of the English Language*   I-636
Norsemen Discover the New World   I-11
Nullification Controversy, The   II-702

Occupation of California and the Southwest   II-818

Opening of the Chisholm Trail and Rise of the Cattle Kingdom   II-1020
Opening of the Metropolitan Opera   II-1135
Opening of the Santa Fe Trade   I-588
Operation of the Pony Express   II-925
Organization of American States   III-1789
Organization of the American Federation of Labor   II-1152
Organization of the National Grange of the Patrons of Husbandry   II-1043
Organization of the People's Party   II-1225
Organization of the Standard Oil Trust   II-1116

Pacific Railroad Surveys   II-865
Passage of the Alien and Sedition Acts   I-414
Passage of the British Navigation Acts   I-121
Passage of the Chinese Exclusion Act and the First Immigration Law   II-1123
Passage of the Dawes Act   II-1161
Passage of the Employment Act of 1946   III-1770
Passage of the Federal Reserve Act   III-1432
Passage of the First National Draft Law   II-991
Passage of the Homestead Act   II-962
Passage of the Indian Removal Act   I-666
Passage of the Interstate Commerce Act   II-1157
Passage of the Judiciary Act   I-345
Passage of the Kansas-Nebraska Act   II-871
Passage of the Maryland Act of Toleration   I-115
Passage of the Morrill Land Grant Act   II-974
Passage of the National Bank Acts of 1863 and 1864   II-985
Passage of the National Labor Relations Act   III-1637
Passage of the National Security Act   III-1783
Passage of the Neutrality Acts   III-1649
Passage of the Northwest Ordinance   I-324
Passage of the Pendleton Act Reforming the Civil Service   II-1128
Passage of the Pre-emption Act of 1841   II-772
Passage of the Reconstruction Finance Corporation Legislation   III-1594
Passage of the Sherman Antitrust Act   II-1206
Passage of the Social Security Act   III-1643
Pershing Military Expedition into Mexico   III-1438
Philippine Insurrection, The   II-1290
Pike's Exploration of the Southwest   I-467
Polarization of American Society in the 1960's   III-1861
Population Explosion and the Move to Suburbia, The   III-1811
Poverty in an Affluent Society   III-1866

Powell Publishes *Report on the Lands of the Arid Region of the United States*   II-1104
Proclamation of 1763   I-207
Propaganda and Civil Liberties in World War I   III-1454
"Pro-Slavery Argument," The   I-648
Publication of Reinhold Niebuhr's *Moral Man and Immoral Society,* and the Rise of Neoörthodoxy   III-1604
Publication of *The Federalist*   I-335
Publication of *The Southern Literary Messenger*   II-725
Publication of Washington's Farewell Address   I-403
Pullman Strike, The   II-1237
Purchase of Alaska   II-1037

Radio Station KDKA Begins Commerical Broadcasting   III-1519
Raleigh's Attempts at Colonization in the New World   I-46
Ratification of the Bill of Rights   I-367
Reconstruction of the South   II-1003
Red Scare, The   III-1491
Republican Congressional Insurgency   III-1390
Republican Resurgence in the Elections of 1918 and 1920   III-1472
Revenue Act of 1767 and the Townshend Crisis   I-225
Rise of Mass Culture, The   III-1501
Rise of the Whig Party   II-690
Rise of Transcendentalism   I-654
Robert Goddard Launches the First Liquid-Fueled Rocket   III-1555

Salem Witchcraft Trials   I-169
Scandals of the Grant Administration   II-1054
Scandals of the Harding Administration   III-1525
Scopes Trial, The   III-1549
Scottsboro Trials, The   III-1588
Second Awakening and Frontier Religious Revival, The   I-420
Settlement of Connecticut   I-91
Settlement of Georgia   I-182
Settlement of Jamestown   I-59
Settlement of the Carolinas   I-132
Sherman's March to the Sea   II-1010
Sixteenth Amendment, The   III-1415
Sociological Jurisprudence Established as a Principle *(Muller* v. *Oregon)*   III-1369
Spanish-American War, The   II-1284
Spanish Civil War and the American Arms Embargo   III-1661
Stamp Act Crisis   I-219
Stephen Crane Publishes *The Red Badge of Courage*   II-1255
Stock Market Crash of 1929   III-1577
Struggle for Oregon, The   II-778

Supreme Court Decisions in Reapportionment Cases   III-1883

Supreme Court Defines Rights of Accused Criminals *(Gideon* v. *Wainright)*   III-1893

Supreme Court Orders Desegregation of the Public Schools *(Brown* v. *Board of Education of Topeka)*   III-1849

Supreme Court Packing Fight   III-1667

Supreme Court's First Exercise of the Right of Judicial Review *(Marbury* v. *Madison)*   I-437

Surrender of Cornwallis at Yorktown   I-294

Texas Revolution   II-736

Theodore Roosevelt Assumes the Presidency   II-1325

Trial of John Peter Zenger and Freedom of the Press   I-188

Truman Doctrine with Its Policy of Containment, The   III-1776

Truman-MacArthur Confrontation, The   III-1829

Twelfth Amendment, The   I-456

United Nations Charter Convention   III-1741

Universal Negro Improvement Association Founded in the United States   III-1444

Upton Sinclair Publishes *The Jungle*   III-1353

V-E Day   III-1748

Voyages of John Cabot, The   I-23

Walter Rauschenbusch and the Social Gospel   II-1195

War in Vietnam, The   III-1906

War Industries Board and Economic Mobilization for War, The   III-1460

War of 1812, The   I-505

War with Mexico   II-825

Watts Riot and Violence in the Ghetto, The   III-1924

Webster-Hayne Debate over States' Rights   I-660

Whiskey Rebellion, The   I-377

White House Conference on Conservation, The   III-1374

Whitney Invents the Cotton Gin   I-371

William Faulkner Publishes *The Sound and the Fury*   III-1571

William Graham Sumner Publishes *Folkways*   III-1357

William James Publishes *Pragmatism*   III-1363

Works Progress Administration Formed   III-1632

World's Columbian Exposition   II-1231

Wright Brothers' First Flight, The   II-1346

XYZ Affair, The   I-408

Yalta Conference, The   III-1736

AMERICAN

KEY WORD INDEX FOR EVENTS

Acts to Assure Loyalty at Home in Wartime, Government   III-1703

Adams-Onís Treaty, Negotiation of the I-558

Adams Publishes *History of the United States of America During the First Administrations of Jefferson, and Madison,* Henry   II-1184

Adoption of the Articles of Confederation I-288

Adoption of the Constitution   I-330

Adoption of the Ordinance of 1785   I-306

Adoption of Virgina Statute of Religious Liberty I-318

Adventures of Huckleberry Finn, Mark Twain Publishes *The*   III-1146

Africa, Invasion of North   III-1715

Alaska, Purchase of   II-1037

Algonquin Indians Sell Manhattan Island for Twenty-Four Dollars   I-80

Alien and Sedition Acts, Passage of the   I-414

Amendment, The Eighteenth   III-1507

Amendment, The Fourteenth   II-1049

Amendment, The Nineteenth   III-1513

Amendment, The Sixteenth   III-1415

Amendment, The Twelfth   I-456

American Anti-Slavery Society, Formation of the   II-719

American Dictionary of the English Language, Noah Webster Publishes *An*   I-636

American Federation of Labor, Organization of the   II-1152

American Fur Company, Chartering of the I-476

American Philosophical Society, Founding of the   I-194

American Renaissance, The   II-848

Anesthetic, Discovery and Demonstration of an Effective   II-791

Anthracite Coal Strike   II-1329

Anti-Slavery Society, Formation of the American   II-719

Antitrust Act, Passage of the Sherman   II-1206

Apollo 11 Lands on the Moon   III-1940

Armory Show, The   III-1411

Arrival of the First Negroes and the Origins of Slavery in British North America   I-69

Arrival of the Indians, the First Americans I-1

Articles of Confederation, Adoption of the I-288

Assassination of Lincoln and the End of the Civil War   II-1014

Assassination of President Kennedy   III-1899

Assassinations of Martin Luther King and Robert F. Kennedy   III-1927

Assemby Line and Adoption of the Five-Dollar-a-Day Minimum Wage, Development of the Ford   III-1421

"Atlanta Compromise" Speech, Booker T. Washington Delivers His   II-1249

Atomic Bomb on Hiroshima, Dropping of the III-1753

Autobiography, Benjamin Franklin Writes His I-236

Awakening and Frontier Religious Revival, The Second   I-420

Awakening, The Great   I-151

Bacon's Rebellion   I-151

Baltimore and Ohio Railroad Begins Operations I-624

Bancroft Publishes *History of the United States from the Discovery of the American Continent* II-730

Bank Acts of 1863 and 1864, Passage of the National   II-985

Bank of the United States, Andrew Jackson's Battle with the Second   II-696

Bank of the United States, Chartering of the Second   I-539

Barnum's Circus, Inauguration of   II-1066

Battle for Leyte Gulf   III-1731

Battle of Bull Run, First   II-952

Battle of Fallen Timbers   I-383

Battle of Guadalcanal   III-1709

Battle of Lexington and Concord   I-251

Battle of the Little Big Horn   II-1094

Battle of Tippecanoe   I-498

Battles of Gettysburg, Vicksburg, and Chattanooga   II-997

Battles of Saratoga   I-277

Beard Publishes *An Economic Interpretation of the Constitution*   III-1426

Bell Invents the Telephone, Alexander Graham II-1089

Berkeley Student Revolt, The   III-1912

Berlin Airlift, The   III-1794

Bible Institute, Founding of the Moody   II-1173

Bill of Rights, Ratification of the   I-367

Black Sox Scandal and the Rise of Spectator Sports   III-1497

Bleeding Kansas   II-889

Boston Massacre   I-231

Boston Tea Party   I-241

Boycott, Montgomery Bus   III-1855

British Conquest of New Netherland   I-140

British Navigation Acts, Passage of the   I-121

Broadcasting, Beginnings of Commercial Television   III-1674

Broadcasting, Radio Station KDKA Begins Commercial   III-1519

Brooklyn Bridge Erected   II-1060

1590

AMERICAN

Key Word Index for Events

(Brown v. *Board of Education of Topeka),* Supreme Court Orders Desegregation of the Public Schools   III-1849

Brown's Raid on Harpers Ferry, John   II-918

Bull Run, First Battle of   II-952

Burr's Conspiracy   I-461

Business, Election of Coolidge to the Presidency, and the Ascendency of Big   III-1542

Cable, Laying of the First Transatlantic   II-895

Cabot, The Voyages of John   I-23

Calendar, The Mayan   I-5

California and the Southwest, Occupation of   II-818

California Gold Rush   II-843

Canal, Construction of the Erie   I-546

Canal Zone, Acquisition of the Panama   II-1339

Capitalism, Howe's Invention of the Sewing Machine Heralding the Rise of Industrial   II-837

Carnegie Publishes *The Gospel of Wealth*   II-1167

Carolina Regulator Movements   I-213

Carolinas, Settlement of the   I-132

Cartier and Roberval Search for a Northwest Passage   I-28

Cases, The Insular   II-1318

Cattle Kingdom, Opening of the Chisholm Trail and the Rise of the   II-1020

Chartering of the American Fur Company   I-476

Chartering of the Second Bank of the United States   I-539

Chattanooga, Battles of Gettysburg, Vicksburg, and   II-997

China, Marshall Mission to   III-1765

Chinese Exclusion Act and the First Immigration Law, Passage of the   II-1123

Chisholm Trail and the Rise of the Cattle Kingdom, Opening of the   II-1020

Circulation War, Hearst-Pulitzer   II-1243

Circus, Inauguration of Barnum's   II-1066

Civil Liberties in World War I, Propaganda and   III-1454

Civil Service, Passage of the Pendleton Act Reforming the   II-1128

Civil War, Assassination of Lincoln and the End of the   II-1014

Clermont, First Successful Voyage of the   I-471

Clinic, Founding of the Mayo   II-1178

Clipper Ships, Era of the   II-807

Closing of the Frontier   II-1213

Coal Strike, Anthracite   II-1329

College, Establishment of Oberlin   II-708

Colonization in the New World, Raleigh's Attempts at   I-46

Columbian Exposition, World's   II-1231

Columbus Lands in the New World   I-17

Commercial Broadcasting, Radio Station KDKA Begins   III-1519

Commercial Oil Well, First   II-912

Commercial Television Broadcasting, Beginnings of   III-1674

Commissioner of Education, Creation of the Office of   II-1031

(Commonwealth v. *Hunt),* Beginnings of Organized Labor   II-785

Communitarian Movement, New Harmony, Indiana, and the   I-511

Completion of the Transcontinental Telegraph   II-930

Compromise of 1850, The   II-854

Concord, Battle of Lexington and   I-251

Confederate States of America, Creation of the   II-941

Confederation, Adoption of the Articles of   I-288

Confederation of the United Colonies of New England   I-109

Congress, First Pan-American   I-1190

Congress of Industrial Organizations Formed   III-1655

Congressional Insurgency, Republican   III-1390

Connecticut, Settlement of   I-91

Conservation, The White House Conference on   III-1374

Conspiracy, Burr's   I-461

Constitution, Adoption of the   I-330

Construction of the Erie Canal   I-546

Construction of the First Transcontinental Railroad   II-969

Construction of the National Road   I-491

Continental Congress, Convening of the First   I-246

Continental Congress, Convening of the Second   I-256

Contracts *(Fletcher* v. *Peck),* Judicial Recognition of the Doctrine of the Sanctity of   I-485

Convention, The Hartford   I-517

Cornwallis at Yorktown, Surrender of   I-294

Coronado's Expedition and the Founding of Santa Fe   I-40

Cotton Gin, Whitney Invents the   I-371

Crane Publishes *The Red Badge of Courage,* Stephen   II-1255

Crash of 1929, Stock Market   III-1577

"Crime of 1873," The   II-1083

Cuban Missile Crisis, The   III-1888

Culture, The Rise of Mass   III-1501

Dawes Act, Passage of the   II-1161

Dawes Plan, Formulation of the   III-1537

Debate over States' Rights, Webster-Hayne   I-660

Debates, Lincoln-Douglas   II-906

Decision on Slavery *(Dred Scott* v. *Sanford),* Dred Scott   II-900

Declaration of Independence   I-261
Demobilization after World War I   III-1478
Demobilization and Reconversion after World War II   III-1759
Democracy, Development of Direct   II-1307
Democracy, Dorr Rebellion and the Growth of Political   II-766
Democratic Revolution of 1928, The   III-1566
Depression, 1929-1939, The Great   III-1582
Desegregation of the Public Schools *(Brown* v. *Board of Education of Topeka),* Supreme Court Orders   III-1849
DeSoto's Expedition and the Founding of St. Augustine   I-33
de Tocqueville's Visit to America, Alexis   II-673
Dewey Publishes *The School and Society*   II-1301
Dictionary of the English Language, Noah Webster Publishes *An American*   I-636
Dingley Tariff, The   II-1273
Diplomacy, Dollar   III-1379
Direct Democracy, Development of   II-1307
Disarmament Conference, Meeting of the Washington   III-1531
Dollar Diplomacy   III-1379
Dominion of New England, Formation of the   I-163
Dorr Rebellion and the Growth of Political Democracy   II-766
Draft Law, Passage of the First National   II-991
Dred Scott Decision on Slavery *(Dred Scott* v. *Sanford)*   II-900
Dust Bowl, The   III-1627

Economic Interpretation of the Constitution, Beard Publishes *An*   III-1426
Edison Demonstrates the First Practical Incandescent Lamp   II-1110
Education, Creation of the Office of Commissioner of   II-1031
Education, Enactment of the G.I. Bill and Federal Aid to   III-1725
Eighteenth Amendment, The   III-1507
Election of 1824   I-607
Election of 1840   II-760
Election of 1884   II-1140
Election of Coolidge to the Presidency, and the Ascendency of Big Business   III-1542
Election of Eisenhower to the Presidency in 1952   III-1843
Election of Franklin D. Roosevelt to the Presidency in 1932   III-1609
Election of Hayes to the Presidency, and the End of Reconstruction   II-1099
Election of Jackson to the Presidency in 1828   I-1828
Election of Jefferson to the Presidency in 1800   I-426

Election of Kennedy to the Presidency   III-1871
Election of Lincoln to the Presidency in 1860   II-935
Election of Lyndon B. Johnson to the Presidency, and the Emergence of the Great Society   III-1918
Election of McKinley to the Presidency in 1896   II-1268
Election of Nixon to the Presidency in 1968   III-1933
Election of Truman to the Presidency, and the Emergence of the Fair Deal   III-1800
Election of Wilson to the Presidency in 1912   III-1405
Elections of 1918 and 1920, Republican Resurgence in the   III-1472
Ellis Island Immigration Station, The New Immigration and the Establishment of   II-1219
Emancipation Proclamation   II-980
Embargo, Spanish Civil War and the American Arms   III-1661
Employment Act of 1946, Passage of the   III-1770
Erie Canal, Construction of the   I-546
Expedition, Lewis and Clark   I-450
Expeditions of John C. Frémont   II-795
Exploration of the Far West, Jedediah Smith's   I-619
Exploration of the Great Lakes, Founding of Quebec and French   I-52
Exploration of the Mississippi Valley, French   I-144
Exploration of the Southwest, Pike's   I-467
Exposition, World's Columbian   II-1231

Fair Deal, Election of Truman to the Presidency, and the Emergence of the   III-1800
Fallen Timbers, Battle of   I-383
Farewell Address, Publication of Washington's   I-403
Faulkner Publishes *The Sound and the Fury,* William   III-1571
Federal Aid to Education, Enactment of the G.I. Bill and   III-1725
Federal Government Assumes Control of Interstate Commerce *(Gibbons* v. *Ogden)*   I-606
Federal Reserve Act, Passage of the   III-1432
Federalist, Publication of *The*   I-335
First Battle of Bull Run   II-952
First Commerical Oil Well   II-912
First Continental Congress, Convening of the   I-246
First Flight, The Wright Brothers'   II-1346
First General Assembly of Virginia, Calling of the   I-65
First Immigration Law, Passage of the Chinese Exclusion Act and the   II-1123
First Pan-American Congress   II-1190

First Practical Incandescent Lamp, Edison Demonstrates the   II-1110
First Showing of *The Great Train Robbery* II-1333
First Successful Voyage of the *Clermont*   I-471
First Test of a Submarine in Warfare   I-267
(Fletcher v. *Peck),* Judicial Recognition of the Sanctity of Contracts   I-485
Flight, The Wright Brothers' First   II-1346
Folkways, William Graham Sumner Publishes III-1357
Ford Assembly Line and Adoption of the Five-Dollar-a-Day Minimum Wage, Development of the   III-1421
Founding of Pennsylvania   I-157
Founding of Quebec and French Exploration of the Great Lakes   I-52
Founding of Rhode Island   I-97
Founding of St. Augustine, DeSoto's Expedition and the   I-33
Founding of San Francisco   I-272
Founding of Santa Fe, Coronado's Expedition and the   I-40
Founding of the American Philosophical Society I-195
Founding of The Johns Hopkins University II-1077
Founding of the Mayo Clinic   II-1178
Founding of the Moody Bible Institute   II-1173
Founding of the Smithsonian Institution   II-831
Founding of the Unitarian Church in the United States   I-570
Fourteenth Amendment, The   II-1049
Franco-American Treaties, Conclusion of   I-282
Franklin Writes His *Autobiography,* Benjamin I-236
Free Public School Movement, The   I-576
Freedom of the Press, Trial of John Peter Zenger and   I-188
Frémont, Expeditions of John C.   II-795
French and Indian War, The   I-200
French Exploration of the Great Lakes, Founding of Quebec and   I-52
French Exploration of the Mississippi Valley I-144
Frontier, Closing of the   II-1213
Fur Company, Chartering of the American I-476

G.I. Bill and Federal Aid to Education, Enactment of the   III-1725
General Assembly in Virginia, Calling of the First   I-65
Georgia, Settlement of   I-182
German and Irish Immigration   II-754
Gettysburg, Vicksburg, and Chattanooga, Battles of   II-997

Ghent, Negotiation of the Treaty of   I-522
Ghetto, The Watts Riot and Violence in the III-1924
(Gibbons v. *Ogden),* Federal Government Assumes Control of Interstate Commerce   I-600
(Gideon v. *Wainright),* Supreme Court Defines Rights of Accused Criminals   III-1893
Goddard Launches the First Liquid-Fueled Rocket, Robert   III-1555
Gold Rush, California   II-843
Gospel of Wealth, Carnegie Publishes *The* II-1167
Grange of the Patrons of Husbandry, Organization of the National   II-1043
Grant Administration, Scandals of the   II-1054
Great Awakening, The   I-176
Great Depression, 1929-1939, The   III-1582
Great Lakes, Founding of Quebec and French Exploration of the   I-52
Great Migration, The   I-527
Great Puritan Migration, The   I-85
Great Society, Election of Lyndon B. Johnson to the Presidency, and the Emergence of the III-1918
Great Train Robbery, First Showing of *The* II-1333
Guadalcanal, Battle of   III-1709

Half-Way Covenant, The   I-127
Hamilton's *Report on Public Credit,* Issuance of Alexander   I-356
Harding Administration, Scandals of the III-1525
Harpers Ferry, John Brown's Raid on   II-918
Hartford Convention, The   I-517
Harvard College and Enactment of the Massachusetts School Law, Establishment of   I-103
Hay Sends His "Open Door Notes," John II-1296
Hearst-Pulitzer Circulation War   II-1243
Hemingway Publishes *The Sun Also Rises,* Ernest   III-1560
Hiroshima, Dropping of the Atomic Bomb on III-1753
History of the United States from the Discovery of the American Continent, Bancroft Publishes II-730
History of the United States of America During the First Administrations of Jefferson, and Madison, Henry Adams Publishes   II-1184
Homestead Act, Passage of the   II-962
Hoover-Stimson Doctrine   III-1599
Howe's Invention of the Sewing Machine Heralding the Rise of Industrial Capitalism II-837
Hudson River School of Painters, The   I-613
Humanitarian Reform Movement, The   I-642

Hundred Days, The   III-1615

Husbandry, Organization of the National Grange of the Patrons of   II-1043

Immigration and the Establishment of Ellis Island Immigration Station, The New   II-1219

Immigration, German and Irish   II-754

Immigration Law, Passage of the Chinese Exclusion Act and the First   II-1123

Impeachment of Andrew Johnson   II-1026

Implied Powers *(McCulloch* v. *Maryland)*, Judicial Recognition of the Doctrine of   I-564

Inauguration of Abraham Lincoln, First   II-946

Inauguration of George Washington as First President   I-341

Incandescent Lamp, Edison Demonstrates the First Practical   II-1110

Independence, Declaration of   I-261

Independent Treasury, Establishment of the   II-748

Indian Removal Act, Passage of the   I-666

Indians Sell Manhattan Island for Twenty-Four Dollars, Algonquin   I-80

Indians, the First Americans, Arrival of the   I-1

Influence of Sea Power upon History, 1660-1783, Mahan Publishes *The*   II-1201

Institute, Founding of the Moody Bible   II-1173

Institution, Founding of the Smithsonian   II-831

Insular Cases, The   II-1318

Insurrection, Nat Turner's Slavery   II-685

Insurrection, The Philippine   II-1290

Interstate Commerce Act, Passage of the   II-1157

Interstate Commerce *(Gibbons* v. *Ogden)*, Federal Government Assumes Control of   I-600

Intervention Short of War, 1939-1941, American   III-1686

Invasion of Normandy: Operation "Overlord," The   III-1721

Invasion of North Africa   III-1715

Irish Immigration, German and   II-754

Jackson's Battle with the Second Bank of the United States, Andrew   II-696

James Publishes *Pragmatism,* William   III-1363

Jamestown, Settlement of   I-59

Jay's Treaty, Negotiation of   I-389

Johns Hopkins University, Founding of The   II-1077

Johnson, Impeachment of Andrew   II-1026

Judicial Recognition of the Doctrine of Implied Powers *(McCulloch* v. *Maryland)*   I-564

Judicial Recognition of the Doctrine of the Sanc-

tity of Contracts *(Fletcher* v. *Peck)*   I-485

Judicial Review *(Marbury* v. *Madison)*, Supreme Court's First Exercise of the Right of   I-437

Judiciary Act, Passage of the   I-345

Jungle, Upton Sinclair Publishes *The*   III-1353

Kansas, Bleeding   II-889

Kansas-Nebraska Act, Passage of the   II-871

Kennedy, Assassination of President   III-1899

Kennedy, Assassinations of Martin Luther King and Robert F.   III-1927

King and Robert F. Kennedy, Assassinations of Martin Luther   III-1927

Knickerbocker School, Appearance of the   I-481

Korean War, The   III-1823

Labor *(Commonwealth* v. *Hunt)*, Beginnings of Organized   II-785

Labor, Organization of the American Federation of   II-1152

Land Grant Act, Passage of the Morrill   II-974

Land Law of 1820   I-582

Landing of the Pilgrims at Plymouth   I-74

Lewis and Clark Expedition   I-450

Lexington and Concord, Battle of   I-251

Leyte Gulf, Battle for   III-1731

Library of Congress Occupies Its Own Building   II-1279

Lincoln and the End of the Civil War, Assassination of   II-1014

Lincoln, First Inauguration of Abraham   II-946

Lincoln-Douglas Debates   II-906

Little Big Horn, Battle of the   II-1094

Louisiana Purchase, The   I-445

Loyalty at Home in Wartime, Government Acts to Assure   III-1703

McCarthy Hearings, The   II-1817

McCormick's Invention of the Reaper   II-679

(McCullock v. *Maryland)*, Judicial Recognition of the Doctrine of Implied Powers   I-564

Mahan Publishes *The Influence of Sea Power upon History, 1660-1783*   II-1201

(Marbury v. *Madison)*, Supreme Court's First Exercise of the Right of Judicial Review   I-437

March to the Sea, Sherman's   II-1010

Marshall Mission to China, The   III-1765

Maryland Act of Toleration, Passage of the   I-115

Mass Culture, The Rise of   III-1501

Massachusetts School Law, Establishment of

Harvard College and Enactment of the I-103

Massacre, Boston   I-231

Mayan Calendar, The   I-5

Mayo Clinic, Founding of the   II-1178

Merrimack, The *Monitor* v. the   II-957

Metropolitan Opera, Opening of the   II-1135

Meuse-Argonne Offensive   III-1466

Mexico, Pershing Military Expedition into III-1438

Mexico, War with   II-825

Migration, The Great   I-527

Migration, The Great Puritan   I-85

Migration to Utah, Mormon   II-812

Military Academy, Establishment of the United States   I-432

Military Expedition into Mexico, Pershing III-1438

Minimum Wage, Development of the Ford Assembly Line and Adoption of the Five-Dollar-a-Day   III-1421

Missile Crisis, The Cuban   III-1888

Mississippi Valley, French Exploration of the I-144

Missouri Compromise, Negotiation of the I-552

Mobilization for War and Formation of the War Production Board, Economic   III-1680

Monitor v. the *Merrimack,* The   II-957

Monroe Doctrine, The   I-593

Montgomery Bus Boycott   III-1855

Moody Bible Institute, Founding of the   II-1173

Moon, Apollo 11 Lands on the   III-1940

Moral Man and Immoral Society, and the Rise of Neoörthodoxy, Publication of Reinhold Niebuhr's   III-1604

Mormon Migration to Utah   II-812

Morrill Land Grant Act, Passage of the   II-974

(Muller v. *Oregon),* Sociological Jurisprudence Established as a Principle   III-1369

National Association for the Advancement of Colored People Formed   III-1384

National Bank Acts of 1863 and 1864, Passage of the   II-985

National Draft Law, Passage of the First II-991

National Grange of the Patrons of Husbandry, Organization of the   II-1043

National Labor Relations Act, Passage of the III-1637

National Road, Construction of the   I-491

National Security Act, Passage of the   III-1783

Navigation Acts, Passage of the British   I-121

Negotiation of Jay's Treaty   I-389

Negotiation of Pinckney's Treaty   I-396

Negotiation of the Adams-Onís Treaty   I-558

Negotiation of the Missouri Compromise   I-552

Negotiation of the Treaty of Ghent   I-522

Negotiation of the Treaty of Paris   I-300

Negotiation of the Treaty of Versailles   III-1484

Negotiation of the Treaty of Washington II-1072

Negotiation of the Webster-Ashburton Treaty II-801

Negro Improvement Association Formed in the United States, Universal   III-1444

Negroes and the Origins of Slavery in British North America, Arrival of the First   I-69

Neoörthodoxy, Publication of Reinhold Niebuhr's *Moral Man and Immoral Society,* and the Rise of   III-1604

Neutrality Acts, Passage of the   III-1649

New England, Confederation of the United Colonies of   I-109

New England, Formation of the Dominion of I-163

New Harmony, Indiana, and the Communitarian Movement   I-511

New Netherland, British Conquest of   I-140

New World, Columbus Lands in the   I-17

New World, Norsemen Discover the   I-11

New World, Raleigh's Attempts at Colonization in the   I-46

Niebuhr's *Moral Man and Immoral Society,* and the Rise of Neoörthodoxy, Publication of Reinhold   III-1604

Nineteenth Amendment, The   III-1513

Normandy: Operation "Overlord," The Invasion of   III-1721

Norsemen Discover the New World   I-11

North Africa, Invasion of   III-1715

North Atlantic Treaty, Negotiation of the III-1806

Northwest Ordinance, Passage of the   I-324

Northwest Passage, Cartier and Roberval Search for a   I-28

Nullification Controversy, The   II-702

Oberlin College, Establishment of   II-708

Office of Commissioner of Education, Creation of the   II-1031

Oil Trust, Organization of the Standard   II-1116

Oil Well, First Commercial   II-912

"Open Door Notes," John Hay Sends His II-1296

Opera, Opening of the Metropolitan   II-1135

Oregon, The Struggle for   II-778

Organization of American States   III-1789

Organized Labor *(Commonwealth* v. *Hunt),* Beginnings of   II-785

Ordinance of 1785, Adoption of the   I-306

Ordinance, Passage of the Northwest   I-324

Pacific Railroad Surveys   II-865

Painters, The Hudson River School of   I-613
Pan-American Congress, First   II-1190
Panama Canal Zone, Acquisition of the   II-1339
Paris, Negotiation of the Treaty of   I-300
Parties, Emergence of the First Political   I-350
Party, Formation of the Republican   II-877
Party, Organization of the People's   II-1225
Party, Rise of the Whig   II-690
Passage, Cartier and Roberval Search for a Northwest   I-28
Pawtucket, Erection of Slater's Spinning Mill at I-362
Peace Corps, Formation of the   III-1877
Pearl Harbor, Bombing of   III-1697
Pendleton Act Reforming the Civil Service, Passage of the   II-1128
Pennsylvania, Founding of   I-157
Penny Press, Beginning of the   II-713
People's Party, Organization of the   II-1225
Perry Opens Japan to American Trade, Commodore   II-884
Pershing Military Expedition into Mexico III-1438
Philippine Insurrection, The   II-1290
Pike's Exploration of the Southwest   I-467
Pilgrims at Plymouth, Landing of the   I-74
Pinckney's Treaty, Negotiation of   I-396
(Plessy v. *Ferguson),* Establishment of Separate but Equal Doctrine for Black and White Public Facilities   II-1261
Plymouth, Landing of the Pilgrims at   I-74
Poetry Movement, The New   III-1399
Polarization of American Society in the 1960's III-1861
Political Democracy, Dorr Rebellion and the Growth of   II-766
Political Parties, Emergence of the First   I-350
Pony Express, Operation of the   II-925
Population Explosion and Move to Suburbia, The   III-1811
Poverty in an Affluent Society   III-1866
Powell Publishes *Report on the Lands of the Arid Region of the United States*   II-1104
Pragmatism, William James Publishes   III-1363
Pre-emption Act of 1841, Passage of the   II-772
Presidency in 1912, Election of Wilson to the III-1405
President, Inauguration of George Washington as First   I-341
Press, Beginning of the Penny   II-713
Press, Trial of John Peter Zenger and Freedom of the   I-188
Proclamation, Emancipation   II-980
Proclamation of 1763   I-207
Propaganda and Civil Liberties in World War I III-1454

"Pro-Slavery Argument," The   I-648
Public Health Service, Establishment of the United States   III-1394
Public School Movement, The Free   I-576
Publication of *The Federalist*   I-335
Publication of *The Southern Literary Messenger* II-725
Publication of Washington's Farewell Address I-403
Pulitzer Circulation War, Hearst-   II-1243
Pullman Strike, The   II-1237
Purchase of Alaska   II-1037
Puritan Migration, The Great   I-85

Quebec and French Exploration of the Great Lakes, Founding of   I-52

Radio Station KDKA Begins Commercial Broadcasting   III-1519
Raid on Harpers Ferry, John Brown's   II-918
Railroad Begins Operations, Baltimore and Ohio I-624
Railroad, Construction of the First Transcontinental   II-969
Railroad Surveys, Pacific   II-865
Raleigh's Attempts at Colonization in the New World   I-46
Ratification of the Bill of Rights   I-367
Rauschenbusch and the Social Gospel, Walter II-1195
Reaper, McCormick's Invention of the   II-679
Reapportionment Cases, Supreme Court Decisions in   III-1883
Rebellion and the Growth of Political Democracy, Dorr   II-766
Rebellion, Bacon's   I-151
Rebellion, The Whiskey   I-377
Reconstruction, Election of Hayes to the Presidency and the End of   II-1099
Reconstruction Finance Corporation Legislation, Passage of the   III-1594
Reconstruction of the South   II-1003
Red Badge of Courage, Stephen Crane Publishes *The*   II-1255
Red Scare, The   III-1491
Reform Movement, The Humanitarian   I-642
Regulator Movements, Carolina   I-213
Renaissance, The American   II-848
Report on Public Credit, Issuance of Alexander Hamilton's   I-356
Report on the Lands of the Arid Region of the United States, Powell Publishes   II-1104
Republican Congressional Insurgency   III-1390
Republican Party, Formation of the   II-877
Republican Resurgence in the Election of 1918 and 1920   III-1472
Revenue Act of 1767 and the Townshend Crisis I-225

Revolt, The Berkeley Student   III-1912
Revolution of 1928, The Democratic   III-1566
Revolution, Texas   II-736
Rhode Island, Founding of   I-97
Rights, Ratification of the Bill of   I-367
Riot and Violence in the Ghetto, The Watts   III-1924
Road, Construction of the National   I-491
Roosevelt Assumes the Presidency, Theodore   II-1325
Rocket, Robert Goddard Launches the First Liquid-Fueled   III-1555

St. Augustine, DeSoto's Expedition and the Founding of   I-33
Salem Witchcraft Trials   I-169
Salk Vaccine, Development of the   III-1835
San Francisco, Founding of   I-272
Santa Fe, Coronado's Expedition and the Founding of   I-40
Santa Fe Trade, Opening of the   I-588
Saratoga, Battles of   I-277
Scandals of the Grant Administration   II-1054
Scandals of the Harding Administration   III-1525
School and Society, Dewey Publishes *The*   II-1301
Scientific Research and Development, Creation of the Office of   III-1692
Scopes Trail, The   III-1549
Scottsboro Trials, The   III-1588
Sea, Sherman's March to the   II-1010
Second Awakening and Frontier Religious Revival, The   I-420
Second Bank of the United States, Andrew Jackson's Battle with the   II-696
Second Bank of the United States, Chartering of the   I-539
Second Continental Congress, Convening of the   I-256
Separate but Equal Doctrine for Black and White Public Facilities *(Plessy* v. *Ferguson),* Establishment of,   II-1261
Settlement of Connecticut   I-91
Settlement of Georgia   I-182
Settlement of Jamestown   I-59
Settlement of the Carolinas   I-132
Sewing Machine Heralding the Rise of Industrial Capitalism, Howe's Invention of the   II-837
Sherman Antitrust Act, Passage of the   II-1206
Sherman's March to the Sea   II-1010
Ships, Era of the Clipper   II-807
Sinclair Publishes *The Jungle,* Upton   III-1353
Sixteenth Amendment, The   III-1415
Slater's Spinning Mill at Pawtucket, Erection of   I-362

Slavery *(Dred Scott* v. *Sanford),* Dred Scott Decision on   II-900
Slavery in British North America, Arrival of the First Negroes and the Origins of   I-69
Slavery Insurrection, Nat Turner's   II-685
Smith's Exploration of the Far West, Jedediah   I-619
Smithsonian Institution, Founding of the   II-831
Social Gospel, Walter Rauschenbusch and the   II-1195
Social Security Act, Passage of the   III-1643
Society in the 1960's, Polarization of American   III-1861
Sociological Jurisprudence Established as a Principle *(Muller* v. *Oregon)*   III-1369
Sound and the Fury, William Faulkner Publishes *The*   III-1571
South, Reconstruction of the   II-1003
Southern Literary Messenger, Publication of *The*   II-725
Southwest, Occupation of California and the   II-818
Southwest, Pike's Exploration of the   I-467
Spanish-American War, The   II-1284
Spanish Civil War and the American Arms Embargo   III-1661
Speech, Booker T. Washington Delivers His "Atlanta Compromise"   II-1249
Sports, Black Sox Scandal and the Rise of Spectator   III-1497
Stamp Act Crisis   I-219
Standard Oil Trust, Organization of the   II-1116
State Universities, Beginnings of   I-312
States' Rights, Webster-Hayne Debate over   I-660
Stock Market Crash of 1929   III-1577
Stowe Publishes *Uncle Tom's Cabin,* Harriet Beecher   II-859
Strike, Anthracite Coal   II-1329
Strike, The Pullman   II-1237
Struggle for Oregon, The   II-778
Student Revolt, The Berkeley   III-1912
Submarine in Warfare, First Test of a   I-267
Suburbia, The Population Explosion and Move to   III-1811
Sumner Publishes *Folkways,* William Graham   III-1357
Sun Also Rises, Ernest Hemingway Publishes *The*   III-1560
Supreme Court Decisions in Reapportionment Cases   III-1883
Supreme Court Defines Rights of Accused Criminals *(Gideon* v. *Wainright)*   III-1893
Supreme Court Orders Desegregation of the Public Schools *(Brown* v. *Board of Education of Topeka)*   III-1849
Supreme Court Packing Fight   III-1667
Supreme Court's First Exercise of the Right of

Judicial Review *(Marbury* v. *Madison)*   I-437

Surrender of Cornwallis at Yorktown   I-294

Surveys, Pacific Railroad   II-865

Tariff, The Dingley   II-1273

Tea Party, Boston   I-241

Telegraph, Completion of the Transcontinental   II-930

Telegraph, Invention of the Electric   II-742

Telephone, Alexander Graham Bell Invents the   II-1089

Television Broadcasting, Beginnings of Commercial   III-1674

Tennessee Valley Authority, Creation of the   III-1621

Texas Revolution   II-736

Tippecanoe, Battle of   I-498

Toleration, Passage of the Maryland Act of   I-115

Townshend Crisis, Revenue Act of 1767 and the   I-225

Trade, Commodore Perry Opens Japan to American   II-884

Trade, Opening of the Santa Fe   I-588

Transatlantic Cable, Laying of the First   II-895

Transcendentalism, Rise of   I-654

Transcontinental Railroad, Construction of the First   II-969

Transcontinental Telegraph, Completion of the   II-930

Treasury, Establishment of the Independent   II-748

Treaties, Conclusion of Franco-American   I-282

Treaty, Negotiation of Jay's   I-389

Treaty, Negotiation of Pinckney's   I-396

Treaty, Negotiation of the Adams-Onís   I-558

Treaty, Negotiation of the Webster-Ashburton   II-801

Treaty of Ghent, Negotiation of the   I-522

Treaty of Paris, Negotiation of the   I-300

Treaty of Versailles, Negotiation of the   III-1484

Treaty of Washington, Negotiation of the   II-1072

Trial of John Peter Zenger and Freedom of the Press   I-188

Trial, The Scopes   III-1549

Trials, Salem Witchcraft   I-169

Trials, The Scottsboro   III-1588

Truman Doctrine with Its Policy on Containment, The   III-1776

Truman-MacArthur Confrontation, The   III-1829

Trust, Organization of the Standard Oil   II-1116

Turner's Slavery Insurrection, Nat   II-685

Twain Publishes *The Adventures of Huckleberry Finn,* Mark   II-1146

Twelfth Amendment, The   I-456

Uncle Tom's Cabin, Harriet Beecher Stowe Publishes   II-859

Unitarian Church in the United States, Founding of the   I-570

United Colonies of New England, Confederation of the   I-109

United Nations Charter Convention   III-1741

United States Military Academy, Establishment of the   I-432

United States Public Health Service, Establishment of the   III-1394

Universal Negro Improvement Association Formed in the United States   III-1444

Universities, Beginnings of State   I-312

University, Founding of The Johns Hopkins   II-1077

Utah, Mormon Migration to   II-812

V-E Day   III-1748

Versailles, Negotiation of the Treaty of   III-1484

Vicksburg, and Chattanooga, Battles of Gettysburg,   II-997

Vietnam, The War in   III-1906

Virginia, Calling of the First General Assembly of   I-65

Virginia Statute of Religious Liberty, Adoption of   I-318

Voyages of John Cabot, The   I-23

War, The French and Indian   I-200

War in Vietnam, The   III-1906

War Industries Board and Economic Mobilization for War, The   III-1460

War of 1812, The   I-505

War Production Board, Economic Mobilization for War and Formation of the   III-1680

War, The Korean   III-1823

War, The Spanish-American   II-1284

War with Mexico   II-825

Washington as First President, Inauguration of George   I-341

Washington Delivers His "Atlanta Compromise" Speech, Booker T.   II-1249

Washington Disarmament Conference, Meeting of the   III-1531

Washington, Negotiation of the Treaty of   II-1072

Washington's Farewell Address, Publication of   I-403

Watts Riot and Violence in the Ghetto, The   III-1924

Webster-Ashburton Treaty, Negotiation of the   II-801

Webster-Hayne Debate over States' Rights   I-660

AMERICAN

Key Word Index for Events

Webster Publishes *An American Dictionary of the English Language,* Noah   I-636

Well, First Commercial Oil   II-912

Whig Party, Rise of the   II-690

Whiskey Rebellion, The   I-377

White House Conference on Conservation, The   III-1374

Whitney Invents the Cotton Gin   I-371

Witchcraft Trials, Salem   I-169

Works Progress Administration Formed   III-1632

World War I, Demobilization after   III-1478

World War I, Entrance of the United States into   III-1450

World War I, Propaganda and Civil Liberties in   III-1454

World War II, Demobilization and Reconversion after   III-1759

World's Columbian Exposition   II-1231

Wright Brothers' First Flight, The   II-1346

XYZ Affair, The   I-408

Yalta Conference, The   III-1736

Yellow Fever Is Spread by a Mosquito, Discovery That   II-1313

Yorktown, Surrender of Cornwallis at   I-294

Zenger and Freedom of the Press, Trial of John Peter   I-188

CONSTITUTIONAL

Adoption of the Articles of Confederation
I-288
Adoption of the Constitution   I-330
Creation of the Confederate States of America
II-1031
Declaration of Independence   I-261
Dred Scott Decision on Slavery *(Dred Scott* v.
Sanford)   II-900
Eighteenth Amendment, The   III-1507
Establishment of Separate but Equal Doctrine
for Black and White Public Facilities *(Plessy*
v. *Ferguson)*   II-1261
Federal Government Assumes Control of Inter-
state Commerce *(Gibbons* v. *Ogden)*   I-600
Fourteenth Amendment, The   II-1049
Inauguration of George Washington as First
President   I-341
Judicial Recognition of the Doctrine of Implied
Powers *(McCulloch* v. *Maryland)*   I-564
Judicial Recognition of the Doctrine of the Sanc-
tity of Contracts *(Fletcher* v. *Peck)*   I-485
Nineteenth Amendment, The   III-1513
Nullification Controversy, The   II-702
Publication of *The Federalist*   I-335
Ratification of the Bill of Rights   I-367
Sixteenth Amendment, The   III-1415
Sociological Jurisprudence Established as a Prin-
ciple *(Muller* v. *Oregon)*   III-1369
Stamp Act Crisis   I-219
Supreme Court Decisions in Reapportionment
Cases   III-1883
Supreme Court Defines Rights of Accused
Criminals *(Gideon* v. *Wainright)*   III-1893
Supreme Court Orders Desegregation of the
Public Schools *(Brown* v. *Board of Education
of Topeka)*   III-1849
Supreme Court's First Exercise of the Right of
Judicial Review *(Marbury* v. *Madison)*   I-
437
Twelfth Amendment, The   I-456

CULTURAL

Alexis de Tocqueville's Visit to America   II-
673
American Renaissance, The   II-848
Appearance of the Knickerbocker School   I-
481
Armory Show, The   III-1411
Bancroft Publishes *History of the United States
from the Discovery of the American Continent*
II-730
Beginning of the Penny Press   II-713
Beginnings of Commercial Television Broadcast-
ing   III-1674
Beginnings of State Universities   I-312

Benjamin Franklin Writes His *Autobiography*
I-236
Black Sox Scandal and the Rise of Spectator
Sports   III-1497
Creation of the Office of Commissioner of Educa-
tion   II-1031
Dewey Publishes *The School and Society*   II-
1301
Ernest Hemingway Publishes *The Sun Also Rises*
III-1560
Establishment of Harvard College and Enact-
ment of the Massachusetts School Law
I-103
Expeditions of John C. Frémont   II-795
First Showing of *The Great Train Robbery*
II-1333
Founding of the American Philosophical Society
I-194
Founding of The Johns Hopkins University
II-1077
Founding of the Smithsonian Institution   II-
831
Great Puritan Migration, The   I-527
Hearst-Pulitzer Circulation War   II-1243
Henry Adams Publishes *History of the United
States of America During the First Administra-
tions of Jefferson and Madison*   II-1184
Hudson River School of Painters, The   I-613
Humanitarian Reform Movement, The   I-
642
Inauguration of Barnum's Circus   II-1066
Library of Congress Occupies Its Own Building
II-1279
Mark Twain Publishes *The Adventures of Huck-
leberry Finn*   II-1146
New Harmony, Indiana, and the Communi-
tarian Movement   I-511
New Poetry Movement, The   III-1399
Noah Webster Publishes *An American Diction-
ary of the English Language*   I-636
Opening of the Metropolitan Opera   II-1135
"Pro-Slavery Argument," The   I-648
Publication of Reinhold Niebuhr's *Moral Man
and Immoral Society* and the Rise of Neoör-
thodoxy   III-1604
Publication of *The Southern Literary Messenger*
II-725
Radio Station KDKA Begins Commercial
Broadcasting   III-1519
Rise of Mass Culture, The   III-1501
Second Awakening and Frontier Religious
Revival, The   I-420
Stephen Crane Publishes *The Red Badge of
Courage*   II-1255
Walter Rauschenbusch and the Social Gospel
II-1195
William Faulkner Publishes *The Sound and the
Fury*   III-1571

World's Columbian Exposition   II-1231

DIPLOMATIC

American Intervention Short of War, 1939-1941
    III-1686
Berlin Airlift, The   III-1794
Commodore Perry Opens Japan to American
    Trade   II-884
Conclusion of Franco-American Treaties   I-282
Cuban Missile Crisis   III-1888
Dollar Diplomacy   III-1379
First Pan-American Congress   II-1190
Formulation of the Dawes Plan   III-1537
Hoover-Stimson Doctrine   III-1599
John Hay Sends His "Open Door Notes"
    II-1296
Louisiana Purchase, The   I-445
Marshall Mission to China, The   III-1765
Meeting of the Washington Disarmament Con-
    ference   III-1531
Monroe Doctrine, The   I-593
Negotiation of Jay's Treaty   I-389
Negotiation of Pinckney's Treaty   I-396
Negotiation of the Adams-Onís Treaty   I-558
Negotiation of the North AtlanticTreaty   III-1806
Negotiation of the Treaty of Ghent   I-522
Negotiation of the Treaty of Paris   I-300
Negotiation of the Treaty of Versailles   III-1484
Negotiation of the Treaty of Washington
    II-1072
Negotiation of the Webster-Ashburton Treaty
    II-801
Organization of American States   III-1789
Passage of the Neutrality Acts   III-1649
Publication of Washington's Farewell Address
    I-403
Purchase of Alaska   II-1037
Spanish Civil War and the American Arms Em-
    bargo   III-1661
Struggle for Oregon, The   II-778
Truman Doctrine with Its Policy of Contain-
    ment, The   III-1776
United Nations Charter Convention   III-1741
XYZ Affair, The   I-408
Yalta Conference, The   III-1736

ECONOMIC

Acquisition of the Panama Canal Zone   II-1339
Adoption of the Ordinance of 1785   I-306
Algonquin Indians Sell Manhattan Island for
    Twenty-Four Dollars   I-80
Andrew Jackson's Battle with the Second Bank
    of the United States   II-696
Anthracite Coal Strike   II-1329

Boston Tea Party   I-241
California Gold Rush   II-843
Chartering of the American Fur Company
    I-476
Chartering of the Second Bank of the United
    States   I-539
Commodore Perry Opens Japan to American
    Trade   II-884
Congress of Industrial Organizations Formed
    III-1655
Construction of the Erie Canal   I-546
Construction of the First Transcontinental Rail-
    road   II-969
Construction of the National Road   I-491
Creation of the Tennessee Valley Authority
    III-1621
"Crime of 1873," The   II-1083
Demobilization After World War I   III-1478
Demobilization and Reconversion after World
    War II   III-1759
Dingley Tariff, The   II-1273
Dust Bowl, The   III-1627
Economic Mobilization for War and Formation
    of the War Production Board   III-1680
Election of Coolidge to the Presidency and the
    Ascendancy of Big Business   III-1542
Enactment of the G.I. Bill and Federal Aid to
    Education   III-1725
Era of the Clipper Ships   II-807
Erection of Slater's Spinning Mill at Pawtucket
    I-362
Establishment of the Independent Treasury
    II-748
First Commercial Oil Well   II-912
First Successful Voyage of the *Clermont*   I-471
Formulation of the Dawes Plan   III-1537
Great Depression, 1929-1939, The   III-1582
Hartford Convention, The   I-517
Hearst-Pulitzer Circulation War   II-1243
Howe's Invention of the Sewing Machine Her-
    alding the Rise of Industrial Capitalism
    II-837
Issuance of Alexander Hamilton's *Report on
    Public Credit*   I-356
John Hay Sends His "Open Door Notes"
    II-1296
Judicial Recognition of the Doctrine of the Sanc-
    tity of Contracts *(Fletcher* v. *Peck)*   I-485
McCormick's Invention of the Reaper   II-679
New Harmony, Indiana, and the Communi-
    tarian Movement   I-511
Opening of the Chisholm Trail and Rise of the
    Cattle Kingdom   II-1020
Opening of the Santa Fe Trade   I-588
Operation of the Pony Express   II-925
Organization of the Standard Oil Trust   II-1116
Pacific Railroad Surveys   II-865
Passage of the British Navigation Acts   I-121

Passage of the Employment Act of 1946   III-1770

Passage of the Federal Reserve Act   III-1432

Passage of the Indian Removal Act   I-666

Passage of the Interstate Commerce Act   II-1157

Passage of the National Bank Acts of 1863 and 1864   II-985

Passage of the Pre-emption Act of 1841   II-772

Passage of the Reconstruction Finance Corporation Legislation   III-1594

Passage of the Sherman Antitrust Act   II-1206

Pullman Strike, The   II-1237

Raleigh's Attempts at Colonization in the New World   I-46

Revenue Act of 1767 and the Townshend Crisis   I-225

Sixteenth Amendment, The   III-1415

Spanish Civil War and the American Arms Embargo   III-1661

Stamp Act Crisis   I-219

Stock Market Crash of 1929   III-1577

Truman Doctrine with Its Policy of Containment, The   III-1776

War Industries Board and Economic Mobilization for War, The   III-1460

Whiskey Rebellion, The   I-377

Whitney Invents the Cotton Gin   I-371

EDUCATIONAL

Beginnings of State Universities   I-312

Creation of the Office of Commissioner of Education   II-1031

Dewey Publishes *The School and Society*   II-1301

Enactment of the G.I. Bill and Federal Aid to Education   III-1725

Establishment of Harvard College and Enactment of the Massachusetts School Law   I-103

Establishment of Oberlin College   II-708

Establishment of the United States Military Academy   I-432

Founding of The Johns Hopkins University   II-1077

Founding of the Moody Bible Institute   II-1173

Free Public School Movement, The   I-576

Passage of the Morrill Land Grant Act   II-974

Scopes Trial, The   III-1549

Supreme Court Orders Desegregation of the Public Schools *(Brown v. Board of Education of Topeka)*   III-1849

INTELLECTUAL

Alexis de Tocqueville's Visit to America   II-673

American Renaissance, The   II-848

Bancroft Publishes *History of the United States from the Discovery of the American Continent*   II-730

Beard Publishes *An Economic Interpretation of the Constitution*   III-1426

Carnegie Publishes *The Gospel of Wealth*   II-1167

Dewey Publishes *The School and Society*   II-1301

Establishment of Oberlin College   II-708

Founding of the American Philosophical Society   I-194

Founding of The Johns Hopkins University   II-1077

Founding of the Unitarian Church in the United States   I-570

Henry Adams Publishes *History of the United States of America During the First Administrations of Jefferson and Madison*   II-1184

Library of Congress Occupies Its Own Building   II-1279

Mark Twain Publishes *The Adventures of Huckleberry Finn*   II-1146

New Poetry Movement, The   III-1399

Rise of Transcendentalism   I-654

Stephen Crane Publishes *The Red Badge of Courage*   II-1255

Walter Rauschenbusch and the Social Gospel   II-1195

William Faulkner Publishes *The Sound and the Fury*   III-1571

William Graham Sumner Publishes *Folkways*   III-1357

William James Publishes *Pragmatism*   III-1363

LEGAL

Adoption of the Ordinance of 1785   I-306

Anthracite Coal Strike   II-1329

Beginnings of Organized Labor *(Commonwealth v. Hunt)*   II-785

Burr's Conspiracy   I-461

Creation of the Office of Commissioner of Education   II-1031

"Crime of 1873," The   II-1083

Development of Direct Democracy   II-1307

Dingley Tariff, The   II-1273

Dorr Rebellion and the Growth of Political Democracy   II-766

Dred Scott Decision on Slavery *(Dred Scott v. Sanford)*   II-900

Establishment of Separate but Equal Doctrine for Black and White Public Facilities *(Plessy v. Ferguson)*   II-1261

Establishment of the Independent Treasury   II-748

Federal Government Assumes Control of Interstate Commerce *(Gibbons v. Ogden)*   I-600

Hundred Days, The   III-1615
Insular Cases, The   II-1318
Judicial Recognition of the Doctrine of Implied
  Powers *(McCulloch* v. *Maryland)*   I-564
Judicial Recognition of the Doctrine of the Sanc-
  tity of Contracts *(Fletcher* v. *Peck)*   I-485
Land Law of 1820   I-582
Nullification Controversy, The   II-702
Passage of the Alien and Sedition Acts   I-414
Passage of the British Navigation Acts   I-121
Passage of the Chinese Exclusion Act and the
  First Immigration Law   II-1123
Passage of the Employment Act of 1946   III-
  1770
Passage of the First National Draft Law   II-
  991
Passage of the Homestead Act   II-962
Passage of the Indian Removal Act   I-666
Passage of the Interstate Commerce Act   II-
  1157
Passage of the Judiciary Act   I-345
Passage of the Maryland Act of Toleration
  I-115
Passage of the National Bank Acts of 1863 and
  1864   II-985
Passage of the National Labor Relations Act
  III-1637
Passage of the Northwest Ordinance   I-324
Passage of the Pendleton Act Reforming the
  Civil Service   II-1128
Passage of the Pre-emption Act of 1841   II-
  772
Passage of the Sherman Antitrust Act   II-
  1206
Propaganda and Civil Liberties in World War I
  III-1454
Ratification of the Bill of Rights   I-367
Reconstruction of the South   II-1003
Salem Witchcraft Trials   I-169
Scopes Trial, The   III-1549
Scottsboro Trials, The   III-1588
Sixteenth Amendment, The   III-1415
Sociological Jurisprudence Established as a Prin-
  ciple *(Muller* v. *Oregon)*   III-1369
Supreme Court Decisions in Reapportionment
  Cases   III-1883
Supreme Court Defines Rights of Accused
  Criminals *(Gideon* v. *Wainright)*   III-1893
Supreme Court Orders Desegregation of the
  Public Schools *(Brown* v. *Board of Education
  of Topeka)*   III-1849
Supreme Court Packing Fight   III-1667
Supreme Court's First Exercise of the Right of
  Judicial Review *(Marbury* v. *Madison)*   I-
  437
Trial of John Peter Zenger and Freedom of the
  Press   I-188

LITERARY

American Renaissance, The   II-848
Appearance of the Knickerbocker School   I-
  481
Benjamin Franklin Writes His *Autobiography*
  I-236
Charles Beard Publishes *An Economic Interpre-
  tation of the Constitution*   III-1426
Ernest Hemingway Publishes *The Sun Also Rises*
  III-1560
Harriet Beecher Stowe Publishes *Uncle Tom's
  Cabin*   II-859
Library of Congress Occupies Its Own Building
  II-1279
Mark Twain Publishes *The Adventures of Huck-
  leberry Finn*   II-1146
Publication of *The Southern Literary Messenger*
  II-725
Stephen Crane Publishes *The Red Badge of Cour-
  age*   II-1255
Upton Sinclair Publishes *The Jungle*   III-
  1353
William Faulkner Publishes *The Sound and the
  Fury*   III-1571

MILITARY

Bacon's Rebellion   I-151
Battle for Leyte Gulf   III-1731
Battle of Fallen Timbers   I-383
Battle of Guadalcanal   III-1709
Battle of Lexington and Concord   I-251
Battle of New Orleans   I-533
Battle of the Little Big Horn   II-1094
Battle of Tippecanoe   I-498
Battles of Gettysburg, Vicksburg, and Chat-
  tanooga   II-997
Battles of Saratoga   I-277
Berlin Airlift, The   III-1794
Bombing of Pearl Harbor   III-1697
Boston Massacre   I-231
Burr's Conspiracy   I-461
Carolina Regulator Movements   I-213
Conclusion of Franco-American Treaties   I-
  282
Creation of the Office of Scientific Research and
  Development   III-1692
Cuban Missile Crisis   III-1888
Dropping of the Atomic Bomb on Hiroshima
  III-1753
Entrance of the United States into World War
  I   III-1450
Establishment of the United States Military
  Academy   I-432
First Battle of Bull Run   II-952
First Test of a Submarine in Warfare   I-267
French and Indian War, The   I-200
Invasion of Normandy: Operation "Overlord,"
  The   III-1721
Invasion of North Africa   III-1715
Korean War, The   III-1823
Mahan Publishes *The Influence of Sea Power
  upon History, 1660-1783*   II-1201
Meuse-Argonne Offensive   III-1466

Monitor v. the *Merrimack,* The   II-957

Negotiation of the North Atlantic Treaty III-1806

Occupation of California and the Southwest III-818

Passage of the First National Draft Law   II-991

Passage of the National Security Act   III-1783

Pershing Military Expedition into Mexico III-1438

Philippine Insurrection, The   II-1290

Pike's Exploration of the Southwest   I-467

Sherman's March to the Sea   II-1010

Spanish-American War, The   II-1284

Surrender of Cornwallis at Yorktown   I-294

Texas Revolution   II-736

Truman-MacArthur Confrontation, The III-1829

V-E Day   III-1748

War in Vietnam, The   III-1906

War of 1812, The   I-505

War with Mexico   II-825

XYZ Affair, The   I-408

PHILOSOPHICAL

Emergence of the First Political Parties   I-350

Founding of the Unitarian Church in the United States   I-570

Publication of Reinhold Niebuhr's *Moral Man and Immoral Society,* and the Rise of Neoörthodoxy   III-1604

Rise of Transcendentalism   I-654

William James Publishes *Pragmatism*   III-1363

POLITICAL

Acquisition of the Panama Canal Zone   II-1339

Adoption of the Articles of Confederation I-288

Adoption of the Constitution   I-330

Andrew Jackson's Battle with the Second Bank of the United States   II-696

Anthracite Coal Strike   II-1329

Assassination of Lincoln and the End of the Civil War   II-1014

Assassination of President Kennedy   III-1899

Assassinations of Martin Luther King and Robert F. Kennedy   III-1927

British Conquest of New Netherland   I-140

Burr's Conspiracy   I-461

Calling of the First General Assembly of Virginia I-65

Chartering of the Second Bank of the United States   I-539

Compromise of 1850, The   II-854

Confederation of the United Colonies of New England   I-109

Congress of Industrial Organizations Formed III-1655

Convening of the First Continental Congress I-246

Convening of the Second Continental Congress I-256

Creation of the Confederate States of America II-941

"Crime of 1873," The   II-1083

Declaration of Independence   I-261

Democratic Revolution of 1928   III-1566

Development of Direct Democracy   II-1307

Dorr Rebellion and the Growth of Political Democracy   II-766

Economic Mobilization for War and Formation of the War Production Board   III-1680

Election of 1824   I-607

Election of 1840   II-760

Election of 1884   II-1140

Election of Coolidge to the Presidency, and the Ascendancy of Big Business   III-1542

Election of Eisenhower to the Presidency in 1952 III-1843

Election of Franklin D. Roosevelt to the Presidency in 1932   III-1609

Election of Hayes to the Presidency, and the End of Reconstruction   II-1099

Election of Jackson to the Presidency in 1828 I-1828

Election of Jefferson to the Presidency in 1800 I-426

Election of Kennedy to the Presidency   III-1871

Election of Lyndon B. Johnson to the Presidency, and the Emergence of the Great Society III-1918

Election of McKinley to the Presidency in 1896 II-1268

Election of Nixon to the Presidency in 1968 III-1933

Election of Truman to the Presidency, and the Emergence of the Fair Deal   III-1800

Election of Wilson to the Presidency in 1912 III-1405

Emancipation Proclamation   II-980

Emergence of the First Political Parties   I-350

First Inauguration of Abraham Lincoln   II-946

First Pan-American Congress   II-1190

Formation of the Dominion of New England I-163

Formation of the Republican Party   II-877

Fourteenth Amendment, The   II-1049

Government Acts to Assure Loyalty at Home in Wartime   III-1703

Hartford Convention, The   I-517

Hundred Days, The   III-1615

AMERICAN

Category Index for Type of Event

Impeachment of Andrew Johnson   II-1026
Inauguration of George Washington as First
   President   I-341
Issuance of Alexander Hamilton's *Report on
   Public Credit*   I-356
Lincoln-Douglas Debates   II-906
Louisiana Purchase, The   I-445
McCarthy Hearings,   III-1817
Negotiation of Jay's Treaty   I-389
Negotiation of the Missouri Compromise   I-552
Nineteenth Amendment, The   III-1513
Nullification Controversy, The   II-702
Organization of the People's Party   II-1225
Passage of the Alien and Sedition Acts   I-414
Passage of the Kansas-Nebraska Act   II-871
Passage of the National Labor Relations Act
   III-1637
Passage of the National Security Act   III-1783
Passage of the Pendleton Act Reforming the
   Civil Service   II-1128
Philippine Insurrection, The   II-1290
Proclamation of 1763   I-207
Propaganda and Civil Liberties in World War I
   III-1454
Publication of *The Federalist*   I-335
Publication of Washington's Farewell Address
   I-403
Purchase of Alaska   II-1037
Raleigh's Attempts at Colonization in the New
   World   I-46
Reconstruction of the South   II-1003
Red Scare, The   III-1491
Republican Congressional Insurgency   III-1390
Republican Resurgence in the Elections of 1918
   and 1920   III-1472
Revenue Act of 1767 and the Townshend Crisis
   I-225
Rise of the Whig Party   II-690
Scandals of the Grant Administration   II-1054
Scandals of the Harding Administration   III-1525
Supreme Court Decisions in Reapportionment
   Cases   III-1883
Supreme Court Packing Fight   III-1667
Texas Revolution   II-736
Theodore Roosevelt Assumes the Presidency
   II-1325
Truman Doctrine with Its Policy of Contain-
   ment, The   III-1776
Truman-MacArthur Confrontation, The
   III-1829
Twelfth Amendment, The   I-456
Webster-Hayne Debate over States' Rights
   I-660
Whiskey Rebellion, The   I-377
White House Conference on Conservation, The
   III-1374

XYZ Affair, The   I-408

POLITICO-ECONOMIC

American Intervention Short of War, 1939-1941
   III-1686
British Conquest of New Netherland   I-140
Cartier and Roberval Search for a Northwest
   Passage   I-28
Columbus Lands in the New World   I-17
Compromise of 1850, The   II-854
Construction of the Erie Canal   I-546
Construction of the National Road   I-491
Dingley Tariff, The   II-1273
Dollar Diplomacy   II-1379
Dorr Rebellion and the Growth of Political De-
   mocracy   II-766
Election of Jackson to the Presidency in 1828
   I-1828
Election of McKinley to the Presidency in 1896
   II-1268
First Pan-American Congress   II-1190
Formation of the Peace Corps   III-1877
Founding of Quebec and French Exploration of
   the Great Lakes   I-52
French and Indian War, The   I-200
Land Law of 1820   I-582
Louisiana Purchase, The   I-445
Negotiation of Jay's Treaty   I-389
Negotiation of the Missouri Compromise   I-552
Passage of the British Navigation Acts   I-121
Passage of the Federal Reserve Act   III-1432
Passage of the Northwest Ordinance   I-324
Rise of the Whig Party   II-690
Settlement of Jamestown   I-59
Struggle for Oregon, The   II-778
War of 1812, The   I-505

POLITICO-RELIGIOUS

Adoption of Virginia Statute of Religious Liberty
   I-318
Columbus Lands in the New World   I-17
Founding of Rhode Island   I-97
Passage of the Maryland Act of Toleration
   I-115

RELIGIOUS

Establishment of Oberlin College   II-708
Founding of Pennsylvania   I-157
Founding of the Moody Bible Institute   II-1173
Founding of the Unitarian Church in the United
   States   I-570
Great Awakening, The   I-176
Great Puritan Migration, The   I-85
Half-Way Covenant, The   I-127
Humanitarian Reform Movement, The   I-642

Landing of the Pilgrims at Plymouth   I-74
Mormon Migration to Utah   II-812
Passage of the Maryland Act of Toleration
    I-115
Publication of Reinhold Niebuhr's *Moral Man
    and Immoral Society,* and the Rise of Neoör-
    thodoxy   III-1604
Second Awakening and Frontier Religious
    Revival, The   I-420
Walter Rauschenbusch and the Social Gospel
    II-1195

SCIENTIFIC

Apollo 11 Lands on the Moon   III-1940
Creation of the Office of Scientific Research and
    Development   III-1692
Development of the Salk Vaccine   III-1835
Discovery and Demonstration of an Effective
    Anesthetic   II-791
Discovery That Yellow Fever Is Spread by a
    Mosquito   II-1313
Edison Demonstrates the First Practical In-
    candescent Lamp   II-1110
Expeditions of John C. Frémont   II-795
Founding of the Mayo Clinic   II-1178
Founding of the Smithsonian Institution   II-
    831
Invention of the Electric Telegraph   II-742
Jedediah Smith's Exploration of the Far West
    I-619
Lewis and Clark Expedition   I-450
Mayan Calendar, The   I-5
Pike's Exploration of the Southwest   I-467
Powell Publishes *Report on the Lands of the Arid
    Region of the United States*   II-1104
Robert Goddard Launches the First Liquid-
    Fueled Rocket   III-1555
Wright Brothers' First Flight, The   II-1346

SOCIO-ECONOMIC

Arrival of the First Negroes and the Origins of
    Slavery in British North America   I-69
Booker T. Washington Delivers His "Atlanta
    Compromise" Speech   II-1249
Congress of Industrial Organizations Formed
    III-1655
Coronado's Expedition and the Founding of
    Santa Fe   I-40
DeSoto's Expedition and the Founding of St.
    Augustine   I-33
Development of the Ford Assembly Line and
    Adoption of the Five-Dollar-a-Day Minimum
    Wage   III-1421
Emergence of the First Political Parties   I-
    350
French Exploration of the Mississippi Valley
    I-144
German and Irish Immigration   II-754
Great Migration, The   I-527
Montgomery Bus Boycott   III-1855

Organization of the American Federation of La-
    bor   II-1152
Organization of the National Grange of the Pa-
    trons of Husbandry   II-1043
Passage of the Homestead Act   II-962
Passage of the National Labor Relations Act
    III-1637
Passage of the Pre-emption Act of 1841   II-
    772
Passage of the Society Security Act   III-1643
Population Explosion and the Move to Suburbia,
    The   III-1811
Poverty in an Affluent Society   III-1866
"Pro-Slavery Argument," The   I-648
Pullman Strike, The   II-1237
Settlement of the Carolinas   I-132
Universal Negro Improvement Association
    Founded in the United States   III-1444
Upton Sinclair Publishes *The Jungle*   III-
    1353
Voyages of John Cabot, The   I-23
Watts Riot and Violence in the Ghetto, The
    III-1924
Works Progress Administration Formed
    III-1632

SOCIOLOGICAL

Alexis de Tocqueville's Visit to America   II-
    673
Arrival of the First Negroes and the Origins of
    Slavery in British North America   I-69
Arrival of the Indians, the First Americans
    I-1
Beginning of the Penny Press   II-713
Berkeley Student Revolt, The   III-1912
Black Sox Scandal and the Rise of Spectator
    Sports   III-1497
Carnegie Publishes *The Gospel of Wealth*
    II-1167
Carolina Regulator Movements   I-213
Closing of the Frontier   II-1213
Demobilization after World War I   III-1478
Demobilization and Reconversion after World
    War II   III-1759
Dust Bowl, The   III-1627
Eighteenth Amendment, The   III-1507
Establishment of Oberlin College   II-708
Establishment of Separate but Equal Doctrine
    for Black and White Public Facilities *(Plessy
    v. Ferguson)*   II-1261
Establishment of the United States Public Health
    Service   III-1394
Formation of the American Anti-Slavery Society
    II-719
Founding of Pennsylvania   I-157
German and Irish Immigration   II-754
Great Depression, 1929-1939, The   III-1582
Great Migration, The   I-527
Humanitarian Reform Movement, The   I-
    642

AMERICAN

Category Index for Type of Event

Landing of the Pilgrims at Plymouth   I-74
Nat Turner's Slavery Insurrection   II-685
New Harmony, Indiana, and the Communitarian Movement   I-511
New Immigration and the Establishment of Ellis Island Immigration Station, The   II-1219
Norsemen Discover the New World   I-11
Organization of the American Federation of Labor   II-1152
Organization of the National Grange of the Patrons of Husbandry   II-1043
Passage of the Chinese Exclusion Act and the First Immigration Law   II-1123
Polarization of American Society in the 1960's   III-1861
Population Explosion and the Move to Suburbia, The   III-1811
"Pro-Slavery Argument," The   I-648
Scottsboro Trials, The   III-1588
Settlement of the Carolinas   I-132
Sociological Jurisprudence Established as a Principle *(Muller v. Oregon)*   III-1369
Upton Sinclair Publishes *The Jungle*   III-1353
Walter Rauschenbusch and the Social Gospel   II-1195
Watts Riot and Violence in the Ghetto, The   III-1924
William Graham Sumner Publishes *Folkways*   III-1357

SOCIO-POLITICAL

Assassination of Martin Luther King and Robert F. Kennedy   III-1927
Bacon's Rebellion   I-151
Bleeding Kansas   II-889
Booker T. Washington Delivers His "Atlanta Compromise" Speech   II-1249
Columbus Lands in the New World   I-17
Creation of the Tennessee Valley Authority   III-1621
DeSoto's Expedition and the Founding of St. Augustine   I-33
Dorr Rebellion and the Growth of Political Democracy   II-766
Election of Jackson to the Presidency in 1828   I-1828
Election of Nixon to the Presidency in 1968   III-1933
Emergence of the First Political Parties   I-350
Founding of San Francisco   I-272
German and Irish Immigration   II-754
Government Acts to Assure Loyalty at Home in Wartime   III-1703
John Brown's Raid on Harpers Ferry   II-918
Montgomery Bus Boycott   III-1855
National Association for the Advancement of Colored People Formed   III-1384
Negotiation of the Missouri Compromise   II-552

Organization of the People's Party   II-1225
Passage of the Dawes Act   II-1161
Passage of the Homestead Act   II-962
Passage of the Indian Removal Act   I-666
Passage of the Northwest Ordinance   I-324
Passage of the Social Security Act   III-1643
Polarization of American Society in the 1960's   III-1861
Poverty in an Affluent Society   III-1866
Red Scare, The   III-1491
Rise of the Whig Party   II-690
Settlement of Connecticut   I-91
Settlement of Georgia   I-182
Voyages of John Cabot, The   I-23

TECHNOLOGICAL

Alexander Graham Bell Invents the Telephone   II-1089
Apollo 11 Lands on the Moon   III-1940
Baltimore and Ohio Railroad Begins Operations   I-624
Beginnings of Commercial Television Broadcasting   III-1674
Brooklyn Bridge Erected   II-1060
Completion of the Transcontinental Telegraph   II-930
Construction of the Erie Canal   I-546
Construction of the First Transcontinental Railroad   II-969
Construction of the National Road   I-491
Creation of the Office of Scientific Research and Development   III-1692
Development of the Ford Assembly Line and Adoption of the Five-Dollar-a-Day Minimum Wage   III-1421
Edison Demonstrates the First Incandescent Lamp   II-1110
Era of the Clipper Ships   II-807
Erection of Slater's Spinning Mill at Pawtucket   I-362
First Showing of *The Great Train Robbery*   II-1333
First Successful Voyage of the *Clermont*   I-471
First Test of a Submarine in Warfare   I-267
Howe's Invention of the Sewing Machine Heralding the Rise of Industrial Capitalism   II-837
Invention of the Electric Telegraph   II-742
Laying of the First Transatlantic Cable   II-895
McCormick's Invention of the Reaper   II-679
Mayan Calendar, The   I-5
Pacific Railroad Surveys   II-865
Radio Station KDKA Begins Commercial Broadcasting   III-1519
Robert Goddard Launches the First Liquid-Fueled Rocket   III-1555
Whitney Invents the Cotton Gin   I-371
Wright Brothers' First Flight, The   II-1346

PRINCIPAL PERSONAGES

Abarca y Bolea, Pedro Pablo (*see* de Aranda, Conde)
Abbey, Henry E. (1846-1896) II-1135
Abbott, Lieutenant H.L. (1831-1927) II-865
Abbott, The Reverend Lyman (1835-1922) II-1161
Aberdeen, Lord (George Hamilton Gordon, Earl and Marquis of Aberdeen) (1784-1860) II-778
Acheson, Dean Gooderham (1893-1971) III-1806
Adams, Charles Francis (1807-1886) II-1072
Adams, Henry Brooks (1838-1918) II-1184
Adams, John (1735-1826) I-194; 231; 246; 256; 261; 300; 341; 350; 403; 408; 414; 426; 432; 437; 456
Adams, John Quincy (1767-1838) I-485; 522; 558; 593; 607; 631; II-673; 831
Adams, Samuel (1722-1803) I-241; 246
Addams, Jane (1860-1935) III-1369
Adet, Pierre (*fl.* 1796) I-403
Agnew, Spiro Theodore (1918-) III-1933
Aguinaldo, Emilio (1869-1964) II-1290
Alcott, Amos Bronson (1799-1888) I-654
Aldrich, Nelson Wilmarth (1841-1915) II-1325; III-1390; 1415; 1432
Aldrin, Jr., Colonel Edwin Eugene (1930-) III-1940
Alexander I, of Russia (1777-1825) I-593
Alexander II, of Russia (1818-1881) II-1037
Alexander, James (1691-1756) I-188
Alexander, James Dallas (1759-1817) I-539
Alfred, Mother (*fl.* 1883) II-1178
Alger, Russell Alexander (1836-1907) II-1284
Allison, William Boyd (1829-1908) II-1325
Alsberg, Henry (*fl.* 1930's) III-1632
Altgeld, John Peter (1847-1902) II-1237
Ames, Fisher (1758-1808) I-350; 356
Ames, Oakes (1804-1873) II-969; 1054
Ames, Oliver (1807-1877) II-969
Amherst, Jeffrey (1717-1797) I-200; 207
"Amos 'n Andy" (Freeman Gosden and Charles Correll) (*fl.* 1920's) III-1501
Andrews, Samuel (*fl.* 1882) II-1116
Andros, Sir Edmund (1637-1714) I-163
Angell, James Burrill (1829-1916) II-1077
Anthony, Susan Brownell (1820-1906) III-1513
de Anza, Juan Bautista (1735-1788) I-272
de Aranda, Conde (Pedro Pablo Abarca y Bolea) (1718-1799) I-300
Argall, Sir Samuel (*fl.* 1609-1624) I-65
Arista, Major General Mariano (1802-1855) II-825
Arkwright, Sir Richard (1732-1792) I-362; 371

Armijo, Manuel (*fl.* 1846) II-818
Armstrong, Edwin H. (1890-1954) III-1674
Armstrong, Neil Alden (1930-) III-1940
Armstrong, Samuel Chapman (1839-1893) II-1249
Arnold, Brigadier General Benedict (1741-1801) I-277
Arthur, Chester Alan (1830-1886) II-1123; 1128
Asbury, Francis (1745-1816) I-420
Ashburton, Baron (Alexander Baring) (1774-1848) II-801
Astley, Philip (1742-1814) II-1066
Astor, John Jacob (1763-1848) I-476; 539
Atchison, David Rice (1807-1886) II-871
Atwood, Luther (*fl.* 1859) II-912
Austin, Stephen Fuller (1793-1836) II-736
de Avilés, Pedro Menendez (1519-1574) I-33
de Ayala, Juan Manuel (*fl.* 1775) I-272
de Ayllón, Lucas Vásquez (?-1526) I-33

Babcock, Orville E. (1835-1884) II-1054
Bacheller, Irving Addison (1859-1950) II-1255
Backus, Isaac (1724-1806) I-318
Bacon, Nathaniel (1647-1676) I-151
Baer, George F. (1842-1914) II-1329
Bailey, Gamaliel (1807-1859) II-859
Bailey, James A. (1847-1906) II-1066
Bailey, Joseph (1863-1929) III-1415
Baird, Spencer Fullerton (1823-1887) II-831
Baker, Edward D. (1811-1861) II-946
Baker, Newton Diehl (1871-1937) III-1466
Baker, Ray Stannard (1870-1946) III-1353
Baldwin, Abraham (1754-1807) I-312
Balfour, Arthur James (First Earl of Balfour) (1848-1930) III-1531
Balfour, First Earl of (*see* Balfour, Arthur James)
Ball, George (1909-) III-1888
Ballinger, Richard Achilles (1858-1922) III-1390
Ballou, Adin (1803-1890) I-642
Ballou, Hosea (1771-1852) I-570
Baltimore, First Lord (*see* Calvert, George)
Baltimore, Second Lord (*see* Calvert, Cecilius)
Bancroft, Aaron (1755-1839) II-730
Bancroft, George (1800-1891) II-730
Banks, Nathaniel Prentiss (1816-1894) II-1037
de Barbé-Marbois, Marquis François (1745-1837) I-445
Baring, Alexander (*see* Ashburton, Baron)
Barkley, Alben William (1877-1956) III-1800
Barlow, Joel (1754-1812) I-194; 636
Barlowe, Arthur (1550?-?1620) I-46
Barnard, Henry (1811-1900) I-576; II-1031

Barnum, Phineas Taylor (1810-1891) II-1066

Barrows, Harlan H. (1877-1960) II-1627

Barth, Karl (1886-1968) III-1604

Baruch, Bernard Mannes (1870-1965) III-1460

Bates, Ruby (*fl.* 1930's) III-1588

Bathurst, Henry (Third Earl Bathurst) (1762-1834) I-533

Bathurst, Third Earl (*see* Bathurst, Henry)

Bayard, James A. (1767-1815) I-426; 522

Bayard, Thomas Francis (1828-1898) II-1190

Beach, Sylvia (1887-1962) III-1560

Beard, Charles Austin (1874-1948) III-1426

de Beaumarchais, Pierre Augustin Caron (1732-1799) I-282

de Beaumont, Gustave (1802-1866) II-673

Beauregard, General Pierre Gustave Toutant (1818-1893) II-952

Beckley, John (*fl.* 1799) I-350

Becknell, William (1790?-1832) I-588

Beckwith, Lieutenant E. G. (*fl.* 1850's) II-865

Beecher, Lyman (1775-1863) I-570; II-859

Belknap, William (1829-1890) II-1054

Bell, Alexander Graham (1847-1922) II-1089

Bell, John (1797-1869) II-935

Bellingham, Richard (1592?-1672) I-103

Belmont, August (1816-1890) II-1135

de Benevant, Prince (*see* de Talleyrand-Perigord, Charles)

Bennett, Hugh Hammond (1881-1960) III-1627

Bennett, James Gordon (1795-1872) II-713

Bennett, John C. (1902-) III-1604

Benton, Thomas Hart (1782-1858) I-582 660; II-696; 772; 865

Berkeley, Sir William (1606-1677) I-132; 151

Berry, Sir John (*fl.* 1666-1667) I-151

von Bethmann-Hollweg, Theobald (1856-1921) III-1450

Beverley, Robert (*fl.* 1675-1677) I-151

Bevin, Ernest (1884-1951) III-1806

Biddle, Nicholas (1786-1844) I-539; II-696

Bierstadt, Albert (1830-1902) I-613

Bingham, John A. (1815-1900) II-1049

Birch, Thomas (1779-1851) I-613

Birney, James Gillespie (1792-1857) I-642; II-719

Bissell, George Henry (1821-1884) II-912

Black, Hugo LaFayette (1886-1971) III-1893

Blackwell, Mrs. Henry Brown (*see* Stone, Lucy)

Blain, James Gillespie (1830-1893) II-1140; 1190

Blair, Montgomery (1813-1883) II-900; 980

Blatch, Harriot Stanton (1856-1940) III-1513

Blatchford, Joseph H. (1934-) III-1877

Blennerhassett, Harman (1765-1831) I-461

Bloomfield, Maurice (1855-1928) II-1077

Blount, William (1749-1800) I-396

Bohlen, Charles Eustis (1904-) III-1736

Bonaparte, Napoleon (*see* Napoleon I)

Bonnet, Georges (1889-1973) III-1806

Booth, John Wilkes (1838-1865) II-1014

Borah, William Edgar (1865-1940) III-1484; 1649

de Bourgmound, Etienne (*fl.* 1714) I-144

Bowles, Chester B. (1901-) III-1759

Bradford, David (*fl.* 1794) I-377

Bradford, William (1590-1657) I-74

Bradley, General Omar Nelson (1893-) III-1720; 1748; 1783

Bradley, Richard (*fl.* 1734) I-188

Bradstreet, Simon (1603-1697) I-169

Bragg, Braxton (1817-1876) II-997

Brandeis, Louis Dembitz (1856-1941) III-1369; 1405

Brannan, Samuel (1819-1889) II-812

Brant, Joseph (Thayendanegea) (1742-1807) I-383

von Braun, Wernher (1912-) III-1940

Breckinridge, John Cabell (1821-1875) II-935

Brewer, Dr. Francis Beattie (*fl.* 1859) II-912

Brewster, William (1567-1644) I-74

Briand, Aristide (1862-1932) III-1531

Bridger, James (1804-1881) II-812

de Brion, Sieur (*see* de Chabot, Philippe)

Brown, Edmund G. (Pat) (1905-) III-1912

Brown, Henry Billings (1836-1913) II-1261; 1318

Brown, Dr. J. A. (*fl.* 1840) II-766

Brown, John (1800-1859) II-889; 918

Brown, Moses (1738-1836) I-362

Brownson, Orestes Augustus (1803-1876) I-654

Brunel, Sir Marc Isambard K. (1769-1849) II-895

Brunner, Emil (1889-1966) III-1604

Bryan, William Jennings (1860-1925) II-1268; 1273; III-1432; 1549

Bryant, William Cullen (1794-1878) I-481

de Buade, Louis (Comte de Frontenac) (1620-1698) I-144

Buchanan, James (1791-1868) II-889; 906; 946; 962; 974

Buckley, Jr., William F. (1925-) III-1861

Bull, William (1710-1791) I-213

Bunau-Varilla, Philippe Jean (1860-1940) II-1339

Bundy, McGeorge (1919-) III-1888

Burchard, Samuel D. (1812-1891) II-1140

Burgess, Ernest W. (1886-1966) III-1357

Burgoyne, General John (1722-1792) I-277

Burke, Edmund (1729-1797) I-241

Burke, Dr. Thomas (1747?-1783) I-288

Burnham, Daniel Hudson (1846-1912) II-1231

Burr, Aaron (1756-1836)   I-350; 426; 456; 461

Burritt, Elihu (1810-1879)   I-642

Bush, Dr. Vannevar (1890-   )   III-1692

Bushnell, David (1742?-1824)   I-267

Bute, Earl of (*see* Stuart, John)

Butler, Benjamin F. (1818-1893)   II-1140

Byers, William Newton (1831-1903)   II-1104

Byrnes, James Francis (1879-1972)   III-1680; 1753; 1776

Cabata, Giovanni (*see* Cabot, John)

Cabeza de Vaca, Álvar Núñez (1490?-1557) I-40

Cabot, George (1752-1823)   I-517

Cabot, John (Giovanni Cabata) (1450-1498) I-23

Cabot, Sebastian (1476?-1557)   I-23

Cabrillo, Juan Rodríguez (?-1543)   I-272

Calhoun, John (1806-1859)   II-889

Calhoun, John Caldwell (1782-1850)   I-539; 546; 558; 607; 648; 660; II-690; 702; 748; 854

Calvert, Cecilius (Second Lord Baltimore) (1605-1675)   I-115

Calvert, George (First Lord Baltimore) (1580?-1632)   I-115

Calvert, Leonard (1606-1647)   I-115

Campbell, John (Earl of Loudon) (1705-1782) I-200

Canning, George (1770-1827)   I-505; 593

Cannon, Bishop James (1864-1944)   III-1566

Cannon, Joseph Gurney (1836-1926)   III-1390

Capone, Alphonse "Al" (1899-1947)   III-1507

Carmichael, Stokely (1941-   )   III-1861

Carnegie, Andrew (1835-1919)   II-1167

de Carondolet, Barón Francisco Luis Héctor (1748?-1807)   I-396

Carranza, Venustiano (1859-1920)   III-1438

Carroll, Charles (1737-1832)   I-288; 624

Carson, Christopher "Kit" (1809-1868)   II-795

Carter, James G. (1795-1849)   I-576

Cartier, Jacques (1491-1557)   I-28

Cartwright, Edmund (1743-1823)   I-371

Carver, John (1576?-1621)   I-74

Casey, Edward Pearce (1864-1940)   II-1279

Casey, General Thomas Lincoln (1831-1896) II-1279

Caso Yrujo, Marquis of (*fl.* 1805-1807)   I-461

de Casson, Dollier (*fl.* 17th Cent.)   I-52

Castlereagh, First Viscount (*see* Stewart, Robert)

Castro, General José (1818-1893)   II-818

Catron, John (1786-1865)   II-900

Catt, Carrie Chapman (1859-1947)   III-1513

Cavelier, René Robert (Sieur do La Salle) (1643-1687)   I-52; 144; 443

de Cermeñon, Sebastian Rodrigues (*fl.* 1595) I-272

Cervera y Topete, Admiral Pasqual (1839-1909) II-1284

Cézanne, Paul (1839-1906)   III-1411

de Chabot, Philippe (Sieur de Brion) (1480-1543) I-28

de Champlain, Samuel (1567?-1635)   I-52

Channing, William Ellery (1780-1842)   I-570

Chanute, Octave (1832-1910)   II-1346

Chaplin, Charles Spencer (1889-   )   III-1501

Charles II, of Great Britain and Ireland (1630-1685)   I-121; 157

Chase, Salmon Portland (1808-1873)   II-871; 877; 980; 985; 1026

Chase, Samuel (1741-1811)   I-288

Chauncy, Charles (President of Harvard College) (1592-1672)   I-127

Chauncy, Charles (Pastor, First Church of Boston) (1705-1787)   I-176; 570

Chávez, Cesar (1927-   )   III-1866

Chester, George F. (*fl.* 1882)   II-1116

Cheves, Langdon (1776-1857)   I-539

Chiang Kai-shek (1887-   )   III-1764

Chicheley, Sir Henry (*fl.* 1677)   I-151

Child, Lydia Maria (1802-1880)   II-719

Chisholm, Jesse (1806-1868)   II-1020

Chou En-lai (1898?-   )   III-1764

Church, Frederick Stuart (1842-1924)   I-613

Churchill, Sir Winston Leonard Spencer (1874-1965)   III-1686; 1715; 1736; 1741; 1748; 1776

Cicotte, Ed (1884-1969)   III-1497

Clarendon, Earl of (Edward Hyde) (1609-1674) I-121

Clark, E. E. (1856-1930)   II-1329

Clark, James Beauchamp "Champ" (1850-1921) III-1405

Clark, William (1770-1838)   I-450

Clarke, Dr. John (1609-1676)   I-97

Clay, Henry (1777-1852)   I-505; 522; 582; 593; 607; II-690; 696; 702; 748; 760; 772; 854

Clay, John (1851-1934)   II-1020

Clay, General Lucius D. (1897-   )   III-1794

Clemenceau, Georges (1841-1929)   III-1484

Clemens, Samuel Langhorne (*see* Twain, Mark)

Cleveland, Stephen Grover (1837-1908)   II-1140; 1157; 1161; 1190; 1237; 1268; 1273; 1307

Clifford, Clark McAdams (1906-   )   III-1800

Clinton, DeWitt (1769-1828)   I-546; 576

Clinton, Lieutenant General Sir Henry (1738?-1795)   I-277; 294

Cobb, Howell (1815-1868)   II-941

Cochrane, Admiral Sir Alexander Forrester Inglis (1758-1832)   I-533

Cockburn, Sir Alexander (1802-1880)   II-1072

Coddington, William (1601-1678)   I-97

Cody, William Frederick "Buffalo Bill" (1846-1917)   II-925

Colbert, Jean Baptiste (1619-1683)   I-52
Colden, Cadwallader (1688-1776)   I-194
Cole, Thomas (1801-1848)   I-613
de Coligny, Gaspard (1519-1572)   I-33
Colleton, Sir John (*fl.* 1660)   I-132
Collier, William (c. 1612-1670)   I-109
Collins, Lieutenant Colonel Michael (1930-   )   III-1940
Columbus, Christopher (1451-1506)   I-17
Commons, John Rogers (1862-1945)   II-1077
Conant, Dr. James Bryant (1893-   )   III-1692
Connally, John Bowden (1917-   )   III-1899
Connally, Tom (1877-1963)   III-1741
Conrad, Frank (1874-1941)   III-1519
Cooke, Jay (1821-1905)   II-985
Cooke, Morris L. (1872-1960)   II-1627
Cooke, Lieutenant Colonel Philip St. George (1809-1895)   II-818
Cooley, Charles H. (1864-1929)   III-1357
Cooley, Thomas M. (1824-1898)   II-1157
Coolidge, Calvin (1872-1933)   III-1472; 1525; 1542
Cooper, Anthony Ashley (*see* Shaftesbury, Earl of)
Cooper, James Fenimore (1789-1851)   I-481
Corbin, Abel Rathbone (*fl.* 1869-1875)   II-1054
Cornwallis, Major General Lord Charles (1738-1805)   I-294
de Coronado, Francisco Vásquez (1510-1554)   I-40
Correll, Charles (*see* "Amos 'n Andy")
Corwin, Jonathan (*fl.* 1692)   I-169
Cosby, William (c. 1690-1736)   I-188
Cotton, John (1584-1652)   I-85
Coudert, Frederic René (1832-1903)   II-1318
Coughlin, Charles Edward (1891-   )   III-1582
Coup, William C. (*fl.* 1870)   II-1066
Couzens, James (1872-1936)   III-1421
Cox, Archibald (1912-   )   III-1883
Cox, James M. (1870-1957)   III-1472
Craig, Thomas (*fl.* 1880's)   II-1077
Crane, Stephen (1871-1900)   II-1255
Crawford, William H. (1772-1834)   I-607
Crazy Horse (1849?-1877)   II-1094
Creel, George (1876-1953)   III-1454
Creighton, Edward (*fl.* 1860-1861)   II-930
Crocker, Charles (1822-1888)   II-969
Crompton, Samuel (1753-1827)   I-371
Cromwell, William Nelson (1854-1948)   II-1339
Crook, General George (1829-1890)   II-1094
Crooks, Ramsey (1787-1859)   I-476
Cullom, Shelby M. (1829-1914)   II-1157
Culpeper, John (*fl.* 1671-1680)   I-132
Cummings, Homer Stillé (1870-1956)   III-1667
Cummins, Albert (1850-1926)   III-1415

Curtis, Benjamin Robbins (1809-1874)   II-900
Curtis, George William (1824-1892)   II-1128
Curtiss, Glenn Hammond (1878-1930)   II-1346
Custer, Colonel George A. (1839-1876)   II-1094
Cutler, Manasseh (1742-1823)   I-306; 312
Czolgosz, Leon (1873-1901)   II-1325

Dallas, Alexander James (1759-1817)   I-539
Damrosch, Dr. Leopold (1832-1885)   II-1135
Darlan, Admiral Jean Louis (1881-1942)   III-1715
Darrow, Clarence Seward (1857-1938)   II-1237; III-1549
Dartmouth, Second Earl of (*see* Legge, William)
Darwin, Charles Robert (1809-1882)   II-1167
Daugherty, Harry Micajah (1860-1941)   III-1472; 1525
Davenport, John (1597-1670)   I-91
Davies, Arthur B. (1862-1928)   III-1411
Davies, Samuel (1723-1761)   I-176
Davis, Chester (1896-1966)   III-1627
Davis, Elmer H. (1890-1958)   III-1703
Davis, Jefferson (1808-1889)   II-865; 871; 941
Davis, Richard Harding (1864-1916)   II-1243
Dawes, Charles Gates (1865-1951)   III-1537; 1594
Dawes, Henry Laurens (1816-1903)   II-1123; 1161
Day, Benjamin Henry (1810-1889)   II-713
Deane, Silas (1737-1789)   I-282
DeBow, J. D. B. (1820-1867)   I-371
Debs, Eugene Victor (1855-1926)   II-1237; III-1454; 1472
Decker, Karl (*fl.* late 19th Cent.)   II-1243
Deere, John (1804-1886)   II-679
De Forest, Lee (1873-1961)   III-1519
De La Warr, Lord (*see* West, Thomas)
Dellenbaugh, Frederick Samuel (1853-1935)   II-1104
Deloria, Jr., Vine (*fl.* 1960's)   III-1866
Dew, Thomas R. (1802-1846)   I-648
Dewey, Commodore George (1837-1917)   II-1284; 1290
Dewey, John (1859-1952)   II-1077; 1301; III-1363
Dewey, Thomas Edmund (1902-1971)   III-1800
De Witt, General John L. (1880-1962)   III-1703
Dickinson, John (1732-1808)   I-225; 288
Diem, Ngo Dinh (*see* Ngo Dinh Diem)
Dingley, Nelson (1832-1899)   II-1273
Dinsmore, William B. (*fl.* 1860)   II-925
Dixon, Archibald (1802-1876)   II-871

Dobrynin, Anatoly F. (1919-   )   III-1888
Dodd, Samuel C. T. (1836-1907)   II-1116
Dodge, Grenville M. (1831-1916)   II-969
Doheny, Edward Laurence (1856-1935)   III-1525
Doniphan, Colonel A. W. (1808-1887)   II-818
Donnelly, Ignatius (1831-1901)   II-1225
Dorr, Thomas Wilson (1805-1854)   II-766
Doughty, Thomas (1793-1856)   I-613
Douglas, Stephen Arnold (1813-1861)   II-854; 871; 889; 906; 935
Douglas, William Orville (1898-   )   III-1883; 1893
Douglass, Frederick (1817?-1895)   II-719
Dow, Neal (1804-1897)   I-642
Downing, Sir George (1623-1684)   I-121
Downshire, Marquis of (Wills Hill) (*see* Hillsborough, Earl of)
Drake, "Colonel" Edwin Laurentine (1819-1880)   II-912
Drouilliard, George (*fl.* early 19th Cent.)   I-450
Drummond, William (*fl.* 1664)   I-132
Duane, William (1760-1835)   I-414
Duane, William John (1780-1865)   II-696
DuBois, William Edward Burghardt (1868-1963)   III-1384
Duchamp, Marcel (1887-1968)   III-1411
Dudley, Thomas (1576-1653)   I-103; 109
Duer, William (1747-1799)   I-306; 356
Dulany, Daniel (1722-1797)   I-219
Dulles, John Foster (1888-1959)   III-1906
Dunk, George Montagu (*see* Halifax, Earl of)
Dunster, Henry (1609?-1659)   I-103
Durand, Asher Brown (1796-1886)   I-613
Durant, Thomas C. (1820-1885)   II-969
Dutton, Captain Clarence Edward (1841-1912)   II-1104
Dwight, Theodore (1764-1846)   I-552
Dwight, Timothy (1752-1817)   I-420; 636
Dzhugashvili, Iosif Vissarionovich (*see* Stalin, Joseph)

Eaton, Dorman B. (1823-1899)   II-1128
Eaton, Nathaniel (1609?-1674)   I-103
Eaton, Theophilus (1590-1658)   I-91; 109
Echeandía, José Mariá (*fl.* 1826)   I-619
Eden, Sir Anthony (1897-   )   III-1736
Edison, Thomas Alva (1847-1931)   II-1089; 1110; 1333
Edwards, Benjamin (*fl.* 1835)   II-736
Edwards, Haden (*fl.* 1835)   II-736
Edwards, Jonathan (1703-1758)   I-176; II-730
Edwards, Ninian (1775-1833)   I-582
Egremont, Earl of (Charles Wyndham) (1710-1763)   I-207
Eisenhower, Dwight David (1890-1969)   III-1715; 1720; 1748; 1806; 1823; 1843; 1849
Eliot, Charles William (1834-1926)   II-1077

Elizabeth I, of England and Ireland (1533-1603)   I-46
Ellet, Charles (1810-1862)   II-1060
Elliott, Matthew (*fl.* 1790-1796)   I-383
Ellsworth, Oliver (1745-1807)   I-345
Emde, Carl (*fl.* 1913-1914)   III-1421
Emerson, Ralph Waldo (1803-1882)   I-613; 654; II-848
Emory, Major William H. (1811-1887)   II-818; 865
En-lai, Chou (*see* Chou En-lai)
Epstein, Abraham (1892-1942)   III-1643
Ericsson, John (1803-1889)   II-957
Eric the Red (982-986)   I-11
Erikson, Thorvald (*fl.* 1000-1010)   I-11
Erskine, George (*fl.* 19th Cent.)   I-505
Espejo, Antonio (*fl.* 1581-1583)   I-40
Estebanico (*also* known as Stephen) (?-1539)   I-40
Evans, George Henry (1805-1856)   II-962
Evans, Oliver (1755-1819)   I-471; 546
Evarts, Jeremiah (1781-1831)   I-666
Eveleth, J. G. (*fl.* 1859)   II-912
Everett, Edward (1794-1865)   I-576

Fages, Pedro (*fl.* 1772)   I-272
Fall, Albert Bacon (1861-1944)   III-1525
Fanning, Edmund (1739-1818)   I-213
Fargo, William George (1818-1881)   II-925
Faris, Ellsworth (1874-1953)   III-1357
Farley, James Aloysius (1888-1941)   III-1609
Farley, James T. (*fl.* 1882)   II-1123
Farmer, Moses G. (1820-1893)   II-1110
Farnsworth, Philo T. (1906-1971)   III-1674
Faulkner, William Cuthbert (1897-1962)   III-1571
Felsch, Oscar "Happy" (1891-1964)   III-1497
Fenner, Charles E. (1834-1911)   II-1261
Fenwick, George (1603-1657)   I-109
Ferdinand VII, of Spain (1784-1833)   I-558
Ferguson, Judge John H. (*fl.* 1892)   II-1261
Fessenden, Reginald Aubrey (1866-1932)   III-1519
Fessenden, William Pitt (1806-1869)   II-1049
Field, Cyrus West (1819-1892)   II-895; 1135
Field, James G. (*fl.* 1890's)   II-1225
Field, Matthew D. (*fl.* 1858)   II-895
Field, Stephen Johnson (1816-1899)   II-1167
Fillmore, Millard (1800-1874)   II-854; 884
Finlay, Carlos Juan (1833-1915)   II-1313
Finney, Charles Grandison (1792-1875)   I-420; 642; II-708
Fish, Hamilton (1808-1893)   II-1072
Fisher, Ames (1758-1808)   I-356
Fisher, Professor Irving (1867-1947)   III-1577
Fitch, John (1743-1798)   I-471
Fitzhugh, George (1806-1881)   I-648
Fitzpatrick, Thomas (1799?-1854)   II-795

Flagler, Henry M. (1830-1913)   II-1116
Flanagan, Hallie (1890-1969)   III-1632
Fletcher, Vice Admiral Frank J. (1885-   )
III-1709
Fletcher, Robert (*fl.* 19th Cent.)   I-485
de Floridablanca, Conde (José Moñino y
Redondo) (1728-1808)   I-282
Foch, General Ferdinand (1851-1929)   III-
1466
Folger, Abiah (1667-1752)   I-236
Fomin, Alexandr S. (*fl.* 1962)   III-1888
Foot, Samuel Augustus (1780-1846)   I-582;
660
Forbes, Charles R. (1878?-1952)   III-1525
Ford, Henry (1863-1947)   III-1421; 1501
Forrestal, James Vincent (1892-1949)   III-
1783
Fortas, Abe (1910-   )   III-1893
Foster, W. H. (*fl.* 1886)   II-1152
Foster, William Zebulon (1881-1961)   III-
1609
Fowler, Jacob (1765-1850)   I-588
Francis, Jr., Dr. Thomas F. (1900-   )   III-
1835
Franco, General Francisco (1892-   )   III-
1661
François I, of France (1494-1547)   I-28
Frankfurter, Felix (1882-1966)   III-1883
Franklin, Benjamin (1706-1790)   I-194; 200;
219; 236; 256; 261; 282; 300
Franklin, Deborah Read (?-1774)   I-236
Franklin, James (1697-1735)   I-236
Franklin, Josiah (1657-1745)   I-236
Franklin, William (1731-1813)   I-236
Franklin, William Temple (1758-?)   I-236
Frelinghuysen, Theodore (1787-1862)   I-666
Frémont, John Charles (1813-1890)   II-795;
818; 877
Frick, Henry Clay (1849-1919)   II-1167
de Frontenac, Comte (*see* de Buade, Louis)
Fry, Colonel James B. (*fl.* 1863)   II-991
Fuchs, Klaus (*fl.* 1940's)   III-1817
Fuller, Margaret (1810-1850)   I-654
Fuller, Melville Weston (1833-1910)   II-1318
Fulton, Robert (1765-1815)   I-471; 600
Funston, General Frederick (1865-1917)   II-
1290; III-1438

Gage, General Thomas (1721-1787)   I-225;
231; 251
Gaitan, Jorge Eliecer (*fl.* 1948)   III-1789
Gale, Dr. Benjamin (1715-1790)   I-267
Gale, Leonard (*fl.* 1835)   II-742
Gall (1840?-1894)   II-1094
Gallatin, Albert (1761-1849)   I-350; 377; 414;
491; 522; 539; 546; 582; II-673
Galloway, Joseph (1729?-1803)   I-246
de Gálvez, José (1729-1787)   I-272
Gamble, James (*fl.* 1860-1861)   II-930
Gandil, Charles Arnold "Chick" (1888-1970)
III-1497

de Gardoqui, Don Diego (*fl.* 1795)   I-396
Garfield, James Abram (1831-1881)   II-1031;
1128
Garfield, James Rudolph (1865-1950)   III-
1390
Garland, Hamlin (1860-1940)   II-1255
Garner, John Nance (1868-1967)   III-1594;
1609; 1667
Garrison, Lloyd K. (1897-   )   III-1637
Garrison, William Lloyd (1805-1879)   I-642;
II-719
Garth, Charles (*fl.* 1770's)   I-213
Garvey, Marcus Moziah (1887-1940)   III-
1444
Gates, Major General Horatio (1728?-1806)
I-277
Geary, John White (1819-1873)   II-889
Geddes, Auckland C. (1879-1954)   III-1531
Genêt, Citizen Edmond (1736-1834)   I-403
George III, of Great Britain and Ireland (George
William Frederick) (1738-1820)   I-251
George IV, of Great Britain and Ireland (1762-
1830)   I-593
George, David Lloyd (1863-1945)   III-1484;
1537
Gerard, James Watson (1867-1951)   III-1450
Germain, George Sackville (*see* Germain, Lord
George)
Germain, Lord George (George Sackville Ger-
main, Viscount Sackville) (1716-1785)   I-
277
Gerry, Elbridge (1744-1814)   I-367; 408
Ghormley, Vice Admiral Robert L. (1883-1958)
III-1709
Gibbon, Edward (1737-1794)   II-1184
Gibbon, Colonel John (1827-1896)   II-1094
Gibbons, Thomas (1757-1826)   I-600
Giddings, Franklin H. (1855-1931)   III-
1357
Gideon, Clarence Earl (*fl.* 1963)   III-1893
Gifford, Walter Sherman (1885-1966)   III-
1582
Gilbert, Grove Karl (1843-1918)   II-1104
Gilbert, Sir Humphrey (1539?-1583)   I-46
Gillespie, Lieutenant Archibald H. (*fl.* 1840's)
II-818
Gilman, Daniel Coit (1831-1908)   II-1077
Girard, Stephen (1750-1831)   I-539
Glass, Carter (1858-1946)   III-1432
Glenn, Hugh (1788-1833)   I-588
Goddard, Morrill (*fl.* late 19th Cent.)   II-
1243
Goddard, Dr. Robert Hutchings (1882-1945)
III-1555
Godey, Alexis (*fl.* 1842)   II-795
de Godoy, Manuel (Manuel de Godoy y Alvarez
de Faria) (1767-1851)   I-396
Goldmark, Josephine (1877-1950)   III-1363
Goldwater, Barry Morris (1909-   )   III-
1918
Gompers, Samuel (1850-1924)   II-1152

Gorchakov, Aleksandr Mikhailovich (1798-1883)   II-1037

Gordon, George Hamilton (*see* Aberdeen, Lord)

Gorgas, Major William Crawford (1854-1920)   II-1313

Gorges, Sir Ferdinando (1566?-1647)   I-59

Gorton, Samuel (1592?-1677)   I-97

Gosden, Freeman (*see* "Amos 'n Andy")

Gouge, William M. (1796-1863)   II-748

Gould, Jay (1836-1892)   II-1135

Granger, Gideon (1767-1822)   I-485

Grant, Ulysses Simpson (1822-1885)   II-997; 1026; 1054; 1072

Gravier, Charles (*see* de Vergennes, Comte)

Greeley, Horace (1811-1872)   II-877; 962; 980

Green, Bernard R. (1843-1914)   II-1279

Green, Nicholas St. John (1830-1876)   III-1363

Green, William (1873-1952)   III-1655

Greene, Major General Nathanael (1742-1786)   I-294

Gregg, Josiah (1806-1850)   I-588

Gregson, Thomas (?-1646)   I-109

Grenville, Baron (*see* Grenville, William Wyndham)

Grenville, George (1712-1770)   I-219

Grenville, Sir Richard (1514?-1591)   I-46

Grenville, William Wyndham (Baron Grenville) (1759-1834)   I-389

Grey, Sir Edward Grey (1862-1933)   III-1450

Griffith, David Lewelyn Wark (1875-1948)   III-1501

Griffiths, John Willis (1809?-1882)   II-807

Griswold, J. N. A. (*fl.* 1880)   II-1135

Groves, Brigadier General Leslie Richard (1896-1970)   III-1692

Guggenheim, Simon (1867-1941)   II-1307

Guilford, Earl of (Lord Frederick North) (1732-1792)   I-225; 241

Guiteau, Charles J. (1840?-1882)   II-1128

Gunnison, Lieutenant John W. (1812-1853)   II-865

Gwin, William McKendree (1805-1885)   II-925

Haig, Field Marshall Sir Douglas (1861-1928)   III-1466

Hakluyt, Richard (1552?-1616)   I-46

Halifax, Earl of (George Montagu Dunk) (1716-1771)   I-207

Hall, Caroline A. (1838-1918)   II-1043

Halleck, Fitz-Greene (1790-1867)   I-481

Halsey, Admiral William F. (1882-1959)   III-1709; 1731

Hamilton, Alexander (1757-1804)   I-330; 335; 350; 356; 377; 389; 403; 408; 426; 432; 582; III-1394

Hamilton, Andrew (?-1741)   I-188

Hamlin, Hannibal (1809-1891)   II-946

Hammond, George (*fl.* 1794-1795)   I-389

Hammond, James Henry (1807-1864)   I-648

Hancock, John (1737-1793)   I-231; 241; 256

Hanna, Marcus (Mark) Alonzo (1837-1904)   II-1268; 1325; 1329; 1339

Harding, Warren Gamaliel (1865-1923)   III-1472; 1525; 1531; 1542; 1560

Hargis, Reverend Billy James (1925-   )   III-1861

Hargreaves, James (?-1778)   I-371

Harlan, John Marshall (Associate Justice of the United States 1877-1911) (1833-1911)   II-1261; 1318

Harlan, John M. (Associate Justice of the United States 1955-1971) (1899-1972)   III-1883

Harmar, Brigadier General Josiah (1753-1813)   I-383

Harriman, William Averell (1891-   )   III-1736; 1753; 1806

Harrington, Michael (1928-   )   III-1866

Harrison, Benjamin (1833-1901)   II-1206

Harrison, William Henry (1733-1841)   I-498; 582; II-690; 760

Harvard, John (1607-1638)   I-103

Haslam, "Pony Bob" (*fl.* 1860)   II-925

Hathorne, John (*fl.* 1692)   I-169

Hawley, Joseph R. (1826-1905)   II-1123

Hawthorne, Nathaniel (1804-1964)   II-848

Hay, John Milton (1838-1905)   II-1296; 1339

Hayden, Tom (1940?-   )   III-1861

Hayes, Rutherford Birchard (1822-1893)   II-1099

Hayne, Robert Young (1791-1839)   I-593; 660; II-702

Haynes, John (1594-1654)   I-109

Haywood, William Dudley "Big Bill" (1869-1928)   III-1454

Hearst, William Randolph (1863-1951)   II-1243; 1284

Heathcoate, Thomas W. (*fl.* 1890's)   II-1237; 1284

von Helmholtz, Hermann Ludwig Ferdinand (1821-1894)   II-1089

Hemingway, Ernest (1899-1961)   III-1560

Henry IV, of France (1553-1610)   I-52

Henry VII, of England (1457-1509)   I-23

Henry, Joseph (1797-1878)   II-742; 831

Henry, Patrick (1736-1799)   I-219; 318

Henshaw, David (*fl.* 1829-1837)   II-696

von Herder, Johann Gottfried (1744-1803)   II-730

Herjolfson, Bjarni (*fl.* 985)   I-11

Herndon, William Henry (1818-1891)   II-906

Herrera, José Joaquín (1792-1854)   II-825

Hertz, Heinrich Rudolph (1857-1895)   III-1519

Heth, Joice (*fl.* 1835)   II-1066

Hickok, James Butler "Wild Bill" (1837-1876)   II-1020

Hillsborough, Earl of *and* Marquis of Downshire (Wills Hill) (1718-1793)   I-207; 231
Hippisley, Alfred E. (*fl.* 1899)   II-1296
Hiss, Alger (1904-   )   III-1817
Hitler, Adolf (1899-1945)   III-1686; 1720; 1748
Hoar, George (1826-1904)   II-1206
Hobart, Garret Augustus (1844-1899)   II-1268
Hobby, Oveta Culp (1905-   )   III-1835
Hobson, Richmond Pearson (1870-1937)   III-1507
Ho Chi Minh (1890-1969)   III-1906
Hoffman, Abbie (*fl.* 1960's)   III-1861
Holmes, Jr., Oliver Wendell (1841-1935)   III-1363
Hood, John Bell (1831-1879)   II-1010
Hooker, Thomas (1586?-1647)   I-91; 109
Hoover, Herbert Clark (1874-1964)   III-1507; 1542; 1566; 1577; 1582; 1594; 1599; 1609
Hoover, J. Edgar (1895-1972)   III-1491
Hopkins, Edward (1600-1657)   I-109
Hopkins, Harry L. (1890-1946)   III-1632; 1686
Hopkins, John P. (*fl.* 1890's)   II-1237
Hopkins, Johns (1795-1873)   II-1077
Horne, Jeremiah (*fl.* 1840's)   II-785
Horton, James E. (*fl.* 1930's)   III-1588
House, Colonel Edward M. (1858-1938)   III-1450
Houston, Samuel (Sam) (1793-1863)   II-736; 941
Howard, Sir Ebenezer (1850-1928)   III-1811
Howard, Colonel John Eager (1752-1827)   I-624
Howard, Oliver Otis (1830-1909)   II-1010
Howe, Elias (1819-1867)   II-837
Howe, Louis McHenry (1871-1936)   III-1609
Howe, Lieutenant General Sir William (1729-1814)   I-277
Howells, William Dean (1837-1920)   II-1255
Hudson, Henry (?-1611)   I-80
Hughes, Charles Evans (1862-1948)   III-1531; 1537; 1667
Hull, Cordell (1871-1955)   III-1649; 1661; 1686; 1741
Humphrey, Hubert Horatio (1911-   )   III-1918; 1933
Hunt, Richard Morris (1827-1895)   II-1231
Hunt, Walter (1796-1859)   II-837
Hunt, Wilson Price (*fl.* 1808)   I-476
Husbands, Hermon (1724-1795)   I-213
Hussey, Obed (1792-1860)   II-679
Hutchins, Thomas (1730-1789)   I-306
Hutchinson, Anne (1591-1643)   I-85; 97
Hutchinson, Elisha (*fl.* 1773)   I-241
Hutchinson, Thomas (1711-1780)   I-241
Hutchinson, Jr., Thomas (*fl.* 1773)   I-241
Hyde, Edward (*see* Clarendon, Earl of)

Hyde, Edward (Governor of North Carolina) (c. 1650-1712)   I-132
Hyde, Orson (*fl.* 1848)   II-812

d'Iberville, Pierre Lemoyne (Sieur d'Iberville) (1661-1706)   I-144
d'Iberville, Sieur (*see* d'Iberville, Pierre Lemoyne)
Ickes, Harold L. (1874-1952)   III-1632
Ide, William B. (1796-1852)   II-818
Ingram, Joseph (*fl.* 1676-1677)   I-151
Intendant, The Great (*see* Talon, Jean Baptiste)
Ireland, William M. (*fl.* 1867)   II-1043
Irving, Washington (1783-1859)   I-481
Isabella I, of Spain (Queen of Castile) (1451-1504)   I-17

Jackson, Andrew (1767-1845)   I-533; 558; 607; 631; 660; 666; II-673; 690; 696; 702; 730; 760
Jackson, Charles Thomas (1805-1880)   II-742; 791
Jackson, James (*fl.* 1790)   I-356
Jackson, "Shoeless" Joe (1887-1951)   III-1497
James II, of England (earlier, Duke of York) (*see* James, Duke of York)
James, Duke of York (Crowned King James II in 1685) (1633-1701)   I-140; 163
James, Thomas (1782-1847)   I-588
James, William (1842-1910)   II-1301; III-1363
Jay, John (1745-1829)   I-300; 335; 345; 389; 403
Jeffers, William Martin (1876-1953)   III-1680
Jefferson, Thomas (1743-1826)   I-194; 256; 261; 288; 306; 312; 318; 350; 356; 389; 403; 414; 426; 432; 437; 443; 450; 456; 461; 491; 505; II-1184
Jeffreys, Herbert (*fl.* 1676-1677)   I-151
Jenckes, Thomas Allen (1818-1875)   II-1128
Jensen, Arthur Robert (1923-   )   III-1866
Jewett, John P. (1814-1884)   II-859
Johnson, Andrew (1808-1875)   II-962; 1003; 1026; 1031; 1049
Johnson, Claudia Alta Taylor (*see* Johnson, "Lady Bird")
Johnson, Hiram Warren (1866-1945)   III-1484; 1649
Johnson, General Hugh Samuel (1882-1942)   III-1637
Johnson, "Lady Bird" (Claudia Alta Taylor) (1912-   )   III-1899
Johnson, Louis A. (1891-1966)   III-1783
Johnson, Lyndon Baines (1908-1973)   III-1866; 1871; 1899; 1906; 1918
Johnson, Richard Mentor (1780-1850)   II-760
Johnson, Samuel (1709-1784)   I-636
Johnson, Thomas (1732-1819)   I-288

Johnson, Sir William (Superintendent of Indian Affairs) (1715-1774)   I-207
Johnson, William (Associate Justice of the United States) (1771-1834)   I-600
Johnston, Alvanley (1875-1951)   III-1759
Johnston, General Joseph Eggleston (1807-1891)   II-952; 997; 1010
Johnston, Samuel (1733-1816)   I-213
Jolliet, Louis (1645-1700)   I-52; 144
Jolson, Al (Asa Yoelson) (1886-1950)   III-1501
Jones, William (1760-1831)   I-539
Joseph, Sister Mary (*fl.* 1889-1919)   II-1178
Judah, Theodore D. (1826-1863)   II-969

Kagi, John H. (*fl.* 1856-1859)   II-918
Kahler, John H. (*fl.* 1910-1920)   II-1178
Kai-shek, Chiang (*see* Chiang Kai-shek)
Karlsefni, Thorfinn (*fl.* 1002-1015)   I-11
Kato, Baron Tomosaburo (1859-1923)   III-1531
Kawaguchi, Major General Kiyotake (*fl.* 1943)   III-1709
Keane, General John (*fl.* 1815)   I-533
Kearney, Denis (1847-1907)   II-1123
Kearny, Brigadier General Stephen Watts (1794-1848)   II-818
Keating, Kenneth B. (1900-   )   III-1888
Keith, Myron R. (*fl.* 1882)   II-1116
Kelley, Florence (1859-1932)   III-1369
Kelley, Oliver Hudson (1826-1913)   II-1043
Kelly, John (1822-1886)   II-1140
Kelvin, Baron (*see* Thompson, William)
Kennan, George F. (1904-   )   III-1776
Kennedy, Jacqueline Lee Bouvier (1929-   )   III-1899
Kennedy, John Fitzgerald (1917-1963)   III-1871; 1877; 1888; 1899; 1906; 1940
Kennedy, Robert Francis (1925-1968)   III-1927
Kennerley, Michael (*fl.* 1910)   III-1399
Kent, James (1763-1847)   I-600; II-673
Kerr, Clark (1911-   )   III-1912
Keynes, John Maynard (1883-1946)   III-1770
Keyserling, Leon H. (1908-   )   III-1770
Khrushchev, Nikita S. (1894-1971)   III-1888
Kieft, William (1597-1647)   I-80
Kier, Samuel M. (1813-1874)   II-912
Kimball, Heber C. (1801-1868)   II-812
Kim Il Sung (*fl.* 1950-1953)   III-1823
Kimmel, Admiral Husband Edward (1882-1968)   III-1697
King, Admiral Ernest J. (1878-1956)   III-1709
King, Jr., Dr. Martin Luther (1929-1968)   III-1855; 1927
King, Richard (1825-1885)   II-1020
King, Rufus (1755-1827)   I-552
King, Samuel W. (1786-1851)   II-766
Kirkland, Moses (*fl.* 1770's)   I-213

Klann, William C. (*fl.* 1913-1914)   III-1421
Knight, Jonathan (1789-1864)   I-624
Knight, Thomas E. (1898-1937)   III-1588
Knox, Henry (1750-1806)   I-383; 432
Knox, John Jay (1828-1892)   II-1083
Knox, Philander Chase (1853-1921)   II-1318; III-1379;1415
Knudsen, William Signius (1879-1948)   III-1680
Komei (1821-1867)   II-884
Kuhn, Walter (1877-1949)   III-1411
Kurita, Vice Admiral Takeo   (*fl.*1944)   III-1731

La Follette, Robert Marion (1855-1925)   II-1307; III-1390; 1484
Lamont, Thomas William (1870-1948)   III-1577
de Lancey, James (1703-1760)   I-188
Land, Admiral Emory Scott (1879-1971)   III-1680
Landis, Judge Kenesaw Mountain (1866-1944)   II-1497
Lane, James Henry (1814-1866)   II-889
Lane, Sir Ralph (1530?-1603)   I-46
Langley, Samuel P. (1834-1906)   II-1346
Lanman, Charles Rockwell (1850-1941)   II-1077
Lansdowne, Marquis of (*see* Petty, William)
Lansing, Robert (1864-1928)   II-1450
Larkin, Thomas O. (1802-1858)   II-843
de La Salle, Sieur (*see* Cavelier, René Robert)
Lattimore, Owen (1900-   )   III-1817
de Laudonnière, René Goulaine (*fl.* 1562-1586)   I-33
de La Vérendrye, Sieur (Pierre Gaultier de Varennes) (1685-1749)   I-144
Laws, Dr. S. S. (1824-1921)   II-1110
Leahy, William Daniel (1875-1959)   II-1736
Lee, Arthur (1740-1792)   I-282
Lee, Ezra (*fl.* 1775-1776)   I-267
Lee, Richard Henry (1732-1745)   I-261; 367
Lee, Robert Edward (1807-1870)   II-918; 997
Lefferts, General Marshall (1821-1876)   II-1110
Legge, William (Second Earl of Dartmouth) (1731-1801)   I-251
Leibowitz, Samuel (1893-   )   III-1588
Leif the Lucky (*fl.* 999-1000)   I-11
LeMay, General Curtis E. (1906-   )   III-1933
Lewis, John L. (1880-1969)   III-1655; 1759
Lewis, Meriwether (1774-1809)   I-450
Lewis, Oscar (1914-1970)   III-1866
Lieber, Francis (1800-1972)   II-673
Lilienthal, David Eli (1899-   )   III-1621
Lilienthal, Otto (1848-1896)   II-1346
Lincoln, Abraham (1809-1865)   II-906; 935; 946; 974; 980; 991; 1003
Lincoln, Major General Benjamin (1733-1810)   I-294

Lind, Jenny (1820-1887)   II-1066

Linderman, Henry Richard (1825-1879)   II-1083

Lindsay, Vachel (1879-1931)   III-1399

Lippitt, Francis (*fl.* 1830)   II-673

Livingston, Edward (1764-1836)   III-1394

Livingston, Robert R. (1746-1813)   I-341; 443; 471; 600

Lloyd, David (1656?-1731)   I-157

Lloyd, Thomas (1640-1694?)   I-157

Locke, John (1632-1704)   I-132

Lodge, Henry Cabot (1850-1924)   II-1201; III-1472; 1484; 1531

Lodge II, Henry Cabot (1902-   )   III-1871

Logan, James (1674-1751)   I-157

de Lome, Dupuy (1816-1885)   II-1243

Long, Crawford Williamson (1815-1878)   II-791

Long, Huey Pierce (1893-1935)   III-1582

Long, Colonel Stephen H. (1784-1864)   I-624

Loudon, Earl of (*see* Campbell, John)

Louis XVI, of France (1754-1793)   I-282

Lowell, Francis Cabot (1775-1817)   III-1811

Lowell, John (Jack) (1769-1840)   I-517

Lowery, Grosvenor (*fl.* 1879)   II-1110

Ludlow, Roger (1590-1664?)   I-91

Ludwell, Philip (*fl.* 1660-1704)   I-132; 151

Lumière, Auguste Marie Louis Nicolas (1862-1954)   II-1333

Lumière, Louis Jean (1864-1948)   II-1333

Lumpkin, Wilson (1783-1870)   I-666

Lundy, Benjamin (1789-1839)   II-719

Luther, Seth (1817-1846)   II-766

de la Luzerne, Chevalier (*fl.*1781)   I-288

Lynd, Staughton (1929-   )   III-1861

Lyon, Matthew (1750-1822)   I-414

Mabini, Apolinario (*fl.* early 20th Cent.)   II-1290

McAdoo, William Gibbs (1863-1941)   III-1432

MacArthur, General Douglas (1880-1964)   I-432; III-1731; 1823; 1829

McCarthy, Eugene Joseph (1916-   )   III-1933

McCarthy, Joseph Raymond (1908-1957)   III-1817; 1843

McClellan, Captain George Brinton (1826-1885)   II-865

McClure, Samuel S. (1857-1949)   III-1353

McCormick, Cyrus Hall (1809-1884)   II-679

McCormick, Mrs. Cyrus Hall (*fl.*1889)   II-1173

McCoy, Joseph Geating (1837-1915)   II-1020

McCulloch, Hugh (1808-1895)   II-985

McCulloch, John (*fl.* 1819)   I-564

McDonald, John (*fl.*1869-1875)   II-1054

McDougall, Alexander (1731?-1786)   I-246

McDowell, Brigadier General Irvin (1818-1885)   II-952

McDuffie, George (1790?-1851)   II-702

McGready, James (1758?-1817)   I-420

McHenry, James (1753-1816)   I-432

McKay, Donald (1810-1880)   II-807

McKean, Thomas (1734-1817)   I-377

McKee, Alexander (*fl.* 1790-1796)   I-383

McKenney, Thomas L. (1785-1859)   I-666

McKim, Charles Follen (1847-1909)   II-1231

McKinley, William (1843-1901)   II-1243; 1268; 1273; 1284; 1290; 1296; 1325

McLane, Louis (1786-1857)   II-696

McLean, John (1785-1861)   II-877; 900

McLeod, Alexander (*fl.*1841)   II-801

McLoughlin, Dr. John (1784-1857)   I-619

Maclure, William (1763-1840)   I-511

McMullin, Fred (1891-1952)   III-1497

McNamara, Robert S. (1916-   )   III-1888

Macon, Nathaniel (1758-1837)   I-552

McQuire, P.J. (*fl.* 1886)   II-1152

Madison, James (1751-1836)   I-194; 318; 330; 335; 350; 356; 367; 389; 403; 414; 437; 443; 456; 505; 517; 522; 539; 546; II-1184

Magoffin, James (1799-1868)   II-818

Mahan, Alfred Thayer (1840-1914)   II-1201

Majors, Alexander (1814-1900)   II-925

Mallet, Paul (*fl.* 1739-1740)   I-144

Mallet, Peter (*fl.* 1739-1740)   I-144

Mallory, Stephen Russell (1813?-1873)   II-957

Mann, Horace (1796-1859)   I-576

Manny, John H. (1825-1856)   II-679

Mao Tse-tung (1893-   )   III-1764

Marbury, William (1761?-1835)   I-437

March, General Peyton (1864-1955)   III-1478

Marconi, Marchese Guglielmo (1874-1937)   III-1519

Markham, William (1635?-1704)   I-157

Marquette, Jacques (1637-1675)   I-52; 144

Marroquin, José Manuel (1827-1908)   II-1339

Marshall, General George Catlett (1880-1959)   III-1686; 1697; 1715; 1764; 1776; 1783; 1789; 1794

Marshall, James (*fl.* 1794)   I-377

Marshall, James Wilson (1810-1885)   II-843

Marshall, John (1755-1835)   I-312; 437; 461; 485; 539; 564; 600; 666

Martin, Edward (*fl.*1847)   II-812

Martin, Homer (*fl.* 1935-1936)   III-1655

Martin, Luther (1748?-1826)   I-485; 564

Martinet, Louis A. (*fl.* 1890)   II-1261

Martyn, Benjamin (*fl.* 1733)   I-182

Mary Joseph, Sister (*see* Joseph, Sister Mary)

Mason, George (1725-1792)   I-367

Mason, Richard B. (1797-1850)   II-843

Masters, Edgar Lee (1869-1950)   III-1399

Mather, Cotton (1663-1728)   I-169

Mather, Increase (1639-1723)   I-127; 163; 169

Mather, Richard (1596-1669)   I-127

Mathew, Father Theobald (1790-1856) II-754

Matisse, Henri Émile Benoit (1869-1954) III-1411

Matteson, Edward E. (*fl.* 1849) II-843

Maury, Lieutenant Matthew Fontaine (1806-1873) II-895

May, Cornelius (*fl.* 1624) I-80

Mayhew, Jonathan (1720-1766) I-194; 570

Mayo, Dr. Charles Horace (1865-1939) II-1178

Mayo, Dr. William James (1861-1939) II-1178

Mayo, Dr. William Worrall (1819-1911) II-1178

Meade, George Gordon (1815-1872) II-997

Melgares, Don Facundo (*fl.* 1806) I-467

Melies, George (*fl.* 1900-1912) II-1333

Mellon, Andrew William (1855-1937) III-1542

Melville, Herman (1819-1891) II-848

Mencken, Henry Louis (1880-1956) III-1566

Mercer, Charles Fenton (1778-1858) I-576

Merriam, Charles (1806-1887) I-636

Merriam, George (1803-1880) I-636

Merry, Anthony (*fl.* 1805-1807) I-461

von Metternich, Prince Klemens (1773-1859) I-593

Meyer, Eugene (1875-1959) III-1594

Middleton, John (*fl.* 1853) II-930

Mier y Teran, Manuel (*fl.* 1835) II-736

Mifflin, Thomas (1744-1800) I-377

Mikawa, Vice Admiral Gunichi (*fl.* 1943) III-1709

Miles, Major General Nelson Appleton (1839-1925) II-1284

Miller, John F. (*fl.* 1882) II-1123

Miller, William (1782-1849) I-420

Miller, William Edward (1914-   ) III-1918

Mills, Caleb (*fl.* early 19th Cent.) I-576

Mills, Darius Ogden (1825-1910) II-1135

Mills, Ogden Livingston (1884-1937) III-1594

Minh, Ho Chi (*see* Ho Chi Minh)

Minor, Benjamin B. (1818-1905) II-725

Minuit, Peter (1580-1638) I-80

Mitchell, John (1870-1919) II-1329

Mohammed, Duse (*fl.* 1907-1916) III-1444

Moley, Raymond (1886-   ) III-1609; 1615

Molotov, Vyacheslav M. (1890-   ) III-1736

Monck, Baron (*see* Monck, George)

Monck, George (Baron Monck, Earl of Torrington) (1608-1670) I-121

Moñino y Redondo, José (*see* de Floridablanca, Conde)

Monroe, Harriet (1860-1936) III-1399

Monroe, James (1758-1831) I-389; 443; 522; 552; 558; 593

de Montcalm de Saint-Véran, Marquis Louis Joseph (1712-1759) I-200

Montgomery, General Bernard Law (First Viscount Montgomery of Alamein) (1887-   ) III-1720; 1748

Montgomery of Alamein, First Viscount (*see* Montgomery, General Bernard)

Montgomery, Olen (*fl.* 1930's) III-1588

Moody, Dwight Lyman (1837-1899) II-1173

Moore, A. Y. (*fl.* 1830's) II-679

Moore, Hiram (*fl.* 1830's) II-679

Moore, John Bassett (1860-1947) II-1296

Moraga, Alfrérez José Joaquin (*fl.*1776) I-272

Morales, Juan Ventura (*fl.* 1803) I-443

Morgan, Arthur Ernest (1878-   ) III-1621

Morgan, Harcourt Alexander (1867-1950) III-1621

Morgan, J. Pierpont (1837-1913) II-1110; 1329

Morgan, John T. (1824-1907) II-1339

Morgenthau, Jr., Henry J. (1891-1967) III-1680; 1686

Morrill, Justin Smith (1810-1898) II-962; 974

Morris, Lewis (1671-1746) I-188

Morris, Robert (1734-1806) I-356

Morse, Jedidiah (1761-1826) I-570

Morse, Samuel Finley Breese (1791-1872) II-742; 895

Morton, William Thomas Green (1819-1868) II-791

Moryson, Francis (*fl.* 1676-1677) I-151

Mott, Lucretia (1793-1880) I-642

Moynihan, Daniel Patrick (1927-   ) III-1866

Murphy, Frank (1890-1949) III-1655

Murray, James E. (1876-1961) III-1770

Murray, Philip (1886-1952) III-1655

Murray, William Vans (*fl.* 1800) I-408

Muskie, Edmund Sixtus (1914-   ) III-1933

Napoleon I, Emperor of France (Bonaparte) (1769-1821) I-443; 505

de Narváez, Pánfilo (1480?-1528) I-33

Nelson, Donald Marr (1888-1959) III-1680

Newport, Christopher (?-1617) I-59

Newton, Huey (1941?-   ) III-1861; 1866

Ngo Dien Dinh (1901-1963) III-1906

Nicholson, Sir Francis (1655-1728) I-132

Nicolet, Jean (1598-1642) I-52

Nicolls, Richard (1624-1672) I-140

Niebuhr, Helmut Richard (1894-1962) III-1604

Niebuhr, Reinhold (1892-1971) III-1604

Nimitz, Admiral Chester W. (1885-1966) III-1709; 1731

Nixon, Richard Milhous (1913-) III-1843; 1866; 1871; 1906; 1933

de Niza, Fray Marcos (?-1558) I-40

Nomura, Kichisaburo (1887-1964) III-1697

Norris, Clarence (*fl.* 1930's) III-1588

Norris, George William (1861-1944) III-1621

North, Lord Frederick (*see* Guilford, Earl of)

Nott, Josiah (1804-1873) I-648

Nourse, Edwin G. (1883-) III-1770

Noyes, John Humphrey (1811-1886) I-420

Noyes, Nicholas (*fl.* 1692) I-169

Nye, Gerald P. (1892-1971) III-1649

Oberth, Hermann (1894-) III-1555

Obregon, General Alvaro (1880-1928) III-1438

O'Connor, Basil (1892-1972) III-1835

Ogden, Aaron (1756-1839) I-600

Oglesby, Carl (*fl.* 1960's) III-1861

Oglethorpe, James Edward (1696-1785) I-182

Ohnishi, Vice Admiral Takijiro (*fl.* 1944) III-1731

Olmsted, Frederick Law (1822-1903) II-1231

Olney, Richard (1835-1917) II-1206; 1237

de Oñate, Juan (1549?-?1624) I-40

de Onís, Luis (1762-1827) I-558

Oppenheimer, Dr. Julius Robert (1904-1967) III-1692

Orlando, Vittorio Emanuele (1860-1952) III-1484

Oswald, Lee Harvey (1939-1963) III-1899

Oswald, Richard (1705-1784) I-300

Otis, Harrison Gray (1765-1848) I-414; 517

Otis, Samuel (*fl.* 1789) I-341

L'Ouverture, Toussaint (*see* Toussaint L'Ouverture)

Owen, Robert (1771-1858) I-511

Owen, Robert Dale (1801-1877) I-511

Owen, Robert Lathan (1856-1947) III-1432

Page, Walter Hines (1855-1918) III-1450

Paine, Thomas (1737-1809) I-194; 261

Pakenham, Major General Sir Edward Michael (1778-1815) I-533

Pakenham, Richard (1797-1868) II-778

Palmer, Alexander Mitchell (1872-1936) III-1491

Palóu, Francisco (1722?-1789) I-272

Paredes y Arrillaga, Mariano (1797-1849) II-825

Park, Robert E. (1864-1944) III-1357

Parker, Francis Wayland (1837-1902) II-1301

Parker, Captain John (1729-1775) I-251

Parker, Samuel D. (*fl.* 1840's) II-785

Parker, Theodore (1810-1860) I-654

Parks, Mrs. Rosa (*fl.* 1955-1956) III-1855

Parris, Samuel (1653-1720) I-169

Paterson, William (1745-1806) I-330

Patterson, Commandant Daniel T. (*fl.* 1815) I-533

Patterson, Haywood (*fl.* 1930's) III-1588

Patterson, Robert Porter (1891-1952) III-1783

Patton, Major General George S. (1885-1945) III-1715

Paul, Alice (1885-) III-1513

Paulding, James Kirke (1778-1860) I-481

Peck, John (*fl.* early 19th Cent.) I-485

Peel, Sir Robert (1788-1850) II-778

Peirce, Charles Sanders (1830-1914) II-1077; III-1363

Pelikan, Jaroslav (1923-) III-1604

Pelz, Paul Johannes (1841-1918) II-1279

Pemberton, Israel (1715-1779) I-157

Pemberton, John Clifford (1814-1881) II-997

Pendleton, George (1825-1889) II-1128

Penn, William (1644-1718) I-157

de Peralta, Pedro (*fl.* 1609-1610) I-40

Perceval, Sir John (1683-1748) I-182

Perkins, Frances (1882-1965) III-1643

Perry, Commodore Matthew Calbraith (1794-1858) II-884

Pershing, General John J. (1860-1948) III-1438; 1466; 1478

Pétain, Marshall Henri Philippe (1856-1951) III-1715

Petty, William (Earl of Shelburne *and* Marquis of Lansdowne) (1737-1805) I-207; 300

Phips, Sir William (1651-1695) I-169

Picasso, Pablo (1881-1973) III-1411

Pickering, Timothy (1745-1829) I-324; 350; 403; 408; 414

Pickford (Smith), Mary (1894-) III-1501

Pierce, Franklin (1804-1869) II-871; 884; 889

Pike, Zebulon Montgomery (1779-1813) I-467

Pilling, James Constantine (1846-1895) II-1104

Pinchot, Gifford (1865-1946) III-1374; 1390

Pinckney, Charles Cotesworth (1746-1825) I-426

Pinckney, Thomas (1750-1828) I-396; 456

de Pineda, Alonzo Alvarez (*fl.* 1519) I-33

Pinkney, William (1764-1822) I-564

Pitcairn, Major John (1722-1775) I-251

Pitt, the Elder, William (1708-1778) I-200; 225

Pitt, the Younger, William (1759-1806) I-389

Platt, Orville Hitchcock (1827-1905) II-1325

du Plessis, Armand-Jean (*see* Richelieu, Cardinal)

Plessy, Homer Adolph (*fl.* 1892-1896) II-1261

Plummer, Dr. Henry S. (1874-1936) II-1178

Principal Personages

Poe, Edgar Allen (1809-1849)   II-725
de Polignac, Auguste Jules Armand Marie (Prince de Polignac) (1780-1847)   I-593
de Polignac, Prince (*see* de Polignac, Auguste)
Polk, James Knox (1795-1849)   II-748; 778; 818; 825; 831
Polk, Leonidas LaFayette (1837-1892)   II-1225
Ponce de León, Juan (1460?-1521)   I-33
Popham, Sir John (1531?-1607)   I-59
Porter, Edwin S. (1870-1941)   II-1333
de Portolá, Gaspar (1723?-?1784)   I-272
Pory, John (1572-1635)   I-65
Pound, Ezra (1885-1972)   III-1399; 1560
Povey, Thomas (*fl.* 1660)   I-121
Powderly, Terence V. (1849-1924)   II-1152
Powell, John Wesley (1834-1902)   II-1104
Powell, Ozie (*fl.* 1930's)   III-1588
Powhatan (1550?-1618)   I-59
Pratt, Orson (1811-1881)   II-812
Pratt, Parley P. (1807-1857)   II-812
Preston, Captain Thomas (*fl.* 1770)   I-231
Preuss, Charles (1803-1854)   II-795
Price, Byron (1891-   )   III-1703
Price, Victoria (*fl.* 1930's)   III-1588
Prophet, The (*see* Tenskwatawa)
Pulitzer, Joseph (1847-1911)   II-1243; 1284
Pullman, George Mortimer (1831-1897)   II-1237
Putnam, Israel (1718-1798)   I-267
Putnam, General Rufus (1738-1824)   I-306

Raleigh, Sir Walter (1552?-1618)   I-46
Randolph, Edward (1632-1703)   I-163
Randolph, John (1773-1833)   I-485; 539
Randolph, Peyton (1721-1775)   I-246
von Ranke, Leopold (1795-1886)   II-1184
Rantoul, Jr., Robert (1805-1852)   II-785
Rapp, George (1757-1847)   I-511
Raskob, John J. (1879-1950)   III-1566; 1577
Raulston, John T. (1868-1956)   III-1549
Rauschenbusch, Walter (1861-1918)   II-1195
Rauschenbush, Paul (*fl.* 1930's)   III-1643
Ray, James Earl (1928-   )   III-1927
de Rayneval, Gérard (1746-1812)   I-300
Reagan, John H. (1818-1905)   II-1157
Reed, James A. (1861-1944)   III-1507
Reed,Thomas Brackett (1839-1902)   II-1273
Reed, Major Walter (1851-1902)   II-1313
Reis, Johann Philipp (1834-1874)   II-1089
Remington, Frederic (1861-1909)   II-1243
Reno, Major Marcus (1835-1889)   II-1094
Reno, Milo (1866?-1936)   III-1582
Revere, Paul (1735-1818)   I-251
Reynolds, General Joseph J. (1822-1899)   II-1094
Rhee, Syngman (*see* Syngman Rhee)
Rhett, Robert Barnwell (1800-1876)   II-941
Ribault, Jan (1520?-1565)   I-33
Rice, Joseph Mayer (1857-1934)   II-1301

Rich, Robert (Second Earl of Warwick) (1587-1658)   I-91
Richards, Willard (1801-1868)   II-812
Richberg, Donald Randall (1881-1960)   III-1637
Richelieu, Cardinal (Armand-Jean du Plessis) (1585-1642)   I-52
Ricketts, John Bill (*fl.* 1793)   II-1066
Ripley, George (1802-1880)   I-654
Risberg, Charles "Swede" (1894-   )   III-1497
Roberson, Willie (*fl.* 1930's)   III-1588
Robinson, Charles (1818-1894)   II-889
Robinson, Edwin Arlington (1869-1935)   III-1399
Robinson, Henry M. (1868-1937)   III-1537
Robinson, Dr. John Hamilton (*fl.* 1806)   I-467
Robinson, Joseph Taylor (1872-1937)   III-1667
de Rochambeau, Brigadier General Comte (Jean Baptiste Donatien de Vimeur) (1725-1807)   I-294
Rockefeller, John D. (1839-1937)   II-1116; 1206
Rockefeller, Nelson Aldrich (1908-   )   III-1918; 1933
Rockefeller, William (1841-1922)   II-1116; 1135
Rockhill, William Woodville (1854-1914)   II-1296
Rockingham, Marquis of (*see* Wentworth, Charles Watson)
Rodriguez, Fray Augustín (?-1518)   I-40
Roebling, Emily (?-1903)   II-1060
Roebling, John Augustus (1806-1869)   II-1060
Roebling, Washington Augustus (1837-1926)   II-1060
Rogers, Harrison G. (*fl.* 1826)   I-619
de la Roque, Jean-François (Sieur de Roberval) (*fl.* 1544)   I-28
Rommel, Field Marshall Erwin (1891-1944)   III-1720
Roosevelt, Franklin Delano (1882-1945)   III-1472; 1566; 1582; 1609; 1615; 1621; 1627; 1632; 1637; 1643; 1649; 1661; 1667; 1674; 1680; 1686; 1692; 1697; 1703; 1715; 1725; 1736; 1741; 1748
Roosevelt, Nicholas J. (1767-1854)   I-471
Roosevelt, Theodore (1858-1919)   II-831; 1201; 1284; 1325; 1329; 1339; III-1353; 1374; 1390; 1399; 1405
Root, Elihu (1845-1937)   II-1329; III-1531
Root, John Wellborn (1850-1891)   II-1231
Rose, Sir John (1820-1888)   II-1072
Ross, Edward A. (1866-1951)   III-1357
Ross, John (1790-1866)   I-666
Ross, Major General Robert (1766-1814)   I-533
Rothstein, Arnold (*fl.* 1919)   III-1497

de Roberval, Sieur (*see* de la Roque, Jean-François)

Rubenstein, Jacob (*see* Ruby, Jack)

Rubin, Jerry (1938-   )   III-1861

Ruby, Jack (Jacob Rubinstein) (1911-1967) III-1899

Ruffin, Edmund (1794-1865)   I-371

Rugg, Harold Ordway (1886-1960)   II-1301

von Rundstedt, Field Marshal Karl Rudolf Gerd (1875-1953)   III-1720

Rush, Benjamin (1745?-1813)   I-194

Rush, Richard (1780-1859)   I-593

Rusk, Dean (1909-   )   III-1888

Russell, Jonathan (*fl.* 1814)   I-522

Russell, William Hepburn (1812-1872)   II-925

Ruth, George Herman "Babe" (1895-1948) III-1497

Rutledge, John (1739-1800)   I-345

Sabin, Dr. Albert Bruce (1906-   )   III-1835

Sacajawea (1787?-1812)   I-450

Sackville, Viscount (*see* Germain, Lord George)

Saint, Thomas (*fl.* 1780's)   II-837

St. Clair, Arthur (1736?-1818)   I-324; 383

Salk, Dr. Jonas Edward (1914-   )   III-1835

Samoset (*fl.* early 17th Cent.)   I-74

Sampson, Admiral William Thomas (1840-1902) II-1284

Sanborn, Franklin Benjamin (1831-1917)   II-918

Sandburg, Carl (1878-1967)   III-1399

Sandys, Sir Edwin (1561-1629)   I-65

Sanford, John F. A. (*fl.* 1857)   II-900

de Santa Anna, Antonio López (1795?-1876) II-736; 825

Sargent, Winthrop (1753-1820)   I-306

Sarnoff, David (1891-1971)   III-1519; 1674

Saunders, William (1822-1900)   II-1043

Savio, Mario (*fl.* 1964)   III-1912

Scali, John (1918-   )   III-1888

Scheele, Dr. Leonard Andrew (1907-   ) III-1835

Schurz, Carl (1829-1906)   II-754; 1128; 1140; 1161

Schwartz, Dr. Fred C. (*fl.* 1960's)   III-1861

Scopes, John Thomas (1900-1970)   III-1549

Scott, Dred (1795?-1858)   II-900

Scott, F. A. (1873-1949)   III-1460

Scott, General Hugh L. (1853-1934)   III-1438

Scott, Thomas A. (1823-1881)   II-1099

Scott, Major General Winfield (1786-1886) II-825

Scripps, William E. (1882-1952)   III-1519

Sedgwick III, Theodore (1811-1859)   II-673

Serra, Junípero (1713-1784)   I-272

Sevier, John (1745-1815)   I-396

Sewall, Arthur (1835-1900)   II-1268

Sewall, Samuel (1652-1730)   I-169

Seward, William Henry (1801-1872)   II-754; 877; 946; 980; 1037

Seymour, Horatio (1810-1886)   II-991

Shafter, General William Rufus (1835-1906) II-1284

Shaftesbury, Earl of (Anthony Ashley Cooper) (1621-1683)   I-132

Shaw, John (*fl.* 1660)   I-121

Shaw, Lemuel (1781-1861)   II-785

Shelburne, Earl of (*see* Petty, William)

Sherman, John (1823-1900)   II-985; 1206

Sherman, William Tecumseh (1820-1891) II-997; 1010

Shidehara, Baron Kijuro (1872-1951)   III-1531

Shipherd, John J. (1802-1844)   II-708

Shirley, William (1694-1771)   I-200

Short, General Walter Campbell (1880-1949) III-1697

Short, William (*fl.* 1795)   I-396

Shreve, Henry Miller (1785-1851)   I-471

Shriver, Jr., David (*fl.* early 19th Cent.)   I-491

Shriver, Jr., Robert Sargent (1915-   )   III-1877

Sibley, Hiram (1807-1888)   II-930

Silcox, Ferdinand A. (1882-1939)   III-1627

Silliman, Jr., Benjamin (1816-1885)   II-912

Sinclair, Harry Ford (1876-1956)   III-1525

Sinclair, Upton Beall (1878-1968)   III-1353

Singer, Isaac Merrit (1811-1875)   III-837

Sirhan, Sirhan Bishara (1944-   )   III-1927

Sitting Bull (1834?-1890)   II-1094

Skidmore, Thomas (*fl.* 1820's)   I-582

Slater, Samuel (1768-1835)   I-362

Slattery, Harry A. (1887-1949)   III-1525

Slidell, John (1793-1871)   II-825

Slocum, Henry Warner (1827-1894)   II-1010

Small, Albion W. (1854-1926)   III-1357

Smith, Alfred Emanuel (1873-1944)   III-1566

Smith, Lieutenant Colonel Francis (*fl.* 1775) I-251

Smith, Francis Ormand Jonathan (*fl.* 1835) II-742

Smith, Gerrit (1797-1874)   II-918

Smith, Howard K. (1914-   )   III-1871

Smith, Jedediah Strong (1798-1831)   I-619

Smith, Captain John (1580-1631)   I-59

Smith, Margaret Chase (1897-   )   III-1817

Smith, W. A. "Uncle Billy" (*fl.* 1859)   II-912

Smithmeyer, John L. (*fl.* 1890's)   II-1279

Smithson, James (1765-1829)   II-831

Smythe, Sir Thomas (1558?-1625)   I-59

Snyder, John W. (1895-   )   III-1759

Somers, Sir George (1554-1610)   I-59

Soong, Tsǔ-wên (1894-1971)   III-1764

Sorensen, Charles (1882-1968)   III-1421

de Sosa, Gaspar Castaño (*fl.* 1590)   I-40

de Soto, Hernando (1500?-1542)   I-33
Southampton, Fourth Earl of (Thomas Wriothesley) (1607-1667)   I-121
Sparks, Jared (1789-1866)   I-570; II-673; 801
Spencer, Herbert (1820-1903)   II-1167
Spofford, Ainsworth Rand (1825-1908)   II-1279
Spooner, John (1843-1919)   II-1325; 1339
Sprague, Rear Admiral Thomas L. (*fl.* 1944)   III-1731
Squanto (?-1622)   I-74
Stalin, Joseph (Iosif Vissarionovich Dzhugashvili) (1879-1953)   III-1736; 1741; 1748; 1794; 1806
Stanford, Leland (1824-1893)   II-969
Stanton, Edwin McMasters (1814-1869)   II-980; 991; 1026
Stanton, Elizabeth Cady (1815-1902)   III-1513
Stark, Admiral Harold R. (1880-1972)   III-1697
Stead, William Thomas (1849-1912)   II-1167
Steffens, Lincoln (1866-1936)   III-1353
Stein, Gertrude (1874-1946)   III-1560
Stephen (*see* Estebanico)
Stephens, Alexander Hamilton (1812-1883)   II-871; 941
Sterne, Simon (1839-1901)   II-1157
Stettinius, Jr., Edward Reilley (1900-1949)   III-1736; 1741
Stevens, Isaac I. (1818-1862)   II-865
Stevens, Thaddeus (1792-1868)   I-576; II-760; 985; 1003; 1026; 1049
Stevenson, Adlai Ewing (1890-1965)   III-1843
Stewart, A. T. (*fl.* 1925)   III-1549
Stewart, Philo P. (1798-1868)   II-708
Stewart, Robert (First Viscount Castlereagh) (1769-1822)   I-522; 593
Stewart, William M. (1827-1909)   II-1083
Stimson, Henry Lewis (1867-1950)   III-1599; 1686; 1753
Stockton, Commodore Robert Field (1795-1866)   II-818
de Stoeckl, Baron Edouard (*fl.* 1865-1867)   II-1037
Stone, Lucy (Mrs. Henry Brown Blackwell) (1818-1893)   III-1513
Stone, William A. (1846-1920)   II-1329
Stone, William J. (1848-1918)   III-1450
Stoughton, William (*fl.* 1692)   I-169
Stowe, Calvin Ellis (1802-1886)   II-859
Stowe, Harriet (Elizabeth) Beecher (1811-1896)   II-859
Strasser, Adolf (*fl.* 1886)   II-1152
Stratton, Charles Sherwood (*see* Thumb, General Tom)
Stringfellow, Thornton (*fl.* 1850)   I-648
Strong, Caleb (1745-1819)   I-517
Strutt, Jedediah (1726-1797)   I-362
Stuart, Charles (1783-1865)   II-708

Stuart, John (Earl of Bute) (1713-1792)   I-200
Stuart, Dr. John Leighton (1876-1962)   III-1764
Stuart, Robert (1785-1848)   I-476
Studebaker, Dr. John W. (1887-   )   III-1725
Stuyvesant, Peter (1592-1672)   I-80; 140
Sullivan, Louis Henri (1856-1924)   II-1231
Sumner, Charles (1811-1874)   II-871; 980; 1003; 1037; 1049; 1072
Sumner, William Graham (1840-1910)   II-1167; III-1357
Sung, Kim I (*see* Kim IL Sung)
Sutter, John Augustus (1803-1880)   II-807; 843
Sylvester, James Joseph (1814-1897)   II-1077
Symmes, John Cleves (1742-1814)   I-306
Syngman Rhee (1875-1965)   III-1823

Taft, Robert Alphonso (1889-1953)   III-1759; 1800; 1843
Taft, William Howard (1857-1930)   II-1290; III-1379; 1390; 1405; 1415
de Talleyrand-Périgord, Charles Maurice (Prince de Bénévent) (1754-1838)   I-408
Tallmadge, Jr., James (1778-1853)   I-552
Tally, Thomas L. (1861-1945)   II-1333
Talon, Jean Baptiste (The "Great Intendant") (1625?-1694)   I-52; 144
Taney, Roger Brooke (1777-1864)   II-696; 900; 946
Tappan, Arthur (1786-1865)   I-642; II-708; 719
Tappan, Lewis (1788-1873)   I-642; II-708; 719
Tarbell, Ida Minerva (1857-1944)   III-1353
Taylor, John (Mormon Leader) (1808-1887)   II-812
Taylor, John (Senator from Virginia) (1753-1824)   I-456
Taylor, John W. (Senator from New York) (*fl.* 1819)   I-552
Taylor, Myron C. (1874-1959)   III-1655
Taylor, Nathaniel William (1786-1858)   I-420
Taylor, Zachary (1784-1850)   II-825; 854
Tecumseh (1768?-1813)   I-498
Teller, Henry M. (1830-1914)   II-1161
Tennent, Gilbert (1703-1764)   I-176
Tennent, William (1673-1745)   I-176
Tenskwatawa, "The Prophet" (1768?-1834)   I-498
Terry, General Alfred (1827-1890)   II-1094
Thacher, Peter O. (*fl.* 1840's)   II-785
Thayendanega (*see* Brant, Joseph)
Thayer, Sylvanus (1785-1872)   I-432
Thimonnier, Barthélemy (1793-1859)   II-837
Thomas, Evan (*fl.* 1828)   I-624
Thomas, George Henry (1816-1870)   II-997
Thomas, George Holt (1869-1929)   II-807

Thomas, Jesse B. (1777-1853)   I-552
Thomas, Norman Mattoon (1884-1968)   III-1609
Thomas, Philip Evan (1776-1861)   I-624
Thompson, Almond H. (*fl.* 1878)   II-1104
Thompson, John Reuben (1823-1873)   II-725
Thoreau, Henry David (1817-1862)   I-654; II-848
Thorndike, Edward Lee (1874-1949)   II-1301
Thumb, General Tom (Charles Sherwood Stratton) (1838-1883)   II-1066
Thurber, F. B. (*fl.* 1887)   II-1157
Thurmond, J. Strom (1902-   )   III-1800
Tilden, Samuel (1814-1886)   II-1099
Tillich, Paul (1886-1965)   III-1604
du Tisné, Charles Claude (*fl.* 1714)   I-144
Tituba (*fl.* 1692)   I-169
de Tocqueville, Alexis (1805-1859)   II-673
Todd, Samuel C. T. (1836-1907)   II-1116
Tojo, General Hideki (1885-1948)   III-1697
Tolstoi, Leo (1828-1910)   II-1184
Tomochichi (1650-1739)   I-182
Toombs, Robert Augustus (1810-1885)   II-941
Torrance, Jared Sidney (1852-1921)   III-1811
Torrey, Reuben A. (1856-1928)   II-1173
Torrington, Earl of (*see* Monck, George)
Toule, Katherine (*fl.* 1964)   III-1912
Tourgée, Albion Winegar (1838-1905)   II-1261
de Tousard, Major Louis (*fl.* early 19th Cent.)   I-432
Toussaint L'Ouverture (1743-1803)   I-443
Townsend, Dr. Francis E. (1867-1960)   III-1582; 1643
Townsend, James M. (*fl.* 1859)   II-912
Townshend, Charles (1725-1767)   I-225
Travis, William Barret (1809-1836)   II-736
Trist, Nicholas Philip (1800-1874)   II-825
Trotter, William Monroe (1872-1934)   III-1384
Truman, Harry S (1884-1972)   III-1680; 1741; 1748; 1753; 1759; 1770; 1776; 1783; 1789; 1794; 1800; 1806; 1817; 1823; 1829; 1843
Trumbull, Jonathan (1710-1785)   I-267
Trumbull, Lyman (1813-1896)   II-906
Tryon, William (1729-1788)   I-213
Tse-tung, Mao (*see* Mao Tse-tung)
Tugwell, Rexford Guy (1891-   )   III-1609; 1615
Tunner, Major General William H. (*fl.* 1948)   III-1794
Turco, El (*fl.* 1540-1541)   I-40
Turner, Frederick Jackson (1861-1932)   II-1077
Turner, Nat (1800-1831)   II-685
Turner, Rear Admiral Richmond K. (1885-1961)   III-1709
Twain, Mark (Samuel Langhorne Clemens) (1835-1910)   II-1146

Tweed, William Marcy (1823-1878)   II-1054
Tydings, Millard (1890-1961)   III-1817
Tyler, John (1790-1862)   II-748; 760; 766; 772; 801; 825

Underwood, Oscar (1862-1929)   III-1405; 1531
U'Ren, William (1850-1949)   II-1307

Vail, Alfred (1807-1859)   II-742
Van Brunt, Henry (1832-1903)   II-1231
Van Buren, Martin (1782-1862)   I-607; II-690; 696; 748; 760; 772
Vandegrift, Major General Alexander A. (1887-1973)   III-1709
Vandenberg, Arthur H. (1884-1951)   III-1741; 1800; 1806
Vanderbilt, William H. (1821-1885)   II-1135
Vane, Sir Henry (1613-1662)   I-103
Van Gough, Vincent (1853-1890)   III-1411
Van Sweringen, Mantis James (1811-1935)   III-1811
Van Sweringen, Oris Paxton (1879-1936)   III-1811
Van Twiller, Wouter (*fl.* 1635)   I-91
Varas, Emilio C. (*fl.* 1890's)   II-1190
de Varennes, Pierre Gaultier (*see* de la Vérendrye, Sieur)
Vaughn, Jack Hood (1900-   )   III-1870
de Vergennes, Comte (Charles Gravier) (1717-1787)   I-282; 300
Verne, Jules (1828-1905)   III-1555
Vernon, James (*fl.* 1733)   I-182
Vilas, George H. (*fl.* 1882)   II-1116
Villa, Francisco "Pancho" (1877-1923)   III-1438
Villard, Oswald Garrison (1872-1949)   III-1384
de Vimeur, Jean Baptiste Donatien (*see* de Rochambeau, Brigadier General Comte)
Vinson, Frederick Moore (1890-1953)   III-1849
Viviani, René Raphaël (1863-1925)   III-1531

Waddell, William B. (*fl.* 1860)   II-925
Wade, Jeptha H. (*fl.* 1860-1861)   II-930
Wagner, Robert Ferdinand (1877-1953)   III-1637
Wait, Isaac (*fl.* 1840's)   II-785
Walker, David (1785-1830)   II-719
Walker, Edwin (*fl.* 1890's)   II-1237
Walker, Frank (1886-1959)   III-1632
Walker, Joseph R. (1798-1876)   II-795
Walker, Robert John (1801-1869)   II-772; 889; 1037
Wallace, George Corley (1919-   )   III-1933
Wallace, Henry Agard (1888-1965)   III-1615; 1800
Walling, William English (1877-1936)   III-1384

Walpole, Sir Robert (1676-1745)   I-182
Walsh, Thomas James (1859-1933)   III-1525
Ward, Lester Frank (1841-1913)   III-1357
Ware, Henry (1764-1845)   I-570
Warren, Earl (1891-1974)   III-1800; 1849; 1883
Warren, Joseph (1741-1775)   I-241
Warwick, Second Earl of (*see* Rich, Robert)
Washington, Booker Taliaferro (1856-1915) II-1249; III-1384; 1444
Washington, George (1732-1799)   I-256; 294; 330; 341; 345; 350; 356; 377; 383; 389; 396; 403; 432
Waters, Walter W. (*fl.* 1920's)   III-1582
Watson, Thomas A. (1854-1934)   II-1089
Watson, Thomas Edward (1856-1922)   II-1225; 1268
Watt, James (1736-1819)   I-371
Wayne, Major General Anthony "Mad Anthony" (1745-1796)   I-383
Weaver, George "Buck" (1890-1956)   III-1497
Weaver, James Baird (1833-1912)   II-1225
Webb, William H. (1816-1899)   II-807
Webster, Daniel (1782-1852)   I-539; 564; 600; 607; 660; II-690; 696; 778; 801; 854
Webster, Noah (1758-1843)   I-636
Weed, Thurlow (1797-1882)   I-607; II-760; 877
Weems, Charlie (*fl.* 1930's)   III-1588
Weinberg, Jack (*fl.* 1964)   III-1912
Welch, Robert (1899-   )   III-1861
Weld, Theodore Dwight (1803-1895)   I-642; II-708; 719
Wells, Gideon (1802-1878)   II-957
Wells, Horace (1815-1848)   II-791
Welsh, Herbert (1851-1941)   II-1161
Wentworth, Charles Watson (Marquis of Rockingham) (1730-1782)   I-219
Wentworth, John (1815-1888)   II-906
West, Thomas (Lord De La Warr) (1577-1618) I-59
Weston, George M. (*fl.* 1873)   II-1083
Weston, Thomas (1575?-?1644)   I-74
Welyer y Nicolau, General Valeriano (1838-1930)   II-1243
Whately, Thomas (*fl.* 1765)   I-219
Wheeler, Burton Kendall (1882-   )   III-1667
Whipple, Lieutenant Amiel Weeks (1816-1863) II-865
White, Andrew Dickson (1832-1918)   II-1077
White, Edward Douglass (1845-1921)   II-1318
White, E. E. (1829-1902)   II-1031
White, John (*fl.* 1585-1593)   I-46
White, Mary Ovington (1865-1951)   III-1384
White, Thomas W. (1788-1843)   II-725
Whitefield, George (1714-1770)   I-176
Whitman, Walt (1819-1892)   II-848

Whitney, A. F. (1873-1949)   III-1759
Whitney, Eli (1765-1825)   I-371
Whitney, Richard (*fl.* 1920's)   III-1577
Wickersham, George Woodward (1858-1936) III-1507
Wiley, Calvin, (*fl.* early 19th Cent.)   I-576
Wilkinson, James (1757-1825)   I-396;461;467
Willard, Daniel (1861-1942)   III-1460
Willard, Henry (*fl.* 1879)   II-1110
William II, Emperor of Germany and King of Prussia (1859-1941)   II-1201
William III, of England, Scotland, and Ireland (1650-1702)   I-163
Williams, Claude "Lefty" (1893-1959)   III-1497
Williams, Eugene (*fl.* 1930's)   III-1588
Williams, Roger (1603?-1683)   I-85; 97; 318
Williamson, Lieutenant R. S. (?-1882)   II-865
Willie, James G. (*fl.* 1847)   II-812
Willis, Henry Parker (1874-1937)   III-1432
Willkie, Wendell Lewis (1892-1944)   III-1621
Wilmot, David (1814-1868)   II-854
Wilson, Henry (1812-1875)   II-991
Wilson, James (1742-1798)   I-330; 345; 367
Wilson, Woodrow (1856-1924)   II-1077; III-1390; 1405; 1432; 1438; 1450; 1454; 1460; 1466; 1472; 1478; 1484; 1491; 1507; 1513; 1560
Wingfield, Edward Maria (1560?-?1613) I-59
Winslow, Edward (1595-1655)   I-91; 109
Winthrop, John (1588-1649)   I-85; 103; 109
Winthrop, Jr., John (1638-1707)   I-91
Wirt, William (1772-1834)   I-564
Wise, Henry Alexander (1806-1876)   II-918
Wolfe, James (1727-1759)   I-200
Wood, Arthur (*fl.* 1920's)   III-1582
Wood, Jethrow (1774-1834)   II-679
Woodbridge, Jr., John (*fl.* 1662)   I-127
Woodmason, Charles (*fl.* 1770's)   I-213
Woodworth, John M. (*fl.* 1870)   III-1394
Wright, Andy (*fl.* 1930's)   III-1588
Wright, Chauncey (1830-1875)   III-1363
Wright, Elizur (1804-1885)   II-719
Wright, Orville (1871-1948)   II-1346
Wright, Roy (*fl.* 1930's)   III-1588
Wright, Silas (1795-1847)   II-748
Wright, Wilbur (1867-1912)   II-1346
Wriothesley, Thomas (*see* Southampton, Fourth Earl of)
Wyndham, Charles (*see* Egremont, Earl of)

Yamamoto, Admiral Isoroku (1884-1943)   III-1697
Yarborough, Ralph Webster (1903-   )   III-1899
Yeamans, Sir John (1610?-1674)   I-132
Yeardley, Sir George (1587?-1627)   I-65
Yeats, William Butler (1865-1939)   III-1399
Yoelson, Asa (*see* Jolson, Al)
York, Duke of (*see* James, Duke of York)

AMERICAN

Principal Personages

Young, Brigham (1801-1877)   II-812
Young, John Russell (1840-1899)   II-1279
Young, Owen D. (1874-1962)   III-1537

Zane, Ebenezer (1747-1812)   I-491

Zenger, John Peter (1697-1746)   I-188
Ziolkovsky, Konstantin Eduardovitch (1857-1935)   III-1555
Zook, George F. (1885-1951)   III-1725
Zworykin, Vladimir (1889-1972)   III-1674

Abbot, Henry L.
Beginning of Modern Submarine Warfare
I-269
Abel, Annie H.
History of Events Resulting in Indian Consolidation West of the Mississippi, The. Annual Report of the American Historical Association for the Year 1906   I-669
Abel, Elie
Missile Crisis, The   III-1890
Abernethy, Thomas P.
Burr Conspiracy, The   I-465
Adams, Henry
History of the United States of America During the Administrations of Jefferson and Madison. Vol. II.   I-445
Adams, James Truslow
Founding of New England, The   I-167
Aguilar, Alonso
Pan-Americanism: From Monroe to the Present
II-1193
Albright, George L.
Official Explorations for Pacific Railroads, 1853-1855   II-868
Alden, John R.
American Revolution, 1775-1783, The   I-259
General Gage in America: Being Principally a History of His Role in the American Revolution   I-253
Alexander, James
Brief Narrative of the Case and Trial of John Peter Zenger, Printer of the New York Weekly Journal, *A*   I-191
Allen, Frederick Lewis
Only Yesterday: An Informal History of the 1920's   III-1579
Since Yesterday: The Nineteen-Thirties in America, September 3, 1929-September 3, 1939   III-1584
Allen, Lee
American League Story, The   III-1500
Alperovitz, Gar
Atomic Diplomacy: Hiroshima and Potsdam
III-1756
Altmeyer, Arthur J.
Formative Years of Social Security, The
III-1646
Alvord, Clarence W.
Mississippi Valley in British Politics, The
I-209
Ambrose, Stephen E.
Duty, Honor, Country: A History of West Point
I-434
Eisenhower and Berlin, 1945: The Decision to Halt at the Elbe   III-1751
Anderson, Troyer S.
Command of the Howe Brothers During the

American Revolution, The   I-279
Andrews, Charles M.
Colonial Period of American History, The.
Vol. II: *The Settlements*   I-94; 99; 118
Colonial Period of American History, The. Vol. IV: *England's Commercial and Colonial Policy*   I-123
Andrews, Matthew P.
Founding of Maryland, The   I-117
Aptheker, Herbert
American Negro Slave Revolts   II-688
Arlen, Michael J.
Living Room War, The   III-1677
Ashabranner, Brent
Moment in History: The First Ten Years of the Peace Corps, A   III-1879
Asinof, Eliot
Eight Men Out: The Black Sox and the 1919 World Series   III-1499

Bagby, Wesley M.
Road to Normalcy: The Presidential Campaign and Election of 1920, The. The Johns Hopkins University Studies in History and Political Science series   III-1475
Bailey, Stephen K.
Congress Makes a Law: The Story Behind the Employment Act of 1946   III-1772
Bailey, Thomas A.
Woodrow Wilson and the Peacemakers
III-1486
Bailyn, Bernard
Ideological Origins of the American Revolution, The   I-264
Bakeless, John
Lewis and Clark: Partners in Discovery
I-452
Baldwin, Leland D.
Keelboat Age on Western Waters, The   I-473
Whiskey Rebels: The Story of a Frontier Uprising   I-380
Bancroft, George
History of the United States of America, from the Discovery of the Continent   I-142
Barker, Eugene C.
Life of Stephen F. Austin, Founder of Texas, 1793-1836, The   II-739
Barnes, Viola F.
Dominion of New England: A Study in British Colonial Policy, The   I-165
Barnouw, Erik
History of Broadcasting in the United States, A. Vol. I: *A Tower in Babel: To 1933*
III-1521
History of Broadcasting in the United States, A. Vol. II: *The Golden Web: 1933 to 1953*
III-1676

AMERICAN

Pertinent Literature Reviewed

Bassett, John S.
  Life of Andrew Jackson, The   I-535
Baxter, James P.
  Memoir of Jacques Cartier, A   I-30
  Scientists Against Time   III-1694
Beale, Howard K.
  Charles A. Beard: An Appraisal   III-1430
Beard, Charles A.
  Economic Origins of Jeffersonian Democracy   I-358
Becker, Carl L.
  Declaration of Independence: A Study in the History of Political Ideas, The   I-263
Bemis, Samuel Flagg
  Diplomacy of the American Revolution, The   I-284
  Jay's Treaty: A Study in Commerce and Diplomacy   I-391
  John Quincy Adams and the Foundations of American Foreign Policy   I-596
  Pinckney's Treaty: A Study of America's Advantages from Europe's Distresses   I-400
Berger, John A.
  Franciscan Missions of California, The   I-275
Berman, Ronald
  America in the Sixties: An Intellectual History   III-1864
Bernstein, Irving
  New Deal Collective Bargaining Policy, The   III-1639
Berryman, John
  Stephen Crane. American Men of Letters series   II-1257
Bestor, Arthur E.
  Backwoods Utopias: The Sectarian and Owenite Phases of Communitarian Socialism in America, 1663-1829   I-515
Beveridge, Albert J.
  Life of John Marshall, The. Vol. IV: Conflict and Construction, 1800-1815   I-487; 565; 603
Billington, Ray Allen
  America's Frontier Heritage   II-1216
Binkley, William C.
  Texas Revolution, The   II-738
Bird, Caroline
  Invisible Scar, The   III-1585
Bishop, Jim
  Day Lincoln Was Shot, The   II-1017
Black, Robert C., III
  Younger John Winthrop, The   I-95
Blair, Anna Lou
  Henry Barnard, School Administrator   II-1034
Blair, Walter
  Mark Twain and Huck Finn   II-1148
Blaustein, Albert P.
  Desegregation and the Law: The Meaning and Effect of the School Segregation Cases   III-1852

Bloss, Roy S.
  Pony Express: The Great Gamble   II-928
Blum, John Morton
  Republican Roosevelt, The   II-1327
Board of Governors, Federal Reserve System
  Federal Reserve System: Purpose and Function, The   III-1434
Bolton, Herbert E.
  Coronado: Knight of Pueblos and Plains   I-43
  Outpost of Empire: The Story of the Founding of San Francisco   I-274
Boorstin, Daniel J.
  Lost World of Thomas Jefferson, The   I-196
Bourne, A. N.
  Voyages and Explorations of Samuel De Champlain, 1604-1616, The. Narrated by Himself   I-55
Bourne, Edward G.
  Voyages and Explorations of Samuel De Champlain, 1604-1616, The. Narrated by Himself   I-55
Boyd, Julian P.
  Anglo-American Union: Joseph Galloway's Plans to Preserve the British Empire, 1774-1788   I-248
Bozell, L. Brent
  McCarthy and His Enemies: The Record and Its Meaning   III-1820
Braddy, Haldeen
  Pershing's Mission in Mexico   III-1442
Bradford, William
  Of Plymouth Plantation, 1620-1647   I-77
Bridenbaugh, Carl
  Myths and Realities: Societies of the Colonial South   I-215
Brock, William R.
  American Crisis: Congress and Reconstruction, 1865-1867, An   II-1007
Brodie, Fawn M.
  Thaddeus Stevens: Scourge of the South   II-1029
Brooke, John
  Charles Townshend   I-229
Brooks, Cleanth
  William Faulkner: The Yoknapatawpha Country   III-1573
Brooks, Van Wyck
  World of Washington Irving, The   I-483
Brown, Milton W.
  Story of the Armory Show, The   III-1413
Brown, Richard M.
  South Carolina Regulators, The   I-216
Brown, Robert E.
  Middle-Class Democracy and the Revolution in Massachusetts, 1691-1780   I-292
Brown, Wilburt S.
  Amphibious Campaign for West Florida and Louisiana, 1814-1815: A Critical Review of Strategy and Tactics at New Orleans, The   I-536

Brubacher, John S.
  Higher Education in Transition: A History of American Colleges and Universities, 1936-1968   I-315
Buck, Solon J.
  Granger Movement: A Study of Agricultural Organization and Its Political, Economic, and Social Manifestations, 1870-1880, The   II-1045
Buckley, William F.
  McCarthy and His Enemies: The Record and Its Meaning   III-1820
Buder, Stanley
  Pullman: An Experiment in Industrial Order and Community Planning, 1880-1930   II-1239
Buley, R. Carlyle
  Old Northwest: Pioneer Period, 1815-1840, The   I-530
Buranelli, Vincent
  Trial of Peter Zenger, The   I-190
Burchard, John
  Architecture of America: A Social and Cultural History, The   II-1233
Burlingame, Roger
  March of the Iron Men: A Social History of Union Through Invention   II-841
Burnett, Edmund C.
  Continental Congress, The   I-258
Burns, James M.
  Roosevelt: The Lion and the Fox   III-1671
Bush-Brown, Albert
  Architecture of America: A Social and Cultural History, The   II-1233
Bushman, Richard L.
  From Puritan to Yankee: Character and Social Order in Connecticut, 1690-1765   I-179

Cameron, E. H.
  Samuel Slater, Father of American Manufactures   I-365
Carlson, Oliver
  Man Who Made News, James Gordon Bennett, The   II-715
Carroll, E. Malcolm
  Origins of the Whig Party   II-692
Carter, Dan T.
  Scottsboro: A Tragedy of the American South   III-1590
Caruso, John Anthony
  Great Lakes Frontier: An Epic of the Old Northwest, The   I-529
Catton, Bruce
  Never Call Retreat   II-1013
  War Lords of Washington, The   III-1684
Caughey, John W.
  Gold Is the Cornerstone   II-846
Chalmers, Allan Knight
  They Shall Be Free   III-1591
Chambers, William N.
  Political Parties in a New Nation: The American Experience, 1776-1809   I-353
Channing, Edward
  Jeffersonian System, 1801-1811, The. Vol. XII: *The American Nation: A History.*   I-428
Chase, Richard
  Melville: A Collection of Critical Essays   II-851
Chatelain, Verne E.
  Defenses of Spanish Florida, 1565-1763, The   I-37
Clapesattle, Helen
  Doctors Mayo, The   II-1181
Clark, Arthur H.
  Clipper Ship Era, The   II-809
Clarke, Dwight L.
  Stephen Watts Kearny, Soldier of the West   II-822
Clarkson, Grosvenor B.
  Industrial America in the World War   III-1462
Claude, Inis L., Jr.
  Swords into Plowshares: The Problems and Progress of International Organization   III-1745
Claude, Richard
  Supreme Court and the Electoral Process, The   III-1885
Cleaves, Freeman
  Old Tippecanoe: William Henry Harrison and His Time   II-763
Clemens, Diane Shaver
  Yalta   III-1738
Clendennen, Clarence C.
  United States and Pancho Villa: A Study in Unconventional Diplomacy, The   III-1441
Coffman, Edward M.
  War to End All Wars: The American Military Experience in World War I, The   III-1469
Coggins, Jack
  Ships and Seamen of the American Revolution   I-270
Cohen, Jerry
  Burn, Baby, Burn: The Los Angeles Race Riots, August, 1965   III-1925
Cole, Arthur C.
  Whig Party in the South, The   II-692
Coleman, Peter J.
  Transformation of Rhode Island, 1790-1860, The   II-769
Condit, Carl W.
  Chicago School of Architecture: A History of Commercial and Public Building in the Chicago Area, The   II-1235
Coolidge, Mary Roberts
  Chinese Immigration   II-1125
Coolidge, Olivia
  Women's Rights: The Suffrage Movement in America, 1848-1920   III-1516
Corey, Albert B.

Crisis of 1830-1842 in Canadian-American Relations, The   II-803
Cornell, Robert J.
  Anthracite Coal Strike of 1902, The   II-1331
Corwin, Edward S.
  Court Over Constitution: A Study of Judicial Review as an Instrument of Popular Government   I-439
  Doctrine of Judicial Review: Its Legal and Historical Basis and Other Essays, The   I-439
Costain, Thomas B.
  Chord of Steel, The   II-1090
Coudert, Frederic R., Jr.
  "Evolution of the Doctrine of Territorial Incorporation, The" in *The American Law Review*   II-1322
Coulter, E. Merton
  Georgia: A Short History   I-184
Cowan, Paul
  Making of an un-American: A Dialogue with Experience, The   III-1881
Crandall, Andrew W.
  Early History of the Republican Party, 1854-1856, The   II-881
Craven, Avery O.
  Growth of Southern Nationalism, 1848-1861, The   II-856
  Soil Exhaustion as a Factor in the Agricultural History of Virginia and Maryland, 1606-1860   I-374
Craven, Wesley F.
  Dissolution of the Virginia Company: The Failure of a Colonial Experiment, The   I-67
  Southern Colonies in the Seventeenth Century, 1607-1689, The   I-61
Cremin, Lawrence A.
  American Common School: An Historic Conception, The   I-578
  Transformation of the School: Progressivism in American Education, 1876-1957, The   II-1303
Cronon, E. David
  Black Moses: The Story of Marcus Garvey and the Universal Negro Improvement Association   III-1447
Cross, Whitney R.
  Burned-Over District: The Social and Intellectual History of Enthusiastic Religion in Western New York, 1800-1850, The   I-423; 644
Crosskey, William W.
  Politics and the Constitution in the History of the United States   I-605
Crowell, Benedict
  How America Went to War: Vol. V: *Demobilization: Our Industrial and Military Demobilization After the Armistice, 1918-1920*   III-1481
Cunningham, Noble E., Jr.

Jeffersonian Republicans: The Formation of Party Organization, 1789-1801, The   I-352
Current, Richard N.
  Daniel Webster and the Rise of National Conservatism   II-805
  Lincoln and the First Shot   II-949
  Secretary Stimson: A Study in Statecraft   III-1602
Curtis, James C.
  Fox at Bay: Martin Van Buren and the Presidency, 1837-1841, The   II-750

Dangerfield, George
  Era of Good Feelings, The   I-520; 560; 611
Darrah, William Culp
  Powell of the Colorado   II-1106
Daum, Arnold R.
  American Petroleum Industry: The Age of Illumination, 1859-1899, The   II-915
Davies, D. W.
  Primer of Dutch Seventeenth Century Overseas Trade, A   I-83
Davison, W. Phillips
  Berlin Blockade: A Study in Cold War Politics, The   III-1798
Dawson, Raymond H.
  Decision to Aid Russia, 1941: Foreign Policy and Domestic Politics, The   III-1690
De Conde, Alexander
  Entangling Alliances: Politics and Diplomacy Under George Washington   I-393
  Quasi-War: The Politics and Diplomacy of the Undeclared War with France, 1797-1801, The   I-412
De Landa, D.
  Landa's Relación de las Coasas de Yucatan: *A Translation*   I-9
De Pauw, Linda G.
  Eleventh Pillar: New York State and the Federal Constitution, The   I-337
Derber, Milton
  Labor and the New Deal   III-1640
Dickerson, Oliver M.
  Navigation Acts and the American Revolution, The   I-234
Dietze, Gottfried
  Federalist: A Classic on Federalism and Free Government, The   I-338
Dillon, Merton L.
  Benjamin Lundy and the Struggle for Negro Freedom   II-721
Dillon, Richard
  Meriwether Lewis: A Biography   I-453
Divine, Robert A.
  Reluctant Belligerent: American Entry into the Second World War, The   III-1651
Dixon, Robert A., Jr.
  Democratic Representation: Reapportionment in Law and Politics   III-1886
Donald, David

Politics of Reconstruction, 1863-1867, The
    II-1108
Downes, Randolph C.
    *Council Fires on the Upper Ohio: A Narrative
    of Indian Affairs in the Upper Ohio Valley
    Until 1795*   I-385
Drago, Harry Sinclair
    Great American Cattle Trails   II-1023
Draper, Theodore
    Roots of American Communism, The   III-
    1495
Duberman, Martin B.
    Charles Francis Adams, 1807-1886   II-
    1075
Duffus, Robert L.
    Santa Fe Trail, The   I-590
Duncum, Barbara M.
    *Development of Inhalation Anaesthesia with
    Special Reference to the Years, 1846-1900,
    The*   II-793
DuPuy, Ernest R.
    *Men of West Point: The First 150 Years of the
    United States Military Academy*   I-435
Durden, Robert F.
    Climax of Populism: The Election of 1896, The
    II-1271

Eaton, Clement
    History of the Southern Confederacy, A
    II-944
Eaton, Quaintaince
    *Miracle of the Met: An Informal History of the
    Metropolitan Opera, 1883-1967, The*   II-
    1138
Edgell, David P.
    William Ellery Channing   I-573
Eisenschiml, Otto
    Why Was Lincoln Murdered?   II-1016
Engleman, Fred L.
    Peace of Christmas Eve, The   I-525
Ettinger, Amos A.
    James Edward Oglethorpe, Imperial Idealist
    I-185
Evans, Rowland
    Lyndon B. Johnson: The Exercise of Power
    III-1921

Farago, Ladislas
    *Broken Seal: "Operation Magic" and the Secret
    Road to Pearl Harbor, The*   III-1701
Faris, Robert E.
    Chicago Sociology, 1920-1932   III-1361
Farrar, Victor J.
    *Annexation of Russian America to the United
    States, The*   II-1039
Fehrenbacher, Don E.
    Prelude to Greatness: Lincoln in the 1850's
    II-908
Feis, Herbert
    *Atomic Bomb and the End of World War II,
    The*   III-1755

Ferguson, Clarence C., Jr.
    *Desegregation and the Law: The Meaning and
    Effect of the School Segregation Cases*
    III-1852
Ferrell, Robert H.
    *American Diplomacy in the Great Depression:
    Hoover-Stimson Foreign Policy, 1929-1933*
    III-1601
    George C. Marshall. Vol. XV of *The American
    Secretaries of State and Their Diplomacy* se-
    ries   III-1796
Filler, Louis
    Crusaders for American Liberalism   III-
    1355
Findlay, James F., Jr.
    *Dwight L. Moody: American Evangelist, 1837-
    1899*   II-1175
    "Moody, 'Gapman,' and the Gospel: The
    Early Days of Moody Bible Institute," in
    Church History   II-1175
Finlay, Carlos E.
    Carlos Finlay and Yellow Fever   II-1315
Fitzhugh, George
    Cannibals All: Or, Slaves Without Masters
    I-651
Fleming, Denna F.
    Cold War and Its Origins, The. Vol. I: *1917-
    1950*   III-1780
Fletcher, Robert S.
    *History of Oberlin College: From Its Founda-
    tion Through the Civil War, A*   II-710
Flexner, Abraham
    *Daniel Coit Gilman: Creator of the American
    Type of University*   II-1080
Flexner, James Thomas
    *That Wilder Image: The Painting of America's
    Native School from Thomas Cole to Winslow
    Homer*   I-615
Fogel, Robert William
    *Union Pacific Railroad: A Case in Premature
    Enterprise, The*   II-972
Foner, Eric
    *Free Soil, Free Labor, Free Men: The Ideology
    of the Republican Party Before the Civil War*
    II-879
Foreman, Grant
    *Indian Removal: The Emigration of the Five
    Civilized Tribes of Indians*   I-670
Foster, Charles H.
    *Rungless Ladder: Harriet Beecher Stowe and
    New England Puritanism, The*   II-861
Francis, Thomas F., Jr.
    *Evaluation of the 1954 Field Trail of Poli-
    omyelitis Vaccine: Final Report*   III-1839
Franklin, Benjamin
    Autobiography of Benjamin Franklin   I-
    238
Franklin, John Hope
    Emancipation Proclamation, The   II-982
Freehling, William W.
    Prelude to Civil War: The Nullification Contro-

versy in South Carolina, 1816-1836   II-705

Freeman, Douglas Southall
   George Washington: A Biography. Vol. VI: *Patriot and President*   I-343
   Lee's Lieutenants: A Multiple Biography of the Military Leaders in Lee's Command During the Civil War. Vol. I: *Manassas to Malvern Hill*   II-955
   Lee's Lieutenants: A Multiple Biography of the Military Leaders in Lee's Command During the Civil War. Vol. II: *Cedar Mountain to Chancellorville*   II-955
   Lee's Lieutenants: A Multiple Biography of the Military Leaders in Lee's Command During the Civil War. Vol. III: *Gettysburg to Appomattox*   II-955
   R. E. Lee: A Biography   II-999

Freidel, Frank
   Franklin D. Roosevelt. Vol. III: *The Triumph*   III-1611
   Splendid Little War, The   II-1287

French, Allen
   Day of Concord and Lexington: Nineteenth of April, 1775, The   I-254

Friedman, Milton
   Monetary History of the United States, 1867-1960, A   II-1087

Fuess, Claude M.
   Daniel Webster   I-662

Furnas, Joseph Chamberlain
   Road to Harpers Ferry, The   II-922

Galbraith, John Kenneth
   Great Crash, 1929, The   III-1579

Galenson, Walter
   CIO Challenge to the AFL: A History of the American Labor Movement, 1935-1941, The   III-1658

Gard, Wayne
   Chisholm Trail, The   II-1022

Garvey, Amy-Jacques
   Garvey and Garveyism   III-1446

Gates, Paul W.
   Farmer's Age: Agriculture: 1815-1860, The. Vol. III: *The Economic History of the United States*   II-682

Gibson, John M.
   Physician to the World   II-1316

Giddens, Paul H.
   Birth of the Oil Industry, The   II-914

Gilbert, Felix
   To the Farewell Address: Ideas of Early American Foreign Policy   I-286; 406

Gilmore, Susan
   Revolution at Berkeley   III-1915

Ginger, Ray
   Six Days or Forever: Tennessee Versus John Thomas Scopes   III-1553

Gipson, Lawrence H.
   British Empire Before the American Revolu-

tion, The. Vol. III: *The Victorious Years, 1758-1760: The Great War for the Empire*   I-204
   British Empire Before the American Revolution, The. Vol. VI: *The Years of Defeat, 1754-1757: The Great War for the Empire*   I-204

Glad, Betty
   Charles Evans Hughes and the Illusions of Innocence: A Study in American Diplomacy   III-1535

Glad, Paul W.
   McKinley, Bryan, and the People   II-1270

Gleason, S. Everett
   Undeclared War, 1940-1941, The   III-1689

Goebel, Dorothy B.
   William Henry Harrison: A Political Biography. Vol. XIV: *The Indiana Historical Collections*   I-501

Goetzmann, William H.
   Exploration and Empire: The Explorer and the Scientist in the Winning of the American West   II-797

Goldmark, Josephine
   Impatient Crusader: Florence Kelley's Life Story   III-1372

Gompers, Samuel
   Seventy Years of Life and Labour   II-1154

Gottmann, Jean
   Megalopolis: The Urbanized Northeastern Seaboard of the United States   III-1815

Govan, Thomas P.
   Nicholas Biddle: Nationalist and Public Banker, 1786-1844   I-542

Graebner, Norman A.
   Empire on the Pacific: A Study in American Continental Expansion   II-782

Granger, Bruce I.
   Benjamin Franklin: An American Man of Letters   I-239

Grebstein, Sheldon N.
   Monkey Trial. Houghton Mifflin Research series   III-1552

Green, Constance M.
   Eli Whitney and the Birth of American Technology   I-373

Greene, Evarts B.
   Religion and the State: The Making and Testing of an American Tradition   I-320

Greene, Lorenzo J.
   Negro in Colonial New England, The   I-72

Greenfield, Kent Roberts
   Command Decisions   III-1723

Gregg, Josiah
   Commerce of the Prairies, The   I-590

Gregory, Horace
   History of American Poetry, 1900-1940, A   III-1403

Griffin, Clifford S.
   Their Brothers' Keepers: Moral Stewardship in the United States, 1800-1865   I-645

Gunderson, Robert G.
  Log-Cabin Campaign, The   II-762
Guttmann, Allen
  Wound in the Heart: America and the Spanish Civil War, The   III-1664

Hafen, Ann W.
  Handcarts to Zion: The Story of a Unique Western Migration, 1856-1860   II-816
Hafen, LeRoy R.
  Handcarts to Zion: The Story of a Unique Western Migration, 1856-1860   II-816
Haines, Charles G.
  Role of the Supreme Court in American Government and Politics, 1789-1835, The   I-347
Hamilton, Holman
  Prologue to Conflict: The Crisis and Compromise of 1850   II-857
Hammar, George
  Christian Realism in Contemporary American Theology: A Study of Reinhold Niebuhr, W. M. Horton, and H. P. Van Dusen, Preceded by a General and Historical Survey   III-1606
Hammond, Bray
  Banks and Politics in America, from the Revolution to the Civil War   I-568; II-699
Hammond, George P.
  Don Juan de Oñate and the Founding of New Mexico   I-44
Hansen, Marcus L.
  Atlantic Migration, 1607-1860: A History of the Continuing Settlement of the United States, The   II-756
Harlan, Louis R.
  Booker T. Washington: The Making of a Black Leader, 1856-1901   II-1252
Harper, Lawrence A.
  English Navigation Laws, The   I-125
Harrington, Michael
  Other America: Poverty in the United States, The   III-1867
Harrison, John F.
  Quest for the New Moral World: Robert Owen and the Owenites in Britain and America   I-515
Hartmann, Susan M.
  Truman and the 80th Congress   III-1802
Hartz, Louis
  Liberal Tradition in America: An Interpretation of American Political Thought Since the Revolution, The   I-651
Harvey, Edmund H., Jr.
  Mission to the Moon: A Critical Examination of NASA and the Space Program   III-1943
Hawkins, Hugh
  Pioneer: A History of The Johns Hopkins University, 1874-1889   II-1079
Haworth, Paul L.

Hayes-Tilden Election, The   II-1101
Hays, Samuel P.
  Conservation and the Gospel of Efficiency: The Progressive Conservation Movement, 1890-1920   III-1376
Heckler, Kenneth W.
  Insurgency: Personalities and Politics of the Taft Era   III-1392
Heimert, Alan E.
  Religion and the American Mind: From the Great Awakening to the Revolution   I-178
Hemingway, Ernest
  Moveable Feast, A   III-1563
Hendrick, Burton J.
  Life of Andrew Carnegie, The   II-1169
Hesseltine, William B.
  Lincoln and the War Governors   II-994
  Ulysses S. Grant, Politician   II-1056
Hibbard, Benjamin H.
  History of the Public Land Policies, A   I-584
Hicks, John D.
  Populist Revolt: A History of the Farmers' Alliance and the People's Party, The   II-1227
  Republican Ascendancy, 1921-1933. New American Nation Series   III-1545
Hidy, Muriel E.
  Pioneering in Big Business, 1882-1911: History of Standard Oil Company, New Jersey   II-1120
Hidy, Ralph W.
  Pioneering in Big Business, 1882-1911: History of Standard Oil Company, New Jersey   II-1120
Hoffman, Frederick J.
  Twenties: American Writing in the Postwar Decade, The   III-1562
Hofstadter, Richard
  Age of Reform: From Bryan to F. D. R., The   II-1228
  Anti-Intellectualism in American Life   II-1304
Hollon, W. Eugene
  Lost Pathfinder, Zebulon Montgomery Pike, The   I-469
Hoogenboom, Ari
  Outlawing the Spoils: A History of the Civil Service Reform Movement, 1865-1883   II-1131
Hopkins, C. Howard
  Rise of the Social Gospel in American Protestantism, 1865-1915, The   II-1198
Hopkins, Vincent J.
  Dred Scott's Case   II-902
Horsman, Reginald
  Matthew Elliott, British Indian Agent: A Study of British Indian Policy in the Old Northwest   I-387
Hosford, Frances J.

AMERICAN

Pertinent Literature Reviewed

Father Shipherd's Magna Charta: A Century of Coeduction in Oberlin College II-711

House, Lolabel
Study of the Twelfth Amendment of the Constitution of the United States, A I-458

Howard, A. Dick
Criminal Justice in Our Time III-1896

Howard, Donald S.
W. P. A. and Federal Relief Policy, The III-1635

Howard, Leon
Connecticut Wits, The I-639

Hughes, Emmet J.
Ordeal of Power: A Political Memoir of the Eisenhower Years, The III-1845

Huie, William Bradford
He Slew the Dreamer: My Search for the Truth About James Earl Ray and the Murder of Martin Luther King III-1929

Hulbert, Archer B.
Cumberland Road, The. Vol. X of *Historic Highways of America* I-494

Hungerford, Edward
Story of the Baltimore and Ohio Railroad, The I-627

Hunter, Louis C.
Steamboats on the Western Rivers: An Economic and Technological History I-474

Hutchins, John G.
American Maritime Industries and Public Policy, 1789-1914, The II-810

Hutchinson, William R.
Transcendentalist Ministers: Church Reform in the New England Renaissance, The I-657

Hutchinson, William T.
Cyrus Hall McCormick II-681

Ingstad, Helge
Westward to Vinland: The Discovery of Pre-Columbian Norse House-Sites in North America I-15

Jackson, David K.
Contributors and Contributions to the Southern Literary Messenger, 1834-1864, The II-727

Jackson, Robert H.
Struggle for Judicial Supremacy, The III-1669

Jacobs, Paul
Prelude to Riot: A View of Urban America from the Bottom III-1926

Jaffa, Harry V.
Crisis of the House Divided: An Interpretation of the Issues in the Lincoln-Douglas Debates II-909

James, Joseph B.
Framing of the Fourteenth Amendment, The II-1051

James, Marquis

Andrew Jackson: The Border Captain I-561

James, Sydney V.
People Among Peoples: Quaker Benevolence in Eighteenth-Century America, A I-161

Jenkins, William S.
Pro-Slavery Thought in the Old South I-650

Jennings, Jesse D.
Prehistory of North America I-3

Jensen, Merrill
Articles of Confederation: An Interpretation of the Social Constitutional History of the American Revolution, 1774-1781, The I-290

New Nation: A History of the United States During the Confederation, 1781-1789, The I-290; 327

Jervey, Theodore D.
Robert Y. Hayne and His Times I-663

Johnson, Charles A.
Frontier Camp Meeting: Religion's Harvest Time, The I-422

Johnson, Vance
Heaven's Tableland: The Dust Bowl Story III-1630

Jonas, Manfred
Isolationism in America, 1935-1941 III-1652

Jones, Bessie Zaban
Lighthouse of the Skies II-833

Jones, Joseph M.
Fifteen Weeks, The III-1779

Jones, Maldwyn Allen
American Immigration. Chicago History of American Civilization series II-1222

Jordan, Philip D.
National Road, The I-493

Jordan, Winthrop D.
White Over Black: American Attitudes Toward the Negro, 1550-1812 I-71

Josephson, Matthew
Edison: A Biography II-1112
Politicos, 1865-1896, The II-1057

Josephy, Alvin M., Jr.
Indian Heritage of America, The I-2

Kahin, George M.
United States in Vietnam, The III-1909

Kaiser, Robert Blair
RFK Must Die: The History of the Robert Kennedy Assassination and Its Aftermath III-1930

Kandel, Isaac L.
Impact of the War upon American Education, The III-1727

Kaufman, Burton Ira
Washington's Farewell Address: The View from the Twentieth Century I-405

Kaul, A. N.
Hawthorne: A Collection of Critical Es-

says   II-851
Keesler, Henry H.
    Peter Stuyvesant and His New York   I-141
Kellogg, Charles Flint
    *NAACP: A History of the National Association
    for the Advancement of Colored People*. Vol.
    I: *1909-1920*   III-1386
Kelly, Fred C.
    *Wright Brothers: A Biography Authorized by
    Orville Wright, The*   II-1348
Kennan, Erlend A.
    *Mission to the Moon: A Critical Examination
    of NASA and the Space Program*   III-
    1943
Kennan, George F.
    American Diplomacy, 1900-1950   II-1298
Keys, Thomas E.
    History of Surgical Anesthesia, The   II-793
Kirkland, Edward Chase
    *Industry Comes of Age: Business, Labor, and
    Public Policy, 1860-1897*   II-1159
Kittredge, George Lyman
    Witchcraft in Old and New England   I-173
Knollenberg, Bernhard
    Origins of the American Revolution, 1759-1766
    I-223
Koch, Adrienne
    *Power, Morals, and the Founding Fathers: Es-
    says in the Interpretation of the American
    Enlightenment*   I-198
Kolko, Gabriel
    Railroads and Regulation, 1877-1916   II-
    1160
    *Triumph of Conservatism: A Reinterpretation
    of American History, 1900-1916, The*
    III-1435
Kolodin, Irving
    Metropolitan Opera, The   II-1137
Konvitz, Milton R.
    Emerson: A Collection of Critical Essays
    II-851
Kraditor, Aileen S.
    *Means and Ends in American Abolitionism:
    Garrison and His Critics on Strategy and
    Tactics, 1834-1850*   II-722
Krout, John Allen
    Origins of Prohibition, The   III-1511
Kurtz, Stephen G.
    *Presidency of John Adams: The Collapse of
    Federalism, 1795-1800, The*   I-410

Labaree, Benjamin W.
    Boston Tea Party, The   I-243
La Feber, Walter
    America, Russia, and the Cold War, 1945-1971
    III-1808
Lamont, Lansing
    Day of Trinity   III-1695
Langer, William L.
    Undeclared War, 1940-1941, The   III-1689
Larson, Cedric

Words That Won the War   III-1456
Larson, Henrietta M.
    Jay Cooke, Private Banker   II-988
Lasswell, Harold D.
    Propaganda Technique in World War I
    III-1458
Lavender, David
    First in the Wilderness, The   I-478
Lefler, Hugh T.
    *North Carolina: The History of a Southern
    State*   I-136
Lehman, Milton
    *This High Man: The Life of Robert H. God-
    dard*   III-1557
Leighton, Alexander H.
    Governing of Men, The   III-1705
Lerner, Max
    Tocqueville and American Civilization   II-
    675
Letwin, William L.
    *Law and Economic Policy in America: The
    Evolution of the Sherman Act*   II-1210
Levenson, Jacob C.
    Mind and Art of Henry Adams, The   II-
    1187
Levin, N. Gordon, Jr.
    *Woodrow Wilson and World Politics: Ameri-
    ca's Response to War and Revolution*
    III-1488
Levy, Leonard W.
    *Law of the Commonwealth and Chief Justice
    Shaw: The Evolution of American Law,
    1830-1860, The*   II-788
Lewis, Anthony
    Gideon's Trumpet   III-1895
    *Portrait of a Decade: The Second American
    Revolution*   III-1850; 1858
Lewis, David L.
    King: A Critical Biography   III-1857
Lewis, John W.
    United States in Vietnam, The   III-1909
Ley, Willy
    Events in Space   III-1944
    Rockets, Missiles, and Men in Space   III-
    1558
Liddell Hart, B. H.
    Sherman, Soldier, Realist, American   II-
    1011
Lilienthal, David E.
    T. V. A.: Democracy on the March   III-
    1623
Lindsey, Almont
    *Pullman Strike: The Story of a Unique Experi-
    ment and of a Great Labor Upheaval, The*
    II-1239
Link, Arthur S.
    *Wilson: Campaigns for Progressivism and
    Peace, 1916-1917*   III-1451
    Wilson: The New Freedom   III-1407
    Wilson: The Road to the White House   III-
    1407

AMERICAN

Pertinent Literature Reviewed

Woodrow Wilson and the Progressive Era. New American Nation series   III-1408
Link, Eugene P.
Democratic-Republican Societies, 1790-1800   I-379
Livermore, Seward W.
Politics Is Adjourned: Woodrow Wilson and the War Congress, 1916-1918   III-1474
Livermore, Shaw, Jr.
Twilight of Federalism: The Disintegration of the Federalist Party, 1815-1830, The   I-609
Livezey, William E.
Mahan on Sea Power   II-1204
Luthin, Reinhard H.
First Lincoln Campaign, The   II-937
Lutz, Harley Leist
Public Finance   III-1418
Lyon, E. Wilson
Louisiana in French Diplomacy, 1759-1804   I-447
Man Who Sold Louisiana: The Career of François Barbé-Marbois, The   I-447

Mabee, Carleton
American Leonardo: A Life of Samuel F. B. Morse, The   II-745
MacArthur, General Douglas
Reminiscences   III-1833
McCague, James
Moguls and Iron Men: The Story of the First Transcontinental Railroad   II-971
McCaleb, Walter F.
Aaron Burr Conspiracy: With a New Light on Aaron Burr, The   I-464
McCarthy, Joseph R.
America's Retreat from Victory: The Story of George Catlett Marshall   III-1767
McCloskey, Robert G.
American Conservatism in the Age of Enterprise, 1865-1910. A Study of William Graham Sumner, Stephen J. Field, and Andrew Carnegie   II-1170
McCormick, Richard P.
Second American Party System, The   II-693
McCormick, Thomas J.
China Market: America's Quest for Informal Empire, 1893-1901   II-1299
McDonald, Forrest
We the People: The Economic Origins of the Constitution   III-1428
McDonald, Philip B.
Saga of the Seas: The Story of Cyrus W. Field and the Laying of the First Atlantic Cable, A   II-898
McFaul, John M.
Politics of Jacksonian Finance, The   II-751
McGeary, M. Nelson
Gifford Pinchot: Forester-Politician   III-1376

Macgowan, Kenneth
Behind the Screen: The History and Techniques of the Motion Picture   II-1335
McGrath, C. Peter
Yazoo: Law and Politics in the New Republic, the Case of Fletcher vs. Peck   I-489
Mack, Gerstle
Land Divided: A History of the Panama Canal and Other Isthmian Canal Projects, The   II-1343
Mack, Maynard
Twentieth Century Views: A Collection of Critical Essays   II-851
McKitrick, Eric L.
Andrew Johnson and Reconstruction   II-1029; 1052
Maclaurin, W. Rupert
Invention and Innovation in the Radio Industry: Massachusetts Institute of Technology Studies of Innovation   III-1523
McLoughlin, William G.
Modern Revivalism: Charles Grandison Finney to Billy Graham   II-1176
McWilliams, Carey
Prejudice: Japanese-Americans, Symbol of Racial Intolerance   III-1706
Malin, James C.
John Brown and the Legend of Fifty-Six   II-893
Nebraska Question, 1852-1854, The   II-873
Malone, Dumas
Jefferson and His Time. Vol. III: *Jefferson and the Ordeal of Liberty*   I-429
Manchester, William
Death of a President, The   III-1902
Marland, E. A.
Early Electrical Communication   II-746
Marnell, William H.
First Amendment: The History of Religious Freedom in America, The   I-321
Mason, Alpheus Thomas
Brandeis: A Free Man's Life   III-1371
Matthews, Herbert L.
United States and Latin America, The   III-1791
Matthiessen, Francis O.
American Renaissance: Art and Expression in the Age of Emerson and Whitman   II-850
May, Ernest R.
World War and American Isolation, 1914-1917, The   III-1452
May, Henry
End of American Innocence: A Study of the First Years of Our Own Time, 1912-1917, The   III-1401
Maynard, Theodore
De Soto and the Conquistadores   I-36
Mayo Clinic Division of Publications
Sketch of the History of the Mayo Clinic and the Mayo Foundation   II-1182

Mearns, David C.
  *Story Up to Now: The Library of Congress,
    1800-1946, The*   II-1280
Mecham, J. Lloyd
  *United States and Inter-American Security,
    1889-1960, The*   III-1792
Meier, August
  *Negro Thought in America, 1880-1915: Racial
    Ideologies in the Age of Booker T. Washing-
    ton*   II-1251
Merk, Frederick
  *Manifest Destiny and Mission in American His-
    tory: A Reinterpretation*   II-828
  *Oregon Question: Essays in Anglo-American
    Diplomacy and Politics, The*   II-781
Merk, Lois Bannister
  *Manifest Destiny and Mission in American His-
    tory: A Reinterpretation*   II-828
Meyer, Donald B.
  *Protestant Search for Political Realism, 1919-
    1941, The*   III-1607
Meyers, Marvin
  Jacksonian Persuasion: Politics and Belief, The
    I-634; II-677
Miller, John, Jr.
  Guadalcanal: The First Offensive, in the series,
    *The United States Army in World War II:
    The War in the Pacific*   III-1712
Miller, John C.
  Crisis in Freedom: The Alien and Sedition Acts
    I-416
  *Federalist Era, 1789-1801, The. New American
    Nation* series   I-343
Miller, Michael V.
  Revolution at Berkeley   III-1915
Miller, Perry
  New England Mind, The. Vol. I: *The Seven-
    teenth Century*   I-129
  New England Mind, The. Vol. II: *From Colony
    to Province*   I-129
Miller, Stuart Creighton
  *Unwelcome Immigrant: The American Image
    of the Chinese, 1785-1882, The*   II-1126
Millis, Walter
  Forrestal Diaries, The   III-1786
  *Martial Spirit: A Study of Our War with Spain,
    The*   II-1288
Milton, George F.
  *Age of Hate: Andrew Johnson and the Radicals,
    The*   II-1028
Milton, Lehman
  *This High Man: The Life of Robert H. God-
    dard*   III-1557
Miner, Dwight C.
  Fight for the Panama Route, The   II-
    1342
Minor, Benjamin B.
  Southern Literary Messenger, 1834-1864, The
    II-728
Mitchell, Broadus
  Alexander Hamilton. Vol. I: *Youth to*

  Maturity, 1755-1788   I-359
Alexander Hamilton. Vol. II: *The National
  Adventure, 1788-1804*   I-359
*Biography of the Constitution of the United
  States: Its Origin, Formation, Adoption, In-
  terpretation, A*   I-332; 369
*Depression Decade: From New Era Through
  New Deal, 1929-1941*   III-1596
Mitchell, Louise P.
  *Biography of the Constitution of the United
    States: Its Origin, Formation, Adoption, In-
    terpretation, A*   I-332; 369
Mock, James R.
  Words That Won the War   III-1456
Moley, Raymond
  After Seven Years   III-1618
Moore, Edmund A.
  *Catholic Runs for President: The Campaign of
    1928, A*   III-1568
Moore, Glover
  Missouri Controversy, 1819-1821, The   I-
    555
Morgan, Dale L.
  Jedediah Smith and the Opening of the West
    I-621
Morgan, Edmund S.
  *Puritan Dilemma: The Story of John Winthrop,
    The*   I-87
  Stamp Act Crisis, The   I-221
  Visible Saints: The History of a Puritan Idea
    I-130
Morgan, Helen M.
  Stamp Act Crisis, The   I-221
Morison, Samuel Eliot
  *Admiral of the Ocean Sea: A Life of Christo-
    pher Columbus*   I-19
  *European Discovery of America: The Northern
    Voyages, A. D. 500-1600, The*   I-25
  Founding of Harvard College, The   I-105
  *Harrison Gray Otis, 1765-1848: The Urbane
    Federalist*   I-519
  *History of United States Naval Operations in
    World War II, The.* Vol. V: *The Struggle for
    Guadalcanal, August, 1942-February, 1943*
    III-1713
  *History of United States Naval Operations in
    World War II, The.* Vol. XII: *Leyte: June,
    1944-January, 1945*   III-1733
  Intellectual Life of Colonial New England, The
    I-106
  *Old Bruin: Commodore Matthew C. Perry,
    1794-1858*   II-887
  Strategy and Compromise   III-1718
Morris, Richard B.
  *Peacemakers: The Great Powers and American
    Independence, The*   I-302
Morton, Richard L.
  Colonial Virginia   I-63
Moulton, Harold G.
  War Debts and World Prosperity   III-1539
Mowry, Arthur M.

Dorr War: Or, the Constitutional Struggle in Rhode Island, The   II-768

Mowry, George E.
California Progressives, The   II-1310
Era of Theodore Roosevelt and the Birth of Modern America, 1900-1912, The. The New American Nation series   II-1327
Theodore Roosevelt and the Progressive Movement   III-1393

Munro, Dana G.
Intervention and Dollar Diplomacy in the Caribbean, 1900-1921   III-1381

Murphy, William S.
Burn, Baby, Burn: The Los Angeles Race Riots, August, 1965   III-1925

Murray, Marian
Circus: From Rome to Ringling   II-1070

Murray, Robert K.
Red Scare: A Study in National Hysteria, 1919-1920, The   III-1494

Mustard, Harry S.
Government in Public Health   III-1397

Muther, Jeannette E.
History of the United Nations Charter, A   III-1744

Muzzey, David S.
James G. Blaine: A Political Idol of Other Days   II-1144; 1192

Namier, Lewis B.
Charles Townshend   I-229
England in the Age of the American Revolution   I-227
Structure of Politics at the Accession of George III, The   I-227

Nash, Gerald
"Herbert Hoover and the Origins of the Reconstruction Finance Corporation," *Mississippi Valley Historical Review*   III-1596

Nelles, Walker
"Commonwealth v. Hunt," in *Columbia Law Review*   II-787

Nelson, Donald M.
Arsenal of Democracy: The Story of American War Production   III-1682

Nelson, William H.
American Tory, The   I-249

Nevins, Allan
Ford: The Times, the Man, the Company   III-1423
Frémont: Pathmarker of the West   II-798
Grover Cleveland: A Study in Courage   II-1142
Ordeal of the Union. Vol. II: A House Dividing, 1852-1857   II-874
Ordeal of the Union. Vol. V: The War for the Union. Part I: The Impoverished War, 1861-1862   II-960
Ordeal of the Union. Vol. VI: The War for the Union Part II: War Becomes Revolution, 1862-1863   II-960
Ordeal of the Union. Vol. VII: The War for the Union. Part III: The Organized War, 1863-1864   II-960
Ordeal of the Union Vol. VIII: *The War for the Union. Part IV: The Organized War to Victory, 1864-1865*   II-960
Study in Power: John D. Rockefeller, Industrialist and Philanthropist   II-1119

Newfield, Jack
Prophetic Minority, A   III-1863

Newman, Alfred H.
Assassination of John F. Kennedy: The Reasons Why, The   III-1903

Newsome, Albert R.
North Carolina: The History of a Southern State   I-136

The New York Times
Portrait of a Decade: The Second American Revolution   III-1850; 1858

Nichols, Roy Franklin
Disruption of American Democracy, The   II-891

Nickerson, Hoffman
Turning Point of the Revolution: Or, Burgoyne in America, The   I-280

Noble, David W.
Historians Against History: The Frontier Thesis and the National Covenant in American Historical Writing Since 1830   II-733

Noggle, Burl
Teapot Dome: Oil and Politics in the 1920's   III-1528

Norris, George W.
Fighting Liberal: The Autobiography of George W. Norris   III-1624

Nourse, Edwin G.
Economics in the Public Service: Administrative Aspects of the Employment Act   III-1773

Novak, Barbara
American Painting of the Nineteenth Century: Realism, Idealism, and the American Experience   I-616

Novak, Robert
Lyndon B. Johnson: The Exercise of Power   III-1921

Nye, Russel B.
George Bancroft: Brahmin Rebel   II-732
Midwestern Progressive Politics, 1870-1958   II-1309

Oates, Stephen B.
To Purge This Land with Blood: A Biography of John Brown   II-921

O'Brien, Frank M.
Story of the Sun, New York: 1833-1928, The   II-717

Olsen, Otto H.
Thin Disguise: Turning Point in Negro History—Plessy vs. Ferguson: A Documentary

Presentation, 1864-1869, The   II-1265
Osgood, Herbert L.
   American Colonies in the Seventeenth Century,
      The   I-113
Osgood, Robert E.
   NATO: The Entangling Alliance   III-1809
Otis, D. S.
   "History of the Allotment Policy," in *Read-*
      justment of Indian Affairs   II-1164
Ottoson, Howard W.
   Land Use Policy and Problems in the United
      States   II-966

Page, Charles Hunt
   Class and American Sociology: From Ward to
      Ross   III-1359
Paige, Glenn D.
   Korean Decision, June 24-30, 1950, The
      III-1827
Parkman, Francis
   Discovery of the Great West: La Salle, The
      I-147
   Montcalm and Wolfe   I-203
   Pioneers of France in the New World   I-31
Parmet, Herbert S.
   Eisenhower and the American Crusades
      III-1846
Parry, J. H.
   Age of Reconnaissance: Discovery, Exploration,
      and Settlement, 1450-1650, The. History of
      Civilization series   I-20
Pasvolsky, Leo
   War Debts and World Prosperity   III-1539
Pattison, William D.
   Beginnings of the American Rectangular Land
      Survey System, 1784-1800   I-310
Paul, Rodman W.
   California Gold: The Beginning of Mining in
      the Far West   II-845
Paul, Sherman
   Thoreau: A Collection of Critical Essays
      II-851
Paxson, Frederic L.
   When the West Is Gone   II-1215
Pearce, Roy H.
   Whitman: A Collection of Critical Essays
      II-851
Perkins, Bradford
   Castlereagh and Adams: England and the
      United States, 1812-1823   I-524
   Prologue to War: England and the United
      States, 1805-1812   I-507
Perkins, Dexter
   History of the Monroe Doctrine, A   I-596
Perkins, Frances
   Roosevelt I Knew, The   III-1645
Perry, Ralph Barton
   Thought and Character of William James:
      Briefer Version, The   III-1366
Pershing, John J.
   My Experience in the World War   III-1470

Philbrick, Francis S.
   Rise of the West, 1754-1830, The. New Ameri-
      can Nation series   I-326
Phillips, Cabell
   Truman Presidency: The History of a Trium-
      phant Succession, The   III-1761
Pike, Zebulon Montgomery
   Journals, with Letters and Related Documents
      I-470
Pogue, Forrest C.
   George C. Marshall: Ordeal and Hope, 1939-
      1943   III-1717
Porter, Kenneth W.
   John Jacob Astor, Business Man   I-479
Potter, David M.
   Lincoln and His Party in the Secession Crisis
      II-948
Pratt, Julius W.
   America's Colonial Experiment: How the
      United States Gained, Governed, and in Part
      Gave Away a Colonial Empire   II-1294;
      1321
Priest, Loring B.
   Uncle Sam's Stepchildren: The Reformation of
      United States Indian Policy, 1865-1887
      II-1163
Puleston, William D.
   Mahan: The Life and Work of Captain Alfred
      Thayer Mahan, U. S. N.   II-1203

Quinn, David B.
   Raleigh and the British Empire   I-48

Rachlis, Eugene
   Peter Stuyvesant and His New York   I-141
Rainwater, Lee
   Moynihan Report and the Politics of Contro-
      versy, The   III-1868
Ramsaye, Terry
   Million and One Nights: A History of the Mod-
      ern Motion Picture Through 1925, A   II-
      1337
Randall, James G.
   Lincoln the President. Vol. I: *Springfield to*
      Bull Run   II-938
   Lincoln the President. Vol. II: *Bull Run to Get-*
      tysburg   II-983
Ratner, Sidney
   Taxation and Democracy in America   III-
      1417
Redlich, Fritz
   Molding of American Banking: Men and Ideas,
      The. History of American Economy series
      I-543
Rees, David
   Korea: The Limited War   III-1826
Reid, James D.
   Telegraph in America: Its Founders, Promot-
      ers, and Noted Men, The   II-933
Remini, Robert V.
   Election of Andrew Jackson, The   I-633

Rhodes, Frederick L.
Beginnings of Telephony   II-1091
Richard, Chase
Melville: A Collection of Critical Essays
    II-851
Robbins, Roy M.
*Our Landed Heritage: The Public Domain,
1776-1936*   II-774
Rohrbough, Malcolm J.
*Land Office Business: The Settlement and Ad-
ministration of American Public Lands,
1789-1837, The*   I-585
Roland, Charles P.
Confederacy, The   II-943
Rose, Barbara
American Art Since 1900: A Critical History
    III-1414
Rosenberg, Bernard
Mass Culture: The Popular Arts in America
    III-1503
Ross, Earle D.
*Democracy's College: The Land-Grant Move-
ment in the Formative Stage*   II-977
Ross, Irwin
*Loneliest Campaign: The Truman Victory of
1948, The*   III-1803
Rovere, Richard H.
Senator Joe McCarthy   III-1819
Rudolph, Frederick
*American College and University: A History,
The*   I-314
Rudwick, Elliott M.
*W. E. B. DuBois: Propagandist of the Negro
Protest*   III-1388
Rudy, Willis
*Higher Education in Transition: A History of
American Colleges and Universities, 1636-
1968*   I-315
Russel, Robert R.
*Improvement of Communication with the
Pacific Coast as an Issue in American Poli-
tics, 1783-1864*   II-868
Russell, Ruth B.
History of the United Nations Charter, A
    III-1744
Rutland, Robert A.
Birth of the Bill of Rights, 1776-1791   I-369
*Ordeal of the Constitution: The Antifederalists
and the Ratification Struggle of 1787-1788,
The*   I-333
Rutman, Darrett B.
*Winthrop's Boston: A Portrait of a Puritan
Town, 1630-1649*   I-88
Ryan, Cornelius
Last Battle, The   III-1750

Saloutos, Theodore
Farmer Movements in the South, 1865-1933
    II-1046
Samuels, Ernest
Henry Adams. Vol. II: *The Middle Years*

II-1186
Schlesinger, Arthur M., Jr.
Age of Jackson, The   II-698
Age of Roosevelt, The. Vol. II: *The Coming of
the New Deal*   III-1619
*Bitter Heritage: Vietnam and American De-
mocracy, 1941-1966, The*   III-1910
*Thousand Days: John F. Kennedy in the White
House, A*   III-1891
Schlesinger, Arthur M., Sr.
*Colonial Merchants and the American Revolu-
tion, 1763-1776, The*   I-244
Schnore, Leo F.
*Urban Scene: Human Ecology and Demogra-
phy, The*   III-1813
Scholes, Marie V.
*Foreign Policies of the Taft Administration,
The*   III-1382
Scholes, Walter V.
*Foreign Policies of the Taft Administration,
The*   III-1382
Schuyler, Hamilton
*Roeblings: A Century of Engineers, Bridge-
Builders, and Industrialists, The*   II-1064
Schwartz, Anna J.
*Monetary History of the United States, 1867-
1960, A*   II-1087
Settle, Mary L.
Saddles and Spurs: The Pony Express Saga
    II-927
Settle, Raymond W.
Saddles and Spurs: The Pony Express Saga
    II-927
Shannon, Fred Albert
*Farmer's Last Frontier: Agriculture, 1860-
1897, The.* Vol. V: *The Economic History of
the United States*   II-964
*Organization and Administration of the Union
Army, 1861-1865, The*   II-993
Sharkey, Robert P.
*Money, Class, and Party: An Economic Study
of Civil War, and Reconstruction*   II-987
Sharpe, Dores R.
Walter Rauschenbusch   II-1197
Shaw, Ronald E.
*Erie Water West: A History of the Erie Canal,
1792-1854*   I-548
Sherman, Paul
Thoreau: A Collection of Critical Essays
    II-851
Sherwood, Robert E.
Roosevelt and Hopkins: An Intimate History
    III-1634
Shy, John
*Toward Lexington: The Role of the British
Army in the Coming of the American Revo-
lution*   I-233
Silva, Ruth C.
Rum, Religion, and Votes: 1928 Re-Examined
    III-1569
Silverberg, Robert

*Light for the World: Edison and the Power In-
dustry*   II-1114
Sinclair, Andrew
*Available Man: The Life Behind the Masks of
Warren Gamaliel Harding, The*   III-
1527
Better Half, The   III-1515
*Era of Excess: A Social History of the Prohibi-
tion Movement*   III-1509
Sinclair, Upton
Autobiography of Upton Sinclair, The   III-
1355
Singletary, Otis A.
Mexican War, The   II-829
Sirmans, M. Eugene
*Colonial South Carolina: A Political History,
1663-1763*   I-137
Small, Herbert
*Handbook of the New Library of Congress in
Washington*   II-1281
Smith, Bradford
Bradford of Plymouth   I-76
Smith, Goldwin A.
*Treaty of Washington, 1871: A Study in Im-
perial History, The*   II-1074
Smith, Henry Nash
*Mark Twain: A Collection of Critical Essays.
Twentieth-Century Views series*   II-1149
Smith, James M.
*Freedom's Fetters: The Alien and Sedition
Laws and American Civil Liberties*   I-
418
Smith, Justin H.
War with Mexico   II-821
Smith, Paul H.
Loyalists and Redcoats   I-297
Sorensen, Theodore C.
Kennedy   III-1874
Sosin, Jack M.
*Whitehall and the Wilderness: The Middle
West in British Colonial Policy, 1760-1775*
I-210
Soule, George
*Prosperity Decade: From War to Depression,
1917-1929.* Vol. VIII: *The Economic History
of the United States*   III-1540; 1546
Spanier, John W.
*Truman-MacArthur Controversy and the Ko-
rean War, The*   III-1831
Stallman, Robert W.
Stephen Crane: A Critical Biography   II-
1258
Stanwood, Edward
*American Tariff Controversies in the Nine-
teenth Century*   II-1276
Starkey, Marion L.
*Devil in Massachusetts: A Modern Enquiry into
the Salem Witch Trials, The*   I-172
Steck, Francis B.
Jolliet-Marquette Expedition, 1673, The   I-
149

Stegner, Wallace
*Beyond the Hundredth Meridian: John Wesley
Powell and the Second Opening of the West*
II-1107
*Gathering of Zion: The Story of the Mormon
Trail, The*   II-815
Steiner, Bernard C.
*Life of Henry Barnard: The First United States
Commissioner of Education, 1867-1870*
II-1033
Stephenson, George M.
*Political History of the Public Lands from 1840
to 1862: From Pre-emption to Homestead,
The*   II-775
Stewart, Edgar I.
Custer's Luck   II-1097
Still, William N., Jr.
*Iron Afloat: The Story of the Confederate Ar-
morclads*   II-958
Stourzh, Gerald
*Benjamin Franklin and American Foreign
Policy*   I-303
Stover, John F.
American Railroads   I-628
Stowe, Harriet Beecher
Uncle Tom's Cabin, or, Life Among the Lowly
II-862
Styron, William
Confessions of Nat Turner   II-686
Sullivan, Maurice S.
Jedediah Smith, Trader, and Trail Breaker
I-622
Svobida, Lawrence
Empire of Dust, An   III-1629
Swanberg, W. A.
*Citizen Hearst: A Biography of William Ran-
dolph Hearst*   II-1245
Sward, Keith
Legend of Henry Ford, The   III-1424
Swisher, Carl B.
Roger B. Taney   II-903

Taft, Philip
*A. F. of L. from the Death of Gompers to the
Merger, The*   III-1657
A. F. of L. in the Time of Gompers, The
II-1155
Taussig, Frank W.
Tariff History of the United States, The
II-1275
Taylor, F. Jay
*United States and the Spanish Civil War, 1936-
1939, The*   III-1663
Taylor, George R.
Transportation Revolution, 1815-1860, The.
Vol. IV: *The Economic History of the United
States*   I-549
Theoharis, Athan G.
*Yalta Myths: An Issue in U. S. Politics, 1945-
1955, The*   III-1739
Thomas, Benjamin Platt

Russo-American Relations, 1815-1867 II-1040

Thompson, J. Eric
Maya Hieroglyphic Writing: An Introduction I-7

Thompson, Robert Luther
Wiring a Continent: The History of the Telegraph Industry in the United States, 1832-1866 II-897; 932

Thorelli, Hans B.
Federal Antitrust Policy: Origination of an American Tradition, The II-1208

Tiedt, Sidney W.
Role of the Federal Government in Education, The III-1729

Tolles, Frederick B.
Meeting House and Counting House: The Quaker Merchants of Colonial Philadelphia, 1682-1763 I-159

Trachtenberg, Alan
Brooklyn Bridge, Fact and Symbol, The II-1062

Treat, Payson Jackson
National Land System, 1785-1820, The I-308

Trelease, Allen W.
Indian Affairs in Colonial New York: The Seventeenth Century I-82

True, Alfred Charles
History of Agricultural Education in the United States, A II-976

True, Webster Prentiss
Smithsonian: America's Treasure House, The II-835

Truman, Harry S
Memoirs by Harry S Truman. Vol. I: *Years of Decision* III-1762
Memoirs by Harry S Truman. Vol. II: *Years of Trial and Hope* III-1785

Tucker, Glen
Tecumseh, Vision of Glory I-500

Tugwell, Rexford Guy
Brains Trust, The III-1612

Unger, Irwin
Greenback Era: A Social and Political History of American Finance, 1865-1879, The II-1085

United States Department of Health, Education and Welfare
Technical Report on Salk Poliomyelitis Vaccine III-1840

United States Department of State
United States Relations with China: With Special Reference to the Period, 1944-1949 III-1766

University of California Academic Senate (Select Committee on Education)
Education at Berkeley III-1914

Urofsky, Melvin I.
Big Steel and the Wilson Administration: A Study in Business Government Relations III-1463

Utley, Robert M.
Custer and the Great Controversy: The Origin and Development of a Legend II-1096

Vickery, Olga W.
Novels of William Faulkner: A Critical Interpretation, The III-1575

Vinson, John Chalmers
Parchment Peace: The United States Senate and the Washington Conference, 1921-1922, The III-1533

Wahlgren, Erik
"Fact and Fancy in the Vinland Sagas," in *Old Norse Literature and Mythology, A Symposium* I-16

Wallace, Willard M.
Sir Walter Raleigh I-50

Walworth, Arthur C.
Black Ships Off Japan: The Story of Commander Perry's Expedition II-886

Ward, Harry M.
United Colonies of New England, 1643-1690, The I-111

Warfel, Harry R.
Noah Webster: Schoolmaster to America I-638

Warren, Charles
"New Light on the History of the Federal Judiciary Act of 1789," in *Harvard Law Review* I-348
Supreme Court in United States History, The Vol. I: *1789-1821* I-441

Warren, Harris G.
Herbert Hoover and the Great Depression III-1596

Warshow, Robert
Immediate Experience: Movies, Comics, Theatre, and Other Aspects of Popular Culture, The III-1505

Washburn, Wilcomb E.
Governor and the Rebel, The I-154

Wecter, Dixon
When Johnny Comes Marching Home III-1482

Weisberger, Bernard A.
They Gathered at the River: The Story of the Great Revivalists and Their Impact upon Religion in America II-1176

Welter, Rush
Popular Education and Democratic Thought in America I-579

Werner, M. R.
Barnum II-1068

Wertenbaker, Thomas J.
Torchbearer of the Revolution: The Story of Bacon's Rebellion and Its Leader I-153
Virginia Under the Stuarts, 1607-1688 I-66

Whicher, Stephen E.
  Emerson: A Collection of Critical Essays
  II-851
  *Freedom and Fate: An Inner Life of Ralph
  Waldo Emerson* I-656
Whitaker, Arthur P.
  *Mississippi Question, 1795-1803: A Study in
  Trade, Politics, and Diplomacy, The* I-398
  Spanish-American Frontier, 1783-1795, The
  I-398
White, David Manning
  Mass Culture: The Popular Arts in America
  III-1503
White, George S.
  *Memoir of Samuel Slater: The Father of
  American Manufactures* I-364
White, Leonard D.
  Republican Era, 1869-1901, The II-1133
White, Patrick
  *Nation on Trial: America and the War of 1812,
  A* I-509
White, Theodore H.
  Making of the President, 1960, The III-1873
  Making of the President, 1964, The III-1920
  Making of the President, 1968, The III-1935
Whitehouse, Arch
  *Early Birds: The Wonders and Heroics of the
  First Decades of Flight, The* II-1350
Wiebe, Robert H.
  "Anthracite Strike of 1902: A Record of Con-
  fusion, The" in *Mississippi Valley Historical
  Review* II-1332
Wiener, Philip P.
  Evolution and the Founders of Pragmatism
  II-1365
Willcox, William B.
  *Portrait of a General: Sir Henry Clinton in the
  War of Independence* I-296
Williams, Kenneth P.
  Lincoln Finds a General II-1001
Williams, Ralph C.
  *United States Public Health Service, 1798-
  1950, The* III-1396
Williams, Stanley T.
  Life of Washington Irving, The I-483
Williams, T. Harry
  Lincoln and His Generals II-954
Williamson, Harold F.
  *American Petroleum Industry: The Age of Il-
  lumination, 1859-1899, The* II-915
Williamson, James A.
  *Cabot Voyages and Bristol Discovery Under
  Henry VII, with the Cartography of the Voy-
  ages by R.A. Skelton, The* I-26
Wills, Garry
  Nixon Agonistes III-1937
Wilmerding, Lucius, Jr.

Electoral College, The I-459
Wilmot, Chester
  Struggle for Europe, The III-1722
Wilson, Mitchell
  *American Science and Invention, a Pictorial
  History: The Fabulous Story of How Ameri-
  can Dreamers, Wizards, and Inspired Tink-
  erers Converted a Wilderness into the Won-
  der of the World* II-840
Wilson, Robert Forrest
  How America Went to War. Vol. VI: *Demobili-
  zation: Our Industrial and Military Demo-
  bilization After the Armistice, 1918-1920*
  III-1481
Wilson, William E.
  *Angel and the Serpent: The Story of New Har-
  mony* I-514
Wiltse, Charles M.
  John C. Calhoun. Vol. I: *Nationalist, 1782-
  1828* I-544
  John C. Calhoun. Vol. II: *Nullifier, 1829-1839*
  II-706
Winslow, Ola E.
  Master Roger Williams I-100
Wisan, Joseph E.
  *Cuban Crisis as Reflected in the New York
  Press, 1895-1898, The* II-1246
Wittke, Carl F.
  *We Who Built America: The Saga of the Emi-
  grant* II-757; 1221
Wohlstetter, Roberta
  Pearl Harbor: Warning and Decision III-1700
Wolff, Leon
  *Little Brown Brother: How the United States
  Purchased and Pacified the Philippine Is-
  lands at the Century's Turn* II-1293
Woodward, C. Vann
  Battle for Leyte Gulf, The III-1734
  "Case of the Louisiana Traveler: *Plessy* vs. *Fer-
  guson*, The" in John A. Garraty's *Quarrels
  That Have Shaped the Constitution* II-1266
  *Reunion and Reaction: The Compromise of
  1877 and the End of Reconstruction* II-1102
Wright, Conrad
  Beginnings of Unitarianism in America, The
  I-572
Wrong, George M.
  Rise and Fall of New France, The I-56

Yancey, William L.
  *Moynihan Report and the Politics of Contro-
  versy, The* III-1868
Young, Edwin
  Labor and the New Deal III-1640

Zaturenska, Marya A.
  History of American Poetry, 1900-1940
  III-1403

Abbott, Grace
From Relief to Social Security: The Development of the New Public Welfare Services and Their Administration III-1647
Abell, Aaron I.
Urban Impact on American Protestantism, 1865-1900, The II-1200
Abels, Jules
Man on Fire: John Brown and the Cause of Liberty II-923
Out of the Jaws of Victory III-1805
Abernethy, Thomas P.
From Frontier to Plantation in Tennessee: A Study in Frontier Democracy I-329; 634
Western Lands and the American Revolution I-211
Acheson, Sam H.
Joe Bailey, the Last Democrat III-1419
Acomb, Frances
Anglophobia in France, 1763-1789 I-287
Adams, Brooks
Emancipation of Massachusetts: The Dream and the Reality, The I-131
Adams, George P., Jr.
Wartime Price Control III-1465
Adams, Henry
History of the United States of America During the Administrations of Jefferson and Madison I-431; 490; 521
John Randolph I-556
Adams, James Truslow
Founding of New England, The I-78; 96; 108; 114
Adams, John R.
Harriet Beecher Stowe II-864
Adams, Randolph G.
Political Ideas of the American Revolution I-250
Adams, Samuel Hopkins
Incredible Era: The Life and Times of Warren Gamaliel Harding III-1530
Adams, William F.
Ireland and Irish Immigration to the New World from 1815 to the Famine II-759
Adkins, Nelson F.
Fitz-Greene Halleck: An Early Knickerbocker Wit and Poet I-484
Adler, Selig
Uncertain Giant: 1921-1941, The. Vol. II: *American Diplomatic History* series III-1536
Agar, Herbert
Price of Power: America Since 1945, The III-1788
Ahlstrom, Sydney E.
"Continental Influence on American Christian Thought Since World War I," in *Church History* III-1608

Ahnebrink, Lars
Beginnings of Naturalism in American Fiction, The II-1260
Aitken, Hugh G.
Welland Canal Company: A Study in Canadian Enterprise, The I-551
Aitken, William
Who Invented the Telephone? II-1093
Albion, Robert G.
Rise of New York Port, 1815-1860, The I-550, II-811
Square-Riggers on Schedule: The New York Sailing Packets to England, France, and Cotton Ports II-811
Alden, John R.
General Gage in America I-235
John Stuart and the Southern Colonial Frontier: A Study of Indian Relations, War, Trade, Land Problems in the Southern Wilderness, 1754-1775 I-211; 218
South in the Revolution, 1763-1789, The I-235
Alderfer, E. Gordon
Witness of William Penn, The I-162
Alexander, Charles C.
This New Ocean: A History of Project Mercury III-1945
Allen, Frederick Lewis
Only Yesterday: An Informal History of the Nineteen-Twenties III-1530
Since Yesterday: The Nineteen-Thirties in America, September 3, 1929-September 3, 1939 III-1636
Allen, Gardner W.
Naval History of the American Revolution, A I-271
Allen, Gay Wilson
Our Naval War with France I-413
Walt Whitman Handbook II-853
William James: A Biography III-1368
Allen, Harry C.
Great Britain and the United States: A History of Anglo-American Relations, 1783-1952 II-1076
Allen, Henry T.
Rhineland Occupation, The III-1483
Allen, Leslie H.
Bryan and Darrow at Dayton: The Record and Documents of the Bible-Evolution Trial III-1554
Alsop, Joseph W.
168 Days, The III-1672
Amacher, Richard E.
Benjamin Franklin I-240
Ambler, Charles H.
History of Transportation in the Ohio Valley, A I-496
Ambrose, Stephen E.

AMERICAN
Literature for Additional Recommended Reading

Halleck: Lincoln's Chief of Staff   II-1013

Anderson, Frederick
Mark Twain-Howells Letters: The Correspondence of Samuel L. Clemens and William Dean Howells, 1872-1910   II-1150

Anderson, Jack
McCarthy: The Man, the Senator, the "Ism"   III-1821

Anderson, Maybelle H.
Appleton Milo Harmon Goes West   II-817

Anderson, Oscar E., Jr.
New World, 1939-1946: A History of the United States Atomic Energy Commission, The   III-1758

Andrews, Charles M.
Colonial Background of the American Revolution: Four Essays in American Colonial History, The   I-224
Colonial Period of American History, The. Vol. I-III: *The Settlements*   I-64; 78; 114; 139
Colonial Period of American History, The. Vol. IV: *England's Commercial and Colonial Policy*   I-64; 143; 168
Narratives of the Insurrections, 1675 to 1690   I-156; 168
Our Earliest Colonial Settlements: Their Diversities of Origin and Later Characteristics   I-51; 101

Andrews, Wayne
Architecture, Ambition, and Americans: A Social History of American Architecture   II-1236

Angle, Paul M.
Created Equal? The Complete Lincoln-Douglas Debates of 1858   II-911
Annual Report of the United States Commissioner of Education for 1902. Vol. I   II-1035

Anshen, Melvin
Wartime Production Controls   III-1685

Anthony, Katherine
Susan B. Anthony: Her Personal History and Her Era   III-1518

Archambault, D. Reginald
John Dewey on Education: Selected Writings   II-1306

Archer, Gleason L.
Big Business and Radio   III-1524

Archibald, Warren S.
Thomas Hooker   I-96

Armstrong, William M.
E. L. Godkin and American Foreign Policy, 1865-1900   II-1194

Arnold, Horace L.
Ford Methods and Ford Shops   III-1425

Arrington, Leonard J.
Great Basin Kingdom: An Economic History of the Latter-Day Saints, 1830-1900   II-817

Asbury, Herbert
Great Illusion: An Informal History of Prohibition, The   III-1512

Ashmore, Harry S.
Negro and the Schools, The   III-1853

Asselineau, Roger
Literary Reputation of Mark Twain from 1910-1950, The   II-1150

Atherton, Lewis
Cattle Kings, The   II-1025

Babbidge, Homer D., Jr.
Federal Interest in Higher Education, The   III-1730

Babcock, F. Lawerence
Spanning the Atlantic   II-899

Bagnall, William R.
Textile Industries of the United States, The. Vol. I: *1639-1810*   I-366

Bailey, Charles W., II
No High Ground: The Story of the Atomic Bomb in World War II   III-1757

Bailey, Stephen Kemp
Congress Makes A Law: The Story Behind the Employment Act of 1946   III-1763

Bailey, Thomas A.
Presidential Greatness: The Image and the Man from George Washington to the Present   I-612

Bailyn, Bernard
Education in the Forming of American Society: Needs and Opportunities for Study   I-108; 580
New England Merchants in the Seventeenth Century, The   I-90
"Political Experience and Enlightenment Ideas in Eighteenth Century America," in American Historical Review   I-199

Baker, Carlos
Ernest Hemingway: A Life Story   III-1564

Baker, Charles W.
Government Control of Operations in Great Britain and the United States During the World War   III-1464

Baker, Melvin C.
Foundations of John Dewey's Educational Theory   II-1306

Baker, Rachel
Dr. Morton: Pioneer in the Use of Ether   II-794

Bancroft, Frederic
Calhoun and the South Carolina Nullification Movement   II-707

Bancroft, George
History of the United States of America, from the Discovery of the Continent   I-223

Bancroft, Hubert H.
History of Arizona and New Mexico, 1530-1888. Vol. XVII: *The Works of Hubert Howe Bancroft*   I-45
History of California, 1542-1800. Vol. XVIII: *The Works of Hubert Howe Bancroft*   I-276

Banning, William P.

Commercial Broadcasting Pioneer: The WEAF Experiment, 1922-1926   III-1524

Barbour, Philip L.
Three Worlds of Captain John Smith, The I-64

Baringer, William E.
House Dividing: Lincoln as President Elect, A II-951
Lincoln's Rise to Power   II-911

Barker, Eugene C.
Mexico and Texas, 1821-1835   II-740

Barker, Virgil
American Painting   I-618

Barnard, Harry
Rutherford B. Hayes and His America   II-1103

Barnes, Harry Elmer
Introduction to the History of Sociology, An III-1362

Barnes, Viola F.
Dominion of New England: A Study in British Colonial Policy, The   I-126

Barnouw, Erik
History of Broadcasting in the United States, A. Vol. II. *The Golden Web: 1933 to 1953* III-1524

Barnum, Phineas T.
Life of P. T. Barnum, The   II-1071

Barrett, Don Carlos
Greenbacks and the Resumption of Specie Payments, 1862-1879, The   II-990; 1088

Barrett, Jay A.
Evolution of the Ordinance of 1787, with an Account of the Earlier Plans for the Government of the Northwest Territory. First American Frontier series   I-329

Barrow, Thomas C.
Trade and Empire: The British Customs Service in Colonial America, 1660-1775 I-235

Barrows, Edward M.
Great Commodore, The   II-887

Barry, Richard H.
Mister Rutledge of South Carolina   I-349

Barth, Alan
Price of Liberty, The   III-1898

Barth, Gunther
Bitter Strength: A History of the Chinese in the United States, 1850-1870   II-1126

Bartlett, Richard A.
Great Surveys of the American West   II-1109

Bartlett, Ruhl J.
League to Enforce Peace, The   III-1536

Baruch, Bernard
American Industry in the War   III-1464

Bassett, John S.
Middle Group of American Historians, The II-735
"Regulators of North Carolina, 1765-1771, The," in *Annual Report for the Year 1894*

I-218

Bates, Daisy
Long Shadow of Little Rock, The   III-1853

Bates, J. Leonard
Origins of Teapot Dome: Progressives, Parties, and Petroleum, 1909-1921, The   III-1530

Battis, Emery
Saints and Sectaries: Anne Hutchinson and the Antinomian Controversy in the Massachusetts Bay Colony   I-89

Baur, John I.
New Art in America   III-1414
Revolution and Tradition in Modern American Art   III-1414

Beach, Sylvia
Shakespeare and Company   III-1564

Beal, John R.
Marshall in China   III-1768

Beale, Howard K.
Critical Year: A Study of Andrew Johnson and Reconstruction, The   II-1009; 1030; 1053

Beaney, William M.
Right to Counsel in American Courts, The III-1898

Beard, Charles A.
American Foreign Policy in the Making, 1932-1940: A Study in Responsibilities   III-1654
Economic Interpretation of the Constitution of the United States, An   I-334
President Roosevelt and the Coming of the War, 1941: A Study in Appearances and Realities   III-1702

Beazley, Charles R.
John and Sebastian Cabot: The Discovery of North America   I-26

Becker, Carl L.
Declaration of Independence: A Study in the History of Political Ideas, The   I-199
History of Political Parties in the Province of New York, 1760-1776, The   I-293

Beer, George L.
British Colonial Policy, 1754-1765   I-224; 235
Old Colonial System, 1660-1754, The   I-126; 168

Beer, Thomas
Stephen Crane: A Study in American Letters II-1259

Bellows, George K.
Short History of Music in America, A   II-1138

Bemis, Samuel Flagg
American Secretaries of State and Their Diplomacy, 1776-1925, The   I-394
Hussey-Cumberland Mission and American Independence: An Essay in the Diplomacy of the American Revolution, The   I-305
John Quincy Adams and the Foundations of American Foreign Policy   I-525; 563

John Quincy Adams and the Union   I-612;
II-805
*Latin American Policy of the United States: An
Historical Interpretation, The*   I-598; III-
1383
Bennett, Charles E.
*Laudonnière and Fort Caroline: History and
Documents*   I-38
Bennett, Hugh Hammond
Elements of Soil Conservation   III-1631
Bennett, Lerone, Jr.
*What Manner of Man: A Biography of Martin
Luther King, Jr., 1929-1968*   III-1860
Benson, Lee
*Concept of Jacksonian Democracy: New York
as a Test Case, The*   II-701
*Merchants, Farmers, and Railroads: Railroad
Regulation and New York Politics, 1850-
1887*   II-1160
*Turner and Beard: American Historical Writ-
ing Reconsidered*   III-1431
Berelson, Bernard
*Voting: A Study of Opinion Formation in a
Presidential Campaign*   III-1805
Berg, Roland H.
Polio and Its Problems   III-1841
Berger, Carl
Korea Knot: A Military-Political History, The
III-1828
Berman, William C.
*Politics of Civil Rights in the Truman Adminis-
tration, The*   III-1805
Bernard, Jessie
*Origins of American Sociology: The Social
Science Movement in the United States*
III-1362
Bernard, L. L.
*Origins of American Sociology: The Social
Science Movement in the United States*
III-1362
Bernstein, Irving
*Lean Years: A History of the American Worker,
1920-1933, The*   III-1586; 1660
*Turbulent Years: A History of the American
Worker, 1933-1941, The*   III-1587; 1660
Bernstein, Richard J.
John Dewey   III-1368
Berwanger, Eugene H.
*Frontier Against Slavery: Western Anti-Negro
Prejudice and the Slavery Extension Contro-
versy, The*   II-894
Best, John H.
*American Legacy of Learning: Readings in the
History of Education, The*   I-108
Beuhrig, Edward H.
Woodrow Wilson and the Balance of Power
III-1410
Beveridge, Albert J.
Abraham Lincoln, 1809-1858   II-882; 911
Life of John Marshall, The. 4 vols.   I-466
Life of John Marshall, The. Vol. IV: *Conflict*

and Construction, 1800-1815   I-442
Beverley, Robert
History and Present State of Virginia, The
I-156
Biddle, Francis
Fear of Freedom, The   III-1821
Biddle, Nicholas
*History of the Expedition Under the Command
of Captains Lewis and Clark*   I-454
Biddle, Richard
*Memoir of Sebastian Cabot, with a Review of
the History of Maritime Discovery, A*
I-27
Bidwell, Percy W.
*History of Agriculture in the Northern United
States, 1820-1860*   II-684
Biggar, H. P.
Voyages of Jacques Cartier, The   I-32
Works of Samuel De Champlain   I-57
Billias, George A.
*George Washington's Opponents: British Gen-
erals and Admirals in the American Revolu-
tion*   I-281
Billington, Ray A.
*Protestant Crusade, 1800-1860: A Study of the
Origins of American Nativism, The*   II-
759
*Westward Expansion: A History of the Ameri-
can Frontier*   I-531
Bing, Rudolph
5000 Nights at the Opera   II-1139
Binkley, Wilfred E.
*American Political Parties: Their Natural His-
tory*   I-355; II-695
Birdsall, Paul
Versailles Twenty Years After   III-1489
Birnbaum, Karl E.
*Peace Moves and U-Boat Warfare: A Study of
Imperial Germany's Policy Towards the
United States, April 18, 1916-January 9,
1917*   III-1453
Bishop, Farnham
Goethals, Genius of the Panama Canal   II-
1345
Story of the Submarine, The   I-271
Bishop, Joseph B.
Goethals, Genius of the Panama Canal   II-
1345
Bishop, Morris
Odyssey of Cabeza de Vaca, The   I-45
Bishop, W. W.
Library of Congress, The   II-1282
Blair, Walter
*Art of Huckleberry Finn: Text, Sources, Criti-
cism, The*   II-1151
Blanshard, Paul
*Religion and the Schools: The Great Contro-
versy*   III-1730
Blau, Joseph L.
*Social Theories of Jacksonian Democracy,
1825-1850*   II-701

Blossom, Virgil T.
  It Has Happened Here   III-1853
Blount, James H.
  American Occupation of the Philippines, 1898-1912, The   II-1295
Blum, John M.
  From the Diaries of Henry Morgenthau, Jr.
  III-1647; 1691
Blumberg, Dorothy R.
  Florence Kelley: The Making of a Social Pioneer   III-1373
Blumenson, Martin
  Breakout and Pursuit   III-1724
Boggs, W. S.
  Pony Express, The   II-928
Boland, Frank Kells
  First Anesthetic: The Story of Crawford W. Long, The   II-794
Bolton, Herbert E.
  Spanish Borderlands: A Chronicle of Old Florida and the Southwest, The. Vol. XXIII: *The Chronicles of America*   I-38; 45
Bond, Beverly W., Jr.
  Monroe Mission to France, 1794-1796, The   I-413
Bonsal, Stephen
  Edward Fitzgerald Beale: A Pioneer in the Path of Empire, 1822-1903   II-869
Bontecou, Eleanor
  Federal Loyalty and Security Program, The   III-1821
Boorstin, Daniel J.
  Americans, The. Vol. I: *The Colonial Experience*   I-240
Borning, Bernard C.
  Political and Social Thought of Charles A. Beard, The   III-1431
Boucher, Chauncey S.
  Nullification Controversy in South Carolina, The   II-707
Boudin, Louis B.
  Government by Judiciary   I-569
Bourne, Kenneth
  Britain and the Balance of Power in North America, 1815-1908   II-806
Bowers, C. A.
  Progressive Educator and the Depression: The Radical Years, The   II-1306
Bowers, Claude G.
  Jefferson and Hamilton, the Struggle for Democracy in America   I-361
  My Mission to Spain   III-1666
  Party Battles of the Jackson Period   I-665
  Tragic Era: The Revolution After Lincoln, The   II-1058
Boxer, Charles R.
  Dutch Seaborne Empire, 1600-1800, The   I-84
Boyd, Julian P.
  Declaration of Independence, The   I-265
Boyer, Barry B.

  Warren Court: A Critical Analysis, The   III-1887
Boykin, Edward C.
  Ghost Ship of the Confederacy: The Story of the Alabama   II-1076
Braasch, W. F.
  Early Days in the Mayo Clinic   II-1183
Bracey, John H.
  Black Nationalism in America   III-1449
Bradford, William
  Of Plymouth Plantation: The Pilgrims in America   I-114
Bradley, Glenn D.
  Story of the Pony Express, The   II-928
Brandes, Joseph
  Herbert Hoover and Economic Diplomacy: Department of Commerce Policy, 1921-1928   III-1541
Brandon, William
  Men and the Mountain, The   II-799
Brant, Irving
  James Madison: Father of the Constitution, 1787-1800   I-340; 355
  James Madison: The President, 1809-1812   I-510
  James Madison: The Virginia Revolutionist   I-245
Branyan, Robert L.
  Urban Crisis in Modern America   III-1816
Brenan, Gerald
  Spanish Labyrinth, The   III-1666
Brennan, Joseph
  Social Conditions in Industrial Rhode Island, 1820-1860   II-771
Bretall, Robert W.
  Charles W. Reinhold Niebuhr: His Religious, Social, and Political Thought   III-1608
Bridenbaugh, Carl
  Mitre and Sceptre: Transatlantic Faiths, Ideas, Personalities, and Politics, 1689-1775   I-224
Bridge, James H.
  Inside History of the Carnegie Steel Company: A Romance of Millions, The   II-1172
Briggs, John
  Requiem for a Yellow Brick Brewery: A History of the Metropolitan Opera   II-1139
Brink, Wellington
  Big Hugh: The Father of Soil Conservation   III-1631
Brock, William R.
  American Crisis: Congress and Reconstruction, 1865-1867, An   II-1053
Brockunier, Samuel H.
  Irrepressible Democrat: Roger Williams, The   I-101
Brodie, Bernard
  Sea Power in the Machine Age   II-1205
Brodie, Fawn M.
  Thaddeus Stevens: Scourge of the South   II-1053

Brogan, George S.
Great American Myth, The   II-1019
Bronner, Edwin B.
*William Penn's Holy Experiment: The Found-
ing of Pennsylvania 1681-1701*   I-162
Brooke, John
Chatham Administration, 1766-1968, The
I-230
Brooks, Charles B.
Siege of New Orleans, The   I-538
Brooks, Juanita
*On the Mormon Frontier: The Diary of Hosea
Stout, 1844-1861*   II-817
Brooks, Philip C.
*Diplomacy and the Borderlands: The Adams-
Onís Treaty of 1819*   I-563
"Spain's Farewell to Louisiana, 1803-1821," in
Mississippi Valley Historical Review   I-
449
Brooks, Thomas R.
Toil and Trouble   III-1660
Brower, C.
*Oberliniana: A Jubilee Volume of Semi-His-
torical Anecdotes Connected with the Past
and Present of Oberlin College*   II-712
Brown, B. Katherine
*Virginia, 1705-1786: Democracy or Aristoc-
racy?*   I-293
Brown, Charles H.
*Correspondent's War: Journalists in the Span-
ish-American War, The*   II-1247
Brown, Claude
Manchild in the Promised Land   III-1926
Brown, Emily C.
*From the Wagner Act to Taft-Hartley: A Study
of National Labor Policy and Labor Rela-
tions*   III-1642; 1763
Brown, Everett S.
*Missouri Compromises and Presidential Poli-
tics, 1820-1825, from the Letters of William
Plumer, Jr., The*   I-556
Brown, Robert E.
Charles Beard and the Constitution   I-334
*Virginia, 1705-1786: Democracy or Aristoc-
racy?*   I-293
Brown, Stuart G.
*First Republicans: Political Philosophy and
Public Policy in the Party of Jefferson and
Madison, The*   I-355
Brown, Wallace
*King's Friends: The Composition and Motives
of the American Loyalist Claimants, The*
I-250
Brown, William G.
Life of Oliver Ellsworth, The   I-349
Bruce, Philip A.
*Institutional History of Virginia in the Seven-
teenth Century*   I-68
Brunhouse, Robert L.
*Counter-Revolution in Pennsylvania, 1776-
1790, The*   I-381

Bryan, George S.
Edison: The Man and His Work   II-1115
Bryan, Mary B.
Memoirs of William Jennings Bryan, The
III-1554
Bryan, William Jennings
Memoirs of William Jennings Bryan, The
III-1554
Bryant, Arthur
Triumph in the West   III-1724
Bryarly, Wakeman
Trail to California: Overland Journal   II-
847
Bryce, James
American Commonwealth, The   II-1134
Buchanan, A. Russell
Navy's Air War: A Mission Completed, The
III-1696
United States and World War II, The   III-
1735
Buck, Solon J.
*Agrarian Crusade: A Chronicle of the Farmer
in Politics, The*   II-1047
Bunau-Varilla, Philippe
*Panama: The Creation, Destruction, and
Resurrection*   II-1345
Bundy, McGeorge
*On Active Service in Peace and War: A Study
of the Life and Times of Henry L. Stimson*
III-1603
Burchard, John E.
Combat Scientists: Science in World War II
III-1696
Burlingame, Roger
*March of the Iron Men: A Social History of
Union Through Invention*   II-747
*Engines of Democracy: Inventions and Society
in Mature America*   II-115
Henry Ford   III-1425
Burner, David
*Politics of Provincialism: The Democratic Party
in Transition, 1918-1932, The*   III-1477
Burnett, Edmund C.
Continental Congress, The   I-250
Burnette, O. Lawrence, Jr.
*Wisconsin Witness to Frederick Jackson
Turner*   II-1217
Burns, James M.
John Kennedy: A Political Profile   III-1876
Roosevelt: The Lion and the Fox   III-1620
Burr, George L.
*Narratives of the Witchcraft Cases, 1648 to
1706*   I-175
Burr, Susan S.
Money Grows Up   II-1088
Burson, Caroline M.
*Stewardship of Don Estaban Miro, 1782-1792,
The*   I-402
Burt, Alfred L.
*United States, Great Britain, and British North
America from the Revolution to the Estab-*

lishment of Peace After the War of 1812, The
I-394; 510; 526

Burton, Theodore E.
John Sherman   II-1212

Bushnell, G. H.
First Americans: The Pre-Columbian Civilizations, The   I-4

Butler, Pierce
Books and Libraries in Wartime   III-1730

Butow, Robert J.
Japan's Decision to Surrender   III-1757

Butterfield, Herbert
George III and the Historians   I-230

Buttinger, Joseph
Vietnam: A Dragon Embattled   III-1910

Byrne, Frank L.
Prophet of Prohibition: Neal Dow and His Crusade   I-647

Cable, Frank T.
Birth and Development of the American Submarine, The   I-271

Cahn, Edmond
Great Rights, The   III-1898

Callaghan, Barbara
"Doctors Mayo and the Sister, The," in *Hospital Progress*   II-1183

Callahan, North
Henry Knox: General Washington's General   I-388

Callcott, Wilfrid H.
Santa Anna: The Story of an Enigma Who Once Was Mexico   II-741

Campbell, Angus
Voters Decide, The   III-1848

Campbell, Charles S., Jr.
Special Business Interests and the Open Door Policy   II-1300

Canby, Courtlandt
History of Rockets and Space, A   III-1559

Cannon, James, Jr.
Bishop Cannon's Own Story: Life as I Have Seen It   III-1570

Cannon, M. Hamlin
Leyte: The Return to the Philippines, in the series *The United States Army in World War II: The Technical Services*   III-1735

Canterbery, E. Ray
President's Council of Economic Advisers: A Study of Its Functions and Its Influence on the Chief Executive's Decisions, The   III-1774

Capers, Gerald M.
John C. Calhoun: Opportunist   II-707
Stephen A. Douglas: Defender of the Union   II-876

Carey, Robert G.
Peace Corps, The   III-1882

Carlson, Theodore L.
Illinois Military Tract: A Study of Land Occupation, Utilization and Tenure, The. University of Illinois Studies in the Social Sciences, Vol. 32.   I-587

Carpenter, Frederic I.
Emerson Handbook   II-853

Carstensen, Vernon
Public Lands: Studies in the History of the Public Domain, The   I-587; II-777; 968

Carter, Paul A.
Decline and Revival of the Social Gospel: Social and Political Liberalism in American Protestant Churches, 1920-1940, The   II-1200

Cary, John
Joseph Warren: Physician, Politician, Patriot   I-245

Catt, Carrie Chapman
Woman Suffrage and Politics: The Inner Story of the Suffrage Movement   III-1518

Cattell, David T.
Communism and the Spanish Civil War   III-1665

Catterall, Ralph C.
Second Bank of the United States, The   I-569; II-701

Catton, Bruce
Mister Lincoln's Army   II-956
Stillness at Appomattox, A   II-1018

Caughey, John W.
Rushing for Gold   II-847

Cauthen, Kenneth
Impact of American Religious Liberalism, The   II-1200

Chadwick, French E.
Relations of the United States and Spain: The Spanish-American War, The   II-1289

Chafee, Zechariah, Jr.
Free Speech in the United States   III-1496

Chamberlain, John
MacArthur: 1941-1951   III-1834

Chamberlain, Neil W.
Collective Bargaining   III-1642

Chamberlain, William Henry
America's Second Crusade   III-1740

Chambers, William N.
Old Bullion Benton, Senator from the New West: Thomas Hart Benton, 1782-1858   I-587

Channing, Edward
History of the United States, A   I-569; II-789

Chapman, Arthur
Pony Express, The   II-928

Chapman, Charles E.
Founding of Spanish California: The Northwestward Expansion of New Spain, 1687-1783, The   I-276

Charles, Joseph
Origins of the American Party System, The   I-361

Chesney, Allen M.
Johns Hopkins Hospital and The Johns Hopkins University School of Medicine: A

Chronicle, The   II-1082

Chester, Lewis
American Melodrama: The Presidential Campaign of 1968, An   III-1939

Chevigny, Hector
Russian America: The Great Alaskan Venture, 1741-1867   II-1041

Chiang Kai-shek
Soviet Russia in China   III-1769

Childs, Francis S.
French Refugee Life in the United States, 1790-1800: An American Chapter of the French Revolution   I-419

Childs, Marquis
Eisenhower: Captive Hero   III-1848

Chinard, Gilbert
Honest John Adams   I-344; 413

Chindahl, George L.
History of the Circus in America, A   II-1071

Chittenden, Hiram M.
American Fur Trade of the Far West, The   I-480

Choate, Julian Ernest, Jr.
American Cowboy: The Myth and the Reality, The   II-1025

Christenson, Reo M.
Brannan Plan: Farm Politics and Policy, The   III-1805

Christie, Ian R.
End of North's Ministry, 1780-1782, The   I-305

Chugerman, Samuel
Lester F. Ward: The American Aristotle: A Summary and Interpretation of His Sociology   III-1362

Church, Leslie F.
Oglethorpe: A Study of Philanthrophy in England and Georgia   I-187

Churchill, Winston S.
Second World War, The. Vol. VI: *Triumph and Tragedy*   III-1740; 1752

Civilian Production Administration
Industrial Mobilization for War, 1940-1945   III-1685

Clapp, Gordon R.
T. V. A.: An Approach to the Development of a Region, The   III-1626

Clark, George N.
Later Stuarts, 1660-1714, The   I-126

Clark, George T.
Leland Stanford   II-973

Clark, J. Stanley
Oil Century: From The Drake Well to the Conservation Era, The   II-917

Clark, John D.
Federal Trust Policy   II-1212

Clark, John G.
Grain Trade in the Old Northwest, The   I-630

Clark, Kenneth B.
Prejudice and Your Child   III-1853

Clark, Thomas D.
Rampaging Frontier, The   I-532

Clark, Victor S.
History of Manufactures in the United States. Vol. I: *From 1607-1860*   II-842

Clay, Lucius D.
Decision in Germany   III-1799

Clayton, William
William Clayton's Journal   II-817

Cleaves, Freeman
Old Tippecanoe: William Henry Harrison and His Time   I-503

Cleland, Robert Glass
From Wilderness to Empire: A History of California, 1542-1900   I-276
History of California: The American Period   II-824
This Reckless Breed of Man: The Trappers and Fur Traders of the Southwest   I-480

Cleveland, Catherine C.
Great Revival in the West, 1797-1805, The   I-425

Cloward, Richard A.
Regulating the Poor: The Functions of Public Relief   III-1870

Cobb, Sanford H.
Rise of Religious Liberty in America: A History, The   I-323

Coben, Stanley A.
Mitchell Palmer: Politician   III-1496

Cochran, Thomas C.
Age of Enterprise: A Social History of Industrial America, The   II-1122; 1172

Coe, Michael D.
Maya, The   I-9

Coffman, Edward M.
War to End All Wars: The American Military Experience in World War I, The   III-1483

Cohen, Mitchell
New Student Left, The   III-1916

Cohen, Warren I.
American Revisionists: The Lessons of Intervention in World War I, The   III-1453

Coit, Margaret L.
John C. Calhoun   II-707

Cole, Wayne S.
America First: The Battle Against Intervention, 1940-1941   III-1691
Interpretive History of American Foreign Relations, An   II-830
Senator Gerald P. Nye and American Foreign Relations   III-1654

Coles, Harry L.
War of 1812, The   I-510; 520; 526

Coles, Robert
Children of Crisis. Vol. I: *A Study of Courage and Fear*   III-1870
Children of Crisis. Vol. II: *Migrants, Mountaineers, Sharecroppers*   III-1870
Children of Crisis. Vol. III: *The South Goes*

North III-1870
Coles, William A.
  Architecture in America: A Battle of Styles
  II-1236
Columbus, Christopher
  Journal of Christopher Columbus (During His First Voyage, 1492-1493) and Documents Relating to the Voyages of John Cabot and Gaspar Corte Real, The I-22
Commager, Henry Steele
  Immigration and American History: Essays in Honor of Theodore C. Blegen II-759
Commons, John R.
  History of Labour in the United States II-790
Compton, Arthur H.
  Atomic Quest: A Personal Narrative III-1696
Conant, James B.
  Shaping Educational Policy III-1730
  Thomas Jefferson and the Development of American Public Education I-316
Condon, Thomas J.
  New York Beginnings: The Commercial Origins of New Netherland I-143
Connell-Smith, Gordon
  Inter-American System, The III-1793
Connelly, Thomas C.
  1932 Campaign: An Analysis, The III-1614
Conot, Robert
  Rivers of Blood, Years of Darkness: The Unforgettable Classic Account of the Watts Riot III-1926
Conrad, Earl
  Scottsboro Boy II-1593
Cooke, Jacob E.
  Federalist, The I-339
Cooke, Philip S.
  Conquest of New Mexico and California: An Historical and Personal Narrative, The II-823
Cordasco, Francesco
  Daniel Coit Gilman and the Protean Ph.D.: The Shaping of American Graduate Education II-1082
Cornish, Dudley T.
  Sable Arm: Negro Troops in the Union Army, 1861-1865, The II-995
Corwin, Edward S.
  Doctrine of Judicial Review, The I-349
  French Policy and the American Alliance of 1778 I-286
  John Marshall and the Constitution I-490; 569
  Total War and the Constitution III-1708
Coser, Lewis A.
  American Communist Party, The III-1821
Coues, Elliott
  Expeditions of Zebulon Montgomery Pike, The I-470

Journal of Jacob Fowler, 1821-1822, The I-592
Coulson, Thomas
  Joseph Henry: His Life and Work II-836
Coulter, E. Merton
  College Life in the Old South I-317
  Confederate States of America, 1861-1865, The II-945
  Journal of Peter Gordon, 1732-1735, The I-187
Cowley, Malcolm
  Black Cargoes: A History of the Atlantic Slave Trade, 1518-1865 I-73
  Exile's Return III-1564
Cox, Archibald
  Warren Court: Constitutional Decision as an Instrument of Reform, The III-1887
Cox, Isaac J.
  West Florida Controversy, 1789-1813, The I-563
Cox, James M.
  Journey Through My Years III-1477
Coy, Owen C.
  Great Trek, The II-847
Crane, Theodore R.
  Colleges and the Public, 1787-1862, The I-316
Crane, Verner W.
  Benjamin Franklin and a Rising People I-240
  Southern Frontier, 1670-1732, The I-187
Craven, Avery O.
  Coming of the Civil War, The II-876; 951
  Growth of Southern Nationalism, 1848-1861, The. Vol. VI: *A History of the South* II-876
  Reconstruction: The Ending of the Civil War II-1009
Craven, Wesley F.
  Southern Colonies in the Seventeenth Century, 1607-1689, The I-51; 73; 119; 139; 156
  " '. . . And so the Form of Government Became Perfect'," in *Virginia Magazine of History and Biography* I-68
Cremin, Lawrence A.
  Republic and the School: Horace Mann on The Education of Free Men, The I-580
  Transformation of the School: Progressivism in American Education, 1876-1957, The III-1730
Crenshaw, Ollinger
  Slave States in Presidential Election of 1860, The II-940
Crone, G. R.
  Discovery of America, The. Turning Points in History series. I-22
Crouse, Nellis M.
  La Vérendrye: Fur Trader and Explorer I-150
  Lemoyne d'Iberville: Soldier of New France I-150

Crowell, Benedict
How America Went to War III-1465
Crowl, Philip A.
U. S. Marines and Amphibious War: Its Theory and Its Practice in the Pacific, The III-1714
Cummings, Milton C., Jr.
National Election of 1964, The III-1923
Cuneo, John R.
Robert Rogers of the Rangers I-206
Cunliffe, Marcus
George Washington: Man and Monument I-344
Cunningham, Noble E., Jr.
Jeffersonian Republicans: The Formation of a Party Organization, 1789-1801, The I-361
Jeffersonian Republicans in Power: Party Operations, 1801-1809, The I-431
Current, Richard N.
Daniel Webster and the Rise of National Conservatism I-665; II-858
Lincoln Nobody Knows, The II-911
Curry, Jesse
Retired Dallas Police Chief Jesse Curry Reveals His JFK Assassination File III-1904
Curti, Merle E.
Social Ideas of American Educators, The II-1305
Curtis, Edward E.
Organization of the British Army in the American Revolution, The I-255
Curtis, James C.
Fox at Bay: Martin Van Buren and the Presidency, 1837-1841, The II-764
Cushing, Caleb
Treaty of Washington: Its Negotiation, Execution, and the Discussions Relating Thereto, The II-1075
Cushman, Robert F.
Cases in Civil Liberties III-1898
Cutler, Carl C.
Greyhounds of the Sea: The Story of the American Clipper Ship II-811
Cutright, Paul R.
Lewis and Clark: Pioneering Naturalists I-455
Theodore Roosevelt, the Naturalist III-1377

Daggett, Stuart
Chapters on the History of the Southern Pacific II-973
Dale, Edward Everett
Range Cattle Industry, The II-1025
Dale, Harrison C.
Ashley-Smith Explorations and the Discovery of a Central Route to the Pacific, 1822-1829, The I-622
Dangerfield, George
Awakening of American Nationalism, 1815-1828, The I-641
Era of Good Feelings, The I-504; 526; 544; 557; 598
"Steamboat Case, The" in John A. Garraty's *Quarrels That Have Shaped the Constitution* I-605
Daniels, Jonathan
Man of Independence, The III-1788
Daniels, Roger
Concentration Camps USA: Japanese-Americans and World War II III-1708
Danzig, Allison
Professional Football III-1500
Darling, Arthur B.
Our Rising Empire, 1763-1803 I-305; 402
Darrow, Clarence
Story of My Life, The III-1554
Dauer, Manning J.
Adams Federalists, The I-413
Daum, Arnold R.
American Petroleum Industry: The Age of Illumination, 1859-1899, The II-1122
David, Jay
Weight of the Evidence: The Warren Report and Its Critics, The III-1905
Davidson, Eugene
Death and Life of Germany, The III-1799
Davidson, John Wells
Crossroads of Freedom: The 1912 Campaign Speeches of Woodrow Wilson, A III-1409
Davidson, Marshall B.
"What Samuel Wrought," in *American Heritage* II-747
Davidson, Robert L.
War Comes to Quaker Pennsylvania, 1682-1756 I-162
Davies, Richard O.
Housing Reform During the Truman Administration III-1805
Davis, Andrew M.
Origin of the National Banking System, The II-990
Davis, David Brion
Ante-Bellum Reform I-646
Davis, George T.
Navy Second to None: The Development of Modern American Naval Policy, A II-1205
Dawes, Charles Gates
Journal of Reparations, A III-1541
Dawes, Henry Laurens
"Have We Failed the Indians?" in *Atlantic Monthly* II-1166
Day, A. Grove
Coronado's Quest: The Discovery of the Southwestern States I-45
De Champlain, Samuel
Voyages of Samuel De Champlain I-57
De Conde, Alexander
Entangling Alliances: Politics and Diplomacy

Under George Washington   I-402
"Washington's Farewell, the French Alliance, and the Election of 1796," in *Mississippi Valley Historical Review*   I-407
Dector, Moshe
   McCarthy and the Communists   III-1822
De Forest, Lee
   Father of Radio: The Autobiography of Lee De Forest   III-1524
DeGrummond, Jane L.
   Baratarians and the Battle of New Orleans, The I-538
Dell, Floyd
   Upton Sinclair: A Study in Social Protest III-1356
Dellenbaugh, Frederick S.
   Canyon Voyage, A   II-1108
Deloria, Vine, Jr.
   Custer Died for Your Sins: An Indian Manifesto   III-1870
De Madariaga, Isabel
   Britain, Russia, and the Armed Neutrality of 1780   I-305
Deming, Dorothy
   Fundamental Orders of Connecticut, The I-96
   Settlement of the Connecticut Towns, The I-96
De Remer, Bernard
   Moody Bible Institute: A Pictorial History II-1176
Destler, Chester M.
   American Radicalism, 1865-1901: Essays and Documents   II-1230
De Voto, Bernard
   Across the Wide Missouri   I-480
   Course of Empire, The   I-39
   Journals of Lewis and Clark, The   I-454
   Year of Decision, 1846, The   II-783; 824
De Weerd, Harvey A.
   President Wilson Fights His War: World War I and the American Intervention   III-1471
Dewey, Davis R.
   First and Second Banks of the United States, The   I-544
   State Banking Before the Civil War   I-544
Dewey, John
   Democracy and Education: An Introduction to the Philosophy of Education   II-1305
DeWitt, David M.
   Assassination of Abraham Lincoln and Its Expiation, The   II-1018
   Impeachment and Trial of Andrew Johnson II-1030
Diamond, Edwin
   Rise and Fall of the Space Age, The   III-1945
Dickerson, Oliver M.
   Navigation Acts and the American Revolution, The   I-126

Dill, Alonzo T.
   Governor Tryon and His Palace   I-218
Dillon, Mary E.
   Wendell Willkie, 1892-1944   III-1626
Divine, Robert A.
   Illusion of Neutrality, The   III-1654
Donald, David
   Charles Sumner and the Coming of the Civil War   II-876; 882
   Lincoln Reconsidered   II-984
Donaldson, Thomas
   Public Domain: Its History with Statistics, The I-311
Donelly, Thomas C.
   1928 Campaign: An Analysis, The   III-1570
Donoughue, Bernard
   British Politics and the American Revolution: The Path to War, 1773-1775   I-245
Donovan, Robert J.
   Eisenhower: The Inside Story   III-1848
   Warren Commission Report on the Assassination of John F. Kennedy, The   III-1904
Donovan, Timothy P.
   Henry Adams and Brooks Adams: The Education of Two American Historians   II-1189
Dorfman, Joseph
   Economic Mind in American Civilization, 1606-1933, The   I-545
Dorr, Rheta
   What Eight Million Women Want   III-1373
Dos Passos, John
   Men Who Made the Nation, The   I-344
Douglas, Paul H.
   Social Security in the United States   III-1648
Douglass, Elisha P.
   Rebels and Democrats: The Struggle for Equal Political Rights and Majority Rule During the American Revolution   I-293
Dowdey, Clifford
   Death of a Nation   II-1002
   Land They Fought For: The Story of the South as the Confederacy, The   II-945
Downes, Randolph C.
   Rise of Warren Gamaliel Harding, 1865-1920, The   III-1477
Downey, Fairfax D.
   Indian-Fighting Army   II-1098
   Storming the Gateway, Chattanooga, 1863 II-1002
Dozer, Donald M.
   Are We Good Neighbors?   II-1793
Draper, Hal
   Berkeley: The New Student Revolt   III-1916
Driggs, Howard R.
   Pony Express Goes Through: An American Saga Told by Its Heroes, The   II-928

Drummond, Donald F.
  *Passing of American Neutrality, 1937-1941,
    The* III-1654; 1691
Duberman, Martin
  *Antislavery Vanguard: New Essays on the Abo-
    litionists, The* II-724
DuBois, William E. B.
  *Dusk of Dawn: An Essay Toward an Autobiog-
    raphy of a Race Concept* III-1389
  Souls of Black Folk: Essays and Sketches, The
    II-1253
Dulles, Foster Rhea
  America's Rise to World Power, 1898-1954
    II-1324
  *History of Recreation: America Learns to Play,
    A* II-1071
  Labor in America: A History III-1642
  *Yankees and Sumurai: America's Role in the
    Emergence of Modern Japan* II-888
Dumbauld, Edward
  *Declaration of Independence and What It
    Means Today* I-266
Dunbar, Seymour
  History of Travel in America I-496
Duncan, Otis Dudley
  *Social Characteristics of Urban and Rural
    Communities* III-1816
Dunn, W. H.
  George Washington I-344
Dunning, William A.
  *Reconstruction: Political and Economic, 1865-
    1877* II-1030; 1053; 1103
Durkin, Joseph T.
  Stephen R. Mallory: Confederate Navy Chief
    II-961
Duroselle, Jean-Baptiste
  *From Wilson to Roosevelt: Foreign Policy of the
    United States, 1913-1945* III-1541
Dykstra, Robert R.
  Cattle Towns, The II-1025

Earle, Edward M.
  *Makers of Modern Strategy: Military Thought
    from Machiavelli to Hitler* II-1205
Eaton, Clement
  Henry Clay and the Art of American Politics
    I-612
  Mind of the Old South, The II-904
Eaton, Herbert
  *Presidential Timber: A History of Nominating
    Conventions, 1868-1960* II-1145
Eccles, William J.
  Canada and Louis XIV, 1663-1701 I-149
  *France in America. New American Nation se-
    ries* I-58
Eckenrode, Hamilton J.
  *Separation of Church and State in Virginia: A
    Study in the Development of the Revolution*
    I-322
Eddy, Edward D., Jr.
  Colleges for Our Land and Time: The Land-

  Grant Idea in American Education II-
    979
Edwards, Marcellus B.
  *Marching with the Army of the West, 1846-
    1848* II-824
Edwards, Newton
  *School in the American Social Order: The Dy-
    namics of American Education, The* I-
    581
Ehrenreich, Barbara
  *Long March, Short Spring: The Student Upris-
    ing at Home, and Abroad* III-1916
Ehrenreich, John
  *Long March, Short Spring: The Student Upris-
    ing at Home, and Abroad* III-1916
Einstein, Charles
  Fireside Book of Baseball, The III-1500
Eisenhower, Dwight D.
  *White House Years: Mandate for Change,
    1953-1956, The* III-1848
Ekirch, Arthur A., Jr.
  Decline of American Liberalism, The III-
    1864
Elkins, Stanley M.
  *Slavery: A Problem in American Institutional
    and Intellectual Life* II-689; 724; 905
Elliott, J. H.
  Old World and the New, 1492-1650, The
    I-22
Elliott, William Y.
  Television's Impact upon American Culture
    III-1679
Ely, Richard T.
  *"Founding and Early History of the American
    Economic Association, The" in American
    Economic Review* II-1212
Emery, Edwin
  *Press and America: An Interpretative History
    of Journalism, The* I-192; II-718
Emme, Eugene M.
  History of Space Flight, A III-1945
Emory, William H.
  *Lieutenant Emory Reports: A Reprint of Lt.
    W. H. Emory's Notes of a Military Recon-
    naissance* II-823
Epstein, Edward Jay
  Inquest III-1905
Epstein, Samuel
  Rocket Pioneers, The III-1559
Esarey, Logan
  *Internal Improvements in Early Indiana. In-
    diana Historical Society Publications* I-
    550
Essien-Udom, E. U.
  *Black Nationalism: A Search for an Identity in
    America* III-1449

Falconer, John I.
  *History of Agriculture in the Northern United
    States, 1820-1860* II-684
Fall, Bernard B.

Essays in Econometric History   I-630

Fogelson, Robert
  Fragmented Metropolis: Los Angeles, 1850-1930, The   III-1926

Folmsbee, Stanley J.
  "Origin of the First 'Jim Crow' Law, The" in *Journal of Southern History*   II-1267

Foner, Philip S.
  History of the Labor Movement in the United States: The Policies and Practices of the American Federation of Labor, 1900-1909   II-1332

Forbes, Esther
  Paul Revere and the World He Lived In   I-255

Ford, Henry
  My Life and Work   III-1425

Foreman, Grant
  Last Trek of the Indians, The   I-671
  Pathfinder in the Southwest: The Itinerary of A. W. Whipple During His Explorations for a Railway Route from Fort Smith to Los Angeles in the Years 1853 and 1854, A   II-869

Forman, Sidney
  West Point: A History of the United States Military Academy   I-436

Forrest, Earle R.
  Missions and Pueblos of the Old Southwest   I-45

Forrestel, E. P.
  Admiral Raymond A. Spruance   III-1735

Fortescue, John W.
  History of the British Army, 1813-1815, A   I-538

Editors of *Fortune* Magazine
  Exploding Metropolis, The   III-1816

Fox, Dixon R.
  Completion of Independence, 1790-1830, The   I-641
  Decline of Aristocracy in the Politics of New York, The   I-381

Francis, Dr. Thomas F., Jr.
  "Evaluation of the 1954 Field Trials of Poliomyelitis Vaccine: Summary Report," in *American Journal of Public Health*   III-1842

Frank, Gerold
  American Death: The True Story of the Assassination of Dr. Martin Luther King, Jr., An   III-1931

Frankfurter, Felix
  Commerce Clause Under Marshall, Taney, and Waite, The   I-606
  Mr. Justice Brandeis   III-1373

Franklin, Benjamin
  Autobiography of Benjamin Franklin   I-240

Franklin, John Hope
  Militant South, 1800-1861, The   II-904
  Reconstruction After the Civil War   II-1009

Frantz, Joe B.
  American Cowboy: The Myth and the Reality, The   II-1025

Freed, Fred
  Decision to Drop the Bomb, The   III-1757

Freeman, Douglas Southall
  George Washington. Vol. V: *Victory with the Help of France*   I-205; 298
  George Washington. Vol. VII: *First in Peace*   I-394

Freeman, Joseph
  Dollar Diplomacy: A Study in American Imperialism. Originally published in 1926 as *American Imperialism: Viewpoints of United States Foreign Policy, 1898-1941*   III-1383

Freidel, Frank
  Franklin D. Roosevelt. Vol. II: *The Ordeal*   III-1477
  Franklin D. Roosevelt. Vol. III: *The Triumph*   III-1620

Frémont, John C.
  Memoirs of My Life   II-799
  Narratives of Exploration and Adventure   II-799

French, Allen
  First Year of the American Revolution, The   I-260

French, John C.
  History of the University Founded by Johns Hopkins, A   II-1082

Friedman, Milton
  Monetary History of the United States, 1867-1960, A   III-1437

Frink, Maurice
  When Grass Was King   II-1025

Fritz, Henry E.
  Movement for Indian Assimilation, 1860-1890, The   II-1166

Frost, Robert
  Complete Poems   III-1404

Frothingham, Octavius Brooks
  Transcendentalism in New England: A History   I-658

Fuess, Claude M.
  Carl Schurz, Reformer   II-1058; 1145
  Daniel Webster   II-805; 858

Fulton, John F.
  Centennial of Surgical Anesthesia, The   II-794

Funston, Fredrick
  Memories of Two Wars   II-1295

Furniss, Edgar S., Jr.
  NATO: A Political Appraisal   III-1810

Gabriel, Ralph H.
  Course of American Democratic Thought, The   II-1172

Galbraith, John S.
  Hudson's Bay Company as an Imperial Factor, 1821-1869, The   II-784

Essays in Econometric History   I-630
Fogelson, Robert
  Fragmented Metropolis: Los Angeles, 1850-1930, The   III-1926
Folmsbee, Stanley J.
  "Origin of the First 'Jim Crow' Law, The" in *Journal of Southern History*   II-1267
Foner, Philip S.
  History of the Labor Movement in the United States: The Policies and Practices of the American Federation of Labor, 1900-1909   II-1332
Forbes, Esther
  Paul Revere and the World He Lived In   I-255
Ford, Henry
  My Life and Work   III-1425
Foreman, Grant
  Last Trek of the Indians, The   I-671
  Pathfinder in the Southwest: The Itinerary of A. W. Whipple During His Explorations for a Railway Route from Fort Smith to Los Angeles in the Years 1853 and 1854, A   II-869
Forman, Sidney
  West Point: A History of the United States Military Academy   I-436
Forrest, Earle R.
  Missions and Pueblos of the Old Southwest   I-45
Forrestel, E. P.
  Admiral Raymond A. Spruance   III-1735
Fortescue, John W.
  History of the British Army, 1813-1815, A   I-538
Editors of *Fortune* Magazine
  Exploding Metropolis, The   III-1816
Fox, Dixon R.
  Completion of Independence, 1790-1830, The   I-641
  Decline of Aristocracy in the Politics of New York, The   I-381
Francis, Dr. Thomas F., Jr.
  "Evaluation of the 1954 Field Trials of Poliomyelitis Vaccine: Summary Report," in *American Journal of Public Health*   III-1842
Frank, Gerold
  American Death: The True Story of the Assassination of Dr. Martin Luther King, Jr., An   III-1931
Frankfurter, Felix
  Commerce Clause Under Marshall, Taney, and Waite, The   I-606
  Mr. Justice Brandeis   III-1373
Franklin, Benjamin
  Autobiography of Benjamin Franklin   I-240
Franklin, John Hope
  Militant South, 1800-1861, The   II-904
  Reconstruction After the Civil War   II-1009

Frantz, Joe B.
  American Cowboy: The Myth and the Reality, The   II-1025
Freed, Fred
  Decision to Drop the Bomb, The   III-1757
Freeman, Douglas Southall
  George Washington. Vol. V: Victory with the Help of France   I-205; 298
  George Washington. Vol. VII: First in Peace   I-394
Freeman, Joseph
  Dollar Diplomacy: A Study in American Imperialism. Originally published in 1926 as *American Imperialism: Viewpoints of United States Foreign Policy, 1898-1941*   III-1383
Freidel, Frank
  Franklin D. Roosevelt. Vol. II: The Ordeal   III-1477
  Franklin D. Roosevelt. Vol. III: The Triumph   III-1620
Frémont, John C.
  Memoirs of My Life   II-799
  Narratives of Exploration and Adventure   II-799
French, Allen
  First Year of the American Revolution, The   I-260
French, John C.
  History of the University Founded by Johns Hopkins, A   II-1082
Friedman, Milton
  Monetary History of the United States, 1867-1960, A   III-1437
Frink, Maurice
  When Grass Was King   II-1025
Fritz, Henry E.
  Movement for Indian Assimilation, 1860-1890, The   II-1166
Frost, Robert
  Complete Poems   III-1404
Frothingham, Octavius Brooks
  Transcendentalism in New England: A History   I-658
Fuess, Claude M.
  Carl Schurz, Reformer   II-1058; 1145
  Daniel Webster   II-805; 858
Fulton, John F.
  Centennial of Surgical Anesthesia, The   II-794
Funston, Fredrick
  Memories of Two Wars   II-1295
Furniss, Edgar S., Jr.
  NATO: A Political Appraisal   III-1810

Gabriel, Ralph H.
  Course of American Democratic Thought, The   II-1172
Galbraith, John S.
  Hudson's Bay Company as an Imperial Factor, 1821-1869, The   II-784

Gans, Herbert J.
  Levittowners: Ways of Life and Politics in a New Suburban Community, The   III-1816
Gardner, Albert Ten Eyck
  American Paintings; A Catalogue of the Collection of the Metropolitan Museum of Art   I-618
Gardner, Charles M.
  Grange, Friend of the Farmer: A Concise Reference History of America's Oldest Farm Organization, and the Only Rural Fraternity in the World, 1867-1947, The   II-1048
Gardner, Lloyd C.
  Architects of Illusion: Men and Ideas in American Foreign Policy, 1941-1949   III-1758
Garnett, James M.
  Hayne's Speech   I-665
Garraty, John A.
  Henry Cabot Lodge: A Biography   III-1489
  New Commonwealth, 1877-1890, The   II-1134; 1160
  Quarrels That Have Shaped the Constitution   I-442
Gass, Patrick
  Journal of the Voyages and Travels of a Corps of Discovery, A   I-455
Gates, Paul W.
  Farmer's Age: Agriculture, 1815-1860, The. Vol. III: *The Economic History of the United States*   I-551; II-777
  Fifty Million Acres: Conflicts Over Kansas Land Policy, 1854-1890   II-968
  Frontier Landlords and Pioneer Tenants   I-587
  Illinois Central Railroad and Its Colonization Work, The   I-630
Gatewood, Willard B., Jr.
  Theodore Roosevelt and the Art of Controversy: Episodes of the White House Years   II-1328
Gaustad, Edwin S.
  Great Awakening in New England, The   I-181
Geffen, Elizabeth M.
  Philadelphia Unitarianism, 1796-1861   I-575
Geiger, Vincent
  Trail to California: Overland Journal   II-847
Genovese, Eugene D.
  Political Economy of Slavery, The   I-376
Gephart, William F.
  Transportation and Industrial Development in the Middle West. Vol. 34: *Studies in History, Economics, and Public Law*   I-496
Gesehr, Wesley M.
  Great Awakening in Virginia, 1740-1790, The   I-181
Geyl, Pieter
  Netherlands in the Seventeenth Century, The   I-83
Ghent, William J.
  Our Benevolent Feudalism   II-1332
Gibson, Donald B.
  Fiction of Stephen Crane, The   II-1260
Gibson, George Rutledge
  Journal of a Soldier Under Kearny and Doniphan, 1846-1847   II-824
Gibson, William M.
  Mark Twain-Howells Letters: The Correspondence of Samuel L. Clemens and William Dean Howells, 1872-1910   II-1150
Giddens, Paul H.
  Early Days of Oil: A Pictorial History of the Beginnings of the Industry in Pennsylvania   II-917
Giedion, Sigfried
  Space, Time, and Architecture: The Growth of a New Tradition   II-1236
Gilman, Daniel C.
  Launching of a University and Other Papers: A Sheaf of Rememberances, The   II-1082
Gilpatrick, Delbert H.
  Jeffersonian Democracy in North Carolina, 1789-1816   I-381
Ginger, Ray
  Altgeld's America: The Lincoln Ideal vs. Changing Realities   II-1242
  Bending Cross: A Biography of Eugene Victor Debs, The   II-1242
Giovannitti, Len
  Decision to Drop the Bomb, The   III-1757
Gipson, Lawrence H.
  British Empire Before the American Revolution, The. Vol. IX: *New Responsibilities Within the Enlarged Empire, 1763-1766: The Triumphant Empire*   I-212
  British Empire Before the American Revolution, The. Vol. XI: *The Rumbling of the Coming Storm, 1766-1770: The Triumphant Empire*   I-218; 230
  Coming of the Revolution, 1763-1775, The   I-224
Girdner, Audrie
  Great Betrayal: The Evacuation of the Japanese-Americans During World War II, The   III-1708
Gish, Lillian
  Movies, Mister Griffith, and Me, The   II-1338
Gladwin, Harold S.
  Men Out of Asia   I-4
Glass, Carter
  Adventure in Constructive Finance, An   III-1437
Glasscock, C. B.
  Gasoline Age, The   III-1425
Gluck, Elsie
  John Mitchell, Miner: Labor's Bargain with the Gilded Age   II-1332

Goddard, Robert H.
  Rocket Development   III-1559
  Rockets   III-1559
Goen, Clarence C.
  Revivalism and Separatism in New England, 1740-1800: Strict Congregationalists and Separate Baptists in the Great Awakening   I-181
Goetzmann, William H.
  Army Exploration in the American West, 1803-1863   II-869
  Exploration and Empire: The Explorer and the Scientist in the Winning of the American West   II-1108
  When The Eagle Screamed: The Romantic Horizon in American Diplomacy, 1800-1860   II-784
Goldfarb, Ronald
  Ransom: A Critique of the American Bail System   III-1898
Goldman, Eric F.
  Crucial Decade and After: America, 1945-1960, The   III-1763
  Rendezvous with Destiny, A   II-1312
  Tragedy of Lyndon Johnson: A Historian's Personal Interpretation, The   III-1923
Goldwater, Barry M.
  Where I Stand   III-1923
Gompers, Samuel
  Seventy Years of Life and Labour   III-1660
Gooding, Robert E.
  Warren Court: A Critical Analysis, The   III-1887
Goodrich, Carter
  Government Promotion of Canals and Railroads, 1800-1890   I-551; II-1160
Goodrich, Leland M.
  Korea: A Study of U.S. Policy in the United Nations   III-1828
Goodrich, M.
  Charter of the United Nations: Commentary and Documents   III-1747
Goodwin, Cardinal L.
  John Charles Frémont: An Explanation of His Career   II-199
Gosnell, H. Allen
  Guns on the Western Waters: The Story of River Gunboats in the Civil War   II-961
Gosnell, Harold F.
  Champion Campaigner: Franklin D. Roosevelt   III-1613
Gottschalk, Louis
  Lafayette and the Close of the American Revolution   I-298
  Lafayette Comes to America   I-287
Gould, E. W.
  Fifty Years on the Mississippi: Or, Gould's History of River Navigation   I-475
Govan, Thomas P.
  Nicholas Biddle: Nationalist and Public Banker, 1786-1844   I-569; II-701

Graebner, Norman A.
  Cold War Diplomacy: American Foreign Policy, 1945-1960   III-1782
Graham, W. A.
  Custer Myth: A Source Book of Custeriana, The   II-1098
Gras, Norman S.
  Massachusetts First National Bank of Boston, 1784-1934, The   II-753
Gray, Lewis C.
  History of Agriculture in the Southern United States to 1860   I-375
Gray, Thomas R.
  Confessions of Nat Turner: The Leader of the Late Insurrection in Southampton, Va., The   II-689
Green, Constance M.
  Ordnance Department I: Planning Munitions for War, The, in the series: *United States Army in World War II: The Technical Services*   III-1696
Green, James A.
  William Henry Harrison, His Life and Times   I-503
Greene, Emily
  Occupied Haiti   II-1317
Greene, Theodore P.
  Roger Williams and the Massachusetts Magistrates   I-102
Greenfield, Kent R.
  American Strategy in World War II: A Reconsideration   III-1719
Greever, William S.
  Bonanza West: The Story of the Western Mining Rushes, 1848-1900, The   II-847
Gregg, Kate L.
  Road to Santa Fe, The   I-592
Gregory, Charles O.
  Labor and the Law   II-790
Gressley, Gene M.
  Bankers and Cattlemen   II-1025
Grimwood, James M.
  This New Ocean: A History of Project Mercury   III-1945
Griswold, A. Whitney
  Far Eastern Policy of the United States, The   II-1300; III-1383
Griswold, Wesley S.
  Work of Giants: Building the First Transcontinental Railroad, A   II-973
Grunder, Garel A.
  Philippines and the United States, The   II-1295
Gunderson, Robert G.
  Log Cabin Campaign, The   II-695
Gwinn, William Rea
  Uncle Joe Cannon, Archfoe of Insurgency: A History of the Rise and Fall of Cannonism   III-1393
Gwirtzman, Milton
  On His Own: Robert F. Kennedy, 1964-1968

III-1932

Haas, William H.
American Empire: A Study of the Outlying Territories of the United States, The   II-1324
Habakkuk, H. J.
American and British Technology in the Nineteenth Century: The Search for Labour-Saving Inventions   II-842
Haber, Samuel
Efficiency and Uplift: Scientific Management in the Progressive Era, 1890-1920   III-1377
Hachiya, Michihiko
Hiroshima Diary: The Journal of a Japanese Physician, August 6-September 30, 1945   III-1757
Hafen, Ann W.
Frémont's Fourth Expedition   II-800
Utah Expedition, 1857-1858, The   II-817
Hafen, LeRoy R.
Frémont's Fourth Expedition   II-800
Overland Mail, 1849-1869, The   II-928
Utah Expedition, 1857-1858, The   II-817
Hagan, William T.
American Indians. Chicago History of American Civilization series   I-388; II-1165
Haines, Charles G.
American Doctrine of Judicial Supremacy, The   I-349; 442
Role of the Supreme Court in American Government and Politics, 1789-1835, The   I-490
Hakluyt, Richard
Divers Voyages Touching the Discovery of America and the Islands Adjacent   I-27
Halberstam, David
Best and the Brightest, The   III-1911
Making of a Quagmire, The   III-1910
Hale, Dennis
New Student Left, The   III-1916
Hall, Clayton C.
Lords Baltimore and the Maryland Palatinate, The   I-119
Narratives of Early Maryland, 1633-1684   I-119
Hall, Michael G.
Edward Randolph and the American Colonies, 1676-1703   I-168
Hall, Stuart
Popular Arts: A Critical Guide to the Mass Media, The   III-1506
Halsey, William F.
Admiral Halsey's Story   III-1735
Hambro, E. I.
Charter of the United Nations: Commentary and Documents   III-1747
Hamilton, Holman
Zachary Taylor: Soldier in the White House   II-858
Hammond, John W.

Men and Volts: The Story of General Electric   II-1115
Hampton, Benjamin B.
History of the Movies, A   II-1338
Handlin, Oscar
Al Smith and His America   III-1570
Boston Immigrants: A Study in Acculturation   II-759
John Dewey's Challenge to Education: Historical Perspectives on the Cultural Context   II-1306
Uprooted, The   II-1224
Handy, Robert T.
Social Gospel in America: Gladden, Ely, and Rauschenbusch, 1870-1920, The   II-1200
Hanley, Thomas
Their Rights and Liberties: The Beginnings of Religious and Political Freedom in Maryland   I-119
Hansen, Alvin H.
Economic Policy and Full Employment   III-1775
Hansen, Chadwick
Witchcraft at Salem   I-174
Hansen, Marcus Lee
Atlantic Migration, 1607-1860: A History of the Continuing Settlement of the United States, The   II-1224
Immigrant in American History, The   II-1224
Refugees of Revolution: The German Forty Eighters in America   II-759
Hanson, Earl P.
Transformation: The Story of Modern Puerto Rico   II-1317
Harbaugh, William H.
Power and Responsibility: The Life and Times of Theodore Roosevelt   II-1328
Harbison, Winfred A.
American Constitution: Its Origins and Development, The   I-442; III-1887
Harlan, Louis R.
Booker T. Washington Papers, The   II-1253
Harlow, Alvin F.
Old Wires and New Waves: The History of the Telegraph, Telephone, and Wireless   II-747
Ringlings: Wizards of the Circus, The   II-1071
Harlow, Vincent T.
Founding of the Second British Empire, 1763-1793, The   I-305
Haroutunian, Joseph
Piety Versus Moralism: The Passing of the New England Theology   I-574
Harper, Lawrence A.
English Navigation Laws, The   I-168
Harrington, Fred Harvey
Fighting Politician, Major General N. P. Banks   II-1042

Harris, D. R.
Signal Corps: The Test, The, in the series, United States Army in World War II: The Technical Services   III-1696
Harris, Marshall D.
Origin of the Land Tenure System in the United States   I-311; 329
Harris, Seymour E.
Economic Planning: The Plans of Fourteen Countries with Analyses of the Plans   III-1775
Harrison, Gordon A.
Cross-Channel Attack   III-1724
Harrisse, Henry
John Cabot: The Discoverer of North America and Sebastian Cabot, His Son, a Chapter in Maritime History of England Under the Tudors, 1496-1557   I-27
Hart, Albert B.
Monroe Doctrine: An Interpretation, The   II-1194
Hartsough, M L.
From Canoe to Steel Barges on the Upper Mississippi   I-475
Hartz, Louis
Economic Policy and Democratic Thought: Pennsylvania, 1776-1860   I-544
Haskins, George L.
"Marshall and the Commerce Clause of the Constitution," in W. Melville Jones' Chief Justice John Marshall: A Reappraisal   I-606
Havighurst, Walter
Long Ships Passing, The   I-475
Voices on the River: The Story of the Mississippi Waterways   I-475
Hawke, David
Transaction of Freemen, A   I-266
Hayden, Ralston
Senate and Treaties, 1789-1817: The Development of the Treaty-Making Functions of the United States Senate During Their Formative Period, The   I-402
Hayes, Carlton J.
United States and Spain: An Interpretation, The   III-1666
Hazelton, John H.
Declaration of Independence: Its History, The   I-265
Hazen, Charles D.
Contemporary American Opinion of the French Revolution   I-413
Heath, M. Sydney
Constructive Liberalism: The Role of the State in Economic Development in Georgia to 1860   I-496
Hedges, James B.
Browns of Providence Plantations, The. Vol. II: The Nineteenth Century   I-366
Hedges, William L.
Washington Irving: An American Study, 1802-

1832   I-484
Hendel, Samuel
Charles Evans Hughes and the Supreme Court   III-1673
Henderson, G. F.
Stonewall Jackson and the American Civil War   II-956
Hendrick, Burton J.
Statesmen of the Lost Cause: Jefferson Davis and His Cabinet   II-945
Henry, Robert S.
Story of the Mexican War, The   II-823
Hepburn, A. Barton
History of Currency in the United States, A   II-990
Herold, Amos L.
James Kirke Paulding: Versatile American   I-484
Hersey, John R.
Hiroshima   III-1757
Herskovits, Melville J.
Myth of the Negro Past, The   I-73
Hess, Stephen
Nixon: A Political Portrait   III-1876; 1939
Hesseltine, William B.
Three Against Lincoln: Murat Halstead Reports the Caucuses of 1860   II-940
Trimmers, Trucklers, and Temporizers: Notes of Murat Halstead from the Political Conventions of 1856   II-882
Hewlett, Richard G.
New World, 1939-1946: A History of the United States Atomic Energy Commission, The   III-1758
Heyerdahl, Thor
Kon-Tiki   I-4
Hibbard, Benjamin H.
History of the Public Land Policies, A   I-311; II-776; 968
Hibben, Paxton
Peerless Leader: William Jennings Bryan, The   III-1554
Hicks, John D.
Republican Ascendancy, 1921-1933   III-1581
Hidy, Ralph W.
House of Baring in American Trade and Finance: English Merchant Bankers at Work, 1763-1861, The   I-375
Higginbotham, Don
Daniel Morgan: Revolutionary Rifleman   I-281
Higham, John
History: The Development of Historical Studies in the United States   III-1431
Strangers in the Land: Patterns of American Nativism, 1860-1925   II-1126; 1224
Hill, Hamlin
Art of Huckleberry Finn: Text, Sources, Criticism, The   II-1151
Hill, Harold

Roosevelt and the Caribbean   II-1345
Hilsman, Roger
  *To Move a Nation: The Politics of Foreign
  Policy in the Administration of John F.
  Kennedy*   III-1892
Hindle, Brooke
  *Pursuit of Science in Revolutionary America,
  1735-1789, The*   I-199
Hine, Robert V.
  Edward Kern and American Expansion
  II-870
Hinton, Richard J.
  *John Brown and His Men: With Some Account
  of the Roads They Traveled to Reach Harp-
  ers Ferry*   II-924
Hipsher, Edward E.
  American Opera and Its Composers   II-
  1138
Hockett, Homer C.
  Constitutional History of the United States, The
  I-334; 460
Hodgson, Godfrey
  *American Melodrama: The Presidential Cam-
  paign of 1968, The*   III-1939
Hoffman, Daniel G.
  Poetry of Stephen Crane, The   II-1260
Hofstadter, Richard
  Age of Reform: From Bryan to F. D. R., The
  II-1312
  *American Political Tradition: And the Men
  Who Made It, The*   ·II-1272
  "Andrew Jackson and the Rise of Liberal
  Capitalism" in *The American Political Tra-
  dition and the Men Who Made It*   I-635
  *Development of Academic Freedom in the
  United States, The*   I-316
  "Free Silver and the Mind of 'Coin' Harvey,"
  in *The Paranoid Style in American Politics
  and Other Essays*   II-1088
  *Progressive Historians: Turner, Beard, Parring-
  ton, The*   II-1218; III-1431
  "Pseudo-Conservatism Revisited-1965," in
  *The Paranoid Style in American Politics and
  Other Essays*   III-1864
  Social Darwinism in American Thought
  II-1172; III-1362
Holdsworth, John T.
  *First and Second Banks of the United States,
  The*   I-544
Hollingsworth, J. Rogers
  *Whirligig of Politics: The Democracy of Cleve-
  land and Bryan, The*   II-1272
Holmes, Maurice G.
  *From New Spain by Sea to the Californias,
  1519-1668*   I-276
Hoopes, Roy
  Complete Peace Corps Guide, The   III-
  1882
Hoover, Herbert
  *Addresses upon the American Road by Herbert
  Hoover, 1933-1938*   III-1598

Memoirs of Herbert Hoover, The. Vol. III: *The
  Great Depression, 1929-1941*   III-1613
Hopkins, Harry L.
  Spending to Save: The Complete Story of Relief
  III-1636
Horn, Stanley F.
  Decisive Battle of Nashville, The   II-1013
Hornberger, Theodore
  Benjamin Franklin   I-240
Horsman, Reginald
  Causes of the War of 1812, The   I-510
  *Frontier in the Formative Years, 1783-1815,
  The. Histories of the American Frontier* se-
  ries   I-388
  War of 1812, The   I-520; 526
Horton, Bayard T.
  "Editorials," in *Minnesota Medicine*   II-
  1183
House Executive Document, 33rd Congress
  *Reports of Explorations and Surveys to Ascer-
  tain the Most Practical and Economical
  Route for a Railroad from the Mississippi
  River to the Pacific Ocean, 1853-1854*
  II-869
Howard, John T.
  Short History of Music in America, A   II-
  1138
Howard, Robert W.
  *Great Iron Trail: The Story of the First Trans-
  Continental Railroad, The*   II-973
Howe, George F.
  *Northwest Africa: Seizing the Initiative in the
  West*   III-1719
Howe, Irving
  American Communist Party, The   III-1821
  UAW and Walter Reuther, The   III-1660
Howe, Mark De Wolfe
  *Garden and the Wilderness: Religion and Gov-
  ernment in American Constitutional History,
  The*   I-323
  Life and Letters of George Bancroft, The
  II-735
Howe, Octavius T.
  American Clipper Ships, 1833-1858   II-811
Howley, Frank L.
  Berlin Command   III-1799
Hoyt, Edwin P., Jr.
  *Jumbos and Jackasses: A Popular History of
  the Political Wars*   II-1145
Hughes, Langston
  Fight for Freedom: The Story of the NAACP
  III-1389
Hume, Robert A.
  *Runaway Star: An Appreciation of Henry
  Adams*   II-1189
Humphrey, Edward F.
  *Nationalism and Religion in America, 1774-
  1789*   I-322
Hunter, Sam
  Modern American Painting and Sculpture
  III-1414

Hunting, Warren B.
Obligation of Contracts Clause of the United States Constitution, The   I-490
Huntington, C. C.
History of the Ohio Canals: Their Construction, Cost, Use, and Partial Abandonment   I-550
Huntington, Samuel P.
Soldier and the State: The Theory and Politics of Civil Military Relations, The   III-1810
Hutchinson, William T.
Lowden of Illinois   III-1477
Hyman, Harold M.
Edwin M. Stanton: The Life and Times of Lincoln's Secretary of War   II-1018; 1030
Hyneman, Charles S.
First American Neutrality: A Study of the American Understanding of Neutral Obligations During the Years, 1792-1815, The   I-413

Ickes, Harold L.
Secret Diary of Harold L. Ickes, The   III-1636
Ingersoll, Ralph
Top Secret   III-1724
Iriye, Akira
After Imperialism: The Search for a New Order in the Far East, 1921-1931   III-1603
Isely, Jeter Allen
Horace Greeley and the Republican Party, 1853-1861: A Study of the New York Tribune   II-882; 904
U. S. Marines and Amphibious War: Its Theory and Its Practice in the Pacific, The   III-1714

Jackson, David K.
"Estimate of the Influence of 'The Southern Literary Messenger' 1834-1864, An," in The (revived) *Southern Literary Messenger*   II-728
"Poe and the 'Messenger,' " in The (revived) *Southern Literary Messenger*   II-728
Poe and The Southern Literary Messenger   II-728
Jackson, Joseph H.
Anybody's Gold: The Story of California's Mining Towns   II-847
Jackson, Sidney L.
America's Struggle for Free Schools: Social Tension and Education in New England and New York, 1827-1842   I-581
Jackson, W. Turrentine
Wagon Roads West: A Study of Federal Road Surveys and Construction in the Trans-Mississippi West, 1846-1869   II-869
When Grass Was King   II-1025
Jacob, P. E.
Conscription of Conscience: The American State and the Conscientious Objector, 1940-1947   III-1708
Jacobs, David
Bridges, Canals, and Tunnels   II-1065
Jacobs, James R.
Beginning of the United States Army, 1783-1812, The   I-388; 436
Tarnished Warrior: Major-General James Wilkinson   I-402
Jacobs, Lewis
Rise of the American Film, The   II-1338
Jacobs, Paul
New Radicals: A Report with Documents, The   III-1864
Jacobs, Wilbur R.
Wilderness Politics and Indian Gifts: The Northern Colonial Frontier, 1748-1763   I-531
Jacobson, David L.
John Dickinson and the Revolution in Pennsylvania, 1764-1776   I-230
Jacoby, Annalee
Thunder Out of China   III-1769
Jaffa, Harry V.
In the Name of the People: Speeches and Writings of Lincoln and Douglas in the Ohio Campaign of 1859   II-911
James, Edmund J.
"Origins of the Land-Grant Act of 1862 (The So-Called Morrill Act) and Some Account of Its Author, Jonathan B. Turner, The," in The University Studies. Vol. IV, No. 1   II-979
James, James A.
Life of George Rogers Clark, The   I-329
"Louisiana as a Factor in American Diplomacy, 1795-1800," in Mississippi Valley Historical Review   I-449
James, Marquis
Andrew Jackson: The Border Captain   I-538
Andrew Jackson: Portrait of a President   II-707
Raven: A Biography of Sam Houston, The   II-741
Jameson, J. Franklin
American Revolution Considered as a Social Movement, The   I-293
Janeway, Eliot
Struggle for Survival, The   III-1685
Jellison, Charles A.
Fessenden of Maine: Civil War Senator   II-1030
Jencks, Christopher
Inequality: A Reassessment of the Effect of Family and Schooling in Ameria   III-1870
Jenks, Leland H.
Migration of British Capital to 1875, The   I-544
Jensen, Arthur L.
Maritime Commerce of Colonial Philadelphia,

AMERICAN

Literature for Additional Recommended Reading

The I-245
Jensen, Merrill
Articles of Confederation: An Interpretation of the Social-Constitutional History of the American Revolution, 1774-1781, The I-260
Making of the American Constitution, The I-334; 370
Johannsen, Robert W.
In the Name of the People: Speeches and Writings of Lincoln and Douglas in the Ohio Campaign of 1859 II-911
Letters of Stephen Arnold Douglas, The II-911; 940
Stephen A. Douglas II-876; 911
Johnson, Charles W.
Proceedings of the First Three Republican National Conventions, 1856, 1860, and 1864 II-883
Johnson, Donald
Challenge to American Freedoms: World War I and the Rise of the American Civil Liberties Union, The III-1459; 1496
Johnson, Huge S.
Blue Eagle from Egg to Earth, The III-1620
Johnson, James W.
Black Manhattan III-1449
Johnson, Paul B.
Land Fit for Heroes: The Planning of British Reconstruction, 1916-1919 III-1483
Johnson, Samuel A.
Battle Cry of Freedom: The New England Emigrant Aid Company in the Kansas Crusade, The II-894
Johnson, Walter
Battle Against Isolation, The III-1691
How We Drafted Adlai Stevenson III-1848
Johnston, Abraham R.
Marching with the Army of the West, 1846-1848 II-824
Johnston, Henry P.
Yorktown Campaign and the Surrender of Cornwallis, 1781, The I-298
Johnston, Robert M.
Bull Run, Its Strategy and Tactics II-956
Johnston, William D.
History of the Library of Congress II-1283
Jones, Archer
Confederate Strategy from Shiloh to Vicksburg II-1001
Jones, Gwyn
Norse Atlantic Saga: Being the Norse Voyages of Discovery and Settlement to Iceland, Greenland, America, The I-16
Jones, Maldwyn Allen
American Immigration II-759; 1126
Jones, Mary J.
Congregational Commonwealth, 1636-1662 I-96
Jones, Stanley L.

Presidential Election of 1896, The II-1272
Jones, Virgil C.
Civil War at Sea, The I-271; II-961
Jones, Wilbur D.
Lord Aberdeen and the Americas II-805
Jordy, William H.
Henry Adams: Scientific Historian II-1189
Jorgenson, Chester E.
Uncle Tom's Cabin as Book and Legend II-863
Josephson, Matthew
Life Among the Surrealists III-1565
Politicos, 1865-1896, The II-1145
Journal of the American Medical Association. Vol. 158 (August 6, 1955) III-1842
Juergens, George
Joseph Pulitzer and the New York World II-1247
Jungk, Robert
Brighter Than a Thousand Suns: A Personal History of the Atomic Scientists III-1757

Kaplan, Justin
Mister Clemens and Mark Twain II-1150
Kaplan, Lawrence S.
Colonies into Nation: American Diplomacy, 1763-1801. American Diplomatic History series I-407
Kauper, Paul G.
"Segregation in Public Education: The Decline of *Plessy* v. *Ferguson,*" in *Michigan Law Review* II-1266
Keats, John
Crack in the Picture Window, The III-1816
Kegley, Charles W.
Charles W. Reinhold Niebuhr: His Religious, Social, and Political Thought III-1608
Kelley, Oliver H.
Origin and Progress of the Order of the Patrons of Husbandry in the United States: A History from 1866 to 1873 II-1047
Kellogg, Louise P.
French Regime in Wisconsin and the Northwest, The I-149
Kelly, Alfred H.
American Constitution: Its Origins and Development, The I-442; III-1887
Kelly, Emmett
Clown II-1071
Kelly, F. Beverly
Clown II-1071
Kelly, Fred C.
Miracle at Kitty Hawk: The Letters of Wilbur and Orville Wright II-1351
Kendall, Amos
Autobiography II-934
Kendrick, Benjamin B.
Journal of the Joint Committee of Fifteen on Reconstruction, The II-1053
Keniston, Kenneth

Young Radicals: Notes on Committed Youth III-1917

Kennan, George F.
Russia, the Atom, and the West III-1810

Kenney, William
Crucial Years, 1940-1945, The III-1708

Kenworthy, E. W.
Pentagon Papers as Published by the New York Times, *The* III-1911

Kenyon, Cecelia M.
Antifederalists, The I-339

Kern, Alexander
"Rise of Transcendentalism, 1815-1860, The," in Harry Hayden Clark's, *Transitions in American Literary History* I-659

Kessler, Henry H.
Peter Stuyvesant and His New York I-84

Ketcham, Ralph L.
Benjamin Franklin I-240

Keynes, John Maynard
Economic Consequences of the Peace, The III-1489

Kimmel, Husband E.
Admiral Kimmel's Story III-1702

Kinley, David
History, Organization, and Influence of the Independent Treasury of the United States, The II-753
Independent Treasury of the United States and Its Relations to the Banks of the Country, The II-753

Kinney, J. P.
Continent Lost—a Civilization Won: Indian Land Tenure in America, A II-1166

King, Martin Luther, Jr.
Stride Toward Freedom: The Montgomery Story III-1860

Kirkland, Edward C.
Industry Comes of Age: Business, Labor, and Public Policy, 1860-1897 II-1122
Men, Cities and Transportation: A Study in New England History, 1820-1900 I-629

Klinck, Carl F.
Tecumseh, Fact and Fiction in Early Records I-503

Knebel, Fletcher
No High Ground: The Story of the Atomic Bomb in World War II III-1757

Knight, Arthur
Liveliest Art: A Panoramic History of the Movies, The II-1338

Knight, Edgar W.
Education in the United States I-108

Knight, Thomas S.
Charles Peirce III-1368

Knoles, George H.
Presidential Campaign and Election of 1892, The II-1230

Knollenberg, Bernhard
Origins of the American Revolution, 1759-1766 I-212; 235

Washington and the Revolution, a Reappraisal: Gates, Conway and the Continental Congress I-260

Knox, John Jay
History of Banking in the United States, A II-753

Kobre, Sidney
Development of the Colonial Newspaper, The I-192

Koch, Adrienne
Philosophy of Thomas Jefferson, The I-199

Koch, G. Alfred
Republican Religion: The American Revolution and the Cult of Reason. Reprinted in 1968 by Thomas Y. Crowell, as *Religion of the American Enlightenment* I-199

Koch, Thilo
Fighters for a New World III-1932

Kolko, Gabriel
Politics of War: The World and United States Foreign Policy, 1943-1945, The III-1740
Triumph of Conservatism: A Reinterpretation of American History, 1900-1916, The II-1328

Konefsky, Samuel J.
Legacy of Holmes and Brandeis: A Study in the Influence of Ideas, The III-1373

Kraditor, Aileen S.
Ideas of the Woman Suffrage Movement, 1890-1920, The III-1518

Kranzberg, Melvin
Technology in Western Civilization. Vol. I: *The Emergence of Modern Industrial Society: Earliest Times to 1900* II-747; 842; 1115

Kraus, Michael
Atlantic Civilization: Eighteenth Century Origins, The I-119
Writing of American History, The II-1189

Krehbiel, Henry E.
Chapters of Opera II-1138
More Chapters of Opera II-1138

Kreiger, Alex D.
"Early Man in the New World," in Jennings' and Norbecks' *Prehistoric Man in the New World* I-4

Kroeber, Clifton B.
Frontier in Perspective, The II-1217

Krooss, Herman E.
Financial History of the United States II-1088

Krout, John A.
Completion of Independence, 1790-1830, The I-641
Origins of Prohibition, The I-647

Kursh, Harry
United States Office of Education: A Century of Service, The II-1035

LaFargue, André
"Louisiana Purchase: The French Viewpoint, The," in *Louisiana Historical Quarterly*

I-449
La Feber, Walter
America, Russia, and the Cold War, 1945-1971
III-1758; 1799; 1864
John Quincy Adams and American Continental Empire: Letters, Papers, and Speeches
I-598
New Empire: An Interpretation of American Expansion, 1860-1898, The II-1205; 1289; 1300
La Follette, Belle Case
Robert M. La Follette: June 14, 1855 to June 18, 1925 III-1393
La Follette, Fola
Robert M. La Follette: June 14, 1855 to June 18, 1925 III-1393
La Follette, Robert M.
Autobiography II-1312
Landau, Saul
New Radicals: A Report with Documents, The III-1864
Lane, Frederick
Ships for Victory III-1685
Lane, Mark
Rush to Judgment: A Critique of the Warren Commission Inquiry into the Murders of President John F. Kennedy, Officer J. D. Tippit, and Lee Harvey Oswald III-1905
Langdon, George D., Jr.
Pilgrim Colony: A History of New Plymouth, 1620-1691, The I-79
Langer, William L.
Our Vichy Gamble III-1719
Larkin, John D.
President's Control of the Tariff, The. Harvard Political Science series II-1278
Larkin, Oliver W.
Art and Life in America I-618; III-1414
Larner, Jeremy
Nobody Knows: Reflections on the McCarthy Campaign of 1968 III-1939
Larsen, Lawrence H.
Urban Crisis in Modern America III-1816
Latane, John H.
America as a World Power, 1897-1907. Vol. 25: The American Nation: A History II-1324
Latham, Earl
Communist Controversy in Washington: From the New Deal to McCarthy, The III-1822
Lattimore, Owen
Ordeal by Slander III-1822
Laughlin, J. Laurence
Federal Reserve Act: Its Origins and Problems, The III-437
History of Bimetallism in the United States, The II-1088
Lazarsfeld, Paul
Voting: A Study of Opinion Formation in a Presidential Campaign III-1805

Leach, Douglas E.
Northern Colonial Frontier, 1607-1763, The I-206
Leckie, Robert
Conflict: The History of the Korean War III-1828
Lee, Gordon C.
Struggle for Federal Aid, First Phase: A History of the Attempts to Obtain Federal Aid for the Common Schools, 1870-1890, The II-1035
Lee, James Melvin
History of American Journalism II-718
Leech, Margaret K.
In the Days of McKinley II-1272
Leigh, Robert D.
Federal Health Administration in the United States III-1398
Lemmon, Sarah M.
"Transportation Segregation in the Federal Courts Since 1865," in Journal of Negro History II-1267
Leopold, Richard W.
Robert Dale Owen: A Biography I-516
Leuchtenburg, William E.
Franklin D. Roosevelt and the New Deal, 1932-1940 III-1620
Perils of Prosperity, 1914-1932, The. Chicago History of American Civilization series III-1548; 1581
Levin, David D.
History as Romantic Art: Bancroft, Prescott, Motley, and Parkman II-735
What Happened in Salem? I-175
Levin, N. Gordon, Jr.
Woodrow Wilson and World Politics: America's Response to War and Revolution III-1410; 1453
Levine, Don I.
Mitchell, Pioneer of Air Power II-1351
Levitt, Leonard
African Season, An III-1882
Levy, Leonard W.
Freedom of Speech and Press in Early American History: Legacy of Suppression I-192; 419
Jefferson and Civil Liberties: The Darker Side I-419
Lewis, Archibald R.
New World Looks at Its History, The II-1217
Lewis, Lloyd
Sherman, Fighting Prophet II-1013
Lewis, Oscar
Big Four: The Story of Huntington, Stanford, Hopkins and Crocker, and of the Building of the Central Pacific, The II-973
Lewis, Richard W.
American Adam: Innocence, Tragedy, and Tradition in the Nineteenth Century, The II-853

Lewis, W. David
From Newgate to Dannemora: The Rise of the Penitentiary in New York, 1796-1848 I-647
Lewitt, Richard
George W. Norris: The Making of a Progressive, 1861-1912 III-1393
Ley, Willy
Rockets, Missiles and Men in Space III-1945
Liddell Hart, B. H.
Real War, 1914-1918, The III-1471
Lie, Trygve
In the Cause of Peace III-1747
Lief, Alfred
Brandeis: The Personal History of an American Ideal III-1373
Lieuwen, Edwin
U. S. Policy in Latin America: A Short History, The III-1793
Lindsay, Vachel
Selected Poems III-1404
Lindsey, Lamont
Pullman Strike: The Story of a Unique Experiment and of a Great Labor Upheaval, The II-1156
Link, Arthur S.
Wilson: Campaigns for Progressivism and Peace, 1916-1917 III-1409
Wilson: Confusions and Crises, 1915-1916 III-1410; 1442
Wilson the Diplomatist: A Look at His Major Foreign Policies III-1409; 1489
Wilson: The New Freedom III-1437
Wilson: The Struggle for Neutrality, 1914-1915 III-1410
Lively, Jack
Social and Political Thought of Alexis de Tocqueville, The II-678
Livezey, William E.
Philippines and the United States, The II-1295
Lockwood, George B.
New Harmony Movement, The I-516
Lodge, Henry Cabot
Works of Alexander Hamilton, The I-361
Loftis, Anne
Great Betrayal: The Evacuation of the Japanese-Americans During World War II, The II-1708
Logan, Rayford W.
Betrayal of the Negro: From Rutherford B. Hayes to Woodrow Wilson, The III-1389
Long, Orie W.
Literary Pioneers I-484
Lora, Ronald G.
Conservative Minds in America. Rand McNally Series on the History of American Thought and Culture III-1864
Lord, Walter

Day of Infamy III-1702
Time to Stand, A II-740
Lorwin, Lewis L.
American Federation of Labor: History, Policies, and Prospects, The II-1156
Lossing, Benson J.
Harper's Encyclopaedia of United States History II-1283
Loth, David G.
Chief Justice: John Marshall and the Growth of the Republic I-606
Lowery, Woodbury
Spanish Settlements Within the Present Limits of the United States: Florida, 1562-1574, The I-38
Lowitt, Richard
George W. Norris: The Persistence of a Progressive, 1913-1933 III-1393; 1626
Lubell, Samuel
Future of American Politics, The III-1570; 1763; 1805; 1848
Ludovici, Laurence J.
Cone of Oblivion: A Vendetta in Science II-794
Lukacs, John A.
New History of the Cold War, A III-1782
Lundberg, Ferdinand
Imperial Hearst: A Social Biography II-1247
Luthin, Reinhard H.
First Lincoln Campaign, The II-882
Lutz, Alma
Susan B. Anthony: Rebel, Crusader, Humanitarian III-1518
Luvaas, Jay
Military Legacy of the Civil War, The II-1013
Lynd, Helen M.
Middletown in Transition: A Study in Cultural Conflicts III-1636
Lynd, Robert S.
Middletown in Transition: A Study in Cultural Conflicts III-1636
Lyon, Peter
"Isaac Singer and His Wonderful Sewing Machine," in *American Heritage* II-842
Success Story: The Life and Times of S. S. McClure III-1356
Lyons, Eugene
Our Unknown Ex-President: A Portrait of Herbert Hoover III-1597
Lyons, Gene M.
America: Purpose and Power III-1788
Lyons, Norbert
McCormick Reaper Legend: The True Story of a Great Invention, The II-684

Mabee, Carlton
American Leonardo: A Life of Samuel F. B. Morse, The II-934
MacArthur, General Douglas

AMERICAN

Literature for Additional Recommended Reading

Reminiscences   I-436

McCary, Ben C.
Indians in Seventeenth-Century Virginia
I-64

Macgowan, Kenneth
Behind the Screen: The History and Techniques of the Motion Picture   III-1506

Mackesy, Piers G.
War for America, 1775-1783, The   I-281;
299

MacLaurin, John
United Nations and Power Politics, The
III-1747

Maclaurin, W. Rupert
Invention and Innovation in the Radio Industry: Massachusetts Institute of Technology Studies of Innovation   III-1678

Maclay, William
Journal of William Maclay: United States Senator from Pennsylvania, 1789-1791
I-361

McClelland, C. P.
History of the Ohio Canals: Their Construction, Cost, Use, and Partial Abandonment   I-550

MacCloskey, Monro
Our National Attic   II-836

McCloskey, Robert G.
American Supreme Court, The   I-349; 442

McCluskey, Neil G.
Catholic Viewpoint in Education   III-1730

McConnell, Roland C.
Negro Troops of Antebellum Louisiana: A History of the Battalion of Free Men of Color
I-538

McCormac, Eugene I.
James K. Polk: A Political Biography   II-783

McCormick, Cyrus
Century of the Reaper, The   II-684

McCormick, Richard P.
Second American Party System: Party Formation in the Jacksonian Era, The   I-355;
II-765

McCoubrey, John W.
American Tradition in Painting   I-618

McCoy, Donald R.
Calvin Coolidge: The Quiet President   III-1530

McCrocklin, James H.
Garde D'Haiti, 1915-1934: Twenty Years of Organization and Training by the United States Marine Corps   II-1317

McCulloch, Hugh
Men and Measures of Half a Century   II-989

McDonald, Forrest
Insull   II-1115

McEvoy, James
Black Power and the Student Rebellion: Conflict on the American Campus   III-1917

McFarland, Marvin W.
Papers of Wilbur and Orville Wright, Including the Chanute-Wright Letters and Other Papers of Octave Chanute, The   II-1351

McGann, Thomas F.
New World Looks at Its History, The   II-1217

McGinniss, Joe
Selling of the President, 1968, The   III-1939

McGrane, Reginald C.
Panic of 1837: Some Financial Problems of the Jacksonian Era, The   II-701

McKay, Claude
Harlem: Negro Metropolis   III-1449

McKay, Richard C.
Some Famous Sailing Ships and Their Builder, Donald McKay   II-811

McKay, Robert B.
Reapportionment: The Law and Politics of Equal Representation   III-1887

McKitrick, Eric L.
Andrew Johnson and Reconstruction   II-1109
Slavery Defended: The Views of the Old South
I-653

McLaughlin, Andrew C.
Constitutional History of the United States, A
I-442

McLoughlin, William G., Jr.
Modern Revivalism: Charles Grandison Finney to Billy Graham   I-425

McLuhan, Marshall
Understanding Media: The Extensions of Man
III-1679

McMaster, John B.
Daniel Webster   I-665
History of the People of the United States, from the Revolution to the Civil War, A   II-771

McMurry, Donald L.
Great Burlington Strike of 1888: A Case Study in Labor Relations, The   II-1156

McPhee, William N.
Voting: A Study of Opinion Formation in a Presidential Campaign   III-1805

McPherson, James M.
Struggle for Equality: Abolitionists and the Negro in the Civil War and Reconstruction, The
II-984

McPherson, Robert G.
Journal of the Earl of Egmont: Abstract of the Trustees Proceedings for Establishing the Colony of Georgia, 1732-1738, The   I-186

Madden, Edward H.
Chauncey Wright and the Foundations of Pragmatism   III-1367

Maddox, William A.
Free School Idea in Virginia Before the Civil War: A Phase of Political and Social Evolution, The   I-581

1667

Magill, Frank N.
Cyclopedia of World Authors   II-853; III-1404
Magnusson, Magnus
Vinland Sagas: The Norse Discovery of America, The   I-16
Magoffin, Susan S.
Down the Santa Fe Trail and into Mexico: The Diary of Susan Shelby Magoffin, 1846-1847   I-592
Mahan, Alfred T.
Sea Power and Its Relations to the War of 1812   I-510
Maher, Marty
Bringing Up the Brass: My 55 Years at West Point   I-436
Mahon, John K.
War of 1812, The   I-510
Main, Jackson T.
Social Structure of Revolutionary America, The   I-293
Malone, Dumas
Jefferson and the Ordeal of Liberty   I-419
Malone, Joseph J.
Pine Trees and Politics: The Naval Stores and Forest Policy in Colonial New England   I-224
Mandel, Bernard
Samuel Gompers: A Biography   II-1156
Mandelbaum, Seymour J.
Boss Tweed's New York   II-1059
Manfield, Harvey
Short History of the O. P. A., A   III-1763
Mannix, Daniel P.
Black Cargoes: A History of the Atlantic Slave Trade, 1518-1865   I-73
Mardock, Robert Winston
Reformers and the American Indian, The   II-1165
Marnell, William H.
Man-Made Morals: Four Philosophies That Shaped America   III-1368
Marquis, Samuel S.
Henry Ford: An Interpretation   III-1425
Marshall, Samuel L.
Night Drop: The American Airborne Invasion of Normandy   III-1724
Marti, Werner H.
Messenger of Destiny: The California Adventures, 1846-1847, of Archibald H. Gillespie, U. S. Marine Corps   II-824
Martin, John Barlow
Deep South Says Never, The   III-1853
Martin, Paul S.
Indians Before Columbus: Twenty Thousand Years of North American History Revealed by Archaeology   I-4
Marx, Leo
Machine in the Garden: Technology and the Pastoral Ideal in America, The   II-853; 1151

Masland, John W.
Soldiers and Scholars: Military Education and National Policy   I-436
Mason, Alpheus Thomas
Brandeis: Lawyer and Judge in the Modern State   III-1373
Harlan Fiske Stone: Pillar of the Law   III-1673
Masters, Edgar Lee
Spoon River Anthology   III-1404
Mathews, Lois K.
Expansion of New England: The Spread of New England Settlements and Institutions to the Mississippi River, 1620-1865, The   I-532
Matthews Frederick C.
American Clipper Ships, 1833-1858   II-811
Matthiessen, Francis O.
American Renaissance: Art and Expression in the Age of Emerson and Whitman   I-658
Oxford Book of American Verse, The   III-1404
Maxson, Charles H.
Great Awakening in the Middle Colonies, The   I-180
May, Earl C.
Circus from Rome to Ringling, The   II-1071
May, Ernest R.
Imperial Democracy: The Emergence of America as a Great Power   II-1289
May, Henry F.
Protestant Churches and Industrial America   II-1176
May, Roland W.
McCarthy: The Man, the Senator, the "Ism"   III-1821
Mayer, Arno J.
Political Origins of the New Diplomacy, 1917-1918   III-1453
Politics and Diplomacy of Peacemaking: Containment and Counterrevolution at Versailles, 1918-1919, The   III-1490
Mayer, George H.
Republican Party, 1854-1966, The   II-1058
Mayer, J. P.
Alexis de Tocqueville: A Biographical Study in Political Science   II-678
Mazlish, Bruce
In Search of Nixon: A Psychological Inquiry   III-1939
Mazo, Earl
Nixon: A Political Portrait   III-1876; 1939
Meier, August
Black Nationalism in America   III-1449
Negro Thought in America, 1880-1915: Racial Ideologies in the Age of Booker T. Washington   III-1389
Meigs, Cornelia L.
Violent Men: A Study of Human Relations in the First American Congress, The   I-250
Mencken, Henry L.

Making a President   III-1614

Mereness, Newton D.
Maryland as a Proprietary Province   I-119

Meriwether, James B.
"Introduction for *The Sound and the Fury,* An" in *Southern Review*   III-1576

Meriwether, Robert L.
Expansion of South Carolina, 1729-1765, The I-218

Merk, Frederick
Monroe Doctrine and American Expansionism, 1843-1849, The   II-830

Merk, Lois Bannister
Monroe Doctrine and American Expansionism, 1843-1849, The   II-830

Merz, Charles
Dry Decade, The   III-1512

Metzger, Walter P.
Development of Academic Freedom in the United States, The   I-316

Merrill, Horace S.
Republican Command, 1897-1913, The   II-1328

Merrill, Marion G.
Republican Command, 1897-1913, The   II-1328

Meyer, Balthaser H.
History of Transportation in the United States Before 1860   I-550

Meyer, Jacob C.
Church and State in Massachusetts from 1740 to 1833: A Chapter in the History of the Development of Individual Freedom   I-323

Meyer, Marvin C.
Jacksonian Persuasion: Politics and Belief, The II-701

Meyers, William Starr
State Papers and Other Public Writings of Herbert Hoover, The   III-1597

Michael, Paul
American Movies Reference Book: The Sound Era, The   II-1338

Miller, Abraham
Black Power and the Student Rebellion: Conflict on the American Campus   III-1917

Miller, Howard S.
Dollars for Research: Science and Its Patrons in Nineteenth-Century America   II-836

Miller, John C.
Alexander Hamilton and the Growth of the New Nation. Originally published as *Alexander Hamilton, Portrait in Paradox*   I-340; 361; 407
Federalist Era, 1789-1801, The   I-361
Sam Adams: Pioneer in Propaganda   I-235

Miller, Loren
Petitioners: The Story of the Negro and the United States Supreme Court, The   III-1853

Miller, Perry
Errand into the Wilderness   I-89; 131; 181

New England Mind, The. Vol. I: *The Seventeenth Century*   I-89
New England Mind, The. Vol. II: *From Colony to Province*   I-168; 175
Orthodoxy in Massachusetts, 1630-1650 I-89
Roger Williams: His Contribution to the American Tradition   I-101
Transcendentalists: An Anthology, The   I-659

Miller, Richard H.
American Imperialism in 1898: The Quest for National Fulfillment   II-1289

Miller, William
Age of Enterprise: A Social History of Industrial America, The   II-1122; 1172

Miller, William Lee
"Rise of Neo-Orthodoxy, The," in *Paths of American Thought*   III-1608

Millgate, Michael
Achievement of William Faulkner, The III-1576

Millis, Harry A.
From the Wagner Act to Taft-Hartley: A Study of National Labor Policy and Labor Relations   III-1642; 1763

Millis, Walter
Martial Spirit: A Study of Our War with Spain, The   II-1247; 1295
This Is Pearl: The United States and Japan III-1702

Mills, C. Wright
New Men of Power, The   III-1660

Milton, George Fort
Eve of Conflict: Stephen A. Douglas and the Needless War, The   II-876

Mims, Edwin
"Southern Magazines," in *The South in the Building of the Nation*   II-729

Minnigerode, Meade
Aaron Burr   I-466

Minott, Rodney G.
Fortress That Never Was: The Myth of Hitler's Bavarian Stronghold, The   III-1752

Mirsky, Jeannette
Westward Crossings, The   I-455

Mitchell, Broadus
Depression Decade, 1929-1941   III-1581; 1642

Mitchell, Stewart
Horatio Seymour of New York   II-996

Mitchell, Wesley C.
History of the Greenbacks with Special Reference to the Economic Consequences of Their Issue, 1862-1865, A   II-989

Mizener, Arthur
Far Side of Paradise: A Biography of F. Scott Fitzgerald, The   III-1565

Mock, James R.
Report on Demobilization   III-1483

Moley, Raymond

After Seven Years   III-1614

Monaghan, Jay
Custer: The Life of General George Armstrong Custer   II-1098

Montross, Lynn
Reluctant Rebels: The Story of the Continental Congress, 1774-1789, The   I-260

Moore, Albert B.
Conscription and Conflict in the Confederacy   II-996

Moore, Edward Carter
American Pragmatism: Peirce, James, and Dewey   III-1367
William James   III-1368

Moorhead, Max L.
New Mexico's Royal Road: Trade and Travel on the Chihuahua Trail   I-592

Morgan, Dale L.
Overland Diary of James A. Pritchard, The   II-847

Morgan, Edmund S.
Roger Williams: The Church and the State   I-102

Morgan, H. Wayne
America's Road to Empire: The War with Spain and Overseas Expansion   II-1295

Morgan, Robert J.
Whig Embattled: The Presidency of John Tyler, A   II-771

Morison, Elting E.
Admiral Sims and the Modern American Navy   III-1471
Letters of Theodore Roosevelt, The   II-1328
Turmoil and Tradition: A Study of the Life and Times of Henry L. Stimson   III-1603

Morison, Samuel Eliot
Builders of the Bay Colony   I-131
European Discovery of America: The Northern Voyages, A. D. 500-1600, The   I-16; 32
"Harvard's Past" in By Land and By Sea   I-108
Operations in North African Waters, October 1942-June 1943. Vol. II: *The History of the United States Naval Operations in World War II*   III-1719
"Pilgrim Fathers: Their Significance in History, The," in By Land and By Sea   I-79
Samuel De Champlain: Father of New France   I-58
Three Centuries of Harvard, 1636-1936   I-108

Morley, Sylvanus G.
Ancient Maya, The   I-10

Morray, Joseph P.
From Yalta to Disarmament: Cold War Debate   III-1782

Morris, Lloyd R.
Ceiling Unlimited: The Story of American Aviation from Kitty Hawk to Supersonics   III-1351
Not So Long Ago   III-1524

Morris, Richard B.
American Revolution Reconsidered, The   I-287

Morrison, Robert
Contemporary University: U. S. A., The   III-1917

Morrow, Ralph E.
"Proslavery Argument Revisited, The," in Mississippi Valley Historical Review   I-653

Morse, Edward Lind
Samuel F. B. Morse, His Letters and Journals   II-899

Morse, John T., Jr.
John Sherman   II-1212

Morse, Samuel F. B.
Samuel F. B. Morse: His Letters and Journals   II-934

Morton, Richard L.
Colonial Virginia. Vol. I: *The Tidewater Period, 1607-1710*   I-68; 156

Mott, Frank L.
American Journalism: A History, 1690-1960   I-192; II-718; 1247
History of American Magazines, 1741-1850, A   II-729

Mowry, George E.
Era of Theodore Roosevelt, 1900-1912, The   II-1312

Mumey, Nolie
John Williams Gunnison   II-870

Murdock, Harold
Nineteenth of April, 1775: Concord and Lexington, The   I-255

Murdock, Kenneth B.
Increase Mather: The Foremost American Puritan   I-131

Murphy, Henry C.
National Debt in War and Transition, The   III-1775

Murphy, Robert D.
Diplomat Among Warriors   III-1719

Murray, Robert K.
Harding Era: Warren G. Harding and His Administration, The   III-1548

Muse, Benjamin
Ten Years of Prelude: The Story of Integration Since the Supreme Court's 1954 Decision   III-1853

Muzzey, David S.
James G. Blaine: A Political Idol of Other Days   II-1058

Myrdal, Gunnar
American Dilemma: The Negro Problem and Modern Democracy, An   III-1860

Nasatir, Abraham P.
Before Lewis and Clark: Documents Illustrating the History of the Missouri, 1785-1804   I-150

Nash, Gary B.

Quaker and Politics: Pennsylvania, 1681-1726
I-162
Nathan, Mel C.
Pony Express, The   II-928
Nathans, Sydney
Daniel Webster and Jacksonian Democracy
II-765
Neal, Harry Edward
Communication: From Stone Age to Space Age
II-1093
*Treasures by the Millions: The Story of The
Smithsonian Institution*   II-836
Nearing, Scott
*Dollar Diplomacy: A Study in American Im-
perialism.* Originally published as *American
Imperialism: Viewpoints of United States
Foreign Policy, 1898-1941*   III-1383
Neihardt, John G.
*Splendid Wayfaring: The Exploits and Adven-
tures of Jedediah Smith and the Ashley-
Henry Men*   I-623
Neilson, James W.
Shelby M. Cullom: Prairie State Republican
II-1160
Neville, Anthony E.
Bridges, Canals, and Tunnels   II-1065
Nevins, Allan
*Abram S. Hewitt: With Some Account of Peter
Cooper*   II-1103
Evening Post: A Century of Journalism, The
II-718
*Hamilton Fish: The Inner History of the Great
Administration*   II-1058; 1076
John D. Rockefeller   II-1122
*John D. Rockefeller: The Heroic Age of Ameri-
can Enterprise*   II-1122
Ordeal of the Union. Vol. III: *The Emergence
of Lincoln.* Part I: *Douglas, Buchanan, and
Party Chaos, 1857-1859*   II-940; 950
Ordeal of the Union. Vol. IV: *The Emergence
of Lincoln.* Part II: *Prologue to Civil War,
1859-1861*   II-923; 940; 950
Ordeal of the Union. Vol. VI: *The War for the
Union.* Part II: *War Becomes Revolution,
1862-1863*   II-984
*Origins of the Land-Grant Colleges and State
Universities: A Brief Account of the Morrill
Act of 1862 and Its Results*   II-978
Polk: The Diary of a President, 1845-1849
II-783; 823
State Universities and Democracy, The   II-
979
Newcomb, Richard F.
*Savo: The Incredible Naval Debacle off Gua-
dalcanal*   III-1714
Nichols, Roy Franklin
Battles and Leaders of the Civil War   II-
956; 961
Disruption of American Democracy, The
II-951
Franklin Pierce: Young Hickory of the Granite

Hills   II-858
"Kansas-Nebraska Act: A Century of Histori-
ography, The," in *Mississippi Valley Histori-
cal Review*   II-876
Nimitz, Chester W.
Sea Power: A Naval History   II-1205
Nixon, Richard M.
Six Crises   III-1876
Noble, Louis Legrando
Life and Works of Thomas Cole, The   I-618
Noblin, Stuart
Leonidas LaFayette Polk: Agrarian Crusader
II-1230
North, Douglass C.
*Economic Growth of the United States, 1790-
1860, The*   I-375
Notestein, Wallace
*English People on the Eve of Colonization,
1603-1630, The*   I-64
Novick, David
Wartime Production Controls   III-1685
Nugent, Walter T.
*Tolerant Populists: Kansas, Populism, and
Nativism, The*   II-1229
Nye, Russel B.
*Fettered Freedom: Civil Liberties and the Slav-
ery Controversy, 1830-1860*   II-905
*Midwestern Progressive Politics: A Historical
Study of Its Origins and Development, 1870-
1958*   III-1393

Oakes, Pauline M.
Signal Corps: The Test, The, in the series
*United States Army in World War II: The
Technical Services*   III-1696
Oates, Stephen B.
*To Purge This Land with Blood: A Biography
of John Brown*   II-894
Odegard, Peter H.
*Pressure Politics: The Story of the Anti-Saloon
League*   III-1512
Odum, Howard W.
*American Sociology: The Story of Sociology in
the United States Through 1950*   III-
1362
Ogg, Frederic A.
*Old Northwest: A Chronicle of the Ohio Valley
and Beyond, The.* Vol. XIX: *The Chronicles
of America* series   I-329
O'Leary, Paul M.
"Scene of the Crime of 1873 Revisited: A
Note, The," in *Journal of Political Economy*
II-1088
Oleson, Tryggvi J.
*Early Voyages and Northern Approaches, 1000-
1632.* Vol. I: *Canadian Centenary* series
I-16; 22
Oliver, Peter
*Peter Oliver's Origin and Progress of the Ameri-
can Rebellion: A Tory View*   I-250
Oliver, Robert T.

Syngman Rhee: The Man Behind the Myth III-1828

Olmsted, Frederick L.
Cotton Kingdom, The I-375

O'Neill, William L.
Coming Apart: An Informal History of America in the 1960's III-1926

Orlikoff, Richard M.
"Coming Vindication of Mr. Justice Harlan, The," in *Illinois Law Review* II-1267

Osgood, Ernest S.
Day of the Cattleman, The II-1025

Osgood, Robert E.
Limited War: The Challenge to American Strategy III-1834

Osofsky, Gilbert
Harlem: The Making of a Ghetto, 1890-1930 III-1449

Ostrander, Gilman M.
Prohibition Movement in California, 1848-1933, The III-1512

Ottley, Roi
New World A-Coming: Inside Black America III-1449

Ottoson, Howard W.
Land Use Policy and Problems in the United States II-776

Overton, Richard C.
Burlington West: A Colonization History of the Burlington Railroad I-630

Owen, Robert D.
Threading My Way: Twenty-Seven Years of Autobiography I-516

Page, Bruce
American Melodrama: The Presidential Campaign of 1968, An III-1939

Palmer, Frederick
Our Greatest Battle III-1471

Palóu, Francisco
Francisco Palóu's Life and Apostolic Labors of the Venerable Father, Junipero Serra I-276

Palsson, Hermann
Vinland Sagas: The Norse Discovery of America, The I-16

Paltsits, Victor Hugo
Washington's Farewell Address, In Facsimile, with Transliterations of All the Drafts of Washington, Madison, and Hamilton I-407

Pares, Richard
King George III and the Politicians I-230

Pargellis, Stanley M.
Lord Loudon in North America I-205

Parish, John Carl
Persistence of the Westward Movement, and Other Essays, The II-1217

Parke, David B.
Epic of Unitarianism: Original Writings from the History of Liberal Religion, The I-574

Parker, William Belmont
Life and Public Services of Justin Smith Morrill, The II-978

Parkman, Francis
La Salle and the Discovery of the Great West I-57

Parks, George B.
Richard Hakluyt and the English Voyages I-51

Parran, Thomas
Aims of the Public Health Service, The III-1398

Parsons, W. Barclay
Robert Fulton and the Submarine I-271

Parton, James
"History of the Sewing Machine, The," in *Atlantic Monthly* II-842
Life and Times of Aaron Burr, The I-466

Paschal, Joel F.
Mister Justice Sutherland: A Man Against the State III-1673

Passer, Harold C.
Electrical Manufacturers, 1875-1900, The II-1115

Patrick, Rembert W.
Jefferson Davis and His Cabinet II-945

Patterson, Gardner
NATO: A Political Appraisal III-1810

Patterson, Haywood
Scottsboro Boy III-1593

Pattison, William D.
"Survey of the Seven Ranges, The," in *Ohio Historical Quarterly* I-311

Paul, Randolph E.
Taxation in the United States III-1420

Paul, Rodman W.
Mining Frontiers of the Far West, 1848-1880 II-847

Paul, Sherman
Emerson's Angle of Vision: Man and Nature in American Experience I-659

Payne, George Henry
History of Journalism in the United States II-718

Peckham, Howard H.
Colonial Wars, 1689-1762, The I-206
Pontiac and the Indian Uprising I-211

Pecora, Ferdinand
Wall Street Under Oath: The Story of Our Modern Money Changers III-1581

Peel, Roy V.
1928 Campaign: An Analysis, The III-1570
1932 Campaign: An Analysis, The III-1614

Pelling, Henry
American Labor II-1156

Pelzer, Louis
Cattleman's Frontier: A Record of the Trans-Mississippi Cattle Industry, 1850-1890, The

II-1025

Pendergast, James F.
Cartier's Hochelaga and the Dawson Site I-32

Penick, James L., Jr.
Progressive Politics and Conservation: The Ballinger-Pinchot Affair III-1393

Penrose, Boies
Travel and Discovery in the Renaissance, 1420-1620 I-22

Perkins, Bradford
Castlereagh and Adams: England and the United States, 1812-1823 I-520; 563; 599
First Rapprochement: England and the United States, 1795-1805, The I-395

Perkins, Dexter
Monroe Doctrine, 1867-1907, The II-1194

Perry, Bliss
American Spirit in Literature: A Chronicle of Great Interpreters, The I-641

Perry, Matthew C.
Narrative of the Expedition of an American Squadron to the China Seas and Japan II-887

Persons, Stow
Free Religion: An American Faith I-575

Pessen, Edward
Jacksonian America: Society, Personality, and Politics II-695
New Perspectives on Jacksonian Parties and Politics II-695

Peterson, H. C.
Opponents of the War III-1459

Peterson, Merrill D.
Jeffersonian Image in the American Mind, The I-431
Thomas Jefferson and the New Nation: A Biography I-431

Pettit, Norman
Heart Prepared: Grace and Conversion in Puritan Spiritual Life, The I-90

Pfeffer, Leo
Church and State in the United States I-323

Philbrick, Francis S.
Rise of the West, 1754-1830, The I-212; 532

Phillips, Cabell
From the Crash to the Blitz, 1929-1939 III-1586
Truman Presidency: The History of a Triumphant Succession, The III-1788

Phillips, Paul C.
Fur Trade, The I-480

Phillips, Ulrich B.
American Negro Slavery: A Survey of the Supply, Employment, and Control of Negro Labor as Determined by the Plantation Regime I-375; II-689
History of Transportation in the Eastern Cotton

Belt to 1860, A I-630

Pierce, Bessie L.
Rise of a Modern City, 1871-1893, The. Vol. III: *A History of Chicago* II-1236

Pierson, George W.
Tocqueville and Beaumont in America II-678

Pike, Zebulon M.
Zebulon Pike's Arkansas Journal I-470

Pinchot, Gifford
Breaking New Ground III-1377

Piven, Francis Fox
Regulating the Poor: The Functions of Public Relief III-1870

Poage, George R.
Henry Clay and the Whig Party II-695; 765

Pochmann, Henry A.
Washington Irving: Representative Selections I-484

Pogue, Forrest C.
George C. Marshall: Organizer of Victory, 1943-1945 III-1769
Supreme Command, The III-1752

Pollack, Norman
Populist Response to Industrial America: Midwestern Populist Thought, The II-1230

Pope, Jannie B.
Rise of New York Port, 1815-1860, The II-811

Pope, Joseph
Jacques Cartier, His Life and Voyages I-32

Pope, Robert G.
Half-Way Covenant: Church Membership in Puritan New England, The I-131

Porter, Kirk H.
History of Suffrage in the United States, A II-771

Posey, Walter B.
Frontier Mission: A History of Religion West of the Southern Appalachians to 1861 I-425

Post, Louis F.
Deportations Delirium of Nineteen Twenty, The III-1496

Potter, Elmer B.
Sea Power: A Naval History II-1205

Pound, Ezra
Cantos of Ezra Pound: One Through One Hundred Seventeen, The III-1404
Personae: Collected Shorter Poems III-1404

Powell, William S.
Proprietors of Carolina, The I-139
Ye Countie of Albermarle in Carolina: A Collection of Documents, 1664-1675 I-139

Pratt, Julius W.
Expansionists of 1898: The Acquisition of Hawaii and the Spanish Islands II-1289

Pressley, James

Center of the Storm: Memoirs of John T. Scopes
III-1554
Pressly, Thomas J.
Americans Interpret Their Civil War II-940
Preston, William, Jr.
Aliens and Dissenters: Federal Suppression of Radicals, 1903-1933 III-1459; 1496
Preuss, Charles
Exploring with Frémont II-799
Priestley, Herbert I.
Tristan de Luna, Conquistador of the Old South: A Study in Spanish Imperial Strategy I-38
Pringle, Henry F.
Life and Times of William Howard Taft: A Biography, The III-1383; 1393
Pritchett, Herman C.
American Constitution, The III-1887
Prothro, James Warren
Dollar Decade: Business Ideas in the 1920's, The III-1548
Prucha, Francis P.
American Indian Policy in the Formative Years: The Indian Trade and Intercourse Acts I-671
Sword of the Republic: The United States Army on the Frontier, 1783-1846, The I-388
Pursell, Carroll W., Jr.
Technology in Western Civilization. Vol. I: *The Emergence of Modern Industrial Society: Earliest Times to 1900* II-747; 842; 1115
Pusey, Merlo J.
Charles Evans Hughes III-1536
Eisenhower, the President III-1848
Supreme Court Crisis, The III-1672
Putnam, James W.
Illinois and Michigan Canal, The. A Study in Economic History. Chicago Historical Society *Collections* I-550
Putnam, Samuel
Paris Was Our Mistress: Memoirs of a Lost and Found Generation III-1565

Quaife, Milo M.
Doctrine of Non-Intervention with Slavery in the Territories, The II-904
Quarles, Benjamin
Black Abolitionists II-724
Lincoln and the Negro II-984
Quirk, Robert E.
Affair of Honor: Woodrow Wilson and the Occupation of Veracruz, An II-1317

Rachlis, Eugene
Peter Stuyvesant and His New York I-84
Radway, Laurence I.
Soldiers and Scholars: Military Education and National Policy I-436
Raesly, Ellis L.
Portrait of New Netherland I-143

Rago, Henry
Poetry: The Golden Anniversary Issue III-1404
Rammelkamp, Julian S.
Pulitzer's Post-Dispatch, 1878-1883 II-1248
Randall, James G.
Constitutional Problems Under Lincoln II-995
Rankin, Hugh F.
Upheaval in Albemarle: The Story of Culpeper's Rebellion, 1675-1689 I-139
Ransmeier, Joseph S.
"Fourteenth Amendment and the 'Separate But Equal' Doctrine, The" in *Michigan Law Review* II-1267
Rappaport, Armin
Monroe Doctrine, The. American Problem Studies, I-598
Rawley, James A.
Race and Politics: Bleeding Kansas and the Coming of the Civil War II-894
Rayback, Joseph G.
History of American Labor, A II-1242
Rayback, Robert J.
Millard Fillmore: A Biography of a President II-858
Read, James Morgan
Atrocity Propaganda, 1914-1919 III-1459
Record, Wilson
Race and Radicalism: The NAACP and the Communist Party in Conflict III-1593
Redkey, Edwin S.
Black Exodus: Black Nationalist and Back-To-Africa Movements, 1890-1910 III-1449
Reed, Henry Hope, Jr.
Architecture in America: A Battle of Styles II-1236
Reed, Merle E.
New Orleans and the Railroads: The Struggle for Commercial Empire, 1830-1860 I-630
Rees, David
Age of Containment: The Cold War, 1945-1965, The III-1782
Korea: The Limited War III-1834
Reese, George H.
Proceedings of the General Assembly of Virginia, July 30-August 4, 1619, Written and Sent from Virginia to England by Mr. John Pory I-68
Reese, Trevor R.
Colonial Georgia: A Study in British Imperial Policy in the Eighteenth Century I-186
Reeves, George S.
Man from South Dakota, A III-1631
Reiger, C. C.
Era of the Muckrakers, The III-1356
Reiss, Albert O.
Social Characteristics of Urban and Rural Communities III-1816

Repplier, Agnes
Junípero Serra: Pioneer Colonist of California
I-276
Resek, Carl
Lewis Henry Morgan, American Scholar
III-1362
Reynolds, Quentin
Courtroom III-1593
Rhodes, James F.
History of the United States from the Compromise of 1850 to the Final Restoration of Home Rule at the South in 1877 II-1103
Rice, Madeleine H.
Federal Street Pastor: The Life of William Ellery Channing I-575
Richardson, Elmo R.
Politics of Conservation: Crusades and Controversies, 1897-1913, The III-1377
Richardson, Leon Burr
William E. Chandler: Republican II-1103
Richey, Herman G.
School in the American Social Order: The Dynamics of American Education, The I-581
Ridge, Martin
Ignatius Donnelly: The Portrait of a Politician II-1229
Riemersma, Jelle C.
Religious Factors in Early Dutch Capitalism, 1550-1650 I-84
Riesman, David
"Tocqueville as Ethnographer," in *Abundance for What? And Other Essays* II-678
Riordon, William L.
Plunkitt of Tammany Hall II-1134
Rippy, James Fred
Globe and Hemisphere III-1793
United States and Mexico, The III-1443
Risch, Erna
Quartermaster Support of the Army: A History of the Corps, 1775-1939 I-388
Risings, Sam P.
Chisholm Trail: A History of the World's Greatest Cattle Trail, The II-1024
Robbins, Caroline
Eighteenth-Century Commonwealthman: Studies in the Transmission, Development, and Circumstances of English Liberal Thought from the Restoration of Charles II Until the War with the Thirteen Colonies, The I-266
Robbins, Lionel
Great Depression, The III-1581
Robbins, Roy M.
Our Landed Heritage: The Public Domain, 1776-1936 I-311; 587; II-968; III-1378
Robert, Joseph C.
Road from Monticello: A Study of the Virginia Slavery Debate of 1832, The II-689
Tobacco Kingdom: Plantation, Market, and Factory in Virginia and North Carolina,

1800-1860, The I-375
Robinson, Edwin Arlington
Collected Poems III-1404
Robinson, Victor
Victory Over Pain: A History of Anesthesia II-794
Robinson, William A.
Thomas B. Reed, Parliamentarian II-1278
Roche, John P.
"*Plessy* v. *Ferguson:* Requiescat in Pacem?" in *University of Pennsylvania Law Review* II-1266
Roesler, Robert C.
"Ecology of the Physical Mayo, The" in *Mayo Clinic Proceedings* II-1183
Rogin, Leo
Introduction of Farm Machinery in Its Relation to the Productivity of Labor in the Agriculture of the United States During the Nineteenth Century, The. University of California Publications in Economics. II-684
Rohrbough, Malcolm J.
Land Office Business: The Settlement and Administration of American Public Lands, 1789-1837, The II-776
Romasco, Albert U.
Poverty of Abundance: Hoover, the Nation, the Depression, The III-1548; 1587
Roosevelt, Theodore
Autobiography II-1345; III-1378
Roots, Peter C.
Ordnance Department I: Planning Munitions for War, The, in the series: *United States Army in World War II: The Technical Services* III-1696
Rorty, James
McCarthy and the Communists III-1822
Rose, Barbara
American Art Since 1900 II-1065
Rose, Thomas
Violence in America: A Historical and Contemporary Reader III-1864
Roseboom, Eugene H.
History of Presidential Elections, A II-1145
Short History of Presidential Elections, A I-460; 612
Rosen, George
History of Public Health, A III-1398
Rosenman, Samuel I.
Public Papers and Addresses of Franklin D. Roosevelt, 1928-1945, The III-1620
Rosenzweig, R. M.
Federal Interest in Higher Education, The III-1730
Rosholt, Robert L.
Administrative History of NASA, 1958-1963, An III-1945
Ross, Earl D.
Democracy's College: The Land-Grant Movement in Its Formative Stage II-979
Rossiter, Clinton

Alexander Hamilton and the Constitution I-361
Seedtime of the Republic I-266
Rothman, David J.
On Their Own: The Poor in Modern America.
Themes and Social Forces in American History series III-1869
Rothman, Sheila M.
On Their Own: The Poor in Modern America.
Themes and Social Forces in American History series III-1869
Rourke, Constance M.
Trumpets of Jubilee II-863
Rovere, Richard H.
General and the President, and the Future of American Foreign Policy, The III-1834
Goldwater Caper, The III-1923
Rowse, A. L.
Elizabethans and America, The I-51
Ruchames, Louis
John Brown: The Making of a Revolutionary.
Originally published as *A John Brown Reader* II-923
Rudin, Harry R.
Armistice, 1918 III-1490
Rudolph, Frederick
American College and University: A History, The II-1082
Rudwick, Elliott M.
Black Nationalism in America III-1449
Rugg, Winnifred K.
Unafraid: A Life of Anne Hutchinson I-102
Ruiz, Ramón Eduardo
Mexican War: Was It Manifest Destiny?, The II-830
Russell, Francis
Shadow of Blooming Grove: Warren G. Harding in His Times, The III-1530; 1548
Russell, John H.
Free Negro in Virginia, 1619-1865, The I-73
Rutherford, Livingston
John Peter Zenger; His Press, His Trial, and a Bibliography of Zenger Imprints I-193
Rutland, Robert A.
Ordeal of the Constitution: The Antifederalists and the Ratification Struggle of 1787-1788, The I-340
Rutman, Darrett B.
Husbandmen of Plymouth I-79
Ryan, Cornelius
Longest Day, The III-1724
Rynearson, Edward H.
"Editorials," in *Minnesota Medicine* II-1183

Salinger, Pierre
With Kennedy III-1892
Salisbury, Albert
Two Captains West I-454

Salisbury, Jane
Two Captains West I-454
Salk, Dr. Jonas E.
"Vaccination Against Paralytic Poliomyelitis: Performance and Prospects," in *American Journal of Public Health* III-1842
Salley, Alexander S., Jr.
Narratives of Early Carolina, 1650-1708 I-139
Sandeen, Ernest R.
"Towards a Historical Interpretation of the Origins of Fundamentalism," in *Church History* II-1176
Sanders, Ronald
Downtown Jews: Portraits of an Immigrant Generation, The III-224
Santa Anna, Antonio López de
Mexican Side of the Texas Revolution, The II-740
Sarratt, Reed
Ordeal of Desegregation: The First Decade, The III-1854
Sarris, Andrew
American Cinema: Directors and Directions, 1929-1968, The II-1338
Savelle, Max
"America and the Balance of Power, 1713-1778," in Richard B. Morris' *The Era of the American Revolution* I-287
Sayler, Richard H.
Warren Court: A Critical Analysis, The III-1887
Scammon, Richard M.
Real Majority, The III-1939
Schachner, Nathan
Aaron Burr: A Biography I-466
Alexander Hamilton: A Biography I-361
Founding Fathers, The I-344; 402
Thomas Jefferson: A Biography I-431; 460
Scharf, J. Thomas
History of the Confederate States Navy II-961
Schattschneider, Elmer E.
Politics, Pressure, and the Tariff II-1278
Scheele, Leonard A.
"Past and Future of the Public Health Service, The," in *American Journal of Public Health* III-1398
Schlesinger, Arthur M., Jr.
Age of Jackson, The I-634; II-765
Age of Roosevelt, The. Vol. I: *The Crisis of the Old Order, 1919-1933* III-1570; 1587; 1614
Age of Roosevelt, The. Vol. II: *The Coming of the New Deal* III-1587; 1626; 1647
Age of Roosevelt, The. Vol. III: *The Politics of Upheaval.* III-1626
General and the President, and the Future of American Foreign Policy, The III-1834
Thousand Days: John F. Kennedy in the White House, A III-1876; 1882

AMERICAN

Literature for Additional Recommended Reading

Schmidt, Karl M.
  Henry Wallace: Quixotic Crusade, 1948
  III-1805
Schulberg, Budd
  From the Ashes: Voices of Watts   III-1926
Schuller, Gunther
  Early Jazz; Its Roots and Musical Development
  III-1506
Schuyler, Hamilton
  *The Roeblings: A Century of Engineers, Bridge-
  Builders, and Industrialists*   II-1065
Schutz, John A.
  *William Shirley: King's Governor of Massa-
  chusetts*   I-206
Schwartz, Anna Jacobson
  *Monetary History of the United States, 1867-
  1960, A*   III-1437
Scopes, John Thomas
  Center of the Storm: Memoirs of John T. Scopes
  III-1554
Scott, James B.
  *International Conferences of American States,
  1889-1928, The*   II-1194
Scudder, Horace E.
  Noah Webster   I-641
Scully, Vincent
  *American Architecture and Urbanism: A His-
  torical Essay*   II-1236
Seabright, Thomas B.
  Old Pike: A History of the National Road, The
  I-496
Sears, Paul B.
  Deserts on the March   III-1631
Seitz, Don C.
  *James Gordon Bennetts, Father and Son: Pro-
  prietors of the New York Herald, The*
  II-718
Seldes, Gilbert
  Seven Lively Arts, The   III-1506
Seligman, Edwin R.
  Income Tax, The   III-1419
Sellers, Charles G.
  *James K. Polk: Vol. II: Continentalist, 1843-
  1846*   II-784; 830
  "Travail of Slavery, The" in Sellers' *The
  Southerner as American*   I-653
Sellers, James B.
  *Prohibition Movement in Alabama, 1702 to
  1943, The*   III-1512
Selznick, Phillip
  *T. V. A. and the Grass Roots: A Study in the
  Sociology of Formal Organization*   III-
  1626
Servin, Manuel P.
  *Mexican-Americans: An Awakening Minority,
  The*   III-1870
Seymour, Harold
  Baseball: The Early Years   III-1500
Shadegg, Stephen
  *What Happened to Goldwater? The Inside
  Story of the 1964 Campaign*   III-1923

Shannon, David A.
  *Decline of American Communism: A History
  of the Communist Party of the United States
  Since 1945, The*   III-1822
  Great Depression, The   III-1587
Shannon, Fred A.
  *Farmer's Last Frontier: Agriculture, 1860-
  1897, The.* Vol. V: *The Economic History of
  the United States*   II-684; 1047
Sheehan, Neil
  Pentagon Papers as Published by the New York
  Times, *The*   III-1911
Shelton, William
  Soviet Space Exploration: The First Decade
  III-1945
Sherman, John
  *Recollections of Forty Years in the House, Sen-
  ate, and Cabinet: An Autobiography.* Ameri-
  can History, Politics, and Law series   II-
  1212
Sherwood, Morgan B.
  Alaska and Its History   II-1041
Sherwood, Robert E.
  Roosevelt and Hopkins: An Intimate History
  III-1691
Shields, Archie W.
  Purchase of Alaska, The   II-1041
Shoemaker, Ervin C.
  Noah Webster: Pioneer of Learning   I-640
Shuler, Nettie R.
  *Woman Suffrage and Politics: The Inner Story
  of the Suffrage Movement*   III-1518
Shulman, Arthur
  *How Sweet It Was. Television: A Pictorial
  Commentary*   III-1679
Shumway, A. L.
  *Oberliniana: A Jubilee Volume of Semi-His-
  torical Anecdotes Connected with the Past
  and Present of Oberlin College*   II-712
Shyrock, Richard Harrison
  Medicine and Society in America, 1660-1860
  II-794
Sibley, Mulford Q.
  *Conscription of Conscience: The American
  State and the Conscientious Objector, 1940-
  1947*   III-1708
Sidey, Hugh
  John F. Kennedy, President   III-1876
Sidwell, Robert T.
  *American Legacy of Learning: Readings in the
  History of Education, The*   I-108
Silvert, Kalman H.
  *Conflict Society: Reaction and Revolution in
  Latin America, The*   III-1793
Simon, George T.
  Big Bands, The   III-1506
Simonds, William A.
  Henry Ford: His Life, His Work, His Genius
  III-1425
Simpson, Alan
  Puritanism in Old and New England   I-90

Simpson, Lewis P.
"Southern Novelist and Southern Nationalism, The" in *The Man of Letters in New England and the South: Essays on the Literary Vocation in America*   III-1576
Sinclair, Andrew
Available Man: The Life Behind the Masks of Warren Gamaliel Harding, The   III-1477
Sitterson, J. Carlyle
Sugar Country: The Cane Sugar Industry in the South, 1753-1950   I-375
Smelser, Marshal
Democratic Republic, 1801-1815, The   I-431; 521
Smillie, Wilson G.
Public Health Administration in the United States   III-1398
Public Health: Its Promise for the Future. A Chronicle of the Development of Public Health in the United States, 1607-1914   III-1398
Smith, Alfred G., Jr.
Economic Readjustment of an Old Cotton State: South Carolina, 1820-1860   I-375
Smith, Alson J.
Men Against the Mountains: Jedediah Smith and the South West Expedition of 1826-1829   I-623
Smith, Bradford
Captain John Smith, His Life and Legend   I-64
Smith, Charles B.
Roger B. Taney: Jacksonian Jurist   II-904
Smith, Charles P.
James Wilson: Founding Father, 1742-1798   I-349
Smith, Daniel M.
Great Departure: The United States and World War I, 1914-1920, The. America in Crisis series   III-1453
Smith, Darrell H.
Bureau of Education: Its History, Activities, and Organization, The   II-1035
Smith, Henry L.
Airways Abroad: The Story of American World Air Routes   II-1351
Airways: The History of Commercial Aviation in the United States   II-1351
Smith, Henry N.
Mark Twain-Howells Letters: The Correspondence of Samuel L. Clemens and William Dean Howells, 1872-1910   II-1150
Mark Twain, The Development of a Writer   II-1150
Smith, Justin H.
War with Mexico, The   II-830
Smith, Page
John Adams   I-305
Smith, Theodore C.
Life and Letters of James Abram Garfield,

The. Vol. II: *1877-1882*   II-1035
Smith, Timothy L.
Revivalism and Social Reform: American Protestantism on the Eve of the Civil War   I-425
Revivalism and Social Reform in Mid-Nineteenth Century America   I-647
Smith, Walter B.
Economic Aspects of the Second Bank of the United States   I-544
Smith, William E.
Francis Preston Blair Family in Politics, The   II-904
Smithe, Kendall
Ceiling Unlimited: The Story of American Aviation from Kitty Hawk to Supersonics   III-1351
Snell, John L.
Meaning of Yalta: Big Three Diplomacy and the New Balance of Power, The   III-1740
Solomon, Eric
Stephen Crane: From Parody to Realism   II-1260
Sonneck, Oscar G.
Early Opera in America   II-1139
Sorensen, Theodore C.
Kennedy   III-1892
Spencer, Benjamin T.
Quest for Nationality: An American Literary Campaign, The   I-641
Spencer, Samuel R., Jr.
Booker T. Washington and the Negro's Place in American Life   I-1254; III-1389
Spofford, Ainsworth R.
New Library Building, The   II-1283
Spring, Agnes W.
When Grass Was King   II-1025
Sprout, Harold H.
Rise of American Naval Power, 1776-1918, The   II-1205
Toward a New Order of Sea Power: American Naval Policy and the World Scene, 1918-1922   III-1536
Sprout, Margaret
Rise of American Naval Power, 1776-1918, The   II-1205
Toward a New Order of Sea Power: American Naval Policy and the World Scene, 1918-1922   III-1536
Squier, George O.
Telling the World   II-1093
Stacey, C. P.
Quebec, 1759: The Siege and the Battle   I-205
Stallings, Laurence
Story of the Doughboys: The AEF in World War I, The   III-1471
Stallman, Robert W.
Stephen Crane: A Critical Bibliography   II-1260
Stephen Crane: An Omnibus   II-1260

AMERICAN

Stampp, Kenneth M.
  And the War Came: The North and the Secession Crisis, 1860-1861   II-951
  Era of Reconstruction, 1865 to 1877, The   II-1009; 1030; 1053; 1103
  Peculiar Institution: Slavery in the Ante-Bellum South, The   I-375; II-689
Stanton, William
  Leopard's Spots: Scientific Attitudes Toward Race in America, 1815-1859, The   I-653
Stanton, Madeline E.
  Centennial of Surgical Anesthesia, The   II-794
Starr, Harris E.
  William Graham Sumner   III-1362
Starr, John
  Teapot Dome   III-1530
Staundenraus, P. J.
  African Colonization Movement, 1816-1865, The   II-724
Stebbins, Richard P.
  United States in World Affairs, 1962, The   III-1892
Steffens, Joseph Lincoln
  Autobiography of Lincoln Steffens, The   III-1356
Steinbeck, John
  Grapes of Wrath, The   III-1631
Steiner, Bernard C.
  Beginnings of Maryland   I-120
Steinman, David B.
  Builders of the Bridge, The   II-1065
Stephenson, G. W.
  George Washington   I-344
Stephenson, George M.
  History of American Immigration, 1820-1924, A   II-1224
  Political History of Public Lands from 1840 to 1862: From Pre-Emption to Homestead, The   II-968
Stephenson, Nathaniel W.
  Nelson W. Aldrich   III-1419
Stern, Bernhard J.
  Lewis Henry Morgan: Social Evolutionist   III-1362
Stettinius, Edward R., Jr.
  Lend-Lease, Weapons for Victory   III-1685
  Roosevelt and the Russians: The Yalta Conference   III-1747
Stevens, Hazard
  Life of Isaac Ingalls Stevens by His Son, Hazard Stevens, The   II-870
Stevenson, Elizabeth
  Henry Adams: A Biography   II-1189
Stevenson, Lloyd G.
  "Editorials," in *Minnesota Medicine*   II-1183
Stewart, Randall
  Nathaniel Hawthorne: A Biography   II-853
Stimson, Henry L.
  On Active Service in Peace and War: A Study

of the Life and Times of Henry L. Stimson   III-1603
Stokes, Anson P.
  Church and State in the United States   I-323
Stone, Irving
  Clarence Darrow for the Defense   II-1242
Stone, Ralph A.
  Irreconcilables: The Fight Against the League of Nations, The   III-1490
Storr, Richard J.
  Beginnings of Graduate Education in America, The   II-1082
Stovall, Floyd
  Eight American Authors   II-853
Stowe, Lyman B.
  Saints, Sinners, and Beechers   II-863
Strout, Cushing
  Pragmatic Revolt in American History: Carl Becker and Charles Beard, The   III-1431
Studenski, Paul
  Financial History of the United States   II-1088
Sullivan, Louis H.
  Autobiography of an Idea, The   II-1236
Sullivan, Mark
  Our Times: The United States, 1900-1925. Vol. I: *The Turn of the Century*   II-1317; 1324
Sutherland, Lucy S.
  East India Company in Eighteenth-Century Politics, The   I-245
Swados, Harvey
  Years of Conscience: The Muckrakers, an Anthology of Reform Journalism   III-1356
Swanberg, W. A.
  Pulitzer   II-1248
Sweet, Frederick A.
  Hudson River School and the Early American Landscape Tradition, The   I-618
Sweet, William W.
  Revivalism in America: Its Origin, Growth, and Decline   I-425
Swenson, Lloyd S.
  This New Ocean: A History of Project Mercury   III-1559; 1945
Swisher, Carl B.
  American Constitutional Development   I-334; 460
Sydnor, Charles S.
  Development of Southern Sectionalism, 1819-1848, The. Vol. V: *A History of the South*   I-557; 665; II-689

Taft, Philip
  A. F. of L. from the Death of Gompers to the Merger, The   II-1156; III-1642
  A. F. of L. in the Time of Gompers, The   II-1332
  Organized Labor in American History   II-1242

Tailfer, Patrick
True and Historical Narrative of the Colony of Georgia: With Comments by the Earl of Egmont, A.   I-187

Tait, Samuel W., Jr.
Wildcatters: An Informal History of Oil-Hunting in America, The   II-917

Tannenbaum, Frank
Mexico: The Struggle for Peace and Bread   III-1443

Tarbell, Ida M.
History of the Standard Oil Company, The   II-1122

Tate, Merze
United States and Armaments, The   III-1536

Taus, Esther Rogoff
Central Banking Functions of the United States Treasury, 1789-1941   II-753

Taussig, Frank W.
Some Aspects of the Tariff Question: An Examination of the Development of American Industries Under Protection   II-1278
Tariff History of the United States, The   II-707; III-1420

Taylor, Carl C.
Farmer's Movement, 1620-1920, The   II-1048

Taylor, George R.
Transportation Revolution, 1815-1860, The   II-811

Taylor, Philip
Distant Magnet: European Immigration to the U.S.A., The   II-1224

Tebbel, John W.
Life and Good Times of William Randolph Hearst, The   II-1248

Teitelbaum, Louis M.
Woodrow Wilson and the Mexican Revolution, 1913-1916   III-1443

Ten Broek, Jacobus
Equal Under Law   II-1053

Terkel, Studs
Hard Times: An Oral History of the Great Depression in America   III-1587

Terrell, John U.
Furs by Astor   I-480
La Salle: The Life and Times of an Explorer   I-150
Six Turnings: Changes in the American West, 1806-1834, The   I-480

Terrett, Dulaney
Signal Corps: The Test, The, in the series: *United States Army in World War II: The Technical Services*   III-1696

Tewksbury, Donald G.
Founding of American Colleges and Universities Before the Civil War with Particular Reference to the Religious Influences Bearing upon the College Movement, The   I-316; II-712

Thayer, James B.
"Dawes Bill and the Indians, The," in *Atlantic Monthly*   II-1166

Thayer, William R.
Life and Letters of John Hay   II-1345

Thernstrom, Stephen
Poverty and Progress: Social Mobility in a Nineteenth Century City   II-1224

Thiesmeyer, Lincoln R.
Combat Scientists: Science in World War II   III-1696

Thomas, Benjamin P.
Abraham Lincoln: A Biography   II-911; 1018
Edwin M. Stanton: The Life and Times of Lincoln's Secretary of War   II-1018; 1030

Thomas, Charles M.
American Neutrality in 1793: A Study in Cabinet Government   I-394

Thomas, Hugh
Spanish Civil War, The   III-1665

Thomas, John
"Romantic Reform in America, 1815-1865," in *American Quarterly*   I-647

Thomas, John L.
Liberator: William Lloyd Garrison, The   II-724

Thompson, Edward
Sir Walter Raleigh: Last of the Elizabethans   I-51

Thompson, George R.
Signal Corps: The Test, The, in the series: *United States Army in World War II: The Technical Services*   III-1696

Thompson, Holland
Age of Invention, The   II-899

Thompson, J. Eric
Rise and Fall of Maya Civilization, The   I-10

Thompson, Mack
Moses Brown: Reluctant Reformer   I-366

Thompson, Oscar
American-Singer: A Hundred Years of Success in Opera, The   II-1139

Thompson, Robert L.
Wiring a Continent: The History of the Telegraph Industry in the United States, 1832-1866   II-747

Thoms, Herbert
Doctors of Yale College, 1702-1815: And the Founding of the Medical Institution   I-271

Thomson, Harry C.
Ordnance Department I: Planning Munitions for War, The, in the series: *United States Army in World War II: The Technical Services*   III-1696

Thorne, Christopher
Limits of Foreign Policy, The   III-1603

Thurber, Evangeline
Report on Demobilization   III-1483

Literature for Additional Recommended Reading

Tindall, George Brown
Emergence of the New South, 1913-1945, The
III-1593
Tinkcom, Harry M.
Republicans and Federalists in Pennsylvania, 1790-1801: A Study in National Stimulus and Local Response, The   I-382
Tinkle, Lon
Thirteen Days to Glory: The Siege of the Alamo
II-741
Tocqueville, Alexis de
Journey to America   II-678
Toland, John
Last Hundred Days, The   III-1752
Rising Sun: The Decline and Fall of the Japanese Empire, 1936-1945, The   III-1714
Tolles, Frederick B.
James Logan and the Culture of Provincial America   I-162
Witness of William Penn, The   I-162
Tomkins, Calvin
Living Well Is the Best Revenge   III-1565
Tompkins, Frank
Chasing Villa   III-1443
Tompkins, Jerry R.
D-Days at Dayton: Reflections on the Scopes Trial   III-1554
Tourtellot, Arthur B.
William Diamond's Drum: The Beginning of the War of the American Revolution   I-255
Trappner, W. C.
Wartime Production Controls   III-1685
Treacy, Mildred F.
Prelude to Yorktown: The Southern Campaign of Nathanael Greene   I-299
Treat, Payson J.
Diplomatic Relations Between the United States and Japan, 1853-1865, The   II-888
National Land System, 1785-1820, The   I-587
Tregaskis, Richard
Guadalcanal Diary   III-1714
Trepaski, John J.
Governorship of Spanish Florida, 1700-1763, The   I-38
Trexler, Harrison A.
Slavery in Missouri, 1804-1865   I-556
Trigger, Bruce G.
Cartier's Hochelaga and the Dawson Site   I-32
Trinterud, Leonard J.
Forming of an American Tradition: A Re-Examination of Colonial Presbyterianism, The   I-180
Trottman, Nelson S.
History of the Union Pacific: A Financial and Economic Survey   II-973
Truman, Harry S
Memoirs of Harry S Truman. Vol. II: The

Years of Trial and Hope   III-1828; 1834
Tsou, Tang
America's Failure in China, 1941-1950
III-1769
Tuchman, Barbara W.
Zimmerman Telegram, The   III-1453
Tucker, Glenn
High Tide at Gettysburg   II-1001
Tugwell, Rexford G.
How They Became President   I-612
Mr. Hoover's Economic Policy   III-1598
Turner, Catledge
168 Days, The   III-1672
Turner, Frederick Jackson
Frontier in American History, The   II-1217
Rise of the New West, 1819-1829. The American Nation series   I-532
Tuttle, William M., Jr.
Race Riot: Chicago in the Red Summer of 1919
III-1926
Twain, Mark (pseud.)
Autobiography of Mark Twain   II-1150
Life on the Mississippi   I-475
Tyler, Alice Felt
Foreign Policy of James C. Blaine, The
II-1194
Freedom's Ferment: Phases of American Social History from the Revolution to the Outbreak of the Civil War   I-516; 646
Tyler, Daniel
Concise History of the Mormon Battalion in the Mexican War, 1846-1847, A   II-816
Tyler, David B.
Steam Conquers the Atlantic   I-475; II-899

Ubbelohde, Carl
Vice-Admiralty Courts and the American Revolution, The   I-230
Underhill, Ruth M.
Red Man's America: A History of Indians in the United States   I-4
United Press International Staff
Assassination: Robert F. Kennedy, 1925-1968
III-1932
Upham, Charles W.
Salem Witchcraft   I-175
United States Department of State
Foreign Relations of the United States: China, 1946   III-1769
U. S. Department of State
Foreign Relations of the United States: Diplomatic Papers: The Conferences at Malta and Yalta 1945   III-1740
U. S. Department of the Interior (Office of Education)
Survey of Land-Grant Colleges and Universities
II-979
U. S. Government Printing Office
Public Health Service Today, The   III-1398
U. S. House Document number 206
United States Constitution, The   I-334; 370

Literature for Additional Recommended Reading

Van Alstyne, Richard
  Empire and Independence: The International History of the American Revolution I-287
Vandenberg, Arthur H., Jr.
  Private Papers of Senator Vandenberg, The III-1746; 1788; 1810
Vanden Heuvel, William J.
  On His Own: Robert F. Kennedy, 1964-1968 III-1932
Van Deusen, Glyndon G.
  Horace Greeley: Nineteenth Century Crusader II-1058
  Jacksonian Era, 1828-1848, The II-701
  Life of Henry Clay, The I-665
  Thurlow Weed: Wizard of the Lobby II-695
  William Henry Seward II-882; 940; 1041
Van Doren, Carl
  Benjamin Franklin I-240
Van Every, Dale
  Disinherited: The Lost Birthright of the American Indian I-671
Van Riper, Paul P.
  History of the United States Civil Service II-1134
Van Schreeven, William J.
  Proceedings of the General Assembly of Virginia, July 30-August 4, 1619, Written and Sent from Virginia to England by Mr. John Pory I-68
Van Tassel, David D.
  Recording America's Past: An Interpretation of the Development of Historical Studies in America, 1607-1884 II-735
Varg, Paul A.
  Foreign Policies of the Founding Fathers I-287
  Making of a Myth: The United States and China, 1897-1912, The II-1300
Vaughn, Jesse W.
  Reynolds Campaign on Powder River, The II-1098
Vestal, Stanley
  Old Santa Fe Trail, The I-592
Villard, Oswald Garrison
  John Brown, 1800-1859: A Biography Fifty Years After II-923
Vincent, Theodore G.
  Black Power and the Garvey Movement III-1449
Visscher, William L.
  Thrilling and Truthful History of the Pony Express, A II-929
Voight, David Quenton
  American Baseball: From Gentlemen's Sport to the Commissioner System III-1500
Volpe, Edmond L.
  Reader's Guide to William Faulkner, A III-1576

Wade, Richard C.
  Urban Frontier: The Rise of Western Cities, 1790-1830, The I-531
Wagenknecht, Edward
  Harriet Beecher Stowe: The Known and the Unknown II-864
Walker, Peter F.
  Vicksburg: A People at War, 1860-1865 II-1002
Wallace, Paul A.
  Muhlenbergs of Pennsylvania, The I-382
Wallace, Willard M.
  Traitorous Hero: Life and Fortunes of Benedict Arnold I-281
Walworth, Arthur
  Woodrow Wilson III-1409; 1477
Wandell, Samuel H.
  Aaron Burr I-466
Wangensteen, Owen H.
  "Editorials," in *Minnesota Medicine* II-1183
Ward, Christopher
  War of the Revolution, The I-255
Ward, John W.
  Andrew Jackson: Symbol for an Age I-635; II-701
Ware, Caroline F.
  Early New England Cotton Manufacturer, The I-366
  Greenwich Village, 1920-1930 III-1564
Warne, Colston E.
  Pullman Boycott of 1894: The Problem of Federal Intervention, The II-1242
Warren, Charles
  Supreme Court in United States History, The I-349; 606; II-1324
Warren, Harris Gaylord
  Herbert Hoover and the Great Depression III-1548; 1587
Warren, Robert Penn
  Faulkner: A Collection of Critical Essays III-1576
  John Brown: The Making of a Martyr II-923
Washburn, Wilcomb E.
  "Joseph Henry's Conception of the Purpose of the Smithsonian Institution," in Whitehill's, *A Cabinet of Curiosities: Five Episodes in the Evolution of American Museums* II-836
Washington, Booker T.
  Up from Slavery: An Autobiography II-1254
Watson, Elmo Scott
  Professor Goes West, The II-1108
Watson, Thomas A.
  Exploring Life II-1093
Watt, Richard F.
  "Coming Vindication of Mr. Justice Harlan, The," in *Illinois Law Review* II-1267
Wattenberg, Ben J.
  Real Majority, The III-1939

Weare, George E.
  Cabot's Discovery of North America   I-27
Wecter, Dixon
  Age of the Great Depression, 1929-1941, The
    III-1587; 1636
  Sam Clemens of Hannibal   II-1150
Weigley, Russell F.
  History of the United States Army   I-436
Weinberg, Albert K.
  Manifest Destiny: A Study of Nationalist Expansion in American History   II-830
  "Washington's 'Great Rule' in Its Historical Evolution," in Goddman's *Historiography and Urbanization: Essays in American History in Honor of W. Stull Holt*   I-407
Weinberger, Andrew D.
  Freedom and Protection: The Bill of Rights
    I-370
Weinstein, James
  Corporate Ideal and the Liberal State, 1900-1918, The   II-1332
Weisberger, Bernard A.
  American Newspaperman, The. The Chicago History of American Civilization series
    II-718
  They Gathered at the River: The Story of the Great Revivalists and Their Impact upon Religion in America   I-425
Weisenburger, Francis P.
  Life of John McLean: A Politician on the United States Supreme Court, The   II-904
Welles, Sumner
  Naboth's Vineyard   II-1317
Wellington, Raynor G.
  Political and Sectional Influence of the Public Lands, 1828-1842   II-777
Wellman, Paul I.
  Glory, God, and Gold: A Narrative History
    I-45
  Indian Wars of the West, The   II-1098
Wendell, Barrett
  Cotton Mather: The Puritan Priest   I-174
Werner, Morris R.
  Teapot Dome   III-1530
Wertenbaker, Thomas J.
  Founding of American Civilization: The Middle Colonies, The   I-143
  Virginia Under the Stuarts, 1607-1688   I-64; 156
West, Richard S., Jr.
  Mister Lincoln's Navy   II-961
Whannel, Paddy
  Popular Arts: A Critical Guide to the Mass Media, The   III-1506
Whitaker, Arthur P.
  Mississippi Question, 1795-1803: A Study in Trade, Politics, and Diplomacy, The   I-449
  United States and the Independence of Latin America, 1800-1830, The   I-563; 598

White, Leonard D.
  Federalists: A Study in Administrative History, The   I-355
  Jeffersonians: A Study in Administrative History, 1801-1829, The   I-431
  Republican Era, 1869-1901, The   II-1059
White, Theodore H.
  Fire in the Ashes: Europe in Mid-Century
    III-1799
  Thunder Out of China   III-1769
White, William Allen
  Puritan in Babylon: The Story of Calvin Coolidge, A   III-1530; 1548
Whitener, Daviel J.
  Prohibition in North Carolina, 1715-1945
    III-1512
Whitney, Courtney
  MacArthur: His Rendezvous with History
    III-1834
Whitney, Simon N.
  Antitrust Policies: American Experience in Twenty Industries   II-1212
Wibberly, Leonard
  Wes Powell: Conqueror of the Grand Canyon
    II-1108
Widick, B. J.
  UAW and Walter Reuther, The   III-1660
Wiebe, Robert H.
  Businessmen and Reform: A Study of the Progressive Movement   II-1332
  Search for Order, 1877-1920, The   II-1176
Wik, Reynold M.
  Steam Power on the American Farm   II-684
Wilbur, Earl M.
  History of Unitarianism in Transylvania, England, and America, A   I-575
Wilder, Lucy
  Mayo Clinic, The   II-1183
Wiley, Bell I.
  Life of Billy Yank and the Life of Johnny Reb, The   II-1013
Wilkins, Thurman
  Cherokee Tragedy: The Story of the Ridge Family and the Decimation of a People
    I-671
Willcox, William B.
  Portrait of a General: Sir Henry Clinton in the War of Independence   I-281
Williams, Benjamin H.
  Economic Foreign Policy of the United States
    III-1541
Williams, Beryl
  Rocket Pioneers, The   III-1559
Williams, Kenneth P.
  Lincoln Finds a General: A Military Study of the Civil War   II-956
Williams, Mary W.
  Anglo-American Isthmian Diplomacy, 1815-1915   II-1345
Williams, Oscar

New Pocket Anthology of American Verse, The
III-1404

Williams, T. Harry
Lincoln and His Generals   II-1001; 1018
Lincoln and the Radicals   II-984
P. G. T. Beauregard: Napoleon in Gray
II-956

Williams, William A.
"Age of Mercantilism, An Interpretation of
the American Political Economy to 1828,
The," reprinted in Williams' *The Shaping of
American Diplomacy*   I-407; 598

Williams, William Carlos
Collected Earlier Poems: Before 1940, The
III-1404
Collected Later Poems: 1940-1950, The
III-1404

Williamson, Chilton
*American Suffrage: From Property to Democ-
racy, 1760-1860*   II-771

Williamson, Harold F.
*American Petroleum Industry: The Age of Il-
lumination, 1859-1899, The*   II-1122

Williamson, James A.
"England and the Opening of the Atlantic,"
in *The Cambridge History of the British Empire*   I-51

Willison, George F.
Saints and Strangers   I-79

Willoughby, Charles A.
MacArthur: 1941-1951   III-1834

Wilson, Carol Green
Herbert Hoover: A Challenge for Today
III-1597

Wilson, Charles
*Profit and Power: A Study of England and the
Dutch Wars*   I-83

Wilson, Edmund
*Patriotic Gore: Studies in the Literature of the
American Civil War*   II-863

Wilson, Forrest
*Crusader in Crinoline: The Life of Harriet
Beecher Stowe*   II-863

Wilson, Harold S.
McClure's Magazine and the Muckrakers
III-1356

Wilson, Robert F.
How America Went to War   III-1465

Wiltse, Charles M.
John C. Calhoun. Vol III: *Sectionalist, 1840-
1850*   II-858
*Jeffersonian Tradition in American Democ-
racy, The*   I-431
New Nation: 1800-1845, The   I-431

Wiltz, John E.
*In Search of Peace: The Senate Munitions In-
quiry*   III-1654

Windmiller, Marshall
Peace Corps and Pax Americana, The   III-
1882

Winkler, John K.

*Incredible Carnegie: The Life of Andrew
Carnegie, 1835-1919*   II-1171

Winks, Robin W.
*Canada and the United States: The Civil War
Years*   II-1076
Cold War: From Yalta to Cuba, The. New Per-
spectives in American History series   III-
1782

Winsor, Justin
*From Cartier to Frontenac: Geographical Dis-
covery in the Interior of North America in Its
Historical Relations, 1534-1700*   I-32; 58
Narrative and Critical History of America
I-27

Winthrop, John
*Winthrop's Journal: History of New England,
1630-1649*   I-114

Wish, Harvey
*American Historian: A Social-Intellectual His-
tory of the Writing of the American Past, The*
II-735; 1189
*George Fitzhugh: Propagandist of the Old
South*   I-653

Witte, Edwin E.
Development of the Social Security Act, The
III-1647
Government in Labor Disputes, The   II-790

Wood, G. C.
*Congressional Control of Foreign Relations
During the American Revolution, 1774-1789*
I-394

Wood, Robert C.
Suburbia: Its People and Their Politics
III-1816

Woodmason, Charles
*Carolina Backcountry on the Eve of the Revolu-
tion: The Journal and Other Writings of
Charles Woodmason, Anglican Itinerant,
The*   I-218

Woodson, Carter G.
Education of the Negro Prior to 1861, The
II-712

Woodward, C. Vann
Strange Career of Jim Crow, The   II-1254;
III-1389
Tom Watson: Agrarian Rebel   II-1229

Woodward, Grace Steele
Man Who Conquered Pain, The   II-794

Woody, Carroll H.
*Growth of the Federal Government, 1915-1932,
The*   III-1598

Woody, Thomas
*History of Women's Education in the United
States, A*   II-712

Wooster, Ralph A.
Secession Conventions of the South, The
II-945

Wright, Benjamin F.
Consensus and Continuity, 1776-1787   I-
329

Wright, Benjamin F., Jr.

Contract Clause of the Constitution, The
    I-490
Wright, Edward N.
    Conscientious Objectors in the Civil War
    II-995
Wright, Louis B.
    *Gold, Glory, and the Gospel: The Adventurous
    Lives and Times of the Renaissance Explor-
    ers*   I-22
Wrong, George M.
    Rise and Fall of New France, The   I-32
Wylie, Max
    *Clear Channels: Television and the American
    People*   III-1679
Wyman, Walker D.
    Frontier in Perspective, The   II-1217

Yearns, Wilfred B.
    Confederate Congress, The   II-945
Youman, Roger
    *How Sweet It Was: Television: A Pictorial Com-
    mentary*   III-1679
Young, Jerimiah S.
    *Political and Constitutional Study of the Cum-
    berland Road, A*   I-496

Young, John R.
    *Report of the Librarian of Congress for the Fis-
    cal Year Ended June 30, 1898*   II-1283
Young, Marilyn Blatt
    *Rhetoric of Empire: America's China Policy,
    1895-1901, The*   II-1300
Young, Mary E.
    *Redskins, Ruffleshirts, and Rednecks: Indian
    Land Allotments in Alabama and Missis-
    sippi, 1830-1860*   I-671
Young, Otis E.
    *First Military Escort on the Santa Fe Trail,
    1829, The*   I-592
Young, Roland
    *Congressional Politics in the Second World
    War*   III-1708

Zahler, Helen S.
    *Eastern Workingmen and National Land
    Policy, 1829-1862*   II-968
Zetterbaum, Marvin
    Tocqueville and the Problem of Democracy
    II-678
Zimmerman, John L.
    Guadalcanal Campaign, The   III-1714